PERSPECTIVES IN BUSINESS ETHICS

"A person can't go out the way he or she came in.
Ben, a person has to add up to something."
Willy Loman in Arthur Miller, *Death of A Salesman* (Penguin Books, 1949) p. 125.
[changed for gender neutrality]

"If a *person* lacks integrity, nothing else matters."
Stephen Carter, Integrity

"My task which I am trying to achieve is, by the power of the
written word, to make you hear, to make you feel—it is,
before all, to make you see. That—and no more—and it is
everything. If I succeed, you shall find there according to your
desserts: encouragement, consolation, fear . . . and, perhaps,
also that glimpse of truth for which you have forgotten to ask."
—*Joseph Conrad, Preface,* The Nigger of the "Narcissus"

PERSPECTIVES IN BUSINESS ETHICS

by Laura Pincus Hartman
DePaul University

Irwin
McGraw-Hill

Chicago • Bogotá • Boston • Buenos Aires • Caracas
London • Madrid • Mexico City • Sydney • Toronto

Irwin/McGraw-Hill

A Division of The **McGraw·Hill** Companies

PERSPECTIVES IN BUSINESS ETHICS

 This book is printed on acid-free paper.

1 2 3 4 5 7 8 9 0 DOC/DOC 9 0 9 8 7

ISBN 0-256-23317-9

Vice president and editorial director: *Michael W. Junior*
Publisher: *Craig S. Beytien*
Sponsoring editor: *Karen Mellon*
Developmental editor: *Catherine Schwent*
Marketing manager: *J. Milletics*
Project manager: *Lynne Basler*
Production supervisor: *Jon Christopher*
Designer: *Larry J. Cope*
Compositor: *Shepherd, Inc.*
Typeface: *10/12 Times Roman*
Printer: *R. R. Donnelley & Sons Company*

Library of Congress Cataloging-in-Publication Data
Pincus, Laura B.
    Perspectives in business ethics / Laura Pincus.
        p. cm.
    Includes index.
    ISBN 0-256-23317-9 (acid-free paper)
    1. Business ethics.   I. Title.
    HF5387.P557 1998
    174' .4—dc21   97–22530

http://www.mhhe.com

To Emma, the gentle wind around my soul that caresses and refreshes my heart.

Note to the Reader

This is a textbook that came to exist because I needed it. It's as simple as that. This approach may seem selfish (see Chapter One), but I have found in my experience that when professors write texts because they themselves have a strong need, the most effective text is usually produced.

The study of ethics includes an analysis of the interests of all of the individuals who hold a stake in the outcome of any dilemma or decision ("stakeholder analysis"). In teaching business ethics at both a graduate and undergraduate level, I found myself walking into the classroom with armloads of articles, cases, and other handouts that I used to present the perspectives of each stakeholder involved in a decision. This text seeks to provide perspectives on ethical issues in a variety of different formats—similar to my efforts involving handouts for class.

The text explores traditional ethics issues by providing multiple perspectives on the same issue. For instance, in dealing with the question of cost/benefit analysis, the text presents not only a standard case discussion of the Ford Pinto case, but also presents a libertarian/economist perspective, the writings of a past Ford owner, and the writings of a past Ford executive. Or, in providing an introduction to critical analysis, the text provides a reading on recent problems at Dow Corning and "where the ethicists went wrong" in their original glowing assessment of Dow Corning.

The materials in this book include:

1. Traditional textual explanations/definitions/discussion of new topics or ideas from a historical and foundational perspective.
2. Reprints of articles, whether seminal (older, traditional), or from present day analysis.
3. Short cases for brief explanatory questions and discussion in class.
4. Full-length cases for analysis with sufficient background information and guiding questions. These cases would also be supplemented either in the text or teachers' manual with projects and exercises.
5. Additional nontraditional materials such as song lyrics, excerpts from classical literature, short stories, and so on.

The varying formats not only present different perspectives, but also provide information and opinions in a manner most accessible by the students. As we all know, many of the more academic-focused articles we have read are difficult, even for seasoned ethicists. The material presented in this text is sophisticated, yet relevant and accessible.

The focus of this approach is to encourage readers to open their minds to the variety of opinions on any given issue. The result of this approach is not to persuade readers that there is no right answer to these issues, but instead to ensure that all stakeholders' perspectives are considered. The readings for each section have been chosen with this representative interest in mind.

In addition, links to sites on the World Wide Web are provided in a fashion similar to margin definitions in other texts. For instance, in the section dealing with Dow Corning, the address of the Dow Corning website is provided. In this way, readers can hear the perspectives of the "players" in the cases in their own words, thus permitting extension of the stakeholder analysis.

As you read, please also consider what opinions or perspectives are not represented in this text. I appreciate any and all suggestions/additions/modifications.

ACKNOWLEDGMENTS

This text is, in truth, the work of a host of scholars and business practitioners who offered their opinions as reviewers early on in the project or who have allowed me to compile their work in order to present a more realistic and multiperspectival approach to the study of ethics in business decision making. I am deeply indebted to these individuals for without their work and consideration this text would not have come to pass. In addition, I would like to thank my research assistant, David Thies, for his timeless energy and exceptional research abilities in connection with locating some of the more exceptional materials in the text, as well as for his work on the thankless task of acquiring all of the permissions for the book. I am grateful to the other David for his willingness to hold my hand tightly while he takes leaps with me. It makes everything else come so much more easily. Finally, I thank Craig Beytien, Karen Mellon, and Catherine Schwent at McGraw-Hill/Irwin for their support of this innovative project and for being willing to take some chances in an industry not always known for its risk-taking character.

Laura Pincus Hartman
LPincus@wppost.depaul.edu
Department of Management
DePaul University
1 E. Jackson Blvd.
Chicago, IL 60604
312/362-6569   FAX 312/362-6973

Contents

PERSPECTIVES IN BUSINESS ETHICS

Part One

ETHICAL THEORIES AND APPROACHES

The purpose of this text is not to teach ethics, but instead to offer a foundation in ethical thought, followed by a variety of perspectives on difficult ethical dilemmas. The reader is encouraged to then critically evaluate each perspective using her or his personal ethical theory base. Using ethics to analyze business issues is merely one form of decision making, similar to profit maximization, legal compliance, or religious beliefs. The difference, however, between ethics and these other bases for decisions is that ethics can serve as the foundation for each of the other methods. Therefore, in reaching decisions, the individual may use ethics as a guide in legal or religious compliance, and even in accomplishing profit maximization.

In fact, we already use ethics as a basis for decision making. Assume your grandmother is on her deathbed. She looks up to you and asks, as her last dying wish, that you follow her and your religion in a devout manner after she passes on. Assume, as well, that you do not plan to do this. Do you tell her that you will abide by her wishes, so that she might die a more peaceful death? Or are you honest with her and admit that you will not follow her wishes? Whichever your answer, consider *why* you feel the way you do. There is no law that requires one answer or another, not even a rule. You might believe that you should act one way or another because it is the right thing to do. This is your personal ethic.

Consider the response of the grandfather of Sir Adrian Cadbury, the owner of the second largest chocolate company in Britain, when the queen sought to purchase tins of chocolates to send to each soldier serving in the Anglo-Boer War in South Africa. Cadbury was opposed to the war and was uncomfortable reaping a profit from such a transaction. On the

1

other hand, he was striving to move forward with the company and this would mean additional work for the firm. He decided to accept the order, but to do so only at cost with no additional amount for profit. The firm benefitted from the work, but he did not reap a financial gain at the expense of the war.[1] Was this ethical? Would it have been unethical to deny the queen's contract simply because he didn't approve of the purpose for which she intended to use the chocolate?

On the other hand, consider the $68 million Bausch & Lomb (B&L) recently agreed to pay to settle a consumer class action lawsuit. The plaintiffs complained that B&L had been selling three identical contact lenses under three different brand names for significantly different prices. B&L had attempted to market the lenses in different ways to different consumer groups at varying prices. Is this wrong, unethical?

Volumes of literature are devoted in general terms to the question of defining ethics. Ethics involves judgments as to good and bad, right and wrong, and what ought to be. As defined by the philosopher Epicurus, ethics "deals with things to be sought and things to be avoided, with ways of life and with the *telos*."[2] (*Telos* is the chief aim or end in life.) An ethical dilemma exists where two or more values are in conflict, and we seek from ethics a resolution to this conflict. Business ethics refers to the measurement of business behavior based on standards of right and wrong, rather than relying entirely on principles of accounting and management. For purposes of this discussion, morals are one's personal guiding principles; ethics are the ways that those morals are applied to decisions.

Finding and following the moral course is not always easy for any of us, but the difficult may be particularly acute for the businessperson. The bottom line is necessarily unforgiving. Hence, the pressure to produce is intense and the temptation to cheat may be great. Although the law provides useful guideposts for minimum behavior, no clear moral guidelines have emerged. Therefore, when the business person is faced with a difficult decision, a common tactic is simply to do what he or she takes to be correct at any given moment. Indeed, in one survey of ethical views in business, 50 percent of the respondents indicated that the word *ethical* means "what my feelings tell me is right."[3]

Philosophers have provided powerful intellectual support for that approach. *Existentialists,* led by the famed Jean-Paul Sartre, believe standards of conduct cannot be rationally justified and no actions are inherently right or wrong. Thus, each person may reach her or his own choice about ethical principles. This view finds its roots in the notion that humans are only what we will ourselves to be. If God does not exist, there can be no human nature, because there is no one to conceive that nature.

In Sartre's famous interpretation, existence precedes essence. First humans exist, then we individually define what we are—our essence. Therefore, each of us is free, with no rules to turn to for guidance. Just as we all choose our own natures, so must we choose

---

1. Sir Adrian Cadbury, "Ethical Managers Make Their Own Rules," *Harvard Business Review,* September/October 1987.
2. Diogenes Laertius, *Lives of Eminent Philosophers* (Cambridge, MA: Harvard University Press, 1925), book 10, chap. 30.
3. Tim Friend, "Western European Kids Get Better Health Care," *USA Today,* Aug. 14, 1991, p. D1.

our own ethical precepts. Moral responsibility belongs to each of us individually, and in our own ways.

But, as we have seen countless times through history, what one woman or man believes is right or just, many others may believe is wrong or evil. Consider, for instance, Germany under Nazi rule. Adolph Hitler believed he was right in his brutal acts and decisions *as strongly as* the rest of the world believed he was wrong. Existentialists would say, perhaps, that there is no right answer in this situation, while others would argue for some universal principles of right and wrong. *Relativists* contend that the ethical answer depends on the situation (that ethics is relative). They may argue that those who followed Hitler were not necessarily unethical because of the circumstances of the situation. What is right in one situation may be wrong in another. The theories discussed below offer guidance in this area, though they are by no means the only routes to decisions.   ■

Chapter 1

TRADITIONAL THEORIES

Until philosophers are kings, or the kings and princes of this world have the spirit and power of philosophy, and political greatness and wisdom meet in one, and those commoner natures who pursue either to the exclusion of the other are compelled to stand aside, cities will never have rest from their evils—no, nor the human race.

PLATO, *Republic*

Ethical theories may be divided into two categories: teleological and deontological. The distinction between the two is that teleological theories determine the ethics of an act by looking to the consequences of the decision (the ends), while deontological theories determine the ethics of an act by looking to the process of the decision (the means).

TELEOLOGICAL ETHICAL SYSTEMS

The teleological morality of a decision is determined by measuring the probable outcome or consequences. The theory most representative of this approach is *utilitarianism,* which seeks as its end the greatest good (or utility) for the greatest number. Jeremy Bentham (1748–1832) and John Stuart Mill (1806–1873) were the chief intellectual forces in the development of utilitarianism. The most basic form of utilitarian analysis is cost-benefit analysis, where one tallies the costs and benefits of a given decision and follows the decision that provides for the greatest overall gain.

While this approach is superficially easy to apply (majority rule, profit/loss statements), there remain complexities. For instance, does one consider the impact on animals as well as humans in adding up the benefits and costs? Or, how does one weigh the good? If an action would render one person exquisitely happy and three people moderately unhappy, does the happiness of that one outweigh the unhappiness of the three? How do we measure happiness?

Utilitarianism is viewed as a strong theory because it is liberal (it appeals to no authority in resolving differences of opinion), and because it is able to describe much of the process of human decision making. On the other hand, its weakness is that there is a possibility of injustice regarding the distribution of goods. In other words, the rights of any one person are not taken into account; no rights have any greater weight than others. Consequently, certain individuals may suffer great harm, while others receive only modest benefits.

Distributive justice is another teleological approach to ethical decision making and one that is based on a concept of fairness. Devised by contemporary Harvard philosopher John Rawls, distributive justice holds that ethical acts or decisions are those that lead to an equitable distribution of goods and services. Therefore, it is critical to determine a fair method for distributing goods and services. Rawls suggests that we consider how we would distribute goods and services if we were under a *"veil of ignorance"* that prevented us from knowing our status in society (i.e., our intelligence, wealth, appearance). He asks that we consider what rules we would impose on this society if we had no idea whether we would be princes or paupers. Would we devise a system of high taxes and expensive welfare projects that, presumably, would benefit the impoverished but prove costly to the wealthy? Or would we advocate a pure market-based system that demanded each of us to be responsible for our own needs and desires?

Rawls argues that we would build a cooperative system in which benefits (e.g., income) would be distributed unequally only where doing so would be to the benefit of all, particularly the least advantaged. All those behind the veil would agree to that standard because they could not know whether they would be among the advantaged or the disadvantaged. From this system of distributive economic justice, it follows that ethical justice is measured by the capacity of the act in question to enhance cooperation among members of society. That which is determined from behind the veil of ignorance is deemed ethical through its fairness.

One way to comprehend the implications of distributive justice is to consider a difficult ethical dilemma and imagine that you don't know what position you hold in connection with the outcome—you don't know whether you are going to be impacted in a beneficial way or a detrimental way by the decision. Now, without that knowledge (under the "veil of ignorance"), what decision would you make? Rawls argues that you will make the most just decision under this framework.

DEONTOLOGICAL ETHICAL SYSTEMS

A deontological system is based on rules or principles which govern decisions. The German philosopher Immanuel Kant (1724–1804) developed perhaps the most persuasive and fully articulated vision of ethics as measured by the rightness of rules, rather than by consequences. In this formalistic view of ethics, the rightness of an act depends little (or, in Kant's view, not at all) on the results of the act. Kant believed in the key moral concept of good will. The moral person is one of good will, and that person renders ethical decisions based on what is right, regardless of the consequences of the decision. Moral worth springs from one's decision to discharge one's duty. Thus, the student who refuses to cheat on exams is morally worthy if her or his decision springs from duty, but morally unworthy if the decision is merely one born of self-interest, such as fear of being caught.

But how does the person of good will know what is right? Here, Kant propounded the *categorical imperative,* the notion that every person should act on only those principles that she or he, as a rational person, would prescribe as *universal laws* to be applied to the whole of mankind. (Therefore, this approach has also been called universalism.) Put into action, the rule asks whether you would feel all right if this rule applied in every situation, to every action. (This concept is similar to a parent's asking a child, "How would you feel if everyone stole candy from their friends?")

The moral rule is categorical rather than hypothetical in that its prescriptive force is independent of its consequences—the rule guides us independently of the ends we seek. For instance, the rule does not say "Do not steal from others *if* you don't want to go to jail"; it merely states "Do not steal." The rule prescribes a rule for the means without concern for the end it produces. Kant believed that every rational creature can act according to his or her categorical imperative, because all such persons have "autonomous, self-legislating wills" that permit them to formulate and act on their own systems of rules. To Kant, what is right for one is right for all, and each of us can discover that right by exercising our rational faculties.

Kantian rules recognize universal rights such as freedom of speech, freedom of consent, the right to privacy, or freedom of conscience. Problems exist, however, when an individual does not know which rules to follow. For instance, you might be faced with a dilemma that pits freedom of speech against the right to privacy. Which rule wins?

Kant was not the only one to prescribe a moral system based on rules and rights. The Chinese scholar Confucius (born in 551 B.C.E.) maintained an enormous set of rules by which he suggested one should live. These rules, or maxims, do not appear to us today to be complicated; instead, they seem not to be commonplace and pedestrian. They include the following:

What you do not wish done to yourself, do not do to others.

Do not wish for quick results, nor look for small advantages. If you see quick results, you will not attain the ultimate goal. If you are led astray by small advantages, you will never accomplish great things.

When you see someone of worth, think of how you may emulate. When you see someone unworthy, examine your own character.

Wealth and rank are what people desire, but unless they be obtained in the right way they may not be possessed.

Feel kindly toward everyone, but be intimate only with the virtuous.[4]

Another deontological approach is from the perspective of religion. No theory or approach to the evaluation of actions is more rule-based than religion. After all, the Ten Commandments are viewed by some as the most basic principles of behavior. Additional rules, such as "Do unto others as you would have them do unto you," also spring directly from religious thought or writings, rather than from reason or logic. The religious point of view is not so different from Kant's perspective, except that the universal principles come directly from religious beliefs. Whether one is of Christian, Jewish, Moslem, Buddhist, or other faith, the deity's laws are viewed as absolutes that must shape the whole of one's life, including work. Faith, rather than reason, intuition, or secular knowledge, provides the foundation for a moral life built on religion.

Finally, some philosophers have argued in recent years for *virtue ethics,* claiming that the key to good ethics lies not in rules, rights, and responsibilities, but in the classic notion of character. As Plato and Aristotle contended, our attention should be given to strategies for encouraging desirable character traits such as honesty, fairness, compassion, and generosity. The primary question in virtue ethics is not, "What actions are universally right?" but, "What is the best sort of life for human beings to live?" Virtue ethics applauds the person who is motivated to do the right thing and who cultivates that motivation in daily conduct. One would know the right thing by exercising judgment, rather than by applying a universal set of rules.

ARISTOTELIAN MORAL VIRTUES	
Courage	Gentleness
Self-Control	Friendliness
Generosity	Truthfulness
Magnificence	Wittiness
High-Mindedness	Modesty[5]

---

4. Confucius, *The Analects,* cited in Huston Smith, *The World's Religions* (San Francisco: HarperSanFrancisco, 1991) p. 159.
5. Steven Mintz, "Aristotelian Virtue and Business Ethics Education," *Journal of Business Ethics* 15, no. 8 (August 1996), pp. 827–38.

St. Thomas Aquinas, too, believed in the quest for the right thing or the good life. Aquinas, however, took the study of virtue one step beyond Aristotle when he divided virtue into the religious or theological virtues of faith, hope, and charity, and the intellectual virtues of prudence (wisdom), justice, temperance, and fortitude.[6] Both Aristotle and Aquinas believed that any individual had the potential for virtue, as virtue was learned or acquired, rather than innate. Could a modern corporation realistically aspire to be virtuous according to Aquinas or Aristotle?

Virtue ethics (with its set of traits) might seem to be closely linked with universalism (with its set of principles). However, a part of the virtue ethics argument is that persons guided by virtue ethics are more morally reliable than those who simply follow the rules but fail to inspect, strengthen, and preserve their own personal virtues.

HYBRID THEORIES

A king had some empty glasses. He said, "If I pour hot water into them they will crack. If I pour ice-cold water into them they will also crack." What did the king do? He mixed the hot and the cold water together and poured it into them and they did not crack. Even so did the Holy One, blessed be He, say, "If I create the world on the basis of the attribute of mercy alone, the world's sins will greatly multiply? If I create the world on the basis of the attribute of justice alone, how could the world endure? I will therefore create it with both the attributes of mercy and justice, and may it endure!"[7]

Certain theories do not fit cleanly into one approach or another. *Personal libertarianism,* conceived by contemporary philosopher Robert Nozick, holds that morality springs from the maximization of personal freedom and that individuals should be free from the interference of others. Justice and fairness, right and wrong are measured not by equality of results (e.g., wealth) for all, but from ensuring equal opportunity for all to engage in informed choices about their own welfare. Hence, Nozick takes essentially a free-market stance toward ethics. One might, at first, say that this is a deontological theory since the primary concern is protecting the right to individual freedom, whatever the consequences. On the other hand, the theory also looks to the results of an act in determining whether freedom has been restricted as a result of the decision.

Closely related to libertarianism is the concept of *ethical egoism.* The primary concern under ethical egoism is the maximization of the individual's self-interest, according to that individual. What is right is that which is right for the individual, while minimizing the impact of her or his choices on the rights of others. Ethical egoism identifies a means toward decision making (do what you want), while also identifying the greatest good as that which is the greatest good for the decision maker, hence a hybrid. Self-interest may be wealth, but it can also be fame, a happy family, a great job, or anything else considered important to the decision maker.

---

6. Caryn Beck-Dudley, "No More Quandaries: A Look at Virtue through The Eyes of Robert Solomon," *American Business Law Journal* 34/1 (Fall 1996), p. 119.

7. Aba Hillel Silver, *Where Judaism Differed* (Northvale, NJ: Jason Aronson 1987). Cited in Huston Smith, *The World's Religions* (San Francisco: HarperSanFrancisco, 1991), p. 292.

Enlightened ethical egoism (also known as *enlightened self-interest*) considers the long-range perspective of others or of humanity as a whole. One might explain this by saying that it is important to the individual that the world is a good world; therefore, the individual may have a *self*-interest in curbing pollution or in community projects, even though she or he may not individually and personally benefit from the decision.

In the readings that follow, consider the authors' contentions about what is right and wrong. Do you agree with one of these approaches more strongly than another? In some readings, the approaches may seem more clearly in line with the theories discussed above than in others. Can you align the others with the traditional theories, or are they more likely hybrids of those discussed?

LEVIATHAN
Thomas Hobbes

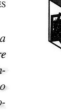

Thomas Hobbes (1588–1679) was viewed as a materialist and as a highly pessimistic philosopher. The Leviathan presents a bleak picture of the innate qualities of human beings in the "state of nature"; without governing rules or laws, a war of all against all is certain to ensue. Hobbes contends that fear of violent death is the primary motive that causes people to create a political state by contracting to surrender their natural rights and to submit to the absolute authority of a sovereign.

Hobbes lived in a time of extreme violence. He was born around the time when Mary, Queen of Scots, was executed by Elizabeth, Queen of England. During his life, the Spanish Armada attacked England and was defeated, and piracy and buccaneering were rampant on the oceans. There was an English Civil war in the 1640s that included the execution of Charles I. London was hit repeatedly with fire and plagues. Women and men were accused of witchcraft and burned at the stake. No wonder he has a dismal view of human nature!

The Hobbesian concept of the social contract led to investigations by other political theorists (Locke, Spinoza, Rousseau) who formulated their own radically different theories of the social contract.

. . . [13] To this war of every man against every man, this also is consequent: that nothing can be unjust. The notions of right and wrong, justice and injustice, have there no place. Where there is no common power, there is no law; where no law, no injustice. Force and fraud are in war the two cardinal virtues. Justice and injustice are none of the faculties neither of the body, nor mind. If they were, they might be in a man that were alone in the world, as well as his senses and passions. They are qualities that relate to men in society, not in solitude. It is consequent also to the same condition that there be no propriety, no dominion, no *mine* and *thine* distinct, but only that to be every man's that he can get, and for so long as he can keep it. And thus much for the ill condition which man by mere nature is actually placed in, though with a possibility to come out of it, consisting partly in the passions, partly in his reason. . . .

[3] But because covenants of mutual trust where there is a fear of not performance on either part (as hath been said in the former chapter) are invalid, though the original of justice be the making of covenants, yet injustice actually there can be none till the cause of such fear be taken away, which, while men are in the natural condition of war, cannot be done. Therefore, before the names of just and unjust can have place, there must be some coercive power to compel men equally to the performance of their covenants, by the ter-

---

Thomas Hobbes, *Leviathan,* pt. I, ch. 13, para. 13; ch. 14, para 3, ch. 15, para. 10.

ror of some punishment greater than the benefit they expect by the breach of their covenant, and to make good that propriety which by mutual contract men acquire, in recompense of the universal right they abandon; and such power there is none before the erection of a commonwealth. And this is also to be gathered out of the ordinary definition of justice in the Schools; for they say the *justice is the constant will of giving to every man his own.* And therefore where there is no *own,* that is, no propriety, there is no injustice; and where there is no coercive power erected, that is, where there is no commonwealth, there is no propriety, all men having right to all things; therefore where there is no commonwealth, there nothing is unjust. So that the nature of justice consisteth in keeping of valid covenants; but the validity of covenants begins not but with the constitution of a civil power sufficient to compel men to keep them; and then it is also that propriety begins. . . .

[10] The names of just and unjust, when they are attributed to men, signify one thing; and when they are attributed to actions, another. When they are attributed to men, they signify conformity or inconformity of manners to reason. But when they are attributed to actions, they signify the conformity or inconformity to reason, not of manners or manner of life, but of particular actions. A just man, therefore, is he that taketh all the care he can that his actions may be all just; and an unjust man is he that neglecteth it. And such men are more often in our language styled by the names of righteous and unrighteous, than just and unjust, though the meaning be the same. Therefore a righteous man does not lose that title by one or a few unjust actions that proceed from sudden passion or mistake of things or persons; nor does an unrighteous man lose his character for such actions as he does or forbears to do for fear, because his will is not framed by the justice, but by the apparent benefit of what he is to do. That which gives to human actions the relish of justice is a certain nobleness or gallantness of courage (rarely found) by which a man scorns to be beholden for the contentment of his life to fraud or breach of promise. This justice of the manners is that which is meant where justice is called a virtue, and injustice a vice. . . .

RELATED WEB SITE

Text of *Leviathan:* gopher://gopher.vt.edu:10010/02/98/1

OF THE STATE
OF NATURE

JOHN LOCKE

John Locke (1632–1704) is considered the father of British empiricism. He was born to a puritan household and it is actually unknown whether Locke ever attended a formal school in his childhood, but he did attend Oxford later in his life. Empiricism is a philosophical doctrine holding that all knowledge is derived from experience, whether of the mind or the senses. Empiricists oppose the rationalist belief in the existence of innate ideas. A doctrine basic to the scientific method, it is associated with the rise of experimental science after the 17th century. It has been dominant in British philosophy, in the works of Hume and Berkeley. Most empiricists acknowledge certain a priori truths (e.g., principles of mathematics and logic), but John Stuart Mill and others have treated even these as generalizations deduced from experience.

Using what he called a "historical, plain method," Locke inquired into the origin, certainty, and extent of human knowledge, together with the grounds and degrees of belief, assent, and opinion. "Our business is not to know all things, but those which concern our conduct."

His Two Treatises on Government *represents the first time that the monarchy had been questioned. The whole concept of human rights and individual freedom had been heard, but Locke was the first to question whether the monarchy had a right to exist, to rule. He supported a popular government answerable to the people with liberty as the overriding value, rather than government by absolute monarchy.*

. . . 4. To understand political power aright, and derive it from its original, we must consider what estate all men are naturally in, and that is, a state of perfect freedom to order their actions, and dispose of their possessions and persons as they think fit, within the bounds of the law of Nature, without asking leave or depending upon the will of any other man.

A state also of equality, wherein all the power and jurisdiction is reciprocal, no one having more than another, there being nothing more evident than that creatures of the same species and rank, promiscuously born to all the same advantages of Nature, and the use of the same faculties, should also be equal one amongst another, without subordination or subjection, unless the lord and master of them all should, by any manifest declaration of

---

John Locke, *Second Treatise on Government*, Ch. II, Of the State of Nature, pars. 4, 6–8, 13–14.

his will, set one above another, and confer on him, by an evident and clear appointment, an undoubted right to dominion and sovereignty. . . .

   . . . 6. The state of Nature has a law of Nature to govern it, which obliges every one, and reason, which is that law, teaches all mankind who will but consult it, that being all equal and independent, no one ought to harm another in his life, health, liberty or possessions; for men being all the workmanship of one omnipotent and infinitely wise Maker; all the servants of one sovereign Master, sent into the world by His order and about His business; they are His property, whose workmanship they are made to last during His, not one another's pleasure. And, being furnished with like faculties, sharing all in one community of Nature, there cannot be supposed any such subordination among us that may authorize us to destroy one another, as if we were made for one another's uses, as the inferior ranks of creatures are for ours. Every one as he is bound to preserve himself, and not to quit his station wilfully, so by the like reason, when his own preservation comes not in competition, ought he as much as he can to preserve the rest of mankind, and not unless it be to do justice on an offender, take away or impair the life, or what tends to the preservation of life, the liberty, health, limb, or goods of another.

   7. And that all men may be restrained from invading others' rights, and from doing hurt to one another, and the law of Nature be observed, which willeth the peace and preservation of all mankind, the execution of the law of Nature is in that state put into every man's hands, whereby every one has a right to punish the transgressors of that law to such a degree as may hinder its violation. For the law of Nature would, as all other laws that concern men in this world, be in vain if there were nobody that in the state of Nature had a power to execute that law, and thereby preserve the innocent and restrain offenders; and if any one in the state of Nature may punish another for any evil he has done, every one may do so. For in that state of perfect equality, where naturally there is no superiority or jurisdiction of one over another, what any may do in prosecution of that law, every one must needs have a right to do.

   8. And thus, in the state of Nature, one man comes by a power over another, but yet no absolute or arbitrary power to use a criminal, when he has got him in his hands, according to the passionate heats or boundless extravagancy of his own will, but only to retribute to him so far as calm reason and conscience dictate, what is proportionate to his transgression, which is so much as may serve for reparation and restraint. For these two are the only reasons why one many may lawfully do harm to another, which is that we call punishment. In transgressing the law of Nature, the offender declares himself to live by another rule than that of reason and common equity, which is that measure God has set to the actions of men for their mutual security, and so he becomes dangerous to mankind; the tie which is to secure them from injury and violence being slighted and broken by him, which being a trespass against the whole species, and the peace and safety of it, provided for by the law of Nature, every man upon this score, by the right he hath to preserve mankind in general, may restrain, or where it is necessary, destroy things noxious to them, and so may bring such evil on any one who hath transgressed that law, as may make him repent the doing of it, and thereby deter him, and, by his example, others from doing the like mischief. And in this case, and upon this ground, every man hath a right to punish the offender, and be executioner of the law of Nature. . . .

13. To this strange doctrine—*viz.,* That in the state of Nature every one has the executive power of the law of Nature—I doubt not but it will be objected that it is unreasonable for men to be judges in their own cases, that self-love will make men partial to themselves and their friends; and, on the other side, ill-nature, passion, and revenge will carry them too far in punishing others, and hence nothing but confusion and disorder will follow, and that therefore God hath certainly appointed government to restrain the partiality and violence of men. I easily grant that civil government is the proper remedy for the inconveniences of the state of Nature, which must certainly be great where men may be judges in their own case, since it is easy to be imagined that he who was so unjust as to do his brother an injury will scarce be so just as to condemn himself for it. But I shall desire those who make this objection to remember that absolute monarchs are but men; and if government is to be the remedy of those evils which necessarily follow from men being judges in their own cases, and the state of Nature is therefore not to be endured, I desire to know what kind of government that is, and how much better it is than the state of Nature, where one man commanding a multitude has the liberty to be judge in his own case, and may do to all his subjects whatever he pleases without the least question or control of those who execute his pleasure? and in whatsoever he doth, whether led by reason, mistake, or passion, must be submitted to? which men in the state of Nature are not bound to do one to another? And if he that judges, judges amiss in his own or any other case, he is answerable for it to the rest of mankind.

14. It is often asked as a mighty objection, where are, or ever were, there any men in such a state of Nature? To which it may suffice as an answer at present, that since all princes and rulers of "independent" governments all through the world are in a state of Nature, it is plain the world never was, nor never will be, without numbers of men in that state. I have named all governors of "independent" communities, whether they are, or are not, in league with others; for it is not every compact that puts an end to the state of Nature between men, but only this one of agreeing together mutually to enter into one community, and make one body politic; other promises and compacts men may make one with another, and yet still be in the state of Nature. The promises and bargains for truck, etc., between the two men in Soldania, in or between a Swiss and an Indian, in the woods of America, are binding to them, though they are perfectly in a state of Nature in reference to one another for truth, and keeping of faith belongs to men as men, and not as members of society. . . .

RELATED WEB SITES

John Locke biography: libertyonline.hypermall.com/Locke/index.html

Explanation of Empiricism:
    www.ilt.columbia.edu/academic/digitexts/notes/empiricism.html

GROUNDING FOR THE METAPHYSICS OF MORALS

IMMANUEL KANT

Immanuel Kant (1724–1804) was intrigued by the bases of human knowledge and understanding. In considering the origin of morals and morality, he concluded that reason is the final authority for morality. Only those actions that are undertaken from a sense of duty dictated by reason are moral; those acts that are dictated only by law or custom cannot be moral. In the following excerpt, Kant explains the categorical imperative, his basis for morality. Consider its close link to what we know as the Golden Rule.

. . . It is clear from the foregoing that all moral concepts have their seat and origin completely a priori in reason, and indeed in the most ordinary human reason just as much as in the most highly speculative. They cannot be abstracted from any empirical, and hence merely contingent, cognition. In this purity of their origin lies their very worthiness to serve us as supreme practical principles; and to the extent that something empirical is added to them, just so much is taken away from their genuine influence and from the absolute worth of the corresponding actions. Moreover, it is not only a requirement of the greatest necessity from a theoretical point of view, when it is a question of speculation, but also of the greatest practical importance, to draw these concepts and laws from pure reason, to present them pure and unmixed, and indeed to determine the extent of this entire practical and pure rational cognition, i.e., to determine the whole faculty of pure practical reason. The principles should not be made to depend on the particular nature of human reason, as speculative philosophy may permit and even sometimes finds necessary; but, rather, the principles should be derived from the universal concept of a rational being in general, since moral laws should hold for every rational being as such. In this way all morals, which require anthropology in order to be applied to humans, must be entirely expounded at first independently of anthropology as pure philosophy, i.e., as metaphysics (which can easily be done in such distinct kinds of knowledge). One knows quite well that unless one is in possiession of such a metaphysics, then the attempt is futile, I shall not say to determine exactly for speculative judgment the moral element of duty in all that accords with duty, but that the attempt is impossible, even in ordinary and practical usage, especially in that of moral instruction, to ground morals on their genuine principles and thereby to produce pure moral dispositions and engraft them on men's minds for the promotion of the highest good in the world. . . .

Everything in nature works according to laws. Only a rational being has the power to act according to his conception of laws, i.e., according to principles, and thereby has he a will. Since the derivation of actions from laws requires reason, the will is nothing but practical reason. If reason infallibly determines the will, then in the case of such a being actions which are recognized to be objectively necessary are also subjectively necessary, i.e., the will is a faculty of choosing only that which reason, independently of inclination, recognizes as being practically necessary, i.e., as good. But if reason of itself does not sufficiently determine the will, and if the will submits also to subjective conditions (certain incentives) which do not always agree with objective conditions; in a word, if the will does not in itself completely accord with reason (as is actually the case with men), then actions which are recognized as objectively necessary are subjectively contingent, and the determination of such a will according to objective laws is necessitation. That is to say that the relation of objective laws to a will not thoroughly good is represented as the determination of the will of a rational being by principles of reason which the will does not necessarily follow because of its own nature. . . .

[I]n the case of this categorical imperative, or law of morality, the reason for the difficulty (of discerning its possibility) is quite serious. The categorical imperative is an a priori synthetic practical proposition, and since discerning the possibility of propositions of this sort involves so much difficulty in theoretic knowledge, there may readily be gathered that there will be no less difficulty in practical knowledge.

In solving this problem, we want first to inquire whether perhaps the mere concept of a categorical imperative may not also supply us with the formula containing the proposition that can alone be a categorical imperative. For even when we know the purport of such an absolute command, the question as to how it is possible will still require a special and difficult effort, which we postpone to the last section.

If I think of a hypothetical imperative in general, I do not know beforehand what it will contain until its condition is given. But if I think of a categorical imperative, I know immediately what it contains. For since, besides the law, the imperative contains only the necessity that the maxim should accord with this law, while the law contains no condition to restrict it, there remains nothing but the universality of a law as such with which the maxim of the action should conform. This conformity alone is properly what is represented as necessary by the imperative.

Hence there is only one categorical imperative and it is this: Act only according to that maxim whereby you can at the same time will that it should become a universal law.

Now if all imperatives of duty can be derived from this one imperative as their principle, then there can at least be shown what is understood by the concept of duty and what it means, even though there is left undecided whether what is called duty may not be an empty concept.

The universality of law according to which effects are produced constitutes what is properly called nature in the most general sense (as to form), i.e., the existence of things as far as determined by universal laws. Accordingly, the universal imperative of duty may be expressed thus: Act as if the maxim of your action were to become through your will a universal law of nature.

We shall now enumerate some duties, following the usual division of them into duties to ourselves and to others and into perfect and imperfect duties.

1.   A man reduced to despair by a series of misfortunes feels sick of life but is still so far in possession of his reason that he can ask himself whether taking his own life would not be contrary to his duty to himself. Now he asks whether the maxim of his action could become a universal law of nature. But his maxim is this: from self-love I make as my principle to shorten my life when its continued duration threatens more evil than it promises satisfaction. There only remains the question as to whether this principle of self-love become a universal law of nature. One sees at once a contradiction in a system of nature whose law would destroy life by means of the very same feeling that acts so as to stimulate the furtherance of life, and hence there could be no existence as a system of nature. Therefore, such a maxim cannot possibly hold as a universal law of nature and is, consequently, wholly opposed to the supreme principle of all duty.

2.   Another man in need finds himself forced to borrow money. He knows well that he won't be able to repay it, but he sees also that he will not get any loan unless he firmly promises to repay it within a fixed time. He wants to make such a promise, but he still has conscience enough to ask himself whether it is not permissible and is contrary to duty to get out of difficulty in this way. Suppose, however, that he decides to do so. The maxim of his action would then be expressed as follows: when I believe myself to be in need of money, I will borrow money and promise to pay it back, although I know that I can never do so. Now this principle of self-love or personal advantage may perhaps be quite compatible with one's entire future welfare, but the question is now whether it is right. I then transform the requirement of self-love into a universal law and put the question thus: how would things stand if my maxim were to become a universal law? He then sees at once that such a maxim could never hold as a universal law of nature and be consistent with itself, but must necessarily be self-contradictory. For the universality of law which says that anyone believing himself to be in difficulty could promise whatever he pleases with the intention of not keeping it would make promising itself and the end to be attained thereby quite impossible, inasmuch as no one would believe what was promised him but would merely laugh at all such utterances as being vain pretenses.

3.   A third finds in himself a talent whose cultivation could make him a man useful in many respects. But he finds himself in comfortable circumstances and prefers to indulge in pleasure rather than to bother himself about broadening and improving his fortunate natural aptitudes. But he asks himself further whether his maxim of neglecting his natural gifts, besides agreeing of itself with his propensity to indulgence, might agree also with what is called duty. He then sees that a system of nature could indeed always subsist according to such a universal law, even though every man (like South Sea Islanders) should let his talents rust and resolve to devote his life entirely to idleness, indulgence, propagation, and, in a word, to enjoyment. But he cannot possibly will that this should become a universal law of nature or be implanted in us as such a law by a natural instinct. For as a rational being he necessarily wills that all his faculties should be developed, inasmuch as they are given him for all sorts of possible purposes.

4.   A fourth man finds things going well for himself but sees others (whom he could help) struggling with great hardships; and he thinks: what does it matter to me? Let everybody be as happy as Heaven will or as he can make himself; I shall take nothing from him nor even envy him; but I have no desire to contribute anything to his well-being or to his assistance when in need. If such a way of thinking were to become a universal

law of nature, the human race admittedly could very well subsist and doubtless could subsist even better than when everyone prates about sympathy and benevolence and even on occasion exerts himself to practice them but, on the other hand, also cheats when he can, betrays the rights of man, or otherwise violates them. But even though it is possible that a universal law of nature could subsist in accordance with that maxim, still it is impossible to will that such a principle should hold everywhere as a law of nature. For a will which resolved in this way would contradict itself, inasmuch as cases might often arise in which one would have need of the love and sympathy of others and in which he would deprive himself, by such a law of nature springing from his own will, of all hope of the aid he wants for himself.

These are some of the many actual duties, or at least what are taken to be such, whose derivation from the single principle cited above is clear. We must be able to will that a maxim of our action become a universal law; this is the canon for morally estimating any of our actions. Some actions are so constituted that their maxims cannot without contradiction even be thought as a universal law of nature, much less be willed as what should become one. In the case of others this internal impossibility is indeed not found, but there is still no possibility of willing that their maxim should be raised to the universality of a law of nature, because such a will would contradict itself. There is no difficulty in seeing that the former kind of action conflicts with strict or narrow [perfect] (irremissible) duty, while the second kind conflicts only with broad [imperfect] (meritorious) duty. By means of these examples there has thus been fully set forth how all duties depend as regards the kind of obligation (not the object of their action) upon the one principle.

If we now attend to ourselves in any transgression of a duty, we find that we actually do not will that our maxim should become a universal law—because this is impossible for us—but rather that the opposite of this maxim should remain a law universally. We only take the liberty of making an exception to the law for ourselves (or just for this one time) to the advantage of our inclination. Consequently, if we weighed up everything from one and the same standpoint, namely, that of reason, we would find a contradiction in our own will, viz., that a certain principle be objectively necessary as a universal law and yet subjectively not hold universally but should admit of exceptions. But since we at one moment regard our action from the standpoint of a will wholly in accord with reason and then at another moment regard the very same action from the standpoint of a will affected by inclination, there is really no contradiction here. Rather, there is an opposition (*antagonismus*) of inclination to the precept of reason, whereby the universality (*universalitas*) of the principle is changed into a mere generality (*generalitas*) so that the practical principal of reason may meet the maxim halfway. Although this procedure cannot be justified in our own impartial judgment, yet it does show that we actually acknowledge the validity of the categorical imperative and (with all respect for it) merely allow ourselves a few exceptions which, as they seem to us, are unimportant and forced upon us.

We have thus at least shown that if duty is a concept which is to have significance and real legislative authority for our actions, then such duty can be expressed only in categorical imperatives but not at all in hypothetical ones. We have also—and this is already a great deal—exhibited clearly and definitely for every application what is the content of the categorical imperative, which must contain the principle of all duty (if there is such a thing at all). But we have not yet advanced far enough to prove a priori that there actually is an imperative of this kind, that there is a practical law which of itself commands absolutely and without any incentives, and that following this law is duty. . . .

If then there is to be a supreme practical principle and, as far as the human will is concerned, a categorical imperative, then it must be such that from the conception of what is necessarily an end for everyone because this end is an end in itself it constitutes an objective principle of the will and can hence serve as a practical law. The ground of such a principle is this: rational nature exists as an end in itself. In this way man necessarily thinks of his own existence; thus far is it a subjective principle of human actions. But in this way also does every other rational being think of his existence on the same rational ground that holds also for me; hence it is at the same time an objective principle, from which, as a supreme practical ground, all laws of the will must be able to be derived. The practical imperative will therefore be the following: Act in such a way that you treat humanity, whether in your own person or in the person of another, always at the same time as an end and never simply as a means. We now want to see whether this can be carried out in practice.

Let us keep to our previous examples.

First, as regards the concept of necessary duty to oneself, the man who contemplates suicide will ask himself whether his action can be consistent with the idea of humanity as an end in itself. If he destroys himself in order to escape from a difficult situation, then he is making use of his person merely as a means so as to maintain a tolerable condition till the end of his life. Man, however, is not a thing and hence is not something to be used merely as a means; he must in all his actions always be regarded as an end in himself. Therefore, I cannot dispose of man in my own person by mutilating, damaging, or killing him. (A more exact determination of this principle so as to avoid all misunderstanding, e.g., regarding the amputation of limbs in order to save oneself, or the exposure of one's life to danger in order to save it, and so on, must here be omitted; such questions belong to morals proper.)

Second, as concerns necessary or strict duty to others, the man who intends to make a false promise will immediately see that he intends to make use of another man merely as a means to an end which the latter does not likewise hold. For the man whom I want to use for my own purposes by such a promise cannot possibly concur with my way of acting toward him and hence cannot himself hold the end of this action. This conflict with the principle of duty to others becomes even clearer when instances of attacks on the freedom and property of others are considered. For then it becomes clear that a transgressor of the rights of men intends to make use of the persons of others merely as a means, without taking into consideration that, as rational beings, they should always be esteemed at the same time as ends, i.e., be esteemed only as beings who must themselves be able to hold the very same action as an end.

Third, with regard to contingent (meritorious) duty to oneself, it is not enough that the action does not conflict with humanity in our own person as an end in itself; the action must also harmonize with this end. Now there are in humanity capacities for greater perfection which belong to the end that nature has in view as regards humanity in our own person. To neglect these capacities might perhaps be consistent with the maintenance of humanity as an end in itself, but would not be consistent with the advancement of this end.

Fourth, concerning meritorious duty to others, the natural end that all men have is their own happiness. Now humanity might indeed subsist if nobody contributed anything to the happiness of others, provided he did not intentionally impair their happiness. But this, after all, would harmonize only negatively and not positively with humanity as an end in itself, if everyone does not also strive, as much as he can, to further the ends of others. For the ends of any subject who is an end in himself must as far as possible be my ends also, if that conception of an end in itself is to have its full effect in me. . . .

RELATED WEB SITES

Discussion of Kantian philosophy:
   www.knight.org/advent/cathen/08603a.htm

Text of Grounding for the Metaphysics of Morals:
   www.swan.ac.uk/poli/texts/

WHEN JUSTICE REPLACES AFFECTION: THE NEED FOR RIGHTS

JEREMY WALDRON

If we didn't have laws, how would we act? Do you believe that our natural affection for other humans would prevail and we would all treat each other in respectful and considerate ways? What might prevent this? In the following piece, Waldron discusses philosophers Kant and Hegel as he considers rights as parameters for natural acts. He uses marriage as his primary example, investigating what happens when affection fades, but when there exist legalistic rights and duties the partners know they can fall back on.

I.

Why do individuals need rights? In a world crying out for a greater emphasis on fraternity and communal responsibility in social life, what is the point of an institution that legitimates the making of querulous and adversarial claims by individuals against their fellows? If human relations can be founded on affection, why is so much made in modern jurisprudence of formal and impersonal rights as a starting point for the evaluation of laws and institutions? In answering these questions, I take as my starting point a disagreement between the philosophers Kant and Hegel regarding the role of rights in marriage.

In his work on the philosophy of law, Immanuel Kant likened marriage to a contract between two people for "life-long reciprocal possession of their sexual faculties."[1] He was quick to add that, though it is a contract, it is "not on that account a matter of arbitrary will"; rather, it is a matter of necessity for anyone who wants to enjoy another person sexually. In sexual relations, Kant says, one party is used as an object by the other, and that *prima facie* is incompatible with the basic "Law of Humanity" prohibiting the use of any human agent as a mere means to the satisfaction of one's desires. That situation can be rectified "only . . . under the one condition that as the one Person is acquired by the other as a *res*, that same Person equally acquires the other reciprocally, and thus regains and re-establishes the rational Personality."[2] Kant went on to say that the reciprocity of rights that this solution presupposes leads to a requirement of monogamy, because in a polygamous regime, one of the partners may be giving more to the other than

Jeremy Waldron, "When Justice Replaces Affection: The Need for Rights." *Harvard Journal of Law and Public Policy* 2, no. (Summer 1988), pp. 625–631, 635–637, 640–642. Reprinted by permission.

1. I. Kant, *The Philosophy of Law: An Exposition of the Fundamental Principles of Jurisprudence as the Science of Right* 110 (W. Hastie trans. 1887).
2. Id. at 110–11.

the other is to her.[3] The contract has got to be a matter of *equal* right in order to satisfy the fundamental test of respect for persons.

Sometimes it seems that Kant was not content with this contractualist characterization of marriage. In one place, he went further and argued that the rights involved are like rights of property:

> *The Personal Right thus acquired is at the same time, real in kind. This characteristic of it is established by the fact that if one of the married Persons runs away or enters into the possession of another, the other is entitled, at any time, and incontestably, to bring such a one back to the former relation, as if that Person were a Thing.*[4]

Many have thought that such ideas are perhaps better ignored in the overall assessment of Kant's philosophy of morals.

The Kantian view of marriage as a purely contractual arrangement was adamantly repudiated by Hegel—"shameful," he said, "is the only word for it."[5] Hegel conceded that marriage originates in a contract between two people and that therefore, in its dependence on their say-so to get it underway, it has some of the contingency and "arbitrariness" that are normally associated with contractual relations.[6] But, according to Hegel, rights and contract are far from telling us the complete story about the institution. For one thing, the public character of the marriage celebration (whether the ceremony is religious or civil)— the procedures of notification, licensing, witnessing, solemnization, registration, and so on—attest to a significance that goes far beyond a mere meeting of the wills or "the mutual caprice" of the prospective partners.[7] For another thing, the parties celebrate their marriage not merely as a *quid pro quo* but in order to attain a union of desire, affection, interest, and identity that goes far beyond anything that could possibly be specified in even the fine print of a contract. There is a world of difference, on this view, between the Kantian "contract for reciprocal use" and the "love, trust, and common sharing of their existence as individuals" which is what married partners commit themselves to.[8] As Hegel puts it, if marriage begins in an agreement, "it is precisely a contract to transcend the standpoint of contract," that is, to transcend the standpoint of "individual self-subsistent units" making claims against one another, which is how contracting parties are normally understood.[9]

There are two distinct aspects to this critique. On the one hand, Hegel is attacking Kant's specific use of *contract* to characterize the marriage bond; the suggestion is that *this* legal concept is inappropriate in the particular context (though I imagine he would take even greater exception to Kant's use of the terminology of property!). On the other hand, he is also attacking the much broader target of Kant's pervasive legalism: the temptation, to which Kantians so often succumb, to reduce social institutions of all kinds to some

---

3. *Id.* at 111–12.
4. *Id.* at 111.
5. G. W. F. Hegel, *Philosophy of Right* 58, at ¶ 75 (T. Knox trans. 1967).
6. *Id.* at 111–12, at ¶ 162.
7. *Id.* at 113–14, at ¶ 164; *id.* at 262, at ¶ 161[A].
8. *Id.* at 112, at ¶ 163.
9. *Id.*

formal array of legalistic rights and duties. Here it is not so much the idea of *contract,* but the more general idea of a *right,* that is out of place. This is the aspect of Hegel's critique that I will focus on, because I think it raises interesting and far-reaching issues about liberal rights-based approaches to social and communal relations.

Few of us would disagree with Hegel's basic point: Claims of right should have little part to play in the context of a normal loving marriage. If we hear one partner complaining to the other about a denial or withdrawal of conjugal *rights,* we know that something has already gone wrong with the interplay of desire and affection between the partners. The same would be true if people started talking about their *right* to a partner's fidelity, their *right* to be freed from child-care or domestic chores once in a while, their equal *right* to pursue a career, their *right* to draw equally on the family income, and so on. In each case, the substance of the claim may be indispensable for a happy and loving marriage in the modern world. But it is its presentation *as a claim*—that is, as an entitlement that one party presses peremptorily, querulously, and adversarially against the other—that would lead to our misgivings. We would certainly look for all these things in a marriage, but we would hope to see them upheld and conceded, not as matters of right, but as the natural outcome of the most intimate mutual concern and respect brought to bear by the partners on the common problems that they face. Even if rights like these were acknowledged as the ground-rules of the relationship in some sort of formal agreement drawn up by the partners, there would still be something unpleasant about their *asserting* them as rights or, as the phrase goes, "*standing on their rights*" in the normal functioning of the relationship. Such behavior would be seen as a way of blocking and preventing warmth and intimacy, replacing relatively unbounded and immediate care and sensitivity with rigid and abstract formulas of justice.

The point can be generalized: To stand on one's rights is to distance oneself from those to whom the claim is made; it is to announce, so to speak, an opening of hostilities; and it is to acknowledge that other warmer bonds of kinship, affection, and intimacy can no longer hold. To do this in a context where adversarial hostility is inappropriate is serious moral failing.[10] As Hegel put it in an Addition to the *Philosophy of Right:* "To have no interest except in one's formal right may be pure obstinacy, often a fitting accompaniment of a cold heart and restricted sympathies. It is uncultured people who insist most on their rights, while noble minds look on other aspects of the thing."[11]

II.

Is there not anything, then, to be said for the Kantian position? I think there is this. Though marriage is certainly more than a matter of rights and correlative duties, and

---

10. *See, e.g.,* Young, *Dispensing with Moral Rights,* 6 *Political Theory* 63, 68 (1978):
    > [O]ften not only is such an appeal to rights otiose, but it is morally jarring (rather than dignified) to insist on one's due . . . . This means of protecting what are conceived to be legitimate interests is, even if understandable, not morally desirable since it does nothing to mend the ruptured relations.
    > *See also* Louden, *Rights Infatuation and the Impoverishment of Theory,* 17 J. *Value Inquiry* 87, 99 (1983) ("In extreme cases [of rights infatuation], a severe form of moral inertia takes over, at which point it becomes difficult to get the rights infatuationist to do anything but claim his rights.")

11. Hegel, *supra* note 5, at 235, at ¶ 37[A].

though one will not expect to hear claims of right in a happily functioning marriage, nevertheless the strength and security of the marriage commitment in the modern world depends in part on there being an array of legalistic rights and duties that the partners know they can fall back on, if ever their mutual affection fades. That is the idea I will consider in this paper.

I want to explore this idea against the background of some criticisms that have been made of rights-based liberalism. In recent years, liberal theories have come under attack from socialists and communitarians for their implausible suggestion that the bonds of social life should be thought of as constituted primarily by the rights and rights-based relations of initially atomistic individuals.[12] I will consider how much of that attack would be mitigated or refuted if liberals were to concede that the structure of rights is not constitutive of social life, but instead to be understood as a position of fall-back and security in case other constituent elements of social relations ever come apart. To go back to the marriage example, I will suggest that there is a need for an array of formal and legalistic rights and duties, not to constitute the affective bond, but to provide each person with secure knowledge of what she can count on in the unhappy event that there turns out to be no other basis for her dealings with her erstwhile partner in the relationship. The importance of rights ought to be much easier to defend from this somewhat less inflated position.

But the argument is not merely a strategic retreat for liberals. Liberals are entitled to ask their communitarian critics how this important function of security is to be performed in a community that repudiates rights and legalism, and under the auspices of a theory that gives individual rights no part to play at all. Is it to be supposed that the intimate and affective relations that characterize various forms of community will never come apart, that affections will never change, and that people will never feel the urge to exit from some relationships and initiate others? If so, communitarianism in the modern world presents itself as naive or desperately dangerous, and probably both. Or is it supposed that a society will be pervaded by such a strong background sense of affection and responsibility, that we will be able to afford to allow people to change their intimate relations as they please without any attempt to articulate formally the terms on which they are to do so? That, for example, in the marriage case, we can somehow count on goodwill to provide for the continued care of person's partner or children if they need it? Again, if this is the view that communitarians rely on, they are dangerously underestimating both the possibility for things to go wrong between human beings, and the human need for some sort of background guarantee, on which, in the last resort, one can rely in the face of that possibility.

Before continuing it may be worth saying a word or two about *communitarianism.* The new communitarianism is by no means a rigidly defined body of thought; the term refers rather to a trend in modern critiques of liberal political philosophy. In the work of writers like Roberto Unger, Michael Sandel, Alasdair Macintyre, and Charles Taylor, liberal theories of rights have been attacked for their individualism, for the way they parade

---

12. *See, e.g., Liberalism and its Critics* (M. Sandel ed. 1984) (hereinafter *Liberalism*); M. Sandel, *Liberalism and the Limits of Justice* (1982); A. Macintyre, *After Virtue: A Study in Moral Theory* (1981); Taylor, *Atomism,* in *Powers, Possessions and Freedom: Essays in Honour of C. B. MacPherson* (A. Kontos ed. 1979); R. Unger, *Knowledge and Politics* (1976).

the desires and interests of the human individual as the be-all and end-all of politics, at the expense of notions like community, fraternity and a shared social good.[13] It is not that liberals ignore those values altogether; but it is alleged that they give them only an instrumental significance or treat them merely as particular moral causes which individuals may or may not espouse. Partly it is a matter of perspective on society. For liberal theories of rights, the point of reference is the "unencumbered" individual, who is free to shrug off his communal and other allegiances whenever he chooses. The relatively unaffectionate and formalistic language of rights and contract theory is said to be an expression of his essential detachability from affective commitments; its formalism expresses the facts deemed most important about his moral status, without reference to any content or community. Communitarians, on the other hand, take as their point of reference the shared lives of people who regard themselves as, in Sandel's words, "defined to some extent by the community of which they are a part"[14]—people who cannot imagine a standpoint of political judgment over and above their particular communal identity.

It is important to stress that community here is not an *abstract* idea; one's communal identity depends on the particularity of one's past. As Macintyre puts it, "I am someone's son or daughter, someone else's cousin or uncle; I am a citizen of this or that city, a member of this or that guild or profession."[15] Apart from the particularity of these attachments, there is said to be no standpoint for abstract political thought, communal or individual. The discourse of this communitarian politics, then, will be informal and engaged rather than impersonal and abstract. Political thought will be a matter of the discovery and recognition of the particular social selves we are, rather than the deliberate choice and articulation of abstract principles of right. There are also other strands in the communitarian literature—notably a strand of civic republicanism that is by no means so clearly incompatible with the traditional liberal point of view—but these are the ones I deal with in this article. . . .[16]

IV.

I have used the marriage example to illustrate these points, but I do not want to give the impression that marriage is my sole concern. There are other areas of law and politics that can be used to make related points about the indispensability of individual rights.

One is the area of welfare rights. It is common to hear laments about the loss of face-to-face charity and caring, whether by individuals or in family groups, and its replacement in modern society by more impersonal systems of welfare agencies and formalized welfare entitlements. Certainly, here is a very important debate to be had about the nature and extent of our provision for need in society—one that I cannot go into here. But it

---

13. There is a good general discussion of the communitarian critique in Gutman, *Communitarian Critics of Liberalism,* 14 Phil. & Pub. Aff. 308 (1985).

14. *See* Sandel, *Introduction,* Liberalism, *supra* note 12, at 5.

15. A. Macintyre, *supra* note 12, 204–05. *See also* M. Sandel, *supra* note 12, at 179.

16. For a discussion of civic republicanism, see H. Arendt, *On Revolution* (1973), B. Smith, *Politics and Remembrance: Republican Themes in Machiavelli, Burke, and Tocqueville* (1985), and *Civic Republicanism and its Critics,* 14 *Political Theory* 423 (1986) (symposium).

may be worth pointing out why the replacement of face-to-face caring by more impersonal structures is not altogether the disaster that some people make it out to be.

Consider care for the elderly. Age brings with it a certain amount of dependence: As
one gets older, one's capacity to secure an income diminishes while one's needs increase.
There have been societies, perhaps ours in an earlier age, or China, both now and in the
past, where the old have been able to count on the support of their adult children as their
needs increase and their capacities diminish. That mode of caring strikes us as an attractive one, for it is based on ties of kinship, affection, and love, and it reciprocates in an almost symmetrical way the care that the parent once lavished on her children.

Moreover, it has the advantage of being personal: The care is between this particular
old person and her children (who can be sensitive to the detail of her needs), rather than
between old people and young people in general. Still, there are good reasons in the modern world why many old people feel less than confident about relying on their children's
support. One problem is demographic: Even in kin-oriented societies such as China, there
are proportionately fewer working adults to support an increasing population of the aged.
But other problems go deeper into modern life. People's lives and careers are complex,
shifting, and often risky and demanding. They cannot always guarantee a secure base for
themselves, let alone provide an assurance of security for their parents. And people are
torn by other motives in modern life which, though not intrinsically hostile to the provision of this care, make it somewhat less certain that this will be something they necessarily want to do.

To insist, then, in a communitarian spirit, that care for the aged should remain the responsibility of the family, we would have to accept either or maybe both of two costs. We
would have to place limits on the *other* demands that adult children would be permitted to
respond to, the risks they could run, and the mobility they could seek. (I suspect, by the
way, that in the present state of things, this would involve limiting once again the capacity
of *women* to move and flourish outside the home. A great many of the concerns about
communitarianism articulated in this paper are above all *feminist* concerns.) Or, if we were
not prepared to do that (and maybe even if we were), we would have to accept the cost of
exposing the elderly to a certain amount of insecurity and uncertainty in addition to the
other burdens of their age. Neither in this country nor in Europe have people been willing
to accept those costs. Instead, we have opted for less personal, less affective modes of
care. People are encouraged to purchase an income for their old age in the marketplace, so
they can rely on a pension check from a finance house even if they cannot rely on the
warm support of their children. And, as a fall-back position, the impersonal agencies of the
state guarantee an income, either to all the elderly, or to those who have not made or have
not been able to make impersonal provision for themselves. Thus, although we may not
care for them on a face-to-face basis, we both provide impersonal structures to enable
them to care for themselves, and respond collectively and impersonally as a society to the
rights that they have to our support. Our choice of this impersonality is well described in
an English context by Michael Ignatieff in his book, *The Needs of Strangers:*

> As we stand together in line at the post office, while they cash their pension cheques,
> some tiny portion of my income is transferred into their pockets through the number-
> less capillaries of the state. The mediated quality of our relationship seems necessary

to both of us. They are dependent on the state, not upon me, and we are both glad of it. . . . My responsibilities towards them are mediated through a vast division of labour. In my name a social worker climbs the stairs to their rooms and makes sure they are as warm and as clean as they can be persuaded to be. When they get too old to go out, a volunteer will bring them a hot meal, make up their beds, and if the volunteer is a compassionate person, listen to their whispering streams of memory. When they can't go on, an ambulance will take them to the hospital, and when they die, a nurse will be there to listen to the ebbing of their breath. It is this solidarity among strangers, this transformation through the division of labour of needs into rights and rights into care that gives us whatever fragile basis we have for saying that we live in a moral community.[17]

It is not that a system of rights is the only imaginable way in which needs could be dealt with in a caring society. We could set things up in a way that encouraged old people to rely on the warm and loving support of their families. But even if we did that, I think we would still want to set up a system of rights as a fall-back—as a basis on which some *assurance* of support could be given, without risking the insecurity, resentment and indignity of leaving the elderly completely at "the uncertain mercy of their sons and daughters. . . ."[18]

---

17. M. Ignatieff, The Needs of Strangers 9–10 (1984).
18. *Id.* at 17.

UTILITARIANISM

JOHN STUART MILL

John Stuart Mill (1806–1873) is most often linked with philosophical empiricism and utilitarianism. As a member of Parliament, he was a staunch defender of individual liberties and argued against state interference. In fact, he was one of the first advocates of women's equality. Mill's concept of utilitarianism was a modification of Jeremy Bentham's version in that Mill enriched the concept of pleasure. While Bentham believed that all pleasures, physical and intellectual, were of equal value, Mill considered the "higher" pleasures of the mind as superior. What are the implications of this belief on decision making?

WHAT UTILITARIANISM IS

The creed which accepts as the foundation of morals "utility" or the "greatest happiness principle" holds that actions are right in proportion as they tend to promote happiness; wrong as they tend to produce the reverse of happiness. By happiness is intended pleasure and the absence of pain: by unhappiness, pain and the privation of pleasure. To give a clear view of the moral standard set up by the theory, much more requires to be said; in particular, what things it includes in the ideas of pain and pleasure, and to what extent this is left an open question. But these supplementary explanations do not affect the theory of life on which this theory of morality is grounded—namely, that pleasure and freedom from pain are the only things desirable as ends; and that all desirable things (which are as numerous in the utilitarian as in any other scheme) are desirable either for pleasure inherent in themselves or as means to the promotion of pleasure and the prevention of pain.

Now such a theory of life excites in many minds, and among them in some of the most estimable in feeling and purpose, inveterate dislike. To suppose that life has (as they express it) no higher end than pleasure—no better and nobler object of desire and pursuit—they designate as utterly mean and groveling, as a doctrine worthy only of swine, to whom the followers of Epicurus were, at a very early period, contemptuously likened; and modern holders of the doctrine are occasionally made the subject of equally polite comparisons by its German, French, and English assailants.

When thus attacked, the Epicureans have always answered that it is not they, but their accusers, who represent human nature in a degrading light, since the accusation supposes human beings to be capable of no pleasures except those of which swine are capable. If this supposition were true, the charge could not be gainsaid, but would then be no longer an imputation; for if the sources of pleasure were precisely the same to human beings and to swine, the rule of life which is good enough for the one would be good enough for the other. The comparison of the Epicurean life to that of beasts is felt as degrading, precisely because a beast's pleasures do not satisfy a human being's conceptions of happiness. Human beings have faculties more elevated than the animal appetites and, when once made conscious of them, do not regard anything as happiness which does not include their gratification. I do not indeed, consider the Epicureans to have been by any means faultless in drawing out their scheme of consequences from the utilitarian principle. To do this in any sufficient manner, many Stoic, as well as Christian, elements require to be included. But there is no known Epicurean theory of life which does not assign to the pleasures of the intellect, of the feelings and imagination, and of the moral sentiments a much higher value as pleasures than to those of mere sensation. It must be admitted, however, that utilitarian writers in general have placed the superiority of mental over bodily pleasures chiefly in the greater permanency, safety, uncostliness, etc., of the former—that is, in their circumstantial advantages rather than in their intrinsic nature. And on all these points utilitarians have fully proved their case; but they might have taken the other and, as it may be called, higher ground with entire consistency. It is quite compatible with the principle of utility to recognize the fact that some kinds of pleasure are more desirable and more valuable than others. It would be absurd that, while in estimating all other things quality is considered as well as quantity, the estimation of pleasure should be supposed to depend on quantity alone.

If I am asked what I mean by difference of quality in pleasures, or what makes one pleasure more valuable than another, merely as a pleasure, except its being greater in amount, there is but one possible answer. Of two pleasures, if there be one to which all or almost all who have experience of both give a decided preference, irrespective of any feeling of moral obligation to prefer it, that is the more desirable pleasure. If one of the two is, by those who are competently acquainted with both, placed so far above the other that they prefer it, even though knowing it to be attended with a greater amount of discontent, and would not resign it for any quantity of the other pleasure which their nature is capable of, we are justified in ascribing to the preferred enjoyment a superiority in quality so far outweighing quantity as to render it, in comparison, of small account.

Now it is an unquestionable fact that those who are equally acquainted with and equally capable of appreciating and enjoying both do give a most marked preference to the manner of existence which employs their higher faculties. Few human creatures would consent to be changed into any of the lower animals for a promise of the fullest allowance of a beast's pleasures; no intelligent human being would consent to be a fool, no instructed person would be an ignoramus, no person of feeling and conscience would be selfish and base, even though they should be persuaded that the fool, the dunce, or the rascal is better satisfied with his lot than they are with theirs. They would not resign what they possess more than he for the most complete satisfaction of all the desires which they have in common with him. If they ever fancy they would, it is only in cases of unhappiness so extreme that to escape from it they would exchange their lot for almost any other, however undesirable in their own eyes. A being of higher faculties requires more to make him happy, is capable probably of more acute suffering, and certainly accessible to it at more points than one of the inferior type; but in spite of these liabilities, he can never really wish to sink into what he feels to be a lower grade of existence. We may give what explanation we please of this unwillingness; we may attribute it to pride, a name which is given indiscriminately to some of the most and to some of the least estimable feelings of which mankind are capable; we may refer it to the love of liberty and personal independence, an appeal to which was with the Stoics one of the most effective means for the inculcation of it; to the love of power or to the love of excitement, both of which do really enter into and contribute to it; but its most appropriate appellation is a sense of dignity, which all human beings possess in one form or other, and in some, though by no means in exact, proportion to their higher faculties, and which is so essential a part of the happiness of those in whom it is strong that nothing which conflicts with it could be otherwise than momentarily an object of desire to them. Whoever supposes that this preference takes place at a sacrifice of happiness—that the superior being, in anything like equal circumstances, is not happier than the inferior—confounds the two very different ideas of happiness and content. It is indisputable that the being whose capacities of enjoyment are low has the greatest chance of having them fully satisfied; and a highly endowed being will always feel that any happiness which he can look for, as the world is constituted, is imperfect. But he can learn to bear its imperfections, if they are at all bearable; and they will not make him envy the being who is indeed unconscious of the imperfections, but only because he feels not at all the good which those imperfections qualify. It is better to be a human being dissatisfied than a pig satisfied; better to be Socrates dissatisfied than a fool satisfied. And if the fool, or the pig, are of a different opinion, it is because they only know their own side of the question. The other party to the comparison knows both sides.

It may be objected that many who are capable of the higher pleasures occasionally, under the influence of temptation, postpone them to the lower. But this is quite compatible with a full appreciation of the intrinsic superiority of the higher. Men often, from infirmity of character, make their election for the nearer good, though they know it to be the less valuable; and this no less when the choice is between two bodily pleasures than when it is between bodily and mental. They pursue sensual indulgences to the injury of health, though perfectly aware that health is the greater good. It may be further objected that many who begin with youthful enthusiasm for everything noble, as they advance in years, sink into indolence and selfishness. But I do not believe that those who undergo this very common change voluntarily choose the lower description of pleasures in preference to the higher. I believe that, before they devote themselves exclusively to the one, they have already become incapable of the other. Capacity for the nobler feelings is in most natures a very tender plant, easily killed, not only by hostile influences, but by mere want of sustenance; and in the majority of young persons it speedily dies away if the occupations to which their position in life has devoted them, and the society into which it has thrown them, are not favorable to keeping that higher capacity in exercise. Men lose their high aspirations as they lose their intellectual tastes, because they have not time or opportunity for indulging them; and they addict themselves to inferior pleasures, not because they deliberately prefer them, but because they are either the only ones to which they have access or the only ones which they are any longer capable of enjoying. It may be questioned whether anyone who has remained equally susceptible to both classes of pleasures ever knowingly and calmly preferred the lower, though many, in all ages, have broken down in an ineffectual attempt to combine both.

From this verdict of the only competent judges, I apprehend there can be no appeal. On a question which is the best worth having of two pleasures, or which of two modes of existence is the most grateful to the feelings, apart from its moral attributes and from its consequences, the judgment of these who are qualified by knowledge of both, or, if they differ, that of the majority among them, must be admitted as final. And there needs be the less hesitation to accept this judgment respecting the quality of pleasures, since there is no other tribunal to be referred to even on the question of quantity. What means are there of determining which is the acutest of two pains, or the intensest of two pleasurable sensations, except the general suffrage of those who are familiar with both? Neither pains nor pleasures are homogeneous, and pain is always heterogeneous with pleasure. What is there to decide whether a particular pleasure is worth purchasing at the cost of a particular pain, except the feelings and judgment of the experienced? When, therefore, those feelings and judgment declare the pleasures derived from the higher faculties to be preferable *in kind,* apart from the question of intensity, to those of which the animal nature, disjoined from the higher faculties, is susceptible, they are entitled on this subject to the same regard.

I have dwelt on this point as being part of a perfectly just conception of utility or happiness considered as the directive rule of human conduct. But it is by no means an indispensable condition to the acceptance of the utilitarian standard; for that standard is not the agent's own greatest happiness, but the greatest amount of happiness altogether; and if it may possibly be doubted whether a noble character is always the happier for its nobleness, there can be no doubt that it makes other people happier, and that the world in general is immensely a gainer by it. Utilitarianism, therefore, could only attain its end by the general cultivation of nobleness of character, even if each individual were only benefited by the nobleness of others, and his own, so far as happiness is concerned, were a sheer deduction from the benefit. But the bare enunciation of such an absurdity as this last renders refutation superfluous.

According to the greatest happiness principle, as above explained, the ultimate end, with reference to and for the sake of which all other things are desirable—whether we are considering our own good or that of other people—is an existence exempt as far as possible from pain, and as rich as possible in enjoyments, both in point of quantity and quality; the test of quality and the rule for measuring it against quantity being the preference felt by those who, in their opportunities to experience, to which must be added their habits of self-consciousness and self-observation, are best furnished with the means of comparison. This, being according to the utilitarian opinion the end of human action, is necessarily also the standard of morality, which may accordingly be defined "the rules and precepts for human conduct" by the observance of which an existence such as has been described might be, to the greatest extent possible, secured to all mankind; and not to them only, but, so far as the nature of things admits, to the whole sentient creation. . . .

ON THE CONNECTION BETWEEN JUSTICE AND UTILITY

In all ages of speculation one of the strongest obstacles to the reception of the doctrine that utility or happiness is the criterion of right and wrong has been drawn from the idea of justice. The powerful sentiment and apparently clear perception which that word recalls with a rapidity and certainty resembling an instinct have seemed to the majority of thinkers to point to an inherent quality in things; to show that the just must have an existence in nature as something absolute, generically distinct from every variety of the expedient and, in idea, opposed to it, though (as is commonly acknowledged) never, in the long run, disjoined from it in fact. . . .

The idea of justice supposes two things—a rule of conduct and a sentiment which sanctions the rule. The first must be supposed common to all mankind and intended for their good. The other (the sentiment) is a desire that punishment may be suffered by those who infringe the rule. There is involved, in addition, the conception of some definite person who suffers by the infringement, whose rights (to use the expression appropriated to the case) are violated by it. And the sentiment of justice appears to me to be the animal desire to repel or retaliate a hurt or damage to oneself or to those with whom one sympathizes, widened so as to include all persons, by the human capacity of enlarged sympathy and the human conception of intelligent self-interest. From the latter elements the feeling derives its morality; from the former, its peculiar impressiveness and energy of self-assertion.

I have, throughout, treated the idea of a *right* residing in the injured person and violated by the injury, not as a separate element in the composition of the idea and sentiment, but as one of the forms in which the other two elements clothe themselves. These elements are a hurt to some assignable person or persons, on the one hand, and a demand for punishment, on the other. An examination of our own minds, I think, will show that these two things include all that we mean when we speak of violation of a right. When we call anything a person's right, we mean that he has a valid claim on society to protect him in the possession of it, either by the force of law or by that of education and opinion. If he has what we consider a sufficient claim, on whatever account, to have something guaranteed to him by society, we say that he has a right to it. If we desire to prove that anything does not belong to him by right, we think this done as soon as it is admitted that society ought not to take measures for securing it to him, but should leave him to chance or to his own exertions. Thus a person is said to have a right to what he can earn in fair professional competition, because society ought not to allow any other person to hinder him from endeavoring to earn in that manner as much as he can. But he has not a right to three hundred a year, though he may happen to be earning it; because society is not called on to provide that he shall earn that sum. On the contrary, if he owns ten thousand pounds three-per-cent stock, he *has* a right to three hundred a year because society has come under an obligation to provide him with an income of that amount.

To have a right, then, is, I conceive, to have something which society ought to defend me in the possession of. If the objective goes on to ask why it ought, I can give him no other reason than general utility. If that expression does not seem to convey a sufficient feeling of the strength of the obligation, nor to account for the peculiar energy of the feeling, it is because there goes to the composition of the sentiment, not a rational only but also an animal element—the thirst for retaliation; and this thirst derives its intensity, as well as its moral justification, from the extraordinarily important and impressive kind of utility which is concerned. The interest involved is that of security, to everyone's feelings the most vital of all interests. All other earthly benefits are needed by one person, not needed by another; and many of them can, if necessary, be cheerfully forgone or replaced by something else; but security no human being can possibly do without; on it we depend for all our immunity from evil and for the whole value of all and every good, beyond the passing moment, since nothing but the gratification of the instant could be of any worth to us if we could be deprived of everything the next instant by whoever was momentarily stronger than ourselves. Now this most indispensable of all necessaries, after physical nutriment, cannot be had unless the machinery for providing it is kept unintermittedly in active play. Our notion, therefore, of the claim we have on our fellow creatures to join in making safe for us the very groundwork of our existence gathers feelings around it so much more intense than those concerned in any of the more common cases of utility that the difference in degree (as is often the case in psychology) becomes a real difference in kind. The claim assumes that character of absoluteness, that apparent infinity and incommensurability with all other considerations which constitute the distinction between the feeling of right and wrong and that of ordinary expediency and inexpediency. The feelings concerned are so powerful, and we count so positively on finding a responsive feeling in others (all being alike interested) that *ought* and *should* grow into *must,* and recognized indispensability becomes a moral necessity, analogous to physical, and often not inferior to it in binding force.

If the preceding analysis, or something resembling it, be not the correct account of the notion of justice—if justice be totally independent of utility, and be a standard *per se,* which the mind can recognize by simple introspection of itself—it is hard to understand why that internal oracle is so ambiguous, and why so many things appear either just or unjust, according to the light in which they are regarded. . . .

It appears from what has been said that justice is a name for certain moral requirements which, regarded collectively, stand higher in the scale of social utility, and are therefore of more paramount obligation, than any others, though particular cases may occur in which some other social duty is so important as to overrule any one of the general maxims of justice. Thus, to save a life, it may not only be allowable, but a duty, to steal or take by force the necessary food or medicine, or to kidnap and compel to officiate the only qualified medical practitioner. In such cases, as we do not call anything justice which is not a virtue, we usually say, not that justice must give way to some other moral principle, but that what is just in ordinary cases is, by reason of that other principle, not just in the particular case. By this useful accommodation of language, the character of indefeasibility attributed to justice is kept up, and we are saved from the necessity of maintaining that there can be laudable injustice.

The considerations which have not been adduced resolve, I conceive, the only real difficulty in the utilitarian theory of morals. It has always been evident that all cases of justice are also cases of expediency; the difference is in the peculiar sentiment which attaches to the former, as contradistinguished from the latter. If this characteristic sentiment has been sufficiently accounted for; if there is no necessity to assume for it any peculiarity of origin; if it is simply the natural feeling of resentment, moralized by being made coextensive with the demands of social good; and if this feeling not only does but ought to exist in all the classes of cases to which the idea of justice corresponds—that idea no longer presents itself as a stumbling block to the utilitarian ethics.

Justice remains the appropriate name for certain social utilities which are vastly more important, and therefore more absolute and imperative, than any others are as a class (though not more so than others may be in particular cases); and which, therefore, ought to be, as well as naturally are, guarded by a sentiment, not only different in degree, but also in kind; distinguished from the milder feeling which attaches to the mere idea of promoting human pleasure or convenience at once by the more definite nature of its commands and by the sterner character of its sanctions.

RELATED WEB SITES

Mill biography: www.utm.edu/research/iep/m/milljs.htm

A discussion of deontological and consequentialist frameworks:
www.princeton.edu/~kenlee/pub/cs291weeks5.html

A Fundamental Objection to Tax Equity Norms: A Call for Utilitarianism:
wuecon.wustl.edu/%7eadnetec/WoPEc/aleapa/aleapa_015.html

Full text of *Utilitarianism:*
www.republic.k12.mo.us/highschool/sstudies/block/eur/mil/util.txt

COST-BENEFIT ANALYSIS: AN ETHICAL CRITIQUE

Steven Kelman

Cost-benefit analysis is one application of utilitarian theory. It is perhaps the one most often used in the business environment, though it is not without its critics. Consider as you read this and the following article what problems are inherent in a strict cost-benefit analysis or where such an analysis might lead to a flawed (or unethical?) result.

At the broadest and vaguest level, cost-benefit analysis may be regarded simply as systematic thinking about decision making. Who can oppose, economists sometimes ask, efforts to think in a systematic way about the consequences of different courses of action? The alternative, it would appear, is unexamined decision making. But defining cost-benefit analysis so simply leaves it with few implications for actual regulatory decision making. Presumably, therefore, those who urge regulators to make greater use of the technique have a more extensive prescription in mind. I assume here that their prescription includes the following views:

1. There exists a strong presumption that an act should not be undertaken unless its benefits outweigh its costs.
2. In order to determine whether benefits outweigh costs, it is desirable to attempt to express all benefits and costs in a common scale or denominator, so that they can be compared with each other, even when some benefits and costs are not traded on markets and hence have no established dollar values.
3. Getting decision-makers to make more use of cost-benefit techniques is important enough to warrant both the expense required to gather the data for improved cost-benefit estimation and the political efforts needed to give the activity higher priority compared to other activities, also valuable in and of themselves.

My focus is on cost-benefit analysis as applied to environmental safety, and health regulation. In that context, I examine each of the above propositions from the perspective of formal ethical theory, that is, the study of what actions it is morally right to undertake. My conclusions are:

1. In areas of environmental, safety, and health regulation, there may be many instances where a certain decision might be right even though its benefits do not outweigh its costs.

Steven Kelman, "Cost-Benefit Analysis: An Ethical Critique," Reprinted with permission of The American Enterprise Institute for Public Policy Research, Washington, DC.

2. There are good reasons to oppose efforts to put dollar values on non-marketed benefits and costs.
3. Given the relative frequency of occasions in the areas of environmental, safety, and
   health regulation where one would not wish to use a benefits-outweigh-costs test as a
   decision rule, and given the reasons to oppose the monetizing of non-marketed benefits or costs that is a prerequisite for cost-benefit analysis, it is not justifiable to devote major resources to the generation of data for cost-benefit calculations or to undertake efforts to "spread the gospel" of cost-benefit analysis further. . . .

II

In order for cost-benefit calculations to be performed the way they are supposed to be, all
costs and benefits must be expressed in a common measure, typically dollars, including
things not normally bought and sold on markets, and to which dollar prices are therefore
not attached. The most dramatic examples of such things is human life itself; but many of
the other benefits achieved or preserved by environmental policy—such as peace and
quiet, fresh-smelling air, swimmable rivers, spectacular vistas—are not traded on markets
either.

Economists who do cost-benefit analysis regard the quest after dollar values for non-
market things as a difficult challenge—but one to be met with relish. They have tried to
develop methods for imputing a person's "willingness to pay" for such things, their approach generally involving a search for bundled goods that *are* traded on markets and that
vary as to whether they include a feature that is, *by itself,* not marketed. Thus, fresh air is
not marketed, but houses in different parts of Los Angeles that are similar except for the
degree of smog are. Peace and quiet is not marketed, but similar houses inside and outside airport flight paths are. The risk of death is not marketed, but similar jobs that have
different levels of risk are. Economists have produced many often ingenious efforts to
impute dollar prices to non-marketed things by observing the premiums accorded homes
in clean air areas over similar homes in dirty areas or the premiums paid for risky jobs
over similar nonrisky jobs.

These ingenious efforts are subject to criticism on a number of technical grounds. It
may be difficult to control for all the dimensions of quality other than the presence or absence of the non-marketed thing. More important, in a world where people have different
preferences and are subject to different constraints as they make their choices, the dollar
value imputed to the non-market things that most people would wish to avoid will be
lower than otherwise, because people with unusually weak aversion to those things or unusually strong constraints on their choices will be willing to take the bundled good in
question at less of a discount than the average person. Thus, to use the property value discount of homes near airports as a measure of people's willingness to pay for quiet means
to accept as a proxy for the rest of us the behavior of those least sensitive to noise, or airport employees (who value the convenience of a near-airport location), or of others who
are susceptible to an agent's assurances that "it's not so bad." To use the wage premiums
accorded hazardous work as a measure of the value of life means to accept as proxies for
the rest of us the choices of people who do not have many choices or who are exceptional
risk-seekers.

A second problem is that the attempts of economists to measure people's willingness to pay for non-marketed things assume that there is no difference between the price a person would require for *giving up* something to which he has a preexisting right and the price he would pay to *gain* something to which he enjoys no right. Thus, the analysis assumes no difference between how much a homeowner would need to be paid in order to give up an unobstructed mountain view that he already enjoys and how much he would be willing to pay to get an obstruction moved once it is already in place. Available evidence suggests that most people would insist on being paid far more to assent to a worsening of their situation than they would be willing to pay to improve their situation. The difference arises from such factors as being accustomed to and psychologically attached to that which one believes one enjoys by right. But this creates a circularity problem for any attempt to use cost-benefit analysis to determine *whether* to assign to, say, the homeowner the right to an unobstructed mountain view. For willingness to pay will be different depending on whether the right is assigned initially or not. The value judgment about whether to assign the right must thus be made first. (In order to set an upper bound on the value of the benefit, one might hypothetically assign the right to the person and determine how much he would need to be paid to give it up.)

Third, the efforts of economists to impute willingness to pay invariably involve bundled goods exchanged in *private* transactions. Those who use figures garnered from such analysis to provide guidance for public decisions assume no difference between how people value certain things in private individual transactions and how they would wish those same things to be valued in public collective decisions. In making such assumptions, economists insidiously slip into their analysis an important and controversial value judgment, growing naturally out of the highly individualistic microeconomic tradition—namely, the view that there should be no difference between private behavior and the behavior we display in public social life. An alternative view—one that enjoys, I would suggest, wide resonance among citizens—would be that public, social decisions provide an opportunity to give certain things a higher valuation than we choose, for one reason or another, to give them in our private activities.

Thus, opponents of stricter regulation of health risks often argue that we show by our daily risk-taking behavior that we do not value life infinitely, and therefore our public decisions should not reflect the high value of life that proponents of strict regulation propose. However, an alternative view is equally plausible. Precisely because we fail, for whatever reasons, to give life-saving the value in everyday personal decisions that we in some general terms believe we should give it, we may wish our social decisions to provide us the occasion to display the reverence for life that we espouse but do not always show. By this view, people do not have fixed-unambiguous "preferences" to which they give expression through private activities and which therefore should be given expression in public decisions. Rather, they may have what they themselves regard as "higher" and "lower" preferences. The latter may come to the fore in private decisions, but people may want the former to come to the fore in public decisions. They may sometimes display racial prejudice, but support antidiscrimination laws. They may buy a certain product after seeing a seductive ad, but be skeptical enough of advertising to want the government to keep a close eye on it. In such cases, the use of private behavior to impute the values that should be entered for public decisions, as is done by using willingness to pay in private transactions, commits grievous offense against a view of the behavior of the citizen that is deeply engrained in our democratic tradition. It is a view that denudes politics of any independent role in society, reducing it to a mechanistic, mimicking recalculation based on private behavior.

Finally, one may oppose the effort to place prices on a non-market thing and hence in effect incorporate it into the market system out of a fear that the very act of doing so will reduce the thing's perceived value. To place a price on the benefit may, in other words, reduce the value of that benefit. Cost-benefit analysis thus may be like the thermometer that, when placed in a liquid to be measured, itself changes the liquid's temperature.

Examples of the perceived cheapening of a thing's value by the very act of buying and selling it abound in everyday life and language. The disgust that accompanies the idea of buying and selling human beings is based on the sense that this would dramatically diminish human worth. Epithets such as "he prostituted himself," applied as linguistic analogies to people who have sold something, reflect the view that certain things should not be sold because doing so diminishes their value. Praise that is bought is worth little, even to the person buying it. A true anecdote is told of an economist who retired to another university community and complained that he was having difficulty making friends. The laconic response of a critical colleague—"If you want a friend why don't you buy yourself one"—illustrates in a pithy way the intuition that, for some things, the very act of placing a price on them reduces their perceived value.

The first reason that pricing something decreases its perceived value is that, in many circumstances, non-market exchange is associated with the production of certain values not associated with market exchange. These may include spontaneity and various other feelings that come from personal relationships. If a good becomes less associated with the production of positively valued feelings because of market exchange, the perceived value of the good declines to the extent that those feelings are valued. This can be seen clearly in instances where a thing may be transferred both by market and by non-market mechanism. The willingness to pay for sex bought from a prostitute is less than the perceived value of the sex consummating love. (Imagine the reaction if a practitioner of cost-benefit analysis computed the benefits of sex based on the price of prostitute services.)

Furthermore, if one values in a general sense the existence of a non-market sector because of its connection with the production of certain valued feelings, then one ascribes added value to any non-marketed good simply as a repository of values represented by the non-market sector one wishes to preserve. This seems certainly to be the case for things in nature, such as pristine streams or undisturbed forests: for many people who value them, part of their value comes from their position as repositories of values the non-market sector represents.

The second way in which placing a market price on a thing decreases its perceived value is by removing the possibility of proclaiming that the thing is "not for sale," since things on the market by definition are for sale. The very statement that something is not for sale affirms, enhances, and protects a thing's value in a number of ways. To begin with, the statement is a way of showing that a thing is valued for its own sake, whereas selling a thing for money demonstrates that it was valued only instrumentally. Furthermore, to say that something cannot be transferred in that way places it in the exceptional category—which requires the person interested in obtaining that thing to be able to offer something else that is exceptional, rather than allowing him the easier alternative of obtaining the thing for money that could have been obtained in an infinity of ways. This enhances its value. If I am willing to say "You're a really kind person" to whoever pays me to do so, my praise loses the value that attaches to it from being exchangeable only for an act of kindness.

In addition, if we have already decided we value something highly, one way of stamping it with a cachet affirming its high value is to announce that it is "not for sale." Such an announcement does more, however, than just reflect a preexisting high valuation. It signals a thing's distinctive value to others and helps us persuade them to value the thing more highly than they otherwise might. It also expresses our resolution to safeguard that distinctive value. To state that something is not for sale is thus also a source of value for that thing, since if a thing's value is easy to affirm or protect, it will be worth more than an otherwise similar thing without such attributes.

If we proclaim that something is not for sale, we make a once-and-for-all judgment of its special value. When something is priced, the issue of its perceived value is constantly coming up, as a standing invitation to reconsider that original judgment. Were people constantly faced with questions such as "how much money could get you to give up your freedom of speech?" or "how much would you sell your vote for if you could?" the perceived value of the freedom to speak or the right to vote would soon become devastated as, in moments of weakness, people started saying "maybe it's not worth *so much* after all." Better not to be faced with the constant questioning in the first place. Something similar did in fact occur when the slogan "better red than dead" was launched by some pacifists during the Cold War. Critics pointed out that the very posing of this stark choice—in effect, "would you *really* be willing to give up your life in exchange for not living under communism?"—reduced the value people attached to freedom and thus diminished resistance to attacks on freedom.

Finally, of some things valued very highly it is stated that they are "priceless" or that they have "infinite value." Such expressions are reserved for a subset of things not for sale, such as life or health. Economists tend to scoff at talk of pricelessness. For them, saying that something is priceless is to state a willingness to trade off an infinite quantity of all other goods for one unit of the priceless good, a situation that empirically appears highly unlikely. For most people, however, the word priceless is pregnant with meaning. Its value-affirming and value-protecting functions cannot be bestowed on expressions that merely denote a determinate, albeit high, valuation. John Kennedy in his inaugural address proclaimed that the nation was ready to "pay any price [and] bear any burden . . . to assure the survival and the success of liberty." Had he said instead that we were willing to "pay a high price" or "bear a large burden" for liberty, the statement would have rung hollow.

III

An objection that advocates of cost-benefit analysis might well make to the preceding argument should be considered. I noted earlier that, in cases where various non-utility-based duties or rights conflict with the maximization of utility, it is necessary to make a deliberative judgment about what act is finally right. I also argued earlier that the search for commensurability might not always be a desirable one, that the attempt to go beyond expressing benefits in terms of (say) lives saved and costs in terms of dollars is not something devoutly to be wished.

In situations involving things that are not expressed in a common measure, advocates of cost-benefit analysis argue that people making judgments "in effect" perform cost-benefit calculations anyway. If government regulators promulgate a regulation that saves 100 lives at a cost of $1 billion, they are "in effect" valuing a life at (a minimum of) $10 million, whether or not they say that they are willing to place a dollar value on a human life. Since, in this view, cost-benefit analysis "in effect" is inevitable, it might as well be made specific.

This argument misconstrues the real difference in the reasoning processes involved. In cost-benefit analysis, equivalencies are established *in advance* as one of the raw materials for the calculation. One determines costs and benefits, one determines equivalencies (to be able to put various costs and benefits into a common measure), and then one sets to toting things up—waiting, as it were, with bated breath for the results of the calculation to come out. The outcome is determined by the arithmetic; if the outcome is a close call or if one is not good at long division, one does not know how it will turn out until the calculation is finished. In the kind of deliberative judgment that is performed without a common measure, no establishment of equivalencies occurs in advance. Equivalencies are not aids to the decision process. In fact, the decision-maker might not even be aware of what the "in effect" equivalencies were, at least before they are revealed to him afterwards by someone pointing out what he had "in effect" done. The decision-maker would see himself as simply having made a deliberative judgment; the "in effect" equivalency number did not play a causal role in the decision but at most merely reflects it. Given this, the argument against making the process explicit is the one discussed earlier in the discussion of problems with putting specific quantified values on things that are not normally quantified—that the very act of doing so may serve to reduce the value of those things.

My own judgment is that modest efforts to assess levels of benefits and costs are justified, although I do not believe that government agencies ought to sponsor efforts to put dollar prices on non-market things. I also do not believe that the cry for more cost-benefit analysis in regulation is, on the whole, justified. If regulatory officials were so insensitive about regulatory costs that they did not provide acceptable raw material for deliberative judgments (even if not of a strictly cost-benefit nature), my conclusion might be different. But a good deal of research into costs and benefits already occurs—actually, far more in the U.S. regulatory process than in that of any other industrial society. The danger now would seem to come more from the other side.

RELATED WEB SITES

Cost-benefit analysis and regulatory reform:
www.riskworld.com/tcnetwrk/riskwrld/nreports/1996/risk_rpt/html/nr6
aa048.htm

Devaluing life: Exposing the flaw of utilitarian ethics:
www.compumedia.com/~treit/files/utility.asc

DEFENDING COST-BENEFIT ANALYSIS: REPLIES TO STEVEN KELMAN

James V. DeLong

Steven Kelman's "Cost-Benefit Analysis—An Ethical Critique" presents so many targets that it is difficult to concentrate one's fire. However, four points seem worth particular emphasis:

(1)   The decision to use cost-benefit analysis by no means implies adoption of the reductionist utilitarianism described by Kelman. It is based instead on the pragmatic conclusion that any value system one adopts is more likely to be promoted if one knows something about the consequences of the choices to be made. The effort to put dollar values on noneconomic benefits is nothing more than an effort to find some common measure for things that are not easily comparable when, in the real world, choice must be made. Its object is not to write a computer program but to improve the quality of difficult social choices under conditions of uncertainty, and no sensible analyst lets himself become the prisoner of the numbers.

(2)   Kelman repeatedly lapses into "entitlement" rhetoric, as if an assertion of a moral claim closes an argument. Even leaving aside the fundamental question of the philosophical basis of those entitlements, there are two major problems with this style of argument. First, it tends naturally toward all-encompassing claims.

Kelman quotes a common statement that "workers have a right to a safe and healthy workplace," a statement that contains no recognition that safety and health are not either/or conditions, that the most difficult questions involve gradations of risk, and that the very use of entitlement language tends to assume that a zero-risk level is the only acceptable one. Second, entitlement rhetoric is usually phrased in the passive voice, as if the speaker were arguing with some omnipotent god or government that is maliciously withholding the entitlement out of spite. In the real world, one person's right is another's duty, and it often clarifies the discussion to focus more precisely on who owes this duty and what it is going to cost him or her. For example, the article posits that an issue in government decisions about acceptable pollution levels is "the right" of such vulnerable groups as asthmatics or the elderly "not to be sacrificed on

"Defending Cost-Benefit Analysis: Replies to Steven Kelman," by James V. DeLong, Reprinted with permission of The American Enterprise Institute for Public Policy Research, Washington, DC.

the altar of somewhat higher living standards for the rest of us." This defends the entitlement by assuming the costs involved are both trivial and diffused. Suppose, though, that the price to be paid is not "somewhat higher living standards," but the jobs of a number of workers?

Kelman's counter to this seems to be that entitlements are not firm rights, but only presumptive ones that prevail in any clash with nonentitlements, and that when two entitlements collide the decision depends upon the "moral importance we attach to the right or duty involved." So the above collision would be resolved by deciding whether a job is an entitlement and, if it is, by then deciding whether jobs or air have greater "moral importance."

I agree that conflicts between such interests present difficult choices, but the quantitative questions, the cost-benefit questions, are hardly irrelevant to making them. Suppose taking X quantity of pollution from the air of a city will keep one asthmatic from being forced to leave town and cost 1,000 workers their jobs? Suppose it will keep 1,000 asthmatics from being forced out and cost one job? These are not equivalent choices, economically or morally, and the effort to decide them according to some abstract idea of moral importance only obscures the true nature of the moral problems involved.

(3)   Kelman also develops the concept of things that are "specially valued," and that are somehow contaminated if thought about in monetary terms. As an approach to personal decision making, this is silly. There are many things one specially values—in the sense that one would find the effort to assign a market price to them ridiculous—which are nonetheless affected by economic factors. I may specially value a family relationship, but how often I phone is influenced by long-distance rates. I may specially value music, but be affected by the price of records or the cost of tickets at the Kennedy Center.

When translated to the realm of government decisions, however, the concept goes beyond silliness. It creates a political grotesquerie. People specially value many different things. Under Kelman's assumptions, people must, in creating a political coalition, recognize and accept as legitimate everyone's special value; without concern for cost. Therefore, everyone becomes entitled to as much of the thing he specially values as he says he specially values, and it is immoral to discuss vulgar questions of resource limitations. Any coalition built on such premises can go in either of two directions: It can try to incorporate so many different groups and interests that the absurdity of its internal contradictions becomes manifest. Or it can limit its membership at some point and decide that the special values of those left outside are not legitimate and should be sacrificed to the special values of those in the coalition. In the latter case, of course, those outside must be made scapegoats for any frustration of any group member's entitlement, a requirement that eventually leads to political polarization and a holy war between competing coalitions of special values.

(4)   The decisions that must be made by contemporary government indeed involve painful choices. They affect both the absolute quantity and the distribution not only of goods and benefits, but also of physical and mental suffering. It is easy to understand why people would want to avoid making such choices and would rather act in ignorance than with knowledge and responsibility for the consequences of their choices. While this

may be understandable, I do not regard it as an acceptable moral position. To govern is to choose, and government officials—whether elected or appointed—betray their obligations to the welfare of the people who hired them if they adopt a policy of happy ignorance and nonresponsibility for consequences.

The article concludes with the judgment that the present danger is too much cost-benefit analysis, not too little. But I find it hard to believe, looking around the modern world, that its major problem is that it suffers from an excess of rationality. The world's stock of ignorance is and will remain quite large enough without adding to it as a matter of deliberate policy.

RELATED WEB SITE

American Enterprise Institute for Public Policy Research: www.aei.org

DISTRIBUTIVE JUSTICE

John Rawls

Contemporary Harvard philosopher John Rawls is known as the father of an ethical theory called distributive justice, which holds that ethical acts or decisions are those that lead to an equitable distribution of goods and services. His description of this approach follows below.

We may think of a human society as a more or less self-sufficient association regulated by a common conception of justice and aimed at advancing the good of its members.[1] As a co-operative venture for mutual advantage, it is characterized by a conflict as well as an identity of interests. There is an identity of interests since social co-operation makes possible a better life for all than any would have if everyone were to try to live by his own efforts; yet at the same time men are not indifferent as to how the greater benefits produced by their joint labours are distributed, for in order to further their own aims each prefers a larger to a lesser share. A conception of justice is a set of principles for choosing between the social arrangements which determine this division and for underwriting a consensus as to the proper distributive shares.

Now at first sight the most rational conception of justice would seem to be utilitarian. For consider: each man in realizing his own good can certainly balance his own losses against his own gains. We can impose a sacrifice on ourselves now for the sake of a greater advantage later. A man quite properly acts, as long as others are not affected, to achieve his own greatest good, to advance his ends as far as possible. Now, why should not a society act on precisely the same principle? Why is not that which is rational in the case of one man right in the case of a group of men? Surely the simplest and most direct conception of the right, and so of justice, is that of maximizing the good. This assumes a prior understanding of what is good, but we can think of the good as already given by the interests of rational individuals. Thus just as the principle of individual choice is to achieve one's greatest good, to advance so far as possible one's own system of rational desires, so the principle of social choice is to realize the greatest good (similarly defined) summed over all the members of society. We arrive at the principle of utility in a natural way: by this principle a society is rightly ordered, and hence just, when its institutions are arranged so as to realize the greatest sum of satisfactions.

The striking feature of the principle of utility is that it does not matter, except indirectly, how this sum of satisfactions is distributed among individuals, any more than it matters, except indirectly, how one man distributes his satisfactions over time. Since certain ways of distributing things affect the total sum of satisfactions, this fact must be taken into account in arranging social institutions; but according to this principle the explanation of common-sense precepts of justice and their seemingly stringent character is

---

John Rawls, "Distributive Justice," Reprinted by permission of the author.

that they are those rules which experience shows must be strictly respected and departed from only under exceptional circumstances if the sum of advantages is to be maximized. The precepts of justice are derivative from the one end of attaining the greatest net balance of satisfactions. There is no reason in principle why the greater gains of some should not compensate for the lesser losses of others; or why the violation of the liberty of a few might not be made right by a greater good shared by many. It simply happens, at least under most conditions, that the greatest sum of advantages is not generally achieved in this way. From the standpoint of utility the strictness of common-sense notions of justice has a certain usefulness, but as a philosophical doctrine it is irrational.

If, then, we believe that as a matter of principle each member of society has an inviolability founded on justice which even the welfare of everyone else cannot override, and that a loss of freedom for some is not made right by a greater sum of satisfaction enjoyed by many, we shall have to look for another account of the principles of justice. The principle of utility is incapable of explaining the fact that in a just society the liberties of equal citizenship are taken for granted, and the rights secured by justice are not subject to political bargaining nor to the calculus of social interests. Now, the most natural alternative to the principle of utility is its traditional rival, the theory of the social contract. The aim of the contract doctrine is precisely to account for the strictness of justice by supposing that its principles arise from an agreement among free and independent persons in an original position of equality and hence reflect the integrity and equal sovereignty of the rational persons who are the contractees. Instead of supposing that a conception of right, and so a conception of justice, is simply an extension of the principle of choice for one man to society as a whole, the contract doctrine assumes that the rational individuals who belong to society must choose together, in one joint act, what is to count among them as just and unjust. They are to decide among themselves once and for all what is to be their conception of justice. This decision is thought of as being made in a suitably defined initial situation one of the significant features of which is that no one knows his position in society, nor even his place in the distribution of natural talents and abilities. The principles of justice to which all are forever bound are chosen in the absence of this sort of specific information. A veil of ignorance prevents anyone from being advantaged or disadvantaged by the contingencies of social class and fortune; and hence the bargaining problems which arise in everyday life from the possession of this knowledge do not affect the choice of principles. On the contract doctrine, then, the theory of justice, and indeed ethics itself, is part of the general theory of rational choice, a fact perfectly clear in its Kantian formulation.

Once justice is thought of as arising from an original agreement of this kind, it is evident that the principle of utility is problematical. For why should rational individuals who have a system of ends they wish to advance agree to a violation of their liberty for the sake of a greater balance of satisfactions enjoyed by others? It seems more plausible to suppose that, when situated in an original position of equal right, they would insist upon institutions which returned compensating advantages for any sacrifices required. A rational man would not accept an institution merely because it maximized the sum of advantages irrespective of its effect on his own interests. It appears, then, that the principle of utility would be rejected as a principle of justice, although we shall not try to argue this important question here. Rather, our aim is to give a brief sketch of the conception of distributive shares implicit in the principles of justice which, it seems would be chosen in the original position. The philosophical appeal of utilitarianism is that it seems to offer a single principle on the basis of which a consistent and complete conception of right can be developed. The problem is to work out a contractarian alternative in such a way that it has comparable if not all the same virtues.

In our discussion we shall make no attempt to derive the two principles of justice which we shall examine; that is, we shall not try to show that they would be chosen in the original position.[2] It must suffice that it is plausible that they would be, at least in preference to the standard forms of traditional theories. Instead we shall be mainly concerned with three questions: first, how to interpret these principles so that they define a consistent and complete conception of justice; second, whether it is possible to arrange the institutions of a constitutional democracy so that these principles are satisfied, at least approximately; and third, whether the conception of distributive shares which they define is compatible with common-sense notions of justice. The significance of these principles is that they allow for the strictness of the claims of justice; and if they can be understood so as to yield a consistent and complete conception, the contractarian alternative would seem all the more attractive.

The two principles of justice which we shall discuss may be formulated as follows: first, each person engaged in an institution or affected by it has an equal right to the most extensive liberty compatible with a like liberty for all; and second, inequalities as defined by the institutional structure or fostered by it are arbitrary unless it is reasonable to expect that they will work out to everyone's advantage and provided that the positions and offices to which they attach or from which they may be gained are open to all. These principles regulate the distributive aspects of institutions by controlling the assignment of rights and duties throughout the whole social structure, beginning with the adoption of a political constitution in accordance with which they are then to be applied to legislation. It is upon a correct choice of a basic structure of society, its fundamental system of rights and duties, that the justice of distributive shares depends.

The two principles of justice apply in the first instance to this basic structure, that is, to the main institutions of the social system and their arrangement, how they are combined together. Thus, this structure includes the political constitution and the principal economic and social institutions which together define a person's liberties and rights and affect his life-prospects, what he may expect to be and how well he may expect to fare. The intuitive idea here is that those born into the social system at different positions, say, in different social classes, have varying life-prospects determined, in part, by the system of political liberties and personal rights, and by the economic and social opportunities which are made available to these positions. In this way the basic structure of society favours certain men over others, and these are the basic inequalities, the ones which affect their whole life-prospects. It is inequalities of this kind, presumably inevitable in any society, with which the two principles of justice are primarily designed to deal.

Now the second principle holds that an inequality is allowed only if there is reason to believe that the institution with the inequality, or permitting it, will work out for the advantage of every person engaged in it. In the case of the basic structure this means that all inequalities which affect life-prospects, say, the inequalities of income and wealth which exist between social classes, must be to the advantage of everyone. Since the principle applies to institutions, we interpret this to mean that inequalities must be to the advantage of the representative man for each relevant social position; they should improve each such man's expectation. Here we assume that it is possible to attach to each position an expectation, and that this expectation is a function of the whole institutional structure: it can be raised and lowered by reassigning rights and duties throughout the system. Thus the expectation of any position depends upon the expectations of the others, and these in turn depend upon the pattern of rights and duties established by the basic structure. But it is not clear what is meant by saying that inequalities must be to the advantage of every representative man. . . . [One] . . . interpretation [of what is meant by saying that inequalities must be to the advantage of every representative man] . . . is to choose some social position by reference to which the pattern of expectations as a whole is to be judged, and then to maximize with respect to the expectations of this representative man consistent with the demands of equal liberty and equality of opportunity. Now, the one obvious candidate is the representative man of those who are least favoured by the system of institutional inequalities. Thus we arrive at the following idea: the basic structure of the social system affects the life-prospects of typical individuals according to their initial places in society, say, the various income classes into which they are born, or depending upon certain natural attributes, as when institutions make discriminations between men and women or allow certain advantages to be gained by those with greater natural abilities. The fundamental problem of distributive justice concerns the differences in life-prospects which come about in this way. We interpret the second principle to hold that these differences are just if and only if the greater expectations of the more advantaged, when playing a part in the working of the whole social system, improve the expectations of the least advantaged. The basic structure is just throughout when the advantages of the more fortunate promote the well-being of the least fortunate, that is, when a decrease in their advantages would make the least fortunate even worse off than they are. The basic structure is perfectly just when the prospects of the least fortunate are as great as they can be.

In interpreting the second principle (or rather the first part of it which we may, for obvious reasons, refer to as the difference principle), we assume that the first principle requires a basic equal liberty for all, and that the resulting political system, when circumstances permit, is that of a constitutional democracy in some form. There must be liberty of the person and political equality as well as liberty of conscience and freedom of thought. There is one class of equal citizens which defines a common status for all. We also assume that there is equality of opportunity and a fair competition for the available positions on the basis of reasonable qualifications. Now, given this background, the differences to be justified are the various economic and social inequalities in the basic structure which must inevitably arise in such a scheme. These are the inequalities in the distribution of income and wealth and the distinctions in social prestige and status which attach to the various positions and classes. The difference principle says that these inequalities are just if and only if they are part of a larger system in which they work out to the advantage of the most unfortunate representative man. The just distributive shares determined by the basic structure are those specified by this constrained maximum principle.

Thus, consider the chief problem of distributive justice, that concerning the distribution of wealth as it affects the life-prospects of those starting out in the various income

groups. These income classes define the relevant representative men from which the social system is to be judged. Now, a son of a member of the entrepreneurial class (in a capitalist society) has a better prospect than that of the son of an unskilled labourer. This will
be true, it seems, even when the social injustices which presently exist are removed and
the two men are of equal talent and ability; the inequality cannot be done away with as
long as something like the family is maintained. What, then, can justify this inequality in
life-prospects? According to the second principle it is justified only if it is to the advantage of the representative man who is worse off, in this case the representative unskilled
labourer. The inequality is permissible because lowering it would, let's suppose, make
the working man even worse off than he is. Presumably, given the principle of open offices (the second part of the second principle), the greater expectations allowed to entrepreneurs has the effect in the longer run of raising the life-prospects of the labouring
class. The inequality in expectation provides an incentive so that the economy is more efficient, industrial advance proceeds at a quicker pace, and so on, the end result of which
is that greater material and other benefits are distributed throughout the system. Of
course, all of this is familiar, and whether true or not in particular cases, it is the sort of
thing which must be argued if the inequality in income and wealth is to be acceptable by
the difference principle.

We should now verify that this interpretation of the second principle gives a natural
sense in which everyone may be said to be made better off. Let us suppose that inequalities are chain-connected: that is, if an inequality raises the expectations of the lowest position, it raises the expectations of all positions in between. For example, if the greater expectations of the representative entrepreneur raises that of the unskilled labourer, it also
raises that of the semi-skilled. Let us further assume that inequalities are close-knit: that
is, it is impossible to raise (or lower) the expectation of any representative man without
raising (or lowering) the expectations of every other representative man, and in particular,
without affecting one way or the other that of the least fortunate. There is no loose-
jointedness, so to speak, in the way in which expectations depend upon one another. Now
with these assumptions, everyone does benefit from an inequality which satisfies the difference principle, and the second principle as we have formulated it reads correctly. For
the representative man who is better off in any pair-wise comparison gains by being allowed to have his advantage, and the man who is worse off benefits from the contribution
which all inequalities make to each position below. Of course, chain-connection and
close-knitness may not obtain; but in this case those who are better off should not have a
veto over the advantages available for the least advantaged. The stricter interpretation of
the difference principle should be followed, and all inequalities should be arranged for
the advantage of the most unfortunate even if some inequalities are not to the advantage
of those in middle positions. Should these conditions fail, then, the second principle
would have to be stated in another way.

It may be observed that the difference principle represents, in effect, an original
agreement to share in the benefits of the distribution of natural talents and abilities, whatever this distribution turns out to be, in order to alleviate as far as possible the arbitrary
handicaps resulting from our initial starting places in society. Those who have been
favoured by nature, whoever they are, may gain from their good fortune only on terms
that improve the well-being of those who have lost out. The naturally advantaged are not

to gain simply because they are more gifted, but only to cover the costs of training and cultivating their endowments and for putting them to use in a way which improved the position of the less fortunate. We are led to the difference principle if we wish to arrange the basic social structure so that no one gains (or loses) from his luck in the natural lottery of talent and ability, or from his initial place in society, without giving (or receiving) compensating advantages in return. (The parties in the original position are not said to be attracted by this idea and so agree to it; rather, given the symmetries of their situation, and particularly their lack of knowledge, and so on, they will find it to their interest to agree to a principle which can be understood in this way.) And we should note also that when the difference principle is perfectly satisfied, the basic structure is optimal by the efficiency principle. There is no way to make anyone better off without making someone worse off, namely, the least fortunate representative man. Thus the two principles of justice define distributive shares in a way compatible with efficiency, at least as long as we move on this highly abstract level. If we want to say (as we do, although it cannot be argued here) that the demands of justice have an absolute weight with respect to efficiency, this claim may seem less paradoxical when it is kept in mind that perfectly just institutions are also efficient.

Our second question is whether it is possible to arrange the institutions of a constitutional democracy so that the two principles of justice are satisfied, at least approximately. We shall try to show that this can be done provided the government regulates a free economy in a certain way. More fully, if law and government act effectively to keep markets competitive, resources fully employed, property and wealth widely distributed over time, and to maintain the appropriate social minimum, then if there is equality of opportunity underwritten by education for all, the resulting distribution will be just. Of course, all of these arrangements and policies are familiar. The only novelty in the following remarks, if there is any novelty at all, is that this framework of institutions can be made to satisfy the difference principle. To argue this, we must sketch the relations of these institutions and how they work together.

First of all, we assume that the basic social structure is controlled by a just constitution which secures the various liberties of equal citizenship. Thus the legal order is administered in accordance with the principle of legality, and liberty of conscience and freedom of thought are taken for granted. The political process is conducted, so far as possible, as a just procedure for choosing between governments and for enacting just legislation. From the standpoint of distributive justice, it is also essential that there be equality of opportunity in several senses. Thus, we suppose that, in addition to maintaining the usual social overhead capital, government provides for equal educational opportunities for all either by subsidizing private schools or by operating a public school system. It also enforces and underwrites equality of opportunity in commercial ventures and in the free choice of occupation. This result is achieved by policing business behaviour and by preventing the establishment of barriers and restriction to the desirable positions and markets. Lastly, there is a guarantee of a social minimum which the government meets by family allowances and special payments in times of unemployment, or by a negative income tax.

In maintaining this system of institutions the government may be thought of as divided into four branches. Each branch is represented by various agencies (or activities thereof) charged with preserving certain social and economic conditions. These branches do not necessarily overlap with the usual organization of government, but should be understood as purely conceptual. Thus the allocation branch is to keep the economy feasibly competitive, that is, to prevent the formation of unreasonable market power. Markets are competitive in this sense when they cannot be made more so consistent with the requirements of efficiency and the acceptance of the facts of consumer preferences and geography. The allocation branch is also charged with identifying and correcting, say, by suitable taxes and subsidies wherever possible, the more obvious departures from efficiency caused by the failure of prices to measure accurately social benefits and costs. The stabilization branch strives to maintain reasonably full employment so that there is no waste through failure to use resources and the free choice of occupation and the deployment of finance is supported by strong effective demand. These two branches together are to preserve the efficiency of the market economy generally.

The social minimum is established through the operations of the transfer branch. Later on we shall consider at what level this minimum should be set, since this is a crucial matter; but for the moment, a few general remarks will suffice. The main idea is that the workings of the transfer branch take into account the precept of need and assign it an appropriate weight with respect to the other common-sense precepts of justice. A market economy ignores the claims of need altogether. Hence there is a division of labour between the parts of the social system as different institutions answer to different common-sense precepts. Competitive markets (properly supplemented by government operations) handle the problem of the efficient allocation of labour and resources and set a weight to the conventional precepts associated with wages and earnings (the precepts of each according to his work and experience, or responsibility and the hazards of the job, and so on), whereas the transfer branch guarantees a certain level of well-being and meets the claims of need. Thus it is obvious that the justice of distributive shares depends upon the whole social system and how it distributes total income, wages plus transfers. There is with reason strong objection to the competitive determination of total income, since this would leave out of account the claims of need and of a decent standard of life. From the standpoint of the original position it is clearly rational to insure oneself against these contingencies. But now, if the appropriate minimum is provided by transfers, it may be perfectly fair that the other part of total income is competitively determined. Moreover, this way of dealing with the claims of need is doubtless more efficient, at least from a theoretical point of view, than trying to regulate prices by minimum wage standards and so on. It is preferable to handle these claims by a separate branch which supports a social minimum. Henceforth, in considering whether the second principle of justice is satisfied, the answer turns on whether the total income of the least advantaged, that is, wages plus transfers, is such as to maximize their long-term expectations consistent with the demands of liberty.

Finally, the distribution branch is to preserve an approximately just distribution of income and wealth over time by affecting the background conditions of the market from period to period. Two aspects of this branch may be distinguished. First of all, it operates a system of inheritance and gift taxes. The aim of these levies is not to raise revenue, but gradually and continually to correct the distribution of wealth and to prevent the concentrations of power to the detriment of liberty and equality of opportunity. It is perfectly true, as some have said,[3] that unequal inheritance of wealth is no more inherently unjust than unequal inheritance of intelligence; as far as possible the inequalities founded on either should satisfy the difference principle. Thus, the inheritance of greater wealth is just as long as it is to the advantage of the worst off and consistent with liberty, including equality of opportunity. Now by the latter we do not mean, of course, the equality of expectations between classes, since differences in life-prospects arising from the basic structure are inevitable, and it is precisely the aim of the second principle to say when these differences are just. Indeed, equality of opportunity is a certain set of institutions which assures equally good education and chances of culture for all and which keeps open the competition for positions on the basis of qualities reasonably related to performance, and so on. It is these institutions which are put in jeopardy when inequalities and concentrations of wealth reach a certain limit; and the taxes imposed by the distribution branch are to prevent this limit from being exceeded. Naturally enough where this limit lies is a matter for political judgment guided by theory, practical experience, and plain hunch; on this question the theory of justice has nothing to say.

The second part of the distribution branch is a scheme of taxation for raising revenue to cover the costs of public goods, to make transfer payments, and the like. This scheme belongs to the distribution branch since the burden of taxation must be justly shared. Although we cannot examine the legal and economic complications involved, there are several points in favour of proportional expenditure taxes as part of an ideally just arrangement. For one thing, they are preferable to income taxes at the level of common-sense precepts of justice, since they impose a levy according to how much a man takes out of the common store of goods and not according to how much he contributes (assuming that income is fairly earned in return for productive efforts). On the other hand, proportional taxes that treat everyone in a clearly defined uniform way (again assuming that income is fairly earned) and hence it is preferable to use progressive rates only when they are necessary to preserve the justice of the system as a whole, that is, to prevent large fortunes hazardous to liberty and equality of opportunity, and the like. If proportional expenditure taxes should also prove more efficient, say because they interfere less with incentives, or whatever, this would make the case for them decisive provided a feasible scheme could be worked out.[4] Yet these are questions of political judgment which are not our concern; and, in any case, a proportional expenditure tax is part of an idealized scheme which we are describing. It does not follow that even steeply progressive income taxes, given the injustice of existing systems, do not improve justice and efficiency all things considered. In practice we must usually choose between unjust arrangements and then it is a matter of finding the lesser injustice.

Whatever form the distribution branch assumes, the argument for it is to be based on justice: we must hold that once it is accepted the social system as a whole—the competitive economy surrounded by a just constitutional legal framework—can be made to satisfy the principles of justice with the smallest loss in efficiency. The long-term expectations of the least advantaged are raised to the highest level consistent with the demands of equal liberty. In discussing the choice of a distribution scheme we have made no reference to the traditional criteria of taxation according to ability to pay or benefits received; nor have we mentioned any of the variants of the sacrifice principle. These standards are subordinate to the two principles of justice; once the problem is seen as that of designing a whole social system, they assume the status of secondary precepts with no more independent force than the precepts of common sense in regards to wages. To suppose otherwise is not to take a sufficiently comprehensive point of view. In setting up a just distribution branch these precepts may or may not have a place depending upon the demands of the two principles of justice when applied to the entire system. . . .

The sketch of the system of institutions satisfying the two principles of justice is now complete. . . .

In order . . . to establish just distributive shares a just total system of institutions must be set up and impartially administered. Given a just constitution and the smooth working of the four branches of government, and so on, there exists a procedure such that the actual distribution of wealth, whatever it turns out to be, is just. It will have come about as a consequence of a just system of institutions satisfying the principles to which everyone would agree and against which no one can complain. The situation is one of pure procedural justice, since there is no independent criterion by which the outcome can be judged. Nor can we say that a particular distribution of wealth is just because it is one which could have resulted from just institutions although it has not, as this would be to allow too much. Clearly there are many distributions which may be reached by just institutions, and this is true whether we count patterns of distributions among social classes or whether we count distributions of particular goods and services among particular individuals. There are definitely many outcomes and what makes one of these just is that it has been achieved by actually carrying out a just scheme of co-operation as it is publicly understood. It is the result which has arisen when everyone receives that to which he is entitled given his and others' actions guided by their legitimate expectations and their obligations to one another. We can no more arrive at a just distribution of wealth except by working together within the framework of a just system of institutions than we can win or lose fairly without actually betting.

This account of distributive shares is simply an elaboration of the familiar idea that economic rewards will be just once a perfectly competitive price system is organized as a fair game. But in order to do this we have to begin with the choice of a social system as a whole, for the basic structure of the entire arrangement must be just. The economy must be surrounded with the appropriate framework of institutions, since even a perfectly efficient price system has no tendency to determine just distributive shares when left to itself. Not only must economic activity be regulated by a just constitution and controlled by the four branches of government, but a just saving-function must be adopted to estimate the provision to be made for future generations. . . .

NOTES

1. In this essay I try to work out some of the implications of the two principles of justice discussed in "Justice as Fairness," which first appeared in the *Philosophical Review,* 1958, and which is reprinted in *Philosophy, Politics and Society,* Series II, pp. 132–57.
2. This question is discussed very briefly in "Justice as Fairness," see pp. 138–41. The intuitive idea is as follows. Given the circumstances of the original position, it is rational for a man to choose as if he were designing a society in which his enemy is to assign him his place. Thus, in particular, given the complete lack of knowledge (which makes the choice one of uncertainty), the fact that the decision involves one's life-prospects as a whole and is constrained by obligations to third parties (e.g., one's descendants) and

duties to certain values (e.g., to religious truth), it is rational to be conservative and so to choose in accordance with an analogue of the maximum principle. Viewing the situation in this way, the interpretation given to the principles of justice earlier is perhaps natural enough. Moreover, it seems clear how the principle of utility can be interpreted; it is the analogue of the Laplacean principle for choice uncertainty. (For a discussion of these choice criteria, see R. D. Luce and H. Raiffa, *Games and Decisions* [1957], pp. 275–98.)

3. Example F. von Hayek, *The Constitution of Liberty* (1960), p. 90.
4. See N. Kaldor, *An Expenditure Tax* (1955).

RELATED WEB SITES

Harvard Philosophy Dept.: www.fas.harvard.edu/~phildept/

Stanford Encyclopedia of Philosophy (Justice, Distributive)
    plato.stanford.edu/entries/justice-distributive/justice-distributive.html

THE ENTITLEMENT
THEORY

ROBERT NOZICK

Nozick's theory is basically ethics according to contract rights. His primary thesis is that liberty upsets patterns. You may have a basic distribution of resources, but given free exchanges, that pattern of distribution will be upset. As long as exchanges are freely entered into, they must (by the definition of free*) be ethical. Can you conceive of situations where this might not be so or where it might cause a conflict?*

Robert Nozick (b. 1938) believes that everyone is entitled to contractual freedom, and that interfering with that freedom would be unethical. Freedom grants individuals the right to self-development and self-fulfillment. Liberty is a greater societal value than justice. Contrast Nozick's concept of freedom and free exchange with Rawls's patterned distribution.

The minimal state is the most extensive state that can be justified. Any state more extensive violates people's rights. Yet many persons have put forth reasons purporting to justify a more extensive state. It is impossible within the compass of this book to examine all the reasons that have been put forth. Therefore, I shall focus upon those generally acknowledged to be most weighty and influential, to see precisely wherein they fail. In this chapter we consider the claim that a more extensive state is justified, because necessary (or the best instrument) to achieve distributive justice; in the next chapter we shall take up diverse other claims.

The term "distributive justice" is not a neutral one. Hearing the term "distribution," most people presume that some thing or mechanism uses some principle or criterion to give out a supply of things. Into this process of distributing shares some error may have crept. So it is an open question, at least, whether *re*distribution should take place; whether we should do again what has already been done once, though poorly. However, we are not in the position of children who have been given portions of pie by someone who now makes last-minute adjustments to rectify careless cutting. There is no *central* distribution, no person or group entitled to control all the resources, jointly deciding how they are to be doled out. What each person gets, he gets from others who give to him in exchange for something, or as a gift. In a free society, diverse persons control different resources, and new holdings arise out of the voluntary exchanges and actions of persons. There is no more a distributing or distribution of shares than there is a distributing of mates in a

---

society in which persons choose whom they shall marry. The total result is the product of many individual decisions which the different individuals involved are entitled to make. Some uses of the term "distribution," it is true, do not imply a previous distributing appropriately judged by some criterion (for example, "probability distribution"); nevertheless, despite the title of this chapter, it would be best to use a terminology that clearly is neutral. We shall speak of people's holdings; a principle of justice in holdings describes (part of) what justice tells us (requires) about holdings. I shall state first what I take to be the correct view about justice in holdings, and then turn to the distribution of alternate views.

THE ENTITLEMENT THEORY

The subject of justice in holdings consists of three major topics. The first is the *original acquisition of holdings,* the appropriation of unheld things. This includes the issues of how unheld things may come to be held, the process, or processes, by which unheld things may come to be held, the things that may come to be held by these processes, the extent of what comes to be held by a particular process, and so on. We shall refer to the complicated truth about this topic, which we shall not formulate here, as the principle of justice in acquisition. The second topic concerns the *transfer of holdings* from one person to another. By what processes may a person transfer holdings to another? How may a person acquire a holding from another who holds it? Under this topic come general descriptions of voluntary exchange, and gift and (on the other hand) fraud, as well as reference to particular conventional details fixed upon in a given society. The complicated truth about this subject (with placeholders for conventional details) we shall call the principle of justice in transfer. (And we shall suppose it also includes principles governing how a person may divest himself of a holding, passing it into an unheld state.)

If the world were wholly just, the following inductive definition would exhaustively cover the subject of justice in holdings.

1. A person who acquires a holding in accordance with the principle of justice acquisition is entitled to that holding.
2. A person who acquires a holding in accordance with the principle of justice in transfer, from someone else entitled to the holding, is entitled to the holding.
3. No one is entitled to a holding except by (repeated) applications of 1 and 2.

The complete principle of distributive justice would say simply that a distribution is just if everyone is entitled to the holdings they possess under the distribution.

A distribution is just if it arises from another just distribution by legitimate means. The legitimate means of moving from one distribution to another are specified by the principle of justice in transfer. The legitimate first "moves" are specified by the principle of justice in acquisition.[1] Whatever arises from a just situation by just steps is itself just. The means of change specified by the principle of justice in transfer preserve justice. As correct rules of inference are truth-preserving, and any conclusion deduced via repeated application of such rules from only true premises is itself true, so the means of transition from one situation to another specified by the principle of justice in transfer are justice-preserving, and any situation actually arising from repeated transitions in accordance with the principle from a just situation is itself just. The parallel between justice-preserving transformations and truth-preserving transformations illuminates where it fails as well as where it holds. That a conclusion could have been deduced by truth-preserving means from premises that are true suffices to show its truth. That from a just situation a situation *could* have arisen via justice-preserving means does *not* suffice to show its justice. The fact that a thief's victims voluntarily *could* have presented him with gifts does not entitle the thief to his ill-gotten gains. Justice in holdings is historical; it depends upon what actually has happened. We shall return to this point later.

Not all actual situations are generated in accordance with the two principles of justice in holdings: the principle of justice in acquisition and the principle of justice in transfer. Some people steal from others, or defraud them, or enslave them, seizing their product and preventing them from living as they choose, or forcibly exclude others from competing in exchanges. None of these are permissible modes of transition from one situation to another. And some persons acquire holdings by means not sanctioned by the principle of justice in acquisition. The existence of past injustice (previous violations of the first two principles of justice in holdings) raises the third major topic under justice in holdings: the rectification of injustice in holdings. If past injustice has shaped present holdings in various ways, some identifiable and some not, what now, if anything, ought to be done to rectify these injustices? What obligations do the performers of injustice have toward those whose position is worse than it would have been had the injustice not been done? Or, than it would have been had compensation been paid promptly? How, if at all, do things change if the beneficiaries and those made worse off are not the direct parties in the act of injustice, but, for example, their descendants? Is an injustice done to someone whose holding was itself based upon an unrectified injustice? How far back must one go in wiping clean the historical slate of injustices? What may victims of injustice permissibly do in order to rectify the injustices being done to them, including the many injustices done by persons acting through their government? I do not know of a thorough or theoretically sophisticated treatment of such issues. Idealizing greatly, let us suppose theoretical investigation will produce a principle of rectification. This principle uses historical information about previous situations and injustices done in them (as defined by the first two principles of justice and rights against interference), and information about the actual course of events that flowed from these injustices, until the present, and it yields a description (or descriptions) of holdings in the society. The principle of rectification presumably will make use of its best estimate of subjunctive information about what would have occurred (or a probability distribution over what might have occurred, using the expected value) if the injustice had not taken place. If the actual description of holdings turns out not to be one of the descriptions yielded by the principle, then one of the descriptions yielded must be realized.

The general outlines of the theory of justice in holdings are that the holdings of a person are just if he is entitled to them by the principles of justice in acquisition and transfer, or by the principle of rectification of injustice (as specified by the first two principles). If each person's holdings are just, then the total set (distribution) of holdings is just. To turn these general outlines into a specific theory we would have to specify the details of each of the three principles of justice in holdings: the principle of acquisition of holdings, the principle of transfer of holdings, and the principle of rectification of violations of the first two principles. I shall not attempt that task here. (Locke's principle of justice in acquisition is discussed below.) . . .

HOW LIBERTY UPSETS PATTERNS

It is not clear how those holding alternative conceptions of distributive justice can reject the entitlement conception of justice in holdings. For suppose a distribution favored by one of these nonentitlement conceptions is realized. Let us suppose it is your favorite one and let us call this distribution D_1; perhaps everyone has an equal share, perhaps shares vary in accordance with some dimension you treasure. Now suppose that Wilt Chamberlain is greatly in demand by basketball teams, being a great gate attraction. (Also suppose contracts run only for a year, with players being free agents.) He signs the following sort of contract with a team: In each home game, twenty-five cents from the price of each ticket of admission goes to him. (We ignore the question of whether he is "gouging" the owners, letting them look out for themselves.) The season starts, and people cheerfully attend his team's games; they buy their tickets, each time dropping a separate twenty-five cents of their admission price into a special box with Chamberlain's name on it. They are excited about seeing him play; it is worth the total admission price to them. Let us suppose that in one season one million persons attend his home games, and Wilt Chamberlain winds up with $250,000, a much larger sum than the average income and larger even than anyone else has. Is he entitled to this income? Is this new distribution, D_2, unjust? If so, why? There is *no* question about whether each of the people was entitled to the control over the resources they held in D_1; because that was the distribution (your favorite) that (for the purposes of argument) we assumed was acceptable. Each of these persons *chose* to give twenty-five cents of their money to Chamberlain. They could have spent it on going to the movies, or on candy bars, or on copies of *Dissent* magazine, or of *Monthly Review*. But they all, at least one million of them, converged on giving it to Wilt Chamberlain in exchange for watching him play basketball. If D_1 was a just distribution, and people voluntarily moved from it to D_2, transferring parts of their shares they were given under D_1 (what was it for if not to do something with?), isn't D_2 also just? If the people were entitled to dispose of the resources to which they were entitled (under D_1), didn't this include their being entitled to give it to, or exchange with, Wilt Chamberlain? Can anyone else complain on grounds of justice? Each other person already has his legitimate share under D_1. Under D_1, there is nothing that anyone has that anyone else has a claim of justice against. After someone transfers something to Wilt Chamberlain, third parties *still* have their legitimate shares; *their* shares are not changed. By what process could such a transfer among two persons give rise to a legitimate claim of distributive justice on a portion of what was transferred, by a third party who had no claim of justice on any holding of the others *before* the transfer? To cut off objections irrelevant here, we might imagine the exchanges occurring in a socialist society, after hours. After playing whatever basketball he does in his daily work, or doing whatever other daily work he does, Wilt Chamberlain decides to put in *overtime* to earn additional money. (First his work quota is set; he works time over that.) Or imagine it is a skilled juggler people like to see, who puts on shows after hours.

Why might someone work overtime in a society in which it is assumed their needs are satisfied? Perhaps because they care about things other than needs. I like to write in books that I read, and to have easy access to books for browsing at odd hours. It would be very pleasant and convenient to have the resources of Widener Library in my back yard. No society, I assume, will provide such resources close to each person who would like them as part of his regular allotment (under D). Thus, persons either must do without some extra things that they want, or be allowed to do something extra to get some of these things. On what basis could the inequalities that would eventuate be forbidden? Notice also that small factories would spring up in a socialist society, unless forbidden. I melt down some of my personal possessions (under D_1) and build a machine out of the material. I offer you, and others, a philosophy lecture once a week in exchange for your cranking the handle on my machine, whose products I exchange for yet other things, and so on. (The raw materials used by the machine are given to me by others who possess them under D_1, in exchange for hearing lectures.) Each person might participate to gain things over and above their allotment under D_1. Some persons even might want to leave their job in socialist industry and work full time in this private sector. . . . Here I wish merely to note how private property even in means of production would occur in a socialist society that did not forbid people to use as they wished some of the resources they are given under the socialist distribution D_1. The socialist society would have to forbid capitalist acts between consenting adults.

The general point illustrated by the Wilt Chamberlain example and the example of the entrepreneur in a socialist society is that no end-state principle or distributional patterned principle of justice can be continuously realized without continuous interference with people's lives. Any favored pattern would be transformed into one unfavored by the principle, by people choosing to act in various ways; for example, by people exchanging goods and services with other people, or giving things to other people, things the transferrers are entitled to under the favored distributional pattern. To maintain a pattern one must either continually interfere to stop people from transferring resources as they wish to, or continually (or periodically) interfere to take from some persons resources that others for some reason chose to transfer to them. (But if some time limit is to be set on how long people may keep resources others voluntarily transfer to them, why let them keep these resources for *any* period of time? Why not have immediate confiscation?) It might be objected that all persons voluntarily will choose to refrain from actions which would upset the pattern. This presupposes unrealistically (1) that all will most want to maintain the pattern (are those who don't, to be "reeducated" or forced to undergo "self-criticism"?), (2) that each can gather enough information about his own actions and the ongoing activities of others to discover which of his actions will upset the pattern, and (3) that diverse and far-flung persons can coordinate their actions to dove-tail into the pattern. Compare the manner in which the market is neutral among persons' desires, as it reflects and transmits widely scattered information via prices, and coordinates persons' activities.

It puts things perhaps a bit too strongly to say that every patterned (or end-state) principle is liable to be thwarted by the voluntary actions of the individual parties transferring some of their shares they receive under the principle. For perhaps some *very* weak patterns are not so thwarted. Any distributional pattern with any egalitarian component is overturnable by the voluntary actions of individual persons over time; as is every patterned condition with sufficient content so as actually to have been proposed as presenting the central core of distributive justice. Still, given the possibility that some weak conditions or patterns may not be unstable in this way, it would be better to formulate an explicit description of the kind of interesting and contentful patterns under discussion, and to prove a theorem about their instability. Since the weaker the patterning, the more likely it is that the entitlement system itself satisfies it, a plausible conjecture is that any patterning either is unstable or is satisfied by the entitlement system.

NOTE

1. Applications of the principle of justice in acquisition may also occur as part of the move from one distribution to another. You may find an unheld thing now and appropriate it. Acquisitions also are to be understood as included when, to simplify, I speak only of transitions by transfers.

RELATED WEB SITES

Libertarian resources: www.libertarian.com

Libertarian Party: www.lp.org

THE ONES WHO WALK AWAY FROM OMELAS

Ursula K. Le Guin

One of the concerns with utilitarian theory is that numbers do not always tell the full story. Le Guin illustrates this problem in the following story where one person's intense suffering is insufficient to outweigh the happiness of many. The story begins with a description of Omelas, one of the happiest cities you can imagine, full of festivals, music, and joy for its inhabitants. This excerpt begins following Le Guin's description of that happiness. Consider how you would modify utilitarian theory to account for problems such as those described in this story.

. . . In a basement under one of the beautiful public buildings of Omelas, or perhaps in the cellar of one of its spacious private homes, there is a room. It has one locked door, and no window. A little light seeps in dustily between cracks in the boards, secondhand from a cobwebbed window somewhere across the cellar. In one corner of the little room a couple of mops, with stiff, clotted, foul-smelling heads, stand near a rusty bucket. The floor is dirt, a little damp to the touch, as cellar dust usually is. The room is about three paces long and two wide: a mere broom closet or disused tool room. In the room a child is sitting. It could be a boy or a girl. It looks about six, but actually is nearly ten. It is feeble-minded. Perhaps it was born defective, or perhaps it has become imbecile through fear, malnutrition, and neglect. It picks its nose and occasionally fumbles vaguely with its toes or genitals, as it sits hunched in the corner farthest from the bucket and the two mops. It is afraid of the mops. It finds them horrible. It shuts its eyes, but it knows the mops are still standing there; and the door is locked; and nobody will come. The door is always locked; and nobody ever comes, except that sometimes—the child has no understanding of time or interval—sometimes the door rattles terribly and opens, and a person, or several people, are there. One of them may come in and kick the child to make it stand up. The others never come close, but peer in at it with frightened, disgusted eyes. The food bowl and the water jug are hastily filled, the door is locked, the eyes disappear. The people at the door never say anything, but the child, who has not always lived in the tool room, and can remember sunlight and its mother's voice, sometimes speaks. "I will be good," it says. "Please let me out. I will be good!" They never answer. The child used to scream for help at night, and cry a good deal, but now it only makes a kind of whining, "eh-haa, eh-haa," and it speaks less and less often. It is so thin there are no calves to its legs; its belly protrudes; it lives on a half-bowl of corn meal and grease a day. It is naked. Its buttocks and thighs are a mass of festered sores, as it sits in its own excrement continually.

They all know it is there, all the people of Omelas. Some of them have come to see it, others are content merely to know it is there. They all know that it has to be there. Some of them understand why, and some do not, but they all understand that their happiness, the beauty of their city, the tenderness of their friendships, the health of their children, the wisdom of their scholars, the skill of their makers, even the abundance of their harvest and the kindly weathers of their skies, depend wholly on this child's abominable misery.

This is usually explained to children when they are between eight and twelve, whenever they seem capable of understanding; and most of those who come to see the child are young people, though often enough an adult comes, or comes back, to see the child. No matter how well the matter has been explained to them, these young spectators are always shocked and sickened at the sight. They feel disgust, which they had thought themselves superior to. They feel anger, outrage, impotence, despite all the explanations. They would like to do something for the child. But there is nothing they can do. If the child were brought up into the sunlight out of the vile place, if it were cleaned and fed and comforted, that would be a good thing, indeed; but if it were done, in that day and hour all the prosperity and beauty and delight of Omelas would wither and be destroyed. Those are the terms. To exchange all the goodness and grace of every life in Omelas for that single, small improvement: to throw away the happiness of thousands for the chance of the happiness of one: that would be to let guilt within the walls indeed.

The terms are strict and absolute; there may not even be a kind word spoken to the child.

Often the young people go home in tears, or in a tearless rage, when they have seen the child and faced this terrible paradox. They may brood over it for weeks or years. But as time goes on they begin to realize that even if the child could be released, it would not get much good of its freedom: a little vague pleasure of warmth and food, no doubt, but little more. It is too degraded and imbecile to know any real joy. It has been afraid too long ever to be free of fear. Its habits are too uncouth for it to respond to humane treatment. Indeed, after so long it would probably be wretched without walls about it to protect it, and darkness for its eyes, and its own excrement to sit in. Their tears at the bitter injustice dry when they begin to perceive the terrible justice of reality, and to accept it. Yet it is their tears and anger, the trying of their generosity and the acceptance of their helplessness, which are perhaps the true source of the splendor of their lives. Theirs is no vapid, irresponsible happiness. They know that they, like the child, are not free. They know compassion. It is the existence of the child, and their knowledge of its existence, that makes possible the nobility of their architecture, the poignancy of their music, the profundity of their science. It is because of the child that they are so gentle with children. They know that if the wretched one were not there snivelling in the dark, the other one, the flute-player, could make no joyful music as the young riders line up in their beauty for the race in the sunlight of the first morning of summer.

Now do you believe in them? Are they not more credible? But there is one more thing to tell, and this is quite incredible.

At times one of the adolescent girls or boys who go to see the child does not go home to weep or rage, does not, in fact, go home at all. Sometimes also a man or woman much older falls silent for a day or two, and then leaves home. These people go out into the street, and walk down the street alone. They keep walking, and walk straight out of the city of Omelas, through the beautiful gates. They keep walking across the farmlands of Omelas. Each one goes alone, youth or girl, man or woman. Night falls; the traveler must pass down village streets, between the houses with yellow-lit windows, and on out into the darkness of the fields. Each alone, they go west or north, towards the mountains. They go on. They leave Omelas, they walk ahead into the darkness, and they do not come back. The place they go towards is a place even less imaginable to most of us than the city of happiness. I cannot describe it at all. It is possible that it does not exist. But they seem to know where they are going, the ones who walk away from Omelas.

RELATED WEB SITES

Society for Utopian Studies: oak.cats.ohiou.edu/~aw148888/sus.html

Unofficial homepage of Ursula Le Guin: www.uic.edu/~lauramd/sf/leguin/

CLOSING ARGUMENT IN LEOPOLD AND LOEB CASE

Clarence Darrow

*Clarence Darrow (1857–1938) was considered one of the most effec-
tive orators of his time. He is perhaps best known for his role as defense attorney during the famous Scopes trial in 1925, during which
he defended the right to teach Charles Darwin's theory of evolution.
The excerpt that follows is taken from Darrow's oral argument to the
court in the appeal for the lives of Richard Loeb and Nathan
Leopold, two affluent young men who were convicted of kidnapping
and murdering Robert Franks, age 14. Darrow's job was not to reverse the conviction but to persuade the court not to impose the death
penalty as a sentence. In doing so (and winning), Darrow discussed
the concept of evil as human nature.*

. . . What do they want? Tell me, is a lifetime for the young boys spent behind prison bars—is that not enough for this mad act? And is there any reason why this great public should be regaled by a hanging?

I cannot understand it, Your Honor. It would be past belief, excepting that to the four corners of the earth the news of this weird act has been carried and men have been stirred, and the primitive has come back, and the intellect has been stifled, and men have been controlled by feelings and passions and hatred which should have died centuries ago.

My friend Savage pictured to you the putting of this dead boy in this culvert. Well, no one can minutely describe any killing and not make it shocking. It is shocking. It is shocking because we love life and because we instinctively draw back from death. It is shocking wherever it is and however it is, and perhaps all death is almost equally shocking.

But here is the picture of a dead boy, past pain, when no harm can come to him, put in a culvert, after taking off his clothes so that the evidence would be destroyed; and that is pictured to this court as a reason for hanging. Well, Your Honor, that does not appeal to me as strongly as the hitting over the head of little Robert Franks with a chisel. The boy was dead.

I could say something about the death penalty that, for some mysterious reason, the State wants in this case. Why do they want it? To vindicate the law? Oh, no. The law can be vindicated without killing anyone else. It might shock the fine sensibilities of the state's counsel that this boy was put into a culvert and left after he was dead, but, Your

Attorney for the Damned, Arthur Weinberg, ed., pp. 42–44, 49–50, 86–88, Copyright 1957, 1989 by Arthur Weinberg. Reprinted with permission of Lila Weinberg.

Honor, I can think of a scene that makes this pale into insignificance. I can think, and only think, Your Honor, of taking two boys, one eighteen and the other nineteen, irresponsible, weak, diseased, penning them in a cell, checking off the days and the hours and the minutes until they will be taken out and hanged. Wouldn't it be a glorious day for Chicago? Wouldn't it be a glorious triumph for the state's attorney? Wouldn't it be a glorious triumph of justice in this land? Wouldn't it be a glorious illustration of Christianity and kindness and charity? I can picture them, wakened in the gray light and morning, furnished a suit of clothes by the State, led to the scaffold, their feet tied, black caps drawn over their heads, stood on a trap door, the hangman pressing a spring so that it gives way under them; I can see them fall through space—and—stopped by the rope around their necks.

This would surely expiate placing Bobby Franks in the culvert after he was dead. This would doubtless bring immense satisfaction to some people. It would bring a greater satisfaction because it would be done in the name of justice. I am always suspicious of righteous indignation. Nothing is more cruel than righteous indignation. To hear young men talk glibly of justice. Well, it would make me smile if it did not make me sad. Who knows what it is? Does Mr. Savage know? Does Mr. Crowe know? Do I know? Does Your Honor know? Is there any human machinery for finding it out? Is there any man who can weigh me and say what I deserve? Can Your Honor? Let us be honest. Can Your Honor appraise yourself, and say what you deserve? Can Your Honor appraise these two young men and say what they deserve? Justice must take account of infinite circumstances which a human being cannot understand.

If there is such a thing as justice it could only be administered by one who knew the inmost thoughts of the man to whom he was meting it out. Aye, who knew the father and mother and the grandparents and the infinite number of people back of him. Who knew the origin of every cell that went into the body, who could understand the structure and how it acted. Who could tell how the emotions that sway the human being affected that particular frail piece of clay. It means more than that. It means that you must appraise every influence that moves men, the civilization where they live, and all society which enters into the making of the child or the man! If Your Honor can do it—if you can do it you are wise, and with wisdom goes mercy.

No one with wisdom and with understanding, no one who is honest with himself and with his own life, whoever he may be, no one who has seen himself the prey and the sport and the plaything of the infinite forces that move man, no one who has tried and who has failed—and we have all tried and we have all failed—no one can tell what justice is for someone else or for himself; and the more he tries and the more responsibility he takes, the more he clings to mercy as being the one thing which he is sure should control his judgment of men.

It is not so much mercy either, Your Honor. I can hardly understand myself pleading to a court to visit mercy on two boys by shutting them into a prison for life.

For life! Where is the human heart that would not be satisfied with that?

Where is the man or woman who understands his own life and who has a particle of feeling that could ask for more? Any cry for more roots back to the hyena; it roots back to the hissing serpent; it roots back to the beast and the jungle. It is not a part of man. It is not a part of that feeling which, let us hope, is growing, though scenes like this sometimes make me doubt that it is growing. It is not a part of that feeling of mercy and pity and understanding of each other which we believe has been slowly raising man from his low estate. It is not a part of the finer instincts which are slow to develop; of the wider knowledge which is slow to come, and slow to move us when it comes. It is not a part of all that makes the best there is in man. It is not a part of all that promises any hope for the future and any justice for the present. And must I ask that these boys get mercy by spending the rest of their lives in prison, year following year, month following month, and day following day, with nothing to look forward to but hostile guards and stone walls? It ought not to be hard to get that much mercy in any court in the year 1924.

These boys left this body down in the culvert, and they came back and telephoned home that they would be too late for supper. Here, surely, was an act of consideration on the part of Leopold, telephoning home that he would be late for supper. Dr. Krohn says he must be able to think and act because he could do this. But the boy who, through habit, would telephone his home that he would be late for supper had not a tremor or a thought or a shudder at taking the life of little Bobby Franks for nothing, and he has not had one yet. He was in the habit of doing what he did when he telephoned—that was all; but in the presence of life and death, and a cruel death, he had no tremor and no thought. . . .

. . . You know it has been done too many times. And here for the first time, under these circumstances, this court is told that you must make an example. . . .

Can you administer law without consideration? Can you administer what approaches justice without it? Can this court or any court administer justice by consciously turning his heart to stone and being deaf to all the finer instincts which move men? Without those instincts I wonder what would happen to the human race?

If a man could judge a fellow in coldness without taking account of his own life, without taking account of what he knows of human life, without some understanding— how long would we be a race of real human beings? It has taken the world a long time for man to get to even where he is today. If the law was administered without any feeling of sympathy or humanity or kindliness, we would begin our long, slow journey back to the jungle that was formerly our home.

How many times has assault with intent to rob or kill been changed in these courts to assault and battery? How many times has felony been waived in assault with a deadly weapon and a man or boy given a chance? And we are asking a chance to be shut up in stone walls for life. For life. It is hard for me to think of it, but that is the mercy we are asking from this court, which we ought not to be required to ask, and which we should have as a matter of right in this court and which I have faith to believe we will have as a matter of right.

Is this new? Why, I undertake to say that even the state's attorney's office—and if he denies it I would like to see him bring in the records—I will undertake to say that in three cases out of four of all kinds and all degrees, clemency has been shown.

Three hundred and forty murder cases in ten years with a plea of Guilty in this county. All the young who pleaded guilty, every one of them—three hundred and forty in ten years with one hanging on a plea of Guilty, and that a man forty years of age. And yet they say we come here with a preposterous plea for mercy. When did any plea for mercy become preposterous in any tribunal in all the universe?

We are satisfied with justice, if the court knows what justice is, or if any human being can tell what justice is. If anybody can look into the minds and hearts and the lives and the origin of these two youths and tell what justice is, we would be content. But nobody can do it without imagination, without sympathy, without kindliness, without understanding, and I have faith that this Court will take this case, with his conscience, and his judgment and his courage and save these boys' lives.

Now, Your Honor, let me go a little further with this. I have gone over some of the high spots in this tragedy. This tragedy has not claimed all the attention it has had on account of its atrocity. There is nothing to that.

What is it?

There are two reasons, and only two that I can see. First is the reputed extreme wealth of these families; not only the Loeb and Leopold families, but the Franks family, and of course it is unusual. And next is the fact it is weird and uncanny and motiveless. That is what attracted the attention of the world.

Many may say now that they want to hang these boys; but I know that giving the people blood is something like giving them their dinner. When they get it they go to sleep. They may for the time being have an emotion, but they will bitterly regret it. And I undertake to say that if these two boys are sentenced to death and are hanged, on that day a pall will settle over the people of this land that will be dark and deep, and at least cover every humane and intelligent person with its gloom. I wonder if it will do good. I wonder if it will help the children—and there is an infinite number like these. I marveled when I heard Mr. Savage talk. I do not criticize him. He is young and enthusiastic. But has he ever read anything? Has he ever thought? Was there ever any man who had studied science, who has read anything of criminology or philosophy—was there ever any man who knew himself who could speak with the assurance with which he speaks? . . .

Your Honor stands between the past and the future. You may hang these boys; you may hang them by the neck until they are dead. But in doing it you will turn your face toward the past. In doing it you are making it harder for every other boy who, in ignorance and darkness, must grope his way through the mazes which only childhood knows. In doing it you will make it harder for unborn children. You may save them and make it easier for every child that sometime may stand where these boys stand. You will make it easier for every human being with an aspiration and a vision and a hope and a fate.

I am pleading for the future; I am pleading for a time when hatred and cruelty will not control the hearts of men, when we can learn by reason and judgment and understanding and faith that all life is worth saving, and that mercy is the highest attribute of man.

I feel that I should apologize for the length of time I have taken. This case may not be as important as I think it is, and I am sure I do not need to tell this court, or to tell my friends that I would fight just as hard for the poor as for the rich. If I should succeed in saving these boys' lives and do nothing for the progress of the law, I should feel sad, indeed. If I can succeed, my greatest reward and my greatest hope will be that I have done something for the tens of thousands of other boys, for the countless unfortunates who must tread the same road in blind childhood that these poor boys have trod; that I have done something to help human understanding, to temper justice with mercy, to overcome hate with love.

I was reading last night of the aspiration of the old Persian poet, Omar Khayyam. It appealed to me as the highest that I can vision. I wish it was in my heart, and I wish it was in the hearts of all.

> So I be written in the Book of Love,
> I do not care about that Book above;
> Erase my name or write it as you will,
> So I be written in the Book of Love.

Tears were streaming down the judge's face as Darrow finished his plea. A newspaper reported, "The stuffed courtroom was like a black hole. Hardly a breath of air moved in it. Yet the crowd that was massed around Darrow sat motionless in attention as the weary old man gathered up all the threads of his argument for the final restatement."

Another newspaper said the lines in Darrow's face were "deeper, the eyes haggard. But there was no sign of physical weariness in the speech, only a spiritual weariness with the cruelties of the world."

Chicago newspapers and many others throughout the country printed Darrow's more-than-twelve-hour plea in full or in part.

A newspaper reporter said, "There was scarcely any telling where his voice had finished and where silence had begun. His own eyes were not the only ones that held tears."

State's Attorney Crowe summed up the case for the State. He talked for two days. Court adjourned.

On September 10, 1924, the Chief Justice of the Criminal Court of Cook County sentenced the defendants to imprisonment for life on the murder indictment and 99 years on the kidnapping charge.

Editorialized the *New York Morning Telegram* the following day: "Law, the bastard daughter of justice, handed her mother a frightful beating in Chicago yesterday."

The New York Times said: "Had the youthful murderers been poor and friendless, they would have escaped capital punishment precisely as Leopold and Loeb have escaped it."

The boys were taken to Joliet penitentiary.

There, twelve years later, Loeb was killed in a prison fight. Leopold, who is still in the penitentiary, has made several unsuccessful pleas for his freedom.

RELATED WEB SITES

The Clarence Darrow Web page: www.brokersys.com/~corny51/darrow.sht

Clarence Darrow misquoted by creationists:
    earth.ics.uci.edu:8080/faqs/darrow.html

Chapter 2

APPLICATION OF TRADITIONAL THEORIES TO MODERN BUSINESS DECISION MAKING

Give each man thy ear, but few thy voice.
Take each man's censure but reserve thy judgment.

POLONIUS'S ADVICE TO HIS
DEPARTING SON, LAERTES, IN
HAMLET, ACT 1, SCENE 3

The person who is trustworthy in very small matters is also trustworthy in great ones; and the person who is dishonest in very small matters is also dishonest in great ones.

LUKE 16:10

MORAL REASONING AND MODELS

In answering the question earlier about your grandmother's request at her deathbed, you resorted to some form of decision making. Perhaps you might call it "gut instinct." Moral reasoning is a more intentional form of decision making where the actor considers the basis for and implications of the decision before acting. The decision maker considers evidence and reaches conclusions, or judgments, about the right and wrong way to act. Moral reasoning can suffer from being too absolute (where one believes that the same rule applies, no matter the circumstances) or from being too relativistic (where the answer always seems to depend entirely on the circumstances).

In order to avoid these two extremes, one might look to a model of reasoning such as the traditional stakeholder model of decision making. Stakeholders include all of the groups and/or individuals affected by a decision, policy, or operation of a firm or individual. Stakeholder theory suggests that, in reaching ethical decisions, we respond to the following inquiries:

A. Seek to recognize the moral dimensions. What is the ethical issue?
B. Who are the interested parties? Who is impacted? What are their relationships?
C. What values are involved?
D. What alternatives do you have in your decision?
E. Weigh the benefits and the burdens of each alternative on each impacted party.
F. Look for analogous cases.
G. Discuss the case with relevant others; gather opinions.
H. Does the decision accord with legal and organizational rules?
I. Am I comfortable with the decision?[1]

Other approaches may prove just as useful. Philosophers/ethicists often ask the decision maker to consider whether she or he would feel all right if the *New York Times* printed this decision as a front-page article, or whether it could be explained to a 10-year-old child so that the child thinks it is the right decision, or whether it will stand the test of time through generations in the firm.

Philosopher Laura Nash suggests asking oneself 12 questions prior to reaching a decision in an ethical dilemma:

1. Have your defined the problem accurately?
2. How would you define the problem if you stood on the other side of the fence?
3. How did the situation occur in the first place?
4. Who was involved in the situation in the first place?
5. What is your intention in making this decision?
6. How does this intention compare with likely results?
7. Whom could your decision or action injure?

---

1. Chris MacDonald, "A Guide to Moral Decision Making," University of British Columbia Centre for Applied Ethics, http://www.ethics.ubc.ca/~chrismac.

8. Can you engage the affected parties in a discussion of the problem before you make your decision?
9. Are you confident that your decision will be as valid over a long period as it seems now?
10. Could you disclose without qualms your decision or action to your boss, your CEO, the board of directors, your family, or society as a whole?
11. What is the symbolic potential of your action if understood?
12. Under what conditions would you allow exceptions to your stand?[2]

A simple, two-step approach seems to consolidate many of the issues and questions raised by the elaborate processes discussed above. In evaluating any decision, consider two elements: *integrity and accountability.* Integrity, meaning consistency in values, would require that the decision maker define her or his values, as well as create a prioritization of those values. Then, when faced with a dilemma or conflict between two or more of these values, the decision maker will have internal guidance regarding the direction her or his decision should take. Second, no matter which direction is taken, the decision maker must be accountable to all stakeholders who are impacted by this decision. That would require a consideration of the alternatives available and the impact of each alternative on each stakeholder.

For instance, assume that times are very tough at your firm and that your superior has informed you that you must cut 10 percent of your present 50-person workforce in order to help the firm avoid a possible bankruptcy filing. You will consider the values at stake and reach some decision about whom to terminate. However, in terminating employees, you offer the employees as much notice as possible, you do not walk them out under armed guard, you offer outplacement counseling to help them to continue their lives, and so on. You accept responsibility for the impact of your decision on those affected.

MORAL DECISION MAKING IN BUSINESS: BUSINESS ETHICS

No one teaches or takes a course in business ethics without hearing the all-too-familiar refrain, "Hey, isn't business ethics an oxymoron?" On the other hand, some argue that ethics is a natural market consequence of business. Scholars George Steiner and John Steiner have identified six primary sources of ethics in the American business arena:

Genetic Inheritance Although the view remains theoretical, sociobiologists have in recent years amassed persuasive evidence and arguments suggesting that the evolutionary forces of natural selection influence the development of traits such as cooperation and altruism that lie at the core of our ethical systems. Those qualities of goodness often associated with ethical conduct may, in some measure, be a product of genetic traits strengthened over time by the evolutionary process.

---

2. Laura Nash, "Ethics Without The Sermon," *Harvard Business Review* 56, no. 6 (1981), pp. 80–81.

Religion Via a rule exemplified by the Golden Rule (or its variations in many religions) and the Ten Commandments, religious morality is clearly a primary force in shaping our societal ethics. The question here concerns the applicability of religious ethics to the business community. The question is all the more relevant since the Golden Rule is not limited to Western thought. Consider these words of Confucius:

> *There are four things in the Way of the profound person, none of which I have been able to do. To serve my father as I would expect my son to serve me. To serve my ruler as I would expect my ministers to serve me. To serve my elder brother as I would expect my younger brothers to serve me. To be the first to treat friends as I would expect them to treat me. These I have not been able to do.[3]*

Could the Golden Rule serve as a universal, practical, helpful standard for the business person's conduct?

Philosophical Systems To the Epicureans, the quality of pleasure to be derived from an act was the essential measure of its goodness. The Stoics, like the Puritans and many contemporary Americans, advocated a disciplined, hardworking, thrifty lifestyle. These philosophies and others, like those cited earlier, have been instrumental in our society's moral development.

Cultural Experience Here, the Steiners refer to the rules, customs, and standards transmitted from generation to generation as guidelines for appropriate conduct. Individual values are shaped in large measure by the norms of the society.

The Legal System Laws represent a rough approximation of society's ethical standards. Thus, the law serves to educate us about the ethical course in life. The law does not and, most would agree, should not be treated as a vehicle for expressing all of society's ethical preferences. Rather, the law is an ever-changing approximation of current perceptions of right and wrong.

Codes of Conduct Steiner and Steiner identify three primary categories of such codes. Company codes, ordinarily brief and highly generalized, express broad expectations about fit conduct. Second, company operating policies often contain an ethical dimension. Express policies as to gifts, customer complaints, hiring, and other decisions serve as a guide to conduct and as a shield by which the employee can protect against unethical advances from those outside the firm. Third, many professional and industry associations have developed codes of ethics, such as the Affirmative Ethical Principles of the American Institute of Certified Public Accountants. (Codes of conduct are further discussed in Chapter 7c.) In sum, codes of conduct seem to be a growing expression of the business community's sincere concern about ethics. However, the utility of such codes remains unsettled.

---

3. Confucius, *The Doctrine of the Mean*, chap. 13; *The Analects*, XIV, p. 28

What forces determine which companies or business persons end up ethical and which do not? Psychologist Lawrence Kohlberg believes that some individuals are simply better prepared than others to make ethical judgments. He built a comprehensive theory of moral development in which he claimed that moral judgment evolves and improves primarily as a function of age and education.

Kohlberg, via interviews with children as they aged, was able to identify moral development as movement through distinct stages, with the later stages being viewed as more advanced than the earlier ones. Kohlberg identified six universal stages grouped into three levels:

Preconventional Level (Level 1)

Stage 1: Obey rules to avoid punishment.

Stage 2: Follow rules only if it is in own interest, but let others do the same. Conform to secure rewards.

Conventional Level (Level 2)

Stage 3: Conform to meet the expectations of others. Please others. Adhere to stereotypical images.

Stage 4: Doing right is one's duty. Obey the law. Uphold the social contract and order.

Postconventional or Principled Level (Level 3)

Stage 5: Current laws and values are relative. Laws and duty are obeyed on rational calculations to serve the greatest number.

Stage 6: Follow self-chosen universal ethical principles. In the event of conflicts, principles override laws.[4]

At the postconventional level, the individual is able to reach independent moral judgments that may or may not be in conformity with conventional societal wisdom. Thus, the Level 2 manager might refrain from sexual harassment because it constitutes a violation of company policy and the law. A manager at Level 3 might reach the same conclusion, but her or his decision would have been based on independently defined, universal principles of justice.

Kohlberg found that many adults never pass beyond Level 2. Consequently, if Kohlberg is correct, many managers may behave unethically simply because they have not reached the upper stages of moral maturity.

Kohlberg's model is based on very extensive longitudinal and cross-cultural studies over a period of more than three decades. For example, one set of Chicago-area boys was interviewed at 3-year intervals for a period of 20 years. Thus the stages of moral growth

---

4. For an elaboration of Kohlberg's stages, see, e.g., W. D. Boyce and L. C. Jensen, *Moral Reasoning* (Lincoln, NE: Univ. of Nebraska Press, 1978), pp. 98–109.

exhibit "definite empirical characteristics" such that Kohlberg was able to claim that his model had been scientifically validated. While many critics remain, the evidence, in sum, is supportive of Kohlberg's general proposition.

Carol Gilligan offers a conception of moral development that runs contrary to Kohlberg's analysis. Instead of finding that individuals grow toward more autonomous, global decision making, Gilligan finds that individuals grow toward more complex webs of "caring" relationships. Gilligan's ethics of care was based on her findings that there exists a way of thinking about moral issues at variance with Kohlberg's sixth stage, and that this alternative was more common among women based on their different life experiences.

Gilligan found the following:

> In a series of studies designed to investigate the relationship between conceptions of self and morality, and to test their association with gender and age, two moral voices could reliably be distinguished in the way people framed and resolved moral problems and in their evaluations of choices they made. One voice speaks of connection, not hurting, care, and response; and one speaks of equality, reciprocity, justice and rights. . . . The pattern of predominance, although not gender specific, was gender related.[5]

Gilligan, therefore had a different conception of moral development:

First focus: Caring for self and ensuring survival.

Transition stage: Self focus as unacceptably selfish.

Second focus: Responsibility and material care for dependent others, self-sacrifice.

Transition stage: Questions illogic of inequality between needs of others and self.

Third focus: Dynamic relationship between self and others.[6]

Consider the similarities and differences between Gilligan's and Kohlberg's analyses. In evaluating the actions of others, is it more helpful to consider their position along Kohlberg's scale or Gilligan's? Which seems more realistic as you apply it to others? Gilligan is often criticized for her general conclusion that women and men (as a result of life experiences) reason differently. Do you agree or disagree with that proposition?

CORPORATE RESPONSIBILITY

A corporation, through its individual decision makers, might be viewed as having reached one of Kohlberg's levels. But is a corporation the same as a moral person? Of course, the corporation has long been treated as a person of sorts in the eyes of the law.

---

5. Carol Gilligan, "Remapping the Moral Domain: New Images of Self in Relationship," in C. Gilligan, J. Ward and J. McClean Taylor, eds., *Mapping the Moral Domain* (Cambridge, MA: Center for the Study of Gender, Education and Human Development, Harvard University Press 1988).
6. Carol Gilligan, *In A Different Voice* (Cambridge: Harvard University Press, 1982).

We can legitimately hold the corporation legally blameworthy for employee wrongs. But can we attribute moral responsibility to the corporation? Ordinarily, we consider an individual morally responsible for act or event X only (1) if the person did X or caused X to occur and (2) if the person's conduct was intentional. Does a corporation ever do or cause any event? And even if a corporation could act, could it do so with intent? In a sense, can a corporation even think?

Philosopher Peter French posits that a corporation can be considered an actor since it has an organizational system of decision making (the organizational chart) and a set of policies and procedures for actions. Thus, the judgments and actions of individuals within the corporation are actually governed by the corporation itself, that is, the will of the corporation. Critics of this approach argue that, while a corporation may be similar to an individual in some ways, it is certainly distinct in others. For instance, the corporation does not have the same rights as individuals, such as the right to life.

Even if we are persuaded that the corporation could be treated as a moral actor, do we want to do so? We might answer yes because, in the event of wrongdoing, we could avoid the nearly impossible task of finding the guilty party within the corporate maze. Why not simply place the blame (or at least part of it) on the organization? But if we were to do so, would we somehow depreciate perhaps the central moral precept in our society—the notion that each of us must accept responsibility for our actions?

BUSINESS ETHICS IN PRACTICE

When questioned regarding the forces that contribute to unethical decision making in working life, managers point to the behavior of their superiors and the nature of company policy regarding wrongdoing. Hence, we assume that an organization committed to ethical quality can institute some structures and procedures to encourage decency. Codes of conduct are a common corporate ethics tool (discussed in further detail in Chapter 7c). But the question remains: can we somehow encourage ethical behavior on the part of managerial decision makers?

As mentioned earlier, ethics is but one mode of decision making in the corporate environment. Is it possible to persuade corporate managers that ethics *should* be the basis of their decisions? Of course, if ethical behavior *always* led to higher profits as well as higher quality products or services, the market would take care of everything. The ethical business person would be more likely to succeed than the unethical business person. However, while higher ethics may lead to higher profits (see Chapter 7), they do not *always* do so. We have all heard tales of those who successfully avoided responsibility for their unethical acts, while reaping millions in the meantime. Or of those that actually go to jail for wrongful conduct, only to have their millions restored to them upon their release. As long as there is some perceived benefit to unethical behavior, some decision makers may be persuaded to leave their ethics at the door.

Modern theories of economics and ethics may prove useful in understanding and encouraging ethical behavior in business. Consider the implications of a lawless system, where we relied solely on market forces to encourage behavior. Would companies be unleashed to act in unethical ways, or would there be any reason to believe that companies would refrain from wrongful conduct (or conduct we considered wrongful, since no law would be broken)? Does the market ensure fairness? Justice? Some scholars believe that the marketplace does, indeed, foster ethical and honest behavior. It is argued that there is some market value to honesty and ethics—that consumers reward firms that are straight with them, firms in which they can place their trust. Consider drugstore giant Walgreen's adage, "The Pharmacy America Trusts," or Johnson & Johnson's "Trust in Tampax." Truth might be the best policy, as the Roman philosopher Seneca noted that "time discovers truth."[7]

Economists Dwight Lee and Richard McKenzie support this contention. They explain that a business person may act honestly because of the high costs of dishonesty.[8] This is not to say that a business person cannot profit through dishonesty, simply that the risks/potential costs of dishonesty are higher than those of honesty.

> *In addition to being a virtue from a strictly moral perspective, honesty is also important for quite instrumental reasons. An economy in which people deal with each other honestly produces more wealth than one in which people are chronically dishonest because more exchanges occur directing resources into their most productive employments.[9]*

An earlier perspective is offered by St. Augustine in his treatise "On Lying," where he explains "when regard for truth has been broken down or even slightly weakened, all things will remain doubtful."

On the other hand, should *all* behavior be regulated, in every situation? Should fairness and justice be completely legislated? Recently, states have enacted laws prohibiting individuals who failed to pay their family support from obtaining drivers licenses. This was considered a crossover of law and behavioral justice. Paying family support really has nothing to do with whether one should be licensed to drive; however, the state is using its muscle to encourage behavior it considers right. In addition, to prevent even the appearance of impropriety, states have enacted conflict-of-interest statutes that prohibit activities by public workers that might *lead* to or give the appearance of wrongful conduct, even where none exists.

Standards of Conduct and Conflict of Interest
Sec. 572.001. Policy; Legislative Intent

(a) *It is the policy of this state that a state officer or state employee may not have a direct or indirect interest, including financial and other interests, or engage in a business transaction or professional activity, or incur any obligation of any nature that is in substantial conflict with the proper discharge of the officer's or employee's duties in the public interest.*

(b) *To implement this policy and to strengthen the faith and confidence of the people of this state in state government, this chapter provides standards of conduct and disclosure requirements to be observed by persons owing a responsibility to the people and government of this state in the performance of their official duties.*

---

7. F. Richard Ciccone, "Truth and The American Way," *Chicago Tribune,* May 12, 1996, sec. 2, p. 8.

8. Dwight Lee, Richard McKenzie, "How the Marketplace Fosters Business Honesty," *Business & Society Review,* Winter 1995, pp. 5–9.

9. Ibid., p. 5.

(c) It is the intent of the legislature that this chapter serve not only as a guide for official conduct of those persons but also as a basis for discipline of those who refuse to abide by its terms. . . .

Sec. 572.051. Standards of Conduct

A state officer or employee should not:

(1) accept or solicit any gift, favor, or service that might reasonably tend to influence the officer or employee in the discharge of official duties or that the officer or employee knows or should know is being offered with the intent to influence the officer's or employee's official conduct;

(2) accept other employment or engage in a business or professional activity that the officer or employee might reasonably expect would require or induce the officer or employee to disclose confidential information acquired by reason of the official position;

(3) accept other employment or compensation that could reasonably be expected to impair the officer's or employee's independence of judgment in the performance of the officer's or employee's official duties;

(4) make personal investments that could reasonably be expected to create a substantial conflict between the officer's or employee's private interest and the public interest; or

(5) intentionally or knowingly solicit, accept, or agree to accept any benefit for having exercised the officer's or employee's official powers or performed the officer's or employee's official duties in favor of another.[10]

SHORT HYPOTHETICAL CASES

Your company's marketing department has placed a classified ad seeking applicants for a job that doesn't exist. The company is not named in the ad. Your company wants to accomplish two things. First, the firm wants to know which of its employees is out looking for a new position. Second, it wants to entice competitors' employees in for an interview, hoping to gain valuable information about the competition. You have been assigned to field calls and to interview the competition. What do you do?

Hypotheticals were written by Catherine Haselden and are included in her unpublished manuscript "The Ethics Game."

---

10. Chapter 572, §001, §051, Texas Government Code (1991); http://gold.utsystem.edu/Ethics/standcon.htm.

BUSINESS AS A SOCIAL
AND MORAL TERRAIN

ROBERT JACKALL

*Jackall lays a foundation for the study of the applied field of research
and analysis: business ethics. While the original domain of ethics lies
in philosophy, ethical theory has consistently been applied to evaluate behavior and decision making in the business environment.*

Corporate leaders often tell their charges that hard work will lead to success. Indeed, this
theory of reward being commensurate with effort has been an enduring belief and a moral
imperative in our society, one central to our self-image as a people, where the main
chance is available to anyone of ability who has the gumption and persistence to seize it.
Hard work, it is also frequently asserted, builds character. This notion carries less conviction because business people, and our society as a whole, have little patience with those
who, even though they work hard, make a habit of finishing out of the money. In the end,
it is success that matters, that legitimates striving, and that makes work worthwhile. What
if, however, men and women in the corporation no longer see success as necessarily connected to hard work? What becomes of the social morality of the corporation—the everyday rules-in-use that people play by—when there is thought to be no fixed or, one might
say, objective standard of excellence to explain how and why winners are separated from
also-rans, how and why some people succeed and others fail? What rules do people
fashion to interact with one another when they feel that, instead of ability, talent, and
dedicated service to an organization, politics, adroit talk, luck, connections, and self-
promotion are the real sorters of people into sheep and goats? . . .

As it happens, the field of business ethics is rapidly becoming big business. Among
other developments, the last fifteen years have seen the proliferation of a great number of
books and articles on ethical problems in business; the emergence of several centers and
institutes at least partly dedicated to the subject or to related problems like the role of values in scientific, technological, or public policy work; the spread of business ethics
courses in both college and business school curricula; and even, in some corporations, the
development of seminars in ethics for executives. This groundswell of attention to ethical
issues in business continues a historical tradition that in different forms dates at least to
the turn of this century, when the big corporation became a paramount institution in our
society. The current upsurge in concern over ethics was prompted undoubtedly by the
Watergate crisis and its spillover into business. It has been stimulated more recently by a
series of corporate and governmental scandals headed by revelations about insider trading
on the stock market and by glimpses of high federal officials illegally diverting funds and

systematically deceiving Congress and the public during the Iran-contra affair. At the same time, the accelerating pace of scientific and technological change that continually overturns taken for granted notions about our universe has prompted widespread discussions of ethical issues. All of this has been a boon to moral philosophers, normally a precariously positioned occupational group in a social order where the mantle of intellectual supremacy has long since passed from a discipline once called the queen of the sciences. With the titles of "ethicist" or even "ethician," moral philosophers have applied their considerable mental acumen to unraveling the conundrums of the fast-paced, hurly-burly worlds of commerce and industry or more sedate scientific milieux. In doing so, they have extended in quite new directions the much longer tradition of moral casuistry, that is, the process of applying general principles to specific situations in order to resolve moral quandaries, an art that may involve the invention of wholly new rules and legitimations for action. Unfortunately, most of this analysis has been of hypothetical cases, of real-life situations abstracted from their intricate organizational contexts, of public testimony before various commissions and hearings by officials who, as it happens, are well-versed in fencing with their adversaries, or of the journalistic accounts of the many highly publicized corporate scandals in recent years. In fact, certain vocabularies have become so institutionalized in some philosophical circles that whole sets of assumptions and taken for granted analyses, often complete with settled moral judgments, are often invoked simply by cryptic references to, say, the "Pinto Case" or the "Dalkon Shield Affair." Despite the emergence of a new industry that one might call Ethics Inc., however, the philosophers at least have done little detailed investigation of the day-to-day operations, structure, and meaning of work in business and of how the conditions of that work shape moral consciousness.

But only an understanding of how men and women in business actually experience their work enables one to grasp its moral salience for them. Bureaucratic work shapes people's consciousness in decisive ways. Among other things, it regularizes people's experiences of time and indeed routinizes their lives by engaging them on a daily basis in rational, socially approved, purposive action; it brings them into daily proximity with and subordination to authority, creating in the process upward-looking stances that have decisive social and psychological consequences; it places a premium on a functionally rational, pragmatic habit of mind that seeks specific goals; and it creates subtle measures of prestige and an elaborate status hierarchy that, in addition to fostering an intense competition for status, also makes the rules, procedures, social contexts, and protocol of an organization paramount psychological and behavioral guides. In fact, bureaucratic contexts typically bring together men and women who initially have little in common with each other except the impersonal frameworks of their organizations. Indeed, the enduring genius of the organizational form is that it allows individuals to retain bewilderingly diverse private motives and meanings for action as long as they adhere publicly to agreed-upon rules. Even the personal relationships that men and women in bureaucracies do subsequently fashion together are, for the most part, governed by explicit or implicit organizational rules, procedures, and protocol. As a result, bureaucratic work causes people to bracket, while at work, the moralities that they might hold outside the workplace or that they might adhere to privately and to follow instead the prevailing morality of their particular organizational situation. As a former vice-president of a large firm says: "What is right in the corporation is not what is right in a man's home or in his church. *What is right in the corporation is what the guy above you wants from you.* That's what morality is in the corporation."* Of course, since public legitimacy and respectability depend, in part, on perceptions of one's moral probity, one cannot admit to such a bracketing of one's conventional moralities except, usually indirectly, within one's managerial circles where such verities are widely recognized to be inapplicable except as public relations stances. In fact, though managers usually think of it as separate from decision making, public relations is an extremely important facet of managerial work, one that often requires the employment of practitioners with special expertise.

Managers do not generally discuss ethics, morality, or moral rules-in-use in a direct way with each other, except perhaps in seminars organized by ethicists. Such seminars, however, are unusual and, when they do occur, are often strained, artificial, and often confusing even to managers since they frequently become occasions for the solemn public invocation, particularly by high-ranking managers, of conventional moralities and traditional shibboleths. What matters on a day-to-day basis are the moral rules-in-use fashioned within the personal and structural constraints of one's organization. As it happens, these rules may vary sharply depending on various factors, such as proximity to the market, line or staff responsibilities, or one's position in a hierarchy. Actual organizational moralities are thus contextual, situational, highly specific, and, most often, unarticulated. . . .

RELATED WEB SITES

Moral mazes: Bureaucracy and managerial work:
  www.hbsp.harvard.edu/bin/showbook?83507

What do eco-anarchists propose instead of capitalism?
  www.geocities.com/CapitolHill/1931/secE1.html

---

*All italics within quotations from interviews represent the subject's own emphasis, as noted by the author.

SOME THOUGHTS ON THE MEANING OF BUSINESS ETHICS

BARBARA LEY TOFFLER

*Toffler is the director of Ethics and Responsible Business Practices
Consulting at Arthur Andersen LLP, New York. This area of Arthur
Andersen's practice helps businesses to address issues related to
ethics. The following article is included in the firm's marketing
materials.*

I. RESPONSIBLE VERSUS COMPLIANT OR ETHICAL

The 1990s have seen an explosion of programs focused on good behavior in both public
and private sector institutions. Most of these activities are called either compliance programs or ethics programs. Compliance programs generally deal with adherence to laws,
regulations, policies and procedures, while ethics programs include compliance issues,
but tend to focus on ethical reasoning and analysis (e.g., rights analysis, which asks who
has rights in a particular situation). Most of the compliance programs are reasonably effective in informing employees of the laws, regulations, etc., and in telling them about the
consequences of noncompliance; and many of the ethics programs do raise ethical awareness. Few of either, however, are successful at weaving those ideas into the fabric of employees' daily work.

Compliance programs usually resemble law enforcement: Participants are potential
offenders who are told by corporate law enforcement officials—lawyers, internal auditors, internal affairs officers—what they must do and what will happen to them if they
disobey. Although usually unintended, the tone is often punitive or paternalistic, neither
of which makes employees feel respected and capable.

Ethics programs, on the other hand, often fall into the Sunday school or sermoniz-
ing category. Often delivered by human resources or a corporate social policy group,
the focus of an ethics program is frequently on being a good person and doing the right
thing, but without attention to institutional realities, the effect of those realities on employee behavior, and how employees can learn to manage the realities—all of which
are essential to behaving ethically. (An example is a business ethics book co-authored
by Kenneth Blanchard and Norman Vincent Peale referred to by many as The One-
Minute Manager Meets the Power of Positive Thinking—in which, if the manager does
the right thing, everything will turn out fine. Real life usually requires more complex
management.)

The word *responsible,* however, encompasses both compliant and ethical, but includes much more. A program that focuses on responsible employee behavior begins with an assumption that employees want to do the right thing, but recognizes that they may face impediments to doing so effectively. It then (1) instructs them in the laws, regulations, policies, and procedures they must know and follow, (2) assists them in understanding the kinds of dilemmas they may face in their jobs and the role their institution plays in those dilemmic situations, (3) guides them in applying the laws, regulations, etc., to their work, and (4) helps them develop skills to resolve their dilemmas. A key message of a responsible business practices program is that the institution respects the employees and their capabilities, and expects them to be responsible and accountable for the actions they take. In other words, the program says they are part of the team.

II. HELPING PEOPLE DO THE RIGHT THING MEANS UNDERSTANDING WHY THEY DO WRONG

Most compliance and ethics programs begin with the assumption that if individuals want to do the right thing, they will do it. But that is not always the case. Let's look at an example:

In 1987, the Internal Revenue Service of the United States discovered that employees in three of its offices—Fresno, Philadelphia, and Andover, Massachusetts—were flushing tax returns and/or related documents down the toilets. Stories appeared in the national media, the Service was embarrassed, and of course, the guilty individuals were terminated. Generally, the focus was on the people who had done wrong and the concern that the IRS had not properly instructed its employees in correct behavior.

But, in reality, why did this unfortunate series of events occur?

The Service needed, and was authorized by Congress, to purchase a new computer system to meet its expanding needs. A system made by a foreign manufacturer was found to best meet the specifications. However, Congress felt it was important that the U.S. government buy American, so the IRS found a U.S. source that claimed the capability of meeting the specs. However, it turned out that not only did the system not have the necessary capacity (it did not meet the specs), it also was of inferior quality—it kept breaking down. Between capacity and quality problems, down-time increased and processing of returns was delayed. When processors came in on weekends to catch up on backlogged work, they often found the system under repair.

At the same time, the evaluation system for these processors measured backlog—what was still piled up on their desks. Since the computer system could not handle the work and supervisors were pressuring processors to get the work off their desks or suffer bad evaluations, processors did get the paper work off their desks—by throwing them into the toilets!

The reason for recounting this story is not to exonerate the return processors. What they did was wrong and they were appropriately disciplined. However, it is critical to note that they did not destroy documents because they did not want to do the right thing, or that they did not know that what they were doing was wrong. Processors destroyed documents because they knew no way to legitimately raise their concerns and be part of finding a solution to the problems, and their supervisors had not been encouraged to be available to subordinates to hear concerns and support problem resolution. Neither processors nor supervisors felt part of a team effort, and all felt that to raise a problem meant that you would be seen as part of the problem (the kill-the-messenger syndrome). Further, the IRS had never stopped to consider the impact of new technology on its employees (which would be significant even with a well-running new system), and to provide avenues for assistance.

There is another example, this one in the private sector, that is worth recalling here:

The public was appropriately horrified when it was discovered that the breast implants made by Dow Corning were leaking silicone into womens bodies. Many said that somebody should have reported the problem when it was seen in the lab, and that here was more evidence of the need for ethics programs. The fact is that Dow Corning had a model ethics program, celebrated in a Harvard Business School case. One element of the program included groups of 35 employees meeting with the CEO, who asked them to tell him of any concerns they had. No one ever raised leaking implants at one of these sessions. Why? In this case, we do not have information on what really happened. But we all must assume that some gap existed in the elegant ethics program—a gap between helping people analyze what was right and wrong in a situation, and helping them do something about it.

III. WHY DO PEOPLE DO WRONG?

There are several reasons why people do wrong:

1. Character Reasons: There are those who do wrong because they do not know right from wrong, they do not care if they do right, they are out for self-gain, or they resent authority. No program will reach such people. An institution hopes to find them and remove them.

2. Information-related Reasons: In these cases, people want to do right, but (1) do not have the information they need (laws, policies, etc.), or (2) have the information they need, but do not understand it, or (3) have the information they need, understand it, but do not know how to apply it, and (4) they do not know where to go for help, or fear that if they ask for help they will be seen as incompetent. Most newcomers to an organization find themselves in this situation. So a good program must provide information in a clear, user-friendly way, with the message: This is what you need to know; this is where you can go to learn what you need to know. Now you are being held accountable.

3. Expectation-related Reasons: In these situations, people know what is right and wrong, and know the laws and policies. But they think one of two things: (*a*) They believe their supervisor or the company expects them to ignore the problem and just get on with the job. This often happens when the problem is relatively small and the cost in time or money is significant. Or (*b*) they experience the Move-it effect, where they feel they are being pressured by superiors to Move it . . . Don't give me an argument, just get it done. In these cases, individuals often believe that if they raise legitimate concerns, they will put themselves at job or career risk.

4. Judgment-related Reasons: In these kinds of cases, people face true dilemmas where there is no clear right answer. Often they are trying to meet two conflicting good values. One company had two statements in its Standards of Conduct: One supported

affirmatively hiring and promoting women and minorities and the other stated there must be no discriminatory behavior. Many felt it was hard to know what was right when hiring. Often dilemmas concern two conflicting regulations. A utility company manager had a hard time deciding how to remove asbestos from scrubbers. To remove asbestos, the scrubbers had to be shut down for longer than EPA allows. To not remove the asbestos would violate EPA regulations. The manager knew the regulations, wanted to do the right thing, and still faced a problem. (The resolution involved working with senior management to approach the regulatory agency for a variance.)

A successful program, a Responsible Business Practices program, must be based on an understanding of why people do wrong things. It must include (1) instruction for all employees—both individual contributors and those with supervisory/managerial responsibilities—in the laws, policies, etc., they must uphold, and (2) skill building, guidance and resources to address the causes of wrongdoing. As well, the company must provide mechanisms to give employees the support and guidance they need, and to enable them to ask for help without feeling foolish or incompetent.

The able employee of the 21st century must be committed to doing right, must have the information necessary to do right, and must have the resources and support essential to solve problems and resolve dilemmas.

RELATED WEB SITE

Arthur Andersen LLP: www.arthurandersen.com

AMERICA'S PERSECUTED MINORITY: BIG BUSINESS

AYN RAND

As will also be discussed in Chapter 3, Ayn Rand is best known for her economic theory, objectivism. Objectivism is a form of ethical egoism which suggests that we accept the fact that we all act in our own self-interest. We should be free to do so, as long as we do not infringe on anyone else's right to act in her or his own self-interest. The following lecture reflects her concern that business is constantly subject to a tolerated persecution, always blamed for the sins, errors, or failures of other groups. It was given at the Ford Hall Forum in Boston, Massachusetts, on December 17, 1961, and at Columbia University in 1962.

If a small group of men were always regarded as guilty, in any clash with any other group, regardless of the issues or circumstances involved, would you call it persecution? If this group were always made to pay for the sins, errors, or failures of any other group, would you call *that* persecution? If this group had to live under a silent reign of terror, under special laws, from which all other people were immune, laws which the accused could not grasp or define in advance and which the accuser could interpret in any way he pleased—would you call *that* persecution? If this group were penalized, not for its faults, but for its virtues, not for its incompetence, but for its ability, not for its failures, but for its achievements, and the greater the achievement, the greater the penalty—would you call *that* persecution?

If your answer is "yes"—then ask yourself what sort of monstrous injustice you are condoning, supporting, or perpetrating. That group is the American businessmen.

The defense of minority rights is acclaimed today, virtually by everyone, as a moral principle of a high order. But this principle, which forbids discrimination, is applied by most of the "liberal" intellectuals in a *discriminatory* manner: it is applied only to racial or religious minorities. It is not applied to that small, exploited, denounced, defenseless minority which consists of businessmen.

Yet every ugly, brutal aspect of injustice toward racial or religious minorities is being practiced toward businessmen. For instance, consider the evil of condemning some

"America's Persecuted Minority: Big Business," lecture given by Ayn Rand at The Ford Hall Forum, Boston, MA, 12/17/61 and Columbia University. Reprinted by permission of the Estate of Ayn Rand.

men and absolving others, without a hearing, regardless of the facts. Today's "liberals" consider a businessman guilty in any conflict with a labor union, regardless of the facts of issues involved, and boast that they will not cross a picket line "right or wrong." Consider the evil of judging people by a double standard and of denying to some the rights granted to others. Today's "liberals" recognize the workers' (the majority's) right to their livelihood (their wages), but deny the businessmen's (the minority's) right to *their* livelihood (their profits). If workers struggle for higher wages, this is hailed as "social gains"; if businessmen struggle for higher profits, this is damned as "selfish greed." If the workers' standard of living is low, the "liberals" blame it on the businessmen; but if the businessmen attempt to improve their economic efficacy, to expand their markets, and to enlarge the financial returns of their enterprises, thus making higher wages and lower prices possible, the same "liberals" denounce it as "commercialism." If a non-commercial foundation—*i.e.,* a group which did not have to *earn* its funds—sponsors a television show, advocating its particular views, the "liberals" hail it as "enlightenment," "education," "art," and "public service"; if a businessman sponsors a television show and wants it to reflect *his* views, the "liberals" scream, calling it "censorship," "pressure," and "dictatorial rule." When three locals of the International Brotherhood of Teamsters deprived New York City of its milk supply for fifteen days—no moral indignation or condemnation was heard from the "liberal" quarters; but just imagine what would happen if *businessmen* stopped that milk supply for one hour—and how swiftly they would be struck down by that legalized lynching or pogrom known as "trust-busting."

Whenever, in any era, culture, or society, you encounter the phenomenon of prejudice, injustice, persecution, and blind, unreasoning hatred directed at some minority group—look for the gang that has something to gain from that persecution, look for those who have a vested interest in the destruction of these particular sacrificial victims. Invariably, you will find that the persecuted minority serves as a scapegoat for some movement that does not want the nature of its own goals to be known. Every movement that seeks to enslave a a country, every dictatorship or potential dictatorship, needs some minority group as a scapegoat which it can blame for the nation's troubles and use as a justification of its own demands for dictatorial powers. In Soviet Russia, the scapegoat was the bourgeoisie; in Nazi Germany, it was the Jewish people; in America, it is the businessmen.

America has not yet reached the stage of a dictatorship. But, paving the way to it, for many decades past, the businessmen have served as the scapegoat for *statist* movements of all kinds: communist, fascist, or welfare. For whose sins and evils did the businessmen take the blame? For the sins and evils of the bureaucrats.

A disastrous intellectual package-deal, put over on us by the theoreticians of statism, is the equation of *economic* power with *political* power. You have heard it expressed in such bromides as: "A hungry man is not free," or "It makes no difference to a worker whether he takes orders from a businessman or from a bureaucrat." Most people accept these equivocations—and yet they know that the poorest laborer in America is freer and more secure than the richest commissar in Soviet Russia. What is the basic, the essential, the crucial principle that differentiates freedom from slavery? It is the principle of voluntary action *versus* physical coercion or compulsion.

The difference between political power and any other kind of social "power," between a government and any private organization, is the fact that *a government holds a legal monopoly on the use of physical force.* This distinction is so important and so seldom recognized today that I must urge you to keep it in mind. Let me repeat it: *a government holds a legal monopoly on the use of physical force.*

No individual or private group or private organization has the legal power to initiate the use of physical force against other individuals or groups and to compel them to act against their own voluntary choice. Only a government holds that power. The nature of governmental action is: *coercive* action. The nature of political power is: the power to force obedience under threat of physical injury—the threat of property expropriation, imprisonment, or death.

Foggy metaphors, sloppy images, unfocused poetry, and equivocations—such as "A hungry man is not free"—do not alter the fact that *only* political power is the power of physical coercion and that freedom, in a political context, has only one meaning: *The absence of physical coercion.*

The only proper function of the government of a free country is to act as an agency which protects the individual's rights, i.e., which protects the individual from physical violence. Such a government does not have the right to *initiate* the use of physical force against anyone—a right which the individual does not possess and, therefore, cannot delegate to any agency. But the individual does possess the right of self-defense and *that* is the right which he delegates to the government, for the purpose of an orderly, legally defined enforcement. A proper government has the right to use physical force *only* in retaliation and *only* against those who initiate its use. The proper functions of a government are: the police, to protect men from criminals; the military forces, to protect men from foreign invaders; and the law courts, to protect men's property and contracts from breach by force or fraud, and to settle disputes among men according to objectively defined laws.

These, implicitly, were the political principles on which the Constitution of the United States was based; implicitly, but not explicitly. There were contradictions in the Constitution, which allowed the statists to gain an entering wedge, to enlarge the breach, and, gradually, to wreck the structure. . . .

A system of pure, unregulated laissez-faire capitalism has never yet existed anywhere. What did exist were only so-called mixed economies, which means: a mixture, in varying degrees, of freedom and controls, of voluntary choice and government coercion, of capitalism and statism. America was the freest country on earth, but elements of statism were present in her economy from the start. These elements kept growing, under the influence of her intellectuals who were predominantly committed to the philosophy of statism. The intellectuals—the ideologists, the interpreters, the assessors of public events—were tempted by the opportunity to seize political power, relinquished by all other social groups, and to establish their own versions of a "good" society at the point of a gun, i.e., by means of legalized physical coercion. They denounced the free businessmen as exponents of "selfish greed" and glorified the bureaucrats as "public servants." In evaluating social problems, they kept damning "economic power" and exonerating political power, thus switching the burden of guilt from the politicians to the businessmen.

All the evils, abuses, and iniquities, popularly ascribed to businessmen and to capitalism, were not caused by an unregulated economy or by a free market, but by government intervention into the economy. The giants of American industry—such as James

Jerome Hill or Commodore Vanderbilt or Andrew Carnegie or J. P. Morgan—were self-made men who earned their fortunes by personal ability, by free trade on a free market. But there existed another kind of businessmen, the products of a mixed economy, the men with political pull, who made fortunes by means of special privileges granted to them by the government, such men as the Big Four of the Central Pacific Railroad. It was the political power behind their activities—the power of forced, unearned, economically unjustified privileges—that caused dislocations in the country's economy, hardships, depressions, and mounting public protests. But it was the free market and the free businessmen that took the blame. Every calamitous consequence of government controls was used as a justification for the extension of the controls and of the government's power over the economy. . . .

What should we do about it? We should demand a reexamination and revision of the entire issue of antitrust. We should challenge its philosophical, political, economic, and *moral* base. We should have a Civil Liberties Union—for businessmen. The repeal of the antitrust laws should be our ultimate goal; it will require a long intellectual and political struggle; but in the meantime and as a first step, we should demand that the jail-penalty provisions of these laws be abolished. It is bad enough if men have to suffer financial penalties, such as fines, under laws which everyone concedes to be non-objective, contradictory, and undefinable, since no two jurists can agree on their meaning and application; it is obscene to impose prison sentences under laws of so controversial a nature. We should put an end to the outrage of sending men to jail for breaking unintelligible laws which they cannot avoid breaking.

Businessmen are the one group that distinguishes capitalism and the American way of life from the totalitarian statism that is swallowing the rest of the world. All the other social groups—workers, farmers, professional men, scientists, soldiers—exist under dictatorships, even though they exist in chains, in terror, in misery, and in progressive self-destruction. *But there is no such group as businessmen under a dictatorship.* Their place is taken by armed thugs: by bureaucrats and commissars. Businessmen are the symbol of a free society—the symbol of America. If and when they perish, civilization will perish. But if you wish to fight for freedom, you must begin by fighting for its unrewarded, unrecognized, unacknowledged, yet best representatives—the American businessmen.

RELATED WEB SITES

Council on Economic Priorities: www.accesspt.com/cep/indexbare.html

About objectivism: www.vix.com/objectivism/

The Ayn Rand Institute: The Center for the Advancement of Objectivism:
    www.aynrand.org/

THE ONE-MINUTE
MORALIST

Robert Solomon

Solomon posits a question that will be asked again and again by authors throughout this text: Does ethics in business lead to profits? Is good ethics good for business?

Once there was a bright young businessman who was looking for an ethical manager.

He wanted to work for one. He wanted to become one.

His search had taken him over many years to the far corners of the business world.

He visited small businesses and large corporations.

He spoke with used-car dealers, chief executive officers of Fortune 500 companies, management-science professors, vice presidents for strategic planning, and one-minute managers.

He visited every kind of office, big and small, carpeted and tiled, some with breath-taking views, some without any view at all.

He heard a full spectrum of ethical views.

But he wasn't pleased with what he heard.

On the one hand, virtually everyone he met seemed frank, friendly, and courteous, adamant about honesty even to the point of moral indignation. People were respectful of one another, concerned about their employees, and loyal to their own superiors. They paid their debts and resented the lawsuits in which they considered themselves the innocent party, victims of misunderstanding and antibusiness sentiment. They complained about regulation and the implied distrust of their integrity. They proudly asserted that they were producing quality products or services that truly did satisfy consumer demand, making the world a better—even if only a very slightly better—place in which to live.

Their superiors were proud of their trustworthiness.

Their subordinates were confident of their fairness.

But, on the other hand, when they were asked for their views about ethics and business, what all of these people had to say was startling, to say the least.

The answers varied only slightly.

"You have to understand that it's a jungle out there!"

"Listen, I'm a survivor."

"If I don't do it, the other guy will."

"You've got to be realistic in this business."

"Profits—that's what it's all about. You do whatever you have to."

"The One-Minute Moralist," from *The New World of Business*. Reprinted by permission of Rowman & Littlefield Publishers.

And when our bright young businessman brought up the topic of business ethics, he invariably heard:

"There aren't any ethics in business"; or . . .

"*Business Ethics*—the shortest book in the world."

The latter usually with a grin.

At the same time, however, many executives shook their heads sadly and expressed the private wish that it were otherwise.

He met a few unscrupulous businessmen who admitted cutting corners, who had made a profit and were proud of it.

He met others who had cut corners and were caught. "This is a cutthroat world," they insisted, often contradicting this immediately by complaining about the injustice of being singled out themselves.

He met several self-proclaimed "ethical managers" who insisted that everyone who worked for them—and of course they themselves—had to be Perfectly Virtuous, to the letter of the Moral Law.

These managers' subordinates generally despised them, and their departments were rife with resentment. More than one employee complained about autocratic management and dogmatic ineffectiveness; a philosophical assistant manager pointed out the difference between morality and moralizing. Almost everyone pointed out that the principles that were so precisely printed out in both memos and plaques above their desks were usually impossible to apply to any real ethical issues. Their primary effect was rather to cast a gray shadow of suspected hypocrisy over everyday business life.

Our bright young businessman was discouraged. He could not understand why the conscientious, sociable, civilized, thoroughly ethical flesh-and-blood managers he met in the office talked in their off moments like the most cynical prophets of corporate Darwinism.

The flesh-and-blood managers complained that the public did not appreciate them.

The cynical prophets joked, "There are no ethics in business," and then wondered why people didn't trust them.

Our bright young businessman was perplexed: Could there be ethics in the real business world? he wondered. Were compromises and cut corners inevitable? he asked. Did the untrammeled pursuit of virtue have to be either hypocrisy or damaging to the bottom line, as he now feared?

And then he met the One-Minute Moralist.

The bright young businessman presented the One-Minute Moralist with his dilemma. The One-Minute Moralist answered him without hesitation.

"You don't understand ethics," he said. "And you don't understand business either.

"You set up an absurd dichotomy between ethical absolutism and the so-called real world, and then you wonder how ethics can possibly be at home in business, and whether business can function without cutting corners and making uneasy compromises. But cutting corners presumes that there are sharply delineated corners. And talking so uneasily of compromise (that is, compromising one's moral principles rather than compromising with other people) seems to assume that ethics consists of engraved principles rather than relations between people who (more or less) share values and interests.

"But ethics isn't a set of absolute principles, divorced from and imposed on everyday life. Ethics is a way of life, a seemingly delicate but in fact very strong tissue of endless adjustments and compromises. It is the awareness that one is an intrinsic part of a social order, in which the interests of others and one's own interests are inevitably intertwined. And what is business, you should ask, if not precisely that awareness of what other people want and need, and how you yourself can prosper by providing it? Businesses great and small prosper because they respond to people, and fail when they do not respond. To talk about being 'totally ethical' and about 'uneasy compromises' is to misunderstand ethics. Ethics is the art of mutually agreeable tentative compromise. Insisting on absolute principles is, if I may be ironic, unethical.

"Business, on the other hand, has nothing to do with jungles, survivalism, and Darwin, whatever the mechanisms of the market may be. The 'profit motive' is an offensive fabrication by people who were out to attack business, which has curiously—and self-destructively—been adopted by business people themselves. Business isn't a single-minded pursuit of profits; it is an *ethos,* a way of life. It is a way of life that is at its very foundation ethical. What is more central to business—any kind of business—than taking contracts seriously, paying one's debts, and coming to mutual agreements about what is a fair exchange? Ethics isn't superimposed on business. Business is itself an ethics, defined by ethics, made possible by ethics. Two hundred years ago, Benjamin Franklin insisted that business is the pursuit of virtue. If you find yourself wondering or doubting whether virtue is possible in business, I suggest you reexamine your ideas about business.

"If you want to talk about hypocrisy, by the way, it is not just to be found in such bloated phrases as 'the untrammeled pursuit of virtue.' There is just as much hypocrisy in the macho, mock-heroic insistence that business is a tough-minded, amoral struggle for survival and profits rather than a staid and established ethical enterprise.

"Now you've had your Minute. When you think about business and ethics, don't worry about whether one is possible along with the other. In America, at least, nothing is more ethical than good business."

PROFIT: SOME MORAL REFLECTIONS

Paul F. Camenisch

The issues of profit, its moral meaning, justification, and role, need careful examination. Mistakes to be avoided in making moral sense of profit include the assumption that profitability establishes a company's moral rectitude. Profit is too complex a phenomenon to establish any such thing. Steps toward clarifying these issues include distinguishing profit as the goal of the corporation from the larger goals of the economy itself, and clarifying what we mean by profit. 'Profit' often includes the moral or value consideration of having been rightly or fairly earned. This provides one starting point internal to business for formulating standards for business ethics.

Profit is only rarely the central focus of business ethics discussions. In fact, when profit *as such* becomes the focus, we are no longer doing business ethics in the usual sense but are rather raising the question of the moral legitimacy of the business system itself. This is quite a different enterprise.

Nevertheless, it would be a mistake to conclude that profit does not play a significant role in business ethics. In fact, it appears to be one of the most important and persistent background elements in such discussions. After all, business ethics currently focuses almost exclusively on for-profit corporations, even though they share many characteristics and problems with not-for-profit enterprises. Apparently profit is widely thought to be a significant, even a *morally* significant distinguishing factor.

In fairness to business ethicists who are often accused of raising the profit issue, it should be noted that the focus on this subject is sometimes sharpened by business people themselves. Aided and abetted by academics such as Peter Drucker (1981), some business people are convinced that the major motivation of business ethicists is an anti-business animus, which presumably translates very easily into a morally based rejection of profits as such. Such persons often concentrate on exposing and discrediting such a bias, or on showing how most measures recommended by ethically concerned critics will threaten profits and thus endanger the corporation itself. At this point the conversation either focuses on profit or comes to an end.

"Profit: Some Moral Reflections," by Paul Camenisch, from *Journal of Business Ethics* 6 (1987), pp. 225–31. Reprinted by permission of Kluwer Academic Publishers.

WHY PROFIT ALWAYS HOVERS
AND SOMETIMES DOMINATES

If we are to get beyond this problem with profits, we must ask why it frequently looms so large, perhaps even larger in popular response to business than in academic discussions. Surveys consistently show that the average citizen greatly overestimates corporate profit. This results in part from the consumer's assumption that any shortfall between the price of goods or services and the perceived value received is the result of corporate profit. Anytime an increasingly demanding and educated buying public feels short-changed in the marketplace, the conviction will grow that profits are soaring beyond all reason. Of course such shortfall actually represents the costs of poor management, inefficient production and marketing, etc. But it is the consumer's perception rather than the reality itself that determines the direction and tone of the discussion.

Profit sometimes becomes an easy target for the critic because of the way it is defined. If profit is what is left of gross receipts after all expenses have been paid, then the critic's obvious question is, "What justifies profit, what is profit repayment for?" Wages and benefits for workers, payment for raw materials, taxes, advertising and other marketing costs, return on needed capital are all generally seen by consumers as costs legitimately passed on as part of the product's price. But if *all* these have been taken care of, and only then is the remainder treated as profit, business is hard pressed to say what profit is payment for, how it is earned, why deserved. The usual move at this point is to define profit as what is left after all *tangible,* or all *specifiable* and *quantifiable* costs have been paid. Thus profit becomes payment or reward for certain intangibles crucial to production and marketing. Risk, entrepreneurial creativity and initiative, uncertainty, deferring use of one's resources to make them available as capital, are some of the possibilities here. While this definition provides a bit more justification for profit, it is still quite an intangible one. Furthermore, the impossibility of measuring such intangible elements makes it difficult if not impossible to answer the almost inevitable next question, "How *much* profit is appropriate?"

Finally, profit is always a potential focus because the solutions to many business ethics problems threaten to eat into profits. Appropriate responses to problems such as pollution, adequate wages and benefits, safe, even pleasant working conditions, non-discriminatory personnel policies backed by appropriate recruitment, training and even retraining programs, careful husbanding of non-renewable resources, honest, informative advertising, production of safe, durable products—all of these frequently involve the expenditure of additional funds which can only come from what was previously treated as profits. Thus, for example, the pollution debate is not between business which favors pollution, and citizens who oppose it. It is between two sides which agree that pollution is undesirable but who will not always agree on what is a tolerable cost for reducing it. Thus while corporations do not pursue profit only (Adam, 1973; Lennox, 1984), that may seem to be the case when other morally indicated goals are resisted in order to protect profits.

Furthermore, business will often be at a significant disadvantage when profits are in this way set in tension with the needs or wants of other constituencies because the intangible elements which might justify profits do not, in the eyes of many persons, stand up well against the more immediate, basic and tangible needs of other claimants, such as more adequate wages and benefits for workers, clean air and water for all, or employee and consumer safety.

MISTAKES TO BE AVOIDED

Premature Defensiveness

There are several pitfalls awaiting persons wishing to make good moral and human sense out of profits in response to the above questions. First, it should be noted that according to the above analysis, profit can end up on the defensive not just because of ill-will, anti-business animus or massive ignorance about economics and the capitalist system. On occasion these factors may contribute to profit's problems. But many problems arise from the response of ordinary persons who predictably identify more easily with those basic interests and needs which often seem to be ranged against profit than they do with profit itself. Thus for business instinctively to charge forth to do battle with ill will and anti-business sentiments when profit is raised as an issue is usually premature, off-target and counter-productive.

Excessive Generalizing

Two other mistakes to be avoided are more conceptual in nature but are still important beyond academic circles. The first is the tack taken by H. B. Acton (1980) and others who argue that the pursuit of profits is simply one manifestation of the desire of everyone—whether investor, wage earner, supplier, or consumer—to possess more than one has. Such a generalizing of the meaning of profit and of profit seeking aims at answering critics of profit in two ways. The first depends on the belief that if a drive can be shown to be universal in humans and therefore apparently innate, it is beyond ethical examination and moral criticism. But this ignores the obvious fact that we are often held responsible for the way we permit even innate and universal traits or drives to shape our conduct. This approach also suggests that even if profit and profit seeking are morally objectionable, it ill behooves any of us to say so since none of our hands are clean in this matter.

But the price paid for any gains in this defense of profit is too high. Such expansion robs the idea of profit of all specificity, and any moral analysis of the central phenomenon in view—the conscious, systematic, and sustained pursuit of increased wealth through investment in capitalistic undertakings—is obstructed in two distinct ways. On the one hand, we find ourselves with traditionally accepted and intuitively persuasive moral distinctions which we can no longer make because this broadened definition reduces these phenomena to a single thing. Thus Rockefeller's (or was it Carnegie's) probably apocryphal response to the question of how much money is enough—"Just a little bit more"—becomes morally indistinguishable from the starving child's plea for his third breadcrust in a week. Both are 'profit' seekers, desiring to increase their share of the available material resources. That equation is not only conceptually unhelpful, it is morally intolerable. On the other hand, this greatly enlarged definition of profit, by tempting us to reduce our defense or profit to the minimalist insistence that everyone does it, removes the motivation for seeking the positive moral points that can be made on behalf of profit in a capitalist or mixed economy.

Profit as Moral Justifier

The second unhelpful move is for business too facilely to appeal to profits as a proof of its integrity and morality so that making a profit serves as a moral vindication—"How could we be doing so well if we weren't doing good?" Such an appeal makes most sense on the assumption that the amount of profit is determined by the workings of some objective laws of nature or of economics which in proper proportion reward some contribution made or some characteristics possessed by the profit maker. Several brief cases show not only why such an appeal is not persuasive, but demonstrate that the very concept of profit itself is becoming problematic. For example, *Crain's Chicago Business* reported that United Airlines "earned only $15.1 million in the first six months despite tax benefits of $148 million" (Merrion, 1983). The obvious question is why we call that a $15.1 million 'earnings' rather than a $132.9 million loss to, or at least subsidy by U.S. taxpayers. Similarly, on February 1, 1984, a *Wall Street Journal* editorial noted that "Federal handouts to agriculture exceeded net farm income in 1983" (Bovard, 1984). Again one might well ask what "net income" means here, or "Whose profit and how earned, and whose loss are we dealing with?"

On September 12, 1983, under a headline reading 'Low-income project turns a profit', *Crain's Chicago Business* reported that on a low income housing rehabilitation project in which it had invested $940,000 in risk capital, and had provided other financing through letters of credit, Indiana Standard estimated its pre-tax profit at $600,000 to $800,000 (Wagner, 1983). The article reports that this project also involved the following elements: the Illinois Housing Development Authority provided a $13.8 million tax-exempt loan; federal subsidies guaranteed that 70 percent of each unit's rent would be paid for up to 30 years; the city of Chicago loaned the partnership $3.3 million at 1.5 percent interest; the congressionally chartered for-profit National Housing Partnership purchased 99 percent of the partnership owned by Rescorp and Indiana Standard and sold 95 percent to investors seeking tax shelters; residents of the development will pay only 30 percent of the rent. By the end of all this, the head of the uninitiated spins as he wonders what it cost the taxpayers to generate that 'profit' for Indiana Standard. No iron laws of economics here! In fact, one can be forgiven for suspecting that to call that money 'profit' is little more than a polite convention.

And finally, financial analysis of some recent corporate earnings statements shows that earnings or profit can be as much an accountant's creation or enhancement of reality as a corporation's reward for performance. For example, according to one analysis, Polaroid's claimed 21 cents a share earnings for the first quarter of 1984 drops to 2 cents a share when one eliminates gains over the previous year from certain non-operating and quite possibly non-repeating items (lower tax rate—5 cents a share; currency gains— 7 cents; lower interest expenses—5 cents; lower depreciation for plant and equipment— 2 cents) (Dorfman, 1984). To what extent then does this 'profit' increase over the year-ago earnings of 7 cents per share accurately inform us about corporate performance in its distinctive task of producing and marketing goods and services, and the appropriate reward for such performance in the competitive market place?

Perhaps these are not typical cases. But at the very least they show that the terms 'profit', 'earnings', and 'net income' are used quite casually. At most, they show that these ideas have been severed from the simple definitions of profit most of us begin with, definitions which underlie most versions of the position that profit is morally justified and morally justifying. Here it becomes clear that profit, at least for major actors in our current economy, is the result of complex interactions among a variety of economic, political and other forces, most of which are beyond the control or even the direct influence of the business, which nevertheless claims the resulting profit as its just reward. Thus, for example, it is virtually impossible in the end to say what the $600,000–$800,000 represents except the amount Indiana Standard is permitted to claim at the end of an extremely complex series of interactions. Whether and why this is an appropriate profit (i.e., whether proportional to any other factor involved or to any actual contribution Standard made) is impossible to establish.

Nor is it only governmental decisions which alter supposedly simple and autonomous economic dynamics to determine profit. The action last year of U.S. auto makers granting their top managers millions of dollars in bonuses shows that certain elements within corporations can simply decree whether certain portions of company assets will be treated as profit or as resources available for meeting other 'expenses' such as executive bonuses. Thus to appeal to profits as a moral vindication of the company and its operations is in at least some cases to pull the rabbit out of the hat only after one—with the help of several allies, both witting and unwitting—has first carefully placed the rabbit there.

HELPFUL WAYS FORWARD

Distinguishing Corporate Goals from the Economy's Goals

How then do we begin to bring greater clarity to the discussion of profit and its moral dimensions? I offer a few modest suggestions. First, it will be helpful to distinguish between the goals or purposes of a corporation and those of business as such, or to make the point clearer still, between those of a corporation and those of the economic system as such. Business leaders, sincerely and with the best of intentions, sometimes state that the primary purpose of a corporation is not to make a profit, but to meet human needs, to serve the consumer, etc. While this may be true of some corporations, and while on some level it may be true of all corporations, the public in general finds such statements unpersuasive, even hypocritical, and many stockholders may possibly see them as indicative of managerial mis- or malfeasance.

However, business persons making such statements are trying to say something which is both true and important. But it is said more clearly and persuasively if the distinction just suggested is observed. It may well help clear the air if corporations would simply acknowledge that their primary purpose is to make a profit and then stood ready to show why and how that is a defensible, a necessary, even a good thing in the present system. But at the same time they should acknowledge—and this would seem to be what executives trying to cast an altruistic light on corporations are trying to say—that the purpose of business, or of the economic system of which the corporation is a part, is not to make profit-making possible, but to fulfill human needs or to provide goods and services which sustain and enhance life (Camenisch, 1981). This identifies profit's proper place within the corporation while acknowledging its subordination to larger societal purposes beyond the corporation.

This distinction between the corporation's internal and external purposes, or perhaps better, between the purpose of the part (the corporation) and that of the whole (the total society and its economic system) may initially seem to raise conceptual as well as practical problems. But in fact we constantly live with this distinction. The purpose or motive of the person who weekly loads my trash onto the sanitation department truck most likely does not coincide either with the department's goal or with the purpose of the city in establishing such a department. But *as long as the individual's goals do not interfere with those of the larger entity,* this need not concern us and we can honestly say that the individual is simultaneously serving both purposes. And this can be said without denying that the individual legitimately has his own distinctive purposes, such as making a living, supporting his family, etc.

We should have no more uneasiness in making parallel statements about the corporation's goal of profit making in relation to the goals of the larger society. The corporation whose pursuit of profit is consistent with, or even is a means to helping society fulfill its economic tasks pursues two different but compatible and entirely honorable sets of goals. This way of seeing things avoids testing the public's credulity by telling it that the primary goal of for-profit corporations is not profit. It would also put corporations and their goals in the appropriate perspective of their relation to the larger society and its needs. Thus profit-making as such might cease to be a moral issue and would raise problems only when it began to jeopardize the larger societal goals to which it is to be subordinated.

Clarifying the Meaning of Profit

The second and more substantive move would be to open the discussion not on whether profit is morally defensible or legitimate, but on what we mean by it. Conceptually it is not always easy to distinguish profit from apparently similar phenomena. How, for example, do 'profits' differ, from lottery winnings, from $10,000 I find on the street, from an inheritance, from income from juice loans, from taking money under false pretenses, from simple theft? After all, all of these frequently leave one with a 'profit'. For the moment let us grant that their illegality eliminates theft, juice loans and taking money under false pretenses as serious comparisons. And yet the recent E. F. Hutton check rigging case cautions us against too facile a dismissal of these comparisons. Thinking now as morally concerned citizens and not simply as accountants, should the gains realized by Hutton in that practice have been considered profits? Were they profits until the scheme was uncovered, at which point they became "ill-gotten gains?" If, after paying the fine, court costs, and refunds to banks, Hutton still comes out ahead—which does not seem unlikely given the length, size, and complexity of the practice—what should their 'profit' be called? Does simply considering it profit in any way taint those profits which were legitimately gained and with which it is now lumped as gross income? Just what are the limits to what can be considered profit.

To return to our list of comparisons, perhaps the element of sheer chance eliminates the $10,000 found on the street from being considered profit. But what about the lottery winnings or the inheritance? No law was broken. I did make some investment and do certain things to attain the goal (I knew aging and wealthy Aunt Gertrude was lonely and enjoyed Sunday drives in the country.) And I profited. Ah, but gains are properly called 'profits' only if they result from 'business activity'. So why then is buying a lottery ticket not 'business', while investing in a highly speculative stock is?

This question of what constitutes 'business activity' is an important one, but more interesting here is another element which is almost invariably introduced to distinguish profit, properly speaking, from some of these other gains, especially the more questionable ones. This is the idea that profit must be *earned,* must even be fairly and justly earned, that it must be a 'reasonable' profit. If we had difficulty defining 'profit' and 'business activity', we can surely expect no fewer problems with such notoriously elusive terms as 'fairly', 'justly', and 'reasonable'.

Profit and Moral Justification

This idea of profit as earned, justified and proportionate is almost certainly behind the invoking of profitability as a moral legitimation of the corporation and its activity that was dismissed above as misleading given the diverse factors now influencing business outcomes. However, it is now time to acknowledge that this group of interconnected ideas does have some role in our understanding of profit and its place in the assessment—moral as well as economic—of corporate performance.

Challenged to explain, even to justify their profit, corporate leaders seem to have four kinds of responses available. The first, which most critical consumers may suspect is descriptively the most accurate one is that the amount of profit is determined by whatever the market will bear. Few business people publicly state this answer since it sounds so much like, "grab all you can and run." But where Adam Smith's "invisible hand" is still thought to function, this answer will be seen not as a license to exploit, but as a realistic recognition of ordinary, even automatic market limitations on over-charging. Nevertheless, because Smith's analysis is unknown to many, and is rejected by many others, and because our economic experience is so different from that represented by Smith's simple model of the market, this answer is usually, and probably wisely avoided by business persons as appearing to legitimate virtually unlimited profit taking without claiming any moral justification for it.

A second answer to the challenge to explain and justify profits, already met above, but mentioned here for the sake of completeness, can be a species of the first. But rather than seeming to remove the limits to profit making, it explicitly invokes such limits in the form of some automatic and impersonal laws of economics which will set limits to what can be charged through the interplay of various market forces. In addition to what was said above about the current inadequacies of this approach, we will here simply note the widely recognized ways such controlling market mechanisms are impeded, obstructed, even defeated by monopoly, oligopoly, various forms of governmental interventions, including subsidy of business, and the difficulty of new producers entering extremely complex and highly technical markets.

A third answer to the questions of justifying profits and their amount is for business to appeal to the public to trust business's own conscience to keep it within appropriate limits specified in part by business's various contributions which ought to be rewarded, and by what business needs to survive. While some persons may find this answer acceptable and while some corporations do deserve to be so trusted, carefully examined this answer finally fails because of its paternalism. Paternalism, which in the present context means the need for some to rely on the voluntary good will and intentions of others, is increasingly out of fashion in this society for a number of good reasons. Thus, at a time when the law, traditional professions, and other agencies in the society are being criticized for their paternalism, it is unlikely that business will be permitted to answer the question of the appropriate limits on profits by appeal to its own internal controls to be exercised on behalf of, but without examination or control by the public.

The fourth answer to our question tries to justify profits in the most direct and usual sense of that term. Here the business person claims that profit and its amount are justified by some contribution of business and/or its owners, for which the profit is an appropriate repayment or reward. For this response to be persuasive, two conditions will have to be met. First and most obviously, that 'contribution' will have to be specifically identified. Otherwise we are back to a paternalism in which we simply take the corporation's own word concerning its virtue, its trustworthiness, or its profit-deserving contribution. The second condition to be met is that the contribution so specified not be so abstract and intangible that it is able to justify virtually any amount of profit, and so leaves unanswered the question of proportionate or appropriate profit.

The frequency with which business persons resort to this last response raises the question of whether "being justified" is helpfully treated as a part of the definition of profit, or whether this element is extraneous to profit so that business gains are properly considered 'profit' even when they cannot be justified in any of the usual ways. This is in part a linguistic or definitional question of how we use the term 'profits'. (Even at this level, however, we ought not to forget that language reflects and perpetuates our moral conceptions and commitments, and thus should be chosen carefully.)

But this is also more than a linguistic issue, for if, according to wide usage, profit is only truly profitable when it is deserved according to some publicly specifiable and generally accepted criteria, then one can begin to argue that at least some of the moral standards applying to business need not be imported from outside business by "business ethicists," but that they are inherent in the very basic concepts, such as 'profit' by which we understand and structure our economic system. I can think of no development which would portend better for progress in business ethics than such a discovery *within* business of some of its governing moral norms. Carefully attended to, the idea of profit as it is frequently used offers an excellent starting point for identifying just such internal moral norms for business. On the other hand, insulated from any such moral considerations and limitations, profit will indeed be difficult for business to defend and, whether explicitly articulated or not, will continue to be a potential obstacle to productive dialogue in business ethics.

REFERENCES

1. Acton, H. B.: 1980, 'The Profit Motive', in M. Missner (ed.), *Ethics of the Business System* (Sherman Oaks, CA: Alfred Publishing Co., Inc.), pp. 21–39.
2. Adam, J., Jr.: 1973, 'Put Profit in Its Place', *The Harvard Business Review* **51,** 150–158.
3. Bovard, J.: February 1, 1984, 'Soaring Succor for Select Business', *Wall Street Journal* **23,** 9.
4. Camenisch, P. F.: 1981, 'Business Ethics: On Getting to the Heart of the Matter', *Business and Professional Ethics Journal* **1,** 59–69.
5. Dorfman, D.: July 28, 1984, '3 Well-known Stocks with Earnings of Dubious Quality', *Chicago Tribune,* Section 2, pp. 1 and 11.
6. Drucker, P.: 1981, 'What is Business Ethics?' *The Public Interest* **63,** 18–36.
7. Lennox, D.: April 3, 1984, 'Ethical Companies Weigh More than Profits', *Crain's Chicago Business* **7,** no. 18, pp. 11–12.
8. Merrion, P.: October 10, 1983, 'UAL sticks to Its Game Plan', *Crain's Chicago Business* **6,** no. 41, pp. 3 and 56.
9. Wagner, L. M.: Sept. 12, 1983, 'Low-Income Project Turns a Profit', *Crain's Chicago Business* **6,** no. 37, p. 22.

THE IDEAS
OF AYN RAND

RONALD MERRILL

Ayn Rand promulgated an economic theory called objectivism and is known for her work incorporating objectivism into novels such as The Fountainhead *and* Atlas Shrugged. *Merrill describes objectivism and compares it to various other theories. Objectivism is really a version of ethical egoism that focuses on self-interested acts because, as Rand contends, all of us always and only act in our own self-interest. Contrary to popular belief, however, Rand sees nothing wrong with selfishness; instead, she berates those who are too selfless, calling them* second-handers. *(See text introduction to this chapter.) Consider for yourself when this has not been the case. (Note that she would claim that even an anonymous donation is selfishly motivated since you would be satisfying some need of your own to help others.)*

THE OBJECTIVIST ETHICS

Rand's most substantial contribution to philosophical thought lies in the field of ethics. It was Ayn Rand who, after 2,000 years of failed attempts, finally proposed a viable solution to the fundamental problem of ethics: deriving normative from factual statements, or, less formally, deriving 'ought' from 'is'. Philosophers have long recognized this as a major problem. Indeed, in the twentieth century most philosophers have despaired of the prospect of developing any sort of logically justifiable ethics. Arguably Ayn Rand's most important accomplishment was producing a solution to this problem. In response, her opponents have concentrated their fire primarily on her ethical reasoning.

I hope, therefore, the reader will forgive me for devoting a great deal of space to this subject. The following discussion will not only present Rand's reasoning, but analyze it in some depth. I will suggest that the Objectivist ethics can be made more rigorous if certain arguments are reformulated. Then I will compare Rand's approach to Aristotle's and show how she can deal with the moral skepticism of Hume. The various arguments of Rand's critics will be surveyed. Finally, I want to look at the implications of the Objectivist ethics and consider some ways in which it may be extended.

Every human society has had ethical precepts, claims that one 'ought' to do, or not do, certain things. How can such claims be justified? The historic justifications have been such as: 'You ought to, because I say so.' Or: 'You ought to because God, speaking through me, says so.' Or: 'You ought to because all the rest of us took a vote and the majority says so.' Or: 'You ought to because if you don't we'll burn you at the stake.'

Excerpts from *The Ideas of Ayn Rand,* by Ronald Merrill. Reprinted by permission of Open Court.

At least in modern times we would not accept any of these modes of argument to settle a factual question such as, say, whether the earth revolves around the sun. Why should we accept them in determining moral questions? But if we don't, just how should we determine the truth of a moral dilemma?

Rand attacks the problem of ethics by going to the root, to a question of 'meta-ethics'. Instead of asking, 'Which morality is correct?' she asks, 'Just what *is* a "morality," anyway?' There are many possible moralities which might be correct: Christian ethics, the Ten Commandments, 'Seek the greatest good of the greatest number', 'Do what thou wilt is the whole of the law', and many others have been asserted. But what do they all have in common? What is a morality?

A morality—any morality—is a set of rules to guide the actions of an individual human being. This—and only this—is what all possible moralities have in common. This is the definition of a morality. (Rand puts it: "A code of values to guide man's choices and actions.")

Well, given this, asks Rand, why should there be any morality at all? This is of course a normative question, so let's rephrase it in factual terms: What would happen to a man who practiced no morality?

A man who practiced no morality would be a man whose behavior was guided by no rules at all. Even Alistair Crowley's morality has a rule ('Do what thou wilt') but our hypothetical literally amoral man could not follow even his whims consistently. He would have to behave as if his brain were connected to a random number generator. What would happen to him? He would of course quickly die.

This suggests that the connection between factual and normative statements is man's life. Man needs morality to live. Man ought to do certain things, because they are necessary in order for him to be. He 'is' because he does what he 'ought'.

Now the skeptic might way, 'You are assuming that I ought to choose life—what if I don't?' It is tempting to reply (as, in effect, John Galt does), 'Fine. If you prefer death, shut up and die.' But this is inadequate; it refutes the arguer, perhaps, but not the argument. It is not enough merely to demonstrate that altruism is a morality based on a premise of death. We need to make a positive argument to show that morality must be based on the standard of human life. To my mind Rand's argument for this position is insufficiently rigorous. However, I will assert that her line of reasoning is basically sound and that it can be put on a very strong footing. . . .

ENDS AND ENDS IN THEMSELVES

The classical philosophical tradition in ethics, tracing back to the Greeks, seeks an 'ultimate end' of human action. The argument typically runs as follows:

Consider a goal, alpha. This goal actually is a means to an end, another goal, beta. But beta is itself a means to another goal, gamma, and so on. Can we find some ultimate goal, call it omega, which is an end in itself, not a means to any other end? If we can, and if we can show that every goal is ultimately a means to omega, then we have a basis for ethics.

Suppose, for instance, that we could establish that every human action is aimed at the individual's happiness. We are compelled to assume this proposition in strong form: A person does nothing, and can do nothing, purposeful unless the purpose is to serve his happiness. Even if he thinks he is doing something for other reasons, his real objective is and must be his own happiness. Then ethics reduces to a matter of engineering, so to speak; one need merely determine the most efficient way to serve one's happiness.

The proposed ethical 'end-in-itself' has been variously identified as justice, love, equality, the greater glory of God, and many other things. But in the end nobody has been able to satisfactorily establish that all goals are means to some end-in-itself.

Has Rand found the answer? It looks problematic at first glance. *Is* life an end-in-itself? Do humans *never* regard life as a means to an end? . . . And is life the *only* end-in-itself? Do humans *never* seek any other value for its own sake? Critics have seen this premise as the crucial weak point of the Randian argument.

Rand's chain of reasoning will not hold unless she can show that, as a matter of metaphysical fact, there is no 'end in itself' other than life. What if there are other ultimate ends, unrelated to, and perhaps even incompatible with, life or survival? Then it will *not* follow that all values must serve to sustain life. So Rand in adopting this argument requires herself to prove a negative.

At best this is going to be difficult, and probably it will be impossible. Take just one prospective counterexample: reproduction. Even with modern medicine a woman faces a noticeable risk of death in having a child. Taking into account economic and other costs, one can scarcely argue that reproduction makes a net contribution to the survival of the parents. It certainly seems plausible to assert that people value their offspring as ends in themselves, and not just as means to the survival of the parents.

Before we can deal with the problem we have identified, we must recognize that Rand is not using the term 'end in itself' in its traditional sense:

> *Metaphysically,* life *is the only phenomenon that is an end in itself: a value gained and kept by a constant process of action.*

Clearly this is not the usual conception of an 'end in itself'. But just what does it mean, then? Here is a paraphrase by Harry Binswanger: ". . . only life is an action directed toward the perpetuation of itself." And illuminating this in more detail:

> *A common misconception is that of thinking of 'survival' as if it were some single vital action that occurs after all the other actions [necessary to life] have been completed. 'Survival', however, means the continuation of the organism's life, and the organism's life is an integrated sum composed of all those specific actions which contribute to maintaining the organism in existence. In this sense in living action the parts are for the sake of the whole: the specific goal-directed actions are for the sake of the organism's capacity to repeat those actions in the future.*
>
> *An ultimate goal, if it is truly ultimate, must be an 'end in itself'. An 'end in itself' gives the appearance of a vicious circle: it is something sought for the sake of itself. This circulatory vanishes when we regard* life *as an end in itself: actions at a given time benefit survival, which means they make possible the organism's repetition of those actions in the future, being then again directed toward survival, which means their repetition, and so on.*

What Rand and Binswanger seem to be saying is that life is an 'end in itself' in an unusual and very special meaning: Life is an ordered collection of activities, which are means to achieving an end, which is—simply those activities. Every action taken to sustain life is simultaneously a means (because it supports life) and an end (because life is by definition simply the collective of such actions).

This conception of life is not only accurate and perceptive, but enormously fruitful for ethics. What's more, it offers a way to escape from the need to prove a negative in the argument for the Objectivist ethics.

THE MEANS TEST

At this point I want to suggest that we can reformulate Rand's argument in a way that leads to the same conclusions, without encountering the difficulty that we discovered above. All we need do is recognize that Rand's idea of 'life' as a sort of self-contained vortex of values which are simultaneously ends and means allows us to reverse the traditional program, as follows.

Consider a goal, Z. Attaining this goal is dependent on another goal, Y, which is a means to Z. Y in turn is dependent on another means, X, and so on. Is there some ultimate *means,* A, which is a means for all other goals? There is indeed: Life is a prerequisite for pursuing any other goal.

We are now in a position to ignore the problem of competing 'ends in themselves'. Let us argue as follows: Man must choose what values to pursue. But can something be a value if its attainment would be such as to eliminate or reduce one's ability to pursue values? To seek an end while rejecting an essential means to that end, is to act (means) to gain and/or keep a value (end) while not so acting—which is a contradiction. So whatever ultimate ends there may be, one can seek them only if, and to the extent that, one values that which serves one's own life. Whether or not life is the *only* ultimate end, it is an end which is a necessary means to any and all other ends.

The Aristotelian flavor of this approach becomes evident if we phrase the argument this way:

> *This goal is a means for all other goals, and not for some special genus apart from others. And all men value it, because it underlies all values. For a value which everyone must hold, who values anything at all, is not arbitrary. Evidently then such a value is the most certain of all; which value this is, let us proceed to say. It is the life of man* qua *man.*

To my mind this line of argument offers the prospect of putting the Objectivist ethics on a truly solid logical footing. . . .

ROBERT NOZICK VERSUS
THE COUNT OF MONTE CRISTO

No philosophical disputation would be complete without an example of the classic meaning-switch cheapo, and in the debate over Objectivist ethics Robert Nozick has provided the most ingenious application of this traditional technique.

Nozick asserts that one cannot derive an ethics from the fact that life is a prerequisite for all other values and cites a counter-example: Being cured of cancer is obviously a value. But having cancer is a prerequisite for being cured of cancer. Does this mean that having cancer is a value?

Well, let us take this sophomore stumper in the spirit in which it is intended and have some fun with it. A dedicated dialectician could dance a pleasant polka with Nozick by taking the affirmative of the question. For instance: Who has not on some occasion abstained from eating before a special meal, in order that hunger may sharpen the appetite and the enjoyment? Perhaps we should go all the way with the Count of Monte Cristo. He asserted that nobody could know true joy who had not experienced the ultimate depths of suffering, and went so far as to let a friend think his fiancée had died so he would be really happy when he learned she hadn't. A professional philosopher no doubt could convince us that it really does make sense to beat your head against a brick wall in order to enjoy the sensation when you stop.

But we must be moving on. Let's point out that Nozick has dropped the context that gives meaning to the value he is invoking. 'Being cured of cancer' is a value only to someone who has cancer. Modern cancer cures range from unpleasant to devastatingly painful; nobody would consider the cure a value in itself.

In short, there is an obvious distinction, which Nozick is fogging, between the circumstances which make something a value, and the means used to attain that value. When we say that Philosophy 101 is a prerequisite for Philosophy 102, we mean that the student will need the information, concepts, and skills taught in the first course in order to profit from the second. We may also say that a certain amount of ignorance of philosophy is a 'prerequisite' for Philosophy 102, in the sense that if the student already knows the material he won't benefit from taking the course—but now we are using 'prerequisite' in an entirely different meaning of the term. . . .

RELATED WEB SITES

"A Culture of Accountability" by Nathaniel Branden:
info-sys.home.vix.com/objectivism/Writing/Nathaniel
Branden/AcultureOfAccountability.html

The Benefits and Hazards of the Philosophy of Ayn Rand
info-sys.home.vix.com/objectivism/Writing/Nathaniel
Branden/BenefitsAndHazards.html

ETHICS OF TOTAL INTEGRITY

STEPHEN R. COVEY

Covey, perhaps best known for his book, The Seven Habits of Highly Effective People, *discusses the critical role of integrity in business decisions and actions. According to Covey, "We can grow our own goodness in our organizations if our integrity is a natural consequence of our humility and courage." Can you think of business situations that might have turned out differently if the decision makers had acted with greater integrity?*

I think that the so-called "ethics movement" of the past few years has taken many organizations down a wrong path. Many leaders confuse ethical with legal issues, or they take a departmental or compartmental approach rather than an integrated and organic approach to ethics.

With an organic approach, an executive naturally sees everything through an ethical lens; consequently, everything is integrated, not seen in different frames.

Also, with an organic approach, a person can be sincere. The Latin word *sinecera* literally means *sine* (without) and *cera* (wax) . . . "without wax." That is to say, without cosmetics, without putting on a face, without relying on personality, public relations, and appearances—or what *seems* to be. The personality ethic is all about *what seems to be.*

Wrestling with issues of integrity, Shakespeare's Hamlet says, "To be or not to be, that is the question." He ponders, "What a piece of work is man!" He counsels, "Suit the action to the word, the word to the action." And he reasons, "What is a man if his chief good and market of his time be but to sleep and feed? He that made us with such large discourse, gave us not that capability and godlike reason to fust in us unused." To his mother, the Queen, Hamlet responds, "Seems, madam? Nay, it is; I know not 'seems'"

For executives who have lost integrity, *seems* is all they know. They live and work in a world of *seeming to be* something they are not. They worry more about how others see them than about who they are. They are actors, who wear wax to cover up covert operations or maintain image.

When I was working in the state of North Carolina recently, I was given a shirt imprinted with the state motto in Latin, *Esse quam videri,* meaning *To be rather than to seem.*

This should be the motto of every executive. Unfortunately, "seeming to be" often substitutes for real integrity. It's "seeming" as opposed to "being." It's neither integral nor integrated, but rather part of a compartment or department.

"Ethics of Total Integrity," by Stephen R. Covey. Reprinted from *Executive Excellence,* August 1995, pp. 3–4. Call Executive Excellence Publishing, 800/304-9782 for reprints.

THREE GENERATIONS

So, how do you arrive at integrity? I see integrity as the child of two primary character traits: the mother of humility and the father of courage.

First Generation: the Mother of Humility   The mother of humility means that you realize that over time principles or natural laws ultimately govern, not social values or personal whims and desires. The prideful, arrogant approach is to claim, "I am in control" and "I am in charge of my destiny." That theme, so common in much of the success literature in recent decades, is a product of the social value system. And, our social values may not be based on rock-solid principles but on the shifting sands of ego and opinion. The president of an international communications firm once told me, "Stephen, our company is value-driven."

I said, "Every company is value-driven. The question is this: are the values based on timeless principles, which ultimately control anyway."

He said, "I think so." He showed me their value statement. It included many ideals, including the following: "We are committed to the practice of all praiseworthy values that enhance the worth of individuals and strengthen our communities."

When I asked him about his core values, he mentioned: *honesty, quality, service, profitability, sensitivity, sincerity, and high ethical and moral standards.*

I said, "There's certainly nothing wrong with this set of corporate values, as they are closely aligned with enduring principles. However, what matters most is how you integrate them into your daily operations."

I was trying to teach what every employee already knows: *an emphasis on high ethical and moral standards is best made not simply with words on a poster in the corporate office but with the attitudes and actions of people at all levels."*

This humble business leader well understood the importance of walking the talk—and making sure that the talk, the corporate value system, is based on principles. He realized that we are not in control, that natural laws and principles control, and that the attitude of humility is, in a sense, the mother of all virtues, because all of them come through that spirit of submission.

The Father of Courage   The father of all virtues is courage, because courage is the quality of every quality at its highest testing point. Eventually every value gets tested. Whether or not we will align our values, our lives, and our habits with those principles is the big question. Again, "to be or not to be" is the big question.

In other words, will we really do it? We may be humble, but are we courageous? Will we, in fact, swim upstream against very powerful social values and also against the internal habituated tendencies of our own nature? Will the "chief good and market of our time" be but to sleep and feed? Or will we put our "infinite faculty, admirable form, and godlike reason" to good use? We won't if we lack the courage to act upon our core beliefs. In fact, our principle-centered initiatives will likely be rolled over and flattened by the latest wave of trendy social values.

Second Generation: the Child of Integrity   When you have both humility and courage, you naturally produce the "second generation" child of integrity. Integrity means that your life is integrated around principles and that your security comes from within, not from without. It also means, as my friend suggested, maintaining "the highest levels of honesty and credibility in all relationships."

You won't have the child of integrity if you lack the mother of humility, or if you have the humility but lack the courage to act on your conviction. Instead, you will have duplicity, hypocrisy, and the personality ethic. False integrity means that your security still lies outside yourself—in the degree to which you are accepted from the outside, and to the degree to which you compare or compete favorably with others.

Third Generation: The Fruits of Integrity   The third generation is the many fruits or children of integrity.

- One child of integrity is *wisdom.* If your security comes from within, you simply have better judgment. You're not in an overreactive state; you don't dichotomize; you don't catastrophize; you're not extreme; you have better overall life balance. With wisdom, you see things in correct perspective and proportion; you don't overreact or underreact. You "suit the action to the word, the word to the action."

- A second child of integrity is the *abundance mentality.* When you get your security from within, you are not in a constant state of comparison from without. Therefore, you can have an abundance mind-set toward life. You see life as an ever-enlarging circle of resources, almost like a cornucopia of resources that get larger and larger. As Hamlet says, "There is nothing either good or bad but thinking makes it so."

- A third child of integrity is *synergy.* You can come up with better ideas, transformational thinking and a spirit of win-win partnering when your security is not a function of how people treat you, or of how you compare with others. You can express your ideas with courage and consideration with the intent of finding the best possible alternative, not simply to please or appease others.

- Another sweet fruit of personal and organizational integrity is *relationships of trust with all stakeholders.* Obviously, trust increases when you create high credibility based on trustworthiness. You simply can't have integral relationships without genuine personal integrity; likewise, corporate relationships with stakeholders will suffer with breaches of ethics. Many bottom-line business benefits—including competitiveness, flexibility, responsiveness, quality, economic value-added, and customer service—depend on relationships of trust.

CORPORATE ETHICS PROGRAMS

With so much riding on integrity and ethics, why are breaches in ethics, both individual and corporate, all too common? Is it partly because well intentioned university ethics courses and organizational ethics programs don't work?

Over the past 15 years, we've seen a heavy emphasis on ethics, as the ethical dimension has been introduced everywhere from MBA programs to government to small business to major corporations.

Organizations spend lots of money on ethics programs. Sadly, according to one recently retired ethics director, *"Some executives are concerned primarily with public image and perceptions. In fact, the ethics program is often started as a response to public outcry or internal inquiry. Ethics directors serve as a point of contact for whistleblowers and for unempowered and uninformed individuals who don't know how else to get a problem resolved. When executives justify the means by the ends, people pick up the signals. They note who is hired, promoted, and rewarded—and why. They see who gets away with murder and who condones inappropriate behavior. Having an ethics program may make people more sensitive to such issues as sexual harassment or sexist language, but they rarely stop or even slow the avalanche of unethical behavior. In fact, the program may just drive unethical behavior further underground, making people even more devious."*

This is a fundamentally flawed approach, because it's not about humility—accepting principles, aligning with those principles, submitting to them, and obeying them. It's more about pride. As universities and corporations add classes or offices on ethics, people begin to see issues through that departmental frame of reference, rather than having their perspectives governed by a central frame of reference, the lens of integrity.

The ethics dilemma is analogous to the quality dilemma. We can't inspect in or manage in quality; rather we must design and build it in from the beginning. Likewise, we can't inspect in ethics. Rather, we must build in an ethical frame of reference, through integrated partnering with all stake holders. When everybody accepts personal responsibility to behave in ethical ways, you then hardly even have to think about it, because ethical behavior is your nature, not some artificial department.

When leaders are open and exact in their observance of ethical codes, they inspire others to do the same. One leader, when stepping down as president of a large university, was commended by the chairman of the board: "A few reach the pinnacle of professional or social or financial success through devious, even evil means. Others may be more virtuous but still show a lack of sensitivity to loved ones, friends, and colleagues as they climb to the top. Those who combine honor, integrity, devotion, and sensitivity to family and friends are rare indeed."

Too often ethics is separate from the reality of the organization. Professional ethicists may huddle and talk, but most of their practice is reactive in response to people not walking their talk, feeling that the only wrong is in getting caught. They may handle a complaint to allay a lawsuit, but they are not preventative or integrative.

As long as there is great disparity and little integration between the corporate ethical stance and individual behavior, the individual will feel no obligation to live by corporate ethical codes.

Your vision, mission, ethics and value statements will be even more valuable if you don't rush the creative process, announce the result, and then ignore or dismiss the document as some meaningless formal exercise. As you involve people in the creation of code and as you review it regularly with them, you build in cultural humility (the acceptance of a value system based on principles) and courage (taking on traditional structures and systems which are contrary to those principles, and aligning your personal style with those structures and systems).

The ethics statement becomes a constitution when it becomes the center from which everything else flows. Then you don't have this "seeming to be" in various areas. In organizations of integrity, ethics is not just another department. The organization serves as a second family. For example, many people who work for Ritz Carlton actually look forward to going to work because they find more harmony, acceptance, integrity, and sense of identity there than they can find even within their own family. People are humble because they know that natural laws and governing principles are in control—not people, programs, and politics. They not only believe in timeless principles, but they have the courage to act on them.

RELATED WEB SITES

Transcript of a live conference with Stephen Covey, hosted by U.S. News Online on CompuServe, February 22, 1995.
www.usnews.com/usnews/TOWN/COVEY.HTM

Covey biography: wyn.com/covey/

Covey's Seven Habits for Life:
ourworld.compuserve.com/homepages/btc/Covey.htm

BETS-L LISTSERVER DISCUSSION/DEBATE ON CONTINUED RELEVANCE OF KOHLBERG

JAMES B. LYTTLE, ROSEMARY GRANT, AND LINDA KLEBE TREVINO

Electronic listservers are often used by academic professionals to discuss issues of interest to a large number of individuals. Often, one scholar makes a statement with which another scholar disagrees, and an electronic discussion ensues. The following discussion addresses the continued relevance of Lawrence Kohlberg's theory on moral development, discussed in this chapter's introduction.

From:	James B Lyttle
To:	Multiple recipients of list BETS-L . . .
Date:	1/19/96 6:32pm
Subject:	Re: Integrity tests

Rosemary Grant writes:
>
>Linda,
>   I didn't know if you are aware that Kohlberg's work has been
>questioned over the last several years, and it is not as reliable as
>it once was. I did quite a bit of research along these lines about
>3 years ago, and few people were relying on him any more.
>

Linda Klebe Trevino is an Associate Professor of Organizational Behavior at Penn State and the co-author of one of the best practical texts in the field IMHO. . . . She is quite well informed about Kohlberg's work. Like all seminal work, it has had its detractors. However, it is still the standard. Since 1969 it has been subject to three main challenges. FIRST, some people claim that there is a Seventh stage, although no two people seem to be able to agree on what that is. Since Kohlberg's longitudinal study lasted only 12 years, it is quite possible that further (later) stages were missed. This in no way detracts from the value of the first six stages. SECOND, some people (most notably his student, Carol Gilligan) claim that girls will develop morally in a different fashion—learning an ethic of care instead of an ethic of justice. Ms. Gilligans's work at Harvard is oft-quoted because it is so unusual and interesting. For example, in the midst of a game with ambiguous rules, boys will tend to argue while girls will tend to put the game away. This research is also unique in another way. Later research has failed to support the idea that there is any discernable difference between the moral reasoning of grown men and women. THIRD, many people worried the Kohlberg's stages would not apply in the modern global environment of business. But recent research has demonstrated the same stages in other cultures. In my opinion, all thinking people should still rely on him.

Jim Lyttle.

From:	Rosemary Grant
To:	Multiple recipients of list BETS-L . . .
Date:	1/20/96 8:11am
Subject:	Re: Integrity tests

Jim,

I think I was just flamed because of the post I wrote yesterday about limitations on Kohlberg. Perhaps I need to explain myself better, and I hope you will not be as upset with me. My research was in ethics education and was not limited to the field of business ethics. Therefore, I am sorry to say that I am not familiar with Linda Trevino's position or work. I would certainly be glad to read it, however.

What I found was that there is much more to ethics education than the ability to reason morally. The case approach that is often used in ethics courses has also been questioned by educational authorities. . . .

Christina Hoff Sommers and William Kilpatrick (authors of ethics texts) argue for an approach to ethics that develops character.

Kohlberg recommended a curriculum based on ethical dilemmas until shortly before his death. He realized after working in prisons that teaching prisoners using the moral dilemma approach would not reduce moral infractions. A person has to care about the kind of person they become before it will work, and that issue is at the crux of the moral life itself. Another one of Kohlberg's detractors Edwin Delattre believes that
relatively few of our moral failings are attributable to inept reasoning about dilemmas. Many more arise from moral indifference, disregard for other people, weakness of will, and bad or self-indulgent habits

What I would like to know is whether the program at Penn State is based on strictly a dilemma approach or not. How about other programs in business ethics? I hope some of these include the option of virtue and character development.
Respectfully,
Rosemary Bradford Grant

From: James B. Lyttle
To: Multiple rcipients of list BETS-L
Date: 1/20/96 5:32pm
Subject: Re: Integrity

Rosemary Grant
>   I think I was just flamed because of the post I wrote yesterday
> about limitations on Kohlberg.

I am sorry, Rosemary. That was just my gut reaction to the remark "nobody listens to Kohlberg anymore" (or words to that effect).

>What I found was that there is much more to ethics education than
>the ability to reason morally.

Agreed. I imagine Kohlberg would agree, too. But his work is simply a description of the states of moral reasoning. We wouldn't expect his work to address anything else.

>Christina Hoff Sommers has done a good job [of debunking Kohlberg]
>in _Ethics and Virtue in Everyday Life_ and William Kilpatrick's
>_Why Johnny Can't Tell Right from Wrong_.
> They argue for an approach to ethics that develops character.

These popular works seem to be calling for us to put "family values" back into the class-room. Admittedly, teaching a set of values to a student is a completely different project from teaching moral reasoning.
It is called indoctrination. The reason we stick to reasoning is that we want to give students a technology or process for discerning right from wrong. While remaining responsible enough to refrain from trying to tell them what is right and what is wrong.

>Edwin Delattre believes that "relatively few of our moral failings are
>attributable to inept reasoning about dilemmas. Many more arise from
>moral indifference, disregard for other people, weakness of will, and
>bad or self-indulgent habits."

I agree with this completely! Philosophers like to debate borderline cases and "interesting" dilemmas, but in most real situations people know exactly what they should do. Nonetheless, they fail to do it.
The key task for us is to support people in taking the "high road."
Why do people fail to make the choices that they know are right?

To some extent, it is due to a lack of moral fortitude. Moral fortitude can be developed at church and, to some extent, through psychotherapy.
As educators, we are not qualified to perform either of those functions, and it would be more than irresponsible for us to pretend otherwise.

In some cases, though, people fail to do the right thing because there are systems in place that discourage moral choices. For example, in business, there may be a drive for increased profits that encourages people to put their morals aside. As academics, we CAN do something about this situation. We can look for, discover, and implement systems to measure and reward ethical behaviour.

In fact, just such a system is now being developed by Tim Bell and Larry Ponemon at the big six accounting firm KPMG Peat Marwick. It is called "ethics process management" and their approach is (in effect) we can't stop bad people from doing bad things, but we might be able to stop good people from being tempted into doing bad things. They hope to establish a kind of ethics accounting that can produce an annual report on ethics performance based on an ethics audit.

I will be following this development closely, and would welcome any constructive discussion on ways to encourage and support people in their attempts to conduct moral lives.

From:	Linda Klebe Trevino
To:	Multiple recipients of list BETS-L . . .
Date:	1/21/96 12:28pm
Subject:	Re: Kohlberg

I agree with Jim.

My own evaluation of Kohlberg's work over the last 10 years suggests that it's absolutely the best research we have. It spans over 30 years and has produced a large volume of empirical research, mostly supportive of

Kohlberg's basic theory. Those who are interested might want to take a look at a paper I wrote that was published in the Journal of Business Ethics in 1992 (vol. 11, pp. 445–459) entitled Moral Reasoning and Business Ethics:

Implications for Research, Education, and Management. It reviewed much of the relevant research at least up to that time.

Kohlberg has received much criticism for a few reasons, I think.

First, he attempted to bridge psychology and philosophy, offering a truly integrative theory. Therefore, he was attacked by both sides and quite vehemently at times. Second, a lot of people didn't like him much as a person. Third, Carol Gilligan got a lot of press when she published her feminist challenge to his work. I think she may be right about young girls. I don't know enough to say. But, the research on adults doesn't support her contention at all. Even if girls & boys are different as children, socialization makes professional men and women quite similar in moral reasoning. In fact, women have generally scored slightly higher on

Kohlberg-based measures of moral development!

I've always been open to the challenges, but I haven't seen evidence to support any of them that compares to the mountain of evidence that supports Kohlberg's theory.

Linda Klebe Trevino

From:	Rosemary Grant
To:	Multiple recipients of list BETS-L . . .
Date:	1/21/96 5:15pm
Subject:	Re: Integrity

James and Linda,

I don't think Christina and Fred Sommers have tried to _debunk Kohlberg_ as you wrote in interpreting my post. And I'm sorry about getting the title of their book wrong. It's _Vice and Virtue in Everyday Life_ -also forgot to mention that she coauthored the book. She also wrote _Right and Wrong:
Basic Readings in Ethics_

I have two hugh boxes of articles about alternatives to Kohlberg in ethics education. You see, I made copies of everything I could find during two years of research in 92–94.

They are all scholarly articles from refereed journals.
Furthermore, I have a long list of books that would also be considered scholarly. I supposed it depends on what you are looking for, and at that time I was interested in character education. I looked at moral development, but that was not my primary interest because I was and still am interested in promoting magnanimity in the professions. There is a school of thought that is based on what is called _virtue theory_. These people think it is valid for a person to consider the shoulds and oughts. Sometimes people choose to do what is right even though they could use their skills from a dilemma oriented ethics course to make a different one.

There are plenty of good arguments out there that could counter the idea that teaching character is not merely _indoctrination_. Furthermore, it has been determined that students who have been presented with a series of moral dilemmas are often more confused about right and wrong than they were before.

Sommers who teaches college ethics opposes a syllabus that focuses strictly on social morality and avoids private morality. I can see that taking time to debate abortion, euthanasia, capital punishment, DNA research, and transplant surgery to the exclusion of topics such as decency, honesty, personal responsibility, and honor is not justified.
IMHO the profs who impose these topics on college students are invading their autonomy much more than a prof who challenges moral relativism.

G. J. Warnock (quoting from Sommers) writes that ethics profs do not need to be bullied out of holding fast to _plain moral facts_. Alasdair
MacIntyre who wrote _After Virtue_ writes that we may be raising a generation of moral stutterers. Michael Josephson (president of an Ethics organization in California) reports that what we have is a hole in our moral ozone.

Sommers recommends a course that focuses on the philosophy of virtue. She begins with Aristotle and argues that her _students find the idea of developing virtuous character traits naturally appealing_. She includes other philosophers in her course on ethics and encourages discussion.

With this guide and others (including moral relativism) her students can choose whether or not they have application for their lives.

At least, it gives them some method to deal with the real world they face everyday.

I don't understand your idea (Jim) that personal ethics should only be offered in the church or at the psychiatrist office. I've been in the classroom over twenty years, and I know my students are not getting much assistance in these places. They are hoping to find assistance at school, and we should be ashamed of ourselves if we always back away from this responsibility.

Jim, you wrote <We can look for, discover, and implement systems
>to measure and reward ethical behaviour.>

What do you offer students to help them understand the rules of the game other than moral reasoning?

Jim, how do people know whether they've done the right thing in the
Bell and Ponemon scheme you describe? You wrote. . . .>we can't stop bad people from doing bad things, but we might be able to >stop good people from being tempted into doing bad things.>____. . . .I ask: How do people in this system know right and wrong? Who sets up the standards? On what basis?

Is this just a punishment and reward system? You wrote __>They hope
>to establish a kind of ethics accounting that can produce an annual
>report on ethics performance based on an ethics audit.>
>

I'd like to know more.

Respectfully,

　　Rosemary Grant

RELATED WEB SITE

Business Ethics Teaching Society: www.usi.edu/bets/index.htm

PSYCHOETHICS: A DISCIPLINE APPLYING PSYCHOLOGY TO BUSINESS ETHICS

TERRI KAYE NEEDLE   MARTIN J. LECKER

The following overviews of four case studies demonstrate the relationship between psychological theory and ethical and moral development. The opinions of these four individuals are those of the authors and are based on research conducted by the authors.

ANITA RODDICK

. . . Anita Roddick's firm philosophy of life is that you can be a business person, make money and use that money to initiate social change. She has become the embodiment of free enterprise, social consciousness, and success. She has become the most outspoken activist businesswoman of the decade.

This once unemployed mother went on to become Businesswoman of the Year, Communicator of the Year, Retailer of the Year, and recipient of the United Nations Environmentalist Award to the Amazon, where she has started cottage industries to help save the rain forest. Profiled by *Time, Newsweek,* and a host of women's magazines, Anita Roddick has become the voice of business in the 90's, an era hungry for principles and change. She took her natural products and $7,000 in borrowed money, built a chain of more than 600 shops, created a franchising system and eventually a public company.

Anita Roddick opened the first Body Shop in Brighton, England, in 1976. She believed in herself from the time she was 18 years old and found out from her mother that her stepfather was really her father. It gave her confidence in her gut feelings because she felt so close to him and not to the other man in her life who was supposed to be her father (Gilligan, Chart I).

Her young-adult life as a hippie, backpacking through Europe, Israel, Greece, Africa, Tahiti, and Australia in the 1960's was unconventional. Although she worked as a teacher, it was only to earn enough money to travel. She met and married a fellow traveler and free spirit, Gordon Roddick, and they had two daughters together. In 1976, Gordon was embarking on a year's journey horsebackriding through South America, and Anita needed to support herself and her two children (Maslow, Chart II).

CHART I

Kohlberg		Gilligan
Decision Based On Justice/Rights		Decision Based on Care/Relationships

Stage 1

Obedience and Punishment
- Decision based on fear and avoidance of punishment.
- Obedience to authority.
- Everyone for himself.
- "I" statements.

- Concern is for self.
- Survival is based on strength, rather than caring.
- "I gotta be tough. I gotta look out for me."

Stage 2

Individualism and Reciprocity
- No thoughts of anyone else except as they serve you.
- Satisfying one's own needs.
- Does not share another's perspective.
- "What's in it for me?"
- "What do I have to give up?"

PRECONVENTIONAL
SELF-FOCUSED

TRANSITION—self-interest is thought of as selfish; starts to be concerned for others.

Stage 3

Interpersonal Conformity

- Takes interpersonal relationships into account.
- Has good intentions.
- Wants to gain approval.
- "Good" and "nice" behavior.
- "How can I do this so most people will like me?"

- Good is equated with caring for others according to conventions of feminine self-sacrifice
- "Always care more for others than for me, no matter what the expense".

Stage 4

Law and Order

- Obeying the law.
- Inflexible.
- "It's always wrong to break the law."

CONVENTIONAL
GROUP-FOCUSED

TRANSITION—word "selfish" reappears when "self-sacrifice" is rejected as unequal.
- "Hey what about me? I'm entitled".

Stage 5

Social Contract

Reasoning, regardless of society.
- Gets away from stage 4 rigidity.
- Protection of individual rights with impartiality.
- Concerned with needs of human beings.
- Rules and laws can be changed.

POST CONVENTIONAL
UNIVERSAL-FOCUSED

- Moral to CARE is obligation extended to oneself on an equal basis with others.
- "How can I resolve this so that everyone is cared for equally?"
- Everyone can't be cared for equally!

Stage 6

Universal Ethical Principles
- Solution is worked out to be just for everyone.
- High principle of preserving life.

CHART II

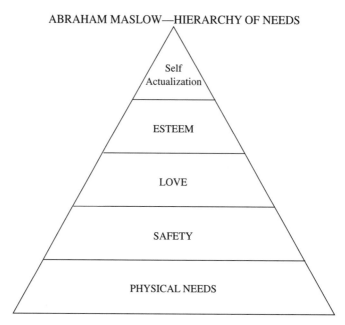

ABRAHAM MASLOW—HIERARCHY OF NEEDS

1. Physical needs are most essential. They include food, clothing, shelter, sleep, activity, water, and biological needs.

2. Safety needs include freedom from fear, pain, failure, punishment, and threats.

3. Love needs involve both giving and receiving love. People need to have a feeling of belonging.

4. Esteem and self-worth needs are related to self-image, confidence, independence, and the need to achieve and feel adequate. Esteem needs also relate to how others see and respect you.

5. Self-actualization needs refer to the desire for self-fulfillment, a desire to become everything one is capable of becoming.

She opened the Body Shop and immediately began to sell the truth about cosmetics, an unheard of practice at that time, that would propel her into the limelight. She gave unconventional people a chance (Gilligan, Chart I). In early 1977, Anita got a call from an herbalist on a pay phone asking if she could market his shampoo. He had trouble selling it because it looked and smelled awful. He was just starting his career and was living in the woods alone—like a hippie, mixing herbs in his kitchen. She gave Mark Constantine his first break (Gilligan, Chart I). She took a chance and he came through. Building on Carol Gilligan's Theory of Care and Response to Need, Anita and her employee, Katie, responded to the needs of the London marathon runners. They stood along the route and handed out samples of peppermint foot lotion, created by Mark Constantine and one of the top selling items in the Body Shop. It not only softened the skin, it also helped with foot odor.

Using Carl Jung's theory of the collective unconscious, Anita and Gordon Roddick were able to team their company, in 1985, with the Greenpeace Mission. They paid for hundreds of posters showing the Greenpeace slogan that said, "You can join Greenpeace at the Body Shop". The socially conscious involvement continues today with involvements in: Save the Whale Campaign, Friends of the Earth, and Amnesty International. A new dimension has been added to the Roddicks' life together. A spiritual dimension has emerged, using their success for promoting social concerns. Anita Roddick said, "You don't have to lose your soul to succeed in business".

BEN COHEN

In 1978, with a $12,000 investment, Ben Cohen and Jerry Greenfield opened a small ice cream parlour. Today, it is a multi-million-dollar, publicly held corporation and is internationally recognized as a benchmark for being socially responsible. Ben Cohen developed the social mission statement, "A business has a responsibility to give back to the community." For this reason, Ben Cohen's psychological background will be analyzed for this research.

As a child, Cohen was highly intelligent, who as the valedictorian of his sixth grade class was voted "most likely to succeed." Placed in an advanced junior high school program, Cohen had to learn things his own way, refused to do his homework, and was perceived by his teachers as being rebellious. Yet, he was extremely creative and excelled in any project that he found interesting. Upon meeting Jerry Greenfield in high school, both were found to possess many common characteristics, including high intelligence, creativity, and a nontraditional work ethic of, "If it's not fun, why do it?" This philosophy would guide Cohen to a multitude of careers, including learning how to produce homemade ice cream via a correspondence course, jointly taken with Greenfield.

Cohen's friendship with Jerry enabled him to feel connected, or as psychologist Carol Gilligan termed it, "an attachment." It was because of this attachment to Greenfield, and Cohen's further perception that he connected (or felt attached) to his customer, that Cohen was able to progress to another ethical level, that psychologist Lawrence Kohlberg called "the sixth stage of universal ethical principles." This sixth stage is part of a justice principle, based upon an agent who makes ethical decisions for himself and everyone else to live by as well. This was exemplified by Cohen's philosophy of putting the community ahead of its stockholders, in what was termed "a linked prosperity."

To further support his socially responsible philosophy, a Ben and Jerry's foundation was developed. Cohen gave the foundation fifty thousand shares of his stock as an initial endowment. Furthermore, Cohen announced that Ben and Jerry's would donate seven and a half percent of its pretax profits to the foundation that in turn would give away the money for projects to nonprofit organizations that were models for social change. All of these social contributions exemplify Kohlberg's sixth stage.

LEONA HELMSLEY

Leona Helmsley was convicted on 33 felony counts, divided into four groups of offenses including: conspiracy, tax evasion, filing false tax returns, and mail fraud. She was sentenced to four years in prison on each group of offenses. This was a total of 16 years, but the sentences would run concurrently and this amounted to 4 years in federal prison.

Her childhood is clouded in obscurity—she changed both her name and the facts of her early life. Lena Rosenthal was one of four children born in 1919. She had two older sisters whom she didn't get along with. Friction between them was so deep that she didn't speak to either of them, and refused to even attend their respective funerals in the early 1980's and mid 1980's (Gilligan/Kohlberg Chart I). Leona didn't relate to either of the two moral objectives in her life: **to treat others fairly** and **not to turn away from those in need.** She married Leo Panzirer, a lawyer, in 1938, who was 12 years her senior. She gave birth to her only child, a son, in 1940. The marriage ended by 1949. She was alone, dependent on minimal child support and alimony. Her family refused to help her. (Maslow, Levels 1, 3, 4). She married and divorced the same man twice, Joseph Lubin, so by 1962 she was on her own again. She was now in her 40's. She got a job in real estate, and she was a natural. Leona began as a receptionist at Pease and Elliman, a prestigious residential brokerage firm. She had no intention of sitting behind the front desk while others were earning commissions selling and renting apartments. Leona was not a team player. She got promoted to showing apartments herself, part-time. She steered clients away from other brokers behind their backs. Leona was out for Leona! (Kohlberg, Chart I, stage 2). She kept moving up. She pressured and bullied tenants to buy apartments in buildings her company owned that were going co-op or condominium in such a harsh and brutal way, that she almost lost her real estate license (Gilligan, Chart I). Some people loved her attention to detail and would work with no one else. Others despised her tactics. After only 10 years in the business she became Vice-President of Pease & Elliman, earning a salary and commission in the six figures. She had made it! Soon after she was introduced to Harry Helmsley who offered her a job as Senior Vice President at a salary of one half of a million dollars. She had come a long way since she started as a low-paid receptionist in a real estate office. She was past 50 when she accepted Harry Helmsley's offer.

MICHAEL MILKEN

In April 1990, Michael Milken pleaded guilty to six felonies—including conspiracy, securities fraud, mail fraud, and filing false tax forms—and agreed to pay $600 million in penalties in return for federal prosecutors' agreement to drop the remaining 92 charges originally brought against him by the federal government in 1989. Seven months later, Federal District Judge Kimba Wood sentenced him to 10 years in prison, three additional years of probation, and 5,400 hours of community service.

Michael Milken's father, Bernard, was an accountant who would be willing to help his wealthy clients locate creative tax solutions to their problems. However, on a personal basis, Bernard Milken was far more risk-averse. Many times, Bernard would reject business opportunities because they appeared too risky. Yet, at home, Michael was taught to share, to help others, but not to receive recognition for his efforts. This covert trait became useful later on, since Milken never personally took credit for any one of his profitable dealings. Nonetheless, he would try to help others and share his own successes with them.

One example of his sharing values was that when he took his college fraternity's funds and invested them, he guaranteed that he would keep 50 percent of the fraternity profits invested, but also pay back 100 percent of any losses. Ironically, this is what he did while at Drexel Burnham Lambert as a junk-bond chief trader. In some instances, Milken would personally guarantee, to a select number of clients that he would pay back 100 percent of any losses when they invested in high-risk junk bonds. However, he refused to file the forms that were legally required of traders who personally guaranteed their clients against unforeseen losses.

However, according to his probation officer, Milken was a product of a deep insecurity. He needed to be needed. As a result, Milken saw himself as the "Candy Man." In a dysfunctional world, he would make everything right for everybody. In essence, two psychological theories may explain his unethical decisions: Maslow's third level of belongingness and Gilligan's theory of attachment. In both theories, Milken displays a proclivity towards pleasing others for purposes of acceptance. Furthermore, a third theory, Kohlberg's stage three, the interpersonal conformity stage, may be used. In this stage a person makes moral decisions because he wants to be a member of the team, and what is right will be determined by what is expected of you by people close to you. Therefore, Kohlberg's third stage personifies the psychological motivation that led to Milken's unethical actions and eventually to his demise.

VENTURING BEYOND COMPLIANCE

Lynn Sharp Paine

Paine identifies two strategems to encourage and support an ethical corporate culture: legal compliance and organizational integrity. Consider which might be more effective from a long-term perspective? Which would be easier to implement? Which do you think is more prevalent in the business environment?

How can managers insure that individuals in their companies conduct business in a way that is responsible and ethically sound? This challenge involves organizational design and a number of specific managerial tasks.

WHY THE ETHICS FOCUS?

In the past decade, a number of factors have brought ethical matters into sharper focus.

Globalization   Global expansion has brought about greater involvement with different cultures and socioeconomic systems. With this development, ethical considerations—such as the different assumptions about the responsibilities of business, about acceptable business practices, and about the values needed to build a cohesive, successful organization—become more important.

Technology   The added capabilities of technology have created a new level of transparency and immediacy to business communication. Now the conduct of businesses around the globe is more exposed than it ever was before.

Competition   Rising competition brings with it added pressure to cut corners. Simultaneously, leaders are looking for new ways to differentiate their companies and move them to a new level of excellence. Some believe that a proactive ethical stance can have a positive impact on the bottom line.

Public Perception and the Law   There is a perceived decline in social ethics that yields uncertainty. Managers are no longer comfortable assuming that employees joining their companies possess the desired ethical values. And public expectations, too, have changed: That which was once deemed acceptable is now more readily scrutinized. New

Lynn Sharp Paine, "Venturing Beyond Compliance," *The Evolving Role of Ethics in Business,* report no. 1141–96-ch, pp. 13–16 (The Conference Board, Inc.: New York, NY 1996) email: info@conference-board.org laws and stepped-up enforcement efforts have increased the risk of personal and organizational liability.

TWO STRATEGIES EMERGE

Most managers are choosing either a *legal compliance* strategy or an *organizational integrity* strategy to support ethics in their companies. These strategies differ markedly in their conception of ethics, human behavior, and management responsibility. While the organizational integrity strategy fully acknowledges the importance of compliance with the law, its aim is to achieve right conduct in general. Thus, it is more comprehensive and broader than the legal compliance strategy. Companies that adopt an organizational integrity strategy are concerned with their identity—who they are and what they stand for—and with how they conduct internal and external affairs. These matters are less clear-cut (and hence, more demanding) than those handled by a legal compliance approach.

These strategies differ in several fundamental ways:

Ethos   The legal compliance strategy regards ethics as a set of limits, boundaries over which we must not cross. The compliance approach is externally driven. Here, ethics is viewed as something that *has* to be done.

The organizational integrity strategy defines ethics as a set of principles to guide the choices we make. Companies that adopt this approach choose their own standards for conducting business on an individual and company-wide basis.

Objectives   The compliance approach is geared toward preventing unlawful conduct and criminal misconduct in particular. The integrity approach, by comparison, has a more lofty goal: to achieve responsible conduct across-the-board, even if not required by law.

Leadership   While companies with a compliance approach place lawyers at the helm, the integrity approach is captained by company managers. To insure that their efforts are thorough and effective, these managers are assisted by lawyers, human resources specialists, and other experts.

Methods   The compliance focus emphasizes the rules people must not violate. It uses increased oversight and stepped-up penalties to enforce these rules. An integrity approach acknowledges the need for a brake on people's behavior from time to time, but treats ethics as a steering mechanism rather than the brake itself. Here, ethics infuses the organization's leadership, its core systems, and its decision-making processes.

Behavioral Assumptions   Finally, the two approaches rest on very different philosophies of human nature. The compliance strategy's ideas are rooted in deterrence theory—how to prevent people from doing bad things by manipulating the costs of misconduct. The integrity strategy views people as having a fuller, richer set of needs and motivations. While it acknowledges that people are guided by material self-interest and the threat of penalties, it also identifies the other drivers of human nature—individual values, ideals, and the influence of peers.

LIMITATIONS OF A COMPLIANCE-BASED APPROACH

Why go beyond compliance? While legal compliance is a must, a legal compliance approach to company ethics has several specific limitations:

- Compliance is not terribly responsive to many of the day-to-day concerns that managers and employees face. It follows the law, which is generally backward looking. For a company on the cutting edge of technology, of new financing mechanisms, of new practices, the law is not very helpful as a guide.

- The majority of hot line calls are not about unlawful or criminal misconduct. They deal with gray areas and with issues of supervisory practice and fair treatment. A legal compliance approach does not provide answers to these types of questions. Therefore, it does not adequately address employees' real concerns and needs.

- The typical legal compliance program runs directly counter to the philosophy of empowerment. Empowerment gives employees discretion, resources, and authority, and then trusts them to make good decisions. Compliance programs, though, reduce discretion, increase oversight, and tighten controls. If a company tries to put forth an empowerment effort and a compliance-driven ethics program at the same time, the two will cancel each other out. This will result in a lot of employee cynicism.

- A legal compliance program is just not very exciting. Compliance is important, but the law was not designed to inspire human excellence so much as to set a floor for acceptable behavior. Since the law has to apply to everyone, its standards are not as demanding as we might choose for ourselves and for our companies.

CHALLENGES TO AN INTEGRITY-BASED APPROACH

If you are really interested in organizational effectiveness and organizational development rather than just avoiding liability, an integrity-driven approach is far more promising. But four challenges must be met before an organizational integrity approach can work:

1. *Developing an ethical framework.* Organizational integrity requires a much more robust concept of organizational identity and responsibility than does compliance.
2. *Aligning practice with principles* This can be very problematic, especially in organizations whose structure, systems, and decision processes run counter to the values and principles espoused by senior management.
3. *Overcoming cynicism.* In *The Cynical Americans,* Donald L. Kanter and Phillip H. Mervis' study of cynicism in the United States (San Francisco, Josey-Bass Publishers, 1989, p. 1), it was revealed that almost 43 percent of Americans fit the profile of the cynic; that is, one who regards selfishness, dishonesty, and fakery as at the core of human behavior. People often adopt cynicism as a self-defense mechanism.

This frame of reference often prevents people from seeing reality, and can act as a barrier to instilling ethical values.

4. *Resolving Ethical Conflicts.* We all have conflicting responsibilities from time to time. If we are very creative, we may be able to solve potential conflicts before they unfold. Sometimes, though, hard trade-offs—between right and right, between two "goods"—must be made.

NAVIGATING WITH THE ETHICAL COMPASS

How do you begin to create an ethical compass or a framework for integrity? A useful starting point is to begin by answering some questions related to the four fundamental sources of responsibility.

- Purpose—What is the organization's fundamental reason for being—its ultimate aims?

- People—Who are the constituencies to whom the company is accountable and on whom it depends for success? What are their legitimate claims and interests?

- Power—What is the organization's authority and ability to act?

- Principles—What are the organization's obligations or duties, as well as its guiding aspirations and ideals?

If used as a set of reference points, these questions can help develop a framework against which to benchmark progress on ethical matters (see Exhibit 1).

The framework of ideas is only a start. Putting it into practice is the difficult part. People often wonder why a gap exists between the espoused values and everyday behavior, when in fact, a gap *should* exist to some degree. If you are fully satisfying your ideals and aspirations, most likely your standards are not high enough. If the gap between principle and practice becomes a chasm, though, it becomes hypocrisy, which is even worse.

MANAGEMENT: PUTTING IT TOGETHER

Integrity-based ethics management efforts have contributed to organizational effectiveness in several fundamental ways. Companies that have adopted such programs report fewer and less serious problems of misconduct. Often this is because problems are caught earlier and are dealt with at the onset. In some cases, an integrity approach can yield strengthened competitiveness: it facilitates the delivery of quality products in an honest, reliable way. This approach can enhance work life by making the workplace more fun and challenging. It can improve relationships with constituencies and can instill a more positive mindset that fosters creativity and innovation. And while an organizational integrity approach cannot guarantee bottom-line performance improvements, it is important to understand that ethics is a very practical matter. The purpose of ethics is to enhance our lives and our relationships both inside and outside of the organization.

Clearly, achieving and maintaining integrity requires intense commitment and involvement from managers company-wide. This goes beyond the so-called "tone" set by

EXHIBIT 1

The Four Points of an Ethical Compass

How can managers develop a framework for integrity?

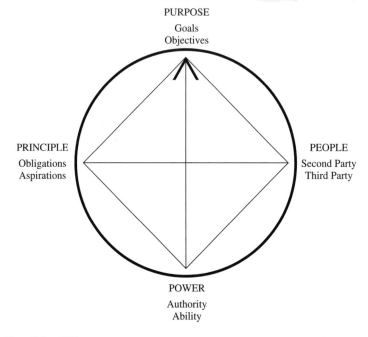

© Lynn Sharp Paine, 1995

senior management. It involves specific leadership tasks and behaviors, starting with the development of the integrity framework. Managers must insure that company systems support responsible behavior. Then they must personally model responsible decision making. These leadership tasks are all essential to building the high-integrity organization.

RELATED WEB SITES

The Organizational Ethics Committee: Roles and Responsibilities:
www.navran.com/Newsletter/94-04/04-94d.html

Sentencing Commission Takes on Corporate Crime:
condor.depaul.edu/ethics/matt2.html

Chapter 3

INDIVIDUAL DECISION MAKING:
Lessons Learned from the Foundations

This above all: to thine own self be true, and it must follow, as the night the day, Thou canst not then be false to any man.

SHAKESPEARE

Jordan Baker: I thought you were rather an honest, straight-forward person. I thought it was your secret pride.
Nick Carraway: I'm thirty. I'm five years too old to lie to myself and call it honor.

F. SCOTT FITZGERALD, *THE GREAT GATSBY*

"To be nothing but yourself, in a world which is doing its best to make you everybody else, means to fight the hardest battle which any human being can fight, and never stop fighting."

E. E. CUMMINGS

In *No Exit* by Sartre, Inez, a lesbian woman who drove her lover's husband to his death says: "One always dies too soon—or too late. And yet one's whole life is complete at that moment, with a line drawn neatly under it, ready for the summing up. You are—your life, and nothing else."

Consider Inez's statement: "You are—your life, and nothing else." Consider how you feel about your accomplishments, your challenges, your actions and decisions. If one were to look at this life from the outside, would that person find it to be worthwhile, good, right, or any other positive judgment? You might believe that a part of our soul is left with each decision we make, and our lasting impact on this earth is evidenced by the "indentations" we make on the lives of others and our environment. If so, then you might also believe that we will all be judged on the basis of these indentations that we leave behind.

Do you consider that you act only in your own self-interest at all times, or would you contend that you ignore your personal interests in order to act in the interests of others at times? When you make a choice that is for your own good but against someone else's are you accountable to that other individual for the impact of your decision. Some theorists argue that we act *only* in our own self interest, that even something like an anonymous donation satisfies your personal need to do that act. Controversial author and philosopher Ayn Rand goes one step further and contends that those who do concern themselves with the interests of others do so to their own detriment or for purely selfish reasons. In discussing this "selflessness," Howard Roark, the protagonist of Rand's novel *The Fountainhead,* says:

> And isn't that the root of every despicable action? Not selfishness, but precisely the absence of a self. Look at them. The man who cheats and lies but preserves a respectable front. He knows himself to be dishonest, but others think he's honest and he derives his self respect from that, second-hand. . . . The frustrated wretch who professes love for the inferior and clings to those less endowed, in order to establish his own superiority by comparison. The man whose sole aim is to make money. Now I don't see anything evil in a desire to make money. But money is only a means to an end. If a man wants it for a personal purpose—to invest in his industry, to create, to study, to travel, to enjoy luxury—he's completely moral. But the men who place money first go much beyond that. Personal luxury is a limited endeavor. What they want is ostentation: to show, to stun, to entertain, to impress others. They're second-handers.[1]

Would you consider yourself someone Rand derides, a "second-hander"?

Ethics demands the integrity to act according to your personal values as well as accountability for each decision that we make in our lives according to those values. If someone were asked to choose between allowing a loved one to die by following the law, or breaking the law in order to allow him or her to live, many may be willing to break the law. Their justification might be "I had no choice—I had to do it" to save the

1. Ayn Rand, *The Fountainhead* (New York: Signet Books, 1971) pp. 606–7.

loved one. The truth is that we all have choices. If you are asked to choose between terminating a subordinate or losing your job, you might fire the worker, claiming, "I have no choice but to do this. Sorry." In fact, you would have a choice—terminate the subordinate or lose your job. You may not like the alternatives offered, but it is a choice nonetheless.

As a student or as an employee or employer, you are faced with a variety of alternatives. It will be up to you to determine the course of your actions. In a well-publicized case involving Electrical Manufacturers, recent college graduates were found guilty of conspiring to fix prices and otherwise violate the antitrust statutes. In response to questions about their guilt, the young employees claimed, "I got out of school and this was how it was done." Does that explain the behavior to you? Consider how you would feel if you were (or had been) asked to do something with which you were uncomfortable during your first year of work. Do you think you would refuse? Would you quit? Of course, your response probably depends on the nature of the request, but questioning accepted business practice is difficult, no matter the cost.

In a 1991 study, researchers determined that business undergraduate students are the most likely to have cheated on a test, when compared to pre-law students and the general population.[2] In response to a statement claiming that *not* cheating is the best way to get ahead in the long run, business students claimed, "This is the Nineties. You snooze, you lose."[3] Does this mean that, perhaps, there is a failure in ethics in the business arena because the people who go into business already cheat? Or is it that business students are aware that the business arena demands this type of unethical conduct to they prepare themselves for it from the start? Competitiveness might make the border between ethical and unethical become blurred. Either way, as our parents once told us, simply because an environment is replete with a certain type of behavior does not mean that we must follow suit, nor does it relieve us of our responsibility for actions in that environment (they would say, "If Janie jumps off a bridge, are you going to follow?").

It may be telling regarding your future decision-making choices whether you believe that you will be held accountable for your actions, whether you believe that you will be caught, or more esoterically, whether you believe that "the world is out to get you," "you should do whatever you can to get ahead," "everyone cheats," "honest people lose in the end," or other cynical doctrines. Are these the type of people with whom you work, or for whom you work? Are these types of individuals more or less likely to act unethically? To be accountable for their actions?

In the readings that follow, a variety of perspectives are offered in connection with this concept of free choice and accountability, beginning with an audit of your own ethical perspective.

---

2. Rick Tetzeli, "Business Students Cheat Most," *Fortune,* July 1, 1991, p. 14.
3. Ibid., p. 18.

Short Hypothetical Cases

A mining company plans to open a gold mine in the area. You are hired by the company to acquire the land. Your commissions and bonuses on this multi-million-dollar deal will be substantial. A large tract of land in the center of the proposed mine is owned by an uneducated farmer who has lived on this land all of his life. He has no knowledge of the plans for the mine. A smaller tract, near the site, but not part of the proposed land purchase, is owned by an influential member of the county council. He knows about the coming development. You know you can acquire the farmer's land for a fraction of its value. The council member has already started raising objections to the mine. What do you do?

Hypotheticals were written by Catherine Haselden and are included in her manuscript "The Ethics Game."

QUIZ YOURSELF
ON BUSINESS ETHICS

Dawn-Marie Driscoll, W. Michael Hoffman, Edward Petry

The following quiz was developed to help you to identify your own ethical awareness and to give you a greater understanding of your personal perspective.

. . . For questions 1 and 2, circle the answers you think are correct. More than one may qualify.

1. **Ethics is** _____
   a.   A branch of philosophy that deals with values as they relate to human conduct.
   b.   The study of what is good and right for people. It asks the question: How should I act, especially when my actions directly or indirectly affect others?
   c.   A fad, a topic that is kept alive by the media on days when there is no hard news to report.

2. **Business ethics is** _____
   a.   The application of ethical principles and methods of analysis to business.
   b.   A topic of study that is now required at all business schools accredited by the American Assembly of Collegiate Schools of Business.
   c.   An oxymoron.

In recent years there have been many tales of moral crises faced by organizations. How many of the following do you recognize? Again, more than one answer may be correct.

3. **Fraud and abuse was so common at NORTEL, Ltd., a giant Canadian telecommunications corporation, that:**
   a.   It was estimated that one indictable offense occurred each and every working day.
   b.   One manager defrauded the company for more than $6 million and then used the company's facilities to engage in widespread wiretapping, all the while amassing a private stockpile of arms.
   c.   The company has since established a remarkably effective fraud prevention program and is emerging as a leader in the Canadian business ethics movement.

4. **For 15 minutes, executives at the Maine shipbuilder Bath Iron Works gave in to the temptation to cheat. Their ethical lapse:**
   a.   Nearly destroyed the company's 100-year-old reputation for integrity.
   b.   Put 8,000 jobs in peril.
   c.   Ended the gubernatorial aspirations of the company's widely admired leader.
   d.   Pushed the company to establish safeguards at the board and officer levels to increase ethical oversight at the top.

5. **A former president of the United Way was:**
   a.   An entrepreneur and business genius who created the "greatest health and human services delivery system in history."
   b.   A flawed leader who misused United Way funds to support a long-distance romance with a young woman just out of high school.
   c.   Both of the above; in fact his successes helped shape an organization that all but made his failures inevitable.

What do business leaders think about the ethics of business? Deloitte & Touche surveyed more than a thousand officers and directors of corporations together with other business leaders. Are your views on the topic in sync with theirs? Circle the answers to questions 6 through 8 that you think are correct.

6. **Is the American business community troubled by ethical problems?**
   a.   Yes
   b.   No

7. **Has the issue of business ethics become overblown?**
   a.   Yes
   b.   No

8. **How do high ethical standards affect a company's competitive position?**
   a.   Strengthen
   b.   Weaken
   c.   No effect

Has the increased acceptance of the concept of business ethics translated into actual changes in the workplace? In the years 1985, 1990 and 1992, the Center for Business Ethics surveyed the Fortune 1000 to find out what changes—if any—were being made to build ethics into corporate policies and programs. Circle the answers you think are correct for questions 9 through 13.

9. **What percentage of the Fortune 1000 are planning to expand efforts to incorporate ethics into their daily operations?**
   a.   More than 90 percent
   b.   About 50 percent
   c.   Less than 25 percent

10. **The most common motive(s) given for implementing ethics initiatives is (are) to:**
    a.   Improve profits
    b.   Provide guidelines for conduct
    c.   Improve public image
    d.   Be socially responsible

11. **What percentage of the Fortune 1000 have written ethics policies?**
    a.   More than 90 percent
    b.   About 50 percent
    c.   Less than 25 percent

12. **What percentage of the Fortune 1000 have employee ethics training?**
    a.   More than 90 percent
    b.   About 50 percent
    c.   Less than 25 percent

13. **Since 1987, the number of large corporations with ethics officers (whose primary function is to create or maintain the company's ethics program) has:**
    a.   Stayed about the same
    b.   Increased slightly
    c.   More than doubled

While there has been a decade of steady growth in the number of corporations implementing corporate ethics policies and programs, the new Federal Sentencing Guidelines for Organizations has certainly piqued the business community's interest and led to a sharp increase in its efforts. Circle the answers you think are correct for questions 14 through 16. More than one answer may be correct.

14. **The Guidelines apply only to large corporations.**
    a.   True
    b.   False

15. **Under the Guidelines organizations may be required to pay restitution and may be placed on probation for up to five years. The Guidelines also cite specific aggravating factors that can increase the organization's fine up to:**
    a.   400 percent
    b.   100 percent
    c.   50 percent

16. **The Guidelines call on organizations to create "effective programs to prevent and detect violations of law." These programs must include:**
    a.   Established compliance standards.
    b.   Specific individual(s) assigned to oversee compliance.
    c.   Due care in delegating discretionary authority.

d.   Steps to communicate standards and procedures, e.g., training programs and publications.

e.   Steps to achieve compliance, e.g., monitoring, auditing, and reporting systems.

f.   A record of consistent enforcement of standards.

g.   Procedures to review and modify the program after an offense.

Hopefully your company is one of those making a serious effort to build ethics into its daily operations. When an ethics dilemma arises, it's unfortunately often the case that, at least initially, you're still facing it alone. What should you do? Circle the answers you think are correct for questions 17 through 20. More than one may be correct.

17. **Possible scenarios: (1) You are an employee at a public utility and discover that rate payers' money is being used illegally to finance political campaigns. (2) You are an employee at a phone company that holds "pervert conventions" every year to "entertain" suppliers. (3) You have a choice of blowing the whistle to your company's officers and possibly facing retaliation or of going outside the company and blowing the whistle to the government and collecting a multi-million-dollar bonus.**

   When faced with such ethical dilemmas, which of the following questions should you ask yourself?

   a.   Have I looked at the problem from the perspective of all the affected parties? Whose interests have priority?

   b.   Who will be harmed and who will be helped? Is there an alternative course of action that will minimize harm?

   c.   If I act unethically, can I get away with it?

   d.   Am I confident that my decision will seem as reasonable over a long period of time as it does now?

   e.   Would I be willing to disclose my decision to my boss, the board, the general public, my family?

18. **If the dilemma is still unresolved, you should:**

   a.   Consult your company's written ethics policies.

   b.   Use your company's hotline or helpline.

   c.   Talk to your company's ethics officer or ombudsman.

   d.   Call your mother.

19. **What companies have faced moral crises, learned their lessons, and now serve as models for how to integrate ethics into their organizations?**

THE BUSINESS ETHICS QUIZ—ANSWERS

Question 1

The study of ethics is at least five thousand years old, and ethics was first explicitly applied to business in the Code of Hammurabi around 2100 BC. If it's a fad, it's the longest one ever. . . . A and B are correct.

Question 2

A and B are correct. If you answered C, you're out of date. Businesses that ignore ethics are businesses at risk.

Questions 3–5

For each, all of the answers are correct.

Questions 6–8

According to the Deloitte & Touche Survey, 94 percent of the business leaders thought the American business community was troubled by ethical problems, only 32 percent thought the issue was overblown, and 63 percent thought high ethical standards strengthened competitiveness.

Questions 9–13

According to the Center for Business Ethics 1990 survey, more than 90 percent of the Fortune 1000 are planning to increase their business ethics efforts. Their principal motives were to provide guidelines for employee conduct and to be socially responsible (about 95 percent each). Only 43 percent said they were doing so to improve public image, and only 30 percent said they were motivated by profit. More than 90 percent of the Fortune 1000 have written ethics policies, and about 50 percent offer ethics training to employees. According to the Center for Business Ethics' Ethics Officer Survey of the Fortune 1000, the number of large corporations with ethics officers has more than doubled since 1987.

Questions 14–16

The Guidelines apply to business organizations of all sizes including those as small as 10 employees. They also apply to unions, governments and political subdivisions, and non-profit organizations. If there is high-level complicity, a prior record of the same offense and obstruction of the investigation, the organization's fine could increase 400 percent above the stipulated base fine. The Guidelines call for an "effective program" that includes all of the listed components. Having such a program can reduce an organization's fine by up to 60 percent.

Question 17

If you answered C, go to jail, go directly to jail, do not pass Go, and take this book with you!

Question 18

All four answers are correct. Answers A through C are the standard steps under any "effective program." Answer D is not required under the Guidelines, but it wouldn't hurt to call your mother more often, would it?

Question 19

A hint: They include one of the "baby bells" [and] a giant in the defense industry. . .

MORALITY:
THE BASIC RULES
ROBERT SOLOMON

*Solomon discusses the importance of moral rules and whether there
may be a list of rules to govern behavior and proposes a definition of
morality—three of the more difficult tasks in ethical theory!*

I don't like violence. I'm a businessman. Blood is a big expense.   MARIO PUZO, *THE GODFATHER*

Ethics is a matter of *ethos,* participation in a community, a practice, a way of life. Business ethics is a function of the business ethos. Within itself, the mentality of business may be a game mentality, but not all of business ethics is defined by this gamelike business *ethos* or by the business community. The nature of business is circumscribed by society, which tends to encourage or discourage particular aspects of business on the basis of its own ideals and well-being. But there is also a more general set of basic rules that are not part of or partial to any particular society, community, or practice. These rules apply everywhere and determine the legitimacy of every practice. These are the rules of *morality.*

Morality is not the same as moralizing, and being moral does not mean being righteous. It means only *doing right.* Most of the time being moral is no big deal. One doesn't praise an accountant for not cheating on the corporation's tax return, and one doesn't praise an employee for not stealing from the company. Morality is most noticeable in its absence, except, perhaps, when a person succeeds in remaining moral under enormous pressure to be otherwise. But morality in general is not heroism; it is simply not doing what no one should think of doing in the first place. In practical business contexts, morality is rarely an issue, not because the possibility of immoral but lucrative behavior does not exist at every turn but because it is assumed—it *must* be assumed—that no amount of gain will justify a breach of morality. Morality and business are mentioned together when a business venture is *immoral,* and there is never a question of which—business or morality—will win that competition. Moral rules are the trump cards of every business transaction.

Given the importance of moral rules, one might like a list of them, but such an exercise is probably a waste of time. Anyone who doesn't know them already isn't going to learn anything. (It's not like learning a new computer language.) But, for starters, how about

Thou shalt not kill

Thou shalt not steal

Robert Solomon "Morality: The Basic Rules," from *The New World of Business.* Reprinted by permission of
Rowman & Littlefield Publishers.

Thou shalt not commit adultery

Thou shalt not bear false witness

Thou shalt not cheat on thy taxes

Thou shalt not knowingly do harm

Don't be cruel

Etc.

We could go on. There are moral rules that are in dispute, such as the morality of premarital sex and the morality of children's advertising. There are moral rules that conflict—especially in times of extreme stress, in wartime or the corporate equivalent thereof. But of morality itself there is surprisingly little to say (until we get to a highly theoretical level, which is not appropriate here). Moral laws are unambiguous and not open to debate. They simply say,

DON'T DO IT!

Against breaches of morality there are no good arguments, whatever a person's status, however powerful the company, however great the profits. In fact, considerable damage may be done by a company spokesman trying to argue against a moral rule, perhaps more damage than the original transgression itself. In this context, we should recall once again the Lockheed spokesman's heedless complaint, defending himself against a morally ambiguous charge: "When a company wants its products to be bought at all costs, [can it] realistically decline the request [for payoffs] on the grounds that it is not a good thing from the ethical point of view?"

The answer to that question is, simply, "Yes."

The practical problem with moral rules is never whether or not to accept them; it is rather how to apply them. Granted that one must accept the principle "Thou shalt not kill," does that include the lives of animals? Does it prohibit any risky industrial activity like mining coal, in which some employees will lose their lives? Does it prohibit the manufacture of any product, like guns or knives, that *might,* if abused, cause fatal injuries? Granted that one accepts the principle that one should not steal—that is, take someone else's property without paying a fair and agreed-upon price for it—does that mean that one should not take advantage of a company in trouble by buying up inventory or perhaps the company itself? Should a business person take advantage of the stupidity or negligence of a supplier or a customer—for example, if the first forgets to send a bill or the second overpays one? Granted that one should tell the truth and ought not to cheat on taxes, does that preclude such common business practices as tax deferrals and shelters?

What is morality, given that it occupies such an unchallengeable place in our (and every) society? Simply stated, morality consists of those rules that circumscribe legitimate activity for every citizen (or visitor). Such rules are the boundaries of a tolerable social life and guarantee the security of those things a society values most—individual life and well-being, obviously, but, in our society at least, extraordinary freedom, private property, personal and social relationships, freedom from terror, and the "pursuit of happiness." But beyond this essential function, the nature of morality is a matter of violent dispute. There are those who insist that morality is inextricably tied to religion—or to a particular religion—and impossible without. There are those who insist on a strict interpretation of an exact set of moral rules, with no room for other interpretations and no exceptions based on current social facts and needs. And there are those who believe that morality is nothing but a set of local social restrictions that (with some risk) can be flouted or bypassed at will. (One sometimes finds people in business who defend the ultrastrict view of morality in their personal lives but are virtually amoral in professional life, thus provoking the most vehement critics of business.) But whatever else it may be, morality is at least the following:

1. MORALITY IS A LIVING PHENOMENON, no matter how ancient its codes and principles. Our primary moral precept is the autonomy of each individual and every generation to rethink and decide for themselves what is right and what is wrong.

2. MORALITY IS WHAT ONES DOES, not what one says or how loudly and publicly one regrets doing wrong afterward—a recent fashion. Apologizing on the national news after being convicted of a crime is not necessarily a mark of morality.

3. MORALITY IS A SHARED SENSE OF VALUES. It is possible that only one person in the company is right and everyone else is wrong, but how do we recognize when that lone voice is indeed correct? Only because that lone voice finds a much larger audience outside the company, and agreement on the moral principles with which the company itself will be condemned.

4. MORALITY ISN'T ACCIDENTAL. It is not what one does that counts but what one does *knowingly*. Promoting the right person by mistake isn't being moral. Giving money to a charity by mistake isn't charity.

5. MORALITY REQUIRES COMPASSION. Cold-blooded obedience of the rules isn't enough.

6. MORALITY IS A WAY OF LIFE, a state of character. It's not a matter of forcing oneself to comply. The self-satisfaction of being a "good person" is motive enough.

7. MORALITY IS NOT A SUBSTITUTE FOR LIFE. We are a "cryptomoral" society that delights in clever criminals and charming con men, and not only in the movies. We are a law-abiding society, but we are also attracted to people who break the rules. No one who knows our society should ever expect a morally perfect business world. But such characters and their stories provide the spice of business life, not its substance. To be moral is an unquestioned good. To be a moralizing bore, a dogmatic stick-in-the-mud in the name of morality, is not good. In the words of Tom Peters, "the line between ethical purity and arrogant egocentrism is a fine one."

SELF-RELIANCE
Ralph Waldo Emerson

Ralph Waldo Emerson (1803–1882) was a primary figure in the Transcendental movement during the mid-19th century, defining "reason" as the highest human faculty. Emerson was originally trained as a Unitarian minister but left the church to pursue his philosophical quests. In his written work, Emerson challenged his audience to be independent thinkers, contending that integrity was of utmost importance. In this, he may be similar to other theorists who believe that universal harmony will be found through each person seeking her or his self-fulfillment.

. . . There is a time in every man's education when he arrives at the conviction that envy is ignorance; that imitation is suicide; that he must take himself for better for worse as his portion; that though the wide universe is full of good, no kernel of nourishing corn can come to him but through his toil bestowed on that plot of ground which is given to him to till. The power which resides in him is new in nature, and none but he knows what that is which he can do, nor does he know until he has tried. Not for nothing one face, one character, one fact, makes much impression on him, and another none. This sculpture in the memory is not without preestablished harmony. The eye was placed where one ray should fall, that it might testify of that particular ray. We but half express ourselves, and are ashamed of that divine idea which each of us represents. It may be safely trusted as proportionate and of good issues, so it be faithfully imparted, but God will not have his work made manifest by cowards. A man is relieved and gay when he has put his heart into his work and done his best; but what he has said or done otherwise shall give him no peace. It is a deliverance which does not deliver. In the attempt his genius deserts him; no muse befriends; no invention, no hope.

Trust thyself: every heart vibrates to that iron string. Accept the place the divine providence has found for you, the society of your contemporaries, the connection of events. Great men have always done so, and confided themselves childlike to the genius of their age, betraying their perception that the absolutely trustworthy was seated at their heart, working through their hands, predominating in all their being. And we are now men, and must accept in the highest mind the same transcendent destiny; and not minors and invalids in a protected corner, not cowards fleeing before a revolution, but guides, redeemers, and benefactors, obeying the Almighty effort and advancing on Chaos and the Dark. . . .

Virtues are, in the popular estimate, rather the exception than the rule. There is the man *and* his virtues. Men do what is called a good action, as some piece of courage or charity, much as they would pay a fine in expiation of daily non-appearance on parade.

Ralph Waldo Emerson, *Self-Reliance.*

Their works are done as an apology or extenuation of their living in the world,—as invalids and the insane pay a high board. Their virtues are penances. I do not wish to expiate, but to live. My life is for itself and not for a spectacle. I much prefer that it should be of a lower strain, so it be genuine and equal, than that it should be glittering and unsteady. I wish it to be sound and sweet, and not to need diet and bleeding. I ask primary evidence that you are a man, and refuse this appeal from the man to his actions. I know that for myself it makes no difference whether I do or forbear those actions which are reckoned excellent. I cannot consent to pay for a privilege where I have intrinsic right. Few and mean as my gifts may be, I actually am, and do not need for my own assurance or the assurance of my fellows any secondary testimony.

What I must do is all that concerns me, not what the people think. This rule, equally arduous in actual and in intellectual life, may serve for the whole distinction between greatness and meanness. It is the harder because you will always find those who think they know what is your duty better than you know it. It is easy in the world to live after the world's opinion; it is easy in solitude to live after our own; but the great man is he who in the midst of the crowd keeps with perfect sweetness the independence of solitude.

The objection to conforming to usages that have become dead to you is that it scatters your force. It loses your time and blurs the impression of your character. If you maintain a dead church, contribute to a dead Bible-society, vote with a great party either for the government or against it, spread your table like base housekeepers,—under all these screens I have difficulty to detect the precise man you are: and of course so much force is withdrawn from your proper life. But do your work, and I shall know you. Do your work, and you shall reinforce yourself. A man must consider what a blind-man's-buff is this game of conformity. If I know your sect I anticipate your argument. I hear a preacher announce for his text and topic the expediency of one of the institutions of his church. Do I not know beforehand that not possibly can he say a new spontaneous word? Do I not know that with all this ostentation of examining the grounds of the institution he will do no such thing? Do I not know that he is pledged to himself not to look but at one side, the permitted side, not as a man, but as a parish minister? He is a retained attorney, and these airs of the bench are the emptiest affectation. Well, most men have bound their eyes with one or another handkerchief, and attached themselves to some one of these communities of opinion. This conformity makes them not false in a few particulars, authors of a few lies, but false in all particulars. Their every truth is not quite true. Their two is not the real two, their four not the real four; so that every word they say chagrins us and we know not where to begin to set them right. Meantime nature is not slow to equip us in the prison-uniform of the party to which we adhere. We come to wear one cut of face and figure, and acquire by degrees the gentlest asinine expression. There is a mortifying experience in particular, which does not fail to wreak itself also in the general history; I mean "the foolish face of praise," the forced smile which we put on in company where we do not feel at ease, in answer to conversation which does not interest us. The muscles, not spontaneously moved but moved by a low usurping wilfulness, grow tight about the outline of the face, with the most disagreeable sensation. . . .

The terror that scares us from self-trust is our consistency; a reverence for our past act or word because the eyes of others have no other data for computing our orbit than our past acts, and we are loath to disappoint them.

But why should you keep your head over your shoulder? Why drag about this corpse of your memory, lest you contradict somewhat you have stated in this or that public place? Suppose you should contradict yourself; what then? It seems to be a rule of wisdom never to rely on your memory alone, scarcely even in acts of pure memory, but to bring the past for judgment into the thousand-eyed present, and live ever in a new day. In your metaphysics you have denied personality to the Deity, yet when the devout motions of the soul come, yield to them heart and life though they should clothe God with shape and color. Leave your theory, as Joseph his coat in the hand of the harlot, and flee.

A foolish consistency is the hobgoblin of little minds, adored by little statesmen and philosophers and divines. With consistency a great soul has simply nothing to do. He may as well concern himself with his shadow on the wall. Speak what you think now in hard words and to-morrow speak what to-morrow thinks in hard words again, though it contradict every thing you said to-day.—"Ah, so you shall be sure to be misunderstood."—Is it so bad then to be misunderstood? Pythagoras was misunderstood, and Socrates, and Jesus, and Luther, and Copernicus, and Galileo, and Newton, and every pure and wise spirit that ever took flesh. To be great is to be misunderstood. . . .

RELATED WEB SITES

Emerson biography:
     www2.lucidcafe.com/lucidcafe/library/96may/emerson.html

Emerson resource site: miso.wwa.com/~jej/lemerson.html

THE REAL LIFE
OF A STUDENT:
TERM PAPERS FOR SALE
WORLDWIDE WEB SITE

The following Internet Web site, www.schoolsucks.com, was created by Kenneth Sahr, a 24-year-old Miami college student. School Sucks is a World Wide Web site for term papers and exams. The site solicits papers and exams from college students who submit them electronically. Sahr collected much of this material by e-mailing fraternities and requesting copies of old term papers, traditionally stockpiled by frats. They are then available to other students who wish to use them. As you might imagine, this site is not favored by academics, who view it as encouraging plagiarism. However, don't judge the site before reviewing some of the materials included below. The administrators of the site believe that it will not lead to plagiarism but instead will force professors to constantly update their courses and exams.

Following the School Sucks information are two e-mail transmissions from professors to an academic listserver discussing the difficult issues raised by a site such as this. What do you think? Is it ethical to coordinate a site such as this? Recall the words of Confucius from The Analects: *"Those who are born with knowledge are the highest. Next come those who attain knowledge through study. Next again come those who turn to study after having been vexed by difficulties. The common people, in so far as they make no effort to study even after having been vexed by difficulties, are the lowest" (chap. XVI, par. 9).*

ELECTRONIC LETTER TO PROFESSORS
FROM SCHOOL SUCKS*

```
Welcome to School Sucks!

I'm sure you've heard lots about School Sucks. It is my pleasure to take
this opportunity to clarify a few matters for you.

Here are a few points:

1. This page, unlike the termpaper mills, does not charge students. There-
   fore both students and professors have full access to School Sucks.
   Students know you are fully aware of this site and therefore should not
   be turning in papers from this site.
```

The Real Life of a Student: Term Papers for Sale.

*www.schoolsucks.com material. Reprinted with permission from Kenny Sahr, creator and publisher of School Sucks.

2. Were this a library of thesis (i.e. graduate level) papers, would there be a problem?

3. The academic world is based on tenure. This is important as it ensures continuity in education. It also poses a great risk—it insulates professors from the "rat race" that their students will soon be joining.

Basic Darwinism tells us that without a struggle there is no progress. No checks and balance. You may or may not be aware of this, but your students feel that many of you are mediocre in your profession.

How much time have you spent on acquiring new teaching methods in the past few years? Compare that to how much time you have spent trying to get your book published.

Granted, not every professor fits in this category—to be fair, this is a minority.

But School Sucks is forcing you to re-evaluate your role as educators. School Sucks is forcing mediocre professors assigning mediocre assignments to wake up. It was you who notified the media of the existence of this site, yet it is you who will benefit the most from the existence of such a popular site.

4. Many of you are reminding School Sucks of the perhaps less than satisfactory level of some the papers featured. School Sucks couldn't agree more—and we point out that the papers featured here are a cross reference of the level of students across the globe. Please do not pass the buck on this one.

I personally believe that the Pandora's box which is now open will further education, not impede it. Did this site make you rethink the roles of many in education? I believe so.

HOW TO USE THE RESOURCES ON SCHOOL SUCKS (AND ELSEWHERE) TO WRITE PAPERS AND NOT GET INTO TROUBLE.

The purpose of this page is to inform you about plagiarism. In her book *A Writer's Reference*, Diana Hacker defines three acts which are considered plagiarism:

(1) failing to cite quotations and borrowed ideas, (2) failing to enclose borrowed language in quotation marks, and (3) failing to put summaries and paraphrases in your own words. (261)

When done intentionally. Plagiarism is a dishonest act; an act of cheating. Dishonesty sucks; plagiarism sucks because it

> cheats the person who plagiarizes because that person does not learn to put ideas into his/her own words which improves thinking and writing skills; cheats other students who took the time and effort to do their own work; cheats the person who did the original work by not giving that person credit for it;

> is not worth the risk of getting caught and getting a zero on the paper, or failing the class, or other disciplinary action. Professors and TA's can find SCHOOL SUCKS as easy as you.

Nobody likes someone who cheats in a game of pick up basketball, or in a game of tennis, or a chess match. And it doesn't feel very good when you have to compete against someone who has gained an unfair advantage over you by cheating. Let the same sense of honor apply when writing a paper.

And don't let flimsy excuses get in the way, either. You know them.

"I will only do it once," "A few sentences won't hurt," or "It's me against the system."

If you are under a lot of *stress* or having problems, ask for help rather than turning to a dishonest act.

Plagiarism can also happen unintentionally when one doesn't know the rules for citation. When this happens, a person can still be held responsible. *Ouch.* Hopefully, this paper will provide you with practical information to understand what plagiarism is and how to avoid it so that you can use the resources on School Sucks (and elsewhere) properly. If you have questions, ask the instructor before you act.

Based on Diana Hacker's definition of plagiarism given above, there are three rules to follow to avoid plagiarism.

> Rule #1:
> Thou shalt not copy someone else's writing, word for word, and claim it as one's own. These words are not yours. When used in a paper, someone else's exact words must have quotation marks and a citation.

> Rule #2:
> Thou shalt cite the source (including page number(s)) of all quotations **as well as** any borrowed ideas in the paper.

> Rule #3:
> If thou summarizes someone else's ideas in a paper, the information has to be put in one's own words in addition to being properly cited. This means you cannot copy some of the author's sentences and add a few of your own to make it sound different, and you cannot use synonyms with the same basic sentence structure as the original work and then claim the work as your own.

SCHOOL SUCKS

BUSINESS

📄 Essay on the Soda Wars

📄 Economic Analysis of Hawaii

📄 Coca-Cola and Its Evolution

📄 Comparison of Mail Communications

📄 Waterford Crystal: a Case Analysis

📄 Corporate Development During the Industrial Revolution

📄 Postal Service as a Monopoly

📄 TQM in Foodservice

📄 Agrarian Discontent in the Late 1800's

📄 Growth of New York's Business between 1825 and 1860

📄 The Fed and Interest Rates

📄 Ethics in Business

📄 Tobacco Advertising and Its Dangerous Effects on Young People

📄 In Search of Excellence

📄 Productivity Growth Hypothesis

History Law Science
Arts Business English

From:	Kent Schenkel*
To:	Multiple recipients of list ALSBTALK
Date:	7/19/96 7:21 am
Subject:	Re: plagiarism and cheating (fwd)

Information from the mail header

Sender:	"Academy of Legal Studies in Business (ALSB) Talk"
Poster:	Kent Schenkel
Subject:	Re: plagiarism and cheating (fwd)

I tell my students that while the law can combat, mitigate, and even practically eradicate many social ills, there are limits to what it can do. High profile examples include the S&L bailout—private civil suits were perceived to be inadequate to correct the problem.

As for the age-old problem of cheating and fraud, resources are always available for those who wish to use them. To cite an example within the scope of the current issue—I remember a guy when I was an undergrad (some 17 years ago) who bought a term paper from a mail-order company, and he got an A on it.

A thought on the issue from a positive perspective: These students are going to be out in the business world where an abundance of opportunities exist for cheating, fraud, etc. To the extent that the same temptations exist in the college environment they get a chance to learn how they would handle them.

And now is our chance to have some influence.

We can (and do) teach ethical approaches to problem-solving and dispute resolution. I, for one, think most students would not buy "canned" term papers.

And for those who would, rules exist to punish those who get caught. But those rules will never be a substitute for an inner sense of right and wrong.

Kent Schenkel
UNC-Wilmington

From:	Kenneth Schneyer*
To:	Multiple recipients of list ALSBTALK
Date:	7/18/96 8:27 pm
Subject:	Re: plagiarism and cheating (fwd)

Information from the mail header

Sender:	"Academy of Legal Studies in Business (ALSB) Talk"
Poster:	Kenneth Schneyer
Subject:	Re: plagiarism and cheating (fwd)

Joan's message led me to explore the site she described, and also to do a Web search for similar sites. There seem to be a number of sites devoted to either selling or writing term papers at costs ranging from $6 to $10 per page.

---

*Responses by Kent Schenkel and Ken Schneyer are reprinted with permission of the authors.

Here are the addresses of some additional sites I found:

http://www.termpaperwarehouse.com/tpw/
http://www.execpc.com/~hppapers/
http://wahoo.netrunner.net/~dolphin/pprs.htm
http://www.termpapersonline.com/

Some of these contain clear, repeated disclaimers indicating that the papers are not intended to be handed in as the student's own work, that the owner will refuse to deliver papers to students if the owner believes that the student will turn it in as his/her own work, that there is no promise that the paper will satisfy the student's course if it is turned in as the students own work, and/or that turning the paper in as the student's own work may violate honor codes etc. (One such site, however, which contained such disclaimers, also contained an offer to provide papers on disks "to avoid time-consuming retyping!" Why would you need to retype a paper that is being used for research purposes only?)

However, the site Joan pointed out, www.schoolsucks.com, contains such a disclaimer only if the student specifically clicks for it. In other words, it is possible for the student to download a paper without seeing the disclaimer. Further, the site contains indications (through words like "cheaters", "scam", and so forth) that it *is* intended to be used for that purpose. This particular site, I think, might be engaged in wire fraud. I have sent an e-mail message to the Justice Department outlining the bare facts and asking whether they will investigate.

In the case of the sites with the repeated disclaimers, it's hard to tell what recourse we have. A site that loudly tells students not to turn papers in as their own work, but to use them as research guides only, probably can't be accused of conspiracy to do anything unless there is some indication that the reader is supposed to know the warning is insincere.

I think, therefore, that this may be a pretty serious situation. You can't get access to the papers on file without paying for them, in most situations, and of course the newly written papers are completely inaccessible. What to do?

Ken Schneyer

RELATED WEB SITES

SchoolSucks.com: www.schoolsucks.com

Blue Ribbon Internet Free Speech Movement: www.eff.org/blueribbon.html

BAD JUDGMENT OR INEXPERIENCE? BUSINESS STUDENTS' ETHICAL DECISIONS

RONALD E. BERENBEIM

How does a business student arrive at an ethical decision? Do you think that business students are actually honest and full of integrity, and unethical decisions occur because of the influence of the evil business environment? Or perhaps you might think that a certain type of individual is attracted to the study and practice of business and they are less likely to make ethical decisions. The Conference Board conducted the following study in order to determine whether bad decisions made by students are made as a result of bad judgment or inexperience.

That's what an executive might wonder, looking at the way business students arrive at ethical decisions.

Do you think that the M.B.A. candidates your company hires this year—its next generation of senior executives—will handle difficult ethical problems in the same way as you and your colleagues would?

- How would you treat a colleague's former confidences if you were now in a position to give him an important promotion?

- How would you respond to requests from Latin American distributors for help in circumventing local tax laws?

- How would you react if you discovered that your predecessor had authorized questionable disbursements?

The Conference Board asked senior business executives and M.B.A. students to analyze these three ethical questions. The U.S. executives were surveyed by mail; 186 responded. The 98 students answered these hypothetical questions after a presentation by Pete Townley, The Conference Board's president, at New York University's Stern Graduate School of Business Administration. Townley appeared there as the 12th annual Stovall Fellow, a program inaugurated by Robert Stovall, president of Stovall/Twenty-First Advisers Inc., a money-management firm.

The senior executives, all of whom work for medium-size to large corporations, were asked for their own views rather than for a statement of their company's policy. Besides being asked to choose from various options for dealing with the ethical problems, the executives and the students were told to rank the three factors that most influenced their thinking. Their answers follow.

DOES CONFIDENTIALITY HAVE LIMITS?

In 1985, Bob Spicer, a 15-year veteran salesman for Archer Corporation and a frequent winner of annual performance awards, told his boss, Joe Sampson, that "I have been drinking a lot because I'm depressed about my personal problems." Sampson referred him to Archer's employee-assistance program, which offers counseling for alcohol and substance abuse and psychiatric problems.

Since that time, Spicer's job ratings have remained consistently superior. The company does not have access to his medical records and does not know whether he has ever obtained or is currently receiving counseling for depression. Joe Sampson, the manager whom Spicer consulted, is now CEO of Archer.

In November 1990, Spicer applied for the high-stress position of vice president of sales, a job that warranted serious consideration of his past performance.

In making their decisions, M.B.A. students tended to focus on giving employees a fair opportunity to be promoted. Senior executives emphasized the company's interest, and, to a lesser but significant degree, their own perceptions of Spicer's interest. More than half of the M.B.A. candidates agreed that "his personal problems are irrelevant in making the promotional decision." A larger percentage of executives believed that Spicer should be asked whether he is still depressed.

The differences between students and senior executives are best illustrated by their rankings of the three factors that most influenced their responses. Both groups agreed that the employee's performance record and general principles of fairness were the two most important considerations, but the students attached a higher priority to employee rights than to the relevance of a medical complaint to job requirements.

"Demonstrated performance is the principal element of job selection," said one M.B.A. candidate. "An employee's civil rights must always be kept in mind." Another student said that using the information would "create an unfair situation for people who are open about personal problems."

One student distinguished between the relevance of health complaints to job performance and the disabling effects of certain conditions. "Health complaints should be considered only when it is known that a person cannot perform a certain function," he argued.

The need for Spicer to understand the high-stress requirements of the new position was a recurring theme among executives who thought the depression incident ought to be discussed. They maintained that such an exchange was in Spicer's best interest. "It would be unfair for a candidate not to seriously consider the potential harmful effects of increased stress," said the personnel manager of a manufacturing company. This arguably paternalistic rationale was rarely cited by students.

Both students and executives who recommended a discussion of the incident cited the relationship between Spicer and Sampson as a justification for it. "Since Spicer was able to talk to Sampson," a financial-services executive said, "the two men obviously have an ideal open relationship. My choice might be more difficult if there was a lower level of trust in the prior relationship." Ultimately, both groups considered Spicer's job performance the decisive factor.

WHAT PRICE "ACCOMMODATION"?

Dagonet, a diversified manufacturer, is undertaking a major effort to introduce its products in Latin American markets. The company has been asked by several poten- tial distributors to overbill and remit the differences to their companies' accounts in Switzerland and the Cayman Islands. The practice is customary in these countries, because local taxes are confiscatory and the local exchange rates make it very diffi- cult for local distributors to achieve profitable results. Dagonet has received similar requests in the past from American and European firms, and has always refused.

The students' responses to this scenario were less dependent on conventional stan- dards of honesty and fidelity to company policy than were the reactions of the senior ex- ecutives. Consequently, the students were more likely to recommend that the company accede to the local distributors' request and to favor allowing the local subsidiaries the latitude to formulate policies based on regional customs and practices.

The students generally challenged the assumption that a corporation should unilater- ally establish ethical business principles in a competitive global environment. The M.B.A. candidates ranked "profitability and sound business practices" third among the factors that most influenced their responses. The students were also much less sensitive than the senior executives to the potentially corrupting effects of agreeing to the distributors' terms. Exec- utives ranked "integrity and morale of company employees" second among the important considerations in making their decision, while students rated it sixth and last.

Reflecting her group's greater concern with profitability in world markets, one stu- dent said, "As long as the firm's practice is in line with the local standards, it's fine. We can't wait for the rest of the world to reach universally acceptable ethical standards be- fore business begins to expand overseas."

The senior executives, on the other hand, considered well-established company pol- icy to be the most important consideration. One M.B.A. candidate shed light on why the students were less likely to factor company policy into their decision. A single policy, he said, might be a luxury that only a large company could afford; "Having one policy worldwide means ignoring all the political, economic, and cultural differences. If Dagonet is a very large and powerful company, such a policy could be feasible; other- wise, probably not."

The students who said that they would deny the distributors' request rejected it for pragmatic rather than principled reasons. The real question, they said, was not what the right or wrong course of action was, but what the effect on the company would be. One stu- dent said, "If you allow it, your U.S. and European sales forces will undoubtedly find out and demand equal treatment for their distributors." Another student warned that "it would be foolish to follow local customs in Latin America because the customs might change and the company could be admonished and thrown out when a new dictator rolls in."

Although senior executives also pointed to the need for flexibility and respect for local customs, their responses suggested that ultimately a company must follow its internal moral compass. A manufacturer's government–business affairs counsel put it this way: "A company should be consistent; its managers should not rely on 'situation ethics'." A general counsel for a bank put it this way: "Without trying to pass judgment on others, ethics decisions must be based on the company's standards."

If there was one point on which the students and the senior executives agreed, it was that it's a lot easier to take a principled stand on a theoretical dilemma than on a real one. "I have no overseas experience," said a vice president of human resources. "I might be less highminded if I had."

SHOULD QUESTIONABLE DISBURSEMENTS BE INVESTIGATED?

Lily Bart's mentor, Lawrence Selden, is promoted, and Bart assumes his post as vice president of the general-services division of Newland Inc. Bart continues to report to Selden. In familiarizing herself with the responsibilities of her new job, Bart discovers that there have been questionable disbursements for travel and entertainment expenses in the past. The company's general counsel assures Bart that there has been no illegal conduct, and that both Selden and his predecessor routinely approved such reimbursements despite their apparent violation of the company's ethics code.

Although students and executives were more likely to agree here than in the two previous scenarios, the M.B.A. candidates showed less enthusiasm for investigation of past practices and a broad interpretation of the general counsel's role in enforcing ethical policies and principles. The students were also less likely than the executives to agree that Bart was confronting ethical as well as business or managerial issues.

Students showed a preference for education and clarification over investigation and enforcement. "The most effective way to correct this kind of misconduct," said one, "is to educate the people involved and increase the awareness of ethical codes among all employees."

Although more of the executives favored investigation and broad powers for the general counsel, many agreed with the students that a nonaccusatory approach should be taken. A bank's senior economist argued in favor of corporate due process: "The travel and expense abuses are 'apparent'—but not facts. Proving that consistent abuse occurred appears difficult and could be disruptive." Even a utility executive who favored an investigation cautioned that "the intent should be to establish a new practice, not to search for the guilty."

One student who said that Bart's career was the most important consideration warned that "for Bart to make too big a commotion about this might be political suicide, in which case she would have no impact on changing the questionable behavior." Executives rated the effect on Bart's career last, and gave it the lowest approval level of any proposed rationale in the three case studies.

WHERE GENERATIONS DIFFER

Students appear to be more concerned than executives about how ethical decisions actually affect people. Will Spicer be judged fairly in his effort to obtain a promotion? Can the manager of the Latin American subsidiary compete for business in his region and for companywide recognition against the heads of U.S. and European units? Should Lily Bart risk her career to enforce the company's policies?

In each of the three cases, the students accorded greater weight to the interests of the individual than did the executives, who were more inclined to emphasize the interests of the company and to be more concerned about exposing it to risk. The Spicer promotion decision best illuminates these contrasting views. Senior executives commented that a discussion of the earlier drinking problem would benefit Spicer because it would help him to understand what the new job required and to determine whether he would be able to handle the stress. Not one student advanced such a rationale for discussing the incident with Spicer. The students' assumption seemed to be that because Spicer had worked for the company in the sales area, he knew the demands of the position he was applying for, and that any further discussion of stress was unnecessary.

It appears, then, that ethical priorities depend on where you sit. If you are responsible for promoting and protecting the company, you are likely to attach the highest priority to the organization's welfare. If you are an ambitious student aspiring to business leadership, you are most concerned that a company offer you opportunity and judge you according to the contribution that you make.

SHOULD ETHICS BE
TAUGHT IN COLLEGE?
David Thies

David Thies, a college senior on his way to law school in a few months, evaluates the role of ethics instruction at the college level. By that time, has students' ethical style or "competency" already been formed, such that a course in ethics will have no bearing? Can ethics be taught at any age? If you were put in charge of a group of 18-year-olds, how would you go about teaching them ethics or ethical behavior? Do you agree with Thies's conclusions?

One enters college with a moral and ethical code developed as a result of the influence of environmental factors such as one's parents, friends, community, and education. But, is ethical development complete by the time one enters college? I believe the answer is a no. Until college, many of us have moral codes developed based upon the consequences of our acts. We looked to teachers, parents, peers, and religious leaders for guidance. Oftentimes, unethical acts were avoided due to the possible consequences imposed by these "guides," similar to the early stages of Kohlberg's moral development scheme. I believe that ethics goes far beyond this fear of retribution or punishment. One's understanding of ethics is complex; situations on the surface may seem to lack a need for ethical evaluation, while careful analysis reveals an underlying dilemma. Ethics, and the critical thinking skills necessary to tackle these difficult moral problems, should be an integral part of every college culture.

Educational institutions should accept their responsibility as educators as well as character developers. An atmosphere of ethics, via a strong code of conduct and an emphasis on ethical development in the classroom and beyond, creates a cultural norm. Those members who may have a less than adequate ethical foundation often conform to this ethical norm in order to be accepted. Engaging students' minds in ethical issues is a powerful way to build an ethical character, and there is no place more appropriate for this challenge than in the universities. Students reflect and become actively aware of the ethical nature of decision making. They often break down and redevelop their own moral code. Maybe they learn that it is no longer acceptable to bend the rules in order to succeed. The creation of this ethical culture will produce graduates with higher ethical standards as they enter public or private professions.

When facing an ethical dilemma in the workplace, these dilemmas are extremely complicated and require split-second decision making. It is because of these circumstances that a strong ethical base must be developed *prior* to entering the work place. Informed decision making at all levels should be the goal of educational institutions. This

Kohlberg

Source: David Thies, "Should Ethics Be Taught in College?" Reprinted by permission of the author.

ability can only be acquired through an ethics course plus the integration of ethics conversations into other courses. The presentation of ethical theories, case studies, and different perspectives on ethics in the classroom environment develops critical thinking skills, moral foundations, and ethical frameworks.

As I leave college, I truly believe my own personal ethic has developed throughout my experiences as a student. When faced with tough moral choices, I now bring to my decision tools I did not have before I started college. I also feel that if I had written this opinion on the teaching of ethics on my first day as a college freshman, it would have been much different. I challenge readers to write down their opinions and to continually readdress this question throughout their academic and professional careers.

GOOD NATURED

Frans de Waal

Do you think that your cat considers your feelings before ignoring your solicitations? Does your dog care about how much time your neighbor has spent encouraging her grass to grow or does he use it for his own purposes nonetheless? Do animals intend, deliberate, and understand right and wrong as we humans (sometimes) do? Frans de Waal's text discusses the origins of right and wrong by looking at the behavior of both humans and other animals. It is helpful to consider animal behavior as we investigate what part of our moral development is innate and what part is nurtured or socialized. In the following selection, de Waal addresses what it takes to be moral and how we, as humans, compare to animals in this area. Of importance to de Waal's analysis is the fact that animals do not take part in deliberations concerning actions of the sort that humans engage in.

Even if animals other than ourselves act in ways tantamount to moral behavior, their behavior does not necessarily rest on deliberations of the kind we engage in. It is hard to believe that animals weigh their own interests against the rights of others, that they develop a vision of the greater good of society, or that they feel lifelong guilt about something they should not have done.

WHAT DOES IT TAKE TO BE MORAL?

Members of some species may reach tacit consensus about what kind of behavior to tolerate or inhibit in their midst, but without language the principles behind such decisions cannot be conceptualized, let alone debated. To communicate intentions and feelings is one thing; to clarify what is right, and why, and what is wrong, and why, is quite something else. Animals are no moral philosophers.

But then, how many *people* are? We have a tendency to compare animal behavior with the most dizzying accomplishments of our race, and to be smugly satisfied when a thousand monkeys with a thousand typewriters do not come close to William Shakespeare. Is this a reason to classify ourselves as smart, and animals as stupid? Are we not much of the time considerably less rational than advertised? People seem far better at explaining their behavior after the fact than at considering the consequences beforehand. There is no denying that we are creatures of intellect; it is also evident that we are born with powerful inclinations and emotions that bias our thinking and behavior.

A chimpanzee stroking and patting a victim of attack or sharing her food with a hungry companion shows attitudes that are hard to distinguish from those of a person picking

EXHIBIT 1

Components of Human Morality

It is hard to imagine human morality without the following tendencies and capacities found also in other species.
Sympathy-Related Traits
Attachment, succorance, and emotional contagion.
Learned adjustment to and special treatment of the disabled and injured.
Ability to trade places mentally with others: cognitive empathy.*
Norm-Related Characteristics
Prescriptive social rules.
Internalization of rules and anticipation of punishment.*
Reciprocity
A concept of giving, trading, and revenge.
Moralistic aggression against violators of reciprocity rules.
Getting Along
Peacemaking and avoidance of conflict.
Community concern and maintenance of good relationships.*
Accommodation of conflicting interests through negotiation.

*It is particularly in these areas—empathy, internalization of rules and sense of justice, and community concern—that humans seem to have gone considerably further than most other animals.

up a crying child, or doing volunteer work in a soup kitchen. To classify the chimpanzee's behavior as based on instinct and the person's behavior as proof of moral decency is misleading, and probably incorrect. First of all, it is uneconomic in that it assumes different processes for similar behavior in two closely related species. Second, it ignores the growing body of evidence for mental complexity in the chimpanzee, including the possibility of empathy. I hesitate to call the members of any species other than our own "moral beings," yet I also believe that many of the sentiments and cognitive abilities underlying human morality antedate the appearance of our species on this planet.

The question of whether animals have morality is a bit like the question of whether they have culture, politics, or language. If we take the full-blown human phenomenon as a yardstick, they most definitely do not. On the other hand, if we break the relevant human abilities into their component parts, some are recognizable in other animals (see Exhibit 1).

Culture: Field primatologists have noticed differences in tool use and communication among populations of the same species. Thus, in one chimpanzee community all adults may crack nuts with stones, whereas another community totally lacks this technology. Group-specific signals and habits have been documented in bonobos as well as chimpanzees. Increasingly, primatologists explain these differences as learned traditions handed down from one generation to the next.

Language: For decades apes have been taught vocabularies of hand signals (such as American Sign Language) and computerized symbols. Koko, Kanzi, Washoe, and several other anthropoids have learned to effectively communicate their needs and desires through this medium.

Politics: Tendencies basic to human political systems have been observed in other primates, such as alliances that challenge the status quo, and tit for tat deals between a leader and his supporters. As a result, status struggles are as much popularity contests as physical battles.

In each of these domains, nonhuman primates show impressive intelligence yet do not integrate information quite the way we do. The utterances of language-trained apes, for example, show little if any evidence of grammar. The transmission of knowledge from one generation to the next is rarely, if ever, achieved through active teaching. And it is still ambiguous how much planning and foresight, if any, go into the social careers of monkeys and apes.

Despite these limitations, I see no reason to avoid labels such as "primate culture," "ape language," or "chimpanzee politics" as long as it is understood that this terminology points out fundamental similarities without in any way claiming *identity* between ape and human behavior. Such terms serve to stimulate debate about how much or little animals share with us. To focus attention on those aspects in which we differ—a favorite tactic of the detractors of the evolutionary perspective—overlooks the critical importance of what we have in common. Inasmuch as shared characteristics most likely derive from the common ancestor, they probably laid the groundwork for much that followed, including whatever we claim as uniquely ours. To disparage this common ground is a bit like arriving at the top of a tower only to declare that the rest of the building is irrelevant, that the precious concept of "tower" ought to be reserved for the summit.

While making for good academic fights, semantics are mostly a waste of time. Are animals moral? Let us simply conclude that they occupy a number of floors of the tower of morality. Rejection of even this modest proposal can only result in an impoverished view of the structure as a whole. . . .

RELATED WEB SITE

Why did kindness evolve?:
www.newciv.org/worldtrans/GIB/diyfut/DIY-29.HTML

OBEDIENCE
TO AUTHORITY
STANLEY MILGRAM

Milgram believed that obedience "is as basic an element in the structure of human life as one can point to." He believed that communal life was not possible without some system of authority. "It is only the man dwelling in isolation who is not forced to respond, through defiance or submission, to the commands of others." Milgram conducted the experiment discussed below in response to his concerns about obedience to Nazi commands during World War II. "These inhumane policies may have originated in the mind of a single person, but they could only have been carried out on a massive scale if a very large number of people obeyed orders."

Consider, as you read the description of the experiment and the responses of the subjects, what you believe your response might have been. Are we as free thinking as we usually believe?

. . . The Nazi extermination of European Jews is the most extreme instance of abhorrent immoral acts carried out by thousands of people in the name of obedience. Yet in lesser degree this type of thing is constantly recurring: ordinary citizens are ordered to destroy other people, and they do so because they consider it their duty to obey orders. Thus, obedience to authority, long praised as a virtue, takes on a new aspect when it serves a malevolent cause; far from appearing as a virtue, it is transformed into a heinous sin. Or is it?

The moral question of whether one should obey when commands conflict with conscience was argued by Plato; dramatized in *Antigone,* and treated to philosophic analysis in every historical epoch. Conservative philosophers argue that the very fabric of society is threatened by disobedience, and even when the act prescribed by an authority is an evil one, it is better to carry out the act than to wrench at the structure of authority. Hobbes stated further that an act so executed is in no sense the responsibility of the person who carries it out but only of the authority that orders it. But humanists argue for the primacy of individual conscience in such matters, insisting that the moral judgments of the individual must override authority when the two are in conflict.

Stanley Milgram, *Obedience to Authority* (Harper & Row: New York: 1974) pp. 1–12, 44–54, 179–80.

. . . In order to take a close look at the act of obeying, I set up a simple experiment at Yale University. Eventually, the experiment was to involve more than a thousand participants and would be repeated at several universities, but at the beginning, the conception was simple. A person comes to a psychological laboratory and is told to carry out a series of acts that come increasingly into conflict with conscience. The main question is how far the participant will comply with the experimenter's instructions before refusing to carry out the actions required of him.

But the reader needs to know a little more detail about the experiment. Two people come to a psychology laboratory to take part in a study of memory and learning. One of them is designated as a "teacher" and the other a "learner." The experimenter explains that the study is concerned with the effects of punishment on learning. The learner is conducted into a room, seated in a chair, his arms strapped to prevent excessive movement, and an electrode attached to his wrist. He is told that he is to learn a list of word pairs; whenever he makes an error, he will receive electric shocks of increasing intensity.

The real focus of the experiment is the teacher. After watching the learner being strapped into place, he is taken into the main experimental room and seated before an impressive shock generator. Its main feature is a horizontal line of thirty switches, ranging from 15 volts to 450 volts, in 15-volt increments. There are also verbal designations which range from SLIGHT SHOCK to DANGER—SEVERE SHOCK. The teacher is told that he is to administer the learning test to the man in the other room. When the learner responds correctly, the teacher moves on to the next item; when the other man gives an incorrect answer, the teacher is to give him an electric shock. He is to start at the lowest shock level (15 volts) and to increase the level each time the man makes an error, going through 30 volts, 45 volts, and so on.

The "teacher" is a genuinely naïve subject who has come to the laboratory to participate in an experiment. The learner, or victim, is an actor who actually receives no shock at all. The point of the experiment is to see how far a person will proceed in a concrete and measurable situation in which he is ordered to inflict increasing pain on a protesting victim. At what point will the subject refuse to obey the experimenter?

Conflict arises when the man receiving the shock begins to indicate that he is experiencing discomfort. At 75 volts, the "learner" grunts. At 120 volts he complains verbally; at 150 he demands to be released from the experiment. His protests continue as the shocks escalate, growing increasingly vehement and emotional. At 285 volts his response can only be described as an agonized scream.

Observers of the experiment agree that its gripping quality is somewhat obscured in print. For the subject, the situation is not a game; conflict is intense and obvious. On one hand, the manifest suffering of the learner presses him to quit. On the other, the experimenter, a legitimate authority to whom the subject feels some commitment, enjoins him to continue. Each time the subject hesitates to administer shock, the experimenter orders him to continue. To extricate himself from the situation, the subject must make a clear break with authority. The aim of this investigation was to find when and how people would defy authority in the face of a clear moral imperative.

There are, of course, enormous differences between carrying out the orders of a commanding officer during times of war and carrying out the orders of an experimenter. Yet the essence of certain relationships remain, for one may ask in a general way: How does a man behave when he is told by a legitimate authority to act against a third individual? If anything, we may expect the experimenter's power to be considerably less than that of the general, since he has no power to enforce his imperatives, and participation in a psychological experiment scarcely evokes the sense of urgency and dedication engendered by participation in war. Despite these limitations, I thought it worthwhile to start careful observation of obedience even in this modest situation, in the hope that it would stimulate insights and yield general propositions applicable to a variety of circumstances. . . .

A commonly offered explanation is that those who shocked the victim at the most severe level were monsters, the sadistic fringe of society. But if one considers that almost two-thirds of the participants fall into the category of "obedient" subjects, and that they represented ordinary people drawn from working, managerial, and professional classes, the argument becomes very shaky. Indeed, it is highly reminiscent of the issue that arose in connection with Hannah Arendt's 1963 book, *Eichmann in Jerusalem.* Arendt contended that the prosecution's effort to depict Eichmann as a sadistic monster was fundamentally wrong, that he came closer to being an uninspired bureaucrat who simply sat at his desk and did his job. For asserting these views, Arendt became the object of considerable scorn, even calumny. Somehow, it was felt that the monstrous deeds carried out by Eichmann required a brutal, twisted, and sadistic personality, evil incarnate. After witnessing hundreds of ordinary people submit to the authority in our own experiments, I must conclude that Arendt's conception of the *banality of evil* comes closer to the truth than one might dare imagine. The ordinary person who shocked the victim did so out of a sense of obligation—a conception of his duties as a subject—and not from any peculiarly aggressive tendencies.

That is, perhaps, the most fundamental lesson of our study: ordinary people, simply doing their jobs, and without any particular hostility on their part, can become agents in a terrible destructive process. Moreover, even when the destructive effects of their work become patently clear, and they are asked to carry out actions incompatible with fundamental standards of morality, relatively few people have the resources needed to resist authority. A variety of inhibitions against disobeying authority come into play and successfully keep the person in his place.

Sitting back in one's armchair, it is easy to condemn the actions of the obedient subjects. But those who condemn the subjects measure them against the standard of their own ability to formulate high-minded moral prescriptions. That is hardly a fair standard. Many of the subjects, at the level of stated opinion, feel quite as strongly as any of us about the moral requirement of refraining from action against a helpless victim. They, too, in general terms know what ought to be done and can state their values when the occasion arises. This has little, if anything, to do with their actual behavior under the pressure of circumstances.

If people are asked to render a moral judgment on what constitutes appropriate behavior in this situation, they unfailingly see disobedience as proper. But values are not the only forces at work in an actual, ongoing situation. They are but one narrow band of causes in the total spectrum of forces impinging on a person. Many people were unable to realize their values in action and found themselves continuing in the experiment even though they disagreed with what they were doing. . . .

George Orwell caught the essence of the situation when he wrote:

> *As I write, highly civilized human beings are flying overhead, trying to kill me. They do not feel any enmity against me as an individual, nor I against them. They are only "doing their duty," as the saying goes. Most of them, I have no doubt, are kind-hearted law abiding men who would never dream of committing murder in private life. On the other hand, if one of them succeeds in blowing me to pieces with a well-placed bomb, he will never sleep any the worse for it.*

From each person in the experiment we derive one essential fact: whether he has obeyed or disobeyed. But it is foolish to see the subject only in this way. For he brings to the laboratory a full range of emotions, attitudes, and individual styles. Indeed, so varied in temperament and manner are the people passing through the laboratory that it sometimes seems a miracle that we emerge with any regularities at all. One subject may be an inarticulate bricklayer, diffident and awkwardly humble in the presence of a scientist. He is followed by a self-assured businessman, who thrusts his cigar at the experimenter to underscore his assertions.

We need to focus on the individuals who took part in the study not only because this provides a personal dimension to the experiment but also because the quality of each person's experience gives us clues to the nature of the process of obedience. . . .

JAN RENSALEER, INDUSTRIAL ENGINEER (IN EXPERIMENT 2)

The subject is a thirty-two-year-old industrial engineer, sporting blond hair and a mustache. He is self-contained and speaks with a trace of a foreign accent. He is neatly dressed. In the interview he tells us that he emigrated from Holland after the Second World War and that he is a member of the Dutch Reformed Church. He is mild-mannered and intelligent.

When the victim complains at the 150-volt level, the subject turns to the experimenter and asks, "What do I do now?"

The experimenter tells him to continue.

The engineer presses his hand to his head and proceeds with the test. He glances more and more often at the experimenter. At 255 volts, he pushes the chair away from the shock generator and turns to the experimenter:

Mr. Rensaleer: Oh, I can't continue this way; it's a voluntary program, if the man doesn't want to go on with it.

Experimenter: Please continue.

(A long pause.)

MR. RENSALEER: No, I can't continue. I'm sorry.

EXPERIMENTER: The experiment requires that you go on.

MR. RENSALEER: The man, he seems to be getting hurt.

EXPERIMENTER: There is no permanent tissue damage.

MR. RENSALEER: Yes, but I know what shocks do to you, I'm an electrical engineer, and I have had shocks . . . And you get real shook up by them—especially if you know the next one is coming. I'm sorry.

EXPERIMENTER: It is absolutely essential that you continue.

MR. RENSALEER: Well, I won't—not with the man screaming to get out.

EXPERIMENTER: You have no other choice.

MR. RENSALEER: I *do* have a choice. (*Incredulous and indignant:*) Why don't I have a choice? I came here on my own free will. I thought I could help on a research project. But if I have to hurt somebody to do that, or if I was in his place, too, I wouldn't stay there. I can't continue. I'm very sorry. I think I've gone too far already, probably.

When asked who was responsible for shocking the learner against his will, he said, "I would put it on myself entirely."

He refused to assign any responsibility to the learner or the experimenter.

"I should have stopped the first time he complained. I did want to stop at that time. I turned around and looked at you. I guess it's a matter of . . . authority, if you want to call it that: my being impressed by the thing, and going on although I didn't want to. Say, if you're serving in the army, and you have to do something you don't like to do, but your superior tells you to do it. That sort of thing, you know what I mean?

"One of the things I think is very cowardly is to try to shove the responsibility onto someone else. See, if I now turned around and said, 'It's your fault . . . it's not mine,' I would call that cowardly."

Although this subject defied the experimenter at 255 volts, he still feels responsible for administering any shocks beyond the victim's first protests. He is hard on himself and does not allow the structure of authority in which he is functioning to absolve him of any responsibility.

Mr. Rensaleer expressed surprise at the underestimation of obedience by the psychiatrists. He said that on the basis of his experience in Nazi-occupied Europe, he would predict a high level of compliance to orders. He suggests, "It would be interesting to conduct the same tests in Germany and other countries."

The experiment made a deep impression on the subject, so much so that a few days after his participation he wrote a long, careful letter to the staff, asking if he could work with us.

"Although I am . . . employed in engineering, I have become convinced that the social sciences and especially psychology, are much more important in today's world. . . ."

RELATED WEB SITES

The Milgram experiment, obedience and individual responsibility:
www.magenta.nl/EyetoEye/milgram.html

Obedience and individual responsibility:
www.sas.upenn.edu/~adlevy/evild.html

The perils of obedience:
jmcneil.sba.muohio.edu/Private/PerilsofObedience_Private.html

THE DAY HAS COME ... TO TAKE AN ACCOUNTING OF MY LIFE

The following poem, of unknown though traditional origins, is reprinted from a prayerbook used by the Makom Shalom congregation in Chicago, Illinois. The prayerbook is meant to be used during the Jewish New Year services for Rosh Hoshanah and Yom Kippur, in early Autumn. During these holidays, called the "high holidays," Jews are asked to review their year and to contemplate those reasons for joy and for atonement, as the poem articulates.

Have I dreamed of late; Of the person I want to be,
Of the changes I would make; in my daily habits,
In the way I am with others; In the friendship I show compassions,
Woman friends, man friends, my partner,
In the regard I show my father and mother; Who brought me out of childhood?

I have remained enchained too often to less than what I am.
But the day has come to take an accounting of my life.

Have I renewed of late; My vision of the world I want to live in,
Of the changes I would make; In the way my friends are with each other,
The way we find out whom we love; The way we grow to educated people,
The way in which the many kinds of needy people; Grope their way to Justice?

I, who am my own kind of needy person, have been afraid of visions.
But the day has come to take an accounting of my life.

Have I faced up of late; To the needs I really have—
Not for the comforts which shelter my unsureness,
Not for the honnors which paper over my self,
Not for the handsome beauty in which my weakness masquarades,
Not for the unattractiveness in which my strengths hide out—

I need to be loved. Do I deserve to be?
I need to love another. Can I commit my love?
Perhaps its object will be less than my visions.
Perhaps I am not brave enough; To find a new vision

"The Day Has Come to Take an Accounting of My Life," in *Gates: A Machzor* (Chicago: Makom Shalom/The Community, 1994). Reprinted with permission of Rabbi Allen Secher.

Through a real and breathing person.

I need to come in touch with my own power,
Not with titles; Not with possessions, money, high praise,
But with the power that is mine; As a child of the Power that is the universe
To be a comfort, a source of honor,
Handsome and beautiful from the moment I awoke this morning
So strong . . . That I can risk the love of someone else
So sure . . . That I can risk to change the world
And know that even if it all comes crashing down
I shall survive it all—
Saddened a bit, shaken perhaps; Not unvisited by tears,
But my dreams shall not crash down. My visions not go glimmering.
So long as I have breath, I know I have the strength, to transform what I can be
To what I am.

The day has come . . . to take an accounting of my life.

BRUCE SPRINGSTEEN AND BUSINESS ETHICS

Patrick Primeaux, S.M.

How do you think you became who you are? Were you born this way, or did you learn to be this way from your parents, friends, education, or other influences? Sometimes it is interesting to review the moral or ethical development of another person in order to better understand our own development. Patrick Primeaux, S.M., has taken such a look at the moral development of music legend Bruce Springsteen. Representative segments of Primeaux's analysis follow. Consider your own personal development and whether you are now where you had hoped to end up, or perhaps only where you had hoped to begin.

What does Bruce Springsteen have to do with business ethics? A quick survey of his music reflects a concern for unemployment and the absence of jobs in manufacturing which once provided paychecks for middle America. In *My Hometown,* for example, he looks around and sees only "Main Street's whitewashed windows and vacant stores."[1] The "textile mill across the tracks" is shutting down leaving little hope as "the jobs are going boy and they ain't coming back."[2] He is concerned about what economic depression does to people, to their shattered hopes and dreams, to their sense of personal dignity.

Springsteen, however, is also concerned about himself, about the meaning of life and about the connection between who he is and what he does. In other words, he wants to identify his own ethics, but not in the usual way we think about ethics. Rather than focusing on ethics as obedience to rules imposed from the outside—from religion, law, and philosophy, for example—he is drawing a connection between life and behavior, between his perception of himself as a person and how that perception translates into his thinking, speaking, and acting. What his music reveals is a person seeking integration and continuity between his own self-identity and his behavior.

Moreover, as we see Springsteen developing from a self-absorbed and inner-focused person into an others-centered and outward-directed person, we'll leverage that progression to propose a similar dynamic for the organizations of business. Within the context of that analogy, we'll also argue that, for both the individual person and the corporate person, ethics is not a matter of reason alone, but of the total person whose behavior is much a concern of the body, heart, and soul as well as of the mind. Before examining Spring-

---

"Bruce Springsteen and Business Ethics," by Patrick Primeaux, S.M. Reprinted by permission of the author.

1. Bruce Springsteen, "My Hometown," *Greatest Hits Bruce Springsteen* (New York: Columbia Records, 1995).
2. Springsteen, "My Hometown."

steen's music, let us consider these assumptions as they apply to Springsteen, to ourselves, and to the organizations in which and for which we work.

We tend to think of ourselves primarily as individuals, especially as individuals isolated from one another. Even within the many relationships of our lives, we focus first on ourselves, our own needs, our own wants, our own concerns. Then, only second, do we consider the needs of others, even those others closest to us and most important to us. From that perspective, we also think of the organizations to which we belong in individual terms. The group, the organization, the company, the corporation is little more than the mathematical sum of the individuals who comprise it.

There is, however, another way of identifying the group. The dictionary definition of the word "corporation" leads us into that other way of thinking. Corporation, as defined by the *American Heritage Dictionary of the English Language,* is "a body of persons granted a charter legally recognizing them as a separate entity having its own rights, privileges, and liabilities distinct from those of its members."[3] This definition has two implications for thinking of groups as other than numerical summations of its individual members. First, the corporation is a "separate entity" having an identity of its own, even an identity "distinct from those of its members." Second, the corporation is "a body of persons" which forms a collective unity of meaning and purpose which, while embracing the totality of its individual members, transcends those individualities and becomes an individual, corporate person with its own identity and its own ethics. . . .

* * *

When Springsteen moves beyond the emotional, and begins to sense a need to include the spiritual for a sense of the whole, his ethics also move. They change as he changes, from interest and concern for the well-being of others into a passionate embrace of identity with others. . . .

Perhaps this absence of the explicitly spiritual in Springsteen's music can move us beyond ourselves as individual persons towards a greater appreciation of the totality of life for corporate business. . . . The incorporation of the spiritual could lead to a greater appreciation of the essential mystery of persons and of the universe to provide a wider and broader perception of the role of the business within the totality of life. It could certainly enhance business ethics, for it would provide a context which moves beyond the limitations of the mind, of the body, or the heart—as important as these are—towards a fuller appreciation of that totality which embraces the spiritual.

In *Secret Garden,* Springsteen reflects that mysterious, spiritual dimension as it is expressed in the intimate relationship of a man and a woman. It does not stand alone, but is always accompanied by the other dimensions of the total person. Physically, "she'll let you in her house," and "she'll let you in her mouth," and "she'll let you deep inside but there's a secret garden she hides."[4] Emotionally, "she'll let you in her heart," but that's a more difficult entry than the physical, accomplished only "if you have a hammer and a

---

3. William Morris, ed., *The American Heritage Dictionary of the English Language* (Boston: Houghton Mifflin, 1976), 298.
4. Springsteen, "Secret Garden."

vise." Even then, "but into her secret garden, don't think twice."[5] Rationally, "she'll let you come just far enough so you know she's really there," but:

> She's got a secret garden
> Where everything you want
> Where everything you need
> Will always stay a million miles away.[6]

The problem for ethics, for individual ethics and for business ethics, arises when so much attention is focused on the physical, or the rational, or the emotional, or even the spiritual, that the other dimensions of the person are ignored or relegated to the periphery. Ethics would include all four of the dimensions and would attest to their interactive presence in all of our decision-making. The choices we make for ourselves and others cannot be determined only rationally. Nor can they be ascribed to emotional well-being, spiritual well-being, or physical well-being alone.

Nor can they be ascribed to an immovable, unchangeable perception of life in all of its complexities. We learn from Springsteen, that our ethics change as we change. There is a dynamic, progressive quality of ethics and values, as there is of our identities as persons. Accordingly, there is also a dynamic quality of the ethics of a business consistent with the identity of the business. As the assumptions, structures, and objectives of a business change, so will its ethics. As that change encompasses the rational, physical, emotional, and spiritual dimensions of the total corporate person the fuller and more adequate the ethics of the business will be. To the extent that the business ignores its mind, body, heart, or soul, to that same degree, its ethics will be incomplete.

---

5. Springsteen, "Secret Garden."
6. Springsteen, "Secret Garden."

Chapter 4

CRITICAL ETHICAL ANALYSIS:
A Decision-Making Model

From here that looks like a bucket of water, but from an ant's point of view, it's a vast ocean; from an elephant's point of view, it's just a cool drink; and to a fish, of course, it's home.   Norton Juster, *The Phantom Toll Booth*

Throughout this text, you are asked to reach your own conclusions and judgments in connection with ethical issues and dilemmas. In earlier sections, we have discussed a variety of models for decision making that may prove fruitful in this effort. In this section, there are several readings which more specifically explain and/or highlight the multiperspectival approach that will be taken throughout the text.

The text presents you with a variety of perspectives in connection with each topic area of business ethics. The basis for this approach is the theory, first propounded by philosopher Ed Freeman, called stakeholder analysis. Stakeholder theory asks a decision maker to consider, in reaching a decision, the interests of each individual or entity that holds a stake in that decision or who will be affected by the decision. The model of this approach was discussed earlier in the section on moral reasoning.

In order to consider the stakeholders of a decision, it is critical to be able to understand the interests of each party, to be able to empathetically evaluate what the potential impact on that stakeholder will be and what the stakeholder's perspective on the decision is likely to be. This is not as easy as it may first appear. For instance, one might not necessarily be able to identify all of the parties who might be impacted, or one might not completely understand the nature of each party's interest, or even the effect the decision will have in the end.

> *It is often difficult for those who look on the tradition of the Red Man from the outside or through the "educated" mind to understand that no object is what it appears to be, but it is simply the pale shadow of a Reality. It is for this reason that every created object is* wakan, *holy, and has a power according to the loftiness of the spiritual reality it reflects. The Indian humbles himself before the whole of creation because all visible things were created before him and, being older than he, deserve respect.[1]*

Several readings included in this section offer a practical application of stakeholder theory. For instance, the seminal business ethics case "The Parable of the Sadhu" offers a specific analysis of the interests and motivations of each decision maker in the parable. Similarly, in "A Jury of Her Peers," Glaspell demonstrates how different individuals may see different implications when viewing the same scene. Werhane's "Rashomon Complex" offers a similar demonstration in connection with the Ford Pinto case, a classic business ethics dilemma. Finally, several interpretations of Dow Corning's experience with silicone implants are included in an effort to illustrate how ethicists have viewed potentially unethical behavior. In reading later segments of this text, try to contemplate the variety of perspectives that may be offered on the same topic and consider your response only after evaluating the anticipated perspectives of each stakeholder in connection with the issue.

---

1. From a letter written by Joseph Epes Brown, cited in Huston Smith, *The World's Religions* (San Francisco, CA: HarperSanFrancisco, 1991), p. 379.

A STAKEHOLDER THEORY OF THE MODERN CORPORATION

R. Edward Freeman

Freeman delineates the basics of stakeholder theory and challenges the primacy of the shareholder in corporate decisions.

INTRODUCTION

Corporations have ceased to be merely legal devices through which the private business transactions of individuals may be carried on. Though still much used for this purpose, the corporate form has acquired a larger significance. The corporation has, in fact, become both a method of property tenure and a means of organizing economic life. Grown to tremendous proportions, there may be said to have evolved a "corporate system"—which has attracted to itself a combination of attributes and powers, and has attained a degree of prominence entitling it to be dealt with as a major social institution.[1]

Despite these prophetic words of Berle and Means (1932), scholars and managers alike continue to hold sacred the view that managers bear a special relationship to the stockholders in the firm. Since stockholders own shares in the firm, they have certain rights and privileges, which must be granted to them by management, as well as by others. Sanctions, in the form of "the law of corporations," and other protective mechanisms in the form of social custom, accepted management practice, myth, and ritual, are thought to reinforce the assumption of the primacy of the stockholder.

The purpose of this paper is to pose several challenges to this assumption, from within the framework of managerial capitalism, and to suggest the bare bones of an alternative theory, *a stakeholder theory of the modern corporation*. I do not seek the demise of the modern corporation, either intellectually or in fact. Rather, I seek its transformation. In the words of Neurath, we shall attempt to "rebuild the ship, plank by plank, while it remains afloat."[2]

My thesis is that I can revitalize the concept of managerial capitalism by replacing the notion that managers have a duty to stockholders with the concept that managers bear a fiduciary relationship to stakeholders. Stakeholders are those groups who have a stake in or claim on the firm. Specifically I include suppliers, customers, employees, stockholders, and the local community, as well as management in its role as agent for these groups.

I argue that the legal, economic, political, and moral challenges to the currently received theory of the firm, as a nexus of contracts among the owners of the factors of production and customers, require us to revise this concept. That is, each of these stakeholder groups has a right not to be treated as a means to some end, and therefore must participate in determining the future direction of the firm in which they have a stake.

The crux of my argument is that we must reconceptualize the firm around the following question: For whose benefit and at whose expense should the firm be managed? I shall set forth such a reconceptualization in the form of a *stakeholder theory of the firm.* I shall then critically examine the stakeholder view and its implications for the future of the capitalist system.

THE ATTACK ON MANAGERIAL CAPITALISM

The Legal Argument

The basic idea of managerial capitalism is that in return for controlling the firm, management vigorously pursues the interests of stockholders. Central to the managerial view of the firm is the idea that management can pursue market transactions with suppliers and customers in an unconstrained manner.

The law of corporations gives a less clearcut answer to the question: In whose interest and for whose benefit should the modern corporation be governed? While it says that the corporations should be run primarily in the interests of the stockholders in the firm, it says further that the corporation exists "in contemplation of the law" and has personality as a "legal person," limited liability for its actions, and immortality, since its existence transcends that of its members. Therefore, directors and other officers of the firm have a fiduciary obligation to stockholders in the sense that the "affairs of the corporation" must be conducted in the interest of the stockholders. And stockholders can theoretically bring suit against those directors and managers for doing otherwise. But since the corporation is a legal person, existing in contemplation of the law, managers of the corporation are constrained by law.

Until recently, this was no constraint at all. In this century, however, the law has evolved to effectively constrain the pursuit of stockholder interests at the expense of other claimants on the firm. It has, in effect, required that the claims of customers, suppliers, local communities, and employees be taken into consideration, though in general they are subordinated to the claims of stockholders.

For instance, the doctrine of "privity of contract," as articulated in *Winterbottom v. Wright* in 1842, has been eroded by recent developments in products liability law. Indeed, *Greenman v. Yuba Power* gives the manufacturer strict liability for damage caused by its products, even though the seller has exercised all possible care in the preparation and sale of the product and the consumer has not bought the product from nor entered into any contractual arrangement with the manufacturer. Caveat emptor has been replaced, in large part, with caveat venditor.[3] The Consumer Product Safety Commission has the power to enact product recalls, and in 1980 one U.S. automobile company recalled more cars than it built. Some industries are required to provide information to customers about a product's ingredients, whether or not the customers want and are willing to pay for this information.[4]

The same argument is applicable to management's dealings with employees. The National Labor Relations Act gave employees the right to unionize and to bargain in good faith. It set up the National Labor Relations Board to enforce these rights with management. The Equal Pay Act of 1963 and Title VII of the Civil Rights Act of 1964 constrain management from discrimination in hiring practices; these have been followed with the Age Discrimination in Employment Act of 1967.[5] The emergence of a body of administrative case law arising from labor-management disputes and the historic settling of discrimination claims with large employers such as AT&T have caused the emergence of a body of practice in the corporation that is consistent with the legal guarantee of the rights of the employees. The law has protected the due process rights of those employees who enter into collective bargaining agreements with management. As of the present, however, only 30 percent of the labor force are participating in such agreements; this has prompted one labor law scholar to propose a statutory law prohibiting dismissals of the 70 percent of the work force not protected.[6]

The law has also protected the interests of local communities. The Clean Air Act and Clean Water Act have constrained management from "spoiling the commons." In an historic case, *Marsh v. Alabama,* the Supreme Court ruled that a company-owned town was subject to the provisions of the U.S. Constitution, thereby guaranteeing the rights of local citizens and negating the "property rights" of the firm. Some states and municipalities have gone further and passed laws preventing firms from moving plants or limiting when and how plants can be closed. In sum, there is much current legal activity in this area to constrain management's pursuit of stockholders' interests at the expense of the local communities in which the firm operates.

I have argued that the result of such changes in the legal system can be viewed as giving some rights to those groups that have a claim on the firm, for example, customers, suppliers, employees, local communities, stockholders, and management. It raises the question, at the core of a theory of the firm: In whose interest and for whose benefit should the firm be managed? The answer proposed by managerial capitalism is clearly "the stockholders," but I have argued that the law has been progressively circumscribing this answer.

The Economic Argument

In its pure ideological form managerial capitalism seeks to maximize the interests of stockholders. In its perennial criticism of government regulation, management espouses the "invisible hand" doctrine. It contends that it creates the greatest good for the greatest number, and therefore government need not intervene. However, we know that externalities, moral hazards, and monopoly power exist in fact, whether or not they exist in theory. Further, some of the legal apparatus mentioned above has evolved to deal with just these issues.

The problem of the "tragedy of the commons" or the free-rider problem pervades the concept of public goods such as water and air. No one has an incentive to incur the cost of clean-up or the cost of nonpollution, since the marginal gain of one firm's action is small. Every firm reasons this way, and the result is pollution of water and air. Since the industrial revolution, firms have sought to internalize the benefits and externalize the costs of their actions. The cost must be borne by all, through taxation and regulation; hence we have the emergence of the environmental regulations of the 1970s.

Similarly, moral hazards arise when the purchaser of a good or service can pass along the cost of that good. There is no incentive to economize, on the part of either the producer or the consumer, and there is excessive use of the resources involved. The institutionalized practice of third-party payment in health care is a prime example.

Finally, we see the avoidance of competitive behavior on the part of firms, each seeking to monopolize a small portion of the market and not compete with one another. In a number of industries, oligopolies have emerged, and while there is questionable evidence that oligopolies are not the most efficient corporate form in some industries, suffice it to say that the potential for abuse of market power has again led to regulation of managerial activity. In the classic case, AT&T, arguably one of the great technological and managerial achievements of the century, was broken up into eight separate companies to prevent its abuse of monopoly power.

Externalities, moral hazards, and monopoly power have led to more external control on managerial capitalism. There are de facto constraints, due to these economic facts of life, on the ability of management to act in the interests of stockholders.

A STAKEHOLDER THEORY OF THE FIRM

The Stakeholder Concept

Corporations have stakeholders, that is, groups and individuals who benefit from or are harmed by, and whose rights are violated or respected by, corporate actions. The concept of stakeholders is a generalization of the notion of stockholders, who themselves have some special claim on the firm. Just as stockholders have a right to demand certain actions by management, so do other stakeholders have a right to make claims. The exact nature of these claims is a difficult question that I shall address, but the logic is identical to that of the stockholder theory. Stakes require action of a certain sort, and conflicting stakes require methods of resolution.

Freeman and Reed (1983)[7] distinguish two senses of *stakeholder*. The "narrow definition" includes those groups who are vital to the survival and success of the corporation. The "wide-definition" includes any group or individual who can affect or is affected by the corporation. I shall begin with a modest aim, to articulate a stakeholder theory using the narrow definition.

Stakeholders in the Modern Corporation

Figure 1 depicts the stakeholders in a typical large corporation. The stakes of each are reciprocal, since each can affect the other in terms of harms and benefits as well as rights and duties. The stakes of each are not univocal and would vary by particular corporation. I merely set forth some general notions that seem to be common to many large firms.

Owners have financial stake in the corporation in the form of stocks, bonds, and so on, and they expect some kind of financial return from them. Either they have given money directly to the firm, or they have some historical claim made through a series of morally justified exchanges. The firm affects their livelihood or, if a substantial portion

FIGURE 1

A Stakeholder Model of the Corporation.

of their retirement income is in stocks or bonds, their ability to care for themselves when they can no longer work. Of course, the stakes of owners will differ by type of owner, preferences for money, moral preferences, and so on, as well as by type of firm. The owners of AT&T are quite different from the owners of Ford Motor Company, with stock of the former company being widely dispersed among 3 million stockholders and that of the latter being held by a small family group as well as by a large group of public stockholders.

Employees have their jobs and usually their livelihood at stake; they often have specialized skills for which there is usually no perfectly elastic market. In return for their labor, they expect security, wages, benefits, and meaningful work. In return for their loyalty, the corporation is expected to provide for them and carry them through difficult times. Employees are expected to follow the instructions of management most of the time, to speak favorably about the company, and to be responsible citizens in the local communities in which the company operates. Where they are used as means to an end, they must participate in decisions affecting such use. The evidence that such policies and values as described here lead to productive company-employee relationships is compelling. It is equally compelling to realize that the opportunities for "bad faith" on the part of both management and employees are enormous. "Mock participation" in quality circles, singing the company song, and wearing the company uniform solely to please management all lead to distrust and unproductive work.

Suppliers, interpreted in a stakeholder sense, are vital to the success of the firm, for raw materials will determine the final product's quality and price. In turn the firm is a customer of the supplier and is therefore vital to the success and survival of the supplier. When the firm treats the supplier as a valued member of the stakeholder network, rather than simply as a source of materials, the supplier will respond when the firm is in need. Chrysler traditionally had very close ties to its suppliers, even to the extent that led some to suspect the transfer of illegal payments. And when Chrysler was on the brink of disaster, the suppliers responded with price cuts, accepting late payments, financing, and so on. Supplier and company can rise and fall together. Of course, again, the particular supplier relationships will depend on a number of variables such as the number of suppliers and whether the suppliers are finished goods or raw materials.

Customers exchange resources for the products of the firm and in return receive the benefits of the products. Customers provide the lifeblood of the firm in the form of revenue.

Given the level of reinvestment of earnings in large corporations, customers indirectly pay for the development of new products and services. Peters and Waterman (1982)[8] have argued that being close to the customer leads to success with other stakeholders and that a distinguishing characteristic of some companies that have performed well is their emphasis on the customer. By paying attention to customers' needs, management automatically addresses the needs of suppliers and owners. Moreover, it seems that the ethic of customer service carries over to the community. Almost without fail the "excellent companies" in Peters and Waterman's study have good reputations in the community. I would argue that Peters and Waterman have found multiple applications of Kant's dictum, "Treat persons as ends unto themselves," and it should come as no surprise that persons respond to such respectful treatment, be they customers, suppliers, owners, employees, or members of the local community. The real surprise is the novelty of the application of Kant's rule in a theory of good management practice.

The local community grants the firm the right to build facilities and, in turn, it benefits from the tax base and economic and social contributions of the firm. In return for the provision of local services, the firm is expected to be a good citizen, as is any person, either "natural or artificial." The firm cannot expose the community to unreasonable hazards in the form of pollution, toxic waste, and so on. If for some reason the firm must leave a community, it is expected to work with local leaders to make the transition as smoothly as possible. Of course, the firm does not have perfect knowledge, but when it discovers some danger or runs afoul of new competition, it is expected to inform the local community and to work with the community to overcome any problem. When the firm mismanages its relationship with the local community, it is in the same position as a citizen who commits a crime. It has violated the implicit social contract with the community and should expect to be distrusted and ostracized. It should not be surprised when punitive measures are invoked.

I have not included "competitors" as stakeholders in the narrow sense, since strictly speaking they are not necessary for the survival and success of the firm; the stakeholder theory works equally well in monopoly contexts. However, competitors and government would be the first to be included in an extension of this basic theory. It is simply not true that the interests of competitors in an industry are always in conflict. There is no reason why trade associations and other multi-organizational groups cannot band together to solve common problems that have little to do with how to restrain trade. Implementation of stakeholder management principles, in the long run, mitigates the need for industrial policy and an increasing role for government intervention and regulation.

The Role of Management

Management plays a special role, for it too has a stake in the modern corporation. On the one hand, management's stake is like that of employees, with some kind of explicit or implicit employment contract. But, on the other hand, management has a duty of safeguarding the welfare of the abstract entity that is the corporation. In short, management, especially top management, must look after the health of the corporation, and this involves balancing the multiple claims of conflicting stakeholders. Owners want higher financial returns, while customers want more money spent on research and development. Employees want higher wages and better benefits, while the local community wants better parks and day-care facilities.

The task of management in today's corporation is akin to that of King Solomon. The stakeholder theory does not give primacy to one stakeholder group over another, though there will surely be times when one group will benefit at the expense of others. In general, however, management must keep the relationships among stakeholders in balance. When these relationships become imbalanced, the survival of the firm is in jeopardy.

When wages are too high and product quality is too low, customers leave, suppliers suffer, and owners sell their stocks and bonds, depressing the stock price and making it difficult to raise new capital at favorable rates. Note, however, that the reason for paying returns to owners is not that they "own" the firms, but that their support is necessary for the survival of the firm, and that they have a legitimate claim on the firm. Similar reasoning applies in turn to each stakeholder group.

A stakeholder theory of the firm must redefine the purpose of the firm. The stockholder theory claims that the purpose of the firm is to maximize the welfare of the stockholders, perhaps subject to some moral or social constraints, either because such maximization leads to the greatest good or because of property rights. The purpose of the firm is quite different in my view.

"The stakeholder theory" can be unpacked into a number of stakeholder theories, each of which has a "normative core," inextricably linked to the way that corporations should be governed and the way that managers should act. So, attempts to more fully define, or more carefully define, a stakeholder theory are misguided. Following Donaldson and Preston, I want to insist that the normative, descriptive, instrumental, and metaphorical (my addition to their framework) uses of 'stakeholder' are tied together in particular political constructions to yield a number of possible "stakeholder theories." "Stakeholder theory" is thus a genre of stories about how we could live. Let me be more specific.

A "normative core" of a theory is a set of sentences that includes among others, sentences like:

(1) Corporations ought to be governed . . .
(2) Managers ought to act to . . .

where we need arguments or further narratives which include business and moral terms to fill in the blanks. This normative core is not always reducible to a fundamental ground like the theory of property, but certain normative cores are consistent with modern understandings of property. Certain elaborations of the theory of private property plus the other institutions of political liberalism give rise to particular normative cores. But there are other institutions, other political conceptions of how society ought to be structured, so that there are different possible normative cores.

So, one normative core of a stakeholder theory might be a feminist standpoint one, rethinking how we would restructure "value-creating activity" along principles of caring and connection.[9] Another would be an ecological (or several ecological) normative cores. Mark Starik has argued that the very idea of a stakeholder theory of the *firm* ignores certain ecological necessities.[10] Exhibit 1 is suggestive of how these theories could be developed.

In the next section I shall sketch the normative core based on pragmatic liberalism. But, any normative core must address the questions in columns A or B, or explain why these questions may be irrelevant, as in the ecological view. In addition, each "theory," and I use the word hesitantly, must place the normative core within a more full-fledged

EXHIBIT 1

A Reasonable Pluralism

	A. **Corporations ought to be governed . . .**	**B.** **Managers ought to act . . .**	**C.** **The background disciplines of "value creation" are . . .**
Doctrine of Fair Contracts	. . . in accordance with the six principles.	. . . in the interests of stakeholders.	—business theories —theories that explain stakeholder behavior
Feminist Standpoint Theory	. . . in accordance with the principles of caring/connection and relationships.	. . . to maintain and care for relationships and networks of stakeholders.	—business theories —feminist theory —social science understanding of networks
Ecological Principles	. . . in accordance with the principle of caring for the earth.	. . . to care for the earth.	—business theories —ecology —other

account of how we could understand value-creating activity differently (column C). The only way to get on with this task is to see the stakeholder idea as a metaphor. The attempt to prescribe one and only one "normative core" and construct "a stakeholder theory" is at best a disguised attempt to smuggle a normative core past the unsophisticated noses of other unsuspecting academics who are just happy to see the end of the stockholder orthodoxy.

If we begin with the view that we can understand value-creation activity as a contractual process among those parties affected, and if for simplicity's sake we initially designate those parties as financiers, customers, suppliers, employees, and communities, then we can construct a normative core that reflects the liberal notions of autonomy, solidarity, and fairness as articulated by John Rawls, Richard Rorty, and others.[11] Notice that building these moral notions into the foundations of how we understand value creation and contracting requires that we eschew separating the "business" part of the process from the "ethical" part, and that we start with the presumption of equality among the contractors, rather than the presumption in favor of financier rights.

The normative core for this redesigned contractual theory will capture the liberal idea of fairness if it ensures a basic equality among stakeholders in terms of their moral rights as these are realized in the firm, and if it recognizes that inequalities among stakeholders are justified if they raise the level of the least well-off stakeholder. The liberal ideal of autonomy is captured by the realization that each stakeholder must be free to enter agreements that create value for themselves, and solidarity is realized by the recognition of the mutuality of stakeholder interests.

One way to understand fairness in this context is to claim *a la* Rawls that a contract is fair if parties to the contract would agree to it in ignorance of their actual stakes. Thus, a contract is like a fair bet, if each party is willing to turn the tables and accept the other side. What would a fair contract among corporate stakeholders look like? If we can articulate this ideal, a sort of corporate constitution, we could then ask whether actual corporations measure up to this standard, and we also begin to design corporate structures which are consistent with this Doctrine of Fair Contracts.

Imagine if you will, representative stakeholders trying to decide on "the rules of the game." Each is rational in a straightforward sense, looking out for its own self-interest. At least *ex ante,* stakeholders are the relevant parties since they will be materially affected. Stakeholders know how economic activity is organized and could be organized. They know general facts about the way the corporate world works. They know that in the real world there are or could be transaction costs, externalities, and positive costs of contracting. Suppose they are uncertain about what other social institutions exist, but they know the range of those institutions. They do not know if government exists to pick up the tab for any externalities, or if they will exist in the nightwatchman state of libertarian theory. They know success and failure stories of businesses around the world. In short, they are behind a Rawls-like veil of ignorance, and they do not know what stake each will have when the veil is lifted. What groundrules would they choose to guide them?

The first groundrule is "The Principle of Entry and Exit." Any contract that is the corporation must have clearly defined entry, exit, and renegotiation conditions, or at least it must have methods or processes for so defining these conditions. The logic is straightforward: each stakeholder must be able to determine when an agreement exists and has a chance of fulfillment. This is not to imply that contracts cannot contain contingent claims or other methods for resolving uncertainty, but rather that it must contain methods for determining whether or not it is valid.

The second groundrule I shall call "The Principle of Governance," and it says that the procedure for changing the rules of the game must be agreed upon by unanimous consent. Think about the consequences of a majority of stakeholders systematically "selling out" a minority. Each stakeholder, in ignorance of its actual role, would seek to avoid such a situation. In reality this principle translates into each stakeholder never giving up its right to participate in the governance of the corporation, or perhaps into the existence of stakeholder governing boards.

The third groundrule I shall call "The Principle of Externalities," and it says that if a contract between A and B imposes a cost on C, then C has the option to become a party to the contract, and the terms are renegotiated. Once again the rationality of this condition is clear. Each stakeholder will want insurance that it does not become C.

The fourth groundrule is "The Principle of Contracting Costs," and it says that all parties to the contract must share in the cost of contracting. Once again the logic is straightforward. Any one stakeholder can get stuck.

A fifth groundrule is "The Agency Principle" that says that any agent must serve the interests of all stakeholders. It must adjudicate conflicts within the bounds of the other principals. Once again the logic is clear. Agents for any one group would have a privileged place.

A sixth and final groundrule we might call, "The Principle of Limited Immortality." The corporation shall be managed as if it can continue to serve the interests of stakeholders through time. Stakeholders are uncertain about the future but, subject to exit conditions, they realize that the continued existence of the corporation is in their interest. Therefore, it would be rational to hire managers who are fiduciaries to their interest and the interest of the collective. If it turns out the "collective interest" is the empty set, then this principle simply collapses into the Agency Principle.

Thus, the Doctrine of Fair Contracts consists of these six groundrules or principles:

(1) The Principle of Entry and Exit
(2) The Principle of Governance
(3) The Principle of Externalities
(4) The Principle of Contracting Costs
(5) The Agency Principle
(6) The Principle of Limited Immortality

Think of these groundrules as a doctrine which would guide actual stakeholders in devising a corporate constitution or charter. Think of management as having the duty to act in accordance with some specific constitution or charter.

Obviously, if the Doctrine of Fair Contracts and its accompanying background narratives are to effect real change, there must be requisite changes in the enabling laws of the land. I propose the following three principles to serve as constitutive elements of attempts to reform the law of corporations.

The Stakeholder Enabling Principle

Corporations shall be managed in the interests of its stakeholders, defined as employees, financiers, customers, employees, and communities.

The Principle of Director Responsibility

Directors of the corporation shall have a duty of care to use reasonable judgment to define and direct the affairs of the corporation in accordance with the Stakeholder Enabling Principle.

The Principle of Stakeholder Recourse

Stakeholders may bring an action against the directors for failure to perform the required duty of care.

Obviously, there is more work to be done to spell out these principles in terms of model legislation. As they stand, they try to capture the intuitions that drive the liberal ideals. It is equally plain that corporate constitutions which meet a test like the doctrine of fair contracts are meant to enable directors and executives to manage the corporation in conjunction with these same liberal ideals.

NOTES

1. Cf. A. Berle and G. Means, *The Modern Corporation and Private Property* (New York: Commerce Clearing House, 1932), 1. For a reassessment of Berle and Means' argument after 50 years, see *Journal of Law and Economics* 26 (June 1983), especially G. Stigler and C. Friedland, "The Literature of Economics: The Case of Berle and Means," 237–68; D. North, "Comment on Stigler and Friedland," 269–72; and G. Means, "Corporate Power in the Marketplace," 467–85.

2. The metaphor of rebuilding the ship while afloat is attributed to Neurath by W. Quine, *Word and Object* (Cambridge: Harvard University Press, 1960), and W. Quine and J. Ullian, *The Web of Belief* (New York: Random House, 1978). The point is that to keep the ship afloat during repairs we must replace a plank with one that will do a better job. Our argument is that stakeholder capitalism can so replace the current version of managerial capitalism.

3. See R. Charan and F. Freeman, "Planning for the Business Environment of the 1980s," *The Journal of Business Strategy* 1 (1980): 9–19, especially p. 15 for a brief account of the major developments in products liability law.

4. See S. Breyer, *Regulation and Its Reform* (Cambridge: Harvard University Press, 1983), 133, for an analysis of food additives.

5. See I. Millstein and S. Katsh, *The Limits of Corporate Power* (New York: Macmillan, 1981), Chapter 4.

6. Cf. C. Summers, "Protecting All Employees Against Unjust Dismissal," *Harvard Business Review* 58 (1980): 136, for a careful statement of the argument.

7. See E. Freeman and D. Reed, "Stockholders and Stakeholders: A New Perspective on Corporate Governance," in C. Huizinga, ed., *Corporate Governance: A Definitive Exploration of the Issues* (Los Angeles: UCLA Extension Press, 1983).

8. See T. Peters and R. Waterman, *In Search of Excellence* (New York: Harper and Row, 1982).

9. See, for instance, A. Wicks, D. Gilbert, and E. Freeman, "A Feminist Reinterpretation of the Stakeholder Concept," *Business Ethics Quarterly,* Vol. 4, No. 4, October 1994; and E. Freeman and J. Liedtka, "Corporate Social Responsibility: A Critical Approach," *Business Horizons,* Vol. 34, No. 4, July–August 1991, pp. 92–98.

10. At the Toronto workshop Mark Starik sketched how a theory would look if we took the environment to be a stakeholder. This fruitful line of work is one example of my main point about pluralism.

11. J. Rawls, *Political Liberalism* (New York: Columbia University Press, 1993); and R. Rorty, "The Priority of Democracy to Philosophy" in *Reading Rorty: Critical Responses to Philosophy and the Mirror of Nature (and Beyond),* ed. Alan R. Malachowski (Cambridge, MA: Blackwell, 1990).

RELATED WEB SITES

Stakeholder theory bibliography:
   www.mgmt.utoronto.ca/~stake/Bibliography.html

Stakeholder theory and a principle of fairness:
   www.darden,virginia.edu/research/olsson/rp_fair.htm

Redefining the Corporation: An International Colloquy:
   www.mgmt.utoronto.ca/~stake/

THE PARABLE
OF THE SADHU

BOWEN H. MCCOY

*This parable is based on the true experience of the author, Bowen
McCoy, a senior executive from Morgan Stanley, who decided that he
needed a sabbatical from the hectic life he had created. His answer
was an extended trek through the Himalayas. The goal of this trek
was to reach Muklinath, an ancient holy village on the other side of
an 18,000-foot ice-covered pass. The parable offers McCoy's reflections upon his return from the experience.*

Last year, as the first participant in the new six-month sabbatical program that Morgan
Stanley has adopted, I enjoyed a rare opportunity to collect my thoughts as well as do
some traveling. I spent the first three months in Nepal, walking 600 miles through 200
villages in the Himalayas and climbing some 120,000 vertical feet. On the trip my sole
Western companion was an anthropologist who shed light on the cultural patterns of the
villages we passed through.

During the Nepal hike, something occurred that has had a powerful impact on my
thinking about corporate ethics. Although some might argue that the experience has no
relevance to business, it was a situation in which a basic ethical dilemma suddenly in-
truded into the lives of a group of individuals. How the group responded I think holds a
lesson for all organizations no matter how defined.

THE SADHU

The Nepal experience was more rugged and adventuresome than I had anticipated. Most
commercial treks last two or three weeks and cover a quarter of the distance we traveled.

My friend Stephen, the anthropologist, and I were halfway through the 60-day Hi-
malayan part of the trip when we reached the high point, an 18,000-foot pass over a
crest that we'd have to traverse to reach the village of Muklinath, an ancient holy place
for pilgrims.

Six years earlier I had suffered pulmonary edema, an acute form of altitude sickness,
at 16,500 feet in the vicinity of Everest base camp, so we were understandably concerned
about what would happen at 18,000 feet. Moreover, the Himalayas were having their
wettest spring in 20 years; hip-deep powder and ice had already driven us off one ridge.
If we failed to cross the pass, I feared that the last half of our "once in a lifetime" trip
would be ruined.

The night before we would try the pass, we camped at a hut at 14,500 feet. In the photos taken at that camp, my face appears wan. The last village we'd passed through was a sturdy two-day walk below us, and I was tired.

During the late afternoon, four backpackers from New Zealand joined us, and we spent most of the night awake, anticipating the climb. Below we could see the fires of two other parties, which turned out to be two Swiss couples and a Japanese hiking club.

To get over the steep part of the climb before the sun melted the steps cut in the ice, we departed at 3:30 A.M. The New Zealanders left first, followed by Stephen and myself, our porters and Sherpas, and then the Swiss. The Japanese lingered in their camp. The sky was clear, and we were confident that no spring storm would erupt that day to close the pass.

At 15,500 feet, it looked to me as if Stephen were shuffling and staggering a bit, which are symptoms of altitude sickness. (The initial stage of altitude sickness brings a headache and nausea. As the condition worsens, a climber may encounter difficult breathing, disorientation, aphasia, and paralysis.) I felt strong, my adrenaline was flowing, but I was very concerned about my ultimate ability to get across. A couple of our porters were also suffering from the height, and Pasang, our Sherpa sirdar (leader), was worried.

Just after daybreak, while we rested at 15,500 feet, one of the New Zealanders, who had gone ahead, came staggering down toward us with a body slung across his shoulders. He dumped the almost naked, barefoot body of an Indian holy man—a sadhu—at my feet. He had found the pilgrim lying on the ice, shivering and suffering from hypothermia. I cradled the sadhu's head and laid him out on the rocks. The New Zealander was angry. He wanted to get across the pass before the bright sun melted the snow. He said, "Look, I've done what I can. You have porters and Sherpa guides. You care for him. We're going on!" He turned and went back up the mountain to join his friends.

I took a carotid pulse and found that the sadhu was still alive. We figured he had probably visited the holy shrines at Muklinath and was on his way home. It was fruitless to question why he had chosen this desperately high route instead of the safe, heavily traveled caravan route through the Kali Gandaki gorge. Or why he was almost naked and with no shoes, or how long he had been lying in the pass. The answers weren't going to solve our problem.

Stephen and the four Swiss began stripping off outer clothing and opening their packs. The sadhu was soon clothed from head to foot. He was not able to walk, but he was very much alive. I looked down the mountain and spotted below the Japanese climbers marching up with a horse.

Without a great deal of thought, I told Stephen and Pasang that I was concerned about withstanding the heights to come and wanted to get over the pass. I took off after several of our porters who had gone ahead.

On the steep part of the ascent where, if the ice steps had given way, I would have slid down about 3,000 feet, I felt vertigo. I stopped for a breather, allowing the Swiss to catch up with me. I inquired about the sadhu and Stephen. They said that the sadhu was fine and that Stephen was just behind. I set off again for the summit.

Stephen arrived at the summit an hour after I did. Still exhilarated by victory, I ran down the snow slope to congratulate him. He was suffering from altitude sickness, walking 15 steps, then stopping, walking 15 steps, then stopping, Pasang accompanied him all the way up. When I reached them, Stephen glared at me and said: "How do you feel about contributing to the death of a fellow man?"

I did not fully comprehend what he meant.

"Is the sadhu dead?" I inquired.

"No," replied Stephen, "but he surely will be!"

After I had gone, and the Swiss had departed not long after, Stephen had remained with the sadhu. When the Japanese had arrived, Stephen had asked to use their horse to transport the sadhu down to the hut. They had refused. He had then asked Pasang to have a group of our porters carry the sadhu. Pasang had resisted the idea, saying that the porters would have to exert all their energy to get themselves over the pass. He had thought they could not carry a man down 1,000 feet to the hut, reclimb the slope, and get across safely before the snow melted. Pasang had pressed Stephen not to delay any longer.

The Sherpas had carried the sadhu down to a rock in the sun at about 15,000 feet and had pointed out the hut another 500 feet below. The Japanese had given him food and drink. When they had last seen him he was listlessly throwing rocks at the Japanese party's dog, which had frightened him.

We do not know if the sadhu lived or died.

For many of the following days and evenings Stephen and I discussed and debated our behavior toward the sadhu. Stephen is a committed Quaker with deep moral vision. He said, "I feel that what happened with the sadhu is a good example of the breakdown between the individual ethic and the corporate ethic. No one person was willing to assume ultimate responsibility for the sadhu. Each was willing to do his bit just so long as it was not too inconvenient. When it got to be a bother, everyone just passed the buck to someone else and took off. Jesus was relevant to a more individualistic stage of society, but how do we interpret his teaching today in a world filled with large, impersonal organizations and groups?"

I defended the larger group, saying, "Look, we all cared. We all stopped and gave aid and comfort. Everyone did his bit. The New Zealander carried him down below the snow line. I took his pulse and suggested we treat him for hypothermia. You and the Swiss gave him clothing and got him warmed up. The Japanese gave him food and water. The Sherpas carried him down to the sun and pointed out the easy trail toward the hut. He was well enough to throw rocks at a dog. What more could we do?"

"You have just described the typical affluent Westerner's response to a problem. Throwing money—in this case food and sweaters—at it, but not solving the fundamentals!" Stephen retorted.

"What would satisfy you?" I said. "Here we are, a group of New Zealanders, Swiss, Americans, and Japanese who have never met before and who are at the apex of one of the most powerful experiences of our lives. Some years the pass is so bad no one gets over it. What right does an almost naked pilgrim who chooses the wrong trail have to disrupt our lives? Even the Sherpas had no interest in risking the trip to help him beyond a certain point."

Stephen calmly rebutted, "I wonder what the Sherpas would have done if the sadhu had been a well-dressed Nepali, or what the Japanese would have done if the sadhu had been a well-dressed Asian, or what you would have done, Buzz, if the sadhu had been a well-dressed Western woman?"

"Where, in your opinion, "I asked instead, "is the limit of our responsibility in a situation like this? We had our own well-being to worry about. Our Sherpa guides were unwilling to jeopardize us or the porters for the sadhu. No one else on the mountain was willing to commit himself beyond certain self-imposed limits."

Stephen said, "As individual Christians or people with a Western ethical tradition, we can fulfill our obligations in such a situation only if (1) the sadhu dies in our care, (2) the sadhu demonstrates to us that he could undertake the two-day walk down to the village, or (3) we carry the sadhu for two days down to the village and convince someone there to care for him."

"Leaving the sadhu in the sun with food and clothing, while he demonstrated hand-eye coordination by throwing a rock at a dog, comes close to fulfilling items one and two," I answered. "And it wouldn't have made sense to take him to the village where the people appeared to be far less caring than the Sherpas, so the third condition is impractical. Are you really saying that, no matter what the implications, we should, at the drop of a hat, have changed our entire plan?"

THE INDIVIDUAL VS. THE GROUP ETHIC

Despite my arguments, I felt and continue to feel guilt about the sadhu. I had literally walked through a classic moral dilemma without fully thinking through the consequences. My excuses for my actions include a high adrenaline flow, a superordinate goal, and a once-in-a-lifetime opportunity—factors in the usual corporate situation, especially when one is under stress.

Real moral dilemmas are ambiguous, and many of us hike right through them, unaware that they exist. When, usually after the fact, someone makes an issue of them, we tend to resent his or her bringing it up. Often, when the full import of what we have done (or not done) falls on us, we dig into a defensive position from which it is very difficult to emerge. In rare circumstances we may contemplate what we have done from inside a prison.

Had we mountaineers been free of physical and mental stress caused by the effort and the high altitude, we might have treated the sadhu differently. Yet isn't stress the real test of personal and corporate values? The instant decisions executives make under pressure reveal the most about personal and corporate character.

Among the many questions that occur to me when pondering my experience are: What are the practical limits of moral imagination and vision? Is there a collective or institutional ethic beyond the ethics of the individual? At what level of effort or commitment can one discharge one's ethical responsibilities?

Not every ethical dilemma has a right solution. Reasonable people often disagree; otherwise there would be no dilemma. In a business context, however, it is essential that managers agree on a process for dealing with dilemmas.

The sadhu experience offers an interesting parallel to business situations. An immediate response was mandatory. Failure to act was a decision in itself. Up on the mountain we could not resign and submit our résumés to a headhunter. In contrast to philosophy, business involves action and implementation—getting things done. Managers must come up with answers to problems based on what they see and what they allow to influence their decision-making processes. On the mountain, none of us but Stephen realized the true dimensions of the situation we were facing.

One of our problems was that as a group we had no process for developing a consensus. We had no sense of purpose or plan. The difficulties of dealing with the sadhu were so complex that no one person could handle it. Because it did not have a set of preconditions that could guide its action to an acceptable resolution, the group reacted instinctively as individuals. The cross-cultural nature of the group added a further layer of complexity. We had no leader with whom we could all identify and in whose purpose we believed. Only Stephen was willing to take charge, but he could not gain adequate support to care for the sadhu.

Some organizations do have a value system that transcends the personal values of the managers. Such values, which go beyond profitability, are usually revealed when the organization is under stress. People throughout the organization generally accept its values, which, because they are not presented as a rigid list of commandments, may be somewhat ambiguous. The stories people tell, rather than printed materials, transmit these conceptions of what is proper behavior.

For 20 years I have been exposed at senior levels to a variety of corporations and organizations. It is amazing how quickly an outsider can sense the tone and style of an organization and the degree of tolerated openness and freedom to challenge management.

Organizations that do not have a heritage of mutually accepted, shared values tend to become unhinged during stress, with each individual bailing out for himself. In the great takeover battles we have witnessed during past years, companies that had strong cultures drew the wagons around them and fought it out, while other companies saw executives, supported by their golden parachutes, bail out of the struggles.

Because corporations and their members are interdependent, for the corporation to be strong the members need to share a preconceived notion of what is correct behavior, a "business ethic," and think of it as a positive force, not a constraint.

As an investment banker I am continually warned by well-meaning lawyers, clients, and associates to be wary of conflicts of interest. Yet if I were to run away from every difficult situation, I wouldn't be an effective investment banker. I have to feel my way through conflicts. An effective manager can't run from risk either; he or she has to confront and deal with risk. To feel "safe" in doing this, managers need the guidelines of an agreed-on process and set of values within the organization.

After my three months in Nepal, I spent three months as an executive-in-residence at both Stanford Business School and the Center for Ethics and Social Policy at the Graduate Theological Union at Berkeley. These six months away from my job gave me time to assimilate 20 years of business experience. My thoughts turned often to the meaning of the leadership role in any large organization. Students at the seminary thought of themselves as antibusiness. But when I questioned them they agreed that they distrusted all large organizations, including the church. They perceived all large organizations as impersonal and opposed to individual values and needs. Yet we all know of organizations where peoples' values and beliefs are respected and their expressions encouraged. What makes the difference? Can we identify the difference and, as a result, manage more effectively?

The word "ethics" turns off many and confuses more. Yet the notions of shared values and an agreed-on process for dealing with adversity and change—what many people mean when they talk about corporate culture—seem to be at the heart of the ethical issue. People who are in touch with their own core beliefs and the beliefs of others and are sustained by them can be more comfortable living on the cutting edge. At times, taking a tough line or decisive stand in a muddle of ambiguity is the only ethical thing to do. If a manager is indecisive and spends time trying to figure out the "good" thing to do, the enterprise may be lost.

Business ethics, then, has to do with the authenticity and integrity of the enterprise. To be ethical is to follow the business as well as the cultural goals of the corporation, its owners, its employees, and its customers. Those who cannot serve the corporate vision are not authentic business people and, therefore, are not ethical in the business sense.

At this stage of my own business experience I have a strong interest in organizational behavior. Sociologists are keenly studying what they call corporate stories, legends, and heroes as a way organizations have of transmitting the value system. Corporations such as Arco have even hired consultants to perform an audit of their corporate culture. In a company, the leader is the person who understands, interprets, and manages the corporate value system. Effective managers are then action-oriented people who resolve conflict, are tolerant of ambiguity, stress, and change, and have a strong sense of purpose for themselves and their organizations.

If all this is true, I wonder about the role of the professional manager who moves from company to company. How can he or she quickly absorb the values and culture of different organizations? Or is there, indeed, an art of management that is totally transportable? Assuming such fungible managers do exist, is it proper for them to manipulate the values of others?

What would have happened had Stephen and I carried the sadhu for two days back to the village and become involved with the villagers in his care? In four trips to Nepal my most interesting experiences occurred in 1975 when I lived in a Sherpa home in the Khumbu for five days recovering from altitude sickness. The high point of Stephen's trip was an invitation to participate in a family funeral ceremony in Manang. Neither experience had to do with climbing the high passes of the Himalayas. Why were we so reluctant to try the lower path, the ambiguous trail? Perhaps because we did not have a leader who could reveal the greater purpose of the trip to us.

Why didn't Stephen with his moral vision opt to take the sadhu under his personal care? The answer is because, in part, Stephen was hard-stressed physically himself, and because, in part, without some support system that involved our involuntary and episodic community on the mountain, it was beyond his individual capacity to do so.

I see the current interest in corporate culture and corporate value systems as a positive response to Stephen's pessimism about the decline of the role in the individual in large organizations. Individuals who operate from a thoughtful set of personal values provide the foundation for a corporate culture. A corporate tradition that encourages freedom of inquiry, supports personal values, and reinforces a focused sense of direction can fulfill the need for individuality along with the prosperity and success of the group. Without such corporate support, the individual is lost.

That is the lesson of the sadhu. In a complex corporate situation, the individual requires and deserves the support of the group. If people cannot find such support from their organization, they don't know how to act. If such support is forthcoming, a person has a stake in the success of the group, and can add much to the process of establishing and maintaining a corporate culture. It is management's challenge to be sensitive to individual needs, to shape them, and to direct and focus them for the benefit of the group as a whole.

For each of us the sadhu lives. Should we stop what we are doing and comfort him; or should we keep trudging up toward the high pass? Should I pause to help the derelict I pass on the street each night as I walk to the Yale Club en route to Grand Central Station? Am I his brother? What is the nature of our responsibility if we consider ourselves to be ethical persons? Perhaps it is to change the values of the group so that it can, with all its resources, take the other road.

THE RASHOMON EFFECT

PATRICIA WERHANE

The abstract of this article offers background to the piece. Consider, in connection with the previous excerpt, how perspective alters judgment. Can you think of times when your perspective may have altered your judgment? What does this say of our justice system? What does it say of our information system as a whole? Do you obtain most of your news from (and therefore base your judgments on) television news shows? the newspaper? How might you ensure that your judgment is based on the most broad and unbiased perspectives?

The Academy Award winning 1960s Japanese movie Rashomon *depicts an incident involving an outlaw, a rape or seduction of a woman, and a murder or suicide of her husband told from four different perspectives; that of the outlaw, the woman, the husband, and a passer-by. The four narratives agree that the outlaw came upon the woman and her husband, the outlaw tied up the husband, sex took place between the woman and the outlaw in front of the bound husband, and the husband was found dead. How these events occurred and who killed the husband (or whether he killed himself) differs with each narrative.*

Applied ethics uses case stories to illustrate ethical issues, and it evaluates the stories or cases through moral theories and moral reasoning. The way we present cases or stories or describe the "facts," that is, the narratives we employ and the mental models that frame these narratives, affect the content of the story, the moral analysis, and subsequent evaluation of events. Indeed, we cannot present a case or tell a story except through the frame of a particular narrative or mental model. When one narrative becomes dominant, we appeal to that story for the "facts," taking it as representing what actually happened. Yet we seldom look at the narrative we use nor are we often aware of the "frame" or mental model at work. If my thesis is not mistaken, then, it is just as important, morally important, to examine different narratives about the cases we use as it is to carry out the ethical analysis.

To demonstrate what I am talking about, I am going to recount narratives of a well-worn case, the Ford Pinto. I shall illustrate how different commentators present what one of them has called "independently supportable facts" (Schmitt and May, 1979, p. 1022). In each instance I cite, the commentator claims that he is presenting facts, not assumptions, commentary, or conjecture. Yet, for some reason, these "facts" seem to differ from each other. The accounts of the case I shall use are Mark Dowie's "Pinto Madness" from September/October 1977 *Mother Jones,* later revised and printed in *Business and Society;* "Beyond Products Liability" by Michael Schmitt and William W. May from the *University of Detroit Journal of Urban Law,* Summer 1979; Manuel Velasquez's treatment of Pinto in his book *Business Ethics* (second ed.); Dekkers L. Davidson and Kenneth Goodpaster's Harvard Business School case, "Managing Product Safety: The Ford Pinto"; Ford Motor Company's statements from their law suit, *State of Indiana* v. *Ford Motor Company;* and Michael Hoffman's case/essay, "The Ford Pinto," printed in *Taking Sides.* It will become evident that one narrative, Mark Dowie's, one of the earliest accounts of the case, becomes the dominant one.

> *There is* one *indisputable set of data upon which all commentators agree. On May 28, 1972, Mrs. Lily Gray was driving a six-month old Pinto on Interstate 15 near San Bernardino, California. In the car with her was Richard Grimshaw, a thirteen-year-old boy. . . . Mrs. Gray stopped in San Bernardino for gasoline, got back onto the freeway (Interstate 15) and proceeded toward her destination at sixty to sixty-five miles per hour. As she approached Route 30 off-ramp, . . . the Pinto suddenly stalled and coasted to a halt in the middle lane . . . the driver of a 1962 Ford Galaxie was unable to avoid colliding with the Pinto. Before impact the Galaxie had been braked to a speed of from twenty-eight to thirty-seven miles per hour.*
>
> *At the moment of impact, the Pinto caught fire and its interior burst into flames. The crash had driven the Pinto's gas tank forward and punctured it against the flange on the differential housing. . . . Mrs. Gray died a few days later. . . . Grimshaw managed to survive with severe burns over 90 percent of his body. (Velasquez, 199, p. 122;* Grimshaw v. Ford Motor Co., *p. 359).*

In 1978 a jury awarded Grimshaw at least 125 million dollars in punitive damages. *Auto News* printed a headline, "Ford Fights Pinto Case: Jury Gives 128 Million" on February 13, 1978. The number $125 million is commonly cited and is in the court records as the sum of the initial punitive award. This award was later reduced on appeal to $3.5 million, a fact that is seldom cited.

What is the background for the development of the Pinto? According to public statements made by Lee Iacocca, then CEO of Ford, to meet Japanese competition Ford decided to design a subcompact car that would not weigh over 2,000 pounds nor cost over $2,000 (Davidson/Goodpaster, 1983). According to Davidson/Goodpaster, Ford began planning the Pinto in June 1967, ending with production beginning in September 1970, a 38-month turn-around time as opposed to the industry average of 43 months for engineering and developing a new automobile (Davidson/Goodpaster, 1983, p. 4). Mark Dowie claims that the development was "rushed" into 25 months (Dowie, p. 20); Velasquez says it occurred in "under two years" (Velasquez, p. 120); Hoffman claims that Ford "rushed the Pinto into production in much less than the usual time" (Hoffman, p. 133). While the actual time of development may seem unimportant, critics of the Pinto design argue that *because* it was "rushed into production" Pinto was not as carefully designed nor checked for safety as a model created over a 43-month time span (Dowie, Velasquez).

The Pinto was designed so that the gas tank was placed behind the rear axle. According to Davidson/Goodpaster, "[a]t that time almost every American-made car had the fuel tank located in the same place" (p. 4). Dowie wonders why Ford did not place the gas tank over the rear axle, Ford's patented design for their Capri models. This placement is confirmed by Dowie, Velasquez and some Ford engineers to be the "safest place." Yet, according to Davidson/Goodpaster other studies at Ford showed that the Capri placement actually increased the likelihood of ignition inside the automobile (p. 4). Moreover, such placement reduces storage space and precludes a hatchback design. Velasquez argues that "[b]ecause the Pinto was a rush project, styling preceded engineering" (p. 120), thus accounting for the gas tank placement. This fact may have been derived from Dowie's quote, allegedly from a "Ford engineer who doesn't want his name used," that "this company is run by salesmen, not engineers; so the priority is styling, not safety" (p. 23).

Dowie argues that in addition to rushing the Pinto into production, "Ford engineers discovered in pre-production crash tests that rear-end collisions would rupture the Pinto's fuel system extremely easily" (p. 18). According to Dowie, Ford crash-tested the Pinto in a secret location and in every test made at over 25 mph the fuel tank ruptured. But according to Ford, while Pinto's gas tank did explode during many of its tests, this was because, following government guidelines, Ford had to test the car using a fixed barrier standard wherein the vehicle is towed backwards into a fixed barrier at the speed specified in the test. Ford argued that Pinto behaved well under a less stringent moving-barrier standard, which, Ford contended, is a more realistic test (Davidson/Goodpaster; *State of Indiana* v. *Ford*).

Ford and the commentators on this case agree that in 1971, before launching the automobile, an internal study was conducted that showed that a rubber bladder inner tank would improve the reliability of Pinto during tests. The bladder would cost $5.08 (Dowie, p. 29; Schmitt and May, 1979, p. 1023), $5.80 (Davidson/Goodpaster) or $11 (Velasquez, p. 120). The $11 figure probably refers to a design adjustment that Ford would have had to make to meet a later new government rollover standard (see below). However, the idea of this installation was discarded, according to Ford because of the unreliability of the rubber at cold temperatures, a conjecture no one else mentions. Dowie also contends that Ford could have reduced the dangers from rear-end collisions by installing a $1 plastic baffle between the gas tank and the differential housing to reduce the likelihood of gas tank perforation. I can find no other verification of this fact.

All commentators claim that Ford did a cost/benefit analysis to determine whether it would be more costly to change the Pinto design or assume the damages for burn victims, and memos to that effect were evidence at the Grimshaw trial (*Grimshaw* v. *Ford Motor Co.,* 570). However, according to Davidson/Goodpaster and Schmitt/May, this estimate was done in 1973, the year *after* the Grimshaw accident, in response to evaluating a proposed new government rollover standard. To meet that requirement would cost $11 per auto, Ford calculated. Ford used government data for the cost of a life ($200,000 per person), and projected an estimate of 180 burn deaths from rollovers. The study was not applicable to rear-end collisions as commentators, following Dowie's story, claimed.

There are also innuendoes in many write-ups of this case that the $200,000 figure was Ford's price of a human life. Dowie says, for example, "Ever wonder what your life is worth in dollars? Perhaps $10 million? Ford has a better idea: $200,000." In fact, it was the U.S. government's 1973 figure.

How many people have died as a result of a rear-end collision in a Pinto? "By conservative estimates Pinto crashes have caused 500 burn deaths to people who would not have been seriously injured if the car had not burst into flames. The figure could be as high as 900," Dowie claimed in 1977 (p. 18). Hoffman, in 1984, repeats those figures word for word (p. 133). Velasquez, more cautious, claims that by 1978 at least 53 people had died and "many more had been severely burnt" (p. 122), and Schmitt and May, quoting a 1977 article in *Business and Society Review,* estimate the number at "at least 32" (p. 1024; May, p. 102 at 16). Davidson/Goodpaster claim that by 1978 NHTSA estimated there were 38 cases which involved 27 fatalities.

There was a second famous Pinto accident that led the State of Indiana to charge Ford with criminal liability. The facts in that case upon which all agree are reported by Hoffman as follows:

> *On August 10, 1978, a tragic automobile accident occurred on U.S. Highway 33 near Goshen, Indiana. Sisters Judy and Lynn Ulrich (ages 18 and 16, respectively) and their cousin Donna Ulrich (age 18) were struck from the rear in their 1973 Ford Pinto by a van. The gas tank of the Pinto ruptured, the car burst into flames, and the three teenagers were burned to death. (p. 132)*

There are two points of interest in this case, points that helped to exonerate Ford in the eyes of the jury in the Indiana trial. First, in June of 1978 Ford recalled 1.5 million of its Pintos to modify the fuel tank. There is some evidence that the Ulrich auto had not participated in the recall. (*State of Indiana* v. *Ford Motor Company*). Secondly, Ulrich's Pinto was hit from behind at 50 miles an hour by a van driven by a Mr. Duggar. Mr. Duggar, who was not killed, later testified that he looked down for a "smoke" when he then hit the car, although the Ulrichs had their safety blinkers on. Found in Duggar's van were at least two empty beer bottles and an undisclosed amount of marijuana. Yet this evidence, cited in the *State of Indiana* v. *Ford Motor Co.* case, are seldom mentioned in the context of the Ulrich tragedy, nor was Duggar ever indicted.

The point of all this is not to exonerate Ford nor to argue for bringing back the Pinto. Rather, it is to point out a simple phenomenon—that a narrative—a story—can be taken as fact even when other alleged equally verifiable facts contradict that story. Moreover, one narrative can become dominating such that what it says is taken as fact. Dowie's interesting tale of the Pinto became the prototype for Pinto cases without many of the authors going back to see if Dowie's data was correct or to question why some of his data contradicts Ford's and government claims. Moreover, Dowie's reporting of Grimshaw becomes a prototype for the narrative of Ulrich case as well, so that questions concerning the recall of the Ulrich auto and Mr. Duggar's performance were virtually ignored. Such omissions not only make Ford look better. They also bring into question these reports and cases.

Let me mention another set of stories, those revolving around the more recent Dow Corning silicone breast implant controversy. From the volumes of reports there are a few facts upon which everyone agrees. Dow Corning has developed and manufactured silicone breast implants since 1962. It is one of a number of manufacturers that include Bristol Myers Squibb, Baxter, and 3M. In 1975 it changed the design of the implant to a thinner shell that, according to the company, was more "natural," thus less likely to harden over time. Out of the almost 2 million women who have had implants, at least 440,000 have joined class action suits or brought individual law suits claiming to have experienced a variety of illnesses, including autoimmune diseases such as lupus and rheumatoid arthritis, connective tissues diseases, scleroderma, cancer, and various other malaises such as pain, fatigue, insomnia, memory loss, and/or headaches. (*New York Times,* 1995, p. C6; Angell, p. 18)

Since this is an evolving case not all the positions and narratives have sufficiently so-lidified to make exhaustive comparisons. But let me focus on three points. First, there is a very simple question, Do silicone breast implants cause cancer and other diseases, in par-ticular connective tissue or autoimmune diseases? Second, did the industry, and Dow Corning in particular, cover up or not inform physicians or women patients of the risks of implantation? Third, did Dow Corning fail "to acknowledge and promptly investigate signs of trouble?" (See bibliography for citations.)

The first question is the most simple and the most puzzling. A seldom cited fact in the case is that pacemakers and a number of other implants are made from silicone, be-cause silicone is thought to be the most inert of all possible implant substances. Yet pace-maker wearers have not sued for illnesses that allegedly result from that implant. Accord-ing to pathologist Nir Kossovsky, however, silicone breast implants can affect the immune system and cause a variety of harms to the system. This is particularly acute when an implant ruptures (Taubes, 1995). Yet in numerous independent epidemiological studies investigators have been unable to establish any but the weakest correlation be-tween breast implants and cancer, connective tissue disease, or autoimmune diseases (Sánchez-Guerrero et al., 1995; Giltay et al., 1994; McLaughlin et al., 1994). The most extensive of these is a longitudinal study by Brigham and Women's Hospital of 87,318 women nurses from the ages of 30 to 55 covering their medical records over a 14-year span. This study, partly funded by the NIH, is the basis for what will be a larger study of 450,000 women. (It should also be noted that silicone breast implants were withdrawn from the market by the FDA, not because they were proven to be harmful but because the FDA concluded that the evidence was not strong enough to show they were not harmful.) Despite what an overwhelming number of scientists consider to be overwhelming evi-dence, a number of lawsuits have been won by claimants who argue they became ill be-cause of implants.

The second question—Did Dow Corning cover up evidence?—is also equally puz-zling. Dow Corning claims, of course, that they did not. This is partly because they insti-gated their own studies that found no conclusive link between implants and disease, and partly because from the very beginning they did in fact inform *physicians* about risks of implants, including possibility of rupture or hardening in some patients. It is only re-cently, since 1985, that Dow Corning has developed brochures to be distributed to candi-dates for implantation.

The third question seems to become moot if implants do not cause disease. Yet more is at stake here. Dow Corning and other silicone breast implant manufacturers depended on the narratives of science. They imagined that scientific evidence and only scientific evidence would count as evidence in the courts, that the media would not print a story to the contrary when such scientific evidence was conclusive, and that the emotional fact that women with implants became ill would become a dominant factor in what appeared to be a matter of science. We have here a number of narratives: the scientific evidence re-ports, Dow Corning's defense of their consent procedures, and lawsuits that focus on the illnesses. There are also a set of media narratives that focus on the emotional reactions of ill women (not all media narratives do this), the dominating examples of which are the *Business Week* article "Informed Consent" (Byrne, 1995) and John Byrne's book, which was produced from this reporting. This article focuses on the emotional trauma of

Colleen Swanson, the wife of a Dow Corning manager, John Swanson, who recently resigned from Dow Corning after 27 years of employment. Colleen Swanson had had implants 17 years ago and has been suffering from a variety of illnesses almost since the end of the operation. While Byrne focuses on Colleen's emotional suffering he cites the epidemiological evidence but puts that evidence in doubt by stating:

> *Recent studies from Harvard Medical School and the Mayo Clinic, among others, have case doubt on the link between implants and disease. But critics have attacked these studies on numerous grounds—among them that they look only for recognized diseases such as lupus, rather than the complex of ailments many recipients complain of. (Byrne, 1995b, p. 116)*

Again I am not trying to whitewash this case. But it is interesting how the fact of illnesses in women with implants has been conflated with the causal claim of "illnesses caused by silicone breast implants." Perhaps it is the notion of causality that should be brought into question. The dominating emotional narratives have simply overshadowed the scientific ones. It is no wonder that Dow Corning cannot figure out what happened since they focused primarily on the scientific narratives. Moreover they seemed to assume that physicians performing implant surgery were all reasonable professionals who would inform their patients uniformly and thoroughly about the risks of implantation. (One cannot even with good conscience construct a narrative that claims that scientists are male-dominated and thus biased in their data analysis, because these studies have been conducted by men and women of a variety of scientific and medical backgrounds and nationalities.)

What can we say about the role of narratives? As I have argued elsewhere (Werhane, 1991, 1995) human beings do not simply perceive the data of their experiences unedited, so to speak. Each of us orders, selects, structures, and even censors our experiences. These shaping mechanisms are mental models or schema through which we experience the world. The selection processes or schema are culturally and socially learned and changed, and almost no perspective or model is permanent or unalterable. But we never see the world except through a point of view, a model, or framing mechanism. Indeed, narratives that shape our experiences and influence how we think about the world are essential to the facts of our experience. At the same time, these mental models or schema and these narratives are not merely subjective. They represent points of view that others share or can share, and they are, or can be, what Amartya Sen calls "positionally objective." Sen writes:

> *[w]hat we can observe depends on our position vis-a-vis the objects of observation. . . . Positionally dependent observations, beliefs, and actions are central to our knowledge and practical reason. The nature of objectivity in epistemology, decision theory, and ethics has to take adequate note of the parametric dependence of observation and inference on the position of the observer.*

Position-dependency defines the way in which the object appears "from a delineated somewhere." This "delineated somewhere," however, is positionally objective. That is, any person in that position will make similar observations, according to Sen. I would add that the parameters of positionality are not merely spatial but could involve a shared schema. For example, managers at Ford had access to a lot of the same data about the

Pinto. Ford's decision not to recall the Pinto despite a number of terrible accidents could be defended as a positionally objective belief based on the ways in which managers at Ford processed information on automobile crashes. (Gioia, 1991) Similarly, Dow Corning's reluctance to stop manufacturing silicone implants could be construed as positionally objective from their focus on scientific evidence and reliance on responsible surgeons. Colleen Swanson and other ill recipients of implants also adopt a positionally objective view, from their perspective as very ill people with implants.

However, a positionally objective point of view could be mistaken in case it did not take into account all available information. Thus, as Sen points out, in most cases one need not unconditionally accept a positionally objective view. Because of the variety of schema with which one can shape a position, almost any position has alternatives, almost every position has its critics. I would qualify that further. Even allegedly positionally objective phenomena are still phenomena that have been filtered through the social sieve of a shared mental model or schema.

As I have just demonstrated, some narratives are more closely based on actual experiences; others are taken from the narratives of others which we have accepted "as true"; still others are in the form of stories. For example, the movie *Wall Street* tells a story about Wall Street that reshapes our perception of investment banking. These perspectives are necessarily incomplete, they can be biased, or they can be constituted by someone else's framing of experience. So, for example, as E. H. Gombrich the art historian relates, following Albrecht Durer's famous etching of a rhinoceros, for a very long time naturalists as well as artists portrayed rhinos with "armored" layers of skin, when in fact, a simple look at a rhino belies that conclusion (Gombrich). Similarly, Dowie's portrayal of the Pinto case became the prototype for other case descriptions. Byrne's *Business Week* article and his subsequent book on the Dow-Corning breast implant controversy appear to be becoming the prototype factual bases for analyzing that case. What happens in these instances is that "life imitates art," or the "grammar," the alleged data of the narrative creates the essence of the story.

Does this mean that one can never arrive at facts or truths? The short answer is "yes" or "no." The longer answer is more complicated. The thesis that experience is always framed by a perspective or point of view is closely related to another thesis, Wittgenstein's claim that "*[e]ssence* is expressed by grammar" (Wittgenstein, §371), that is, in short, that all our experiences are framed, organized, and made meaningful only through the language we employ to conceive, frame, think, describe, and evaluate our experiences. Whether or not all experiences are linguistically constituted is a topic for another essay. What is important is what Wittgenstein does not say, that "essence is *created* by grammar" (Anscombe, p. 188). Nor did he hold that view, as I have argued in detail elsewhere (Werhane, 1992). To put the point in more Kantian terms, there is data or "stuff" of our experience that is not created or made up (although sometimes we can and do make up the content of our experiences when we envelop ourselves in fantasy) and indeed, the distinction between "reality" and "fantasy" may be just that—that we do not make up the content of our experience. Nevertheless, that data or content or "stuff" is never pure—it is always constituted and contaminated by our perspective, point of view, or mental model.

At the same time, we are able to engage in "trans-positional" assessments or what Sen has called a "constructed 'view from nowhere.'" A trans-positional view from nowhere is a constructed critique of a particular conceptual scheme, and no positionally objective view is merely relative nor immune from challenge. This sort of assessment involves comparing various positionally objective points of view to see whether one can make coherent sense of them and develop some general theories about what is being observed. These trans-positional assessments, are *constructed* views, because they too depend on the conceptual scheme of the assessors. From a trans-positional point of view conceptual schemes themselves can be questioned on the basis of their coherence and/or their explanatory scope. Although that challenge could only be conducted from another conceptual scheme, that assessment could take into account a variety of points of view. Still, revisions of the scheme in question might produce another conceptual scheme that more adequately or more comprehensively explained or took into account a range of phenomena or incidents. Together, studying sets of perspectives can get at how certain events are experienced and reported, and even, what mental models, scheme, or narratives are at work in shaping the narratives about these experiences. While one can never get at those from a purely *tabula rasa,* nevertheless one can achieve a limited, dispassionate view from somewhere.

Near the end of *Rashomon* the narrator of the tale, who is also the bystander, decries the lack of trust in society engendered from the impossibility of ascertaining the truth. The cases we develop must be done with care. In using others' cases and narratives one should study not just the facts as presented in the case narratives. Rather, we need to examine the ways in which the facts are constituted to make a story or a case, and one should become aware of how some of those cases can become prototypical narratives that we imitate. The so-called "classics" like Pinto need to be revisited or they will become cliched prototypes. And we need to be wary of assumptions generated by these prototypes such as the assumption that Dow Corning caused egregious harms, perhaps even deliberately, to the over 2 million women who have their breast implants. While we cannot arrive at The Truth we can at least approximate it more fully. Only then will we who teach and write in applied ethics become, in the words of Henry James, "finely aware and richly responsible" (James/Nussbaum).

BIBLIOGRAPHY

Angell, Marcia. 1995. "Are Breast Implants Actually OK?" *The New Republic.* September 11, 17–21.

_____. 1996. *Science on Trial.* New York: W. W. Norton & Co.

Anscombe, G. E. M. 1976. "The Question of Linguistic Idealism." *Essays on Wittgenstein in Honour of G. H. Von Wright.* Acta Philosophica Fennica, Vol. 28. ed. Jaakko Hintikka. Amsterdam: North Holland Publishing Co., 181–215.

Byrne, John A. 1995. "Informed Consent," *Business Week,* October 2, pp. 104–116.

_____. 1996. *Informed Consent: A Story of Personal Tragedy and Corporate Betrayal.* New York, McGraw-Hill Companies.

Davidson, Dekkers and Goodpaster, Kenneth E. 1983. "Managing Product Safety: The Ford Pinto." Harvard University Graduate School of Business Administration Case #9–383–129. Boston: Harvard Business School Press.

Dowie, Mark. 1977a. "Pinto Madness." *Mother Jones.* September/October. 18–32.

_____. 1977b. "How Ford Put Two Million Firetraps on Wheels." *Business and Society Review,* 23, 46–55.

"Ford Fights Pinto Case: Jury Gives 128 Million." 1978, *Auto News.* February 13, 1.

Gabriel, S. E., et al. 1994. "Risk of Connective-Tissue Diseases and Other Disorders After Breast Implantation." *New England Journal of Medicine.* 330: 1697–1702.

Giltay, Erik J., et al. 1994. "Silicone Breast Protheses and Rheumatic Symptoms: A Retrospective Follow Up Study." *Annals of Rheumatic Diseases.* 53, 194–196.

Gioia, Dennis. 1991. "Pinto Fires and Personal Ethics: A Script Analysis of Missed Opportunities." *Journal of Business Ethics,* 11, 379–389.

Gombrich, E. H. 1961. *Art and Illusion.* Princeton: Princeton University Press.

Grimshaw v. *Ford Motor Co.* 1978. No. 197761. Super CT. Orange County, CA, February 6.

Hoffman, Michael. 1984; "The Ford Pinto." rpt. in *Taking Sides.* ed. Lisa H. Newton and Maureen M. Ford. Dushkin Publishing Group. 132–137.

Kolata, Gina. 1995. "Proof of a Breast Implant Peril is Lacking, Rheumatologists Say." *New York Times.* October 25.

McLaughlin, Joseph K. and Fraumeni, Joseph F. Jr. 1994. "Correspondence Re: Breast Implants, Cancer, and Systemic Sclerosis." *Journal of the National Cancer Institute.* 86, 1424.

Nussbaum, Martha. 1990. *Love's Knowledge.* New York: Oxford University Press.

Sanchez-Guerrero, Jorge, et al. 1995. "Silicone Breast Implants and the Risk of Connective-Tissue Diseases and Symptoms." *New England Journal of Medicine.* 332: 1666–1670.

Schmitt, Michael A. and May, William W. 1979. "Beyond Products Liability: The Legal, Social, and Ethical Problems Facing the Automobile Industry in Producing Safe Products." *University of Detroit Journal of Urban Law.* 56: 1021–1050.

Sen, Amartya. 1993. "Positional Objectivity." *Philosophy and Public Affairs.*

State of Indiana v. *Ford Motor Co.* (179) No. 11-431, Cir. Ct. Pulaski, IN.

Taubes, Gary. 1995. "Silicone in the System." *Discover.* December, 65–75.

Velasquez, Manuel. 1988. *Business Ethics,* second edition. Englewood Cliffs: Prentice-Hall, Inc.

Werhane, Patricia H. 1991. "Engineers and Management: The Challenge of the Challenger Incident." *Journal of Business Ethics.* 10, 605–616.

_____, _____. 1992. *Skepticism, Rules, and Private Languages.* Atlantic Highlands, NJ: Humanities Press.

_____. 1998. "Moral Imagination and Management Decision-Making." *New Avenues of Research in Business Ethics.* Edited by R. Edward Freeman. New York: Oxford University Press, forthcoming.

Wittgenstein, Ludwig. 1953. *Philosophical Investigations.* trans. G. E. M. Anscombe. New York: Macmillan and Co.

RELATED WEB SITES

Information on the film "Rashomon":
www.mhs.schnet.edu.au/endzone/rashomon.htm

Conflicting testimony in Rashomon:
www.creativeloafing.com/newsstand/at1090995/B_RASH.HTM

A JURY OF HER PEERS

Susan Glaspell

In the following short story, Martha Hale and her husband are taken by the sheriff and his wife to the Wrights' home, where Mrs. Hale had found Mr. Wright strangled to death the previous morning. Mrs. Wright, pleading ignorance, was arrested and is awaiting charges. The women were at the house to gather Mrs. Wright's clothes and to see to her preserves. The men mocked the women's "trifles" and teased them about not missing any "clues" while they were to go about their more serious business of finding a motive. In a basket of patches waiting to be quilted, the women find a canary, strangled. The following excerpt discusses why they decide to conceal this evidence that might incriminate her.

Consider why the women notice some of these clues, but the men ignore the same evidence. Is it relevant that this story was written before women were allowed to sit on juries? Is justice blind, or gender-specific? Should it matter in our system who is the judge and who is the judged?

"Mrs. Peters!"

"Yes, Mrs. Hale?"

"Do you think she—did it?"

A frightened look blurred the other things in Mrs. Peters' eyes.

"Oh, I don't know," she said, in a voice that seemed to shrink away from the subject.

"Well, I don't think she did," affirmed Mrs. Hale stoutly. "Asking for an apron, and her little shawl. Worryin' about her fruit."

"Mr. Peters says—" Footsteps were heard in the room above; she stopped, looked up, then went on in a lowered voice: "Mr. Peters says—it looks bad for her. Mr. Henderson is awful sarcastic in a speech, and he's going to make fun of her saying she didn't—wake up."

For a moment Mrs. Hale had no answer. Then, "Well, I guess John Wright didn't wake up—when they was slippin' that rope under his neck," she muttered.

"No, it's *strange,*" breathed Mrs. Peters. "They think it was such a—funny way to kill a man."

She began to laugh; at sound of the laugh, abruptly stopped.

"That's just what Mr. Hale said," said Mrs. Hale, in a resolutely natural voice. "There was a gun in the house. He says that's what he can't understand."

"Mr. Henderson said, coming out, that what was needed for the case was a motive. Something to show anger—or sudden feeling."

"Well, I don't see any signs of anger around here," said Mrs. Hale. "I don't—"

She stopped. It was as if her mind tripped on something. Her eye was caught by a dish towel in the middle of the kitchen table. Slowly she moved toward the table. One half of it was wiped clean, the other half messy. Her eyes made a slow, almost unwilling turn to the bucket of sugar and the half empty bag beside it. Things begun—and not finished.

After a moment she stepped back, and said, in that manner of releasing herself:

"Wonder how they're finding things upstairs? I hope she had it a little more red-up up there. You know,"—she paused, and feeling gathered,— "it seems kind of *sneaking;* locking her up in town and coming out here to get her own house to turn against her!"

"But, Mrs. Hale," said the sheriff's wife, "the law is the law."

"I s'pose 'tis," answered Mrs. Hale shortly.

She turned to the stove, saying something about that fire not being much to brag of. She worked with it a minute, and when she straightened up she said aggressively:

"The law is the law—and a bad stove is a bad stove. How'd you like to cook on this?"—pointing with the poker to the broken lining. She opened the oven door and started to express her opinion of the oven; but she was swept into her own thoughts, thinking of what it would mean, year after year, to have that stove to wrestle with. The thought of Minnie Foster trying to bake in that oven—and the thought of her never going over to see Minnie Foster—.

She was startled by hearing Mrs. Peters say: "A person gets discouraged—and loses heart."

The sheriff's wife had looked from the stove to the sink—to the pail of water which had been carried in from outside. The two women stood there silent, above them the footsteps of the men who were looking for evidence against the woman who had worked in that kitchen. That look of seeing into things, of seeing through a thing to something else, was in the eyes of the sheriff's wife now. When Mrs. Hale next spoke to her, it was gently:

"Better loosen up your things, Mrs. Peters. We'll not feel them when we go out."

Mrs. Peters went to the back of the room to hang up the fur tippet she was wearing. A moment later she exclaimed, "Why, she was piecing a quilt," and held up a large sewing basket piled high with quilt pieces.

Mrs. Hale spread some of the blocks on the table.

"It's log-cabin pattern," she said, putting several of them together. "Pretty, isn't it?"

They were so engaged with the quilt that they did not hear the footsteps on the stairs. Just as the stair door opened Mrs. Hale was saying:

"Do you suppose she was going to quilt it or just knot it?"

The sheriff threw up his hands.

"They wonder whether she was going to quilt it or just knot it!"

There was a laugh for the ways of women, a warming of hands over the stove, and then the county attorney said briskly:

"Well, let's go right out to the barn and get that cleared up."

"I don't see as there's anything so strange," Mrs. Hale said resentfully, after the outside door had closed on the three men—"our taking up our time with little things while we're waiting for them to get the evidence. I don't see as it's anything to laugh about."

"Of course they've got awful important things on their minds," said the sheriff's wife apologetically.

They returned to an inspection of the blocks for the quilt. Mrs. Hale was looking at the fine, even sewing, and preoccupied with thoughts of the woman who had done that sewing, when she heard the sheriff's wife say, in a queer tone:

"Why, look at this one."

She turned to take the block held out to her.

"The sewing," said Mrs. Peters, in a troubled way. "All the rest of them have been so nice and even—but—this one. Why, it looks as if she didn't know what she was about!"

Their eyes met—something flashed to life, passed between them; then, as if with an effort, they seemed to pull away from each other. A moment Mrs. Hale sat there, her hands folded over that sewing which was so unlike all the rest of the sewing. Then she had pulled a knot and drawn the threads.

"Oh, what are you doing, Mrs. Hale?" asked the sheriff's wife, startled.

"Just pulling out a stitch or two that's not sewed very good," said Mrs. Hale mildly.

"I don't think we ought to touch things," Mrs. Peters said, a little helplessly.

"I'd just finish up this end," answered Mrs. Hale, still in that mild, matter-of-fact fashion.

She threaded a needle and started to replace bad sewing with good. For a little while she sewed in silence. Then, in that thin, timid voice, she heard:

"Mrs. Hale!"

"Yes, Mrs. Peters?"

"What do you suppose she was so—nervous about?"

"Oh, *I* don't know," said Mrs. Hale, as if dismissing a thing not important enough to spend much time on. "I don't know as she was—nervous. I sew awful queer sometimes when I'm just tired."

She cut a thread, and out of the corner of her eye looked up at Mrs. Peters. The small, lean face of the sheriff's wife seemed to have tightened up. Her eyes had that look of peering into something. But the next moment she moved, and said in her thin, indecisive way:

"Well, I must get those clothes wrapped. They may be through sooner than we think. I wonder where I could find a piece of paper—and string."

"In that cupboard, maybe," suggested Mrs. Hale, after a glance around.

One piece of the crazy sewing remained unripped. Mrs. Peters' back turned, Martha Hale now scrutinized that piece, compared it with the dainty, accurate sewing of the other blocks. The difference was startling. Holding this block made her feel queer, as if the distracted thoughts of the woman who had perhaps turned to it to try and quiet herself were communicating themselves to her.

Mrs. Peters' voice roused her.

"Here's a birdcage," she said. "Did she have a bird, Mrs. Hale?"

"Why, I don't know whether she did or not." She turned to look at the cage Mrs. Peters was holding up. "I've not been here in so long." She sighed. "There was a man round last year selling canaries cheap—but I don't know as she took one. Maybe she did. She used to sing real pretty herself."

Mrs. Peters looked around the kitchen.

"Seems kind of funny to think of a bird here." She half laughed—an attempt to put up a barrier. "But she must have had one—or why would she have a cage? I wonder what happened to it."

"I suppose maybe the cat got it," suggested Mrs. Hale, resuming her sewing.

"No; she didn't have a cat. She's got that feeling some people have about cats—being afraid of them. When they brought her to our house yesterday, my cat got in the room, and she was real upset and asked me to take it out."

"My sister Bessie was like that," laughed Mrs. Hale.

The sheriff's wife did not reply. The silence made Mrs. Hale turn round. Mrs. Peters was examining the birdcage.

"Look at this door," she said slowly. "It's broke. One hinge has been pulled apart."

Mrs. Hale came nearer.

"Looks as if someone must have been—rough with it."

Again their eyes met—startled, questioning, apprehensive. For a moment neither spoke nor stirred. Then Mrs. Hale, turning away, said brusquely:

"If they're going to find any evidence, I wish they'd be about it. I don't like this place."

"But I'm awful glad you came with me, Mrs. Hale." Mrs. Peters put the birdcage on the table and sat down. "It would be lonesome for me—sitting here alone."

"Yes, it would, wouldn't it?" agreed Mrs. Hale, a certain determined naturalness in her voice. She picked up the sewing, but now it dropped in her lap, and she murmured in a different voice: "But I tell you what I *do* wish, Mrs. Peters. I wish I had come over sometimes when she was here. I wish—I had."

"But of course you were awful busy, Mrs. Hale. Your house—and your children."

"I could've come," retorted Mrs. Hale shortly. "I stayed away because it weren't cheerful—and that's why I ought to have come. I"—she looked around—"I've never liked this place. Maybe because it's down in a hollow and you don't see the road. I don't know what it is, but it's a lonesome place, and always was. I wish I had come over to see Minnie Foster sometimes. I can see now—" She did not put it into words.

"Well, you mustn't reproach yourself," counseled Mrs. Peters. "Somehow, we just don't see how it is with other folks till—something comes up."

"Not having children makes less work," mused Mrs. Hale, after a silence, "but it makes a quiet house—and Wright out to work all day—and no company when he did come in. Did you know John Wright, Mrs. Peters?"

"Not to know him. I've seen him in town. They say he was a good man."

"Yes—good," conceded John Wright's neighbor grimly. "He didn't drink, and kept his word as well as most, I guess, and paid his debts. But he was a hard man, Mrs. Peters. Just to pass the time of day with him—." She stopped, shivered a little. "Like a raw wind that gets to the bone." Her eye fell upon the cage on the table before her, and she added, almost bitterly: "I should think she would've wanted a bird!"

Suddenly she leaned forward, looking intently at the cage. "But what do you s'pose went wrong with it?"

"I don't know," returned Mrs. Peters; "unless it got sick and died."

But after she said it she reached over and swung the broken door. Both women watched it as if somehow held by it.

"You didn't know—her?" Mrs. Hale asked, a gentler note in her voice.

"Not till they brought her yesterday," said the sheriff's wife.

"She—come to think of it, she was kind of like a bird herself. Real sweet and pretty, but kind of timid and—fluttery. How—she—did—change."

That held her for a long time. Finally, as if struck with a happy thought and relieved to get back to everyday things, she exclaimed:

"Tell you what, Mrs. Peters, why don't you take the quilt in with you? It might take up her mind."

"Why, I think that's a real nice idea, Mrs. Hale," agreed the sheriff's wife, as if she too were glad to come into the atmosphere of a simple kindness. "There couldn't possibly be any objection to that, could there? Now, just what will I take? I wonder if her patches are in here—and her things."

They turned to the sewing basket.

"Here's some red," said Mrs. Hale, bringing out a roll of cloth. Underneath that was a box. "Here, maybe her scissors are in here—and her things." She held it up. "What a pretty box! I'll warrant that was something she had a long time ago—when she was a girl."

She held it in her hand a moment; then, with a little sigh, opened it.

Instantly her hand went to her nose.

"Why—!"

Mrs Peters drew nearer—then turned away.

"There's something wrapped up in this piece of silk," faltered Mrs. Hale.

"This isn't her scissors," said Mrs. Peters in a shrinking voice.

Her hand not steady, Mrs. Hale raised the piece of silk. "Oh, Mrs. Peters!" she cried. "It's—"

Mrs. Peters bent closer.

"It's the bird," she whispered.

"But, Mrs. Peters!" cried Mrs. Hale. "*Look* at it! Its neck—look at its neck! It's all—other side *to.*"

She held the box away from her.

The sheriff's wife again bent closer.

"Somebody wrung its neck," said she, in a voice that was slow and deep.

And then again the eyes of the two women met—this time clung together in a look of dawning comprehension, of growing horror. Mrs. Peters looked from the dead bird to the broken door of the cage. Again their eyes met. And just then there was a sound at the outside door.

Mrs. Hale slipped the box under the quilt pieces in the basket, and sank into the chair before it. Mrs. Peters stood holding to the table. The county attorney and the sheriff came in from outside.

"Well, ladies," said the county attorney, as one turning from serious things to little pleasantries, "have you decided whether she was going to quilt it or knot it?"

"We think," began the sheriff's wife in a flurried voice, "that she was going to—know it."

He was too preoccupied to notice the change that came in her voice on that last.

"Well, that's very interesting, I'm sure," he said tolerantly. He caught sight of the birdcage. "Has the bird flown?"

"We think the cat got it," said Mrs. Hale in a voice curiously even.

He was walking up and down, as if thinking something out.

"Is there a cat?" he asked absently.

Mrs. Hale shot a look up at the sheriff's wife.

"Well, not *now,*" said Mrs. Peters. "They're superstitious, you know; they leave."

She sank into her chair.

The county attorney did not heed her. "No sign at all of anyone having come in from the outside," he said to Peters, in the manner of continuing an interrupted conversation. "Their own rope. Now let's go upstairs again and go over it, piece by piece. It would have to have been someone who knew just the—"

The stair door closed behind them and their voices were lost.

The two women sat motionless, not looking at each other, but as if peering into something and at the same time holding back. When they spoke now it was as if they were afraid of what they were saying, but as if they could not help saying it.

"She liked the bird," said Martha Hale, low and slowly. "She was going to bury it in that pretty box."

"When I was a girl," said Mrs. Peters, under her breath, "my kitten—there was a boy took a hatchet, and before my eyes—before I could get there—" She covered her face an instant. "If they hadn't held me back I would have"—she caught herself, looked upstairs where footsteps were heard, and finished weakly—"hurt him."

Then they sat without speaking or moving.

"I wonder how it would seem," Mrs. Hale at last began, as if feeling her way over strange ground—"never to have had any children around?" Her eyes made a slow sweep of the kitchen, as if seeing what that kitchen had meant through all the years. "No, Wright wouldn't like the bird," she said after that—"a thing that sang. She used to sing. He killed that too." Her voice tightened.

Mrs. Peters moved uneasily.

"Of course we don't know who killed the bird."

"I knew John Wright," was Mrs. Hale's answer.

"It was an awful thing was done in this house that night, Mrs. Hale," said the sheriff's wife. "Killing a man while he slept—slipping a thing round his neck that choked the life out of him."

Mrs. Hale's hand went out to the birdcage.

"His neck. Choked the life out of him."

"We don't *know* who killed him," whispered Mrs. Peters wildly. "We don't *know.*"

Mrs. Hale had not moved. "If there had been years and years of—nothing, then a bird to sing to you, it would be awful—still—after the bird was still."

It was as if something within her not herself had spoken, and it found in Mrs. Peters something she did not know as herself.

"I know what stillness is," she said, in a queer, monotonous voice. "When we homesteaded in Dakota, and my first baby died—after he was two years old—and me with no other then—"

Mrs. Hale stirred.

"How soon do you suppose they'll be through looking for evidence?"

"I know what stillness is," repeated Mrs. Peters, in just that same way. Then she too pulled back. "The law has got to punish crime, Mrs. Hale," she said in her tight little way.

"I wish you'd seen Minnie Foster," was the answer, "when she wore a white dress with blue ribbons, and stood up there in the choir and sang."

The picture of that girl, the fact that she had lived neighbor to that girl for twenty years, and had let her die for lack of life, was suddenly more than she could bear.

"Oh, I *wish* I'd come over here once in a while!" she cried. "That was a crime! That was a crime! Who's going to punish that?"

"We mustn't take on," said Mrs. Peters, with a frightened look toward the stairs.

"I might 'a' *known* she needed help! I tell you, it's *queer,* Mrs. Peters. We live close together, and we live far apart. We all go through the same things—it's all just a different kind of the same thing! If it weren't—why do you and I *understand?* Why do we *know*— what we know this minute?"

She dashed her hand across her eyes. Then, seeing the jar of fruit on the table, she reached for it and choked out:

"If I was you I wouldn't *tell* her her fruit was gone! Tell her it *ain't.* Tell her it's all right—all of it. Here—take this in to prove it to her! She—she may never know whether it was broke or not."

She turned away.

Mrs. Peters reached out for the bottle of fruit as if she were glad to take it—as if touching a familiar thing, having something to do, could keep her from something else. She got up, looked about for something to wrap the fruit in, took a petticoat from the pile of clothes she had brought from the front room, and nervously started winding that round the bottle.

"My!" she began, in a high, false voice, "it's a good thing the men couldn't hear us! Getting all stirred up over a little thing like a—dead canary." She hurried over that. "As if that could have anything to do with—with—My, wouldn't they *laugh?*"

Footsteps were heard on the stairs.

"Maybe they would," muttered Mrs. Hale—"maybe they wouldn't."

"No, Peters," said the county attorney incisively; "it's all perfectly clear, except the reason for doing it. But you know juries when it comes to women. If there was some definite thing—something to show. Something to make a story about. A thing that would connect up with this clumsy way of doing it."

In a covert way Mrs. Hale looked at Mrs. Peters. Mrs. Peters was looking at her. Quickly they looked away from each other. The outer door opened and Mr. Hale came in.

"I've got the team round now," he said. "Pretty cold out there."

"I'm going to stay here awhile by myself," the county attorney suddenly announced. "You can send Frank out for me, can't you?" he asked the sheriff. "I want to go over everything. I'm not satisfied we can't do better."

Again, for one brief moment, the two women's eyes found one another.

The sheriff came up to the table.

"Did you want to see what Mrs. Peters was going to take in?"

The county attorney picked up the apron. He laughed.

"Oh, I guess they're not very dangerous things the ladies have picked out."

Mrs. Hale's hand was on the sewing basket in which the box was concealed. She felt that she ought to take her hand off the basket. She did not seem able to. He picked up one of the quilt blocks which she had piled on to cover the box. Her eyes felt like fire. She had a feeling that if he took up the basket she would snatch it from him.

But he did not take it up. With another little laugh, he turned away, saying:

"No; Mrs. Peters doesn't need supervising. For that matter, a sheriff's wife is married to the law. Ever think of it that way, Mrs. Peters?"

Mrs. Peters was standing beside the table. Mrs. Hale shot a look up at her; but she could not see her face. Mrs. Peters had turned away. When she spoke, her voice was muffled.

"Not—just that way," she said.

"Married to the law!" chuckled Mrs. Peters' husband. He moved toward the door into the front room, and said to the county attorney:

"I just want you to come in here a minute, George. We ought to take a look at these windows."

"Oh—windows," said the county attorney scoffingly.

"We'll be right out, Mr. Hale," said the sheriff to the farmer, who was still waiting by the door.

Hale went to look after the horses. The sheriff followed the county attorney into the other room. Again—for one moment—the two women were alone in that kitchen.

Martha Hale sprang up, her hands tight together, looking at that other woman, with whom it rested. At first she could not see her eyes, for the sheriff's wife had not turned back, since she turned away at that suggestion of being married to the law. But now Mrs. Hale made her turn back. Her eyes made her turn back. Slowly, unwillingly, Mrs. Peters turned her head until her eyes met the eyes of the other woman. There was a moment when they held each other in a steady, burning look in which there was no evasion nor flinching. Then Martha Hale's eyes pointed the way to the basket in which was hidden the thing that would make certain the conviction of the other woman—that woman who was not there and yet who had been there with them all through the hour.

For a moment Mrs. Peters did not move. And then she did it. With a rush forward, she threw back the quilt pieces, got the box, tried to put it in her handbag. It was too big. Desperately she opened it, started to take the bird out. But there she broke—she could not touch the bird. She stood helpless, foolish.

There was the sound of a knob turning in the inner door. Martha Hale snatched the box from the sheriff's wife, and got it in the pocket of her big coat just as the sheriff and the county attorney came back into the kitchen.

"Well, Henry," said the county attorney facetiously, "at least we found out that she was not going to quilt it. She was going to—what is it you call it, ladies?"

Mrs. Hale's hand was against the pocket of her coat.

"We call it—knot it, Mr. Henderson."

WHERE AND WHY DID BUSINESS ETHICISTS GO WRONG? THE CASE OF DOW CORNING CORPORATION

DARYL KOEHN

Dow Corning is a contradiction in itself: it was one of the first firms to institute a senior level code of conduct committee and received accolades from ethicists for forging ahead in this area, while it also declared bankruptcy after some claimed it ignored numerous complaints of serious medical problems in connection with its products: silicone breast implants. Later, it was alleged that Dow even destroyed a survey that disclosed the medical issues customers had with the implants. John Byrne was an engineer who expressed concern early on for the lack of safety testing.

Update to Dow Corning: In 1993, Dow Corning unveiled a $4.25 billion plan—the largest mass injury settlement ever—to settle all silicone breast implant claims (Thomas Burton, "Adding Insult to Injury," Progressive, July, 1994, p. 8). Individual women would receive between $200,000 and $2 million each. Many criticized the plan as being extravagantly generous to certain claimants and "stingy" to others. By 1995, 440,000 women had joined in the settlement. However, 15,000 women decided to try their luck filing individual suits against Dow and opted out of the settlement (Michael Hoffman et al., The Ethical Edge, p. 134). Dow filed for bankruptcy in 1995, effectively freezing all claims and delaying payment to claimants for years. Four months after Dow's filing, a federal judge declared the original settlement dead.

In the following analysis, Koehn describes the history of the Dow Corning case and discusses why ethicists may originally have been misled regarding the ethical culture at Dow.

In the early 1980's, it seemed Dow Corning Corporation (DCC) could do no wrong. It hit the billion dollar sales mark in 1986. What is more, it maintained its competitiveness while

---

acting in a fashion many judged ethically exemplary. In fact, a highly complimentary case study was done in 1984 by a Harvard business ethicist lauding various of the company's ethical initiatives. Yet by 1989, the company was in the midst of a public relations fiasco over its manufacture and marketing of silicone breast implants or "mammaries." The company had been found guilty of fraud for suppressing internal memos suggesting that these implants were less safe than the company's marketing literature represented them to be. Juries had awarded several multimillion dollar awards to women who claimed to have been seriously harmed by their implants. A criminal investigation had been launched into DCC's business practices. Although this investigation was subsequently dropped for lack of evidence, fifteen members of Congress urged (in July 1995) Janet Reno, the U.S. Attorney General, to examine whether a senior manager of DCC had perjured himself when testifying before Congress several years earlier. In 1995, DCC filed for bankruptcy, claiming it did not have the funds necessary to fund the $4.23 billion settlement that had been reached for paying women who had been part of class action lawsuits against the company.

Whether or not silicone implants are safe is a highly contested matter. Some of DCC's own studies suggest they may not be safe. In particular, leaked silicone may harm the immune system. Later DCC studies seem to indicate that silicone is inert within the human body. Studies by researchers at University of Michigan and Mayo Clinic have been interpreted as showing that there is no link between silicone breast implants and autoimmune disease. However, critics have charged that these studies are suspect because the samples used were too small to be statistically significant and because the research was funded in part by DCC and the plastic surgeons who have a financial interest in showing that these implants are safe. While many women with implants firmly believe these implants to be the cause of their problems, their symptoms are diverse. Removal of the implants has not always improved their condition. Although the United States declared a moratorium on cosmetic surgeons implanting this product, the British government chose to leave them on the market after deciding women with implants were at no greater risk of contracting autoimmune disease than those without the implants.

This paper does not aim at resolving the scientific controversy regarding the safety of the implants. Nor does it try to build a case that DCC's production and manufacture of these implants was unethical. While I would question the goodness of many of DCC's reported actions, I am less interested in passing judgment on this company than in discovering what we can learn from its difficulties. To this end, I want to consider, first, why DCC won praise for its ethics initiatives; and second, what factors and forces, if any, business ethicists failed to consider when assessing the ethical goodness of DCC. I am interested in what mistakes business ethicists made in thinking about DCC's ethics and in learning what we can from these errors.

PART 1: THE ETHICS PROGRAM AT DCC

DCC sponsored many ethics initiatives. The company wrote and published a corporate code of ethics as early as 1977. While many codes emphasize matters of etiquette or remaining within the law, DCC's code was noteworthy for stressing integrity and respect.

The 1977 code read: "The watchword of Dow Corning worldwide activities is integrity . . . We believe that business is best conducted and society best served within each country when business practice is based on the universal principles of honesty and integrity." The code goes on to say that "We recognize that our social responsibilities must be maintained at the high standards which lead to respect and trust by society. A clear definition of our social responsibilities should be an integral part of our corporate objectives and be clearly communicated to every employee."

Furthermore, the code was widely disseminated and was hung in the corridors of the corporation. The then CEO of the company, Jack Ludington, sent a letter to every employee urging him or her to read the code and to contact Ludington if they had any questions. Ludington and other managers of DCC consistently referred to the code of ethics in their speeches. Since various areas faced different ethical challenges, the areas were allowed to devise their own separate codes, although these codes still needed to be consistent with DCC's corporate code. Efforts were made to solicit employee feedback concerning the code and to keep the code current by revising it every two years. As John Swanson, the manager–business communications specialist who was the only permanent member of the Business Conduct Committee, put it, "The code of conduct is a 'living' statement, one that can change as accepted business practices change."

In addition, DCC instituted annual audits beginning in 1977 both to communicate the code and to solicit feedback as well as to monitor compliance. The audits were conducted by a newly created committee at DCC—the Business Conduct Committee. Up to 40 audits per year were conducted at the area level (e.g., in Mexico City, Toronto, Brussels, Hong Kong). Since different areas had different concerns (e.g., requests for bribes were more prevalent in Asia than in some other areas), the audits were tailored to the area being evaluated. Every effort was made to include regional personnel who were actually dealing with problems in the day to day business operation of the company. The results of the audit were documented and kept on file at headquarters, but the intent was not punitive. Rather the audits were an attempt to educate employees concerning the code and to highlight potential problems or ambiguities with the code itself. Some of the audit sessions were videotaped. These tapes were then shared with area personnel to educate them concerning the audit process.

Finally, the BCC developed corporate training modules on the code and a semi-annual opinion survey. The survey attempted to measure whether employees knew about the code and whether DCC's ethics initiatives were making a real difference in the life of the corporation.

Business ethicists praised DCC for its meaningful code and for its serious commitment to making ethics a regular part of business practice. It certainly looked as though management was serious about these various initiatives. Rising executives were regularly assigned to do a stint on the rotating Business Conduct Committee and were expected to spend up to 15% of their time per week on ethical issues. However, initiatives by themselves do not make a company ethical. In the next section, I explore several important dimensions of corporate life that were completely ignored by the *Harvard Business Review* study, dimensions that played a pivotal role in how DCC handled the growing public concern regarding the safety of silicone breast implants manufactured by the company.

PART 2: WHAT BUSINESS ETHICISTS FORGOT TO CONSIDER

Factor 1: Managerial Hubris

Although the CEO of DCC supported the ethics initiative, he met with some resistance from senior area personnel who believed that DCC was already a thoroughly ethical company. For example, Phil Brooks, a senior employee in Hong Kong, wrote a memo to Ludington arguing that DCC had no problem "and that our house doesn't need putting in order. Therefore we need to agree on the purpose of any Code and that purpose must arise from some need. What is the need if we already believe (as I do) that we are morally, legally, and ethically correct in all aspects of our business conduct?"

The certainty implicit in this claim is remarkable. Given that DCC had just begun ethics audits to uncover what various managers' actual practices were, it seems odd to claim that one already knows that DCC is behaving completely correctly—legally, ethically, and morally. The certainty that DCC was an entirely ethical company is doubly striking because it seems to have been widely held. As the controversy surrounding silicone breast implants deepened, another senior manager, Silas Braney, would proclaim, "I can say, without any qualification, that never in my 30 years at Dow Corning did I ever know of anyone doing anything illegal, unethical, or immoral." His sentiments echo those of CEO Ludington who, in the late 1970's, claimed that his corporate managers "would not intentionally do anything questionable and would even blow the whistle if they learned of any actual wrongdoing within the company." Again, the certainty seems rather misplaced, given that the company experienced a good deal of resistance to some parts of the code from some of its managers who believed that the code was making DCC uncompetitive. It is doubtful whether Ludington was warranted in asserting that DCC's employees would definitely blow the whistle on unethical practices by corporate employees if these employees in many cases (see Brooks quote above) did not accept that some of their past practices were in fact unethical.

More generally, such certainty on the part of management evinces an attitude that is antithetical to ethical reasoning. As Aristotle puts it, the "stuff" of ethical discourse is controversy because practical matters do not admit of the same degree of certainty as mathematical or scientific subjects. To reason ethically, therefore, consists at least in part in being willing to submit one's beliefs to the scrutiny and challenges of others. If agents begin with the position that they and their company have done no wrong, this very process of discussion is shortcircuited. This shutting off of the possibility of discussion may itself be an ethical wrong, yet this possibility cannot get raised in this atmosphere of certainty.

All of the processes in the world will make little difference if people are fundamentally committed to the proposition that neither they nor their colleagues have done any wrong. One sees the consequences of this certainty quite clearly in the book on the breast implant controversy to which DCC insider John Swanson contributed. Key players at DCC are certain that the breast implants they helped to design and manufacture are absolutely safe. Indeed, they are so certain of their moral rectitude that they dismiss as "crazy" all of the women who think they have been harmed by their implants. Even after the Federal Drug Administration ordered companies manufacturing breast implants to prove that they were safe, some senior managers at DCC insisted that there was no ethical issue connected with the marketing of silicone breast implants. While the implants may turn out not to be the cause of these women's health problems, such demonizing of these women hardly seems consistent with DCC's professed commitment to respect the dignity of employees and of customers and to treat them fairly. It is, however, consistent with a certain hubris that appeared as early as 1977 in DCC's managers' view of the company's ethics initiatives. To the extent business ethicists quoted these hubristic claims but ignored the arrogance implicit in them, they were misled in their judgment of the company.

Factor 2: Corporate History

Another striking feature of HBR's analysis of DCC's ethics was the total disregard of the company's history. The case study looked at DCC at just one point in time—the late 1970's. While the case study was updated in the 1980's it still made no mention of the company's history. This oversight is striking because Dow Corning is a subsidiary of Dow Chemical. Managers moved between the two companies. Indeed, Keith McKennon, the manager brought in as the new CEO to provide decisive leadership at DCC as the lawsuits and bad publicity began to mount, was formerly an executive vice-president at Dow Chemical. Dow Chemical, in turn, had invented and marketed napalm, Agent Orange and, along with Merill-Dow, Benedictin, a morning sickness pill suspected of causing birth defects. These products all proved tremendously controversial in the late 1960's and 1970's. I do not here want to argue the morality of Dow Chemical's decision to produce these products nor the way in which the company responded to criticism of these products. It may be that any company in the chemical and pharmaceuticals business runs certain risks by producing powerful compounds whose long-term effects may not be immediately obvious. However, I do want to insist that this history and the behavior of the players in these earlier controversies is relevant to judging the ethics of Dow Corning because some of these same people were responsible for deciding how to respond to the press, whether to voluntarily pull the implants, how aggressively to respond to lawsuits, etc. In fact, CEO McKennon was apparently appointed to head DCC because he was internally regarded as the consummate "fireman" who successfully put out the Agent Orange controversy when it threatened to flame out of control.

A corporation is like a living organism. It has a history, and how it behaves in the present is a function of its past experiences, acquired habits and attitudes and the stories it tells itself concerning the past. To ignore such matters and to merely focus on the present behavior of corporate employees can and likely will lead both the business ethicist and the company astray. For if a company's management behaved questionably in the past, and if the company showed no willingness to engage in any soul-searching regarding these past actions, what reason is there to think that management will suddenly mend its ways and its habits just because a company institutes a code of conduct and sets up some ethics training sessions?

This tendency to ignore corporate history is endemic in the business ethics literature. We philosophers report some event or action. We raise a number of questions about behavior in this event, yet we rarely situate this event in the company's history or relate it to the company's past deeds. While this isolation of an action may give the illusion of analytic clarity, it seriously falsifies the actual process of choice. Choices are always made by human beings who have acquired certain habits of choice by dint of dealing with past crises and problems. To describe ethics processes such as DCC's "ethics audits" in isolation from the people doing and undergoing the audit will tell us little about the real value of these processes.

Factor 3: Corporate Culture

A third factor is the company's internal culture. By "culture," I mean both the totality of factors (history, environment, sanctions, etc.) that lead employees to embrace certain characteristic ways of viewing the world and this worldview itself, since, as it develops, it, too, becomes a controlling factor. The HBR case study attempts to characterize this culture. We read that "DCC's culture was open, informal, and relaxed; little emphasis was placed on official status or a traditional organizational chart with clear-cut reporting relationships." As far as it goes, this judgment appears sound. DCC was known for being a highly matrixed company with many dotted line reporting relations. Employees routinely met in the halls to informally share information and to make decisions. The problem with this assessment of culture is not so much that it was wrong but that it was very incomplete. The HBR article assessed culture entirely in light of the company's reporting structure. However, we can also get a feel for culture by examining where people spend most of their time and energy, what behaviors are rewarded, and who the heroes of the company are. When these are considered, we get a rather different view of DCC's culture.

At the time the HBR article was written, one out of every ten employees of DCC was involved in new product development. This number is relatively high and suggests that there was a great deal of interest in not merely developing but also probably a good bit of pressure to successfully market new products to the consumer. Such pressure can result in a company rushing products to market before the product's safety has been adequately established. Swanson tells the story of how he had been sent to publicly announce a new silicon handwash; however, at the last minute he received a panicked call cancelling the product rollout because the product adversely affected monkeys. The rollout of breast implants may also have been premature. It appears, for example, that DCC provided implants to surgeons who placed them in women while the company was still doing initial safety testing on animals.

DCC was also distinguished by a tendency to lionize its scientists. The company's "hall of fame" featured pictures of the chemists who had made new discoveries concerning silicone or who had invented silicone-based products. There was a widespread perception among employees that to advance one had to be a scientist. The non-scientists within the company seemed to take the scientists' word as gospel. John Swanson relates how psychologically difficult it was for him to even consider the possibility that silicone might not be inert because he and his colleagues had been told for years by scientists that the material did not react with the body in any way. In short, the culture at DCC was one that prided itself on being scientifically expert.

On the one hand, a culture of people who pride themselves on their expertise may be driven by professional self-esteem to produce products that can be trusted not to harm the end-users. On the other hand, expertise may feed arrogance and lead employees to feel contempt for those who are not experts like them. At one point, DCC refused to take any questions from reporters on the ground that such people lacked scientific credentials. There is also a danger that expertise will lead those who view themselves as professionals to overlook the client's needs entirely. Thus we have doctors speaking of curing AIDs or the virus rather than the patient. A similar displacement seems to have occurred at DCC where both the surgeons and apparently the company itself restrictively defined a "failed implant" as one damaged in manufacture. The patient might experience pain or discomfort or require surgery to implant a new device, but these cases were not counted as failed implants. It was not until several years into the controversy over the implants that a CEO at DCC finally would say that the company's overriding responsibility was to women who had the implants. Although DCC's own code of corporate ethics gives priority to treating the customer fairly and with respect, the code proved no match for the corporate culture of expertise.

It might be objected that it is unfair to criticize business ethicists for failing to fully comprehend a corporation's culture. Persons who write case studies and consultants rarely have access to the corporate memos and jokes that often prove so revealing of a company's culture. Nor are they around long enough to get much of a feel for how the company operates. There is some truth in this objection but it does not completely exonerate business ethicists. These facts suggest that we business ethicists need to be extremely circumspect when praising a company as ethically good. We need to be aware of our limitations and do the most we can to widen our focus to include other features of the culture, features of the sort described above.

Factor 4: The Wider Culture

The culture of a particular corporation is not freestanding. It is always embedded in the larger national culture (and global one, too, to the extent that it makes sense to speak of a global culture). Whether a corporation will act ethically depends at least in part on what pressures and expectations the wider culture brings to bear on the corporation and the way in which the corporation responds to them. In some cases, refusing to meet these expectations may be the most ethical response, especially if these expectations are ill-formed, unrealistic, or the product of suspect motivations. Business ethicists need to consider, therefore, whether the company in question has shown itself willing to sometimes say "no" to people.

In the case of DCC, the company faced pressure from plastic surgeons to develop a host of products they could use. In some cases, the silicone products were clearly of use in promoting people's health (e.g., a shunt used to drain fluid from the brain). However, breast implants did not unambiguously fall into this category. Although they could be, and were, used to rebuild the breasts of women who had mastectomies, most implants were used for purely cosmetic reasons. The plastic surgeons knew there was a huge market for these mammaries and that there was big money to be made because a surgeon could do up to six implants per day at a charge of $1000/implant (1970's dollar value). Furthermore, the plastic surgeons had the money and connections to increase this market. They lobbied hard to have small breasts defined as a disease so that insurance companies would pay for the breast enlargements the plastic surgeons were promoting.

From almost the moment DCC entered the implant market, it was involved with a product that was of questionable value and that was being promoted by doctors who had a vested interest in having women come to see themselves as defective. Although some women with small breasts may very well have low self-esteem, this condition hardly qualifies as a "disease" in the normal sense of the term. Many women with small breasts do not lack self-esteem so the symptomology is questionable. Furthermore, the condition generally is not debilitating in the way cancer or polio is. Even if some small-breasted women were to have difficulty functioning because of a lack of self-confidence, the "cure" arguably lies not in encouraging them to have surgery (with its attendant possible complications) but in fighting the propaganda that would have such women view themselves as inferior. It could be argued that this "disease" was manufactured to play on the fears of vulnerable parties who perhaps are already short on self-esteem. If this logic is sound, then DCC was in the business of not just manufacturing breast implants but of manipulating vulnerable people as well. DCC failed to ask itself early on: Why are we in this business anyway? The business ethicists who evaluated the ethics program at DCC also failed because they did not examine whether DCC product rollout process was thoughtful. Instead, they focused largely on the existence of a code of conduct and audits, neither of which directly speaks to the question of how DCC was dealing with external pressures and expectations.

Factor 5: Good Time Ethics

As I noted earlier, the HBR case study focused on processes of ethical review at DCC but did not consider in any detail exactly what cases were coming up for review. From the code, it was clear that DCC thought that it was most exposed in the area of bribery, kickbacks or political contributions in its foreign operations. Swanson characterized the cases he dealt with as ranging from instances of alleged sexual harassment to cases where an employee was arrested for brawling in a barroom. What is most striking about this list is that many of charges were one-time violations by a single employee. The cases did not involve systemic wrongdoing nor did they threaten any of the company's core business lines. After he left the company, Swanson himself characterized the company as having a "good time" ethics program—i.e., a program that functioned well only as long as the sums of money involved were not very large.

Philosophers surely need to be sensitive to the likelihood that acting well may be appealing to a company and its employees only as long as doing the right thing is not an expensive proposition. Before praising a corporation as ethical, business ethicists need to examine whether the company has faced any hard tests. Johnson and Johnson showed it was truly concerned about the customer when it recalled all of its Tylenol product after a customer had died from ingesting some of this product. One could argue that DCC's decision not to stop selling the silicone implants was of a different order. Both Johnson and Johnson and the police knew that the death was the result of some Tylenol having been tampered with, while the evidence linking the implants to many of the reported conditions was ambiguous. Given that there were risks as well in having the implants removed, DCC might have caused more harm by unduly alarming women and frightening them into "ex-plants." Still, the basic point remains: When evaluating a company's behavior, it is necessary to consider the extent to which the company has faced significant temptations not to do the right thing.

Factor 6: Character and Commitment

This last comment brings me to the sixth and final factor that business ethicists have tended to overlook in their case study—the issue of character and commitment. Paper codes and conduct committees are virtually worthless if people within the firm are not committed to avoiding wrongdoing. In fact, without such a commitment, a structure such as a business conduct committee may wind up being pernicious. Members may use the committee to avoid having to assume personal responsibility for their acts. Some literature suggests that people are less likely to do the right thing when they are a member of a group and take their cues from the collective than when they are confronting a crisis alone. This is not to say that, for people who are genuinely committed to acting well, the committee may provide a valuable sounding board for thinking through choices. But much will depend on the character and motivations of those on the board.

The problem thus becomes one of assessing the commitment of employees and management to acting well. All of the factors mentioned above need to be considered in arriving at a thoughtful judgment of this commitment. The DCC case suggests several other considerations especially relevant to the question of commitment. It is interesting that DCC was originally driven to adopt its ethical initiative only after Congress passed the Foreign Corrupt Practices Acts in 1977. This act imposed fines on corporations and up to $10,000 in fines or five years in prison on individuals convicted of violating the act. The prospect of prison time no doubt proved sobering to many CEO's who were criminally liable if they "knew or had reason to know that their agents used the payments received from the U.S. concern to pay a foreign official for a prohibited purpose." The original impulse behind a move to develop an ethics initiative does not necessarily taint the entire resulting ethics initiative. Swanson, for example, apparently initially thought of the Business Conduct Committee as so much window dressing but over the years the committee and the rest of DCC's ethics program came to symbolize for him a genuine commitment to do the right thing. Nevertheless, if senior management understands its ethics program merely or largely as a strategy for avoiding getting into legal trouble, the company is not likely to do the right thing in those cases where it thinks it either will not be caught or can use the legal system to its advantage.

The corporate compensation system should be considered as well. At DCC, people were told, on the one hand, that they should avoid paying bribes to officials in order to get business; but, on the other hand, they believed they would be evaluated entirely on their contribution to the bottom line. The employees received a dual signal. Under such circumstances, employees may justifiably wonder about the sincerity of the company's commitment to doing the right thing.

Third, business ethicists should look to the possible effects of ownership structure (public vs. private) on a company's ethics. No doubt there are decent family-owned businesses. Clearly public ownership is neither a necessary nor a sufficient condition for encouraging ethically good behavior. Nevertheless, it may be that a company like DCC, which was accountable only to Dow Chemical and Corning Inc., will be less responsive to concerns about its actions than it would be if it were forced to confront and report to shareholders directly. Corporate structure does have ethical implications and should not be ignored.

Finally, it may prove insightful to ask employees who is responsible for ethics within their company. The right answer surely is: "I am." Every person who performs a deed places himself or herself within the ethical realm and becomes accountable for the actions he or she voluntarily initiates. Yet, at DCC, one man—Swanson—was viewed as "Mr. Ethics" and the "guardian of the company's ethics." The fact that Swanson apparently accepted these titles and the fact that they were given to him in the first place should have been a sign that something was seriously awry. No single person can know what others are doing around the world. Nor can he justly be held responsible for actions beyond his control that others initiate. Business ethicists seem to have been so impressed by Swanson's integrity that they forgot that one person does not a corporation make.

Conclusion

Although I have been critical of business ethicists' praise of Dow Corning, I am aware that I, too, might have spoken of the company's code and ethics program in glowing terms had I been the one writing a case study of the company back in 1977. However, the issue is not whether business ethicists sometimes err in their judgments but whether they show themselves willing to learn from their past errors. Like companies, we are judged by our histories and by our character and commitments. While it is the human condition to err, it is also part of our condition to be able to identify our mistakes as such and to learn from them. The above analysis represents one answer to the question of where and why we philosophers erred in our judgment of one company. The errors are generic in the sense that they are the sort we might make when evaluating any company and its actions. The good news is that, since these errors are generic, we can taken the lesson learned from DCC to heart and do better the next time.

RELATED WEB SITES

FDA: Use Saline Implants or Enroll Patients in Silicone Trials:
  http://www.genderweb.org/~julie/medical/breasts/fdause10.html

A Call for Higher Standards for Breast Implants:
  http://www.genderweb.org/~julie/medical/breasts/acallf02.html

Update on Breast Implants: The New Evidence Against DOW Chemical:
  http://seamless.seamless.com/alexanderlaw/txt/article/dow.shtml

An Update on the Lawsuits Filed Against Breast Implant Manufacturers:
  http://web-cr01.pbs.org/newshour/bb/health/may96/breast_implants_
  5-30.html

Chapter 5

ETHICS, BUSINESS, AND RELIGION
Is There a Crossroads?

It is the way of heaven to show no favouritism.
It is for ever on the side of the good man.

Lao Tzu, *Tao Te Ching*

What can business learn from religion, or vice-versa? Oftentimes, individuals in business believe that there is no room for such personal issues as religion in business decision making, while others believe that there is no way to make difficult decisions without its guidance. Given the pressures of today's workplace, perhaps a bit of spirituality is necessary in order to balance one's personal life with one's work life. But through what door should religion enter the work environment?

Consider the advent of industrial chaplains—these are ministers who are hired by a firm to work with employees. Since employers are asking more and more from their employees in terms of time and commitment, it seems to follow that employees are forced to satisfy more of their needs during that extended workday. Consequently, some workers may find it helpful, if not comforting, that there is a minister in the workplace available to them. On the other hand, given employee concerns about personal privacy, especially with technological advances allowing intrusions never before considered, employees may reasonably be disturbed by their employer's "involvement" in this intimate area of their life. Robert Bruce, vice president for labor relations at ServiceMaster, responds to some of these concerns in his selection.

Aside from the integration of active religion in the business environment, what guidance can religious theory offer to business decision makers? In 1980, a committee of the National Conference of Catholic Bishops drafted a pastoral letter on the American economy that was finally approved in 1986. The letter criticized the American economy for failing to appropriately provide for the poor in this country. The Bishops suggested a focus on human dignity and community social responsibility. They contended that justice exists only where the community meets the needs of its poorest components (termed a *preferential option for the poor*) and maintains human dignity for all. The principal themes of the letter included:

- Every economic decision and institution must be judged in light of whether it protects or undermines the dignity of the human person.

- Human dignity can be realized and protected only in community.

- All people have the right to participate in the economic life of society.

- All members of society have a special obligation to the poor and vulnerable.

- Human rights are the minimum conditions for life in community.

- Society as a whole, acting through public and private institutions, has the moral responsibility to enhance human dignity and protect human rights.[1]

Is an economy such as that supported by the pastoral letter realistic? What would be some of its greatest obstacles? A commission made up of lay Catholics who had originally criticized the pastoral letter during its drafting later released its own concerns about the Bishops' position, claiming that the pastoral letter suffered from "serious intellectual defects," including a

---

1. United States Catholic Conference, *Economic Justice for All: Pastoral Letter on Catholic Social Teaching* (1986).

*failure to grasp what makes poor nations into developed nations; deficient under-
standings of political economy; excessive trust in the state and its officials; an inadequate grasp of crucial concepts such as enterprise, markets, and profits; significant
confusions about economic rights; fateful confusions between defense spending and
spending on weapons; a preference for solidarity over pluralism; and an inadequate
exposition of 'liberty.'*[2]

Consider as you read the following selections whether concepts borne in religious
thought and applicable to our personal lives are equally applicable to our professional
lives. If not, where are the distinctions?

---

2. W. Simon and M. Novak, "Liberty and Justice for All," *Crisis Magazine,* November 1986. Messrs. Simon
and Novak are cochairmen of the Lay Commission on Catholic Social Teaching and the U.S. Economy.

THE TEN COMMANDMENTS

As discussed earlier, one of the earliest recorded codes of conduct is found in the Bible: the Ten Commandments. If you were given the opportunity to write 10, and only 10, commandments today, do you think that these would be the ones that you would choose? Are these sufficient? Are they realistic? In your opinion, is a good person one who follows these commandments?

1 Then God delivered all these commandments:

2 "I, the LORD, am your God, who brought you out of the land of Egypt, that place of slavery. 3 You shall not have other gods besides me. 4 You shall not carve idols for yourselves in the shape of anything in the sky above or on the earth below or in the waters beneath the earth; 5 you shall not bow down before them or worship them. For I, the LORD, your God, am a jealous God, inflicting punishment for their fathers' wickedness on the children of those who hate me, down to the third and fourth generation; 6 but bestowing mercy down to the thousandth generation, on the children of those who love me and keep my commandments.

7 "You shall not take the name of the LORD, your God, in vain. For the LORD will not leave unpunished him who takes his name in vain.

8 "Remember to keep holy the sabbath day. 9 Six days you may labor and do all your work, 10 but the seventh day is the sabbath of the LORD, your God. No work may be done then either by you, or your son or daughter, or your male or female slave, or your beast, or by the alien who lives with you. 11 In six days the LORD made the heavens and the earth, the sea and all that is in them; but on the seventh day he rested. That is why the LORD has blessed the sabbath day and made it holy.

12 "Honor your father and your mother, that you may have a long life in the land which the LORD, your God, is giving you.

13 "You shall not kill.

14 "You shall not commit adultery.

15 "You shall not steal.

16 "You shall not bear false witness against your neighbor.

17 "You shall not covet your neighbor's house. You shall not covet your neighbor's wife, nor his male or female slave, nor his ox or ass, nor anything else that belongs to him."

RELATED WEB SITE

The Bible: www.sni.net/advent/cathen/02543a.html

The Ten Commandments, Exodus 20: 1–17. The Bible

CONNECTING: TRUST AND FAITH FOR RELIGION AND BUSINESS

PATRICK PRIMEAUX, S.M.

Primeaux explains what business can learn from a religious or spiritual perspective. While some may argue that there is no room or role for religion in the business world, perhaps a spiritual approach to some business decisions can prove to be enlightening.

Norman Lear, the television producer who brought Archie Bunker, Fred Sanford, and Mary Hartman into our homes, claims that "American business . . . is now the fountainhead of values in our society."[1] Not only has business become the most powerful institution of the contemporary social order, it has surpassed the influence of religion and politics in scope and reference. He cites Joseph Campbell's historical and architectural metaphor to ground this contention:

> *In medieval times . . . as one once approached a city, the tallest structure on the skyline was the church and its steeple. Subsequently, as the power and influence of the church gave way to kings and rulers, the castle dominated the skyline. Today, as one approaches a city, the most commanding structures are the skyscrapers, the cathedrals of modern business.[2]*

As the physical structures of business dominate the skyline, their organizational structures dominate the values of our social order. So powerful and pervasive has business become in our world that its values surpass those of families, churches, schools, and governments. Although Lear is confident in that assertion, he is less so about the values of business, precisely because the values of business are devoid of any spiritual content. That neglect of the spiritual has resulted in an overwhelming preoccupation with mathematics, especially those of "number systems" which have "become the new currency of

Patrick Primeaux, S.M., "Connecting: Trust & Faith for Religion & Business." Reprinted by permission of the author.

1. Norman Lear, "The Cathedral of Business: The Fountainhead of Values in America Today," *New Oxford Review,* April, 1993, 7.

2. Lear, 8. See Joseph Campbell with Bill Moyers, *The Power of Myth* (New York: Doubleday, 1988), 95–96. Lear paraphrases Campbell: "You can tell what's informing a society by what the tallest building is. When you approach a medieval town, the cathedral is the tallest thing in the place. When you approach an eighteenth-century town, it is the political palace that's the tallest thing in the place. And when you approach a modern city, the tallest places are the office buildings, the centers of economic life."

public values."[3] For Lear, this means that "we define our values by SAT scores, Nielsen ratings, box office grosses, public opinion polling, throw weights, cost benefit analyses, quarterly reports, bottom lines."[4] The person, then, is only as valuable as his or her status within a numerical listing, i.e., objectified as a number. Human dignity has been relegated to statistical analysis. We can readily see that Lear's perspective is consistent with Milton Friedman's well-known ethical imperative defining the social responsibility of business primarily in terms of increased profits.[5]

This emphasis on numbers, and on profits, necessarily results in a personal alienation and isolation, a personal emptiness.[6] To fill that emptiness, Lear recommends a greater appreciation of "the spirit-led or spiritual life of our species":

I'm talking about the mysterious inner life, the fertile invisible realm that is the well-spring for our species' creativity and morality. It is that portion of ourselves that impels us to create art and literature, and study ethics, philosophy, and history. It is that portion of our being that gives rise to our sense of awe and wonder and longing for truth, beauty, and a higher order of meaning. For want of a better term, one could call it the spirit-led or spiritual life of our species.[7]

This is the closest Lear comes to defining spirituality. If that is what spirituality is, we can all agree that it is woefully lacking in business. As a clergyman and a teacher, I also find this sense of mystery, wonder, and awe missing in our churches and classrooms as well. Rather than contemplating the majesty of God, we concentrate on the overwhelming demands of ordinary life, and use religion as an escape, a respite, a diversion, a consolation. I fear that, for Lear, as for many of us, religion is little more than a useful antidote offering momentary release from all that preoccupies us. Below the surface of his inspiring thoughts is a shadowy identification of religion with utility. It is useful to fill a void.

Inadvertently, Lear is confirming his own assumptions. Business is not only defining the values of our world and its people. It is also redefining religion within a utilitarian emphasis on bottom-line profit maximization. Richard P. Niebuhr expresses that same concern for Christian faith in his examination of the Jesus of History/Christ of Faith debate. Tracing the growing emphasis on reason from the Enlightenment, and into the nineteenth century, he demonstrates how the physical sciences framed the scientific method, joining absolutist laws of cause-and-effect to rational objectivity, how it entered into historical and sociological methods of interpretation, and how it became adopted by scriptural and theological investigation.[8] Accordingly, "there is a strong tendency among many theologians to subject historical statements to the criteria of classical, syllogistic logic or to the sanctions of methods of verification appropriate to natural science."[9] So?

3. Lear, 10.
4. Lear, 10.
5. Milton Friedman, "A Friedman Doctrine: The Social Responsibility of Business is to Increase its Profits," *New York Times Magazine,* September 13, 1978, 32ff.
6. Lear, 8–9.
7. Lear, 12.
8. Richard R. Niebuhr, *Resurrection and Historical Reason* (New York: Scribner's, 1957).
9. Richard R. Niebuhr, *Experiential Religion* (New York: Harper and Row, 1972), 60.

For Niebuhr, this means that the biblical witness to the resurrection, so central to Christian faith and practice, has actually been relegated to the periphery or rendered insignificant. Why? Because it simply does not fit the criteria of rational objectivity and causality. Likewise, as we are arguing, belief in God does not fit the criteria of cost-benefit analysis, and when pursued from this utilitarian frame of reference, that faith is reduced and minimized. God is reduced to a utilitarian function: What can God do for me? If nothing, God does not exist or is irrelevant. She does not fill the emptiness in my life. He does not cure my sick mother's cancer. He did not give me the job I wanted. She did not help me pass the exam.

In other words, we use God to do for us what we are unwilling to do for ourselves or cannot do for ourselves. But, what are we really talking about? Clearly we're not discussing the existence of God, or the identity of God, or the attributes of God. We are discussing faith in God, our faith in God. We are discussing a relationship with God. As we do that, however, let us also examine our relationships with ourselves and our relationships with others. The first question, then, is how we know ourselves? Surely, we do not know ourselves as purely or primarily rational. We know ourselves as rational beings, but also as spiritual, emotional, and physical beings as well. Actually, we know ourselves at that point where the mind, the body, the heart, and the soul connect; at that point where the rational, the physical, the emotional, and the spiritual conjoin in a dynamic interaction of the total, integrated person.

Totality and integration are familiar, perhaps overused words and concepts. They warrant discussion because they are also often used in a misleading way. Philosophy, for example, will appeal to totality and integration, but on its terms. The emotional, the physical, and the spiritual have to fulfill the requirements of the rational. The emotions, then, are defined and regulated by the mind. They have no value or positive existence within themselves. Whatever integration is acclaimed, it is a false integration because it subsumes the body, the heart, and the soul within the dictates of the mind. We do the same in theology, interpreting the rational, the physical, and the emotional according to the principles and conclusions of theological methodology and assumptions. The body, then, becomes irrelevant, as does the physical universe, or becomes relegated to secondary significance. The natural sciences, as well as psychology, do the same within their respective disciplines.

How do we relate to others? We relate to others as ourselves as total, integrated persons to other total, integrated persons—physically, emotionally, spiritually, and rationally. Likewise, consistently and simultaneously, we relate to God. At the heart of that totality and integration is the wonder, awe, and mystery of which Lear speaks. We may not know why or how, we may not be able to prove—emotionally, rationally, physically, or spiritually—that conjunction of the heart, the mind, the body, and the soul. But we do know ourselves to be so. We also know others to be so. We do not know why we are attracted to some people and repelled by others—at least not fully or comprehensively—but we know that we are. So wonder, awe, and mystery belong not only to relationships with God, but to relationships with others, and to relationships with ourselves. So does love. So does trust. . . .

Richard R. Niebuhr, writing fifteen years after his study of the resurrection—and having studied Jonathan Edwards, Friedrich Schliermacher, Martin Buber, as well as

Luther and Calvin—defines faith with respect to relationships, and also with respect to trust.[10] For Niebuhr, though, faith is not confined to the spiritual; nor is it confined to relationships with God. Likewise, trust arises from the total person, from that conjunction of the heart, soul, body, and mind, and is an attribute of all relationships—to ourselves, to others, and to God. Actually, Niebuhr does not use the word faith. His word is "believing," which, on the one hand, removes the concept from its static, rational implications, and which, on the other hand, stresses its progressive, evolutionary, dynamic and energizing connotations.[11] Believing does not belong to a realm of abstraction or definition, but to the active life, i.e., to behavior—morality and ethics.

When Niebuhr describes believing, he does so in terms of "trust" and "confidence."[12] The *Oxford English Dictionary* does the same. Trust is defined as having "faith or confidence;" confidence as "firm trust, reliance, faith;" faith as "confidence, reliance, trust."[13] The question, then, for theology and for business, is not the meaning of these words in abstraction, but in practical behavior, especially the behavior of relating to one's self, to others, and to God. In her recent book, *Jerusalem,* Karen Armstrong underscores this behavioral relatedness, claiming that during the Axial Age of the seventh century B.C.E., "true faith had to be characterized by practical compassion."[14] This was a time during which the "Hebrew prophets began to insist on the prime importance of social justice," realizing that "it was all too easy for a religious symbol such as the Temple to become a fetish, an end in itself and an object of false security and complacency."[15] Armstrong is inadvertently asking the pivotal question of human relationships: do we direct our trust towards relationships with one another, or towards relationships with the institutions and structures which organize those relationships? To whom or to what is that trust, faith, or confidence directed?

Those questions arise from business management rather than from theological inquiry. They become even more poignant if we accept Lear's observation that business has become more pervasive and influential than religion for defining moral values. It is the ethical imperatives implicit in our organizational structures which are determinative of our ethics. That insight has been advanced in Rensis Likert's ground-breaking study of organizational structures.

Likert examines four organizational structures and aligns them progressively along a continuum with the *exploitative authoritative* at one extreme and the *participative-group* at the other. Between the two are the *benevolent authoritative* (a softened form of the exploitative authoritative) and then the *consultative* (a transitional stage from the authoritative organizations towards the participative-group).

Likert's analysis of the authoritative organizational structure provides a context for this discussion because it demonstrates a continuity between the hierarchical organizational

---

10. Richard R. Niebuhr, *Experiential Religion* (New York: Harper and Row, 1972), 60.
11. Niebuhr, 51–76.
12. Niebuhr, 64, 75
13. J. A. Simpson and E. S. C. Weiner, eds. *The Oxford English Dictionary,* Second Edition (Oxford: Clarendon Press, 1989).
14. Karen Armstrong, *Jerusalem: One City, Three Faiths* (New York: Alfred A. Knopf, 1996), 64.
15. Armstrong, 64.

structure and an authority-obedience ethical nexus demanded of scientific, rational control. It also provides a context for this discussion because the authoritative organizational structure is anchored in tenets of philosophical inquiry which, according to the principle of cause and effect, proscribes both universal laws and compliance to those laws. Moreover, someone will have to enforce that compliance. Who will do that? Within the authoritative organization the goals of the organization, and its operating principles and expectations, are defined at the highest level of management, and communicated and enforced through a series of descending levels of authority and compliance.[16] The expected response on each level is obedience. On that basis, good and evil, right and wrong, rewards and punishments, promotions and dismissals, are defined and conditioned. Authority and obedience are not only the primary virtues of the authoritative organizational structure; they are necessary for its maintenance and survival.

Within Likert's analysis, the authoritative organization can assume two forms, "exploitative" or "benevolent," to the degree it demands compliance.[17] In either case, though, because of its dual caste structure, the authoritative organization necessarily enlists not only distinctions of rank and function, but conflict and dissension occasioned by these distinctions. Attitudes towards other members of the organization are, consequently, those of observable subservience "toward superiors coupled with hostility" and "contempt for subordinates."[18] The role of managers is to impose; that of workers to obey. Authority's expectation of compliance on the part of subordinates, claims Likert, translates into directives being "overtly accepted, but . . . covertly resisted" by subordinates.[19]

We can then conclude that it is in the best interest of managers to maintain and perpetuate that structure and their respective roles within it. It translates directly into prestige and salaries in direct proportion to their own compliance as well as their ability to exact compliance from subordinates. It is in the best interest of subordinates to obey, for failure to do so can only result in dismissal or denial of promotion.[20] The motivational forces within this organization are "physical security, economic security, and some use of the desire for status."[21]

Ethical expectations are tied to this authority-obedience nexus, and defined, contextualized, and conditioned by its structure. "Distrust is widespread," maintains Likert, and, because of its absence, "fear, threats, punishments, and occasional rewards" are used to enforce and exact compliance.[22] Human relationships are also contextualized and limited by the differentiation of roles and responsibilities of individuals within the organization. Individuals are boxed, categorized, and separated from one another by role and function,

---

16. Rensis Likert, *New Patterns of Management* (New York: McGraw-Hill, 1961), 226.
17. Likert, 224, 226. For the "exploitive authoritative" organizational structure, communication is initiated only at the top of the organization; in the "benevolent authoritative," primarily at the top. In the first, the "bulk of decisions" is at the top of the organization; in the second, "policy at the top" and a framework is provided for lower-level decisions.
18. Likert, 225.
19. Likert, 231.
20. Likert, 223.
21. Likert, 223.
22. Likert, 225, 223.

detached and isolated, so that there is "little interaction" between organizational levels, and, even then, "fear and distrust" mark what interaction there is.[23]

This fear and distrust between managers and workers results in hidden divisions within the larger organization, for an "informal" organization comes into existence to "counteract and oppose the goals of the formal organization."[24] The more the formal organization's goals and objectives are directed towards the requirements and conditions of utility, the more the informal organization concentrates on those of human dignity. We can then expect that the more the formal organization promotes separate and division, the more the informal organization encourages solidarity and community. The structures and values of the formal organization are so powerful, however, that they precede those of the informal organization, at least on the surface.

Within this authoritative organizational structure productivity is mediocre at best, loss and waste high, and absences excessive.[25] Yet, the reason the organization exists in the first place, and for which it was created and structured, is precisely that of production. The reason for the descending levels and ranks of authority and obedience is maximum utility. Not only are people used to fulfill that production objective, they are organized to do so within a structure built on individual fear and distrust accompanied by an ethical code anchored in obedience to authority. It's a vicious circle: fear and distrust elicit authority and obedience; authority and obedience elicit fear and distrust.

The conflicts inherent to this authoritative organizational structure are not caused simply by individuals, but by the corporate structure which separates and distinguishes, isolates and detaches individuals from one another. The individual has no value other than that of usefulness to the organization's goals and objectives, and, as those goals and objectives are imposed, so also is the ethical expectation of obedience and compliance. It is this perspective which underlies Lynn Sharp Paine's argument for managerial responsibility for ethical violations by employees.[26] Assuming the separations and divisions between managers and workers, she is implicitly recommending a continuation of the distrust and hostility between the two, for it is those "managers who fail to provide proper leadership and to institute systems that facilitate ethical conduct" who should "share responsibility with those who conceive, execute, and knowingly benefit from corporate misdeeds."[27] It is managers who make decisions for others to obey.

Clearly, within Likert's authoritative organizational structure, trust is not of primary significance, at least not the appreciation of trust which is synonymous with faith, confidence, and love. From another perspective, when trust is elicited it is conditioned and contextualized not only by the organizational structure, but by the ethical imperatives of that structure. It is defined with respect to, and in terms of, obedience and compliance. Trust becomes little more than valuing the decision-making role of senior managers and their directives and policies.

---

23. Likert, 228.
24. Likert, 233.
25. Likert, 233.
26. Lynn Sharp Paine, "Managing for Organizational Integrity," *Harvard Business Review,* March-April, 1994, 106ff.
27. Paine, 106.

Inherent to, and implicit in, the authoritative, hierarchical organizational structure is a dynamic that divides leaders and followers, defines leadership with respect to authoritative decision-making and membership with respect to compliance. That authority-obedience nexus determines and defines not only the organizational structure, but the decisions of its leaders and the obedience of its members. It also dismisses trust as insignificant, except with respect to the person and office of leadership. Trust has been stripped of everything but its rational dimension, and defined with respect to utilitarian authority and obedience.

There is, however, another approach or method which releases trust from hierarchical control and from the limitations of philosophical reason alone. Its danger is that it would demand a new organizational structure. Its attribute is that it would restore a more comprehensive identification of trust as a virtue of reason, emotion, body, and spirit, i.e., of the total, integrated person. That method is perhaps most clearly stated by Andrew Greeley in his description of Bruce Springsteen as a "Catholic meistersinger."[28]

For Greeley, we become aware of ourselves, know ourselves, first through a "preconscious, creative intuition" or "poetic imagination" or an "agent intellect—the 'active' intellect that rushes out and grabs images."[29] He describes it as "the scanner that collects images from the outside world and juxtaposes them with images in our memories so as to provide raw material for reflection and abstraction."[30] It is a "metaphor maker."[31] What is a metaphor? For Wayne Koestenbaum, it is "the urge to compare unlike things, to yoke incommensurables together, the desire to be wrong, wrong-tongued; the craving to avoid literality and law."[32] It moves beyond a slavish adherence to reason as the ultimate bonding agent, and, from our perspective, yokes the body, the heart, the mind, and the soul one to another. Human knowledge is first total and integrated, and only second divided, and only third reduced to reason.

That theological perspective is not original to Greeley. I first became aware of it studying sacraments and Mariology in the early seventies, reading Otto Semmelroth's *Mary, Archetype of the Church.*[33] For Semmelroth, and for the literature of early Christianity, Mary is not a "figure venerated through the practice of a devotion," but rather "an object of theological speculation."[34] He describes the assumptions of his theological method:

> *First, it can mean the personification or representation of a spiritual entity through some sort of image. Second, it can mean a real bond between one entity and another as the objective foundation of this relationship. And finally, it can be a moral example as a result of this relationship.*[35]

On this basis, Semmelroth describes Mary as the archetype of the Church representing "the united multiplicity of the church" such that "every kind of existence is in effect

28. Andrew Greeley, "The Catholic Imagination of Bruce Springsteen," *America,* February 6, 1988, 110ff.
29. Greeley, 111.
30. Greeley, 111.
31. Greeley, 111.
32. Wayne Koestenbaum, "Obscenity: A Celebration," *New York Times Magazine,* May 21, 1995, 46.
33. Otto Semmelroth, *Mary, Archetype of the Church* (New York: Sheed and Ward, 1963).
34. Semmelroth, 7–8.
35. Semmelroth, 28.

an appeal to the moral behavior of the human being coming in contact with it."[36] Semmelroth is proposing a theological and scriptural image for ecclesial identity which assumes an emphasis not only on the personal, but on the personal as total and integrated. It is also an image which ties morality and ethics to that total integration of the personal, and which implies an organizational structure which has both affectional and rational components, encouraging unity rather than division, commonality rather than distinction, and togetherness rather than separation. From a theological perspective, Greeley and Semmelroth are proposing a metaphorical basis which has the same assumptions as Likert's *participative-group* organizational structure wherein trust—as defined in terms of faith and confidence—becomes more than rational assent to authority, but a primary virtue of the organization and its members.

Likert's *participative-group* organizational structure, as we'll see, is an alternative to the traditional authoritative, hierarchical structure. The participative organizational structure enlists an ethical emphasis on relationships and cooperation rather than on authority and obedience. Lines of authority for setting goals and objectives, for dictating operations and procedures, are blurred almost to the point of obliteration. Communication and decision-making move from top to bottom, from bottom to top, sideways, and every which way.[37] Right and wrong are grounded in cooperation arising from interpersonal relationships and interactions.[38] The primary value is cooperation grounded in what Likert calls "ego motives."[39]

Likert's preference for this second organizational structure is based on measured increases in the quantity and quality of productivity, as well as in high rates of job satisfaction and personal happiness.[40] Why? Conflict and tension are diffused as caste distinctions between leaders and followers, authority and obedience are no longer valued.[41] The distrust and hostility implicit within the authoritative organization no longer exist because the authority-obedience nexus which contextualizes that response is replaced by a cooperative-relational nexus which diffuses distinctions and divisions. Rather, there exists "extensive, friendly interaction with a high degree of confidence and trust."[42] Conflicts which do emerge are resolved within cooperative, interpersonal processes rather than in appeal to the rationally mandated legalisms of authority and obedience. And, as the authoritative organizational structure cannot tolerate disobedience, the participative organizational structure cannot tolerate hostility and distrust.

This second of Likert's organizational structures not only represents a change from an authority-obedience ethic to one of relational cooperation. It also implies a change of

---

36. Semmelroth, 32.

37. Likert, 225.

38. Likert, 225. There exist "favorable, cooperative attitudes throughout the organization with mutual trust and confidence."

39. Likert, 225. The primary motivational forces of the "authoritative organization" are physical and economic security coupled with a desire for status. In the "participative," these are economic, as well as those "ego" motives tied to group process relationships.

40. Likert, 233. Productivity moves from "mediocre" to "excellent."

41. Likert, 233. The "informal and formal organization are one and the same; hence all social forces support efforts to achieve the organization's goals."

42. Likert, 228.

emphasis from the isolated, detached individual to the social, relational group. More than simply an emphasis on the interaction of persons within the group, it concentrates on the organization itself and its ethics, even apart from the values of individual members of the group. Moreover, it incorporates a fuller appreciation of the person as not only relational, but as affectively cooperative. In other words, it considers the person's, as well as the group's, affective dimension to be significant for an appreciation of the dignity of the person.

In participative organizations, decisions are made by all of the members, and that decision-making role designates every member of the organization as both leader and owner. The participative organization, then, gives new meaning to a virtue like trust. No longer subjugated to the demands of rational compliance, trust becomes not only a rational virtue, but an affective one as well. It becomes a virtue of the total integrated person, given a physical, spiritual, emotional dimension as well as a rational dimension. It also becomes a virtue of group relationships rather than of individual compliance. We could even say that it anchors or grounds relational cooperation, and becomes absolutely necessary for organizational integrity.

Trust, especially as appreciated with respect to faith and confidence in oneself, others, and (perhaps) even God, becomes an attribute of the total, integrated person. It also becomes the primary virtue of the total, integrated organization. It also becomes the basis for decision making, now a prerogative of every member of the organization rather than of a managing elite. It also redefines leadership as facilitating decision making and the trust required of cooperative relationships.

A RELIGIOUS APPROACH TO BUSINESS ETHICS

PAUL F. CAMENISCH

In discussing the life of his father, a small businessman, Camenisch illustrates what Protestant teachings might look like as applied to life experiences and challenges the suggestion that such religious teachings are impossible to take seriously (or have no role) in contemporary business.

Religious faith and practice make their most fundamental contribution to business ethics by asking what the role and significance of economic activity are and ought to be in the lives of persons and communities, and then offering guidance on how to shape one's life accordingly. Presbyterian Christianity shares the widespread conviction that economic activity must be in the service of the total lives of persons and communities, or better still, of persons in community. Persons and communities are not to be understood primarily as being in the service of economics, whether as consumers, workers, managers, or investors. Few people explicitly deny this. But in the contemporary United States, or perhaps in "western" style consumer societies generally, the shape of our lives increasingly suggests that to assert the subordinate role of economics is not to belabor the obvious.

Theologian Paul Tillich armed mainline Protestants with a guiding principle in such matters: "The Protestant principle, in name derived from the protest of the 'protestants' against decisions of the Catholic majority, contains the divine and human protest against any absolute claim made for a relative reality."

The most fundamental assumption of this essay is that a Presbyterian Christian perspective on business and economic activity—or perhaps simply a truly humane perspective on them—can ground a life of resistance to the largely implicit, but still very influential "absolute claims" often made for the relative reality of contemporary business and/or of economic activity as such.

Such a life involves several strands which John Calvin brought together in his foundational *Institutes of the Christian Religion:*

> *But Scripture . . . reminds us, that whatever we obtain from the Lord is granted on the condition of our employing it for the common good of the Church, and that, therefore, the legitimate use of all our gifts is a kind and liberal communication of them with others. . . . [W]e are taught that all the endowments which we possess*

Paul Camenisch, "A Presbyterian Approach to Business Ethics," Reprinted by permission of the author.

*are divine deposits entrusted to us for the very purpose of being distributed for the
good of our neighbour. . . . [I]n regard to everything which God has bestowed
upon us, and by which we can aid our neighbour, we are his stewards, and are
bound to give account of our stewardship.*

Calvin also speaks to how we understand our role in this world, including our economic
role:

*[T]he Lord enjoins every one of us, in all the actions of life, to have respect to our
own calling. . . . Every man's mode of life . . . is a kind of station assigned him by
the Lord, that he may not be always driven about at random. . . . [I]n following
your proper calling, no work will be so mean and sordid as not to have a splendour
and value in the eye of God.*

Often in matters of ethics, however, the lived text speaks more persuasively than
does the written one. For me the life of my deceased father illustrates with great clarity
the multiple implications of seeing economic activity as a subordinate or relative matter.
This is also one helpful way to present the way religious faith and moral seriousness most
often shape the lives of ordinary people who lack opportunity for, and/or interest in, abstract approaches to religion or morality. For them, religion and morality have less to do
with doctrines and moral principles than they do with seeing the world, the self and others in a certain way, and then living accordingly.

I saw in Dad not only an approach to business—more accurately an approach to life,
which, for him, happened to include business—but a faith lived out, a faith which can be
characterized in several ways moving from the more specific to the more general, as
Presbyterian, Reformed, mainline Protestant, or Christian. In that combination of faith
and business we can see how, in at least one time and place, religious belief and practice
could not only be joined but could help shape a life in business. I believe an examination
of his life can raise illuminating, even provocative questions about the currently dominant
ways of doing business.

"Business ethics" would have struck Dad as a strange idea. If one ran one's business
as one lived the rest of one's life, why would business ethics ever arise as a separate
issue? Business was simply another arena in which to be the person one already was. The
most basic message I learned from him was that owning and running Swiss Sanitary Milk
Company was only a means to the larger ends of being a responsible member of a
family—as son, brother, husband, father—a church, and a community. I learned that message not from his lips, but from a thousand daily choices and the resulting actions and
patterns that were his life.

For him business was no false god. He was *in* business, but he was not *of* it. It defined neither his world nor him. It was a way to support his family. But beyond that, it
was, in more traditional theological language, a calling—a set of opportunities which became a trust and a responsibility because of the things it made possible for him and for
others he could serve through it. Those good things included offering employment and
fair treatment to the twenty-five to thirty persons who worked there, and the chance to be
a good steward of the resources involved in the business and of the opportunities for himself and others that the business made possible.

BEING IN BUT NOT OF BUSINESS

"One thing I always said about Johnny, he was a good provider." Mother's oldest sister certainly got it right about Dad when she said "provider" and not "businessman." The two were linked, but the former was the key for Dad. He was in business because that was the opportunity that had come along and offered a way to care for his family and to do other worthwhile things.

Dad got an eighth-grade education before it became clear that as the oldest child, he was needed on his immigrant parents' and grandparents' small Kentucky farm if it was to support the three generations dependent on it. After several years of virtually managing the farm, the family's continuing economic struggle, the maturing of younger brothers who could take his place, and a sunstroke that made the open fields inhospitable for him led Dad to take a technical course in Cincinnati and then to seek his fortune in the tire factories of Akron. After a brief stint there, he returned to the small town of Danville, eighteen miles from the home place, married, and went to work for his cousin in the last surviving dairy of the several started by members of that Swiss colony. His growing familiarity with the business and his growing confidence in his own abilities enabled him to seize the opportunity created by a disagreement with his cousin. "Sell me Swiss or run it without me," Dad had said. Thus did the young family man with virtually no capital, become his own boss.

Some time later he took in his younger brother Paul, just out of the Navy, as boarder and worker, and eventually as partner, and settled in to raise a family, to be a faithful member of his church and to be a good citizen of the community.

Given the subsidiary role economic activity played in his life, was Dad really engaged in business? Technically of course it was business of the small, entrepreneurial variety. A modest amount of capital, virtually all of it from the business itself, was dedicated to producing and marketing products that generated enough income for the business to survive from the mid 1930's until the early sixties when Dad died, and for a brief period thereafter. Dad knew about competition and dealt with it. For most of his business life it was only moderate competition from small local firms such like Swiss. In that largely live-and-let-live economy, beating out the competition was not a major part of the game. But eventually he bought out two small competitors after years of peaceful, even cooperative co-existence. He probably could simply have taken over their customers as they fell victim to the growing complexity of the business and to the limits of their own capital. But in that time and place—for Dad at least—one conducted business as honorably as one conducted the rest of one's life. So he paid a modest price for what would probably have come his way anyway.

He planned for growth by purchasing three small houses next to the plant. He later moved one to make room for a larger production facility. He understood about changing markets and product diversity. The move to paper packaging of liquid products was expensive for that size of operation, but he knew he had no choice. He tried jobbing frozen biscuits and orange juice along with the dairy products. In the early fifties he and Paul began making their own frozen novelties.

So Dad was truly in business and he knew the rules by which it worked. But even in high school I began to chafe against Dad's rather gentle approach to business and competition, and his willingness in some transactions to let other kinds of considerations override strictly business concerns. I thought him at least imprudent when I learned that he serviced weekend church carnivals thirty-five and forty miles away at considerably less than his cost, Catholic carnivals which included small-time gambling and the sale of beer. In my mind, whatever the church connection did to justify Dad's generosity was largely canceled by the knowledge that our church would never have sponsored such a function.

I was even more indignant when Meadow Gold, which entered the area in the late fifties, began returning our ice cream cabinets to our warehouse after having switched our customers to their products. "Can't you sue them for messing with your property?" I asked, indignant at the way Dad and Paul were being treated after years' of loyal service to their customers. "Why," responded Dad, "so we can go pick up the cabinets ourselves?"

In Dad's complex world of multiple values, profit maximization did not automatically hold first place. He was free to choose his response to such events and did not pretend that their economic implications dictated the "only possible" response.

CALLING

Any adequate mainline Protestant approach to business must include the idea of a calling. While almost certainly unknown to Dad in its theological sense, calling is still one appropriate window through which to view his life in business.

I doubt Dad ever entertained any idea that God had, in any specific way, called him and Paul to run Swiss Sanitary Milk Company. If it was a call, it came to him through very ordinary choices made in the normal course of events. But clearly he did feel called to use the opportunities the dairy offered in ways consistent with his faith. The dairy was not simply to be a way to pay the family's bills. He was to make of it an opportunity for service to others. He was to transform who he was and where he found himself into a calling, into a way of serving God by serving others.

Of course Dad's ability to turn his business life into a calling was in part a function of the small scale and relative simplicity of the business, as well as of his own location as senior partner in it. While the dairy consumed what many would now consider a disproportionate amount of his time and energy, it still made possible a freedom that few in today's much larger and more complex business organizations will find possible. That freedom enabled him to choose just how he would live out that calling.

STEWARDSHIP WITHIN BUSINESS

A significant part of that calling is reflected in the fact that Dad seemed to see himself as a steward of the opportunities the business offered him and others. Once when the question of selling the dairy came up, Dad noted that a number of the minimally skilled workers he and Paul employed would probably have real difficulty finding and holding jobs elsewhere.

As a serious man—some would even say somber—Dad clearly valued fairness toward his employees over an artificial camaraderie. But he could also be firm, even hard when he thought it was appropriate. One day I stumbled into a heated exchange with a clearly agitated employee. Dad's explanation later was brief and to the point: "He lied to me. I fired him." And when Dad caught his man Friday filling up his own car at the company pump, Dad figured what such filching had probably cost him over several months and presented the man with the choice of paying up through payroll deductions or moving on. That may now sound unacceptably unilateral, even draconian. But Dad was also very concerned, although helpless to provide any remedy, when the same man lost his small, hard-won house in divorce proceedings.

Dad's fairness was sometimes costly. In the days before insurance cushioned us against all the ills of this life, one of his drivers' legs was crushed when his skidding truck met an oncoming Greyhound bus. Dad made room for him in the office until his legs healed, even though Swiss hardly needed another pencil-pusher. When the ten-gallon batch freezer had to be replaced with a much faster and more demanding continuous freezer, there was some question as to whether Frank—the freezer man for as long as I could remember—would be able to keep up with the faster equipment. But there was no question about whether Frank would still have a job.

Dad met a more difficult choice in the elderly tenant couple living on the small farm he bought. After months of struggle with the old man's irreformable ways of farming, Dad sadly concluded that he had to let the man go. But first he made sure the couple would not be destitute by helping them qualify for Social Security, a boon they had never dreamt of. One might have to let people go, but one did not abandon them.

My most ambiguous memory about Dad's loyalty was his rising early several Sunday mornings to get his early morning home delivery man out of jail where he'd landed after what Dad simply called too much Saturday night celebrating. I never knew if Dad got him out for the driver's sake, for Dad's sake, or for the customers' sake. But Dad stuck with him until he turned his life around and became as upright, hard-working, and reliable a citizen as anyone could wish.

Dad also tried to cultivate talent where he saw it. One truck driver, probably the best educated man Dad ever employed, was offered a job in the office, in the hope that he would later pick up some managerial responsibilities. But it turned out that he liked the road and the interaction with customers more. So Dad, somewhat reluctantly, gave him his truck back. Another driver Dad got with one of the small dairies he purchased proved to be quite energetic and self-reliant. Dad soon had him working his small farm along with running his milk route, a combination that pleased them both. When Dad and Paul bought a second small dairy, they gave the driver the territory to develop. He moved his family to the neighboring town and built the business up far beyond what it had ever been, eventually going into business for himself.

Dad knew it took people to run a business. But, it was always clear to him that no one was simply part of the machinery needed to make the dairy work. Dad never read Buber's *I and Thou* nor thought much about the *imago dei* in each of us. But had he done so, he would have found little there that he had not already discovered through instinct or experience.

Nor would he have had much to say about a doctrine of creation, or an eco-theology that had not yet emerged to tell us of our responsibilities for the earth and its resources. But he knew these were good gifts for which we were responsible. He smiled when he recalled the old farmer who tried to prove his knowledge of farming by citing the three farms he'd farmed to death.

For most of the years Dad and Paul ran the dairy, skim milk not incorporated into some other product was run down the drain. There was simply no market for "blue john" before the low-fat craze. But on many days when my older brother or I, or the general handy man would be available at the end of the day, the skim was caught in milk cans and hauled out to the farm Dad and Paul had left behind, to be fed to the pigs their brother Richard still raised there, pigs which helped Rich pay Dad and Paul back for the loan with which he had built the new silo when the old metal plate one had been damaged by the wind.

I do not know how contemporary accounting standards or even the tax code would deal with such transfers of value from the business to the personal or family realm. Dad dealt with it simply by seeing his life and its various realms as a whole. If the good stewardship one was called to practice in all areas of activity could be advanced in one realm with resources drawn from another, why would one hesitate to do it?

BUSINESS AND COMMUNITY

Dad and Paul's way of doing business also had positive impacts outside the business. One of those was the sustaining of a small interdependent community of economic activity where, otherwise, there would have been none. Swiss had twenty-five to thirty milk producers scattered over three or four of Kentucky's small counties. These were not simply cogs in the productive machinery. Dad and Paul knew the producers and their situations personally. One early spring morning passing one of the pasteurizing vats, Dad caught the aroma of green onions. "Better call Holtzclaw and tell him his cows have gotten into that lower pasture again," he said. When Swiss stepped up to Grade A, Dad and Paul made sure the producers could arrange financing for the required upgrading of their milking parlors. They knew that the milk money was important, perhaps even crucial in keeping those modest multipurpose family farms solvent.

When Swiss stopped processing milk after Dad's and Paul's deaths in the early sixties, some of the producers joined a co-op that trucked the milk into Virginia. But the transportation costs proved too great. Now many of their former producers' barns stand empty as they decline toward demolition or are used for storage.

Dad's and Paul's relations with their retailers also went beyond mere business transactions. A couple of years ago I discovered just how deep a loyalty such personal care had fostered among some of their retailers. My search for one of the few surviving Swiss ice cream signs took me to a rural general store and used car lot combination where the only Swiss sign I have found sits back on a shelf to protect its colors from the harsh sun. Three subsequent visits and offers of over a hundred dollars have not moved the septuagenarian owner to sell the sign. But I never leave without hearing again the several stories that still tie him to Dad and Swiss Sanitary even though all the ice cream had been gone for over twenty-five years when we first talked. "I remember the day in '45 when your Dad called me up and said, 'Jack, I've got an ice cream box for you if you can come and get it.'" And he tells me again about the late March blizzard that almost stranded him in his pickup truck hauling his new cabinet home.

Nor did the smallest customer escape his attention. One of the clerks in the retail store offered Dad some business one hot summer day. "You know, you're not making a thing on those one-dip nickel cones. If you dropped them, folks would just have to spend a dime for the double dip." "Well," Dad said, "I remember when I only had a nickel in my pocket. There're still a lot of kids like that out there. So we'll just keep on dipping the nickel cones."

STEWARDSHIP IN THE WIDER COMMUNITY

Dad and Paul's philanthropy was modest in any absolute terms, but in relation to their means and to their lifestyles it was a significant part of who they were. Seen from the outside, their lifestyles might seem to have been shaped by Max Weber's classic discussion of that complex of beliefs and patterns he labeled "the Protestant Ethic," especially the this-worldly asceticism which prompted believers to the simple life, thus freeing up additional monies for investment. While I sensed a connection in Dad's and Mom's minds between a modest lifestyle and their religious beliefs, their general style was probably shaped more by having lived through the Depression, and by the general patterns of small-town, middle-class families of the time.

In any case, their lifestyle was not determined simply by their living to the outer limits of whatever means became available. Their patterns remained unchanged even after the house was paid for and all the children but one had completed college. Dad worked hard and provided for us a comfortable and secure, but by no means extravagant life. And while I have no evidence that he could have earned significantly more money if he had wished, it always seemed to me that our modest life style was as much a question of choice as it was of limited means. Consumption was not the engine that drove his and the family's life. It is surely not irrelevant that over the years Mom and Dad had heard more than a few sermons on Jesus' warning that one cannot serve God and mammon (Matthew 6:24/Luke 16:13).

Paul, who sometimes seemed not quite to share Dad's enthusiasm for the business, said one day after some new difficulty had arisen: "Maybe we should just get out and go back to farming."

"Maybe so. But then we wouldn't have the little bit of money we do now to do the kind of things we want to."

Dad didn't list those things. But Paul and I knew they didn't include a big, fancy house, family vacations, or even a modest boat out on the lake. But they did include participating, financially and otherwise, in the church, in the Gideons, and in the Salvation Army. Before his own children went to college, they included helping needy students at the local college and in later years helping his youngest brother and some of his classmates with their seminary expenses. I have no idea how much money Dad put into such causes, and I doubt he kept very good track of it. In my first year at Yale Divinity School, a Brooklyn minister, a total stranger to me, invited me down for Thanksgiving weekend. I later learned that I owed that enlightening weekend to the fact that Dad had helped my host through college. Dad had no memory of him.

Dad's stewardship went beyond giving his money. Being his own boss permitted him to take occasional days off to help the Synod oversee a farm it had inherited several counties away. He served on the boards of the local Salvation Army and of a Presbyterian orphanage in the Kentucky mountains, and as an elder in the local church for years.

He was also a citizen of the larger community. He was for some years a member of the city council, a post he would probably never have sought had he not been appointed to fill an unexpired term. For several years he was regularly seen sitting with the mayor at one of the small tables in the retail part of the dairy discussing city business.

Of course such stewardship or philanthropy can also be good public relations and good for business. In that small town Dad's various involvements, as a matter of course, would have been known to most others active in the town's life. But given Dad's natural reticence and modesty, I doubt there were any ulterior motives at work in those activities. It took a patient minister several years of coaxing to get him to offer even the simplest prayer at a meeting of the church Session.

THE SELF BEHIND THE ACTION

There is no foolproof way to get at the person at the center of the acts and patterns we observe. But sharing in that person's life for twenty-four years is a good start. Dad worked hard all his life. He got tired, frustrated, and sometimes impatient. But through it all—arriving at the plant at 6:30 A.M. seven days a week until the later years, the nightly checking of the refrigeration equipment before bedtime, and only two short weekend vacations during his entire adult life—I never heard him complain about having to work so hard for a living. Instead, he seemed grateful, grateful that with only an eighth-grade education and a brief technical course he had been able to do as well as he had, to support his family, send his older three children to college, and provide for Mom's and his youngest son's future security, to contribute to the community and the church, to help causes and individuals who needed help and to have even a seventy-acre farm—scrub land though it was—as his only personal diversion. I doubt Dad thought God had singled him out for such blessings. But I am confident that one of the objects of his gratitude was the God who, in ways Dad probably never worried much about, presided over a world in which such lives as he was living were possible. While the idea of gratitude may seem remote from business conduct, I believe that such appreciation for what one has may be the best antidote to the seemingly insatiable desire for more that plagues so many of us today, and to our resentment at what we have to do to earn that more.

The last time I saw Dad alive I was again leaving for school out of state. "Don't be surprised if Swiss isn't here when you come back," he said. He was much calmer in saying it than I was in hearing it. It was an eminently sensible thing to say. Swiss's production volume, its product mix, its way of doing business were clearly not competitive with the larger metropolitan dairies that were beginning to show an interest in the territory. But without the dairy what would be left of . . . of what? Of Dad? Gradually it dawned on me. The man knew who he was. However much energy and time and worry he had put into the dairy, that was not who he was. And he was perfectly willing, as I was not, to let that part of him slip away, because all the important facets of who he was would still be there—husband and father, brother and grandfather, citizen and churchman, and a farmboy who still liked to go down to the local Monday morning stock auction and buy a bushel of peaches or tomatoes from some farmer's flatbed truck, or to walk the fields of his modest farm in the evening to see how the corn and sheep were doing. With an untutored wisdom wiser than all my years of schooling, he knew that the dairy had been only a means, and that when the time came, he was ready to move on.

CAN THIS PAST INFORM THE PRESENT?

How much can this quaint picture of small-town small business in the fifties and sixties teach us about the possibility of linking religious faith and business today? Clearly business for most of us will not be today what it was then. Few will have the sort of autonomy Dad had in dealing with his own time and the resources of the company. Changes in the nature and setting of business mean that any guidance we derive from such examples will be less about specific conduct than about the more encompassing issues of how we see the world and the self. But messages of this scope may be obscured when we break a life down into its constituent parts. As I search for the key to what we can learn from lives such as Dad's and Paul's, I am driven back to the Reformed tradition and to what many see as the key to Calvin's theology, to what in some respects is simply Tillich's Protestant Principle in another language—the sovereignty of God.

> *After learning that there is a Creator, [faith] must forthwith infer that he is also a Governor and Preserver, and that, not by producing a kind of general motion in the machine of the globe as well as in each of its parts, but by a special Providence sustaining, cherishing, superintending, all the things which he has made.*

Some will always hear in such a statement the threat of an omnipresent, omniscient judge. But others will hear there the comforting message that all of the world and all of their activities in it form a coherent, meaningful whole, that there is an integrity, a continuity in the world that means that we do not have to transfer our loyalties from one sovereign to another as we move from realm to realm. There is one providential God who is the source and sustainer and yes, ultimately, the judge of all that is.

The Protestant Principle cautions us to keep all relative realities in their places. Calvin's doctrine of divine sovereignty tells us why we must do that. In the world of the one sovereign God there are no "autonomous spheres" permitted to operate on their own distinctive rules which excuse them from the moral imperatives operative in other spheres. This means that business is part of God's one world, part of God's one plan for prospering God's people, for building and sustaining community on the earth. This understanding of God's sovereignty simply disqualifies the idea that business can play by different rules, or that *we* can play by different rules in business.

This integrity or wholeness which characterizes the world under God's sovereignty means that all our various activities can—indeed, that they should—reflect that same integrity, wholeness, and connectedness. Life for Dad and Paul as family members and citizens, as business persons and Christians, and simply as human beings was of a piece. The perceiving of obligations and duties, the movement of benefits, and the extending of a helping hand across what would for others have been sovereign borders between business, civic, family, and personal domains, was easy and natural. There was an integrity, a wholeness, a consistency to their lives that today's compartmentalization makes very difficult for most of us. They had not yet learned from a fragmented culture to build impermeable walls between different spheres of conduct. It is perhaps not our fault today if we cannot avoid such fragmentation, but it is our fault if we too readily consent to it, reinforce it and, when convenient, hide behind it.

Of course this portrait of Reformed Christian life may not offer any insights into or guidance for contemporary business, for there is no guarantee that values derived from a Christian outlook on the world will finally be compatible with contemporary institutions and practices such as business. The Gospel rightly understood may put one in tension, even in conflict with any such practice or with the dominant culture as a whole. I do not think that is the case here, but it should not be dismissed out of hand. If currently there is no way to succeed or even to survive in business without consenting to being a business person first, and everything else only thereafter, then the sort of life Dad and Paul led is no longer possible. In that case, we learn from such examples not how to run our business lives today, but how much we all must sacrifice for whatever benefits the current way of doing business yields.

In Dad's and Paul's lives we can see how, for some persons, business, personal life, community, and the entirety of their lives once fit together, and did so in ways consistent with a Protestant understanding of the role and significance of economic activity in the lives of persons and of communities. That fit was perhaps as much the result of the simpler times and structures within which they lived as it was of the decisions and virtues of the individuals involved. However, we should not entirely discredit the latter, lest we provide ourselves with too easy an excuse for consenting to the hegemony currently so often claimed for economic activity, for reinforcing the compartmentalizations of world and self we have learned to live with, and for too facilely rejecting alternative visions of ourselves and our economic activity as being impossibly unrealistic.

BIBLIOGRAPHY

Buber, Martin (1958). *I and Thou*. New York: Scribners.
Calvin, J. (1962). *Institutes of the Christian Religion*. Grand Rapids, MI: Wm. B. Eerdmans Publishing Company. (Originally published in 1536)
Jackall, Robert. (1988), *Moral Mazes: The World of Corporate Managers*. New York: Oxford University Press.
Reich, Robert. (1992). *The Work of Nations*. New York: Vintage Books.
Tillich, P. (1957). *The Protestant Era*. Chicago: University of Chicago Press.
Weber, M. (1958). *The Protestant Ethic and the Spirit of Capitalism*. New York: Charles Scribner's Sons.

THE CONSTITUTION AND SERVICEMASTER'S FIRST COMPANY OBJECTIVE

THE SERVICEMASTER COMPANY

The ServiceMaster Company was founded in 1929 as a moth-proofing company by Marion Wade, a former minor league baseball player. Now it is one of America's largest service companies, serving more than 6 million customers through companies such as Trugreen Chemlawn, Terminix, Merry Maids, and American Home Shield. ServiceMaster's objectives include four areas of focus: "To honor God in all we do, to help people develop, to pursue excellence, and to grow profitably." The first objective has an impact on every aspect of the firm's business. "We believe that every person—regardless of personal beliefs or differences—has been created in the image and likeness of God. We seek to recognize the dignity, worth and potential of each individual and believe that everyone from service worker to company president has intrinsic worth and value."

Integrating God into the workplace, however, has the potential to conflict with a person's First Amendment right to the free exercise of religion. ServiceMaster addresses this concern in the following material.

INTRODUCTION

The ServiceMaster Enterprise exists, first and foremost, for the purpose of our four Company objectives. The philosophy of our Company demands that we have absolute standards for determining what is right and good in the way we treat our employees, our customers, and our vendors. We believe strongly that our objectives and standards do not waver or change depending on the exigencies of a particular issue or the day to day pressure to meet customer expectations and to reach short term financial goals. Rather, our business depends on seeing the truth through the distractions of an aggressive service business. We are deeply committed to the vision of ServiceMaster and the fact that our business is in reality "training and developing people" to make them the best that they can be.

We are not afraid to state our first Company objective in terms of "God." We believe strongly in the right of companies and individuals to express their religious beliefs freely as mandated by our Constitution. The following represents ServiceMaster's analysis of the interplay between our first Company objective and the Constitution.

Pursuant to the Constitution, all individuals, as well as companies, have a right to religious freedom. This principle is encompassed in our vision of our first Company objective.

TO HONOR GOD IN ALL WE DO

What It Means

It means that employees, partners, and representatives must conduct themselves in the marketplace according to the highest moral and ethical standards. It also means that employees, partners, and representatives must treat fellow employees, customers, and vendors, really anyone we deal with, with respect and dignity. There are absolutes, right and wrong, and we commit ourselves to doing business the "right" way.

What It Does Not Mean

It does not mean that employees, partners, and representatives have to believe in God or any particular God. It does not mean that anyone is forced to choose between their religion and their job. It is the outward manifestation of the objective in terms of conduct and treatment of others that cannot be compromised, not the personal beliefs of any particular employee.

Why We Articulate It in Terms of God

Our founders believed, and our current leadership continue to believe, that a "reference point" of God that is unwavering is the best way to set the course for our business. Contrary to current societal trends we do not believe it is necessary to secularize everything. Indeed, we strongly believe in the provisions of the constitution that grant us all religious freedom. In fact, in stating our first Company objective as we do we recognize, respect, and promote everyone's right to religious freedom.

THE GOOD SAMARITAN
LUKE

The Bible offers us parables in order to teach lessons. The following story is related by Jesus in the Gospel according to Luke. Many people do not even know that the "good samaritan" has its origins in the Bible. Instead, they look at a good samaritan as someone who, for better or worse, helps another out of civic compassion. Do you know people who act like this? Would the world be a better place if everyone acted as the good samaritan? Why doesn't everyone (or every organization) act like the good samaritan? What is there to lose?

30 Jesus replied: "There was a man going down from Jerusalem to Jericho who fell prey to robbers. They stripped him, beat him, and then went off leaving him half-dead. 31 A priest happened to be going down the same road; he saw him but continued on. 32 Likewise there was a Levite who came the same way; he saw him and went on. 33 But a Samaritan who was journeying along came on him and was moved to pity at the sight. 34 He approached him and dressed his wounds, pouring in oil and wine. He then hoisted him on his own beast and brought him to an inn, where he cared for him. 35 The next day he took out two silver pieces and gave them to the innkeeper with the request: 'Look after him, and if there is any further expense I will repay you on my way back.'

36 "Which of these three, in your opinion, was neighbor to the man who fell in with the robbers?" 37 The answer came, "The one who treated him with compassion." Jesus said to him, "Then go and do the same."

The Good Samaritan, Luke 10: 30–37. The Bible

Chapter 6

ETHICS AND CORPORATE SOCIAL RESPONSIBILITY
One and the Same?

Business has to take account of its responsibilities to society in coming to its decision, but society has to accept its responsibilities for setting the standards against which those decisions are made.

SIR ADRIAN CADBURY[1]

---

1. "Ethical Managers Make Their Own Rules," *Harvard Business Review,* September/October 1987.

*By "social responsibility," we mean the intelligent and objective con-
cern for the welfare of society that restrains individual and corporate
behavior from ultimately destructive activities, no matter how immediately profitable, and leads in the direction of positive contributions
to human betterment, variously as the latter may be defined.*   KENNETH R. ANDREWS[2]

*"Look at a well-run company and you will see the needs of its stock-
holders, its employees, and the community at large being served   —ARNOLD HIATT, FORMER
simultaneously."*   CEO, STRIDE RITE CORP.

*Fill your bowl to the brim
and it will spill.
Keep sharpening your knife
and it will be blunt.
Chase after money and security
and your heart will never unclench.
Care about people's approval
and you will be their prisoner.
Do your work, then step back.
The only path to serenity.*   LAO TZU, *TAO TE CHING*

Is there a social responsibility of business? This question has been asked numerous times
in a variety of ways, with just as many answers. Central to this question is perhaps the
underlying determination of what responsibility business has at all. Do you ask yourself
whether your friends, colleagues, parents, or others have a social responsibility? Probably, at some point. You might see your colleague drop some trash on the floor and walk
on. You may feel that this person should stop and pick it up instead of continuing. Your
belief about the responsibility of business may be no more than this—a firm should clean
up after itself, so to speak. On the other hand, there are some theorists who believe that
firms owe something back to the society that supports it, and that this debt is greater than
the debt of the individual members of society.

The article by Milton Friedman in this section is perhaps the best known argument
for a purely *profit-based* social responsibility of business (though Adam Smith was probably among the first to articulate this concept). Friedman is not ignoring ethical responsibility in his analysis; he is merely suggesting that decision makers are acting ethically if
they follow their firm's self-interest. Primeaux expands on Friedman's analysis in order to
find a corporate social responsibility within a profit-maximizing framework. Consider the
qualities of a successful firm—it meets the needs of its market. If the market demands socially responsible behavior, a firm may only be successful by demonstrating this behavior.
On the other hand, if the market places no value at all on socially responsible behavior, it
is unlikely that a firm would be encouraged by profit to exhibit this behavior. Professor
James Wilson explains that, "while free markets will ruthlessly eliminate inefficient firms,

---

2. *The Concept of Corporate Strategy* (Burr Ridge, IL: Richard D. Irwin, 1971) p. 120.

the moral sentiments of man will only gradually and uncertainly penalize immoral ones. But, while the quick destruction of inefficient corporations threatens only individual firms, the slow anger at immoral ones threatens capitalism, and thus freedom itself."[3]

The general public seems to disagree with Friedman's underlying presumption. A *BusinessWeek*/Harris poll of over one thousand Americans found that 95 percent reject the notion that a corporation's role is limited to profit maximization.[4] Further, there may be other arguments for a socially responsible firm. Employees who are well treated in their work environments may prove more loyal, more effective, and productive in their work. Liz Bankowshi, director of social missions at Ben & Jerry's Homemade Ice Cream Company, claims that 80 to 90 percent of their employees work at Ben & Jerry's because "they feel they are part of a greater good.[5] The impact on the bottom line, therefore, stems not only from customer preference but also from employee preference. The problem with a focus on preference, however, is that social responsibility becomes merely social marketing. That is, a firm may use the image of social responsibility to garner customer support or employee loyalty while the facts do not evidence a true commitment. Are motivations relevant? Paul Hawken, co-founder of Smith & Hawken gardening stores and an advocate of business social responsibility, reminds us that

> you see tobacco companies subsidizing the arts, then later you find out that there are internal memos showing that they wanted to specifically target the minorities in the arts because they want to get minorities to smoke. That's not socially responsible. It's using social perception as a way to aggrandize or further one's own interests exclusively.[6]

On the other hand, if the market does not encourage responsibility for social causes, should a firm engage in this behavior? And, indeed, is this responsibility only that of firms, or are we responsible for supporting firms that fail to exhibit socially responsible behavior? If we stand by and allow irresponsible actions to take place using profits garnered by our purchases, do we bear any responsibility? Consider this dilemma as you read George Orwell's "A Hanging."

Disagreements exist even among scholars who advocate social responsibility. For instance, to whom does the firm owe this responsibility? To the employees? The community? The consumers? All stakeholders? As we have seen in previous sections, it may be impossible to satisfy the needs of every stakeholder in a situation. Therefore, what is the prioritization of this social responsibility? Consider the case of the spotted owl and the loggers in the Pacific Northwest, discussed later in connection with ethics and the environment. Logging poses a danger of extinction to the spotted owl, but discontinuing logging activities poses a hardship on the logging communities and those connected with them. Animal rights activists consider the interests of society in preserving the spotted owl to be predominant, while others consider the interests of the loggers and their communities to be predominant. Whether you are persuaded because this is a conflict

---

3. James Wilson quoted by Elmer W. Johnson, "Corporate Soulcraft in The Age of Brutal Markets," the Hansen-Wessner Memorial Lecture, Northwestern University, May 2, 1996.

4. *Business Ethics,* November/December 1996, p. 6.

5. Joel Makower, *Beyond The Bottom Line* (New York: Simon & Schuster 1994), p. 68.

6. Ibid, p. 15.

between humans and animals or because a species might be endangered, the answer is found only in your personal prioritization scheme.

Finally, what is the nature of this responsibility? In a case study in this section involving British Petroleum and TONASCO, you are asked to consider a firm's responsibility to a community where operations are discontinued. Is profit for the firm the only guiding principle, or should the impact of its decision on others be considered, even where the law allows the decision? Perhaps the answer lies somewhere in the middle of all of these arguments. Philosopher Ayn Rand contends that our only social responsibility is to ourselves, but that this concern does not act as a barrier to helping others:

> *The moral purpose of one's life is the achievement of happiness. This does not mean that he is indifferent to all men, that human life is of no value to him, and that he has no reason to help others in an emergency—but it does mean that he does not subordinate his life to the welfare of others, that he does not sacrifice himself to their needs, that the relief of their suffering is not his primary concern, that any help he gives is an act of generosity, not of moral duty.[7]*

In the end, does good ethics mean good business? Does corporate social responsibility translate into fiscal responsibility? A landmark study by Stephen Erfle and Michael Frantantuono found that firms that ranked highest on a variety of social issues (including charitable contributions, community outreach programs, environmental performance, advancement of women, and promotion of minorities) had greater financial performance as well. Financial performance was better in terms of operating income growth, sales-to-assets ratio, sales growth, return on equity, earnings-to-asset growth, return on investment, return on assets, and asset growth.[8]

Previous studies had found both supporting and conflicting results (though supporting seems to outweigh conflicting). Professor Ullman summarizes the results of previous empirical studies on the relationship between social and financial performance as follows:

- Seven showed a positive relationship between social and financial performance.

- Three showed a negative relationship between social and financial performance.

- One showed a positive relationship between the promotion of women and financial performance and a negative relationship between charitable contributions and financial performance.

- One showed a U-shaped relationship, meaning that extreme social performance (good or bad) was negatively related to financial performance.

- Two found no effect.[9]

The jury therefore remains out on a concrete linkage between social performance and financial performance.

---

7. Ayn Rand, *The Virtue of Selfishness*, p. 49.
8. Joel Makower, *Beyond The Bottom Line* (New York: Simon & Schuster 1994), pp. 70–71.
9. A. Ullman, "Data in Search of a Theory: A Critical Examination of the Relationships among Social Performance, Social Disclosure and Economic Performance of U.S. Firms," *Academy of Management Review,* July 1985, pp. 545–57.

THE SOCIAL RESPONSIBILITY OF BUSINESS IS TO INCREASE ITS PROFITS

Milton Friedman

In perhaps the seminal article in the challenge to corporate social responsibility, Nobel Prize–winning economist Milton Friedman articulates his objections to the presumption that business owes something extra to our social environment. Consider the recent influx of "socially conscious" firms (or at least those that appear socially conscious) in the marketplace: Ben & Jerry's, The Body Shop, Working Assets Long Distance, and others. Is this the direction of the future? **Should** *this be the direction of the future?*

When I hear businessmen speak eloquently about the "social responsibilities of business in a free-enterprise system," I am reminded of the wonderful line about the Frenchman who discovered at the age of 70 that he had been speaking prose all his life. The businessmen believe that they are defending free enterprise when they declaim that business is not concerned "merely" with profit but also with promoting desirable "social" ends; that business has a "social conscience" and takes seriously its responsibilities for providing employment, eliminating discrimination, avoiding pollution and whatever else may be the catchwords of the contemporary crop of reformers. In fact they are—or would be if they or anyone else took them seriously—preaching pure and unadulterated socialism. Businessmen who talk this way are unwitting puppets of the intellectual forces that have been undermining the basis of a free society these past decades.

The discussions of the "social responsibilities of business" are notable for their analytical looseness and lack of rigor. What does it mean to say that "business" has responsibilities? Only people can have responsibilities. A corporation is an artificial person and in this sense may have artificial responsibilities, but "business" as a whole cannot be said to have responsibilities, even in this vague sense. The first step toward clarity in examining the doctrine of the social responsibility of business is to ask precisely what it implies for whom.

Presumably, the individuals who are to be responsible are businessmen, which means individual proprietors or corporate executives. Most of the discussion of social responsibility is directed at corporations, so in what follows I shall mostly neglect the individual proprietors and speak of corporate executives.

Milton Friedman, "The Social Responsibility of Business Is to Increase Its Profits," Reprinted by permission of *The New York Times*.

In a free-enterprise, private-property system, a corporate executive is an employee of the owners of the business. He has direct responsibility to his employers. That responsibility is to conduct the business in accordance with their desires, which generally will be to make as much money as possible while conforming to the basic rules of the society, both those embodied in law and those embodied in ethical custom. Of course, in some cases his employers may have a different objective. A group of persons might establish a corporation for an eleemosynary purpose—for example, a hospital or a school. The manager of such a corporation will not have money profit as his objectives but the rendering of certain services.

In either case, the key point is that, in his capacity as a corporate executive, the manager is the agent of the individuals who own the corporation or establish the eleemosynary institution, and his primary responsibility is to them.

Needless to say, this does not mean that it is easy to judge how well he is performing his task. But at least the criterion of performance is straightforward, and the persons among whom a voluntary contractual arrangement exists are clearly defined.

Of course, the corporate executive is also a person in his own right. As a person, he may have many other responsibilities that he recognizes or assumes voluntarily—to his family, his conscience, his feelings of charity, his church, his clubs, his city, his country. He may feel impelled by these responsibilities to devote part of his income to causes he regards as worthy, to refuse to work for particular corporations, even to leave his job, for example, to join his country's armed forces. If we wish, we may refer to some of these responsibilities as "social responsibilities." But in these respects he is acting as a principal, not as an agent; he is spending his own money or time or energy, not the money of his employers or the time or energy he has contracted to devote to their purposes. If these are "social responsibilities," they are the social responsibilities of individuals, not of business.

What does it mean to say that the corporate executive has a "social responsibility" in his capacity as businessman? If this statement is not pure rhetoric, it must mean that he is to act in some way that is not in the interest of his employers. For example, that he is to refrain from increasing the price of the product in order to contribute to the social objective of preventing inflation, even though a price increase would be in the best interests of the corporation. Or that he is to make expenditures on reducing pollution beyond the amount that is in the best interests of the corporation or that is required by law in order to contribute to the social objective of improving the environment. Or that, at the expense of corporate profits, he is to hire "hard-core" unemployed instead of better qualified available workmen to contribute to the social objective of reducing poverty.

In each of these cases, the corporate executive would be spending someone else's money for a general social interest. Insofar as his actions in accord with his "social responsibility" reduce returns to stockholders, he is spending their money. Insofar as his actions raise the price to customers, he is spending the customers' money. Insofar as his actions lower the wages of some employees, he is spending their money.

The stockholders or the customers or the employees could separately spend their own money on the particular action if they wished to do so. The executive is exercising a distinct "social responsibility," rather than serving as an agent of the stockholders or the customers or the employees, only if he spends the money in a different way than they would have spent it.

But if he does this, he is in effect imposing taxes, on the one hand, and deciding how the tax proceeds shall be spent, on the other.

This process raises political questions on two levels: principle and consequences. On the level of political principle, the imposition of taxes and the expenditure of tax proceeds are governmental functions. We have established elaborate constitutional, parliamentary, and judicial provisions to control these functions, to assure that taxes are imposed so far as possible in accordance with the preferences and desires of the public—after all, "taxation without representation" was one of the battle cries of the American Revolution. We have a system of checks and balances to separate the legislative function of imposing taxes and enacting expenditures from the executive function of collecting taxes and administering expenditure programs and from the judicial function of mediating disputes and interpreting the law.

Here the businessmen—self-selected or appointed directly or indirectly by stockholders—is to be simultaneously legislator, executive, and jurist. He is to decide whom to tax by how much and for what purpose, and he is to spend the proceeds—all this guided only by general exhortations from on high to restrain inflation, improve the environment, fight poverty, and so on and on.

The whole justification for permitting the corporate executive to be selected by the stockholders is that the executive is an agent serving the interests of his principal. This justification disappears when the corporate executive imposes taxes and spends the proceeds for "social" purposes. He becomes in effect a public employee, a civil servant, even though he remains in name an employee of a private enterprise. On grounds of political principle, it is intolerable that such civil servants—insofar as their actions in the name of social responsibility are real and not just window-dressing—should be selected as they are now. If they are to be civil servants, then they must be elected through a political process. If they are to impose taxes and make expenditures to foster "social" objectives, then political machinery must be set up to make the assessment of taxes and to determine through a political process the objectives to be served.

This is the basic reason why the doctrine of "social responsibility" involves the acceptance of the socialist view that political mechanisms, not market mechanisms, are the appropriate way to determine the allocation of scarce resources to alternative uses.

On the grounds of consequences, can the corporate executive in fact discharge his alleged "social responsibilities"? On the other hand, suppose he could get away with spending the stockholders' or customers' or employees' money. How is he to know how to spend it? He is told that he must contribute to fighting inflation. How is he to know what action of his will contribute to that end? He is presumably an expert in running his company—in producing a product or selling it or financing it. But nothing about his selection makes him an expert on inflation. Will his holding down the price of his product reduce inflationary pressure? Or, by leaving more spending power in the hands of his customers, simply divert it elsewhere? Or, by forcing him to produce less because of the lower price, will it simply contribute to shortages? Even if he could answer these questions, how much cost is he justified in imposing on his stockholders, customers and employees for this social purpose? What is his appropriate share and what is the appropriate share of others?

And, whether he wants to or not, can he get away with spending his stockholders', customers', or employees' money? Will not the stockholders fire him? (Either the present

ones or those who take over when his actions in the name of social responsibility have reduced the corporation's profits and the price of its stock.) His customers and his employees can desert him for other producers and employers less scrupulous in exercising their
social responsibilities.

This facet of "social responsibility" doctrine is brought into sharp relief when the
doctrine is used to justify wage restraint by trade unions. The conflict of interest is naked
and clear when union officials are asked to subordinate the interest of their members to
some more general purpose. If the union officials try to enforce wage restraint, the consequence is likely to be wildcat strikes, rank-and-file revolts, and the emergence of strong
competitors for their jobs. We thus have the ironic phenomenon that union leaders—at
least in the U.S.—have objected to Government interference with the market far more
consistently and courageously than have business leaders.

The difficulty of exercising "social responsibility" illustrates, of course, the great
virtue of private competitive enterprise—it forces people to be responsible for their own
actions and makes it difficult for them to "exploit" other people for either selfish or un-
selfish purposes. They can do good—but only at their own expense.

Many a reader who has followed the argument this far may be tempted to remon-
strate that it is all well and good to speak of Government's having the responsibility to
impose taxes and determine expenditures for such "social" purposes as controlling pollution or training the hard-core unemployed, but that the problems are too urgent to wait on
the slow course of political processes, that the exercise of social responsibility by businessmen is a quicker and surer way to solve pressing current problems.

Aside from the question of fact—I share Adam Smith's skepticism about the benefits
that can be expected from "those who affected to trade for the public good"—this argument must be rejected on grounds of principle. What it amounts to is an assertion that
those who favor the taxes and expenditures in question have failed to persuade a majority
of their fellow citizens to be of like mind and that they are seeking to attain by undemoc-
ratic procedures what they cannot attain by democratic procedures. In a free society, it is
hard for "evil" people to do "evil," especially since one man's good is another's evil.

I have, for simplicity, concentrated on the special case of the corporate executive, except only for the brief digression on trade unions. But precisely the same argument applies
to the newer phenomenon of calling upon stockholders to require corporations to exercise
social responsibility (the recent G.M. crusade for example). In most of these cases, what is
in effect involved is some stockholders trying to get other stockholders (or customers or
employees) to contribute against their will to "social" causes favored by the activists. Insofar as they succeed, they are again imposing taxes and spending the proceeds.

The situation of the individual proprietor is somewhat different. If he acts to reduce
the returns of his enterprise in order to exercise his "social responsibility," he is spending
his own money, not someone else's. If he wishes to spend his money on such purposes,
that is his right, and I cannot see that there is any objection to his doing so. In the process,
he, too, may impose costs on employees and customers. However, because he is far less
likely than a large corporation or union to have monopolistic power, any such side effects
will tend to be minor.

Of course, in practice the doctrine of social responsibility is frequently a cloak for
actions that are justified on other grounds rather than a reason for those actions.

To illustrate, it may well be in the long-run interest of a corporation that is a major employer in a small community to devote resources to providing amenities to that community or to improving its government. That may make it easier to attract desirable employees, it may reduce the wage bill or lessen losses from pilferage and sabotage or have other worthwhile effects. Or it may be that, given the laws about the deductibility of corporate charitable contributions, the stockholders can contribute more to charities they favor by having the corporation make the gift than by doing it themselves, since they can in that way contribute an amount that would otherwise have been paid as corporate taxes.

In each of these—and many similar—cases, there is a strong temptation to rationalize these actions as an exercise of "social responsibility." In the present climate of opinion, with its widespread aversion to "capitalism," "profits," the "soulless corporation," and so on, this is one way for a corporation to generate goodwill as a by-product of expenditures that are entirely justified in its own self-interest.

It would be inconsistent of me to call on corporate executives to refrain from this hypocritical window-dressing because it harms the foundations of a free society. That would be to call on them to exercise a "social responsibility"! If our institutions, and the attitudes of the public make it in their self-interest to cloak their actions in this way, I cannot summon much indignation to denounce them. At the same time, I can express admiration for those individual proprietors or owners of closely held corporations or stockholders of more broadly held corporations who disdain such tactics as approaching fraud.

Whether blameworthy or not, the use of the cloak of social responsibility, and the nonsense spoken in its name by influential and prestigious businessmen, does clearly harm the foundations of a free society. I have been impressed time and again by the schizophrenic character of many businessmen. They are capable of being extremely far-sighted and clear-headed in matters that are internal to their businesses. They are incredibly short-sighted and muddle-headed in matters that are outside their businesses but affect the possible survival of business in general. This short-sightedness is strikingly exemplified in the calls from many businessmen for wage and price guidelines or controls or income policies. There is nothing that could do more in a brief period to destroy a market system and replace it by a centrally controlled system than effective governmental control of prices and wages.

The short-sightedness is also exemplified in speeches by businessmen or social responsibility. This may gain them kudos in the short run. But it helps to strengthen the already too prevalent view that the pursuit of profits is wicked and immoral and must be curbed and controlled by external forces. Once this view is adopted, the external forces that curb the market will not be the social consciences, however highly developed, of the pontificating executives; it will be the iron fist of government bureaucrats. Here, as with price and wage controls, businessmen seem to me to reveal a suicidal impulse.

The political principle that underlies the market mechanism is unanimity. In an ideal free market resting on private property, no individual can coerce any other, all cooperation is voluntary, all parties to such cooperation benefit or they need not participate. There are no values, no "social" responsibilities in any sense other than the shared values and responsibilities of individuals. Society is a collection of individuals and of the various groups they voluntarily form.

The political principle that underlies the political mechanism is conformity. The individual must serve a more general social interest—whether that be determined by a church or a dictator or a majority. The individual may have a vote and say in what is to be done, but if he is overruled, he must conform. It is appropriate for some to require others to contribute to a general social purpose whether they wish to or not.

Unfortunately, unanimity is not always feasible. There are some respects in which conformity appears unavoidable, so I do not see how one can avoid the use of the political mechanism altogether.

But the doctrine of "social responsibility" taken seriously would extend the scope of the political mechanism to every human activity. It does not differ in philosophy from the most explicitly collectivist doctrine. It differs only by professing to believe that collectivist ends can be attained without collectivist means. That is why, in my book "Capitalism and Freedom," I have called it a "fundamentally subversive doctrine" in a free society, and have said that in such a society, "there is one and only one social responsibility of business—to use its resources and engage in activities designed to increase its profits so long as it stays within the rules of the game, which is to say, engages in open and free competition without deception or fraud."

ARGUMENTS FOR AND AGAINST CORPORATE SOCIAL RESPONSIBILITY

N. Craig Smith

Smith responds to Friedman's contentions in the following excerpt.

There are five principal arguments against corporate social responsibility: the problem of competing claims (the role of profit), competitive disadvantage, competence, fairness, and legitimacy. Each will be considered in turn.

COMPETING CLAIMS—THE ROLE OF PROFIT

Friedman argues that the notion of social responsibility in business 'shows a fundamental misconception of the character and nature of a free economy'. Business's function is economic, not social. Accordingly, it should be guided and judged by economic criteria alone. Action dictated by anything other than profit maximisation, within the rules of the game, impairs economic efficiency and represents a taxation on those bearing the costs of such inefficiency, most notably the stockholders. The role of the corporation is to make a profit and maximise social welfare through the efficiency which that entails, and as Simon *et al.* put it, 'consideration of any factors other than profit-maximising ones either results in a deliberate sacrifice of profits or muddies the process of corporate decision-making so as to impair profitability'. So, to quote Silk and Vogel, 'In short, the corporation will best fulfill its obligation to society by fulfilling its obligation to itself.' However, this argument falls down in a number of ways. Simon *et al.* identify four reasons. First, it emphasises the profits of the individual firm as opposed to the corporate sector, which may not mean the highest efficiency from society's point of view. Second, there is the distinction between the short term and the long term. Social goals may be profitable in the long term, for the reasons . . . of enlightened self-interest. Third, there are other indicators of well-being besides profitability. Because of the uncertainty about what will be profitable, corporate goals in practice place profitability second, seeking an assurance of a required minimum profit. Fourth, and finally, there is the concern for the efficient use of national resources. Because of social costs, profitability is not necessarily the best measure of effectiveness. Indeed, they argue, 'the argument for efficient allocation of resources would appear to require the corporation to locate and regulate the social consequences of its own conduct'.

N. Craig Smith, "Arguments for and Against Corporate Social Responsibility," excerpted from *Morality and The Market* (Routledge: New York: 1990), pp. 69–76.

Furthermore, Simon *et al.* suggest that if these arguments are not accepted, the negative injunction against social injury would, at least, have to be respected. In other words, Friedman ignores the moral minimum: 'most of the debate on corporate responsibility, by rather carelessly focusing on what we have termed affirmative duties . . . has obscured what seems to be the fundamental point: that economic activity . . . can have unwanted and injurious side-effects, and that the correction of these indirect consequences require self-regulation.' (There are some similarities here with Heilbroner's point that pure profit-maximisation could amount to social irresponsibility. . . . Essentially, the main criticism of this argument against corporate social responsibility—the need for profit maximisation—is its basis in an inappropriate economic model, the competitive model of capitalism; particularly because of social costs and the question of who the profits are for. Noting the argument about the separation of ownership and control and the consequent limited influence of shareholders over the conduct of professional managers, Ackerman quotes a statement by the chairman of Xerox which pointedly illustrates the inapplicability of the notion of profit-maximisation for shareholders: 'If we ran this business Wall Street's way, we'd run it into the ground . . . We're in this business for a hell of a long time and we're not going to try to maximise earnings over the short run.'

COMPETITIVE DISADVANTAGE

The competitive disadvantage argument against corporate social responsibility suggests that because social action will have a price for the firm it also entails a competitive disadvantage. So, either such works should be carried out by government or, at least, legislated for so that all corporations or industries will be subject to the same requirements. Mintz and Cohen show that such a consideration was paramount in Alfred Sloan's 1929 decision not to fit safety glass to Chevrolets, 'one of the single most important protections ever devised against avoidable automotive death, disfigurement and injury'. Sloan was concerned about public anxiety over automobile safety and did not wish to publicise hazards. In his correspondence with Lammont du Pont over the possible supply of safety glass he observes that despite General Motors La Salles and Cadillacs being equipped with safety glass, sales by Packard, one of their competitors, had not been materially affected. So Sloan wrote, 'I do not think that from the stockholder's standpoint the move on Cadillac's part has been justified.' Sloan was still reluctant even when he recognized that such a feature would come in the end, he did not want to hurry it along: 'The net result would be that both competition and ourselves would have reduced the return on our capital.' Even when Du Pont noted that Ford had started to fit safety glass in the windshields of all their cars, Sloan observed: 'it is not my responsibility to sell safety glass.'

Green notes that Sloan's rejection of safety glass because it would add slightly to price and because his competitors lacked the 'lifesaving technology' should not be possible today because companies could go to the government to urge minimum standards and thereby avoid placing the firm at a competitive disadvantage. And as Simon *et al.* observe, the competitive disadvantage argument against social responsibility is difficult to accept when the social injury is caused by one firm but not its industry peers—as in Sloan's refusal to fit safety glass even after it was fitted to the windshields of all Ford cars. But if the social injury is not unique to one firm then 'the individual corporation can at least be expected to work for industrywide self-regulation within the limits of anti-trust laws; or the individual firm can work for government regulation'. What this ignores, however, is that many industries are ultimately in competition with other industries and there may then be a competitive disadvantage for the industry as a whole in relation to substitution goods. This issue of inter-industry competition aside, the criticism of the competitive disadvantage argument is essentially sound. In approbation of his position, Friedman quotes Adam Smith's comment: 'I have never known much good done by those who affected to trade for the public good.' While healthy skepticism might be desirable, the oligopolistic form of most markets and increased consumer knowledge and awareness makes such a position inappropriate. There are other reasons besides. Ackerman's observations on the advantages and disadvantages of early corporate response to social demands suggest that an early response, while it may seem unnecessary, does provide flexibility. Perhaps more significant, though, is his recognition that the area of discretion within which managers act is quite broad and as competition is conducted on many fronts there is scope for an early response, particularly when the potential benefits are also considered.

COMPETENCE

Friedman asks, 'If businessmen do have a social responsibility other than making maximum profits for stockholders, how are they to know what it is?' This implies the competence argument against corporate social responsibility. Simon *et al.* identify three ways in which, it may be claimed, a firm is not competent to deal with social issues. First, there is the claim that corporations do not have the technical skills to deal with social issues. This, they suggest, will vary from case to case and, given the notion of last resort in the Kew Gardens Principle . . . can only be valid if some other party can do the job better. Second, there is the claim that corporations do not know what is good for society and some other institution, such as government, knows better. But, they observe, 'a corporation's alleged lack of insight into the nature of the good is not a reason for objecting to its social activities unless they are deliberately coercive'. Third, there is the claim that incompetent attempts to resolve social issues waste shareholders' money. But, suggest Simon *et al.,* this is only true if management needs to be made more accountable to the shareholder. Alternatively, such a claim could be countered by pointing to the separation of ownership and control and the role of the professional manager. These factors notwithstanding, the argument of competence can only be applicable to affirmative actions; there is still, as Simon *et al.* note, the moral minimum of the negative injunction against social injury, for which competence cannot be an issue.

Bradshaw, a practitioner writing in this area (as President of Atlantic Richfield Company), does point out that 'corporations cannot cure all social ills, and, indeed, in many areas should not even try . . . This nation is richly endowed with many and varied institutions. Social change is, I believe, accomplished through these many institutions and not through any one.' He goes on to argue that business people should stick to their competencies, but, bearing in mind his observation that the rules of the game are changing, work 'within those competencies [and] become a prime mover for change at the rule-making level, whether it is in national government, regional areas or states'. Similarly,

Silk and Vogel report the comments of the executives at the Conference Board meetings who contended that if they try to operate outside their special area of competence they will invariably get into trouble: 'We shouldn't accept responsibility for what we don't know about.' Elsewhere, Vogel observes that many social issues do not present much scope for solution by business. Moreover, it is not realistic to expect the business community to assume a leading role in balancing social needs with economic imperatives, because it would be inconsistent with the political views of business: 'The social reforms whose enactment have so dramatically improved the lot of the average American over the last 75 years mostly were adopted in spite of business lobbying, not because of it . . . if business is to perform as well as it can, it requires pressure from those outside it.'

So on the competency argument one must conclude that while there is the moral minimum, social actions beyond this are constrained by what business is able, competent, and willing to do. As Rockefeller notes: 'No one sector of our society is competent to deal with these problems . . . The only answer is that all sections must become involved, each in its own distinctive way, but in full and collaborative relationship with the others.'

FAIRNESS—DOMINATION BY BUSINESS

Friedman asks, 'is it tolerable that these public functions of taxation, expenditure, and control be exercised by the people who happen at the moment to be in charge of particular enterprises, chosen for those posts by strictly private groups?' This is the fairness argument against corporate social responsibility. Heilbroner's concern about corporations playing God has already been noted. In a similar vein, Davis and Blomstrom observe, 'combining social activities with the established economic activities of business would give business an excessive concentration of power . . . [which] would threaten the pluralistic division of powers which we now have among institutions, probably reducing the viability of our free society'. As Levitt notes, 'The corporation would eventually invest itself with all-embracing duties, obligations, and finally powers—ministering to the whole man and molding him and society in the image of the corporation's narrow ambitions and its essentially unsocial needs.' Big business acting in accord with notions of social responsibility gives managers more discretionary power over the lives of others in three ways, as Simon *et al.* observe: by political action (lobbying), the creation of private government (within the organisation), and by a smothering effect—domination by business values.

However, they counter, if business does have this power then the problem is to control it, not think it presents a problem only in the social policy context. One must also consider what is worse: a lack of self-regulation may be more arbitrary in its effects:

> *We grant that even corporate self-regulation may have some spill-over effect—that the attempt to avoid or correct a self-caused social injury may have some influence on the freedom of action of others. Such effects will, we think, be relatively insignificant when compared to the benefits of self-correction.*

Moreover, they ask that even if affirmative modes of corporate social responsibility involve manipulation, should one fault genuine efforts to help? Besides which, the distinction between leadership and manipulation is a fine one. They conclude on this issue: 'we are convinced that the type of corporate self-regulation we have proposed will help to limit the arbitrary and oppressive impact of corporate activity, rather than the opposite, and therefore does not present a fairness problem.'

LEGITIMACY—THE ROLE OF GOVERNMENT

The final principal argument against corporate social responsibility is legitimacy: social issues are the concern of government. Or, as one executive commented at the Conference Board meetings: 'We pay the government well. It should do its job and leave us alone to do ours.' As Silk and Vogel comment, the business person feels 'non business' contributions should be voluntary and government has legitimate social concerns which business supports in the payment of taxes. Simon *et al.* identify three positions in this argument. First, unless business acts then government will act, with all the attendant disadvantages of government intervention cited by critics of government encroachment of private spheres. Moreover, corporate social problem-solving may be preferable because it is pluralistic and is therefore likely to be preferred by the people. This position seeks to minimise the role of government. Second, as Levitt and Friedman suggest, corporate involvement in social problems is likely to be bungled, which in itself will lead to government intervention. This has the disadvantages of both government and business interference in the private sphere: again, a position which can be employed to support business action to minimise government's role. The third position claims that only government can deal with market imperfections. This is because some encroachment is viewed as necessary (the mixed market position) and there needs to be an orderly division of labour. They counter that again these positions against corporate social responsibility reflect only on the affirmative duty and not on the negative injunction against social injury. In any event, there is still a case for self-regulation because the duplication of effort cannot in itself be harmful, federal agencies tend to represent industry interests anyway, and much corporate activity is overseas and outside government jurisdiction.

Simon *et al.* conclude on these five principal arguments against corporate social responsibility:

> *These points do carry weight with respect to some affirmative modes of corporate social action, but we find these objections unpersuasive in application to self-regulating activity. Whatever debate there may be over more expansive notions of corporate responsibility, a self-policing attempt to take into account the social consequences of business activity and at least an attempt to avoid or correct social injury represents a basic obligation.*

The problem of competing claims, competitive disadvantage, competency, fairness, and legitimacy are the principal arguments against corporate social responsibility. Other arguments include: the public being misled about who bears the cost of corporate social action, believing it to be free; the problem of determining benefits, costs, and priorities; the weakened international balance of payments—reduced efficiency raises costs and may put companies at a competitive disadvantage internationally; and the lack of a broad base of support among all groups in society. Also, as Beesley and Evans observe, Friedman's argument must be seen within the context in which it is presented, as 'part of an argument holding that property rights, as for instance manifest in company shareholdings, and, more fundamentally, the right to engage freely in economic activity are necessary (but admittedly not sufficient) conditions for the maintenance of Western-style political freedom' . . . Essentially this argument, the others briefly mentioned, and the principal arguments have been answered and found to be lacking. This is due mainly to their dependence on an inappropriate socioeconomic model of contemporary society, and their failure to account for social costs and the moral minimum of the negative injunction against social injury.

The arguments for corporate social responsibility are implied above. They emphasise changes in public expectations of business; enlightened self-interest; the avoidance of government intervention; the extent of corporate power and the need to balance this with responsibility in self-regulation; and business resources. It is worth concluding this chapter by quoting Steiner and Steiner's summary in review of the arguments for and against corporate social responsibility:

> *Business decision making today is a mixture of altruism, self-interest, and good citizenship. Managers do take actions that are in the social interest even though there is a cost involved and the connection with long-range profits is quite remote. These actions traditionally were considered to be in the category of 'good deeds'. The issue today is that some people expect—and some managers wonder whether they should respond to the expectation—that business should assume a central role in resolving major social problems of the day in the name of social responsibility . . . Business cannot do this, nor should it try. Larger corporations, however, clearly feel that the old-fashioned single-minded lust for profits tempered with a few 'good deeds' must be modified in favour of a new social concern. Society also expects its business leaders to be concerned. The issue is not whether business has social responsibilities. It has them. The fundamental issue is to identify them for business in general and for the individual company.*

The identification of these responsibilities and ensuring they are met—as well as the continuing problem of corporate power ignored by Steiner and Steiner—demands social control of business. . . .

MAXIMIZING ETHICS AND PROFITS
PATRICK PRIMEAUX, S.M.

Primeaux offers a practical rejoinder to critics of Friedman, arguing for the possibility of a balance between money and ethics that is based on a theory of profit maximization.

Business is the highest level of human activity and the highest level of social good. Some of the greatest pieces of art the world has ever known are a good meal, a Boeing 747, a BMW, a PC, a CAT scanner, a refrigerator. By any measure, the kind of behavior needed to produce these works of art constitutes the highest level of human activity and the highest level of social good. After all, it is people engaged in business who deliver all the goods and services the community wants—better health care, schools for our children, food for our tables, and shelter for our families.

Business demands excellence and creativity. Men and women in business are artists and scientists. The activities in which they engage are like those required to produce a great symphony, a well-written play, a fine painting, a vintage wine, or a new scientific discovery. These activities demand excellence and require an abundance of creativity.

These words appear in the opening chapter of a book John Stieber and I wrote about business ethics.[1] Stieber and I want to reflect a positive and optimistic evaluation of business and of the men and women in business. However, when we read newspapers, watch television, or listen to business people conversing, we know that this positive evaluation of business is not universally accepted. Everyone knows that men and women in business are interested in one thing: money. And, as everyone also knows, men and women in business will do anything that has to be done to make money. That's the name of the game. That's what business is really all about.

If that's the case, why bother talking about ethics? When Milton Friedman claims that the ethical mandate of business is to increase shareholder profit, he's talking about money and he's talking about ethics. Connecting the two, he probably did more than any other theorist to advance business ethics. Now we hear executives of major corporations giving commencement speeches about ethics. "What will it look like on the front page of the *New York Times?*" and "Think of yourself as running for mayor" they propose as guiding principles for ethics in business. What they are advising is business as usual. Do what you have to do to maximize profits, but make it look good to the public and to the

Patrick Primeaux, S.M., "Maximizing Ethics and Profits." Reprinted by permission of the author.

1. For a fuller examination of the theory and implications of the argument reflected in this essay, see Patrick Primeaux and John Stieber, *Profit Maximization: The Ethical Mandate of Business* (San Francisco: Austin & Winfield, 1995) and an article of the same title in *The Journal of Business Ethics* 13; no. 4 (1994), pp. 287–94.

Securities and Exchange Commission. We might commend them for their practicality, but why not ask them to become even more practical? Why don't they recommend, as Charles E. Quinn does, that everyone simply invest in a personal paper shredder?

The problem for business and for business ethics is the equation of business with money, specifically bottom-line accounting profits, and the pressure to increase those profits quarterly or annually. That motivating objective is itself reflective of an ethical code. It consists of an ethical principle, and demands a certain kind of behavior consistent with that principle. The organization is structured, people are hired, jobs are described, managers are held accountable, raw materials are acquired, and technology engaged to increase that bottom line. Everything and everybody within the company is directed by that profit-maximizing principle and expected to conform to its demands.

Stieber and I want to create another ethical code for business, one which still takes money seriously. We also want to provide a framework or blueprint for business and for people in business to be able to appreciate the ethics of business, and to regulate themselves rather than waiting for political, legal, and religious demands to be imposed on them from the outside. In other words, we want to tie business ethics to profit maximization, but to a broader understanding of profit maximation than that usually ascribed to rational, numerical bottom-line accounting profits.

When numbers become more important than anything else, everything and everyone in the company becomes valued in those same mathematical and numerical terms. When people or things are valued for their contribution to increased profit margins, they are identified numerically and treated as such. They are themselves valued simply with respect to their contribution to profits. The philosopher would say that they are objectified for utility. They are treated as objects and valued simply for their contribution to production. It is when this happens that business and men and women in business leave themselves wide open to criticism and to regulation from the law, from philosophy, or from religion.

That's the problem with Friedman's ethical imperative. It is too myopic, too focused on bottom-line accounting profits alone and, because of that, values the factors of production only insofar as they are useful for production and for rationally-and-numerically determined profits. It also reflects Friedman's values, what is important to him, how he views people and the world, especially the world of nature which provides the raw resources which go into productivity. It is evident that the values he wants to encourage are focused exclusively on utility, on usefulness to production. Is there not another value system which appreciates people and things for their own positive existence, their own presence in the world, rather than how they can be useful to us? Asking that question raises questions about ourselves.

What are our values? What do we value? Who do we value? How do we value ourselves? The subject and objects of each of these questions, as well as the contexts of the questions themselves, suggest that we are presuming different meanings of the word *value*. In the first case, we're asking about morals or ethics, about behavior. In the second question, we're inquiring about objects. In the third, the focus is on people other than ourselves. The fourth question is about ourselves, about self-identity. However, although used in different ways to ask different questions, the contextual nuances suggest a commonality and continuity of behavior, possessions, others, and ourselves. How can all of these be connected?

They are connected by value, and value suggests relationship. To ask questions about value is to ask questions about relationship, about how we perceive ourselves, others—perhaps God—and the objects we possess. Value not only suggests relationships, but similarity and continuity within our perceptions and considerations of the things we have, the people we meet, and the persons we are becoming. Today, in our world, that bonding is primarily economic.

The first meaning of the word *value* in *Webster's* is "a fair return or equivalent in goods, services, or money for something exchanged," and the second is "the monetary worth of something: marketable price."[2] The third meaning is "relative worth, utility, or importance," and the fourth is "a numerical quantity assigned or computed." These definitions not only provide answers to our questions, but lead us to conclude that who and what we value, as well as our values, are defined primarily in economic terms: money, utility, numerical quantity. Not only is money an object, it is an object that can be quantified numerically. Its utility, its usefulness, is also quantified numerically.

But, let's not focus on money alone. Surely what we value, as well as our values, cannot be determined by money alone. They can also be determined by what money can buy and what money can provide. Even then, that focus on money is too myopic, as would be any appreciation for economics that would concentrate on money alone, or even on what money can buy. It is that understanding of economics which is misleading, for it subjects economics to numbers and accounting principles.

Profit maximization is not, however, only an accounting notion. There is also an economic definition of profit maximization which is much broader in scope and reference than any accounting formulation. Actually, the two are almost identical, defining profits as total revenues minus total costs (TR − TC). The real difference surfaces within total costs. The accountant would define total costs with respect to fixed costs and variable costs (TC = FC + VC). The economist would widen that definition to include opportunity costs so that total costs involves fixed costs, variable costs, and opportunity costs (TC = FC + VC + OC).

So what? The inclusion of opportunity costs within decision-making opens the doors to a broader perspective. That broader perspective goes beyond money and numbers. It moves beyond the bottom line to question a whole list of concerns which go into, and contribute to, that bottom-line maximization of profits. In other words, economic profit maximization is not content to focus on the numbers. Economic profit maximization wants to know how those profits are realized.

What are opportunity costs? Opportunity costs are usually defined as the forgone goods and services that could have been produced from a given set of scarce resources that was used to produce some other goods and services. There are two key phrases in this definition of opportunity costs that should help us understand their role in business decision-making. The two phrases are "the forgone goods and services" and "from a given set of resources."

---

2. Henry Bosley Woolf, ed., *Webster's New Collegiate Dictionary* (Springfield: G. & C. Merriam Company, 1981).

Assume that a business has a fixed amount of money from the earnings it has retained to invest for its owners. Further, suppose it decides to start a used car lot in an Amish town. Once these resources ("a given set of resources") are committed to the project, they can never be used to produce any other goods and services for the community such as health care, education, or housing ("forgone goods and services").

Besides the usual kinds of business considerations associated with this decision (location, lease, hiring, taxes, etc.), there is a serious ethical consideration to be addressed. The Amish do not drive cars. Were the decision makers insensitive to this ethical behavior, the project would fail and the resources would be lost.

If the project were to fail because the management of this company was insensitive to the ethics of the situation, the opportunity costs for the community would be that of a whole set of scarce resources used to produce something consumers did not want, i.e., did not value. These wasted resources can never be used to produce anything else. The opportunity cost for the firm is the loss of money from a set of scarce resources that could have been used for another project.

From a more philosophical perspective there are some implications of opportunity costs we can apply to ourselves as men and women in business as well as to the business itself. First, opportunity costs imply that in every decision, in every choice, there is a negation, a rejection. This means that statements like "it's OK as long as no one gets hurts" become downright silly. Someone or something is always hurt, negated, or rejected in any choice to pursue one opportunity rather than another. Second, opportunity costs remind us that we can't have or do everything because resources are scarce. In other words, opportunity cost decision making serves to make the obvious even more so. Anything and everything is a scarce resource. Third, opportunity costs suggest that every decision about anything is an ethical decision. To choose one thing over another, or one course of action in preference to another, implies values. It also implies good and bad, right and wrong. This is especially the case when decisions are made about scarce resources. The very appreciation of scarcity suggests that any abuse or misuse of any resource is wrong. Fourth, opportunity-cost decision making opens wide the horizons of consideration. It moves beyond any immediate and short-term concerns to refer to implications and considerations for the widest possible scope of reference. It moves beyond numbers to encompass the whole of human experience, the whole of the world's ecology. That is, it encourages us to consider anything and everything that could possibly affect profits—both within and without the company. The establishment of a used-car lot in an Amish community fails precisely because the religious traditions of the people of that community were ignored. In opportunity-cost decision making, nothing can be ignored. To do so would incur opportunity costs, waste scarce resources, and would, for that reason, provide the grounding for unethical behavior.

How do we know whether a company is being ethical or not? To do so we would have to investigate its use of scarce resources. Within economics, we have a framework of reference within which to pursue that investigation. We can isolate the factors of production, and examine the costs associated with those factors. The factors of production are, of course, the scarce resources that enter into production.

The factors of production are usually described as four: land, labor-time, creativity/entrepreneurship, and capital. The costs associated with land are paid as rent, to labor-time as wages, to creativity-entrepreneurship as profit, to capital as interest. Tying the costs of production to the factors of production implies an ethical imperative based in efficiency. To use these resources inefficiently leads to waste, abuse, and misuse. That inefficiency translates into unnecessary costs, and reflects not only inefficiency, but waste of scarce resources.

Since the time of Adam's and Eve's eviction from the Garden of Eden, everything and anything has become a scarce resource. While in the Garden, they had everything they wanted. Why? They had an infinite number of resources available to them. Outside the Garden, they found that resources were limited. Moreover, they quickly discovered that to acquire the things they wanted, these scarce resources had to be used efficiently.

They also quickly discovered that once an animal was slaughtered for food and clothing, that animal would never be able to provide additional food and clothing. There would be other animals, though, and for a time it might have seemed that these existed in limitless, infinite numbers. As time progressed, and as the earth became more and more populated, the number of animals available for food and clothing became more and more scarce. In today's world, we can easily argue from casual observation and ordinary experience, that anything and everything is a scarce resource; that once used for one purpose, the resource no longer exists for any other purpose.

In economics, that realization of the scarcity of resources is translated into the principle of opportunity costs. Actually, the monetary value we attach to human labor and time, as well as to personal creativity, land, and even money, is itself an indication of scarcity. Once any of these resources is brought into production, any opportunity for an alternative use is forgone. Measuring its actual use with respect to its potential use, provides an indication of the value of a given resource, i.e., a measure of whether or not the person or thing is employed towards its maximum value or potential. To do otherwise would prove inefficient, for it would involve waste, abuse, or misuse of a valuable and scarce resource. It would also be inefficient, for it would result in unwarranted costs.

The principle of opportunity costs can be assessed personally as well as corporately. Given the many choices we have in life, the college student can choose between preparing for an exam the following day or socializing with friends. As opportunity-cost decision making implies both choice and negation, to choose to spend time and expend energy poring over class notes and text books necessitates the rejection of the company of one's friends. The costs of studying are weighed with the costs of socializing for the scarce resources of time and energy require a choice. To choose one requires the negation of the other. The question to ask is, which will be more efficient? Another question to ask is, which will cost more in the long run?

We need to ask the same question when choosing between two desirable alternatives in business. A really intelligent, responsible, and productive secretary who is paid a salary commensurate with market standards, even though contributing more than required or expected of that standard, provides a practical and common example. The decision hinges on capital and the most efficient use of that capital. Should he receive a higher salary, or should that same money—a scarce resource—be used to increase bottom-line accounting profits? Choosing to direct the money towards profits could mean the secretary leaving the firm for higher-salaried employment by another firm. The costs of hiring and training a replacement, perhaps one contributing less than the former secretary, could exceed the costs of a salary raise. In that case, the scarce resource of the original secretary, as well as the scarce resource of capital, would be wasted and misused, especially in the long run. Directly pertaining to ethics, no one would consider the decision bearing on this case to be a good one. With respect to costs, no one would judge this use of the person as well as of capital to be good and efficient.

Perhaps the most abused of the factors of production is that of creativity/entrepreneurship. Although afforded a market-level salary, our exceptionally efficient secretary is not rewarded. Only senior managers and directors are considered worthy of pay for the creativity of their decisions, especially those of bringing creative people into the firm. A creative and entrepreneurial spirit can, however, be found at every level of the organizational structure and also rewarded in a manner proportionate to contribution to profit. Our exemplary secretary should be compensated for her creativity. So also should the janitor who saves the company money by using cleaning supplies sparingly while, at the same time, complying with the dictates of her job description.

Opportunity-cost decision making leads to profit-maximization insofar as it recognizes the scarcity of all of its resources, and uses those resources as efficiently as possible. To evaluate whether a company is profit-maximizing, then, one needs to look beyond bottom-line accounting profits to identify what those profits represent. To do that, one would have to study the costs incurred by each of the factors of production, to assess those costs in terms of opportunity costs, and to evaluate those opportunity costs from a long-term perspective. This kind of assessment would answer the most important question of practical and ethical concern: Are all of the factors of production being used as efficiently as possible?

This perspective commends itself for good business and good business ethics because it originates directly within business theory and practice. It also commends itself because it encourages business to move beyond bottom-line accounting profits to consider people and things not only as valuable for production, but also as valuable in themselves—as scarce resources having value and dignity. It also commends itself because we could then equate good business and good business ethics.

IN DEFENSE OF NON-DIVERSITY

T. J. RODGERS

T. J. Rodgers is the president and chief executive officer of Cypress Semiconductor. He wrote the following letter in response to a letter from Doris Gormley, OSF, the director of corporate social responsibility for the Sisters of St. Francis of Philadelphia. Sr. Doris Gormley had told him that her order would vote against the Cypress board of directors because it lacked women and minority members. The Wall Street Journal *reported that he wrote the first draft of this letter to Sr. Gormley on his way home from work the day he received it, "clamping his teeth down on the microcassette recorder when he had to change gears." The letter from Rodgers was sent not only to Sr. Gormley but also to all of Cypress's shareholders. Rodgers received hundreds of replies from shareholders, almost all positive (91 percent of 605 letters). Do you agree? Would Rodgers' letter encourage you to support him, and even to purchase Cypress stock?*

May 23, 1996

Doris Gormley, OSF
Director, Corporate Social Responsibility
The Sisters of St. Francis of Philadelphia
Our Lady of Angeles Convent—Glen Riddle
Aston, PA 19014

Dear Sister Gormley:

Thank you for your letter criticizing the lack of racial and gender diversity of Cypress's Board of Directors. I received the same letter from you last year. I will reiterate the management arguments opposing your position. Then I will provide the philosophical basis behind our rejection of the operating principles espoused in your letter, which we believe to be not only unsound, but even immoral, by a definition of that term I will present.

The semiconductors business is a tough one with significant competition from the Japanese, Taiwanese, and Koreans. There have been more corporate casualties than survivors. For that reason, our Board of Directors is not a ceremonial watchdog, but a critical management function. The essential criteria for Cypress board membership are as follows:

- Experience as a CEO of an important technology company.

- Direct expertise in the semiconductor business based on education and management experience.

Letter from T. J. Rodgers to Doris Gormley, OSF. Dir., Corporate Social Responsibility, The Sisters of St. Francis of Philadelphia Our Lady of Angels Convent, May 23, 1996. Reprinted by permission of the author.

- Direct experience in the management of a company that buys from the semiconductor industry.

A search based on these criteria usually yields a male who is 50-plus years old, has a Masters degree in an engineering science, and has moved up the managerial ladder to the top spot in one or more corporations. Unfortunately, there are currently few minorities and almost no women who chose to be engineering graduate students 30 years ago. (That picture will be dramatically different in 10 years, due to the greater diversification of graduate students in the '80s.) Bluntly stated, a "woman's view" on how to run our semiconductor company does not help us, unless that woman has an advanced technical degree and experience as a CEO. I do realize there are other industries in which the last statement does not hold true. We would quickly embrace the opportunity to include any woman or minority person who could help us as a director, because we pursue talent— and we don't care in what package that talent comes.

I believe that placing arbitrary racial or gender quotas on corporate boards is fundamentally wrong. Therefore, not only does Cypress *not* meet your requirements for boardroom diversification, but we are unlikely to, because it is very difficult to find qualified directors, let alone directors that also meet investors' racial and gender preferences.

I infer that your concept of corporate "morality" contains in it the requirement to appoint a Board of Directors with, in your words, "equality of sexes, races, and ethnic groups." I am unaware of any Christian requirements for corporate boards; your views seem more accurately described as "politically correct," than "Christian."

My views aside, your requirements are—in effect—immoral. By "immoral," I mean "causing harm to people," a fundamental wrong. Here's why:

- I presume you believe your organization does good work and that the people who spend their careers in its service deserve to retire with the necessities of life assured. If your investment in Cypress is intended for that purpose, I can tell you that each of the retired Sisters of St. Francis would suffer if I were forced to run Cypress on anything but a profit-making basis. The retirement plans of thousands of other people also depend on Cypress stock—$1.2 billion worth of stock—owned directly by investors or through mutual funds, pension funds, 401(k) programs, and insurance companies. Recently, a fellow 1970 Dartmouth classmate wrote to say that his son's college fund (Dartmouth, Class of 2014," he writes) owns Cypress stock. Any choice I would make to jeopardize retirees and other investors from achieving their lifetime goals would be fundamentally wrong.

- Consider charitable donations. When the U.S. economy shrinks, the dollars available to charity shrink faster, including those dollars earmarked for the Sisters of St. Francis. If all companies in the U.S. were forced to operate according to some arbitrary social agenda, rather than for profit, all American companies would operate at a disadvantage to their foreign competitors, all Americans would become less well off (some laid off), and charitable giving would decline precipitously. Making Americans poorer and reducing charitable giving in order to force companies to follow an arbitrary social agenda is fundamentally wrong.

- A final point with which you will undoubtedly disagree: Electing people to corporate boards based on racial preferences is demeaning to the very board members placed under such conditions, and unfair to people who are qualified. A prominent friend of mine hired a partner who is a brilliant, black Ph.D. from Berkeley. The woman is constantly insulted by being asked if she got her job because of preferences; the system that creates that institutionalized insult is fundamentally wrong.

Finally, you ought to get down from your moral high horse. Your form letter signed with a stamped signature does not allow for the possibility that a CEO could run a company morally and disagree with your position. You have voted against me and the other directors of the company, which is your right as a shareholder. But here is a synopsis of what you voted against:

- Employee ownership. Every employee of Cypress is a shareholder and every employee of Cypress—including the lowest-paid—receives new Cypress stock options every year, a policy that sets us apart even from other Silicon Valley companies.

- Excellent pay. Our employees in San Jose averaged $78,741 in salary and benefits in 1995. (That figure excludes my salary and that of Cypress's vice presidents; it's what "the workers" really get.)

- A significant boost to our economy. In 1995, our company paid out $150 million to its employees. That money did a lot of good: it bought a lot of houses, cars, movie tickets, eyeglasses, and college educations.

- A flexible health-care program. A Cypress-paid health-care budget is granted to all employees to secure the health-care options they want, Including medical, dental, and eye care, as well as different life insurance policies.

- Personal computers. Cypress pays for half of home computers (up to $1,200) for all employees.

- Employee education. We pay for our employees to go back to school, and we offer dozens of internal courses.

- Paid time off. In addition to vacation and holidays, each Cypress employee can schedule paid time off for personal reasons.

- Profit sharing. Cypress shares its profits with its employees. In 1995, profit sharing added up to $5,000 per employee, given in equal shares, regardless of rank or salary. That was a 22% bonus for an employee earning $22,932 per year, the taxable salary of our lowest-paid San Jose employee.

- Charitable work. Cypress supports Silicon Valley. We support the Second Harvest Food Bank (food for the poor), the largest food bank in the United States. I was chairman of the 1993 food drive, and Cypress has won the food-giving title three years running. (Last year, we were credited with 354,131 pounds of food, or 454 pounds per employee, a record.) We also give to the Valley Medical Center, our Santa Clara-based public hospital, which accepts all patients without a "VISA check."

Those are some of the policies of the Board of Directors you voted against. I believe you should support management teams that hold our values and have the courage to put them into practice.

So, that's my reply. Choosing a Board of Directors based on race and gender is a lousy way to run a company. Cypress will never do it. Furthermore, we will never be pressured into it, because bowing to well-meaning, special-interest groups is an immoral way to run a company, given all the people it would hurt. We simply cannot allow arbitrary rules to be forced on us by organizations that lack business expertise. I would rather be labeled as a person who is unkind to religious groups than as a coward who harms his employees and investors by mindlessly following high-sounding, but false, standards of right and wrong.

You may think this letter is too tough a response to a shareholder organization voting its conscience. But the political pressure to be what is euphemized as a "responsible corporation" today is so great that it literally threatens the well being of every American. Let me explain why.

In addition to your focus on the racial and gender equality of board representation, other investors have their pet issues; for example, whether or not a company:

- is "green," or environmentally conscious.

- does or does not do business with certain countries or groups of people.

- supplies the U.S. Armed Forces.

- is "involved in the community" in appropriate ways.

- pays its CEO too much compared with its lowest-paid employee.

- pays its CEO too much as declared by self-appointed "industry watchdogs."

- gives to certain charities.

- is willing to consider layoffs when the company is losing money.

- is willing to consider layoffs to streamline its organization (so-called downsizing).

- has a retirement plan.

- pays for all or part of a health-care plan.

- budgets a certain minimum percentage of payroll costs for employee training.

- places employees on its Board of Directors (you forgot this one).

- shares its profits with employees.

We believe Cypress has an excellent record on these issues. But that's because it's the way we *choose* to run the business for ourselves and our shareholders—not because we run the business according to the mandates of special-interest groups. Other companies, perhaps those in older industries just trying to hold on to jobs, might find the choices our company makes devastating to their businesses and, consequently, their employees.

No one set of choices could be correct for all companies. Indeed, it would be impossible for any company to accede to all of the special interests, because they are often in conflict with one another. For example, Cypress won a San Jose Mayor's Environmental Award for water conservation. Our waste water from the Minnesota plant is so clean we are permitted to put it directly into a lake teeming with wildlife. (A game warden station is the next door neighbor to that plant.) Those facts might qualify us as a "green" company, but some investors would claim the opposite because we adamantly oppose wasteful, government-mandated, ride-sharing programs and believe that car-pool lanes waste the time of the finest minds in Silicon Valley by creating government-inflicted traffic jams—while increasing pollution, not decreasing it, as claimed by some self-declared "environmentalists."

The May 13, 1996 issue of *Fortune* magazine analyzed the "ethical mutual funds" which invest with a social-issues agenda, and currently control $639 billion in investments. Those funds produced an 18.2% return in the last 12 months, while the S&P 500 returned 27.2% The investors in those funds thus lost 9% of $639 billion, or *$57.5 billion in one year,* because they invested on a social-issues basis. Furthermore, their loss was not simply someone else's gain; the money literally vanished from our economy, making every American poorer. That's a lot of houses, food, and college educations that were lost to the "higher good" of various causes. What absurd logic would contend that Americans should be harmed by "good ethics"?

Despite our disagreement on the issues, The Sisters of St. Francis, the ethical funds, and their investors are merely making free choices on how to invest. What really worries me is the current election-year frenzy in Washington to institutionalize "good ethics" by making them law—a move that would mandate widespread corporate mismanagement. The "corporate responsibility" concepts promoted by Labor Secretary Reich and Senator Kennedy make great TV sound bites, but if they were put into practice, it would be a disaster for American business that would dwarf the $57 billion lost by the inept investment strategy of the "ethical funds." And that disaster would translate into lost jobs and lost wages for all Americans, a fundamental wrong.

One Senate proposal for "responsible corporations," as outlined in the February 26 issue of *Business Week,* would grant a low federal tax rate of 11% to "responsible corporations," and saddle all other companies with an 18% rate. One seemingly innocuous requirement for a "responsible corporation," as proposed by Senators Bingaman and Daschle, would limit the pay of a "responsible" CEO to no more than 50 times the company's lowest-paid, full-time employee. To mandate that a "responsible corporation" would have to limit the pay of its CEO is the perfect, no-lose, election-year issue. The rule would be viewed as the right thing to do by voters who distrust and dislike free markets, and as a don't-care issue by the rest. But the following analysis of this proposal underscores the fact that the simplistic solutions fashioned by politicians to provide fear and anger against America's businesses often sound reasonable—while being fundamentally wrong.

Consider the folly of the CEO pay limit as it applies to Intel: the biggest semiconductor company in the world, the leader of America's return to market dominance in semiconductors, the good corporate citizen, the provider of 45,325 very high-quality jobs, the inventor of the random-access memory, the inventor of the microprocessor, and the manufacturer of the "brains" of 80% of the world's personal computers. Suppose that Intel's lowest-paid trainee earns $15,000 per year. The 50 to 1 CEO salary rule would mandate that the salary of Intel's co-founder and CEO, Andy Grove, could be no more than $750,000. Otherwise, Intel would face a federal tax rate of 18% rather than 11%. Last year, Andy Grove earned $2,756,700, well over that $750,000 limit, and Intel's pre-tax earnings were $5.6 billion. Seven percentage points on Intel's tax rate translates into a whopping $395 million tax penalty for Intel. Consequently, the practical meaning of this "responsible corporation" law to Intel would be this gun-to-the-head proposition: "Either cut the pay of your Chief Executive Officer by a factor of four from $2,756,700 to $750,000, or pay the federal government an extra $395 million in taxes."

The Bingaman-Daschle proposal would limit the pay of the CEO of the world's most important semiconductor company to less than that of a second-string quarterback in the NFL! That absurd result is not about "responsible corporations," but about two leftist senators, out of touch with reality, making political hay, causing harm, and labeling it "good." Their plan is particularly immoral in that it would cause the losses inherent in practicing their newly invented false moral standard to fall upon all investors in American companies, even though the government itself had not invested in those companies.

Meanwhile, my current salary multiple of 25 to 1 relative to our lowest-paid employee would qualify Cypress as a "responsible corporation," only because we are younger and not yet as successful as Intel—a fact reflected by my lower pay. If Cypress had created as much wealth and as many jobs as Intel, and if my compensation were higher for that reason, then, according to the amazingly perverse logic of the "responsible corporation," Cypress would be moved from the "responsible" to the "irresponsible" category for having been more successful and for having created more jobs! A final point: Why should either Intel or Cypress, both companies making 30% pre-tax profit, be offered a special tax break by the very politicians who would move on to the next press conference to complain about "corporate welfare?"

How long will it be before Senators Kennedy, Bingaman, and Daschle hold hearings on "irresponsible corporations" that pay tens of millions of dollars to professional athletes? Or are athletes a "protected group," leaving CEOs as their sole target? If not, which Senate Subcommittee will determine the "responsible" pay level for a good CEO with 30% pre-tax profit, as compared to a good pitcher with 1.05 earned run average? These questions highlight the absurdity of trying to replace free market pricing with the responsible-corporation claptrap proposed by Bingaman, Daschle, Kennedy, and Reich.

In conclusion, please consider these two points: First, Cypress is run under a set of carefully considered moral principles, which rightly include making a profit as a primary objective. Second, there is a fundamental difference between your organization's right to vote its conscience and the use of coercion by the federal government to force arbitrary "corporate responsibilities" on America's businesses and shareholders.

Cypress stands for personal and economic freedom, for free minds and free markets, a position irrevocably in opposition to the immoral attempt by coercive utopians to mandate even more government control over America's economy. With regard to our shareholders who exercise their right to vote according to a social agenda, we suggest that they reconsider whether or not their strategy will do net good—after all of the real costs are considered.

Sincerely,
T. J. Rodgers
President CEO

DODGE V. FORD MOTOR CO.

Hon. J. Ostrander

Henry Ford believed that there should be a Ford in every garage; in other words, that Ford cars should be made for and affordable by everyone. At the time of this case, that meant a reduction in the price of a Ford automobile from $440 to $360 and a refusal to pay stock dividends. John and Horace Dodge were shareholders in Ford's company and believed that Ford's primary responsibility was to make a profit for his shareholders. Dodge sued (and eventually opened his own firm producing Dodge automobiles!). Do you agree with the majority or with the concurrence (or with neither)?

. . . The plan, as affecting the profits of the business for the year beginning August 1, 1916, and thereafter, calls for a reduction in the selling price of the cars. It is true that this price might be at any time increased, but the plan called for the reduction in price of $80 a car. The capacity of the plant, without the additions thereto voted to be made (without a part of them at least), would produce more than 600,000 cars annually. This number, and more, could have been sold for $440 instead of $360, a difference in the return for capital, labor and materials employed of at least $48,000,000. In short, the plan does not call for and is not intended to produce immediately a more profitable business but a less profitable one; not only less profitable than formerly but less profitable than it is admitted it might be made. The apparent immediate effect will be to diminish the value of shares and the returns to shareholders.

It is the contention of plaintiffs that the apparent effect of the plan is intended to be the continued and continuing effect of it and that it is deliberately proposed, not of record and not by official corporate declaration, but nevertheless proposed, to continue the corporation henceforth as a semi-eleemosynary institution and not as a business institution. In support of this contention they point to the attitude and to the expressions of Mr. Henry Ford.

Mr. Henry Ford is the dominant force in the business of the Ford Motor Company. No plan of operations could be adopted unless he consented, and no board of directors can be elected whom he does not favor. One of the directors of the company has no stock. One share was assigned to him to qualify him for the position, but it is not claimed that he owns it. A business, one of the largest in the world, and one of the most profitable, has been built up. It employs many men, at good pay.

"My ambition," said Mr. Ford, "is to employ still more men, to spread the benefits of this industrial system to the greatest possible number, to help them build up their lives

---

Dodge v. Ford Motor Co., 204 Mich. 459; 170 N.W. 668 (1919), excerpt.

and their homes. To do this we are putting the greatest share of our profits back in the business."

"With regard to dividends, the company paid sixty per cent on its capitalization of two million dollars, or $1,200,000, leaving $58,000,000 to reinvest for the growth of the company. This is Mr. Ford's policy at present, and it is understood that the other stockholders cheerfully accede to this plan."

He had made up his mind in the summer of 1916 that no dividends other than the regular dividends should be paid, "for the present."

QUESTION: For how long? Had you fixed in your mind any time in the future, when you were going to pay —

ANSWER: No.

QUESTION: That was indefinite in the future?

ANSWER: That was indefinite, yes, sir."

The record, and especially the testimony of Mr. Ford, convinces that he has to some extent the attitude towards shareholders of one who has dispensed and distributed to them large gains and that they should be content to take what he chooses to give. His testimony creates the impression, also, that he thinks the Ford Motor Company has made too much money, has had too large profits, and that although large profits might be still earned, a sharing of them with the public, by reducing the price of the output of the company, ought to be undertaken. We have no doubt that certain sentiments, philanthropic and altruistic, creditable to Mr. Ford, had large influence in determining the policy to be pursued by the Ford Motor Company—the policy which has been herein referred to.

It is said by his counsel that—

"Although a manufacturing corporation cannot engage in humanitarian works as its principal business, the fact that it is organized for profit does not prevent the existence of implied powers to carry on with humanitarian motives such charitable works as are incidental to the main business of the corporation."

And again:

"As the expenditures complained of are being made in an expansion of the business which the company is organized to carry on, and for purposes within the powers of the corporation as hereinbefore shown, the question is as to whether such expenditures are rendered illegal because influenced to some extent by humanitarian motives and purposes on the part of the members of the board of directors."

In discussing this proposition, counsel have referred to decisions such as Hawes v. Oakland . . . ; Taunton v. Royal Ins. Co. . . . . ; Henderson v. Bank of Australasia . . . ; Steinway v. Steinway & Sons . . . ; People, ex rel. Metropolitan Life Ins. Co., v. Hotchkiss. . . . These cases, after all, like all others in which the subject is treated, turn finally upon the point, the question, whether it appears that the directors were not acting for the best interests of the corporation. We do not draw in question, nor do counsel for the plaintiffs do so, the validity of the general propositions stated by counsel nor the soundness of the opinions delivered in the cases cited. The case presented here is not like any of them. The difference between an incidental humanitarian expenditure of corporate funds for the benefit of the employees, like the building of a hospital for their use and the employment of agencies for the betterment of their condition, and a general purpose and plan to benefit mankind at the expense of others, is obvious. There should be no confusion (of which there is evidence) of the duties which Mr. Ford conceives that he and the stockholders owe to the general public and the duties which in law he and his codirectors owe to protesting, minority stockholders. A business corporation is organized and carried on primarily for the profit of the stockholders. The powers of the directors are to be employed for that end. The discretion of directors is to be exercised in the choice of means to attain that end and does not extend to a change in the end itself, to the reduction of profits or to the nondistribution of profits among stockholders in order to devote them to other purposes.

There is committed to the discretion of directors, a discretion to be exercised in good faith, the infinite details of business, including the wages which shall be paid to employees, the number of hours they shall work, the conditions under which labor shall be carried on, and the prices for which products shall be offered to the public. It is said by appellants that the motives of the board members are not material and will not be inquired into by the court so long as their acts are within their lawful powers. As we have pointed out, and the proposition does not require argument to sustain it, it is not within the lawful powers of a board of directors to shape and conduct the affairs of a corporation for the merely incidental benefit of shareholders and for the primary purpose of benefiting others, and no one will contend that if the avowed purpose of the defendant directors was to sacrifice the interests of shareholders it would not be the duty of the courts to interfere.

We are not, however, persuaded that we should interfere with the proposed expansion of the business of the Ford Motor Company. In view of the fact that the selling price of products may be increased at any time, the ultimate results of the larger business cannot be certainly estimated. The judges are not business experts. It is recognized that plans must often be made for a long future, for expected competition, for a continuing as well as an immediately profitable venture. The experience of the Ford Motor Company is evidence of capable management of its affairs. It may be noticed, incidentally, that it took from the public the money required for the execution of its plan and that the very considerable salaries paid to Mr. Ford and to certain executive officers and employees were not diminished. We are not satisfied that the alleged motives of the directors, in so far as they are reflected in the conduct of the business, menace the interests of shareholders. It is enough to say, perhaps, that the court of equity is at all times open to complaining shareholders having a just grievance. . . .

The decree of the court below fixing and determining the specific amount to be distributed to stockholders is affirmed. In other respects, except as to the allowance of costs, the said decree is reversed. Plaintiffs will recover interest at five per cent per annum upon their proportional share of said dividend from the date of the decree of the lower court. Appellants will tax the costs of their appeal, the two-thirds of the amount thereof will be paid by plaintiffs. No other costs are allowed.

STEERE, FELLOWS, BROOKE, and STONE, J. J., concurred with OSTRANDER, J.

CONCUR: MOORE, J. (concurring). I agree with what is said by Justice OSTRAN-DER upon the subject of capitalization. I agree with what he says as to the smelting enterprise on the River Rouge. I do not agree with all that is said by him in his discussion of the question of dividends. I do agree with him in his conclusion that the accumulation of so large a surplus establishes the fact that there has been an arbitrary refusal to distribute funds that ought to have been distributed to the stockholders as dividends. I therefore agree with the conclusion reached by him upon that phase of the case.

BIRD, C. J., and KUHN, J., concurred with MOORE, J.

COMPARING BRITISH PETROLEUM IN SOUTH WALES AND TONASO IN THE CZECH REPUBLIC

MICHAEL BODDINGTON, ALAN BROWN,
ROBIN HEAL, MARIE BOHATA

What is a firm's responsibility to communities where operations are discontinued? Does that firm owe anything back to the community? Some might argue that it does because it has been willing to take advantage of the community's resources while it was there (human resources and others). However, others say that firms pay for what they use and that creating any additional obligation would, in effect, make them pay a second time. In each of the companies discussed below, what ethical obligations, if any, does the management have to its employees, the community, or its investors?

PART A

Two plants, one in the United Kingdom and the other in the Czech Republic, faced similar challenges during the past decade. In the mid-1980s, British Petroleum (BP) managers at the Llandarcy refinery in South Wales faced the need to discontinue operations. With a major presence in the community dating back to the 1920s, BP had to consider what its obligations to the community and its workers were as it closed its operations.

In the early 1990s the TONASO plant in Nestemice, Czech Republic, faced two options: either close or restructure and downsize. If this state-owned company were to overcome significant economic and environmental problems, as well as address the uncertainties of impending privatization, its new director would need to develop and implement a far-reaching strategy.

BP in South Wales

BP established its Llandarcy refinery in 1922. The complex expanded until its facilities stretched from Milford Haven, 64 miles away, through the refinery site (274 hectares) and the associated 696 hectares of land, to the ports at Swansea and the petrochemical works at Baglan Bay, for which it provided feedstock. It is fair to say that BP effectively built the town and moved people there to work. In the mid-1970s, the refinery was the hub of a major source of employment and industrial activity in South Wales, involving as many as 3,000 jobs.

By the mid-1980s, though, the area around Neath and Swansea reeled from redundancies in coal, steel, and other industries. The area had the lowest rate of company formation in the country (6.8 percent of the existing stock of businesses) and the highest rate of business failure (91.5 percent of business start-ups failed). It was an area where employment had been dominated by large companies and there was no culture of self-employment.

At the same time, BP determined that the development of North Sea oil and the increased use of its Rotterdam refinery made the Llandarcy refinery largely superfluous. BP decided to close the operation except for a small lubrication oil facility. Some 750 people would lose their jobs.

BP managers were concerned about the impact of their decision in light of the long history and important role BP played in the community's economy. Beyond legally required payments to redundant workers, what more, if anything, should BP do to mitigate the impact of its plant closing?

TONASO in the Czech Republic

TONASO was established in 1905 as a joint venture between the Belgium firm Solvay & Co. and the Austrian Association for Chemical and Metallurgical Production. The initial soda ash plant was located in Nestemice in the heart of the glass region, where good transportation and convenient energy generation from nearby brown coal mines kept costs low. Over time, the company enlarged its capacity by building plants for other products.

Following the 1989 revolution, it became evident that the anticipated national move to a market economy would bring TONASO increased competition from cheaper imports and drastically higher input prices. The Czech Republic Ministry for Industry realized the company needed to close or undergo major restructuring; it chose the latter and organized a search for a new director capable of leading the change needed for the company to survive.

Prior to reform TONASO controlled domestic soda ash production and provided considerable employment to local citizens (employment in 1989 was about 1,000 including seasonal workers). Given the company's role in the community, the newly hired director understood that social responsibility and employee involvement would be important considerations in TONASO's future. His strategic objectives, in order of priority, were: survival, long-term stability, employment generation, profitability, and environmental protection.

In 1991 TONASO decided to close its main soda ash plant because the technology had become outdated and its negative environmental impact was deemed unacceptable. The resulting downsizing produced redundant workers, excess capacity, and other unused facilities.

During 1992, as part of a comprehensive privatization process, the state-owned TONASO was transformed into TONASO, a joint-stock company. Former divisions were converted into limited (daughter) companies. To transfer ownership from the state to shareholders, management participated in a national voucher program where each Czech citizen exchanged his/her allotment of vouchers for shares (as it happened, most shares among companies were acquired by "privatization funds," i.e., groups of citizen investors, rather than individually). Management established a regional privatization fund that acted on behalf of TONASO employees willing to commit their investment vouchers. The ultimate ownership of TONASO was primarily privatization funds like the regional fund (81 percent of shares were spread across 10 funds) and individual owners (some 5,400 persons).

All in all, it was clear that TONASO management faced a formidable challenge in finding a way to move the company forward.

PART B

The Main Lines of Change

At TONASO, the director quickly moved to develop cooperative relationships of trust with employees and managers. Working closely with municipal authorities, management began an active policy of inviting entrepreneurs in the area to use a variety of support services provided by TONASO. The company also developed new production programs. The results of these efforts was approximately 350 new jobs, largely employing redundant TONASO workers. In addition, the company successfully privatized without being sold to foreign investors.

BP determined that the shutdown of its south Wales refinery would not be just another plant closure. The company instituted a range of remedial measures including job counseling, job search assistance, and a study to determine whether the surplus assets of the refinery could be reused to help the local economy. This study recommended establishing a separate company to undertake redeployment and redevelopment of the site, offering a range of activities to give local people support to rebuild their business lives. BP agreed to adopt these recommendations, which led, over seven years, to measures that have generated 70 new businesses and more than 500 jobs.

Restructuring at TONASO

Immediately after his appointment, the new director began a dialogue with employees. With the assistance of the labor union he organized an internal survey to find competent people whom employees trusted. From this process a new management team was created, which then contributed to the development of the company's transformation strategy. The management team devoted significant time and energy toward making the strategy as transparent as possible and continually explained its main principles to employees.

After the soda ash plant was closed, management offered local entrepreneurs an existing infrastructure, services from specialized TONASO departments, and available workers. This process led to the establishment of a so-called industrial zone. The company also began to restructure its production. The local community resisted inorganic chemical production (Nestemice was the most polluted part of the country), so management developed new, environment-friendly specialty chemical plans. Some TONASO daughter companies pursued modernization opportunities to ensure competitive quality, while others turned to energy production, substituting cleaner (but more expensive) natural gas for brown coal.

An Innovation Center under the TONASO holding company began addressing pollution problems by treating waste from past production. Near the company site, a large waste-water treatment plant is being built. And plans are underway for additional sewage construction that will dispose of chemical wastes at their source. The whole industrial zone now provides approximately 800 jobs.

Privatization at TONASO

Following the restructuring, TONASO was privatized (as described in Part A). The pattern that resulted—several independent companies entering their markets while paying for centralized services from the holding company—allowed the companies to focus more aggressively on external markets. Management concepts that focused on profits and cash flow, along with delegation of more power to lower levels, resulted in a high level of independence, responsibility, and innovation. There is currently an active recruiting campaign to find highly qualified professionals for technical management positions.

The holding company provides its daughter companies financial resources, covers most of the Innovation Center's R&D costs, and operates the industrial zone support services—all for profit. The Center works on the same principle as most technology parks, with services and products that meet the needs of the daughter companies on a market basis. Overall, privatization has produced shifts in attitudes about TONASO priorities, most notably a stronger emphasis on profitability.

Current Challenges at TONASO

As it moves forward, a number of new challenges confront TONASO's management:

- increased emphasis on profitability may reduce interest in environmental protection and job creation;

- changes in the macroeconomy and a heavier emphasis on cost could severely damage some TONASO businesses where prices remain uncompetitive, and

- recruitment of highly qualified professionals is proving to be a bottleneck for the entire strategy, due to unexpectedly low unemployment and a negative perception of the region among university graduates (mainly because of its environmental problems).

BP's D'Arcy Development Limited

In 1987 BP established D'Arcy Development Limited (DDL) as a wholly owned subsidiary of BP Oil UK Ltd. It placed the redundant refinery assets in DDL and provided an endowment of one million pounds, along with a half-million-pound Small Business Loan Fund (SBLF). This represented nearly one-half the total capital requirement estimated in the study recommendations, and it was anticipated that the other 50 percent would be available from grants.

The DDL board consisted of BP personnel and leaders of groups in the local community, including a labor union representative, the chief executive of the borough council, the director of a local enterprise trust, and a representative of the Welsh Development

Agency. The chair was the head of BP's Community Affairs Department. An important early decision was that DDL staff would be recruited based on job qualifications rather than preference going to redundant workers. Only one of the six long-term staff members was formerly employed by BP.

Under a 125-year lease, BP passed all rights over a range of buildings and land to DDL, giving it complete freedom of action over those assets. DDL, itself a government-registered Enterprise Agency, now has Neath Development Partnership on site with its business advisory service, as well as a business center with 39 small industrial and office units. Also included are a refurbished office block with 20 self-contained suites, a seminar and conference center, a small industrial park with 12 units, some old industrial buildings that have been recycled, and 40 acres of land where companies can build their own units to specification.

Implementation and Impact of the DDL Strategy

In 1987 DDL immediately set to work generating income from its most-easily realized assets. Early efforts were made to raise cash from the sale of DDL's interests, but this did not produce results in the depressed market of South Wales.

Through leases on some existing buildings and the conversion of the office block and several other buildings, the development got under way. It was much-heralded in the area and there appeared to be a good supply of waiting entrepreneurs.

DDL's objective was to generate sufficient economic activity on the site to employ more people in the new businesses than had been laid off by the closing of the refinery. The first business came on-site in 1988 and, by the end of 1992, the Business Development Center had an 87 percent occupancy and the Britannic House office complex 80 percent. The total number of on-site jobs in 1994 was 503. In addition, the SBLF granted 227 loans amounting to over one million pounds, assisting in the creation of 1,408 jobs in both off-site and on-site small businesses. The conference center is also a growing success.

The new employment community that has emerged is robust and has managed the current recession well. Most of the businesses (90 percent) have been originated by entrepreneurs from the Swansea area; they are committed to the area and unlikely to leave. If a business does leave or fail, it will not threaten the whole community because of the number and diversity of small businesses.

Among the factors judged especially important to success in the DDL experience that might be transferable elsewhere are:

• entrepreneurial ability in the population, assisted by a wide range of support services

• treating tenants in a caring manner without suggesting a free ride (e.g., up-front subsidies for rent and interest/loan repayment are counter-productive)

• involving local people is crucial

• employing people suited to the job of building and running the center, rather than finding jobs for senior people who were made redundant

• concentrating on helping local businesses grow

- close working relationships between the executive team and the policy makers and the ability of the whole team to move entrepreneurially

- partnership among all interests

- secure funding base

- atmosphere of mutual support among the businesses on-site.

Implications for BP beyond South Wales

BP's success with D'Arcy Development Limited poses dilemmas for the company regarding associated publicity and its implications for BP operations elsewhere that downsize or close.

In a European environment where corporate downsizing, staff reductions, and plant closures are becoming increasingly common, a successful initiative that regenerates the community's economic base and maintains the company's reputation is a powerful example. Indeed, during the 1993–94 European Commission's discussion of actions to counter the corrosive effects of long-term unemployment, the DDL example was highlighted as one of a small number of examples of best practice. In 1995, the Commission president announced that he wished to encourage similar initiatives throughout Europe and to cite BP as one of the leading companies in a joint Commission/business drive to resolve economic and social problems.

BP will continue to reduce employment levels in its operations in many Member States and would ordinarily implement such steps gradually through attrition and retrenchment, without major disruptions and publicity. While there are obvious benefits to BP's reputation as a result of the publicity surrounding its DDL initiative, widespread awareness of the example could raise public expectations, stimulate union pressure, and increase the cost of other reorganizations.

The company devolves power as much as possible to its operational units. Many of these local units are opposed to publicity regarding the DDL experience and to BP taking such a proactive role. Others counter-argue that positive evidence of responsible social and business policies will help the company when seeking contracts in some countries.

RELATED WEB SITE

Community resource center: www.lamendola.com/crc/

THE DOMINI SOCIAL INDEX AND SOCIAL RATING CRITERIA, ANALYSIS YEAR 1996

KINDER, LYDENBERG, DOMINI & CO.

The Domini Social Index (DSI) is a market capitalization–weighted common stock index that monitors the performance of 400 U.S. corporations that pass multiple, broad-based screens founded on a social consciousness. The materials that follow describe the index's creation and reason for existence.

CREATION OF THE DSI

. . . The Domini Social Index (DSI) was created to fill two primary needs:

- To create a diversified benchmark against which social investors can measure the investment performance of socially screened portfolios. The DSI is constructed to represent the broad market available to the social investor.

- To provide a resource for social investors wishing a broad index of companies in a variety of industries that pass commonly applied social screens.

In creating the DIS, Kinder, Lydenberg, Domini & Co., Inc. (KLD) employed a combination of exclusionary and qualitative social screens. *The exclusionary screens:*

- Eliminated companies that derive two percent or more of sales from military weapons systems; derive any revenues from the manufacture of alcoholic or tobacco products; or derive any revenues from the providing of gaming products or services. It also eliminated companies with equity interests in South Africa, but this screen was dropped in November 1993.

- Eliminated electric utilities that own interests in nuclear power plants or derive electricity from nuclear power plants in which they have an interest.

The qualitative screens:

- Evaluated companies' records in areas such as diversity, employee relations, the environment, and product. KLD made an effort to exclude companies whose records were on balance negative in these areas and to include companies whose

---

EXHIBIT 1

Domini Social Index Statistical Review

Comparison of fundamentals as of 11/30/96.

	DSI 400	**S&P 500**	**S&P Midcap**
Median Market Cap ($billions)	2.55	5.62	1.39
5yr Book Value Growth	9.47%	7.88%	14.23%
5yr Earnings Growth	11.26%	11.52%	8.69%
5yr Return on Equity	19.72%	20.14%	13.88%
5yr Dividend Growth	3.24%	3.54%	2.13%
5yr Payout Ratio	27.62%	30.29%	21.33%
Current Dividend Yield	1.64%	1.96%	1.52%
Current Price/Earnings	21.60	20.80	21.50
Current Price/Book	4.98	4.74	4.19
Current Price/Sales	2.67	2.99	2.99
%NYSE	88.42%	91.65%	73.34%
%AMEX	0.73%	0.43%	1.36%
%OTC	10.85%	7.91%	25.29%

records were on balance positive in these areas. Problems in one area did not automatically eliminate a company. KLD instead sought to balance the mixed records of concerns and strengths that companies often have within these areas.

In creating the DSI, KLD started by screening the companies in the Standard & Poor's 500 Index at that time. It eliminated those companies that failed to qualify under the exclusionary and qualitative screens. Firms with stock prices below $5 per share were eliminated, as were firms with financial problems so serious that their long term viability was questionable. Approximately 250 companies were eliminated through this process.

KLD then surveyed non-S&P companies, looking for a combination of large market capitalization and industry representation. Approximately 100 companies that fit these criteria were added. Finally, KLD sought firms with exceptional social characteristics. Approximately 50 companies were added as a result of that search (see Exhibit 1). . . .

1996 Social Rating Criteria: Community

Strengths:

Generous Giving.   The company has consistently given over 1.5% of trailing three-year net earnings before taxes (NEBT) to charity, or has otherwise been notably generous in its giving.

Innovative Giving.   The company has a notable innovative giving program that supports nonprofit organizations such as those promoting self-sufficiency among the economically disadvantaged. Companies that permit nontraditional federated charitable giving drives in the workplace are often noted in this section as well.

Support for Housing.   The company is a prominent participant in public/private partnerships that support housing initiatives for the economically disadvantaged, e.g., the National Equity Fund or the Enterprise Foundation.

Support for Education.   The company has either been notably innovative in its support for primary- or secondary-school education, particularly for those programs that benefit the economically disadvantaged, or the company has prominently supported job training programs for youth.

Other Strength.

Concerns:

Controversies.   The company has recently paid substantial fines or civil penalties, or was involved in major litigation or controversies, relating to a community in which it operates. Or, the company is a financial institution whose local investment practices have led to controversies, particularly ones related to the Community Reinvestment Act.

Breach of Agreements.   The company's relations with a community in which it operates have become notably strained due to a recent plant closing or to a general breach of its agreements with the community.

Other Concern.

1996 Social Rating Criteria: Diversity

Strengths:

CEO. The company's chief executive officer is a woman or a member of a minority group.

Promotion. The company has made notable progress in the promotion of women and minorities, particularly to line positions with profit-and-loss responsibilities within the corporation.

Board of Directors. Women, minorities, and/or the disabled hold four seats or more (with no double counting) on the board of directors, or one-third or more of the board seats if the board numbers less than 12.

Family Benefits. The company has outstanding employee benefits or other programs addressing work/family concerns, e.g., child care, elder care, or flextime.

Women/Minority Contracting. The company does at least 5% of its subcontracting, or otherwise has a demonstrably strong record on purchasing or contracting, with women- and/or minority-owned businesses.

Employment of the Disabled. The company has implemented innovative hiring programs or other innovative human resource programs for the disabled.

Progressive Gay/Lesbian Policies. The company has implemented notably progressive policies toward its gay and lesbian employees.

Other Strength.

Concerns:

Controversies. The company has either paid fines or civil penalties as a result of affirmative action controversies, or has otherwise been involved in major controversies related to affirmative action issues.

Non-Representation. The company has no women on its board of directors or among its senior line managers.

Other Concern.

1996 Social Rating Criteria: Employee Relations

Strengths:

Strong Union Relations. The company has a history of notably strong union relations.

Cash Profit Sharing. The company has a cash profit-sharing program through which it has recently made distributions to a substantial portion of its workforce.

Employee Involvement. The company strongly encourages worker involvement and/or ownership through gain sharing, stock ownership, sharing of financial information, or participation in management decision making.

Strong Retirement Benefits. The company has maintained a notably strong retirement benefits program.

Other Strength.

Concerns:

Poor Union Relations. The company has a history of notably poor union relations.

Safety Controversies. The company recently has either paid substantial fines or civil penalties for willful violations of employee health and safety standards, or has been involved in other major health and safety controversies.

Workforce Reductions. The company has reduced its workforce by 15% in the most recent year or by 25% during the past two years, or it has announced plans for such reductions.

Pension/Benefits Concerns.   The company has either a substantially under-funded defined benefit pension plan, or an inadequate retirement benefits program.

Other Concern.

1996 Social Rating Criteria: Environment

Strengths:

Beneficial Products and Services.   The company derives substantial revenues from innovative remediation products, environmental services, or products that promote the efficient use of energy, or it has developed innovative products with environmental benefits. The term "environmental services" does not include services with questionable environmental effects, such as landfills, incinerators, waste-to-energy plants, and deep injection wells.

Pollution Prevention.   The company has notably strong pollution prevention programs including both emissions reductions and toxics-use reductions programs.

Recycling.   The company either is a substantial user of recycled materials as raw materials in its manufacturing processes, or a major factor in the recycling industry.

Alternative Fuels.   The company derives substantial revenues from alternative fuels. The term "alternative fuels" includes natural gas, wind power, and solar energy.

Communications.   The company is either a signatory to the CERES Principles or publishes a notably substantive environmental report.

Other Strength.

Concerns:

Hazardous Waste.   The company's current liabilities for hazardous waste sites exceed $50 million, or the company has recently paid substantial fines or civil penalties for waste management violations.

Regulatory Problems.   The company has recently paid substantial fines or civil penalties for violations of air, water, or other environmental regulations, or has a pattern of regulatory controversies under the Clean Air Act, Clean Water Act, or other major environmental regulations.

Ozone Depleting Chemicals.   The company is among the top manufacturers of ozone depleting chemicals such as HCFCs, methyl chloroform, methylene chloride, or bromines.

Substantial Emissions. The company's legal emissions of toxic chemicals (as defined by and reported to the EPA) into the air and water are among the highest of the companies followed by KLD.

Agricultural Chemicals.   The company is one of the largest U.S. producers of agricultural chemicals (pesticides or chemical fertilizers).

Other Concern.

1996 Social Rating Criteria: Non-U.S. Operations

Strengths:

General Non-U.S. Operations Strength.   The company's non-U.S. operations have been praised for their community relations, employee relations, environmental impact, or product innovation.

Community.   The company has established substantial, innovative charitable giving programs outside the U.S.

Other Strength.

Concerns:

Burma.   The company has operations in Burma.

Mexico.   The company's operations in Mexico have had major recent controversies, especially those related to the treatment of employees or degradation of the environment.

General Non-U.S. Operations Concern.   The company's non-U.S. operations have been the subject of major recent controversies related to community relations, employee relations, environmental impact, or product safety or quality.

Other Concern.

N.B.: Data for these issues are less complete, less reliable, and more difficult to interpret than the data underlying ratings for U.S. operations.

THE WEALTH
OF NATIONS
ADAM SMITH

Adam Smith (1723–1790) is perhaps best known as the father of modern capitalism and the market approach to decision making through his seminal text, A Wealth of Nations. *Less known is his work on values entitled* A Theory of Moral Sentiments *where he provides a value base for his market. Justice and fairness serve as the bases of Smith's theories and he believes that society could exist without any mutual love or affection. However, in* Moral Sentiments, *Smith articulates his belief that humankind has a fundamental concern for others and beneficence, without which the market could not operate.*

> How selfish soever man may be supposed, there are evidently some principles in his nature, which interest him in the fortune of others, and render their happiness necessary to him, though he derives nothing from it, except the pleasure of seeing it. (*Theory of Moral Sentiments,* p. 9)

Smith introduced a concept of the "impartial spectator," a type of conscience that functions as an inner disinterested judge, encouraging empathy within the decision maker. In other words, the decision maker, in reaching a decision, would consider the perspective of the impartial spectator and evaluate the impact of her or his possible decision on others (compare the impartial spectator to its later incarnation as stakeholder theory and Rawls's distributive justice). Smith also introduced the idea of the "invisible hand," a force that guides our decisions to a market-based end in the public interest. In fact, Smith contends that we are more likely to act in the public interest unintentionally guided by the invisible hand than if we intended it in the first place! Consider this oft-cited quote from Smith's Wealth of Nations:

> Every individual . . . neither intends to promote the public interest, nor knows how much he is promoting it. . . . [B]y directing [his] industry in such a manner as its produce may be of the greatest value, he intends only his own gain, and he is in this, as he is in many other cases, led by an invisible hand to promote an end which was no part of his intention. Nor is it always the worse for society that it was no part of it. By pursuing his own

---

Adam Smith, *The Wealth of Nations,* book I, ch. 1, "Of the Division of Labor," ch. 2, "Of the Principle Which Gives Occasion to the Division of Labor.

interest he frequently promotes that of society more ef-
fectually than when he really intends to promote it. I
have never known much good done by those who affected to trade for the public good. It is an affectation,
indeed, not very common among merchants, and very
few words need to be employed in dissuading them
from it. (*An Inquiry into the Nature and Causes of the
Wealth of Nations,* edited by R. Campbell, A. Skinner,
W. Todd (Oxford: Clarendon Press, 1976), book IV,
chap. ii, para. 9)

*According to Smith, capitalism (as we now call his market-based
system) is not without its flaws. Smith admitted that a division of
labor where individuals do those tasks for which they are best
"suited" might cause atrophy in the minds of those confined to simple, repetitive tasks. Relevant to our purposes here, he also admitted
that the privileges afford the rich and famous might make them less
prone to virtue. Smith's answer to these and other concerns was
public education. Education could provide breadth to an otherwise
regimented mind. How could this concept be applied to our present
corporate society?*

BOOK I

*Of the causes of improvement in the productive powers of labor and of the order ac-
cording to which its produce is naturally distributed among the different ranks of the
people*

Chapter I Of the Division of Labor

The greatest improvement in the productive powers of labor, and the greatest part of the
skill, dexterity, and judgment with which it is anywhere directed, or applied, seem to
have been the effects of the division of labor. . . .

To take an example, therefore, from a very trifling manufacture; but one in which the
division of labor has been very often taken notice of, the trade of the pin-maker; a workman not educated to this business (which the division of labor has rendered a distinct
trade), nor acquainted with the use of the machinery employed in it (to the invention of
which the same division of labor has probably given occasion), could scarce, perhaps,
with his utmost industry, make one pin in a day, and certainly could not make twenty.
But in the way in which this business is now carried on, not only the whole work is a peculiar trade, but it is divided into a number of branches, of which the greater part are likewise peculiar trades. One man draws out the wire, another straightens it, a third cuts it, a
fourth points it, a fifth grinds it at the top for receiving the head; to make the head requires two or three distinct operations; to put it on is a peculiar business, to whiten the
pins is another; it is even a trade by itself to put them into the paper; and the important

business of making a pin is, in this manner, divided into about eighteen distinct operations, which in some manufactories, are all performed by distinct hands, though in others the same man will sometimes perform two or three of them. I have seen a small manufactory of this kind where ten men only were employed, and where some of them consequently performed two or three distinct operations. But though they were very poor, and therefore but indifferently accommodated with the necessary machinery, they could, when they exerted themselves, make among them about twelve pounds of pins a day. There are in a pound upwards of four thousand pins of a middling size. Those ten persons, therefore, could make among them upwards of forty-eight thousand pins in a day. Each person, therefore, making a tenth part of forty-eight thousand pins, might be considered as making four thousand eight hundred pins in a day. But if they had all wrought separately and independently, and without any of them having been educated to this peculiar business, they certainly could not each of them have made twenty, perhaps not one pin in a day; that is, certainly, not the two hundred and fortieth, perhaps not the four thousand eight hundredth part, of what they are at present capable of performing in consequence of a proper division and combination of their different operations.

In every other art and manufacture, the effects of the division of labor are similar to what they are in this very trifling one; though in many of them, the labor can neither be so much subdivided, nor reduced to so great a simplicity of operation. The division of labor, however, so far as it can be introduced, occasions, in every art, a proportionate increase of the productive powers of labor. . . .

This great increase of the quantity of work, which in consequence of the division of labor, the same number of people are capable of performing, is owing to three different circumstances: first, to the increase of dexterity in every particular workman; secondly, to the saving of the time which is commonly lost in passing from one species of work to another; and lastly, to the invention of a great number of machines which facilitate and abridge labor, and enable one man to do the work of many.

First, the improvement of the dexterity of the workman necessarily increases the quantity of the work he can perform; and the division of labor, by reducing every man's business to some one simple operation and by making this operation the sole employment of his life, necessarily increases very much the dexterity of the workman. A common smith, who, though accustomed to handle the hammer, has never been used to make nails, if upon some particular occasion he is obliged to attempt it, will scarce, I am assured, be able to make about two or three hundred nails in a day, and those too very bad ones. A smith who has been accustomed to make nails, but whose sole or principal business has not been that of a nailer, can seldom with his utmost diligence make more than eight hundred or a thousand nails in a day. I have seen several boys under twenty years of age who had never exercised any other trade but that of making nails, and who, when they exerted themselves, could make, each of them, upwards of two thousand three hundred nails in a day. The making of a nail, however, is by no means one of the simplest operations. The same person blows the bellows, stirs or mends the fire as there is occasion, heats the iron, and forges every part of the nail: In forging the head too he is obliged to change his tools. The different operations into which the making of a pin or of a metal button is subdivided, are all of them much more simple; and the dexterity of the person, of whose life it has been the sole business to perform them, is usually much greater. The rapidity with which some of the operations of those manufacturers are performed exceeds what the human hand could, by those who had never seen them, be supposed capable of acquiring.

Secondly, the advantage which is gained by saving the time commonly lost in passing from one sort of work to another is much greater than we should at first view be apt to imagine it. It is impossible to pass very quickly from one kind of work to another, that is carried on in a different place, and with quite different tools. A country weaver who cultivates a small farm must lose a good deal of time in passing from his loom to the field, and from the field to his loom. When the two trades can be carried on in the same workhouse, the loss of time is no doubt much less. It is even in this case, however, very considerable. . . .

Thirdly, and lastly, every body must be sensible how much labor is facilitated and abridged by the application of proper machinery. . . .

. . . A great part of the machines made use of in those manufactures in which labor is most subdivided were originally the inventions of common workmen, who, being each of them employed in some very simple operation, naturally turned their thoughts toward finding out easier and readier methods of performing it. Whoever has been much accustomed to visit such manufacturers must frequently have been shown very pretty machines which were inventions of such workmen in order to facilitate and quicken their own particular part of the work. In the first fire-engines, a boy was constantly employed to open and shut alternately the communication between the boiler and the cylinder, according as the piston either ascended or descended. One of those boys, who loved to play with his companions, observed that, by tying a string from the handle of the valve which opened this communication to another part of the machine, the valve would open and shut without his assistance, and leave him at liberty to divert himself with his play-fellows. One of the greatest improvements that has been made upon this machine, since it was first invented, was in this manner the discovery of a boy who wanted to save his own labor. . . .

It is the great multiplication of the productions of all the different arts, in consequence of the division of labor, which occasions, in a well-governed society, that universal opulence which extends itself to the lowest ranks of the people. Every workman has a great quantity of his own work to dispose of beyond what he himself has occasion for; and every other workman being exactly in the same situation, he is enabled to exchange a great quantity of his own goods for a great quantity, or, what comes to the same thing, for the price of a great quantity of theirs. He supplies them abundantly with what they have occasion for, and they accommodate him as amply with what he has occasion for, and a general plenty diffuses itself through all the different ranks of the society. . . .

Chapter II   Of the Principle Which Gives Occasion to the Division of Labor

This division of labor, from which so many advantages are derived, is not originally the effect of any human wisdom which forsees and intends that general opulence to which it gives occasion. It is the necessary, though very slow and gradual, consequence of a certain propensity in human nature which has in view no such extensive utility: the propensity to truck, barter, and exchange one thing for another.

. . . In almost every other race of animals each individual, when it is grown up to maturity, is entirely independent, and in its natural state has occasion for the assistance of no other living creature. But man has almost constant occasion for the help of his brethren, and it is in vain for him to expect it from their benevolence only. He will be more likely to prevail if he can interest their self-love in his favor, and show them that it is for their own advantage to do for him what he requires of them. Whoever offers to another a bargain of any kind, proposes to do this. Give me that which I want, and you shall have this which you want, is the meaning of every such offer; and it is in the manner that we obtain from one another the far greater part of those good offices which we stand in need of. It is not from the benevolence of the butcher, the brewer, or the baker, that we expect our dinner, but from their regard to their own interest. We address ourselves, not to their humanity but to their self-love, and never talk to them of our own necessities but of their advantages. Nobody but a beggar chooses to depend chiefly upon the benevolence of his fellow-citizens. Even a beggar does not depend upon it entirely. The charity of well-disposed people, indeed, supplies him with the whole fund of his subsistence. But though this principle ultimately provides him with all the necessaries of life which he has occasion for, it neither does nor can provide him with them as he has occasion for them. The greater part of his occasional wants are supplied in the same manner as those of other people, by treaty, by barter, and by purchase. With the money which one man gives him he purchases food. The old clothes which another bestows upon him he exchanges for other old clothes which suit him better, or for lodging, or for food, or for money, with which he can buy either food, clothes, or lodging, as he has occasion.

As it is by treaty, by barter, and by purchase that we obtain from one another the greater part of those mutual good offices which we stand in need of, so it is this same trucking disposition in which originally gives occasion to the division of labor. In a tribe of hunters or shepherds a particular person makes bows and arrows, for example, with more readiness and dexterity than any other. He frequently exchanges them for cattle or for venison with his companions; and he finds at last that he can in this manner get more cattle and venison than if he himself went to the field to catch them. From a regard to his own interest, therefore, the making of bows and arrows grows to be his chief business, and he becomes a sort of armorer. Another excels in making the frames and covers of their little huts or moveable houses. He is accustomed to be of use in this way to his neighbors, who reward him in the same manner with cattle and with venison till at last he finds it his interest to dedicate himself entirely to this employment, and to become a sort of house carpenter. In the same manner a third becomes a smith or a brazier; a fourth a tanner or dresser of hides or skins, the principal part of the clothing of savages. And thus the certainty of being able to exchange all that surplus part of the produce of his own labor, which is over and above his own consumption, for such parts of the produce of other men's labor as he may have occasion for, encourages every man to apply himself to a particular occupation, and to cultivate and bring to perfection whatever talent or genius he may possess for that particular species of business.

The difference of natural talents in different men is, in reality, much less than we are aware of; and the very different genius which appears to distinguish men of different professions, when grown up to maturity, is not upon many occasions so much the cause as the effect of the division of labor. The difference between the most dissimilar characters, between a philosopher and a common street porter, for example, seems to arise not so much from nature as from habit, custom, and education. When they came into the world, and for the first six or eight years of their existence, they were, perhaps, very much alike, and neither their parents nor play-fellows could perceive any remarkable difference. About that age, or soon after, they come to be employed in very different occupations. The difference of talents comes then to be taken notice of, and widens by degrees, till at last the vanity of the philosopher is willing to acknowledge scarce any resemblance. But without the disposition to truck, barter, and exchange, every man must have procured to himself every necessary and convenience of life which he wanted. All must have had the same duties to perform, and the same work to do, and there could have been no such difference of employment as could alone give occasion to any great difference of talents. . . .

A HANGING

George Orwell

Do we feel a responsibility for that which occurs in front of us, though not as a result of us? This story discusses the response to that question. Does it matter more to you that something happens to someone you know, rather than to a complete stranger? Or that the person impacted by an event will know if it was your responsibility, rather than some stranger's? In "The Hanging," do you wonder about the nature of the prisoner's offense? Should it matter or do you take the state's decision as to his guilt as sufficient justification? If you were called to serve on a jury and, prior to hearing the case or the nature of the alleged offense, were asked if you would be willing to impose the death penalty under certain circumstances, what would be your response?

"The Hanging" is relevant to our ethics inquiry for its perspective on accountability. If you disagree with an event, how far will you go (if at all) to stop that event from occurring?

It was in Burma, a sodden morning of the rains. A sickly light, like yellow tinfoil, was slanting over the high walls into the jail yard. We were waiting outside the condemned cells, a row of sheds fronted with double bars, like small animal cages. Each cell measured about ten feet by ten and was quite bare within except for a plank bed and a pot of drinking water. In some of them brown silent men were squatting at the inner bars, with their blankets draped round them. These were the condemned men, due to be hanged within the next week or two.

One prisoner had been brought out of his cell. He was a Hindu, a puny wisp of a man, with a shaven head and vague liquid eyes. He had a thick, sprouting moustache, absurdly too big for his body, rather like the moustache of a comic man on the films. Six tall Indian warders were guarding him and getting him ready for the gallows. Two of them stood by with rifles and fixed bayonets, while the others handcuffed him, passed a chain through his handcuffs and fixed it to their belts, and lashed his arms tight to his sides. They crowded very close about him, with their hands always on him in a careful, caressing grip, as though all the while feeling him to make sure he was there. It was like men handling a fish which is still alive and may jump back into the water. But he stood quite unresisting, yielding his arms limply to the ropes, as though he hardly noticed what was happening.

Eight o'clock struck and a bugle call, desolately thin in the wet air, floated from the distant barracks. The superintendent of the jail, who was standing apart from the rest of

---

us, moodily prodding the gravel with his stick, raised his head at the sound. He was an army doctor, with a grey toothbrush moustache and a gruff voice. "For God's sake hurry up, Francis," he said irritably. "The man ought to have been dead by this time. Aren't you ready yet?"

Francis, the head jailer, a fat Dravidian in a white drill suit and gold spectacles, waved his black hand. "Yes sir, yes sir," he bubbled. "All iss satisfactorily prepared. The hangman iss waiting. We shall proceed."

"Well, quick march, then. The prisoners can't get their breakfast till this job's over."

We set out for the gallows. Two warders marched on either side of the prisoner, with their rifles at the slope; two others marched close against him, gripping him by arm and shoulder, as though at once pushing and supporting him. The rest of us, magistrates and the like, followed behind. Suddenly, when we had gone ten yards, the procession stopped short without any order or warning. A dreadful thing had happened—a dog, come goodness knows whence, had appeared in the yard. It came bounding among us with a loud volley of barks, and leapt round us wagging its whole body, wild with glee at finding so many human beings together. It was a large woolly dog, half Airedale, half pariah. For a moment it pranced round us, and then, before anyone could stop it, it had made a dash for the prisoner, and jumping up tried to lick his face. Everyone stood aghast, too taken aback even to grab at the dog.

"Who let that blood brute in here?" said the superintendent angrily. "Catch it, someone!"

A warder, detached from the escort, charged clumsily after the dog, but it danced and gambolled just out of his reach, taking everything as part of the game. A young Eurasian jailer picked up a handful of gravel and tried to stone the dog away, but it dodged the stones and came after us again. Its yaps echoed from the jail walls. The prisoner, in the grasp of the two warders, looked on incuriously, as though this was another formality of the hanging. It was several minutes before someone managed to catch the dog. Then we put my handkerchief through its collar and moved off once more, with the dog still straining and whimpering.

It was about forty yards to the gallows. I watched the bare brown back of the prisoner marching in front of me. He walked clumsily with his bound arms, but quite steadily, with that bobbing gait of the Indian who never straightens his knees. At each step his muscles slid neatly into place, the lock of hair on his scalp danced up and down, his feet printed themselves on the wet gravel. And once, in spite of the men who gripped him by each shoulder, he stepped slightly aside to avoid a puddle on the path.

It is curious, but till that moment I had never realized what it means to destroy a healthy, conscious man. When I saw the prisoner step aside to avoid the puddle, I saw the mystery, the unspeakable wrongness, of cutting a life short when it is in full tide. This man was not dying, he was alive just as we were alive. All the organs of his body were working—bowels digesting food, skin renewing itself, nails growing, tissues forming—all toiling away in solemn foolery. His nails would still be growing when he stood on the drop, when he was falling through the air with a tenth of a second to live. His eyes saw the yellow gravel and the grey walls, and his brain still remembered, foresaw, reasoned—reasoned even about puddles. He and we were a party of men walking together, seeing, hearing, feeling, understanding the same world; and in two minutes, with a sudden snap, one of us would be gone—one mind less, one world less.

The gallows stood in a small yard, separate from the main grounds of the prison, and overgrown with tall prickly weeds. It was a brick erection like three sides of a shed, with planking on top, and above that two beams and a crossbar with the rope dangling. The hangman, a grey-haired convict in the white uniform of the prison, was waiting beside his machine. He greeted us with a servile crouch as we entered. At a word from Francis the two warders, gripping the prisoner more closely than ever, half led, half pushed him to the gallows and helped him clumsily up the ladder. Then the hangman climbed up and fixed the rope round the prisoner's neck.

We stood waiting, five yards away. The warders had formed in a rough circle round the gallows. And then, when the noose was fixed, the prisoner began crying out to his god. It was a high, reiterated cry of "Ram! Ram! Ram! Ram!", not urgent and fearful like a prayer or a cry for help, but steady, rhythmical, almost like the tolling of a bell. The dog answered the sound with a whine. The hangman, still standing on the gallows, produced a small cotton bag like a flour bag and drew it down over the prisoner's face. But the sound, muffled by the cloth, still persisted, over and over again: "Ram! Ram! Ram! Ram! Ram!"

The hangman climbed down and stood ready, holding the lever. Minutes seemed to pass. The steady, muffled cry from the prisoner went on and on, "Ram! Ram! Ram!" never faltering for an instant. The superintendent, his head on his chest, was slowly poking the ground with his stick; perhaps he was counting the cries, allowing the prisoner a fixed number—fifty, perhaps, or a hundred. Everyone had changed colour. The Indians had gone grey like bad coffee, and one or two of the bayonets were wavering. We looked at the lashed, hooded man on the drop, and listened to his cries—each cry another second of life; the same thought was in all our minds; oh, kill him quickly, get it over, stop that abominable noise!

Suddenly the superintendent made up his mind. Throwing up his head he made a swift motion with his stick. "Chalo!" he shouted almost fiercely.

There was a clanking noise, and then dead silence. The prisoner had vanished, and the rope was twisting on itself. I let go of the dog, and it galloped immediately to the back of the gallows; but when it got there it stopped short, barked, and then retreated into a corner of the yard, where it stood among the weeds, looking timorously out at us. We went round the gallows to inspect the prisoner's body. He was dangling with his toes pointed straight downwards, very slowly revolving, as dead as a stone.

The superintendent reached out with his stick and poked the bare body; it oscillated, slightly. "*He's* all right," said the superintendent. He backed out from under the gallows, and blew out a deep breath. The moody look had gone out of his face quite suddenly. He glanced at his wrist-watch. "Eight minutes past eight. Well, that's all for this morning, thank God."

The warders unfixed bayonets and marched away. The dog, sobered and conscious of having misbehaved itself, slipped after them. We walked out of the gallows yard, past the condemned cells with their waiting prisoners, into the big central yard of the prison. The convicts, under the command of warders armed with lathis, were already receiving their breakfast. They squatted in long rows, each man holding a tin pannikin, while two warders with buckets marched round ladling out rice; it seemed quite a homely, jolly scene, after the hanging. An enormous relief had come upon us now that the job was done. One felt an impulse to sing, to break into a run, to snigger. All at once everyone began chattering gaily.

The Eurasian boy walking beside me nodded towards the way we had come, with a knowing smile: "Do you know, sir, our friend (he meant the dead man), when he heard his appeal had been dismissed, he pissed on the floor of his cell. From fright.—Kindly take one of my cigarettes, sir. Do you not admire my new silver case, sir? From the boxwallah, two rupees eight annas. Classy European style."

Several people laughed—at what, nobody seemed certain.

Francis was walking by the superintendent, talking garrulously: "Well, sir, all hass passed off with the utmost satisfactoriness. It wass all finished—flick! like that. It iss not always so—oah, no! I have known cases where the doctor wass obliged to go beneath the gallows and pull the prisoner's legs to ensure decease. Most disagreeable!"

"Wriggling about, eh? That's bad," said the superintendent.

"Ach, sir, it iss worse when they become refractory! One man, I recall, clung to the bars of hiss cage when we went to take him out. You will scarcely credit, sir, that it took six warders to dislodge him, three pulling at each leg. We reasoned with him. 'My dear fellow,' we said, 'think of all the pain and trouble you are causing to us!' But no, he would not listen! Ach, he wass very troublesome!"

I found that I was laughing quite loudly. Everyone was laughing. Even the superintendent grinned in a tolerant way. "You'd better all come out and have a drink," he said quite genially. "I've got a bottle of whisky in the car. We could do with it."

We went through the big double gates of the prison, into the road. "Pulling at his legs!" exclaimed a Burmese magistrate suddenly, and burst into a loud chuckling. We all began laughing again. At that moment Francis's anecdote seemed extraordinarily funny. We all had a drink together, native and European alike, quite amicably. The dead man was a hundred yards away.

TOM'S OF MAINE STATEMENT OF BELIEFS AND MISSION STATEMENT

TOM CHAPPELL

Tom Chappell is the founder and president of Tom's of Maine, a company known for its environmentally correct cosmetics and bath products. Its mission statement has been cited, not necessarily as one of the best in the business (though it is very good), but as one of the ones that is sincerely adhered to by the company that created it. Tom's of Maine is known for placing its mission first, which, it believes, allows for greater profits in the long run.

WE BELIEVE that both human beings and nature have inherent worth and deserve our respect.

WE BELIEVE in products that are safe, effective, and made of natural ingredients.

WE BELIEVE that our company and our products are unique and worthwhile, and that we can sustain these genuine qualities with an ongoing commitment to innovation and creativity.

WE BELIEVE that we have a responsibility to cultivate the best relationships possible with our co-workers, customers, owners, agents, suppliers, and our community.

WE BELIEVE in providing employees with a safe and fulfilling work environment, and an opportunity to grow and learn.

WE BELIEVE that our company can be financially successful while behaving in a socially responsible and environmentally sensitive manner.

our mission

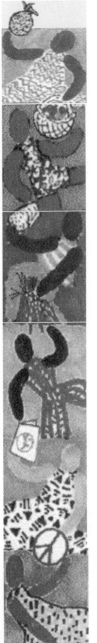

TO SERVE our customers by providing safe, effective, innovative, natural products of high quality.

TO BUILD relationships with our customers that extend beyond product usage to include full and honest dialogue, responsiveness to feedback, and the exchange of information about products and issues.

TO RESPECT, value, and serve not only our customers, but also our co-workers, owners, agents, suppliers, and our community; to be concerned about and contribute to their well-being, and to operate with integrity so as to be deserving of their trust.

TO PROVIDE meaningful work, fair compensation, and a safe, healthy work environment that encourages openness, creativity, self-discipline, and growth.

TO CONTRIBUTE to and affirm a high level of commitment, skill, and effectiveness in the work community.

TO RECOGNIZE, encourage, and seek a diversity of gifts and perspectives in our worklife.

TO ACKNOWLEDGE the value of each person's contribution to our goals and to foster teamwork in our tasks.

TO BE DISTINCTIVE in products and policies which honor and sustain our natural world.

TO ADDRESS community concerns in Maine and around the globe, by devoting a portion of our time, talents, and resources to the environment, human needs, the arts, and education.

TO WORK TOGETHER to contribute to the long-term value and sustainability of our company.

TO BE A PROFITABLE and successful company while acting in a socially and environmentally responsible manner.

Chapter 7a

CORPORATE STRATEGY AND DECISION MAKING
Actions and Repercussions

The trouble with the rat race is that, even if you win, you're still a rat. LILY TOMLIN

Take care to guard against all greed, for though one may be rich, one's life does not consist of possessions. LUKE 12:15

Good ethics is good business. Have you heard that before? Did you believe it? Theorists argue about whether ethical decisions lead to higher profits than unethical decisions. While we are all familiar with examples of unethical decisions leading to high profits, there is general agreement that, in the long run, ethics pays off. But the question of what is an ethical decision remains. Lao Tzu in the *Tao Te Ching* (Chapter 46) contends that there is no crime greater than having too many desires and no misfortune greater than being covetous. How would Taoism view the acts and intentions of a profit-maximizing firm in today's market?

Consider the demise of small bookstores all over the country. In the past several years, large, multipurpose bookstores such as Crown Books and Barnes & Noble have seemed to take over the literary consumption landscape. For example, Chicago has seen the collapse of a number of old standbys, bookstores that had been in the city for years serving a specific, sometimes idiosyncratic, population rather than the entire book-purchasing community. These stores (Krochs and Brentanos, Stuart Brent, Guild Books, and others) could not survive next to chain superstores that provide a greater selection of low-priced alternatives.

Stuart Brent, a longtime bookseller on prestigious Michigan Avenue in Chicago, recently was forced out of business by competition from Borders and other chain bookstores opening right down the street from him. Brent's store was one where the salespeople could remember your name, where there were large, comfy chairs in which to peruse the books, where there were experts available on literary issues, and where they knew just the right book for your Uncle Gordy. Brent's sales went down 30 percent with the opening of Borders Bookstore three blocks away. "Supermarkets," he snorts, "philistines. My father used to speak of 'men you'd have to stand on tiptoes to talk to.' Where are those men today?" Even Mayor Richard Daley mourned the loss in a telegram sent to Brent on closing day: "Michigan Avenue will miss you, as much as it was enhanced by your fine store and elegant presence."[1] A traditional tale of David and Goliath?

The chain superstores argue that it is not. Instead, these stores contend that they are merely serving the needs of their customers in a more effective, efficient manner, and therefore deserve a larger share of the market. "It's no longer simply the big, stupid bestseller stores and the small, elegant, literary bookstores," says shopper and northwestern University professor Joseph Epstein. "Places like Barnes & Noble and Borders stock the good books, too. I doubt that Stuart Brent had anything these stores don't, except in his specialty of psychoanalytic books."[2] Perhaps these larger bookstores aren't so much predators as they are simply players—answering the needs of the public.

Does a large chain store have any particular responsibility when it enters a market in a small community? Consider as well the tales of Walgreens stores entering small towns where there is one established pharmacy equipped with a pharmacist who has been serving that public for many years. The pharmacist cannot compete with the economies of scale available to a large firm like Walgreens, so she closes her doors. Is Walgreens to blame? Perhaps. But is it at *fault?* Is it using its size as a competitive advantage to reap greater profits for its owners?

---

1. Jeff Lyon, "For Starters," *Chicago Tribune, Sunday Magazine,* January 14, 1996, p. 6.
2. Epstein quoted in John Blades, "Staying Alive," *Chicago Tribune,* March 20, 1996, sec. 5, pp. 1, 4.

Consider what ethical and unethical steps might be taken in the name of profits. Is offering a larger selection, lower prices, and a different ambience unethical? Is an act ethical because it results in higher profit or in spite of it? The readings in this topic area are divided into three subchapters. The first segment contains readings relating directly to corporate decision making, profit maximization, and cost reduction. The second group comprises a discussion of a controversy surrounding the Ford Pinto automobile and other cases. The Pinto case is considered a seminal case in ethics—one that pits profits against human lives, but one that also evidences the benefits of long-term ethical thinking. The group of materials also includes a scenario similar to the Ford Pinto: the space shuttle *Challenger* disaster. Do you see similarities in the handling of the two cases? What should those involved in the latter case have learned from the former? The group finally addresses ethical issues in a traditional cost-cutting activity: employee downsizing.

Finally, the third segment takes a look at the corporate response to public demands for ethical behavior and the concern for the "appearance of propriety," the corporate reputation. As you review the readings in this last group, ponder the following (facetious and sarcastic) recommendations for leadership offered by Colin Powell as a result of the frustration he experienced during the mishandling of the Iranian hostage crisis:

1. Release facts slowly, behind the pace at which they are already leaking to the public.
2. Don't tell the whole story until forced to do so.
3. Emphasize what went well and euphemize what went wrong.
4. Become indignant at any suggestion of poor judgment or mistakes.
5. Disparage any facts other than your own.
6. Accuse critics of Monday-morning generalship.
7. Accept general responsibility at the top, thus clearing everybody at fault below.[3]

SHORT HYPOTHETICAL CASES

a. Four of the original owners of a metal fabricating company are selling out to the fifth owner. The company has been successful and, after 25 years, employs 250 people in the plant and 150 in the office. In evaluating the company, the new sole owner sees much duplication: five accountants could do the job that 20 now handle. In every office department, the company has overhired. Cutting back would dramatically improve the company's profits. But the company is a small, close-knit community and the employees have long service records and are extremely loyal. As the new sole owner, what do you do?

---

3. Colin Powell and Joseph Persico, *My American Journey* (New York: Random House, 1995), p. 250.

b. You are a project manager for a recliner manufacturer. A young child died after his head was caught in the leg rest on a recliner of the same design as yours. You learn that several children have died in this manner; you did not manufacture any of the recliners involved. A federal regulatory agency has studied the problem and has determined that a safeguard would cost $0.25 per chair. However, the agency estimates that lawsuits for all anticipated deaths and injuries will only cost $0.11 per chair. The agency therefore will not require the safeguards to be installed. Your major competitors have decided it is not cost-effective to install the safeguard. What will you do?

Hypotheticals were written by Catherine Haselden and are included in her manuscript "The Ethics Game."

PROFITABLE ETHICAL PROGRAMS

JASON LUNDAY

In response to a previous e-mail to a listserver on teaching business ethics, Lunday identifies some apparently successful ethical business practices from the annals of business history.

. . . Some apparently successful ethical business practices:

(In some cases, the companies claim a very direct bottom-line effect to certain ethical practices. Others claim that their ethical practices contribute to an overall corporate climate which cuts waste, encourages efficiency, promotes community/marketplace goodwill, allowing the company a healthy bottom line.)

1. 3M—through its Pollution Prevention Program (3P), initiated in the mid-1970s, the corporation claims to have decreased its production and emission of air, solid, and water pollutants by billions of lbs. AND saved the company over $500 million during its first 15 years. It did so by using its expertise in innovation to find new ways of manufacturing which led to fewer pollutants. To qualify for the 3P program, ideas had to meet three of four measures, only one of which was cost savings. [See Alfred Marcus, *Business and Society: Strategy, Ethics, and the Global Economy,* Irwin, Chicago, 1996.]

While 3M was considered the first, I understand that a large number of companies have successfully accomplished similar environmental initiatives, reducing pollutants and saving money. Contact the Management Institute for Environment and Business, Washington, DC, for examples.

2. Levi Strauss—with a strong history of employee goodwill, LSCO has worked for numerous years to insure that its employee policies demonstrate respect for workers and their lives. It has consistently paid workers at the top of the industry and granted benefits uncommon among its competitors (like year-round employment). Further, it has encouraged strong employee communication and idea-sharing. It has expected that such treatment would create mutual respect. This apparently came true when a South American operation effectively communicated one of its new product launches to headquarters during a time of overall lagging sales. The idea, Dockers, became the biggest product introduction in U.S. history and reinvigorated the company. [See Jeffrey Edwards and Jason Lunday, *Levi Strauss & Co.: The South Zarzamora Street Plant,* Darden Graduate Business School Case Bibliography.]

Ethics and Profits: Mutually Exclusive? Email from Jason Lunday, "Profitable Ethical Programs," Email, June 18, 1996. Reprinted by permission of the author.

There are other stories of how factory employees have taken pay cuts, done without raises, and accepted other risks at certain times because of the company's fair treatment and with an expectation that such a well-managed company will overcome periodic difficulties.

3.   South Shore Bank—the company came up with the great idea to help its local community, a depressed area of Chicago, where few could get back loans. In finding ways to grant credit where other banks would not, South Shore not only helped a community pick itself back up, it increased bank earnings.

[Sorry, don't have a reference handy. South Shore has won Business Ethics Magazine's annual award in recent years, so a past edition of the magazine will overview the company's story.]

4.   Johnson & Johnson—need we say more on this one? For a treatment of this, see *Managing Corporate Ethics,* Francis Aguilar, Oxford University Press, New York, 1994.

5.   Delta Air Lines—Delta also has a strong history of employee relations, to the extent that, for years, it was the only non-unionized airline. This allowed the carrier flexibility during recessions to move workers around in order to maximize manpower in key areas. It also traditionally allows the airline to have employees perform multiple tasks so that it does not have to hire additional workers. The airline had, for many years, consistently been at the top of the Dept. of Transportation's lowest complaint list. It generally is still there, occasionally being beat out by Southwest. Employee goodwill because of the company's treatment also helps the company keep a very low employee/seat miles ratio. Some years back, because of exceptional treatment, the employees chipped in and bought the company a passenger jet. Delta has also ended up as one of the country's most admired companies for many years. [Personal unpublished research—if you want article references, just ask. I've got a lot.]

6.   Lincoln Electric—arc welding. Company claims that strong employee orientation has allowed it to earn exceptional profits. [See *Managing Corporate Ethics,* Francis Aguilar, Oxford University Press, New York, 1994.]

7.   Honda—attention to customer quality allowed it strong entrance into U.S. market. [*Business and Society . . . ,* Alfred Marcus, Irwin, Chicago, 1996.]

8.   BFI—effort to help New York rid itself of corruption in the trash hauling business gave the company early entry into a lucrative market. [See recent *Fortune* cover story.]

9.   Socially responsible companies Body Shop, Ben & Jerry's, Tom's of Maine, etc.: each claims that their orientation to meeting stakeholder needs—in a variety of forms—allowed them to become large players in their respective markets. [See *Body and Soul,* Anita Roddick, *The Soul of a Business,* Tom Chappell, don't know Ben & Jerry's book.]

10.   Merck—another company at the very top of Fortune's Most Admired Companies. The company ended up paying millions of dollars to formulate, manufacture, and distribute a drug which cures river blindness, which is generally found in poor regions of lesser developed countries. The goodwill alone from this has apparently, like J&J and Tylenol, given it many consumers' trust. Granted, it would be difficult to quantify how much that is worth, but I doubt that Vagelos or the current chairman would deny it has been worth a lot.

11.   Sears, Roebuck—when questions arose about possible inappropriate sales practices of product warranties, which, by the way, were making BIG money for the retailer, they retrained their associates to ensure that the warranties were not being pushed on customers or otherwise sold unethically. Expecting a drop in warranty sales, they instead were hit with a sizeable increase.

[See *Ethikos* back issue, can't remember the date. Also, personal consulting experience with them.]

Business ethics books are generally filled with cases of companies which have gotten into trouble. We don't see enough of the good stories since, I suppose, we simply expect this. However, the positive examples can go a long way in encouraging prosocial behavior, which, like deterrence theory, is another aspect of business ethics.

MORAL LEADERSHIP AND BUSINESS ETHICS

AL GINI

How do you judge the ethics of a leader? What makes one leader ethical and another unethical? Does it depend on the impact of that leader on her or his followers? Gini identifies the parameters within which we might appropriately judge a leader and the structural restraints imposed upon corporate leadership. Consider the impact of these restraints on the decisions and actions of leaders. Do they justify any (or all) leadership decisions?

. . . How do we judge the ethics of a leader? Clearly, no leader can be expected to be perfect in every decision and action made. As John Gardner has pointed out, particular consequences are never a reliable assessment of leadership.[1] The quality and worth of leadership can only be measured in terms of what a leader intends, values, believes in or stands for—in other words, character. In *Character: America's Search for Leadership,* Gail Sheehy argued, as did Aristotle before her, that character is the most crucial and most elusive element of leadership. The root of the word "character" comes from the Greek word for engraving. As applied to human beings, it refers to the enduring marks or etched-in factors in our personality, which include our in-born talents as well as the learned and acquired traits imposed upon us by life and experience. These engravings define us, set us apart and motivate behavior.

In regard to leadership, said Sheehy, character is fundamental and prophetic. The "issues (of leadership) are today and will change in time. Character is what was yesterday and will be tomorrow."[2] For Sheehy, character establishes both our day-to-day demeanor and our destiny. Therefore, it is not only useful but essential to examine the character of those who desire to lead us. As a journalist and longtime observer of the political scene, Sheehy contends that the Watergate affair of the early 1970s serves as a perfect example of the links between character and leadership. As Richard Nixon demonstrated so well, said Sheehy: "The Presidency is not the place to work out one's personal pathology."[3] Leaders rule us, run things, wield power. Therefore, said Sheehy, we must be careful whom we choose as leaders. Because who we choose, is what we shall be. If, as Heraclitus wrote, "character is fate," the fate our leaders reap will also be our own.

Al Gini, "Moral Leadership and Business Ethics." Reprinted by permission. Al Gini is an associate professor of philosophy at Loyola University of Chicago and managing editor of *Business Ethics Quarterly.*
1. John W. Gardner, *On Leadership* (New York: The Free Press, 1990), p. 8.
2. Gail Sheehy, *Character: America's Search for Leadership* (New York: Bantam Books, 1990), p. 311.
3. *Ibid.,* p. 66.

Putting aside the particular players and the politics of the episode, Watergate has come to symbolize the failings and failures of people in high places. Watergate now serves as a watershed, a turning point, in our nation's concern for integrity, honesty and fair play from all kinds of leaders. It is not a mere coincidence that the birth of business ethics as an independent, academic discipline can be dated from the Watergate affair and the trials that came out of it. No matter what our failings as individuals, Watergate sensitized us to the importance of ethical standards and conduct from those who direct the course of our political and public lives. What society is now demanding, and what business ethics is advocating, is that our business leaders and public servants should be held accountable to an even higher standard of behavior than we might demand and expect of ourselves.

Mutual Purposes and Goals   The character, goals and aspirations of a leader are not developed in a vacuum. Leadership, even in the hands of a strong, confident, charismatic leader remains, at bottom, relational. Leaders, good or bad, great or small, arise out of the needs and opportunities of a specific time and place. Leaders require causes, issues and, most importantly, a hungry and willing constituency. Leaders may devise plans, establish an agenda, bring new and often radical ideas to the table, but all of them are a response to the milieu and membership of which they are a part. If leadership is an active and ongoing relationship between leaders and followers, then a central requirement of the leadership process is for leaders to evoke and elicit consensus in their constituencies, and conversely for followers to inform and influence their leaders. This is done in at least two ways, through the use of power and education.

The term "power" comes from the Latin *posse:* to do, to be able, to change, to influence or effect. To have power is to possess the capacity to control or direct change. All forms of leadership must make use of power. The central issue of power in leadership is not, "Will it be used?" but, rather, "Will it be used wisely and well?" According to James MacGregor Burns, leadership is not just about directed results; it is also about offering followers a choice among real alternatives. Hence, leadership assumes competition, conflict and debate whereas brute power denies it.[4] "Leadership mobilizes," said Burns, "naked power coerces."[5] But power need not be dictatorial or punitive to be effective. Power can also be used in a noncoercive manner to orchestrate, direct and guide members of an organization in the pursuit of a goal or series of objectives. Leaders must engage followers, not merely direct them. Leaders must serve as models and mentors, not martinets. "Power without morality," said novelist James Baldwin, "is no longer power."

For Peter Senge teaching is one of the primary jobs of leadership.[6] The "task of leader as teacher" is to empower people with information, offer insights, new knowledge, alternative perspectives on reality. The "leader as teacher" said Senge, is not just about "teaching" people how "to achieve their vision" but, rather, is about fostering learning, offering choices and building consensus.[7] Effective leadership recognizes that in order to

---

4. James MacGregor Burns, *Leadership* (New York: Harper Torchbooks, 1979), p. 36.

5. *Ibid.,* p. 439.

6. For Senge the three primary tasks of leadership include: leader as designer; leader as steward; leader as teacher.

7. Peter M. Senge, *The Fifth Discipline* (New York: Double/Currency Books, 1990), p. 353.

build and achieve community, followers must become reciprocally coresponsible in the pursuit of a common enterprise. Through their conduct and teaching, leaders must try to make their fellow constituents aware that they are all stakeholders in a conjoint activity that cannot succeed without their involvement and commitment. Successful leadership believes in and communicates some version of the now famous Hewlett Packard motto: "The achievements of an organization are the results of the combined efforts of each individual."

In the end, says Abraham Zaleznick, "leadership is based on a compact that binds those who lead with those who follow into the same moral, intellectual and emotional commitment."[8] However, as both Burns and Rost warned us, the nature of this "compact" is inherently unequal because the influence patterns existing between leaders and followers are not equal. Responsive and responsible leadership requires, as a minimum, that democratic mechanisms be put in place which recognize the right of followers to have adequate knowledge of alternative options, goals and programs, as well as the capacity to choose between them. "In leadership writ large, mutually agreed upon purposes help people achieve consensus, assume responsibility, work for the common good and build community."[9]

STRUCTURAL RESTRAINTS

There is, unfortunately, a dark side to the theory of the "witness of others." Howard S. Schwartz in his radical, but underappreciated, managerial text *Narcissistic Process and Corporate Decay,*[10] argued that corporations are not bastions of benign, other-directed ethical reasoning. Nor can corporations, because of the demands and requirements of business, be models and exemplars of moral behavior. The rule of business, said Schwartz, remains the "law of the jungle," "the survival of the fittest," and the goal of survival engenders a combative "us against them mentality" which condones the moral imperative of getting ahead by any means necessary. Schwartz calls this phenomenon "organizational totalitarianism": Organizations and the people who manage them create for themselves a self-contained, self-serving world view, which rationalizes anything done on their behalf and which does not require justification on any grounds outside of themselves.[11] The psychodynamics of this narcissistic perspective, said Schwartz, impose Draconian requirements on all participants in organizational life: do your work; achieve organizational goals; obey and exhibit loyalty to your superiors; disregard personal values and beliefs; obey the law when necessary, obfuscate it whenever possible; and, deny internal or external discrepant information at odds with the stated organizational worldview. Within such a "totalitarian logic," neither leaders nor followers, rank nor file, operate as independent agents. To "maintain their place," to "get ahead," all must conform. The agenda of "organizational totalitarianism," said Schwartz, is always the preservation of the *status quo.* Within such a logic, like begets like, and change is rarely possible.

8. Abraham Zaleznik, "The Leadership Gap," *Academy of Management Executive* (1990), V.4, N.1, p. 12.

9. Joseph C. Rost, *Leadership for the Twenty-First Century,* p. 124.

10. Howard S. Schwartz, *Narcissistic Process and Corporate Decay* (New York: New York University Press, 1990).

11. Howard S. Schwartz, "Narcissism Project and Corporate Decay: The Case of General Motors," *Business Ethics Quarterly,* V.1, N.3, p. 250.

Except for extreme situations in which "systemic ineffectiveness" begins to breed "organization decay," transformation is never an option.

In *Moral Mazes* Robert Jackall, from a sociological rather than a psychological perspective, parallels much of Schwartz's analysis of organizational behavior. According to critic and commentator Thomas W. Norton, both Jackall and Schwartz seek to understand why and how organizational ethics and behavior are so often reduced to either dumbloyalty or the simple adulation and mimicry of one's superiors. While Schwartz argued that individuals are captives of the impersonal structural logic of "organizational totalitarianism," Jackall contends that "organizational actors become personally loyal to their superiors, always seeking their approval, and are committed to them as persons rather than as representatives of the abstractions of organizational authority." But in either case, both authors maintain that organizational operatives are prisoners of the systems they serve.[12]

According to Jackall, all organizations (to be exact, he is specially referring to American business organizations) are examples of "patrimonial bureaucracies" wherein "fealty relations of personal loyalty" are the rule and the glue of organizational life. Jackall argued that all corporations are like fiefdoms of the middle ages, wherein the Lord of the Manor (CEO, President) offers protection, prestige and status to his vassals (managers) and serfs (workers) in return for homage (commitment) and service (work). In such a system, said Jackall, advancement and promotion are predicated on loyalty, trust, politics and personality as much as, if not more than, on experience, education, ability and actual accomplishments. The central concern of the worker/minion is to be known as a "can-do-guy," a "team player," being at the right place at the right time and master of all the social rules. That's why in the corporate world, says Jackall, 1,000 "atta-boys" are wiped away with one "oh, shit!"

As in the model of a feudal system, Jackall maintains that employees of a corporation are expected to become functionaries of the system and supporters of the *status quo*. Their loyalty is to the powers that be; their duty is to perpetuate performance and profit; and their values can be none other than those sanctioned by the organization. Jackall contends that the logic of every organization (place of business) and the collective personality of the workplace conspire to override the wants, desires and aspirations of the individual worker. No matter what a person believes off the job, said Jackall, on the job all of us to a greater or lesser extent are required to suspend, bracket or only selectively manifest our personal convictions.

> *What is right in the corporation is not what is right in a man's home or his church.*
> *What is right in the corporation is what the guy above you wants from you.*[13]

For Jackall the primary imperative of every organization is to succeed. This logic of performance, what he refers to as "institutional logic," leads to the creation of a private moral universe. A moral universe that, by definition, is totalitarian (self-sustained), solipsistic (self-defined) and narcissistic (self-centered). Within such a milieu truth is socially

---

12. Thomas W. Norton, "The Narcissism and Moral Mazes of Corporate Life: A Commentary on the Writings of H. Schwartz and R. Jackall," *Business Ethics Quarterly,* V.2, N.1, p. 76.
13. Robert Jackall, *Moral Mazes* (New York: Oxford University Press, 1988), p. 6.

defined and moral behavior is determined solely by organizational needs. The key virtues, for all alike, become the virtues of the organization: goal-preoccupation, problem solving, survival/success and, most importantly, playing by the "house rules." In time, said Jackall, those initiated and invested in the system come to believe that they live in a self-contained worldview which is above and independent of outside critique and evaluation.

For both Schwartz and Jackall, the logic of organizational life is rigid and unchanging. Corporations perpetuate themselves, both in their strengths and weakness, because corporate cultures clone their own. Even given the scenario of a benign organizational structure which produces positive behavior and beneficial results, the etiology of the problem, and the opportunity for abuse that it offers, represents the negative possibilities and inherent dangers of the "witness of others" as applied to leadership theory. Within the scope of Schwartz's and Jackall's allied analysis, "normative" moral leadership may not be possible. The model offered is both absolute and inflexible, and only "regular company guys" make it to the top. The maverick, the radical, the reformer are not long tolerated. The "institutional logic" of the system does not permit disruption, deviance or default. . . .

The term moral leadership often conjures up images of sternly robed priests, waspishly severe nuns, carelessly bearded philosophers, forbiddingly strict parents and something ambiguously labeled the "moral majority." These people are seen as confining and dictatorial. They make us do what we should do, not what we want to do. They encourage following the "superego" and not the "id." A moral leader is someone who supposedly tells people the difference between right and wrong from on high. But there is much more to moral leadership than merely telling others what to do.

The vision and values of leadership must have their origins and resolutions in the community of followers, of whom they are a part, and whom they wish to serve. Leaders can drive, lead, orchestrate and cajole, but they cannot force, dictate or demand. Leaders can be the catalyst for morally sound behavior, but they are not, by themselves, a sufficient condition. Leaders by means of their demeanor and message must be able to convince, not just tell others, that collaboration serves the conjoint interest and well-being of all involved. Leaders may offer a vision, but followers must buy into it. Leaders may organize a plan, but followers must decide to take it on. Leaders may demonstrate conviction and willpower, but followers, in the new paradigm of leadership, should not allow the leader's will to replace their own.[14] To reiterate the words of Abraham Zaleznick: "Leadership is based on a compact that binds those that lead with those who follow into the same moral, intellectual and emotional commitment."

Joseph C. Rost has argued, both publicly and privately, that the ethical aspects of leadership remain thorny. How, exactly, do leaders and collaborators in an influence relationship make a collective decision about the ethics of a change that they want to implement in an organization or society? Some will say, "Option A is ethical," while others will say, "Option B is ethical." How are leaders and followers to decide? As I have suggested, ethics is what "ought to be done" as the preferred mode of action in a "right-vs.-right," "values-vs.-values" confrontation. Ethics is an evaluative enterprise. Judgments

---

14. Garry Wills, *Certain Trumpets*, p. 13.

must be made in regard to competing points of view. Even in the absence of a belief in the existence of a single universal, absolute set of ethical rules, basic questions can still be asked: How does it impact on self and others? What are the consequences involved? Is it harmful? Is it fair? Is it equitable? Perhaps the best, but by no means definitive, method suited to the general needs of the ethical enterprise is a modified version of the scientific method: A) *Observation,* the recognition of a problem or conflict; B) *Inquiry,* a critical consideration of facts and issues involved; C) *Hypothesis,* the formulation of a decision or plan of action consistent with the known facts; D) *Experimentation and Evaluation,* the implementation of the decision or plan in order to see if it leads to the resolution of the problem. There are, of course, no perfect answers in ethics or life. The quality of our ethical choices cannot be measured solely in terms of achievements. Ultimately and ethically, intention, commitment and concerted effort are as important as outcome: What/why did leader/followers try to do? How did they try to do it?

Leadership is hard to define, and moral leadership is even harder. Perhaps, like pornography, we only recognize moral leadership when we see it. The problem is, we so rarely see it. Nevertheless, I am convinced that without the "witness" of moral leadership, standards of ethics in business and organizational life will not occur or be sustained. Leadership, even when defined as a collaborative experience, is still about the influence of individual character and the impact of personal mentoring. Behavior does not always beget like behavior on a one-to-one ratio, but it does establish tone, set the stage and offer options. Although it is mandatory that an organization as a whole—from top to bottom— make a commitment to ethical behavior to actually achieve it, the model for that commitment has to originate from the top.[15] Labor Secretary Robert Reich recently stated: "The most eloquent moral appeal (argument) will be no match for the dispassionate edict of the market."[16] Perhaps, the "witness" of moral leadership can prove to be more effective.

---

15. Dolecheck, *"Ethics: Take It From the Top,"* p. 14.
16. William Pfaff, "It's Time For a Change in Corporate Values," *Chicago Tribune,* Jan. 16, 1996, p. 17.

WHAT MAKES FOR SUCCESS?
DAVE THOMAS

Dave Thomas, the founder of Wendy's International, who describes himself as a "hamburger cook," believes that there are no secrets to being successful. He sets forth below his plain and simple principles for success.

A FIRST WORD

There are all kinds of success and all kinds of ways to achieve it. I know bus drivers who are as successful as bankers. I know anonymous computer programmers who are now more successful than some of the biggest sports celebrities. I also know glamorous Hollywood stars and leading political figures who are failures. Sometimes you can spot true success. Sometimes you can't. Success can take many forms, but one thing's for sure: There are certain ingredients that are necessary in any recipe for success, and they may be applied by anyone.

In other words, success comes through doing the right things—developing proper skills, attitudes, and values. As I've thought this through from an ordinary guy's perspective (which, above all else, I am; Lord knows, I'm no scholar), I have come to identify twelve ingredients. We know them as "character traits" or "values" or "virtues." People have been making lists of these ingredients ever since the Bible was written—and even before then. I've seen lists that are longer and some that are shorter, but twelve feel just about right to me. They are the ones that have made the most sense and have proved most valuable in my walk through life.

But I should warn you, making lists is not enough to achieve success. You have to *show* people what success is. For example, I don't think that we really need to define generosity; we need to show what it means to be more generous—with our time, our talents, and our treasures.

My list of ingredients for success is divided into four basic groups:

Inward—these have to do with getting your own act together successfully.

Outward—these are all about treating people right.

Upward—these are skills you need to know if you want to go beyond just doing an okay job and truly excel.

Onward—these are attitudes you need to have in order to put yourself second and other people first. I think that onward values may be the toughest and the most rewarding values of all.

Added on to these ingredients are some others. Since I'm a hamburger cook, I call them "toppings." They are the pickles and onions of how I look at success:

Anything is possible within the laws of God and man.

You can't cut corners on quality.

Give back—early and often.

When you help someone, you really help yourself.

Pay attention to the basics.

You can't make much progress walking forward if you don't keep your balance, and that means balance in every part of your life.

Have a sense of urgency about most things you do, and you won't end up as the caboose.

Focus on only one thing at a time, and on just a few things in a lifetime.

Don't waste time trying to do things you know nothing about: Either learn the basics or steer clear.

Remember that life is short and fragile. Live it as if you don't know if you are going to be around for the next breath.

Don't take the people of our nation—or their freedom—for granted.

Be yourself—don't take yourself too seriously.

Do the right thing—even when it may seem like the hardest thing in the world.

Put more into life than you get out of it. . . .

OUTWARD: TREATING PEOPLE RIGHT

Success may start inside, but it doesn't mean anything until you draw other people into the picture. The key is whether you are going to be fair to other folks—will you treat people right? If you are to treat people right, you have to master three fundamentals: caring, teamwork, and support. Most of us are lucky enough to learn these basic ideas from our parents and should be pros at them by the time we are in nursery school. (But I have met some Ph.D.s and millionaires who have never learned the words or have forgotten what they mean, and I bet that you know people like that, too.) Not taking people for granted is a great way to steer a straight outward course and to do right by your fellow human beings.

Caring

Caring is the rock that love is built upon. Caring is feeling what another person feels. Some people call it "empathy." Genuinely caring about people usually leads to success. And really successful people widen the circle of people they care about more and more as they grow older. Mary Kay Ash, founder of Mary Kay Cosmetics, once told me something

I'll never forget. She said the one suggestion she got in life that helped her most was to "pretend that every single person you meet has a sign around his or her neck that says, 'Make me feel important.'"

Why aren't we just nice to people? One year, shortly before Christmas, I went to a Wendy's restaurant in Albuquerque to film a television program about adoption with two youngsters. The little girl, who was about seven, had a fresh scar where her father had walloped her with a beer bottle. That scar wasn't going to go away. As we ate lunch along with a friend of mine, the girl and her older brother, who was about nine, finally started to look us in the eyes, and that was none too easy for them. We talked about how important it is to stick together when you don't have other family. And then the boy said: "I don't want to be adopted with her. Just look at her ugly scar!"

It may seem cruel, but he was right. The boy knew his sister's appearance would turn off many possible adoptive parents. And before you condemn him, think back for a minute: Were you any less selfish when you were nine? I doubt that I was. My friend—who is smart in a low-key way and who made it big-time by building a big business over the years—reached into his wallet and pulled out two crisp one hundred dollar bills. "You kids," he said in a real quiet voice, "don't have any money to buy Christmas presents. It's plain to see that. So I want you to buy some Christmas presents, but there's a catch. You can't buy anything for yourself. Think hard about what your brother or sister might like or need and buy that instead. Finally, you have to write me a letter about what you got each other."

That five-minute course in caring outdid the best universities anywhere. The brother and sister made up. In January, my friend received a letter reporting what they bought each other, and he sent a copy to me. Then we learned that they had been adopted by a family. As I hear it, they're quite a team, and their new parents are proud to have them—because of the way that they care for each other and for lots of other reasons, too.

Teamwork

Teamwork is the starting point for treating people right. Most people think that teamwork is only important when competing against other teams. But competition is only part of the picture. In most things we do in life, people have to work with rather than against each other to get something done. Win-win situations and partnerships are the most important results of teamwork. The best teams in the world are the ones that help people become better and achieve more than they ever thought they could on their own.

One place people learn teamwork from is their families. Children get their first lesson watching how their parents behave toward each other. So, if you're a parent, you are also a teacher of teamwork—for good or ill—every day. Your sons and daughters learn from what you do. For me, the people I've worked with have become my family, too. Throughout my career, my "second family" has taught me a whole lot about teamwork.

There are little teams and there are big teams. Your community is a team, for example. My daughter Pam organizes volunteer work for the city of Columbus, so she knows a lot about how to get different kinds of teams to work together, on projects ranging from recreation centers to hospital boards. Teams can work together, and teams can compete, too, even when they are not rivals. Why aren't Pam's kids jealous when she spends so much of her time on community work? There is a simple answer: The kids are all involved in community work themselves, and they have been from an early age. Pam and her husband, Steve, endorse it and encourage it. The community team isn't a rival or an opponent of the family team—it's an extension of it. Neat idea, don't you think?

Many people believe that support is something you give to someone you feel sorry for or that it means propping someone up who would fail unless you were there to give him a boost. But that's not the way I see it. Support is the boost you give someone who can help himself but who needs a partner to open a window or to push aside a roadblock. Support isn't a bunch of reckless advice, either. It's real help—commitment and effort. Support is "teamwork plus." Support is also sharing feelings and insights with other people. It's helping others with their level of awareness and making your own awareness stronger at the same time.

The best way to get support is to give it. Wendy's President Gordon Teter likes to remind people of a saying that Jack Mollenkopf, his college coach at Purdue, often used: "Meet me halfway, and it's amazing what can happen." It *is* amazing what can be done when you treat people with respect. Respect goes both ways, too. Just as the players need it from the coach, the coach needs it from the players.

Support is also easier if things aren't too complicated. Gordon believes in what he calls "The Law of the Lowest Common Denominator," and it has nothing to do with arithmetic. It goes like this: "The simpler you can keep it, the better you can execute it." It's that way for a department and its boss, for a congregation and its minister, and for a volunteer group and its chairperson. If you want to give and get support, it's a lot more likely to come and keep coming if the rules are simple and clear. . . .

ONWARD: PUTTING YOURSELF SECOND AND OTHERS FIRST

If going upward and reaching for excellence is where success gets tricky, going onward by putting yourself second and others first is where success really gets tough. Most books on success tell you that you have really "arrived" when you win the race. That's wrong. Truly successful people are the ones who help others cross the finish line. People who make this last big step toward success really have three things: responsibility, courage, and generosity. Onward is the direction Success Soldiers follow—Christian or any other kind.

Responsibility

We try to teach children responsiblity, and that's good, but, as I have already said, most of us don't learn the full meaning of responsibility until we are older and have gained solid experience, made some decisions, and learned from our mistakes—not the simple mistakes we make when "following orders" but mistakes we make when trying to do something really hard or trying to excel. Making these sorts of mistakes teaches us judgment, and it helps toughen our backbone.

Mature responsibility means realizing that no single person can be responsible for everything. You can't be successful if you are stumbling around trying to juggle the whole world on your shoulders. Responsible people refuse to take shortcuts, even though they are almost always available. They make sure that others with duties act responsibly, too. And they use whatever recognition or honor they may have earned not to further their own ends but on behalf of good causes. Instead of stealing the limelight, they allow it to shine upon a good cause.

My son Kenny says that the most important piece of advice I ever gave him came in 1979 as the two of us were driving over the Oakland Park Bridge in Ft. Lauderdale. He was thinking about becoming a Wendy's franchisee. I gave him my opinion; I was against it. I didn't come out and say why, but my feeling was that he wasn't ready for that kind of responsibility, and I didn't want to see him fail. When he told me his mind was made up, I said, "Don't ever forget how you got here, and don't ever let yourself become complacent." Kenny went on to become pretty successful in the restaurant business. He says my advice really helped him. But I could have summed up everything I said that day in just two words: Be responsible.

Courage

We tend to make courage too dramatic. Courage is often doing something simple, unpleasant, or boring again and again until we get it down pat. People who are physically challenged and who have the determination to get around their handicaps are great examples because their courage makes them test their limits every day in a way that the rest of us write off as small-time or insignificant. Lois Gruenbaum grew up in Cleveland and went to work in a hospital kitchen when she was fifteen. During World War II, she became a nurse's aide and worked in an army hospital. After a shift, she would say to herself, "Hey, things are bad, but there's always someone who is worse off. All you need to do is find out what you can and can't do and then go ahead and do what you can do."

Great lesson—Lois learned it not long before she needed to put it to use. In 1955, she was diagnosed with cancer. Operation after operation followed, but the cancer always came back. Finally, she lost one leg and half of the pelvic bone and was forced to drag herself around on crutches. She came home from the hospital faced with the challenge of taking care of her husband, a seven-year-old, a four-year-old, and two-year-old twins. She says she cut a deal with the Lord: "I promised that if He let me live to raise my children, I would not vegetate. I would be a contributing person." It was a good deal. Forty years later, the family is flourishing, and Lois is one of the most active and happy people you could ever hope to meet. And there are thousands of such quiet, unsung heroes in every town. I'll bet you know lots of people with the courage of Lois Gruenbaum.

FEDERAL SENTENCING GUIDELINES

If the profit argument is insufficient to encourage ethical decision making, consider the impact of the federal sentencing guidelines. The guidelines, enacted in 1991 to assist federal judges in sentencing convicted individuals and organizations, require judges to consider "aggravating and mitigating" circumstances in determining sentences and fines. Many companies claim that they were generally law abiding, that one "bad apple" created the problem. The United States Sentencing Commission (USSC) allows these firms to show that, in effect, they tend the rest of their orchard well.

These guidelines apply both to large corporations and to small organizations that might not have initiated an ethics program. Between 1991 and 1995, 56 percent of all sentenced organizations had fewer than 20 employees (Linda Farrell and O. C. Ferrell, "Ethics Training: Its Time Has Come," *Forum* 80, no. 9 [October 1996], p. 8).

The fine range for corporate unethical and illegal behavior is based on the seriousness of the offense (a base fine) multiplied by some figure representing the culpability of the organization. For instance, a score is modified based on the level of authority and size of the organization (one to five points), the prior history (one or two points), any violation of an order (one or two points), obstruction of justice (three points), whether there exists an effective program to prevent and detect violations (deduction of three points), and whether there is self-reporting, cooperation, and acceptance of responsibility (deduction of five points, two points, or one point). Where a firm has a culpability score of 10 or more, the fine will range from $20 million to $40 million. Where a firm has a culpability score of zero or less, the fine will range from $500,000 to $2 million. (All data is taken from USSC, "Corporate Crime in America: Strengthening the Good Citizen Corporation," Proceedings of the Second Symposium on Crime and Punishment in the United States, Sept. 7–8, 1995 [Washington, DC]. See also USSG, sec. 8C2.7; chap. 8, introductory comment.)

In addition, the guidelines suggest a seven-step plan toward due diligence in preventing and detecting criminal conduct by a firm's employees and agents (see three-point reduction of culpability above). In this section, you will read several discussions, both pro and con, relating to the guidelines and their anticipated impact.

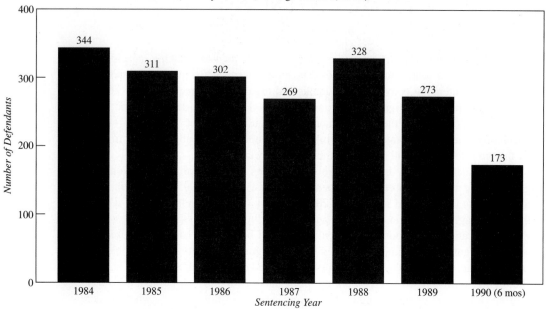

Organizational Defendants Sentenced Prior to the Guidelines
(January 1, 1984, through June 30, 1990)

SOURCE: United States Sentencing Commission.

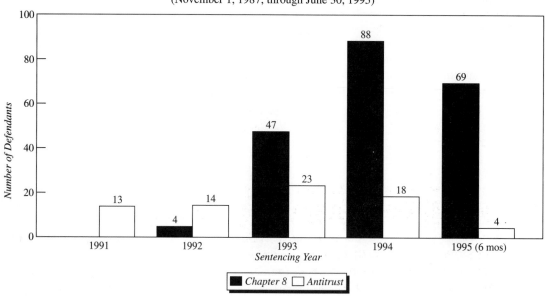

Organizational Defendants Sentenced Pursuant to the Guidelines
(November 1, 1987, through June 30, 1995)

■ *Chapter 8* □ *Antitrust*

SOURCE: United States Sentencing Commission.

Number of Employees for Organizations Sentenced Pursuant to the Guidelines
(November 1, 1987, through June 30, 1995)

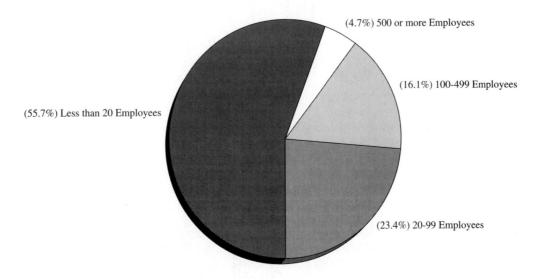

(4.7%) 500 or more Employees

(16.1%) 100-499 Employees

(55.7%) Less than 20 Employees

(23.4%) 20-99 Employees

"Organizational Defendants Sentenced Prior to the Guidelines," "Organizational Defendants Sentenced Pursuant to the Guidelines," "Number of Employees for Organizations Sentenced Pursuant to the Guidelines." Reprinted from "Corporate Crime in America: Strengthening the 'Good Citizen' Corporation," *Proceedings of the Second Symposium on Crime and Punishment in the United States,* United States Sentencing Commission, September 7–8, 1995 (Washington, DC) pp. 247–48.

WHY DAIWA BANK WILL PAY $340 MILLION UNDER THE SENTENCING GUIDELINES

JEFFREY M. KAPLAN

The following article evidences the application of the federal sentencing guidelines in practice. Daiwa Bank was ordered to pay the largest criminal fine in the history of the United States, even though it was essentially the "victim" of an employee's crime.

Since the organizational (or "corporate") sentencing guidelines went into effect in November 1991, some observers have questioned just how real was its threat of enormous fines. On February 28, 1996, all such doubts were put to rest. A Manhattan federal court sentenced Daiwa Bank to pay a fine of $340 million under the guidelines. This was the largest criminal fine in the history of U.S. law.

Beyond confirming for skeptics that the law means what it says, the *Daiwa Bank* case carries important lessons for companies that might otherwise pay insufficient attention to the guidelines' mandate to develop and implement effective compliance programs. Specifically, the bank was essentially the *victim* of an employee's crime. However, because of the bank's lack of a meaningful compliance program and its consequent failure to report the employee's wrongdoing, it became the target of the prosecution itself.

A $1.1 BILLION LOSS IN UNAUTHORIZED TRADING

In late July of 1995 senior management of Daiwa received a series of letters from a trader in its New York branch, Toshihide Iguchi. In these letters, Iguchi confessed to losing more than $1.1 billion in unauthorized, concealed securities trading that he had conducted for the previous eleven years. He had covered those losses by selling, without authorization, government bonds held in custody on behalf of the bank and pension fund accounts.

(In the interests of disclosure, the author wishes to note that his law firm represents a former branch manager of Daiwa Bank who has also pleaded guilty and is cooperating with the government's ongoing investigation. This article, however, is based solely upon publicly available facts in the case.)

Jeffrey M. Kaplan, "Why Daiwa Bank Will Pay $340 Million under the Sentencing Guidelines," reprinted with permission from *Ethikos,* v. 9, n. 6 (May/June 1996).

In late July and early August 1995 the bank investigated and confirmed the broad outlines of this remarkable confession. Daiwa quickly replaced the lost pension account funds with its own money. However, it decided not to disclose Iguchi's crimes to the public or to the U.S. government until the end of September so that it could do so as part of its scheduled financial reporting. This decision formed the basis for the charges against Daiwa, as U.S. regulations require banks to file a "Criminal Referral Form" within 30 days of learning of an employee's offense.

The reasons for the bank's unfortunate choice were several. On one level, Iguchi's scheme was so complex that the bank felt that it needed weeks of intense investigation to grasp fully what had occurred. However, the bank also wished to delay reporting out of concern for what immediate disclosure might do to its stock price. Disclosing later, when it could demonstrate its continued financial security by writing off the losses at one time, was seen as advantageous from a business perspective.

Perhaps most significantly, the Japanese Ministry of Finance, which was informed of the loss in early August, suggested to Daiwa management that immediate disclosure could have adverse consequences on that country's financial markets (which were then being rocked by other events). In sum, the bank made a business decision to delay reporting Iguchi's losses based partly on legitimate concerns (the time needed to investigate), partly self-serving ones (demonstrating financial security), and partly out of deference to the wishes of its principal regulator. Had the bank had an effective compliance program in place, however, it would have quickly understood that none of these reasons justified the risks entailed by delayed reporting.

FALSIFYING RECORDS

One consequence of the decision to maintain confidentiality was that bank executives felt compelled to falsify certain records to conceal Iguchi's losses from internal auditors until the scheduled time for disclosure. Under U.S. law, such falsification is itself a serious felony.

After meeting with its U.S. lawyers, the bank did disclose Uguchi's crimes on September 18, although the prosecutors contended that even this disclosure was somewhat incomplete. The government also learned that Daiwa had failed to disclose a second unauthorized trading incident in the 1980s and made another misrepresentation to regulators in the early 1990s.

At Daiwa's sentencing, the bank was taken to task for failing to develop and implement adequate compliance measures. Assistant U.S. Attorney Reid Figel told the court: "[I]t is virtually impossible for any financial institution to protect itself against every potential criminal act by its employees, particularly given the highly specialized nature and complexity of the securities now traded in the world's capital markets. It is precisely because of this complexity, however, that it is essential that corporations institute and insist upon a corporate culture of absolute compliance with the rules and regulations of the marketplace. One of the most important ways to do this is to establish and enforce a system of internal controls and checks and balances that are designed to protect against the criminal acts of corporate employees."

Figel continued, "[f]rom the perspective of corporate citizenship" the bank's conduct "was intolerable . . . . Far from establishing a culture of corporate compliance, the management of the bank directed its employees to engage in criminal acts."

THE IMPORTANCE OF SELF-REPORTING

What can one learn from *Daiwa Bank?* While one lawyer jokingly called it "the largest late fee in history," the case does underscore, to an extent that was previously unthinkable, the tremendous importance of corporations self-reporting employee offenses.

As a purely legal matter, self-reporting is often not required when companies learn of an employee's offense. Affirmative self-reporting obligations analogous to that of banking law's Criminal Referral Form are still relatively rare. (Environmental and securities law are among the few other areas with self-reporting requirements.)

However, federal law does contain a little-used offense called "misprision of felony," which was one of the charges against Daiwa Bank and which could, in theory, apply to any type of business.

According to prosecutor Figel, to be guilty of this offense "only requires proof of knowledge of a crime and efforts to conceal that crime." Figel said that his office hoped that "Daiwa's plea to [misprison] will serve as a stark reminder to the corporate community, and particularly regulated entities that have an affirmative duty to disclose material events, of their need to comply scrupulously with their disclosure obligations, and that the failure to make timely disclosure, coupled with attempts at concealment, constitutes a violation of federal criminal law."

Beyond strictly enforcing affirmative obligations to report for regulated entities like banks and utilizing the previously-neglected misprison of a felony statute, the government is increasingly making such self-reporting a priority as a matter of policy for companies in all areas of business. Under the corporate sentencing guidelines, even an organization with an effective compliance program does not receive mitigation credit if "after becoming aware of an offense, [it] unreasonably delayed reporting the offense to the appropriate governmental authorities." (The guidelines note, however, "that an organization will be allowed a reasonable period of time to conduct an internal investigation." Additionally, if, based upon the information available to it at the time, a corporation erroneously but in good faith concludes that no offense was committed, it's failure to report may be excused.)

Self-reporting was also a major theme of the four top federal prosecutors who spoke at the U.S. Sentencing Commission's September 1995 conference, "Corporate Crime in America: Strengthening the 'Good Citizen' Corporation." The Deputy Assistant Attorney General for the Criminal Division, the Chief of the Environmental Crimes section, the top prosecutor in the Antitrust Division and the Justice Department's head of food and drug prosecutions all indicated that corporations that self-reported employees' offenses were significantly less likely to be charged themselves. (See *ethikos,* January/February 1996.)

Mary Jo White, chief prosecutor in the U.S. Attorney's office that brought the *Daiwa Bank* case, has noted that timely self-reporting helps to prevent witness collusion and the destruction of documents. In other words, it enables the government to bring more and better cases (and so might be viewed as part of the Justice Department's "business development" efforts).

And yet, the extraordinary emphasis on self-reporting is somewhat new. For example, in 1991, Salomon Inc. waited longer than Daiwa Bank did to report violations of law that had occurred in its government securities trading, yet neither Salomon nor its top managers were prosecuted for this. Thus, managers and their advisors should be particularly mindful of the *Daiwa Bank* case because failure to meet this new standard of accountability—of which many corporations are doubtless still unaware—could have devastating consequences.

INTERNAL SELF-REPORTING POLICIES

Should a corporation, as part of its compliance program, create a formal written *policy* requiring disclosure? By itself, the presence of such a policy is likely to mean little to prosecutors, who are accustomed to judging corporate targets by their deeds rather than their words. Additionally, if for some reason such a policy is not strictly adhered to a corporation would likely be *worse* off for having adopted it.

On the other hand, having a self-reporting policy could remind management—in a time of crisis, when clear thinking does not always prevail—of where a corporation's interests generally lie. The issue for a given company is whether having a such policy will in fact impact its decision making. Another important question in determining whether to draft such a policy is to what extent a company can think through all of the types of situations that could give rise to disclosure issues, which is necessary to create a meaningful but not inflexible policy.

A LESSON FOR FOREIGN COMPANIES

Beyond underscoring the importance of self reporting, *Daiwa Bank* carries a lesson of special importance for foreign companies doing business in the U.S. Specifically, the entire disaster occurred not because the bank was greedy or malevolent, *but simply because it failed to accord due weight to U.S. regulatory mandates.*

In this regard, although its punishment was record-breaking, Daiwa Bank itself may not have been unique. Lori Tansey, of the Washington D.C.-based International Business Ethics Institute, told *ethikos,* "Without question many foreign companies doing business in the United States fail to understand the requirements of United States law. Most are not aware of the sentencing guidelines or their implications. Nor are many aware of the fact that if they are listed on a United States stock exchange, a significant body of American law—such as the Foreign Corrupt Practices Act—creates special obligations for them."

It is not only the specific substantive requirements of U.S. law that many foreign companies fail to appreciate adequately. According to Tansey, "They also, from a cultural perspective, often don't understand the litigious nature of United States society. They are used to a different—less adversarial—relationship with regulators."

In *Daiwa Bank* a misperception such as this resulted in a $340 million dollar fine. One wonders how many foreign companies will learn from Daiwa's mistakes, and how many will be forced to learn the hard way.

BEATING THEM WITH CARROTS AND FEEDING THEM STICKS

JOSEPH E. MURPHY

Joseph Murphy is a senior attorney at Bell Atlantic, where he specializes in compliance issues. He wrote the following three articles "from the future" in connection with his comments made during the United States Sentencing Commission's Symposium on Crime and Punishment in the United States. The fictitious articles were drafted in order to express his concerns with the federal sentencing guidelines.

SYNERGY CORP TO PAY $120 MILLION FINE

Assistant US Attorney John Fox announced today that Synergy Corporation had agreed to plead guilty to a 20-count indictment and to pay a total of $120 million in fines. This penalty was the largest ever imposed against a business in this district. Fox stated:" "This will send a message to others in industry."

Industry observers noted that Synergy had been reputed to have one of the most highly praised compliance programs in the country. Ironically, the government's case began with a voluntary self-disclosure by Synergy, based on the findings of its own compliance audit. Synergy's spokesperson stated that the company had cooperated fully with the government investigation.

In a press briefing, prosecutor Fox noted that this was a clear-cut case. The Company's own investigation notes provided conclusive details. Moreover, Fox observed that the legal and ethical lapses in the company were extensive. Notes obtained from the compliance training seminars showed managers did not really understand key areas of the law. Said Fox: "That was the company's job, to make sure everyone got it right." The government also reviewed years of hotline records. Fox remarked that this was a company with a pattern of misconduct.

Company insiders, who asked not to be identified, said they had warned management about implementing a so-called interactive compliance program. The company had appointed a high level compliance officer who gave detailed reports to the board, publicized a compliance hotline, conducted interactive, experimental training, and had an active compliance audit program. Even the annual assessments of managers covered compliance

---

Joseph E. Murphy, "Beating Them with Carrots and Feeding Them Sticks," in United States Sentencing Commission, "Corporate Crime in America: Strengthening the 'Good Citizen' Corporation," *Proceedings of the Second Symposium on Crime and Punishment in the United States,* September 7–8, 1995 (Washington, DC) pp. 396–97.

and ethics. Insiders told the story of a top sales manager who was kept away from a Company trip to Hawaii because he let his people miss the antitrust seminar.

Skeptics in the industry stated that it was this program that brought the prosecutors gunning for Synergy. One member of the US Attorney's staff described it as a ready-made case. "The compliance program's material gave us everything we needed."

When questioned about this point, prosecutors scoffed at the program. Said Fox: "A criminal is a criminal. We would have caught them sooner or later anyway." Court records indicate that the Company's fine was so high because one of the managers implicated in the violation headed a district with 220 employees; this canceled out the "mitigating factor" of the program. In commenting on the government's approach, editors at Rutgers University's Corporate Conduct Quarterly observed "no good deed goes unpunished."

Others React

A task force of the attorneys general from 17 states has announced a coordinated attack based on the information uncovered by the federal prosecutors. State Attorney General Marybeth Adams said she expects to review all of the company's compliance materials for more leads. Although the state has a compliance audit shield law, she said the company waived any protection in disclosing so much to the federal enforcers. Adams said: "There's no Fifth Amendment privilege for corporations."

Consumer groups also have launched three separate class action cases. In Washington, the federal office of contract compliance has begun debarment proceedings against the company.

When asked their views about the reasons for operating voluntary compliance programs, spokespersons for most companies in the industry declined to comment. Omnitech Industries, Synergy's largest competitor, did disclose that it had eliminated its compliance office six months ago, when the Synergy probe was announced. Omnitech's spokesperson said competitive pressures and the need to keep costs down in a competitive international marketplace, made the cuts necessary.

Synergy's former complacence officer, Marsha Downs, expressed surprise at the government's position. Speaking from her home . . .

(NOTE: This story is a fictitious account. No person, company or event mentioned in the story is real. It is the author's hope that this story never happens to a real company.)

FASTTECH ELUDES PROSECUTION

Congressman John ("Jack") Lynch, Chairman of the House Oversight Committee, today announced that his committee would begin hearings into the now-closed investigation of alleged wrongdoing at Fasttech Industries. That probe, which lasted three years, came to a successful end for the Company when the government failed to return an indictment in the case. Shortly after the government's task force was disbanded, it was announced that the Assistant US Attorney responsible for the case, John Fox, would be reassigned from a litigation position to research and support in Washington.

According to Congressional staff investigators, what had started as a potentially major criminal case was derailed by clever maneuvering by Fasttech's lawyers, using shield and immunity laws, and the technical standards for an "effective" compliance program.

Prosecutors had been led to believe Fasttech had voluntarily disclosed a minor violation, when in fact related and much more serious violations were about to fall into prosecutors' hands with no help from Fasttech. But by the time word of a whistleblower's allegations reached the government, the prosecutors' best experts were hopelessly compromised by the information "voluntarily" disclosed by the Company, which fell within a statutory immunity provision.

It is expected that prosecutors will testify before the Oversight Committee that the evidence they would have needed to make out a serious case was entangled in a web of attorney-client confidences and statutory protections.

Most embarrassing to the government was the prosecutors' apparent gullibility in responding to the Company's compliance program. An unnamed source in Fox's office told the Congressional staffers that Fasttech's general counsel, Lawrence Badger, put on quite a show. "He showed us a 47-page Code of Conduct, and went through a punch list of Sentencing Guidelines compliance elements." When questioned about this, Badger said: "We have one of everything on the list."

Company insiders and industry observers were said to be prepared to tell the Oversight Committee a different story. One high-level Fasttech manager stated: "Sure, the policy binder has all the right things—but no one else other than Badger even knew it existed."

Compliance in a Can

Knowledgeable sources described compliance training at Fasttech as "a canned lecture, including warnings to toss out all records and not to take notes." Leaked copies of an interview transcript quote one sales manager as telling one of Congressman Lynch's staffers: "You knew you were unimportant if you got stuck going to 'the Lecture'. No one important ever did."

One plant manager did recall seeing the Code once. She reportedly had smirked and said: "Yeah, we got that with a box of other stuff. It reminded me of my insurance policies; it meant nothing to me so I tossed it in a file somewhere."

Other insiders tell the story of one foolhardy manager who insisted on citing the Code in staff meetings. After his dismal annual review for failure to be a team player and poor judgment in setting priorities, the Code was not mentioned again.

Fasttech's competitors called that company's program "the best program on the shelf." In a year when Fasttech's costcutting helped it reach record earnings, other companies were said to be studying carefully Fasttech's successful, cost-free compliance approach.

When pressed on these points, prosecutors said the three years of investigation took enormous resources. "How were we to investigate the Company's in-house compliance program, too?" But according to the Oversight Committee's investigators, everyone in the industry knew it was just window dressing.

Former Assistant US Attorney Fox expressed surprise at the reports about Fasttech's compliance program. Speaking from his home, Fox said . . .

(NOTE: This story is a fictitious account. No person, company or event mentioned in the story is real. It is the author's hope that this story never happens to a real prosecutor.)

SKYSOFT WINS INTEGRITY AWARD

Uncle Sam Picks Best in Class

"It's how we do things here"

Skysoft Services, Inc., CEO Westin Chandler announced today that the Company will receive the coveted President's Business Integrity Award, in recognition of its Ethics and Compliance Program. The Company's stock, already at a two-year high, was up 1 1/2 points on the news.

This award caps a three-year effort by Skysoft, described as a comprehensive management and culture change process. Wall Street analysts had pointed to the Company as a rising star, driven by its management strength and a cohesive vision of the Company's direction. Earnings had shown consistently solid growth in this period.

Skysoft's Compliance Officer, CFO James Overton, explained that the program took the US Sentencing Commission's standards as the template, but then applied fundamental management techniques to drive implementation, test for results, and continuously improve the process.

Industry observers noted that Skysoft had developed a reputation for dealing exclusively with suppliers and agents who instituted similar approaches. Company purchasing personnel said it was an integral part of Skysoft's quality standards.

Skysoft's program, according to Overton, relies heavily on reaching managers and employees throughout the Company. Compliance and ethics are made core parts of annual appraisals and objective setting. Awards recognition for outstanding performers and work groups made it a point of pride for business units to best their peers. Insiders told of one district manager whose work group scored so high in the integrity measures that he earned a two-step promotion—unheard of in his department.

When asked her views on the Company Program, a first line manager, Marjory Killen, said: "That's just the way we do things here." She said she had left Xycor, Skysoft's chief competitor, to join Skysoft because it was a better place to work.

A Government Commitment

In 1991, Skysoft's general counsel had instituted a program to meet the US Sentencing Guidelines standards. At first, company management had considered it an insurance policy. But an innovative, inter-agency program, leading up to the President's Integrity Award, helped change Skysoft's lawyer-driven program into a management one.

The government initiative was multi-pronged, starting with legislation protecting companies' voluntary compliance audits and granting immunity for self-disclosure. This blunted the initial resistance of Skysoft's lawyers to instituting a more aggressive program.

But, according to Overton, the major break came when the government put money on the table, and made a real commitment. Congress let the agencies offer substantial bidding preferences and other bottom line benefits as incentives. And the President's Award, to single out the "Best in Class," touched off industry-wide competition that was intense.

In its award application, Skysoft revealed that it had disclosed to the US Attorney's office that a mid-level manager had been colluding with Xycor on a pending bid. Although this would have technically been a disqualifier for sentencing relief because of the manager's position, the Department of Justice had set firm immunity standards for self-disclosing companies with effective compliance programs. Skysoft was treated as a cooperating witness.

Assistant US Attorney John Fox described the information obtained from Skysoft as "highly useful" in the pending investigation of Xycor. Separately, Xycor announced a sharp dip in its quarterly net income, stemming from reserves taken for potential liability in pending investigations. Insiders report that Xycor is spending as much as $200,000 per month to defend against the government's probe and to prepare for anticipated private claims.

A Profit Center

Skysoft has seen its insurance premiums drop significantly in the last year, after agency pressure on insurers convinced them to include the impact of compliance programs in underwriting analyses. Overton also reports that outside counsel fees have fallen off. Jokes CEO Chandler: "Overton seems to have developed his own profit center with this."

Insiders report that the Program has changed dramatically over the three years. Compliance audits used to be the exclusive domain of lawyers; said one auditor: "They were more secret than the formula for Coca-Cola." Today, even a casual visitor will see the reports posted on plant bulletin boards for all employees to view. Said one plant worker, after reading a new report: "Boy, I hope we never pull a corker like they did in the Indianapolis plant." These postings started immediately after the audit privilege legislation was enacted.

The Company now also publishes a newsletter reporting on actual hotline cases (names omitted) telling employees what conduct gets punished and why. Until the new government commitments Skysoft's lawyers had squashed this idea. Skysoft has also initiated an industry compliance practices forum to exchange ideas on what has worked and what has not in the compliance business. Some industry members were skittish at first because of antitrust concerns, but agency endorsement of the meetings and the lure of gaining valuable insights has moved numerous companies to join the forum.

Also receiving recognition at the Award ceremony is newly-promoted Agency Deputy Chief Sandra Fisher, who acted as liaison for Skysoft's compliance office.

Xycor's former general counsel, Charles "Chip" Blunt, expressed surprise at Skysoft's success. Speaking from his home, Blunt said . . .

(NOTE: Unfortunately, this story is a fictitious account. No person, company or event in the story is real. It is the author's hope that industry and government, working together, will turn this into tomorrow's news report.)

THE PRINCE
NICCOLÒ MACHIAVELLI

Niccolò Machiavelli (1469–1527) was born to a Florentine family distinguished by its history of political prominence. Unfortunately for Niccolò, his father (an unsuccessful lawyer) and his immediate family were beset by chronic financial woes. Machiavelli held significant positions in the government of Florence. As an ambassador, he was able to gather information about the chaotic world of international and Italian politics. He was also a military technician responsible for overseeing the city's military preparedness. As the defense minister, he was known for substituting a citizen's militia for the mercenary system. His power and influence ended in 1512, when the Spanish, in league with the pope, attacked Florence.

Machiavelli's writings were shocking and highly controversial. The Prince *was banned by the pope; some critics contend that he led to modern totalitarianism. But Machiavelli saw* The Prince *as a realistic account of the qualities necessary for political success. He believed that although some common virtues (e.g., moderation, clemency, chastity, gentleness, generosity, vigor, religion, and devotion) might be praiseworthy, they were not what the real world required. A person with these virtues would be good—but too good for this world, and a disastrous leader. Instead, a leader would need qualities like energy, boldness, and shrewdness.*

Compare this philosophy to that of Lao Tzu, who wrote in Tao Te Ching:

> A leader is best
> When people barely know that he exists.
> Of a good leader, who talks little,
> When his work is done, his aim fulfilled,
> They will say, "We did this ourselves." (Chapter 17)

Machiavelli believed in divorcing ethics from politics, contending that "a weak Christian makes a better president than a strong one. . . . [A president] needs to be unscrupulous, without strong standards and beliefs." Since public acts often have unforeseen consequences, Machiavelli believed that a political agent may be excused for performing certain acts that would be ethically indefensible in private life.

. . . Going further down our list of qualities, I recognize every ruler should want to be thought of as compassionate and not cruel. Nevertheless, I have to warn you to be careful about being compassionate. Cesare Borgia was thought of as cruel; but this supposed cruelty of his restored order to the Romagna, united it, rendered it peaceful and law-abiding. If you think about it, you will realize he was, in fact, much more compassionate than the people of Florence, who, in order to avoid being thought cruel, allowed Pistoia to tear itself apart.[1] So a ruler ought not to mind the disgrace of being called cruel, if he keeps his subjects peaceful and law-abiding, for it is more compassionate to impose harsh punishments on a few than, out of excessive compassion, to allow disorder to spread, which leads to murders or looting. The whole community suffers if there are riots, while to maintain order the ruler only has to execute one or two individuals. Of all rulers, he who is new to power cannot escape a reputation for cruelty, for he is surrounded by dangers. Virgil has Dido say:

> Harsh necessity, and the fact my kingdom is new, oblige me to do these things,
> And to mass my armies on the frontiers.[2]

Nevertheless, you should be careful how you assess the situation and should think twice before you act. Do not be afraid of your own shadow. Employ policies that are moderated by prudence and sympathy. Avoid excessive self-confidence, which leads to carelessness, and avoid excessive timidity, which will make you insupportable.

This leads us to a question that is in dispute: Is it better to be loved than feared, or vice versa.[3] My reply is one ought to be both loved and feared; but, since it is difficult to accomplish both at the same time, I maintain it is much safer to be feared than loved, if you have to do without one of the two. For of men one can, in general, say this: They are ungrateful, fickle, deceptive and deceiving, avoiders of danger, eager to gain. As long as you serve their interests, they are devoted to you. They promise you their blood, their possessions, their lives, and their children, as I said before, so long as you seem to have no need of them. But as soon as you need help, they turn against you. Any ruler who relies simply on their promises and makes no other preparations, will be destroyed. For you will find that those whose support you buy, who do not rally to you because they admire your strength of character and nobility of soul, these are people you pay for, but they are never yours, and in the end you cannot get the benefit of your investment. Men are less nervous of offending someone who makes himself lovable, than someone who makes himself frightening. For love attaches men by ties of obligation, which, since men are wicked, they break whenever their interests are at stake. But fear restrains men because they are afraid of punishment, and this fear never leaves them. Still, a ruler should make himself feared in such a way that, if he does not inspire love, at least he does not provoke hatred. For it is perfectly possible to be feared and not hated. You will only be hated if you seize the property or the women of your subjects and citizens. Whenever you have to kill someone, make sure you have a suitable excuse and an obvious reason; but, above all else, keep your hands off other people's property; for men are quicker to forget the death

---

1. In 1501.
2. Virgil, *Aeneid,* I, 563–4.
3. Cicero, *De officiis,* bk. 2, ch. 7, § 23–24.

of their father than the loss of their inheritance. Moreover, there are always reasons why you might want to seize people's property; and he who begins to live by plundering others will always find an excuse for seizing other people's possessions; but there are fewer reasons for killing people, and one killing need not lead to another.

When a ruler is at the head of his army and has a vast number of soldiers under his command, then it is absolutely essential to be prepared to be thought cruel; for it is impossible to keep an army united and ready for action without acquiring a reputation for cruelty. Among the extraordinary accomplishments of Hannibal, we may note one in particular: He commanded a vast army, made up of men of many different nations, who were fighting far from home, yet they never mutinied and they never fell out with one another, either when things were going badly, or when things were going well.[4] The only possible explanation for this is that he was known to be harsh and cruel. This, together with his numerous virtues [*virtù*], meant his soldiers always regarded him with admiration and fear. Without cruelty, his other virtues [*virtù*] would not have done the job. Those who write about Hannibal without thinking things through both admire the loyalty of his troops and criticize the cruelty that was its principal cause. If you doubt my claim that his other virtues [*virtù*] would have been insufficient, take the case of Scipio.[5] He was not only unique in his own day, but history does not record anyone his equal. But his army rebelled against him in Spain.[6] The sole cause of this was his excessive leniency, which meant his soldiers had more freedom than is compatible with good military discipline. Fabius Maximus criticized him for this in the senate and accused him of corrupting the Roman armies. When Locri was destroyed by one of his commanders,[7] he did not avenge the deaths of the inhabitants, and he did not punish his officer's insubordination. He was too easygoing. This was so apparent that one of his supporters in the senate was obliged to excuse him by saying he was no different from many other men, who were better at doing their own jobs than at making other people do theirs. In course of time, had he remained in command without learning from his mistakes, this aspect of Scipio's character would have destroyed his glorious reputation. But, because his authority was subordinate to that of the senate, not only were the consequences of this defect mitigated, but it even enhanced his reputation.

I conclude, then, that, as far as being feared and loved is concerned, since men decide for themselves whom they love, and rulers decide whom they fear, a wise ruler should rely on the emotion he can control, not on the one he cannot. But he must take care to avoid being hated, as I have said.

RELATED WEB SITE

"The Executive: An Updated Version of *The Prince*"

www.proaxis.com/~pharmon/contents.html

---

4. Hannibal (247—ca. 183 B.C.) campaigned in Italy from 218 to 203 B.C. Machiavelli's source is Polybius, bk. 11, ch. 19.
5. Scipio (ca. 236—183 B.C.) defeated Hannibal at Zama in North Africa (202 B.C.).
6. In 206 B.C. Livy, bk. 28, chs. 24—29.
7. In 205 B.C

ETHICAL DILEMMAS REGARDING COMPETITIVE INTELLIGENCE

Thomas Furtado

How far should a company go in seeking sensitive information about competitors? What are the parameters for ethical competition? The following case asks you to consider these and other issues surrounding the nature of free market competition. Do you do something simply because you can? Imagine you are in a competitor's office and you see confidential information related to your industry sitting on her desk. She leaves the room for a moment to speak with someone. Do you take a look? What factors would enter into your decision? Does it matter whether "anyone else would do it"?

PART A

Gathering and Using Competitor Information

Transformations in the technology of generating and storing information, and the increasing reliance on "knowledge workers" in business and commerce, mean that timely information and creative ideas are often the key differentiators in competitive industries like high-tech engineering and manufacturing, computers, financial services, and industrial and commercial electronics. In an age when clones can appear overnight, companies must take all possible precautions to protect their information from competitors for as long as possible. Likewise, successful businesses will vigorously seek to learn as much as possible about competitors' products and plans.

What are appropriate principles to follow in gathering and using competitive information? Is anything acceptable as long as it is not illegal? Does it matter in what industry and/or in what region of the world we do business?

What Is Competitive Information?

One major U.S. corporation with worldwide business activities defines competitive information as follows: It "includes anything related to the competitive environment or to a competitor—for example, information related to products, markets, pricing, or business

Thomas Furtado, "Ethical Dilemmas Regarding Competitive Intelligence," published by the Council for Ethics in Economics (Case 3, 1995). Copyright (c) 1995 Council for Ethics in Economics.

plans. This information could be drawn from published sources or could otherwise be widely available to the public. Some of this information will be oriented to a specific competitor ('competitor information') and some competitor information would be considered 'proprietary,' 'business confidential,' or 'trade secret' which a business would attempt to hold closely."

As this definition suggests, much competitive information exists in public channels and can be obtained legitimately. For instance, traditional techniques for protecting information have been patents, copyrights and trademarks. While these provide legal protection, the information is in the public domain. By following the patent applications of a firm's employees, a competitor could quickly get a picture of their research. In fact, many companies openly discuss competitive intelligence and some have departments well known in the industry which are dedicated to gathering such information.

Legal gathering of information readily available in the public domain, then, does not raise any ethical concerns. Just as clearly, on the other side, obviously illegal activities such as break-ins, computer hacking, and wiretaps are not ethically ambiguous. Even the people who commit such actions are fully aware they are breaking the law. The tough ethical questions arise when information is gathered in ways that do not fit neatly into either of these categories.

Sources of Competitive Information

One of the most frequent sources of competitive information, especially proprietary information, is a company's own employees. Despite intellectual property agreements intended to establish company ownership of creative efforts funded by the firm, employees still sometimes turn over proprietary information to a competitor. Bitter, disillusioned employees, who have perhaps been by-passed for promotions and other opportunities, see giving confidential data to a competitor as rectifying past wrongs done to them.

Company employees may also be negligent. Extremely sensitive data are left exposed on a desk while the employee goes elsewhere. Folders are left on someone else's desk while attending a meeting. Sales reps leave their briefcases in a customer's office while they go out for lunch. Phone conversations that can be overheard in a public place are often the source of confidential data for someone who happens to be at the right place at the right time.

Customers can also be a source of competitive information. In many cases they are as negligent with the supplier's data as they sometimes are with their own. In other cases, the customer may deliberately give one supplier's proprietary information to another during a bidding process. Some customers choose instead to give all the information from all bidders to the others in an effort to make the process more competitive. They may do so even when the data were furnished to them by the suppliers with "proprietary" and "secret" markings.

Another source of competitive information is technical seminars and conferences. Often attendees target speakers at breaks and attempt to learn critical information. They are most successful at this when they misrepresent themselves, either with a fake name badge or no badge at all, letting the target person think they are merely curious participants and certainly not a competitor.

What Actions Are Ethically Appropriate?

As these examples illustrate, managers in highly competitive industries are faced with numerous opportunities both to actively gather competitive information and to use information that may have been given to them. Consider the following example:

You are the engineering director of a large international firm working on a new compact disk that will be able to produce high-quality video on the same size surface as an audio disk. You have two formidable competitors and the stakes are enormous. Not only must this small disk be capable of playing movies up to three hours duration, but to capture the video market from cassette tape, the equipment must have recording capability. All three of you have solved the first challenge, but no one seems to be breaking through on the recording issue. Your own engineers have had little success in this regard.

While attending a technical seminar on the subject whose participants also include representatives from your competitors, you listen to a presentation by an engineer from one of the competitors. The presentation touches on the recording problem in a way that makes you think they may have solved the problem.

PART B

Protecting Competitive Information: The Lopez Case

Part A of this case focused generally on how competitor information is gathered, received and used. But when a firm seeks to protect its own information, complications can sometimes arise when the "giver" and the "receiver" disagree over the facts and over the extent and limits of what can be protected. A case in point is the incident concerning Mr. José Ignacio Lopez de Arriortua, the head of global purchasing at General Motors who left to join Volkswagen in a similar position in March 1993.

Within a month, GM claimed that Mr. Lopez had taken with him highly secret information about their Opel division in Germany. Shortly thereafter, GM filed a complaint with the German courts alleging industrial spying and theft. In subsequent months, General Motors went to court to prevent Mr. Lopez from working for Volkswagen, and also attempted to prevent seven other GM employees who had left with him from working for VW. At the time of this writing, many of the issues are still in the courts awaiting decisions. The German courts ruled, however, that Mr. Lopez and his team could begin work at Volkswagen.

Although the details are not entirely clear and the situation may be resolved through legal remedies or an out-of-court settlement by mid-year 1995, the following general account based on published reports provides a springboard for considering important ethical issues in cases like this.

Background at General Motors

General Motors has been the largest auto manufacturer in the world for several decades. In the 1980s, however, GM began to lose market share to Japanese and German auto makers, and by the early 1990s, it was also dealing with a strong resurgence of Ford and Chrysler.

In particular, GM had been slow to change its manufacturing processes, and consequently found itself competing with higher cost structures than many of its competitors.

One bright spot in the GM story was the performance of its German company, Adam Opel AG, which had slashed costs considerably through a very aggressive approach to its suppliers. The architect of this initiative was José Ignacio Lopez, Opel's head of purchasing. Through what some called heavy-handed tactics, Mr. Lopez had successfully renegotiated many supplier contracts to provide much lower costs, and he was given much of the credit for the turnaround of GM in Europe. By 1993, General Motors was a very close second to Volkswagen in auto production in Europe.

In the meantime, GM had brought Mr. Lopez to Detroit in May 1992 to replicate his achievements as the head of global purchasing for the entire organization. Using the same aggressive approach, he soon began to make a difference in the company and was named the auto industry's "Man of the Year" for 1992 by a major trade publication in Detroit. Ironically, only a few months later, he was the center of a major confrontation between General Motors and Volkswagen.

Lopez Moves to Volkswagen

Volkswagen, the largest auto producer in Europe, had fallen on hard times in the early 1990s. Like GM, it was having a difficult time keeping its costs in line and staying competitive. Over the past several years, it had seen General Motors and its Open company cut into its market share. Obviously, VW was well aware of the role Mr. Lopez had played in the GM resurgence.

Some time in early 1993, Volkswagen and Mr. Lopez began to talk. Mr. Lopez had reportedly become disenchanted with his employer over what he saw as a broken promise. Apparently feeling betrayed, he decided to leave GM.

General Motors Reaction

Once Mr. Lopez told GM Chief Executive John Smith that he was leaving, events moved swiftly. A week later, on March 16, 1983, Mr. Lopez was appointed head of purchasing and production for Volkswagen, and within another week, seven of his colleagues, who had followed him from Opel to Detroit, resigned from General Motors to join him at VW. On April 7, Mr. Smith made the first serious allegation that Mr. Lopez may have stolen secret documents and plans about future GM and Opel products and strategies, a charge Mr. Lopez denies. Six weeks later, GM went to court in Germany alleging that Lopez and others had stolen secret competitive information.

In the two years since, charges and countercharges have been made by individuals and the companies concerned. Boxes of documents were found and seized by the courts. Volkswagen denied the material was secret and went so far as to suggest the documents were planted by Opel security forces. Opel and GM attempted to ban Lopez and the other seven from working for VW, but they lost this case in the German Labor Law court in Wolfsburg in September 1994. At this point, Mr. Lopez had been on the job for over a year and was receiving full support over the incident from the Volkswagen head, Ferdinand Piëch.

AIRLINE TRAVEL: SAFETY AT WHAT PRICE?

Kenneth K. Boyer

You want a low-price ticket to your favorite destination, but how low? How do you think airlines lower their prices? The following article cautions that sometimes the lowest price to the consumer is not the best option.

Many people take the convenience and ease of air travel for granted. . . . The growth of air travel is largely based on two factors: low prices and excellent safety. Greater competition among airlines has generated low fares which benefit the consumer, allowing passengers to travel long distances quickly and cheaply. In fact, low prices can be viewed as one of the major factors fueling the boom in air travel. Yet, while low prices may lure passengers away from other modes of travel (train, automobile, boat), safety remains a critical qualifier. Without a good safety record, airlines would not be able to attract customers at any price. In fact, commercial airline travel is one of the safest modes of travel: according to the National Safety Council the fatality rate for people traveling by automobile was 37 times greater than that for people traveling on U.S. airlines during the period from 1980 to 1992.

Several discount airlines such as Southwest, Valujet and America West have prospered by offering very low prices for air travel, while at the same time larger airlines such as United, American and Delta have been forced to lower their prices to remain competitive. How have these airlines managed to cut costs in order to fund reductions in prices? Several techniques have been used, including outsourcing of maintenance activities, labor savings through new contracts with airline personnel, and increasing the lifetime of airplanes.

The issue of airline safety has recently become a hotly debated topic following a spate of recent crashes, including TWA flight 800 (230 passengers killed) off Long Island and Valujet flight 592 (110 passengers killed) in the Everglades. The Federal Aviation Administration (FAA) thoroughly investigates every accident and incident in order to identify causes, and prevent future accidents. The FAA also regulates U.S. airports, commercial airlines, pilots, etc., in an attempt to ensure safe airline travel. The ultimate goal is to achieve a 100% safety record, yet the reality is that some accidents are likely to occur despite the best efforts of every agency associated with airline travel. Greater regulation and attention to safety should result in improved safety, yet may also result in increased costs. There is an inherent trade-off between low cost and safety. How should a balance be struck between the two objectives? The following discussion examines two factors that affect both cost and safety.

MAINTENANCE OF AIRCRAFT

Airplane maintenance accounts for 15% to 20% of an airline's direct operating costs. For instance, American Airlines spends approximately $1.5 billion per year on maintenance. Because maintenance represents such a large cost, reducing these costs has become a primary means for airlines to decrease their operating costs. Larger airlines often enjoy certain economies of scale based on the ability to build dedicated maintenance facilities and spread the huge costs incurred over a large fleet of planes. Many smaller airlines such as Valujet have opted to outsource much of their maintenance in an effort to reduce costs. This practice can lead to saving between 20% and 30% on maintenance costs, but at what price in terms of safety?

A major trade-off associated with outsourcing maintenance is that the airline no longer directly controls this critical safety element. The risk of mistakes or poor quality repairs increases as the number of companies involved grows. Outsourcing also adds an additional layer of communication, forcing airlines to expend additional energy monitoring not only their own personnel, but also the work performed by an external organization. For many smaller airlines this additional coordination may simply be too great a challenge. In fact, several airlines have experienced close calls due to poor maintenance. For example, in June 1996 an engine on a Valujet flight at Atlanta exploded. The engine had been overhauled and sold to Valujet by a repair station in Turkey that lacked FAA approval.

The safety concerns associated with outsourcing are compounded by the increasing use of counterfeit, or bogus, parts. Numerous FAA inspectors say the problem of substandard parts has grown dramatically over the past five years. This growth is in part because the nation's aging airline fleet needs more parts. Cash-strapped small and start-up airlines are more likely to be hit with bogus parts because their extensive outsourcing of maintenance makes quality assurance much more difficult. Bogus parts played a role in at least 166 U.S.-based aircraft accidents or less serious mishaps from 1973 to 1993 according to *Business Week*. Yet, the actual number may have been far greater since it is impossible to determine the cause of a crash in many cases.

WHY ARE BOGUS PARTS A GROWTH BUSINESS?

A single Boeing 747 has approximately 6 million parts. Many of these parts will have been replaced five times or more by the time the plane is ten years old. Airlines, which lose between $20,000 and $100,000 in revenue for each day a plane is grounded, must depend on a mostly unregulated network of 5,000 dealers to keep spare parts in stock. Opportunities for unscrupulous dealers to cut corners or blatantly falsify records abound in this system. For example, a broker can buy scrap compressor blades for jet engines for as little as $1 each. Once smoothed and coated, these blades can then be sold for $1200. One repair station rewelded worn-out turbine blades. The blades then broke off, damaging the engine on a commuter aircraft.

The potential profit from supplying bogus parts is so large that Detective Luis Vergera, a bogus parts specialist in Miami's Dade County Police Departments, says, "I know of people who quit running drugs and switched to aircraft parts because it was more profitable." So, what can be done to stem the tide of bogus parts? Requiring every part to be traced back to an approved manufacturer would be prohibitively expensive and "we'd all go out of business tomorrow," according to Michael Rioux, vice-president of engineering and maintenance at the Air Transport Association, an industry group representing 21 major airlines. While the FAA says it recognizes "the need for additional guidance dealing with the issue of documentation of parts," it has failed to act decisively in moving toward new standards.

The question of how to deal with the problem of bogus parts highlights a fundamental conflict within the FAA. In essence FAA has a dual mission to both promote the business of aviation and ensure public safety. Critics contend that the FAA has historically erred on the side of commerce.

While airline safety overall is very good, there certainly are some problems and risks associated with air travel. There are several questions which the FAA must grapple with: What approach should be used to monitor and ensure safety when airlines outsource their maintenance and to prevent the use of bogus parts? How much effort would be allocated to safety—in other words, what is the break-even point between cost and safety? How should a balance be struck between low-cost travel and greater safety? After all, while perfect safety is in theory attainable, it may come at a prohibitive cost.

REFERENCES

1. Zimba, S., "Preventive Maintenance Keeps Planes Airworthy," *Chicago Tribune,* September 15, 1996, sect. 5, pp. 1, 4.
2. Dahl, J. and Miller, L., "Which Is the Safest Airline? It all Depends . . .", *The Wall Street Journal,* July 24, 1996, p. B1.
3. Stern, W., "Warning! Bogus Parts Have Turned Up in Commercial Jets. Where's the FAA," *Business Week,* June 10, 1996, pp. 84–92.
4. Condom, P., "Is Outsourcing a Winning Solution," *Interavia Business and Technology,* May, 1994, p. 34.

Chapter 7b

CORPORATE STRATEGY AND DECISION MAKING
Select Topic Analyses

THE FORD PINTO CASE

There is generally a right way to do something and a wrong way. The problem is that we are not always sure which is which, especially before the fact. In hindsight, we can usually figure it out—or someone is bound to tell us. That was the Ford Motor Company's experience with the Pinto case. Ford executives thought that they were doing the right thing, that their position was defensible. But once the decision was made, it was unacceptable to the public. Perhaps Ford should have considered one of the telltale signs of decision making. How would you feel if your decision were publicized on the cover of a national paper tomorrow? Would you be proud, humiliated, ashamed? Sometimes the answer offers some guidance.

WHAT'S YOUR LIFE WORTH?
Douglas Birch

In order to clearly present the costs and benefits of the Pinto decision regarding the fuel leakage, a representative from Ford Motor Company prepared the following chart in conjunction with an internal memo entitled "Fatalities Associated with Crash-Induced Fuel Leakage and Fires." The second chart is drawn from a federal study that showed how the National Highway Traffic Safety Administration calculates the value of a human life. The chart shows the estimated cost to society every time someone is killed in an auto accident. This estimate was developed as a result of auto industry pressure. Ford used the chart in its arguments that certain safety measures are not worth the savings in human lives.

"What's Your Life Worth" (chart), "$11 vs. a Burn Death" (memorandum), from Douglas Birch, *The Ford Pinto Case.* Reprinted by permission of SUNY Press.

$11 VS. A BURN DEATH

Benefits and Costs Relating to Fuel Leakage Associated with the Static Rollover Test Portion of FMVSS 208

Benefits

Savings: 180 burn deaths, 180 serious burn injuries, 2,100 burned vehicles.
Unit Cost: $200,000 per death, $67,000 per injury, $700 per vehicle.
Total Benefit: $180 \times (\$200,000) + 180 \times (\$67,000) + 2,100 \times (\$700)$ = **$49.5 million.**

Costs

Sales: 11 million cars, 1.5 million light trucks.
Unit Cost: $11 per car, $11 per truck.
*Total Cost: $11,000,000 \times (\$11) + 1,500,000 \times (\$11)$ = **$137 million.***

WHAT'S YOUR LIFE WORTH?

Societal Cost Components for Fatalities, 1972
NHTSA Study

Component	1971 Costs
FUTURE PRODUCTIVITY LOSSES	
Direct	$132,000
Indirect	41,300
MEDICAL COSTS	
Hospital	700
Other	425
PROPERTY DAMAGE	1,500
INSURANCE ADMINISTRATION	4,700
LEGAL AND COURT	3,000
EMPLOYER LOSSES	1,000
VICTIM'S PAIN AND SUFFERING	10,000
FUNERAL	900
ASSETS (Lost Consumption)	5,000
MISCELLANEOUS ACCIDENT COST	200
TOTAL PER FATALITY:	$200,725

THE FORD PINTO
W. Michael Hoffman

Hoffman's case study describes Ford's experience with its Pinto automobile. This case is often cited as evidence that a financial decision cannot be made in a vacuum, that factors other than money must be taken into account in many decisions.

I

On August 10, 1978, a tragic automobile accident occurred on U.S. Highway 33 near Goshen, Indiana. Sisters Judy and Lynn Ulrich (ages 18 and 16, respectively) and their cousin Donna Ulrich (age 18) were struck from the rear in their 1973 Ford Pinto by a van. The gas tank of the Pinto ruptured, the car burst into flames, and the three teenagers were burned to death.

Subsequently an Elkhart County grand jury returned a criminal homicide charge against Ford, the first ever against an American corporation. During the following twenty-week trial, Judge Harold R. Staffeldt advised the jury that Ford should be convicted of reckless homicide if it were shown that the company had engaged in "plain, conscious and unjustifiable disregard of harm that might result (from its actions) and the disregard involves a substantial deviation from acceptable standards of conduct."[1]

The key phrase around which the trial hinged, of course, is "acceptable standards." Did Ford knowingly and recklessly choose profit over safety in the design and placement of the Pinto's gas tank? Elkhart County prosecutor Michael A. Cosentino and chief Ford attorney James F. Neal battled dramatically over this issue in a rural Indiana courthouse. Meanwhile, American business anxiously awaited the verdict which could send warning ripples through boardrooms across the nation concerning corporate responsibility and product liability.

II

As a background to this trial some discussion of the Pinto controversy is necessary. In 1977 the magazine *Mother Jones* broke a story by Mark Dowie, general manager of *Mother Jones* business operations, accusing Ford of knowingly putting on the road an unsafe car—the Pinto—in which hundreds of people have needlessly suffered burn deaths and even more have been scarred and disfigured from burns. In his article, "Pinto Madness," Dowie charges that:

- Fighting strong competition from Volkswagen for the lucrative small-car market, the Ford Motor Company rushed the Pinto into production in much less than the usual time.

- Ford engineers discovered in preproduction crash tests that rear-end collisions would rupture the Pinto's fuel system extremely easily.

- Because assembly-line machinery was already tooled when engineers found this defect, top Ford officials decided to manufacture the car anyway—exploding gas tank and all—even though Ford owned the patent on a much safer gas tank.

- For more than eight years afterward, Ford successfully lobbied, with extraordinary vigor and some blatant lies, against a key government safety standard that would have forced the company to change the Pinto's fire-prone gas tank.

  By conservative estimates Pinto crashes have caused 500 burn deaths to people who would not have been seriously injured if the car had not burst into flames. The figure could be as high as 900. Burning Pintos have become such an embarrassment to Ford that its advertising agency, J. Walter Thompson, dropped a line from the ending of a radio spot that read "Pinto leaves you with that warm feeling."

  Ford knows that the Pinto is a firetrap, yet it has paid out millions to settle damage suits out of court, and it is prepared to spend millions more lobbying against safety standards. With a half million cars rolling off the assembly lines each year, Pinto is the biggest-selling subcompact in America, and the company's operating profit on the car is fantastic. Finally, in 1977, new Pinto models have incorporated a few minor alterations necessary to meet that federal standard Ford managed to hold off for eight years. Why did the company delay so long in making these minimal, inexpensive improvements?

- Ford waited eight years because its internal "cost-benefit analysis," which places a dollar value on human life, said it wasn't profitable to make the changes sooner.[2]

Several weeks after Dowie's press conference on the article, which had the support of Ralph Nader and auto safety expert Byron Bloch, Ford issued a news release attributed to Herbert T. Misch, vice president of Environmental and Safety Engineering, countering points made in the *Mother Jones* article. Their statistical studies conflict significantly with each other. For example, Dowie states that more than 3,000 people were burning to death yearly in auto fires; he claims that, according to a National Highway Traffic Safety Administration (NHTSA) consultant, although Ford makes 24 percent of the cars on American roads, these cars account for 42 percent of the collision-ruptured fuel tanks.[3] Ford, on the other hand, uses statistics from the Fatality Analysis Reporting System (FARS) maintained by the government's NHTSA to defend itself, claiming that in 1975 there were 848 deaths related to fire-associated passenger-car accidents and only 13 of these involved Pintos; in 1976, Pintos accounted for only 22 out of 943. These statistics imply that Pintos were involved in only 1.9 percent of such accidents, and Pintos constitute about 1.9 percent of the total registered passenger cars. Furthermore, fewer than half of those Pintos cited in the FARS study were struck in the rear.[4] Ford concludes from this and other studies that the Pinto was never an unsafe car and has not been involved in some 70 burn deaths annually, as *Mother Jones* claims.

Ford admits that early-model Pintos did not meet rear-impact tests at 20 mph but denies that this implies that they were unsafe compared with other cars of that type and era. In fact, according to Ford, some of its tests were conducted with experimental rubber "bladders" to protect the gas tank, in order to determine how best to have its future cars meet a 20-mph rear-collision standard which Ford itself set as an internal performance goal. The government at that time had no such standard. Ford also points out that in every model year the Pinto met or surpassed the government's own standards, and

> *it simply is unreasonable and unfair to contend that a car is somehow unsafe if it does not meet standards proposed for future years or embody the technological improvements that are introduced in later model years.*[5]

Mother Jones, on the other hand, presents a different view of the situation. If Ford was so concerned about rear-impact safety, why did it delay the federal government's attempts to impose standards? Dowie gives the following answer:

> *The particular regulation involved here was Federal Motor Vehicle Safety Standard 301. Ford picked portions of Standard 301 for strong opposition way back in 1968 when the Pinto was still in the blueprint stage. The intent of 301, and the 300 series that followed it, was to protect drivers and passengers after a crash occurs. Without question the worst post-crash hazard is fire. So Standard 301 originally proposed that all cars should be able to withstand a fixed barrier impact of 20 mph (that is, running into a wall at that speed) without losing fuel.*
>
> *When the standard was proposed, Ford engineers pulled their crash-test results out of their files. The front ends of most cars were no problem—with minor alterations they could stand the impact without losing fuel. "We were already working on the front end," Ford engineer Dick Kimble admitted. "We knew we could meet the test on the front end." But with the Pinto particularly, a 20 mph rear-end standard meant redesigning the entire rear end of the car. With the Pinto scheduled for production in August of 1970, and with $200 million worth of tools in place, adoption of this standard would have created a minor financial disaster. So Standard 301 was targeted for delay, and with some assistance from its industry associates, Ford succeeded beyond its wildest expectations: the standard was not adopted until the 1977 model year.*[6]

Ford's tactics were successful, according to Dowie, not only due to their extremely clever lobbying, which became the envy of lobbyists all over Washington, but also because of the proindustry stance of NHTSA itself.

Furthermore, it is not at all clear that the Pinto was as safe as comparable cars with regard to the positioning of its gas tank. Unlike the gas tank in the Capri, which rode over the rear axle, a "saddle-type" fuel tank on which Ford owned the patent, the Pinto tank was placed just behind the rear bumper. According to Dowie,

> *Dr. Leslie Ball, the retired safety chief for the NASA manned space program and a founder of the International Society of Reliability Engineers, recently made a careful study of the Pinto. "The release to production of the Pinto was the most reprehensible decision in the history of American engineering," he said. Ball can name more than 40 European and Japanese models in the Pinto price and weight range with safer gas-tank positioning.*
>
> *Los Angeles auto safety expert Byron Bloch has made an in-depth study of the Pinto fuel system. "It's a catastrophic blunder," he says. "Ford made an extremely irresponsible decision when they placed such a weak tank in such a ridiculous location in such a soft rear end. It's almost designed to blow up—premeditated."*[7]

Although other points could be brought out in the debate between *Mother Jones* and Ford, perhaps the most intriguing and controversial is the cost-benefit analysis study that Ford did entitled "Fatalities Associated with Crash-Induced Fuel Leakage and Fires," released by J. C. Echold, director of automotive safety for Ford. This study apparently convinced Ford and was intended to convince the federal government that a technological improvement costing $11 per car which would have prevented gas tanks from rupturing so easily was not cost-effective for society. The costs and benefits are broken down in the following way:

Benefits:

Savings:	180 burn deaths, 180 serious burn injuries, 2,100 burned vehicles
Unit Cost:	$200,000 per death, $67,000 per injury, $700 per vehicle
Total Benefit:	$180 \times \$200,000 + 180 \times \$67,000 + 2,100 \times \$700 = \$49.5$ *million*

Costs:

Sales:	11 million cars, 1.5 million light trucks
Unit Cost:	$11 per car, $11 per truck
Total Cost:	$11,000,000 \times \$11 + 1,500,000 \times \$11 = \$137$ *million*

And where did Ford come up with the $200,000 figure as the cost per death? This came from a NHTSA study which broke down the estimated social costs of a death as follows:

Component	1971 Costs
Future productivity losses	
Direct	$132,000
Indirect	41,300
Medical costs	
Hospital	700
Other	425
Property damage	1,500
Insurance administration	4,700
Legal and court	3,000
Employer losses	1,000
Victim's pain and suffering	10,000
Funeral	900
Assets (lost consumption)	5,000
Miscellaneous	200
Total per fatality	$200,725

(Although this analysis was on all Ford vehicles, a breakout of just the Pinto could be done.) *Mother Jones* reports it could not find anybody who could explain how the $10,000 figure for "pain and suffering" had been arrived at.[8]

Although Ford does not mention this point in its news release defense, one might have replied that it was the federal government, not Ford, that set the figure for a burn death. Ford simply carried out a cost-benefit analysis based on that figure. *Mother Jones,* however, in addition to insinuating that there was industry-agency (NHTSA) collusion, argues that the $200,000 figure was arrived at under intense pressure from the auto industry to use cost-benefit analysis in determining regulations. *Mother Jones* also questions Ford's estimate of burn injuries: "All independent experts estimate that for each person who dies by an auto fire, many more are left with charred hands, faces and limbs." Referring to the Northern California Burn Center, which estimates the ratio of burn injuries to deaths at ten to one instead of one to one, Dowie states that "the true ratio obviously throws the company's calculations way off."[9] Finally, *Mother Jones* claims to have obtained "confidential" Ford documents which Ford did not send to Washington, showing that crash fires could largely be prevented by installing a rubber bladder inside the gas tank for only $5.08 per car, considerably less than the $11 per car Ford originally claimed was required to improve crashworthiness.[10]

Instead of making the $11 improvement, installing the $5.08 bladder, or even giving the consumer the right to choose the additional cost for added safety, Ford continued, according to *Mother Jones,* to delay the federal government for eight years in establishing mandatory rear-impact standards. In the meantime, Dowie argues, thousands of people were burning to death and tens of thousands more were being badly burned and disfigured for life, while many of these tragedies could have been prevented for only a slight cost per vehicle. Furthermore, the delay also meant that millions of new unsafe vehicles went on the road, "vehicles that will be crashing, leaking fuel and incinerating people well into the 1980s."[11]

In concluding his article Dowie broadens his attack beyond just Ford and the Pinto.

> *Unfortunately, the Pinto is not an isolated case of corporate malpractice in the auto industry. Neither is Ford a lone sinner. There probably isn't a car on the road without a safety hazard known to its manufacturer. . . .*

Furthermore, cost-valuing human life is not used by Ford alone. Ford was just the only company careless enough to let such an embarrassing calculation slip into public records. The process of willfully trading lives for profits is built into corporate capitalism. Commodore Vanderbilt publicly scorned George Westinghouse and his "foolish" air brakes while people died by the hundreds in accidents on Vanderbilt's railroads.[12]

Ford has paid millions of dollars in Pinto jury trials and out-of-court settlements, especially the latter. *Mother Jones* quotes Al Slechter in Ford's Washington office as saying: "We'll never go to a jury again. Not in a fire case. Juries are just too sentimental. They see those charred remains and forget the evidence. No sir, we'll settle."[13] But apparently Ford thought such settlements would be less costly than the safety improvements. Dowie wonders if Ford would continue to make the same decisions "were Henry Ford II and Lee Iacocca serving twenty-year terms in Leavenworth for consumer homicide."[14]

III

On March 13, 1980, the Elkhart County jury found Ford not guilty of criminal homicide in the Ulrich case. Ford attorney Neal summarized several points in his closing argument before the jury. Ford could have stayed out of the small-car market, which would have been the "easiest way," since Ford would have made more profit by sticking to bigger cars. Instead, Ford built the Pinto "to take on the imports, to save jobs for Americans and to make a profit for its stockholders."[15] The Pinto met every fuel-system standard of any federal, state, or local government, and was comparable to other 1973 subcompacts. The engineers who designed the car thought it was a good, safe car and bought it for themselves and their families. Ford did everything possible to recall the Pinto quickly after NHTSA ordered it to do so. Finally, and more specifically to the case at hand, Highway 33 was a badly designed highway, and the girls were fully stopped when a 4,000-pound van rammed into the rear of their Pinto at least 50 miles an hour. Given the same circumstances, Neal stated, any car would have suffered the same consequences as the Ulrich's Pinto.[16] As reported in the *New York Times* and *Time,* the verdict brought a "loud cheer" from Ford's board of directors and undoubtedly at least a sigh of relief from other corporations around the nation.

Many thought this case was that of a David against a Goliath because of the small amount of money and volunteer legal help Prosecutor Cosentino had in contrast to the huge resources Ford poured into the trial. In addition, it should be pointed out that Cosentino's case suffered from a ruling by Judge Staffeldt that Ford's own test results on pre-1973 Pintos were inadmissible. These documents confirmed that Ford knew as early as 1971 that the gas tank of the Pinto ruptured at impacts of 20 mph and that the company was aware, because of tests with the Capri, that the over-the-axle position of the gas tank was much safer than mounting it behind the axle. Ford decided to mount it behind the axle in the Pinto to provide more trunk space and to save money. The restrictions of Cosentino's evidence to testimony relating specifically to the 1973 Pinto severely undercut the strength of the prosecutor's case.[17]

Whether this evidence would have changed the minds of the jury will never be known. Some, however, such as business ethicist Richard De George, feel that this evidence shows grounds for charges of recklessness against Ford. Although it is true that there were no federal safety standards in 1973 to which Ford legally had to conform and although Neal seems to have proved that all subcompacts were unsafe when hit at 50 mph by a 4,000-pound van, the fact that the NHTSA ordered a recall of the Pinto and not other subcompacts is, according to De George, "*prima facie* evidence that Ford's Pinto gas tank mounting was substandard."[18] De George argues that these grounds for recklessness are made even stronger by the fact that Ford did not give the consumer a choice to make the Pinto gas tank safer by installing a rubber bladder for a rather modest fee.[19] Giving the consumer such a choice, of course, would have made the Pinto gas tank problem known and therefore probably would have been bad for sales.

Richard A. Epstein, professor of law at the University of Chicago Law School, questions whether Ford should have been brought up on criminal charges of reckless homicide at all. He also points out an interesting historical fact. Before 1966 an injured party in Indiana could not even bring civil charges against an automobile manufacturer solely because of the alleged "uncrashworthiness" of a car; one would have to seek legal relief from the other party involved in the accident, not from the manufacturer. But after *Larson v. General Motors Corp.* in 1968, a new era of crashworthiness suits against automobile manufacturers began. "Reasonable" precautions must now be taken by manufacturers to minimize personal harm in crashes.[20] How to apply criteria of reasonableness in such cases marks the whole nebulous ethical and legal arena of product liability.

If such a civil suit had been brought against Ford, Epstein believes, the corporation might have argued, as it did to a large extent in the criminal suit, that the Pinto conformed to all current applicable safety standards and with common industry practice. (Epstein cites that well over 90 percent of United States standard production cars had their gas tanks in the same position as the Pinto.) But in a civil trial the adequacy of industry standards are ultimately up to the jury, and had civil charges been brought against Ford in this case the plaintiffs might have had a better chance of winning.[21] Epstein feels that a criminal suit, on the other hand, had no chance from the very outset, because the prosecutor would have had to establish criminal intent on the part of Ford. To use an analogy, if a hunter shoots at a deer and wounds an unseen person, he may be held civilly responsible but not criminally responsible because he did not intend to harm. And even though it may be more difficult to determine the mental state of a corporation (or its principal agents), it seems clear to Epstein that the facts of this case do not prove any such criminal intent even though Ford may have known that some burn deaths and injuries could have been avoided by a different placement of its Pinto gas tank and that Ford consciously decided not to spend more money to save lives.[22] Everyone recognizes that there are trade-offs between safety and costs. Ford could have built a "tank" instead of a Pinto, thereby considerably reducing risks, but it would have been relatively unaffordable for most and probably unattractive to all potential consumers.

To have established Ford's reckless homicide it would have been necessary to establish the same of Ford's agents, since a corporation can only act through its agents. Undoubtedly, continues Epstein, the reason why the prosecutor did not try to subject Ford's officers and engineers to fines and imprisonment for their design choices is "the good faith character of their judgment, which was necessarily decisive in Ford's behalf as well."[23] For example, Harold C. MacDonald, Ford's chief engineer on the Pinto, testified that he felt it was important to keep the gas tank as far from the passenger compartment as possible, as it was in the Pinto. And other Ford engineers testified that they used the car for their own families. This is relevant information in a criminal case which must be concerned about the intent of the agents.

Furthermore, even if civil charges had been made in this case, it seems unfair and irrelevant to Epstein to accuse Ford of trading cost for safety. Ford's use of cost-benefit formulas, which must assign monetary values to human life and suffering, is precisely what the law demands in assessing civil liability suits. The court may disagree with the decision, but to blame industry for using such a method would violate the very rules of civil liability. Federal automobile officials (NHTSA) had to make the same calculations in order to discharge their statutory duties. In allowing the Pinto design, are not they too (and in turn their employer, the United States) just as guilty as Ford's agents?[24]

IV

The case of the Ford Pinto raises many questions of ethical importance. Some people conclude that Ford was definitely wrong in designing and marketing the Pinto. The specific accident involving the Ulrich girls, because of the circumstances, was simply not the right one to have attacked Ford on. Other people believe that Ford was neither criminally nor civilly guilty of anything and acted completely responsibly in producing the Pinto.

Many others, I suspect, find the case morally perplexing, too complex to make sweeping claims of guilt or innocence.

Was Ford irresponsible in rushing the production of the Pinto? Even though Ford violated no federal safety standards or laws, should it have made the Pinto safer in terms of rear-end collisions, especially regarding the placement of the gas tank? Should Ford have used cost-benefit analysis to make decisions relating to safety, specifically placing dollar values on human life and suffering? Knowing that the Pinto's gas tank could have been made safer by installing a protective bladder for a relatively small cost per consumer, perhaps Ford should have made that option available to the public. If Ford did use heavy lobbying efforts to delay and/or influence federal safety standards, was this ethically proper for a corporation to do? One might ask, if Ford was guilty, whether the engineers, the managers, or both are to blame. If Ford had been found guilty of criminal homicide, was the proposed penalty stiff enough ($10,000 maximum fine for each of the three counts equal $30,000 maximum), or should agents of the corporations such as MacDonald, Iacocca, and Henry Ford II be fined and possibly jailed?

A number of questions concerning safety standards are also relevant to the ethical issues at stake in the Ford trial. Is it just to blame a corporation for not abiding by "acceptable standards" when such standards are not yet determined by society? Should corporations like Ford play a role in setting such standards? Should individual juries be determining such standards state by state, incident by incident? If Ford should be setting safety standards, how does it decide how safe to make its product and still make it affordable and desirable to the public without using cost-benefit analysis? For that matter, how does anyone decide? Perhaps it is putting Ford, or any corporation, in a catch-22 position to ask it both to set safety standards and to make a competitive profit for its stockholders.

Regardless of how we answer these and other questions it is clear that the Pinto case raises fundamental issues concerning the responsibilities of corporations, how corporations should structure themselves in order to make ethical decisions, and how industry, government, and society in general ought to interrelate to form a framework within which such decisions can properly be made in the future.

NOTES

1. *The Indianapolis Star,* Sunday, Mar. 9, 1980, Section 3, p. 2.
2. Mark Dowie, "Pinto Madness," *Mother Jones,* September–October, 1977, pp. 18, 20. Subsequently Mike Wallace for "Sixty Minutes" and Sylvia Chase for "20-20" came out with similar exposés.
3. *Ibid.,* p. 30.
4. Ford news release (Sept. 9, 1977), pp. 1–3.
5. *Ibid.,* p. 5.
6. Dowie, p. 29.
7. *Ibid.,* pp. 22–23.
8. *Ibid.,* pp. 24, 28.
9. *Ibid.,* p. 28.
10. *Ibid.,* pp. 28–29.
11. *Ibid.,* p. 30.
12. *Ibid.,* p. 32. Dowie might have cited another example which emerged in the private correspondence which transpired almost a half-century ago between Lammot du Pont and Alfred P. Sloan, Jr., then president of GM. Du Pont was trying to convince Sloan to equip GM's lowest-priced cars. Chevrolets, with safety

glass. Sloan replied by saying: "It is not my responsibility to sell safety glass. . . . You can say, perhaps, that I am selfish, but business is selfish. We are not a charitable institution—we are trying to make a profit for our stockholders." [Quoted in Morton Mintz and Jerry S. Cohen, *Power, Inc.* (New York: The Viking Press, 1976), p. 110.]

13. *Ibid.,* p. 31.

14. *Ibid.,* p. 32.

15. Transcript of report of proceedings in *State of Indiana v. Ford Motor Company,* Case No. 11-431, Monday, Mar. 10, 1980, pp. 6202–6203. How Neal reconciled his "easiest way" point with his "making more profit for stockholders" point is not clear to this writer.

16. *Ibid.,* pp. 6207–6209.

17. *Chicago Tribune,* Oct. 13, 1979, p. 1, and Section 2, p. 12; *New York Times,* Oct. 14, 1979, p. 26; *The Atlanta Constitution,* Feb. 7, 1980.

18. Richard De George, "Ethical Responsibilities of Engineers in Large Organizations: The Pinto Case," *Business and Professional Ethics Journal,* vol. 1., No. 1 (Fall 1981), p. 4. *The New York Times,* Oct. 26, 1978, p. 103, also points out that during 1976 and 1977 there were thirteen fiery fatal rear-end collisions involving Pintos, more than double that of other United States comparable cars, with VW Rabbits and Toyota Corollas having none.

19. *Ibid.,* p. 5.

20. Richard A. Epstein, "Is Pinto a Criminal?" *Regulation,* March–April, 1980, pp. 16–17.

21. A California jury awarded damages of $127.8 million (reduced later to $6.3 million on appeal) in a Pinto crash in which a youth was burned over 95 percent of his body. See *New York Times,* Feb. 8, 1978, p. 8.

22. Epstein, p. 19.

23. *Ibid.,* pp. 20–21.

24. *Ibid.,* pp. 19–21.

FORD REBUTS PINTO CRITICISM AND SAYS ARTICLE IS DISTORTED

The following article discusses a press release from Ford Motor Company that defends Ford's Pintos and rebuts challenges to their safety.

Allegations that Ford Pintos have faulty fuel tanks which make them firetraps and cause the death of some 70 people each year is pure exaggeration, a spokesman for the automaker said last week.

In an eight-page statement released nearly a month after a highly publicized news conference held by the magazine *Mother Jones* (NU, Aug. 19), Vice President Herbert L. Misch said statistical evidence "totally discredits the opinions of the alleged safety experts quoted by Mother Jones."

In the article, author Mark Dowie wrote "by conservative estimates, Pinto crashes were responsible for 500 burn deaths to people who would not have been seriously injured if the car had not burst into flames." Mr. Dowie added that the "figure could be as high as 900."

Mr. Misch, however, claimed the article contained "half-truths and distortions."

CITES STATISTICS

He said nationwide accident statistics maintained by the National Highway Traffic Safety Administration show that in 1975, for example, "there were 848 deaths associated with passenger-car accidents in which fires also occurred in some parts of the vehicles. Only 12 of these 848 reported fatalities involved occupants of Pintos, including two who had been ejected from their cars. In 1976, the number of occupant fatalities in fire-associated passenger-car accidents in which Pintos were involved was 11 out of 942."

Mr. Misch, referring to further "distortions," said "it is true, for example, that early model Pintos did not pass rear-impact tests at 20 mph. It is not true, however, that these test results mean the early Pintos were unsafe compared with the range of other cars of that era, or on any basis of rational judgment."

According to Mr. Misch, some of Ford's tests on 1971 Pintos were conducted "to learn what revisions would be required to make our cars meet rear-impact requirements prepared by the Federal government for future cars."

The truth, he said, is that "in every model year the Pinto has been tested and met, or surpassed, the Federal fuel-system-integrity standard applicable to it."

Mr. Misch further said that in 1976, while Pintos accounted for about 2 percent of all cars in operation, their involvement rate in fire-associated fatality reports was only 1.17 percent.

"This is evidence with substance—objective statistics on how the Pinto performs in real-world accidents—and it totally discredits the opinions of the alleged safety experts quoted by Mother Jones."

Mr. Dowie also charged in the article that Ford lobbied for eight years to prevent the implementation of a Federal safety standard for fuel-integrity in rear impacts, and opposed such standards on grounds their implementation would have cost $11 per vehicle.

The facts, according to Mr. Misch, are that as early as March 18, 1968, Ford recommended an "early adoption of a Federal fuel-integrity standard incorporating rear moving-barrier impact requirements at 20 miles per hour, and reiterated to the government its support for such a standard on two other occasions during the next two and a half years."

What Ford did oppose, Mr. Misch admitted, were "certain excessive testing requirements involving 20- or 30-mile-per-hour rear crashes into a massive, fixed barrier and a post-crash rollover test which we viewed as imposing wastefully expensive costs. We suggested that, considering the total spectrum of safety improvement, this might be an unwise allocation of resources for a single type of hazard. In the end, a rollover requirement was retained in the final standards, and a 30-mile-per-hour rear impact by a 4,000 pound barrier was specified."

Mr. Misch also contested Mr. Dowie's assertion that a plastic fuel tank baffle had been tested and found effective in preventing fuel tank punctures prior to introduction of the first Pinto in the fall of 1970, but was discarded by Ford.

Ford tests report, said Mr. Misch, that "the fuel tank baffle in question was first tested in 1974. And the stopped Pinto involved in the collision described in the article appears to be the same car that Ford investigation revealed was struck so severely by a vehicle weighing more than 3,900 pounds that the fuel tank was massively crushed by the impact forces that demolished the car.

"It appears," Mr. Misch said, "the author has misinterpreted the Ford test reports on which he says his article was based."

The government's data show that "the performance of the Pinto's fuel tank system in actual accidents appears to be superior to that which might be expected of cars of its size and weight."

RICHARD GRIMSHAW, MINOR, ETC., PLAINTIFF AND APPELLANT

V.

FORD MOTOR COMPANY, ETC., ET AL., DEFENDANTS AND APPELLANTS

The Ford Motor Company was sued in a product liability action brought by a passenger who suffered severely and permanently disfiguring burns on his face and entire body as a result of an automobile accident, as well as by the heirs of the driver of the car, who suffered fatal burns in the accident. The court entered a judgment in favor of the plaintiffs but required the passenger to remit all but $3.5 million of the original $125 million jury award as a condition of his refusal to grant a new trial. Ford still appealed. In the following appeal, the court determined, among other matters, that the punitive damage award of $3.5 million was not excessive and that the lower court judge's reduction of the jury's original award was not an abuse of discretion.

. . . *Amount of Punitive Damage Award:* Ford's final contention is that the amount of punitive damages awarded, even as reduced by the trial court, was so excessive that a new trial on that issue must be granted. Ford argues that its conduct was less reprehensible than those for which punitive damages have been awarded in California in the past; that the 3½ million dollar award is many times over the highest award for such damages ever upheld in California; and that the award exceeds maximum civil penalties that may

Grimshaw v. Ford Motor Co., 119 Cal.App.3d 757 (4th Dist. 1981).

be enforced under federal or state statutes against a manufacturer for marketing a defective automobile. We are unpersuaded.

In determining whether an award of punitive damages is excessive, comparison of the amount awarded with other awards in other cases is not a valid consideration. . . . Nor does "[t]he fact that an award may set a precedent by its size" in and of itself render it suspect; whether the award was excessive must be assessed by examining the circumstances of the particular case. . . . In deciding whether an award is excessive as a matter of law or was so grossly disproportionate as to raise the presumption that it was the product of passion or prejudice, the following factors should be weighed: The degree of reprehensibility of defendant's conduct, the wealth of the defendant, the amount of compensatory damages, and an amount which would serve as a deterrent effect on like conduct by defendant and others who may be so inclined. . . . Applying the foregoing criteria to the instant case, the punitive damage award as reduced by the trial court was well within reason.

In assessing the propriety of a punitive damage award, as in assessing the propriety of any other judicial ruling based upon factual determinations, the evidence must be viewed in the light most favorable to the judgment. . . . Viewing the record thusly in the instant case, the conduct of Ford's management was reprehensible in the extreme. It exhibited a conscious and callous disregard of public safety in order to maximize corporate profits. Ford's self-evaluation of its conduct is based on a review of the evidence most favorable to it instead of on the basis of the evidence most favorable to the judgment. Unlike malicious conduct directed toward a single specific individual, Ford's tortious conduct endangered the lives of thousands of Pinto purchasers. Weighed against the factor of reprehensibility, the punitive damage award as reduced by the trial judge was not excessive.

Nor was the reduced award excessive taking into account defendant's wealth and the size of the compensatory award. Ford's net worth was 7.7 billion dollars and its income after taxes for 1976 was over 983 million dollars. The punitive award was approximately .005% of Ford's net worth and approximately .03% of its 1976 net income. The ratio of the punitive damages to compensatory damages was approximately 1.4 to one. Significantly, Ford does not quarrel with the amount of the compensatory award to Grimshaw.

Nor was the size of the award excessive in light of its deterrent purpose. An award which is so small that it can be simply written off as a part of the cost of doing business would have no deterrent effect. An award which affects the company's pricing of its product and thereby affects its competitive advantage would serve as a deterrent. . . . The award in question was far from excessive as a deterrent against future wrongful conduct by Ford and others.

Ford complains that the punitive award is far greater than the maximum penalty that may be imposed under California or federal law prohibiting the sale of defective automobiles or other products. For example, Ford notes that California statutes provide a maximum fine of only $50 for the first offense and $100 for a second offense for a dealer who sells an automobile that fails to conform to federal safety laws or is not equipped with required lights or brakes . . . ; that a manufacturer who sells brake fluid in this state failing to meet statutory standards is subject to a maximum of only $50 . . . ; and that the maximum penalty that may be imposed under federal law for violation of automobile safety standards is $1,000 per vehicle up to a maximum of $800,000 for any related series of offenses. . . . It is precisely because monetary penalties under government regulations prescribing business standards or the criminal law are so inadequate and ineffective as deterrents against a manufacturer and distributor of mass produced defective products that punitive damages must be of sufficient amount to discourage such practices. Instead of showing that the punitive damage award was excessive, the comparison between the award and the maximum penalties under state and federal statutes and regulations governing automotive safety demonstrates the propriety of the amount of punitive damages awarded. . . .

Finally, Grimshaw contends the court abused its discretion in reducing the award to 3½ million dollars as a condition of its new trial order and urges this court to restore the jury award or at least require a remittitur of substantially less than that required by the trial court.

In ruling on a motion for new trial for excessive damages, the trial court does not sit "in an appellate capacity but as an independent trier of fact. . . ."

Here, the judge, exercising his independent judgment on the evidence, determined that a punitive award of 3½ million dollars was "fair and reasonable." Evidence pertaining to Ford's conduct, its wealth and the savings it realized in deferring design modifications in the Pinto's fuel system might have persuaded a different fact finder that a larger award should have been allowed to stand. Our role, however, is limited to determining whether the trial judge's action constituted a manifest and unmistakable abuse of discretion. Here, the judge referred to the evidence bearing on those factors in his new trial order and obviously weighed it in deciding what was a "fair and reasonable" award. We cannot say that the judge abused the discretion vested in him by Code of Civil Procedure section 662.5 or that there is "no substantial basis in the record" for the reasons given for the order. Finally, while the trial judge may not have taken into account Ford's potential liability for punitive damages in other cases involving the same tortious conduct in reducing the award, it is a factor we may consider in passing on the request to increase the award. Considering such potential liability, we find the amount as reduced by the trial judge to be reasonable and just. We therefore decline the invitation to modify the judgment by reducing the amount of the remittitur. . . .

FINANCING OF THE U.N. PEACEKEEPING OPERATIONS: DEATH AND DISABILITY BENEFITS

This table lists the compensation rates the United Nations pays to soldiers who are injured on peacekeeping missions. Consider whether this table represents a type of analysis that is different from the one conducted by the Ford Motor Company in connection with the Pinto. Are you comfortable with this type of table, or do you believe that each case should be valued individually?

Loss	Payment
Both arms or both hands, or both legs or both feet, or sight in both eyes	$50,000
Hearing	$17,500
Sight in one eye (presuming other eye is normal)	$12,000
Arm (at shoulder)	$30,000
Arm (at or below elbow)	$28,500
Hand (at or below wrist)	$27,000
Thumb	$11,000
Index finger	$7,000
Middle finger	$5,500
Ring finger	$2,500
Fourth finger	$1,500
Leg (above the knee)	$20,000
Leg (at or below knee)	$18,000
Foot (at or below ankle)	$14,000
Big toe	$2,500
Any other toe	$500

SPACE SHUTTLE CHALLENGER DISASTER

SPACE SHUTTLE CHALLENGER:

MISSION 51-L LAUNCH DECISION

KURT HOOVER AND WALLACE T. FOWLER

In the following materials published on the Web site of the University of Texas, Hoover and Fowler describe the events that led to the space shuttle Challenger disaster in 1986. Consider whether there are any similarities between this case and the Ford Pinto case. What would you have hoped that decision makers had learned from the Pinto case that may have helped in this case?

On January 28, 1986, the Space Shuttle Challenger was launched for the last time. The decision to launch the Challenger was not simple. Certainly no one dreamed that the Shuttle would explode less than two minutes after lift-off. Much has been said and written about the decision to launch. Was the decision to launch correct? How was the decision made? Could anyone have foreseen the subsequent explosion? Should the decision-making procedure have been modified? These questions are examined in this case study.

BACKGROUND

The Space Shuttle

The Space Shuttle is the most complicated vehicle ever constructed. Its complexity dwarfs any previous project ever attempted, including the Apollo project. The Apollo project possessed a very specific goal—to send men to the moon—whereas the Space Shuttle program has a wide variety of goals, some of which conflict. The attempt to satisfy conflicting goals is one of the chief roots of difficulty with the design of the Space Shuttle. Originally, the design was to be only a part of NASA's overall manned space transportation system, but because of politics and budget cuts, it was transformed from an integral component of a system to the sole component of the manned space program.

Kurt Hoover and Wallace T. Fowler, "Space Shuttle Challenger: Mission 51-L Launch Decision."
http://www.ac.utexas.edu/~lehman/ethics/challeng.htm#back. Reprinted by permission of the authors.

The Space Shuttle was the first attempt to produce a truly reusable spacecraft. All previous spacecraft were designed to fly only a single mission. In the late 1960's, NASA envisioned a vehicle which could be used repeatedly, thus reducing both the engineering cost and hardware costs. However, the resulting vehicle was not as envisioned. It had severe design flaws, one of which caused the loss of the Challenger.

NASA Planning and Politics

NASA's post-Apollo plans for the continued manned exploration of space rested on a three-legged triad. The first leg was a reusable space-transportation system, the Space Shuttle, which could transport men and cargo to low earth orbit (LEO) and then land back on Earth to prepare for another mission. The second leg was a manned orbiting space station that would be resupplied by the Shuttle and would serve as both a transfer point for activities further from Earth and as a scientific and manufacturing platform. The final leg was the exploration of Mars, which would start from the Space Station. Unfortunately the politics and inflation of the early 70's forced NASA to retreat from its ambitious program. Both the Space Station and the Journey to Mars were delayed indefinitely, and the United States manned space program was left standing on one leg—the Space Shuttle. Even worse, the Shuttle was constantly under attack by a Democratic Congress and poorly defended by a Republican president.

To retain Shuttle funding, NASA was forced to make a series of major concessions. First, facing a highly constrained budget, NASA sacrificed the research and development necessary to produce a truly reusable shuttle and instead accepted a design that was only partially reusable, eliminating one of the features that made the shuttle attractive in the first place. Solid rocket boosters (SRBs) were used instead of safer liquid fueled boosters because they required a much smaller research-and-development effort. Numerous other design changes were made to reduce the level of research and development required.

Second, to increase its political clout and to guarantee a steady customer base, NASA enlisted the support of the United States Air Force. The Air Force could provide the considerable political clout of the Defense Department and had many satellites which required launching. However, Air Force support did not come without a price. The Shuttle payload bay was required to meet Air Force size and shape requirements, which placed key constraints on the ultimate design. Even more important was the Air Force requirement that the Shuttle be able to launch from Vandenburg Air Force Base in California. This constraint required a larger cross range than the Florida site, which in turn decreased the total allowable vehicle weight. The weight reduction required the elimination of the design's air-breathing engines, resulting in a single-pass unpowered landing that greatly limited the safety and landing versatility of the vehicle.

FACTORS AFFECTING THE LAUNCH DECISION

Pressures to Fly

As the year 1986 began, there was extreme pressure on NASA to "Fly out the Manifest." From its inception the Space Shuttle program had been plagued by exaggerated expectations, funding inconsistencies, and political pressures. The ultimate design was shaped almost as much by politics as physics. President Kennedy's declaration that the United States would land a man on the moon before the end of the decade had provided NASA's Apollo program with high visibility, a clear direction, and powerful political backing. The Space Shuttle program was not as fortunate; it had neither a clear direction nor consistent political backing.

System Status and Competition

In spite of all its early difficulties, the Shuttle program looked quite good in 1985. A total of 19 flights had been launched and recovered, and although many had experienced minor problems, all but one of the flights could rightfully be categorized as successful. However, delays in the program as a whole had led the Air Force to request funds to develop an expendable launch vehicle. Worse still, the French launch organization Arianespace had developed an independent capability to place satellites into orbit at prices the Shuttle could not hope to match without greatly increased federal subsidization (which was not likely to occur as Congress was becoming increasingly dissatisfied with the program). The Shuttle was soon going to have to begin showing that it could pay for itself. There was only one way this could be done—increase the number of flights.

For the Shuttle program, 1986 was to be the year of truth. NASA had to prove that it could launch a large number of flights on time to continue to attract customers and retain Congressional support. Unfortunately, 1986 did not start out well for the Shuttle program. Columbia, Flight 61-C, had experienced a record four on-pad aborts and had three other schedule slips. Finally, on Mission 61-C, Columbia was forced to land at Edwards Air Force Base rather than at Kennedy Space Center as planned. The delays in Columbia's launch and touchdown threatened to upset the launch schedule for the rest of the year.

Not only did Columbia's landing at Edwards require it to be ferried back to the Cape, but several key shuttle parts had to be carried back by T-38 for use on the other vehicles. These parts included a temperature sensor for the propulsion system, the nose-wheel steering box, an air sensor for the crew cabin, and one of the five general-purpose computers. At the time of the Challenger explosion, NASA supposedly had four complete shuttles. In reality there were only enough parts for two complete shuttles. Parts were passed around and reinstalled in the orbiters with the earliest launch dates. Each time a part was removed or inserted, the shuttles were exposed to a whole host of possible servicing-induced problems.

In addition to problems caused by the Flight 61-C of Columbia, the next Columbia flight, 61-E, scheduled for March, also put pressure on NASA to launch the Challenger on schedule. The March flight of Columbia was to carry the ASTRO spacecraft, which had a very tight launch window because NASA wanted it to reach Halley's Comet before a Russian probe arrived at the comet. In order to launch Columbia 61-E on time, Challenger had to carry out its mission and return to Kennedy by January 31.

Politics

NASA had much to gain from a successful Flight 51-L. The "Teacher in Space" mission had generated much more press interest than other recent shuttle flights. Publicity was and continues to be extremely important to the agency. It is a very important tool that

NASA uses to help ensure its funding. The recent success of the Space Shuttle program had left NASA in a Catch-22 situation. Successful Shuttle flights were no longer news because they were almost ordinary. However, launch aborts and delayed landings were more newsworthy because they were much less common.

In addition to general publicity gained from flight 51-L, NASA undoubtedly was aware that a successful mission would play well in the White House. President Reagan shared NASA's love of publicity and was about to give a State of the Union speech. The value of an elementary teacher giving a lecture from orbit was obvious and was lost neither on NASA nor on President Reagan.

SEQUENCE OF EVENTS

Monday, January 27

On Monday NASA had attempted to place Challenger in orbit, only to be stymied by a stripped bolt and high winds. All preliminary procedures had been completed and the crew had just boarded when the first problem struck. A microsensor on the hatch indicated that it was not shut securely; it turned out that the hatch had been shut securely and that the sensor was malfunctioning, but valuable time was used determining that the sensor was the problem.

After the hatch was closed, the external hatch handle could not be removed. The threads on the connecting bolt were stripped, and instead of cleanly disengaging when turned, the handle simply spun around. Attempts to use a portable drill to remove the handle failed. Technicians on the scene asked Mission Control for permission to saw the bolt off. Fearing some form of structural stress to the hatch, engineers made numerous time-consuming calculations before giving the go-ahead to cut off the bolt. The entire process consumed almost two hours before the countdown was resumed.

Misfortunes continued. During the attempts to verify the integrity of the hatch and remove the handle, the wind had been steadily rising. Chief Astronaut John Young flew a series of approaches in the Shuttle training aircraft and confirmed the worst fears of Mission Control. The crosswinds at the Cape were in excess of the level allowed for the abort contingency. The opportunity had been missed and the flight would have to wait until the next possible launch window, the following morning. Everyone was quite discouraged, especially since extremely cold weather was forecast for Tuesday, which could further postpone the launch.

Tuesday, January 28

After the canceled launch on Monday morning there was a great deal of concern about the possible effects of weather. The predicted low for Tuesday morning was 23° F, far below the nominal operating temperature for many of the Challenger's subsystems. Undoubtedly, as the sun came up and the launch time approached, both air temperature and vehicle would warm up, but there was still concern. Would the ambient temperature become high enough to meet launch requirements? NASA's Launch Commit Criteria stated that no launch should occur at temperatures below 31° F. There was also concern over any permanent effects on the Shuttle due to the cold overnight temperatures.

All NASA centers and subcontractors involved with the Shuttle were asked to determine the possible effects of cold weather and present any concerns. In the meantime Kennedy Space Center went ahead with its freeze-protection plan. This plan included the use of using anti-freeze in the huge acoustic damping ponds and allowing warm water to bleed through pipes, showers, and hoses to prevent freezing.

The weather for Tuesday morning was to be clear and cold. Because the overnight low was forecast at 23° F, there was doubt that Challenger would be much above freezing at launch time. The Launch Commit Criteria included very specific temperature limits for most systems on the shuttle. A special wavier would be required to launch if any of these criteria were not met. Although these criteria were supposedly legally binding, Marshall Space Flight Center administrator Larry Mulloy had been routinely writing waivers to cover the problems with the SRBs on the recent Shuttle flights.

Engineers at Morton-Thiokol, the SRB manufacturer in Utah, were very concerned about the possible effects of the cold weather. The problems with the SRBs had been long known to engineers Roger Boisjoly and Allan McDonald, but both felt that their concerns were being ignored. They felt that the request by NASA to provide comment on the launch conditions was a golden opportunity to present their concerns. They were sure that Challenger should not be launched in such conditions as those expected for Tuesday morning. Using weather data provided by the Air Force, they calculated that at the 9:00 A.M. launch time the temperature of the O-rings would be only 29° F. Even by 2:00 P.M., the O-rings would have warmed only to 38° F.

The design validation tests originally done by Thiokol covered only a very narrow temperature range. The temperature data base did not include any temperatures below 53° F. The O-rings from Flight 51-C, which had been launched under cold conditions the previous year, showed very significant erosion. This was the only data available on the effects of cold, but all the Thiokol engineers agreed that the cold weather would decrease the elasticity of the synthetic rubber O-rings, which in turn might cause them to seal slowly and allow hot combustion gas to surge through the joint.

Based on these results, the engineers at Thiokol recommended to NASA Marshall that Challenger not be launched until the O-rings reached a temperature of 53° F. The management of Marshall was flabbergasted, and demanded that Thiokol prove that launching was unsafe. Such a response was a complete reversal of normal procedure. Normally, NASA required its subcontractors to prove that something was safe. Now they were requiring their subcontractors to prove that something was unsafe. Faced with this extreme pressure, Thiokol management asked its engineers to reconsider their position. When the engineers stuck to their original recommendations not to fly, Thiokol management overruled them and gave NASA its approval to launch.

Rockwell, the company that manufactured the Orbiter, also had concerns about launching in cold and icy conditions. Their major concern was the possibility of ice from either the Shuttle or the launch structure striking and damaging the vehicle. Like Thiokol, they recommended against the launch, and they too were pressed to explain their reasoning. Instead of sticking with their original strong recommendation against launch, the Rockwell team carefully worded their statement to say that they could not fully guarantee the safety of the Shuttle.

In its desire to fly out its manifest, NASA was willing to accept Rockwell's statement as a recommendation. The final decision to launch, however, belonged to Jesse

Moore. He was informed of Rockwell's concerns, but was also told that they had approved the launch. The engineers and management from NASA Marshall chose not to even mention the original concerns of Thiokol. Somehow, the warnings and concerns were diminished as they were communicated up each step of the ladder of responsibility.

Late Monday night the decision to push onward with the launch was made. Despite the very real concerns of some of the engineers familiar with the actual vehicle subsystems, the launch was approved. No one at NASA wanted to be responsible for further delaying an already delayed launch. Everyone was aware of the pressure on the agency to fly out the manifest, yet no one would have consciously risked the lives of the seven astronauts. The potential rewards had come to outweigh the potential risks. Clearly, there were many reasons for launching Challenger on that cold Tuesday morning, and a great deal of frustration from the previous launch attempt remained.

Pre-Launch Events

Although the decision to launch on Tuesday had been made late on Monday night, it was still possible that something might force NASA to postpone the launch. However, the decision to launch had been made, and nothing was going to stand in the way; the "press on" mentality was firmly established, and even if all of Florida froze over, Challenger would launch.

The pre-launch inspection of Challenger and the launch pad by the ice-team was unusual to say the least. The ice-team's responsibility was to remove any frost or ice on the vehicle or launch structure. What they found during their inspection looked like something out of a science-fiction movie. The freeze protection plan implemented by Kennedy personnel had gone very wrong. Hundreds of icicles, some up to 16 in. long, clung to the launch structure. The handrails and walkways near the shuttle entrance were covered in ice, making them extremely dangerous if the crew had to make an emergency evacuation. One solid sheet of ice stretched from the 195-ft. level to the 235-ft. level on the gantry. However, NASA continued to cling to its calculations that there would be no damage due to flying ice shaken loose during the launch.

The Launch

As the SRBs ignited, the cold conditions did not allow the O-rings to properly seat. Within the first 300 milliseconds of ignition, both the primary and secondary O-rings on the lowest section of the right SRB were vaporized across 70° of arc by the hot combustion gases. Puffs of smoke with the same frequency as the vibrating booster are clearly present in pictures of the launch. However, soon after the Challenger cleared the tower, a temporary seal of glassy aluminum-oxides from the propellant formed in place of the burned O-rings and Challenger continued skyward.

Unfortunately, at the time of greatest dynamic pressure, the shuttle encountered wind shear. As the Challenger's guidance control lurched the Shuttle to compensate for the wind shear, the fragile aluminum-oxide seal shattered. Flame arched out of the joint, struck the external tank and quickly burned through the insulation and the aluminum structure. Liquid hydrogen fuel streamed out and was ignited. The Challenger exploded.

When the remains of the cabin were recovered, it became apparent that most of the crew survived the explosion and separation of the Shuttle from the rest of the vehicle. During the 2-min.-45-sec. fall to the ocean, at least four of the personal egress packs were activated and at least three were functioning when the Challenger struck the water. The high-speed impact with the water produced a force of 200g and was undoubtedly the cause of death for all the crew.

Post-Crash Events

Since the crash of Challenger, NASA and external investigators have taken a look at both the shuttle and the sequence of events that allowed it to be launched. The SRBs have gone through significant redesign and now include a capture feature on the field joint. The three Marshall administrators most responsible for allowing the SRB problems to go uncorrected have all left NASA. Following the recommendations of the Rogers commission, NASA has attempted to streamline and clean up its communication lines. A system for reporting suspected problems anonymously now exists within NASA. In addition, the astronauts themselves are now much more active in many decision-making aspects of the program. The former NASA Administrator, Admiral Richard Truly, is a former shuttle astronaut.

SAFETY AND ETHICS ISSUES

There are many questions involving safety and/or ethics that are raised when we examine the decision to launch the Challenger. Obviously, the situation was unsafe. The ethics questions are more complex. If high standards of ethical conduct are to be maintained, then each person must differentiate between right and wrong and must follow the course that is determined to be the right, or ethical, course. Frequently, the determination of right or wrong is not simple, and good arguments can be made on both sides of the question. Some of the issues raised by the Challenger launch decision are listed below.

1. Are solid rocket boosters inherently too dangerous to use on manned spacecraft? If so, why are they a part of the design?
2. Was safety traded for political acceptability in the design of the Space Shuttle?
3. Did the pressure to succeed cause too many things to be promised to too many people during the design of the Space Shuttle?
4. Did the need to maintain the launch schedule force decision makers to compromise safety in the launch decision?
5. Were responsibilities being ignored in the writing of routine launch waivers for the Space Shuttle?
6. Were managers at Rockwell and Morton Thiokol wise (or justified) in ignoring the recommendations of their engineers?
7. Did the engineers at Rockwell and Morton Thiokol do all that they could to convince their own management and NASA of the dangers of launch?
8. When NASA pressed its contractors to launch, did it violate its responsibility to ensure crew safety?
9. When NASA discounted the effects of the weather, did it violate its responsibility to ensure crew safety?

REFERENCES

1. "Actions to Implement the Recommendations of the Presidential Commission of the Space Shuttle Challenger Accident," National Aeronautics and Space Administration, Washington, DC, July 14, 1986.
2. *Challenger: A Major Malfunction.* Malcolm McConnell. Doubleday & Company, Inc. Garden City, NY. 1987.
3. *Prescription for Disaster.* Joseph J. Trento. Crown Publishers Inc. New York, NY. 1987.
4. "Report of the Presidential Commission of the Space Shuttle Challenger Accident," The Presidential Commission of the Space Shuttle Challenger Accident, Washington, DC, June 6, 1986.

ROGER BOISJOLY ON THE SPACE SHUTTLE DISASTER
ROGER BOISJOLY

The following information regarding Roger Boisjoly introduces his materials on the World Wide Web:

Roger Boisjoly had over a quarter century's experience in the aerospace industry in 1985 when he became involved in an improvement effort on the O-rings which connect segments of Morton Thiokol's Solid Rocket Booster, used to bring the Space Shuttle into orbit. Boisjoly has spent his entire career making well-informed decisions based on his understanding and belief in a professional engineer's rights and responsibilities. For his honesty and integrity leading up to and directly following the shuttle disaster Roger Boisjoly was awarded the Prize for Scientific Freedom and Responsibility from the American Association for the Advancement of Science.

It is interesting to note Roger Boisjoly's concerns regarding the Hoover and Fowler materials that precede these. Boisjoly, in a telephone conversation with me, expressed his concern over Hoover and Fowler's characterization of the Challenger events in the beginning of their materials. After reading their statement that "no one dreamed that the Shuttle would explode less than two minutes after lift-off," Boisjoly asked me, "What am I, a hologram?" He also indicated that the claim that NASA had Launch Commit Criteria of 31° F or higher was merely heresay and that he didn't believe that this standard ever existed. Instead, he said that there was an actual performance criterion for the booster of 40° F, which certainly would not have been met.

In the following materials, Boisjoly explains the nature of his involvement in the O-ring decision and his reaction to NASA's handling of this issue. In addition, you will find interoffice Morton Thiokol memoranda discussing the "potential failure criticality" of the O-ring problem and encouraging postponement of the shuttle mission.

"Roger Boisjoly on the Space Shuttle Disaster." Roger Boisjoly, Reprinted by permission of the author.
http://web.mit.edu/ethics/www/boisjoly

III. BEING ASKED TO SOFTEN THE URGENCY OF THE O-RING PROBLEM

My notebook entry on August 15, 1985, reads as follows: "An attempt to form the team (referring to the Solid Rocket Motor seal erosion team) was made on 19 July 1985. This attempt virtually failed and resulted in my writing memo 2870:FY86:073. This memo finally got some response and a team was formed officially. The first meeting was held on August 15, 1985, at 2:30 P.M." The memo referred to is the one I read to the Presidential Commission on February 25, 1986, which was written to the vice president of engineering at Morton Thiokol on July 31, 1985. The memo ended by saying, "It is my honest and very real fear that if we do not take immediate action to dedicate a team to solve the problem, with the field joint having the number one priority, then we stand in jeopardy of losing a flight along with all the launch pad facilities."

During this July period, NASA headquarters in Washington, D.C., asked Morton Thiokol to prepare a presentation on the problems with all the booster seals. The presentation was prepared on August 19, 1985, with Morton Thiokol personnel in attendance.

Morton Thiokol was then asked in September to send a representative to a conference in October to discuss the seals and solicit help from the experts. I prepared and presented a six page overview of the joints and the seal configuration to approximately 130 technical experts on October 7, 1985. However, I was given strict instructions, which came from NASA, not to express the critical urgency of fixing the joint but only to emphasize the joint improvement aspect during my presentation.

VI. A MANAGEMENT DECISION OVERRIDES A RECOMMENDATION NOT TO LAUNCH

The major activity that day focused upon the predicted 18 degrees Fahrenheit overnight temperature and meeting with engineering management to persuade them not to launch. The day concluded with the hurried preparation of fourteen viewgraphs which detailed our concerns about launching at such a low temperature. The teleconference started with a history of O-ring damage in field joints. Data was presented showing a major concern with seal resiliency and the change to the sealing timing function and the criticality of this on the ability to seal. I was asked several times during my portion of the presentation to quantify my concerns, but I said I could not since the only data I had was what I had presented and that I had been trying to get more data since last October. At this comment, the general manager of Morton Thiokol gave me a scolding look as if to say, "Why are you telling that to them?" The presentation ended with the recommendation not to launch below 53 degrees. This was not well received by NASA. The Vice President of Space Booster Programs, Joe Kilminster, was then asked by NASA for his launch decision. He said he did not recommend launching based upon the engineering position just presented. Then Larry Mulloy of NASA asked George Hardy of NASA for his launch decision. George responded that he was appalled at Thiokol's recommendation but said he would not launch over the contractor's objection. Then Larry Mulloy spent some time giving his interpretation of the data with his conclusion that the data presented was inconclusive.

Just as he finished his conclusion, Joe Kilminster asked for a five-minute off-line caucus to re-evaluate the data and as soon as the mute button was pushed our general manager, Jerry Mason, said in a soft voice, "We have to make a management decision." I became furious when I heard this because I knew that an attempt would be made by management to reverse our recommendation not to launch.

Some discussion had started between the managers when Arnie Thompson moved from his position down the table to a position in front of the managers and once again tried to explain our position by sketching the joint and discussing the problem with the seals at low temperature. Arnie stopped when he saw the unfriendly look in Mason's eyes and also realized that no one was listening to him. I then grabbed the photographic evidence showing the hot gas blow-by and placed it on the table and, somewhat angered, admonished them to look and not ignore what the photos were telling us, namely, that low temperature indeed caused more hot gas blow-by in the joints. I too received the same cold stares as Arnie with looks as if to say, "Go away and don't bother us with the facts." At that moment I felt totally helpless and that further argument was fruitless, so I, too, stopped pressing my case.

What followed made me both sad and angry. The managers were struggling to make a pro-launch list of supporting data. . . . During the closed managers' discussion, Jerry Mason asked in a low voice if he was the only one who wanted to fly. The discussion continued, then Mason turned to Bob Lund, the vice-president of engineering, and told him to take off his engineering hat and put on his management hat. The decision to launch resulted from the yes vote of only the four senior executives since the rest of us were excluded from both the final decision and the vote poll. The telecon resumed, and Joe Kilminster read the launch support rationale from a handwritten list and recommended that the launch proceed. NASA promptly accepted the recommendation to launch without any probing discussion and asked Joe to send a signed copy of the chart.

The change in decision so upset me that I do not remember Stanley Reinhartz of NASA asking if anyone had anything else to say over the telecon. The telecon was then disconnected so I immediately left the room feeling badly defeated.

MEMO ON O-RING EROSION

Interoffice Memo

31 July 1985

TO: R. K. Lund
             Vice President, Engineering

CC: B. C. Brinton, A. J. McDonald,
             L. H. Sayer, J. R. Kapp

FROM: R. M. Boisjoly
             Applied Mechanics—Ext. 3525

SUBJECT: SRM O-Ring Erosion/Potential Failure Criticality

This letter is written to insure that management is fully aware of the seriousness of the current O-ring erosion problem in the SRM joints from an engineering standpoint.

The mistakenly accepted position on the joint problem was to fly without fear of failure and to run a series of design evaluations which would ultimately lead to a solution or at least a significant reduction of the erosion problem. This position is now drastically changed as a result of the SRM 16A nozzle joint erosion which eroded a secondary O-ring with the primary O-ring never sealing.

If the same scenario should occur in a field joint (and it could), then it is a jump ball as to the success or failure of the joint because the secondary O-ring cannot respond to the clevis opening rate and may not be capable of pressurization. The result would be a catastrophe of the highest order—loss of human life.

An unofficial team [a memo defining the team and its purpose was never published] with leader was formed on 19 July 1985 and was tasked with solving the problem for both the short and long term. This unofficial team is essentially nonexistent at this time. In my opinion, the team must be officially given the responsibility and the authority to execute the work that needs to be done on a non-interference basis (full time assignment until completed.)

It is my honest and very real fear that if we do not take immediate action to dedicate a team to solve the problem with the field joint having the number one priority, then we stand in jeopardy of losing a flight along with all the launch pad facilities.

R. M. Boisjoly

Concurred by:
J. R. Kapp, Manager
Applied Mechanics

MEMO FROM A. R. THOMPSON ON THE FLIGHT SEAL
Interoffice Memo

2871:Fy86:141
22 August 1985

TO: S. R. Stein
               Project Engineer

CC: J. R. Kapp, K. M. Sperry, B. G. Russell, R. V. Ebeling,
               H. H. McIntosh, R. M. Salita, D. M. Ketner

FROM: A. R. Thompson, Supervisor
               Structures Design

SUBJECT: SRM Flight Seal Recommendation

The O-ring seal problem has lately become acute. Solutions, both long and short term are being sought, in the mean time flights are continuing. It is my recommendation that a near term solution be incorporated for flights following STS-27 which is currently scheduled for 24 August 1985. The near term solution uses maximum possible shim thickness and a .292 +.005/-.003 inch dia O-ring. . . . A great deal of effort will be required to incorporate these changes. However, . . . the O-ring squeeze is nearly doubled for the example (STS-27A). A best effort should be made to include a max shim kit and the .292 dia O-ring as soon as it is practical. Much of the initial blow-by during O-ring sealing is controlled by O-ring squeeze. Also more sacrificial O-ring material is available to protect the sealed portion of the O-ring. The added cross-sectional area of the .292 dia O-ring will help the resilience response by added pressure from the groove side wall.

Several long term solutions look good; but, several years are required to incorporate some of them. The simple short term measures should be taken to reduce flight risks.

A. R. Thompson

ART/jh

REPORT OF THE PRESIDENTIAL COMMISSION ON THE SPACE SHUTTLE CHALLENGER ACCIDENT

These materials are located at the World Wide Web site for the official Presidential Commission report on the Challenger accident.

CHAPTER 8: PRESSURES ON THE SYSTEM

With the 1982 completion of the orbital flight test series, NASA began a planned acceleration of the Space Shuttle launch schedule. One early plan contemplated an eventual rate of a mission a week, but realism forced several downward revisions. In 1985, NASA published a projection calling for an annual rate of 24 flights by 1990. Long before the Challenger accident, however, it was becoming obvious that even the modified goal of two flights a month was overambitious.

In establishing the schedule, NASA had not provided adequate resources for its attainment. As a result, the capabilities of the system were strained by the modest nine-mission rate of 1985, and the evidence suggests that NASA would not have been able to accomplish the 14 flights scheduled for 1986. These are the major conclusions of a Commission examination of the pressures and problems attendant upon the accelerated launch schedule.

FINDINGS

1. The capabilities of the system were stretched to the limit to support the flight rate in winter 1985/1986. Projections into the spring and summer of 1986 showed a clear trend; the system, as it existed, would have been unable to deliver crew training software for scheduled flights by the designated dates. The result would have been an unacceptable compression of the time available for the crews to accomplish their required training.
2. Spare parts are in critically short supply. The Shuttle program made a conscious decision to postpone spare parts procurements in favor of budget items of perceived higher priority. Lack of spare parts would likely have limited flight operations in 1986.

"Pressures on the System," "Recommendations of the Presidential Commission," from the *Report of the Presidential Commission on the Space Shuttle Challenger Accident*.
http://www.ksc.nasa.gov/shuttle/missions/51-1/docs/rogers-commission/table-of-contents.html.

3. Stated manifesting policies are not enforced. Numerous late manifest changes (after the cargo integration review) have been made to both major payloads and minor payloads throughout the Shuttle program.

Late changes to major payloads or program requirements can require extensive resources (money, manpower, facilities) to implement.

If many late changes to "minor" payloads occur, resources are quickly absorbed.

Payload specialists frequently were added to a flight well after announced deadlines.

Late changes to a mission adversely affect the training and development of procedures for subsequent missions.

4. The scheduled flight rate did not accurately reflect the capabilities and resources.

The flight rate was not reduced to accommodate periods of adjustment in the capacity of the work force. There was no margin in the system to accommodate unforeseen hardware problems.

Resources were primarily directed toward supporting the flights and thus not enough were available to improve and expand facilities needed to support a higher flight rate.

5. Training simulators may be the limiting factor on the flight rate: the two current simulators cannot train crews for more than 12–15 flights per year.
6. When flights come in rapid succession, current requirements do not ensure that critical anomalies occurring during one flight are identified and addressed appropriately before the next flight.

RECOMMENDATIONS OF THE PRESIDENTIAL COMMISSION

The Commission has conducted an extensive investigation of the Challenger accident to determine the probable cause and necessary corrective actions. Based on the findings and determinations of its investigation, the Commission has unanimously adopted recommendations to help assure the return to safe flight.

The Commission urges that the Administrator of NASA submit, one year from now, a report to the President on the progress that NASA has made in effecting the Commission's recommendations set forth below:

I. DESIGN

The faulty Solid Rocket Motor joint and seal must be changed. This could be a new design eliminating the joint or a redesign of the current joint and seal. No design options should be prematurely precluded because of schedule, cost or reliance on existing hardware. All Solid Rocket Motor joints should satisfy the following requirements:

The joints should be fully understood, tested and verified.

The integrity of the structure and of the seals of all joints should be not less than that of the case walls throughout the design envelope.

The integrity of the joints should be insensitive to:

Dimensional tolerances.

Transportation and handling.

Assembly procedures.

Inspection and test procedures.

Environmental effects.

Internal case operating pressure.

Recovery and reuse effects.

Flight and water impact loads.

The certification of the new design should include:

Tests which duplicate the actual launch configuration as closely as possible.

Tests over the full range of operating conditions, including temperature.

Full consideration should be given to conducting static firings of the exact flight configuration in a vertical attitude.

Independent Oversight

The Administrator of NASA should request the National Research Council to form an independent Solid Rocket Motor design oversight committee to implement the Commission's design recommendations and oversee the design effort. This committee should:

Review and evaluate certification requirements.

Provide technical oversight of the design, test program and certification.

Report to the Administrator of NASA on the adequacy of the design and make appropriate recommendations.

II. SHUTTLE MANAGEMENT STRUCTURE

The Shuttle Program Structure should be reviewed. The project managers for the various elements of the Shuttle program felt more accountable to their center management than to the Shuttle program organization. Shuttle element funding, work package definition, and vital program information frequently bypass the National STS (Shuttle) Program Manager.

A redefinition of the Program Manager's responsibility is essential. This redefinition should give the Program Manager the requisite authority for all ongoing STS operations. Program funding and all Shuttle Program work at the centers should be placed clearly under the Program Manager's authority.

Astronauts in Management

The Commission observes that there appears to be a departure from the philosophy of the 1960s and 1970s relating to the use of astronauts in management positions. These individuals brought to their positions flight experience and a keen appreciation of operations and flight safety.

NASA should encourage the transition of qualified astronauts into agency management positions.

The function of the Flight Crew Operations director should be elevated in the NASA organization structure.

Shuttle Safety Panel

NASA should establish an STS Safety Advisory Panel reporting to the STS Program Manager. The Charter of this panel should include Shuttle operational issues, launch commit criteria, flight rules, flight readiness and risk management. The panel should include representation from the safety organization, mission operations, and the astronaut office.

III. CRITICALITY REVIEW AND HAZARD ANALYSIS

NASA and the primary Shuttle contractors should review all Criticality 1, 1R, 2, and 2R items and hazard analyses. This review should identify those items that must be improved prior to flight to ensure mission safety. An Audit Panel, appointed by the National Research Council, should verify the adequacy of the effort and report directly to the Administrator of NASA.

IV. SAFETY ORGANIZATION

NASA should establish an Office of Safety, Reliability and Quality Assurance to be headed by an Associate administrator, reporting directly to the NASA Administrator. It would have direct authority for safety, reliability, and quality assurance throughout the agency. The office should be assigned the work force to ensure adequate oversight of its functions and should be independent of other NASA functional and program responsibilities.

The responsibilities of this office should include:

The safety, reliability and quality assurance functions as they relate to all NASA activities and programs.

Direction of reporting and documentation of problems, problem resolution and trends associated with flight safety.

V. IMPROVED COMMUNICATIONS

The Commission found that Marshall Space Flight Center project managers, because of a tendency at Marshall to management isolation, failed to provide full and timely information bearing on the safety of flight 51-L to other vital elements of Shuttle program management.

NASA should take energetic steps to eliminate this tendency at Marshall Space Flight Center, whether by changes of personnel, organization, indoctrination or all three.

A policy should be developed which governs the imposition and removal of Shuttle launch constraints.

Flight Readiness Reviews and Mission Management Team meetings should be recorded.

The flight crew commander, or a designated representative, should attend the Flight Readiness Review, participate in acceptance of the vehicle for flight, and certify that the crew is properly prepared for flight.

VI. LANDING SAFETY

NASA must take actions to improve landing safety.

The tire, brake and nosewheel steering systems must be improved. These systems do not have sufficient safety margin, particularly at abort landing sites.

The specific conditions under which planned landings at Kennedy would be acceptable should be determined. Criteria must be established for tires, brakes and nosewheel steering. Until the systems meet those criteria in high fidelity testing that is verified at Edwards, landing at Kennedy should not be planned.

Committing to a specific landing site requires that landing area weather be forecast more than an hour in advance. During unpredictable weather periods at Kennedy, program officials should plan on Edwards landings. Increased landings at Edwards may necessitate a dual ferry capability.

VII. LAUNCH ABORT AND CREW ESCAPE

The Shuttle program management considered first-stage abort options and crew escape options several times during the history of the program, but because of limited utility, technical infeasibility, or program cost and schedule, no systems were implemented. The Commission recommends that NASA:

Make all efforts to provide a crew escape system for use during controlled gliding flight.

Make every effort to increase the range of flight conditions under which an emergency runway landing can be successfully conducted in the event that two or three main engines fail early in ascent.

VIII. FLIGHT RATE

The nation's reliance on the Shuttle as its principal space launch capability created a relentless pressure on NASA to increase the flight rate. Such reliance on a single launch capability should be avoided in the future.

NASA must establish a flight rate that is consistent with its resources. A firm payload assignment policy should be established. The policy should include rigorous controls on cargo manifest changes to limit the pressures such changes exert on schedules and crew training.

IX. MAINTENANCE SAFEGUARDS

Installation, test, and maintenance procedures must be especially rigorous for Space Shuttle items designated Criticality 1. NASA should establish a system of analyzing and reporting performance trends of such items.

Maintenance procedures for such items should be specified in the Critical Items List, especially for those such as the liquid-fueled main engines, which require unstinting maintenance and overhaul.

With regard to the Orbiters, NASA should:

Develop and execute a comprehensive maintenance inspection plan.

Perform periodic structural inspections when scheduled and not permit them to be waived.

Restore and support the maintenance and spare parts programs, and stop the practice of removing parts from one Orbiter to supply another.

CONCLUDING THOUGHT

The Commission urges that NASA continue to receive the support of the Administration and the nation. The agency constitutes a national resource that plays a critical role in space exploration and development. It also provides a symbol of national pride and technological leadership.

The Commission applauds NASA's spectacular achievements of the past and anticipates impressive achievements to come. The findings and recommendations presented in this report are intended to contribute to the future NASA successes that the nation both expects and requires as the 21st century approaches.

DOWNSIZING

Right before Christmas in 1995, AT&T announced that it would lay off 40,000 workers in an effort to cut costs and to boost revenues. At that time, its stock was trading at around $65 per share. By September 1996, when, hopefully, AT&T expected to show some positive results of this massive action, its stock was trading at just above $50 per share—a loss of 23 percent in less than a year ("Watch Out, Widows," *Newsweek,* October 7, 1996, p. 59). If downsizing is presumably detrimental to those who lose their jobs, one would expect there to be large gains somewhere to justify the cuts. Unfortunately (for both terminated employees as well as shareholders), the connection between downsizing and increased profits is not so clear.

To present downsizing in a more positive light, companies are continually creating new ways to refer to the practice, for example: release of resources, career-change opportunities, reshaping, schedule adjustments, involuntary separation from payroll, and elimination of employment security policy (see William Lutz, *The New Doublespeak* [New York: HarperCollins, 1996]).

METAPHOR OF THE SURVIVING CHILDREN
David Doer

In order to better understand the emotional and other effects of downsizing, David Doer offers the following metaphor. Take a moment to consider its implications. Do you believe that it is a fitting metaphor? What parts of it work and what parts do not ring true? What can we learn from this type of exercise? Do you think that it helps us to be a bit more compassionate when we are asked to actually "feel" something in this way?

Imagine a family: a father, a mother, and four children. The family has been together for a long time, living in a loving, nurturing, trusting environment. The parents take care of the children, who reciprocate by being good.

Every morning the family sits down to breakfast together, a ritual that functions as a bonding experience, somewhat akin to an organizational staff meeting. One morning, the children sense that something is wrong. The parents exchange furtive glances, appear nervous, and after a painful silence, the mother speaks. "Father and I have reviewed the

---

family budget," she says, looking down at her plate, avoiding eye contact, "and we just don't have enough money to make ends meet!" She forces herself to look around the table and continues, "As much as we would like to, we just can't afford to feed and clothe all four of you. After another silence she points a finger. "You two must go!"

"It's nothing personal," explains the father as he passes out a sheet of paper to each of the children. "As you can see by the numbers in front of you, it's simply an economic decision—we really have no choice." He continues, forcing a smile, "We have arranged for your aunt and uncle to help you get settled, to aid in your transition."

The next morning, the two remaining children are greeted by a table on which only four places have been set. Two chairs have been removed. All physical evidence of the other two children has vanished. The emotional evidence is suppressed and ignored. No one talks about the two who have disappeared. The parents emphasize to the two remaining children, the survivors, that they should be grateful, "since, after all, you've been allowed to remain in the family." To show their gratitude, the remaining children will be expected to work harder on the family chores. The father explains that "the workload remains the same even though there are two less of you." The mother reassures them that "this will make us a closer family!"

"Eat your breakfast, children," entreats the father. "After all, food costs money!"

. . . [Now, consider the following questions:]

1. *What were the children who left feeling?* Most managers say, "anger," "hurt," "fear," "guilt," and "sadness."
2. *What were the children who remained feeling?* Most managers soon conclude that the children who remain have the same feelings as those who left. The managers also often report that the remaining children experience these feelings with more intensity than those who left.
3. *What were the parents feeling?* Although the managers sometimes struggle with this question, most of them discover that the parents feel the same emotions as the surviving children.
4. *How different are these feelings from those of survivors in your organization?* After honest reflection, many managers admit that there are striking and alarming similarities.
5. *How productive is a work force with these survivor feelings?* Most managers conclude that such feelings are indeed a barrier to productivity. Some groups move into discussions about effects of survivor feelings on the quality of work life and share personal reflections.

U.K. BUSINESS ETHICS ESSAY COMPETITION

PAUL WHYSALL

Whysall describes a competition sponsored by Natwest (one of the United Kingdom's largest banks) and The Times newspaper. He includes the winning essay. Do you agree?

From:	Paul Whysall, Nottingham Business School
To:	Multiple recipients of list BETS-L <BETS-L@UICVM.C...
Date:	4/30/96 5:29am
Subject:	U.K. Business Ethics Essay Competition

Last year (to a closing date of 31.1.96) a competition was run for U.K. undergraduate students under the slogan "Could you solve an ethical dilemma?"

The competition (described as a Business Ethics Competition) invited students to submit an essay of up to 1000 words setting out a response to a fictitious ethical dilemma. . . .

The brochure promoting the competition said the sponsors were "committed to opening up the ethical debate. Business Ethics is on the agenda of major companies, discussed in corporate boardrooms and in universities and is on the curricula of students world-wide. So what practical use is Business Ethics and how can companies balance the interests of stakeholders such as customers, staff, suppliers, shareholders and the community?"

The scenario entrants were to respond to was that of a company called Food Chain Stores (chief executive, John Smith) who were a week away from closing a suburban store. Hundreds of protest letters had been received, and on visiting the area, Smith had been met by protestors and the news media.

Protestors argued that low income families could not afford to travel to other stores and that old people could not carry shopping from the city centre. The protest organizer (Jane Care) also pointed out that the opening of the store had resulted in the closure of all other such local shops.

"U.K. Business Ethics Essay Competition," E-mail transmission from Paul Whysall, 4/30/96. Reprinted by permission of the author.

Food Chain's strategy, strongly supported by shareholders, was to overhaul its operations replacing most old stores with larger outlets carrying a wider range of lines than the basic range at this particular store. Renovations to this store are impractical, being costly and unable to offer more sales space.

Jane Care felt a large company like this could easily absorb costs of running one lower revenue outlet, asking only for minimal service and that the store remain open for the sake of the community.

What should Smith recommend to his board? . . .

The Times of yesterday printed the winning essay (winner of 3000 pounds sterling and the same sum for his university) . . . and this (together with other details of judges etc) can be accessed on the Internet at the following URL:

http://www.the-times.co.uk/news/pages/tim/96/04/29/timbizbiz02010html?1070963

(hope I got that right!)

I was rather disappointed by the winning essay, which seemed to be more an exercise in corporate public relations than business ethics. The winner 'invents' various initiatives (such as loyalty cards, which are currently big in UK food retailing) to show the company is responsive to customer needs. He portrays any change as being threatening to the corporate strategy.

The store closure is to be delayed for 2 months to allow bus services to be set up to and from the city centre (by negotiation with local bus companies).
Bus users will get reductions on presentation of tickets at Food Chain stores (we didn't know others were accessible!)—which may also encourage others to use their stores.

Food Chain and bus staff are to be trained to be helpful in carrying shopping for the elderly and less mobile. Food Chain will also approach the local council and convenience store chains to 'ensure a replacement store is in operation before the original outlet closes'. . . .

As I said earlier, I was rather disappointed in the judges decision, notwithstanding a most imaginative, well structured, and aware effort by the winner. I have several reservations about the style and approach of the winning entry, but most fundamentally am very worried that what seems to me at best a very clever tactical response may be seen as an example of 'practical' business ethics—let alone a good example.

Anyone else with any thoughts on this? I'm thinking of a response to the Times, and wonder if others would agree that we need to be careful of such rather opportunist exercises masquerading as business ethics?

THE WORKERS
IN THE VINEYARD
MATTHEW

In the following parable, the early workers who toiled the whole day long in the brutal heat are paid what they originally agreed to, while workers who did not work as long also received this full day's wage. Is this fair? Does that matter? To whom? What would be the impact of this practice if it were to become universal? Why might a manager practice a wage plan such as this? Is there any such thing as a fair daily wage or is it determined merely by market forces?

1 "The kingdom of heaven is like a landowner who went out at dawn to hire laborers for his vineyard. **2** After agreeing with them for the usual daily wage, he sent them into his vineyard. **3** Going out about nine o'clock, he saw others standing idle in the marketplace, **4** and he said to them, 'You too go into my vineyard, and I will give you what is just.' **5** So they went off. [And] he went out again around noon, and around three o'clock, and did likewise. **6** Going out about five o'clock, he found others standing around, and said to them, 'Why do you stand here idle all day?' **7** They answered, 'Because no one has hired us.' He said to them, 'You too go into my vineyard.' **8** When it was evening the owner of the vineyard said to his foreman, 'Summon the laborers and give them their pay, beginning with the last and ending with the first.' **9** When those who had started about five o'clock came, each received the usual daily wage. **10** So when the first came, they thought that they would receive more, but each of them also got the usual wage. **11** And on receiving it they grumbled against the landowner, **12** saying, 'These last ones worked only one hour, and you have made them equal to us, who bore the day's burden and the heat.' **13** He said to one of them in reply, 'My friend, I am not cheating you. Did you not agree with me for the usual daily wage? **14** Take what is yours and go. What if I wish to give this last one the same as you? **15** [Or] am I not free to do as I wish with my own money? Are you envious because I am generous?' **16** Thus, the last will be first, and the first will be last."

"The Workers in the Vineyard," Matthew 20: 1–16, *The Bible.*

THE ETHICS
OF DOWNSIZING
FRANK NAVRAN

*Navran addresses some of the primary concerns about downsizing
practices.*

IS DOWNSIZING EVER ETHICAL?

Organizations in every segment of business, industry, government and education are
downsizing. The very act of forcing people to leave their employment is rife with ethics-
related questions. In this article, we will consider one of the most fundamental questions:
Is downsizing ever ethical?

The truth is that unless an organization was designed expressly and overtly for the
purpose, it is not in business to provide employment. Jobs are the by-product of successful organizational endeavors, not their intended output.

Furthermore, downsizing is not necessarily a desperate move on the part of failing
organizations. It can be, and probably should be, a strategic choice designed to serve the
best interests of an organization. We should not be constrained by the false belief that
current organizational effectiveness or financial success is a de facto argument against
doing what is necessary to ensure continuing success. A healthy profit picture and downsizing are not mutually exclusive.

But this is only a partial answer to the question. We have merely said that organizational downsizing is not intrinsically unethical. To answer more fully, we have to look at
a number of issues. First, some definitions:

> *Values*—this term refers to a set of beliefs. Values are how one defines what is
> right, fair and good. This definition applies whether we consider individual val-
> ues, organizational values or societal values.

> *Ethics*—here we mean choices and the observable, behavioral manifestation of
> values-based decisions.

> *Ethical dilemma*—this is a situation where every viable option requires the
> decision maker to choose between conflicting values. Under these conditions,
> any decision under consideration will violate one or more values even as it hon-
> ors others.

> *Ethical congruence*—a situation where one's decision is consistent with, aligns
> with, the applicable set(s) of values. Under these circumstances, a choice to take
> some action will harmonize with the decision maker's values.

Bearing these definitions in mind, we find that determining whether the decision to downsize is ethical means determining whether that choice is congruent with the values of at least two different constituencies:

Those who must leave the organization against their will.

Those who remain after the downsizing.

To frame the ethical issues faced by these two constituencies, we must first agree on a set of values to use as a reference point. For this discussion, we will employ four values suggested by Kenneth W. Johnson, JD. He uses the acronym EPIC to define the values set:

E = Empathy: Caring about the consequences of one's choices as they affect others. Being concerned with the effect one's decisions have on those who have no say in the decision itself.

P = Patience: Taking time to consider and deliberate the long-term consequences of a choice before making that choice and acting upon it.

I = Integrity: Making choices that are consistent with each other and with the stated and operative values one espouses. Striving for ethical congruence in one's decisions.

C = Courage: Choosing to do what one believes is right even if the result will not be to everyone's liking or may lead to personal loss.

THOSE WHO MUST LEAVE

Being forced to leave a job, irrespective of separation allowances, pension enhancements or any of the other tools used by organizations to soften the blow, feels wrong. It feels like it must violate some values, and typically it does.

Empathy—the act of dismissal can be unempathetic, since it negatively affects those who are forced to give up their chosen path, no matter what future success may await them and since they typically feel as though they had no voice in the decision.

Patience—if the decision to downsize is perceived to be a faddish response to competitive pressures it will appear impatient or premature to those who must leave. If it is perceived as anything less than a well-developed, strategic response to demands on the organization, then it fails the patience criterion.

Integrity—where there was either an implied or spoken promise of continuing employment as the repayment for employee loyalty and/or the successful completion of assigned work, the decision—and hence the organization and its leaders—may be thought to lack integrity.

Courage—downsizing can sometimes be seen to be about creating victims and displacing blame rather than accepting responsibility and choosing the more difficult, moral high ground.

THOSE WHO REMAIN

Surviving a downsizing has its own ethical issues. Surviving employees will often share perceptions about the ethics of this decision with those who are being forced to leave. They also experience their own emotional reactions—anger, guilt, fear and depression—when asked to take up the slack by doing more work, learning new tasks, and all for the same or less money than before the downsizing occurred.

Empathy—asking people to do more with less and for less can seem unfair. Downsizing organizations put terrible pressures on their surviving employees, and that often affects their families as well. This can seem to show a lack of caring on the part of decision makers, an insensitivity to the reality that employees are people with full lives and responsibilities outside of work.

Patience—organizations which downsize often have a sense of urgency about realizing the promised benefits of doing more with less. If this rush to a new order is seen to be without a basis in fact, and if the decision makers are viewed as being unaware of what is needed to get the job done, then the decision can be seen to violate the patience ethic.

Integrity—in organizations where downsizing is imposed at the same time that executive and/or stockholders are receiving substantial bonuses, there can be the perception of a double standard. When the organization's stated values include an assertion that "we value our employees," downsizing can be seen to violate the integrity value.

Courage—if executives blame their superiors (CEO's, boards of directors, special interests or stockholders) for the necessity to downsize, and speak or act as though they had no choice, the message can be that they lacked the courage to do what is right, to stand up for those who have served them loyally, no matter the personal risk. This is viewed as cowardice.

CONCLUSION

As with most complex organizational issues, the question of whether downsizing is ethical has no easy answer. Perhaps the best that can be hoped for is that the decision makers apply the EPIC test to their choice:

That they demonstrate empathy for all of those affected by their decision: the employees who leave and those who remain behind. That they displace patience, avoiding a premature knee-jerk reaction. That the decision be based on a critical understanding of its stimuli and its consequences. That they show integrity as they strive to live according to their word and match their actions to their professions of belief. And finally that they have the courage to do the right thing, even when the right thing may be the more difficult thing to do.

GENERAL MOTORS CORPORATION AND THE ART OF TRUTH-TELLING[1]

JASON DRUCKER

Michael Moore's popular documentary, Roger and Me, *exposes the impact of the General Motors downsizing plan on Flint, Michigan, a midwestern town that relied in great part on GM's presence in its town for employment and community support. Drucker discusses the issue of trust and truth-telling as it is reflected in GM's actions.*

The exchange of sentiments is the guiding factor in social intercourse, and truth must be the guiding principle herein. Without truth social intercourse and conversation becomes valueless. We can only know what a man thinks if he tells us his thoughts, and when he undertakes to express them he must really do so, or else there can be no society of men.

IMMANUEL KANT[2]

I.

No doubt, the imperative to "tell the truth" is a commonplace platitude and for the most part such an injunction pervades the moral atmosphere. As little children we are urged to tell the truth about naughty things we have done. As young adults we are told that we have to tell the truth about evenings that have extended hours beyond curfews. And, as adults we are confronted by friends, colleagues, and lovers who expect, even demand, the truth from us—the truth of our feelings and opinions, perhaps our misdeeds. Yet, as much as we think the truth *should* be told, what exactly does it mean to tell it—the whole truth and nothing but the truth? Businessmen and other professionals, it would seem, are not exempt from the obligation of truthtelling. Or are they? This lack of truth-telling seems to be one of the many themes of "Roger & Me,"[3] Michael Moore's sensational 1989 hit-movie depicting the situation in Flint, Michigan, when General Motors Corporation laid

---

"General Motors and the Art of Truth-Telling," by Jason Drucker. Reprinted by permission of the author.

1. Thanks to Daryl Koehn for her helpful comments on an earlier draft of this manuscript.

2. Immanuel Kant, "Ethical Duties Towards Others: Truthfulness," in *Lectures on Ethics,* trans. Louis Infield (New York: Harper & Row, 1963), 224.

3. Produced, directed, and written by Michael Moore. Distributor: Warner Brothers. Video distributor: Warner Home Video. A Dog-Eat-Dog Film Production.

off thousands of workers in the late 1980s.[4] It's not only what General Motors' *does say* about the layoffs that seems to be particularly troubling for the film-maker—in other words, the "official story" of the General Motors pullout—but also, what the corporation *failed to say* or *said in an unsatisfactory way.*

But before we get there, we might want to ask: why should we pay attention to what a corporation says? After all, don't people speak, not corporations? Actually, representatives of corporations, in the form of lobbyists and public relations specialists, are paid to speak on behalf of the interests of the corporation; they are charged with making statements that reinforce the image of the corporation, or rather, the image that a company would like to project. Advertisements also speak in the sense that they make claim to what we—the consumers—can expect from a product or a service. The law itself recognizes advertising as an act of speech and requires that advertisers not intentionally misrepresent their products. According to the Advertising Code of American Business, "advertising shall tell the truth, and shall reveal significant facts, the concealment of which would mislead the public."[5] But here, once again, the notion of truth seems fairly flexible and less than comprehensive, especially if it is to be taken as a regulative ideal or model form of speech conduct. After all, how many products are there that claim to be "the best"?

Perhaps the truth is never expected to be told in the course of normal business transactions and all claims should be measured with a healthy degree of skepticism.[6] We seldom feel empathy for the person who is misled by the everyday slogans of an advertisement or the routine pitches of a salesperson. How, then, do we determine the ethical parameters of a speech act if we normally expect everything to be less than the full truth? What kind of provisional understanding can we have of a legitimate speech-act? For instance, if a lobbyist knows that he needs to promote the interests of a corporation, but also recognizes that it is self-interested to speak both persuasively and truthfully, he still has a great degree of latitude in positioning his remarks. How, then, are we to know what counts as an appropriate way for him to speak?

Tom Kay, a lobbyist for General Motors, appears to be remarkably forthright throughout the movie. He tells Michael Moore that:

> *[GM] is a corporation that is in business to make a profit and it does what it has to do to make a profit. That is the nature of corporations or companies. It's why people take their own money and invest it in a business so they can make money. It isn't to honor their hometown.*

---

4. See Ronald Edsforth, "Review of 'Roger & Me'" *American Historical Review* 96 (October 1991): 1145–1147. "Michael Moore's subject is the decline of his hometown, Flint, Michigan, the birthplace and largest production center of the General Motors Corporation. From the mid-1970s to the late 1980s, Flint was rocked by corporate decisions that closed several major factories and moved other important GM product lines out of the city. Together, General Motors' plant closings and modernization programs reduced its Flint-area work force from a peak of 79,000 in the early 1970s to just 49,000 in 1989" (1145).

5. See "The Advertising Code Case," in *Ethical Theory and Business,* eds. Tom L. Beauchamp and Norman E. Bowie (Englewood Cliffs, NJ: Prentice Hall, 1988), 186.

6. See Albert Z. Carr, "Is Business Bluffing Ethical?" in *Ethical Theory and Business,* eds. Tom L. Beauchamp and Norman E. Bowie (Englewood Cliffs, NJ: Prentice Hall, 1988), 438–442.

However, while the lobbyist does provide us with a fairly honest bottom-line, his truth-telling quickly spirals into empty rhetoric. He continues to tell us:

> *I'm sure that Roger Smith [the CEO of General Motors] has a social conscience as strong as anybody else in the country. . . . Because a guy is an automobile executive does not make him inhuman. . . . He has as much concern about these people as you do. . . . Nobody likes to see anybody laid off or put in a hardship situation.*

The viewers are, or course, fairly dubious about Roger Smith's intense concern for the workers of Flint. In fact, Michael Moore attempts to validate this skepticism by interviewing Smith, but the CEO is less than amenable to this prospect and successfully manages to avoid the filmmaker throughout the movie. From Moore's perspective, perhaps no one likes to see hardship, but as long as one doesn't have to serve as a witness to inhumanity, he may remain morally exempt.

Now, what exactly do we expect to hear from the lobbyist or representative of a corporation, and more importantly, what *should* we expect? As Immanual Kant has indicated, truthtelling may be the most legitimate form of conduct in speech, but the idea that we should "tell the truth" begs the question about what constitutes the truth that is to be told. As most people know, we regularly distort, alter, manipulate information in order to better tailor it to our circumstances. And this applies not only to *what* we say, but to *how* we say it. For instance, how would a woman narrate to a police officer that she just ran a red-light and how would she tell the same story to her friend? What elements in the story would she emphasize, and then, de-emphasize, based on who she was talking to? How would we tell a child that her dog was hit by a car? What aspects of the story would be omitted altogether and where would we most significantly alter details in our enterprise of "truthtelling"? We may understand the imperative to "tell the truth" but the presentation of truth is a little more tricky and takes a bit of practice. Indeed, if there was only one way to be truthful, we wouldn't need public relations specialists, advertising firms, or lobbyists.

Kant believes that we typically "arrange our conduct either to conceal our faults or to appear other than we are. We possess the art of simulation."[7] And Michael Moore seems to concur with this estimation, especially in the case of General Motors. For instance, how would we evaluate the following statement, made by what appears to be another bureaucratic flunky:

> *I think most of you are aware that this is the first major plant closing to take place in Flint. Let me rephrase that: this is not a plant closing, it's the loss of one product line.*

For all ostensible purposes, though, it certainly appears that plants are shutting down. After all, we do get to see Michael Moore inside a plant as the last car is being sent down the assembly line and we do witness a spokeswoman for General Motors tell Moore that this last day at the plant is a very private time for the laid-off workers. If these plants aren't being closed down, why are people not coming to work the following morning?

---

7. Kant, "Truthfulness," 224.

Why are people upset? Why are plants being demolished or boarded up? Why are people moving out of Flint? Perhaps he is self-deluded and really believes that General Motors is simply eliminating a product, but I suspect that this is not the case. Especially when he continues in his muddled way to say that "I'm trying to impress upon the employees that are being laid off that there is nothing out there for them to depend upon for the future."

Clearly there is more going on here than the closing of a product line and this latter comment is more to the point. When a product line is abolished customers are restricted from purchasing a product that was once available for consumption. When a plant closes, people lose jobs. The shift in speech intends to ultimately evade responsibility for the shutting down of the plants. But the extent of General Motors' responsibility to keep the plants viable is one of the tacit questions being asked in this movie. What the transition in speech appears to do is to actively disclaim the lived experiences of the workers, the stories of which Michael Moore has attempted to recover. The workers who are laid off from General Motors do not experience the "closing of a product line," and [they do experience] the harsh reality of the plant's being shut down. Notice how the language itself skirts the issue that is central to the workers' concerns. From the perspective of the workers, and that is what I contend "Roger & Me" tries to represent, such language attempts to minimize the extent to which a potential offense is perpetuated against them. That effacement in the language manages to perpetuate the affront or, as one might say, add insult to injury.

An analysis of corporate rhetoric appears to be particularly needed here. What has occurred in Flint is certainly the "closing of a product line," *but is that really the truth?* Michael Moore's footage here is particularly revealing since he catches the manager restating the frame for the event, drawing the viewer into the inconsistencies of the corporate narrative. What is characterized first as a "plant closing" has been strategically restated to be the "closing of the product line." Do both descriptions adequately reflect the fundamental reality here at the plant? Is one proposition more truthful than the other, or do they both say something about different people's perspectives of the truth itself?

One might similarly analyze the word "downsize," another "happier-sounding phrase" that is meant to sugarcoat a less than desirable state of affairs: being fired.[8] At least from the perspective of the workers, the truth is apparent, and the words are meant to shield General Motors' management who may have the less than fulfilling job of delivering termination notices to their soon-to-be-ex-colleagues and staff. On the other hand, Deputy Sheriff Fred Ross, given the responsibility of evicting delinquent tenants from their homes in Flint, makes no attempt to poeticize the harshness that words are sometimes used to cover over. There is no cloaking of the truth here since the deputy has no public relations man to speak for him, and even if he did have this mediator, the soon-to-be-evicted tenants would ultimately understand the message delivered at their doorstep when he knocks: "Get out."

Michael Moore effectively presents a number of instances in which the exercise of truthtelling becomes foregrounded. While the examples he presents suggest a certain degree of humor in comparison to the general indictment against General Motors, they

---

8. See William Safire, "Downsized," *New York Times Magazine,* May 26, 1996: 12.

make a singular and consistent point: that the way one frames an issue or event can be fundamentally misleading, but it can also be plainly offensive. It may even make some acts like firing tens of thousands of workers appear morally permissible. Bob Eubanks, the star-host of the Newlywed game and one of the most well-known ex-residents of Flint, implicitly understands these conventions of normal and proper discourse, and this is the reason, no doubt, that Moore includes footage of his appearance at the local country fair into the final version of the film. Consider the following exchange about what constitutes an acceptable question:

> *Michael Moore: What about questions like: How heavy are your breasts?*
> *Bob Eubanks: I never ask that question. I will say: How much does your wife's chest weigh? But there's a lot of difference in that question you just asked. A hell of a lot of difference. . . . I wouldn't ask that question for anything in the world. I wouldn't even say breast.*

At least Bob Eubanks would like us to think he has high standards. He knows how far he can go in order to communicate a meaning without saying what he shouldn't, and that's why the game-show host is able to get a rise out of his audience.

Is there a correct way to frame a certain issue? Does language naturally conform to certain situations so that we can deem language an appropriate description of a state of affairs? If corporate language is part of the problem, it doesn't strike me as an incidental fact that Moore records these disparate moments when speech itself seems to break down or when an event's characterization in language seems particularly apt, or conversely, wholly inappropriate. Take the case of the "bunny lady" (as my students call her), a resident of Flint who is currently unemployed, on welfare, and clearly struggling to make ends meet. In order to supplement her already meager income, she breeds rabbits and sells them to anyone who is willing to provide her with some additional money. What is so revealing about Moore's analysis is that the rabbits themselves don't come unmediated to their new owners. Rather, the rabbits themselves are available as either "pets" or "meat"—two very different and perhaps contradictory ways of framing the rabbit in language. What does it mean for a rabbit to be a "pet" as opposed to "meat"? I think that the analogy is very transparent, and while it may be heavy-handed, it shows the extreme options we have when we choose our language to describe our situations, or in this case, the rabbit's predicament. As the bunny lady states so eloquently: "If you don't sell them as pets, you've got to get rid of them as meat." I guess it should come as no surprise that the cages the rabbits are kept in look a lot like the General Motors' plants.

Is there a legitimate and illegitimate form of speech, then? If only our situation was as simple as the Scrabble player who comes to the now defunct Hyatt hotel in Flint and finds that her word, "partier," is not considered acceptable since the "official" Scrabble dictionary does not list it. We, on the other hand, have no manual or guidebook that will tell us what kind of language is off-limits. As she tells us, "parties" and "partied" are her best alternatives, but "partier" will not cut it. She does not seem particularly distraught at her situation even though she seems convinced that "partier" is, in fact, a word in the English language (I couldn't find it in the dictionary either). Then again, why should she be upset? Remember: Scrabble is just a game.

A philosopher like Immanuel Kant is less than helpful in telling us how a corporation or corporate representative should speak since he argues for the absoluteness of his dictum to tell the truth,[9] even though he is quick to tell us that the smart man, and especially the good conversationalist, will never find himself in this position. Rather than lying, he will "invent on the spur of the moment something noncommittal."[10] He thus avoids having to be deceptive. On the other hand, Kant does admit that we can be deceptive by not saying anything, for instance, in the case of packing a bag in order to give people the impression that I am going on vacation.[11] The point is clear: not every untruth counts as a lie, and it is only those active deceptions that we intend to communicate to another that are particularly problematic. Kant states as much when he writes that:

> *Not every untruth is a lie; it is a lie only if I have expressly given the other to understand that I am willing to acquaint him with my thought. Every lie is objectionable and contemptible in that we purposely let people think that we are telling them our thoughts and do not do so. We have broken our pact and violated the right of mankind.*[12]

But if we can avoid difficult questions—in other words, if we refuse to answer the questions that are put to us—are we in the clear? If we can avoid situations that oblige us to tell the truth are we exempt from ethical considerations? Does self-insulation serve as a moral cure-all?

Perhaps Roger Smith has done the most appropriate thing by keeping his mouth shut, and not letting his language compound the damage his actions have done in the public eye. And, by Kant's estimation, this is the best idea: "If a man tries to exhort the truth from us and we cannot tell it to him and at the same time do not wish to lie, we are justified in resorting to equivocation in order to reduce him to silence and to put a stop to his questionings. If he is wise, he will leave it at that."[13] Roger Smith appears to understand the prudence of Kant's remarks since he refuses to engage with Moore during a stockholder's meeting and turns off Moore's microphone so he can avoid being asked difficult questions.

While Michael Moore, no doubt, has exaggerated certain elements of the General Motors "story" in order to more effectively package his own message—paradoxically, what he criticizes General Motors for doing—his insights are still significant, even if they've only been thematized (as opposed to documented) in "Roger & Me." If these attempts to ask Roger Smith honest questions about the shutdown of the plants are indeed staged, as I am persuaded they must be, these various instances are not meant to serve as examples of when Roger has been evasive. Michael Moore is making his point a bit more indirectly and allegorically: there are no forthcoming questions because corporate

---

9. For Kant, lying or false promising is only possible because of the assumption that normal discourse will be truthful. See *The Moral Law: Kant's Groundwork of the Metaphysics of Morals,* trans. H. J. Paton (New York: Barnes and Noble, Inc., 1948).
10. Kant, "Truthfulness," 226.
11. Kant says that it "is possible to deceive without making any statement whatever." See "Truthfulness," 226.
12. Kant, "Truthfulness," 228.
13. Kant, "Truthfulness," 229.

bureaucrats effectively hide themselves from watching the very misery that they wreak on others' lives in the pursuit of profit. There is, in fact, no need to tell the truth because Roger Smith, for instance, has insulated himself from being asked questions to which he would know how to respond. As Ronald Edsforth says, while these various encounters to speak with Roger Smith are indeed staged, "they also effectively disclose the way that corporate decision makers . . . who have the power to make or break a community, insulate themselves from the injuries, the pain, and the anger their policies may create."[14] And, if he is asked, Kant has indicated to us his likely ignorance or non-response.

But, as we know, remaining silent itself sends a certain kind of message; sometimes it is ambiguous, but in many cases, words are not needed. One ex-worker at a General Motors plant, when asked what he has to say to Roger Smith, proclaims, "I can't mention it on TV." Unquestionably we can fill in the bleeps for him. Similarly, Moore portrays a typical, understanding Flint resident who has quite a few things that she *could* say about the "fat cats" at General Motors, but chooses not to. She proclaims herself a "lady" because she will not sink so low as to demean herself and say what she thinks. The implication is clear: she has no intention to deceive and would prefer to maintain her composure in the face of immoral conduct:

> *[Roger Smith can] get off his big bucks and start giving some of it back to [his] workers. I'm sick and tired of these damn fat cats. I could say a few choice words, but I'm a lady and I was raised a lady so I won't say what I really feel but I could use some very unsavory language as far as fat cats.*

Whereas General Motors, on the other hand, has remained noticeably silent about the plant closings—and in this case, silence is an admission of certain guilt. As Kant tells us, the silent individual is usually considered to be "suspect."[15]

The same is true of the spokeswoman for General Motors, who, as an appointed "voice" of the corporation, refuses to speak to Michael Moore because, in her estimation, he doesn't represent anyone. Silence, then, is a powerful weapon. As Kant reminds us, "we are, for instance, not naturally tempted to speak about and to betray our own misdemeanors."[16] From the perspective of the workers which Moore wants to represent, the spokeswoman can hardly avoid hanging her own neck if she talks. Consider the following exchange:

> *Michael Moore: Why can't we talk to you if you're the spokesperson?*
> *Spokesperson: You can talk to me . . .*
> *MM: We will go down there if you'll come down and talk to us.*
> *S: No, I don't think I'll talk to you.*
> *MM: You're the spokesperson and you will not speak to us about why the plant is closing?*
> *S: You don't represent anybody and you're a private interest and no I won't speak to you.*
> *MM: We happen to be citizens of this community here; it's not a private interest.*

14. Ronald Edsforth, "Review of 'Roger & Me'," 1146.
15. Kant, "Truthfulness," 226.
16. Kant, "Truthfulness," 225.

This silencing takes place on a number of levels . . . throughout the narrative. One African-American woman who raises vocal objections to her imminent eviction is temporarily allowed to stay in her home because Michael Moore's camera has captured the despair of her voice. Once out of the camera lights, though, her eviction is reinstated, and so the viewer learns that without a forum to capture her voice, life proceeds along its self-interested way. Without a microphone or a camera that can record her story for an audience comprised of people who can hold others accountable, she too, then, is effectively silenced and by all accounts, mute.

II.

One of the most remarkable features of "Roger & Me" is Moore's capacity to produce a film that is mediated through the perspective of the workers who are not normally given the channels in order to address their concerns, especially to the impersonal corporation. The film is an opportunity for viewers to witness truthtelling from the perspective of the poor and disenfranchised and not solely from the vantage points of the wealthy and powerful. Humbly asking what the working-man would want to know, Michael Moore asks the questions that have strategically not been answered:

> *Maybe I got this wrong but I thought companies lay off people when they've hit hard times. GM was the richest company in the world and it was closing factories when it was making profits in the billions.*

And by asking questions and giving some preliminary responses, Moore is able to begin a dialogue that never got started. As he puts it in his own words, what is so successful about this movie is that "[t]he working person [finally] gets to give a Bronx cheer to management. I think people left 'Roger & Me' with that sense of 'Yeah! Finally, one for our side'."[17]

Is the movie, though, just a trophy for the working class that narrates without regard for what is true? Has Michael Moore himself been co-opted by his own desire to stick it to General Motors? Throughout the film, Michael Moore seemed to suggest the ethical obligation to speak properly about what we describe; that legitimacy in speech requires a willingness to accurately narrate or express a state of affairs. While the imperative to tell the truth seems by all standards to be logically and necessarily ethical, it also has a double requirement: to respond with words that encourage such a reciprocal "exchange of sentiments." But too often we return a falsehood with a falsehood. We're more likely to respond to an abuse with another abuse, and with what seems to be good reason since anger generally provokes strong emotions. "Why shouldn't I be angry," Moore said in another context. "Why can't we look at these corporations who in the eighties and nineties have got filthy rich at the expense of millions of people losing their jobs? Why shouldn't I use every device I can to go after them?"[18] But if this is the case, hasn't Michael Moore gone against his own criticisms of General Motors? And if Moore is

---

17. Jolie Solomon, " 'Roger & Me' Redux" *Newsweek,* October 5, 1992: 79.
18. "Success," *The New Yorker* 68 (October 12, 1992): 45.

going to use any device to satisfy his anger against General Motors, how reliable are we to take his indictment of the company? Does using every device mean that he can also be deceptive in his practices, just like he has accused General Motors of doing? And if Moore, too, is being deceptive in his presentation of the case against General Motors, is he excused because, as one critic put it, Moore is "openly one-sided"[19] whereas General Motors is just plain manipulative?

I might be inclined to argue that Michael Moore symptomatically reproduces some of the ills of which he criticizes General Motors, and in the end, it is the "official story" of General Motors, "Roger & Me," and the stories of Flint residents seen in tandem with each other that provides for a more dynamic version of the truth. Perhaps what the narrative poses for the viewer is the question about how much truth one person could ever possibly reveal. In other words, we must wonder how anyone could ever tell the truth on his own. For instance, take the case where a young child in tears runs up to his parent and declares, "Johnny hit me." On face value, the statement itself explains fairly little about the events that have just transpired, but based on a parent's love for a child, a mother may judge that the action was done with malice. What the parent may not know is that the child solicited the abuse or that it was, in fact, an accident. Only by rounding out the statement, through a series of questions and exchanges with other parties directly concerned with the event, does the truth itself begin to emerge. While the statement itself—Johnny hit me—may be true and quite accurately reflect what has occurred, the proposition is what I might characterize as "impoverished" since it doesn't sufficiently reveal the "whole story." It may turn out that everyone has been convinced by their own impoverished versions of the truth. And isn't this exactly the problem: that everyone has been hijacked by their own true stories?

In the case of the upwardly-mobile resident of Flint who seem untouched by the ills of the city, truthtelling probably means something very different for them than for the laid-off workers. In one instance, a socialite at a Great Gatsby party tries to argue that Flint is a great place to live. Michael Moore's film shows us that this is probably true, but only for her and her friends. Similarly, an older woman relaxing on a golf course thinks that many of the laid-off workers are just lazy and "some of them . . . just want to take the easy way out." After all, she tells us, "we have such a good welfare system." And, from her perspective, that is probably true. At the end of "Roger & Me," Moore catches up with Roger Smith at a General Motors' Christmas party. When asked if he will come to Flint to meet with former General Motors' workers, many of whom have been evicted from their homes, Smith's response is that General Motors did not evict them. Indeed, we would have to agree with Smith's statement. But to claim an utterly disinterested, and ultimately disingenuous pose of non-responsibility, is similarly illegitimate. Perhaps we have caught Roger Smith at a bad moment, perhaps there are a number of logical explanations for the erosion of Flint, but, inevitably, Smith takes Kant's advice: if you know that you are going to be forced to lie, try to avoid the interlocutor! It is not surprising, then, that we watch Smith scurry off after pleading his ignorance and providing his own impoverished form of the truth. In Moore's estimation, it isn't that the truth hasn't been

---

19. Annette Insdorf, "Who Made 'Roger & Me'?" *American Film* 15 (November 1989): 14.

told, but not everyone's version of the truth has been given adequate expression nor are the ideas of the workers regularly given an opportunity for airing.

If "Roger & Me" is a heavy-handed, one-sided account of the General Motors' situation, then maybe this is exactly the point. As Miles Orvell has suggested, we expect the truth from documentary but not from satire, and "Roger & Me" is more like the latter than the former, maybe even a combination of the two.[20] But the notion of documentary is certainly relevant here, since "Roger & Me" is no doubt consistent with *the truth claims of the workers* who have every reason to justifiably believe that they are getting screwed over by management. While the full picture may in fact be impoverished, "Roger & Me" is a true account of the Flint workers' self-perception of their predicament.

I have tried to argue that we have an imperative to try our language and engage in dialogue with other individuals in order to best express the reality of a situation. There may be no explicit legitimacy assigned to the actual content of our speech, but we may be obliged to "manage" our speech with the self-consciousness that our words may be disrespectful to others and perhaps not adequately or sufficiently conform to the reality our words purport to describe. It is only by essaying or assessing the statements of a number of parties or stakeholders that this truthtelling might take its place. While it would be difficult to weigh these various responsibilities without further investigation of the purported offenses, it seems to me worthwhile to consider the speech-acts of various parties and consider the extent to which they may be considered justifiably offensive.

Certainly "Roger & Me" prompts a number of interesting questions about the legitimacy of GM's actions: Did the company treat its employees appropriately? Did General Motors encourage the Flint community to have a false sense of reliance upon the company for endlessly meeting its needs? Or, was Flint short-sighted in not considering a future without General Motors? In my estimation, no one party can successfully illuminate these issues. Rather, as Kant says, it is "[f]reedom of investigation [that] is the best means to consolidate the truth."[21] The truth itself needs to be negotiated by all these various perspectives, and without the viewpoints of the workers, the fuller picture may never have been told. In this sense, Moore's willingness to narrate another side of the story provides us with a rounder, more balanced sense of the Flint, Michigan, layoffs. In the end, this may only show that truth and discourse can never seamlessly coincide.

RELATED WEB SITE

General Motors: www.gm.com

---

20. Miles Orvello, "Documentary Film and the Power of Interrogation: American Dream & Roger and Me," *Film Quarterly* 48 (Winter 1994): 10–18.

21. Kant, "Truthfulness," 235.

Chapter 7c

CORPORATE STRATEGY AND DECISION MAKING:
Reputation Management

CORPORATE CODES, OMBUDSPERSONS AND ASSOCIATIONS

In order to act with integrity, as discussed earlier, a firm must first articulate its values, its priorities. The most prevalent form of values articulation and communication is a corporate mission, code of conduct, or code of ethics. Once the firm has defined its individual value structure, individual decision makers within the firm have guidance in connection with difficult dilemmas. Codes may refer to general areas of business conduct or may apply to a specific area of the firm's business. Reebok, for example, has Human Rights Production Standards that assist it in ensuring that the factories it uses have humane working conditions.

Other strategies exist to communicate corporate values as well as to continually update corporate programs and make them more effective. Some firms have used corporate ombudspersons. An ombudsperson is someone who is neither an advocate for the firm nor for the employee; instead, she or he often administers a general reporting structure that holds fairness to all parties as its most important goal. A firm may also serve as part of an association such as the Ethics Officers Association, which allows representatives to continually explore developing issues that face the firm.

CORPORATE CODES AND ETHICS PROGRAMS
MICHAEL C. DECK

In the following selection, Michael Deck explains research conducted to gather and to analyze 200 codes of conduct. The researcher found that while many firms have codes, they are not always communicated to stakeholders, nor are they always adhered to. Consider whether any firm you have worked for has had a code and whether you felt it was completely integrated into the decision-making functions of the firm.

Michael C. Deck, "Corporate Codes and Ethics Programs," www.kpmg.ca/ethics/eth_clks.htm First presented at "Business Practices under NAFTA: Developing Common Standards for Global Business," University of Colorado-Denver, December 8–10, 1994. Reprinted by permission of the author.

STAKEHOLDER THEORY

Our research program has examined more than seventy Canadian corporations over the last ten years. As we studied the data, it became clear that the managers of successful companies no longer regard shareholders as the sole and necessarily most important stakeholders in the corporation. The concept of shareholders endowed with a right to the maximization of profits is being replaced by the concept of stakeholders, of which shareholders comprise only one group. The shareholder is no longer the preeminent stakeholder, to be rewarded at the expense of other stakeholders. . . .

What this research shows is that when management or the board of a company favour one group of stakeholders at the expense of other primary stakeholder groups, difficulties always develop. When shareholders are favoured unfairly, when maximizing the bottom line takes full priority, customers or employees or suppliers invariably will be shortchanged. . . .

MANAGING ETHICS IN THE WORKPLACE

If we agree that values, ethics, and moral principles are essential to sound decision making, how does a manager go about managing that aspect of the organization?

In looking for an answer to that question, we thought it would make sense to begin looking for the values, ethics, and moral principles of an organization in its Code of Ethics. Beginning three years ago, our Centre undertook to gather and to analyse 200 corporate codes. We learned that while corporations do indeed have values, ethics, and moral principles, these are not always communicated in a code of ethics and may in fact be quite different from what the code might lead one to believe.

While it would be ingenuous to think that ethical behavior within an organization can be changed simply by posting a list of high sounding principles, it is equally naive to imagine that the ethics of an organization "just happens and there's nothing to be done about it."

Every organization, as Steven Brenner points out, has an ethics program, whether it knows it or not.[1] The ethics program is that set of factors both explicit and implicit which communicate corporate values, define parameters of decision making, and establish the ground rules for behaviour. This is similar to what Robert Jackall has described as "institutional logic." An effective ethics program encourages behaviour consistent with corporate principles.

Explicit elements of a corporate ethics program include the things which an organization says it believes in, and the efforts made to communicate those principles directly. The centerpiece of the explicit components is the corporate code. In order to evaluate the effectiveness of a corporate code, the purpose of the code must be considered. Corporate codes can serve a variety of purposes: from "image enhancing" to "due diligence defense," from guidance for employees who want to "do the right thing" to helping an employee resist pressure from a superior. The corporate code and its implementation can raise issues of ethics to a conscious level and legitimate discussion.[2]

Our research on about 200 corporate codes revealed some interesting details about their nature and purpose.[3] Using the Stakeholder Model, we sorted out the statements made in these codes according to which stakeholder's interests were being addressed.

One observation is that most of the text in these codes is concerned with the duty and responsibility of the employee to the company. Put more strongly, it seems that the most common purpose of a corporate code is to protect the firm from its employees. This is borne out by the observation that the most frequently cited "reason why" for ethical behaviour is that violations will hurt the company. The problem with this approach is that if the possibility of getting caught (and incurring the penalty) is apparently small, then the reason for ethical behaviour evaporates. . . .

The analysis of these codes also looked at the "approach" used for each statement, categorizing each as Guiding Principle, Act & Disclose, Seek Advice, or Rule. These categories lie along a scale which we describe as "Source of Control."

. . . This analysis [made it] clear that there were really three basic types of codes, differentiated by the source of control.

The terms *"Code of Ethics," "Code of Conduct,"* and *"Code of Practice"* are often used interchangeably. It is useful, however, to distinguish among these terms in order to establish a basic typology. Each basic code type has a different intent and purpose.

Codes of Ethics are statements of values and principles which define the purpose of the company. These codes seek to clarify the ethics of the corporation and to define its responsibilities to different groups of stakeholders as well as defining the responsibilities of its employees. These codes are expressed in terms of credos or guiding principles. Such a code says: "This is who we are and this is what we stand for," with the word "we" including the company and all its employees, whose behaviour and actions are expected to conform to the ethics and principles stated in the code.

Codes of Practice are interpretations and illustrations of corporate values and principles, and they are addressed to the employee as individual decision maker. In effect they say: "This is how we do things around here." Such a code seeks to shape the expression of the corporation's stated values through the practices of its employees. Codes of practice tend to rely on guidelines for decision making, using such rules of thumb as "act and disclose" or "seek advice." This approach takes a view of ethics as "what we do because it is our character."

Codes of Conduct are statements of rules: "This is what you must (or must not) do," as distinct from the code of ethics, which is stating: "This is how we expect you to behave." Codes of conduct typically are comprised of a list of rules, stated either affirmatively or as prohibitions. Penalties for transgressions may be identified and systems of compliance and appeal defined. Potential conflicts of interest are often described, with appropriate rules for guidance. This approach takes a view of ethics as what is not to be done (or seen not to be done) in view of the consequences.

In practice, corporate codes tend to include elements of all three types, but for analytical purposes it is helpful to consider these three basic types as benchmarks. Each of the three types is useful and each can be appropriate or necessary in particular business and organizational settings. For example, in a divisionalised corporation, it would be appropriate to draft a Code of Ethics in order to enunciate the company's overall purpose and the guiding principles and ethics that govern its actions and behavior. At the divisional and functional area levels, different and divisionalised Codes of Conduct and Practice are appropriate, so long as the rules, examples, and guidelines are not in conflict with the statement of the corporation's guiding principles and ethics. . . .

HAVE ETHICS PROGRAMS FAILED?

It is interesting to note at this point that recent research has found no significant correlation between corporations having a code of ethics and a reduction in ethical violations.[4] Is the problem that the code was badly written? Probably not. Is there a problem with implementation? A more likely suspect, since, of the 90% of companies that have codes, only 28% do any training. There is, however, another factor which, I would suggest, accounts for these findings. I referred earlier to the implicit components of an ethics program. It may well be that the failure of the explicit components to produce results is the result of their having to fight an uphill battle against the implicit components.

If the goal is to produce behaviour which is in line with the explicit values, principles, and ethics of the organization, then congruency between the explicit and implicit components of the ethics program is essential.

To evaluate the potential effectiveness of an ethics program we propose several criteria which can be applied to the explicit components, beginning with the published code of ethics/practice/conduct. Assuming that the corporate code is satisfactory, the next step is to evaluate implementation efforts. Ultimately, the success and effectiveness of the program will depend on the next step, which is an honest and objective audit of the "implicit" components.

One danger of using a phrase such as "ethics program" is that it might suggest a requirement for a large scale, disruptive, and expensive process. Just the opposite is true. As I said at the beginning of this section, every corporation already has an ethics program. What is proposed here is a framework for looking at the effectiveness of what is already in place and for identifying what, if any, aspects need strengthening or modification. The ethical ground rules, values, and practices of an organization develop incrementally over time and will require time to change.

NOTES

1. Brenner, S. N., "Ethics Programs and Their Dimensions," *Journal of Business Ethics,* Vol. 11: 391, 399, 1992.
2. Metzger, M., D. R. Dalton, and J. W. Hill, "The Organization of Ethics and the Ethics of Organizations: The Case for Expanded Organizational Ethics Audits," *Business Ethics Quarterly,* Vol. 3, Issue 1, 1993, pp. 27–43.
3. The details of this research are expanded in M. B. E. Clarkson and M. C. Deck, "Applying the Stakeholder Management Model to the Analysis and Evaluation of Corporate Codes," in *Business and Society in a Changing World Order,* pp. 55–76 (Best Papers volume of the 1992 Conference of the International Association for Business and Society), Dean C. Ludwig, Editor. Edwin Mellen Press, New York. 1993.
4. Rich, A. J., C. S. Smith, and P. H. Mihalek: 1990, "Are Corporate Codes of Conduct Effective?" *Management Accounting* (September), pp. 34–35.

ETHICS OFFICERS ASSOCIATION

W. MICHAEL HOFFMAN

The Ethics Officers Association (EOA) is one response to the growing need for firms to learn about ways in which they might be able to create an ethical corporate environment. Michael Hoffman, a member of the association's board of directors, explains the activities and objectives of the EOA.

The Ethics Officer Association (EOA) started in the summer of 1991. At least, the seeds of it were planted then, when about 40 to 45 ethics officers came to the Center for Business Ethics at Bentley College and began to meet each other, some of them for the first time. The day-and-a-half's very unstructured workshop was so successful that the ethics officers that were there said, "Let's keep this going."

So we had a planning committee meeting at Raytheon a couple of months later and then another planning committee meeting at Honeywell about six months after that. We became a chartered 501(c)(3) non-profit organization about a year after we started the planning. So the EOA is now about three years old. . . .

The mission of the Ethics Officers Association is dedicated to promoting ethical business practices and serving as a forum for the exchange of information and strategies among individuals responsible for ethics programs. To be a member of the Ethics Officers Association—I will call it EOA for short—you have to be involved in some managerial responsibility for an ethics/compliance program in your organization. I will talk about membership in just a minute; the growth of the EOA has been quite dramatic.

Here is a list of services and projects. We have Sponsoring Partner Forums. There is a category in the Ethics Officers Association for a company to become a Sponsoring Partner Organization, and for just the Sponsoring Partner Organizations, there are special forums which are smaller than our general conferences.

We have had four Sponsoring Partner Forums. The first in 1992 and the second in 1993, both held at Raytheon outside of Boston. The third in 1994 held at Levi Strauss in San Francisco, and the fourth this past April at Sears in Chicago. We try to spread our forums around.

We also have conferences. We have had two general conferences so far. The first one in 1993 at the Center for Business Ethics at Bentley College, and the second one in 1994 in Dallas, hosted by Texas Instruments. Our next conference is going to be in Toronto in October, hosted by NORTEL. In 1994 in Dallas, we had about 165 registrants. We anticipate that the Toronto conference will be at close to 200.

W. Michael Hoffman "Ethics Officers Association," (during the Second Symposium on Crime and Punishment in the United States, September 7–8, 1995, Washington, DC).

Professional development courses (PDC) have just started within the Ethics Officers Association. Our first PDC course, jointly sponsored by the EOA and the Center for Business Ethics, is being held September 17 through September 22 at the Center for Business Ethics at Bentley College. We wanted to have 35 participants in this first executive development course. We have as of now 37. It is closed for September, but we will be offering another one in May of 1996. We already have a waiting list for the May PDC course.

The PDC course is called "Managing Ethics in Organizations," and has more than 25 faculty members. Seventeen or 18 of those faculty are experienced ethics officers from different companies, talking about different areas in that course.

These ethics officers are flying in from all over the country at their own expense because they feel that this executive development initiative for present and future ethics officers is extremely important. So we have people coming from all kinds of different corporations to participate, giving their time freely, to make this professional development program a success.

The EOA also plans to work with the Center for Business Ethics in a strategic alliance to continue to offer such professional development courses. This week-long intensive course will continue, but we will also have one-day intensive courses that will focus on a specific subject matter, exploring in more depth a particular area that the week-long course touched upon but couldn't deal with thoroughly.

The Ethics Officer Association hopes, within the next year or so, to be offering credentials for ethics officers. For example, if a person takes the week-long intensive course, and perhaps three one-day intensive courses, he or she would receive credentials for being an ethics officer from the EOA. The EOA intends to provide some professional credentialing for this very new profession.

The EOA is really very similar to the DII (Defense Industry Initiative), which started in 1986. We started in 1991/92. One of the main differences is the fact that the EOA is open to corporations from all industries instead of just the defense industry, even though we have as many defense companies as members of the EOA.

In fact, just as a change of pace, I wonder if all the members of the EOA who are here today would stand up or those people who know that their corporations have a representative in the EOA. Would you stand up just for a couple of seconds?

That's a good representation of the EOA at this symposium. I'm pleased to see that all our panelists stood, too. So if you saw people stand and would like to know more about the EOA, please go up to them and ask them what they think of it. I think you will find that they are pleased with what they have been receiving from the services of the EOA.

There are some other EOA services, and I'll go quickly. There is resource assistance with the Ethics Officer Association. The Center for Business Ethics and the EOA maintain a very extensive research library at Bentley College. It is very similar, I suspect, to the DII's research library. We have both EOA company materials, approximately 1,500 to 2,000 books on business ethics, the best journals on business ethics are there, and many videos on business ethics.

We have networking assistance. Quite often, members will call EOA headquarters at the Center for Business Ethics to find out who to benchmark with in regard to a safe reporting system? Who can we benchmark with in terms of our training programs? And in addition to being able to come to the Center and look over the materials that are there, we can put people in touch with companies that have some of the best ethics programs in a particular area.

The growth of the EOA has been excellent. These numbers may not jump out at you right away, but for us, they're very exciting. As of today, we have 84 Sponsoring Partner corporations and 119 individual members. You can be an individual member (IM) even if your organization chooses not to become a Sponsoring Partner (SP), at least not initially. We have 119 in this category. So that puts us over 200 members, including SPs and IMs, in the EOA.

The EOA has numerous plans for future development. We now have a full-time Executive Director. I was more of a part-time Executive Director. Now I have been invited to join the Board of Directors. I think they didn't know what else to do with me, but I am honored.

I would like to introduce you to our new Executive Director, Ed Petry, who you will be hearing from after lunch. And the Chairman of our Board who has been the EOA President, Bill Redgate. Bill is Vice President of Business Practices at Dun & Bradstreet. Ed Petry is still a tenured faculty member at Bentley College and works with the Center for Business Ethics, but he will be the full-time Executive Director at the Center. A full-time Executive Director of the EOA is now needed because of its growth in membership and services.

The future development of the EOA certainly involves improving benefits and services for its members. It has now struck up a strategic alliance with the Center for Business Ethics. The Center is no longer just the administrative headquarters of the EOA, but it is also a strategic partner, an example of which is the professional development course being offered in September, which is jointly sponsored by EOA and CBE [Center for Business Ethics].

We are certainly going to continue the progress with the executive education program. We are also going to start carving inroads into the international arena. The EOA has already scheduled conference panels in Tokyo, Germany, and Great Britain, so that we can spread the EOA mission of building best-practice ethics and compliance programs abroad.

The final comment I will make is this. If anything distinguishes the EOA from other organizations it is stressing the importance of ethics/compliance programs not being just compliance driven. We feel that a truly successful compliance program must be value driven, integrity driven. There is too much to lose in an ethics/compliance program not stressing the good things that come about in raising the level of ethical awareness of all members of the company and in providing all employees with the tools to make intelligent ethical business decisions.

If anything could characterize the efforts of the EOA, it would be that out of that effort to raise the level of ethical awareness and to provide the educational tools for making intelligent ethical business decisions, a good compliance program will follow. Thank you.

ETHICS IN AMERICAN BUSINESS: POLICIES, PROGRAMS, AND PERCEPTIONS

ETHICS RESOURCE CENTER, INC.

The Ethics Resource Center conducted the following study of the impact of ethics policies and programs on a firm's reputation.

CHAPTER 1: OVERALL FINDINGS

Ethics Programs in American Business

A growing number of companies have ethics programs: 60% of respondents reported that their companies had a code of conduct; 33% reported that their companies had training on business ethics; and, 33% reported that their companies had an ethics office or ethics ombudsman.

Utilization of all these program elements was high. Well over half of respondents relied on their codes of conduct, and a similar proportion found the ethics training useful. Nearly one-quarter of respondents with ethics offices had turned to them for advice or to report concerns about misconduct. Of those who had turned to their ethics offices, the vast majority were not satisfied with how their concerns were addressed. Ethics offices, however, do not weaken the relationship between supervisors and their employees, but may serve as a "safety-valve" in situations where it may be inappropriate to take matters elsewhere in the company.

Personal Ethics on the Job

Nearly half of respondents claimed that their business ethics had improved during the course of their careers. Nonetheless, nearly one in ten admitted that they had done things at work in the last year about which they would be ashamed or embarrassed to tell their children.

Employees expressed a certain amount of skepticism about their fellow employees' ethics. More than half of respondents regarded their own business ethics as higher than those of their peers and their direct subordinates, but not different from their senior management.

Companies' Ethical Performance

Although employees had positive perceptions of their own business ethics, they tended to be more critical of the ethics of the companies for which they worked.

On the positive side, most respondents thought their companies fulfilled their ethical obligations to stakeholder groups *adequately* or even *exceptionally*. Similarly, a majority of respondents believed that the amount of commitment to ethical business conduct exhibited by their companies was *about right.*

However, one-fourth of respondents believed that their companies sometimes ignore unethical conduct to meet business objectives, and nearly one employee in six stated that their companies encourage misconduct to meet business objectives.

Almost one-third of respondents indicated that they feel pressured at times by other employees or management to engage in conduct which violates their companies' standards of conduct. Achieving business goals—either schedule deadlines or overly-aggressive financial or business objectives—was the most common motive for misconduct.

Encountering Misconduct on the Job

Although perceptions of employee misconduct appear to be widespread in the U.S. workplace, American workers are still reluctant to blow the whistle on fellow employees. In the last year, nearly one in three respondents observed conduct at work which he or she believed violated the law or company policy, but more than half did not report their observation to their company.

Of the respondents who did report their observations of misconduct to their companies, most were not satisfied with the outcome of their report. The most common unsatisfactory responses to employee reports of misconduct were that: *nothing happened; their concerns did not remain confidential; their report was not taken seriously;* and, *they were not given a prompt or satisfactory response.* For those who did not report their observation of misconduct, the most common reasons cited for their reluctance were that: *they did not believe the company would take corrective action; they feared retaliation from superiors;* and, *they did not trust the company to keep their report confidential.*

Lying appeared to be the most common type of misconduct observed by employees. A majority of respondents who observed misconduct had witnessed lying to supervisors (56%) and other employees lying on reports or falsifying records (41%). One-third of respondents who had observed misconduct witnessed: *sexual harassment, stealing/theft, drug/alcohol abuse* and *conflicts of interest.* Ten percent reported that their companies had violated environmental laws or regulations, nearly half of them (8%) in serious enough ways to cause harm to the health or safety of employees or the public.

Employees demonstrated skepticism about the ethics of fellow employees compared to their own. Very few respondents admitted to having misrepresented information to their supervisors (3%), but were much more likely to believe their peers did so (42%).

More than one-quarter of respondents believed that they had been the victims of some sort of discrimination in important ways during the course of their careers. Gender discrimination was the most common form of discrimination reported. Nearly one-third of female survey respondents claimed to have been victims of gender discrimination. Age and racial discrimination were the next most commonly cited types of discrimination.

Business Law and Ethics

Overall, survey respondents appeared to lack knowledge and understanding of key areas of business law and ethics such as overseas bribery, gathering competitive intelligence, anti-trust, unfair sales practices, insider trading and sexual harassment.

CHAPTER 2: EFFECT OF ETHICS PROGRAMS

Ethics Programs in American Business

At least one in five survey respondents worked in a company which had a comprehensive program: a code of conduct, ethics training and an ethics office. Ethics training, as a supplement to a code of conduct, appeared to increase substantially the effectiveness of a corporate code of conduct in guiding business decisions and behavior. Comprehensive ethics programs appear to correlate strongly with improved employee attitudes toward the ethics of their own organization and its management.

Personal Ethics on the Job

Employees in companies with comprehensive ethics programs had better views of their own business ethics than employees in companies with fewer program elements. They believed that their business ethics had improved in the course of their careers. In addition, employees in companies with comprehensive ethics programs indicated that they saw less difference between their business and personal ethics and that their business ethics can positively affect their personal ethics. Corporate ethics initiatives also appeared to correlate with improved employee perceptions of senior management: employees in companies with no ethics programs were much more likely to see their own ethics as distinctly different from and higher than their senior management's.

Companies' Ethical Performance

Employees who worked for companies with comprehensive ethics programs were much more likely to rate their companies' fulfillment of ethical obligations to various stakeholders as *exceptional.* They were also much more likely to consider the commitment to ethical conduct by others in their companies to be *about right,* with the most dramatic differences seen in the more positive opinions of higher levels of management. Employees who worked for companies with comprehensive ethics programs were nearly two-and-one-half times as likely to believe that the amount of unethical conduct in their companies had decreased in the last five years. A code of conduct as the sole component of an ethics initiative seemed to produce employee attitudes and perceptions more negative than where nothing was done.

Encountering Misconduct

The likelihood that employees would report the misconduct they observed increased in companies with comprehensive ethics programs. Additionally, respondents in companies with comprehensive programs were more likely to be satisfied with the outcome of their report than those respondents in companies without ethics programs (58% vs. 46%).

Business Law and Ethics

The responses to the six hypothetical questions regarding legal and ethical behavior (questions 34–39), reflected few significant differences when comparing the responses of employees with and without ethics programs, with the exception of the responses to the hypothetical question about sexual harassment. Seven of the nine situations described in the sexual harassment question yielded statistically significant differences, as did the "I don't know" response. In each case, employees of companies with comprehensive ethics programs were more likely to view the described behavior as harassment. Also, in the responses to five of the six legal questions (including the question on sexual harassment) a higher percentage of respondents in organizations with no ethics program responded that they *did not know* what was acceptable in the scenarios presented. . . .

CHAPTER 4: DIFFERENCES BY JOB FUNCTION

Ethics in American Business

Employees in technical positions were the most likely to report that their companies had ethics programs. Nearly one-fifth of those in manufacturing positions said that they did not know if their companies had codes, training or ethics offices; nonetheless, those employees in manufacturing jobs who did have an ethics office were the most likely of any job function to have reported utilizing it. However, employees in administration, human resources and public relations positions found their companies' codes and training the most useful.

Personal Ethics on the Job

Respondents in manufacturing positions appeared to be the most skeptical about ethics generally. They were more likely than any group to report that their business ethics were not as rigorous as their personal ethics, that they could keep their personal and business ethics separate at all times, and that they had engaged in business conduct about which they would be ashamed to tell their children. In fact, they were not only skeptical about their own business ethics, but they also had the most negative opinion of the ethics of their companies and fellow employees. Respondents in product and customer service often barely trailed those in manufacturing and quality control in their negative assessments. In contrast, those in administration, human resources and public relations generally were the most likely to report that their business ethics had improved in the course of their careers, and that they did not separate their business and personal ethics.

Companies' Ethical Performance

Employees in administration, human resources and public relations had the best perceptions of their companies' commitment to ethical business conduct and of their companies' unwillingness to ignore or encourage misconduct to achieve business objectives. Again, manufacturing, quality control and product/customer service employees had negative perceptions in these areas and reported the highest levels of pressure from their companies to engage in misconduct to meet business objectives.

Encountering Misconduct on the Job

Employees in manufacturing and quality control positions were slightly more likely than other respondents to observe behavior which they thought violated the law or company policy. Of those who observed misconduct, those in administration, human resources and public relations were the most likely to report the misconduct they observed to their companies. Those in technical and product/customer service positions were the least likely to report observed misconduct. Respondents in manufacturing were the least likely to believe they had been discriminated against in their careers. However, this may be due in part to the fact that respondents overall cited gender discrimination as the most common form of discrimination suffered, and manufacturing respondents were disproportionately male.

Business Law and Ethics

In answering questions on basic business law, respondents in job functions to which certain areas of law related more than others (e.g., anti-trust and competitive intelligence for sales and marketing employees), tended to believe most actions were acceptable, including those actions which would be considered more legally questionable. . . .

THE PRINCE
Niccolò Machiavelli

This excerpt from Machiavelli's The Prince *discusses how a prince (or person with governing power, generally) gains his reputation. Machiavelli concludes that dignity is the most important quality. Based on this, do you think that Machiavelli would be impressed by our business and government leaders today? Do you agree with his contentions? If not, why not?*

CHAPTER TWENTY-ONE: WHAT A RULER SHOULD DO IN ORDER TO ACQUIRE A REPUTATION

Nothing does more to give a ruler a reputation than embarking on great undertakings and doing remarkable things. In our own day, there is Ferdinand of Aragon, the present King of Spain. He may be called, more or less, a new ruler, because having started out as a weak ruler he has become the most famous and most glorious of all the kings of Christendom. If you think about his deeds, you will find them all noble, and some of them extraordinary. At the beginning of his reign he attacked Granada, and this undertaking was the basis of his increased power.[1] In the first place, he undertook the reconquest when he had no other problems to face, so he could concentrate upon it. He used it to channel the ambitions of his Castilian barons, who, because they were thinking of the war, were no threat to him at home. Meanwhile, he acquired influence and authority over them without their even being aware of it. He was able to raise money from the church and from his subjects to build up his armies. Thus, this lengthy war enabled him to build up his military strength, which has paid off since. Next, in order to be able to engage in more ambitious undertakings, still exploiting religion, he practiced a pious cruelty, expropriating and expelling from his kingdom the Marranos:[2] an act without parallel and truly despicable. He used religion once more as an excuse to justify an attack on Africa.[3] He then attacked Italy and has recently[4] invaded France. He is always plotting and carrying out great enterprises, which have always kept his subjects bewildered and astonished, waiting to see what their outcome would be. And his deeds have followed one another so closely that he has never left space between one and the next for people to plot uninterruptedly against him.

The Prince, Chapter 21, by Niccolò Machiavelli, translated by David Wootton. Copyright (c) 1995 Hackett Publishing Co. Reprinted by permission.

1. The muslim state of Granada was conquered between 1480 and 1492.

2. The Marranos were Jews who had been forced to convert to Catholicism. On misinterpretations of this term, see Edward Andrew, "The Foxy Prophet: Machiavelli Versus Machiavelli on Ferdinand the Catholic," *History of Political Thought* 11 (1990), 409–22.

3. In 1509.

4. In 1512.

It is also of considerable help to a ruler if he does remarkable things when it comes to domestic policy, such as those that are reported of Mr. Bernabò of Milan.[5] It is a good idea to be widely talked about, as he was, because, whenever anyone happened to do anything extraordinary, whether good or bad, in civil life, he found an imaginative way to reward or to punish them. Above all a ruler should make every effort to ensure that whatever he does it gains him a reputation as a great man, a person who excels.

Rulers are also admired when they know how to be true allies and genuine enemies: That is, when, without any reservations, they demonstrate themselves to be loyal supporters or opponents of others. Such a policy is always better than one of neutrality. For if two rulers who are your neighbors are at war with each other, they are either so powerful that, if one of them wins, you will have to fear the victor, or they are not. Either way, it will be better for you to take sides and fight a good fight; for, if they are powerful, and you do not take sides, you will still be preyed on by the victor, much to the pleasure and satisfaction of his defeated opponent. You will have no excuse, no defense, no refuge. For whoever wins will not want allies who are unreliable and who do not stand by him in adversity; while he who loses will not offer you refuge, since you were not willing, sword in hand, to share his fate.

The Aetolians invited Antiochus to Greece to drive out the Romans.[6] Antiochus sent an ambassador to the Achaeans, who were allies of the Romans, to encourage them to remain neutral; while the Romans urged them to fight on their side. The ruling council of the Achaeans met to decide what to do, and Antiochus's ambassador spoke in favor of neutrality. The Roman ambassador replied: "As for what they say to you, that it would be sensible to keep out of the war, there is nothing further from your true interests. If you are without credit, without dignity, the victor will claim you as his prize."

It will always happen that he who is not your ally will urge neutrality upon you, while he who is your ally will urge you to take sides. Rulers who are unsure what to do, but want to avoid immediate dangers, generally end up staying neutral and usually destroy themselves by doing so. But when a ruler boldly takes sides, if your ally wins, even if he is powerful, and has the ability to overpower you, he is in your debt and fond of you. Nobody is so shameless as to turn on you in so ungrateful a fashion. Moreover, victories are never so overwhelming that the victor can act without any constraint: Above all, victors still need to appear just. But if, on the other hand, your ally is defeated, he will offer you refuge, will help you as long as he is able, and will share your ill-fortune, in the hope of one day sharing good fortune with you. In the second case, when those at war with each other are insufficiently powerful to give you grounds to fear the outcome, there is all the more reason to take sides, for you will be able to destroy one of them with the help of the other, when, if they were wise, they would be helping each other. The one who wins is at your mercy; and victory is certain for him whom you support.

Here it is worth noting a ruler should never take the side of someone who is more powerful than himself against other rulers, unless necessity compels him to, as I have already implied. For if you win, you are your ally's prisoner; and rulers should do

---

5. Bernabò Visconti ruled Milan from 1354 to 1385.
6. 192 B.C. The source is Livy, bk. 35, chs. 48, 49.

everything they can to avoid being at the mercy of others. The Venetians allied with the King of France against the Duke of Milan, when they could have avoided taking sides; they brought about their own destruction.[7] But when you cannot help but take sides (which is the situation the Florentines found themselves in when the pope and the King of Spain were advancing with their armies to attack Lombardy)[8] then you should take sides decisively, as I have explained. Do not for a moment think any state can always take safe decisions, but rather think every decision you take involves risks, for it is in the nature of things that you cannot take precautions against one danger without opening yourself to another. Prudence consists in knowing how to assess risks and in accepting the lesser evil as a good.

A ruler should also show himself to be an admirer of skill [*virtù*] and should honor those who are excellent in any type of work. He should encourage his citizens by making it possible for them to pursue their occupations peacefully, whether they are businessmen, farmers, or are engaged in any other activity, making sure they do not hesitate to improve what they own for fear it may be confiscated from them, and they are not discouraged from investing in business for fear of losing their profits in taxes; instead, he should ensure that those who improve and invest are rewarded, as should be anyone whose actions will benefit his city or his government. He should, in addition, at appropriate times of the year, amuse the populace with festivals and public spectacles. Since every city is divided into guilds or neighborhoods, he ought to take account of these collectivities, meeting with them on occasion, showing himself to be generous and understanding in his dealings with them, but at the same time always retaining his authority and dignity, for this he should never let slip in any circumstances.

---

7. In 1499.
8. In 1512.

Part Two

ETHICS IN THE BUSINESS DISCIPLINES

411

Chapter 8

ETHICS AND HUMAN RESOURCES MANAGEMENT
The Employment Relationship

Cartoon	PETE MUELLER
"Some Issues in Employment Discrimination on Grounds of Race, Sex, and Age"	RICHARD POSNER
"Affirming Affirmative Action"	JESSE L. JACKSON
"Hiring/Firing, Sexism/Racism Ethics Cases"	DENIS COLLINS'S STUDENTS

We can invest all the money on Wall Street in new technologies, but we can't realize the benefits of improved productivity until companies rediscover the value of human loyalty.   FREDERICK REICHHELD, DIRECTOR, BAIN & CO.

In 1960, about one-third of the American workforce was represented by unions. Today, that figure is about 11 percent. Collective bargaining, established to protect the interests of workers, has proven inadequate to the task. Not surprisingly, the number of federal and state regulations governing work practices has exploded. The variety of protections is prodigious: antidiscrimination laws, wage and hour laws, worker safety laws, unemployment compensation, workers' compensation, and social security, to name a few.

The purpose of this section is to present ethical dilemmas that face the worker, whether as an employee on an assembly line, the manager of a restaurant, or the CEO of a large corporation. While the perspectives change, similar conflicts (and stakeholders) exist. The predominant theme is that at some point, almost everyone will be an employee or an employer, and it is critical to recognize the stakes each player may have in any given dilemma. The chapter will provide a textual background relating to the employment relationship, its origins and its regulation, as well as readings relevant to this topic. Articles are also included that address the issue of the balance of power within the employment relationship, drug testing, employee privacy rights, and compensation issues.

Drug Testing   Whether an employer tests its employees for drug usage requires a delicate balance between the right of the employer to protect its interests and the right of the employee to be free from wrongful intrusions into her or his personal affairs. Since the employer is often responsible for legal violations of its employees committed in the course of their job, the employer's interest in retaining control over every aspect of the work environment increases. On the other hand, employees may argue that their drug usage is only relevant if it impacts their job performance. Until it does, the employer should have no basis for testing.

Country singer Tom T. Hall would likely advocate drug testing as he croons, "If you hang all the people, you'll get all the guilty." Consider the possibilities of incorrect presumptions in connection with drug testing. For instance, in his book, *Drug Abuse in the Workplace: An Employer's Guide for Prevention,* Mark de Bernardo suggests that crudely wrapped cigarettes, razor blades, eye droppers, frequent trips to the bathroom, or dressing inappropriately for the season may be warning signs of drug use.[1] On the other hand, it does not take a great deal of imagination to come up with other, more innocuous alternative possibilities. Yet, an employer may decide to test based on these "signs."

In a study examining the attitudes of college students to drug testing programs, researchers found that "virtually all aspects of drug testing programs are strongly accepted by some individuals and strongly rejected by others."[2] The only variable that the researchers found indicative of a student's attitude was whether the student had ever used drugs in the past. Where a student had never used drugs, she or he was more likely to find drug testing programs acceptable.[3] In general, the following factors contribute to greater acceptance and approval by workers: programs that use a task force made up of employees and their supervisors, a completely random program, effective communication of procedures, programs that offer treatment other than termination for first-time offenders, and programs with no distinction between supervisory and other workers.

Compensation   One of the most heated issues in any discussion of human resource management is salary. Often workers believe that they are underpaid for their work, that employers might not always treat them fairly, or that they are not appreciated. One of the most sensitive areas in connection with salary and fairness is gender discrimination. Title VII of the 1964 Act places race, color, and national origin among those "protected classes" against which discrimination is forbidden. The act was directed primarily to improving the employment opportunities of blacks, but it applies to all races and colors (including whites and Native Americans). The national origin provision forbids discrimination based on one's nation of birth, ancestry, or heritage. Therefore, an employment office sign reading "Mexicans need not apply" would clearly be unlawful. In addition, the Equal Pay Act of 1963 specifically provides that men and women must be paid equal pay for equal work. Accordingly, failure to fairly compensate workers may constitute both a legal and ethical breach.

The fact is, when any employment decision is made, discrimination exists. Does that surprise you? Isn't it appropriate for an employer to discriminate based on actual qualifications such as education and experience (for some jobs)? In fact, employers can, should, and do discriminate based on perfectly acceptable grounds. You wouldn't find it strange or wrong for a business to require a human resources degree for applicants to a position as vice president of human resources. American law merely forbids discrimination on a *few, specific, non-job-related* factors (such as religion and race), as you will see below.

An employer seeking to avoid a violation of Title VII or the Equal Pay Act can adjust its wage structure by raising the pay of the disfavored sex. Lowering the pay of the favored sex violates the act. Paying women and men the same amount for the same work is simple enough in principle, but the legal issues have proved slippery, indeed. For example:

1. Mark A. de Bernardo, *Drug Abuse in the Workplace: An Employer's Guide for Prevention,* available from the U.S. Chamber of Commerce, 1615 H Street, NW, Washington, DC 20062.
2. Kevin Murphy, George Thornton, and Douglas Reynolds, "College Students' Attitudes Toward Employee Drug Testing Programs," *Personnel Psychology* 43 (1990), p. 615.
3. Ibid.

1. Is travel reimbursement a "wage"? Maternity payments? (According to the federal government—no.)
2. Must the plaintiff establish a *pattern* of sex-based wage discrimination? (According to the federal government—no.)
3. Are jobs unequal in effort and thus "unequal work" when a part of one job includes tasks that females are physically unable to perform? (No, if those tasks do not constitute a substantial part of the job.)

In the leading case of *Corning Glass Works* v. *Brennan,* the Supreme Court was faced with the question of whether different shifts constituted differing "working conditions." Women had been engaged in glass inspection on the day shift. Corning added a night shift of inspectors, which, due to state "protective" laws, was composed entirely of males. The night shift demanded and receiver higher wages than the female day inspectors. The Supreme Court held that the time of day in and of itself is not a *working condition.* That term, the Court said, refers to "surroundings" and "hazards." However, shift differentials could lawfully constitute a "factor other than sex" if established by the employer.

Comparable Worth   Equal pay for equal work is hardly a radical notion, but equal pay for work of comparable value would, if fully realized, dramatically alter the nature of the American labor market. *Comparable worth* calls for determining the compensation to be paid for a position based on the job's intrinsic value in comparison to wages being paid for other jobs requiring comparable skills, effort, and responsibility and having comparable worth to the organization.

The argument is that the dollar value assigned to jobs held predominantly by men is higher than the value assigned to jobs held predominantly by women. To proponents of comparable worth, such disparities cannot be explained by market forces. They argue that women are the continuing victims of sex discrimination in violation of Title VII of the Civil Rights Act of 1964.

A variety of studies have contrasted pay scales in traditionally female jobs with those in traditionally male jobs where the jobs are judged to be of comparable worth. For example, licensed practical nurses in Illinois in 1983 earned an average of $1,298 per month, while electricians earned an average of $2,826. A 1987 Child Welfare League study fixed the median salary of garbage collectors at $14,872 annually, as compared with $12,800 for child care workers. The same study found social workers with master's degrees earned about $21,800 per year, while auto salespeople averaged $22,048.

There may be market explanations for the inequality between wages in occupations which are traditionally male-dominated as opposed to those jobs which are traditionally female-dominated. Economist and jurist, Judge Richard Posner, explains:

[While] irrational or exploitive discrimination is one possibility[,] another is that male wages include a compensatory wage premium for the dirty, disagreeable and often strenuous jobs that men dominate presumably because their aversion to such work is less than women's. Another (these are not mutually exclusive of course) is differences in investments in market-related human capital (earning capacity). If a woman allocates a substantial part of her working life to household production, including child care, she will obtain a substantially lower return on her market human

capital than a man planning to devote much less time to household production, and she will therefore invest less in that human capital. Since earnings are in part a return on one's human capital investments (including education), women's earnings will be lower than men's. In part this will show up in the choice of occupations: Women will be attracted to occupations that don't require much human capital. Of course the amount of time women are devoting to household production is declining, so we can expect the wage gap to shrink if the economic model is correct.[4]

Posner concludes by qualifying his comments, "if the economic model is correct." Why might you believe that this model would not be correct or that the wage gap may not shrink completely? If actual prejudice (i.e., pre-judging) exists, that is, women are *believed* to be less valuable as workers than men, regardless of their *actual* abilities, then employers may continue to hire men at higher wages. In other words, even though women are actually spending less time at home and the household and child care duties are more likely to be split, employers may still *believe* that women will get pregnant and quit. Given this prejudice, employers will not pay women commensurate with men, notwithstanding market influences. Do you agree?

A number of companies and state governments and several foreign countries practice some form of comparable worth, but most continue to rely on the market as the best measure of worth. The U.S. Supreme Court has yet to directly explore the substance of the comparable worth debate. In the *Gunther* case, the Court held, in effect, that Title VII does not forbid the comparable worth theory. However, the federal appeals court decisions to date have rejected the comparable worth theory in the context of Title VII sex discrimination.

Can the Market "Fix" Discrimination?   If the market were left to its own devices, wouldn't you expect firms that discriminate to fall by the wayside? That is, if a firm hires its employees based on prejudices and discriminatory views (e.g., women can't do a certain job), then it is limiting its pool of possible employees. Another firm that does not discriminate can choose from the larger pool and is more likely to obtain the *most* qualified individual for the job. Judge Richard Posner explains the economic impact of this theory in terms of race discrimination as follows:

In a market of many sellers, the intensity of the prejudice against blacks will vary considerably. Some sellers will have only a mild prejudice against them. These sellers will not forgo as many advantageous transactions with blacks as their more prejudiced competitors (unless the law interferes). Their costs will therefore be lower, and this will enable them to increase their share of the market. The least prejudiced sellers will come to dominate the market in much the same way as people who are least afraid of heights come to dominate occupations that require working at heights: they demand a smaller premium.[5]

Under what circumstances would Posner's argument fail? Consider the implications if the discriminating firm held a monopoly on its good or service. What is the effect of

---

4. Richard Posner, *Economic Analysis of Law* (Boston: Little, Brown, 1986), p. 313–14.
5. Ibid., p. 616.

regulation such as Title VII on Posner's argument? Consider his approach above as you read the excerpt from his text later in this section.

Discrimination and Affirmative Action   Efforts toward the elimination of discrimination in employment over the past 30 years have, indeed, resulted in a more diverse workforce. Diversity refers to the presence of differing cultures, languages, ethnicities, races, affinity orientations, genders, religious sects, abilities, social classes, ages, and national origins of the individuals in a firm. Diversity has brought countless benefits to the workplace, but also conflicts that were not previously present. Where individuals from different backgrounds are brought together for the first time, *and* where negative stereotypes previously ruled interactions between these two groups, sensitivity to the potential for conflict is necessary. Efforts at multiculturalism, defined as the acknowledgement and promotion of diversity through celebration and appreciation of various cultures in the work place, is one response.

Other problems exist that one might not necessarily consider. For example, reflect on a report by the U.S. Commission on Civil Rights that addresses the unique predicament of Asian Americans. The report documents widespread discrimination against Asian Americans, who have long been considered to have escaped the national origin barriers that face other cultures. The report contends that the typical Asian stereotype of being hardworking, intelligent, and successful is actually a detriment to Asian Americans. This stereotype results in the problems of poor Asians being overlooked, in preventing successful Asian Americans from becoming more successful, in placing undue pressure on young Asian Americans to succeed in school, and in discrediting other minorities by arguing that "if Asian Americans can succeed, so can other minorities."[6] In an article highlighting the report, *Fortune* magazine intuits that the problem is really that the commission is "being driven crazy by the fact that Asian Americans have been succeeding essentially *without the benefit of affirmative action*. The ultimate problem is not that they may make other minorities look bad—it is that they are making the civil rights bureaucracy look irrelevant."[7] Some theorists argue that formal affirmative action measures have often served to create a greater divide rather than to draw people closer.

The struggle for civil rights in the workplace sometimes cannot be achieved, in the short run, simply by avoiding discriminatory practices. Obviously, obeying the law is expected of all. However, as a matter of social policy, we have decided that mere compliance with the civil rights laws, guaranteeing equal opportunity in the workplace, is not always adequate to correct the wrongs of discrimination. Among other problems, much time ordinarily would need to pass before the lingering effects of past discrimination would no longer be felt if we were to do nothing more than not practice discrimination. Therefore, we have decided as a society to implement the policy that we label **affirmative action** as a means of remedying past wrongs and preventing the same in the future. In following an affirmative action plan, employers consciously take positive steps to seek out minorities and women for hiring and promotion opportunities, and they often employ goals and timetables to measure progress toward a workforce that is representative of the qualified labor pool.

---

6. "Up From Inscrutable," *Fortune,* April 6, 1992, p. 20.
7. Ibid.

Affirmative action efforts arise in two ways: (1) courts may order implementation of affirmative action after a finding of wrongful discrimination, and (2) employers may voluntarily adopt affirmative action plans. Some do so because they believe it is a wise management strategy or because they approve of affirmative action as a matter of social policy, or both. Others may adopt affirmative action because they wish to do business with the federal government. All government contractors must meet the affirmative action standards of the Office of Federal Contract Compliance Programs. As discussed above, those standards consist essentially of established goals and timetables for strengthening the representation of "underutilized" minorities and women.

Good Policy?   Affirmative action is one of the most hotly disputed social issues in contemporary life. Minorities and women have been the victims of discrimination. Should white males "pay" for those wrongs? Critics decry affirmative action as "reverse discrimination." They argue that affirmative action is paternalistic and encourages the view that minorities and women can progress only with the aid of white males. Studies confirm that affirmative action plans stigmatize minorities and women in the minds of coworkers. Minorities and women are often assumed to have achieved their positions via "quotas" and not as the result of their efforts and abilities.

Now, many white males feel that they are surrounded and under siege by the forces of affirmative action and multiculturalism. Even if so, *Newsweek* argues that being a white man is still a very comfortable role in contemporary America:

> *But is the white male truly an endangered species, or is he just being a jerk? It's still a statistical piece of cake being a white man, at least in comparison with being anything else. White males make up just 39.2 percent of the population, yet they account for 82.5 percent of the Forbes 400 (folks worth at least $265 million), 77 percent of Congress, 92 percent of state governors, 70 percent of tenured college faculty, almost 90 percent of daily-newspaper editors, 77 percent of TV news directors. They dominate just about everything but NOW and the NAACP.*

Affirmative Action in Practice   *United Steelworkers of America* v. *Weber* is perhaps the clearest Supreme Court statement to date about the permissible boundaries of affirmative action. Weber, a white male, challenged the legality of an affirmative action plan that set aside for black employees 50 percent of the openings in a training program until the percentage of black craft workers in the plant equaled the percentage of blacks in the local labor market. Weber was denied entry to the training program. The federal district court and the federal court of appeals held for Weber, but the U.S. Supreme Court reversed. Therefore, under *Weber,* race-conscious affirmative action remedies *can* be permissible. Several qualities of the Steelworkers' plan were instrumental in the Court's favorable ruling:

1. The affirmative action was part of a plan.
2. The plan was designed to "open employment opportunities for Negroes in occupations which have been traditionally closed to them."
3. The plan was temporary.
4. The plan did not unnecessarily harm the rights of white employees. That is:
    a.   The plan did not require the discharge of white employees.
    b.   The plan did not create an absolute bar to the advancement of white employees.

Therefore, affirmative action in situations like that in *Weber* does not constitute unlawful reverse discrimination. The Supreme Court clarified the law's affirmative action commands a bit further in the *Burdine* case, in which the Court asserted that Title VII does not require the employer to hire a minority or female applicant whenever that person's objective qualifications were equal to those of a white male applicant. Therefore, "the employer has discretion to choose among equally qualified candidates, provided the decision is not based upon unlawful criteria."

Sexual Harassment   One additional area of recent concern is sexual harassment. Sexual harassment evolved through a traditional application of Title VII: treating someone differently because of her or his gender is unlawful under Title VII. Two types of sexual harassment fit within this broad prohibition: quid pro quo and hostile environment. Quid pro quo exists where a supervisor offers an employment benefit in exchange for sexual activity or where a supervisor refuses to give deserved benefits unless an employee engages in sexual activity. Hostile environment sexual harassment is not so easily defined. The Supreme Court, through a host of cases, explains that a hostile environment exists where a work environment is severely or pervasively altered such that a reasonable person would find it offensive or abusive.

The Court's definition of a hostile environment is thus rather complicated and amorphous, a hybrid of a subjective and objective test. First, the plaintiff must show that the environment would be considered offensive to a reasonable person (objective analysis); then the plaintiff must *also* show that she or he, individually, was offended by the situation (subjective analysis). For this reason, it is difficult to state conclusively whether any given circumstance might be considered sexual harassment. On the other hand, we are given some parameters. The facts that give rise to the claim must be severe or pervasive. A one-time event would not constitute sexual harassment unless it is severe; and a relatively benign event might become sexual harassment where it is pervasive. In order to shed more light on this characterization, *Harris* v. *Forklift* is included in the readings that follow.

SHORT HYPOTHETICAL CASES

a. You recently started working in the personnel department of a large company. The personnel manager has asked you to tell any black applicants that the company is not hiring; if the person fills out an application, you are to tell the personnel manager that the applicant is black. What do you do?

b. Your department manager has asked you to be her confident and to relay to her any complaints or problems you overhear from your coworkers. She assures you that the information will be kept highly confidential. She says that she is doing this in an effort to improve her effectiveness and to address the issues that workers may not be willing to bring to her attention. The department's performance in the past has been poor. If she can turn it around, she'll be in line for a promotion, you would be in line for her job, and no cutbacks in staff would need to be made. What do you do?

Hypotheticals were written by Catherine Haselden and are included in her manuscript "The Ethics Game."

THE NATURE
OF THE RELATIONSHIP

THE ETHICS
OF EMPLOYMENT
LAW: WHOSE POWER
IS IT ANYWAY?

ROGER J. JOHNS, JR.

INTRODUCTION

In this essay, the system of state and federal employment discrimination laws in the United States will be subjected to analysis under the Utilitarian theory of ethics, in order to develop some insight into modeling the ethicality of the exercise of governmental authority to alter the balance of power between the owners of the firm and its employees. It is not, however, intended as a criticism of the philosophical motive of this system of laws, because it is this writer's belief that the principle of equal opportunity is essential to the vitality of society.

A fundamental premise of this analysis is that this alteration of the balance of power between the employer and the employee is actually a transfer, to some degree, of ownership of the firm from the owner-employer to the employee. Ownership, as that term is used in a strict legal sense, is the "[c]ollection of rights to use and enjoy property . . . the exclusive right of possession, enjoyment, and disposal; involving as an essential attribute the right to control, handle, and dispose."[1] To the extent the balance of power is altered in favor of the employee, there is a transfer of control, and to the extent there is a transfer of control, there is, by definition, a transfer of some part of ownership. The idea that property ownership can be transferred simply by a regulatory deprivation of a significant measure of control, has a long history in the Due Process jurisprudence under the United States Constitution.[2] While it is beyond the scope of this writing to subject particular anti-discrimination laws to scrutiny under the Due Process Clause, in order to determine whether there has been a taking sufficient to warrant a payment of compensation, the idea of a regulatory taking is raised here to provide a foundation in law for the premise that transfers of control, by operation of law, can constitute transfers of ownership.

1. *Black's Law Dictionary* 712 (5th ed. 1979).
2. *See, e.g., Pennsylvania Coal* v. *Mahon Co.,* 260 U.S. 393 (1922).

   The system of employment discrimination law in this country consists of a collection of state and federal statutes, and regulations, and the administrative and court cases decided thereunder, as well as local ordinances. Together, these laws prohibit discrimination in the workplace on the basis of a variety of traits like race, color, religion, national origin, sex,[3] age,[4] disability,[5] sexual orientation, medical condition, marital status,[6] and others—traits considered by the enactors of these rules to be irrelevant to decisions by the employer regarding various aspects of the employer-employee relationship such as whom to hire, fire, promote, demote, train, compensate, interview, discipline, or lay off. . . .

   The desired effect of all of these various forms of anti-discrimination law is to eliminate workplace discrimination on the basis of the traits specified in the law. In order to accomplish this purpose, anti-discrimination laws use two general techniques: (1) the law deprives the employer of the power to make decisions about individuals on the basis of the traits specified in the law free of legal consequences, and (2) the law provides the employee some legal or regulatory mechanism for enforcing the law against employers that the employee believes have violated it. Without debating, for the moment, the propriety or necessity of the deprivation, it is important to focus on the fact that the deprivation and the enforcement mechanism exist. And, it is important to focus on the fact that, absent the law, the employer would retain the legal authority to make employment decisions on the basis of any trait of an employee or applicant, regardless of the relevance of the trait to the job held or applied for, or the employment benefit involved, and without fear of legal consequences. Again, without, at this point, debating the propriety or necessity of using these techniques, it is important to recognize that these techniques accomplish a transfer of control over, and, therefore, ownership of some aspect of the firm from the owner-employer to the employee.

ETHICAL THEORIES

Typically, theories of ethics are divided into two broad categories: teleological, and deontological. Teleological theories measure the ethics or correctness of an act by the amount of good it produces. Deontological theories, on the other hand, are unconcerned with the consequences of an act, and judge its ethicality, instead, on the basis of the duty or obligation out of which the impulse to act arises. The ethicality of the system of employment laws described above, and the premise that the enactment and implementation of these laws constitute a transfer of ownership of the firm from the owner-employer to the employee, will be assessed under the teleological theory known as utilitarianism.

---

3. *See,* 42 U.S.C. § 2000e-2 (Title VII of the Civil Rights Act of 1964) for the prohibition against using race, color, religion, sex, or national origin in employment decisions.

4. *See,* 29 U.S.C. § 623 (Age Discrimination in Employment Act).

5. *See,* 29 U.S.C. § 791, 793, and 794 (Rehabilitation Act of 1973), and 42 U.S.C. § 12112 (Americans With Disabilities Act of 1990).

6. Although there are no federal statutes prohibiting workplace discrimination on the basis of these traits, there are state and local laws, in some places which prohibit workplace discrimination on the basis of these, and other traits. *See, e.g.,* 28 N.M. Stat. Ann. § 28-1-7, and the regulations promulgated thereunder.

UTILITARIANISM AND THE LAW OF EMPLOYMENT DISCRIMINATION

. . . The first element of the analysis of any action under the theory of utilitarianism must be a precise identification of the action under consideration. In a field as complex as law creation and implementation, this would be difficult at best since the process involves hundreds of discrete component acts. So, for present purposes, it will be necessary to confine the analysis to a distillation of the component acts, represented by an expression of the common character of the acts. To this end, the thesis stated above, of the transfer of power and ownership from the employer-owner to the employee, will serve as a proxy for all of the component acts in the process of creating and implementing employment discrimination laws. Proceeding from this point, the next logical step in the calculus of utilitarianism is to identify the elements of pleasure and the elements of pain generated by this transfer of power and attempt to quantitatively compare them. In order to do this in an orderly fashion, it will be necessary to first identify the members of the population under consideration, and then to identify the explicit pluses and minuses that accrue to each member or to various groups of members.

The entirety of the population under consideration here is the entire population of the country. To simplify the analysis, the population can be categorized into two fairly distinct subgroups and one *in globo* group, on the ground that each group has, to some degree, different interests, and would seem to experience qualitatively distinct, but sometimes overlapping consequences of the ownership transfer. The *in globo* group is the entire population of the country (Society) and the subgroups are (1) Employers, and (2) Employees. Beginning with the group containing the most direct beneficiaries, Employees, we can develop a list of at least some of the pleasures (or goods) and the painful consequences that they derive from the transfer of ownership.

Employee Goods

Freedom from discrimination by employers on the basis of traits irrelevant to ability.

The ability to access a government operated system of administrative investigation, and conciliation of claims of discrimination, at no cost to the employee.

Participation in a workplace in which overt discrimination is more likely to be held in check.

Employer Goods

Presence of a clearly stated public policy.

The presence of legal forces in the market place tending to ensure the most qualified workforce.

Employee Pain

Fear of retaliation in the wake of the assertion of a claim.

In cases where affirmative action played a part, uncertainty over whether one's status is a result of one's abilities.

Possibility of ostracism by other employees, in the wake of the assertion of a claim.

Employer Pain

Fear of the assertion of false claims

The expenditure of monetary, human, and temporal resources in order to ensure compliance

The expenditure of monetary, human, and temporal resources in responding to claims.

The financial and other rewards of operating with the most qualified workforce.

Societal Goods

The presence of legal forces in the market place tending to ensure the most qualified workforce.

The presence of legal forces in the market place tending to promote tolerance and a sense of community and the attendant benefits thereof.

Resentment at having to expend resources on compliance or defense.

Resentment over feeling forced to comply.

Societal Pain

The expenditure of monetary, human, and temporal resources in order to ensure compliance.

The presence of legal forces in the market place tending to promote resentment among those groups whose members feel victimized by law.

For purposes of comparison of the relative goods and pain, three paired groupings are useful: (I) Employer-Employee, (II) Employer-Society, and (III) Employee-Society. While comparisons and evaluations of the specific goods and pain experience by each group are important, and will be taken up eventually, some conceptual analysis must be done first.

Beginning with Pair I, one will immediately recognize that the number of employees will be vastly greater than the number of employers, and, consequently, there will be a greater number of beneficiaries over which to spread any net good or pain. Keeping the *greatest good for the greatest number* idea in mind, we can simplify our analysis by positing certain generic situations, which can be expressed mathematically. For instance, note that in the situation described by the equations below, the mere fact that Employees constitute a numerically larger group than Employers, means that, with respect to pair I, the ethicality of the employment discrimination is somewhat ambiguous.

Assume that:

1. Employer Goods – Employer Pain = A
2. Employee Goods – Employee Pain = B

If $A - B = 0$ (i.e., $A = B$), and N_E and N_R are the number of Employees and Employers, respectively, then $B/N_E < A/N_R$. But the interpretation of this will be at best, inconclusive because one is now faced with choosing which of two situations is ethically preferable. With respect to the Employer group, a given amount of good will be distributed over a smaller population resulting in a greater amount of good per person. With respect to the Employee group, the same amount of good that was available to the Employers will be distributed over a much larger group, resulting in a much lower amount of good per person, but at least some good accruing to each member of the much larger group. Thus, one must decide whether the ethical ideal is achieved where there is a great amount of good for a small group or a lesser amount of good for a larger group. Since this is a personal preference, on the part of each observer, the analysis herein will proceed, for the present, on the assumption that the potential of a situation to achieve the ideal of the greatest good for the greatest number is the ethically preferable situation.

Assume, now, that the difference between A and B is such that the good available to the Employee group is the greater. In this situation, the greater amount of good, distributed over the larger population will result in the greatest good for the greatest number, only if the magnitude of the good per person ratio is great enough to overcome the dilution of the larger group. Thus, even when the difference between A and B is such that the amount of good available to the Employee group is greater, achievement of the greatest good for the greatest number occurs only when the difference between A and B is huge. In other words, when we require satisfaction of both the *greatest good* and the *greatest number* elements of the analysis, the ethical ideal is achieved only when the difference between A and B is great enough that $B/N_E > A/N_R$. This occurs only when the amount of good accruing to the Employee group is greater than $(B)(N_R)$.

When the difference between A and B is such that the good accruing to the Employer group is greater, the greatest good per person is most readily achieved, because of the numerical inferiority of the group, but this same numerical inferiority precludes satisfaction of the *greatest number* aspect of the analysis.

At first blush, it seems that if achieving the greatest good for the greatest number is the ideal, then systems which result in $A/N_R > B/N_E$, which can never have the potential to bring about the ideal, should not be the goal. But this is true only when the calculation is made over an infinitely short time horizon. Once the time factor is taken into account, interpretations of the calculations change. For instance, if, at every given moment, the system of employment discrimination law results in $B/N_R > A/N_E$ (i.e., the greater good accrues to the Employee group), the *greatest good for the greatest number* ideal will remain constantly satisfied, but only so long as the Employee group constitutes the larger group and the difference between A and B is great enough so that $B/N_E > A/N_R$. Over time, however, the extent to which the Employee group is consistently favored with the greater good will be positively related to the extent to which the Employer group is discouraged from creating new employment opportunities. If, over time, this sufficiently reduces the business formation impulse, the size of the Employee group, or the degree to which A exceeds B, then the potential for $B/N_E > A/N_R$ to produce the greatest good for the greatest number declines. The somewhat paradoxical result is that in the short run $A/N_R > B/N_E$ can never result in the ideal, but it can, in the long run, foster the ability of $B/N_E > A/N_R$ to achieve the ideal, and while $B/N_E > A/N_R$ will always produce the ideal in the short run, it will defeat itself in the long run. Obviously, what is called for is an exquisite balance. Given the vagaries of human nature, it is not likely that any sort of static balance could be hoped for, but a dynamic balance, over time, in which both $B/N_E > A/N_R$ and $A/N_R > B/N_E$ are adequately nurtured by the system probably could be approached.

It is interesting to note, that, at least conceptually, analysis using Employer-Society and Employee-Society pairs arrive at the same point. While it may be analytically useful to describe and treat the Employee and Employer groups as distinct in all interests and goals, the reality is obviously very different. As an observer of the twists and turns in the relationships between the different immigrant and ethnic groups in the United States recently stated, "We may not have all come over on the same ship, but we're all in the same boat now." The point of relating this observation here is that while the Employee and Employer groups may have different characteristics, interests, and goals, in the long run, the success of each will be dependent upon the success of the other.

By definition, the size of the combined groups will always constitute the largest group, a state of affairs that presents, again by definition, the greatest potential to satisfy the *greatest number* aspect of the analysis. The remaining aspect, *greatest good,* then becomes likelier as A + B increases. The sum A + B will increase even if one of the terms tends toward or becomes zero, so long as the other term grows in value. However, as the analysis of the Employer-Employee pair revealed, there can come a point beyond which the growth in B, to the exclusion of A, can result, in the long run, in a diminution of B, and vice-versa. Thus, without a great deal of analysis, it seems fairly reasonable to conclude that the ethical ideal is achieved by pursuing the same balance across every grouping.

COMPARING SPECIFIC GOODS AND PAIN

In order to arrive at any sort of practical understanding of the effect of the system of employment discrimination laws, the goods and pain listed above will need to be quantified and plugged into the variables A and B, in order to determine whether $B/N_E > A/N_R$, $A/N_R > B/N_E$, or $A/N_R = B/N_E$. Some of these factors will obviously confound any attempt at meaningful quantification. The fear factors and resentment fall into this category. Some factors, however, such as expenditure of monetary, human, and temporal resources, will yield, at least to some degree, to a quantitative approach. In any event, it is important to recognize from the outset that with respect to the monetary, human and temporal factors, virtually all of the resource movements resulting from the operation of the law will be away from the employer in the form of tax dollars, defense costs, record keeping costs, payments of judgments and settlements, employee and management time that could have been spent on revenue-producing activities, and the like. Once the claim process is initiated by the employee, the best outcome the employer can hope for is that no liability will be found. The employer will, nevertheless, have expended some resources in pursuit of this result. There are no scenarios in which the immediate net resource position of the employer will be greater after the conclusion of a claim, regardless of the outcome. For the employee, on the other hand, there are many scenarios in which the net resource position of the employee could be enhanced as a result of the claim/litigation/settlement process. From the employer's perspective, then, the best that can be hoped for under the current system, is that the process will be efficient and will produce some form of benefit in excess of the other resources it consumes.

With respect to the efficiency of the process, it is surprisingly good. For the six years 1989 to 1994, the EEOC received 824,201 charges to process, and, during the same period, it resolved 741,688, or 89% of its inventory. During the same period, its budget appropriations totalled $1,230,839,000 and it recovered $973,300,369 in monetary benefits for individuals who had filed claims, 31% of which was recovered through litigation, and all of which was paid by employers or their insurers. Overall, the EEOC spent $1.27 in tax dollars for each dollar it recovered for individuals who filed claims. Stated differently, the EEOC produced a 79% return on investment, which by probably any standard, is amazingly high, and amazingly costly to employers.

The benefits that employers might expect to enjoy from this efficiency, would be the increased revenues and profits resulting from the enhanced productivity of the most efficient work force that non-discrimination could produce. But, even if the only monetary expenditures on the part of employers were the payment of judgments and settlements (which is obviously not the case), the enhancements to productivity would need to be about $162,000,000 per year. Factoring in the cost to employers of dollars spent on legal fees and costs, or on preventive training, or record keeping, or time spent responding to or taking preventive measures to avoid claims, would require the enhancements to produce considerably more than $162 million. This may be possible, but to the extent it is, such benefits would accrue to employers as a group. It would not be the case that each employer would receive enhancements in an amount equal to the resources expended. Thus, many individual employers will suffer. And, maybe they should. From a deontological[7] perspective such considerations as cost are irrelevant, so long as justice is produced.

Looked at from a more cold-eyed perspective, the benefits to individual employees, recovered through the EEOC claim process, constitute transfers of money from the capital-creating employer to the employee. Individual employees benefit directly, and society benefits in some intangible, and probably unmeasurable, ways, but the productive capacity of employers is impaired. In a healthy economy, though, the productive capacity can probably withstand a great deal of this sort of stress before its viability is visibly compromised. Ultimately, the ethicality of the system of employment discrimination laws, at least from a utilitarian point of view, will come down to how it affects the country's competitive advantage in the global marketplace, and solutions will, as they inevitably do, arise out of necessity. Perhaps the focus will be shifted from the workplace to the early classroom. Perhaps disincentives for frivolous claims should be built into the system. Perhaps empirical study will show that there are already sufficient increases in societal goods, in the form of increases in productivity, greater social harmony, and other benefits, to justify the current system. Perhaps a body of wisdom that flourished here in times past can provide guidance.

A VOICE FROM THE PAST

As occasionally occurs, the profundity of some past thinker's observations about the age in which he or she writes can be gauged by the relevance of those thoughts to the present day. An example of such a thinker particularly appropriate for discussion here is the nineteenth century economist Frederic Bastiat. In Bastiat's short book, *The Law,*[8] the idea of legal plunder is articulated to describe the actions of a government gone completely awry. He begins by defining the purpose of government as a mechanism, ordained by the governed through a limited surrender of individual liberty and authority, and set up for the sole purpose of interposing the pooled protective powers of all citizens between the innocent and the predatory. He proceeds from this minimalist premise to a justification of the idea that, in practice, government should exercise this function only in response to an affirmative act of plunder committed by one citizen or group against another, with plunder being defined as the taking by force, of the life, liberty or property of another. Any other

---

7. Under deontological theories of ethics the rightness of actions is judged on the basis of the worthiness of the duty or motive behind the act, regardless of the consequence.
8. Citation to the book, generally.

use of governmental power, he argued, goes beyond the government's authority, and constitutes what he terms legal plunder—the taking, by the government, of that which belongs to one, and giving it to another. He expressed much chagrin at the double standard, at work in France at the time of his writing, of criminalizing the act of an individual taking that which does not belong to him from its rightful owner, while clothing the same act in legality when accomplished by legislation, to serve the interests of a politically favored segment of the population.

The obvious difficulty with Bastiat's approach is that there is no way to limit which rights or things fits within the definitions of liberty and property, without injecting the bias of the definer. For instance, one could, with little effort, argue persuasively that the right to a job is a legitimate property right of every member of society, the protection of which is within the sphere of what Bastiat considered to be government's appropriate domain. This is, of course, a giant loophole through which the spirit of Bastiat's philosophy could be subverted by the mores of whoever exerts sufficient control over the machinery of government. Nevertheless, conceding the inherent limitation imposed by the Theorem of Incompleteness,[9] regarding the ability of any system to yield only intended results, it would seem that Bastiat's philosophical and moral stance of strictly limited governmental action provides some useful guidance in achieving balance the system of employment discrimination laws. The most practical reason that comes to mind for adopting such a stance is unreliability of the political winds. A fair wind today could sweep one onto the rocks tomorrow.

CONCLUSIONS AND PROGNOSTICATIONS

Of late, two competing phenomena indicate a shift from the typical scenario of the past where the majority of the skirmishes along legislatively drawn employment discrimination lines were carried out mostly by individual plaintiff's pursuing individual actions against individual employers. One of these phenomena is the concerted action by large voter-blocs to roll back the heretofore seemingly endlessly advancing frontier of employee rights. Proposition 209, passed by the voters of California in 1996, essentially outlawed affirmative action in the state. The premise underlying this assault on affirmative action by the California voters, and others, is based largely on affirmative action's somewhat contradictory nature: it permits,[10] and in some cases mandates[11] that discrimination be practiced for the purpose of ending discrimination. More precisely, it is argued by opponents of affirmative action, that affirmative action employs politically-favored discrimination as a weapon to combat politically-disfavored discrimination. In nature, when two antithetical phenomena encounter each other, such as matter and antimatter, there is a violent reaction resulting in the annihilation of both. Within the human sphere, however, all

---

9. Kurt Gödel, developed the Theorem of Incompleteness, which, in a very non-technical formulation, holds that no system of rules can be devised in which even a correct application of the rules to the field over which the rules were designed to operate will invariably yield a result within the intended domain. In other words, paradoxical results are an inherent inevitability in the operation of every system. *See generally,* Hofstadter, Douglas R., *Gödel, Escher, Bach: An Eternal Golden Braid,* Basic Books, New York, 1979.

10. *See,* 42 U.S.C. 2000e–5(g)(1).

11. *See* 29 U.S.C. § 793 and, Exec. Order 11,246, 30 F.R. 12319, September 28, 1965.

we have gotten so far is the violent reaction, in the form of heated rhetoric and the phenomenon of so-called reverse-discrimination litigation, with each side of the issue insisting that the tactics of the other are unfair. Instead of annihilating discrimination, it appears that affirmative action, and, for that matter, other antidiscrimination measures, have, if the increasing frequency of litigation is any indication, simply exposed the extent to which employment discrimination is occurring or is believed to be occurring. Another, high-profile example of concerted voter action occurred when, in 1993, the voters of Colorado amended the state's constitution to make it illegal to protect individuals from employment discrimination based upon their sexual orientation.

The other of these phenomena is concerted action by plaintiffs in employment discrimination lawsuits in the form of the relatively recent proliferation of class-action employment discrimination lawsuits arising in the wake of the Civil Rights Act of 1991. The Mitsubishi and Texaco class-action suits are just two of the more prominent examples of this. While individual action under the antidiscrimination laws, will never become atypical, the phenomena cited above can certainly be viewed as an indictment by both those who stand to gain (i.e., the individual beneficiaries of these legislative power transfers) and those who are at some risk of losing out (i.e., defendant-employers, potential defendants, and those adversely affected by affirmative action) of the ineffectiveness of individual action.

Both phenomena are costly reactions to the current system. Neither phenomenon portends harmony. Both involve manipulations of government-created processes from a reactive posture, and it seems likely that the propagation of both will lead to more resentment and mistrust. It is ironic that in Bastiat's exposition on the miscast role of the French government of his times, he cites, with great envy, the fledgling government of the United States as the acme of a properly confined system. Perhaps these phenomena are the indicators that the societal experience necessary to an understanding of the need for balance is accumulating.

MANAGING CONSULTANTS AND TRAINERS: A COMMUNICATION PERSPECTIVE

DANIEL J. MONTGOMERY AND STEPHEN MACNAMARA

Human resource management includes the management of employees as well as other forms of human resources, such as consultants and trainers. Montgomery and MacNamara identify some of the ethical issues surrounding this area of human resource management and discuss strategies for maintaining an ethical approach through effective communication.

Over the past several decades, we have witnessed an exponential increase in "the advice industry" (Seitel, 1989, p. 62). As organizations sought new ways to stay one step ahead of their competition, they have increasingly turned to outside consultants for help. The result has been a surfeit of strategic initiatives, including Quality Circles, Total Quality Management, Reengineering, Empowerment and Team Building to mention a few.

These initiatives were launched with considerable fanfare, great expectations and significant capital outlays. Considerable sacrifice went into ensuring their success. Nevertheless, in many instances the initiatives failed or were abandoned a few years later, leaving behind little except cynicism, employee and management mistrust, and considerable finger pointing (Brandon, 1989; Daniels, 1994).

How could something that seemed so right go so wrong? Were managers sold a "bill of goods"? Were the consultants and "gurus" little more than "snake oil salesmen" in designer suits? Did consultants act unethically by promising too much too fast? Or, perhaps the fault rests with the exaggerated expectations of management, their naivete regarding the difficulties and hazards of organizational change, or their unwillingness to follow consultant advice.

In this article, the authors suggest how managers might avoid some of the myriad of ethical problems one encounters when working with consultants. Unlike much of the literature on this topic, our focus will not be on "consultant ripoffs" (Seitel, 1989, p. 62), but rather on managing the relationship between the well intended, qualified consultant and the organization. Our thesis is that many of the problems associated with the management fads of the 80's and 90's are the fault of neither management nor the consultants. We conjecture that a number of these failures may have arisen as a result of misunderstandings—misunderstandings that both parties might have avoided if they had been clear about what they wanted, what they could or could not do, and if they had taken the time to ask the right questions and communicate their expectations. In this article, we will provide managers with a checklist of issues and questions designed to help clarify their expectations, communicate clearly about what they want and do not want, and construct safeguards to prevent ethical breeches and keep the consultancy "off the rocks."

1.   Clarifying expectations. It all begins with the manager: Knowing what you want is the first step in organizational change. In the authors' experience, we have found that many managers have only a vague idea of what they want. They know something is wrong; they know that they are losing their competitive edge; or they are intrigued by a new management "fad;" but they do not know what they want or how to achieve it. When this occurs, managers do the equivalent of dropping off a car to be fixed without knowledge of the garage, the mechanics, the possible alternatives or whether the car requires repair. In short, they abdicate their responsibility, and the result is a failed consultancy. To avoid such problems, managers need to ask themselves: What do I want to change? They need to be specific about what they want to change and the steps they need to take to effect the change. Before they hire a consultant, they should define the desired goal or outcome and behaviors necessary to achieve the goal. For example, if your desired outcome is to develop "teamwork," ask yourself: What exactly is "teamwork"? How would I know if "teamwork" were achieved? If I were to observe "teamwork," what exactly would team members do that they are not doing now? Is this something I "want" or a passing fad?

2.   Is change necessary? We may feel that we "should" change but is it necessary? Competitors, for example, are using teams, but is it necessary? Where is the evidence that teams actually enhance the "bottom line"? Perhaps, there is evidence to suggest teams work in industry X, but are they appropriate in our operation? What would happen if we did nothing? When managers are instituting change for "change's sake" alone, they may find themselves enmeshed in ethical a "folie-a-deux" with their consultants: "We will pretend that we want to change, and you can pretend you can help us. If you don't challenge our sincerity as managers, we won't question your competence as consultants." The result: money and time are spent with few if any meaningful results.

3.   Organizational support. Next, managers must ask what their colleagues and workers want. Does anyone else want to achieve this objective? Do they want to change the behaviors necessary to accomplish the goal? Will you have the support you need? If not, can they get "buy in"? A "No" response to any of these questions is reason enough to pause and reconsider the proposed changes. Without employee support the consultancy is likely to fail.

4.   Capacity and resources. Do we have the capacity, resources and talent to make the changes? Or are we buying something we cannot afford or will not be able to implement? Can we follow through? Again, "No" answers are yellow flags.

Lack of capacity and resources will hinder the consulting effort and will increase the probability that management and/or the consultants will engage in less than ethical behavior. In order to achieve organizational goals, managers and consultants may take short-cuts. For example, knowing that funds are short, managers may make unwise decisions in order to appear to accomplish goals or take unwarranted and questionable actions to achieve organizational objectives. Consultants, on the other hand, knowing that the project is under-funded, may turn in less than adequate work products in order to complete their portion of the contract.

5.   Selecting a consultant. Identifying and enlisting the help of a qualified expert require careful consideration of a number of important questions. Some of these are: (*a*) What are the consultants' background, training and experience? (*b*) Have they successfully executed similar projects? Who are their references? Do they have empirical support for their claims (i.e., can they point to concrete tangible results)? If not, be careful. Many change agents will say that what they do "cannot be measured." But, if this is the case, how will management know if their consultants are making progress? How will management know if they have succeeded? Look for consultants who use a systematic, data based approach to change. When you can measure and track what consultants are doing, you are likely to avoid questionable claims and ambiguous results. Management will know when consultants are performing as promised. (*c*) Beware of anything that seems "too good to be true." Again, even the well intentioned and honest consultant may, for a variety of reasons, create ethical problems by offering services they cannot provide. Most of us have fantasies of hiring a good consultant who will achieve fast results for very little money. In reality, we are more often than not faced with a more difficult decision, one illustrated by this old conundrum: If we want "good," "fast" and "cheap," but could only select two, which would we choose? If we choose "good" and "fast," then we cannot have "cheap." If we want "fast" and "cheap," then we cannot have "good." And if we want "cheap" and "good," then we cannot have "fast" (author unknown). Quality work requires adequate time and you will, more than likely, pay the market rate.

6.   Informed consent. Before entering into a contract, you have the right to know the costs and benefits, the possible risks as well as the alternatives. As a manager you should insist on knowing the following: What will the project cost? What are the tangible benefits and the possible risks to your organization? What are the costs, the benefits and the risks of the available alternatives including doing nothing? Insist that the consultant put this information in writing. Without it you cannot make a fully informed, rational decision about what is or is not in your best interest.

7.   Negotiating a contract. This is a critical point. All too often managers turn the work over to legal. Don't do it. Include legal, but be an active part of the process. Specifically, you should make sure that you can say "yes" to the following questions: (*a*) Does the contract specify who is going to do the work? Too often the "guru" that sells the service is not the one who delivers it. He or she simply turns it over to underlings. Who are they and are they qualified? (*b*) Is remuneration contingent upon results and within a specified time frame? Many professionals charge by the hour. Try and find someone who works by the job—either payment for completion of the overall job or payment at the completion of each stage. If possible pay for results and not for time. (*c*) Are consultants willing to sign non-competition and non-disclosure agreements? Are they willing to promise not to provide similar services to your competition for a specified period of time (generally a year) without your consent? Are they willing to promise confidentiality and to insure that confidentiality will be maintained by all their employees, from management

to the secretarial staff? (*d*) Are there frequent checkpoints or "exit clauses" in the contract, i.e., Are there points where you can check on progress and if need be terminate the relationship (Montgomery, Heald, MacNamara, and Pincus, 1995)? (*e*) Does the contract spell out specific, measurable, target objectives? By "specific," we mean "very specific." Many of the ethical problems that arise during a consultancy stem from simple misunderstandings. For example, If you hire someone to do eight hours of management skills training, does the eight hours include lunch? Coffee breaks? Or, do you mean eight hours of classroom time? (*f*) Does the contract specify how both parties will know when and if the objectives have been met? Managers and consultants should agree in advance how to measure success. (*g*) Does the contract include provisions and terms for follow-up work if the initial successes are not maintained? What are they? What is the cost?

8.   Letting the expert be the expert. The success of the consultancy depends on creating a substantive dialogue around the above critical issues. However, remember you hired outside experts, because you wanted their expertise. Ask questions, demand answers, make certain that you are fully informed, but do not "back seat drive." If you want to perform the task and you know how, you may not need a consultant.

These eight points and the related questions can serve as a checklist for avoiding potential ethical and legal problems as well as avoiding costly disasters. The list is not exhaustive nor does it apply to every consultancy. But, if you address the issues and questions outlined above, they should help you reduce the chances of misunderstandings, avoid ethical pitfalls, and allow you to exit the consultancy before the "train wreck." In short, attention to above questions and issues should increase the probability of a successful, mutually beneficial outcome for all concerned.

REFERENCES

1.   Brandon, J. (1989, May) Where consultants fall down, *Management Today,* pp. 109–110.
2.   Daniels, A. C. (1994). *Bringing out the best in people.* New York: McGraw-Hill.
3.   Montgomery, D. J., Heald, G. R., MacNamara, S. R. & Pincus, L. B. (1995). Malpractice and the communication consultant. *Management Communication Quarterly,* 8, 368–364.
4.   Seitel, F. P. (1989, June) Consultant ripoffs. *United States Banker,* pp. 62–63.

THE BALANCE OF POWER

HARRIS V. FORKLIFT SYSTEMS, INC.

One of the areas most discussed in employee training these days is sexual harassment, which was relatively unheard of prior to the Anita Hill–Clarence Thomas incident several years ago. Subjects of sexual harassment are now filing suits against their employers in record numbers. Defining what constitutes sexual harassment or what is a "hostile environment" is difficult and circumstantial. The following case exemplifies some of these challenging issues.

. . . JUSTICE O'CONNOR delivered the opinion of the Court.

In this case we consider the definition of a discriminatorily "abusive work environment" (also known as a "hostile work environment") under Title VII of the Civil Rights Act of 1964.

I

Teresa Harris worked as a manager at Forklift Systems, Inc., an equipment rental company, from April 1985 until October 1987. Charles Hardy was Forklift's president.

The Magistrate found that, throughout Harris' time at Forklift, Hardy often insulted her because of her gender and often made her the target of unwanted sexual innuendos. Hardy told Harris on several occasions, in the presence of other employees, "You're a woman, what do you know" and "We need a man as the rental manager"; at least once, he told her she was "a dumb ass woman." Again in front of others, he suggested that the two of them "go to the Holiday Inn to negotiate [Harris'] raise." Hardy occasionally asked Harris and other female employees to get coins from his front pants pocket. He threw objects on the ground in front of Harris and other women, and asked them to pick the objects up. He made sexual innuendos about Harris' and other women's clothing.

In mid-August 1987, Harris complained to Hardy about his conduct. Hardy said he was surprised that Harris was offended, claimed he was only joking, and apologized. He also promised he would stop, and based on this assurance Harris stayed on the job. But in early September, Hardy began anew: While Harris was arranging a deal with one of Forklift's customers, he asked her, again in front of other employees, "What did you do, promise the guy . . . some [sex] Saturday night?" On October 1, Harris collected her paycheck and quit.

Harris then sued Forklift, claiming that Hardy's conduct had created an abusive work environment for her because of her gender. The United States District Court for the

---

Sexual Harassment: *Harris* v. *Forklift Systems, Inc.*, 510 U.S. 17 (1993).

Middle District of Tennessee, adopting the report and recommendation of the Magistrate, found this to be "a close case," but held that Hardy's conduct did not create an abusive environment. The court found that some of Hardy's comments "offended [Harris], and would offend the reasonable woman," but that they were not

> *so severe as to be expected to seriously affect [Harris'] psychological well-being. A reasonable woman manager under like circumstances would have been offended by Hardy, but his conduct would not have risen to the level of interfering with that person's work performance.*
>
> *Neither do I believe that [Harris] was subjectively so offended that she suffered injury. . . . Although Hardy may at times have genuinely offended [Harris], I do not believe that he created a working environment so poisoned as to be intimidating or abusive to [Harris].*

In focusing on the employee's psychological well-being, the District Court was following Circuit precedent. The United States Court of appeals for the Sixth Circuit affirmed in a brief unpublished decision.

We granted certiorari to resolve a conflict among the Circuits on whether conduct, to be actionable as "abusive work environment" harassment (no quid pro quo harassment issue is present here), must "seriously affect [an employee's] psychological well-being" or lead the plaintiff to suffer injury. . . .

II

Title VII of the Civil Rights Act of 1964 makes it "an unlawful employment practice for an employer . . . to discriminate against any individual with respect to his compensation, terms, conditions, or privileges of employment, because of such individual's race, color, religion, sex, or national origin." As we made clear in Meritor Savings Bank v. Vinson, this language "is not limited to 'economic' or 'tangible' discrimination. The phrase 'terms, conditions, or privileges of employment' evinces a congressional intent 'to strike at the entire spectrum of disparate treatment of men and women' in employment," which includes requiring people to work in a discriminatorily hostile or abusive environment. When the workplace is permeated with "discriminatory intimidation, ridicule, and insult" that is "sufficiently severe or pervasive to alter the conditions of the victim's employment and create an abusive working environment," Title VII is violated.

This standard, which we reaffirm today, takes a middle path between making actionable any conduct that is merely offensive and requiring the conduct to cause a tangible psychological injury. As we pointed out in Meritor, "mere utterance of an . . . epithet which engenders offensive feelings in a employee" does not sufficiently affect the conditions of employment to implicate Title VII. Conduct that is not severe or pervasive enough to create an objectively hostile or abusive work environment—an environment that a reasonable person would find hostile or abusive—is beyond Title VII's purview. Likewise, if the victim does not subjectively perceive the environment to be abusive, the conduct has not actually altered the conditions of the victim's employment, and there is no Title VII violation.

But Title VII comes into play before the harassing conduct leads to a nervous breakdown. A discriminatorily abusive work environment, even one that does not seriously affect employees' psychological well-being, can and often will detract from employees' job performance, discourage employees from remaining on the job, or keep them from advancing in their careers. Moreover, even without regard to these tangible effects, the very fact that the discriminatory conduct was so severe or pervasive that it created a work environment abusive to employees because of their race, gender, religion, or national origin offends Title VII's broad rule of workplace equality. The appalling conduct alleged in Meritor, and the reference in that case to environments " 'so heavily polluted with discrimination as to destroy completely the emotional and psychological stability of minority group workers' " merely present some especially egregious examples of harassment. They do not mark the boundary of what is actionable.

We therefore believe the District Court erred in relying on whether the conduct "seriously affected plaintiff's psychological well-being" or led her to "suffer injury." Such an inquiry may needlessly focus the factfinder's attention on concrete psychological harm, an element Title VII does not require. Certainly Title VII bars conduct that would seriously affect a reasonable person's psychological well-being, but the statute is not limited to such conduct. So long as the environment would reasonably be perceived, and is perceived, as hostile or abusive, there is no need for it also to be psychologically injurious.

This is not, and by its nature cannot be, a mathematically precise test. We need not answer today all the potential questions it raises, nor specifically address the EEOC's new regulations on this subject. But we can say that whether an environment is "hostile" or "abusive" can be determined only by looking at all the circumstances. These may include the frequency of the discriminatory conduct; its severity; whether it is physically threatening or humiliating, or a mere offensive utterance; and whether it unreasonably interferes with an employee's work performance. The effect on the employee's psychological well-being is, of course, relevant to determining whether the plaintiff actually found the environment abusive. But while psychological harm, like any other relevant factor, may be taken into account, no single factor is required.

III

Forklift, while conceding that a requirement that the conduct seriously affect psychological well-being is unfounded, argues that the District Court nonetheless correctly applied the Meritor standard. We disagree. Though the District Court did conclude that the work environment was not "intimidating or abusive to [Harris]," it did so only after finding that the conduct was not "so severe as to be expected to seriously affect plaintiff's psychological well-being," and that Harris was not "subjectively so offended that she suffered injury." The District Court's application of these incorrect standards may well have influenced its ultimate conclusion, especially given that the court found this to be a "close case."

We therefore reverse the judgment of the Court of Appeals, and remand the case for further proceedings consistent with this opinion.

So ordered. . . .

RELATED WEB SITE

Policies against sexual harassment:

www.abanet.org/genpractice/compleat/w96shi.html

ISSUES IN DRUG TESTING FOR THE PRIVATE SECTOR

GEORGE R. GRAY AND DARREL R. BROWN

Gray identifies some of the key issues related to drug testing for the private sector.

A recent survey of Fortune 500 companies on the use of workplace drug testing indicates that illegal drug use among employees remains a serious concern for employers.

Eighty-eight percent of the responding companies currently conduct drug testing of applicants as part of the preemployment physical examination. Of the companies that did not conduct drug tests, 80 percent indicated that they have plans to begin applicant testing.

Virtually all employers conducting applicant testing indicated that the tests were administered during the final stages of processing. When questioned on what actions the company took when an applicant tested positive, all employers responded that they did not hire the individual, although many volunteered that they would consider the applicant after a period ranging from 30 days to one year. Only one company mentioned that they would retest at the applicant's expense. No companies suggested the options of conducting a second test or using a more accurate type of test.

The survey found that 60 percent of companies test current employees, and a majority of those firms (75 percent) conduct those tests for cases of suspected abuse. Twenty-one percent said they conduct routine, periodic tests of all employees in sensitive positions, and 8 percent test randomly among workers in sensitive positions. Another 8 percent of employers said they conduct routine, periodic tests for all employees.

When a current employee tests positive, the most frequent course of action taken by companies involves referral to an employee assistance program. Retesting, testing after rehabilitation, termination and other disciplinary actions were mentioned less frequently. The practice, however, clearly varies with the sensitivity of the position in relation to security and the safety of other individuals.

ISSUES OF CONCERN

Right to privacy: Despite the fact that the constitutional right to privacy does not apply to private-sector employment, many people feel strongly that drug testing is too "invasive" and violates an important right. This is probably the primary impetus behind local and state legislative efforts to ban drug testing among current employees. San Francisco, for example, has barred employers from ordering urinanlysis and other tests on current employees unless "clear evidence" exists that the worker's drug use endangers others. Some observers have predicted that other cities—even some states—could restrict or prohibit random testing of current employees, except when safety is the issue.

Although such proposals have been introduced in several states, these legislatures have not yet adopted them as laws. Employers convinced of the need for testing should consider taking a more active role in their area when such legislation is proposed. This could include employee education, public awareness campaigns and testimony before legislative bodies.

Testing error: Much has been written about the validity and reliability of tests, the debate over broad-spectrum versus narrow-spectrum tests and incompetent testing laboratories.

Drug-testing laboratories, however, may be the weakest link in the system since these companies operate in an unregulated environment. The proliferation of new firms, many lacking in expertise and often overloaded by the increase in corporate drug testing, add to the problem. A Centers for Disease Control study of 13 laboratories, for example, reported in 1988 that error rates up to 66 percent were found. The report concluded that none of the labs studied were reliable. It is in every employer's interest to work for testing standards, to insist that certain quality standards be adhered to by laboratories working for them, and to make sure those standards are met.

Testing costs: The most commonly used screening tests are relatively inexpensive, reportedly on the order of $5 per sample. High error rates, however, have led toxicologists to recommend confirmatory testing for all positive samples. Such tests are more sophisticated to ensure greater accuracy and, in turn, can cost about $90. For a large corporation with a lot of testing activity, this becomes truly expensive. For small employers, such testing may seem prohibitive.

Employee morale: Testing current employees seems to promote a statement that employers do not trust their workers to behave responsibly regarding drug use. Although such perceptions cannot be avoided totally, careful education efforts about the need for testing can help prepare workers for a new program. A program directed toward sensitive positions or departments, tailored to a company's specific problems, and carefully designed to avoid communicating a feeling of mistrust among all employees appears to be a company's best approach in drug testing.

RELATED WEB SITES

"Urinalysis or Uromancy: Costs of Drug Testing Abuse":

www.natlnorml.orgtesting/untold.txt

ACLU on drug testing: www.aclu.org/library/pbr5.html

IS EMPLOYEE DRUG
TESTING THE ANSWER?
THOMAS GOLLOT, MARK COHEN, AND ERIC FILLMAN

Gollot, Cohen, and Fillman debate the appropriateness of drug testing in the workplace.

POINT
BY THOMAS A. GOLLOT

Everyone seems to be in agreement that we have a drug problem in America and we need to do something about it. But people disagree on solutions for this national crisis. Some are choosing to confront the problem through drug testing.

Drug testing is a means of identifying the user and scaring the naive experimenter into staying straight. Drug testing is not a solution to the drug problem, but it does give the nation a better handle on it.

Those opposed to drug testing have voiced four primary objections: inaccuracy of the tests, inconvenience and possible violations of privacy, fear of job loss on detection and the overall cost.

Two things are important concerning these arguments: the integrity of the laboratory and the employer. Laboratory integrity is easier to monitor than employers' integrity but there are proper procedures for checking both. The percentage of misdiagnoses caused by human error is minimal compared to the benefits of drug testing. Most employers are ethical. They care about their employees and want to prevent drug addiction. In addition, training new labor costs the company more money than rehabilitation.

It is an inconvenience to submit to a drug test. Nobody likes to give urine specimens. It's aggravating. My employees at Gollot and Sons Transfer and Storage Co. must submit to drug testing if they want to work for my company—or any other trucking company. Starting Dec. 21, drug testing will be required by the U.S. Department of Transportation for the trucking industry, regardless of the size of the carrier. It's too bad that people have to be inconvenienced like this.

It's also too bad that more than 80 percent of the people serving time in state prisons are there because of drug-related crimes. Maybe if they had been inconvenienced by a drug test, they wouldn't be where they are now.

As far as invasion of privacy is concerned, it's a weak excuse. Urine samples can be collected and validated without direct observation. An inexpensive dye can be used to confirm that the sample is genuine, temperature checks can be made of urine samples and "specific gravity" analysis and other methods can ensure validity while maintaining privacy. The fear of observation or undignified positioning while urinating should not be given as a reason to avoid drug testing.

Testing can be a legitimate concern for people who abuse illegal drugs. Their fears of detection and job loss are what deter drug use. But states also must mandate rehabilitation programs for drug-addicted workers. Drug users are not going to submit to treatment unless it's mandatory.

The initial drug screening of an employee costs about $20. A more detailed identification of drug substance costs more. For example, the Gas Chromatography and Mass Spectrophotometry tests cost more than $70 a person. The Baumgartner chronological hair sampling test costs about $30 per substance identified.

Yes, testing costs money. But we can afford the cost. What we can't afford is the continued drain and waste of the nation's talent and the weakening and corruption of people.

I have introduced legislation in the Mississippi Senate that would require all elected and appointed state officials to submit to a drug test. Government leaders need to show leadership. We represent the public's trust and we have a responsibility that goes with that trust.

We don't want government officials who might be abusing drugs making policy decisions, just as we do not want to be on an airplane with a pilot tampering with drugs. The Federal Aviation Agency has mandated regular random drug checks for all commercial pilots. State governments should follow the FAA's lead.

In addition, the U.S. Air Force requires random drug testing for all military personnel. The FBI also requires that all agents be routinely tested for drug use. As one agent said, "I wouldn't want my life to depend on an agent on drugs."

We need to make drug testing mandatory for public officials, not only to set an example, but because it makes sense.

COUNTERPOINT
BY MARK B. COHEN AND ERIC S. FILLMAN

Drug use is a great threat to the health of millions of Americans, and the crime that drug use generates is a threat to millions more.

That is why in our battle against drugs we must not subject innocent lives to further risks. The danger with drug testing is that, without appropriate safeguards, it can become a means of harassment and a series of booby traps for non-drug-using workers.

If it leads to the firing, instead of the rehabilitation, of an occasional drug user, it can push that person deeper into the drug culture.

Legislators should examine not only the goals behind drug testing, but how these programs actually function.

This topic was studied in-depth by the Pennsylvania House Labor Relations Committee before legislation was introduced requiring companies using drug testing to offer employee assistance programs, more rigorous confirmation tests and opportunities for workers to reform themselves.

At one public hearing, James Moran, executive director for the Philadelphia Project on Occupational Safety and Health, graphically depicted the scene of a worker in a bathroom stall and the physical, undignified stance she had to position herself in to give a urine sample while being observed for security reasons. "Suppose this was your mother," Moran asked.

Attempting to verify drug use by way of blind, random, arbitrary testing of individuals without some standard of probable or just cause can damage the fabric of workplace dignity and morale. A constructive alternative lies in testing only under circumstances where there is a reasonably articulable suspicion of intoxication causing impaired ability to perform normal duties.

Testing in this manner will help ensure that the innocent worker is not unjustly forced through the indignity of drug testing at the whim of a supervisor.

Employee assistance programs designed to meet the unique needs of specific businesses and employees must serve as functional, integrated parts of the workplace. If employers intend to test for drug use, they should be adequately prepared for the results of such tests and use such results in a socially responsible manner.

Failing their initiative to do so, legislatures have a responsibility to regulate this practice to guarantee the proper use of such testing and the availability of counseling and treatment programs for those who need them.

We all must remember that drug abuse is a health and social problem, not just a police problem. Employers genuinely interested in combating the drug problems of the workplace have the responsibility to make a sincere effort to help troubled employees.

The continued success and proliferation of employee assistance programs in recent years suggest that such programs respond to the true needs of employers and chemically dependent persons alike.

Training new employees is costly. Employers should not pursue the wasteful approach of discharging employees in their efforts to combat drug abuse in the workplace. Health professionals have long recognized that job security is positively related to treatment of chemically dependent persons.

The ultimate goal of employers should be to prevent further drug use, not to reinforce its abuse by adding reasons for an employee to turn to drugs, such as the loss of a job.

Firing otherwise productive workers on the basis of drug tests is not a satisfactory answer to the problem of drug abuse in the workplace.

As far as legal remedies are concerned, constitutional attacks on drug testing speak only to public employers, not private employers. But privacy is compromised with involuntary testing, regardless of the nature of employment.

Urine samples contain a vast amount of personal information to which an individual has a legitimate expectation of privacy. In addition to detecting drugs, urine can identify an employee's medical history, including such conditions as venereal disease, epilepsy and schizophrenia, as well as an employee's susceptibility to diseases such as heart attacks and sickle cell anemia.

The implications of obtaining such information from a urine bottle are staggering. Employers possess a great, unchecked potential to weed out employees unjustly on the basis of health risks completely dissociated with job responsibilities. Again, proper regulation will ensure that injustices like this do not occur on the basis of the limited technology used by employers.

The limited technology of today does not do what employers need it to do: establish or verify worker impairment.

RELATED WEB SITE

A leading drug testing company: www.psychemedics.com/main.htm

HOW TO PASS
A URINALYSIS
CANNABIS ACTION NETWORK

Should this item even have been included in this volume? Perhaps it is unethical to broadcast this material, even when it is readily available on the World Wide Web. On the other hand, if you believe that testing employees for drugs is not ethical, then would avoiding detection be ethical?

During the later part of the twentieth century, the once mighty and proud but by then petty and third rate nation state of USA declared war on living plants, strange as it seems. Because certain growing plants and flowers were sometimes used by people for relaxation or to enhance their perception, the police-state government of USA outlawed the plants and harassed, incarcerated, and even killed people who used or possessed the plants. The leaders of this strange nation, angered that anyone could even relax at all, ignored the fact that these plants could feed, clothe, and heal the people, and banned all use of the plants. The soldier-robots of this peculiar state were sent across the land to destroy the plants with fire and with chemicals, and to steal the homes, cars, and businesses of people who used the plants. During this dark and backward time, a certain level of "technology" had been reached, which enabled the bureaucrats to devise a scheme whereby people, if they wanted to eat, had to prove their innocence of any use of, or contact with, the forbidden plant materials—by urinating on command!

Cannabis Action Network believes that urine drug testing violates your Fourth Amendment right against unreasonable searches and your Fifth Amendment right against self incrimination. The Federal court system has upheld them as constitutional, however, and companies are under increasing pressure to comply with the Drug Free Workplace Act.

Drug tests have something in common with other physical searches in that you have more rights if you do not consent to the search. When you consent, you surrender your rights. Should you be forced by economic pressure to work for a company that does drug testing or by court order undergo regular tests there are many things you should know.

Marijuana is detectable for up to six weeks in the urine of regular users.

Drug testing laboratories have fewer quality control regulation than restaurants.

Your urine sample will change hands many times before the actual analysis. There is a high probability of mix-ups and errors due to this "chain of custody" issue.

The chemical agents used in testing have a limited shelf life, which can cause false positives. Many over-the-counter medications, foods, and environmental factors can also cause false positives. When you are aware that you will be tested, there are a number of things to keep in mind.

Don't give urine samples from the first urination of the day as the metabolite concentration is higher. Urinate a couple of times before giving the sample to be tested.

There are many old wives' tales concerning what works and what doesn't. People who claim to have drunk vinegar and passed, or other such nonsense, probably received false negative results. Goldenseal is currently being tested for, along with recreational drugs, so don't use it.

Natural diuretics like caffeine and cranberry juice will stimulate flushing of your system. Use them prior to a test, but not the night before. Over-the-counter and prescription diuretics are dangerous and should not be used.

Sabotaging your sample with bleach or Drano will only require another humiliating session of peeing on command.

Substituting someone else's urine is tricky. Many employers and labs check for color, temperature, and sediment in samples. Approximate age and sex of the urine provider can be determined, so choose your donor carefully.

PRODUCTS THAT CAN PROTECT YOUR PRIVACY

Part One: Pre-employment and Scheduled Tests

Proven results have been obtained for many years by users of Houston Enterprises' powdered drink mix "The Stuff." This product works by forming a gelacious barrier in the bladder temporarily retaining all solids while clean water colored by B vitamins to look like normal urine passes. This blocks detection not only of actual drug use of all kinds, but also all environmental factors known to cause false positives. Because the "jello" is broken down and expelled by the body after three hours, the timing of the use of this product is crucial. Directions are included in the package and should be followed precisely to avoid failure. Use of "The Stuff" on an empty stomach is mandatory, so care should be taken to ingest nothing orally for eight hours prior to it's use. Houston Enterprises guarantees the effectiveness of "The Stuff" when used as directed. Many other products also come with this pledge of effectiveness, but we are not convinced because we don't know anyone who has used them. Over one thousand people have been referred to Houston Enterprises products by us and no one has come back to kill us, so we feel confident recommending them to you.

Part Two: Random Tests

Proven results have been obtained by building trades workers, truck drivers and military personnel subject to random testing on the job with a combination of Houston Enterprises

Naturally Klean Herbal Tea and Daily Detox products. Used carefully, these two products allow anyone subject to random tests to use any recreational drugs on the weekends and pass urinalysis any work day. Naturally Klean Herbal Tea works in three ways: Diuretic, liver stimulant, and zinc supplement. The metabolites of most recreational drugs are quite small and are only present in the urine because they are too small for elimination via the liver and colon. The zinc supplement in Naturally Klean binds with the drug metabolites in the blood stream forming a much larger molecule which the liver can then clean from the blood and deposit in the feces. This ensures the urine will not show traces of drug use. The liver stimulant aids this process. The diuretic flushes all drug traces from the bladder that may have been deposited prior to the product's use and dilutes the concentration of the urine to further make detection of drug use impossible. Workers subject to random testing should use the tea as a quick flush on the evening before or morning they return to work. This is done simply by brewing one gallon of tea and drinking it continuously for three hours.

Timing is important; one must have finished the tea by the time the test could possibly be administered. One drawback to this program is that the tea's diuretic action creates copious quantities of urine. Workers without easy bathroom access on demand are urged to complete the tea regimen four hours before going to work to avoid suspicion. The effects of the tea can be continued indefinitely by consuming one Daily Detox tablet or cup of tea every twelve hours beginning four hours after the end of the Naturally Klean Herbal Tea drinking period and continuing for at least thirty days. Any time in the thirty day period the worker gets high, they must drink the gallon of Naturally Klean Herbal Tea before returning to the job and resume the Daily Detox regimen. This program requires abstinence from all drugs during the work week. Houston Enterprises has guaranteed the effectiveness of their products for over seven years and we recommend them with utmost confidence.

COMPENSATION:
COMPARABLE WORTH

AMERICAN NURSES'
ASSOCIATION V.
STATE OF ILLINOIS

The following Seventh Circuit decision is one of the few written court decisions to specifically address comparable worth. In this case, a nurses association brought a claim for discrimination in the wages of its members, claiming that they were underpaid because they were in traditionally female-dominated positions. Judge Posner (a University of Chicago professor and free market advocate) held that no cause of action exists on a comparable worth theory. Posner refuses to apply comparable worth theory because he says that "it is not the sort that judges are well equipped to resolve intelligently." Do you agree? Who would be better equipped than a judge who can sit and hear all of the facts? Are you persuaded by comparable worth theory?

. . . POSNER, Circuit Judge.

    This class action charges the State of Illinois with sex discrimination in employment, in violation of Title VII of the Civil Rights Act of 1964, and the equal protection clause of the Fourteenth Amendment. The named plaintiffs are two associations of nurses plus 21 individuals, mostly but not entirely female who work for the state in jobs such as nursing and typing that are filled primarily by women. The suit is on behalf of all state employees in these job classifications. . . . [T]he [plaintiffs] charge that the state pays workers in predominantly male job classifications a higher wage not justified by any difference in the relative worth of the predominantly male and the predominantly female jobs in the state's roster. . . .

    Comparable worth is not a legal concept, but a shorthand expression for the movement to raise the ratio of wages in traditionally women's jobs to wages in traditionally men's jobs. Its premises are both historical and cognitive. The historical premise is that a society politically and culturally dominated by men steered women into certain jobs and kept the wages in those jobs below what the jobs were worth, precisely because most of the holders were women. The cognitive premise is that analytical techniques exist for determining the

American Nurses Association, 783 F.2d 716 (7th Cir. 1986).

relative worth of jobs that involve different levels of skill, effort, risk, responsibility, etc. These premises are vigorously disputed on both theoretical and empirical grounds. Economists point out that unless employers forbid women to compete for the higher-paying, traditionally men's jobs—which would violate federal law—women will switch into those jobs until the only difference in wages between traditionally women's jobs and traditionally men's jobs will be that necessary to equate the supply of workers in each type of job to the demand. Economists have conducted studies which show that virtually the entire difference in the average hourly wage of men and women, including that due to the fact that men and women tend to be concentrated in different types of job, can be explained by the fact that most women take considerable time out of the labor force in order to take care of their children. As a result they tend to invest less in their "human capital" (earning capacity); and since part of any wage is a return on human capital, they tend therefore to be found in jobs that pay less. Consistently with this hypothesis, the studies find that women who have never married earn as much as men who have never married. To all this the advocates of comparable worth reply that although there are no longer explicit barriers to women's entering traditionally men's jobs, cultural and psychological barriers remain as a result of which many though not all women internalize men's expectations regarding jobs appropriate for women and therefore invest less in their human capital.

On the cognitive question economists point out that the ratio of wages in different jobs is determined by the market rather than by any a priori conception of relative merit, in just the same way that the ratio of the price of caviar to the price of cabbage is determined by relative scarcity rather than relative importance to human welfare. Upsetting the market equilibrium by imposing such a conception would have costly consequences, some of which might undercut the ultimate goals of the comparable worth movement. If the movement should cause wages in traditionally men's jobs to be depressed below their market level and wages in traditionally women's jobs to be jacked above their market level, women will have less incentive to enter traditionally men's fields and more to enter traditionally women's fields. Analysis cannot stop there, because the change in relative wages will send men in the same direction: fewer men will enter the traditionally men's jobs, more the traditionally women's jobs. As a result there will be more room for women in traditionally men's jobs and at the same time fewer opportunities for women in traditionally women's jobs— especially since the number of those jobs will shrink as employers are induced by the higher wage to substitute capital for labor inputs (e.g., more word processors, fewer secretaries). Labor will be allocated less efficiently; men and women alike may be made worse off.

Against this the advocates of comparable worth urge that collective bargaining, public regulation of wages and hours, and the lack of information and mobility of some workers make the market model an inaccurate description of how relative wages are determined and how they influence the choice of jobs. The point has particular force when applied to a public employer such as the State of Illinois, which does not have the same incentives that a private firm would have to use labor efficiently.

[1] It should be clear from this brief summary that the issue of comparable worth . . . is not of the sort that judges are well equipped to resolve intelligently or that we should lightly assume has been given to us to resolve by Title VII or the Constitution. An employer (private or public) that simply pays the going wage in each of the different types of job in its establishment, and makes no effort to discourage women from applying

for particular jobs or to steer them toward particular jobs, would be justifiably surprised to discover that it may be violating federal law because each wage rate and therefore the ratio between them have been found to be determined by cultural or psychological factors attributable to the history of male domination of society; that it has to hire a consultant to find out how it must, regardless of market conditions, change the wages it pays, in order to achieve equity between traditionally male and traditionally female jobs; and that it must pay backpay, to boot. We need not tarry over the question of law presented by this example because as we understand the plaintiffs' position it is not that a mere failure to rectify traditional wage disparities between predominantly male and predominantly female jobs violates federal law. The circuits that have considered this contention have rejected it; see the *AFSCME* case discussed below; we shall see shortly that this rejection may be compelled by the Supreme Court's decisions in the *Davis* and *Feeney* cases.

The next question is whether a failure to achieve comparable worth—granted that it would not itself be a violation of law—might permit an inference of deliberate and therefore unlawful discrimination, as distinct from passive acceptance of a market-determined disparity in wages. The starting point for analyzing this question must be *County of Washington v. Gunther.* Women employed to guard female prisoners were paid less than men employed to guard male prisoners. Since male prison inmates are more dangerous than female ones and since each male guard on average guarded ten times as many prisoners as each female guard, the jobs were not the same. Therefore, paying the male guards more could not violate the Equal Pay Act of 1963, which requires equal pay only for equal work. The issue was whether it could violate Title VII, and the Court held that it could. A comparable worth study figured in this conclusion. The plaintiffs had alleged (and the allegation had to be taken as true for purposes of appeal, because the complaint had been dismissed, as in this case, for failure to state a claim) that the county had conducted a comparable worth study and had determined that female guards should be paid 95 percent of what male guards were paid; that it had then decided to pay them only 70 percent; "and that the failure of the county to pay [the plaintiffs] the full evaluated worth of their jobs can be proved to be attributable to intentional sex discrimination. Thus, [the plaintiffs'] suit does not require a court to make its own subjective assessment of the value of the male and female guard jobs, or to attempt by statistical technique or other method to quantify the effects of sex discrimination on the wage rates." . . .

The *AFSCME* case resembles our hypothetical case of the firm accused of sex discrimination merely because it pays market wages. *AFSCME* shows that such a case is not actionable under Title VII even if the employer is made aware that its pattern of wages departs from the principle of comparable worth to the disadvantage of women (plus the occasional male occupant of a traditionally woman's job) and even if the employer is not so much a prisoner of the market that it cannot alter its wages in the direction of comparable worth, as eventually the State of Washington did. The critical thing lacking in *AFSCME* was evidence that the state decided not to raise the wages of particular workers *because* most of those workers were female. Without such evidence, to infer a violation of Title VII from the fact that the state had conducted a comparable worth study would, again, just discourage such studies.

. . . The plaintiffs can get no mileage out of casting a comparable worth case as an equal protection case. . . . that the equal protection clause is violated only by intentional discrimination; the fact that a law or official practice adopted for a lawful purpose has a racially differential impact is not enough.

IS PAY EQUITY EQUITABLE?

Laura B. Pincus and Nicholas J. Mathys

In the following article, Mathys and I argue that a simplistic evaluation of pay equity does not consider the intrinsic rewards offered by some positions. These rewards might include greater autonomy, flexibility, different work tasks, or others. When these intrinsic rewards are coupled with the salary paid in those positions, perhaps the compensation is similar to a higher-paying job with fewer intrinsic rewards.

. . . Much has been written about the disparity in wages between men and women. The familiar phrase, "70 cents on the dollar" has been repeated as the basic comparison between the value of women in employment to that of men.[1] However, though allegedly slightly higher today than at the time of its first calculation, it is the contention of these authors that this figure overstates the compensation disparity which exists between male and female workers. Furthermore, the extent of that disparity has been greatly exaggerated by prior research and writing that has failed to recognize all of the variables that must be considered in the determination of "compensation." Instead, prior research has focused on the *specific* disparity between the dollar amount of the wages paid to women and the wages paid to men in similar positions. It has failed to adequately answer the question: "Why are people paid what they are paid?" As one researcher states: "whereas women may feel underpaid, they may not feel undercompensated."[2] For instance, as women are more likely to be the individuals who care for children, women may place a higher value on positions which offer flexible hours, work at home possibilities, or day care centers at the workplace.

The Equal Pay Act as it was originally envisioned applied only to workers performing the *same* job. As the comparable worth movement developed, the Act took on a broader application; equal pay was now arguably warranted for "similar" jobs. The definition of "similar" was expanded to include not only equal positions but also jobs that had equal worth as defined by job evaluation analyses. The authors are in entire agreement with the original, narrow application of the Equal Pay Act, requiring that individuals in the same position should be paid equal compensation, regardless of their gender. It is the determination of what constitutes equal compensation that begs the question.

"Is Pay Equity Equitable?" by Laura Pincus, Nick Mathys. Reprinted by permission of the authors.

1. Kleiman, "Women's Lower Pay Adds Up to Lower Pensions," *Chicago Tribune* (November 18, 1991). B. Norris, "Comparable Worth, Disparate Impact, and The Market Rate Salary Problem: A Legal Analysis and Statistical Application," *California Law Review,* 71, 730 (1983). G. Meng, "All the Parts of Comparable Worth" *Personnel Journal,* 99 (November, 1990). J. Hollenbeck, D. Ilgen, C. Ostroff, J. Vancouver, "Sex Differences in Occupational Choice, Pay and Worth: A Supply-Side Approach to Understanding The Male-Female Wage Gap," *Personnel Psychology,* 40, 715 (1987).

2. Hollenbeck et al., pp. 715, 717.

The issue which serves as the focal point in this paper is not whether the jobs are similar, but whether the areas in which the positions are dissimilar constitute, in themselves, a difference in compensation. In other words, the functional responsibilities of a male-dominated position and a female-dominated position may be similar (as determined by job evaluation techniques), but the female may receive greater intrinsic compensation (as explained below) and less renumerative compensation than the male. Therefore, the employer's defense under the Equal Pay Act is not that the male and female employee are performing different jobs, but instead that the compensation received is actually of equal value though not in equal ratios of monetary gain and other benefits. . . .

WHAT CONSTITUTES COMPENSATION?

Compensation, at least in theory, represents the reward to an individual for contributions made to the organization—first for job-related contributions and second (at least for some jobs) for performance contributions. *Equity theory* holds that there is a large number of potential contributions and benefits that are recognized and considered relevant to both parties in the employment exchange. It is the sum total of all these contributions made by the individual employee and rewards (financial and otherwise) offered by the organization that goes into the determination of equity (see Figure 1). It is our contention that the proponents of pay equity focus almost exclusively on pay to determine whether people are being "treated equitably," when it is obvious that pay (or compensation) is only one motivation (albeit a major one) why people accept a position or desire a particular career.

Let's expand on this. The variety of rewards offered in the employment exchange is large. However, they fall into two general categories: those that are *intrinsic* (provided by the job itself) and those that are *extrinsic* (provided by factors outside the job). Examples of extrinsic rewards include pay, fringe benefits, job security, social satisfaction, and recognition by one's supervisor. Examples of intrinsic rewards include a sense of accomplishment attained from the job, its challenge, variety, and degree of autonomy.

In determining the variants of pay equity, organizations and unions (along with economists) have tended to focus their attention on the economic basis of the employment exchange. On the other hand, psychologists and other behavioral scientists have taken a broader view by identifying a sizable number (over 100) of nonfinancial rewards in studies on job satisfaction.[3] Following are some examples of nonfinancial rewards desired by individuals.

To some employee groups, job security and safety issues may be important. The pleasant, sanitized working conditions in many office settings attract more job candidates than do more hazardous, less-skilled jobs resulting in lower pay being offered to those candidates. Also, many positions in governmental agencies are viewed as more secure against layoffs than "equivalent" private sector positions. Greater job security along with better fringe benefits usually offered by the public sector can explain much of the seeming disparity between the pay of jobs in the public and private sector.

Other people look for friendships and sociability from their job. For these people, jobs that allow for social interaction will be viewed more favorably than those that require individual work.

---

3. E. E. Lawler, *Pay and Organizational Effectiveness: A Psychological View* (New York: McGraw-Hill, 1971). F. Herzberg, *Work and The Nature of Man* (Cleveland: World Books, 1966).

FIGURE 1

Equity Model for Employment Exchange

Contributions	Rewards (Benefits)
Being Brought to	Being Offered to
Organization by	Individual by
Individual	Organization

Balance Needed

Skills/Abilities	∧	A. *Extrinsic*
Education		—Pay
Experience		—Fringe Benefits
"Potential"		—Job Security
Performance		—Promotion Opportunities
Personality Traits		—Social Relations
Energy Level		—Closeness to Home
Values		—Organization Culture
Flexibility		—Organization Working
		Relationships
		B. *Intrinsic*
		—Challenge
		—Variety
		—Autonomy
		—Significance of Task
		—Sense of Achievement

Some workers desire scheduling flexibility as an important nonfinancial reward and may trade this for (be satisfied with) less pay. Students, spouses with small children, and individuals holding two or more jobs, among others, are often found in this group.

Another nonfinancial reward factor is job status. Many financial institutions have many layers of "vice-presidents" who are not paid at the levels suggested by the title. The title can be viewed as "psychic" pay.

Finally, to some the job may be seen as a "cause" or "calling." The sense of achievement and satisfaction of fulfilling a desired purpose in life or the emotional significance of the task may "compensate" for lower than normal financial rewards. Examples of some occupational groups affected are artists, many jobs dealing with social issues and causes, and educators.

The conclusion drawn from the above is that comparable worth exponents ignore the differences in intrinsic and nonfinancial rewards offered by jobs of "comparable worth" even in the same organization. These differences need much further study rather than assuming away all things but pay, and calling it equity.

Worse yet, comparable worth proponents constantly use misleading comparisons such as "women are paid approximately 70¢ per $1 paid to men."[4] These differences are

---

4. U.S. Bureau of the Census, *Current Population Reports,* Series P-60, No. 174 (Washington, D.C.: U.S. Printing Office, 1992), pp. 112–118.

the result of so many factors (such as type/level of jobs, experience differences, industry differences, personal characteristics, etc.) that one cannot assume the "unexplained" difference is proof of discrimination.

FACTORS AFFECTING PAY DIFFERENCES

Even if only pay is looked at, we believe pay equity proponents drastically overstate the extent of pay differences between men and women. In order to determine the extent of pay differences in similar jobs, one needs to hold constant the effects of factors such as the following.

Type of industry and company: Studies suggest that employees in some jobs can receive as much as a 20 percent increase simply by switching industries in the same geographic area while performing basically similar jobs.[5] Also, firms and industries that have a greater ability to pay their employees should not be compared with those that are less profitable.[6] For example, in Chrysler's efforts to stave off bankruptcy, the company requested and obtained pay concessions from UAW workers.

Size of organization: Research indicates that small companies usually pay less than large organizations.[7] Other research suggests that women "like" smaller companies.[8] Pay differences between genders may result, but are women less satisfied?

Marital Status: Macro economic data shows that the economic effects of marriage and parenthood are significant and often directly opposite in their effects on men and women. For instance, marriage increases a man's participation rate in the labor force compared to single men and reduces a woman's labor force participation rate compared to single women.[9] Also, a married man's hours worked annually increase with the number of children, while a married woman's hours tend to decrease with more children.[10] Thus married men with children work more and earn more than single men, while the reverse is true for women. In fact, women who remain single earn over 93 percent of the income of single men (18 years old and over).[11] In the end, the major difference is *not* between men and women but between married women and everyone else.

5. E. Groshen, "Sources of Wage Dispersion: How Much Do Employers Matter?" Working paper, Harvard University Department of Economics (1985).

6. G. Bahar, M. Jensen, K. Murphy, "Compensation and Incentives: Practice vs. Theory," *Journal of Finance,* 593–616. B. Gerhardt, G. Milkovich, "Organizational Differences in Managerial Compensation and Financial Performance," F. Foulkes, Ed., *Executive Compensation in 1990s* (Boston: Harvard Business School Press, 1990).

7. W. Mellow, "Employer Size and Wages," *Review of Economics and Statistics,* 495–501 (1982). D. Evans, L. Leighton, "Why Do Smaller Firms Pay Less?" *Journal of Human Resources, 26* 3, 562–580 (1989). A. Weiss, H. Landau, "Wages, Hiring Standards and Firm Size," *Journal of Labor Economics, 2,* 4, 477–479 (1984).

8. W. Oi, "Neglected Women and Other Implications of Comparable Worth," *Contemporary Policy Issues,* 4, 2, 21–32 (1986).

9. W. Bowen, T. Finegan, *The Economics of Labor Force Participation* (Princeton: Princeton University Press, 1969).

10. S. Smith, "Estimating Annual Hours of Labor Force Activity," *Monthly Labor Review,* (February, 1983), p. 19.

11. U.S. Bureau of The Census, pp. 124–127.

Age group: Research indicates that the gender wage gap is larger for older than younger workers. At age 20–24 the gap is 89 percent and widens to 65 percent for those 55–64 years of age. Factors accounting for this gap could include a greater career orientation of the post-Civil Rights age group and the fact that women bear the brunt of child care responsibility, resulting in pay erosion over time because of being placed on the "mommy track."[12]

Experience: We have already noted that, on the average, men work more hours per week than women (roughly 6 percent more). Although the gap is narrowed over time, this results in the fact that after 16 years out of school, women still average half as much labor market experience as men.[13] Since women still lag behind men in the total work force experience (especially in older age groups), it is important that age cohort studies take this into account. This can be done by comparing younger age groups (20–30 years old) to reduce the effect or by comparing men and women with the same years of experience. Research shows that the male/female pay differential is reduced by about half when years of experience rather than age cohorts are used.

Education: Currently men and women are graduating from college in nearly equal numbers. The careers women are entering are changing and so too are the college majors chosen by women. This is significant, since a college major is the strongest factor affecting income of college graduates. A major in engineering or accounting brings the highest income for both men and women while a major in education brings the lowest.[14] In 1964, nearly half (42.5 percent) of all bachelors degrees earned by women were in education. By 1981 it declined to 18 percent. Today the fields attracting women are those that were traditionally male-dominated, especially in the professional areas. In 1964, women earned fewer than 5 percent of medical, law, and MBA degrees. In 1984, one-fourth of medical degrees, one-third of law degrees and one-fourth of MBAs were earned by women.

These facts are significant, since research shows clearly that it is *type* of education not *years* of education that matters. Common sense suggests that a degree in the humanities is not equivalent to a degree in electrical engineering. Research studies that use years of education as proxies for all the differences in an individual's skills, abilities, and quality of education received are doomed to reach erroneous conclusions. . . .

DIRECTION FOR FURTHER RESEARCH

The failure of researchers to properly identify the extent of disparity and to recognize the degree of equality actually evidenced in the area of gender compensation results in negative consequences. Through increased awareness, continued education and greater opportunities for women, the magnitude of gender-based employment discrimination is being reduced.

First, the continued use of statistics such as "women are paid 70 cents on the dollar compared to men" fosters an atmosphere of distrust in the workplace. When added to the

---

12. E. Erlich, "The Mommy Track," Business Week, (March 20, 1989) 123–128.

13. V. Fuchs, "Women's Quest for Economic Equality," *Journal of Human Resources, 26,* 3,562–580 (1991).

14. J. Estelle, N. Abraham, J. Conaty, D. To, "College Quality and Future Earnings," Working Paper, SUNY-Stonybrook Department of Economics (1989).

normal secrecy of most organizational compensation systems, the chance for heightened barriers between men and women is increased. It is time for responsible people to discuss the gender-based pay issue on grounds that take into account all relevant reward factors and sound statistical bases. Lacking an understanding of statistics, many women are led to believe that they are underpaid compared to men doing the same job.

Second, researchers need to undertake studies that hold constant factors known to affect compensation besides gender. These factors were discussed above and include types of industries and companies, size of organization, and a variety of personal work-related characteristics such as age, years of work experience, type and extent of education, and marital status. In addition, the effect that intrinsic reward factors have on market forces that may affect pay should be considered and evaluated.

Third, requiring employers to increase the amounts they pay to women will critically reduce the opportunities available to women who are marginal performers.[15] If an employer is compelled to raise the wages of any of its employees, that employer may not be able to afford the same number of employees. The added cost is likely to force the employer to reduce the number of people employed. In determining which employees to discharge, the employer likely will retain the best performers and terminate those whose performance is marginally adequate. Unfortunately, among this group will be women who are most in need of protection against discrimination. In addition, this solution reduces the flexibility of other benefit options. These options include flexible hours and day care programs, which may be valued as compensatory benefits, but employers will lose the incentive to provide women and others benefits which they actually value greatly.

REDUCING GENDER-BASED WAGE DIFFERENCES

In lieu of a pay equity analysis, there are a number of solutions that would help to reduce any actual disparities which remain between the compensation of men and women. First, the education of women in the United States must begin to emphasize career opportunities for women in non-traditional occupations at an early age.[16] Our conventional pigeonholing of women in certain career paths and men in others must be removed in favor of a more balanced approach based on skill and potential rather than preconceived, traditional expectations. Women should receive similar educational preparation and counseling for any occupation and be equally equipped to obtain similar positions as men, allowing them to more effectively exert their market power. Ironically, many of the counselors giving advice in our primary and secondary schools are themselves women.

Second, there is a need to emphasize the societal need as well as the economic benefit to the employer to provide day care, parental leave, flexible hours/shifts, and other non-monetary compensation which allow women to remain in employment positions instead of following the "mommy track" and retreating from their positions at the onset of children. If one accepts the reality that women are equally qualified for almost every position as men, then the inability to retain women upon the birth of their children must be

---

15. L. Fischel, "Comparable Worth and Discrimination in Labor Markets," *U. Chi. L. Rev.,* 53, 891.
16. Hollenbeck et al., 1987, p. 715, 718.

seen as the loss to the workforce of valuable resources. As women (and their spouses) advance to higher decision-making levels in organizations, these benefits are more often being implemented. If employers were to provide support for working mothers, these individuals would not suffer the economic and social pressure felt by many to leave the workforce, and employers would benefit from the increased pool of potential employees. In addition, research has shown that firms which provide this support report strengthened employee loyalty, decreased absenteeism and increased productivity.[17]

Third, women must be increasingly aware of the value of their market power. In the long run, pay equity and comparable worth will not assist the greatest population of female workers, individuals who have merely adequate abilities. Firms may be less willing to take a chance with a potential employee if employers believe that they will have difficulty terminating them because of potential liability. For instance, suppose an employer has the option of hiring a female applicant or a male applicant, both of whose applications evidence adequate abilities. The employer may hesitate in hiring the female applicant because, if she does not work out and is terminated, there is a greater risk of a discrimination action. In addition, the employer could hire the male applicant at a lower wage than his other employees until such time as that individual proves himself, even though he would generally hire all workers at the same wage. On the other hand, the employer does not have this flexibility in hiring the female applicant because the law requires the employer to pay to her the same wage as a male in the position for which he is hiring her.

Wages are determined by the market, not by any ex ante determination of relative merit. As stated earlier, if women act rationally as a group, they would be able to create a supply and demand ratio that would force the wages for women up to meet that lack of supply. Women are forced to make decisions with which, perhaps, men have not traditionally been faced. What must be understood is that, in the past, women were willing to accept low paying positions because, as a general rule, they had husbands who would support them. The ones that did not were forced to take positions solely based on the salaries offered, and may have foregone portions that they truly would have preferred. Now, more women do not have that marital support and may be forced into certain positions due to the salaries offered.

The answer to this market imperfection, therefore, is not only to require employers to provide women wages equal to those men receive (as this would lead to a supply and demand curve that is superficially supported), but also to encourage women to identify and exercise their market power, as do other underrepresented classes.

RELATED WEB SITE

Equal Pay Act: www.law.cornell.edu/uscode/29/206.html

---

17. W. List, "Employers Find Rewards in Employment Equity," *Canadian Business Review,* 35 (Spring, 1989).

A FREE MARKET APPROACH TO COMPARABLE WORTH

LAURA B. PINCUS

The following article supports Posner's criticisms of comparable worth theory. I argue that the market should be able to correct any discrepancy between male and female wages and that, if it does not correct this difference, there are other means by which women (using market power) may be able to argue for increased wages.

The issue of comparable worth exemplifies the imperfection of market effects. The argument made by proponents of comparable worth is that women earn between 59% to 65% of men's earnings because they are systematically segregated into jobs that are traditionally held by women and traditionally underpaid. Champions of comparable worth argue that each job has an inherent value irrespective of the market, that the market thus is imperfect in its valuation of females in these positions, and that the law should create a hierarchy of job positions that are comparable in worth and set wages accordingly. They refuse to accept that an employee's economic worth is determined by his or her salary. Due to this flawed approach, they fail to recognize that incomparable wages derive not from faulty wage-value scales but from the supply and demand curves that are formed.

Proponents argue instead that the supply curve for female employees is skewed in certain positions due to discrimination in the marketplace. Assume that nursing and auto maintenance require approximately the same skill level (I am making no realistic comment, this is only an example). Next assume that female nurses comprise 90% of the nurses in this country and that male auto mechanics comprise 90% of the mechanics in this country. Proponents of a comparable worth system would contend that these percentages (or similar ones) exist due to two related reasons: Women are forced into nursing because this is accepted as a job which "should" be staffed by women, and they are forced out of other positions that are predominantly male because of similar discriminatory employment barriers. As the employers know that the women have no bargaining power because they have no other jobs to go to that will pay more, they do not have to pay women as much as they would have to pay men to lure them to the same positions.

The purpose of this paper is to address the arguments proposed by proponents of a comparable worth system using the analytical approach defined as "objectivism" and to explain why regulation of employment decisions is best left to market forces. Objectivism is a political and social philosophy first developed and cultivated by author and philosopher, Ayn Rand. The essence of objectivism is the recognition that Woman or

Man is an end in herself or himself. One applies this concept through the utilization of an "objective absolute", which regards reality as set by the Reason of Nature. Facts are recognized as independent of one's emotions or influences [i.e. wishing it will happen does not make is so]. No one person decides what is right or wrong, nature does not decide; Man and Woman merely observe and attempt to act in furtherance of what is right. While some may identify this conclusion as moral realism, this is incorrect as morality is subjective while "right" and "wrong", according to Rand, are objective.

As there is one set of absolutes by which all are governed, the distinctions among individuals exist by virtue of characteristics unique to each individual. Objectivism thus encourages every individual to realize his or her own independence, a right derived from his or her nature as a rational being. This does not mean, as most critics believe, that one naturally has the right to do as he or she pleases, no matter the cost to others or to society. What it does mean is that individuals have the right to exist for their own sakes, neither sacrificing their selves to others nor requiring the sacrifice of others to themselves. The individual recognizes all others' right to the same freedom and may not restrict that right.

The most volatile topic of objectivism, and of Rand's writings, is her concept of "egoism" or "rational selfishness." Rand explains that an "egoist" is one who does not sacrifice others but instead stands above the need of using others in any manner.[1] She contends that this is the only form of close association and mutual respect possible between individuals.[2] "Rational selfishness" is a concept that does not embrace a moral evaluation of good or evil but merely acknowledges that selfishness, by definition, is a concern with one's own interests. As long as one is a rational being, he or she will act at all times in his or her own best interest, within the confines of his or her power. This concept is best defined by examining the difference between one's interest in creation and one's interest, instead, in theft. The distinction between the two lies in the object of the pursuit, the object each actor values and each actor's conception of his or her own self-interest. Rand argues that, as there is a set of absolute rules, a rational person motivated by self interest will view creation of the object as a proper goal, as opposed to theft of the object.

Critics view such support of selfishness as detrimental to our fundamental social structure as there will be no charity, no giving of one's self for the benefit of others. However, the critics incorrectly assume that one cannot gain from the activities mentioned, that pure altruism exists and that such altruism is good (in its meaning as "opposed to evil"). These assumptions are not logical conclusions. First, one gives to charity or helps one in need because he or she has a desire to do so. Failure to act upon the desire precludes self-satisfaction. The impetus behind charitable acts is therefore satisfaction of the actor through satisfaction of the desires of the recipient. There is personal gain to the actor. Second, due to the fact that one's motivation for all that he or she does during his or her lifetime is self-interest, altruism, in its most strict sense of selflessness, cannot possibly exist. Third, altruism in this traditional sense is insulting to rational minds as it permits no concept of humans except as "sacrificed animals and profiteers-on-sacrifice, as

---

1. Ayn Rand, *For The New Intellectual* (Random House: New York, 1961), p. 94.
2. Ibid.

victims and parasites" as opposed to a more genuine and realistic portrayal of men and women as self-supporting and self-respecting individuals.[3]

The moral obligation owed by one human being to another is only the obligation of rationality one owes to himself or herself. This rationality comes only through thought. The egoist is the creator, and the selfless man is the one who does not think but instead learns from the thought others. Man and Woman have the power to be independent thinkers, individuals and free, self-interested actors in their lives. Any denial of these freedoms will also deny our society of the whole of its parts.

Society, accordingly, can benefit from the exercise of self-interest on the part of all of its members. The American governmental system encourages self-interested behavior through its political-economic system: laissez-faire capitalism. The American system is one which prescribes that individuals do not act as victims and slayers but instead as equal traders, by free, voluntary exchanges for their mutual benefit.[4] The role of the capitalist government is merely to protect individual rights, requiring a complete separation of the government and the country's economics. This has not, and potentially may not, be accomplished in the United States. Yet, this is the ideal system in which to protect one's rights.

As can be inferred from objectivist theory, it is not the duty of the government to exercise an individual's rights, it is the duty of each individual to assert those rights, and the government only will intervene in situations where one's rights infringe upon another's. In a perfect capitalist society, the market controls all that is produced, the price at which it is produced, and the manner in which it is produced. There should be no outside influences that dictate some conclusion other than that reached by clear market demands. Critics argue that the market may lead to unfair consequences; yet, it is the concept of "unfair" that is the issue, not the market. An actor will act in such a way that he or she will influence the market to some extent; yet, due to the fact that he or she is behaving rationally, these influences must be fair by definition. That which is rational and logical must be fair. Without this certainty, there could be no objective determination of "equity." Therefore, the imperfections of market effects occur solely due to irrational decisions made by players in that market.

In connection with the concept of comparable worth, and applying the fundamental theories of objectivism, the argument that all women are trapped in "female occupational ghettos" appears insupportable. First, there are positions open to women in areas which may be dominated by men. If women cannot obtain those positions, there is already a legal remedy against that type of discrimination through enforcement of Title VII of the Civil Rights Act.

Second, it is not a valid argument that women have been in certain positions for many years and thus should not have to change their jobs merely to obtain a higher paying job. This is the nature of the market. If women act rationally as a group, they might be able to create a supply and demand ratio that would force the wages for nurses up to meet that lack of supply. What these women are contending, however, is that they would like to stay in their present positions and also make the amount of money they feel that they deserve. The employers obviously do not feel threatened that these women will leave if they pay them a low salary, NOT because they know that the women have nowhere else to go, but because this has been their experience.

---

3. Ayn Rand, *The Virtue of Selfishness* (New American Library: New York, 1964), p. xii.
4. "Introducing Objectivism," *The Objectivist Newsletter* (Aug. 1962), p. 35.

What must be realized under such a scenario is that, in the past, women were willing to accept low paying positions because, as a general rule, they had husbands who would support them. The ones that did not were forced to take positions solely based on the salaries offered, and may have foregone positions that they truly would have preferred. Now, more women do not have that marital support and may be forced into certain positions due to the salaries offered. Men must do this also; it is naive to believe that this is not the case.

The answer to this market imperfection, therefore, is not to provide women with higher wages in certain positions which they claim are undervalued. This would lead to a supply and demand curve that is superficially supported, forcing resources into areas where the demand is slight and leaving other areas which are objectively valued by participants in the market without sustenance. Without voluntary exchange by independent judgment there could be no trade, save for that which was dictated. An actor acts in her or his own self interest and is therefore attracted by the full scope of rewards of a particular activity or job. If there is an intrinsic value to each position in employment, given to it my market definition of priority of resource allocation, is there not also an intrinsic value to other things? And therefore, prices, too, must be set. Why are women's shoes more expensive than men's? Women's clothes? Women's soap? If we intend to retain a free market economy, the question of value of services or of goods must be left for the market.

Objectivism does not oppose the reality that women are as valuable as are men in the perfect employment market. While there are irrational actors who play in this market, they will not prevail. The rational profit seekers, acting in their self interest, will realize the potential of women. Females continue to be viewed by some remnants of the historical discriminators as less able to participate. To force a specific treatment of these new entrants without allowing the market to respond on its own will do nothing more than prove to these traditionalists that the problem of discrimination cannot be handled on a rational level of reason. "To deal with men [women] by force is as impractical as to deal with nature by persuasion."[5] All that is necessary to some demonstration of the value of the female worker, of which there has been much, in order to force a market response. I refuse to demean women to the extent that I feel do these critics. Women are capable of asserting their independence and in doing so, they will vie for positions that are traditionally male-dominated, and if refused they will use the law to prevent their discrimination. Their sense of self must be exalted, not the value that they feel our male-dominated society should place on them. There are examples of this everywhere one looks, yet many simply claim that this is not enough and that more should be done to pave their way to independence. Until they begin to act in their own self-interest, and use the market that exists to further their position in this society, they will continue to be treated as if they are not independent, and as if they have no selves.

RELATED WEB SITE

"Comparable Worth: Are Women Worth as Much as Men?"

www.duke.edu/~jrd4/djgula7.htm

---

5. Ayn Rand, *Philosophy: Who Needs It?* (New American Library: New York), p. 32.

EMPLOYEE PRIVACY RIGHTS

FEDERAL SUIT QUESTIONS WORKER PRIVACY RIGHTS

Ben Dobbin

Similar to the controversy surrounding employee drug testing, employee privacy rights also engender philosophical arguments on both sides. Employees have an interest in protecting personal information from unwarranted intrusions, while employers have an interest in determining all relevent data from their employees. From the face of it, these interests don't seem to be in conflict. However, problems arise where the employer believes that certain information is relevant to the job, while the employee does not. Dobbin discusses a federal lawsuit that asks the court to determine those protections to which employees are entitled, as well as how far employers can go in monitoring their staff.

It was a short-lived, middle-distance love affair.

They worked at McDonald's restaurants in towns 60 miles apart. So, to fill the void between their amorous get-togethers, Michael Huffcut and Rose Hasset left messages for each other on their voice mail at work.

Then, everything came unstuck. Their boss allegedly monitored the lovey-dovey whisperings, recorded them and played them back to Huffcut's wife, Lisa. Huffcut was soon fired.

The two-month liaison is long over and the Huffcuts are back together, but a legal question is left hanging: How private is the American workplace?

In a federal lawsuit, Huffcut is seeking $1 million in damages from McDonald's Corp., Harry Harvey III, a fellow McDonald's supervisor who was a family friend, and longtime employer Fred Remillard, who operates 12 McDonald's franchises in western New York. Lisa Huffcut is suing for the same amount.

The couple contend Remillard violated privacy rights guaranteed them by federal law and intentionally inflicted emotional anguish, embarrassment and loss of reputation and income. The case could become the nation's first to test whether conversations recorded in electronic voice-mail boxes are granted the same confidentiality protections as live telephone calls or postal mail.

It also delves into the ill-charted terrain of how far an employer can go in eavesdropping at work for "quality assurance" or other business reasons.

The American Civil Liberties Union argues that covert electronic monitoring generally should be avoided. The U.S. Chamber of Commerce counters that employers should not be legally restrained in trying to ensure that their telephones, computers and other property are used strictly for business.

"When people speak privately, they must be free of uninvited scrutiny and detection," said the couple's lawyer, Raymond M. Schlather. "We've got to build a wall around that kind of private communication."

Robert Ellis Smith, publisher of Privacy Journal, a monthly newsletter based in Providence, R.I., said "employers certainly have the right to listen in on business-related conversations. They probably don't . . . have the right to listen further when it's clearly private and personal."

The defendants have until Monday to reply to the lawsuit. If a trial is ordered, it would probably not begin for another six to 12 months.

"Our answer will speak for itself," said Edward C. Hooks, a lawyer for Remillard. "We're still in the process of reviewing and analyzing."

McDonald's executives declined to comment.

Huffcut, now 41, joined McDonald's out of high school, starting at the counter and working his way up to regional supervisor in Elmira. Hasset was one notch below store manager in a McDonald's in Binghamton when their dalliance turned serious in the fall of 1993.

The lawsuit alleges that Harvey, another of Remillard's area supervisors, intercepted the lovers' intimate messages and transmitted them to Remillard's voice mail. Huffcut says he had been told his voice mail was private.

It claims Harvey, at his boss' direction, played a tape of the messages for Lisa Huffcut in December, 1993. When Huffcut found out, he confronted Remillard about the propriety of his action and was fired. Later, Hasset was promoted to store manager.

Why Lisa Huffcut was told of the affair "is one of the dark mysteries of all this," Schlather said. "From our perspective, it was totally unnecessary."

With counseling, the couple's relationship is now "stronger than ever," he said. The Huffcuts, who were married 14 years ago and have two children, did not respond to a telephone message seeking comment.

Milind Shah, a spokesman for the ACLU's National Task Force on Civil Liberties in the Workplace, said the federal Electronic Communications Privacy Act prohibits employers from using "information gathered from private calls for business reasons, for employment purposes."

That law, which updated the Federal Wiretapping Statute, protects electronic communications and electronic storage of information. Schlather argues that this covers voice mail, although it was not specified.

The ACLU believes employees "should be told how they're going to be monitored, when they're going to be monitored and how that information will be used," Shah said.

"You'd be amazed at how many different ways your privacy can be violated when you walk into the workplace—video cameras, sound bugging, keyboard and e-mail monitoring. According to the law, you effectively check your privacy rights at the door."

Peter J. Eide, manager of human resources for law and policy at the U.S. Chamber of Commerce, said Fourth Amendment privacy rights do not apply in the private-sector workplace.

Employers ought to give new employees notice that phones must be monitored. "But that is as far as we can go," Eide said.

"The employer paid for the phone, paid for the computer, paid for the voice mail. It seems reasonable to say that the employers, since they own the . . . stuff, ought to be able to regulate its use and monitor its use.

"And if the employee is bothered by that, then the employee can buy their own equipment! It's a property rights issue."

STATE V. BONNELL

The defendants/employees moved to suppress evidence that was obtained as a result of warrantless covert surveillance of them in their "break room" during work hours in the post office. The court held that, since the employees had a reasonable expectation of privacy in their break room, the surveillance was inappropriate. Do you think that this is the right result? Do you expect privacy in all areas of your workplace or just certain areas? Should an employer have the right to know what's going on in its workplace, no matter where the activity is taking place?

I. BACKGROUND

The defendants are postal workers employed at the United States Post Office located in downtown Lahaina, on the Island of Maui. All were charged on November 22, 1991, with one or more counts of gambling (a misdemeanor) in violation of Hawaii Revised Statutes (HRS) § 712–1223 (1985). Maielua was also charged with three counts of promoting gambling in the second degree (a misdemeanor) in violation of HRS § 712–1222 (Supp. 1992) and one count of possession of gambling records in the second degree (a misdemeanor) in violation of HRS § 712–1225 (1985).

The defendants' motions to suppress were heard by the district court on February 21, 1992. The State elicited testimony from three witnesses: United States Postal Inspectors Keith Silva (Inspector Silva) and Chuck Rader (Inspector Rader), and MPD Officer Benjamin Nu (Officer Nu). Inspector Silva testified that his supervisor in the United States Postal Service, Paul Smith (Smith), had received two anonymous letters alleging that gambling, involving Sylva and Maielua, was taking place in the downtown Lahaina post office (post office). Smith first brought the letters to Inspector Silva's attention in January 1990. By this time, Inspector Silva had heard similar rumors of gambling activity in the post office. Smith turned the letters over to MPD Sergeant Higgins.

Inspector Silva took no further action until October 1990 when, having been advised by Sergeant Higgins that the MPD was interested in pursuing the matter, he met with Higgins and several other officers of the MPD in order to plan an investigation. Inspector Silva decided for the first time in his four-and-a-half years as a postal inspector to utilize hidden video cameras as a means of conducting the covert surveillance. Inspector Silva, Inspector Rader, and members of the MPD inspected the post office to determine where to place the video cameras. No effort was made to obtain a search warrant authorizing the installation. From this point, Inspector Silva's only continuing involvement in the investigation was to assist periodically in changing the videotapes.

Inspector Rader testified that, in late October and early November 1990, he and "his" technicians installed the video system at the post office. The process consumed four days.

State v. Bonnell, 856 P.2d 1265 (Ha. 1993).

Post office employees were falsely advised that the technicians were installing smoke detectors and a burglar alarm.

The surveillance system's hidden cameras were strictly visual; there was no audio component. A total of four cameras were installed. Two were placed in a position to record events at the public counter area. A third was placed in the ceiling of the supervisor's office. The final camera was placed inside a smoke detector in the break room and focused on the area of the break room table. Once installed, the cameras ran twenty-four hours a day for the duration of the investigation.

The data received from the four cameras was routed to a "switcher," which cycled among the images received from the cameras. The switcher was necessary because there was only one recorder for the surveillance system; the switcher enabled the operator to circumvent any particular camera transmission at any particular time. The switcher and recorder were concealed in a nondescript yellow box atop a vending machine outside the post office. A microwave transmitter broadcasted the cameras' images to a receiver unit as they cycled through the switcher. The transmitter was in constant operation and enabled the officers monitoring the receiver to observe the video images within a radius of one hundred feet of the post office.

Officer Nu testified that he was one of the two MPD police officers assigned to investigate the alleged gambling. Nu and the other officer monitored the video data being transmitted via a receiver and television screen located inside a van that was parked outside the post office. The two police officers recorded activity they deemed to be suspicious. For an entire year—November 13, 1990, through sometime in November 1991—they conducted covert video surveillance five days a week (Mondays through Fridays) during regular work hours, from 7:00 or 7:30 A.M. until 4:30 or 5:00 P.M. Officer Nu periodically replaced full videotapes with new ones at 2:00 or 3:00 in the morning in order to insure the secrecy of the operation. The MPD officers accumulated roughly fifty videotapes containing approximately twelve hundred hours of footage, of which the portions recorded during the regular working day (when the post office was lit) were visible. Officer Nu testified that only a minute fraction of the videotaped conduct reflected any gambling activity.

Following the completion of the State's case, the district court requested an offer of proof from defense counsel as to "what . . . your witnesses [are] going to tell us[.]" Among other things, defense counsel represented that each of the defendants would testify that, during the relevant period, he or she had an actual subjective expectation of privacy in the break room for the following reasons: (1) the break room was not a public place; rather, access was limited to post office employees and authorized visitors; (2) the break room was not visible to the public service area of the post office or from outside the building; (3) "activities" in the break room could not be "overheard" by persons not present; (4) there were no catwalks or galleries within the post office from which the break room could be observed; (5) none of the defendants had ever heard of video surveillance by the police being used as an investigative technique in the post office or anywhere else; (6) a person in the break room could observe anyone approaching and could avoid being inadvertently seen or overheard; (7) there was no provision in the employee manual or collective bargaining agreement addressing or authorizing the use of video surveillance; (8) the break room was used only for breaks from work and to store employees' personal belongings; and (9) the defendants did not believe that they were subject to police video surveillance in that location. . . .

Defense counsel completed his case with the testimony of an elementary school special education assistant, a mechanic employed by the County of Maui, a Maui Fire Department captain, an account clerk employed by the State of Hawaii, and the office manager of the Maui Medical Group. In substance, all of these "community members" testified that, because the break rooms were the only locations in the workplace where employees could relax and discuss private matters, they would not expect to encounter covert police surveillance there. . . .

II. DISCUSSION

The dispositive question presented in this appeal is whether the covert video surveillance of the employee break room of the post office constituted an illegal search within the meaning of the fourth amendment to the United States Constitution[1] and/or article I, section 7 of the Constitution of the State of Hawaii.[2]

Like the fourth amendment to the United States Constitution, article I, section 7 of the Hawaii State Constitution protects people from unreasonable government intrusions into their legitimate expectations of privacy. "And, as 'the ultimate judicial tribunal in this state,' this court has final, unreviewable authority to interpret and enforce the Hawaii Constitution." *Quino*, "'The basic purpose . . . [of these constitutional provisions] is to safeguard the privacy and security of individuals against arbitrary invasions by government officials.'" The constitutional proscription . . . that the person and effects of individuals are considered to be sacrosanct and may not be the object of unreasonable searches . . . draws no distinction in its application between an individual suspected of criminal activity and one who is not." "Thus, article I, section 7 of the Hawaii Constitution was 'designed to protect the individual from arbitrary, oppressive, and harassing conduct on the part of government officials'.

---

1. The fourth amendment to the United States Constitution provides:

    The right of the people to be secure in their persons, houses, papers, and effects, against unreasonable searches and seizures, shall not be violated, and no Warrants shall issue, but upon probable cause, supported by Oath or affirmation, and particularly describing the place to be searched, and the persons or things to be seized.

    U.S. Const. amend. IV. Because we resolve the present appeal on state constitutional grounds, we need not (and do not) decide whether a federal constitutional violation has occurred.

2. Article I, section 7 of the Constitution of the State of Hawaii provides:

    The right of the people to be secure in their persons, houses, papers and effects against unreasonable searches, seizures, *and invasions of privacy* shall not be violated; and no warrants shall issue but upon probable cause, supported by oath or affirmation, and particularly describing the place to be searched and the persons or things to be seized *or the communications sought to be intercepted.*

    Haw. Const. art. I, § 7 (emphasis added). The words "invasions of privacy" were added to article I, section 7 by the 1968 Constitutional Convention. *State v. Roy,* 54 Haw. 513, 518, 510 P.2d 1066, 1069 (1973) (Levinson, J., concurring). The Convention's Standing Committed Report No. 55 explained in relevant part that "[t]he proposed amendment [was] intended to include *protection against indiscriminate wiretapping.* . . ." *Id.* (emphasis added).

It is well settled that an area in which an individual has a reasonable expectation of privacy is protected by article I, section 7 of the Hawaii Constitution and cannot be searched without a warrant. . . .

"'[A] search is not . . . made legal by what it turns up. In law it is good or bad when it starts and does not change character from its success.'" Moreover, "no amount of probable cause can justify a warrantless search or seizure absent 'exigent circumstances'" or some other recognized exception to the warrant requirement.

Given the deliberation with which the videotape surveillance was undertaken and its yearlong duration, there were obviously no special or exigent circumstances that would have justified a warrantless search in this case; it can hardly be said that the MPD was faced with any sort of "emergency." It therefore follows that if the warrantless and covert video surveillance of the employee break room was a search in the constitutional sense, then the videotapes and any other evidence obtained as a result thereof are tainted by the surveillance and must be suppressed as "fruits of the poisonous tree."

A. The Defendants Had a Reasonable Expectation of Privacy Regarding Activities of Employees in the Break Room.

This Court has adopted the following two-part test, borrowed from the concurring opinion of Justice Harlan in *Katz,* to determine when a person's expectation of privacy may be deemed reasonable: "First, one must exhibit an actual, subjective expectation of privacy. Second, that expectation must be one that society would recognize as objectively reasonable." Accordingly, we must ascertain whether the record before us supports the district court's findings and conclusion that the defendants had such reasonable expectations with respect to their activities in the post office break room.

1. The defendants exhibited an actual subjective expectation of privacy.

Regarding the first prong of the two-part test, the State challenges the district court's FOF No. 13, in which it found that "[t]he [d]efendants demonstrated subjective expectations that they would not be covertly viewed and videotaped by government agents in their employee breakroom . . . and that their activities in that area would remain private." The State argues that

> *the existence of an actual subjective expectation is . . . not to be presumed in the absence of some affirmative evidence. . . . Here, the only defendant to testify was . . . Gonsalves. She asserted her own personal expectations of privacy. . . . Accordingly, the [district] court had no evidence upon which to base a factual finding as to actual expectations of privacy on the part of [the other defendants]. . . .*

We believe that the State's argument is without merit.

As noted above, the district court expressly requested that defense counsel make an offer of proof as to "what your witnesses [are] going to tell us?" Defense counsel complied by proffering a detailed list of factual matters, which, if believed, would definitively establish the defendants' actual subjective expectations of privacy regarding the break room and as to which each of the defendants would testify. He then validated his offer of proof through Gonsalves's testimony, at the conclusion of which he renewed his offer—to which the State did not object and which the record confirms that the district court accepted. As a direct result, defense counsel did not adduce any testimony from the other defendants, all of whom were present at the hearing, but rather moved on to other witnesses. . . .

2. The defendants' expectation of privacy is one that society would recognize as objectively reasonable. . . .

"[A] person has a 'halo' of privacy wherever he goes and can invoke a protectable right to privacy wherever he may legitimately be and reasonably expect freedom from governmental intrusion."

> *the test is . . . one of reasonable expectations of privacy. Every individual has expectations of privacy with regard to his* person *wherever he may go, be it a public park or a private place; yet this is not so with regard to* places *where an individual happens to be. The place must be of such a character as to give rise reasonably to these expectations of privacy.*

In assessing the reasonableness of an expectation of privacy, we consider, *inter alia,* "the nature of the area involved, the precautions taken to insure privacy," and the "type and character of [the] governmental invasion" employed.

A person may have a subjective expectation of privacy that is objectively reasonable in some area of his or her workplace. Such an expectation is not defeated merely because the area is accessible to others. This is precisely because what a person " 'seeks to preserve as private, even in an area accessible to the public, may be constitutionally protected.' "

> *Privacy does not require solitude. . . . [E]ven "private" business offices are often subject to the legitimate visits of coworkers, supervisors, and the public, without defeating the expectation of privacy unless the office is "so open to fellow employees or the public that no expectation of privacy is reasonable."*

In the present case, the employee break room was neither a public place nor subject to public view or hearing. Only postal employees and invited guests were allowed in it. Accordingly, the defendants were in a position to regulate their conduct as a function of present company. Moreover, when seated in the break room, the defendants could see anyone approaching and could avoid being surprised by an untrusted intruder. . . .

Whatever the general privacy interest the defendants may or may not have had in the break room, they had an actual and objectively reasonable "expectation of privacy against being videotaped in it."[3]

RELATED WEB SITES

ACLU on electronic monitoring:

www.aclu.org/library/pbr2.html

"Can Voicemail, Email, Phonecalls be Monitored by your Boss?"

www.uniontrib.com/reports/privacy/950703privacy.html

---

3. Persons may create temporary zones of privacy within which they may not reasonably be videotaped, . . . even when that zone is [in] a place they do not own or normally control, and in which they might not be able reasonably to challenge a search at some other time or by some other means. *Taketa,* 923 F.2d at 677 (citation omitted).

SOROKA V. DAYTON HUDSON CORP.

Dayton-Hudson, a department store, had a policy of administering psychological screening test to applicants. Plaintiffs were applicants for a store security officer positions who were asked to undergo these tests. They claimed that, because the questions on the test referred to their sexual orientation and religious beliefs, they were justified in refusing to take the test. The court addresses their claim that the test constituted an invasion of their privacy.

I. FACTS

Respondent Dayton Hudson Corporation owns and operates Target Stores throughout California and the United States.[1] Job applicants for store security officer (SSO) positions must, as a condition of employment, take a psychological test that Target calls the "Psychscreen." An SSO's main function is to observe, apprehend and arrest suspected shoplifters. An SSO is not armed, but carries handcuffs and may use force against a suspect in self-defense. Target views good judgment and emotional stability as important SSO job skills. It intends the Psychscreen to screen out SSO applicants who are emotionally unstable, who may put customers or employees in jeopardy, or who will not take direction and follow Target procedures. . . .

The test includes questions about an applicant's religious attitudes, such as: "[¶] 67. I feel sure that there is only one true religion. . . . [¶] 201. I have no patience with people who believe there is only one true religion. . . . [¶] 477. My soul sometimes leaves my body. . . . [¶] 483. A minister can cure disease by praying and putting his hand on your head. . . . [¶]486. Everything is turning out just like the prophets of the Bible said it would. . . . [¶]505. I go to church almost every week. [¶] 506. I believe in the second coming of Christ. . . . [¶] 516. I believe in a life hereafter. . . . [¶] 578. I am very religious (more than most people). . . . [¶] 580. I believe my sins are unpardonable. . . . [¶] 606. I believe there is a God. . . . [¶] 688. I believe there is a Devil and a Hell in afterlife."

The test includes questions that might reveal an applicant's sexual orientation, such as: "[¶] 137. I wish I were not bothered by thoughts about sex. . . . [¶] 290. I have never been in trouble because of my sex behavior. . . . [¶] 339. I have been in trouble one or more times because of my sex behavior. . . . [¶] 466. My sex life is satisfactory. . . . [¶] 492. I am very strongly attracted by members of my own sex. . . . [¶] 496. I have often wished I were a girl. (Or if you are a girl) I have never been sorry that I am a girl. . . . [¶] 525. I have never indulged in any unusual sex practices. . . . [¶] 558. I am worried

---

Soroka v. Dayton Hudson Corp., 1 Cal. Rptr. 2d 77 (Cal. App. 1st Dist. 1991).

1. For convenience, the opinion refers to Dayton Hudson Corporation, doing business as Target Stores, as "Target."

about sex matters. . . . [¶] 592. I like to talk about sex. . . . [¶] 640. Many of my dreams are about sex matters."[2]

An SSO's completed test is scored by the consulting psychologist firm of Martin-McAllister. The firm interprets test responses and rates the applicant on five traits: emotional stability, interpersonal style, addiction potential, dependability and reliability, and socialization—i.e., a tendency to follow established rules. Martin-McAllister sends a form to Target rating the applicant on these five traits and recommending whether to hire the applicant. Hiring decisions are made on the basis of these recommendations, although the recommendations may be overridden. Target does not receive any responses to specific questions. It has never conducted a formal validation study of the Psychscreen, but before it implemented the test, Target tested 17 or 18 of its more successful SSO's.

Appellants Sibi Soroka, Susan Urry and William d'Arcangelo were applicants for SSO positions when they took the Psychscreen. All three were upset by the nature of the Psychscreen questions. Soroka was hired by Target. Urry—a Mormon—and d'Arcangelo were not hired. In August 1989, Soroka filed a charge that use of the Psychscreen discriminated on the basis of race, sex, religion and physical handicap with the Department of Fair Employment and Housing. . . .

A. Constitutional Claim

First, Soroka argues that he is likely to prevail at trial on his constitutional right to privacy claim. The parties dispute the standard to be applied to determine whether Target's violation of Soroka's privacy was justified. In order to understand the various legal issues underlying this contention, a review of the basic legal concepts that guide us is in order.

1. The Right to Privacy

The California Constitution explicitly protects our right to privacy. Article I, section 1 provides: "All people are by nature free and independent and have inalienable rights. Among these are enjoying and defending life and liberty, acquiring, possessing, and protecting property, and pursuing and obtaining safety, happiness, and privacy." "By this provision, California accords privacy the constitutional status of an inalienable right, on a par with defending life and possessing property." Before this constitutional amendment was enacted, California courts had found a state and federal constitutional right to privacy even though such a right was not enumerated in either constitution, and had consistently given a broad reading to the right to privacy. Thus, the elevation of the right to privacy to constitutional stature was intended to expand, not contract, privacy rights.

Target concedes that the Psychscreen constitutes an intrusion on the privacy rights of the applicants, although it characterizes this intrusion as a limited one. However, even the constitutional right to privacy does not prohibit *all* incursion into individual privacy. The parties agree that a violation of the right to privacy may be justified, but disagree about the standard to be used to make this determination. At trial, Target persuaded the court to apply a reasonableness standard because Soroka was an applicant, rather than a Target

---

2. Soroka challenges many different types of questions on appeal. However, we do not find it necessary to consider questions other than those relating to religious beliefs and sexual orientation.

employee. On appeal, Soroka and the ACLU contend that Target must show more than reasonableness—that it must demonstrate a compelling interest—to justify its use of the Psychscreen. . . .

4. Application of Law

Target concedes that the Psychscreen intrudes on the privacy interests of its job applicants. Having carefully considered *Wilkinson,* we find its reasoning unpersuasive. As it is inconsistent with both the legislative history of article I, section 1 and the case law interpreting that provision, we decline to follow it. Under the legislative history and case law, Target's intrusion into the privacy rights of its SSO applicants must be justified by a compelling interest to withstand constitutional scrutiny. Thus, the trial court abused its discretion by committing an error of law—applying the reasonableness test, rather than the compelling interest test.[3]

While Target unquestionably has an interest in employing emotionally stable persons to be SSO's, testing applicants about their religious beliefs and sexual orientation does not further this interest. To justify the invasion of privacy resulting from use of the Psychscreen, Target must demonstrate a compelling interest and must establish that the test serves a job-related purpose. In its opposition to Soroka's motion for preliminary injunction, Target made no showing that a person's religious beliefs or sexual orientation have any bearing on the emotional stability or on the ability to perform an SSO's job responsibilities. It did no more than to make generalized claims about the Psychscreen's relationship to emotional fitness and to assert that it has seen an overall improvement in SSO quality and performance since it implemented the Psychscreen. This is not sufficient to constitute a compelling interest, nor does it satisfy the nexus requirement. Therefore, Target's inquiry into the religious beliefs and sexual orientation of SSO applicants unjustifiably violates the state constitutional right to privacy.[4] Soroka has established that he is likely to prevail on the merits of his constitutional claims.

---

3. We note that the trial court, faced with a single appellate case setting out the standard to be applied to a privacy violation alleged by a job applicant, did what it had to do—it applied that case. Trial courts must accept the law as declared by appellate courts. It is not a trial court's function to attempt to overrule decisions of a higher court. (*Auto Equity Sales, Inc. v. Superior Court* (1962) 57 Cal.2d 450, 455, 20 Cal.Rptr. 321, 369 P.2d 937.) However, as an appellate court, we are not compelled to apply the law as interpreted by a court of equivalent jurisdiction if we find that court's reasoning unpersuasive.

4. In light of this ruling, we need not address the question of whether the means chosen to achieve a compelling interest must be the least intrusive means. (See, e.g., *Luck v. Southern Pacific Transportation Co., supra,* 218 Cal. App.3d at p. 24, fn. 15, 267 Cal.Rptr. 618.)

EMPLOYEE LOYALTY
WHISTLEBLOWING

Do you feel that you have a right to take a pen or two home from work because you give so much to your boss that goes unrewarded? Of 1,423 individuals surveyed, About Work found that 49 percent felt that it was acceptable to take home staplers from work, 14 percent felt that pens were appropriate, and 13 percent felt that it was all right to take home computer disks for personal use (http://www.aboutwork.com/bon/poll_ad.cgi.). Does your firm owe you anything in exchange for your performance, devotion, and loyalty? That is, does your firm owe you anything in addition to your salary? Do you feel a loyalty to the firm? What might serve to increase or decrease the amount of loyalty you feel?

WHISTLEBLOWING AND TRUST: SOME LESSONS FROM THE ADM SCANDAL
DARYL KOEHN

"Whistleblowing" occurs when an employee informs the public of inappropriate activities going on inside the organization. More limited definitions of the term include the requirement that the whistleblowing relate to an activity requested of the whistleblower, such as when an individual is asked to lie on federal reporting documents to protect the firm. Philosopher Norman Bowie contends that whistleblowing is not justified unless the following characteristics are present:

1. *It is done based on an appropriate moral motive.*
2. *The individual has exhausted all internal channels for dissent.*
3. *The individual's belief regarding the inappropriate conduct is based on evidence that would persuade a reasonable person.*
4. *The individual has carefully analyzed the situation to determine the serious nature of the violation, the immediacy of the violation, and the specificity of the violation.*
5. *The individual's action is commensurate with responsibility for avoinding and/or exposing moral violations.*

"Whistleblowing and Trust: Some Lessons from the ADM Scandal," by Daryl Koehn. Reprinted by permission of the author.
(http://condor.depaul.edu/ethics/beat.html)

*6. The individual's action has some chance of success, exposing
and/or avoinding the moral violation (Norman Bowie, Business
Ethics [Englewood Cliffs, NJ: Prentice Hall, 1982], pp. 142–43).*

*"No servant can serve two masters. He will either hate one and love
the other, or be devoted to one and despise the other (Luke 16: 13).
Koehn evaluates the concept of trust as it applies to the Archer Daniels
Midland whistleblowing case. In doing so, she highlights the responsibilities of both the whistleblower and the firm. Interestingly enough,
she concludes that there are times when whistleblowing is not ethically
correct. Do you agree with her conclusion? Is she persuasive?*

The 1980's witnessed a flurry of articles regarding the ethics of whistleblowing. These
articles tended to focus on three issues: (1) the definition of whistleblowing; (2) whether
and when it was permissible to violate one's obligations of loyalty to colleagues or one's
profession/corporation; and (3) whether a threat to the public interest actually obligates
someone with knowledge of this threat to make this knowledge public.[1] These same issues have surfaced in recent discussions of the act of whistleblowing by Mark Whitacre
at Archer Daniels Midland. While I do not think these three issues are morally irrelevant
to a discussion of whistleblowing, I am troubled by the fact that the entire discussion to
date has focused on the issue of duty. In this commentary, I want to focus less on the
question of duty and more on the question of personal, corporate, and public trust: Does
whistleblowing foster or destroy moral trust? What makes whistleblowers and the companies for whom they work worthy of employee and public trust?

I shall use the alleged events at ADM to explore these questions. The reader should
keep in mind that I am not writing a case history of whistleblowing at ADM. At the time
of this writing, we have yet to hear much of the company's side of the story nor do we
know exactly what evidence Whitacre has to support his allegation that the company engaged in price-fixing with their competitors. What matters for my purposes here is not
that these events did occur but that they could have occurred and they raise serious and
interesting questions for corporate, individual and public behavior.

PART ONE: WHISTLEBLOWING
AND ITS EFFECTS ON TRUST

It will be helpful to begin with a working definition of a whistleblower. Following Sissela
Bok, I shall define whistleblowers as persons who "sound an alarm from within the very
organization in which they work, aiming to spotlight neglect or abuses that threaten the
public interest."[2] Several features of this definition are relevant to thinking about trust.
First, the whistleblower claims to be acting in the public interest. He or she tries to occupy the moral highground by calling attention to some matter the whistleblower thinks
the public will be, or should be, concerned about. I say "concerned about" rather than
simply "interested in" because the whistleblower claims to be more than a mere tattler. If

I were to disclose the religious preferences of my boss, we would not think such disclosure constituted whistleblowing because it is hard to see what public interest is involved. Given the very real risks of being fired, demoted, ostracized, or attacked by those the whistleblower is accusing of negligence or abuse, the whistleblowers generally must think of themselves as on something akin to a mission. They try to portray themselves as acting on behalf of an interest higher than their own—the public interest.

I dwell on this point to emphasize that the whistleblower has made some assumptions as to what constitutes the public interest. He may have erred in his assessment of the nature of the public interest. Or he may have misevaluated his "facts." The facts may be unsound, or they may be sound yet irrelevant to the public interest. If we take trust as the trustor's belief that he or she is the recipient of the good will of the trusted party, the whistleblower can be thought of as portraying himself as a trustworthy person who has acted in good will toward the public and who merits the public's trust. Mark Whitacre, for example, portrayed himself as the white knight of the consumer, a consumer whom ADM had allegedly declared to be the enemy.[3] However, if Whitacre's accusations result in the demise of ADM and the loss of a major supplier of consumer goods, we may well wonder whether Whitacre has acted in fact in the public's interest. Moreover, Whitacre himself arguably has something of a skewed view of public interest since he seems perfectly willing to engage in predatory, monopolistic pricing.[4] According to his own account, he balked at his company's pricing policy only when his colleagues tried to engage in price-fixing.[5] Given that the customer is hurt by monopolistic pricing as well as price-fixing, his whistleblowing at this late date may be less an attempt to aid the customer and the public than to save his own skin. More generally, if and when a whistleblower's motives are mixed, we have some reason to wonder, on the one hand, whether he is trustworthy and, on the other hand, to perhaps be more sympathetic to a company who charges that the whistleblower has betrayed it and the public as well.

Second, the whistleblower believes that there is a substantial audience who will attend to her disclosures. If an employee calls up the press and discloses that the CEO wears blue shirts to work every day, his announcement is likely to be greeted by the reporter with a stifled yawn, if not a burst of profanity. To say that the whistleblower's disclosure is in the public interest just is to say that it has the makings of a good story. The tale, therefore, will likely attract the press and maybe the regulatory authorities as well. It can quickly become sensationalized as people begin to speculate on the extent and magnitude of the alleged corporate misconduct. Furthermore, the regulatory authorities may begin an elaborate investigation on the theory that any abuse known by one individual may just be the tip of the iceberg. The Federal authorities, for example, are not merely subpoenaing many of ADM's records; they have also asked for the records of many of ADM's competitors.[6] There is a very real danger of a witchhunt, for as Bok reminds us, secret police almost always rely on informers and have a history of widening the charges against those accused.[7] Such reflections suggest that it is incumbent upon a whistleblower who truly wants to merit the public's trust to try to explore issues internally before going public with her accusations.

There are, of course, difficulties associated with going public internally. I shall say more about these shortly. My point here is that whistleblowing may harm public trust in our institutions, rather than restore it, if whistleblowing creates a whirlwind of suspicion and the impression that corruption is everywhere. Fellow employees of whistleblowers may be justifiably irritated at a colleague who makes accusations to the press without ever running these same charges by them or without seeking their interpretation of actions and events within the corporation. It may be unfair for the corporation to try to dismiss a whistleblower as a troublemaker with few social skills. On the other hand, the whistleblower may very well be someone who is overly suspicious or inclined to make wild accusations without verifying her facts. Moreover, if the whistleblower does not try to work internally first to try to resolve what she perceives as a problem, it is difficult to see how she can claim to be trying to right the problem. It is striking that Whitacre, by his own account, had heard allegations of price-fixing for many years and had simply ignored them,[8] treating them as though they were someone else's problem. But if he really cared for the company and for the public interest, why did he not investigate these charges when he first heard them? Given that he was in line to be president of ADM, he surely should have worried about this problem and taken steps to address a problem that he was bound to inherit. Conversely, one wonders why he would have wanted to be president of a company that was in his judgment engaged in dastardly deeds. At a minimum, it seems as though he should have interested himself many years ago in the question of whether and why ADM had a history of tolerating price-fixing.

Another way of putting the point is as follows: Whistleblowers are part and parcel of the corporate culture on which they blow the whistle. They are often rather senior because it is those issuing orders who usually have the most control over and the most knowledge about what is occurring within the corporation. At the point of public disclosure, the whistleblower assigns responsibility for the abuse to someone else and thereby distances himself from any responsibility. But matters are rarely so clean. If one has worked many years for a company, taken a salary from them, followed their policies, then one is arguably complicitous in the practices of that corporation. The traditional discussion of whistleblowing pits the individual's loyalty to the company against his loyalty to himself. But this formulation presupposes that that self is a private self, totally independent of the company. I am saying that the self is a company self as well. And while it may be convenient for the whistleblower to talk as though it is him against the big bad company, such talk is suspect to the extent that the whistleblower has supported that company. Blowing the whistle may not increase public trust to the extent the public is rightly suspicious of the whistleblower's own history within the corporation.

Third, the whistleblower is levelling an accusation of neglect or abuse at particular persons within the corporation. These accusations are not pleasant for the accused whose lives may be permanently disrupted by what may turn out to be false charges. At a minimum, the lives of the accused will be unsettled for a substantial amount of time as the press picks up the story and as investigations run their course. While no one should be above the law, we also should not be insensitive to the need for due process. We should also remember that passions almost always run high around whistleblowers' accusations because the whistleblower's charge applies to present activities of a corporation or profession.[9] No one blows the whistle or shows much interest in past abuses with few present effects or in remote, unlikely future events. The alleged danger is present and person's emotions are engaged, which is all the more reason for exercising extreme caution in making charges and in evaluating them.

The above observations suggest that corporate employees and leaders rightly are concerned about the effect of whistleblowing not merely on corporate morale but on the ability of employees to work together in relative harmony. This harmony becomes close to impossible when the atmosphere is a highly charged one of mutual suspicion. Note that I am not saying that an employee has an overriding loyalty of duty to the group for which he works. It may well be, as Ronald Duska has argued, that the corporation is not the kind of group to which one can be loyal.[10] In any case, there is no prima facie duty to be loyal to any group. A profession such as medicine is worth serving not because it is a group but because its end—the health of individuals—is a genuine good. The end, not the group per se, commands group members' loyalty. We do not, for example, say that agents have a prima facie duty to the Ku Klux Klan or the mafia. The person who leaves such a group does not override a prima facie duty. Rather, there never was a duty to be a part of a group engaged in unethical behavior.

My point then is not that the employee acts wrongly because whistleblowing is disloyal. The wrongness in the whistleblowing consists instead in acting to destroy the workplace atmosphere if and when this destruction could have been avoided by adopting a less accusatory stance or by working within the corporation. Whistleblowing may destroy trust. And trust within a corporation is good when the trust is a reasoned trust, born of open and probing discussions with one's peers regarding matters of joint concern. Whistleblowing should be evaluated in light of its consequences for this reasoned trust, not in light of its effects on irrational loyalty or its relation to a non-existent prima facie duty of group loyalty.

PART TWO: RESPONSIBILITIES OF BOTH WHISTLEBLOWER AND CORPORATION

This last comment raises what I take to be the central moral issue connected with whistleblowing: What can both whistleblower and corporation do to foster reasoned trust and to avoid a situation in which employees feel they have to go outside the company to get their concerns addressed?

Given the very real dangers associated with whistleblowing and the all-too-human propensities toward self-righteousness and misinterpretation, it is clear that the would-be whistleblower and corporation alike should make every effort to discuss perceived abuses and negligence before it gets to the point where the whistleblower thinks a public accusation must be made. The corporation thus has a responsibility to provide a regular forum for free and open discussion of possible abuses. Participants should have equal and reciprocal rights to question one another, to bring evidence, etc. They should not be penalized in any way for participation in this forum. It is striking that ADM had no such forum. In fact, communication was so bad within the company that the CEO's own son apparently did not know until after the fact that the father had called in the FBI to help investigate whether production at ADM was being sabotaged.[11]

Conversely, the whistleblower must be willing to come forward and be identified. It is close to impossible for the accused to mount a defense or even seek clarification when the accuser is anonymous. This requirement to publicly participate increases the odds that the would-be whistleblower will doublecheck her facts before going public. Discussion will also tend to dispel employees' perception that corruption is everywhere. In fact, regular discussion should deflate a good deal of the anger and anxiety regarding corporate problems. Employees will come to see that, yes, their corporation has problems and oversights but, yes, their corporation is routinely and professionally addressing these difficulties. Participation in such a forum will require a good deal of courage on the part of employees and a good bit of restraint on the part of a corporate hierarchy tempted to retaliate against any and all perceived threats.

Second, it is incumbent on corporate leadership to examine the tasks they impose on their employees. An employee can only be morally required to do that which is possible. If the employee is placed in an untenable position, then he will feel anxious, trapped, and may be driven to try to escape from this position by taking his predicament public in an effort to gain public sympathy and support. Whitacre, for example, apparently was expected to do cut-rate pricing with a view to grabbing a large market share while at the same time showing either minimal losses or a profit.[12] Price-fixing becomes a temptation in a corporate environment with these unreasonable expectations, and reasoned trust is not given much of a chance to flourish. For their part, the employees must critically examine the position they are being asked to assume. It is curious that Whitacre professed unease about recruiting competitors for their expertise when he himself seems to have been recruited from a German competitor precisely for his expertise![13] Uncritical naivete on the part of employees becomes morally culpable to the extent that they fail to raise objections that would promote in-house discussion of possible unethical practices.

Third, a company that desires the reasoned trust of its employees must grant the employees access to information about the company's practices. When a whistleblower accuses a company of malpractice, all employees of the corporation feel slightly tainted and anxious. They may feel betrayed not just by the whistleblower but also by the company whom they perceive as having hid relevant information from them. Secrecy encourages corporate paranoia. One of the best ways to combat it is to run as open a corporation as possible. The more access employees have, the more the corporation can legitimately hold them accountable for their actions and the more responsibility the employees will feel for actions they have known about and have had a chance to discuss. If there is genuine access to information about corporate practices, employees have a responsibility to seek out and to consider the implications of this information. It becomes less legitimate for them to bury their heads in the sand and then at some late date cry "Foul!" And this is how it should be in corporations where all parties are genuinely committed to acting well.

Fourth, and finally, all members of the corporation have a responsibility to critically examine their actions, even if they have been taught to perform these acts and been rewarded for doing so. A recent study comparing Japanese and American managers' attitudes towards ethics showed that the American managers were far more focussed on marketing than their foreign competitors and tended to think of immorality as occurring largely within marketing. This focus is problematic in several ways. It encourages managers to overlook ways in which they are treating their employees badly (e.g., by imposing unreasonable job requirements upon them). Furthermore, to the extent that American managers see only particular marketing practices as immoral, they fail to consider whether marketing itself may not be in some ways immoral. For example, does the idea of "targeting" specific groups of people for specific products wind up instrumentalizing the customer? If this customer is little more than a means to selling this product, it is not much of a leap to begin to think (as ADM allegedly did) of the customer as an enemy whose demand for low prices is keeping the company from attaining maximal profit.[14] More thought needs to be given to the nature of the core practices of business and less attention devoted to the bribery, price-fixing, etc., which may merely be symptoms of a sick practice. Unless and until these practices are well-scrutinized by the people who are engaged in them and who have the most knowledge about them, we should expect to continue to have a series of nasty abuses springing up and surprising us.

The corporate atmosphere also should be scrutinized. ADM's anti-bureaucratic rhetoric is a case in point. Whitacre mentions it several times and indicates that ADM has historically prided itself on its ability to get things done.[15] However, what gets dismissed as bureaucracy is often the system of checks and balances within the firm. Anti-bureaucratic rhetoric may encourage, at worst, an attitude of lawlessness and at best, a "can-do" approach which may, as in the case of Whitacre, breed enthusiasm but not do much for thoughtfulness.

CONCLUSION

While whistleblowing sometimes may be the only way to call attention to serious abuses by professions or corporations, whistleblowing is not unambiguously ethically good. It is perhaps best seen as an option of last recourse. Rather than concentrating on when whistleblowing is moral, our time would be better spent thinking about how to improve corporate and professional environments so that employees and clients will not be driven to adopt this strategy.

NOTES

1. Ronald Duska, "Whistleblowing and Employee Loyalty," in Tom L. Beauchamp and Norman E. Bowie, *Ethical Theory and Business* (Englewood Cliffs, NJ: Prentice Hall, 1993), pp. 312–316.
2. Sissela Bok, "Whistleblowing and Professional Responsibility," in Beauchamp, op.cit.
3. Mark Whitacre as told to Ronald Henkoff, "My Life as a Corporate Mole for the FBI" in *Fortune,* Sept. 4, 1995, pp. 56–62.
4. Ibid.
5. Ibid. Ronald Henkoff comments that Whitacre's preferred approach to pricing "sounds a lot like predatory pricing," in Henkoff, "So Who Is This Mark Whitacre, and Why Is He Saying These Bad Things about ADM," in *Fortune,* Sept. 4, 1995, pp. 64–67.
6. See "Suicide Hurts Government's ADM Case," Monday, August 14, 1995 at clari.news.crime.murders on the Worldwide Web.
7. Bok, op.cit.
8. Whitacre. op.cit.
9. Bok also discusses the fact that the charges apply to present wrongdoing. Bok, op.cit.
10. Duska, op.cit.
11. Whitacre, op.cit.
12. Ibid.
13. Ibid.
14. Ibid.
15. Ibid.

THE CASE OF GEORGE AND THE MILITARY AIRCRAFT

M. C. McFarland

George knows that a plane that passed all of its tests might still be defective; his employer plans to go forward with flight-testing. George struggles between his conflicting duties—he feels obligated to his employer but he also feels a duty to protect public safety. How would you resolve this dilemma?

The past several months, George, an electrical engineer working for an aerospace contractor, has been the quality control manager on a project to develop a computerized control system for a new military aircraft. Early simulations of the software for the control system showed that, under certain conditions, instabilities would arise that would cause the plane to crash. The software was subsequently patched to eliminate the specific problems uncovered by the tests. After the repairs were made, the system passed all of the required simulation tests.

George is convinced, however, that those problems were symptomatic of a fundamental design flaw that could only be eliminated by an extensive redesign of the system. Yet, when he brought his concern to his superiors, they assured him that the problems had been resolved, as shown by the tests. Anyway, to reevaluate and possibly redesign the system would introduce delays that would cause the company to miss the delivery date specified in the contract, and that would be very costly.

Now, there's a great deal of pressure on George to sign off on the system and allow it to be flight-tested. It has even been hinted that, if he persists in delaying release of the system, the responsibility will be taken away from him and given to someone who is more compliant.

What make the situation so difficult for George is that he must choose between conflicting duties: loyalty to self, family, employer, and superiors versus the obligation to tell the truth and protect others from harm.

"The Case of George and the Military Aircraft" in "Urgency of ethical standards intensifies in computer community," by M.C. McFarland. Portions reprinted, with permission, from *IEEE Computer,* volume 23, pp. 77–81 (1990).

DISCRIMINATION AND AFFIRMATIVE ACTION: LEGISLATED ETHICS?

CARTOON
PETE MUELLER

Some people argue that we have gone too far as a society in terms of what is "P.C.," or politically correct. Cartoonist Pete Mueller offers his opinion of the situation in this drawing.

RELATED WEB SITE

Title VII: www.law.cornell.edu/uscode/42/ch21.html

SOME ISSUES IN EMPLOYMENT DISCRIMINATION ON GROUNDS OF RACE, SEX, AND AGE

RICHARD POSNER

Seventh Circuit Court Judge and lecturer at the University of Chicago Richard Posner offers his market theory as applied to discrimination. Posner addresses three issues: why unions have long refused to admit black workers, comparable worth, and mandatory retirement. Posner is known for his logical, well-reasoned analyses, though they are not always in line with society's preferred result. Are you persuaded by the judge's arguments? If you were asked to debate him on these issues, what would be your arguments or criticisms of his reasoning?

. . . Racial discrimination in employment is a part of a larger issue—that of the causes and cures of racial discrimination. . . . Here we shall discuss one specialized topic in racial discrimination and also employment discrimination against women and the aged.

Many unions long refused to admit black workers. Why? Economics suggests an answer. As we have seen, unions seek to raise the wage rate above the competitive level; and to the extent they succeed, an excess demand for union jobs is created. There are various ways in which this excess demand could be eliminated. One would be by auctioning off union membership. The successful bidders would be those willing to pay an entrance fee equal to the present value of the difference between the union wage scale and the wages in their next best employment. This would be the method of rationing used if unions were simply firms enjoying monopoly power over labor—firms that bought labor at the competitive wage and resold it to employers at a monopoly wage. But unions are not firms; they are representatives (however imperfect) of the workers, and they will not adopt a rationing method that would deny the union membership any net wage gains from membership. The problem with nonmonetary rationing methods, however, is that they induce applicants to expend real resources. If admission to the union is based on work skills, for example, applicants will incur real costs to obtain the requisite skills, and the competition in obtaining skills may result in eliminating the expected monopoly profits of union membership . . . What makes criteria involving race or some other relatively immutable status (such as being the son of a union member) attractive is that they do not invite heavy expenditures on qualifying; the costs of changing one's race or parents are prohibitive.

The central economic question relating to employment discrimination against women is explaining the persistently higher average wage of men compared to women (women's wages per hour are on average about 60 percent of men's wages).[1] Irrational or exploitive discrimination is one possibility. Another is that male wages include a compensatory wage premium for the dirty, disagreeable, and strenuous jobs that men dominate presumably because their aversion to such work is less than women's. Another (these are not mutually exclusive possibilities, of course) is differences in investments in market-related human capital (earning capacity). If a woman allocates a substantial part of her working life to household production, including child care, she will obtain a substantially lower return on her market human capital than a man planning to devote much less time to household production, and she will therefore invest less in that human capital. Since earnings are in part a return on one's human capital investments (including education), women's earnings will be lower than men's.[2] In part this will show up in the choice of occupations: Women will be attracted to occupations that don't require much human capital. Of course the amount of time women are devoting to household production is declining for reasons explained in Chapter 5, so we can expect the wage gap to shrink if the economic model is correct.

Comparable worth refers to the movement, now being pressed in courts and legislatures, for raising the wage level of job classifications filled primarily by women (e.g., secretarial work) to that of predominantly male job classifications (e.g., truck driving).[3] The proposal is to determine the actual worth of the different jobs, and if the worth is the same equalize the wages (by raising the lower wage level) regardless of the market conditions. The effort to divorce worth from market value is troubling to an economist. If a truck driver is paid more than a secretary, even though the secretary works just as long hours and has as good an education, the economist's inclination will be to assume that the market is compensating a skill that is in shorter supply, or is offsetting a disamenity, rather than making arbitrary distinctions based on fast-vanishing stereotypes. The economist would therefore assume that if measurements of comparable worth failed to pick up the different worths of the two types of job, this was because of the crudeness of the measuring devices rather than the absence of real differences.

1. With certain adjustments the real percentage is estimated for 1974 at 66 percent, in Improvements in the Quality of Life: Estimates of Possibilities in the United States, 1974–1983, at 194 (Nestor E. Terleckyj ed. 1975).
2. See Jacob Mincer & Haim Ofek, Interrupted Work Careers: Depreciation and Restoration of Human Capital, 17 J. Human Resources 3 (1982); Jacob Mincer & Solomon W. Polachek, Family Investments in Human Capital: Earnings of Women, 82 J. Pol. Econ. S76 (1974); Trends in Women's Work, Education, and Family Building, 3 J. Labor Econ. S1 (1985).
3. See June O'Neill, Comparable Worth (Urban Institute and U.S. Commn. on Civil Rights, unpublished, Jan. 29, 1985); June O'Neill & Hal Sider, The Pay Gap and Occupational Segregation: Implications for Comparable Worth (Urban Institute and U.S. Commn. on Civil Rights, unpublished, Dec. 29, 1984); Comparable Worth: Issue for the 80's (U.S. Commn. on Civil Rights 1984); Comparable Worth: An Analysis and Recommendations (U.S. Commn. on Civil Rights 1985).

In any event, consider what the consequences will be if comparable worth is implemented. If wages in jobs now dominated by women are raised, the number of jobs available will shrink, as employers seek to substitute other, and now cheaper, inputs (e.g., word processors for typists), and as customers substitute other products for those made by firms whose wage bills and hence prices have risen because of comparable worth. At the same time, men will start competing more for those jobs, lured by the higher wages. So female employment in a job classification that had been (for whatever reason) congenial to women may (why not will?) drop. Some displaced women will find new employment in the predominantly male occupations such as truck driving—perhaps replacing men who have become secretaries! But these women may not be happier in their new jobs; after all, there is nothing to stop a woman today from becoming a truck driver if that is what she wants to be. Finally, under comparable worth the incentives of women to invest in human capital usable in the traditional men's jobs will drop as the relative wages in those jobs drop, so that in the end occupational sex segregation may not be greatly affected.

Federal law forbids public or private employers to force their employees to retire before the age of 70, with the exception of a few job classifications such as airline pilot. The economist is naturally troubled by the government's intervening in the decision of a private employer to use age as a basis for terminating employment either on a retail or wholesale (mandatory retirement age) basis. The reply is that the use of age is arbitrary. Although this is true, it does not provide a good economic reason for government intervention in the employment market. The use of a single, readily determinable characteristic such as age as the basis for an employment decision economizes on the costs of information. True, there is diseconomy as well as economy: Sometimes a more competent older worker will be replaced by a less competent younger one. But that does not make the employer's use of age as a proxy for competence, crude as the proxy is, inefficient. The employer's objective is to minimize the sum of the costs of suboptimal retention decisions resulting from lack of individualized assessment of workers' abilities and the information costs of making such assessments.[4] If the sum is minimized by having a mandatory retirement age, the employer will have a mandatory retirement age; otherwise he will not. There is no externality calling for government intervention.

---

4. This decisional problem is strikingly like that of deciding how much procedure to provide to litigants.

AFFIRMING
AFFIRMATIVE ACTION
JESSE L. JACKSON

Rev. Jesse Jackson, president and founder of the Rainbow/PUSH Coalition, first became involved in the civil rights movement in the mid-1960s when he worked with Martin Luther King, Jr., and the Southern Christian Leadership Conference. Since then, he has focused his energy on advocating for minority rights and the rights of the disadvantaged. In the following press release, Jackson articulates his perspective on controversial issues surrounding affirmative action. The release is a response to arguments put forth by the Republican majority elected to Congress in 1994, which advocated abolishing affirmative action programs. He believes that critics of affirmative action have capitalized on the fears of the American public regarding the competition of the global marketplace. Do you agree with Jackson's discussion of myths versus facts? Given that you are reading this several years after Jackson's statistics were compiled, do you notice any recent changes since the material was released in 1995? Are you convinced that affirmative action is still mandated by public fears and biased attitudes, or has this country come to a place and time where such programs are no longer necessary?

There is great tension in our country today. There are economic fears and insecurities that are real and must be corrected. But there are the hostile voices of fear and demagoguery using the tactic of scapegoating, turning American against American, neighbor against neighbor.

SCAPEGOATING THE DISADVANTAGED

We have a smiling face on our economy—the stock market has hit its all-time high, Wall Street is booming, the top 20% of all Americans are doing very well. But there is beneath that face a nauseous stomach, the underbelly of our economy, that is not as fortunate. Our rank-and-file workers are feeling insecure and with good reason. For the past two years, they've been working longer and making less at less stable jobs. America once exported products; we now export jobs and plants.

Workers feel the pain of the globalization of the economy, the impact of competing with cheaper, less secure, more vulnerable workers. When you combine this with the

"Affirming Affirmative Action," by Jesse L. Jackson, from a press release to National Press Club, March 1, 1995.

impact of "reinventing" or reducing government, exporting jobs, downsizing corporations, ending the Cold War (there is nobody to fight), closing military bases, plants, and family farms, while increasing the military budget, it is not surprising that we, as a nation, are feeling anxious.

Nike, Reebok, LA Gear, Westinghouse, Smith Corona, and many of our other manufacturing companies have moved offshore. RCA, once symbolized by the dog listening to its master's voice, is an image which no longer applies. Today, the master speaks a language the dog cannot understand.

In the face of this profound structural crisis in our national economy, we need leadership to provide a clear analysis and constructive solutions to appease our anxieties. Instead, women and people of color are being used as scapegoats and objects of vilification.

While we witness congressional attacks on Aid to Families with Dependent Children, Congress blindly embraces Aid for Dependent Corporations. There is an attack on welfare but tiptoeing around S&L thieves, buccaneer bankers, a trillion and one-half dollar military budget to defend Europe, Japan, and South Korea at a time when they are able to share the burden of their own defense.

Instead of identifying these real problems and finding real solutions, many are perpetrating falsehoods and spreading myths blaming the weakest in our society for the excesses of the few. The new Republican congressional majority is using affirmative action to divide our nation for political gain.

MYTH VERSUS FACT

Affirmative Action is under attack. The Republicans want to rip it. The President wants to review it. We must look at America before Affirmative Action and since Affirmative Action. We must look at the remaining gap in wages between men and women, whites and people of color. We must determine its necessity by data, not by anecdotes.

It is a myth that white males are being hurt and discriminated against because of Affirmative Action Programs. White males are 33% of the population, but

- 80% of Tenured Professors

- 80% of the U.S. House of Representatives

- 90% of the U.S. Senate

- 92% of the Forbes 400

- 97% of School Superintendents

- 99.9% of Professional Athletic Team Owners; and

- 100% of U.S. Presidents

Since the inception of this nation, white males were given preferential or deferential treatment—for the right to vote, the right to own land, to apply for loans and institutions of higher education. In the late 1800's white males were given a million acres of oil and soil-rich land under the Homestead Act as a bonus to go west and replace Native Americans. As current statistics show, such preferential treatment carries over to 1995.

It is a myth that Affirmative Action creates preferences for women and people of color. After 250 years of slavery, 100 years of apartheid, and 40 years of discrimination—history, of course, is unbroken continuity—we cannot burn the books, we cannot scorch the Earth. This unbroken record of race and sex discrimination has warranted a conservative remedy— Affirmative Action. Those who have been locked out need the law to protect them from the "tyranny of the majority." That is the genius of our Constitution, with its checks and balances and balance of power. We need not be race neutral, but race inclusive. We need not be color and gender blind, but color- and gender-caring. The Good Samaritan was not blind to a damaged man of another race, another religion, and another language; he was caring.

The conservative remedy of affirmative action seeks to repair the effects of past and *present* discrimination. It creates equal opportunities for people who have been historically and currently discriminated against. Affirmative Action does not mean "quotas"— in point of fact, it is *illegal* for employers to prefer *unqualified* applicants over qualified ones. What Affirmative Action mandates is the use of goals and timetables to diversify our workforce and universities.

It is a myth that Affirmative Action has hurt people of color, women, or the nation. Affirmative Action has benefitted our entire nation. The first beneficiaries are U.S. corporations. We have the strongest, most diversified workforce in the world. We urge the President to convene corporate leaders and let them assume the burden and the obligation to make a statement sharing their experience of the advantages of having a diversified, educated workforce. Affirmative Action has benefitted white women and their families as a result of two-wage earners in their households. It has benefitted blacks, browns, Native Americans, Asians, veterans, and the disabled. It has turned tax consumers into taxpayers and revenue-generators. It has created a new middle class. It has diversified our workforce and has made us a better nation. I literally went to jail to open up building trades unions so that we might become carpenters and brickmasons and glazers and have the right to work with a skill, and earn a livable wage.

REVIEW MUST BE BASED ON DATA, NOT MYTH

As the President pursues his review it must be based on data, not myth. We urge him to convene the Chair of the EEOC [Equal Employment Opportunity Commission], a rather invisible position, the Chair of the Office of Contract Compliance, and indeed the Chair of the U.S. Civil Rights Commission. And let's have a review, not a retreat. A review to renew a commitment to fairness and to complete unfinished business.

The President is calling for a review. When he does his review, he will discover that Department of Labor statistics illustrate clear disparities in the representation of women and people of color in the American workforce as compared to white men.

In the 1994 labor market, while women represented 51.2% of the U.S. adult population, African Americans 12.4%, and Latinos 9.5%.

- 22% of all doctors were women, 4% African American, 5% Latino

- 24% of all lawyers were women, 3% African American, 3% Latino

- 42% of all professors were women, 5% African American, 2% Latino

- 16% of all architects were women, 1% African American, 3% Latino

- 31% of all scientists were women, 4% African American, 1% Latino

- 8% of all engineers were women, 4% African American, 3% Latino

In May 1994, the National Rainbow Coalition [a civil rights organization] released a study of the National Broadcast Corporation (NBC) which highlights a pattern of racial and gender discrimination in hiring practices in its New York division. ABC and CBS do not vary very much. We found:

- Out of 645 employees of the News Division, 354 were white males, 261 were white females (a total of 96%), 8 were black males, 8 black females, 7 Latino females, 1 Latino male, 3 Asian males and 3 Asian females, 0 Native Americans.

- Of the key employee positions, 142 were white males, 121 were white females, 3 black males, 2 black females, 1 Latino male, 1 Latino female, 0 Asians, and 0 Native Americans.

- Out of 386 employees in NBC's East Coast Entertainment Division, 237 were white males, 130 white females, 6 black males, 3 black females, 5 Latino males, 1 Latino female, 4 Asian males, 0 Asian females and 0 Native Americans.

Patterns of present-day discrimination—of being locked out. This is not a gene factor. This is a pattern based upon cultural, race, and sex bias.

AFFIRMATIVE ACTION IS STILL NEEDED

We cannot fall prey to the inane notion that discrimination is an evil of the past. It is today a very painful reality. As the figures above demonstrate, representation of women and people of color in the American workforce has improved, but is hardly sufficient. We still have a long way to go. When Affirmative Action was being enforced, gains were made, but during Reagan-Bush years, many of the gains were lost. One need look no further than the well-documented disparity in pay between white men, women, and people of color:

- In 1975, median income as a *percentage of white men's salaries* was 74% for African American men, 72% for Latino men, 58% for white women, 55% for African American women, and 49% for Latino women.

- At the height of the Reagan-Bush years in 1985, median income for African American men had dropped to 70%, for Latino men to 68%, rose for white women to 63%, and nominally increased to 57% for African American women and 52% for Latino women.

- In 1993, the figures reflect an increase for African American men to 74%, the rate for Latino men fell to 64%, 70% for white women, and 53% for African American women.

When the President reviews college and professional athletics, he will find great disparities in the positions of power between women, people of color, and white men:

- When the Chargers and the Super Bowl champion 49ers met on Super Bowl Sunday in 1994, there were no people of color or women in positions of power. Yet over 60% of those on the field were African Americans. But beyond the playing field, from coaches to athletic directors, to owners, the same situation is evident in NCAA [National Collegiate Athletic Association] athletic programs. We have effectively gone from picking cotton balls to picking basketballs, baseballs, and footballs. Upward mobility is severely limited.

When the President reviews institutions of higher education, he will find an attack on scholarships and, in effect, the globalization of American doctoral degrees according to a NAFEO (National Association For Equal Opportunity) report:

- Today African Americans comprise only 9.9% of the 12 million students enrollment in two- and four-year undergraduate institutions.

- In 1993, of the 6,496 doctorates awarded in physical sciences only 41 (0.6%) were awarded to African Americans, 89 (1.4%) were awarded to Latinos, and 2,818 (43.3%) were awarded to foreign students (whose countries we subsidize).

- Of all of the 39,754 doctorates awarded in 1993, African Americans received 1,106 (2.8%), Latinos received 834 (2.1%), and foreign students received 12,173 (30.6%).

Lest we forget, forms of preferences have traditionally been granted in higher education on non-racial grounds. For example, we have not yet heard the call to deny children of alumnae special consideration in the admissions process.

When the President reviews government contracting practices, he will find empirical proof that when controls are eliminated, we witness a return to pre-Affirmative Action underrepresentation in our economy. Since the *Croson* decision, minority contracting in the city of Richmond, Virginia—a city of about 70% African American—went from 35% to 1%—reverting back to its pre-Affirmative Action levels.

When the President reviews lending practices, he will find that access to capital and credit is denied to women and people of color because lending decisions are so arbitrary and subjective. Unless there is a reinvestment plan with goals, targets and timetables, the traditionally locked out will never gain access to capital. The contract is useless without the capital. Women and minorities have often had to joint venture with larger, white male firms in order to obtain the necessary capital.

A RENEWED COMMITMENT

Upon completion of his review, we urge the President to renew his commitment to Affirmative Action and enforce Affirmative Action laws as a way of expanding our economy and making us bigger and better and stronger. We hope that he will make the Equal Employment Opportunity Commission and the Office of Contract Compliance and Civil Rights Commission visible agencies and forces for good. The falsely accused need protection, and hope, and opportunity, not scapegoating, and review, and divisiveness, and undue blame.

HIRING/FIRING, SEXISM/RACISM ETHICS CASES

Denis Collins's Students

In his ethics courses, Professor Denis Collins asks his students to describe ethical dilemmas they have encountered; they submitted the following items in connection with human resources decisions. Do they seem realistic to you? How would you respond in each case?

- You are the regional manager for a restaurant chain that serves wines. Restaurants in your area employ servers who are below the legal drinking age of 21. A manager in one of your stores has been fined by the police for allowing an 18-year-old to taste a new wine that customers are likely to ask about. When you threaten to fire him he tells you that this occurs in all of your restaurants and that his wife is pregnant. What would you do?

- You are brought in to reorganize the transportation department for a tourist firm. The restructuring gives you the flexibility to fire some old employees, hire new ones, and change existing job contracts so they are more favorable to the firm. One of the current employees is undergoing kidney dialysis treatment every other day. He has no formal education, minimum work skills beyond driving a bus, and is the sole wage earner in his family. You contact his doctor who certifies that if you reduce his workload by one-third and keep track of his medical condition he will not be endangering the life of any customers. What would you do?

- You are the manager for a company that has recently received a tremendous amount of nationwide positive publicity because the owner decided to give full pay for 30 days and medical benefits for 90 days to the 2,400 employees who lost their jobs due to a fire that severely damaged the plant. After thirty days the owner offers another 30 days of full pay to the unemployed workers. One month later he considers making the offer again. This policy has already cost the firm $10 million at a time when you have no sales and the former employees could be collecting unemployment insurance. What would you recommend?

- You are the owner of a funky business that has an international reputation for social responsibility. In need of a CEO, the firm creates a publicity stunt offering the job to the best 100-word essay under the title "Yo, I'm Your CEO." 20,000 applications pour in, none of them the person you need. Then a CEO search firm says they have

---

just the person you are looking for, but he doesn't want to mislead the public by writing and winning the 100-word essay. What would you do?

• Due to your influential contacts, you are brought in as a new partner to a very successful accounting firm. You realize that the new hires are the best and brightest. They also work 80 hours a week, are highly stressed-out, and only 1% make it to partner. As a result, most do top quality work for 3 years, get paid very well, make contacts, and obtain very good jobs with other accounting firms. One of the older partners asks if you think this very successful work culture should stay the way that it is, or be changed. What would you recommend?

• You are a young woman employed as a furniture salesperson immediately out of college. The District Manager who you are assigned to makes a comment about you being too young for the job and then tells you to look more risque when you conduct sales calls. A short time later he threatens to fire you for not fitting in with the company image. What would you do?

• You manage a manufacturing facility that has a night-shift in a nation with no anti-discrimination laws. Your plant is located thirty minutes outside of a city. The road to the facility crosses a very unsafe and dangerous neighborhood. A few months ago a manager had his car stolen at gunpoint when he stopped for gas at night. The most qualified person for a night-shift management opening is a woman. Is it socially responsible or irresponsible to hire her?

• You are hired and enter a company's management training program. You notice that high profile volunteer tasks are given to white-male friends of the training program coordinator. At the end of the training session the higher level jobs are assigned to the white-males. You consider telling the training manager's boss about this blatant racism/sexism, but the boss is a known bigot. What should you so?

• You manage a local movie theater that is part of a national chain that has a "no-dating" policy for employees because it employs many teenagers. In addition, the company has a "promotion within" policy and dating among employees could result in a major conflict of interest in the future. Because many of the employees socialize with one another after work hours, you have ignored the no-dating policy. Then your assistant manager informs you that she has fallen madly in love with one of the ticket-takers. You can continue to ignore the no-dating policy, fire your assistant manager and/or ticket-taker or transfer the less valuable employee (the ticket-taker). What would you do?

Chapter 9

ETHICS AND SALES/ MARKETING
The Value of Truth?

488

In a survey of 1,076 marketing professionals asking for the most difficult ethical issues they face in their work, respondents cited the following: bribery (gifts, questionable payments), fairness (conflicts of interest, manipulation), honesty (lying, misrepresentation), price issues (differential or predatory pricing), products (safety, infringement), personnel, confidentiality, advertising (puffing versus misrepresentation), manipulation of data and purchasing (reciprocity in supplier selection).[1]

One response to many of these issues is that marketing has such a bad reputation in certain areas that consumers expect deception and prepare themselves against it. For instance, no reasonable person would believe absolutely everything we were told by a used-car salesperson. For that reason, many of the statements uttered by car salespeople are considered to be mere "puffing" rather than true misrepresentation—a reasonable person would not be misled.

Consider the following advertising techniques and whether they are unethical. Some marketing material uses vague claims such as "fights odors," "best at cleaning tough kitchen stains," "tastes good like a cigarette should." What about claims that offer no comparison, such as "more body and shine to your hair," "life is better with. . . ."? Advertisers may also claim that a product has a quality that every product of its type contains. Is this misleading? Some products are said to contain special ingredients about which no one really knows anything. Have you ever considered what benefit a breath freshener product has if it contains a "sparkling drop of retsyn?" Would a reasonable person be misled by any of these claims, and is that the appropriate standard for the ethical content of these claims?

The issue of the "battling claims," where similarly believable sources make competing claims about products or services is best exemplified by the materials on The Body Shop in this section. A reputable magazine first printed what was considered an "expose" on claims of the socially and environmentally conscious Body Shop store chain. The Body Shop responded, as did the critics. The Body Shop produced a social audit of the firm and the critics produced their own. In reading these materials, it becomes impossible to ascertain where the truth actually exists.

Marketing Tobacco   485,000,000,000 cigarettes. That's a lot of zeros. That is the number of cigarettes Americans consumed during 1994. That doesn't include the amount of tobacco used in cigars, cigarillos, pipes, self-rolled, chewing tobacco, and snuff. U.S. expenditures for tobacco products during that same year totaled $47.1 billion, paying for the salaries of almost 700,000 workers.[2] In the meantime, the United States has a $50 billion medical bill for tobacco-related illnesses, and 153,000 people died from lung cancer.[3]

Is it ethical for companies to continue to market a product which has been shown to be hazardous to one's health? Is the sale of tobacco any different from the sale of guns? Beyond any discussion of the ethics of marketing cigarettes in general lies the

---

1. Lawrence Chonko and Shelby Hunt, "Ethics and Marketing Management: An Empirical Investigation," *Journal of Business Research* 13 (1985), pp. 339–59.
2. The Tobacco Institute, *Tobacco Industry Profile: 1995* (1995).
3. American Cancer Society, "Cancer Facts and Figures—1994."

controversy surrounding the marketing of tobacco products to underage smokers. The federal government is seeking to further regulate the sale of tobacco products. If a manufacturer complies with regulation in this area, do you consider it ethical? Consider the lobbying efforts by tobacco companies seeking to influence the regulatory environment surrounding tobacco sales. Thomas Lauria, spokesperson for the Tobacco Institute, the industry's lobbying group, claims that the anti-smoking lobbyists go too far—"We are only strong because 700,000 people [are employed in the tobacco industry] and 50 million customers choose to buy these products. That's more people than voted for Bill Clinton."[4]

The Body Shop Controversy   Many readers will be familiar with The Body Shop's trademark green stores selling all sorts of bath and cosmetic items for men and women. You might not be so familiar with the controversy surrounding The Body Shop's claims of environmentally and socially friendly business tactics. After Jon Entine, a newspaper journalist, first uncovered and revealed some startling details disputing The Body Shop's claims in *Business Ethics* magazine, Gordon Roddick, chairman of the Body Shop and husband of Body Shop owner Anita Roddick, responded by sending a letter to all *Business Ethics* subscribers defending The Body Shop and chastising both the magazine and Entine for shoddy reporting. His letter is reproduced below, along with additional information from both sides.

The interesting part about this controversy is that one might expect the dispute to concern facts that can be verified—does The Body Shop misrepresent its activities or not? However, in reading the audits and the contentions below, you may find yourself persuaded by one argument, only to be dissuaded by the next piece.

Notwithstanding this introduction, be wary of concern for either side. As mentioned in an informal review of this text by Kevin Gibson, an ethics professor at Marquette University:

> *I'm not sure if this is a personal bias, but this might not be as significant a case as it first appears. The Body Shop and Ben & Jerry's are the acknowledged paragon cases of selling social responsibility. The emperors turned out to have less fancy clothes than promised, and so the market did a reality check resulting in (somewhat) lower sales. Entine's article is marketplace information resulting in a market correction. My problem in both these cases is that they are selling luxury items to folks with disposable incomes, and so many of the problems with caveat emptor disappear. To elaborate: "buyer beware" has its problems when we are dealing with a market that has little relative power and little access to information. The Body Shop and Ben & Jerry's lied (or "spun" the truth) and this has a chilling effect on the market, but still those who were hurt are not homeless as a result. I find my students to be very cynical about marketing anyway, and most sympathetic when powerless people are ripped off. However, they have no great problem with exploiting the rich or ignorant rich.[5]*

4. Christina Kent, "Daunting Hurdles Ahead: Tobacco Industry Declares War on FDA Regulation," American Medical News 38 (Sept. 11, 1995), p. 1(4).
5. Kevin Gibson, review comments to Irwin Co., October 5, 1996, p. 3.

We can all agree that the generic purpose of marketing and advertising efforts is to sell more of the specific product or service discussed. The question in marketing ethics is how far one may go in her or his efforts before those efforts become unethical.

SHORT HYPOTHETICAL CASE

You publish a successful teen magazine. Magazines are, at best, barely profitable, and you rely on attracting and keeping major advertisers. Over the years, you have bowed to pressure from tobacco company advertisers and have not run antismoking articles in your magazines. Now, however, you are increasingly concerned that tobacco ads are targeting teens, and preteens are more likely to smoke or to use smokeless tobacco. At the same time, major tobacco companies have merged with food companies. In the past, these food and tobacco companies have accounted for a large part of your advertising sales. Do you continue to omit antitobacco articles?

Source: Hypotheticals were written by Catherine Haselden and are included in her manuscript "The Ethics Game."

MARKETING ETHICS

MARKETING ETHICS: SOME DIMENSIONS OF THE CHALLENGE

PAUL F. CAMENISCH

Camenisch contends that marketing should enhance the information and the freedom of decision of the potential customer. Marketers suggest that the market drives out those that violate this goal, but Camenisch is unconvinced. Instead, he believes that marketers are tempted to appeal to our baser, darker side. Notwithstanding these influences, Camenisch advocates a marketing environment of self-regulation guided by a vision of advertising and business in the service of society and by the marketer's sense of personal integrity, rather than through external controls. Given the admitted tension between our integrity and our "darker" side, do you agree that this is the best solution?

The tension between the imperatives of economic survival in the competitive marketplace and ethics is a very real one for many individuals and corporations. Any such tensions can be magnified and complicated in marketing since the marketing firm must not only survive in its own market, but must, as one factor in that survival, deal with the question of what it must do, or what its clients *think* it must do to ensure the clients' survival in their marketplaces. Practitioners must vividly portray these complex and difficult situations for academic ethicists from time to time, lest the ethical analysis and recommendations offered by the latter lose all touch with the harsh realities business people actually face.

At the same time, the integrity of the ethicists' own profession requires that they keep pressing practitioners not to relax the tension they feel by abandoning ethics and capitulating to the demands of the marketplace. Confronting practitioners with hard questions about such matters is not, or certainly need not be, the attack of hostile outsiders determined to expose the soft underbelly of business to a critical public. It can also be the challenge of the loyalist who believes that businesspersons are often sufficiently sensitive to such issues and that business can be sufficiently creative to find ways to be simultaneously successful and ethical.

Paul F. Camenisch, "Marketing Ethics: Some Dimensions of the Challenge." Reprinted by permission of Kluwer Academic Publishers from the *Journal of Business Ethics*, v. 10 (1992).

One way to press such a concern about ethics in business, and specifically in marketing is by holding up the issue of the social responsibility of business, which I understand to refer to the doing of societal good unrelated or minimally related to the business activity in view. It is in some ways a kind of "add-on" ethic for business. Following Milton Friedman many business persons dismiss such social responsibility as an inappropriate add-on for business people and organizations operating in the competitive marketplace. They often maintain not that business does no social good, but that business that does its business well is already performing a number of positive services to society and its members through the creation of jobs, the paying of taxes, and the generating of beneficial and/or desired products and services. Additional social responsibility is simply seen as excessive and inappropriate. While I think the issue of corporate social responsibility cannot be dismissed this easily, I will here focus on another dimension of the business-society relationship by raising the question of the ethics of business activity itself, the question of the ethics which is in some sense internal to that activity. In our current case, that means the ethic that is internal to marketing. Here we deal not with some add-on to business but with an element integral to business activity.

One can begin thinking about an ethic internal to a given kind of activity by asking what the goal or purpose of that activity is. By this I mean not the goals or purposes of the various parties engaged in that activity; those are almost unlimited in their variety. I mean rather the purpose or goal of the activity itself, specifically its *societal* purpose, the reason that society permits, encourages, even facilitates such activity.

The goals of marketing have been variously stated and I will not here conclusively answer the question of which is its definite goal. The goal perhaps most often assumed and supported by commonsense observation of the business enterprise is that marketing's goal is to increase the company's profits by increasing the sales of its product. Some students of business and marketing, either because they fear that a focus on profit will give too much of a toehold to the critic, or because they know a company's profits depend on many factors other than marketing, prefer to see the goal of marketing as creating a market, or creating a customer. But to this amateur observer such ideas do not really change the thrust of the first answer. They only buffer it by putting another layer between the activity and its ultimate goal. Why does a company want to create a market except to increase its sales? And why create a customer except to buy its products or services?

However put, such answers may be more or less adequate when marketing is viewed from the side of the marketer. But marketing is a societal enterprise. It occurs in society, with society's permission and support, and purportedly, in part for society's benefit. Presumably it is therefore to some extent subject to the moral regulations and expectations society and potential customers attach to it.

But what is marketing's purpose when seen from other perspectives, specifically those of the larger society and of the customer? These two perspectives are not identical. But given that all of us are customers in much of our lives, this perspective represents the larger society better than does the perspective of businesspersons who represent only a portion of the population.

To speak of the goal of marketing from this perspective we must go beyond the simple idea of moving the product or increasing sales, since these as such serve the larger society only indirectly at best. One might attempt to bring together the goals of marketing as seen by business and as seen by the customer or the larger society by suggesting that the goal of responsible marketing is to inform the customer about the product so that sales will increase. This goal of informing the potential customer can be brought one step closer to specifically moral considerations by drawing on philosopher Richard DeGeorge and others who have suggested that transactions are more likely to be morally defensible if both parties enter it freely and fully informed. Assuming that marketing and marketers want to be part of morally defensible transactions, one might then say that viewed societally, the goal of marketing should be to increase the likelihood and frequency of free and informed transactions in the marketplace. Or, to put it negatively, marketing ought not to decrease the likelihood of such free and informed market transactions.

The information requirement is easy enough to state, even if determining what constitutes being fully informed is not. Unfortunately we are also familiar with the various ways it can be compromised. Blatant untruths would seem to be relatively rare in current advertising. But partial truths, the misleading embellishing of the facts (the fixed focus camera becomes "focus free," the unsized bathrobe becomes "one-size-fits-all"), propositions intentionally implied to be true but not actually stated, still abound. Here we meet a variety of unresolved and perhaps unresolvable matters: How much hard information do customers want and deserve? How much of the relevant information are marketers obligated to provide and how much should potential customers be left to seek out on their own? In planning advertising so as not to mislead the public, are marketers to envision the average citizen, however that elusive will 'o the wisp is defined, or the especially vulnerable or gullible citizen—the child, the aged, the simple-minded? How much of the policing of advertising should be taken on by the government and how much left up to the industry.

But in spite of these and related questions, the most complex part of the problem of morally defensible transactions probably has to do with the question of freedom. Clear, honest information relevant to the goods or services being marketed is almost certain to enhance the potential customer's freedom in the transaction, or at least it will not diminish that freedom. But except for the highly technical information aimed at limited markets such as stereophiles, and price advertising of grocery specials and automobile deals, very little of marketing has to do with hard information about the product. Any student of marketing knows that much of contemporary marketing consists of techniques which can be used to "hook" the potential customer on the product in a way that potentially diminishes clear, rational decision making about the product or service being offered. These of course include enhancing the symbolic value of products by associating them with celebrities, including them in sexually provocative advertising campaigns, linking them with deeply held values and commitments, or presenting them as solutions to widely shared insecurities and fears. This is not to say that all puffery is inappropriate. But it is to say that the lines between legitimate puffery, distortion, deception and the psychological "hooking" of the potential customer are not easy to draw, and that the more the interaction is cluttered by irrelevant "information," the more likely the seller is trying to prevent a fully informed and free decision by the customer.

Of course some will dismiss this goal of marketing as the recommendation of a well-meaning but idealistic academician. But before doing that, one should consult that almost perennial final appeal of the defender of the marketplace, Adam Smith. The market he was willing to defend is one in which there is no fraud or coercion and in which all participants are adequately informed about the transaction. Of course we will not always agree on what constitutes adequate information. But here we are more interested in the principle of adequate information for the participant than we are in the details of definition or the mechanics of enforcement.

But perhaps most decisive for the argument being made here is the point made by many marketers that the marketplace is not turned into a moral reality only by moral considerations brought to it from the outside—the moral convictions of the various participants, or the societal guidelines established for its conduct. Rather, the marketplace is itself already a moral as well as an economic mechanism even prior to any externally imposed moral requirements. There are moral constraints built into the very dynamics through which marketing works. For example, contemporary marketing practitioners often argue that dishonest marketing will be unsuccessful marketing, that the market will weed out those who violate the common morality. I am not entirely convinced that that is true, at least in the short run. Products that conspicuously and almost immediately fail to perform have been rejected by the public in spite of aggressive and clever marketing campaigns. But that is a very limited category of test cases. Increasingly we deal more in very complex products and services whose performance, especially long-run performance, and potential negative impacts are not easily assessed by the layperson. Just what sort of performance level, length of service, and maintenance and repair costs are reasonable for such products as modern automobiles, or the electronic products which now flood our lives? What are the truly significant potential harms of the countless chemical products from pharmaceuticals to fertilizers we now scatter freely through our lives and our environment? These are much more complex judgments than whether the miracle knife advertised on television can slice both tin cans and ripe tomatoes in that order with equal aplomb, or whether the new copier really does produce X copies per minute with greater clarity than the old machine. The variety and complexity of products most of us now purchase in the consumer society mean that virtually no unassisted layperson can make truly informed rational decisions about such purchases. The question then is whether marketing will be an ally or an obstacle in our making such decisions. Where it is the latter it is clearly morally indefensible on the criteria suggested here. But even if marketing is merely neutral in terms of its impact on the freedom and informed character of the transaction, it is not clear how one would justify the increase it generates in the ultimate cost of the product.

There is another set of concerns which are an element in the issues raised above, but which also have a life of their own in the discussion of advertising ethics. These concerns arise in relation to advertising that critics see as appealing to our baser, darker, less admirable side—our penchant towards violence, exploitative sex, and the desire to control and manipulate other persons. The usual defense of such advertising is that marketers here are simply offering us what we want, whether in the product or service offered, or in the marketing which sells it. Such a defense is backed up by the claim that they have discovered what we want both by experience and by marketing research through surveys and focus groups. But given the more than 100 billion dollars poured annually into advertising and the shaping of the consumer's view of the world, it should hardly surprise us that advertisers find in the minds and psyches of many consumers what they have been helping put there for decades. It is no trick to pull a rabbit from a hat as long as one chooses the hat into which one has previously put the rabbit. Nor are advertisers cleared of responsibility for such advertising even if this baser side is rooted in something other than prior marketing efforts, which it no doubt is. The question still remains whether marketing and its clients should not only exploit that side of us for the sake of sales, but legitimate it and give it respectable, public standing by making it seem to be not only a natural and universal, but even the dominant dimension of the human self.

Of course if these questions are to be answered and the answers then enforced by agencies outside the marketing enterprise, we encounter the very complex and troubling issues of censorship in a free society. It is much to be preferred for everyone's sake that marketers and their clients raise these questions in a serious manner that can, where indicated, lead to self-regulation. This is most likely to happen if they look at these issues not just from the perspective of business, but as responsible citizens of a society in which they, their children, families and friends must also joint with the rest of us in building and sustaining liveable, humane communities.

This raises the issue, met by many occupational and professional groups, of how we relate our work or our professional roles to our other roles in the society—our roles as responsible citizens, as members of communities responsible for the raising and moral formation of children, as members of religious communities and other voluntary associations. Do these other dimensions of our selves figure into our reflections on appropriate marketplace activity? If so, then economic survival, whether individual or corporate, cannot be the only, or even the last and decisive consideration. Or do we recommend a compartmentalization, a walling off of these various roles from each other that denies the marketer a consistency, an integrity among the various things she is and does? Little need be said here about the individual and societal pathologies that result from such an approach. The only viable alternative seems to be a proper vision of the world which subordinates marketing to business, and business to the goals and purposes of the larger society, so that the tensions among these and the other spheres of one's life are reduced to a minimum and one can fulfill one's various roles with a sense of personal integrity.

My focus has been on the possible moral problems posed by contemporary marketing. That is not because there is no positive case to be made for marketing. It rather reflects my assigned task and the fact that the interesting ethical discussions occur there rather than around the positive side of advertising, such as its alerting us to the availability of new products, the helpful information it does sometimes convey, and the possible reduction in price resulting from the larger volume of sales generated.

It would be an impossible and a pointless task to attempt a cost/benefit analysis on the basis of the above considerations to decide if advertising as a whole is morally defensible. It should be neither impossible nor pointless to do such a calculus about some specific forms of advertising for those who are prepared to acknowledge that marketing must be seen in the context of the larger society, of the sorts of human communities we are trying to build and of the sorts of persons we are trying to become.

BENEFITING SOCIETY AND THE BOTTOM LINE

PAUL BLOOM, PATTIE YU HUSSEIN, AND LISA SZYKMAN

In the past, most "social marketing" campaigns came from the non-profit or government sectors. In the last decade, these authors argue, many private corporations have moved to the forefront of promoting social causes, reaping substantial benefits. The authors sought to identify and to evaluate the success of several social marketing initiatives, with a primary focus on whether society is better off because of the program and whether corporate involvement allowed the program to perform better than if it were managed by a nonprofit or governmental agency. If the answer to both questions was yes, the researchers concluded that the program would be both efficient and effective. Examples of these effective and efficient programs follow below.

. . . A corporate social marketing program is an initiative in which marketing personnel who work for a corporation or one of its agents devote significant amounts of time and effort toward persuading people to engage in a socially beneficial behavior. . . .

FIBER CONSUMPTION

One of the most widely publicized and extensively examined corporate social marketing programs—based on our definition of such a program—is the All-Bran cereal campaign conducted by Kellogg Co. in collaboration with the National Cancer Institute. Started in the mid-1980s, this campaign encouraged the eating of a high-fiber, low-fat diet (in part by consuming Kellogg's All-Bran) as a means of reducing the risks of some types of cancer. Print ads, television spots, mailings to health professionals, and public speaking engagements all were used to deliver this basic message. The toll-free telephone number of the National Cancer Institute's Information Service was placed on the back panel of the All-Bran box.

As a first attempt to incorporate a very strong, credible, preventive health message in an ad for a commercial product, this campaign attracted considerable comment and review. Several studies looked at the campaign's impact on consumer knowledge, attitudes, and behavior.

Paul Bloom, Pattie Yu Hussein, Lisa Szykman, "Benefiting Society and the Bottom Line," reprinted from *Marketing Management,* Winter 1995, by permission of the American Marketing Association.

"All of these studies confirm that the Kellogg campaign had significant impact on consumers' knowledge, attitudes, and practices regarding consumption of fiber," according to communications researchers Vicki Friemuth and her colleagues. "Although it is not possible to attribute these changes to the Kellogg campaign directly, given the extensive exposure of the campaign, it seems reasonable to assume the campaign was quite influential."

"The Cancer Information Service data provide an opportunity to directly link the campaign to the consumer reaction," Friemuth et al. said in a 1988 American Journal of Public Health article. "Nearly 20,000 calls were made to the CIS in the first year after the campaign by individuals who specifically identified either the cereal box or the TV commercial as the motivation for their call."

Additionally, the business press reported that the campaign was associated with a substantial boost in All-Bran's sales as well as an increase in sales and share for all Kellogg cereals.

The results achieved by this campaign are generally recognized to be something that could not have been achieved by the National Cancer Institute or any other nonprofit group acting alone. The funding and know-how provided by Kellogg's marketing people, coupled with the credibility of the National Cancer Institute, created positive outcomes for both Kellogg and society.

BENEFITS OF WALKING

A good example of a social marketing campaign that has many direct benefits plus strong ties to the product is Rockport Co.'s campaign to educate Americans on the health benefits of walking.

In 1982, Rockport (now a division of Reebok) began the campaign to give "a corporate soul for its comparatively pedestrian walking shoe business," said Don Oldenburg in a Fall 1992 Business and Society Review article, "Big Companies Plug Big Causes for Big Gains."

As part of the campaign, Rockport distributed over 2 million brochures and founded the Rockport Walking Institute, dedicated to studying and promoting fitness walking.

Rockport's campaign has been credited with starting the fitness walking craze. In addition, today's sales reflect a twentyfold increase over the company's sales in 1982, and many consumers relate the Rockport brand name with walking and good health.

CHANGE YOUR BATTERY

The roots of Eveready's "Change Your Clock, Change Your Battery" campaign came from a simple yet highly compelling finding that no other group had addressed: One-third of all smoke alarms in place do not work because their batteries are worn out or missing. This situation, according to the International Association of Fire Chiefs (IAFC), is to blame for the majority of deaths, serious injuries, and property damage caused by fires every year.

Armed with this information, Eveready Battery Co., the leader in the 9-volt battery category used by most smoke detectors, launched a public education campaign in 1988 to encourage Americans to change their smoke detector barriers once a year when they change their clocks from daylight-saving time every fall.

To strengthen the programs's credibility, Eveready recruited the IAFC as a cosponsor, and fire chiefs in 37 target cities participated during the first year. A multitiered publicity campaign created exclusive exposure, including placements on TV networks and nationally syndicated talk shows at both the national and local levels. Since then, more than 4,000 fire departments across the country have adopted the program, and the number continues to grow.

The campaign has so far generated 1 billion media impressions with an advertising equivalency of $20.9 million. Coverage highlights included six national wire placements, features in *USA Today,* and reports by "Dear Abby," "The Today Show," "Good Morning America," "Larry King Live," "Regis & Kathie Lee," "CNN Headline News," "CBS Weekend News," *Parade* magazine, the Mutual Broadcasting Network, 1,772 local newspapers, more than 500 local TV stations, and 1,000 radio shows.

Now in its seventh year, the promotion boosted overall category sales by 8% during its first year alone, with Eveready garnering most of those sales. From a qualitative standpoint, "Change Your Clock, Change Your Battery" has received outstanding coverage because it's an important news story. More important, response to the program indicates that the campaign is well on its way toward institutionalizing a new home safety habit. . . .

GETTING 'INN' SHAPE

An example of a program that is not tied to product sales but does urge people to engage in behaviors that provide direct personal benefits is the "Inn Shape with Residence Inn" campaign run by Marriott's chain of extended-stay hotels. Using media stories and brochures, Residence Inns have been urging people to eat better and exercise more, at the hotel and at all times.

Working with the American Heart Association to develop recipes (for in-room cooking) and exercises (for in-room workouts), the chain has obtained considerable publicity and distribution of materials. However, we were not able to find out whether the program has motivated changes in the diets or exercise habits of the hotels' guests.

BREAST CANCER CRUSADE

Avon's Breast Cancer Crusade is an example of a social marketing campaign that is not directly tied to the company's product, but does have direct benefits to consumers. Avon initiated the five-year marketing campaign in 1993 to educate women about breast cancer and encourage them to follow the guidelines for early detection.

As part of the campaign, Avon makes extensive use of its sales representatives. They sell pink enamel breast cancer awareness ribbons (modeled after the red AIDS awareness ribbons), the proceeds of which go to fund local education programs and early-detection programs for low-income and minority women, and distribute brochures and information about the benefits of early detection. And, because many of the interactions between sales reps and customers occur on a one-to-one basis, sales representatives are trained to offer support and guidance about breast cancer.

Avon also uses its catalog and advertising to promote the crusade. For example, in a 30-second Avon commercial that aired during a one-hour ABC special on breast cancer, viewers were given a toll-free number to call for more information. In October 1993, Avon underwrote a one-hour PBS program, entitled "The Breast Cancer Test." In conjunction with the special, Avon sales reps distributed more than 15 million educational fliers discussing the 10 most-asked questions about breast cancer. . . .

TREAD LIGHTLY!

Jeep, a company that prides itself on its longstanding effort to be environmentally responsible, was a founding member of Tread Lightly! a nonprofit organization started by the U.S. Forest Service and Bureau of Land Management to protect the environment by encouraging ethical and responsible off-road practices. Tread Lightly! reminds off-roaders to consider the potential impact of their actions on the environment. The organization's pledge can be easily summarized in a few main points:

- Never venture off established trails.

- Respect the rights of hikers, skiers, and campers to enjoy their activities undisturbed.

- Educate yourself by obtaining travel maps and regulations from public agencies, comply with signs and barriers, and ask owners' permission to cross private property.

- Avoid streams, lake shores, meadows, muddy roads and trails, steep hillsides, wildlife, and livestock.

- Drive responsibly to protect the environment and preserve opportunities to enjoy your vehicle on wildlands.

Jeep reinforces the Tread Lightly! message in several different ways. First of all, in its advertising, vehicles are shown only on approved roads or trails. Second, each year the company organizes several "Jeep Jamborees," gathering together Jeep owners and experts for several days of off-road adventure and education. Finally, Jeep incorporates the Tread Lightly! message into product brochures and videos that Jeep owners receive with their vehicles. . . .

BENEFITS AND DRAWBACKS

Even though social marketing programs benefit society, corporations must weigh the societal benefits provided by a particular program against the costs of persuading people to perform socially beneficial behaviors. Some social marketing programs achieve the desired results very efficiently while others end up being too expensive for what they accomplish. Still others may never attain the level of commitment and resources needed to raise awareness, stimulate action, or encourage repeated behavior in significant ways.

   In some situations, corporations might be less capable than nonprofit organizations or government agencies to change behavior or control costs. Nevertheless, many corporations have the following comparative advantages in managing social marketing programs:

- Corporate marketers often have done extensive consumer research, giving them a level of understanding of consumer behavior in a certain context or market that makes them better able to design and place persuasive messages about socially beneficial behaviors for a particular target audience. For example, companies such as Kellogg or Quaker have knowledge of consumer eating habits that might help in determining the best way to promote healthier diets.

- Corporate marketers have more experience putting together the kind of multifaceted, comprehensive marketing programs that are needed to achieve significant changes in behavior. Many nonprofit and government programs have limited resources at their disposal, restricting the number of marketing tools they can deploy for each campaign (e.g., only public service announcements or pamphlets). Increased repetition of the social message, using a variety of techniques, can probably lead to more change in behavior, thereby making the campaign more successful.

- Corporate marketers have substantial credibility on certain topics, giving them an edge on persuasion. For example, a company such as Johnson & Johnson has several highly successful and popular health care brands (e.g., Band-Aid, Tylenol, K-Y Jelly), and the company's ties with the Robert Wood Johnson Foundation, which is well-known for its philanthropic activities in health care, further enhance credibility in this arena.

- Corporate marketers don't have the same political pressures as nonprofits and government agencies. The need to answer to legislators, advisory committees, or nonprofit board members on issues such as "wasting money on marketing" can inhibit the success of social marketing programs. Additionally, corporate marketers might not have to pay as much attention to being politically correct by ensuring a campaign's relevancy to all minority segments and special interest groups. Efforts that try to be everything to everybody become diluted—and therefore ineffective. A corporate social marketing campaign can target a specific audience, define the promise, and deliver a power message.

While nonprofit organizations (including government agencies) often have limited resources, they also have their own comparative advantages:

- Society already has trust and confidence in many nonprofit organizations. Because most nonprofits exist for the sole benefit of society, and not to make money, most people do not question their motives. Therefore, when delivering messages to the public, nonprofit organizations may be viewed as more credible than their corporate counterparts.

- Nonprofits have more experience in their own causes than do corporations. This knowledge could help them tailor more effective messages to specific audiences.

- Experts in the field might be more willing to share crucial information with nonprofit organizations than with corporations. Like the general public, field experts may question the motives of the corporations, especially if the company's bottom line is directly tied to its social marketing campaign. . . .

AMERICAN MARKETING ASSOCIATION CODE OF ETHICS

AMERICAN MARKETING ASSOCIATION

One option for self-regulation is adherence to the Code of Ethics promulgated by the American Marketing Association.

Members of the American Marketing Association (AMA) are committed to ethical professional conduct. They have joined together in subscribing to this Code of Ethics embracing the following topics:

RESPONSIBILITIES OF THE MARKETER

Marketers must accept responsibility for the consequences of their activities and make every effort to ensure that their decisions, recommendations, and actions function to identify, serve, and satisfy all relevant publics: customers, organizations, and society.

Marketers' professional conduct must be guided by:

1. The basic rule of professional ethics: not knowingly to do harm.
2. The adherence to all applicable laws and regulations.
3. The accurate representation of their education, training, and experience.
4. The active support, practice, and promotion of this Code of Ethics.

HONESTY AND FAIRNESS

Marketers shall uphold and advance the integrity, honor, and dignity of the marketing profession by:

1. Being honest in serving consumers, clients, employees, suppliers, distributors, and the public.
2. Not knowingly participating in conflict of interest without prior notice to all parties involved.
3. Establishing equitable fee schedules, including the payment or receipt of usual, customary, and/or legal compensation for marketing exchanges.

RIGHTS AND DUTIES OF PARTIES
IN THE MARKETING EXCHANGE PROCESS

Participants in the marketing exchange process should be able to expect that:

1. Products and services offered are safe and fit for their intended uses.
2. Communications about offered products and services are not deceptive.
3. All parties intend to discharge their obligations, financial and otherwise, in good faith.
4. Appropriate internal methods exist for equitable adjustment and/or redress of grievances concerning purchases.

It is understood that the above would include, *but is not limited to,* the following responsibilities of the marketer:

In the Area of Product Development and Management.

- Disclosure of all substantial risks associated with product or service usage.

- Identification of any product component substitution that might materially change the product or impact on the buyer's purchase decision.

- Identification of extra-cost added features.

In the Area of Promotions.

- Avoidance of false and misleading advertising.

- Rejection of high-pressure manipulations, or misleading sales tactics.

- Avoidance of sales promotions that use deception or manipulation.

In the Area of Distribution.

- Not manipulating the availability of a product for purpose of exploitation.

- Not using coercion in the marketing channel.

- Not exerting undue influence over the reseller's choice to handle a product.

In the Area of Pricing.

- Not engaging in price-fixing.

- Not practicing predatory pricing.

- Disclosing the full price associated with any purchase.

In the Area of Marketing Research.

- Prohibiting selling or fund raising under the guise of conducting research.

- Maintaining research integrity by avoiding misrepresentation and omission of pertinent research data.

- Treating outside clients and suppliers fairly.

ORGANIZATIONAL RELATIONSHIPS

Marketers should be aware of how their behavior may influence or impact on the behavior of others in organizational relationships. They should not demand, encourage, or apply coercion to obtain unethical behavior in their relationships with others, such as employees, suppliers, or customers.

1. Apply confidentiality and anonymity in professional relationships with regard to privileged information.
2. Meet their obligations and responsibilities in contracts and mutual agreements in a timely manner.
3. Avoid taking the work of others, in whole or in part, and representing this work as their own or directly benefiting from it without compensation or consent of the originator or owners.
4. Avoid manipulation to take advantage of situations to maximize personal welfare in a way that unfairly deprives or damages the organization or others.

Any AMA members found to be in violation of any provision of this Code of Ethics may have his or her Association membership suspended or revoked.

HOW FAR SHOULD YOU GO TO ACT AS A CORPORATE SPY?

KIRK O. HANSON

Hanson relates an incident where an individual is faced with the classic ethical dilemma: do what you think is right and, perhaps, not end up with the best result or do what you know is bending the rules but end up in a "better" position. The following circumstances may present themselves to you, no matter what your industry. How would you react?

ACU
student
in Ft Worth

There are always opportunities to get ahead by cutting an ethical corner here and there. An incident related by one of my former students demonstrates this:

George, who had recently completed his degree, was hired by a small software firm to help prepare its marketing plans for a new product. George's boss asked him to find out what he could about the future product plans of the company's two competitors.

George asked two co-workers how he should go about this.

"Call them up and tell them you are a student doing a paper at State," one suggested. "They'll be a lot looser talking to a student than they would to a competitor."

"Don't you know some old friends who have gone to work at the other two companies?" the other said. "Just go have lunch with them and trade some information about our new product for some information about their future plans. You can be a star here, and they can earn some brownie points at their company, too. That is the way things work now. We all help each other out. You never know when your company is going to go under, and you will need a friend elsewhere."

George certainly wanted to impress his boss with his ability to get the information on the competitors, but he was worried about how far he should go to get it.

He is facing one of the fundamental realities of business life: There is always an easier way of getting things done, if you're willing to skirt the boundary of acceptable behavior and compromise your own integrity.

Misrepresenting yourself when talking to a competitor is simply wrong. Every firm has the obligation to protect its confidential information but can't do so if you are engaged in deception. The case is less clear if the company representative started talking without knowing who George was. Some consulting firms now require their researchers to state, "We are doing a study for a competitor in your industry" before having a conversation.

Trading confidential information is to me an even more serious issue. George would be enticing a friend to violate his or her obligation to protect proprietary information—

and George himself would be violating his own obligation to protect information about his employer's product plans. Though company loyalty is clearly eroded today, the obligation to protect proprietary information is fundamental. George is not in a position to judge whether he is getting better information than he is giving—and certainly has not been authorized to do so.

Beyond the specific decision George is making, he is deciding at the outset of his career whether his personal style will be one of expediency or one of integrity.

We all have had bosses and co-workers who always choose the easy way out. Such a boss manipulates monthly reports to look good and blames his or her failings on subordinates. The expedient boss is obvious to those who work for him or her, if not to the more senior managers in the company.

The expedient co-worker is the one who is always looking out for No. 1. He may fudge on expense reports to "reward" himself for all his hard work. Or puff up his contribution to projects to take more of the credit than he deserves. Or dump the tough problems on co-workers. You can work with such a person, but you can never trust him completely.

What did George do in our situation above? He felt uncomfortable about "trading" confidential information with old friends, but he did call the competitors and claim to be a student doing a paper for class. The competitors were very talkative and gave him information he did not think he could have gotten any other way. But George felt queasy about what he had done.

When a similar assignment came up a couple of weeks later, he resolved to handle it without subterfuge and told his co-workers so. They kidded him that he had "lost his nerve" and was "naive." But George kept his promise to himself and today remains wary of temptations to "do it the easy way."

NESTLÉ AND THE CONTROVERSY OVER THE MARKETING OF BREAST MILK SUBSTITUTES

CHARLES MCCOY, SHEILA EVERS, MEINOLF DIERKES, AND FRED TWINING

How should a firm respond to protests against the ethics of its marketing programs? Nestlé had to face this issue in connection with the marketing of its breast milk substitutes for infants in developing countries. This controversy has raged for more than two decades and centers on Nestlé's claim that its milk substitute should be used in the early months of a baby's life. In fact, babies in developing countries often suffered from fatal diarrhea and other ailments as a result of mixing the formula with unsafe water. What, if anything, should Nestlé be doing now toward resolving this controversy? Should it take any actions in relation to its critics, governments, the World Health Organization, or the public? How could effective, independent monitoring be achieved at this point?

PART A

Once known in the United States as the Swiss company that sold coffee and chocolate, Nestlé may be better known today as the center of a 21-year-old controversy over the ethics of its infant formula marketing practices. This short case focuses on Nestlé's role, but attention should also be given to the actions of all parties in the conflict:

- other manufacturers of infant formula,

- action groups that have been critical of Nestlé,

- UNICEF and the World Health Organization.

The controversy has gone through five distinct stages as described in the following sequence of events:

Case Study: Charles McCoy, Sheila Evers, Meinolf Dierkes, Fred Twining, "Nestle and the Controversy over the Marketing of Breast Milk Substitutes," published by the Council for Ethics in Economics (Case 6, 1995). Copyright (c) 1995 Council for Ethics in Economics.

1968–1976

Bottle feeding as a dangerous substitute for breast feeding in the developing world emerged as an issue. An action group in Britain published *The Baby Killers* in 1974; it was translated into German by a Swiss group as *Nestlé totet babys* (*Nestlé Kills Babies*). Nestlé sued and won in court. However, the worldwide publicity was a victory for the critics; Nestlé became the focus of the controversy.

1977–1980

An international boycott of Nestlé products was organized by INFACT (Infant Formula Action Coalition). U.S. Senate hearings, presided over by Ted Kennedy, further damaged Nestlé's reputation. In response, Nestlé begins to make policy changes. The United Methodist Church (U.S.) sets up a task force to investigate the controversy and make recommendations on appropriate action. After study, the task force reported that Nestlé is changing its policies and recommended against joining the boycott.

1981–1988

The World Health Organization adopts an International Code of Marketing of Breast-milk Substitutes (1981). New Nestlé management declares its intention to follow the WHO Code. The company's two top leaders meet with the Methodist Task Force in the U.S. In an important strategic move Nestlé forms an independent commission, chaired by former U.S. Senator Edmund Muskie, to monitor Nestlé compliance with the WHO Code. Its members were chosen to represent a broad spectrum of constituencies and technical expertise.

1988–1992

Disagreements over the integration of the WHO Code and Nestlé's compliance with it lead to a resumption of the boycott in 1988 by some action groups. The Muskie Commission sponsored an extensive study of hospitals in Mexico which discovered that health care organizations in developing countries discourage breast feeding. The Muskie Commission dissolves itself in 1991, saying that Nestlé is in compliance with the WHO Code.

1993–1995

Reports from action groups, based on surveys by their world-wide network of observers, accuse the infant formula industry of multiple violations of the WHO Code. Nestlé management investigated the charges and denied most of the findings of the action group studies. These results intensified the growing distrust between the action groups and Nestlé.

Background of the Controversy

Nestlé was founded in 1867 by Henri Nestlé, a chemist who developed a breast-milk substitute. "During the first months," Nestlé wrote, "the mother's milk will always be the most natural nutriment" but "there will never be enough woman's milk to nourish all the children that are born. We must then seek some suitable substitute. . . . I have endeavored to make a food suitable for infants, and fulfilling all the conditions sought for by physicians."[1]

Nestlé, S.A., is now a huge multinational corporation with annual sales of nearly $50 billion and more than 200,000 employees. Nestlé is the world's largest producer and distributor of infant formula, with 37% of the market in 20 developing nations and 39% of the market in five European countries in 1992. Nestlé's worldwide share of the infant formula market declined, however, from 40% in 1981 to 27% in 1992. Sales of infant formula are less than 2% of its annual total sales. Profit percentages are reported as 1% in developed nations and .5% in developing countries. The ratio of Nestlé infant formula sales to live births in developing countries is far lower than the ratio in developed nations.

Using infant formula as a substitute for breast milk in the early months of a baby's life is the center of the controversy. In 1972, the U.N. Protein Advisory Group stated: "It is clearly important to avoid actions that would accelerate the trend away from breast feeding. . . . At the same time, it is essential to make formulas, foods, and instructions for good nutrition of their infants available to those mothers who do not breast feed for various reasons."[2] Nestlé says it endorses this view. In the 1970s, action groups, concerned about the people of developing countries, charged that the marketing of infant formula led to a decline in breastfeeding and that the use of breast-milk substitutes in developing societies caused infant deaths from diarrhea and other ailments. This is because users did not understand the dangers of bottle-feeding when formula was mixed with unsafe water. Research has confirmed the danger of bottle-feeding.[3] In 1974, a pamphlet critical of the baby food industry was published in Britain with the title *The Baby Killers.* A group in Switzerland published it in German as *Nestlé totet babys (Nestlé Kills Babies.)* Nestlé leaders expressed their shock, affirmed Nestlé's support for breastfeeding, and sued the Swiss group. Though Nestlé won the case in court, the judge said that Nestlé should review its marketing practices to avoid criticism in the future. The worldwide publicity given the case was a victory for the critics and placed Nestlé at the center of the controversy.

In 1977, advocacy groups led by the Infant Formula Action Coalition (INFACT) organized a boycott of Nestlé products. In May 1978, Senator Edward M. Kennedy chaired U.S. Senate hearings on the infant formula industry, resulting in further damage to Nestlé's reputation. Many religious, educational, and labor groups joined the boycott, which was effective enough to get Nestlé's attention.

In the early 80s, the course of the controversy changed.

- *First, in 1981, the WHO Code was adopted.* This landmark action provides criteria for judging infant formula marketing practices. It did not resolve all controversy: (a) because differences of definition and interpretation remain, and (b) because adoption and enforcement is needed by WHO member nations, most of which have been slow to act.

- *Second, the United Methodist Church (U.S.) declined to join the boycott* and set up a Task Force (MTF) to investigate and recommend appropriate action. The MTF reported that Nestlé was changing its policies, recommended against the boycott, and questioned the fairness and truthfulness of the charges made by some critics.[4]

- *Third, new leadership emerged at Nestlé.* Helmut Maucher, CEO, and Dr. Carl Angst, Executive Vice President, announced their intention to follow the WHO Code and, in 1982, met directly with the MTF to discuss Nestlé's revised marketing policies and practices.

- *Fourth, Nestlé established an independent commission to monitor the company's compliance with the WHO Code,* chaired by former U.S. Senator Edmund S. Muskie. In 1984 the INFACT-led boycott was suspended.

The Activities of the Muskie Commission

Commission membership included critics of the infant food industry, religious leaders, and scholars from public health and related disciplines. The Commission investigated alleged violations of the WHO Code by Nestlé, clarified ambiguities, checked on Code infractions, sponsored studies of health and nutritional issues affecting mothers and children in the Third World, and met with Nestlé management to evaluate policy and suggest changes.

In 1991, the Muskie Commission dissolved, stating that Nestlé was in compliance with the WHO Code and had internal means to investigate and resolve complaints. Also, the International Association of Infant Food Manufacturers had appointed an ombudsman to deal with allegations against its members.

The Boycott Renewed

Though Nestlé and the industry were changing their practices toward conformity with the WHO Code, criticism continued and has been increasing. In 1988, the boycott was renewed, led by the International Boycott Committee (INBC), International Baby Food Action Network (IBFAN), Baby Milk Action (United Kingdom), and Action for Corporate Accountability (U.S.). IBFAN issues periodic reports called *Breaking the Rules,* accusing the infant food industry of multiple violations of the WHO Code. The gulf between Nestlé and its critics is shown in that, after investigation of the alleged violations, only 3 of 455 charges were found by Nestlé to be accurate and these 3 were reported as corrected.

PART B

Nestlé Corporate Culture, Ethical Values, and Strategies

The infant formula controversy has been unsettling for a Nestlé management group that takes pride in its strong corporate culture and ethics.

The current Nestlé organization is both centralized and decentralized. As a multinational, Nestlé operates with subsidiaries that have considerable freedom within firm overall policies. Company-wide management functions are located in Vevey, Switzerland: top line managers, financial control and administration, strategic business groups, research and development, purchasing and export, and the zone managers for the five operating areas around the globe. Each zone has its own decentralized operating groups, able to adapt to the diverse cultures of each zone and country. In the view of its managers, the growth and success of Nestlé is based upon its strong corporate culture and capable leadership, with high levels of mutual trust and loyalty among managers drawn from the many nations in which Nestlé conducts business. But one wonders, has the strength of its culture led to internal rigidity, an inability to learn as an organization, and an inability to adapt to changing social conditions? All the attention given the infant formula controversy by Nestlé seems to some to have been greater than is warranted by the volume of sales or profits. A few Nestlé managers would prefer to drop the product, but most say the commitment to market infant formula in developing countries, based on company tradition and values more than on profit, is too strong.

Nestlé managers believe the company is highly ethical, making many contributions to third-world communities. Senior management today regards the hostile reactions to critics in the 1970s as mistakes, fostering an atmosphere of distrust and mutual suspicion, and they believe that many marketing practices in the 1970s were wrong. Nestlé says it has supported the WHO Code from the time it was adopted and has been implementing the Code ever since. Nestlé managers regret that the infant formula issue continues to hurt the company's reputation and express willingness to work with critics to improve the health and nutrition of children and mothers around the world. They believe that the company has learned from past experience and has adopted more responsible policies toward developing nations. One executive said: "We came to the conclusion that to serve the developing countries we should . . . develop, manufacture, and sell low-cost products, including infant formula, based on local raw materials fitted to the tastes and nutritional needs of children up to age five, not just for charitable reasons. We believe it will serve the long-term interests of Nestlé. And I am very happy that at the same time we can do some good for the people of those countries."

Views of Nestlé's Critics

The scholar who conducted the most extensive study of the infant formula controversy, S. Prakash Sethi, says that Nestlé's actions in the 1970s "could not have been better designed to play into the hands of its adversaries." And further: "The company was a prisoner of its own values set and operational philosophy. Nestlé's values set revolved around conventional business values: a good product, efficiently sold, in every possible market and with flexible marketing and promotional strategies that would adapt to the needs of individual country markets, and by people who were both dedicated to the company and proud of their ability to perform successfully under various operating and competitive conditions. Nestlé's management was also insular and looked to its own traditions for guidance. The company jealously guarded its freedom to manage its far-flung world-wide operations as it saw fit as long as they were in harmony with local laws. The preservation of maximum management discretion was one of the core values of the company, reinforced by the fact that it was also in harmony with the intellectual and cultural orientation of the Swiss-based management and the personal inclinations of its then top management."[5]

In his subsequent evaluation of the company's performance in relation to the controversy until 1994, Sethi sees no substantial improvements with reference to environmental scanning for new constituencies, corporate communications dealing with external issues-related constituencies, the development of strategic assets related to the controversy, or organizational structure and decision-making processes—that is, Nestlé's organizational learning.[6]

The action groups that have led the renewed boycott see Nestlé still as placing profit above humane values. They believe that Nestlé and the entire infant formula industry could take far greater initiative in controlling the free and low-cost distribution of infant formula. The view of some critics is that infant formula should be treated as a drug that is dangerous if misused. If not entirely withdrawn from the market, it should be available only on prescription and used under controlled conditions. Any vendor of dangerous drugs must take responsibility in relation to its eventual end use.

In addition, the industry is seen by some as slippery, not to be trusted. Indeed, industry managers are seen as trying to discredit their critics and trusting neither the action groups nor UNICEF and WHO.

The action groups are especially critical of the continued giving of free and low-cost samples that they regard as blatant violations of the WHO Code. Though having far fewer resources than industry, the action groups regard as a breakthrough the network of sources in the developing world that has enabled them to publish the multiple violations cited in *Breaking the Rules.* The action groups want independent and more effective monitoring.

Health Care Practices in Developing Countries: The Mexico Study and the Baby Friendly Hospital Initiative

A major study of health care sponsored by Nestlé through the Muskie Commission investigated the hospital procedures for newborns in Mexico and how these practices influenced breast feeding by mothers while in the hospitals and later *(Infant Feeding in Mexico, 1991).* Directed by Sheldon Margen, M.D., and V. J. Melnick, M.D., the study involved 59 hospitals in three widely separated regions in Mexico and concluded that existing hospital practices discourage breast feeding and influenced mothers to adopt bottle feeding using infant formula. This study and others in Thailand and Cote d'Ivoire made it clear that health care practices must be changed if the health and nutrition of children and mothers in developing countries are to be improved.

In 1991, WHO and UNICEF launched the Baby Friendly Hospital Initiative with Ten Steps to promote health care practices that support and encourage breast feeding. The Baby Friendly Hospital Initiative is a promising approach in promoting better health and nutrition for infants and mothers. The infant food industry's role so far has been to agree to remove all free supplies of infant formula from hospitals in developing nations on a country-by-country basis.

In 1995, follow-up research by Enrique Rios, M.D., Dr.P.H., found that the Mexico Study had influenced important policy changes and practices toward promoting breast-feeding in two major health care systems in Mexico, with 234 Mexican hospitals now certified as Baby Friendly Hospitals, and had contributed to the creation of a National Breastfeeding Committee. This update suggests that cooperation among industry, critics, and academic researchers as represented in the Mexico study can produce positive changes, though much more remains to be done.[7]

Divergent Points of View

The following significant quotes have been drawn from the many interviews and sources consulted on which this case is based:

An industry executive: "Whatever our viewpoint, most can agree that our major aim ought to be improving the health and nutrition of mothers and children everywhere. That's the central problem."

An industry critic: "The baby food people are slippery. If they would stop giving free or low-cost infant formula, as they promised, we might be able to cooperate on basic problems of health care, with Baby Friendly Hospitals at the center of our efforts."

A health care expert: "Poverty, disease, bad water, inadequate education, and poor health practices are pervasive obstacles to overcoming malnutrition and bad health of children and mothers in the Third World. Our highest priority should be getting good information on problems and cooperation toward improving the situation."

A Nestlé executive: "I believe it is ethical for Nestlé to produce infant formula. But from a business perspective, there are too many problems. It would be better to drop it. That is *my* opinion. But there's no easy way Nestlé will go against its commitment."

Senator Edward M. Kennedy (1978): "Can a product that requires clean water, good sanitation, adequate family income, and literate parents to follow printed instructions be properly and safely used in areas where water is contaminated, sewage runs in the streets, poverty is severe, and illiteracy is high?"

Two involved Britons: "There must be other ways than confrontation through advocacy groups to achieve better health and nutrition for mothers and children." "The issue is multinational accountability. They are a law unto themselves and find ways to evade responsibility. The voluntary groups bring them to account."

A Nestlé manager: "There is no point in fighting or continuing to throw bricks; we have to gain some minimal level of trust. The company was overly aggressive in its marketing in the early 70s. But we began improving and, with the passage of the WHO Code, have really been *trying*. We don't, however, get much credit for it."

A woman's view: "To the extent that the boycotts succeed in their purpose of restricting access to formula, they serve to take the choice to breastfeed or not out of the hands of women . . . and have doctors and scientists in the developing countries decide if *this* bottlefeeding is 'necessary,' or if *that* woman is an 'appropriate' receiver of infant formula."

A UNICEF spokesperson: "Because of the widespread abandonment of breastfeeding, 1.3 million infant deaths occur each year. Countless more survive the fatal odds but suffer impaired growth and development because their mothers were not informed about the lifesaving properties of breastfeeding."

A scholarly observer: "In the process of emphasizing extremes, a vast middle ground is lost to inflaming rhetoric with results that are neither enlightening nor conducive to reaching consensus on implementable public policy options."

WHO Executive Director, January 1994: "It is considered that the underlying principles governing relevant national measures should include clear definitions, which are communicated to and understood by all parties: transparent monitoring and reporting procedures to determine whether alleged violations contravene national measures; and a monitoring authority established under government responsibility. It is hoped that this longstanding and contentious issue can be resolved rapidly."

A management academician: "Organizational learning begins by producing different perceptions of the organization's internal and external environments. New perceptions are followed by development of a new vision, mission, and strategy and by their implementation."

ENDNOTES

1. Henri Nestlé, chemist. *Memorial on the Nutrition of Infants.* Vevey, Switzerland: Loertscher & Son, 1869: 1, 3.
2. Statement 23, Protein Advisory Group of the United Nations, 18 July, 1972.
3. See Roy E. Brown, "Breast Feeding in Modern Times," *The American Journal of Clinical Nutrition,* 26:485–6 (May 1973) and Carol Adelman, "Infant Formula, Science and Politics," *Policy Review,* Winter 1988:107–126.
4. "Recommendations of the United Methodist Infant Formula Task Force, October, 1982," and "Fourth Report of the Infant Formula Task Force, April 28, 1982."
5. Sethi, *Multinational Corporations,* 68, 69.
6. *Ibid.,* 351–352, 371–377.
7. Enrique Rios, "A Follow-Up Study on Current Policies and Practices of Infant Feeding in Mexican Hospitals," April 1995.

MARKETING AND THE VULNERABLE

GEORGE BRENKERT

In line with the previous case study, Brenkert discusses the particular responsibilities of marketers who serve vulnerable communities. Brenkert identifies who those vulnerable populations might be, discusses the nature of marketing campaigns to these select groups, and discusses the ethics of those schemes.

I. INTRODUCTION

Contemporary marketing is commonly characterized by the marketing concept which enjoins marketers to determine the wants and needs of customers and then to try to satisfy them. This view is standardly developed, not surprisingly, in terms of normal or ordinary consumers. Much less frequently is attention given to the vulnerable customers whom marketers also (and increasingly) target. Though marketing to normal customers raises many moral questions, marketing to the vulnerable also raises many moral questions which are deserving of greater attention.

This paper has three objectives. First, it explores the notion of vulnerability which a target audience might (or might not) have. I argue that we must distinguish those who are specially vulnerable from normal individuals, as well as the susceptible and the disadvantaged—two other groups often distinguished in marketing literature. Second, I contend that marketing to the specially vulnerable requires that marketing campaigns be designed to ensure that these individuals are not treated unfairly, and thus possibly harmed. Third, I maintain that marketing programs which violate this preceding injunction are unethical or unscrupulous whether or not those targeted are harmed in some further manner. Accordingly, social control over marketing to the vulnerable cannot simply look to consumer injury as the measure of unfair treatment of the vulnerable.

The upshot of my argument is that, just as we have a doctrine of product liability to which marketers are accountable, we also need a corresponding doctrine of client liability to which marketers should be held. By this I refer to the moral liability of marketers for the manner in which they market to consumers. Marketing to the specially vulnerable without making appropriate allowances for their vulnerabilities is morally unjustified.

II. ON BEING VULNERABLE

The notion of vulnerability is complex and slippery. Most simply, to be "vulnerable" is to be "susceptible to being wounded; liable to physical hurt" (Barnhart, 1956). More generally being vulnerable is being susceptible to some harm or other. One can be vulnerable

---

to manmade or natural harms; one can also be vulnerable to harms from actions or omissions (Goodin, 1985: 110). In each of these cases, the threatened harm is to one's "welfare" or "interests."

The vulnerability of the person may be a permanent, or temporary, condition. Clearly, vulnerability is a matter of degree. Typically only those who are subject to some substantial level of harm are referred to as "vulnerable." This vulnerability may arise due to their own peculiar characteristics, those of the agents who are said to impose the harm on them, or the system within which certain acts impose harm on them. Accordingly, vulnerability is a four place relation: some person (P) is vulnerable to another (moral or causal) agent (A) with respect to some harm (H) in a particular context (C). As such "vulnerability is inherently object and agent specific" (Goodin, 1985: 112).

We can further clarify the nature of vulnerability by briefly noting its relation to two related concepts—susceptibility and disadvantage—which are used in marketing literature.

Vulnerability is distinct from susceptibility, in that a person might be susceptible to something or someone and still not be vulnerable to that thing or person. "Susceptibility" merely implies that one is "capable of being affected, especially easily" by something or someone. It is true that one who is susceptible may also be vulnerable. Clearly, one who is vulnerable is susceptible. But one need not be vulnerable if one is susceptible, since one's susceptibility may not be to some harm or other. An overweight, under-exercised adult might be susceptible through flattery or positive remarks to certain suggestions made by friends to exercise and moderate food intake. But this person would not, thereby, be vulnerable to such suggestions. Hence, vulnerability and susceptibility are different.

The vulnerable also differ from those with "unusual susceptibilities," a term of art in marketing for those "who have idiosyncratic relations to products that are otherwise harmless when used by most people" (Morgan et al., 1995: 267). People who are "unusually susceptible" are those who are atypically harmed by various products. Accordingly, "unusual susceptibility" has been linked with vulnerability. However, in any ordinary sense, a person might have "unusual susceptibilities" to some experiences (e.g., changes in air pressure or moisture), the suggestions of others, clothing styles, etc. Further, people may be vulnerable in ways other than that they may be atypically harmed by the products they use. Vulnerable groups such as young children, the grieving or the elderly, are not necessarily atypically harmed by the products they use. Nevertheless, they are vulnerable.

Finally, the vulnerable are also distinct from the disadvantaged. Though marketers quite frequently speak of disadvantaged populations or market segments, they have given little analysis of this concept. Most discussants simply give examples of those whom they consider to be disadvantaged. This extensive, diverse and confused list includes: the poor, immigrants, the young married, teenagers, the elderly, children, racial minorities, the physically handicapped, ethnic minorities, and even women shopping for automobiles.

Generally, we are told that members of this list are disadvantaged because they are impaired in their transactions in the marketplace. For some this means not getting their full consumer dollar (Andreasen, 1975: 6). For others this means confronting an imbalance in the marketplace (Barnhill, 1972; Morgan and Riordan, 1983). Andreasen says "the disadvantaged" are "those who are unequal in the marketplace because of characteristics that are not of their own choosing, including their age, race, ethnic minority status, and (sometimes) gender" (Andreasen, 1993: 273).

It is clear, then, that the vulnerable and the disadvantaged also constitute different, though overlapping, groups. The disadvantaged are impaired or unequal with regard to their attempt to obtain various goods and services. This may occur relative to other groups (normal consumers) competing for various goods, or to those from whom they seek to purchase those goods. On the contrary, those who are vulnerable are not vulnerable with regard to others who are competing for similar goods, but with regard to the harm they might suffer from those who market those goods to them. As such, the notion of vulnerability suggests the harm which one might receive, whether or not one is competing for a particular good, but due to the manner of obtaining some good (or service). Further, this harm need not come from paying more or being deceived. The vulnerable may get exactly what they want, but what they want may unwittingly and unfairly harm them (as well as their family and/or community).

Accordingly, the vulnerable are not simply the susceptible or the disadvantaged. They constitute a distinct group which deserves our close attention.

III. VULNERABILITY AND MARKETING

What moral responsibilities do marketers have when they consider marketing to the vulnerable? Since anyone might be said to be vulnerable in a variety of ways, and since some people might willingly place themselves in competitive situations where their vulnerabilities are exposed, we must specify the manner(s) in which various forms of vulnerability are significant from the standpoint of marketing. Otherwise, if it were morally unjustified to market to those who are vulnerable in any sense, moral marketing would not exist. It would be an oxymoron.

We might begin by reflecting on the fact that vulnerability is not simply a relational but also a relative notion. Individuals may be more or less vulnerable. It might be claimed, then, that those who are vulnerable to an especial degree are those to whom marketers owe a special responsibility of protection and avoidance. Drawing upon this characteristic of vulnerability, Goodin has proposed a general analysis of our responsibility to the vulnerable.[1] He defends the following basic moral principle: "If A's interests are vulnerable to B's actions and choices, B has a special responsibility to protect A's interests; the strength of this responsibility depends strictly upon the degree to which B can affect A's interests" (Goodin, 1985: 118). Thus, if the interests of children, the poor, and the grieving are vulnerable to the actions of marketers, then they have a special responsibility to protect the interests of those individuals. Accordingly, society might seek to control those marketers who, by imposing substantial harm on consumers, violate this special responsibility.

There are, however, at least two problems with adopting Goodin's suggestion for present purposes. First, his principle is not, as formulated, applicable to the marketplace. For example, a competitor's interests might well be specially vulnerable to the actions and choices of another competitor. The first firm's interests include gaining a certain amount of market share; but the second firm might be a much larger firm which can undercut the first competitor and prevent it from gaining market share. Surely it does not follow that the second firm has a special responsibility to protect the first firm's interests.

Second, if a consumer's interests are vulnerable to some marketer, it does not follow that the marketer has a special responsibility to protect that consumer's interests simpliciter.

Suppose a person's health interests are vulnerable to a tobacco marketer's actions and choices. It is far from obvious that the tobacco marketer now has a special responsibility to protect that person's health interests without any further specification. At most, a marketer has a responsibility not to harm those interests which may be affected by that marketer's marketing campaign.

Another standard to which we might turn for the responsibilities of marketers to the vulnerable refers not to the degree of their vulnerability, but to the effects on all those relevantly affected by marketing to these individuals. In short, harm to the vulnerable by marketing programs might be balanced by countervailing benefits for all other consumers and competitors. Thus, the responsibilities of marketers to the vulnerable would depend upon which course of action would maximize all relevant utilities.

However, appeal to a simple utilitarian standard is ethically unacceptable in that it would allow a few vulnerable individuals to substantially suffer because a certain action or policy maximized total utilities. For example, it might be that other marketers are more vulnerable (they might go out of business) than some of the individuals (they might be harmed by the products or the form of marketing targeting them) to whom those marketers and others sought to sell their goods. Hence, in order to protect vulnerable marketers (and their employees, suppliers, etc.), the proposed standard might permit targeting various vulnerable market segments because the total harm they sustained was less than that of those engaged in producing and marketing products to them. This could unleash a tide of manipulative and exploitative marketing.

Similarly, suppose that a particular means of marketing did not make allowances for the fact that those targeted were vulnerable in that they significantly lacked a capacity to make judgments regarding economic exchanges (e.g., children, the senile, or the retarded). Though the marketing efforts took advantage of this vulnerability, it nevertheless maximized total utilities. We might suppose that these customers were not dissatisfied and the marketers were pleased with their successes. To argue that this means of marketing is, nevertheless, morally acceptable runs afoul of important moral and market principles. To begin with, those targeted are not competent to evaluate the product marketed to them. They might not be aware of problems with the products they use. As such, this justification of marketing to the vulnerable permits treating some individuals simply as means to the ends of others. It denies them moral respect. It runs afoul of basic ethical and market principles, even though those targeted do not suffer a direct harm.

The difficulty with Goodin's approach is that he treats vulnerability as simply a quantitative matter without recognizing that each form of vulnerability occurs within a particular context. The market is one such context. In it some individuals may justifiedly seek, in recognized forms of competition, to exploit the vulnerabilities of others. The problem with the consequentialist approach is that it does not consider the nature of people's vulnerabilities except insofar as they portend certain consequences for everyone. Not the ability of the person to participate, but the effects on society are its concern. Instead, we need to be able to identify those who are specially vulnerable within a market situation, but whose vulnerability is not the occasion for justified competitive attacks. In short, we need a different approach which takes account both of the context within which marketers address the vulnerable as well as the nature of their vulnerabilities.

MARKETING TO THE VULNERABLE

The necessary features for morally (not merely legally) justified market relations are commonly stated in terms of the nature of the relations or interactions which participants in the market enjoy.[2] Thus, we are told that among the relevant characteristics a morally justified market requires are the following: (*a*) Competition is free, i.e., participants in the market do so voluntarily, when each believes they can benefit; (*b*) competition is open; i.e., "access to the market is not artificially limited by any power, government, or group" (DeGeorge, 1982: 101); and (*c*) deception or fraud are not used in market competition (Friedman, 1962).

These conditions spell out some of the necessary conditions for a justified form of competition among those we may call "market participants," i.e., those who willingly and knowingly engage in market relations. The activity of these marketplace competitors is strongly determined by their need to derive a profit. To be a market participant is to place oneself in competition with other participant capitalists in which one recognizes that one may succeed or fail. It is to engage in these relations in order to produce various goods or services for sale. It is to acknowledge that all participants, including oneself, have strengths and weaknesses, formidable powers and vulnerabilities. The endeavor of each participant is to compete such their own strengths and powers will outweigh those of others, or that their weaknesses and vulnerabilities are less significant than those of others.

Second, though these conditions are important for a morally justified market, they make no direct reference to the conditions or characteristics which those individuals who engage in market relations as ultimate consumers—call them "market clients"—must have in order to do so. However, morally and legally justified market relations also make assumptions about the nature of these participants since not just anyone can be a market client. To take the most obvious cases, the severely mentally ill, incompetent elderly and young children cannot be market clients. Someone else must visit the market on their behalf.

Those who would visit the market as clients do so not under a concern to derive a profit or to compete, but in order to satisfy various needs and wants they have. Accordingly, they must have certain cognitive, motivational and material market competencies: (*a*) They have knowledge of the products and their characteristics. According they know they should shop around and are able to do so. (*b*) They are competent to determine differences in quality and best price. Thus, they are also able to exercise physical and emotional control; i.e., they are not simply subject to their impulses, but can evaluate the various goods in the market. (*c*) They are aware of their legal rights (cf. Schnapper). (*d*) They are capable of being satisfied, in some broad sense, by the products offered in the market. (*e*) They have the resources to enter into market relations.[3]

These conditions, conjoined with the preceding, spell out essential requirements for individuals to be market clients. It is assumed that those who fulfill these conditions are able to protect their own interests and that their self-interested behavior in the market will work towards greater wealth or well-being for all. Accordingly, when these conditions are fulfilled (ceteris paribus), market relations between market participants and clients will be fair or just. Thus, these conditions for market clients have been recognized not simply as moral restrictions, but also as the source of various legal regulations regarding children, the elderly, and the grieving.

Third, the preceding market client conditions are not fulfilled by consumers wholly independently of marketers. On the contrary, marketers seek to foster the fulfillment of these conditions. "Ultimately," a marketing text reminds us, "the key objective [for marketers] must be to influence customer behavior" (Assael, 1993: 592). Thus, marketers extend credit or loans to prospective individuals so that they may have the needed resources to enter the market. They advertise to foster the knowledge and desire of their products. They seek to identify unfulfilled needs, wants and interests among potential clients, and endeavor to find ways to ensure that their products satisfy them. Marketers seek to draw into the market those who might not otherwise enter the market, or do so only in different ways and under different conditions. Thus, one marketing researcher comments that "marketers have failed to develop strategies designed to attract the elderly consumer market" (Bailey, 1987: 213). In short, marketers create not only products, but seek to create clients out of ordinary, non-market interested, people. This is not to say that they create clients out of whole cloth, as it might seem that they do a product. Nor is it to say that they are always successful, or that whenever a person becomes a market client it is because of some specific action of a marketer. Still, marketers not only create products for clients, but they also have a hand in creating clients for their products.

In these various efforts, the marketer has a number of advantages over even the most reasonable client. These include greater knowledge of the product; expertise on how to market to individual customers and targeted groups; knowledge of what interests, fears, wants and/or needs motivate various market segments; and resources to bring that knowledge to bear on behalf of persuading a customer to buy a product. Indeed, the marketer may be aware of attributes of potential clients of which they are themselves unaware. These special characteristics, powers and abilities of marketers create special responsibilities for them in the relationships they create with clients.[4]

Fourth, when marketers, or market participants, compete with each other, the fact that one has a vulnerability may be viewed as an opportunity for another who seeks to take advantage of that vulnerability. There are, obviously, legal and moral limits here. If one firm has temporarily lost its security force and its headquarters are unguarded one evening, this does not imply that another firm may use that opportunity to sneak into those headquarters to steal important files. Thus, competing firms ought not to try to exploit those vulnerabilities which would require illegal or immoral acts. On the other hand, vulnerabilities linked to market performance may be the occasion for other firms to try to outperform the vulnerable firm when the acts involved do not transgress the preceding limits. Accordingly, if market participants fail to compete aggressively out of laziness or are indifferent to quality differences, they may be harmed as a result. This is acceptable to the market, since it is intended to encourage participant competitiveness.

However, when a marketer confronts a market client, i.e., an ordinary consumer, the situation is different. Individuals must fulfill the above conditions to be market clients. Those that do so may also be lazy shoppers or indifferent to quality differences. As a consequence, they too may suffer. This is also acceptable within the market. However, some individuals may suffer not through such circumstances, but because they fail to fulfill, in ways which render them specially vulnerable, various conditions to be market clients.

I suggest that we may initially characterize this specially vulnerable group as being constituted by those individuals who are particularly susceptible to harm to their interests because the qualitatively different experiences and conditions that characterize them (and on account of which they may be harmed) derive from factors (largely) beyond their control.

Accordingly, there are three conditions for the specially vulnerable:

1. They are those, in contrast to other normal adults, who are characterized by qualitatively different experiences, conditions and/or incapacities which impede their abilities to participate in normal market activities. These characteristics may render them vulnerable (assuming the following two conditions are also fulfilled) in any of four different ways:

    (a) They may be **physically vulnerable** if they are unusually susceptible due to physical or biological conditions to products on the market, e.g., allergies or special sensitivity to the chemicals or substances which are marketed.[5]

    (b) They may be **cognitively vulnerable** if they lack certain levels of ability to cognitively process information or to be aware that certain information was being withheld or manipulated in deceptive ways. This may occur because these abilities have not been (sufficiently) developed or they are (at least temporarily) impaired. Children, the senile elderly, and even those who lack education and shopping sophistication have been included here.[6]

    (c) They may be **motivationally vulnerable** if they could not resist ordinary temptations and/or enticements due to their own individual characteristics. Under the motivationally vulnerable might be brought the grieving and the gravely ill.[7]

    (d) They may be **socially vulnerable** when their social situation renders them significantly less able than others to resist various enticements, appeals or challenges which may harm them. Some of those who have been included here are certain groups of the poor, the grieving, new mothers in developing countries.

2. The qualitatively different conditions and incapacities of specially vulnerable individuals are ones they possess due to factors (largely) beyond their control. In addition, they may be largely unaware of their vulnerability(ies). In either case, they are significantly less able (in any normal sense) to protect themselves against harm to their interests as a result. Thus, the allergic, the child, the elderly, and the grieving all experience their vulnerabilities due to reasons (largely) beyond their control. In certain situations this may also be true of various racial groups. The fact that these factors are largely beyond their control may be due to the weaknesses or inabilities these individuals themselves possess, due to the greater power of marketers which render their characteristics specially weak or incapable, or due to the system within which they find themselves.

3. These special conditions render them particularly susceptible to the harm of their interests by various means which marketers (and others) use but which do not (similarly) affect the normal adult. In short, it is the combination of their special characteristics and the means or techniques which marketers use that render them specially vulnerable. This emphasizes the relational nature of vulnerability.

As so identified, the specially vulnerable are significantly less able than others to protect their own interests and, in some cases, even to identify their own interests. Consequently, they are considerably less able to take appropriate measures to satisfy or fulfill those interests. Central to these difficulties is the special liability (or susceptibility) they have to be swayed, moved or enticed in directions which may benefit others but which may harm their interests.

Accordingly, when market participants face individuals who do not qualify or pass a certain threshold for market competition, the latter are unable to protect their interests in a manner comparable to that of ordinary market clients. If the fulfillment of these conditions or threshold is required to be treated as a market client, then these individuals may not morally be treated as other clients in the market. Further, when this situation arises because these individuals have special vulnerabilities, then to market to them in ways which take advantage of their vulnerabilities, i.e., to seek to engage them in the competitive effort to sell them goods through the weaknesses characterizing their vulnerabilities, is to treat them unfairly. Regardless of whether they are actually harmed, they are being taken advantage of. They have little or no control over these features of their behavior. The fact that they may take fun or pleasure in being targeted by marketers is, then, irrelevant since they do not qualify as market clients.[8] And it is this situation which has been cited as one of the criteria for determining unfairness in advertising, i.e., advertising (or marketing) makes unfair claims when those claims " . . . cause especially vulnerable groups to engage in conduct deleterious to themselves" (Cohen, 1974: 13).[9]

Consequently, since moral marketing must exclude treating clients unfairly, marketers need to "qualify" those they propose to target as genuine market clients before they introduce marketing campaigns which target them. This might involve helping them to become qualified clients, avoiding marketing to them, or marketing to them in ways which are compatible with their limited abilities and characteristics.

As such, moral marketing requires a theory of client liability analogous to the products liability, to which marketers are presently held responsible. A theory of client liability would elaborate on and operationalize the conditions noted above under which individuals may play full roles as market clients as well as what lesser roles they may play. In any case, it would tell us what relationships marketers might have with them.

V. IMPLICATIONS

What are the implications of the preceding analysis? A first interpretation might be that marketers may not market to the specially vulnerable at all. This is mistaken. There are obviously cases in which those who are specially vulnerable, e.g., the elderly or the grieving, require various products and services and would benefit from learning about them. The preceding argument contends that any marketing to the vulnerable cannot morally be undertaken in a way which trades upon their vulnerabilities.

In cases when the special vulnerability is temporary, measures could be taken to restrain marketing to them until after such period. Accordingly, the legislatures of some states have introduced and/or passed legislation prohibiting lawyers ". . . from soliciting the business of victims until 30 days after accidents, wrongful deaths and workplace injuries (Ferrar, 1996). Similarly, for the grieving, some have suggested that "insurance companies may need to be restricted through legislation regarding the nature of their contacts with those in grief; specifically, the payoff of a life insurance policy should not be accompanied by an immediate attempt to encourage the survivor to re-invest. A period of time (i.e., at least a month) should elapse before the insurance company initiates a sales contact" (Gentry et al, 1994: 139). When it is desirable that individuals in this group have certain products or services prior to the vulnerability creating situation abating, other arrangements can be made for advisors to the specially vulnerable to be present or for restraints on the marketing to them.

The situation is different when the vulnerability is not temporary or relatively short-term. In such cases, it might be contended that the preceding analysis implies that the success of moral marketing cannot rely on those characteristics that render individuals specially vulnerable. Once again, this does not follow. This is too weak a claim, since the reasons for the success or failure of any marketing campaign may be difficult to determine. Further, this interpretation would also prevent a marketing program from trying to sensitively adapt to the vulnerabilities of these individuals. Finally, marketing programs which failed could not be criticized on this view. Consequently, it would permit a wide assortment of marketing approaches which attempted to tie into the client's vulnerabilities.

Instead, a third, stronger interpretation of the above argument is required. This might be that marketers may not target those who are specially vulnerable in ways such that their marketing campaign depends upon the vulnerabilities of that specially vulnerable group. That is, in the case of the specially vulnerable, no significant aspect of a marketing campaign may rely upon the characteristics that render those individuals specially vulnerable in order to sell a product. Hence, because children are cognitively vulnerable due to their undeveloped abilities, any marketing to children must be done in ways which do not presuppose those vulnerabilties. As such, the FCC's limit on the amount of advertising on children's television programming does not directly address this issue. Instead, the content of those advertisements must be monitored so that children's special vulnerabilities are not taken advantage of. The removal of ads for vitamins and drugs from children's television programming does directly respond to the present point (Guber and Berry, 1993: 145). However, it does not go far enough. Since young children do not understand the purpose of ads (cf. McNeal, 1987: 186), they do not fulfill the qualifications of market clients. Accordingly, it is mistaken to speak of restrictions on marketing to the vulnerable (and particularly children) as violating their rights as consumers (cf. McNeal, 1987: 185). Since vulnerable children do not qualify as market clients, they cannot be said to have consumers' rights.

Admittedly, vulnerable individuals such as children will witness marketing to competent market clients. There is no way to stop this, though there may be ways to limit it. In any case, this does not mean that, in marketing to genuine clients, marketers can invoke images, symbols, etc., which are, however, designed to persuade or influence a group of non-competent vulnerable individuals to purchase products (or influence those who do) through the very characteristics which render them unfit to be market clients.

Accordingly, it is not morally acceptable to market goods to specially vulnerable individuals with the intention that they bring pressure to bear on genuine market clients to buy those products and with the expectation that those genuine clients will curb any problems which the use or possession of those products by the specially vulnerable would raise. Such marketing continues to target those who are not fully competent market clients. Further, to depend upon others to prevent harm which the marketing techniques may potentially engender through the purchase of various products is to seek to escape from the responsibility marketers have for the consequences of their actions. It is a case of displaced moral responsibility.

However, the interpretation of the above argument is still incomplete. What about those cases in which marketing takes place to genuine market clients, but the campaigns are (unavoidably) witnessed by the specially vulnerable who positively react upon these campaigns and seek out the marketers' products? Let us assume that R. J. Reynolds' use of "Old Joe" is such an example.[10]

If the effects on the specially vulnerable in such cases were not harmful, then few moral problems would be raised. However, when they are harmful, one must ask whether there are other means of marketing the product which would not have these secondary effects? If marketers, as other individuals, are under the general obligation of doing no harm, or minimizing harm, then they should seek to alter those marketing methods even if the harm is an indirect result of the marketer's intentions. On the other hand, if it is not possible to alter the marketing methods, then means might be sought to limit the exposure to those who are specially vulnerable to these marketing measures. In short, moral marketing requires some response other than simply ignoring the harm done to the vulnerable.

I suggest, then, that a more complete account of marketing and the vulnerable is that marketers may not market their products to target groups (specially vulnerable or not) in such a way that their marketing campaigns significantly affect vulnerable groups through their vulnerabilities. That is, there is nothing in the preceding that says that we must limit the effects of marketers' programs to their intentional aims with regard to a particular target segment. When significant spillover effects arise, they too must be taken into account.

Finally, is it morally justified to use marketing techniques which take advantage of the vulnerabilities of the specially vulnerable but which promote products which members of this group are widely acknowledged to need? For example, may marketers use techniques which young children cannot understand in order to get them to exercise properly or to eat a healthy diet? Or, may marketers use fear appeals to get the elderly to use their medications in a proper manner? Bailey has suggested that public service appeals might use fear appeals to warn certain groups of the elderly about dangers to them (Bailey, 1987: 242). But this misses the point three ways. First, if the use of such appeals violates those who have been rendered specially susceptible to it, then they ought not to be used for good (public service messages) or bad (confidence games) or even ordinary marketing. Second, if some of the elderly are so specially susceptible to messages including fear, then the use of ordinary messages concerning their problems should also reach them. Fear is not needed. They are already concerned about the content of the appeal. Third, public service messages are one kind of "communication," whereas those messages which seek to sell a product or a service are very different. Since the marketing concept speaks of marketers seeking to satisfy consumer needs some seek to use this to slide over into the public message realm. However, this is a slide that rests on an equivocation: public messages solely for the good of the recipient and private messages for the good of the sender, which may also be good for the recipient. In short, if a group is specially vulnerable, the use of unfair techniques which would not ultimately cause them harm is still the use of techniques which treat such individuals unfairly through manipulating them through their vulnerabilities. Only in very special circumstances should such marketing techniques be employed.

VI. CONCLUSION

A number of years ago Morgan and Riordan noted that "certain [market] segments, because of their unique characteristics or particular problems, may have to be treated with extra care" (Morgan and Riordan, 1983: 88). They went on to note that "the next logical step from a marketing perspective would be to see if the 'garden variety' category [of consumer, as opposed to commercial buyers] could be further subdivided, perhaps into normal and disadvantaged subsets" (Morgan and Riordan, 1983: 88). I have argued that we must at least distinguish between normal and vulnerable subsets.

Those who are vulnerable are subject to significant harm to their interests. However, in a market setting responsibilities to this group cannot be identified simply on the basis of the degree of harm they might experience or the total effects on all those in the market. Instead, we must look to various special conditions which render them particularly susceptible to harm and over which they have little control. Individuals so characterized are unable to fulfill additional conditions required to be market clients.

Accordingly, marketers who treat the vulnerable like other market participants or clients treat them unfairly when they take advantage of those characteristics which render them vulnerable. Such unfairness does not require that they be actually harmed, only that they are treated like other qualified market clients. As such, marketers must attempt to understand the behavior of those market segments (or people) which are specially vulnerable and to foresee the kinds of problems which they will have with their products and marketing programs. In short, marketers must first "qualify" as genuine market clients those whom they target through advertisements, promotions, as well as in personal sales.

It follows that the marketing concept must be framed so as to recognize cases involving groups that are specially vulnerable. As marketers, and business more generally, are subject to product liability so too they should be subjected to client liability. This moral doctrine would formulate the nature of marketers' responsibilities to the vulnerable. It is an account of marketing moral responsibility that deserves our considerable attention.[11]

ENDNOTES

1. Goodin claims that "A is more vulnerable to B (1) the more control B has over outcomes that affect A's interests and (2) the more heavily A's interests are at stake in the outcomes that B controls. B is defined as having 'less control' the more likely it is that the outcome will occur (or not occur) whatever B does . . ." (Goodin, 1985: 118). Accordingly, vulnerability is to be interpreted in terms of the lack of control which one agent might have vis-a-vis another agent with regard to the fulfillment of the first agent's interests.
2. I wish to capture here not the ideal market, but a morally justified imperfect market, filled with real participants. Further, I do not attempt to state all the necessary conditions for a capitalist market system, but only to highlight those most important for present purposes.
3. I intend that this allows for the use of credit, loans, etc.
4. It is conceivable that they could transform the vulnerabilities of a normal consumer into special vulnerabilities.
5. Physical vulnerability is *not* being equated here with "unusual susceptibility to physical or biological conditions." These special circumstances render a person specially physically vulnerable only when the following two conditions are also fulfilled.
6. Andreasen writes that "the swindler finds particularly good customers among the disadvantaged, since he expects the consumer not to understand much about contracts and 'formalities,' such as confessions of judgment, and to be unlikely to read legal language carefully or to peruse contracts disguised as receipts" (Andreasen, 1975: 204).

7. Vulnerability, in the grieving, involves a transformation of the self that forces people to face new consumer or market roles when they are least prepared to do so because of the associated stresses (Gentry et al, 1994: 129). This state involves "traumatic confusion" (*Ibid.*); a passage between two worlds; a "marginalized experience often accompanied by isolation and suspension of social status" (*Ibid.*).

8. See McNeal who notes the objection that limited market exposure of children would rob them of "the joy of being a consumer" or "the fun and pleasure that comes with being a consumer" (McNeal, 1987: 183–184).

9. Amongst the members of these specially vulnerable groups which may be treated unfairly by marketers Cohen lists "children, the Ghetto Dweller, the elderly, and the handicapped" (Cohen, 1974: 11).

10. There is much dispute over whether this is the case. For present purposes I will assume that R. J. Reynolds has not directly targeted children.

11. I have benefitted from helpful comments from Françoise Baylis and Jessie Taylor in my preparation of this paper.

REFERENCES

Andreasen, A. R. 1975. *The Disadvantaged Consumer.* New York: The Free Press.

Andreasen, A. R. 1993. Revisiting the Disadvantaged: Old Lessons and New Problems. *Journal of Public Policy & Marketing,* 12: 270–275.

Assael, H. 1993. *Marketing: Principles & Strategy.* Second edition; Fort Worth, Texas: The Dryden Press.

Bailey, J. M. 1987. The Persuasibility of Elderly Consumers. *Current Issues in Research in Advertising,* 10, 1:213–247.

Barnhill, J. A. 1972. Market Injustice: The Case of the Disadvantaged Consumer. *Journal of Consumer Affairs,* 6, 1: 78–83.

Barnhart, C. L. (ed.). 1956. American College Dictionary. New York: Random House.

Cohen, D. 1974. The Concept of Unfairness as It Relates to Advertising Legislation. *Journal of Marketing,* 38: 8–13.

DeGeorge, R. T. 1982. *Business Ethics.* New York: Macmillan Publishing Co. Inc.

Ferrar, R. 1996. Bill Seeks to Reduce 'Ambulance Chasing'. *Knoxville News Sentinel,* January 18, 1996: A3.

Friedman, M. 1962. *Capitalism and Freedom.* Chicago: The University of Chicago Press.

Gentry, J. W., P. F. Kennedy, K. Paul, and R. P. Hill. The Vulnerability of Those Grieving the Death of a Loved One: Implications for Public Policy. *Journal of Public Policy & Marketing,* 13, 2: 128–142.

Goodin, R. E. 1985. *Protecting the Vulnerable.* Chicago: The University of Chicago Press.

Guber, S. S. and Berry, J. 1993. *Marketing to and Through Kids.* New York: McGraw-Hill, Inc.

McNeal, J. U. 1987. *Children as Consumers.* Lexington, Mass., Lexington Books.

Morgan, F. W., Schuler, D. K., Stoltman, J. J. 1995. A Framework for Examining the Legal Status of Vulnerable Consumers. *Journal of Public Policy & Marketing,* 14, 2: 267–277.

Morgan, F. W. and Riordan, E. A. 1983. The Erosion of the Unusual Susceptibility Defense: The Case of the Disadvantaged Consumer. *Journal of the Academy of Marketing Science,* 11, 2: 85–96.

Schnapper, R. 1967. Consumer Legislation and the Poor. *The Yale Law Journal,* 76, 4: 1967: 745–792.

RELATED WEB SITE

Let's Hear it for ethics in marketing: www.stellar.org/global/e-mktg4.html

MARKETING
ETHICS CASES
Denis Collins's Students

In his ethics courses, Professor Denis Collins asks his students to relay ethical dilemmas they have come into contact with; they submitted the following items. Do they seem realistic to you? How would you respond in each case?

- You are a product brand manager for a formerly very successful family firm that was recently bought out by an international firm. For sixty years the family-owned policy was that whenever product expenses were reduced due to new technology, all of the savings were passed on to the consumer to build long-term brand loyalty. The new corporate owners are very sensitive about maximizing short-term profits and increasing stock dividend payments. Should you lower the price and reward consumers, or let the price remain the same and reward stockholders?

- You switch jobs for higher pay and are employed as an engineering manager for one year-old start-up firm. Your new firm employs mostly foreign students right out of college because they are willing to work many hours for low pay in order to stay in the United States. You join the owner to visit a potential new customer. The owner tells the potential customer that the firm has many experienced engineers with high-level abilities, neither of which is true. The customer signs a contract with your firm for its services. When you mention this concern to the owner after the sales meeting he tells you that it works all the time. What would you do? Is this misrepresentation an acceptable exaggeration or an unacceptable lie?

- You are a manager at a bank that is feeling competitive pressures as a result of deregulation. Another manager proposes changing many previous "free" offerings to "fee-based" offerings, such as automatic-teller usage, teller services and check overdrafts. Competitors are charging their customers $20 for overdrafts, a process which only costs $2. The primary customer who has check overdrafts are poor people, who are least able to afford this cost. Low-income customers also use many teller services. What would be your recommendations regarding the proposal to charge $20 for overdrafts and nominal fees for teller services?

- You manage a software store in a shopping mall for a national chain. Managers are paid $20,000 plus a bonus based on the percentage increase over the previous year's sales. The national software chain also sells its product in a national book store chain, which is opening a mega-store on the other side of the shopping mall. You tell corporate headquarters this isn't fair and recommend that the book store sell a different product mix than what you are already offering, and a change in your bonus calculation. Corporate headquarters says that it cannot do these things. What would you do?

THE BODY SHOP CONTROVERSY

BODY SHOP SCRUTINIZED

JOAN BAVARIA, ERIC BECKER AND SIMON BILLENNESS

The following article offers a brief overview of the controversy sur-
rounding cosmetic and body care retailer The Body Shop and its
claims of social responsibility. The story unfolds as you continue to
the following material which includes a letter from Gordon Roddick
of The Body Shop to the subscribers of Business Ethics *magazine*
after the magazine published an expose of The Body Shop's allegedly
false claims. Business Ethics *magazine publisher Marjorie Kelly's*
response to that letter (standing behind the facts as stated in the orig-
inal article) follows. After that letter, you will find Body Shop mission
and principles, as well as social audit material published by both The
Body Shop and its independent auditor, Kirk Hanson. The final judg-
ment is really up to you. What do you believe? Who is credible and
how do you decide? What additional information would you need to
make up your mind?

In the past few weeks the British press has focused on the Body Shop's social record with
an intensity normally reserved for the Royal Family. Since the story broke, Body Shop's
stock has fallen from almost 250 pence to a low of 205 pence. Recently, the stock has recovered to 216 pence.

Two main questions emerge from this debate:

• Why did this issue reach such a boiling point?

• What is the Body Shop's social record?

HOW THE STORY STARTED . . .

In September 1991 *Franklin's Insight* profiled the Body Shop, awarding the company our
highest social ratings. However, since then, we have received information that challenges
our initial assessment of the company. A German newsletter noted that the Body Shop
uses non-plant derived ingredients in its products. A British animal rights organization
criticized the company's animal testing policy. Early this year, investigative reporter Jon

Joan Bavaria, Eric Becker, Simon Billenness, "Body Shop Scrutinized," from *Insight,* published by Franklin
Research and Development. Reprinted by permission of Franklin Research and Development.

Entine provided us with considerable information about apparent contradictions between the Body Shop's image and its actual record on social issues. As we independently investigated, we verified some of Entine's claims.

As 1994 progressed, we also became concerned about the growth prospects of the Body Shop's stock. In early June, *Franklin's Insight* lowered its stock recommendation to a "hold," citing a rise in the stock's price and expansion plans by a competitor. At an early June Social Investment conference in Toronto, Jon Entine discussed the results of his research on the firm. On June 14, callers to *Franklin's Insight's* weekly hotline heard that Body Shop stock had been further downgraded from a "hold" to a "sell" recommendation. On June 17 and on June 22, Franklin Research & Development Corporation sold all 45,950 of its clients' shares in the Body Shop. The following July 15 issue of *Franklin's Insight* stated:

> *Last month we lowered Body Shop to a hold based on concerns that its major competitor [Bath & Body Works] was accelerating its growth in the U.S. and Europe. Given this concern and fears that a fairly negative upcoming magazine article may put some near-term price pressure on the stock, we are lowering our rating to a sell.*

For a while all was quiet. Then on August 19, *Financial Times* reporter Andrew Jack wrote about Franklin Research's decision to sell its Body Shop stock two months before. The London edition's headline, somewhat inaccurately read, "US ethical fund turns against Body Shop." At that point, we had simply "turned against" the Body Shop *stock*. We had still not reached a conclusion on the company's overall social performance.

Then the British Press seemed to declare open season on the Body Shop fueled in part by leaks from Entine's story. Journalists followed the gyration of the stock, probed into the background of Entine and speculated as to the contents of his forthcoming article for the U.S. magazine *Business Ethics,* which was published September 1.

The Body Shop has come to its own defense. The company has released a 32-page "Memorandum of Response to the Allegations of Jon Entine." The Body Shop later released a strong reply to the *Business Ethics* article, which it labeled "recycled rubbish." Anita Roddick was quoted calling one animal rights group which criticized the Body Shop "a bunch of babies."

As the issue has died down a bit in the mainstream media, the debate has intensified within the progressive investment and business community. We hope that our following findings help to shed some light on the Body Shop's social record and serve as another chapter in the emerging profile of the company.

LIMITATIONS

The staff of Franklin Research & Development have spent an extraordinary amount of time verifying the information used in this article. We strive to avoid using inflammatory language or assuming the motives of others. We print information that we believe to be true. But we are not chemists, lawyers or anthropologists, nor do we have the resources and contacts of an investigative news organization. It is also hard to establish the facts of an issue that is being so hotly debated. Consequently, we do not attempt to reach a definitive conclusion, but we try instead to state the facts of the issue as we have been able to ascertain them.

THE BODY SHOP: AS WE SEE IT NOW

Our view of the Body Shop's social record has undergone considerable changes since our last profile. The issue is not necessarily just whether the Body Shop has a good or bad relative record of corporate responsibility. The Body Shop has clearly set for itself high standards. However, the company has also enjoyed positive tangible benefits from those publicly espoused standards while, apparently, failing to meet many of them.

Moreover, and perhaps more importantly, the company has compounded what otherwise might be isolated and curable difficulties by repeatedly failing to provide material information to back up its claims and by repeatedly taking a combative stance with its critics. This defensive and almost secretive posture violates what we consider to be cornerstones of social responsibility: openness and accessibility at the highest level of management. We believe we should hold even the most well-intentioned company accountable to this standard. We hope that the following article fairly represents the record of the Body Shop in several key areas.

FRANCHISES

Since the Body Shop is largely a wholesaler and franchisor, the company's dealings with its franchisees are an important part of the firm's record of corporate responsibility. We have no evidence of problems between the company and its British franchisees. However, there appear to be serious disputes between the Body Shop and some overseas franchisees.

In June 1994, the Body Shop settled a breach of contract suit with its former Norwegian franchisee. In a counterclaim, the Body Shop's former Asian head franchisee is suing the company for conspiracy and breach of obligation. In March 1994, the U.S. Federal Trade Commission (FTC) began an investigation of the Body Shop. According to the U.S. General Accounting Office, in the period 1989–92, the FTC received more than 1,360 complaints but began only 78 franchise rule and business opportunity investigations. Of the 78 cases, the FTC filed 14 court cases, closed 31 cases and continued investigating 33 cases.

The FTC has issued a civil investigation demand (CID), to at least one former Body Shop franchisee. The Body Shop confirms that current franchisees have also received FTC questionnaires. FTC Franchise Rule Director Steven Toporoff told *Insight* that there is no clear distinction between an FTC inquiry and an investigation. He added that the FTC uses CID's "fairly frequently" and in instances where the FTC is unable to obtain information voluntarily. In a letter from the FTC, purported to be to a former Body Shop franchisee, it is revealed that the franchisee was concerned that providing information to the FTC would violate a provision in the contract for the resale of the franchise to the franchisor that requires the franchisee "not to write about or speak about or do or perform directly or indirectly, any act injurious or prejudicial to the good will associated with franchisors' proprietary marks or business."

Susan Kezios, president of the American Franchisee Association, told *Insight* she has received complaints from about 10 of the Body Shop's 58 franchisees. It is unclear whether the franchisees are complaining about the conduct of Body Shop employees or company head franchisees. However, some of the complaints include allegations that prospective franchisees were misled about their expected earnings when they were quoted the lower merchandise prices charged to head franchisees when, in fact, they later had to pay the higher price charged to franchisees. Both Kezios and a staff member of the House Committee on Small Business—which investigates franchising—told *Insight* that the Body Shop treats its franchisees no better than most franchisors. Kezios added that the Body Shop franchisees that contacted her insisted on anonymity and seemed "more fearful" than franchisees she had spoken to at other companies.

Body Shop investor relations manager Angela Bawtree told *Insight* of steps the company had recently taken to improve its relationship with franchisees. Over the last year, the Body Shop has set up a committee of franchisees and corporate management. In addition, in some cases, the company now provides loan guarantees for franchisees. The Body Shop has also decided in some cases to open stores in more marginal locations itself before selling them to franchisees. As a measure of franchisee satisfaction with the Body Shop, Bawtree cited the firm's low turnover of franchisees.

We hope that the Body Shop works to resolve the apparent problems with its franchisees. However, the existence of the FTC investigation and the lawsuits do force us to question the Body Shop's reputation as a responsible business partner.

PRODUCT QUALITY

There is evidence that challenges the Body Shop's claim that its products are of "high quality." Letters between the Body Shop and its franchisees dating from 1990 and 1991 mention problems with old and contaminated products. In 1993, a batch of 151 bottles of contaminated banana shampoo were sold to U.S. consumers. According to documents obtained through the Freedom of Information Act, the Food & Drug Administration (FDA) inspected the Body Shop's new headquarters in North Carolina on October 7, 8 and November 12 of 1993. The inspectors found seven irregularities including improper sampling for bacteria in bulk containers, skipped tests and failure to follow-up bacteria problems with its product filling jets, missing records to document proper cleaning and sanitizing of its equipment and inconsistent handling of consumer complaints.

According to Angela Bawtree, the banana shampoo incident occurred at a time when the Body Shop was moving operations from New Jersey to North Carolina. She also notes that, while the FDA made recommendations after its inspection, it did not issue a notice of violation. According to Bawtree, over 60% of such inspections result in the issuance of a notice of violation and, in the last three years, more than 100 such notices have been issued to cosmetics firms. The Body Shop also claims that the FDA inspection was prompted by Jon Entine. We would feel much more comfortable with the Body Shop's response to the issue of product quality if the company focused more on what actions it has taken to prevent future problems and less on trying to discredit Jon Entine.

NATURAL PRODUCTS

In the Body Shop's early years, its products were described as "natural" even though they contained chemical and synthetic ingredients. Several years ago the Body Shop started to more accurately describe its products as "naturally-based." However, as recently as September 1992, Anita Roddick said in an interview with *Business Ethics* that the Body Shop "just [used] food stuffs rather than chemical formulas."

Angela Bawtree told *Insight* that the dominant ingredient in many Body Shop products is water, which is natural. However, using this standard, almost any personal care product could be labeled "naturally-based." In fact, while the company's products derive their names, if not their fragrance or color, from flowers, vegetables or fruits, one is hard pressed to find Body Shop products without synthetic ingredients. For example, the Aloe Hair Gel label reads "Water, Rosewater, SD Alcohol 40-B, Aloe Vera Gel, PVP (setting agent), Triethanolamine, PEG-75 Lanoline, Propylene Glycol, Carbomer 940, Phenoxyethanol, Polysorbate 20, Methylparaben, Benzophenone-4, Disodium EDTA, Sodium Dehydroacetate, Propylparaben, Fragrance, FD&C Yellow No. 5, FD&C Blue No. 1."

While we cannot pretend to have done any more than the most cursory research on this point, *Insight* observes that two readily available competing products, "Shampure," by Aveda and Tom's of Maine's "natural shampoo," both appear to use all natural ingredients and, unlike the Body Shop, make it clear on the product label where the ingredients were obtained.

We cannot determine if the Body Shop intentionally misrepresented the nature of its products. The question that we pose is whether the Body Shop should be held responsible for the public perception of its products if that perception diverges from the truth?

We would answer "yes" to the question even though this means holding the Body Shop to a higher standard. In today's marketplace, companies regularly employ exaggeration and allow misinterpretation as a general practice. However, Anita Roddick has clearly denounced this standard puffery and has portrayed the Body Shop as "the most honest cosmetics company in the world." Since the Body Shop has recently stated that it is "a leader in product disclosure" and since we believe that the Body Shop has benefited from subtle public misperceptions, we feel that it should, at least, join Aveda and Tom's of Maine in stating the source of each ingredient on its product packaging.

ENVIRONMENT

There has been much media coverage of three leaks of product from the Body Shop's former New Jersey warehouse. According to the records of the company and the local Hanover Sewerage Authority, at least 62 gallons of shampoo and shower gel were released. It also appears that the spills were first identified by the officials of the Hanover Sewerage authority and traced back to the Body Shop. Although the pattern of spills suggests that management at the Body Shop's facility was lax in its safeguards and tardy in its reporting, the severity of the incidences is immaterial compared to the company's overall environmental record.

The Body Shop's record of environmental auditing and disclosure is impressive. The Body Shop is a signatory of the CERES Principles, an environmental code of conduct created by environmentalists and social investors including the Franklin Research. Moreover, the Body Shop is also the only company that we know of to have set up environmental management systems and an annual environmental audit that follows the voluntary European Union Eco-Management and Audit Regulation. The Body Shop has made efforts to comply with the regulation since it was available in draft form in 1991. In its 1993/94 "Green Book" the Body Shop provides an independently verified environmental statement according to EU regulation standards for the company's main UK Watersmead facility. The statement includes comparable information on energy efficiency, water usage and waste generation going back three years. The Green Book also contains information on product stewardship, training and some information on the environmental impact of its facilities around the world. While we question whether the Body Shop has lived up to its claims in other areas of its business, we find its stated efforts on environmental disclosure to be well founded.

TRADE NOT AID

"Trade Not Aid" (recently renamed "Direct Trading") has been a high-profile Body Shop slogan. It refers to the firm's "direct sourcing projects," which according to the Body Shop "create livelihoods for economically stressed communities. . . ." Images of Anita Roddick traveling the world and developing products using ingredients from indigenous communities have been at the heart of the Body Shop's public relations efforts. Gordon Roddick claims that "Trade Not Aid is quickly growing into a cornerstone for the Body Shop. . . . The next ten years will see a huge development in this part of our business." But Trade Not Aid has come under fire from some activists and anthropologists who feel the projects are, in fact, patronizing and exist more for the benefit of the Body Shop's image than for the communities they purport to assist. Others have criticized the Body Shop for focusing so much attention on a program which accounts for a small percentage of its business.

Fair trade initiatives are inherently complex and are easy targets for critics who feel that it is "neo-colonialism." But it is a relatively new field, especially for corporate involvement, and we would withhold judgment about the overall impact of such programs until there is further evidence that they are either constructive or destructive.

We see three issues at the heart of the debate. First, is Trade Not Aid based on a well researched understanding of economic, environmental and anthropological issues? Second, has the Body Shop worked sensitively with communities in implementing its projects? Third, has the Body Shop accurately represented its Trade Not Aid activities? While it is hard to characterize the whole program based on one or two projects, because of space and time considerations we will focus principally on the Body Shop's project with the Kayapo Indians in Brazil.

In 1991 the Body Shop began working with the Kayapo to harvest Brazil Nut oil which is used in its bestselling Brazil Nut Hair Conditioner. The Body Shop also buys beaded wristbands made by Kayapo women. In its promotional materials the Body Shop states that the harvest of Brazil Nuts is "a viable and sustainable alternative to cutting down their forests." But according to Terence Turner, an anthropologist at the University of Chicago, the Kayapo make the bulk of their income from selling logging and mining concessions on their lands, precisely the activities that the Body Shop claims it is preventing. Turner told *Insight* that the money the Kayapo make from the Brazil Nut oil and wristbands is just supplemental income that could never match the level of income achieved by selling logging and mining rights.

But Darrell Posey, an Oxford anthropologist who has worked with both the Kayapo and the Body Shop, told *Insight* that "the forces are great and the subversion by logging companies is irresistible. It is unfair to expect that the Body Shop project could offset these forces. We all underestimated the power and ruthlessness of the logging mafia. . . . They will stop at nothing." Given the complexity of the issue, we question whether it is appropriate for the Body Shop to claim that purchases of Brazil Nut Conditioner "give [the Kayapo] an income to help protect the Amazon rainforest," as stated in Body Shop stores. But we find it difficult to fault the Body Shop merely for participating in an effort to assist indigenous peoples through trade agreements.

Turner told *Insight* that the Body Shop set up the Brazil Nut Oil project as a "commercial operation" managed by a non Indian Brazilian, Saulo Petean, rather than as a trade arrangement between two equal parties. He says that the Kayapo make fair wages, but that they are not in control of the project, which is run in an authoritarian manner by Petean. Turner says the Kayapo have called repeatedly for his removal, to no avail.

The Body Shop responds that Petean is "an ally of indigenous peoples," and that "he has to act as the liaison and organizational instructor for the Kayapo to help them control the use of the airplane, keep the accounts, . . . appoint officers and register the businesses for export." Posey says that the Body Shop "sent a person as experienced as existed to work and live with the Kayapo and guide both sides in this project." Nevertheless, according to the Body Shop, Petean "is scheduled to turn over all aspects of the trade links in August of 1995." But the question raised is whether the Body Shop's Trade Not Aid programs "give people control over their resources, land and lives," as claimed. Posey states that "the Body Shop has done as good a job as anyone could expect." Another anthropologist told *Insight,* "If the Kayapo had run the project from day one, it probably would have failed."

Turner states that the firm's work with the Kayapo is "a public relations ploy above all" which aids the Body Shop in promoting its image while offering the Kayapo little trade in return. The Body Shop has used images of the Kayapo extensively in its stores and its "information broadsheets." According to Turner, the Kayapo have not been compensated for these images, which have furthered the Body Shop's corporate image as an environmentally and culturally sensitive company.

In response, the Body Shop claims that it pays the Kayapo well above market price for Brazil Nut oil, thereby implicitly compensating the Kayapo for the use of their images. But Turner says there is no true market price, as there is only one other producer of Brazil Nut oil worldwide. According to the Body Shop's Mark Johnston, the images have been shown to and approved by Kayapo representatives. The Body Shop also agreed to a broad covenant with the Kayapo that outlines a set of principles for any future trading arrangements, including clauses covering intellectual property rights (IPR). It aims to ensure that future commercial development of products based on Kayapo knowledge would be implemented in full and equal cooperation with the Kayapo. The covenant was not signed by either party and is not a legal document. Mark Johnston of the Body Shop told *Insight* it would be used as a template for trading contracts. To date the Body Shop has signed no formal IPR agreements with its Trade Not Aid partners, despite publicizing a May 1993 announcement that it intended to sign an IPR agreement with an indigenous group.

Despite the difficulties with these projects, all parties acknowledge that the Kayapo do not want the Body Shop to pull out. In fact, other Kayapo villages have asked the Body Shop to establish new projects. A Kayapo statement released by the Body Shop says, "The chiefs are pleased with the businesses they make with the Body Shop because it is a way for the community to earn money to buy the things they need without having to work in the city. . . . We discuss our business with the Body Shop, as equals, from company to company."

Other Trade Not Aid projects offer fewer obstacles, such as the Body Shop's purchases of organic Blue Corn flour from the Santa Ana Pueblo in New Mexico. Jerry Kinsman, the manager of the project told *Insight* the tribe has had a "very honest, straightforward relationship" with the Body Shop. But we find it misleading when the Body Shop claims that the project "indirectly" affects 3 villages and 500 Native Americans. Kinsman told *Insight* that the project employs 9 full time equivalent Native American employees and that all profits (which are tiny) are reinvested in the project, not distributed to the community.

Richard Adams of New Consumer, a British consumer advocacy group, has criticized the Body Shop for sourcing a tiny fraction of its ingredients through Trade Not Aid, yet publicizing the projects heavily. The Body Shop admits that, "Although direct sourcing from such communities is currently just a small percentage of all our trade, we intend to increase this practice wherever possible." Adams has repeatedly requested the Body Shop to disclose what percentage of its raw materials purchases are obtained through Trade Not Aid projects. While it has not responded directly to this request, the Body Shop states that its Trade Not Aid purchases from producers amounted to £1.2 million in FY1994, double that of the previous year. Based on those figures, Adams has calculated that in FY1993 just 0.165% of gross retail sales ended up in the pockets of Trade Not Aid producers.

The Body Shop states that it is increasing the number of ingredients sourced through Trade Not Aid, citing recent purchases of cocoa butter and shea butter from cooperatives. Adams has stated that he is encouraged by the Body Shop's commitment to working with alternative trade organizations and non-government organizations involved in fair trade initiatives.

As in other areas *Insight* examined, we found the Body Shop less than forthright when presenting its Trade Not Aid program in company materials. Though its flyers may be factually accurate, they leave the impression that the Body Shop ethically sources all or most of its ingredients, rather than the tiny number that are part of Trade Not Aid. For example, in a Spring 1994 publication the Body Shop offered the headline "How We Do Business: DIRECT TRADING." In much smaller print, the flyer acknowledged that direct sourcing is "just a small percentage of all our trade." We feel that the language that the Body Shop uses in its literature still requires revision if it is to truly reflect the scale of the projects it supports.

CHARITABLE GIVING

Over the past year, the Body Shop's level of charitable giving has increased dramatically, from 0.89% of pretax profits in the fiscal year ending February 1993 to nearly 3% of pretax profits in 1994. This new figure compares well to the average annual U.S. corporate giving figure of 1.9% but falls short of the level of contributions made by such socially responsible corporation as Dayton Hudson (5%), Ben & Jerry's (7.5%) and Patagonia

(10%). However, it should be noted that the Body Shop's figure does not take into account its employees' voluntary activities taken on company time as well as the publicity provided by the Body Shop to organizations like Amnesty International in its company campaigns.

CORPORATE GOVERNANCE

As both investors and as a company that has taken the effort to recruit an active board made up of a majority of qualified outside directors, we are frankly not impressed by the Body Shop's inability thus far to name a single independent board member. The Body Shop currently does not comply with the British "Code of Best Practice" recommended by the Report of the Committee on the Financial Aspects of Corporate Governance. Consequently, the company's stockholders lack such independent checks and balances as an independent audit and remuneration committee. The Body Shop has repeatedly promised that the appointment of independent directors will be forthcoming.

RESPONSE TO CRITICISM

The issue that has concerned us the most is the Body Shop's extremely combative response to criticism and its readiness to use legal action or threats of legal action. For instance, in its replies to the article in *Business Ethics,* the Body Shop repeatedly attacks the credibility of its critics, sometimes using invective, rather than just addressing the criticism.

Since our first contact with the Body Shop on this issue in March, the Body Shop has stated consistently that they first encountered Jon Entine when he was preparing a story for ABC's Primetime but that ABC decided not to run the story and Jon Entine no longer works for ABC. We feel this statement strongly implies that ABC fired Entine, a point that ABC has denied. We feel that Jon Entine's background is irrelevant.

In a recent press release, the Body Shop characterized the recent *Business Ethics* article on the company as "a poorly researched piece in a tiny newsletter." According to *Business Ethics,* the magazine received letters from the Body Shop's attorneys threatening possible legal action for libel before the article was even published. According to Angela Bawtree, the Body Shop is still reviewing its legal position in regard to the magazine. If, as it claims, *Business Ethics* checked and published the article in good faith and a lawsuit would bankrupt the magazine, we would consider a lawsuit by the Body Shop as unfair and likely to stifle further legitimate public discussion of the company.

We are also particularly concerned at the way in which the Body Shop has treated Richard Adams, Director of New Consumer, a British non-profit that publishes research on corporate responsibility issues. In our view, Adams has, since the fall of last year, made legitimate requests to the Body Shop for information that backs up the company's claims. The Body Shop has refused to provide what we would consider to be readily obtainable and non-proprietary information, such as the amount of goods bought through its Trade Not Aid programs, stating: "[Adams'] close relationship with, and support for, Entine's 'investigation' over the past year makes all his opinions highly suspect. "We find this claim of "guilt-by-association" unwarranted considering the thoughtful and fair tone of Adams' writing for New Consumer and his extensive experience in the field of alternative trading relationships with developing countries.

CONCLUSION

After months of research, *Insight* has come to believe that certain recent criticism of the Body Shop is justified. In our view, the problems are quite correctable and there is evidence that the company is currently making improvements in almost all areas. Two important points remain unresolved.

The first is the gap between the Body Shop's image and its reality. We believe that any company seeking public approval must accept responsibility not only for what is said literally but also for the impression that is left. Through clever public relations, the Body Shop carefully cultivated an image which is inconsistent with the company's sometimes less than impressive performance, and we believe that the company should take measures to close the gap.

The second major problem we have with the Body Shop is its response to criticism, particularly in the press. Although there is a cultural difference between practices in Britain and practices in America where the First Amendment guarantees free speech, the Body Shop's consistent use of character assassination and its habit of assuming motives is offensive and virtually unheard of in our experience. The Body Shop's bombastic tactics have set back any legitimate attempts by the company to change and seem to be currently triggering a backlash. In our opinion, it is important that the company be much more constructive with its critics. The wounds left by the company's defensiveness will be hard to heal. But nothing is impossible.

LETTER TO BUSINESS
ETHICS SUBSCRIBERS
GORDON RODDICK

Shortly after the publication of Body Shop criticism in an article in Business Ethics *magazine, Gordon Roddick sent the following letter to its subscribers, in defense of The Body Shop. How Mr. Roddick obtained the list of subscribers is still in controversy.*

22 September 1994

Dear fellow *Business Ethics* subscriber,

I sit down to write this letter with some anger and considerable sadness. It concerns the article "Shattered Image," which appeared in the September/October issue of *Business Ethics.* As you are probably aware, that article contained allegations that maligned and defamed our company, my wife and me. Although a representative of The Body Shop is quoted in the article, making it appear that we were given an opportunity to respond, in fact we were not informed of most of the charges prior to publication. Such treatment would be indefensible under any circumstances, but it is especially troubling when the right to a fair hearing is denied by a magazine with "ethics" in its title.

It has become clear that writing to you personally is the only way we can be sure you will have the chance to hear our side of the case. Hence, this letter.

Frankly, it is difficult to know where to begin rebutting an article filled with as many lies, distortions, and gross inaccuracies as this one. I suppose we have to give the author some credit for throwing together such an impressive volume of information. It is his attempt to confuse and misrepresent the reality of a company that has struggled hard for 18 years to be in the forefront of a movement seeking a different way of doing business.

Where the information comes from is another matter. Of the 22 sources named in the article, 10 are disgruntled former employees or franchisees, current competitors, or disappointed bidders for our business, all of whom obviously have personal reasons for wanting to make The Body Shop look bad. Four other sources have either strenuously denied their quotes or said their words have been used out of context in a way that entirely distorts their meaning. Yet another five sources are cited for opinions they expressed about social investment in general, opinions that have been turned around so as to make them appear to be highly critical of The Body Shop.

There is, in fact, almost no attempt to observe the normal standards of journalism. The article cites two people as "independent experts," for example, without mentioning

Letter to *Business Ethics* magazine subscribers from Gordon Roddick, chairman of The Body Shop, dated Sept. 22, 1994.

that they are among our competitors. Elsewhere, a competitor's marketing newsletter is used to provide "expert analysis," again without noting the obvious conflict of interest. And another alleged "source," The Federal Trade Commission, has already issued a flat-out denial that is has commented on The Body Shop practices in any way, shape, or form. We understand from the FTC that *Business Ethics* have agreed to print a correction in the next issue.

But to see what is really going on here, it is necessary to look at some of the specific allegations in detail. Consider the opening snapshot of two former franchisees, Stacy and Larry Benes, who are portrayed as terrified, bankrupt people somehow done in by our malfeasance. The implication is that such stories are common throughout our organization. Nothing could be further from the truth.

To begin with, there is more to the Beneses' story than the author chose to report. Stacy and Larry Benes were like many other people who come to us for a franchise, whenever we begin trading in a country or a region. They bring us their hopes and dreams, which may or may not be achievable. We try to select franchisees with realistic expectations and the ability to fulfill them. It is very much in our interest as a franchisor to do so. Sometimes we make mistakes in our selection.

In the case of the Beneses, we were led to believe that Larry had a full-time job and Stacy would run the shop, which would thus have to provide income for just one person. Whatever they say now, they were clearly told at the time that a single shop in Charlottesville, Va., could not possibly do more, at least in the first few years. Whether it could do even that well depended to a great degree on what the Beneses were prepared to put into it. Sadly, they turned out to be neither good franchisees nor good retailers. They so mismanaged the business that a group of their employees came to us to complain about their behavior and their values. Meanwhile, they were taking out more than $80,000 a year for themselves in their first year of operations—somewhat more than either Anita or I were paid annually during The Body Shop's first decade. Eventually, they wound up in financial difficulty, owing the company more than $200,000 for products they had bought from us on credit and then sold. Rather than sue them for payment, we agreed to repurchase the store.

As unfortunate as such episodes are, it is ridiculous to suggest they are typical of our relationships with franchisees. Within 24 hours of this article's publication, 95% of our U.S. franchisees signed a letter repudiating the accusations in it. The fact is that we operate on a worldwide basis trading either directly or through head franchisees in more than 40 countries with more than 1,100 stores, of which 1,000 are owned by approximately 650 franchisees. There are always some disputes between franchisor and franchisees. That's the nature of business. But our disputes have actually been far milder than is common. In 18 years of operation, we have terminated the contract of only one franchisee, and that was in England. (She had fired all her employees on grounds that could only be described as lunatic. We put them on our payroll, some 50 people in all, many of whom had mortgages and other financial obligations, and we kept paying them until the dispute was resolved.) In addition, we had litigation in Norway that was settled amicably. There is presently litigation in Singapore, but we are hopeful it, too, can be settled.

Such conflicts are the daily bread of any business. The unusual part is that we have had so few of them, as *Business Ethics* would surely have discovered had it checked the facts of this article with independent franchising experts. Instead, it appears to have relied on the author's own biased sources, who naturally confirmed what they's already said to him.

The same pattern repeats itself throughout the article. There is, for example, the assertion that we stole The Body Shop's name, concept, and products from Jane Saunders and Peggy Short, who had a natural cosmetic business of the same name based in Berkeley, Ca. The charge is pure rubbish. Jane and Peggy do not make such claims. They have stated that the company "didn't rip us off" and that there have always been "fundamental differences" between their stores and ours. (I am using their words here.) Had they thought otherwise, we would probably not have been able to develop the warm and cordial relationship we have with them and their companies, a relationship that continues to this day.

Indeed, the fundamental differences in our retail styles and appearance are instantly obvious to anyone who visits the two companies' shops. After the author of "Shattered Image" showed up at the Saunders', we heard from Jane Saunder's daughter, Ann, who wrote us saying a man named Jon Entine (the author of the *Business Ethics* article) had "barged in" on her and starting making claims about our supposed larceny. She told him she "had no knowledge of anything he was talking about." She said "his 'facts' are wrong." Entine has since alleged that there is a gag order preventing Jane Saunders, Peggy Short, and others from commenting on the relationship. In her letter, Ann wrote that she specifically told him there was no such gag order.

Another person supposedly under a gag order is Mark Constantine, who was a major supplier to us for more than a decade and whom we worked with to develop many of our early products. He wrote me after reading the opinions ascribed to him in the article. Judge his remarks about Entine for yourself:

> It would appear that he has edited, or, worse, twisted my comments. Taking a few of the points, "Roddick's first business partner, cosmetologist Mark Constantine (who is under a gag order prohibiting him from discussing it)," . . . "suggest that Anita knew about the Berkeley company."
>
> Oh how I wish I had been your business partner! . . . "cosmetologist," I am not a cosmetologist.
>
> "Under a gag order", no gag order. See the interview in last Sunday's Mirror as an example. Anyway, how can I suggest something if I'm under a gag order?
>
> He suggested that Anita knew about the Berkeley company, and I was shocked when he asked me. I didn't deny it because I did not know. I was entertained to see the examples he chose of similarities: "loofah sponges and glycerin and rosewater lotion."
>
> I take offense at the next paragraph, "The Body Shop's most basic myth." Anita was the first person to recognize that the products that I formulated had a greater amount of "naturals" than any others on the market, then or now. She gave me a much needed break at a time when no one was interested in natural ingredients as anything but label claims. I went to great pains to explain this, and the guy phoned me back and read this paragraph to me. It was rubbish then, and I told him, and it's still rubbish now.

Mark's letter reflects the frustration we have all felt in trying to deal with this article. There are sensible questions that could be raised, and we would all learn from such a discussion. I make no appeal for The Body Shop to be exempt from criticism or scrutiny. We are happy to open up our hearts, our minds, and our company to those who wish to examine us, provided they accept their responsibility to be balanced and fair.

But I am at a loss to find *anything* balanced or fair in this article. In its zeal to impugn our commitment to our principles, it goes after our Trade Not Aid program, building its attack around an utterly irrelevant statistic—the percentage of our ingredients that come from Trade Not Aid projects. What is this number supposed to reveal? It certainly tells nothing about the effectiveness of our efforts. Or the amount of time and energy we have put into nurturing these projects. Or the obstacles we have had to overcome due to the lack of infrastructure in disenfranchised, Third World communities—transport difficulties, investment problems, absence of technological capabilities, cultural issues, the need to build trust and personal relationships, and so on. One single ingredient, such as Brazil nut oil or cocoa butter, may take two years or more to source and develop. Believe me, there are much easier ways to do business than by taking on the problems of such projects. We don't do it to "save the planet." In most cases, we do it because we are asked to help by the disenfranchised communities themselves. The only significant measure of our success is the number of people who are directly and beneficially affected by our activities. That number, I am proud to say, runs into the thousands. It can best be verified by talking to the communities we have assisted—another thing *Business Ethics* neglected to do.

A letter was written to *Business Ethics* on 26th August 1994 from Jerry Kinsman, the program manager of Santa Ana Agricultural Enterprises (The Pueblo of Santa Ana is a federally recognized American Indian Tribe located in New Mexico). In this letter he says: "*I hope you will give some importance to what representatives of Body Shop's trading partners have to say about that company.*"

However, *Business Ethics* chose to ignore that request.

Kinsman writes:

> *Be assured that the people of Santa Ana Pueblo are very pleased with and proud of the connection with Body Shop. Whereas the direct profit from sales to BSI [The Body Shop] has been very beneficial, it should be noted that the relationship has had an indirect multiplier effect on the Tribe's Blue Corn business. Public notice from the association, in and of itself, has brought in more public notice—and more business. Santa Ana has become* the *place to observe successful Native American development efforts. Has Body Shop been the singular cause of that accomplishment? Clearly not! More than any other factor, the Tribe's achievements are a function of some very savvy people knowing what they want for themselves. Has Body Shop been important? Clearly yes! . . . I must inform you that Santa Ana is not a victim of BSI. Rather, the Tribe is an ardent supporter of its approach to trade.*

And let me tell you about a Trade Not Aid project that produces *no* ingredients for our products. It is called *The Big Issue,* and it is a newspaper sold by about 2,000 vendors, almost all of them homeless people, in London, Edinburgh, Glasgow, Manchester, and several other cities in our own backyard. Its average weekly circulation is 200,000. It has been going for three years now and has been financially self-sufficient on an operating basis for some time. Recently it moved into a new building with a print shop, meeting rooms, and a cafe.

I myself started this project after seeing the homeless newspaper called *Street News* being sold in New York. I persuaded an old friend of mine to be the editor. Together we launched *The Big Issue* despite a feasibility study warning against the idea. The Body Shop put in $450,000 over two years, and The Body Shop Foundation contributed another $350,000. As large as the investment was, the possibility of losing the money was not, in fact, the greatest risk we faced. Far more serious was the risk that the project might go wrong and wind up harming our reputation. That is always a danger when you work with disadvantaged people. In the case of the homeless, you are wide open to accusations of promoting drug abuse, violence, alcoholism, welfare fraud, and so on—all issues around which passions run high. The possibility of scandal is a given. You can't avoid it, especially in the early phases of a project, when you are feeling your way and haven't yet figured out the necessary controls. So far we have been lucky. We have also had an enormous amount of help—from the police authorities, commercial businesses, and non-profit foundations. We have thanked them all in the newspaper itself. Still the fact remains that the risk was, and is, ours. If scandal comes, if the project fails, The Body Shop will take the heat.

We are not looking here for credit, or recognition. I would not have brought it up at all but for this unscrupulous attack in a magazine called *Business Ethics.* I mention *The Big Issue* only because it is one of several projects that we talk little about, but that have provided some small measure of hope or work for a lot of people. Those people are the entire reason for doing these things. Yet they are the ones who get lost when high-minded organizations quibble about the percentage of ingredients produced under our Trade Not Aid policy.

I could go on and on cataloguing the error and misrepresentation in this article, but it would take a small book to answer every one of Entine's allegations. We have, in fact, prepared such a document and would be happy to send it to you if you are interested. Meanwhile, there are a couple of other matters I must address, including the charge by Entine, and the editors of *Business Ethics,* and others that we have used thuggery and legal threats to suppress legitimate criticism of The Body Shop.

Let me say straight off that Anita and I are very protective of the business we have built, and we have probably been oversensitive and overdefensive to criticism at times. But look at the history.

In 1992, representatives of a company called Fulcrum Productions approached us about a program on The Body Shop they wanted to make for Channel 4, a British television channel. They asked for our help, assuring us they would produce a fair and balanced piece. We let them film at our headquarters in England and our Soapworks factory in Glasgow. We gave them volumes of printed material as well as in-house videos, films, and stills that they wound up using in the program. They had full access to the company. We answered every question they raised. Both Anita and I made ourselves available for interviews on camera. Subsequently, the producer admitted, under oath, that we had been very cooperative.

The program Fulcrum produced was a shamefully biased piece that defamed The Body Shop, Anita, and me. In order to keep it from being sold into the 40-odd other countries where we trade, we decided after lengthy deliberation to sue Channel 4 and Fulcrum Productions.

We won the libel action after a grueling six-week trial in the British High Court. Thousands of documents, internal memos, position papers, and videos were paraded before the jury, along with every other scrap of information that might possibly be relevant. Anita and I and others in the company were cross-examined for days on end. I personally put in four days in the witness box. The intensity of the process made a social audit look like a day at the fairground.

Contrary to what you may have heard, truth *is* a defense against libel in the U.K. Had the charges in the program proved to be truthful, Fulcrum and Channel 4 would have won the case, and we would have had to pay their legal bills. Instead, we were completely vindicated. The jury found in favor of Anita, myself, and The Body Shop. The defendants had to pay damages of 276,00 pounds plus our court costs. Our total award required them to pay us in excess of one and a half (1.5) million dollars. In addition, they were served with an injunction forbidding them from repeating any of the defamatory statements they were found to have made, including those concerning our public positions on environmental, human rights, and animal testing issues.

It would be difficult to imagine a more public airing of the issues surrounding The Body Shop. It would be equally unimaginable that rational human beings would willingly subject themselves twice to the level of stress involved in such a court action.

Four weeks after the end of the trial, Jon Entine showed up at our headquarters in England, saying he was working on a piece about The Body Shop for ABC's Prime Time Live. We gave him hundreds of pages of documents and offered to provide more. Within days, however, we began hearing from suppliers, franchisees, and independent organizations about his investigation of us. His technique was literally to harass people until he got something he could use. He called one of our suppliers more than seven times in two days. Whenever he got hold of somebody, he would misrepresent what another person had said in an aggressive attempt to elicit "on-the-record" responses from the person he was talking to. These remarks he would then repeat to his next subject, distorting them as necessary. In this manner, he created a maelstrom of misinformation and fear wherever he went.

We eventually got fed up with all this and contacted people at ABC to advise them of their producer's outrageous behavior. Entine left ABC with the program unfinished. He alleges, of course, that we intimidated the network. It is hard to believe that a major news organization with a reputation for hard-nosed investigative journalism would be intimidated by the likes of The Body Shop, especially if we are as supposedly evil and as despicable as he had said on many occasions. Then again, we do not know for sure what happened at ABC. Our best source is the deputy editor of *The Sunday Times,* England's leading weekend newspaper, who wrote me a letter on October 8, 1993, after we had questioned a story the newspaper had run on the proposed Prime Time Live piece following its cancellation: In his letter he said:

> We *[The Sunday Times] have now established what we did not know then, that ABC discovered Entine had made a number of mistakes in his methodology, so serious that they had in effect fired him some 10 days before. Entine, probably unknown to ABC, was however picking up his messages from a phone on his old desk in the ABC building. We now understand from ABC sources that Entine is regarded as out of control and has been running around saying some wild things.*

So, whatever may have happened inside ABC, Entine was misrepresenting himself as part of ABC to a journalist at *The Sunday Times* after he had already left the network. Moreover, he was telling the journalist that the Prime Time Live segment would be shown when he knew it would not. As it turned out, he was playing much the same game with the Food and Drug Administration.

Unbeknownst to us, Entine, while still at ABC, had gone to the FDA with a number of untrue allegations, leading inspectors to make a surprise visit to our new headquarters in Wake Forest, N.C. They issued no citations or violation notices. Undeterred, Entine, now gone from ABC, but leaving the FDA inspector with the impression that he was still with them and headed our way with hidden cameras—got the FDA to make a second inspection. Again, no citations. Having failed twice, Entine did not give up—he obtained a copy of the internal FDA notes of their visits and leaked them to other journalists, trying to start a story that we had problems with the FDA.

There was one problem with his strategy, however, and he was well aware of it. The internal documents made it absolutely clear that the FDA inspections were initiated "*in response to allegations made by a Prime Time news reporter.*" Entine found a simple solution to his problem. By his own admission, he falsified the FDA documents to blot out his name and all references to himself as the source of the "complaints"; he circulated the FDA documents that directly misled other reporters to believe he, Jon Entine, was not at the start, middle and end of this whole episode.

Let's face it: this is not the behavior of a responsible journalist. I dare say it is not the behavior of a journalist at all. I certainly cannot imagine a real journalist launching a campaign to drive down the share price of a company he was writing about. Yet Entine did just that, even calling up Peter Lynch's office to urge him to dump Fidelity's holdings of The Body Shop stock. Entine also showed up in Toronto at a meeting of the Social Investment Forum and harangued the assembly about The Body Shop until he was told to sit down. He then proceeded to hand out copies of a grossly defamatory article he had written about us for *Vanity Fair,* which had rejected it. This same article he circulated to social activists, fair trade organizations, animal rights advocates, and others on both sides of the Atlantic. Still others he called up and harangued about "*the most evil corporation* [he had] *encountered in twenty years of reporting,*" as he described us to Jay Harris, the publisher of *Mother Jones,* a magazine that has tangled with some pretty evil corporations in its day. Entine was quoted in one newspaper saying that his impending revelations would be "*the story of the century,*" putting us right up there with the moon landing, two world wars, the Holocaust, the war in Vietnam, the end of the Soviet Union, and countless human and ecological disasters. All of which would have been worth a good laugh had he not also taken to harassing Anita in public and in private. At that point, his obsession became both unnerving and a bit frightening.

In the face of such attacks, I make no apologies for anything we have done to protect ourselves. It is not "legal thuggery" to defend your family, your employees, your friends and associates, your principles, and your reputation from someone who is hell-bent on doing as much damage to them as he can. There is a difference between criticism and character assassination. Just as there are environmental laws to stop polluters, so there are libel laws to stop irresponsible and damaging reports. Yet, we protested vigorously to *Vanity Fair* for assigning an article on The Body Shop to Jon Entine. We told the magazine we would cooperate with any responsible journalist they cared to have write about us, but we would not deal with Entine under any circumstances. *Vanity Fair* dropped the article. *Business Ethics* picked it up.

I cannot tell you how disheartening it is to find the attack on us coming now from people with whom we had always supposed we shared common commitments and common values. That Entine succeeded in driving down our share price was thanks largely to Franklin Research and Development, whose President, Joan Bavaria, wrote a column for *Business Ethics* in the same issue. Franklin sold 50,000 shares of The Body Shop stock on the strength of Entine's rejected *Vanity Fair* article. This information was relayed to the *Financial Times* in London, which ran an article about it, setting off a firestorm in the British press. Only later did Franklin even make a pretense of investigating Entine's charges. How this qualifies as "ethical investing" is beyond me.

Which brings us to *Business Ethics*. When we learned of the magazine's intention to publish a version of Entine's article, we informed the editors of our history with him and asked for an opportunity to review the piece for factual inaccuracies. The editors declined. One of our staff, Angela Bawtree, then visited the *Business Ethics* offices, but very few of the allegations contained in the article were put to her. Editor Craig Cox later refused her offer of follow-up information.

The editors have since tried to portray themselves as crusading journalists standing up to a bullying corporation. They have boasted loudly about taking out libel insurance. They have made much of their fear of publishing in Britain and their insistence that distributors sign pledges not to sell the magazine in any Commonwealth country. But, as noted above, truth is a defense against libel under British law. They face no risk if their article is factual. If we did sue them (something we have not threatened to do), they could recover all their legal expenses—assuming, that is, they could prove the accuracy of Entine's charges. So why didn't they publish in the U.K.? And what were their motives in publishing the article at all?

Perhaps the answer lies in a letter that Marjorie Kelly, publisher and editor-in-chief of *Business Ethics,* sent to her financial backers in August, just prior to publication of the Entine article.

> *This piece will be talked about,"* she wrote. *"It will create a stir. . . .* It's the best thing we've ever done. It could put us on the map.

The emphasis, I'm afraid, is hers.

Let me reiterate in closing that we have a detailed response to every single allegation Entine makes in his article and elsewhere. We will happily provide those responses to all who care to read them, but now we wish to get back to work. We have taken a severe kicking from the press on both sides of the Atlantic and elsewhere in the world. Perhaps there is some balance in that. We have also had a lot of good press over the years, some of it excessive in its enthusiasm. I suppose we should learn to live with excessive attacks as well.

In the future, I hope there will be objective and detailed reporting on our business. Some of the conclusions would no doubt be critical, but I am also certain a fair analysis would reveal a company that has tried very hard and has much to be proud of. We chose a difficult and thorny path. With the help of many others, we will continue to tread that path with pride and vigor.

In any event, the time for anger is past. We know the world is filled with businesses concerned with "putting something back." We hope they will not sit around too long in detailed analysis and therapy as a result of the hoopla created by this attack on us.

After the Channel 4 libel case, we ourselves began the process of producing a methodology for a definitive social audit of our company, following the lead of Ben & Jerry's and other companies. It is a mammoth undertaking, aimed at analyzing our social performance against the expectations created by ourselves and others. Along with our financial and environmental reports, it should provide a complete picture of the business, available to all. We expect to have a report by mid 1995. It will come as a great relief, most of all to us, who will use it to improve on the shortcomings it will undoubtedly highlight.

And what of *Business Ethics*? To date, two prominent members of its editorial advisory board have resigned, questioning the ethics of the magazine. We wonder if Marjorie Kelly has achieved the circulation boost she was counting on. The episode has certainly provided a reminder of the potential conflict between business needs and editorial principles. Perhaps Marjorie's words at the end of her "Musings" piece in the same issue of *Business Ethics* should now be read in a new light.

> *What we may have neglected in our enthusiasm is ethics. Good, old-fashioned ethics. Also known as integrity. It's not something to shout about in our marketing packages, but if we can't live up to it, we won't have much to shout about for long.*

We agree entirely. Enthusiasm in the pursuit of greater circulation is no substitute for ethics. I can only hope that the standards Marjorie articulates will be applied to *Business Ethics* magazine in the future.

Yours truly,

Gordon Roddick
Chairman

LETTER FROM
MARJORIE KELLY

Marjorie Kelly

January 13, 1995

From: Marjorie Kelly, Publisher and Editor-in-Chief, *Business Ethics*

"Shattered Image: Is The Body Shop Too Good to Be True?" was the cover story of the September/October 1994 issue of *Business Ethics,* the magazine of socially responsible business, read by progressive businesspeople and investors nationwide.

In my twenty years in journalism, I have never before seen a piece so *difficult to investigate and yet so* well-researched, so path-breaking, and so wide-reaching in its impact. *It is being discussed in boardrooms across the country.* It promises to change social investing, to lead to an increase in independent social audits, and in general to help business toward a greater social maturity. After The Body Shop article, I think you'll be seeing far less puffery in corporate ethics claims, and more hard facts to back up claims that are made.

You may have heard about The Body Shop article, for hundreds of reports about it have been published in the U.S., Great Britain, and as far away as Australia and Nigeria. I am honored to have published this piece, and honored to have worked with Jon Entine. I commend him to you as a truly extraordinary investigative journalist. He published this story against almost overwhelming opposition, yet he prevailed. . .

SUMMARY OF THE ARTICLE

"Shattered Image" reported on how the international franchisor and natural cosmetics maker The Body Shop—a $700 million firm known internationally as a premier socially responsible company—has for years secretly engaged in business practices that fall far short of its exaggerated social claims. Entine's evidence shows *that in area after area, The Body Shop's social reputation has been more image than reality:* its "natural" cosmetics contained numerous petrochemicals and preservatives, stories about the exotic origins of products were fabricated, environmental practices and charitable contributions fell far short of company statements. Third World sourcing of ingredients was greatly exaggerated, and franchisee relations were so troubled as to merit an FTC investigation.

Despite this dubious history, The Body Shop enjoyed worldwide prestige as a premier ethical company. *Ralph Nader called founder Anita Roddick "the most progressive business person I know. Inc. magazine featured Roddick on the cover, saying, "This Woman Has Changed Business Forever." USA Today dubbed her "The Mother Theresa*

Memorandum from Marjorie Kelly, publisher and editor, *Business Ethics,* for public consumption, Jan. 13, 1995. Reprinted by permission of the author.

of Capitalism." Whenever journalists sniffed a bit of the contrary truth and attempted to publish it, the company used heavy-handed legal threats to keep the stories under wraps. Among the publishers who backed off negative stories because of libel threats were *Vanity Fair, International Management,* the *London Daily Mail,* the *London Daily Telegraph,* and ABC. . . .

OBSTACLES OVERCOME IN THE REPORTING

Jon Entine was the first to uncover and tell this story in its entirety. It is a story no one expected and few were willing to believe. And Entine reported it against great odds—including fourteen libel threats in writing from the company, a slanderous campaign against him by the company's PR firm Hill and Knowlton, a campaign by The Body Shop to get sources to recant (several did right before press time), the imposition of gag orders on franchisees and employees, and the apparent hiring of a private investigation firm to follow Entine (as well as my staff at *Business Ethics*).

Business Ethics also received written libel threats from the Body Shop, as well as a campaign attacking us—directed at our editorial advisory board (one advisory board member quit: Ben Cohen of Ben & Jerry's, a personal friend of The Body Shop). After the story was published, the company obtained the *Business Ethics* subscriber list—by renting it under the name "Hoffman and Associates," purporting to mail a nonprofit fundraising catalogue—and used the list to mail a 10-page letter to our subscribers, accusing us of publishing lies and distortions. They conducted a similar campaign of vilification against Jon Entine, through numerous press releases and statements.

As Jon Entine went out on a limb to report this story, I put my company on the line to publish it. Facing a threat of libel, my staff and I were under fierce pressure to fact-check everything in the article. We consulted closely with a libel lawyer, and spent weeks fact-checking; we have an entire banker's box of documents from Jon Entine as evidence. Yet I know these are but a fraction of the materials he himself has. Whenever Entine's story and The Body Shop's story conflicted, we checked it out—and Entine's facts invariably were solid. Whenever we had any doubt about a fact or a source, we pulled it—and Entine always had another source, another fact, which made precisely the same point.

When we were reluctant to quote a franchisee called The Body Shop a "Gambino crime family," Entine showed us two other sources who had used uncannily similar language. When it seemed heavy-handed to use a quote saying the company's products were like those of "Payless Drug Story" (though selling at two or three times the price), Entine showed us three other sources who had said, literally, the products were of "drug store quality." When several sources recanted at the last minute, under pressure from The Body Shop, we pulled them—and Entine had other sources at the ready, so there was no harm to the story.

The depth and quality of Entine's research was extraordinary. I've never seen anything like it.

The wealth of sources and material Entine had was staggering. Though fully half his sources were not willing to have their names used, Entine succeeded in putting together a densely factual story using *only one unnamed source.* It is a testimony to his skill as a reporter that he got so many sources on the record, using their names in print—despite The Body Shop's fiercely litigious reputation. . . .

ACTION RESULTING FROM PUBLICATION
OF THE INVESTIGATION

As the editor who founded *Business Ethics* nine years ago, and a journalist who has followed the development of socially responsible business for over a decade, I can say unequivocally that Entine's article has changed the face of business ethics forever. It marks a turning point, a painful but necessary loss of naivete. Society no longer can pretend to draw a line between the "good guy" corporations like Ben & Jerry's, and "bad guy" corporations like Dow Chemical. Entine's article obliterated that line.

As Joan Bavaria, creator of the CERES Principles and president of Franklin Research (a social investing firm), wrote: "We are entering a new era in the world of socially responsible managing and investing. It is not a black world or a white world with neat and crisp lines of demarcation, and it doesn't lend itself to sound bites. It is the real world of complex systems, internal contradictions, and uneven, interrupted progress."

She called for the abandonment of "screening" in social investing, and for the invention of a system "beyond screens." This is very significant, coming from the woman who founded the Social Investment Forum—the central trade group for social investing professionals—because screening has been the central premise of social investing for thirty years. Bavaria's change of heart on this point was a direct result of Jon Entine's article.

A second major impact of Entine's article is the rising call for independent social audits. Should such a practice take root, companies could no longer garner points simply for making social claims. They would have to back them up. A call for such audits was made by Gary Hirshberg—founder of Stonyfield Yogurt, and chairman of the prestigious Social Venture Network—as a direct result of Entine's article.

As Hirshberg wrote: "The recent media frenzy regarding the Body Shop is an inevitable phase in the evolution of the corporate social responsibility concept . . . the issues are *measurement* and *disclosure,* and I believe that our businesses' chances for success as change catalysts hinge on our moving decisively toward a uniform, independent auditing methodology that accomplishes both."

Another, surprising, effect of Entine's story has been seen within The Body Shop itself: it has increased charitable giving, hired a new coordinator for Third World trade, and pledged to do a complete internal social audit and to publish the results.

Employees who had tried to tell The Body Shop the truth, over the years, had been fired. A quality control manager who spoke to the FDA was fired. Others were threatened into silence. Jon Entine broke that silence, and his words have been heard. And remarkably, the company is acknowledging the need for change.

Donald David, editor of *Drug & Cosmetic Industry,* [a] trade journal, said Entine's piece was "the best researched and lucidly written expose on any cosmetic company I have ever read in my 39 years of covering that business."

The article led to a firestorm of press coverage, including NPR coverage, articles in the *New York Times, USA Today, Financial Times* of London, *New York* magazine, and countless other media, as well as a major symposium in the *Utne Reader.*

In addition to the hundreds of articles that have been published, Entine has been invited to speak about the article to the National Conference on Ethics, the National Association for

Biomedical Research, Loyola University Center for Values in Business, Bentley College, Columbia School of Journalism, and many other places.

Entine's investigation of The Body Shop is truly a watershed event in the history of socially responsible business. I believe this story will become a "business parable" for years to come—much as Johnson and Johnson and the Tylenol incident has become a business parable. It is through vivid stories like these that we learn the truth of our world. And this story would not have been told were it not for the courage and professionalism of Jon Entine.

Sincerely,

Marjorie Kelly
Publisher and Editor-in-Chief

THE BODY SHOP
SOCIAL STATEMENT
WEB SITE

Welcome to **The Values Report,** an independently verified assessment of how The Body Shop impacts on the environment and society, and on the Company's animal protection policy.

Our approach to auditing follows the sequence of THINK-ACT-CHANGE. We THINK about the issues facing our business and industry today and reflect these in our policies; we ACT by monitoring our impact on the environment and publishing details of these; and we will CHANGE and reduce our impacts in the future by setting ourselves targets and campaigning in order to achieve continuous improvement.

Also explore *our approach* to ethical auditing, *our reason for being,* 20 years of *defining moments,* a special letter for *American readers* and a *summary* of the report. You can also read a copy of an *independent social assessment of The Body Shop by Kirk Hanson,* business ethics and social responsibility professor at Stanford University Graduate School of Business, USA

MISSION STATEMENT

Our Reason for Being:

To dedicate our business to the pursuit of social and environmental change.

To Creatively balance the financial and human needs of our stakeholders: employees, customers, franchisees, suppliers and shareholders.

To Courageously ensure that our business is ecologically sustainable: meeting the needs of the present without compromising the future.

Materials from The Body Shop Social Statement Web Site, http://www.think-act-change.com. Reprinted by permission of The Body Shop.

To Meaningfully contribute to local, national and international communities in which we trade, by adopting a code of conduct which ensures care, honesty, fairness and respect.

To Passionately campaign for the protection of the environment, human and civil rights, and against animal testing within the cosmetics and toiletries industry.

To Tirelessly work to narrow the gap between principle and practice, whilst making fun, passion and care part of our daily lives.

THE BODY SHOP BILL OF RIGHTS AND RESPONSIBILITIES

The Rights of the Company:

To make the final decision.

To recruit the best people for the job.

To dismiss people when justified.

To expect a high level of contribution, performance and commitment.

To expect respect for its values.

The Responsibilities of the Company:

To do its best to provide a secure environment for its employees.

To look for new ways of doing things.

To educate employees about the Company's culture and values.

To educate employees about the Company's business.

To provide adequate induction and training.

To consider existing employees first when looking at new opportunities.

To meet all relevant employment legislation.

To be honest to employees about what we are offering.

To listen, care and support.

To be fair.

To walk the talk.

To say thank you.

The Rights of the Individual:

To have a voice, to challenge.

To have equality of opportunity.

To be trained to do your job.

To be developed as an individual.

To be rewarded fairly for the work you do; to understand how your pay is determined.

To know how the business is doing.

To be told the truth about things that will affect you.

To have a piece of the action.

To have the opportunity to do your best.

The Responsibilities of the Individual:

To think.

To learn.

To be honest.

To try your hardest, to do your best.

To treat others with trust and respect.

To take responsibility for your own actions.

To acknowledge the efforts of others.

To obey the rules.

To stand against injustice.

This Mission Statement and Bill of Rights and Responsibilities is the driving force for everything we do, and is the yardstick against which the Human Resources function, and the Company Culture function, and indeed The Body Shop as a whole, can be measured in its dealing with its people.

It covers all aspects of the Human Resources function from Training and Development to Pay and Remuneration, from Recruitment to Pensions, from Induction to Appraisals, from Equal Opportunities to Administration systems. It recognises and publishes the special nature of The Body Shop's relationship with its employees, in which they are not just resources for the Company, but are people whose own needs and aspirations are recognised and taken seriously.

At its heart is the phrase "meeting each other's needs" which in four words incorporates virtually the whole of our behaviour and actions whilst working at The Body Shop.

SOCIAL STATEMENT

The publication of this Social Statement marks the first attempt by The Body Shop to systematically audit, verify and disclose the Company's performance on social matters. But it is just the beginning. It is the starting point for more effective dialogue and communication with all our stakeholders. The entire process has taken us about three years: researching, planning, and implementing. The methodology we have adopted is described in detail in an accompanying document, 'The Body Shop Approach to Ethical Auditing,' setting out all of our ethical auditing and reporting practices, but it is important to recognise here what have been our major influences. Certainly, we have taken as our philosophical starting point the belief that all stakeholders should have an effective voice in commenting upon and shaping a company's behaviour. We do not believe that a company is only in business to serve the interests of a limited number of stakeholders.

Our methodology has drawn heavily on our own research into the history of private and public sector social accounting, auditing and assessment. We have also learned a great deal from the recent experiences of organisations like the Sbn Bank in Denmark, Traidcraft in the UK and Ben and Jerry's in the U.S. In learning from these examples we have endeavoured to synthesise and develop an approach which makes sense not just for The Body Shop, but, we hope, for other organisations too.

We have systematically collected the views of key stakeholders by techniques not dissimilar to those used by market researchers: open meetings, interviews, confidential focus groups and large scale surveys. In designing survey questionnaires our Ethical Audit department has observed rigorous standards to ensure that all issues of relevance to stakeholders or raised by them, e.g., in focus groups, were included. And we took professional advice from the Institute for Employment Studies (IES) to ensure clarity in questionnaire design and analysis. All surveys were conducted anonymously and confidentially, with completed forms returned directly to IES; stakeholders were also invited to make direct contact with our audit verifiers, the New Economics Foundation (NEF).

We have also tried to report on quantitative indicators of social performance relevant to stakeholder groups. In selecting performance indicators we have been mindful of the types of information often requested by the ethical investment community and by consumer interest organisations such as the Council for Economic Priorities in the U.S. In trying to collect these data we have become aware of the limitations of some of our own internal information systems. We will endeavour to improve on our reporting of these performance standards in future years.

The purpose of our social audit was not to focus on specific criticism or issues. It was to deal broadly with only one accounting period and not the entire history of the Company. Thus we have not investigated individual allegations of wrong doing or inefficiency, but we have provided a platform for all views, including critical and minority views.

Our audit and disclosure processes have been subject to independent verification by the New Economics Foundation (NEF). They have engaged, in turn, an Audit Review Panel, whose names are listed on the verification page of this Statement, to advise them.

Our advisers and consultants have been very influential in shaping our social audit and indeed this Statement. Our experience has been positive, but it is clear that there is still much work to be done to develop the practice of social auditing to the standards now being followed for environmental auditing. However, we now have four years' experience in implementing the EU Eco-management and Audit Regulation and three years' experience in researching, developing and applying a social audit methodology. So we are able to confirm that the two audit processes are compatible, that measurement techniques (though different) can produce useful data in both cases, and that it is possible to independently verify audit procedures and produce public statements of performance for both environmental and social issues.

EMPLOYEES

Good News:

83% of employees agreed with the founders' statement that "Our success depends on the commitment, skill, creativity, and good humour of our employees."

93% of employees either agreed or strongly agreed that The Body Shop lives up to its mission on the issues of environmental responsibility and animal testing.

79% of employees either agreed or strongly agreed that working for The Body Shop has raised their awareness of pressing global issues.

75% of employees say they are proud to tell others they are part of The Body Shop.

71% of employees enjoy their job.

Bad News:

45% of employees were quite or very dissatisfied with the way The Body Shop encourages them to obtain qualifications.

26% of employees could not recall ever having a job appraisal.

23% of employees felt the best way for them to develop their career was to change companies.

53% of employees either disagreed or strongly disagreed that the behaviour and decision-making of managers was consistent throughout the Company.

The Future:

A new strategy for learning and development (including the issue of in-service qualifications).

Reinforcement of career development.

Reinforcement of new appraisal procedures.

Improved internal communications, particularly via managers in New initiatives on equal opportunities. . . .

SHAREHOLDERS

Good News:

90% of shareholders agreed or strongly agreed that The Body Shop takes active steps to make its business more environmentally responsible.

76% of shareholders agreed or strongly agreed that the Company's business practices reflect a high standard of ethics.

78% of shareholders were satisfied with the information they receive on The Body Shop's financial performance.

75% of shareholders either agreed or strongly agreed that the Company's annual report and accounts provide a comprehensive picture of The Body Shop's over-all performance.

Bad News:

29% of shareholders either disagreed or strongly disagreed that the Company enjoys the trust of the financial community.

33% of shareholders either had no opinion or disagreed that The Body Shop has a clear long-term business strategy. The Body Shop share price fell from a high of £2.63 on 11 May 1994 to a low of £1.68 on 8 February 1995, ending the financial year 1994/95 at £1.82.

The Future: While The Body Shop remains a public company it will:

Aim to maximize shareholder interests while also balancing the needs of other stakeholders.

Develop and build relationships with shareholders and prospective shareholders.

Operate a progressive dividend policy.

COMMUNITY INVOLVEMENT

Good News:

In 1994/95 The Body Shop's directly employed staff gave an estimated 19,500 hours to projects in the community.

87% of recipients of funding from The Body Shop Foundation ('The Foundation') either agreed or strongly agreed that The Body Shop takes active steps to make its business more environmentally responsible.

More than 90% of The Foundation grantees were satisfied with: i) the dedication to issues, ii) integrity and transparency and iii) clarity and competence of individuals whom they dealt with in The Body Shop Foundation.

In 1994, The Body Shop donated 2.3% of pre-tax profits to charity. This compares favourably with other UK companies, eg: 2.16% for the Co-operative Bank and 0.44% for Boots.

Bad News:

75% of The Body Shop employees do not participate actively in the community volunteering programme.

Nearly half of grantees either disagreed or strongly disagreed that it was easy to identify the right decision-makers in The Body Shop Foundation.

Nearly one-third of grantees felt The Body Shop Foundation communicates its grant making policy clearly in selected areas.

The Future:

Launch of a new six-point plan for the encouragement of community volunteering.

Formalisation of arrangements for community liaison around The Body Shop's principal operating sites.

Implementation of a ten-point plan by The Body Shop Foundation to improve effectiveness and communications.

Introduction of better performance indicators and service standards for the Foundation Campaigns (and relations with non-governmental organisations).

THE BODY SHOP INTERNATIONAL SOCIAL EVALUATION, 1995

KIRK O. HANSON

INTRODUCTION

This report presents the results of an independent evaluation of the social practices, performance and impact of The Body Shop International (referred to as The Body Shop in this report). The Board of The Body Shop commissioned this study late in 1994 and it was conducted between January and December 1995. This report evaluates the social performance of the company during the 1994-1995 period. Kirk O. Hanson, the author, is Senior Lecturer at the Stanford Graduate School of Business in California and has worked in the field of business responsibility for almost thirty years.

The company requested an examination of its social performance on those dimensions addressed in its Mission Statement and Trading Charter, but authorized me to include any other dimensions which I felt were critical to an assessment of its social impact and the fulfillment of its mission.

This report has limitations. At this time, there is no generally accepted methodology for a social audit or social assessment. This report draws upon the work done by many others to develop criteria and standards for social performance, but is still dependent to a significant extent upon my own experience and judgment regarding good social practice. Secondly, one cannot hope to examine all aspects of the behavior of a worldwide enterprise like The Body Shop, nor document every instance of exemplary or deficient behavior, even if given unlimited time to do so. Therefore, this evaluation rests upon the examination and tests which can be done in the 60 working days I spent on the project. While I may have issued individual acts which are significant, I believe I have captured accurately the overall social performance of the company. I hope this report will be useful to The Body Shop in its own efforts to improve its social performance and to others who wish to evaluate its behavior. I also hope this report will be useful to those who are committed to extending the methodology of social assessment and to improving the social performance of their own companies. The Body Shop encouraged me to approach this project in a way that it might advance our collective understanding of social auditing. I am grateful to them for the extra time and expense this entailed.

Overall, I believe The Body Shop demonstrates greater social responsibility and better social performance than most companies of its size. Certain dimensions of its social behavior, however, raise concerns and should be addressed promptly by the company.

Excerpts from Kirk Hanson, *Social Evaluation: The Body Shop International, 1995*. Reprinted by permission of the author.

Other aspects of its social record are about the same as other companies and must be improved if the company seeks to distinguish itself as a leader in social responsibility. The Body Shop has made mistakes in the past, but its management today has committed itself to correcting those errors. This report is part of that process. The social performance measured in this report benefits greatly from the substantial efforts already launched by the company in 1994 and 1995 to address areas of weakness.

I believe the social record of The Body Shop must be viewed with the perspective that this is by any measure a large company—with 1995 turnover (sales) of £220 million ($352 million). Retail sales totaled £500 million ($800 million) in 1210 stores in 45 countries. Company employment totalled 3300. The Body Shop has 572 independent franchisees and sub franchisees operating stores around the world and employing several thousand employees. Achieving outstanding social performance in a rapidly growing, large and global business is a very difficult task.

This evaluation can be viewed as a complement to the company's internally developed Values Report released late in January 1966. My report takes advantage of the data collected for that Values Report, but addresses a broader set of performance issues and the worldwide operations of the company. . . .

I sought to evaluate the record of The Body Shop against "comparable companies," against the company's own values and goals, against the practices of the most outstanding companies ("best practice"), and against the company's claims regarding its social performance. While detail on various of these standards is presented in the text of this report, I have chosen to present a "score" of one to five stars based on how The Body Shop compares to "comparable" companies or the "average company" in the UK and the U.S.

To present my evaluations, I have used the following five star system:

***** Performance Much Better than Comparable Companies.

**** Performance Better than Comparable Companies.

*** Performance Similar to Comparable Companies.

** Performance Worse than Comparable Companies.

* Performance Much Worse than Comparable Companies.

A three rating is therefore "average." Given the stated goal of The Body Shop to be a leader in social responsibility, there is still room for significant improvement in those dimensions rated three. Even in those areas rated four, there are usually aspects of performance which fall short of "best practice," of the company's own aspirations, and sometimes of the company's public statements about itself. . . .

After preparing drafts of this evaluation, I presented the highlights of this evaluation orally at the December 1995 meeting of the Board of Directors and written drafts subsequently to selected company officials. I listened to their reactions and feedback but, following the ground rules established at the outset of the project, made my own decisions about whether to incorporate these additional perspectives. I alone determined the content of this final report.

GENERAL SUMMARY

The Body Shop International is a company publicly committed to social values and to having a substantial and positive impact on society. Its Memorandum of Association (similar to U.S. company's articles of incorporation and by-laws), Mission Statement and Trading Charter are exemplary documents, committing the company to a vision of responsible enterprise that is uncommon among businesses, particularly larger businesses such as The Body Shop has become. The goals of the company embrace both social as well as economic objectives. The Trading Charter extends this dual commitment to the core business of the company, highlighting the pursuit of economic and environmental sustainability, economic development for the disadvantaged, and respect for the rights and human rights of all who trade with the company.

The company's social campaigns, conducted through the medium of the retail shop and shop windows, represent in effect a second "product line," one designed to leverage the shop space and customer traffic for social change. Some campaigns, such as the company's plea for Nigerian Ken Saro-Wiwa, have been fought in the public press and through high profile speeches by founder Anita Roddick and other company executives.

The company's record of social performance has been strongest in areas where it has pursued social causes independent of the traditional trading and commercial activities of the company. Over the past ten years, the company has made significant contributions to the animal welfare movement, to environmental awareness, to communities in which it operates, and to the human rights movement.

The social impact of the company's day-to-day business activities, by contrast, is mixed—outstanding in some areas and in need of significant management attention in others. Some weaknesses have their origins in the rapid growth of the company over the past ten years. Management talent, time and systems have been stretched very thinly in some key areas. This is due in part to the fact that The Body Shop has been growing into a global enterprise of almost 1400 stores in 45 countries which works through 21 head franchisees and over 500 sub franchisees, each of which is an independent business. Nonetheless, I believe that until very recently the company has given more attention to its "social campaigns" than it has to improving the social impact of its day-to-day business dealings with its shareholders, employees, franchisees, customers, local communities and suppliers.

The company has not made the relationship with its shareholders a priority concern. The combined holdings of founders Anita and Gordon Roddick and early partner Ian McGlinn, whose interest is represented on the Board of Directors by the Roddicks, total about 52% of the company's stock. On key dimensions of concern to shareholders, such as financial performance, governance structure, and maintaining the quality of management, The Body Shop has demonstrated mixed performance. Disclosure to minority shareholders and the compensation of executives has generally been acceptable.

The company's relations with its employees have also been mixed. On one hand the company has good benefits and an open and enthusiastic culture. Employees in the UK and in the U.S. report that they are proud to tell others that they work for The Body Shop. On the other hand, it has done less well in defining the jobs of employees, in helping employees plan careers, and in keeping them informed about company developments. Many basic management tasks of importance to employees have not been well executed.

The company's relations with head franchisees and sub franchisees, its most important business partners, have also been varied. Some of the same failings which affect shareholders—particularly inconsistent management—are of importance to franchisees as well. Of most concern, however, has been the day-to-day working relationships between The Body Shop and its franchise system. Many franchisees believe they do not receive enough and timely information and believe their complaints/suggestions are not taken seriously enough by the company.

The company's relations with its customers are generally good, though some of its past promotional claims and follow-up on consumer complaints raise concerns. The company is working hard to reduce the hype and exaggeration which had crept into the company's public statements, but still has work to do. In many areas of the world, there are no effective systems for following up on consumer complaints and feedback.

Supplier relationships are generally good, though a few suppliers indicate that they have been approached by company representatives with unethical proposals, always a risk in purchasing and a cause for concern.

Relations with local communities are generally strong. Company philanthropic contributions are above average, but as yet are not as strategically planned and executed as they might be. The employee benefit by which employees can volunteer locally on company time is innovative, but has not yet been well promoted or widely used.

Relations with the public and the media are an area of substantial concern. In the past the company has not demonstrated adequate openness and transparency, accuracy in its general communications and willingness to entertain constructive criticism. This report and other corporate efforts, however, demonstrate a commitment to change this record.

As noted earlier, the company's record is most outstanding in its contributions to social change. However, even in the company's chosen areas of priority concern—environmental sustainability, animal rights and human rights—there is room for improvement.

The company has been subject to many charges of irresponsible behavior over the past two years. Many of these charges have no merit whatsoever. Others I have been unable to verify and have found still others to be accurate but greatly overblown in their significance. A few of the charges do have substance and are addressed in this report. Some have even argued that the company has cynically used claims of social concern for pure commercial advantage. I am convinced the company and its employees are genuinely committed to making The Body Shop a force for social change.

Finally, The Body Shop has been an important and powerful example to many other businesses and to consumers that it is possible to serve both social as well as economic goals. It has also pioneered many social innovations that have stimulated others to try similar efforts. The company's impact as an exemplary business, however, has at times been weakened by some of the behaviors noted in this report.

RATINGS BY DIMENSIONS OF SOCIAL PERFORMANCE

Company Values and Mission

Company Purpose *****

The company's strong commitment to both commercial success and to social betterment is exceptional among larger companies. The Memorandum of Association was amended by the company in 1994 to state clearly that the objectives of the company include supporting campaigns and educational programs for human and civil rights, establishing trading relationships with communities in need, implementing policies aimed at protecting the natural environment and supporting campaigns against animal testing in the cosmetics industry.

The Body Shop Mission Statement . . . states the company will "balance the financial and human needs of our stakeholders." It states further that The Body Shop will "passionately campaign for the protection of the environment, human and civil rights and against animal testing within the cosmetics and toiletries industry." The deliberate blend of commercial product and social campaign is unique in my experience, at least at the scale it is pursued by The Body Shop.

The Trading Charter, . . . adopted in 1994, makes more explicit the values and standards to be achieved in business and trading relationships. While other parts of this report will conclude the company does not fully achieve its aspirations, the goals and enabling documents are exceptional among any set of comparable companies.

Advocacy of Responsible Business ****

Company founder Anita Roddick is an extraordinary advocate for corporate responsibility and a vision of business as an agent of social betterment and change. Many of the company's activities and much of its communication are geared to encouraging other companies to emulate the model The Body Shop has developed. At the same time, the company and its founder are sometimes too critical of the behavior of other companies and institutions and fail to acknowledge and encourage the efforts and accomplishments of others.

The company has been in the forefront of developments regarding social auditing and the development of a definition of responsible business behavior. The company's own Values Report, published in January 1996, addresses and evaluates many dimensions of corporate behavior. This report, with its measures of social responsibility, is another demonstration of the company's commitment to promoting standards for responsible business. Ms. Roddick has, in the past year, spearheaded the development of the New Academy of Business, a seminar program to teach principles of responsible business. While all these efforts can be improved, they demonstrate a continuing advocacy of responsible business.

Relations with the Public

Accuracy of Communication **

The Body Shop's leadership has long been committed to honest and straightforward communication—in its promotional claims and all its public statements. Unfortunately, there has been a pattern of exaggeration and occasional failure to substantiate many statements made for and by The Body Shop. Some of this pattern is traceable to the company's natural ebullience and enthusiasm, some to the eagerness to "sell" the company's message and products, and some to an inaccurate assumption that ideas developed by top managers have been instantly implemented by the organization.

Some company representatives have been too quick to present every action of the company as the "first, best and most socially conscious." Some statements and publications of the company have so emphasized the use of "natural" ingredients and the indigenous origins of ingredients and accessories that many customers have assumed the products were "all natural" or "mostly sourced in the Third World." The Body Shop bears some of the responsibility for these assumptions, though a close reading of company statements indicates most claims were worded to avoid direct misrepresentation. Nonetheless, store visits demonstrated that a significant minority of shop clerks, in both company-owned and franchised stores, misrepresent the naturalness and origins of products. The problem was somewhat more pronounced in stores visited in the greater London area than in stores visited in the greater San Francisco area.

This pattern has weakened the credibility of the company and the impact of its actual accomplishments. Weeding out this pattern takes long term attention and effort. The company has initiated an "information audit" designed to preview and verify any written document or oral presentation to be made by the company. The system has not yet been completely effective.

One charge which has attracted recent comment is that the concept and products of The Body Shop were not conceived of entirely by the founders. I found no evidence to prove the founders knew of a California-based company known as The Body Shop before opening their first shop. However, it is clear, and the founders have verified, that they learned of the California company during the first year of the company's existence and used promotional and product ideas from the California company in early merchandising and catalogs. There was nothing illegal in such imitation, though statements of The Body Shop have not fully disclosed the creative inspiration provided by the California company. When The Body Shop entered the U.S. in 1988, it paid the owners of the California based company more than $3.5 million (£2.2 million) for the name "The Body Shop" in the U.S., Japan and elsewhere. It also offered to make them the head franchisee for a portion of the U.S., an offer they accepted but eventually sold back to the company. Additional royalties will be paid over a 10 year period. The total of all payments to the end of 1995 was $4.4 million (£2.75 million).

Reaction to Criticism *

The most serious concern to be raised regarding the company's record of social responsibility is its reaction to criticism. It is the one area I feel compelled to give a single star rating for the 1994–1995 period, though the publication of this Social Evaluation and the recently released "Values Report" represent a new willingness to confront criticism openly.

In the past, The Body Shop has reacted strongly and defensively to reports that it may not live entirely up to its values or claims. The record of the company's dealings with the media over the past several years clearly shows this defensiveness. It has at times been unwilling to entertain even valid concerns, and has been inclined to use legal warnings to dampen criticism of the company. While it must be stated in the company's defense that few companies have faced such determined and persistent attacks as has The Body Shop, the company has reacted poorly to criticism even from "friends," franchisees and employees.

There are differences in libel law between the UK and the U.S., and British companies are generally more aggressive in pressing for corrections in published and broadcast reports. Even by UK standards, however, the company's reactions have been stronger and more defensive than the "average" company. Company officials today suggest their attitudes were shaped by the 1993 Channel 4 libel case in the UK and subsequent attacks by an American journalist. In the Channel 4 case, the company sued the independent network and proved in court the broadcast was inaccurate and malicious. By U.S. standards, the Channel 4 broadcast was relatively mild and the inaccuracies typical of "entertainment" television. But in the UK context and for The Body Shop, the impact was traumatic.

In responding to the critical article "Shattered Image" in the U.S. magazine *Business Ethics* in September 1994, and to coverage of the article's charges as reported in the British press, the company overreacted badly. Company officials today regret some aspects of their own behavior during this intense period, though they argue they had a right to defend themselves against inaccurate charges. I do not question this right, but believe the strong language used in many company statements and other steps taken were unnecessary and overly defensive.

It is undoubtedly difficult to face criticism after being hailed uncritically for so many years as the embodiment of a new way of doing business. Part of the defensiveness results from a real concern that criticism will damage the interests of the franchisees and the social agenda being pursued by the company.

The Body Shop has, in my view, encouraged criticism from others by being excessively critical of other companies and institutions. The Body Shop executives have at times stated that others—in the investment community, in the media, in industry, and in business schools (!)—are motivated solely by baser concerns and are doing nothing of social usefulness. This has unfortunately encouraged many to look for and to welcome criticism of the company.

It is also true that any company which makes socially responsible claims a key element in its marketing will be scrutinized to a much greater extent and will be held to a higher standard than a company which does not. Under these circumstances, the company must demonstrate extraordinary transparency and a willingness to hear and act on criticism of any dimension of its behavior.

ADVERTISING

IS IT EVER RIGHT
TO LIE? (ON TRUTH
IN ADVERTISING)

ROBERT SOLOMON

*Ask yourself Solomon's first question: Is it ever right to lie? Do you
answer that immediately, from your gut, with no? Most of us would
instead offer qualifying comments, then say that (generally) we think
it is a bad idea. Now, do you expect advertisers to lie? Do you answer yes immediately? Maybe. Many of us take advertisements with a
grain of salt, and Solomon addresses this phenomenon.*

Is it ever right to lie?

No.

Now, let's get down to business.

It may never be right to tell a lie, but nevertheless it is often prudent, preferable,
and—if the way people behave is any indication at all of morals—popular as well.

Consider the familiar dilemma of HGT sales representative John G., who is asked
whether his product is in fact as good as a Xerox. One curious fact is that John G. owns a
Xerox himself, but another not insignificant fact is that he is employed by the HGT company to sell their line of products, not to express his personal preferences or conduct a
neutral survey of product quality. What does he do? What can he do? Of course, he says,
"Yes—and better besides." Is he lying? Or just doing his job? He is doing both, of
course, but should we say that he is thereby doing wrong?

"Truth" and "falsehood" are evasive qualities even in an academic seminar or a scientist's laboratory; they are even more so in the real world. Is a lover lying to himself
when he says that his love is the "most wonderful woman in the world"? Is a salesman
lying to a customer when he praises an imperfect product? To be sure, there is such a
thing as outright deception—the standard care in which a used-car salesman insists that in
old convertible is an excellent mechanical condition, knowing full well that the unhappy
new owner will be lucky to get the heap off the lot. But one can also argue that shopping
at certain used-car lots (the kind advertised by a hand-painted sign that says,—"Honest
Harry Has the Bargains") carries with it the knowledge of risk on the part of the buyer,
risking a trade-off for the bargain. What counts as "honest" is already put into question.

Of course, there are outright lies—falsification of the odometer reading or the false claim that the engine was overhauled 3,000 miles ago, but there is a certain latitude in lying that depends on the context, the customer, and the costs. Not only lying but giving misleading information is intolerable in the health-care industry—for example, not mentioning the side effects of a new drug. Showing hyperdramatic demonstrations of "action" toys to children or giving technical information to people who cannot possibly understand it may involve neither false nor misleading information but nevertheless may be morally dubious (given the huge proportion of the adult population that can be swayed by mere adjectives such as "scientific" or "natural"). Cost counts, too. Exaggerated claims for the cleaning powers of an inexpensive soap product or the convenience of a household gadget advertised on TV for (inevitably) $19.95 are more easily forgiven than even mildly bloated praise for the value of a new house or bulldozer. On the other hand, it is clear that it is not only self-defeating but cruel to tell a customer *everything* horrible that might befall him with his product. (Imagine the warnings that would have to accompany even such a simple household appliance as a food processor.)

Lying may always be wrong, but some lies are much more wrong than others. Truth may always be desirable, but the "whole truth and nothing but the truth" is just as likely to be a nightmare.

To say that it is never right to lie is not the same as to say that one should never lie. It is rather to say that a lie is always a later resort, a strategy that is not a first choice. If the salesman could sell his wares by saying nothing but the truth, he could, should, and would do so. But one must always excuse a lie, by showing that some greater evil would result from telling the truth or, most often, simply by showing that there is minimal harm done by lying and that, in this context, the lie is not wholly inappropriate. The one thing that a person cannot do is to think that telling a lie—*any* lie—is just as good or right as telling the truth, and so needs no special justification for doing so.

Lying has almost always been considered a sin or an immoral act. In a best-selling book, Sissela Bok has argued that lying is always wrong because, in a variety of ways, it always has bad consequences—worse, that is, than if the lie had not been told. Common experience indicates otherwise, perhaps, for the general attitude both in business and in society is that lies have a perfectly proper social place. Indeed there are clearly contexts in which it would be wrong *not* to lie. Lies can prevent family fights and quarrels among couples. They can prevent bad feelings and help avoid misunderstandings. And, often, they can help an employee keep his or her job. ("I was caught in traffic" is a transparent lie but sometimes an acceptable excuse for being late; "I hated the idea of coming to work so much that I forgot to set the alarm" is, though true, utterly unacceptable.)

We can all agree, looking only at short-term and immediate benefits, that the harm done by some lies is considerably less than the harm that would be done by telling the "unvarnished truth." An employer forced to fire a mediocre worker is certainly not to be blamed for saying that "financial exigencies" have forced him to lay off several low-seniority personnel, instead of telling the truth, which is that the fellow borders on incompetence and doesn't have either the charm or the imagination of a pocket calculator. An advertiser would be judged an idiot, not honest, if he baldly stated that this pain remedy is no more or less effective than any other on the market, though its packaging is prettier. Nevertheless, there are reasons for saying that lying is always wrong.

The first reason has to do with the enormous amount of effort involved in telling a lie—any lie. The truth—even the incomplete truth—is an enormously complex network of interlocking facts. Anyone who has found himself caught in the nervous web of fabrications involved in even such a simple lie as, "We don't know a thing about what our competitors are doing" ("Then how to you know that. . . ?") knows how many seemingly disparate facts can come crashing in when a lie has torn just a small piece out of the truth. As recent national politics has so prominently displayed, the cost of a cover-up is often many times more than the damage done by the lie itself, even if the cover-up is successful.

The second reason looks beyond the short-term benefits of lying to the longer-term damage, which may be harder to see. Every lie diminishes trust. A lie discovered is guaranteed to undermine faith in the liar, but, more subtly, *telling* a lie diminishes one's trust in others. ("If I'm lying to them, they are probably lying to me as well.") Most Americans now look at television advertising as if it were nothing but a tissue of lies—ironically making the more successful ads just those that ignore substantial content and concentrate on memorable associations and effects. A businessman may make many a profit through deception—for a while—but unless one wants to keep on the road for the rest of one's life (sounds good at twenty, not so good at forty), deception almost always catches up and destroys just the business it once ensure. As long-term investments, lies are usually a bad risk.

The third and strongest reason for thinking that it is never right to lie was suggested by Kant. He asked himself the question, "What would happen if lying were generally accepted? For example, "What would happen if it were an everyday and unexceptional feature of the business world that one person would borrow money from another with no intention whatever of repaying the loan?" His answer was that telling the truth and, in the example, borrowing money would both become impossible, so that if I were to approach you and ask for a $10,000 loan, which I would promise to repay on the first of the year, you would simply laugh in my face, since everyone by then would know that such promises were not to be taken seriously. Lying, in other words, must always be wrong, since to treat lying as acceptable undermines just that trust that makes telling the truth meaningful.

Does this mean that one should never lie? Well, no. But it does mean that it is never right to tell a lie; that telling a lie always requires extra thought and some very good reasons to show that this cardinal violation of the truth should be tolerated.

This said, perhaps we should clear up a few common misconceptions about the place of lying in business. It is sometimes suggested that advertising is always a lie, since it tells only one side of the story and that side, needless to say, in the best possible light. But now it is important to distinguish—in facing any such accusation—among the following:

1. telling less than the whole truth;
2. telling a biased truth, with one's own interests in mind;
3. idealizing one's products or services;
4. giving misleading information; that is, true statements that are intended to be misunderstood or misinterpreted;
5. stating obvious falsehoods;
6. stating vicious falsehoods.

An obvious falsehood, for example, is the displayed claim of some toothpaste manufacturers—that use of a certain gel will overnight convert Shy Sam or Plain Jane to

Fabulous Fred or Super Sally, the heartthrob of the high-school prom. One might object to other aspects of such advertising, but "It isn't true" seems too silly to say.

Vicious falsehoods, on the other hand, are those that are not at all obvious and are a deliberate and possibly dangerous form of deception. Saying that a product will do such and such when it will not is vicious deception, as is intentionally withholding information—for example, the flammability of children's pajamas or the side effects of a popular over-the-counter drug. Misleading information can be as vicious as false information—indeed it is only a matter of logical nuance that allows us to distinguish between the two.

It is impossible to tell the "whole story," especially in the limited time of a fifteen-second radio or TV slot or in the small space available on a paper package. But advertising isn't supposed to be a scientific study, even if it utilizes some (more or less) scientific evidence on the product's behalf. Of course advertising expresses a bias on the behalf of the product. Of course it idealizes the product in its presentation. But neither bias nor idealization is lying, and it is surely foolish to insist that advertising, unlike almost every other aspect of social life, be restricted to the simple, boring truth—that is, that this product is not much different from its competitors and that people have lived for hundreds of thousands of years without any of them.

It is often challenged—these days with Orwellian overtones—that advertising in general and TV advertising in particular have turned the American consumer into something of a supermarket zombie, without a will of his or her own, without judgment, buying hundreds of innocuous but sometimes tasteless products that no one really needs. But the zombie image contradicts precisely what lies beneath the whole discussion of truth—namely, the confidence that we are, more or less, capable of making value judgments on our own, and that if we buy or even need to buy products that are of no particular cosmic importance, this does not signal either the end of civilization or the disintegration of the human mind. Encouraging someone to buy a product that is only a fad or a mark of status is not deception, and to call it that tends to undermine the ethical distinction that is of enormous importance—between vicious falsehoods and any number of other "varnishings" of the truth. These may be vulgar. They may encourage us to compete for some pretty silly achievements—the shiniest (and most slippery) floor, a car that can win the grand prix (to be driven in bumper-to-bumper traffic up and down the freeway), a soap that makes one speak in a phony Irish brogue. But to condemn all advertising is to make it impossible to attack vicious advertising and thus to bring about the logical conclusion imagined by Kant—an entire world in which no one believes anything, in which advertising serves at most as a source of amusement and seduction of the feeble-minded.

Let's end our discussion of lying by commenting once again on Alfred Carr's suggestion that business is like poker, that it has its own rules, which are different from ordinary ethics. One of these rules, supposedly, is the permissibility of lying. But business (like poker) forbids lying. Contrary to Carr, a generally accepted practice of lying would undermine the business world faster than any external threat that has ever faced it. Promises and contracts, if not good faith, are the presuppositions of all business. The exact nature of truth in advertising may be controversial, but advertising in general must be not only based on fact but believable and truthworthy. If it were not, the commercial world in America would be about as effective as the provocations of Hari Krishnas in America's airports—an annoyance to be ignored as we all go on with the rest of our lives.

Honesty isn't just the best policy in business; it is, in general, the only possible policy.

SUMMA THEOLOGICA
St. Thomas Aquinas

Aquinas addresses a question similar to that posed by Solomon. Are you persuaded by Aquinas's logic?

WHETHER EVERY LIE IS A MORTAL SIN?

We proceed thus to the Fourth Article:—

Objection 1. It seems that every lie is a mortal sin. For it is written (Ps. vi. 7): *Thou wilt destroy all that speak a lie,* and (Wis. i. II): *The mouth that belieth killeth the soul.* Now mortal sin alone causes destruction and death of the soul. Therefore every lie is a mortal sin.

Obj. 2. Further, whatever is against a precept of the decalogue is a mortal sin. Now lying is against this precept of the decalogue: *Thou shalt not bear false witness.* Therefore every lie is a mortal sin.

Obj. 3. Further, Augustine says (*De Doctr. Christ.* i. 36): *Every liar breaks his faith in lying, since forsooth he wishes the person to whom he lies to have faith in him, and yet he does not keep faith with him, when he lies to him: and whoever breaks his faith is guilty of iniquity.* Now no one is said to break his faith or *to be guilty of iniquity,* for a venial sin. Therefore no lie is a venial sin.

Obj. 4. Further, the eternal reward is not lost save for a mortal sin. Now, for a lie the eternal reward was lost, being exchanged for a temporal meed. For Gregory says (*Moral.* xviii) that *we learn from the reward of the midwives what the sin of lying deserves: since the reward which they deserved for their kindness, and which they might have received in eternal life, dwindled into a temporal meed on account of the lie of which they were guilty.* Therefore even an officious lie, such as was that of the midwives, which seemingly is the least of lies, is a mortal sin.

Obj. 5. Further, Augustine says (*Lib. De Mend.* vxii) that *it is a precept of perfection, not only not to lie at all, but not even to wish to lie.* Now it is a mortal sin to act against a precept. Therefore every lie of the perfect is a mortal sin: and consequently so also is a lie told by anyone else, otherwise the perfect would be worse off than others.

On the contrary, Augustine says on Ps. v. 7, *Thou wilt destroy,* etc.: *There are two kinds of lie that are not grievously sinful yet are not devoid of sin, when we lie either in joking, or for the sake of our neighbor's good.* But every mortal sin is grievous. Therefore jocose and officious lies are not mortal sins.

I answer that, A mortal sin is, properly speaking, one that is contrary to charity whereby the soul lives in union with God, as stated above (**Q. 24, A.** 12; **Q. 35, A.** 3). Now a lie may be contrary to charity in three ways: first, in itself; secondly, in respect of the evil intended; thirdly, accidently.

St. Thomas Aquinas, "Whether Every Lie Is a Mortal Sin," *Summa Theologica,* 2.2, ques. 110, art. 4, cited in *Lying: Moral Choice in Public and Private Life.*

A lie may be in itself contrary to charity by reason of its false signification. For if this be about divine things, it is contrary to the charity of God, whose truth one hides or corrupts by such a lie; so that a lie of this kind is opposed not only to the virtue of charity, but also to the virtues of faith and religion; wherefore it is a most grievous and a mortal sin. If, however, the false signification be about something the knowledge of which affects a man's good, for instance if it pertain to the perfection of science or to moral conduct, a lie of this description inflicts an injury on one's neighbor, since it causes him to have a false opinion, wherefore it is contrary to charity, as regards the love of our neighbor, and consequently is a mortal sin. On the other hand, if the false opinion engendered by the lie be about some matter the knowledge of which is of no consequence, then the lie in question does no harm to one's neighbor; for instance, if a person be deceived as to come contingent particulars that do not concern him. Wherefore a lie of this kind, considered in itself, is not a mortal sin.

As regards the end in view, a lie may be contrary to charity, through being told with the purpose of injuring God, and this is always a mortal sin, for it is opposed to religion; or in order to injure one's neighbor, in his person, his possessions or his good name, and this also is a mortal sin, since it is a mortal sin to injure one's neighbor, and one sins mortally if one has merely the intention of committing a mortal sin. But if the end intended be not contrary to charity, neither will the lie, considered under this aspect, be a mortal sin, as in the case of a jocose lie, where some little pleasure is intended, or in an officious lie, where the good also of one's neighbor is intended. Accidentally a lie may be contrary to charity by reason of scandal or any other injury resulting therefrom: and thus again it will be mortal sin, for instance if a man were not deterred through scandal from lying publicly.

Reply Obj. 1. The passages quoted refer to the mischievous lie, as a gloss explains the words of Ps. v. 7, *Thou wilt destroy all that speak a lie.*

Reply Obj. 2. Since all the precepts of the decalogue are directed to the love of God and our neighbor, as stated above (**Q.** 44, **A.** 1, *ad* 3: **I-II, Q.** 100, **A.** 5 *ad* I), a lie is contrary to a precept of the decalogue, in so far as it is contrary to the love of God and our neighbor. Hence it is expressly forbidden to bear false witness against our neighbor.

Reply Obj. 3. Even a venial sin can be called *iniquity* in a broad sense, in so far as it is beside the equity of justice; wherefore it is written (I John iii. 4): *Every sin is iniquity.* It is in this sense that Augustine is speaking.

Reply Obj. 4. The lie of the midwives may be considered in two ways. First as regards their feeling of kindliness towards the Jews, and their reverence and fear of God, for which their virtuous disposition is commended. For this an eternal reward is due. Wherefore Jerome (in his exposition of Isa. ixv. 21, *And they shall build houses*) explains that God *built them spiritual houses.* Secondly, it may be considered with regard to the external act of lying. For thereby they could merit, not indeed eternal reward, but perhaps some temporal meed, the deserving of which was not inconsistent with the deformity of their lie, though this was inconsistent with their meriting an eternal reward. It is in this sense that we must understand the words of Gregory, and not that they merited by that lie to lose the eternal reward as though they had already merited it by their preceding kindliness, as the objection understands the words to mean.

Reply Obj. 5. Some say that for the perfect every lie is a mortal sin. But this assertion is unreasonable. For no circumstance causes a sin to be infinitely more grievous unless it transfers it to another species. Now a circumstance of person does not transfer a sin to another species, except perhaps by reason of something annexed to that person, for instance if it be against his vow: and this cannot apply to an officious or jocose lie. Wherefore an officious or a jocose lie is not a mortal sin in perfect men, except perhaps accidentally on account of scandal. We may take in this sense the saying of Augustine that *it is a precept of perfection not only not to lie at all, but not even to wish to lie:* although Augustine says this not positively but dubiously, for he begins by saying: *Unless perhaps it is a precept,* etc. Nor does it matter that they are placed in a position to safeguard the truth: because they are bound to safeguard the truth by virtue of their office in judging or teaching, and if they lie in these matters their lie will be a mortal sin: but it does not follow that they sin mortally when they lie in other matters. . . .

LYING

St. Augustine

Augustine perhaps puts an end to this quandary about whether it is right to lie by defining several different types of lies. Which of his arguments is most persuasive?

ON LYING

. . . The first type of lie is a deadly one which should be avoided and shunned from afar, namely, that which is uttered in the teaching of religion, and to the telling of which no one should be led under any condition. The second is that which injures somebody unjustly: such a lie as helps no one and harms someone. The third is that which is beneficial to one person while it harms another, although the harm does not produce physical defilement. The fourth is the lie which is told solely for the pleasure of lying and deceiving, that is, the real lie. The fifth type is that which is told from a desire to please others in smooth discourse. When these have been avoided and rejected, a sixth kind of lie follows which harms no one and benefits some person, as, for instance, when a person, knowing that another's money is to be taken away unjustly, answers the questioner untruthfully and says that he does not know where the money is. The seventh type is that which is harmful to no one and beneficial to some person, with the exception of the case where a judge is questioning, as happens when a person lies because he is unwilling to betray a man sought for capital punishment, that is, not only a just and innocent person but even a criminal, because it belongs to Christian discipline never to despair of the conversion of anybody and never to block the opportunity for repentance. Now, I have spoken at length concerning these last two types, which are wont to evoke considerable discussion, and I have presented my opinion, namely, that by the acceptance of sufferings which are borne honorably and courageously, these lies, too, may be avoided by strong, faithful, and truthful men and women. The eighth is that type of lie which is harmful to no one and beneficial to the extent that it protects someone from physical defilement, at least, from that defilement which we have mentioned above. Now, the Jews considered a defilement to eat with unwashed hands. If anyone considers that as defilement, then a lie must not be told in order to avoid it. However, we are confronted with a new problem if a lie is such that it brings injury to any person, even though it protects another person from that defilement which all men detest and abhor. Should such a lie be told if the injury resulting from it is not in the nature of the defilement of which we have been treating? The question here does not concern lying; rather, it is whether harm should be done to any person, not necessarily through a lie, so that such defilement may be warded off from another person. I am definitely inclined to oppose such license. Even though the most trivial injuries are proposed, such as that one which I mentioned above in regard to the one lost measure of grain, they disturb me greatly in this problem as to whether we ought to do injury to one

St. Augustine, "Lying," from *Treatises on Various Subjects.*

person if, by that wrong, another person may be defended, or protected against defilement. But, as I have said, that is another question. . . .

AGAINST LYING

You have sent me much to read, dear brother Consentius, you have sent me much to read. [. . .] I am quite delighted with your eloquence, with your memory of sacred Scripture, with your adroitness of mind, with your distress in stinging indifferent Catholics, with your zeal in raging against even latent heretics. But I am not persuaded that they should be drawn out of hiding by our lies. For, why do we try with so much care to track them and hunt them down? Is it not so that, when they have been caught and brought into the open, we may either teach them the truth themselves or else, by convicting them of error, keep them from harming others? Is it not, in short, so that their falsehood may be blotted out or guarded against and God's truth be increased? Therefore, how can I suitably proceed against lies by lying? Or should robbery be proceeded against by means of robbery, sacrilege by sacrilege, and adultery by adultery? 'But if through my lie the truth of God has abounded,' are we, too, going to say, 'why should we not do evil that good may come from it?' You see how much the Apostle detests this. But what is it to say: "Let us lie in order to bring lying heretics to the truth, if not the same as saying, "Why should we not do evil that good may come from it?' Or is lying sometimes a good, or sometimes not an evil? Why, then, has it been written: 'Thou hatest all the workers of iniquity: thou wilt destroy all that speak a lie'? He has not made exception of some or said indefinitely: 'Thou wilt destroy tellers of lies,' so as to allow that certain ones be understood, but not every one. But he has brought forth a universal proposition, saying: 'Thou wilt destroy all that speak a lie.' Or, because it has not been said: 'Thou wilt destroy all that speak any lie or that speak any lie whatsoever,' are we to think, therefore, that room has been made for a certain kind of lie and that God will not destroy those who tell a certain kind of lie, but only those who tell unjust lies, not any lie whatsoever, because there are found just lies, too, which ought actually to be matter for praise rather than reproach?

(2) Do you not see how much this argument supports the very ones whom we are trying to catch as great quarry by our lies? That, as you yourself have shown, is precisely the opinion of the Priscillianists. To establish this opinion they produce evidence from Scripture, urging their followers to lie as if in accordance with the example of the Patriarchs, Prophets, Apostles, and angels, not hesitating to add even Christ our Lord Himself, thinking that they cannot otherwise prove their falsehood to be true except by saying that the Truth is mendacious. They must be refuted, not imitated. We must not participate with the Priscillianists in that evil in which they are proved to be worse than all other heretics, for they alone, or at least they especially, in order to hide what they think is their truth, are found to give dogmatic sanction to lying. And this great evil they deem just, for they say that what is true must be kept in the heart, but that it is no sin to utter what is false with the tongue to strangers. They say that it has been written: 'He that speaketh truth in his heart,' as if that were sufficient for justice, even if one tells a lie with his tongue when a stranger and not a neighbor is listening. On this account they even think that the Apostle Paul, when he had said: 'Put away lying and speak truth,' at once added: "each one with his neighbor, because we are members of one another,' so that it plainly might be

lawful and dutiful to tell a lie to those who are not our neighbors in the community of truth and not, as it were, our comembers.[. . .]

(36) But, because we are men and live among men, I confess that I am not yet in the number of those who are not troubled by compensatory sins. Often, in human affairs, human sympathy overcomes me and I am unable to resist when someone says to me: 'Look, here is a patient whose life is endangered by a serious illness and whose strength will not hold out any longer if he is told of the death of his dearly beloved only son. He asks you whether the boy is still alive whose life you know is ended. What will you answer when, if you say anything except "He is dead" or "He is alive" or "I don't know," the patient will believe that he is dead, because he realizes that you are afraid to say and do not want to lie? It will be the same no matter how hard you try to say nothing. Of the three convincing answers, two are false: "He is alive" and "I don't know," and you cannot utter them without lying. But, if you make the one true answer, namely, that he is dead, and if the death of the anguished father follows hard upon it, people will cry that he was slain by you. And who can bear to hear them exaggerate the evil of avoiding a beneficial lie and of loving homicide as truth?' I am moved by these arguments—more powerfully than wisely! For, when I put before my mind's eye the intellectual beauty of Him from whose mouth nothing false proceeded, then, although my weakness reverberates in palpitation before the radiance of the truth shining ever more brightly, I am so inflamed by love of such great beauty that I despise all human considerations that call me back from there. It is hard for this feeling to persist so far that its effect is not lost in time of temptation. Indeed, when I am contemplating the luminous good on which there is cast no shadow of a lie, I am not moved by the fact that, when we are unwilling to lie and men die upon hearing what is true, truth is called homicide. Why, if a shameless woman expects to be defiled and then dies of her fierce love because you do not consent, will chastity also be homicide? Or, indeed, because we read: 'We are the fragrance of Christ for God, alike as regards those who are saved and those who are lost; to these an odor that leads to death, but to those an odor that leads to life,' shall we also pronounce the fragrance of Christ to be homicide? But, because we are men and because human sympathy generally overcomes or harasses us amid such questions and objections, therefore, he, too, added, And for such offices; who is sufficient?

(37) Besides these there is the more distressing fact that, if we grant that we ought to lie about the son's life for the sake of that patient's health, little by little and bit by bit this evil will grow and by gradual accessions will slowly increase until it becomes such a mass of wicked lies that it will be utterly impossible to find any means of resisting such a plague grown to huge proportions through small additions. Hence, it has been most providentially written: 'He that contemneth small things, shall fall by little and little.' What of the fact that such lovers of this life as do not hesitate to prefer it to the truth want us not only to lie but also to perjure ourselves in order that a man may not die, nay, in order that a man who must sooner or later die may die a little later? They would have us take the name of the Lord our God in vain in order that the vain health of a man may not pass away a little sooner. And there are in these matters learned men who even make rules and set limits for when we ought and when we ought not to be perjured. O where are you, ye fountains of tears? And what shall we do? Where shall we go? Where shall we hide ourselves from the wrath of truth, if we not only disregard the avoidance of lies, but venture

in addition to teach perjuries? Let the advocates and defenders of lies look to what kind or kinds of lying it pleases them to justify! Only in the worship of God may they grant that we must not lie; only from perjuries and blasphemies may they restrain themselves; only where God's name, God's testimony, God's oath is introduced, only where talk of divine religion is brought forth, may no one lie, or praise or teach or enjoin lying or say that lying is just. About other kinds of lies, let him who believes that we ought to lie choose for himself what he thinks is the mildest and most innocent kind of lying. This much I know, that even he who teaches that we ought to lie wants to appear to be teaching the truth. For, if what he teaches is false, who would want to study the false doctrine where the teacher deceives and the learner is deceived? But if, in order that he may be able to find some pupil, he declares that he is teaching the truth when he teaches that we ought to lie, how will that lie be of the truth, since John the Apostle protests that no lie is of the truth?' Therefore, it is not true that sometimes we ought to lie. And what is not true we should never try to persuade anyone to believe.

RELATED WEB SITE

The works of St. Augustine: ccat.sas.upenn.edu/jod/augustine.html

---

Chapter 10

ETHICS AND FINANCE

Over 17 percent of respondents to a large-scale survey of investment analysts about ethical behavior reported that they failed to use diligence and thoroughness in making investment recommendations.[1] That's almost one in five. How would you feel if one of the five recommendations you received from your investment counselor was not thoroughly researched? Should it be "buyer beware" or do you rely on the analyst in making all of your investment decisions? Fifteen percent of the analysts surveyed also admitted to communicating inside information and writing reports to support predetermined conclusions. Yet, in the same survey, these analysts rated themselves higher on an ethical scale than politicians, attorneys, corporate bankers, and corporate managers!

Obviously, trust is an integral issue for all involved in the finance industry. After all, what more can an analyst offer than integrity and trustworthiness? There is no real, tangible product to sell, nor is there the ability to "try before you buy." Therefore, treating clients fairly and building a reputation for fair dealing may be the finance professional's greatest assets. Harvard Professor Greg Dees highlights some of these critical issues in his essay, "Deciding What Is Fair," where he discusses the unique finance issues that might arise in the area of entrepreneurship. The following are a few ethically challenging areas of finance.

Insider Trading   Insider trading is an area that, on the surface and from a legal perspective, seems black and white. If someone trades based on inside information, it's illegal and wrong. On the other hand, if someone has worked very hard to obtain a certain position in a firm and, by virtue of being in that position, is privy to inside information, isn't it just for that person to take advantage of the information since she or he has worked so hard to obtain the position? Is it really wrong? Unethical? Consider an issue that might be closer to home. If your brother has always been successful in whatever he does in the business world, is it unethical to purchase stock in the company he just acquired. Others don't know quite how successful he has been, so are you trading on inside information? Would you tell others?

In many circumstances, not only in finance but also in other areas of business, the actors believe that their actions are justified and that they are staying on the *right* side of the line dividing ethical and unethical behavior. Dennis Levine, convicted for insider trading, was one of those people. Consider his discussion that follows and what might have prevented him (or would prevent others) from getting into this treacherous spot in the first place.

Ethical Investing   There is another side to ethical investing—the obligations of the individual investor. Does the investor have a duty to invest in socially responsible firms? That would seem a bit far-fetched. But isn't it a bit hypocritical for someone to complain a great deal about the lack of social responsibility in corporate America, but then to refuse to financially support the firms who *are* socially responsible? Investors show their support by choosing their investments. If socially responsible firms fail in the public stock exchanges, they will have no capital with which to conduct socially responsible

---

[1]E. Theodore Veit and Michael Murphy, "Ethics Violations: A Survey of Investment Analysts," *Journal of Business Ethics* (1996) 15, pp. 1287–97.

acts—a clear correlation. On the other hand, the complexity of markets and firm activities make it extremely difficult to make wise investment choices in this regard.

Takeovers, Mergers, and Leveraged Buyouts (LBOs)   Are we a better society because we allow hostile takeovers than we would be if we did not? Companies may perform more efficiently as a result of the threat of a takeover looming at their door. On the other hand, perhaps companies perform efficiently *despite* the threat of takeovers. How well do you work when you know that someone else is after your job? Sometimes better, sometimes worse. Since the market often reflects short-term judgments of long-term decisions, hostile takeovers have been criticized as forcing short-term solutions where a more effective solution would be preferable. In addition, in order to finance the takeovers, many firms take on huge internal debts, paid off only as long as the company is doing well but left as a market loss when the company is threatened with higher costs.

When a firm is threatened with a takeover, decision makers sometimes react by attempting to take the company private through the issuance of bonds. This is often accomplished by issuing high-risk, or "junk," bonds in order to repurchase stock. Does this satisfy the directors' fiduciary duty to shareholders? The decision makers have a duty to the shareholder to increase stock price, but also a self-interest in keeping stock prices low for repurchase. Utilitarian theory may be best applied here. When the public hears of an LBO or restructuring, it is often assumed that jobs may be lost and the rich will just get richer. But people often fail to realize that the money of the rich is not just sitting under a mattress somewhere—it is invested in the market. LBOs often trim the fat of companies and make them more efficient (through increased productivity, lower prices, and an increase in *long-term* employment).

Another vexing market issue in connection with takeovers is **greenmail.** You decide to buy some shares of a company. After purchasing those shares, you find out some information related to this firm which, when made public, causes an extreme rise in the stock price. Have you done anything wrong by making this information public? It doesn't appear so. Greenmail is not much different. Greenmail occurs where a potential takeover agent purchases stock in a company. After the purchases have totaled 5 percent, the agent must announce its intention to take over the company, if that is its intent. The stock price goes up in anticipation of the takeover battle. The takeover agent ends up selling its shares back to the firm for this increased price (or sometimes a higher, negotiated price) when the attacked company struggles to thwart the takeover. Is this any different from the facts in the first scenario? Is this unethical?

Some contend that the ethics of the situation depend on the real intent of the takeover agent. If there was never any real intent to complete the takeover, but instead merely to increase the price and sell back, then the practice would be considered unethical. They argue that someone with a real intent may propose a restructuring plan and, if management adopts it, the agent would withdraw its offer. The profit received from selling the shares back to the firm would be not unethical but a "consultant's fee" for offering assistance to the firm! Are you convinced? What is the key problem with this argument? Aren't you bothered that the firm didn't have the free choice of whether to "hire" this assistance or not? It was forced on them and they were threatened to "use it or lose it." Free choice is nonexistent.

How could this type of behavior be prevented? Legislation has been proposed to thwart these attempts at greenmail, requiring for instance that proposed takeover agents have 100 percent of funding available for the takeover at the time of the announcement. Can you think of other mechanisms or would you argue that the free market should prevail without any regulation of this type? Is this evidence of a free market success or breakdown?

Something that might be justified by free market theory is **golden parachutes.** The term *golden parachute* refers to the guarantee to the chief executives of a firm that they will be "taken care of" in the event of a takeover. This provision is often in the bylaws of the firm long before it becomes a takeover target and may actually serve to dissuade certain takeover agents because of the potential costs involved. Some theorists argue that golden parachutes preserve the integrity of the executives' fiduciary duties because they know that they will be taken care of whether the firm, or their jobs, remain in existence or not. On the other hand, should corporate funds really go to this end? Aren't executives paid awfully well in some cases precisely because they are willing to take these risks?

Financial issues may pose the greatest ethical dilemmas simply because they frequently pit money against other priorities. Perhaps the best way to solve these ethical issues in finance is to consider your personal priority scheme long before the dilemma presents itself. Money is seductive, sometimes more so than the "right" thing to do.

SHORT HYPOTHETICAL CASES

a. Garcia Corporation is a 20-year-old, publicly traded company that generates $50,000,000 in annual sales of commercial food prep equipment. Most of Garcia's sales growth has come from selling the same basic product line to newly opened restaurants. Consequently, Garcia has managed to modestly increase its profits over the previous year's performance and declare a higher dividend for its shareholders during most years.

In the past five years, however, the restaurant industry in which most Garcia customers compete has suffered from a major shake-up. Several established restaurant chains and more than a few new start-ups have failed. As a result, the restaurant equipment market has been flooded with used goods, which sell for half the cost of new equipment. Garcia's equipment sales this year have declined while it waits for this temporary glut to disappear, and the company may post a slight loss (the company's first) as a result.

Most of Garcia's stockholders are investors who expect the company's profits, share value, and dividends to increase. Although they are sympathetic to tough economic times, the stockholders will sell off their shares and refuse to buy additional shares in the future if the company's fortunes decline. To keep its stockholders content, Garcia plans to make an accounting change in its depreciation policy on its auto fleet from double-declining-balance to straight-line. The company would show a slight profit this year and hopefully give its management time to boost the company's sales and profitability the next year.

Are these plans ethical, given the fact that the change would be disclosed and that shareholders are still getting the same information? Are the shareholders' expectations realistic? Does this matter?

b. Since 1894, ABC Steel Company has manufactured and distributed sheet metal fabricated in its mills to many American and foreign companies. Until the mid-1970s, this family-operated company had been a very healthy and profitable operation, but the company's fortunes began to change when it faced stiff quality and price competition from foreign steel manufacturers. ABC suffered a strong decline in sales and closed several plants as a result.

During the early 1980s, ABC replaced both its aging plant equipment and its aging management team. Most of the equipment ABC once used in its manufacturing process was installed during the 1950s and had been repaired, modified, and expanded, but never replaced. By closing more than half of its existing operations, ABC concentrated on its remaining facilities and purchased $50,000,000 of modern equipment that allowed it to successfully compete with foreign steelmakers.

The stockholders also replaced the family that started the company with a younger, more aggressive management team. The stockholders paid the managers competitive salaries but also realized that good managers frequently changed positions every few years.

As an incentive to encourage the management's loyalty and performance, the stockholders also offered them $3,000,000 in lucrative stock options that could be exercised when the earnings per share (EPS) first exceeded $2 per share, a rather sizable increase to expect at that time.

By November 1994, the company projected annual earnings of $20,000,000 and had 11,000,000 shares outstanding and $18,000,000 in cash reserves for future investment. Since the 1980s and 1990s, the company's sales steadily grew to a respectable amount, but the manufacturing equipment once again began to show signs of its age. The management team was faced with a decision: Should it recommend that the company spend the $18,000,000 in available cash on the more modern equipment or use it to repurchase 1,500,000 shares of stock? What would be the consequences if the management team repurchased the stock? How might this decision affect the stockholders? What would you do if you were a member of the management team?

From *Essentials of Managerial Accounting* by James Don Edwards, Roger Hermanson, and Michael Maher. Copyright © 1994 Business One Irwin. Reprinted by Permission.

ETHICAL INVESTMENT

INTEGRATIVE INVESTING
THE GREENMONEY ON-LINE JOURNAL

Should you invest according to your values? Electronic magazine
The GreenMoney On-Line Journal *offers its guidance as to why your*
values matter in the world of money.

Whenever you make important decisions in your life, you act in accordance with your values and beliefs. Why would it be any different when making investment decisions?

Integrative Investing allows people to invest in a manner consistent with their values and beliefs concerning a variety of social and environmental issues. Another term used to describe this global movement is Socially Responsible Investing (SRI).

When you invest in a socially and environmentally responsible mutual fund, you are putting your money to work towards a better world and a more just society. You are voicing an opinion for positive social change, while helping to make it happen. You also know your money isn't going to finance businesses engaged in poor social and environmental practices. You are helping to create a sound and sustainable future. Investing for profit with principles.

The stock market moved up throughout 1995. Ten of the 41 socially responsible mutual funds returned more than 30%. The top fund was Citizens Trust Emerging Growth Fund with a total return of 40.7%. You can be ethical and make money.

Information on SRI is now available around the world, 24-hours a day. The Internet's world wide web is an exciting new medium for the exchange of information. We stepped into this arena during 1995 by launching The GreenMoney On-Line Journal. The web site address is http://www.greenmoney.com.

As SRI continues to gain financial creditability and moves forward with conviction and commitment, it will increase its influence in the national and global conversation.

SCREENS

Investment screening integrates your values and your money. The complexity of our world is reflected in the following questions. The choices you make reflect your values and beliefs. You can screen in the positive and screen out the company or activities you don't want to support.

Do you want to avoid certain companies because of their products and corporate behavior? Do you want to be involved in shareholder activism using shareholder resolutions to change corporate behavior? What is the composition of a company's Board of Directors—do they represent a cross section of customers, community, employees, and shareholders? Is a company advertising in publications or on TV/Radio programs that you don't want to support? . . .

Approximately half of the largest 1,000 publicly traded U.S. companies meet most socially responsible mutual funds screening criteria. The Domini 400 Social Index contains 250 companies from the Standard & Poor's 500 (S&P 500). The new Citizens 300 Index contains 200 companies from the S&P 500.

Are there performance sacrifices when investing in socially and environmentally responsible ways? No. Consider these numbers: The Domini 400 Social Index (DSI) was launched in May 1990 by Kinder, Lydenberg and Domini (KLD) to track 400 companies that pass multiple social screens. From May 1990 through December 1995, the DSI returned 135.5% compared to 120.5% for the S&P 500. The DSI had its fifth anniversary last May. It demonstrated the long-term profitability of SRI, during the five-year period May 1, 1990–April 30, 1995. Total return for the DSI was 92.64% vs. 81.13% for the S&P 500. The annualized return for the DSI was 12.5% vs. 11.4% for the S&P 500. For more information call Karen Pratt of KLD at (617) 547–7479.

CASES IN VENTURE CAPITAL ETHICS

J. GREGORY DEES

Dees offers the following case studies as examples of the moral and ethical dilemmas facing entrepreneurs and venture capitalists.

The following examples are fictionalized representations of real situations. The names are made up and any similarity to existing individuals or firms is unintended. Each case is sketched with very limited background information. If you think something is crucial is missing, fill it in with "what if" assumptions. If the missing information makes a difference to you, make note of how and why it makes a difference.

CASE 1—SKINFUSION, INC.

You are in the midst of due diligence concerning a major investment in SkinFusion, Inc., a company specializing in transdermal drug delivery systems. SkinFusion has an exciting new technology that company executives claim is lower cost, safer, and more precise than currently popular systems. This could be a big winner, if they are right. You have signed a term sheet, and, so far, you are pleased with what you are turning up on the due diligence. However, it is hard to find out what sort of competing technology is under development. In the midst of the due diligence, you receive a business plan from Patchaderm Pharmaceuticals, a direct competitor of SkinFusion with its own new technology. The plan came in unsolicited, but directed to your attention. The cover letter indicates that the CEO of Patchaderm read an article you wrote for a medical technology trade journal on methods of financing entrepreneurial ventures. He liked what he read and wants you to consider investing in his business.

1. Do you read the Patchaderm business plan? Do you pass it on to the associate helping with the due diligence? What is your rationale?
2. Do you respond to the CEO's letter? What do you say?
3. Would your behavior change if you were not so happy with what was turning up in the SkinFusion due diligence? Would it change if you had already closed the SkinFusion deal?
4. Assume that you are unable to resist a peak at the plan. After all, the SkinFusion investment could be a large and risky one. You are intrigued by what you read, but the plan just does not include enough information to decide who has the superior technology. The letter from Patchaderm's CEO invited you to come to the company. Do you accept Patchaderm's invitation? If so, what do you tell Patchaderm about your

---

J. Gregory Dees, "Cases in Venture Capital Ethics," reprinted by permission of the author.

intentions in making the visit? How would you respond if Patchaderm's CEO asks you to sign a confidentiality agreement?

5. Suppose that you visit Patchaderm and the issue of confidentiality is never discussed. Perhaps it just slipped their minds. After the visit, you are still convinced that Skin-Fusion is the best bet. However, you have gained valuable competitive information. After closing the deal, do you share any of this information with the SkinFusion management team? What would you share and how?

6. Suppose that after your visit you decide that Patchaderm would be a better investment than SkinFusion. Do you walk away from the SkinFusion deal? How do you explain this to SkinFusion management? If you invest in Patchaderm, do you share any of your knowledge about SkinFusion with Patchaderm management? Where do you draw the line?

CASE 2—PORTERWAVE, INC.

Your firm was a seed investor in PorterWave, Inc., putting up $100,000 of the initial $275,000 capitalization. The remainder was invested by the founder, her family and friends. The founder was Jane Porter, a brilliant engineer from Cal Tech who is pioneering the technology for portable, battery operated microwave ovens. After two years, she has produced a working prototype, and it is time for a major capital infusion. At least $5 million is needed to convert the prototype into a commercially viable design that might be sold or licensed to a major appliance manufacturer. Your firm is willing to invest more money, another $1 million, but you cannot be the lead investors in this next round. For a number of reasons, you simply do not have the funds available.

After a search for funding partners, Bluebird Ventures (BV) emerges as a strong potential lead. They would invest $3.2 million and bring in a third investor for the remaining $800,000. BV is a relatively new firm. You have not worked with any of its principals. They have a reputation for being smart and driving tough deals. You were not totally surprised when BV initially proposed a relatively low value for PorterWave stock. The PorterWave board (on which you sit) was disappointed with the offer, but, in the absence of any viable alternative, agreed to move forward with BV, into due diligence.

After taking an unusually long time to conclude the due diligence, BV announces that it must renegotiate the deal. Concerns about safety, competition, and time to market have led them to an even lower valuation, significantly lower. You are shocked. Their new assumptions seem far too pessimistic, but BV is adamant. This new deal would essentially wash-out the early investors. Even Jane Porter's share would be diluted to 5%. To add insult to injury, BV insists that Porter be put on a vesting schedule. She would have to earn her 5% by seeing the company through some key milestones. All this strikes you as grossly unfair. Your firm would never propose such a harsh deal. During your time on the board, you have developed a particularly close, friendly relationship with Porter and the other seed investors. For each of them, PorterWave was a significant personal investment. They trust you, as one of the second round investors, to see to it that they get a fair deal.

On the other hand, BV's new proposal, if accepted, would result in your firm gaining a larger share of PorterWave, more than enough to compensate for the dilution of your seed investment. PorterWave is running very low on cash, and you need to decide what to do about BV's new proposal.

1. Where are your primary loyalties and responsibilities in this situation?
2. If Porter comes to you (as a friend) asking for personal advice, what do you say? Do you confess that you think the deal is unfair?
3. Do you complain to BV about the new valuation? If so, how do you justify a better deal for seed investors and the founder?
4. Is there anything wrong with what BV did? If so, what? If you are not sure, what would you need to know to decide?

CASE 3—DESK BEAUTIFUL CORPORATION

Your firm is heavily invested in Desk Beautiful Corporation (DBC), a manufacturer and distributor of furniture systems for small businesses. These systems are designed to allow the offices to have a warm, home-style look. Electronic equipment can be easily hidden from view. The desks, shelves, and file cabinets are made of wood. Chairs and sofas are nicely upholstered in quality fabrics. DBC has been able, through efficient design, strategic procurement, and state-of-the-art production and distribution systems, to keep costs down. Its systems are priced to compete with the better-quality metal and laminated office systems. When DBC started up, it was alone in this niche, and it grew rapidly. However, in the last two years, three new competitors have entered the same niche. One of them is a division of a major office furniture manufacturer. As a result of the new competition, prices have been driven down further and margins have been squeezed. DBC is still the market leader and is profitable, but it has fallen slightly behind its original plan.

Six months ago, the CEO of DBC, Ralph Veneer, attended a seminar entitled "Beyond Compliance: Leading the Furniture Business Out of the Tropical Rain Forest." The seminar convinced Veneer that DBC was contributing to global environmental problems by purchasing timber harvested from tropical rain forests. At the last board meeting, Veneer gave a powerful multi-media presentation about the disastrous destruction of rain forests and its potential impact on the global environment and on indigenous people living in the forests. The DBC management team then presented a proposal for using less wood and switching to more environmentally friendly woods. Even with aggressive "green" marketing, the management team projected some continued loss of market share, increased costs, and a decline in profits as a result of this new strategy, at least in the near term. The impact could be as much as a twenty percent loss in the value of the firm, and it might mean a delay of a couple of years in the public offering that would provide your exit.

Veneer argued that DBC, as a profitable industry leader, should set a positive example. His conscience will not let him continue with the old practices. You were personally moved by his presentation. You have also become more deeply concerned about environmental issues in recent years. However, the other venture capitalists on the board are opposed to a change in policy. Your vote could well be the swing vote.

1. How do you vote on DBC's new "green" strategy? Why?
2. Do you consult anyone on this? Do you listen to your own conscience?

3. If the strategy is passed by the board, do you write down the investment in statements to your limited investors? How do you explain the write down?

4. Does your decision about this strategy depend at all on who your limited partners are and what they might want? Does it depend on the view of the principals in your firm?

5. What would you do if Veneer simply implemented the strategy without bringing it to the board? Would this be grounds for firing him?

6. Would your views change if DBC was wildly profitable and far ahead of plan?

ETHICS AND INSIDER TRADING

THE INSIDE STORY
OF AN INSIDE TRADER
Dennis B. Levine

In his letter granting permission to reprint the following article,
Levine stated that, in writing the article, "it was my sincere desire
that other young people could learn from my mistakes and not suc-
cumb to the pressures of the work place in advancing their careers."
Levine, a partner to Ivan Boesky, was arrested for insider trading,
setting off a barrage of arrests, including his partner, Ivan Boesky,
and Michael Milkin. Levine traded on the stocks of soon-to-be-an-
nounced merger targets using mainly offshore bank accounts. His
Nabisco trades reaped him a $2.7 million profit. In this article,
Levine tells his personal story.

Waking early in my Park Avenue apartment on May 12, 1986, I read the morning papers, checked on the European securities markets, and ate breakfast with my wife, Laurie, then six weeks pregnant, and my son, Adam, who was 4. By 8 A.M. I was in downtown Manhattan, meeting with my staff at Drexel Burnham Lambert. At 33, I was a leading merger specialist and a partner in one of the most powerful investment banks on Wall Street. Among the many appointments on my calendar that day were meetings with two CEOs, including Revlon's Ronald Perelman, to discuss multibillion-dollar takeovers. I was a happy man.

In midafternoon two strangers, one tall and one short, came looking for me at Drexel. They didn't identify themselves, but the receptionist said they weren't dressed like clients. For ten months, I knew, the Securities and Exchange Commission had been investigating the Bahamian subsidiary of Bank Leu, the Swiss bank that had executed insider stock trades for me since 1980. That very morning I had spoken on the phone with one of the bank's employees, who reassured me that everything was under control. Still, I knew something was wrong, and I fled. While the authorities searched for me, I drove around New York in my BMW, making anxious calls on the car phone to my wife, my father, my boss. Before leaving the car, I hired a legal team headed by superstar lawyer Arthur Liman, who went on to serve as chief Senate counsel in the Iran-contra investigation and is now representing Michael Milken.

By the time I had hired Liman, my darkest secret was being broadcast by TV stations across the country. Early in the evening, I drove alone to the U.S. Attorney's office in lower Manhattan, expecting only to be served with a subpoena. The federal officers read me my rights instead. At the nearby Metropolitan Correctional Center, they locked me up with a bunch of drug dealers in a cell whose odor I won't soon forget. It was like an out-of-body experience. As I ate cornflakes at the prison cafeteria the next morning, I watched the story of my arrest on a TV wake-up show. My carefully orchestrated career, years of planning and sacrifice, thousands of hours of work that had lifted me from Bayside, Queens, to the pinnacle of Wall Street—all reduced to nothing. Just like that.

I have had four years to reflect on the events leading up to my arrest. Part of that time—15 months and two days—I spent in Lewisburg federal prison camp in Pennsylvania. Getting your comeuppance is painful, and I have tried to take it on the chin. Unfortunately, my family also had to endure the trauma of humiliation, disgrace, and loss of privacy—and they did nothing to deserve it.

I will regret my mistakes forever. I blame only myself for my actions and accept full responsibility for what I have done. No one led me down the garden path. I've gained an abiding respect for the fairness of our system of justice: For the hard work and creativity I brought to my investment banking career, I was well rewarded. When I broke the law, I was punished. The system works.

People always ask, *Why would somebody who's making over $1 million a year start trading on inside information?* That's the wrong question. Here's what I thought at the time, misguided as I was: When I started trading on nonpublic information in 1978, I wasn't making a million. I was a 25-year-old trainee at Citibank with a $19,000 annual salary. I was wet behind the ears, impatient, burning with ambition. In those days people didn't think about insider trading the way they do now: You'd call it "a hot stock tip." The first U.S. criminal prosecution for insider trading wasn't until around that time, and it was not highly publicized. In the early years I regarded the practice as just a way to make some fast money. Of course I soon realized what I was doing was wrong, but I rationalized it as harmless. I told myself that the frequent run-ups in target-company stock prices before merger announcements proved others were doing it too.

Eventually insider trading became an addiction for me. It was just so easy. In seven years I built $39,750 into $11.5 million, and all it took was a 20-second phone call to my offshore bank a couple of times a month—maybe 200 calls total. My account was growing at 125% a year, compounded. Believe me, I felt a rush when I would check the price of one of my stocks on the office Quotron and learn I'd just made several hundred thousand dollars. I was confident that the elaborate veils of secrecy I had created—plus overseas bank-privacy laws—would protect me.

And Wall Street was crazy in those days. These were the 1980s, remember, the decade of excess, greed, and materialism. I became a go-go guy, consumed by the high-pressure, ultracompetitive world of investment banking. I was helping my clients make tens and even hundreds of millions of dollars. I served as the lead banker of Perelman's nearly $2 billion takeover of Revlon, four months of work that enabled Drexel to earn $60 million in fees. The daily exposure to such deals, the pursuit of larger and larger transactions, and the numbing effect of 60- to 100-hour work-weeks helped erode my values and distort my judgment. In this unbelievable world of billions and billions of dollars, the millions I made by trading on nonpublic information seemed almost insignificant.

At the root of my compulsive trading was an inability to set limits. Perhaps it's worth noting that my legitimate success stemmed from the same root. My ambition was so strong it went beyond rationality, and I gradually lost sight of what constitutes ethical behavior. At each new level of success I set higher goals, imprisoning myself in a cycle from which I saw no escape. When I became a senior vice president, I wanted to be a managing director, and when I became a managing director, I wanted to be a client. If I was making $100,000 a year, I thought, *I can make $200,000.* And if I made $1 million, *I can make $3 million.* And so it went. . . .

It was at Citibank that I met Robert Wilkis. A fit, balding junior officer a few years older than I, Bob struck me as terribly urbane when he introduced himself at a meeting for new employees. He was a Harvard grad with a Stanford MBA who spoke five languages. Bob shared my love of the stock market, and we became close friends. We would meet at the fourth-floor stock-quote terminal, where he monitored his personal portfolio while I tracked the latest M&A deals.

As a lending officer in the world corporate group, Bob had routine access to sensitive information about mergers Citibank might finance. Early in 1978 he told me he had identified a major U.S. company—let's call it ChemCorp—as a takeover target. He said he had bought its shares and recommended I do the same. I did: Borrowing on margin, I purchased $4,000 of ChemCorp stock. The merger never materialized and I sold the stock for about what I paid for it. To this day I'm not sure the transaction was illegal; Bob never told me he had inside information about ChemCorp. But it was well over a year before I dared make another such trade. . . .

During the year [I worked in Paris for Smith Barney], Bob Wilkis and I kept in touch by telephone, and in the spring of 1979 he visited Paris on business. Bob had also moved into investment banking by then, as an associate in international finance at Blyth Eastman Dillon. We talked at length about trading on the inside information we came across at work. By nature, investment banking requires that even junior people encounter nonpublic information as they work on prospective deals; both Bob and I learned of transactions long before they were announced.

When Bob was in Paris we decided to open accounts at Swiss banks. I borrowed as much as I could from my Ready Credit account and my family, telling them only that I had found some promising investment opportunities. With the $39,750 I raised, I opened a numbered account at Pictet & Cie in Geneva; Bob's was at Crédit Suisse. I didn't really begin buying stocks until Smith Barney moved me back to its New York office a few months later. I went to great lengths to avoid creating a paper trail for investigators to follow. Accustomed to confidential arrangements, Pictet's bankers suggested I use the code name Milky Way. *When you call,* they said, *why don't you just say it's Mr. Way?* They sent me no bank statements. I called in my trades from public phones—collect. (The bank extracted a service charge of about $20 per call.)

Bob and I tried to avoid linking our trading activities or creating noticeable patterns. That way, if one of us was found out, the other would be safe. We agreed to pool our information but to avoid any financial relationship. According to our pact, we would keep our trading secret, never share our stock tips with anyone else, and never trade in the U.S.

Bob came up with the code name Alan Darby, which each of us used when calling the other at work.

The procedure was simple. In the normal course of business Bob might learn that Blyth—or his next employer, Lazard Frères—was representing one company in a prospective takeover of another. Let's call the target Flounder Corp. Bob would phone me at work, identifying himself as Darby if anyone other than I answered. We would set up a meeting, often a quick lunch of pizza or Chinese food. Between bites, he would tell me the inside dope on Flounder. We would also chat about work, family, movies—we were friends, remember—then say goodbye.

Before buying any shares, I would do enough research on Flounder to assure myself that its stock was worth buying at current prices even if the takeover never materialized. (Inside information is not always a sure thing: I lost as much as $250,000 on some trades.) If Flounder's fundamentals looked good enough, I would find a moment to step out to a pay phone and call my bank with a buy order. Once the public got wind of the takeover and bid up the stock, I would telephone again with a sell order. It was that simple. As often as not, of course, I'd provide information and Bob would trade.

My initial uneasiness gradually ebbed—there were no inquiries, and all of a sudden the balance in my account was over $125,000. . . .

My relationship with Ivan Boesky began innocently enough. Having learned to listen to the market's tom-toms as part of my legitimate career, I developed a network of sources that eventually included the man considered America's boldest and most influential stock speculator. Like the CIA, Ivan seemed to have sources everywhere: His intelligence was extremely valuable. And he was an important Drexel client. . . .

Ivan's attentions were flattering. He invited me to lunch at "21." He would telephone me at home, at work, even when I was on business trips or vacations, seeking information about deals. My home phone would ring well before 6 A.M.; Laurie would answer and hand me the receiver, saying, *It's Ivan,* rolling her eyes. He had such a insatiable desire for information that he would call me up to a dozen times a day. With Bob's knowledge, I began giving him tips in exchange for access to the vast store of market information in Ivan's head.

I wasn't telling Ivan anything very specific—it was more a matter of suggesting that, say, his investment in XYZ Corp. seemed worth holding on to. I never told him my oblique suggestions were based on nonpublic information, but over time he evidently learned their value. Then Ivan drastically changed the nature of our relationship by offering to pay for the information I was giving him, based on a percentage of his trading profits. He said something like, *You seem to have very, very good information. You should be compensated for it.*

Despite my own illicit activities, I was flabbergasted. I couldn't believe he would risk exposing himself so blatantly, by proposing something clearly illegal on its face. I already had a secret life, and it was not something I was anxious to expand: My safety depended on keeping the number of people who knew of my insider trading to a minimum. Besides, by then I had millions in my account at Bank Leu. I turned Ivan down and resisted his overtures for weeks.

I'm not quite sure why I finally accepted. Stupidity, I guess. And I don't know why Ivan engaged in illegal activities when he had a fortune estimated at over $200 million.

I'm sure he derived much of his wealth from legitimate enterprise: He was skilled at arbitrage and obsessed with his work. He must have been driven by something beyond rational behavior. In any case, I never received a penny from him, though I was due $2.4 million under our formula when I was arrested.

When my scheme fell apart, it did so quickly. In the summer of 1985, Merrill Lynch received an anonymous letter accusing two of its brokers in Caracas, Venezuela, of insider trading; only one was subsequently charged. Unbeknownst to me, for years several Bank Leu executives had been making trades that mimicked mine, for their own accounts or for others'—apparently, the bank's policies condoned this. Disregarding my instructions to spread my orders among several brokers, they had funneled much of the business through Merrill Lynch. At least one trader there, in Caracas, apparently piggybacked on my trades too. Somebody blew the whistle, perhaps out of jealousy. Merrill Lynch, it seems, then informed the SEC, and just as my legitimate career was reaching its peak, the government began its ten-month investigation of Bank Leu. . . .

The day the government came looking for me, I was petrified about Laurie's reaction. Laurie is wonderful. Tutoring our daughter, Sarah, with flashcards or playing softball with Adam, she shows the patience of a grade school teacher, a career she gave up to raise our children. She is also assertive: She lets you know exactly what she thinks. Certain that she wouldn't approve and meaning to shield her from any legal consequences of my actions, I had never told her about my insider trading. It was a secret big enough to strain any marriage: Some spouses use drugs, others have extramarital affairs, I secretly traded stocks.

Laurie had no reason to suspect: We had always lived within my means. We stayed in a cramped one-bedroom apartment for almost three years after Adam was born, though I could have paid for almost any apartment in Manhattan with my offshore trading profits. . . .

The death blow came when Bob Wilkis asked to meet with me. To my amazement, he told me that he had tipped others, including a member of his family, and had been executing trades in the U.S. all along. That had created an easily detected trading pattern nearly identical to mine—more than enough to nail me. I knew I was finished and in the end my attorneys advised me that I had no choice but to settle with the government and tell the truth about everything and everybody involved in my case.

I pleaded guilty to four criminal charges related to my insider trading and settled civil charges with the SEC. Turning over cash and other assets, I made full restitution of my $11.5 million in trading profits. Everyone else involved in the case also entered guilty pleas and cooperated. Ivan Boesky turned himself in, pleading guilty to one criminal count and turning over $100 million. At that point I assumed the investigation was closed, but apparently Ivan's illicit activities extended far beyond his involvement with me. I had no inkling of his secret relationship with Marty Siegel, whose office was right next to mine at Drexel. The revelations of Ivan's paying Siegel off for inside information with suitcases of cash surprised me as much as anyone. So did Drexel's collapse and Michael Milken's settlement with the government. I don't think the firm's ethics were materially different from any other investment bank's.

On February 20, 1987, I pulled up to the federal courthouse in White Plains, New York, with my wife and lawyers. As our car approached I noticed dozens of reporters and camera crews standing outside. It reminded me of a lynch mob. Once inside, I learned that few experiences are more humbling than standing before a federal judge, publicly acknowledging guilt and being sentenced to jail. Less than four months after Sarah's birth, I began serving my sentence. Saying goodbye to your family is painful enough, but imagine having to explain to your 5-year-old son why his father is going to prison.

Although minimum-security prison camps have no walls, you are constantly reminded of your separation from family and society. I had no privacy, my moves were monitored, and my daily routine was controlled by others. I went from never having enough time to a place where everyone kills time. I mopped floors and mowed grass and spent hours just thinking. At first I could not come to grips with the turbulent changes in my life; I was burning with anger at myself. Eventually I decided to change my priorities and try to regain control over my life. I had entered prison grossly overweight, at 241 pounds. One outward sign of my new resolve: I lost 67 pounds in prison.

I got along all right with the other prisoners, many of them drug offenders with no convictions for violence; nobody bothered me. They loved TV shows like *Wiseguy* and *Miami Vice*—and the inmates always rooted for the crook. Having experienced prison, I'm saddened that most Americans apparently believe we can solve our drug problems by building more jails and locking more people up. From what I've seen, prisons don't solve social problems.

The other prisoners called me "Mr. Wall Street" and asked me for market advice. I always said no.

Money had little value, but there was a lively barter economy: If you were long on cigarettes, you could often buy a plate of linguini with clam sauce, heated in an aluminum pie tin over an electric iron. As one of the few nonsmokers in an institution that rationed cigarettes, I was a wealthy man. Laurie sent me a copy of *Bonfire of the Vanities,* Tom Wolfe's novel about a Wall Streeter who gets thrown in jail. I never felt quite like a Master of the Universe, but I saw parallels. . . .

I am rebuilding my life. I still feel the consequences of my mistakes and doubtless will forever. But I've been granted a precious second chance. This time around, I'm spending far more time at home with my family than ever before. I love the investment-banking business—it's in my blood—but as part of my settlement I agreed never to work for a securities firm again. I can still advise companies about raising money or doing deals, so I have started my own New York advisory firm, named Adasar Group after my children. My clients are smaller than they used to be, but much to my surprise, most people have treated my reentry into business with fairness and compassion. . . .

ETHICS, ECONOMICS, AND INSIDER TRADING: AYN RAND MEETS THE THEORY OF THE FIRM

JONATHAN R. MACEY

Macey responds to Lawson's discussion of the moral basis of insider trading.

I. ETHICS VS. IDEOLOGY IN THE DEBATE AGAINST INSIDER TRADING

It is not difficult to confuse ethical judgments with ideological beliefs. Indeed, in close cases the distinction is quite subtle. At the extremes, however, the analysis is easy. Ethics has to do with the establishment of individual, moral standards of conduct. The goal of ethical theory is to arrive at clearly delineated moral standards from carefully constructed premises, which themselves are subject to justificatory critique.[1] Ideology, on the other hand, is merely a descriptive term for the prejudices of a particular class or group that are reflected in their doctrines and opinions. While ethical theory starts from the bottom and seeks to construct a set of principles from first premises, ideology starts at the top with its conclusions and proceeds downward to justify these results on sociological,[2] cultural,[3] psychological,[4] or epistemological[5] grounds. While ethical theory seeks to ground moral judgments on carefully constructed logical hypotheses, "[i]deology is an emotion-laden,

---

Jonathan R. Macey, "Ethics, Economics and Insider Trading: Ayn Rand Meets the Theory of the Firm." Reprinted by permission from *Harvard Journal of Law and Public Policy* (Summer 1988).

1. D. LYONS, ETHICS AND THE RULE OF LAW 11–35 (1984).
2. Karl Marx and Friedrich Engels were the initial proponents of this approach.
3. Examples of the cultural, sometimes called "psychocultural," approaches to ideology are contained in the work of Clifford Geertz and Leon Dion:

   Our hypothesis is that political ideology is a cultural and mental complex which mediates between the norms associated with given social attitudes and conduct and the norms which the political institutions and mechanisms tend to crystallize and propagate. In other terms, political ideology is a more or less integrated system of values and norms, rooted in society, which individuals and groups project on the political plane in order to promote the aspirations and ideals they have come to value in social life.

   Dion, *Political Ideology as a Tool of Functional Analysis in Socio-Political Dynamics: An Hypothesis* v. 25 CANADIAN J. ECON. POL. SCI. 47, 49 (1959): *see also* Geertz, *Ideology as a Cultural System*, in IDEOLOGY AND DISCONTENT 47 (D. Apter ed. 1964) (examining the cultural elements embodied in ideology).
4. Needless to say, the leading proponent of the psychological approach to ideology was Freud, who expounded the view that ideological is "essential to man's psychological well-being as well as to the continuity of culture," Rejai, *Ideology*, in 2 DICTIONARY: THE HISTORY OF IDEAS 552, 557 (1973).
5. Etienne Bonnet de Condillac is "widely acknowledged as the founder of [the] school of ideology." *See id.* at 553.

myth-saturated, action-related system of beliefs and values about man and society, legitimacy and authority, acquired as a matter of routine and habitual reinforcement."[6]

Mr. Lawson fails to recognize that when commentators such as William Painter, Louis Loss, and Ralph Nader decry any and all forms of insider trading, they are not advancing any theory at all, much less an ethical theory. Rather, they are condemning insider trading on the basis that it is antithetical to a set of cultural norms that were acquired through routine and habitual reinforcement, and therefore are nothing more than ideologically-based belief systems. Professor Painter is particularly honest about the origins of his beliefs regarding insider trading. He scoffs at moral philosophy,[7] choosing instead to ground his arguments purely in emotional terms.[8] Indeed, in a triumph of anti-intellectual sophistry over reasoning and analysis, he defends arguments against insider trading on the grounds that they contain elements of "simplicity and immediacy which make up for their lack of theoretical respectability."![9]

Far from objecting to such anti-intellectualism, Mr. Lawson actually refers to such ramblings as "fair" questions with which all "legal scholarship must, at some point, come to grips."[10] Because the vast majority of Mr. Lawson's essay is a critique of the existing moral notions about insider trading, he ultimately ends up doing more to legitimize these empty ideas than to expand our understanding of insider trading.

Mr. Lawson thus appears to have exceedingly low standards for what constitutes ethical theory. It is therefore not surprising that he weaves his ideas rather confusingly throughout a discussion of the writings of others instead of expressing his own ideas about the ethics of insider trading in any systematic fashion.

Taken as a whole, what emerges from Mr. Lawson's effort is an analysis, albeit a highly inconclusive one, based on classical egoism, which he summarizes in a subsection titled "An Egoistic Interlude."[11] Egoism is the belief, which Mr. Lawson traces back to the classical Greek tradition of eudaimonism, that the individual's highest moral calling is to himself.[12] In essence, it seems, the egoist's moral calling in life is to "identify

---

6. *Id.* at 558. *See also* R. Guess, The Idea of a Critical Theory 4–12 (1981).

7. But, after all, what is morality? Attempts to provide a "rational" foundation for moral judgments have a way of being unconvincing. The whole philosophy of ethical judgments has a pedantic quality which escapes the ordinary individual who merely stamps his or her foot and declares, inarticulately that "I don't care, it's just not right."

8. Painter, *Book Review,* 35 Geo. Wash. L. Rev. 146, 159 (1966). "Even if the content of moral statements be primarily emotive, which is doubtful, a satisfactory morality must be emotionally satisfying. . . ." *Id.*

9. *Id.* at 159.

10. Lawson, *The Ethics of Insider Trading,* v. 11, Harv. J. L. & Pub. Pol'y, 727, 775–83 (1988).

11. *Id.* at 747. At one point Mr. Lawson includes a Lockean theory of insider trading, which I discuss in the following section. *See id.* at 763–69. Because Mr. Lawson believes that "something like a Lockean . . . approach flows from eudaimonism [classical egoism]," *id.* at 768, little is lost by not treating his Lockean arguments here.

12. *Id.* at 748.

Because of the highly individualistic nature of egoism, this belief system does not provide an acceptable basis for actually solving moral problems. The reason is that such problems characteristically involve conflicts of interest; the moral problem is to provide a fair solution. Imagine a judge deciding a case in a particular way on the ground that the outcome promotes her (the judge's) best interest! Egoism can be saved from irrelevancy only if it can be shown to require acts and decisions that involve a due concern for others. I am grateful to David Lyons for this point.

that human excellence that is distinctively his own—that is, his daimon—and the principles of conduct that allow him to develop that excellence and flourish as a person."[13] Unfortunately, of course, because "each person has unique potentialities that, in the particular circumstances in which he finds himself, ought to be actualized if he is to flourish as a person,"[14] it is not possible to construct any universally applicable principles of moral conduct. Thus, to mention but a few, Aristotle and Hegel are out, and Kant and Hume obviously are out also. Locke should be out too, but for some reason he is not.[15]

Mr. Lawson's idea is that most of the criticisms of insider trading are, in the final analysis, grounded on notions of altruism and are therefore unacceptable. Mr. Lawson finds it important to rehabilitate egoism because of the lack of good argument in favor of altruism.[16] This line of reasoning has two flaws that relate specifically to the insider trading debate.

First, as Mr. Lawson himself at times seems to recognize, there may not be a conflict between egoism and altruism.[17] Egoism at least pretends to concern itself with individual flourishing, not simply short-term with fulfillment at the expense of others. To say that someone is an egoist does not necessarily mean that he is not altruistic, particularly if altruism is the means through which he best can flourish. Indeed if one's "unique potentialities" are altruistic in nature, then the tenets of egoism and altruism would dictate the same conduct.

Second, and perhaps more importantly, it is not clear precisely what egoistic theory implies for insider trading besides a seemingly absurd result. If we take Mr. Lawson's suggestion seriously and look at the insider trading controversy by invoking an egoistic ethic, the analysis becomes virtually comic. Mr. Lawson appears to say that the egoist who finds himself in possession of material, non-public information about a particular firm must decide whether trading on the basis of that information is "self-fulfilling," that is, whether it "will allow him to develop . . . and flourish as a person.[18] Mr. Lawson defends this position against the straw-man argument that self-fulfillment is a better guide to human action than peer pressure. The more difficult question is whether self-fulfillment is a better guide to human action than one's own sense of individual duty and moral responsibility.

Frankly, the unrefined argument that acquiring money is good is not really worthy of discussion, because all sides—yes, even the egoists—agree that there is a significant difference between making money in some wealth-creating activity like investment or entrepreneurship and making money by stealing it.[19] The only moral (or economic) question worth asking is where insider trading lies along the continuum that runs from wealth cre-

---

13. *Id.* at 748.
14. *Id.* at 749.
15. *See infra* note 27 (discussing application of Locke's work to insider trading).
16. Lawson, *supra* note 10, at 747.
17. *Id.* at 751–52.
18. *See id.* at 748.
19. *See id.* at 762 (The statement that "Theft is wrong" is "as close to an uncontroversial moral proposition as one is going to get").

ation to theft. Mr. Lawson does nothing to help us sort this out. Similarly, Mr. Lawson explains that refraining from insider trading might be a good idea if one has agreed not to engage in insider trading prior to disclosure, or if failure to disclose prior to trading would "seriously damage someone of great [objective] importance to him."[20] But these are precisely the situations that those of us who have been engaged in the study of insider trading have been studying. What constitutes an "agreement" not to engage in insider trading? Is such an argument an implicit part of every manager's employment agreement? And if it isn't, why not?

The freedom given to corporate officers and directors as a manifestation of the separation of ownership and management in the large, publicly held corporation, makes contractarian analysis of insider trading issues very difficult.[21] Reasonable people, who agree on a wide range of corporate law matters, divide on the seemingly intractable issue of how to allocate the privilege to trade on material, non-public information.

As Mr. Lawson himself appears to suggest at various points in his article,[22] "[t]he moral inquiry with respect to insider stock trading thus centers on where the network of contracts between the firm and its shareholders, suppliers, lawyers, accountants, investment bankers, printers, and so on, places the right to trade on the information."[23] This is a point that has been made both implicitly and explicitly by many, including myself.[24] But it is not at all obvious what this inquiry has to do with egoism—or with altruism for that matter.[25]

To take a very simple example of the difficulty of determining whether a particular corporate act is consistent with ethical norms, suppose we observe a Harvard law student leaving Langdell Hall late one snowy evening. Shrouded beneath his parka is an electric typewriter that belongs to the law school. Is the student doing anything wrong in removing this typewriter? The answer depends on whether someone with legitimate authority (that is, the owner of the typewriter or his agent) has given the student permission to take the machine. The analysis is the same for traders who use inside information. In the first step of the analysis we invoke Locke to determine who has legitimate ownership rights over the relevant information. If it is the person trading in the information, there is no ethical problem whatsoever. We are simply observing a person making proper use of his assets. So, for example, there is no ethical issue when a tender offeror purchases stock in a target company before disclosing his plans to the target's shareholders. The tender

---

20. *Id.* at 752.

21. Frank Easterbrook has been particularly alert to this problem. *See* Easterbrook, *Insider Trading as an Agency Problem,* in PRINCIPALS AND AGENTS: THE STRUCTURE OF BUSINESS 81–98 (Pratt & Zeckhauser eds. 1985).

22. *See, e.g.,* Lawson, *supra* note 10, at 767–73.

23. *Id.* at 766.

24. *See* Haddock & Macey, *A Coasian Model of Insider Trading,* 80 Nw. U.L. REV. 1449 (1986).

25. Mr. Lawson tells us that the contraction approach to insider trading finds is intellectual roots in Locke. *See* Lawson, *supra* note 10, at 769. Having said this, he then asserts that "something like a Lockean approach flows from eudaimonism [classical egoism]." But he declines to tell us how or why this connection is made.

offeror, as the creator of the news that there will be a tender offer, is the rightful owner, according to a Lockean analysis, of this information.[26] The problem arises when the person trading on the information is not its rightful owner. In such a case, we must first determine whether the trader has the actual or implied authority of the owner to use the information before we can know whether or not his actions are ethically justified. Thus, as is explored more fully below, the dichotomy between efficiency principles and the ethical norms implied by natural rights analysis is a false one. . . .

---

26. Macey, *supra* note 24, at 28 n.98 ("because a corporation that makes a tender offer expends great resources to do so, information that a target company is an appropriate target may be said to exist in a 'state of nature,' to use Locke's analysis").

CODE OF ETHICS
& STANDARDS
OF PRACTICE
ASSOCIATION FOR INVESTMENT MANAGEMENT AND RESEARCH

Take a look at the code of ethics of the Association for Investment Management and Research, the Federal Analysts Federation, and the Institute of Chartered Financial Analysts. Do you think this code is sufficient and addresses the necessary sensitive areas?

All members of the Association for Investment Management and Research, the Financial Analysts Federation, and the Institute of Chartered Financial Analysts and the holders of and candidates for the Chartered Financial Analyst designation are obligated to conduct their activities in accordance with the following Code of Ethics and Standards of Professional Conduct. Disciplinary sanctions may be imposed for violations of the Code and Standards.

THE CODE OF ETHICS

A financial analyst should conduct himself with integrity and dignity and act in an ethical manner in his dealings with the public, clients, customers, employers, employees, and fellow analysts.

A financial analyst should conduct himself and should encourage others to practice financial analysis in a professional and ethical manner that will reflect credit on himself and his profession.

A financial analyst should act with competence and should strive to maintain and improve his competence and that of others in the profession.

A financial analyst should use proper care and exercise independent professional judgment.

RELATED WEB SITE

Association for Investment Management and Research.
www.aimr.com/aimr/profconduct/pro_cesc.html

"Code of Ethics and Standards of Practice." Reprinted by permission of the Association for Investment Management and Research.

Chapter 11

ETHICS, ACCOUNTING, AND THE TECHNOLOGY OF BUSINESS

From mainframe through personal computer to internet, the electronic computer has transformed information and human communication in unanticipated ways that are giving birth to what has been variously termed cyberspace, virtual reality or hyperreality. To live in this new milieu, however, requires not virtual but real ethics, grounded in practical and public reflection on the new technolife world.[1]

---

1. Carl Mitcham, "Current Issues in Modern Thought," *World & I* 11, no. 3 (March 1996), p. 314.

Ethics and Accounting   If you were to look in a standard business textbook, you might find the following definition of accounting: "the process by which any business keeps track of its financial activities by recording its debits and credits and balancing its accounts." Accounting offers us a system of rules and principles which govern the format and content of financial statements. Accounting, by its very nature, is a system of principles applied to present the financial position of a business and the results of its operations and cash flows. It is hoped that adherence to these principles will result in fair and accurate reporting of this information.

There is a distinction between an accountant who works for a company and has an obligation as an employee to that company, and an independent certified public accountant (CPA) who may be hired by a company as outside counsel. In the second case, that individual comes in to perform an audit for the benefit, in truth, of the public, the shareholders, and the government in order to maintain the public's confidence. In that regard, companies would love to be able to direct what that outside accountant says because people believe the "independent" nature of the audit. On the other hand, if accountants were merely rubber stamps for the word of the corporation, they would no longer be believed or considered "independent."

Now, would you consider an accountant to be a watchdog or a bloodhound? Does an accountant stand guard or instead seek out problematic reporting? The answer to this question may depend on whether the accountant is employed internally by a firm or works as outside counse.

The ethical issues surrounding accounting practices are varied. They include underreporting income, falsifying documents, allowing or taking questionable deductions, illegally evading income taxes and engaging in fraud. In order to prevent accountants from being put in these types of conflicts, the American Institute of CPAs publishes professional rules. In addition, accounting practices are governed by generally accepted accounting principles (GAAP), established by the Financial Accounting Standards Board, that stipulate the methods by which accountants gather and report information. However, the International Accounting Standards Committee is in the process of developing standards (to be completed by 1998) that would allow foreign companies to sell securities in the United States as long as their accounting conforms to the international standards, even if it does not comply with the GAAP.[2]

Imagine the consternation of U.S. firms that would be required to comply with GAAP while foreign firms could merely comply with the new standards. The difference could be great. The international standards allow firms far more discretion in the manner of reporting, permitting the accountant to choose which accounting practice to apply in a given situation. Since different accounting practices may place a firm in a better or worse light, the onus of standing up to firms who want to use the discretion to report misleading figures would be on the accountant.

Accountants are also governed by the American Institute of Certified Public Accountants (AICPA) which has a Code of Professional Conduct. The code relies on the judgment

---

2. Floyd Norris, "Will U.S. Accounting Rules Be Irrelevant?" *New York Times,* December 29, 1996, Sect. 3, p. 1.

of accounting professionals in carrying out their duties rather than stipulating a set of extremely specific rules. In any case, are standards enough? As you will see from the cases that follow, the answers to ethical dilemmas are not always so easily found within the rules and regulations governing the industry.

Ethics and Technology   With the advent of new technology, new ethical issues emerge. That is because we consider the advances of the technology first, then consider the implications. A *Worklife Report* survey of 300 American businesses in a variety of industries indicates that over 20 percent search their employees' E-mail, computer files, or voice mail.[3] Do you think about who will see the E-mails you send? How do you know that your boss will not forward your disparaging remarks about a colleague directly to that colleague? It can be done with the touch of a key. Are different issues raised by that concern as opposed to those that arose with a traditional written letter?

The above concern raises but one potential dilemma in connection with new technology. In order to address some of the issues that are presented by computers specifically, the Computer Ethics Institute has created "The Ten Commandments of Computer Ethics." The commandments include the following:

3. Thou shalt not snoop around in other people's computer files.
9. Thou shalt think about the social consequences of the program you are writing or the system you are designing.
10. Thou shalt always use a computer in ways that insure consideration and respect for your fellow humans.

Unfortunately, many of the ethical issues that arise in the area of managing information are not readily visible. When we don't completely understand the technology, we might not understand the ethical implications of our decisions. Can your employer read your E-mail? Your first response might be, "No, not without my secret password." However, experts tell us that any system is penetrable. Employers have been known to randomly read E-mails in order to ensure that the system is being used for business purposes. Is this ethical? Does it matter if there is a company policy that systems must only be used for business purposes, or that the employees are given notice that their E-mail will be read? These ethical issues may be compounded by the fact that there exists a knowledge gap between people who *do* understand the technology, and others who are unable to protect themselves precisely because they do *not* understand.

The law offers little protection or guidance in this area, especially given how new these issues really are. The Constitutional protections against unreasonable searches and seizures (through the Fourth Amendment) apply only to public-sector employees and, to date, there has been no precedent in connection with Fourth Amendment protection of E-mail transmissions. State constitutions, such as California's, may provide protection against invasions of privacy but, again, there has been no precedent in this area. Exceptions

---

3. "The Electronic Invasion of Workplace Privacy," *Worklife Report* 9, no. 5(1995), pp. 4–5. Also see Bonnie Glassberg, William Kettinger, and John Logan, "Electronic Communication: An Ounce of Policy Is Worth a Pound of Cure," *Business Horizons* (July/August 1996), p. 74.

in the Electronic Communications Privacy Act of 1986 leave E-mail privacy without protection and the proposed Privacy for Consumers and Workers Act has been subject to congressional debate barring its passage since 1991.

All that an employee may be left with is state common law protection against intrusion into seclusion; this protection guards against invasions into areas where the individual has a reasonable expectation of privacy or invasions that would be highly offensive to a reasonable person[4] Since the "reasonableness" of one's expectation of privacy regarding E-mail has yet to be determined, even this general protection offers little guidance.

Electronic Performance Monitoring   Technology invades and affects the employment relationship in an additional way: employee electronic performance monitoring. Considerable controversy surrounds the issue of whether it is ethical for an employer to monitor the actions of employees through electronic surveillance. This type of monitoring may take the form of recording telephone calls of customer service representatives, electronically counting the number of keystrokes a word processor makes during the day, installing video cameras in the workplace, and so on. While the employer may claim the right to monitor in order to adequately and accurately appraise its employees and maintain quality levels, employees argue that the monitoring causes undue stress and is too invasive.

Where should the line be drawn? Most of us would agree that installing video cameras in the washrooms of the workplace may be going a bit too far to prevent theft, but knowing where to draw the line before that might be more difficult. As long as technology exists to allow for privacy invasions, should the employer have the right to use it? What constitutes humane or inhumane use of this technology?

Consider whether invasive monitoring could be made ethical or humane. Ethical problems might be removed by giving employees due notice that they will be monitored plus the opportunity to avoid monitoring in certain situations. For instance, if an employer randomly monitors phone calls made by its customer service representatives, it could so notify the workers and monitored calls could be signified by a beep on the line during the monitoring. In addition, a worker could use a nonmonitored phone for personal calls and avoid a wrongful invasion of privacy.

However, this may not solve all of the concerns about monitoring. Suppose you are the employer and you want to make sure that your service representatives handle calls in a patient, tolerant, and affable manner. By telling the worker which calls you are monitoring, your employees may be sure to be on their best behavior during those calls. Random, anonymous monitoring may better resolve your concerns (but not those of the worker). A recent study found that electronic performance monitoring has undesirable impacts on monitored workers, such as a lower perception of the fairness of the evaluation, health problems, and increased stress.[5]

---

4. Restatement (2d) of Torts 652B (1977).
5. Stephen Hawk, "The Effects of Computerized Performance Monitoring: An Ethical Perspective," *Journal of Business Ethics* 13(1994), pp. 949–57.

SHORT HYPOTHETICAL CASES

a. Maria and Sam were having lunch at the University Coffee House. "I have a problem that I'd like your advice about," said Sam. "I prepare all of the expense reports in the department. Most of the time when people travel or have business meals, they exceed the limits."

"Do you mean the university limits on amounts reimbursed per person per meal and the daily limits on hotel accommodations?" asked Maria.

"That's right," said Sam. "When people exceed the university limits, my supervisor has me add fictitious tips and taxi fares on business trips to increase the expense reimbursement. My supervisor claims that the university limits are just too low. Everyone knows that, so everyone 'pads' expense accounts."

"But I just don't feel good about this situation," Sam continued. "Normally, if I have a question about the ethics of certain practices, I would talk to my supervisor."

"That probably won't accomplish much in this case. Perhaps you could talk to your supervisor's boss," Maria suggested.

"If my supervisor found out, I'd be in big trouble," said Sam. "Besides, maybe all the higher-ups condone this practice. Maybe everyone pads the expense accounts. Maybe I have to go along with the practice to keep my job." What should Sam do?

b. Bill Merino works in the inventory control group at a company that produces stone-washed jeans. A good friend of Bill's manages the stitching department at the same company. At the end of a recent month, Bill reviewed the stitching department's production cost report and found the department has no beginning work in progress inventory, had started 27,000 pairs of jeans, and had produced only 24,000 pairs. "That leaves 3,000 pairs in ending inventory," Bill thought. "That's a lot of jeans they didn't finish."

Later, Bill visited his friend who managed the stitching department. "Why all this ending inventory?" Bill asked.

"One of the new workers set several machines wrong, and the stitching was bad on 2,400 pairs," the manager replied. "We set those aside and we'll fix them when we have some free time. The other 600 pairs are complete now and have been transferred out. Our entire operation was slower because of the machine problem."

"Company policy is to send all defective products to the rework department. They can fix the jeans. That's their job," Bill said.

"No way!" exclaimed the stitching department manager. "We'd all be in trouble if plant management found out. The worker who messed up would probably be fired. I don't want that. This is our little problem and we'll take care of it."

What should Bill do? Would your answer change if Bill learned that the stitching department had fixed the jeans and had sent them on to the next department?

From *Essentials of Managerial Accounting* by James Don Edwards, Roger Hermanson, Michael Maher. Copyright (c) 1994 Business One Irwin. Reprinted by Permission.

ETHICS AND ACCOUNTING

TEST YOUR KNOWLEDGE OF PROFESSIONAL ETHICS
SUSAN COFFEY

Are you aware of the ethical issues in accounting? When you first looked at the title of this section, were you convinced that there are no real ethical issues in accounting because, perhaps, accounting is based on specific principles and formulas? Take a look at the following test in order to help you to identify some of accounting's more sensitive areas.

QUESTIONS

Rule 101—Independence

1. A member's spouse is employed as an accountant by a client. Would this relationship impair the independence of the member or member's firm?
   ❏ Yes   ❏ No
2. A member's client has not paid fees for tax services provided during the past two years. Would the member's independence be impaired with respect to the client's current-year audit?
   ❏ Yes   ❏ No
3. A member has been asked to perform bookkeeping services for an audit client, including printing the client's presigned checks. Would the performance of the bookkeeping services impair the member's independence?
   ❏ Yes   ❏ No
4. A member has been asked to perform payroll preparation services for an audit client, which include preparing and signing payroll checks using either a laser printer or a client-provided signature stamp. The member also is responsible for mailing the checks to employees or authorizing a transfer of funds from a client bank account to employees' bank accounts. Would such services impair the member's independence?
   ❏ Yes   ❏ No

5. CPA & Co.'s independence is considered impaired with respect to Company B in accordance with Rule 101. Can an owner, partner or shareholder of CPA & Co. establish a sole proprietorship to perform services requiring independence for Company B?
   ❏ Yes   ❏ No

Rule 505—Form of Organization and Name

6. May a member form a partnership with a non-CPA for the practice of public accounting?
   ❏ Yes   ❏ No

7. If a member's state law permits mixed partnerships, may the member form a partnership with a non-CPA in which each partner owns 50% of the firm?
   ❏ Yes   ❏ No

8. May John Smith, a sole proprietor who employs no professional employees, name his firm "John Smith & Company, Certified Public Accountant?"
   ❏ Yes   ❏ No

9. If an owner, partner or shareholder in a CPA firm resigns from membership in the AICPA, may the firm continue to designate itself as "Members of the American Institute of Certified Public Accountants"?
   ❏ Yes   ❏ No

ANSWERS

1. Possibly. The performance of accounting services by the member would not impair independence if performed in accordance with the requirements of Interpretation 101-3–Accounting services (ET §101.05). Therefore, a member's spouse could perform the same functions without impairing the independence of the member or member's firm. If, however, the spouse's functions were not in compliance with Interpretation 101-3, independence may be impaired and should be considered under Interpretation 101-9—Spouses and dependent persons (ET §101.11).

2. Yes. Independence of the member's firm is considered to be impaired if, when the report on the client's current year is issued, fees remain unpaid—whether they are billed or unbilled—for *any* professional services provided more than one year prior to the report date. Such amounts assume the characteristics of a loan within the meaning of Rule 101 and its interpretations.

3. Yes. The preparation of presigned checks for a client would impair the member's independence. However, bookkeeping services, in general, normally would not impair independence provided the member meets the requirements identified in Interpretation 101-3.

4. Yes. If the member has the authority to sign client checks or has custody of a client's signature via either laser printer or signature stamp, his or her independence would be impaired. Likewise, if a member is given the authority to transfer client funds from one bank account to another or from a client bank account to an employee's bank account, independence would be impaired. However, payroll preparation services, in general, normally would not impair independence provided the member meets the requirements identified in interpretation 101-3.

5. No. An owner, partner or shareholder of a CPA firm who is not independent with respect to an entity would not be independent of that entity, even as a sole practitioner.
6. Yes. Rule 505 does not prohibit a member from forming a partnership with a non-CPA provided that mixed partnerships are permitted by state law or regulation and the characteristics of the partnership conform to the May 1994 resolution of AICPA Council (see JofA, Oct. 94, page 135). The partnership, however, would not be permitted to represent itself as a partnership of CPAs.
7. No. Although the AICPA permits mixed partnerships if allowed by state law or regulation, the characteristics of the partnership must conform to the May 1994 Council resolution, which provides that a super majority (66 2/3%) of firm ownership in terms of financial interests and voting rights must belong to CPAs.
8. Yes. The use of the term "& Company, Certified Public Accountant" may be used by a sole proprietor in the firm's name. However, the use of the term "Certified Public Accountants" to imply that more than one CPA is an owner of, or is employed by, the firm would be considered a knowing misrepresentation of fact in violation of Rule 102—Integrity and objectivity of the Code of Professional Conduct.
9. No. The designation "Members of the American Institute of Certified Public Accountants" can be used by a firm only if all of its owners are members.

ACCOUNTING ETHICS AND THE TRADITIONAL JEWISH PERSPECTIVE

RABBI GORDON M. COHN

In line with an attempt to present varying perspectives on traditional ethical issues, the following is an analysis of accounting ethics from a traditional Jewish perspective. What can we learn from the Jewish perspective that might assist us (Jew and non-Jew) in understanding the ethics of accounting?

INTRODUCTION

Considerable research has focused on whether investors are fooled by misleading corporate earnings information.[1] However, there has been less investigation of the ethical implications of such reporting. This chapter represents such an examination. It focuses on ethical dilemmas that result from the economic harm caused by reporting misleading accounting earnings. Talmudic[2] sources are used as a framework to analyze ethical issues.

The [article] does not present definitive opinions as to the ethically correct behavior in specific situations. Rather, it conveys a feeling for the Talmudic view of business conduct. An exposure to the traditional Jewish approach can benefit a wide range of readers. Gaining a familiarity with other cultural positions provides improved understanding of societal norms. The traditional Jewish view is particularly informative due to the Judeo-Christian influence on Western societal mores. In addition to discussing the Talmudic view, the chapter uses Rabbinical teachings to identify and reflect on general ethical issues which are connected to earnings manipulations and misrepresentations. . . .

Talmudic law (*halakhah*) and its derivatives offer a well-articulated and thorough approach to proper business behavior. The observant Jew is required to follow these statutes. However, the universality and Biblical derivation of these laws enables the *halakhah* to provide the Jewish and non-Jewish, religious and nonreligious with insights regarding appropriate business demeanor.

Before [we begin] this discussion, it is important to understand the actual process of a Talmudic legal analysis. The analysis involves a Rabbinical authority analyzing particular actions to determine if they violate specific religious laws. There are several Jewish legal codes which present an overall legal framework. (Rabbis Caro and Asher's are the two principal codes). If the exact case being analyzed is not explicitly discussed, the Rab-

Rabbi Gordon M. Cohn, "Accounting Ethics and the Traditional Jewish Perspective," from *The Ethics of Accounting and Finance,* edited by W. Michael Hoffman, Judith Brown Kamm, Robert E. Frederick, and Edward S. Petry (Westport, CT: Quorum Books 1996), from the Tenth National Conference on Business Ethics sponsored by the Center for Business Ethics at Bentley College.

binical analyst combines the codes' frameworks with his general knowledge of Talmudic principles. The multifaceted legal analysis of a law's applicability also elucidates fundamental ethical quandaries.

This discussion assumes the following scenario. An observant Jewish person works as a company's certified public accountant. This company has just adopted a new accounting procedure which will increase accounting earnings without affecting future cash flows.[3] The accountant is troubled by a possibility that the new earnings report might inappropriately increase the company's stock market price. The company is about to issue new stock and would directly benefit by an increased stock market price. The accountant suspects that the sudden decision to make an accounting change is related to the new stock issue. He goes to a Rabbinical authority and asks if his approval of the reported accounting earnings is a violation of any *halakhic* (Jewish legal) principals. The nature of accounting earnings and their correlations to stock market performance is explained to the Rabbi. The following is a possible description of the Rabbi's analysis.

After hearing the accountant's concern the Rabbi decided that laws related to overcharging are a logical place to begin an investigation. There is a Talmudic prohibition of overcharging based on the verse from Leviticus 25:14. The verse says, "When you buy or sell to your people you should not afflict your brother." From this verse the Talmud derives regulations about *ona'ah* (overcharging).[4] The ordinances are expanded upon in Chapter 227 of the *Choshen Mishpat* section of the *Shulchan Arukh* (the business section of the *Code of Jewish Laws*).

THE PHILOSOPHY UNDERLYING THE ONA'AH PROHIBITION

The analysis could [begin] by reflecting on the general characteristic of the overcharging transgression. Rabbi Asher explains that *ona'ah* is a type of stealing since it extracts an unfair price. Furthermore, the word *ona'ah* used in the Pentateuch literally means afflict. Overcharging, besides causing financial loss, also precipitates psychological distress.[5] The anguish is caused by the victim's awareness that he foolishly and willingly gave the "thief" his money. The verse thus teaches that when someone is unexpectedly injured by a trusted merchant, he is both psychologically and financially abused.

It is important for accountants to realize that there are similar feelings of betrayal and loss of confidence when, for example, bankers and investors are duped as a result of an audit which allows misleading information on a company prospectus. These feelings can be as significant as the accompanying financial loss.

Supported by the above mentioned verse, the *halakhah* stresses the importance of merchants upholding public trust. A merchant can be guilty of fraud even though the victim suffers no loss and does not realize he is being deceived. An example would be a customer being made to think that he received a bargain when he actually paid a fair price. Rabbi Epstein explains how, even if no mispricing occurs, it is forbidden for a businessman to artificially improve an item's appearance for the purpose of implying that it is of a higher quality. He says that, for example, a slave's hair cannot be dyed in order for him to appear younger and that an animal can not be fed bran-water to look fatter.

An accountant who comprehends his Pentateuchal responsibility to prevent fraud will perform his duties with an increased carefulness. As indicated above, accountants can be violating their ethical responsibilities even if no scandal or loss results from their negligence. A financial statement which misleads investors to think that they are receiving a bargain for a fairly priced stock is an example of such a transgression. Thus, according to the Pentateuchal position, the Generally Accepted Accounting Principles (GAAP) charge for faithful representation is an ethical requirement even if no mispricing occurs.

Chief Justice Burger has expressed a similar view of the auditor's responsibility to insure accurate reporting.

> *By certifying the public reports that collectively depict a corporation's financial status, the independent auditor assumes a public responsibility transcending any employment relationship with the client. The independent public accountant performing this special function owes ultimate allegiance to the corporation's creditors and stockholders, as well as to the investing public. This "public watchdog" function demands that the accountant maintain total independence from the client at all times and requires complete fidelity and public trust.[6]*

In contrast to the Pentateuchal position, Benston presents another approach to accounting ethics. He asserts that the accountant's expected diminished profits due to exposure of wrongdoings is greater than potential profits from such activities. Benston uses fear of lawsuits and loss of clients as sufficient motivations for insuring ethical behaviors. However, the above discussion has emphasized that the *halakhah* requires accountants to avoid endorsing misleading financial statements even if they know that no monetary loss will occur and that no negligence will be uncovered. It is obvious that such high standards of behavior cannot be established through fear of law suits and loss of reputation. Thus, it can be seen that Benston's notion of automatic regulation has only limited potential to insure ethical standards which are in accordance with *halakhic* opinions.

THE TALMUDIC LEGALITY OF EARNINGS MISREPRESENTATIONS

After the above attempt to gain a philosophical perspective, the Rabbinical authority would focus on the legality of earnings misrepresentation. His goal is to determine if earnings misrepresentation violates the *ona'ah* prohibition. The Rabbi examines all aspects of the potential infractions with the same precision as a secular judge. The Rabbi's examination could probe four independent issues.

The first is the issue of corporate versus individual corporate responsibility. There is broad discussion in both the secular and Talmudic literature as to the extent that corporate entities are bound by the same moral statutes as individuals. Schweiker asserts that even if the corporations have more limited ethical responsibilities, they are no less than an aggregate of managers, each socially obligated to the larger public.

However, evaluating an individual corporate manager's community obligation is problematic. Since single corporate activities can be performed by numerous individuals, it is difficult to allocate responsibility. Each person may claim that another member was the culprit. For example, suppose a corporate accountant misrepresents earnings while someone else in the corporation sells the company's stock at an inflated price. The accountant might claim that only the actual seller of the new issue is guilty of the *ona'ah* prohibition.[7]

The Rabbinic literature provides a framework for exploring the culpability of each of the above individuals. However, the complexity of analysis creates another obstacle. Due to the lack of straightforward guidelines, a corporate actor who is confronted by a subtle ethical dilemma may easily succumb to the less ethical alternative.

The second issue deals with indirect damages. While the Rabbinic law is strict with respect to direct damage, it is more lenient in terms of indirect damages. For example, if someone cuts a hole in a fence through which an animal escapes, there is a requirement to pay for the value of the lost animal.[8] The hole only indirectly caused the animal's disappearance, since the animal ran through the hole on its own volition. However, even though the courts cannot legally obligate payment, such action is forbidden and there is a moral obligation to pay for indirect damages.

Recapitulating, the legal standards for indirect damages are lower than for direct damages. If this logic is applied to earnings misrepresentations it mitigates the *ona'ah* prohibition. Assume that as a result of the misrepresentation the stock price increased. However, the accountant did not personally set the higher price. Rather, his earnings misrepresentation only caused the stock market to wrongly conclude that the company was financially strong. The stock market then independently raised the price. When the company sells additional corporate shares at an increased price, it is only a passive price taker. It did not fix the inflated price. Thus, the accountant has limited culpability for the higher price. The accountant's earnings misrepresentation is comparable to making the hole in the fence. In summary, although the accountant is prohibited from causing damages, ex post facto, he is only morally, but not legally, responsible.

Third, the prohibition of *ona'ah* implies that an article was sold for more than fair value. In the classic case, value is determined by examining the competitive market price.[9] For homogeneous goods, such as a bushel of wheat, the market price is readily available. However, corporations have unique stock market prices which are not directly comparable.[10] Thus, since a company's stock price has no readily available benchmark, its fair price cannot be established. An increase due to misleading information is not a violation of the *ona'ah* prohibition.

Fourth, *ona'ah* implies that the buyer was hurt by the merchant's actions. One can argue the stock purchaser's dominant interest is not whether a share of the company is worth what she is paying, rather, her consideration is if her investment will be profitable. The buyer wants to estimate the "true" value of the company only to the extent that true value is a predictor of shares' appreciation. The investor may be indifferent to misrepresented accounting earnings increasing the stock price as long as the price will not collapse to its "true" value.

Kaplan and Roll and Hand, for example, claim that stock prices rise as a result of misleading accounting earnings. However, according to the analysis, only if the artificially inflated price eventually falls is there a transgression of the *ona'ah* prohibition. To this writer's knowledge, there has been no research which examines the ethically significant point of whether prices return to their nonmanipulated levels. Thus, the lack of evidence on investors being damaged by earnings misrepresentations is another source of leniency in terms of a violation of the *ona'ah* prohibition.

Nevertheless, one might speculate that the artificially induced price changes must eventually reverse. If a company in one period uses all its income increasing accruals, in the next period, having expended these accruals, ceteris paribus it should report a lower income. Just as announcing higher income increased the stock price, reporting lower income in the subsequent period should decrease it.

Second, assume that manipulating accounting procedures causes unsophisticated investors to inflate the stock price. One would expect that prices eventually return to a level which is commensurate with the company's true value. Further analysis is required to determine if the above conjectures are sufficient to establish a potential *ona'ah* transgression.

CONCLUSION

In conclusion, this chapter explored whether someone who misrepresents earnings has violated the Pentateuchal transgression of *ona'ah*. It found four reasons for leniency. They included the difficulty of pinpointing the transgressor in the corporate context, indirectness of the damages, the lack of a standard market price for a share of stock, and the problem of proving that investors are actually damaged. These reasons for leniency also represent general ethical issues involving the culpability of someone who misrepresents earnings.

This discussion could be expanded to analyze the applicability of other Talmudic business-related laws. Furthermore, there would be value in comparing the issues raised by the Talmudic approach with those espoused by both secular and religious theorists. It is hoped that this chapter's examination demonstrates the possibilities of using Talmudic analysis to illuminate accounting ethical issues. . . .

NOTES

1. It is assumed that investors are nonsophisticated (Hand 1990) and that there is not a strongly efficient market (Fama 1970). Appendix 1 presents a description of relevant accounting theory concepts.
2. Talmudic law is a highly intertextual literature. It was written and developed over a 2,000-year period. The Talmud exists in two versions. The first version is the shorter, Jerusalem edition. The second version is the more extensive, Babylonian edition. The Talmud was written between 300 B.C.E. and 500 C.E. It records and synthesizes previous centuries of Rabbinical discourse. The contents of these volumes were later categorized and catalogued into easier to understand legal guides. These guides also expanded on the Talmudic discussions in order to consider a broad range of contemporary issues.
3. This chapter makes two assumptions concerning public disclosures of these procedural changes. First, there is an inefficient capital market such that many investors are not aware of these changes. For example, footnotes in financial statements may not be examined. Second, the disclosures are not publicized until after the initial earnings announcement. As a result of the second assumption, the reason for an earnings increase can be initially misunderstood. A topic for future discussion is the extent that the above-mentioned types of disclosures fulfill a company's ethical obligations. Perhaps it can be claimed that it is an investor's responsibility to utilize all publicly available information or to wait until an explanation of earnings changes is released before she purchases stock.

4. Babylonian Talmud Tractate Bava Mezia folios 50–59. Although the Hebrew word *ona'ah* literally means afflict, for the purpose of this discussion it is used in its legalistic sense to mean overcharging.

5. This psychological interpretation of the term *ona'ah* in a nonfinancial context is explicit in verse #17, which refers to exclusively emotional damage.

6. *The United States v. Arthur Young & Co. et al.,* 104 S. Ct. 1495, 465 U.S. 805 (1984), p. 1503.

7. The hierarchical design of a corporation necessitates that many positions have extensive support personnel. An analysis could examine the degree of liability of passive supervisory personnel. A more subtle question is ascertaining the culpability of a person in the organization who is not directly involved, but could have prevented the earnings misrepresentation.

8. The Babylonian Talmud, Tractate Bava Kammah, folio 57.

9. Rabbi Epstein, *Arukh Halshulchan, Choshen Misphat,* chapter 227.

10. It might be possible to develop a mathematical model which uses Betas, returns, ratios, and so on, to determine a standard price for each corporation. This price might be used as a benchmark for measuring the amount of overcharges.

THE ETHICAL TEMPERATURE AT ARCTICVIEW

GRANT RUSSELL

The following two case studies address some of the more difficult personal issues accountants might face. With both cases, it is important to place yourself in the position of the protagonist and to consider what you would do in similar circumstances.

"I don't know what to do, John."

Mary Benninger, in obvious discomfort, was discussing her employment situation with John Chu, an old friend from university. Both had graduated in the class of 1985 from Mackenzie King University and had then proceeded to complete their CMA's [Certified Management Accountants], graduating in 1987. John had been promoted quickly and now held the position of controller for Ace Seating Company, a division of a large multinational auto supplier. Mary, on the other hand, had removed herself from full-time employment to raise her children and had only recently taken up her current position.

"I thought this was an ideal position: controller/office manager of a small growing company, full of new ideas, flexible on working hours, and Bob and I can really use the cash now, since he has been unable to work since his illness. But the situation sure turned sour quickly, and I really don't know who to talk to. In fact, I'm not sure that I should be talking to you!"

"Don't worry about that," John replied reassuringly. "You know that you can trust me—after all, I never did tell Bob about your adventure in Mabel MacKay Residence!"

Mary laughed. "That's okay, because I did . . . and I told him it was all your fault! But this situation is well beyond anything I think I can handle."

"I joined the company about six months ago. The company is a small, privately-held manufacturer that makes specialty chemicals in small quantities for testing labs, other manufacturing firms, etc. Most of our production and sales are so small that none of the big chemical companies wanted to enter the market. Henson Chemical grew rapidly and had increasing sales up to 2 years ago, when Dusque, the big integrated chemical company, set up a small subsidiary to do exactly what we are doing. I guess we shouldn't have been so successful! Dusque's sub must be losing money like crazy, since we've taken a real hit in sales and profits. Our business is down 30%, and the new plant that we built in Brampton 3 years ago is operating at 50% of capacity.

Grant Russell, "The Ethical Temperature at Arcticview." Reprinted by permission of the author and the Centre for Accounting Ethics, School of Accountancy, University of Waterloo, Ontario, Canada. Copyright (c) 1996 Grant Russell.

"I gather we were never very good at cost control and internal controls were virtually non-existent. When we were growing so quickly, sales were more important than costs. When things got tough, they dismissed my predecessor and hired me. They told me that I could have free rein to implement what I thought was necessary. Wow, is it necessary! The senior staff really don't know the difference between personal and corporate assets. I've got some really tough problems just in terms of separating personal and corporate expenses. Our sales and marketing expenses are double what I think they should be. But I think I can get this under control.

"The really big problem is our Northern Development grant. When business fell off, Brian Henson, our president, attended a seminar on how to get government grants. He discovered that a matching program was available for firms to establish northern manufacturing facilities. So Brian, and Herb Ottely, our VP Manufacturing, submitted a proposal to manufacture chemicals in Arcticview, where the mines have been playing out. The proposal had been prepared by a consultant for another unsuccessful grant application previously, and Brian and Herb simply updated it, changing the location of operations from Brampton to Arcticview. Arcticview is a really remote village, with 2,500 people and 5,000 caribou! The government must have been really desperate for anyone to locate there since they accepted the proposal very quickly, and both levels of government have provided matching funds of $750,000 for our new plant there, a total of $1,500,000 of government money. They have also guaranteed a bank loan for us of $750,000. We used the loan proceeds as our contribution."

"Well, that sounds great, Mary. What's the problem?"

"The problem is that after the funds were provided, we rented a temporary facility in Arcticview, and we hired a few staff there to maintain the building. However, we told the Ministry of Northern Development that the new equipment needed to be tested and the manufacturing process needed to be developed further. So the equipment was delivered to our Brampton facility. The equipment is currently being used to manufacture a new line of chemicals for us, one that will allow us to regain much of the market share we had lost to Dusque. The problem is that the grant requires us to use the funds in Arcticview."

John's reply was quick: "But will anybody check on how the funds are really being used?

"That's what I'm worried about, John. At the present time, one of my tasks is to ensure that optimistic reports are sent about how development work is coming. In the short run, I can handle this, since there is a real need to shake down this new equipment. The supplier of the equipment had suggested 2 months, but the company has already been "testing" the equipment for 6 months in Brampton and are hoping that they can "test" the equipment for a full year."

"Well, after the year, they'll simply move the equipment up to Arcticview, and your problems will be over?" John responded.

"No, that's when my problems will really start. You see, there is absolutely no way that they can turn a profit up in Arcticview. We have to transport all the raw materials up there, and then ship the finished product back here. Even though it is new technology we are using, Dusques will be able very quickly to beat us on delivery costs."

"I see. Then you'll have to shut down operations and return the funds?"

Mary's reply was terse. "We can't. If we shut down operations here, we don't have enough funds to repay the loan and the resale value of the equipment is very low. Besides, we would be operating below breakeven on the balance of our operations."

"Wow! Major problems. What do they plan to do then?

"Well, the equipment is actually relatively small and quite portable since only small quantities of the chemicals are produced in each batch. Brian plans to ship the equipment to Arcticview for a startup phase, and move workers temporarily from the Brampton plant, while the government publicity pictures are being taken. After a discreet period of time, they'll return the equipment to Brampton, and bring the workers back down. They'll continue to "produce" chemicals in Arcticview with a few local workers. However, the real operations will be here in Brampton. The grant contract states that the company is obligated to produce in Arcticview for only 3 years; they figure that if they can last for 2 years past the testing period, they will be able to keep the equipment and keep the company viable.

"But surely some government audits are necessary, Mary. What will they do then?

"Believe it or not, John, the only audited statements the government requires is our financial statements from our external auditors. Brian figures that the auditors aren't particularly concerned about where we manufacture, since the financial statements don't show that detail anyway. As long as we can document all the equipment, inventory and labour, we'll probably be okay with the auditors. Brian and Herb have to complete an annual written report on how the grant is being used, but all I have to contribute is a brief statement on the "testing and setup" part, and, yes, provide the financials. I'm hoping that I won't have to even see their finished report! One of the things I can do is bill as much of our supplies as possible to the Arcticview Plant and minimize the amount billed through the Brampton plant. Some of our labour costs in the Brampton plant will be billed through Arcticview as well. They'll serve as consultants to the Brampton operation, but be based in Arcticview. Because the equipment is portable, and the auditors really don't know the technical aspects of our business, we'll ship some equipment north for the audit, along with staff, to give the impression of a high level of activity.

"Brain and Herb tell me not to worry, that everybody does this for tax reasons, but I'm really confused on this point. The financial statements will be perfectly accurate and consistent with previous years, so I don't think anyone could nail me for my ethics here.

Mary continued, "Brian figures that nobody really could operate a manufacturing facility in Arcticview since both suppliers and markets are too far away. Training costs up there alone would blow our grant budgets. I agree with him that the government just wants to wave the flag a little bit for votes, and they must know or at least suspect what we are going to do. Besides, we are giving a few local people employment as custodians and also managing to keep Henson Chemical afloat during this tough time. Both Brian and Herb are upset that Dusque's subsidiary got a major government supply contract away from us, and are arguing that this government grant merely put us back on a level playing field.

"I've talked to both Brian and Herb about trying to get more government money to underwrite our transportation costs, but they are concerned about drawing attention to our situation. The grant also prohibits us from selling the equipment and using the funds for operating expenses.

"John, I'm really bewildered here. I signed a labor *contract* and it states that I can't talk to anyone. I've violated it already, talking to you, but I can't talk to anyone else. I signed a very restrictive employment contract (see box). Besides, I think that talking to the government would violate my professional code of ethics. Bob and I need the money to survive, and Henson has 60 employees that need their jobs. I'm having difficulty sleeping, but Bob keeps telling me to simply ignore the issue and do what I'm told. In all other aspects, this is a great job. Brian is wonderful to work for. If we can pull this off, he'll cut me in for equity participation. If I quit, I'll be a long time getting another job, and you'd better believe that Brian would not be helpful in getting me placed."

THE CONTRACT SIGNED BY MARY BENNINGER

The Employee expressly covenants and agrees that he/she will not at any time during or after the termination of his employment with the Company:

(A) reveal, divulge or make known to any person, firm or corporation, the contents of any formula, chemical compound, product or other substance owned or developed by the Company or the method, process or manner of manufacturing, compounding or preparing any of such formulae, compounds, products or substances or sell, exchange or give away, or otherwise dispose of any formula, compound, product or substance now or hereafter owned by the Company whether the same shall or may have been originated, discovered or invented by the Employee or otherwise;

(B) reveal, divulge or make known to any person, firm or corporation any secret or confidential information whatsoever, in connection with the company or its business, or anything connected therewith, or the name or any other information pertaining to its customers or suppliers;

(C) solicit, interfere with or endeavour to entice away from the Company any customer or supplier or any other person, firm or Corporation having dealings with the Company, or interfere with or entice away any other officer or employee of the Company.

THE ETHICAL DILEMMA AT NORTHLAKE

GRANT RUSSELL

Our story opens with an irate Jim McIntosh confronting his manager of corporate reporting: "I thought we had an understanding on this issue, Frank. Tina tells me that you are threatening to go public with your stupid statements about the report. For Pete's sake, Frank, wake up and smell the coffee! You're about to damage all the important things in your life: your career, your friendships, and your company!"

Frank sat quietly in the overstuffed sofa in his V.P.'s expansive office. He thought that the pale green report lying on the desk looked innocent enough but it certainly had provided the basis for some serious turmoil. Jim stood by his desk trembling with rage. His face was bright red and mottled with anger. Frank had often seen Jim upset, but never in a temper such as this.

"I'm sorry, Jim," Frank replied softly, "I know how much this means to you, but I don't think that I have a choice in this matter. I can't sit idle while you and that twit from financial analysis allow this report to go forward. You both know that these numbers have no foundation in fact."

The report, entitled, "Endangered Species: The Pulp and Paper Industry in the Upper Peninsula," laid out the industry's response to the new government proposals to put effluent controls on the discharge of waste water from pulp and paper mills in environmentally sensitive regions of the province. One section of the report detailed the financial consequences of the emission controls as determined by each of the five pulp and paper companies operating in the region. Amalgamated Forest Products had taken the industry lead in developing the report, and the company president, Jean Letourneau, was scheduled to testify before a legislative sub-committee next week, giving the industry perspective on the proposed legislation.

Amalgamated had three major mills, located in some of the more remote locations in the province. The firm had been facing difficult financial times due to the recession, and this had caused substantial hardship in the three small communities where the mills were located. Corporate offices were located in Northlake, a town of approximately 10,000 people.

The section of the report dealing with the dollar impact to Amalgamated Forest Products of installing the emission control equipment had been prepared by Tina Pacquette. Tina, a long-term employee of the firm, had risen through the accounting department to

Grant Russell, "The Ethical Dilemma at Northlake." Reprinted by permission of the author and the Centre for Accounting Ethics, School of Accountancy, University of Waterloo, Ontario, Canada. Copyright (c) 1996 Grant Russell.

become the manager of financial analysis. While Tina and Frank were at equal levels in the organizational structure, their working relationship had not been particularly cordial. In Frank's opinion, Tina's work was barely adequate, but then, no one asked for his opinion.

"Well, Frank, your pig-headedness has really caused a problem for all of us! Wait here! I'll get Jean Letourneau, and we'll see what he thinks about your efforts!" Jim exited the office and slammed the door.

As he waited in the silence of his boss's beautifully decorated office, Frank looked back over his 10 years with Amalgamated Forest Products. Just like his father before him, Frank started with the firm after completing high school and his first job was as a yard man calling out damaged logs before processing. That's when Frank severely damaged his right leg on the job. He had been celebrating the birth of his son the night before and he was unable to manoeuvre his footing with the dexterity required. Surgery saved the leg and he was extremely grateful that the company had brought him inside to the accounting office. An accounting clerk's salary was low compared to being a yard helper, but in a short time his natural talent for analysis brought him to the attention of the vice-president, finance. Within two years, Jim McIntosh had arranged for him to go to university, complete his CMA designation after graduation, and then return to Amalgamated. The financial support provided by the firm had been adequate but not lavish by any means, and Jim had done well in his studies. He was the gold medalist for his province on the CMA examinations, and he had returned to Northlake in triumph. With three young children and a proud wife, Frank had been appointed to a new position in corporate reporting. After a year of having Jim as his mentor, he rose to the position of manager of corporate reporting.

The office door opened abruptly and Jim entered with the company president. Jean Letourneau was a distinguished man of approximately 60 years of age. He had a long history with Amalgamated and a solid reputation in the pulp and paper industry.

"What's the problem, Frank?" Jean's voice broke into the silence. "Jim tells me that you have a few concerns about the report that we're submitting to the legislative committee."

"Well, Mr. Letourneau, I think we—the company—have some major problems here. The report indicates that we'll have severe financial problems if we're forced into building a lagoon for waste water treatment. In fact, the report says we are likely to be pushed into bankruptcy if the legislation is passed. But we all know these estimates of costs are highly inflated. There's no way that our operating costs would be raised by 30 per cent. I could see our operating costs rising by only 8–10 per cent. That's what the internal report Tina wrote a year ago predicts and there's really been no significant change. Moreover, you have to testify before the legislative committee as to the truthfulness of this report—and there's not a shred of truth in it. The other cost estimates are all high, and the prediction of our product demand is based upon a further deepening of the recession. For our internal purposes, we have been using an estimated increase of 10 per cent in demand."

"Slow down, son," Letourneau's calm voice broke in, "we have to use different figures for different purposes. When we report to our shareholders, we give them numbers that are substantially altered from the internal documents, right? In this case, we have to make those dunderheads in the government see what all this regulation is doing to us. Besides, they know we're going to use the most effective numbers to justify our position."

"But this isn't simply a matter of different figures," Frank sputtered. "These numbers have been totally fabricated. And they don't take into account the damage that we're doing to the Wanawashee River. The same stuff we're dumping was cleaned up by our competition years ago. The aboriginal community downstream is still drinking this garbage. We're going to be subject to a huge lawsuit if they ever trace it to us. Then, where will we be? I've got to worry about my professional obligations as well. If this blows up, you could go to jail, and I could get my designation revoked."

"We'll cross that bridge when we come to it," Jim McIntosh interjected. "You've got to remember what's at stake here. Northlake's totally dependent on the mill for its economic survival. As the mill goes, so goes the town. It's your buddies you'd be threatening to put out of work, Frank. This legislation may not bankrupt us, but it will certainly put a squeeze on profits. If profits are gone, no more reinvestment by Chicago. Head office is putting lots of pressure on us to improve the bottom line since the takeover last year. They're talking about cutting all of that new production line equipment we requested."

"The bottom line is this, Frank," Letourneau spoke softly. "You're an important part of our team—we've invested a lot in you. Jim was talking about working you into a new role: V.P.-controller. We'd hate to let you go because of this small issue. However, we need to have everybody working on the same goal. Besides, Jim tells me this isn't even your responsibility. If you hadn't picked up the copy of the report on Tina's desk, we wouldn't have even involved you. Now take the rest of the day off, go home to Cheryl and the kids, and take out that new speed boat of yours. Think the problem through, and I'm sure you'll see the long-term benefit of what we're doing. This pollution problem is a 'Northern problem' that we can resolve here, not in some fancy legislature in the south. Besides, we've had the problem for as far back as I can remember. So a few extra years certainly won't hurt."

ETHICS AND BUSINESS TECHNOLOGY

IN CYBERSPACE, EVERYONE CAN HEAR YOU SCREAM

DANIEL S. LEVINE

Levine describes circumstances between Smith Barney and one of its ex-employees, Michael Lissack. The interaction became more extreme as a result of Lissack's use of a web site to distribute information about his employment situation. It is interesting to note that Lissack has now removed the information referred to in this article from the web.

Smith Barney, Inc., the New York investment banking firm, isn't too happy that Michael Lissack has set up a web site.

Lissack, a whistleblower who gave up a 13-year career at Smith Barney, where he rose to become a managing director in the investment bank's public finance department, now continues his crusade against his former employer and others in the industry he says are cheating the public out of millions of dollars.

Earlier this month, attorneys for the investment firm sent letters to Lissack and his attorneys, accusing Lissack of infringing on the trademarks of Smith Barney and its parent Travelers Group, Inc.

Among other things, his web site Municipal Bond Scandals features The Smith Barney Page, which includes a drawing of a pickpocket at work next to text that reads, "Making money the 'old fashioned way,' " a play on the company's slogan.

The case is another example of the equalizing effects of the Internet that allows a whistleblower to be heard as loudly as the multibillion dollar target of his alarm and the difficulties people have when they try to stifle free expression on the medium.

Even though Lissack responded to the first letter by taking down a Smith Barney logo from his site to avoid another legal battle, the letters persisted. Lissack said he believes Smith Barney's big concern is that as they push forward to make a big splash on the Internet, web search engines will carry people interested in Smith Barney to his page.

In fact, that is a concern that Smith Barney's attorneys at Orrick, Herrington & Sutcliffe make clear in their letters. They want all references to Smith Barney struck from his pages. They accused him of repeatedly using the firm's name to cause search engines to find his page "as one of the most relevant on the subject of the 'Smith Barney.' "

Ironically, in their efforts to silence Lissack, they've merely spread references to the controversy throughout the web and Usenet, expanding the chances that a search engine will point someone interested in Smith Barney to Lissack.

Lissack said he will not remove the Smith Barney references from his pages. He doesn't believe he is violating the company's trademark. Smith Barney intends to pursue further actions according to a representative quoted in The Bond Buyer.

Smith Barney is currently involved in a New York Stock Exchange arbitration case in which Lissack alleges the firm wrongfully discharged him for his whistleblowing and also defamed him. He is seeking $75 million in damages. Smith Barney filed a $15 million counterclaim charging that Lissack has tried to damage their business by spreading false and derogatory information.

He began supplying information to the FBI anonymously in Dec. 1993, 14 months before going public and being fired. He said he waited until then because he wanted to get as much of his deferred compensation as possible.

"Most of the people who blow the whistle are not in a financial position where they would still do it if they understood the consequences," said Lissack. "I, on the other hand, am still very comfortable."

That's not to say his whistleblowing experiences have been a lot of fun. During the ordeal and since, Lissack survived a suicide attempt, a divorce, the loss of his job as well as many friends.

On February 1, 1995, he informed his employer that he did not plan to remain silent when called before a grand jury. He was fired days later.

In a piece in the *New York Times,* Lissack shed light on what is known as "yield burning," a practice of charging excessive markups on government securities that are sold to municipalities. It has been estimated that in the early 1990s, Wall Street firms made an extra $1 billion from this practice.

Unlike refinancing a mortgage where a homeowner can retire high interest debt with new, lower-interest debt, because of the way deals are structured, municipalities usually have to wait at least 10 years before they can pay off bondholders. If interest rates fall, municipalities will refinance their debt and purchase Treasury securities with the proceeds and hold them in an escrow account until the higher interest bonds can be retired.

Under law, though, they are prohibited from profiting on those escrow accounts. So, Lissack said, the investment firms decided to capture that profit for themselves by marking up the Treasury securities and then getting opinions from friendly competitors that the securities were being sold at fair market price.

Lissack said his whistleblowing has been involved in more than one dozen civil and criminal investigations by the U.S. Securities and Exchange Commission, Internal Revenue Service and the U.S. Department of Justice. Smith Barney has previously denied any wrong doing.

Though Smith Barney maintains a prominent place on his web site, Lissack said he is trying to show the range of illegal and unethical activity investment firms perpetuate in the municipal bond market and to offer a source of broad and alternative coverage to the limited news people usually get about public finance.

One unexpected consequent of his web site is that it has become a direct line for whistleblowers to pass on information about other Municipal Bond Scandals to authorities, while protecting their anonymity.

"The part I hadn't given any thought to is that I've created a safety net for people," he said. "They look at the page and get stuff to me to pass on."

RELATED WEB SITE

Computer Professionals for Social Responsibility:
   snyside.sunnyside.com/home/

ETHICAL E-MAIL ISSUES

JANE HALPERT

Halpert prepared the following material for a presentation to the board of directors of the Institute for Business & Professional Ethics. Her purpose was to highlight issues of growing concern and controversy in connection with e-mail transmissions in the employment context.

THE ETHICS OF ELECTRONIC COMMUNICATION

*   Is e-mail the same as hard copy? As a phone call?

*   What expectations should the e-mail sender have?

*   How do we deal with the issue of confidentiality?

*   Is there an ethical right to privacy here?

*   What should employees be told about their e-mail access?

SCENARIO A

Mark was appointed manager of the Employee Training group six months ago, and has just done his first set of yearly performance appraisals on the people in his group. Several individuals were unhappy about the way Mark arrived at his ratings of their performance, and have been discussing it among themselves. Sue went to speak to Mark about her rating and they had an argument. Returning to her office, Sue detailed her complaints in an angry e-mail to Mark. Mark did not respond directly to Sue, but forwarded her e-mail to the rest of the people in the group, stating the he was putting the issue of the performance appraisal process on the agenda for the next group staff meeting in two weeks.

SCENARIO B

(Same incident as in Scanario A.) During the two weeks before the staff meeting, a number of e-mails concerning individual employees' dissatisfaction with their performance ratings are sent to Mark, and he responds to the people who sent them. At the meeting, Mark reveals that he has also been sending blind copies of all the e-mails, both his staff's and his own, to his boss.

SCENARIO C

You work for a company which provides you with e-mail and Internet access. The company pays their Internet Service Provider (ISP) a flat yearly fee for this access.

- Is it acceptable for you to use your company access to send e-mail back and forth with your brother in Denver?

- Does your answer change depending on whether this is done on your own time or on company time?

- Does your answer change if the company paid the ISP a charge per message or per byte rather than a flat fee?

THE ETHICS OF E-MAIL

The proliferation of devices and resources for electronic communication has raised issues with respect to the ethical standards that pertain to this mode of interaction. Many organizations now provide their employees with e-mail access in order to facilitate work-related communication. E-mail can be sent to, and received from, others in the same organization as well as individuals from the outside (e.g., clients, suppliers, regulatory agencies, etc.).

At first glance, it seems reasonable that the same ethical standards that apply to regular mail should be used in this new context. Thus, if it is unethical and inappropriate to read another person's mail (incoming or outgoing), it should be equally wrong to read their e-mail. If an employee is permitted to lock his or her file cabinets so that documents cannot be read without the employee's knowledge, then computer files should be similarly protected. Most companies would frown (at least) on an employee putting company postage on a personal letter; the parallel would be that Internet access is to be used only for business purposes and not for communicating with relatives or surfing the 'Net.

There are, however, several significant differences between paper and electronic documents. With the help of a good computer consultant (or a typical teenager) it's not at all difficult for a supervisor to get access to an employee's computer files. Moreover, this can usually be done without the employee's knowledge. Unlike the file cabinet, it is not necessary to ask the employee for the key. Employees are typically surprised and dismayed to discover that their boss has been reading their e-mail ("I didn't know he could even do that!"). In addition, employees are normally assigned a password to ostensibly protect their computer account from intrusion, giving the illusion that such intrusion is impossible.

Employees need to be made aware that their company-provided e-mail access is company property and not a personal perk. They should know that electronic communications can be monitored and electronic documents retrieved, and that abuse of these resources may bring penalties. At the same time, organizations need to exercise restraint in looking over their employees' electronic shoulders. The technology makes it very easy to read documents and e-mail while leaving no trace, but abuse of this ability will create an atmosphere of mistrust and hostility. As with most ethical issues, the governing concern should be mutual respect, and mutual accountability.

RELATED WEB SITE

Company E-mail Policies: www.io.com/SS/email-policy.html

THE ETHICAL
AND LEGAL QUANDARY
OF E-MAIL PRIVACY

JANICE C. SIPIOR AND BURKE T. WARD

Were you perfectly clear on the appropriate response to Halpert's cases mentioned earlier? If so, you were probably in the minority. Most of us have never considered some of these issues, much less decided how we feel about them or know how our employer might feel about them. Sipior and Ward address some of these ethical issues and discuss how they might be resolved.

How private are employees' e-mail messages? The answer is unclear. This lack of clarity means that protection of employee e-mail will be at the forefront of legal controversy for at least the rest of the decade.

Privacy protection is not a new issue, and employee privacy encompasses a spectrum of issues, including:

- Drug testing;

- Searches of employees and their work areas;

- Psychological testing;

- Telephone, computer, and electronic monitoring; and

- Other types of employee surveillance.

The controversial nature of these areas demands that employers and employees, as well as those with whom they interact—consultants, information service support personnel, suppliers, and customers—be aware of, and responsive to, expectations of and concerns about privacy. Users and organizations naive about ethical conduct and the legal parameters concerning e-mail privacy are vulnerable to harm caused by intrusions. This article examines the potentially conflicting expectations of employers and employees regarding the ethical and legal aspects of privacy invasions in e-mail communications. It also examines the U.S. legal system to determine the applicability of federal and state constitutional law, state common law, and federal and state statutory sources in protecting e-mail privacy.

E-MAIL AND ETHICS

Organizations have an obligation to their employees, business partners, customers, and society, as well as to themselves, to act ethically. However, ethical behavior is often difficult to achieve. A primary concern is actual or potential harm to individuals and groups. What is ethical and what is unethical? Answers are not straightforward. Societal standards of "good," "right," and "moral" help guide our behavior, but do not provide definitive answers for all situations. The political debate on individual and workplace privacy highlights the lack of consensus of opinion with respect to ethics and privacy. Legislatures and courts are being asked to resolve the ethical and legal questions raised by drug testing, physical searches of persons and places, electronic surveillance, and other privacy issues. This article seeks to raise awareness of the ethical issues of e-mail privacy by identifying the vulnerabilities plaguing e-mail and the privacy expectations of employers and employees regarding their use of e-mail.

The increasing number of computer users, applications, and system interconnections, along with the increasing complexity of overall technological capabilities means a greater chance for e-mail privacy to be compromised. E-mail privacy invasions are characterized along two dimensions: sources of invasion and types of invasion. E-mail communications are at risk for interception from sources both internal and external to the organization. Internal sources are people employed by the organization, including executives, managers, and co-workers. External sources are people with whom the organization interacts, through formal and informal relationships. Formal relationships can link service providers, consultants, suppliers, and customers. Interaction may also occur in the absence of formal relationships—with competitors, corporate spies, and hackers.

An invasion may be authorized or unauthorized—that is, it may be condoned by an internal authority, such as a manger, an external authority, such as a law-enforcement agency, or may be a totally unauthorized privacy violation. These combinations are organized into four cells. This article focuses on internally authorized interception of e-mail messages.

EMPLOYERS' VIEW OF E-MAIL PRIVACY

E-mail monitoring in organizations may be viewed by employers as a necessity, as well as a right. As owners of the resources, employers may assume the right to monitor e-mail. Such monitoring may or may not be ethically acceptable or legally permissible. But the reasons offered by employers for doing so may appear ethical and legal, including prevention of personal use or abuse of company resources, the prevention or investigation of corporate espionage or theft, cooperation with law-enforcement officials in investigations, the resolution of technical problems, or other special circumstances.

A grayer area is when internal e-mail monitoring is used to track worker performance. In this case, it is not just suspected individuals whose e-mail is read. Hardworking employees might use e-mail to help make a sale or to meet work deadlines; if not for their record of correspondence, their productivity and accomplishments may otherwise go unnoticed.

For publicly traded companies, an employer must ensure that employees abide by Securities and Exchange Commission rules. A company that fails to monitor performance by examining e-mail messages sent to external destinations might be failing to protect trade secrets and proprietary information.

To achieve the positive results in these examples, all messages sent and received by employees would be subject to scrutiny. Some may regard this as an unethical disregard of employee privacy. Information an employee intends to keep private and confidential may be examined. However, an employer could argue that since the e-mail system is owned by the employer and is to be used for the employer's purposes, the employee should not expect communications to be private. The employer would conclude that e-mail monitoring is not unethical because employees have no reasonable expectation of privacy with respect to the employer's e-mail system. Conversely, some may argue that monitoring is indeed an unethical invasion of an individual's privacy in light of the potential for negative consequences.

Monitoring can be a double-edged sword for those being monitored. Productive and exceptional employees, as well as employees who are unproductive, could be readily identified throughout the organization.

EMPLOYEES' VIEW OF E-MAIL PRIVACY

From the employees' perspective, the content—even the existence—of e-mail messages may be regarded as confidential, private correspondence between sender and receiver(s). This perception seems reasonable, given that e-mail is accessed as a facility in users' computer accounts, to which access is password-controlled, providing a sense of confidentiality. Further, most people are familiar with the privacy protection of the U.S. mail and may assume it applies to e-mail as well. Thus, users can mistakenly and reasonably assume that e-mail messages are free from interception.

Electronic surveillance for the purpose of improving job performance, product quality, and productivity takes many forms. For example, e-mail messages are usually sent and received in directly readable, unencrypted alphanumeric form, intended for immediate reading. Employee computer screens may be viewed or messages may be intercepted without employee knowledge or consent. E-mail messages are thus exposed to employer scrutiny. At Epson America, Inc., an e-mail system administrator, Alana Shoars, claimed to have been terminated in 1991 for protesting the routine practice of intercepting and printing employees' MCI e-mail. In her case, *Shoars v. Epson America, Inc.,* she claimed Epson's invasion of privacy and her termination violated California law [16]. In another 1991 case, *Bourke v. Nissan Motor Corp.,* two software specialists contended they were forced to quit after a supervisor read their personal e-mail correspondence, which included sexual statements [3]. They also claimed invasion of privacy and wrongful termination in violation of California law.

In both cases, the companies' right to manage their e-mail systems was legally recognized. But because both were tried in lower-level California state courts and have not yet worked their way through the appellate process, they are of minimal value as precedents. The question remains: Were the companies' actions ethical?

Many users expect that when they press the delete key on their computers, an e-mail message is actually deleted. However, user deletions are often archived on tape and stored for years. For example, a former employee of Borland International Inc. found, to his dismay, that deleted messages can be retrieved from the archives [14]. The employee was suspected of using a Borland-supplied MCI e-mail account to divulge trade secrets to his future employer—and Borland rival—Symantec Corp. Borland asked MCI Communications Corp. to retrieve the former employee's deleted messages. This alleged intrusion was viewed as a property right by Borland. Since Borland paid for the e-mail service, the employee's account became Borland's property upon his departure. The result: pending criminal investigations of both the sender and recipient, as well as a civil suit, *Borland v. Symantec.*

Perhaps the most infamous example of retrieval of deleted messages occurred in 1987–89 during Congress's Iran-Contra investigations. Deleted IBM PROFS e-mail correspondences between Oliver North and John Poindexter were retrieved from White House backup tapes. In testimony before the Senate, North said, "We all sincerely believed that when we sent a PROFS message to another party and punched the button 'delete' that it was gone forever. Wow, were we wrong."[9].

Regardless of the type or characteristics of e-mail system used, the question remains: what privacy protection, if any, does an employee have in e-mail communications? Such communications are usually made on the employer's premises, with the employer's equipment, on the employer's time, and at the employer's cost—to further the employer's objectives. With such a substantial employer investment, do employees have a legitimate expectation of e-mail privacy?

Despite employers' significant proprietary interests, employees do have expectations of privacy [10]. Given the potentially differing perceptions of employers and employees regarding e-mail privacy and the potential problems that can result from privacy intrusions, employees and employers both need to understand the privacy protection provided by the U.S. legal system. Although ethics and law are not identical, they do come in close contact. Law is often the vehicle for formally implementing ethics into social guidelines and procedures. . . .

ELECTRONIC COMMUNICATIONS PRIVACY ACT

In an influential 1985 study, the Congressional Office of Technological Assessment (OTA) found approximately 50% of the U.S. population believed computers threaten privacy rights and supported further action to protect these rights [10]. This study inspired Congress to enact the Electronic Communications Privacy Act (ECPA) of 1986 [19]. As a society, Americans generally value privacy. However, if a societal value, such as personal privacy, is not legally protected, is it a right? By implication, the American people seem to assume they are already endowed with this right. With respect to e-mail, the OTA stated "the existing protections are weak, ambiguous, or nonexistent" [10]. This lack of protection is significant because e-mail is vulnerable to interception, as identified by the OTA, at five specific stages:

- At the sender's terminal or electronic file;

- While being transmitted;

- When accessing the recipient's mailbox;

- When the communication is printed in hard copy; and

- When retained in the files of the e-mail service.

Relying on the 1985 study, the OTA concluded internal company e-mail systems were not covered by federal statute [10]. Congress used the ECPA to amend existing federal wiretap protection law to include most electronic communications. Its purpose was to extend privacy protections against wiretapping to new forms of electronic communications, including e-mail, cellular telephones, and data transmission, from improper interception.

Broadly, the ECPA prohibits interception of wire, oral, and electronic communications, as well as disclosure or use of such intercepted communications. The statute's broad definition of electronic communication includes e-mail. Further, in Title II, the EPA, subject to significant exceptions, prohibits access to and disclosure of stored electronic communications.

Two Exceptions

Whether coverage extends to monitoring the e-mail of private-sector employers is unclear because of two exceptions in the ECPA that were part of earlier federal wiretap protection law:

Business Use or Business Extension   This exception is the basis for most of the cases brought under the ECPA [5]. To be an effective defense against employee claims of e-mail privacy invasion, employers must demonstrate that a business use was the reason for the interception and that monitoring was conducted within the ordinary course of business [22]. In a 1983 case [22], brought under the prior federal wiretap protection law, an employer notified an employee that telephone sales calls were being monitored. This notification was interpreted to mean that the specific interception was in the ordinary course of business. The business purpose ended when it became apparent the telephone communication was personal. This exception, which can be applied to telephone communications, would seem to apply to e-mail. If an employer wants to ensure its e-mail system is used solely for work-related purposes, routine monitoring of the content of e-mail messages might be included under this exception.

Prior Consent   This exception may permit telephone and e-mail monitoring. Under it, employers may be able to protect themselves against the risk of liability by notifying employees their e-mail may be examined. Such consent may be expressed or implied but is limited to the scope of the consent. In the aforementioned 1983 case, the consent was only to the monitoring of business calls. The court refused to extend this consent to all telephone calls.

The issue of whether the ECPA protects the privacy of e-mail is unclear and is currently under debate in the courts. A review of relevant legal research seems to conclude that the ECPA does not afford significant privacy protection to employee e-mail communications [5, 6]. . . .

CONCLUSIONS

Various courts and legislative bodies have sought to balance employees' expectations of personal privacy with employers' proprietary and access interests. From a managerial perspective, e-mail—an increasingly important organizational resource touted as contributing to worker productivity—must be used in an ethical and legal manner. Since clear guidance is not provided by our legal system, organizations must formulate their own internal e-mail privacy policies. Lacking a formal policy, employee expectations of privacy may differ from their employers' perspectives. Even with a formal policy, this balance is not easily achieved because of the dynamic nature of information technology capabilities. The rapid pace of technological advances forces the legal system to resolve conflicts for which there is no precedent.

REFERENCES

1. Baumhart, J. T. The employer's right to read employee e-mail: Protecting property or personal prying? *The Labor Lawyer 8,* 4 (Fall 1992), 923–948.
2. Bloustein, E. J. Privacy as an aspect of human dignity: An Answer to Dean Prosser. *39 NYU Law Review, 962* 1001, (1964).
3. *Bourke v. Nissan Motor Corp.,* No. YC 003979 (Super. Ct. Cal. filed Jan. 4, 1991).
4. *Ettore v. Philco Television Broadcasting Co.,* 229 F. 2d 481 (3d Cir. 1956).
5. Griffin, J. J. The monitoring of electronic mail in the private sector workplace: An electronic assault on employee privacy rights. *Software Law Journal IV* (1991), 493–527.
6. Addressing the new hazards of the high technology workplace. *Harvard Law Review,* 104, 8 (June 1991), 1898–1916.
7. Heredia, H. F. Is there privacy in the workplace?: Guaranteering a broader privacy right for workers under California law. *Southwestern University Law Review, 22* 1 (1992), 307–335.
8. *Luck v. Southern Pacific Transportation Co.,* 267 Cal. Rptr. 618 (Ct. App. 1990), cert. denied, 111 S. Ct. 344 (1990).
9. National Public Radio news broadcasts (1992).
10. Office of Technology Assessment (OTA), Federal Government Information Technology: Electronic Surveillance and Civil Liberties (1985).
11. *O'Connor v. Ortega,* 480 U.S. 709 (1987).
12. Privacy for Consumers and Workers Act, S. 984, H.R. 1900, (1993).
13. Restatement (Second) of Torts 652B (1977).
14. Shieh, J. and Ballard, R. E-mail privacy. *Educom Review* (March/April 1994), 59–62.
15. *Shoars v. Epson America, Inc.* No. SWC 112749 (Cal. Sup. Ct. filed July 30, 1990).
16. *Shoars v. Epson America, Inc.* No. BC 007036 (Cal. Sup. Ct. filed March 12, 1991).
17. *Skinner v. Railway Labor Executives Association,* 489 U.S. 602 (1989).
18. *Soroka v. Dayton Hudson Corp.,* 7 Cal. App. 4th 203, review granted, 4 Cal. Rptr. 2d 180 (1992).
19. 18 USC 2510–2521, 2701–1711 (1988).
20. *Vernars v. Young,* 539 F. 2d 966 (3d Cir., 1976).
21. Warren, S. D. and Brandeis, L. D. The right of privacy. *Harvard Law Review* (December 1890), 193–220.
22. *Watkins v. L. M. Berry & Co.,* 704 F. 2d 577 (11th Cir. 1983).
23. *Wilkinson v. Times Mirror Corp.,* 215 Cal. App. 3rd 1034 (Cal. App. 1 Dist. 1989).

Part Three

SELECTED EMERGING ISSUES IN ETHICS

Chapter 12

ETHICS IN THE PROFESSIONAL AND TECHNICAL ARENAS
Selected Issues

"All progress depends on the unreasonable man. The reasonable man adapts himself to the world. The unreasonable man persists in trying to adapt the world to himself."

GEORGE BERNARD SHAW

The purpose of this section is to apply the decision-making model to broad issues raised in particular professions. Medicine, law, and journalism, after all, are but businesses with a specific purpose. The decisions made in these professions, therefore, are subject to many of the same concerns, motivations, and ramifications as decisions in traditional corporate settings. Accordingly, the articles in this section will address the business aspect of these professions rather than those ethical issues that might be raised by the nature of that business. Note that this section will merely touch upon the many issues and dilemmas presented by each of these professions, rather than provide an intricate and comprehensive review of *all* ethical issues in the area.

The health care profession has been very much in the news in the past several years, and many ethical issues have been at the center of these articles and discussions. Health care is a unique business in that it seeks to make a profit in an area that is supposed to be concerned with social welfare. Consider, for example, the quandary of pharmaceutical companies that have invested a great deal of funds in the research and development of drugs for AIDS and HIV. Since the time the drugs first hit the market, many individuals afflicted with HIV and AIDS have not been able to afford the high-priced drugs. (In fact, though the make-up of the AIDS/HIV population has shifted, the price of drugs remains of infinite concern to patients.) A pharmaceutical firm has a familiar conflict between its interest in profits and its interest in serving the public through drug research and development.

The cost of traditional health care has increased to a level that is prohibitive for many Americans. Researchers point to three areas of ethical conflict that have contributed to the increase in health care costs: (1) violations of traditional business ethics by fraud, deception, theft, waste, and conflicts of interest; (2) deliberate distortions of the market by use of power and deceptive marketing; and (3) imperfections in the market, such as the irrationality introduced by ignorance and emotions that reduce rationality.[1] Private health insurance fraud has been estimated as high as $75 billion per year.[2] These and other issues are addressed in the articles that follow.

Ethics in the legal "business" is a stormy area. National opinion polls rank lawyers among the lowest in terms of professional conduct, and the media and Hollywood do nothing to ameliorate this impression. (See Lyttle's "Shortest Ethics Case Ever.") Yet, is this characterization warranted? Indeed, lawyers are subject to a code of professional responsibility that uses stronger language than most corporate codes of conduct and are regulated by the law in connection with their practices. On the other hand, much of the law is left to discretion or the perspective of the "reasonable person." Thus, lawyers must use their individual judgment in many cases to determine the propriety of an act or omission. The law does not provide answers to every dilemma and, often, when it does, those answers may not be considered ethical. Consider the fact that the Nazi genocide was conducted by representatives of the German government under the auspices of German law. Can you imagine other, less-extreme, circumstances where a lawyer would be more ethical by *not* following the law?

---

1. Thomas Garrett, Richard Klonoski, and Harold Baillie, "American Business Ethics and Health Care Costs," *Health Care Management Review* 18, no. 4 (1993), pp. 44–50.
2. T. Donlan, "Unsure Insurers: They're Holding the Bag on Health Care Schemes," *Security Management* 70 (1990), p. 28.

SHORT HYPOTHETICAL CASE

You are a surgical nurse with 15 years of experience. During surgery, you argued with a surgeon about a procedure he was about to perform. You knew the procedure might endanger the patient. The surgeon got angry, performed the procedure, and the patient died as a result. The family is suing the surgeon. You have talked to no one about what happened during surgery. The family's lawyer has scheduled your deposition. The hospital and the doctor have subtly pressured you to take a "no comment" stance during the deposition. Medicine is a closed community. If you "blow the whistle," you'll be fired and probably won't be able to find another job in this locale. What do you do?

Hypotheticals were written by Catherine Haselden and are included in her manuscript "The Ethics Game."

ETHICS IN THE MEDICAL
OR HEALTH CARE BUSINESS

BENEFITS MANAGERS AND THE RESPONSIBILITY FOR RATIONING HEALTH CARE

DAVID T. OZAR

BEFORE MANAGED CARE

The structures through which health care is distributed in the United States have undergone dramatic changes since the early 1980's. By the early 1980's it was a well established pattern that most people's hospital bills and most of their doctor bills were paid through "third-party payers," namely private insurance programs and government programs like Medicare and Medicaid. But up until the early 1980's, such third-party payers exerted very little control over the charges of hospitals and doctors. Admittedly, there was a standard requirement that reimbursed charges not exceed the "usual and customary." There often were yearly or lifetime limits on the payers' outlays; sometimes there were co-payments by those insured; and there were a number of kinds of treatment that might not be covered in a particular insurance program. But these constraints had relatively little effect on caregivers' decisions about treatment and on doctors' and hospitals' approaches to pricing their services.

The reason there was so little effect, to oversimplify greatly, is that the third-party payers rarely looked *prospectively* at the *details* of health care costs. In formulating their programs for coverage and reimbursement, most third-party payers looked at health care only in terms of very large categories of health care costs, and doctors and hospitals, the general public and those who made public policy, all generally looked at it this way as well.

It is not surprising that most Benefits Departments of that era did much the same, considering health care costs almost exclusively in terms of large, broadly defined categories of health care and the total dollars spent on them. They did negotiate with insurance companies about co-payments and yearly and lifetime limits and the kinds of care

David Ozar, "Benefits Managers and the Responsibility for Rationing Health Care," reprinted by permission of the author.

excluded from coverage; but they generally paid no more prospective attention to the details of health care costs and usage than anyone else.

This is why the "R" word, *"rationing,"* was rarely spoken at that time. The United States health care system had never met all the health care needs of all its citizens. But up into the early 1980's, the way in which the impact of limited health care resources was felt was in the exclusion of whole classes of people (most obviously, the uninsured) from the health care system. It was not generally by creating limits on the use of particular forms of therapy. That is, prior to the early 1980's, most of the rationing that went on in American health care did not look like rationing because it chiefly took place "at the door."

THE ARRIVAL OF MANAGED CARE

In 1983, under the pressure of years of double digit inflation in health care costs, the federal Medicare program changed its reimbursement structure. Its reimbursements for hospitals' charges were fixed in each instance to a certain amount of money per admitting diagnosis. All of patients' common admitting diagnoses were categorized into DRG's, *Diagnosis Related Groups;* and Medicare would, with some narrowly drawn exceptions, pay a hospital no more and no less for a given patient's hospital stay than the amount assigned in advance—that is, prospectively—to the patient's DRG. (The amounts to be paid for each DRG were based on average costs for hospitalization for the relevant admitting diagnosis in that region of the country.) If the hospital spent more than this amount caring for the patient, the hospital lost money on the case; it if spent less—for example, if it was able to send the patient home safely a day or two early—then it made money on the case because it still received the same amount, fixed for that patient by his admitting diagnosis.

For the first time, a major payer in the system was looking *prospectively* at the *details* of health care costs, setting the reimbursement level for a particular diagnosis under particular circumstances ahead of time. The result was that Medicare thereby began to put pressure on the providers of care, hospitals and doctors, to manage the care they would give accordingly; that is, *prospectively* and in terms of particular treatments and other *details* of the care they offer.

Before long, all third-party payers, public and private, were seeing the possibility of setting prospective limits on reimbursement on the basis of the details care. These groups were also responding to inflation in health care costs both directly and under pressure from employers seeking to control the costs of health care benefits. Payment structures like the DRG's, as well as a new kind of payer, the Health Maintenance Organization, or HMO, which also puts prospective pressure on health care providers to manage the care they give so it fits into already understood fiscal limits, became increasingly common during the 1980's and early 1990's. For a brief time, doctors and hospitals tried to resist payers' efforts to get them to prospectively limit the resources expended on their patients. But they did not have the economic power to resist altogether and, before long, they found a way of responding that proved more effective. Rather than trying to flatly resist such influence from payers, the providers of care began to look at the details of care from their own perspective and began to prospectively negotiate reimbursement rates with payers on a detail-by-detail basis. If a payer's cost projections about a certain form of care did not mesh with the providers' projections, the two parties could now negotiate their way to an agreement about it on the basis of data from both points of view. Soon, various kinds of caregivers began to organize together—for example, in PPO's and hospital networks—in order to negotiate more effectively with the payers; and some of the payers in turn moved to consolidate their position in these negotiations by uniting into larger groups. In addition, a new kind of organization came into being which neither provided care nor sold health insurance, but which instead focused its attention on brokering between the provider groups and the payer groups.

These new structures for the distribution of health care in the United States are collectively known as "Managed Care."

BENEFITS MANAGERS AS RATIONERS

While all this was going on, the benefits managers could see that employers who simply remained passive to this whole process would likely lose out as a result. Merely pressuring the other players in the system to reign in increasing health care costs was not very effective. Large employers, and later groups formed by smaller employers, realized that they controlled enough economic resources for health care that their Benefits Departments could negotiate with provider groups directly, and they began to do so. Some larger employers also moved to self-insure their own health care programs, using insurance companies services at most to manage these operations for them, but using their own Benefits Departments to determine patterns of coverage and reimbursement prospectively and in terms of the details of care for themselves.

By the middle 1990's, all of these activities—the various components of Managed Care and Benefits Departments' efforts to respond to them—were in full flow. The attention of Benefits Departments, like that of the hospitals and doctors and the established third-party payers, was now focused on prospective determinations of costs and coverage based on detailed categorizations of the types and circumstances of health care.

When a person is in charge of a supply of some very important resource for human life and the available supply of that resource is not sufficient to fully meet the needs of those to whom it will be distributed and the person's decisions affect not just large categories of resources but the specific details of who gets what, then the distributive decisions that this person makes *are rationing.* That is, those who are making health care benefits decisions in the Managed Care environment are, like some other important players in the health care system, engaged in *rationing* health care resources. This raises the following question for consideration: *How should those making health care benefits decisions conduct themselves if they want to perform this task of health care rationing responsibly?*

One possibility is that this task is really no different from any other that an employee undertakes for an employer. That is, there are *no special responsibilities* that come with the activity of rationing health care resources. Another possibility, which can be viewed in two different ways, is that this task has special characteristics that differentiate it from many other employment tasks and that imply *special responsibilities* for those making decisions about health care benefits.

PROPOSAL #1: HEALTH CARE RATIONING INVOLVES NO SPECIAL RESPONSIBILITIES

Some people hold that, apart from an obligation not to interfere in others' own freedom, no one has any responsibilities to anyone else unless he or she has freely and explicitly contracted to have those responsibilities. On this view, unless a benefits decision maker had explicitly (and freely) contracted with his or her employer to exercise special and explicitly identified responsibilities in relation to the rationing aspect of this role, the fact that health care benefits decisions can properly be viewed as rationing decisions is of no special moral significance. Like all employees in Benefits Departments, the proper aim of one who makes decisions about health care benefits is, in a nutshell, to balance the employer's ability to succeed in the employment market against the employer's ability to make a profit (or provide a service, in the case of public sector employers), taking both long-term and short-term considerations into effect on both sides. Once that has been said, Proposal #1 claims, there is nothing more to say, regardless of the fact that rationing health care resources is part of the job.

PROPOSAL #2: HEALTH CARE RATIONING INVOLVES SPECIAL RESPONSIBILITY TO THE RECIPIENTS

The economist Arthur Okun once wrote that some things are too important for us to trust the market place to distribute them properly. Whether he would have included health care among the things that should not be entrusted simply to market forces to distribute, there are many people who believe health care is one of the resources so essential to our lives that distributing them properly takes moral priority over the ordinary workings of the marketplace. If this is true, then a person who is in the position of rationing health care has special responsibilities because of the special nature of the resource that his or her decisions control. Simply doing whatever advances the employer's long-term success is not enough.

One way in which this perspective might be proposed focuses on the immediate recipients of the health care that a Benefits Department serves, namely the employees covered by its health care programs. It might be argued that, as the gatekeepers of access to health care for a group of employees, those making benefits decisions are obligated to try to maximize these employees' access to health care resources. That is, given that health care resources have special moral import in human lives as (one) means by which people are enabled to (or preserved in the ability to) pursue all their other goals, those who control a group of employees' access to these resources must strive to maximize that access to the greatest extent possible.

Suppose, for example, that a particular labor market of interest to an employer was, at a certain point in time, a "buyer's market." That is, there was a surplus of potential employees, and employers therefore could fill their employment needs while offering lower salaries and less comprehensive benefits packages than in other situations. If Proposal #1 is correct, then the Benefits Department should develop the least comprehensive health care benefits package that will still fill the employer's hiring needs. But if Proposal #2 is correct, then benefits decision makers would have a special responsibility to try to maximize employees' access to health care, because it is such an essential and therefore it is also a morally special resource for human life. In practice, of course, the Benefits Department would still have to persuade management of the merits of their proposals in terms of many other criteria; and it might be very rare that they could actually succeed in getting the very best access to health care for employees. But their view of their role under Proposal #2 would be very different from what it would be under Proposal #1 because of their special responsibilities to the recipients of the health care that they control.

PROPOSAL #3: HEALTH CARE RATIONING INVOLVES SPECIAL RESPONSIBILITY TO THE WHOLE COMMUNITY

Another way of holding that a person who is in the position of rationing health care has special responsibilities—because of the special moral importance of the resource that his or her decisions control—sees these special responsibilities as responsibilities to the whole community rather than only to the direct recipients. The third proposal stresses two factors about resources that are viewed as essential to humans' ability to pursue any kind of goals or purposes that they might have.

First, because resources of this sort are so essential to individuals—i.e., that individuals cannot function at all without them—these resources are also radically essential to the existence and functioning of the community as well. That is, every aspect of our collective lives, on which so much of our ability to function as individuals depends, is in turn dependent on individuals at least having the basic ability to function, no matter what particular goals or abilities that individual might have. Proposal #2 stressed how important health care and certain other kinds of essential resources are to particular individuals; this proposal stresses how important they are to the existence of all our communal activities, in fact to our having any collective life at all. Therefore, the argument concludes, anyone who controls the distribution of resources so essential to the community as a whole has a responsibility to the community for distributing these resources with their community's best interest in mind.

Secondly, the health care goods and services that a particular Benefits Department distributes by its decisions are not produced directly by that Department's employer, but by a very complex social process involving not only many individuals throughout the community, but also many complex institutions of the community, they depend on financial and human resources from many corners of the community and across significant stretches of time. Health care, in other words, is not properly viewed as an isolatable commodity, but is rather the complex product of a whole community's effort. Admittedly, the funds that an employer pays out for health care may be legitimately thought of as the employer's own funds to spend as the employer chooses. But when it is health care resources that are being purchased and distributed with these funds, then what is being purchased and distributed is not something that is wholly the employers' own, but something in which the whole community is already intimately involved.

Therefore, Proposal #3 maintains, those who exercise control over the distribution of this communal resource owe it to the community as a whole to distribute it with the whole community's needs in mind, not merely for the long-term success of the employer or even for the maximal well-being of the employees who will be its direct recipients.

TWO CLOSING COMMENTS

The question of how responsible rationers of health care would act if they took the responsibilities of Proposal #3 seriously is a very difficult one. Few theorists about justice have explored the topic of just rationing at the broad social level, where the rationing scheme needs to take account of every citizen in the community. Such discussions and social experiments as have taken place have generally stressed universal access to limited amounts of the scarce resource rather than permitting some people to be passed over so that others might have their needs more fully met. But this leaves a great many questions still to be discussed for the responsible rationer to know how to carry out this task properly.

It is important to stress, finally, that it is not only the Benefits Departments of private and public sector institutions that make decisions about health care benefits. Everything that has been said here also applies to everyone up the chain of command who reviews, evaluates, or eventually accepts or rejects the recommendations of Benefits Departments. Everyone involved in decisions about health care benefits, whatever their title or role, is *rationing* health care and should consider carefully what is the proper way to carry out this task.

ETHICAL ISSUES IN MANAGED CARE

JOHN LAPUMA, DAVID SCHIEDERMAYER, AND MARK SEIGLER

The authors identify some of the most troubling ethical issues facing the health care profession as a result of managed care initiatives.

INTRODUCTION

Medicine is a moral enterprise, and managed care organizations (MCOs), because they are involved in the delivery of medical care, have moral responsibilities to others. Managed care also recognizes the dual concepts of appropriateness and scarcity. Managed care's goals of quality health care delivery, cost-containment, and equality-of-access demand that physicians be both patient advocate and organization advocate, even when these roles seem to conflict. We believe that a re-emphasis of managed care's moral mission is essential in enabling physicians, patients, payers and policy-makers to fulfill their new roles, and to preserve the fidelity of the doctor-patient relationship.[1]

Here, we review two key assumptions that underlie managed care, its benefits and burdens, and its continuing impact on the doctor-patient relationship.

Managed care systems share a general philosophy of care which prizes appropriateness, necessity and cost-effectiveness.[2] Managed care systems which strive to deliver excellent service and achieve high patient satisfaction will be the model health care systems of the 21st century.

Managed care and managed competition recognize the dual concepts of appropriateness and scarcity: if all care were of high quality and appropriate,[3] and if resources were unlimited, managed care would be unnecessary. Managed care requires primary physicians to be resource agents and assumes that physicians will be both patient advocates and MCO advocates, even when these roles seem to conflict. British generalists perform both roles implicitly, and invoke medical reasons to deny medical treatment to patients "too old, too sick, or too unlikely to benefit."[4,5] Patients generally are not told that the resource is relatively scarce.

Although managed care methods are touted to reduce costs and ensure quality, reports exist of patient dissatisfaction,[6] financial conflicts in decision making,[7] physician discontent with MCOs and the gatekeeper role,[8] legal challenges to MCO review and reviewer authority,[9] and mixed cost and quality effects.[10] Below, we further delineate the ethical assumptions of managed care and managed competition, and then attempt to identify some of the benefits and burdens of managed care for patients, physicians and payers.

John LaPuma, David Schiedermayer, Mark Seigler, "Ethical Issues in Managed Care" from *Trends in Health Care, Law & Ethics*, v. 10, No. 1/2 (Winter/Spring 1995). Reprinted by permission of the Robert Wood Johnson Medical School.

THE ETHICAL ASSUMPTIONS OF MANAGED CARE

MCOs are founded on at least two ethical assumptions: the doctor-patient relationship will be fiduciary and non-adversarial; and equality of access is the proper ethical concept for resolving allocation dilemmas.

1. Managed care also relies on the principle that **doctor-patient relationships will be trusting and covenantal,** even when contractually based. Physicians will act with goodwill and will be patient advocates: e.g., when appropriate, they will appeal economic constraints on an individual patient's care. Accordingly, patients will trust their physicians to work with them within the system.

2. **Equality of access** for all MCO members is more important than the option of all-out, expensive treatment for one member. This concept of equality requires that MCO physicians will be consistent decision makers, and will make the same decisions for individual patients as they would for groups of comparable patients.

The traditional goals of managed care have been to improve access, prevent disease, promote health and contain costs. MCOs' goals, however, should not center around simply controlling providers' practices and containing costs.Without attention to its ethical underpinnings, managed care may not resolve policy dilemmas of justice, may adversely affect quality, and may not reduce costs in the long run.[11]

The ethical constraints in managed care result in specific benefits and burdens to all parties.[12]

Benefits—Patients   The benefits to patients in MCOs are substantial. Although various MCOs differ in structure and function, the philosophy of managed care discourages overtreatment, encourages general preventive care, and attempts to promote both cost-containment and quality healthcare delivery. MCOs integrate the financing and delivery of health services, provide services at a discount and minimize paperwork. Co-payments and deductibles are low or non-existent. In one study, the quality and quantity of ambulatory care for HMO patients was judged equal to or better than that of fee-for-service patients.[13]

Benefits—Physicians   MCOs also have benefits for physicians. MCOs limit practice start-up costs and many MCOs can offer dependable incomes, regular practice hours and structured practices. MCOs also review and validate physician credentials, setting a minimum standard of practice for their organizations. MCOs give financial incentives to physicians to deliver care to enrollees in an efficient, cost-effective manner. Physicians are assured a patient population, albeit at volume discount.

Benefits—Payers   MCOs offer equal access for all members, provide financial reimbursement for administrators and others, and allow payers to use developed business principles and test those principles in new markets. For example, the principles of continuous quality improvement have been used in the auto industry since the 1970s and are now being applied to the administration of health care by many MCOs.

Burdens—Patients   Given medicine's traditional focus on the individual patient, MCO emphasis on group benefit may seem utilitarian and even impersonal. Some patients receive incomplete or incomprehensible information when they are offered an MCO plan or when it is advertised:[14] restrictions on care are de-emphasized, and patients must at least consider scrutinizing both payer and physician. These and other practical questions arise about patient autonomy,[15] and patients' ability to access particular providers and services which may not be covered by their MCO plan.

Burdens—Physicians   Managed care presents moral and professional challenges to medicine's virtue-based ethics, including the fundamental values and assumed prerogatives of clinical practice.[16] Managed care's administrative controls may change doctor/patient relationships to businessperson/consumer relationships.[17,18] The administrative complexity and standardization of MCO processes do not easily accommodate differences between individual patients, stifling flexibility.[19] The physician is increasingly caught between patient expectations of more and higher-tech care and the MCOs expectations of cost-containment.

Burdens—Payers   MCOs are often financially risky enterprises; they are responsible for an enormous array of services. MCOs also suffer from a dearth of outcome data, and are often unable to substantiate their protocols and procedures with valid, reliable medical data. MCOs may be liable in several areas, including breach of contract, breach of warranty, breach of the implied covenant of good faith and fair dealing, and breach of the relationship between patient and physician. Finally, payers are responsible for attracting and credentialing credible, respected clinicians as reviewers, heightening administrative and professional regulation.

THE DOCTOR-PATIENT RELATIONSHIP IN MCOs

The nature of the doctor-patient relationship in the MCO is not intended to be ethically distinct from the doctor-patient relationship in indemnity systems. It is still a fiduciary relationship. The doctor still treats patients on his or her panel one at a time as unique and valued individuals; the doctor is still a prudent steward judging wisely the limits of care.

Most physicians and patients want to have trusting, mutually rewarding relationships. Unfortunately, a contractual ethos can fit poorly within the established doctor-patient relationship norms of fidelity and honesty.[20] MCOs have strong incentives to discover "confidential" information about HIV status, for example. MCO interviews with patients may subjugate informed consent, breach confidentiality overtly,[21] and reveal more concern for limiting care than providing it.[22] The working doctor-patient relationship[23] is sometimes transformed into a dysfunctional doctor-patient-MCO *menage a trois*. Instead of a convenantal medical ethics based on trust, MCOs can rely on wariness, accountability and documentation; they have sometimes forced a reconsideration of fidelity, and endorsed a colder, more contractual medico-legal ethic.

The relationship in managed care will change, and move us from a personal, subjective standard of decision making to an objective one. The previous standard, in which the doctor and patient engage in value choices based on the rights of patients and of physicians to reach reasonable medical decisions, is now supplanted by an objective standard, in which various approaches will be used to override both patient and physician autonomy in achieving decisions. Decision-making authority now lies in the hands of new third-parties—not physicians and nurses and family, but payers and regulators and the courts.

The doctor-patient-MCO relationship requires that physicians hold the organization to its own moral responsibilities of facilitating members' access to needed health care and handling confidential information carefully.[24] Physicians can help design systems of managed care that permit ethical practice overall; even so, unfair constraints may occur in individual cases. Physicians have previously successfully appealed constraints on out-of-plan services.[25] Appealing these constraints is a newly explicit burden, which is likely to become more commonplace;[26] whether doctors will continue to help patients appeal these constraints will depend in part on the strength and depth of their relationships, and on the effect of constraints on the quality of care.

PRACTICE GUIDELINES: THE BEGINNING OF A NEW RELATIONSHIP

Physicians have tended to view socio-economic considerations in patient care as external[27] to ethical decisionmaking, perhaps because of a tradition of self-identification as their patient's primary advocate, fear of becoming agents of an inequitable distribution of social resources, or a sense of relatively unrestricted access to medical care through third-party payers.

In a recent study of 562 consecutive patients' visits to a medical office, however, 56 ethical problems involving medical care costs were present.[28] Even though cost constraints in the MCO setting are widely discussed, our experience suggests that the economic motivation underlying requests for ethics consultation may not be apparent or may even be concealed in the consultation request.

Reconciling individual variability and preferences with managed care's efforts at standardization will be difficult. Such standardized protocols have immediate bedside implications for doctors and patients. Practice guidelines can be educational, but they are a double-edged sword which can just as easily be used against physicians who do not advocate for care when it is medically necessary but not within the guideline. It is one thing to use practice guidelines to teach, to practice, to consult. It is another thing to adopt a particular one among the thousands that exist as a mandatory, national standard of practice.

No two patients are precisely the same; no two patients have identical backgrounds, values or even physiologic status. Guidelines do not necessitate much communication between doctors and patients. The application of guidelines can rely primarily on physiologic parameters that do not necessarily include wishes, desires, values or preferences of patients or physicians.

In the age of the payer, economic and decision-making power has already shifted from those who provide medical care and those who receive medical care to those who pay for that care. The system is increasingly based on institutional and societal efficiency as well as on cost concerns, which have now emerged as the central elements in medical decision making.

When conflicts of interest are present, the patient or proxy should be informed. While such disclosure by itself may be insufficient, patients and their families must be aware of financial constraints so they can search for alternative funding, rearrange personal assets, or appeal the constraints directly. Patients who are being denied access to medically indicated treatment for financial reasons should not be led to believe the denial is for medical reasons. Explicit financial information is necessary if patients and their families are to make fully informed choices between alternative medical treatments. The federal requirements that emergency patients be informed when transferred for financial reasons are examples of this new aspect of informed consent.[29]

EQUALITY OF ACCESS

MCOs require that doctors will provide all members with equal access to the MCO's medical resources, and still prescribe care on the basis of an individual member's medical needs.

MCOs depend on physicians to protect the financial well-being of the MCO, and to have the medical and financial interests of all MCO members in mind when seeing an individual patient. Most MCOs could ill afford to care for patients with all the medical needs of persistent-vegetative-state patients, no matter how vocal their proxies.[30] For MCOs, equality of access means that if one patient's needs are huge, providing resources to meet those needs makes it much more difficult to meet the needs of other patients. To provide basic care to all members, certain very expensive benefits are often excluded from MCO care, such as liver or bone marrow transplantation.

For many physicians, the primary obligation is still to the health of an individual patient, rather than the medical and financial well-being of all MCO members or the MCO itself.[31] To meet MCO expectations, some physicians may limit the appropriate care given to a specially medically needy patient so that scarce resources will be available to other patients.[32] Indigent MCO patients, for example, may receive fewer resources than non-indigent MCO patients, and have a higher prevalence of serious symptoms and more hospital bed-days than other non-MCO patients.[33]

To increase the appropriateness of care, and to provide equal access to care which has reasonable efficacy, few untoward effects and low costs, MCOs advocate the standardization of clinical protocols for the individual physician to follow.[34] Patients and doctors view clinical medicine, however, as an effort of particularities. Physicians who treat both managed care and fee-for-service patients may use different rationales for determining whether to refer patients for procedures or desired services: whether MCO patients actually receive fewer services than patients with indemnity insurance is debated.[35] The ethical practice of MCO medicine is similar in many ways to the ethical practice of medicine in other systems. The issue of referring patients for consultation and procedures can arise both in high technology medicine and in everyday office practice. Ethical issues in managed care, however, seem to focus more directly on access and cost issues because they are more explicitly imbedded in the organizational structure of the MCO system.

NEW ETHICAL RESPONSIBILITIES FOR PATIENTS AND PHYSICIANS IN MANAGED CARE

Patients who enroll in MCOs and physicians who care for them have several new responsibilities.

1. As individuals, patients must take greater charge of their own health, especially to prevent diseases for which they are at special risk.

2. As MCO members, they must acknowledge their decision to forgo some explicitly excluded services or to pay for them out-of-pocket. They must also acknowledge that the MCO will work to disallow expensive treatments, even if not explicitly excluded.
3. Patients must be responsible, with their doctors, for appealing unfair economic constraints on their care, beginning with their point of MCO entry (often their place of employment).
4. As members of society, MCO members have civic responsibilities to speak in public health debates, including those on access to basic care.

Physicians also have several new responsibilities.

1.   Physicians must be able to do their work as financial advocates, while maintaining good professional relationships with their patients under managed care; if they cannot, managed care will ultimately fail.

2.   When necessary, physicians must become more informed about their patients' MCO policies, so they can identify areas of interference and red tape, and keep straight the difference between what is medically indicated and medically available.

3.   Referrals to specialists, pre-authorizations for surgery or hospitalization, and required follow-up visits all are within a gatekeeper's control. Primary physicians can develop this role into one of clinical authority, and wear it as a mantle of advocacy.

CONCLUSION

The ethical and economic aspects of treatment decisions are intimately entwined. The end of good medical practice is best served by acknowledging rather than denying the influence of economic realities on clinical practice, and warding off distortions of good judgment.

Patients should be informed of conflicts of interest and of the impact of these constraints on treatment recommendations and patient care. Professional advocacy means that physicians should assist patients with financial issues which are unreasonable, discriminatory, or would injure a patient's medical interests.

A simple cost-containment agenda is neither physicians' nor patients' preferred course of action. The promises of managed care depend on equal access, disease prevention and health promotion, but the economic pressures of the current health care environment threaten to distort these concepts and destroy the fidelity of the doctor-patient relationship.

Medical professionals should not be interchanged as if they were cogs without therapeutic value. Their relationships with patients are the best way to provide good care for patients. Relationships are the optimal way to control bureaucratic officiousness, and probably the best way to protect American values of liberty, self-determination and freedom of choice.

Our best defense against the moral challenges of managed care is to safeguard the view that the doctor-patient relationship is the central process in practicing good medicine. While equality of access and responsible cost-containment are worthwhile goals for any health care organization, the people who are that organization must be able to act honestly and faithfully with the patient, irrespective of the finance and delivery system in which they work.

ENDNOTES

1. LaPuma J. Anticipated changes in the doctor-patient relationship in the managed care and managed competition of the Health Security Act of 1993. *Arch Fam Med* 1994; 3:665–671.

2. Povar G, Moreno J. Hippocrates and the health maintenance organization: A discussion of the ethical issues. *Ann Intern Med* 1988; 109:419–424.

3. Brook RH. Quality of care: do we care? *Ann Intern Med* 1991; 115:486–490.

4. Aaron HJ, Schwartz WB. *The Painful Prescription: Rationing Health Care.* Washington D.C., The Brookings Institution, 1984.

5. LaPuma J, Lawlor E. Quality Adjusted Life Years: Implications for clinicians and policymakers. *JAMA* 1990;263:2917–2921.

6. Mechanic D. The growth of HMOs: issues of enrollment and disenrollment. *Medical Care* 1983;21:338–347.

7. Hillman AL, Pauly MV, Kerstein JJ. How do financial incentives affect physicians' clinical decisions and the financial performance of health maintenance organizations? *N Eng J Med* 1989;321:86–92.

8. Scovern H. A physician's experience in a for-profit staff-model HMO. *N Eng J Med* 1988;319:787–90.

9. *Wickline v. California,* 192 Cal. App 3d 1630, 239 *Cal. Rptr* 810 (1986).

10. The Agency for Health Services Research in Primary Care. Mayfield J, Grady ML, eds. *Conference Proceedings: Primary Care Research: An Agenda for the 90s.* Report No. AHCPR 90–17, Rockville M.D., 1990.

11. Dorwart RA. Managed mental health care: myths and realities in the 1990s. *Hosp and Comm Psych* 1990;41:1087–1091.

12. LaPuma J, Schiedermayer D. *Minimanual of Managed Care,* Gaithersburg, MD: Aspen Publishers, 1994.

13. Udvarhelyi IS, Jennison K, Phillips RS, Epstein AM. Comparison of the quality of ambulatory care for fee-for-service and prepaid patients. *An Intern Med* 1991;115:394–400.

14. Brett AS. The case against persuasive advertising by health maintenance organizations. *N Engl J Med* 1992;326:1353–1357.

15. Danis M, Churchill LR. Autonomy and the commonweal. *Hastings Center Rep* 1991;21(1):25–31.

16. Jonsen AR. *The New Medicine and the Old Ethics.* Cambridge: Harvard University Press, 1990.

17. Morreim EH. Cost containment: issues of moral conflict and justice for physicians. *Theor Med* 1985;6:257–79.

18. Levinsky NG. The doctor's master. *N Eng J Med* 1984;311:1573–5.

19. Siegler M. The progression of medicine: from physicians paternalism to patient autonomy to bureaucratic parsimony. *Ann Intern Med* 1985;145:713–5.

20. Quill TE. Recognizing and adjusting to barriers in doctor-patient communications. *Ann Intern Med* 1989;111:51–58.

21. Freundenheim M.Guarding medical confidentiality. *The New York Times* 1991 January 1, p. 24.

22. Borenstein DJ. Managed care: a means of rationing psychiatric treatment. *Hosp and Comm Psych* 1990;41:1095–1098.

23. Siegler M. The physician-patient accommodation: a central event in clinical medicine. *Arch Intern Med* 1982;142:1899–1902.

24. Institute of Medicine Committee on Utilization Management by Third Parties: *Controlling costs and changing patient care? The role of utilization management.* Gray BH, Field MJ, eds. Washington D.C.: National Academy Press, 1989, p. 153.

25. Schiedermayer DL, LaPuma J, Miles SH. Ethics consultation masking economic dilemmas in patient care. *Arch Intern Med* 1989;149:1303–1305.

26. LaPuma J, Cassel CK, Humphrey H. Ethics, economics and endocarditis: the physician's role in resource allocation. *Arch Intern Med* 1988;148:1809–1811.

27. Siegler M. Decision-making strategy for clinical ethical problems in medicine. *Arch Intern Med* 1982;142:2178–2179.

28. Connelly JE, Campbell C. Patients who refuse treatment in medical offices. *Arch Intern Med* 1987;147:1829–1833.

29. Schiff RL, Ansell DA, Schlosser JE, et al. Transfers to a public hospital: a prospective study of 467 patients. *N Eng J Med* 1986;314:552–557.

30. Miles SH. Requested nonbeneficial treatment: the case of Helga Wanglie. *N Eng J Med* 1991;325.

31. Redelmeier DA, Tversky A. Discrepancy between medical decisions for individual patients and for groups. *N Eng J Med* 1990;322:1162–4.

32. Levinson DF. Toward full disclosure of referral restrictions and financial incentives by prepaid incentives by prepaid health plans. *N Eng J Med* 1987;317:1729–1731.

33. Ware JE Jr, Brook RH, Rogers WH, et al. Comparison of health outcomes at a health maintenance organization with those of fee-for-service care. *Lancet* 1986;1:1017–1022.

34. Eddy DM. The challenge. *JAMA* 1990;263:287–290.

35. Epstein AM, Begg CB, McNeil BJ. The use of ambulatory testing in prepaid and fee-for-service group practice: relations to perceived profitability. *N Eng J Med* 1986;314:1089–1094.

WHEN OPPORTUNITY KNOCKS

Robert A. Berenson and David A. Hyman

As a prelude to articles discussing the controversy from an academic and professional perspective, consider the following case of physician entrepreneurship and the opinions offered by its respondents.

Dr. A is a general practitioner in a small city. He was recently approached by a promoter who offered him the opportunity to invest in a free-standing radiology center. The center, to be staffed by a qualified radiologist, will provide x-rays and diagnostic imaging for all of Dr. A's patients.

Dr. A is asked to put up $10,000 per share. He is told that he will earn 25 percent or more annually on his investment. The promoter tells him that the rest of the doctors in town are investing and shows him financial data from another facility that earned 80 percent annually after two years of operation. Dr. A's return will be calculated based on his investment. However, the profitability of the center will depend on the total number of patients that are referred—a fact that the promoter makes crystal clear to Dr. A.

Dr. A already owns stock in several publicly traded companies that sell drugs he prescribes to his patients. He has always told himself that the companies are so large (and his practice so small) that his judgment could never be affected by stock ownership. Furthermore, medicine is a field in which he has special knowledge—why shouldn't he use that knowledge to pick a good stock?

Dr. A is less certain about investing in an imaging center, even though he has often been envious of the income of radiologists. The promoter reassures him that everything is legal and the American Medical Association (AMA) is on record that these arrangements are not unethical. "Everyone is doing it—opportunity knocks only once" are the last words Dr. A hears from the promoter.

What should Dr. A do? Are there any ethical or legal limits on physician investments of this sort?

COMMENTARY
by Robert A. Berenson

For all the delivery system variations in an increasingly complex, pluralistic health structure, the activity characterizing American medicine today is entrepreneurship, and a focus on the bottom line. It is debateable whether the public is well served by having physician

Robert A. Berenson, David A. Hyman, "When Opportunity Knocks" from *Hastings Center Report* (Nov/Dec 1990). Reprinted by permission of The Hastings Center.

energies spent pursuing entrepreneurial activities. However, the premises for this debate should not presuppose a simplistic dichotomy between serving the public good versus professional avarice; the Federal Republic of Germany provides health insurance for its citizens, directly controls physician spending and, nevertheless, permits vigorous entrepreneurial competition among nonhospital-based physicians. The relevant point here is, as the promoter correctly suggests to Dr. A, that in the United States health care system today virtually everybody is involved in entrepreneurialism. The deal proposed by the promoter, while more visible than other entrepreneurial activities and therefore a target of scrutiny, is refreshingly wholesome compared to other kinds of current economic practices in health care.

What are some of the structural and systemic parameters within which Dr. A must make his decision? A typical, small-city general practitioner such as Dr. A will earn about $90,000 for working a 58-hour week, or about $32 per hour. A radiologist in the center that currently provides radiology services in his small city will earn nearly two and a half times more per hour. So it is little wonder that Dr. A occasionally finds himself envious. In addition, the disparity in earnings between the two will show a continual increase.

In all likelihood, many of Dr. A's primary-care colleagues perform x-rays in their own offices. No ethical problems arise in this situation, they inform him. After all, internal self-referral is an accepted professional activity; one cannot be accused of kickbacks to oneself. Notwithstanding their lack of training, they interpret their own x-rays because their license to practice medicine gives them that privilege. Indeed, providing in-office x-rays has become a major profit center for many primary care physicians.

Dr. A's income may also have declined in recent years partly because he has entered contracts with managed care organizations that use marketplace leverage to have him discount his services. In contrast, the radiology center may have the franchise for radiology services in the city's hospital and therefore control a major barrier to market entry of potential competitors. The center would effectively have a monopoly on radiology services for the area, and their prices will reflect a monopoly market, not a competitive one.

In short, general physicians who perform x-rays in their own offices and radiology facilities with market dominance are able to engage in entrepreneurial activities and generate income in ways that appear ethically acceptable but may not serve the public interest.

With these systemic constraints and realities in mind, is the proposed deal jaywalking or crossing with the light? Nothing in the arrangement resembles a kickback, because Dr. A's prospective profits are neither directly nor indirectly dependent on the volume of his own referrals. Importantly, his share of profits appears to be proportional to his own equity in the company. Nevertheless, would his financial interest in the radiology center provide Dr. A an unsavory inducement to generate referrals?

Assuming the quality of the center is acceptable, ethical concern would be focused not on the existing volume of Dr. A's x-ray referrals, but primarily with the marginal referral, the one that he otherwise would not have made. In fact, Dr. A's benefit from a marginal referral is negligible, at most coming to a few cents, because his $10,000 investment certainly cannot represent even 1 percent of the equity in such an enterprise. This entrepreneurial arrangement is thus not dissimilar to his owning shares in the publicly traded pharmaceutical companies where his own prescribing pattern produces a negligible impact on his own investment. By comparison, Dr. A's colleagues who perform their own x-ray procedures by self-referral achieve marginal profits close to 100 percent of reimbursement.

Dr. A, being an ethical physician and a smart businessman, would still demand a series of additional safeguards about the referral arrangement. First, no physician investor can own more than, say, 5 percent of the outstanding shares. Second, physicians as a group should make up a minority interest of shareholders, and have minority representation on the Board of Directors, but should be encouraged to advise directly on the clinical aspects of the center's operations. Third, physician investors must prominently disclose their investment to all patients whom they might refer to the center, in the knowledge that patients may request referral elsewhere. Finally, the center must conduct quality assurance and utilization review programs open to outside scrutiny.

Even with these protections in place, Dr. A would refer his patients to the center only if it provided quality services; the loss of his investment would be insignificant compared to patient perceptions that he was compromising their care to foster an investment. With the requisite safeguards, Dr. A should have no *ethical* qualms about investing in the center. The test of whether society would benefit from Dr. A's investment is whether the new facility has a pro-competitive impact on health-care delivery in his city. Given the utter lack of competition for radiology services in most areas, it is just possible that Dr. A and his patients would benefit together.

COMMENTARY
by David A. Hyman

Any system for compensating physicians necessarily creates a conflict of interest and some inappropriate incentives. Critics have long recognized this problem, although its importance has grown as cost containment has become a significant issue. The difficulty was acidly stated by George Bernard Shaw in his introduction to the (aptly titled) *Doctor's Dilemma:*

> *That any sane nation, having observed that you could provide for the supply of bread by giving bakers a pecuniary interest in baking for you should go on to give a surgeon a pecuniary interest in cutting off your leg, is enough to make one despair of political humanity. But that is precisely what we have done. And the more appalling the mutilation, the more the mutilator is paid. He who corrects the ingrowing toenail receives a few shillings: he who cuts your inside out receives hundreds of guineas, except when he does it to a poor person for practice.*

Against this backdrop, what is one to make of the promoter and his arrangement? Is this just a variant of fee-for-service practice, raising no new issues? Or is it something altogether less acceptable?

Professional organizations have attempted to provide some guidance as to the ethical acceptability of these "deals." The AMA has sanctioned such arrangements, noting that "physician ownership interest in a venture with the potential for abuse is not in itself unethical." However, the AMA does require full disclosure of the economic interest to all referred patients, a fact conspicuously omitted from the promoter's prospectus. The AMA also has the most entrepreneurially inclined ethical code of any physician organization. The American College of Physicians is less enthusiastic about such arrangements, concluding that "the physician must avoid any personal commercial conflict of interest that might compromise his loyalty and treatment of the patient." Similarly, the American College of Radiology (ACR) recently stated that "referring physicians should not have a direct or indirect financial interest in diagnostic or therapeutic facilities to which they refer patients." The ACR's position is markedly less compelling if one recalls that arrangements like Dr. A's have dramatically cut into radiologists' income and referral base.

The most fundamental criticisms of these arrangements point to their effect on Dr. A's professionalism, and on the difficulty Dr. A will experience trying to disassociate the patient's medical needs from his own economic interests. Two related but distinct arguments inform this point of view. The most obvious argument against these ventures is financial— critics fear that the cost of health care will skyrocket as more and more tests are ordered. Economic incentives exist because they influence behavior, and the effect on Dr. A is likely to be substantial. What empirical evidence there is tends to confirm the obvious conclusion—rewarding a particular clinical decision (such as ordering an x-ray) tends to result in that decision being made more frequently. The dramatic growth in the Medicare budget indicates that physicians do not routinely violate the predictions of economists.

Although Dr. A's return does not vary directly with his referral behavior, such ventures typically have mechanisms such as peer pressure to encourage high utilization. Encouragement may not even be necessary in many instances—"a piece of the action" has always helped ensure maximal effort. Having just learned an expensive lesson the hard way about the effects of a system of open-ended reimbursement, it seems fool-hardy to repeat the same mistake. A study performed by the Inspector General of HHS concluded that excessive testing by physicians with ownership interests in facilities to which they referred patients cost the Medicare program $28 million in 1987. More of these facilities will only worsen the pressure on the budget, and money that could have been spent on necessary health care will be diverted to non-costworthy testing. Efforts at cost containment will be unsuccessful unless they can counter the effect of these ownership interests— presumably by providing still more incentive payments, which will worsen the budgetary constraints even more.

One can also argue that these arrangements will corrupt the decision-making process and undermine professionalism. The full implications of this claim must be understood in the context of a typical doctor-patient relationship. A physician in some ways is nothing more than the agent of his patients, providing services that the principal desires or requires. Like all employees, the physician deserves compensation for his efforts, and, like all dealings between agent and principal, compensation creates a variety of incentives, for both good and evil. Yet, the situation has an implicit conflict of interest because a physician is more than just an agent. Because a physician recommends services and then provides them (or at least stands to profit by the recommendation), he is at once agent and principal, counselor and consumer. Even without this duality, treating physician and patient as arms' length contracting parties is simply misplaced, because patients rarely have the knowledge or inclination to monitor their physician's performance or scrutinize his recommendations. Fiduciary obligations bind the physician because trust is fundamental to the doctor-patient relationship.

Because of the duality of the physician's role, any form of compensation creates an unavoidable conflict of interest. Yet that observation is not a license to create any compensation system. Conflict of interest admits of degrees—of better and worse. The question reduces to a more pragmatic one: what sort of conflict will we tolerate? We allow fee-for-service practice and capitated care even though they create unhealthy incentives for over- and underutilization. However, patients are quite familiar with the ways in which the physician's judgment may be affected in these circumstances, and they consider it when they assess his recommendations. Entrepreneurial activities are rarely disclosed. Even if they were, few patients understand that the physician receives an increased economic return for every patient he refers.

What does all this mean in practical terms? Suppose Dr. A is following a patient with yearly CT scans. Might the patient now require biannual or quarterly scans? After all, Dr. A is simply being more cautious. If the only available appointment is at 2:00 A.M. three weeks later, while another facility is perpetually vacant, well, Dr. A simply has a great deal more confidence in the skill and professionalism of his own imaging center. Certain types of facilities will be "overbuilt," as every physician with a referral pool seeks to enter these arrangements. Skimming of paying patients to these facilities is also likely. What one means by "abuse" is likely to require a new definition, to account for the subtle (and not so subtle) effects of these ownership interests.

Perhaps Shaw, once again, understood the difficulty best—

What other men dare pretend to be impartial when they have a strong pecuniary interest on one side? Nobody supposes that doctors are less virtuous than judges, but a judge whose salary and reputation depended on whether the verdict was for plaintiff or defendant, prosecutor or prisoner, would be as little trusted as a general in the pay of the enemy. To offer me a doctor as my judge and then to weight the decision with a bribe of a large sum of money and a virtual guarantee that if he makes a mistake it can never be proved against him, is to go wildly beyond the ascertained strain which human nature will bear.

Shaw is perhaps too pointed—it is foolish to suggest that physicians should receive no payment for their treatment of patients. Yet he is also perfectly accurate—it is foolhardy to allow these sorts of conflict of interest and expect the quality and cost of health care to remain stable, or to expect the public to esteem those with such conflicting allegiances. Dr. A's misgivings are well founded. If this is opportunity, he should be glad it only knocks once, and might have hoped it never knocked at all.

PHYSICIAN SELF-REFERRAL ARRANGEMENTS: LEGITIMATE BUSINESS OR UNETHICAL "ENTREPRENEURIALISM"

THEODORE N. MCDOWELL, JR.

McDowell presents a variety of diverging opinions on self-referral, arguing that the most effective regulation would be extensive structural guidelines that focus on the physician's referral behavior and limit restrictions on investment procedures, thus minimizing referral abuses and conflict of interest concerns while promoting business and competitive freedom. What are the limits of this approach? Does the AMA's result (following) satisfy McDowell's recommendation?

II. BACKGROUND

Physician self-referral arrangements typically involve physician investment in nonhospital facilities such as clinical laboratories, ambulatory surgery centers, outpatient diagnostic and imaging centers and durable medical equipment companies.[1] The investment generally consists of ownership of corporate stock or partnership interests in a corporation or partnership which operates a health care facility. Perhaps the most controversial structure for this type of venture is a limited partnership, in which physicians typically purchase limited partnership interests. The limited partnership form allows the physician investors to obtain an equity interest in the facility and also to minimize their liability.

The proliferation of self-referral arrangements is predominantly the result of the significant restructuring of the health care industry which has occurred, and continues to occur, in the 1980s. The guiding policy underlying the various changes is cost containment through competition. Competitive pressures aimed at cost containment, such as Medicare's prospective payment system, are forcing physicians, hospitals and other health care providers to develop new strategies to provide efficient medical services while raising revenues. Many of these strategies involve the provision of medical services

"Physician Self-Referral Arrangements: Legitimate Business or Unethical 'Entrepreneurialism'" by T. N. McDowell, Jr. Reprinted with permission by the American Society of Law, Medicine & Ethics from the *American Journal of Law & Medicine*, v. 15, no. 1 (1989), pp. 61–109 (excerpted).

1. Extensive explanatory references have been deleted from this excerpt for reasons of space.

in nonhospital settings. Medical care is being shifted to ambulatory surgery centers, outpatient diagnostic and imaging centers and other nonhospital facilities. The rapid development of diagnostic and therapeutic technology has facilitated this trend.

Physician involvement and investment in the above type of venture may serve a number of purposes. Common purposes are to obtain sources of capital, to increase returns on capital investment, to reduce the risk of the investment, to take advantage of professional skills and expertise, to increase the utilization of a facility, to expand the scope of medical services to the community, to respond to competition, to obtain referrals and to increase or retain market share. Certainly, the fact that physicians largely control access to medical services is a primary reason for their involvement in many ventures.

While physician self-referral arrangements are a natural outgrowth of the competitive health care industry and the physician's unique position in the industry, like many other new business practices, such arrangements are not without dangers. For instance, such arrangements may alter the character of the medical profession. The current policy debate regarding this growing business practice explores the benefits and disadvantages of such arrangements.

III. THE POLICY DEBATE

A. Policy Arguments against Self-Referral Arrangements

Critics have attacked physician referrals to health care facilities or businesses in which the referring physician has a financial or ownership interest as encouraging overutilization of medical services and creating an ethical conflict of interest. The incentive to overutilize services and the conflict of interest may have the negative effect of increasing Medicare costs, jeopardizing the quality of patient care and improperly influencing the physician's exercise of his independent professional judgment. . . .

2. Ethical Conflicts of Interest

Another negative consequence of physician self-referral arrangements is that they present an ethical conflict for the physician between entrepreneurialism and professionalism. The threat accompanying the growing business orientation among physicians is that financial self-interests will be placed above patient interests. The consequences of a shift away from professionalism and toward a business orientation include compromises in quality of care, loss of the crucial moral component inherent in the concept of medicine as a profession and loss of trust by patients and society.

Relman, who is perhaps the most outspoken critic of entrepreneurialism among physicians, argues that physician self-referral arrangements unacceptably compound the conflict of interest that has always existed in the traditional fee-for-service medical practice. Under the fee-for-service arrangement, which involves personal services delivered directly to a patient, the self-interest/patient interest conflict is minimized by the nature of the patient-physician relationship. In contrast, when the physician refers a patient to a facility in which such physician has an investment interest, income to the referring physician is generated by the services of others. As one commentator points out, "[t]his distance, it is feared, may reduce the altruistic component of [the referring physician's] decisions because of the absence of a personal relationship with the patient.

In order to maintain the integrity and autonomy of the medical profession, Relman has urged the medical profession to "clearly separate itself from the health care industry." Such a position translates into a recommended prohibition against physicians referring patients to a health care entity in which they have a financial or ownership interest.

Other commentators have taken a more moderate approach by calling for controls over self-referral arrangements in order to minimize and protect against the potential negative effects. For example, the American Medical Association (AMA) currently authorizes self-referrals as long as certain ethical guidelines, such as disclosure by the physician of his ownership interest to the patient, are followed.

B. Policy Arguments Supporting Self-Referral Arrangements

In response to arguments against self-referral arrangements, proponents argue that such arrangements have numerous pro-competitive effects. These proponents also state that the risks of referrals resulting in "unnecessary, inappropriate, or more expensive care [exist in] many other common practices in the health care field . . . that have never been considered to be unlawful." As with these other common practices, the risks surrounding physician self-referral arrangements can be adequately minimized or prevented through specific limitations and guidelines.

1. Pro-Competitive Effects

The pro-competitive effects of physician self-referral arrangements have been examined by the Federal Trade Commission's (FTC) Bureaus of Competition, Consumer Protection and Economics in two letters. The first letter is a response to a request by the Florida Attorney General's Office for comments on whether Florida's fee splitting statute implicitly prohibits dentists from investing in other dental practices to which they refer patients. The second letter responds to HHS' request for public comments regarding proposed regulations under the Medicare and Medicaid fraud and abuse provisions.

First, the FTC views self-referral arrangements as possessing the potential to improve quality of care "because an investment interest may lead to a stronger, more permanent working relationship between the referring practitioner and the entity in which he has a financial interest." Further, the practitioner's investment interest creates a direct economic interest in ensuring that the facility will provide quality services. If a facility develops a reputation for performing unnecessary or poor quality services, it is likely to lose patients as well as referral business from other providers and ultimately may lose money.

Second, the FTC asserts that self-referral arrangements facilitate the identification of community health care needs as well as experienced, qualified responses to these needs. The FTC suggests that established practitioners in a community are in a unique position to detect and respond to the health care needs of the community, "for example, the need for a certain type of medical laboratory." Prohibiting a practitioner from referring patients to a project may make him "reluctant to invest time, money and experience in such a project." As a result, certain beneficial medical services may remain unavailable in a community, creating serious patient access problems.

A third pro-competitive effect suggested by the FTC and other commentators relates to equity capital resources. A prohibition against investment by referral sources in health care facilities would "eliminate an entire category of potential investors." Consequently, a major source of equity capital would be lost to the health care market. In fact, a prohibition might eliminate the very investors who are most knowledgeable concerning the potential gains and risks involved in a project and who are most willing to take the risk of investing in such a project.

As a final point, the FTC and other commentators purport that certain self-referral arrangements have the potential to reduce medical costs. Established practitioners can use their expertise to reduce costs. For example, "their experience may enable them to organize a new practice efficiently by procuring office space and equipment and hiring [practitioners] and office personnel in a manner that reduces costs and thus may result in lower prices for medical care." In addition, the creation of new health care facilities through self-referral arrangements may provide an alternative to pre-existing facilities in a community, and the resulting competition may reduce the overall price for medical services. . . .

C. Summary

The above policy debate reveals why physician self-referral arrangements have generated so much controversy. The problems associated with such arrangements—overutilization, increased Medicare costs and reduced quality of care—are some of the most controversial issues presently facing the health care industry. The positive aspects of such arrangements, however, comport with the policy of encouraging competition within the industry.

Given the strength of the arguments on both sides of the debate, both complete prohibition and complete freedom regarding self-referral arrangements seem unjustified. Complete business and competitive freedom ignores the significant risks inherent in this type of business practice, while complete prohibition would negate the positive, pro-competitive aspects of such arrangements.

Complete prohibition seems justifiable only by accepting the view that in order for physicians to maintain their role as "professionals," the medical profession must totally reject and dissociate itself from new business arrangements emerging in the health care industry or by believing that the risks of overutilization and increased costs are so dramatic and uncontrollable in self-referral arrangements that the only way to avoid these risks is complete prohibition. If, however, it is possible to maintain the core ethical components associated with the medical profession, prevent or avoid the risks associated with self-referrals, and simultaneously promote the possible benefits of self-referral arrangements through the establishment of guidelines and limitations, then complete prohibition becomes unnecessary. The mere potential for overutilization or unethical conduct should not lead to a *per se* prohibition of self-referral arrangements.

In order to minimize risks and still promote the pro-competitive effects of physician self-referral arrangements, most commentators, including the FTC, suggest guidelines to cover such arrangements. . . .

CONFLICTS OF INTEREST: PHYSICIAN OWNERSHIP OF MEDICAL FACILITIES

COUNCIL ON ETHICAL AND JUDICIAL AFFAIRS,
AMERICAN MEDICAL ASSOCIATION

The federal government has prescribed certain restrictions on the ability of physicians to refer their patients to independent "free-standing" facilities in which the physician has a financial interest. While the issue itself presents a difficult dilemma, it is also interesting to look at the American Medical Association's response to the dilemma. While it originally came down on one side of the issue, it later reversed itself. The AMA Council on Ethical and Judicial Affairs issued a report warning physicians of the potential for conflicts of interest in physician entrepreneurship and advising physicians against self-referral; the AMA approved the report without dissent. The recommendation specifically stated, "In general, physicians should not refer patients to a health care facility outside their office practice at which they do not directly provide care or services when they have an investment in the facility." Six months later, the AMA House of Delegates reversed its opinion, approving a new resolution declaring self-referral to be ethical as long as the patient is fully informed about the physician's financial interest in the facility (John Iglehart, "Health Policy Report, Efforts to Address the Problem of Physician Self-Referral," New England Journal of Medicine, *325 (19, 1991), p. 1820).*

BACKGROUND[1]

The Council issued a major report on conflicts of interest in the practice of medicine in 1986.[2] The Council's view then was that conflicts are inherent in the practice of medicine and that the problem of referral of patients to outside facilities in which physicians have

Council on Ethical and Judicial Affairs, American Medical Association, "Conflicts of Interest: Physician Ownership of Medical Facilities." Reprinted from the Code of Medical Ethics Current Opinions of the Council on Ethical and Judicial Affairs of the American Medical Association, American Medical Association, copyright © 1992.

1. Opening paragraphs of article have been omitted.
2. Council on Ethical and Judicial Affairs, American Medical Association. Conflicts of Interest. In: Proceedings of the House of Delegates, 40th Interim Meeting, December 7–10, 1986; Chicago,Ill: 216–228.

an investment ("self-referral") was not significantly different in principle from other conflicts presented by fee-for-service medicine. In a report in 1990 the Council also identified the conflicts of interest presented by certain managed care arrangements, particularly health maintenance organizations that reward physicians for providing less care.[3]

With all of these arrangements, the Council's primary guidance was to remind physicians that the profession of medicine is unique and that physicians are expected to put their patients' interests first. Thus, when a physician's financial interest may conflict with the best interests of the patient, it is assumed that the physician will not take advantage of the patient.

The Council did recognize that some arrangements may present too great a conflict to be appropriate, but with regard to self-referral the Council issued a list of safeguards to help ensure that the patient's interests would not be jeopardized. That list was most recently updated in 1989.[4]

Since these reports and opinions were issued, several studies have been performed that analyze self-referral and draw conclusions with regard to increased utilization and cost of the practice.

At the request of the Council, the AMA's Center for Health Policy Research reviewed this evidence. . . .

Although the Center found that all of these studies have flaws, several important points could be made with regard to their findings.

- In the neighborhood of 10% of physicians nationwide have ownership interests in health care entities that have been associated with potential self-referral issues. However, not all of the physicians with such ownership interests engage in self-referral, so other motivations exist for physicians to make such investments. Indeed, there is significant geographic variation in the extent of physician ownership of health entities that is not readily explained by differences in the opportunities of physicians to self-refer.

- For several important classes of services for which physicians make referrals, patients of physicians who self-refer have higher utilization rates than other patients. None of the studies, however, examined the appropriateness of the utilization levels of physicians who self-refer and those who refer to other sources.

The study by the Department of Health and Human Services found that self-referring physicians referred patients for clinical laboratory testing at a 45% higher rate than noninvesting physicians; the Florida study concluded that physicians' utilization of clinical laboratories, diagnostic imaging centers, and physical therapy/rehabilitation centers was "significantly higher" where physicians are owners; the study by Hillman et al[5]

---

3. Council on Ethical and Judicial Affairs, American Medical Association. Financial incentives to limit care: ethical implications for HMOs and IPAs. In: Proceedings of the House of Delegates, 139th Annual Meeting, June 24–28, 1990; Chicago, Ill: 228–242.

4. Council on Ethical and Judicial Affairs, American Medical Association. Conflicts of interest; update. In: Proceedings of the House of Delegates, 138th Annual Meeting, June 18–22, 1980; Chicago, Ill: 188–190.

5. Hillman BJ, Joseph CA, Mabry MR, Sunshine JH, Kennedy SD, Noether M. Frequency and costs of diagnostic imaging in office practice—a comparison of self-referring and radiologist-referring physicians. *N Engl J Med.* 1990; 323: 1604–1808.

concluded that physicians with a financial interest in diagnostic imaging facilities referred patients at a rate of four to 4.5 times that of noninvesting physicians.

- There is no evidence in these sources on the extent to which physicians may profit from self-referrals, so the degree of the conflict is not known, except anecdotally. . . .

A NEW APPROACH RECOMMENDED BY THE COUNCIL

The Council believes that it is necessary to strengthen its opinion on self-referral. It believes that physicians in general can be trusted to deal appropriately with the conflicts presented by self-referral. Indeed, the Council believes that physician investment and self-referral have, on balance, been positive for patients and the nation's health care system. But anecdotes of excessive profit and utilization have been widespread, and the formal studies that have been done strongly suggest, although they do not actually prove, inherent problems with the practice.

In addition, the Council takes notice of the change in our nation's health care priorities and, in particular, of our patients' expectations about physicians. In the 1990s and beyond, the growth in the costs of health care is likely to be a dominant concern of our patients. The nation has today, and is likely to continue to have, unparalleled availability of health care facilities and technology of all varieties.

In this environment, the Council believes that the issue of self-referral is a part of the larger issue of physicians' commitment to professionalism. As professionals, physicians are expected to devote their energy, attention, and loyalty fully to the service of their patients. This does not mean they cannot have outside investments and activities or that they should not invest in health care facilities. It does mean that, to the extent possible, physicians should not be in the business of profiting purely from their ability to refer patients to outside facilities. Such a practice is fundamentally different from deriving financial reward from treating patients in their offices or in outside health care facilities they have invested in at which they care for, or provide services to, their patients. When physicians provide care or services, they have direct responsibility for, and control over, the quality of the facility at which the care or services are provided.

At the heart of the Council's view of this issue is its conviction that, however others may see the profession, physicians are not simply businesspeople with high standards. Physicians are engaged in the special calling of healing, and, in that calling, they are the fiduciaries of their patients. They have different and higher duties than even the most ethical businessperson. This is the teaching of the Hippocratic oath and of the great modern teachers of ethical behavior. There are some activities involving their patients that physicians should avoid whether or not there is evidence of abuse. . . .

RECOMMENDATIONS

Accordingly, the Council on Ethical and Judicial Affairs recommends the following:

Recommendation 1

Physician investment in health care facilities can provide important benefits for patient care. However, when physicians refer patients to facilities in which they have an ownership interest, a potential conflict of interest exists. In general, physicians should not refer patients to a health care facility outside their office practice at which they do not directly provide care or services when they have an investment interest in the facility.

Clarification of Recommendation 1

Facilities in Which the Physician Directly Provides Care or Services   Under the guidelines, physicians may refer their patients to facilities in which they have an ownership interest if the physician directly provides care or services at the facility. The Council drew a distinction between the physician who benefits financially from services that the physician actually provides and the physician who benefits purely from the ability to refer patients for services. Thus, for example, a surgeon may operate on a patient at an ambulatory surgical facility in which the surgeon has an investment interest. While self-referral is permissible, there is still an obligation to comply with recommendation 2.b. through 2.j.

The requirement that the physician *directly* provide the care or services should be interpreted as commonly understood. The physician needs to have personal involvement with the provision of care on site.

Recommendation 2

Physicians may invest in and refer to an outside facility, whether or not they provide direct care or services at the facility, if there is a demonstrated need in the community for the facility and alternative financing is not available. There may be situations in which a needed facility would not be built if referring physicians were prohibited from investing in the facility. Need might exist when there is no facility of reasonable quality in the community or when use of existing facilities is onerous for patients. In such cases, the following requirements should also be met:

a.   Individuals who are not in a position to refer patients to the facility should be given a bona fide opportunity to invest in the facility, and they should be able to invest on the same terms that are offered to referring physicians. The terms on which investment interests are offered to physicians should not be related to the past or expected volume of referrals or other business from the physicians.

b.   There should be no requirement that any physician investor make referrals to the entity or otherwise generate business as a condition for remaining an investor.

c.   The entity should not market or furnish its items or services to referring physician investors differently than to other investors.

d.   The entity should not loan funds or guarantee a loan for physicians in a position to refer to the entity.

e.   The return on the physician's investment should be tied to the physician's equity in the facility rather than to the volume of referrals.

f.   Investment contracts should not include "noncompetition clauses" that prevent physicians from investing in other facilities.

g.   Physicians should disclose their investment interest to their patients when making a referral. Patients should be given a list of effective alternative facilities if any such facilities become reasonably available, informed that they have the option to use one of the alternative facilities, and assured that they will not be treated differently by the physician if they do not choose the physician-owned facility. These disclosure requirements also apply to physician investors who directly provide care or services for their patients in facilities outside their office practice.

   h.   The physician's ownership interest should be disclosed, when requested, to third-party payers.

   i.   An internal utilization review program should be established to ensure that investing physicians do not exploit their patients in any way, as by inappropriate or unnecessary utilization.

   j.   When a physician's financial interest conflicts so greatly with the patient's interest as to be incompatible, the physician should make alternative arrangements for the care of the patient.

Clarification of Recommendation 2

Demonstrated Need   Demonstrated need might exist (*a*) when there is no facility or reasonable quality in the community or (*b*) when use of existing facilities is onerous for patients.

No Facility of Reasonable Quality   Self-referral cannot be justified simply if the facility would offer some marginal improvement over the quality of services in the community. The potential benefits of the facility should be substantial to justify assuming the risks of self-referral. The question is whether the community has any facilities that can provide medically appropriate services.

The Community   The community should be defined liberally, since concerns about patient convenience are included in the next criterion. Thus, the community would be the metropolitan area for a city, or the county for a rural area.

Use of Existing Facilities Is Onerous   This guideline permits new facilities when use of existing facilities creates too great a hardship for patients. This might occur, for example, if existing facilities are so heavily used that patients face undue delays in receiving services. A delay would become undue if putting off the service would compromise the patient's care, i.e., it would affect the curability or reversibility of the patient's condition. There would also be too great a hardship if patients had long travel times that made it very difficult for them to receive services. The appropriateness of the travel time would depend in part on the frequency of the service. Longer travel times would be acceptable if patients tended to use the facility rarely, while longer travel times would be unacceptable if patients tended to use the facility more regularly.

Alternative Financing   The requirement that alternative financing not be available carries a burden of proof. If the facility serves a real need and is financially viable, then capital should generally be available to support it. The burden on the builder of the facility is to show that adequate capital could not be raised without turning to self-referring physicians. As to the kind of efforts that must be made to secure alternative financing, the builder would have to undertake the usual steps that entrepreneurs undertake, including efforts to secure funding from banks, other financial institutions, and venture capitalists. . . .

ETHICS IN THE LEGAL BUSINESS

SHORTEST ETHICS CASE EVER
JAMES LYTTLE

I am a scholar and professor in the area of business ethics. As I have mentioned, I have heard all too often that my area of interest is an oxymoron. Much as that is irritating, I suffer the extended abuse of also having a law degree. Therefore, I bear some sensitivity to the following comments by Lyttle on a business ethics listserver. (I like to consider myself a "recovering attorney.") From a realistic perspective, is this all merely humorous or do you believe that any attorney would have the inappropriate approach to ethical issues in business?

From: James B Lyttle
To: Multiple recipients of list BETS-L
Date: 3/13/96 7:46 P.M.
Subject: Discussion Topic

Here is a very brief case study. A company announces a commitment to business ethics, and hires a lawyer to head up its new ethics office. Comments?

Jim Lyttle.

RELATED WEB SITE

American Bar Association Center for Professional Responsibility:
   www.abanet.org/cpr/home.html

SUMMA THEOLOGICA
St. Thomas Aquinas

Aquinas, in pondering the essence of law, considers whether law has anything to do with reason or the common good. Should it? After reading Aquinas, is the answer as clear as you first imagined?

WHETHER LAW IS SOMETHING PERTAINING TO REASON

Objection 1. It would seem that law is not something pertaining to reason. For the Apostle says (Rm. 7:23): "I see another law in my members," etc. But nothing pertaining to reason is in the members; since the reason does not make use of a bodily organ. Therefore law is not something pertaining to reason.

Objection 2. Further, in the reason there is nothing else but power, habit, and act. But law is not the power itself of reason. In like manner, neither is it a habit of reason: because the habits of reason are the intellectual virtues of which we have spoken above. Nor again is it an act of reason: because then law would cease, when the act of reason ceases, for instance, while we are asleep. Therefore law is nothing pertaining to reason.

Objection 3. Further, the law moves those who are subject to it to act aright. But it belongs properly to the will to move to act, as is evident from what has been said above. Therefore law pertains, not to the reason, but to the will; according to the words of the Jurist (Lib. i, ff., De Const. Prin. leg.i): "Whatsoever pleaseth the sovereign, has force of law."

On the contrary, It belongs to the law to command and to forbid. But it belongs to reason to command, as stated above. Therefore law is something pertaining to reason.

I answer that, Law is a rule and measure of acts, whereby man is induced to act or is restrained from acting: for "lex" [law] is derived from "ligare" [to bind], because it binds one to act. Now the rule and measure of human acts is the reason, which is the first principle of human acts, as is evident from what has been stated above; since it belongs to the reason to direct to the end, which is the first principle in all matters of action, according to the Philosopher. Now that which is the principle in any genus, is the rule and measure of that genus: for instance, unity in the genus of numbers, and the first movement in the genus of movements. Consequently it follows that law is something pertaining to reason.

Reply to Objection 1. Since law is a kind of rule and measure, it may be in something in two ways. First, as in that which measures and rules: and since this is proper to reason, it follows that, in this way, law is in the reason alone. Secondly, as in that which is measured and ruled. In this way, law is in all those things that are inclined to something by reason of some law: so that any inclination arising from a law, may be called a law, not essentially but by participation as it were. And thus the inclination of the members to concupiscence is called "the law of the members."

St. Thomas Aquinas, *Summa Theologica,* Question 90: Of the essence of law; Art. 1: Law is not something pertaining to reason; Art. 2: The law is not always directed at the common good.

Reply to Objection 2. Just as, in external action, we may consider the work and the work done, for instance the work of building and the house built; so in the acts of reason, we may consider the act itself of reason, i.e., to understand and to reason, and something produced by this act. With regard to the speculative reason, this is first of all the definition; secondly, the proposition; thirdly, the syllogism or argument. And since also the practical reason makes use of a syllogism in respect of the work to be done, as stated above and since as the Philosopher teaches; hence we find in the practical reason something that holds the same position in regard to operations, as, in the speculative intellect, the proposition holds in regard to conclusions. Such like universal propositions of the practical intellect that are directed to actions have the nature of law. And these propositions are sometimes under our actual consideration, while sometimes they are retained in the reason by means of a habit.

Reply to Objection 3. Reason has its power of moving from the will, as stated above: for it is due to the fact that one wills the end, that the reason issues its commands as regards things ordained to the end. But in order that the volition of what is commanded may have the nature of law, it needs to be in accord with some rule of reason. And in this sense is to be understood the saying that the will of the sovereign has the force of law; otherwise the sovereign's will would savor of lawlessness rather than of law.

WHETHER THE LAW IS ALWAYS SOMETHING DIRECTED TO THE COMMON GOOD

Objection 1. It would seem that the law is not always directed to the common good as to its end. For it belongs to law to command and to forbid. But commands are directed to certain individual goods. Therefore the end of the law is not always the common good.

Objection 2. Further, the law directs man in his actions. But human actions are concerned with particular matters. Therefore the law is directed to some particular good.

Objection 3. Further, Isidore says: "If the law is based on reason, whatever is based on reason will be a law." But reason is the foundation not only of what is ordained to the common good, but also of that which is directed private good. Therefore the law is not only directed to the good of all, but also to the private good of an individual.

On the contrary, Isidore says that "laws are enacted for no private profit, but for the common benefit of the citizens."

I answer that, As stated above, the law belongs to that which is a principle of human acts, because it is their rule and measure. Now as reason is a principle of human acts, so in reason itself there is something which is the principle in respect of all the rest: wherefore to this principle chiefly and mainly law must needs be referred. Now the first principle in practical matters, which are the object of the practical reason, is the last end: and the last end of human life is bliss or happiness, as stated above. Consequently the law must needs regard principally the relationship to happiness. Moreover, since every part is ordained to the whole, as imperfect to perfect; and since one man is a part of the perfect community, the law must needs regard properly the relationship to universal happiness. Wherefore the Philosopher, in the above definition of legal matters mentions both happiness and the body politic: for he says that we call those legal matters "just, which are adapted to produce and preserve happiness and its parts for the body politic": since the state is a perfect community.

Now in every genus, that which belongs to it chiefly is the principle of the others, and the others belong to that genus in subordination to that thing: thus fire, which is chief among hot things, is the cause of heat in mixed bodies, and these are said to be hot in so far as they have a share of fire. Consequently, since the law is chiefly ordained to the common good, any other precept in regard to some individual work, must needs be devoid of the nature of a law, save in so far as it regards the common good. Therefore every law is ordained to the common good.

Reply to Objection 1. A command denotes an application of a law to matters regulated by the law. Now the order to the common good, at which the law aims, is applicable to particular ends. And in this way commands are given even concerning particular matters.

Reply to Objection 2. Actions are indeed concerned with particular matters: but those particular matters are referable to the common good, not as to a common genus or species, but as to a common final cause, according as the common good is said to be the common end.

Reply to Objection 3. Just as nothing stands firm with regard to the speculative reason except that which is traced back to the first indemonstrable principles, so nothing stands firm with regard to the practical reasons, unless it be directed to the last end which is the common good: and whatever stands to reason in this sense, has the nature of a law.

ETHICS IN THE MEDIA

ETHICS AND THE MEDIA
RICHARD CUNNINGHAM

Cunningham identifies some of the more pressing ethical issues in journalism as he contemplates CBS's order to Mike Wallace to cancel an interview with an anonymous tobacco company executive, and Wallace's acquiescence.

When CBS lawyers warned Mike Wallace to kill a "60 Minutes" interview with an anonymous tobacco company executive—and he obeyed them—it was frightening.

When Wallace along with his "60 Minutes" colleague Morley Safer and former *Washington Post* editor Ben Bradlee all dumped on the lawyers, it was comforting.

But when it came out that the lawyers were right and that Wallace may have known they were right—then it was more than frightening; it was disillusioning.

Why frightening? For one thing, the lawyers' order came on the heels of ABC News' capitulation before Philip Morris' libel suit for $10 billion, an amount more than the net worth of the company. Lawyers in the CBS case warned that the tobacco company might sue—successfully—for $10 billion to $15 billion, more than twice the worth of CBS.

ABC was in the final stages of being acquired by Disney when it capitulated. The CBS lawyers' warning came only days before CBS was to be acquired by Westinghouse. The question in each case seemed to be: "Would a network with a multi-billion-dollar libel suit hanging over its head become less attractive to a buyer?"

It all echoed Ben Bagdikian's predictions that news operations would lose their integrity as they were scooped into the toy boxes of a decreasing number of huge conglomerate corporations.

But it was worse. As we read Bagdikian over the years, we imagined the news corporation emerging on some high ground from which it could fight a Davidian battle against a Goliath who was clearly the bad guy. Instead, as the CBS drama played out in recent weeks, we could not get mad at the corporation. The corporation itself appeared powerless, given the outrageously high stakes the conglomerates could play for. We had expected some kind of a bang when the end came. Instead all we heard was a whimper.

And then it got worse. Safer accused his colleague of more than a quarter of a century of misleading him—and by extension all of us—who had joined in dumping on the lawyers.

Richard Cunningham, "Ethics and the Media." Reprinted by permission of Society for Professional Journalists.

The events went this way. On November 9, the *New York Times* published a story based on a leak from CBS that lawyers had ordered the interview killed lest CBS expose itself to a suit for "litigious interference," that is, inducing the tobacco executive to break his contract pledge not to talk about his company's business.

November 12: "60 Minutes" went on the air without the interview but with a segment designed to show the lengths the tobacco industry goes to block information about the dangers of its products.

November 13: Wallace and Safer assured New York's popular public television interviewer Charlie Rose that CBS made no offer of money to induce the tobacco executive to violate his contractual pledge not to talk about his company's business. Safer said, "He wasn't paid; he wasn't threatened; he wasn't promised anything other than an opportunity to speak, an opportunity to exercise his First Amendment rights on our air."

Bradlee, who was a telephone guest on the Rose program, said, "If you guys didn't hustle this fella, give him money, pay him something, it seems to me that you are OK."

Then everyone on the program went on a dirge for the good old days of new gathering.

Bradlee and Wallace recalled the courage of Bradlee's publisher, Katharine Graham, in going against the advice of lawyers to fight the government for the right to publish the Pentagon Papers. Safer said the "character" has changed at CBS and other networks "because of a kind of corporate ownership. I mean . . . the people at NBC [owned by General Electric] might as well be making Twinkies. It's just one more part of a huge conglomerate.

But the networks have always been publicly owned, said Rose; what's different?

The old time owners were broadcasters, said Safer; Disney is not. General Electric is not, and Westinghouse, generally speaking, is not.

Wallace said broadcasters made money in the old days, but there was a "different sense of responsibility."

"I don't think that Mr. Tisch [Laurence Tisch, chairman of CBS] ever fully understood . . . the responsibility of a man who owns one of the major networks in America to the public health, the public welfare, public understanding, or whatever."

Safer said broadcasters have to have in their blood "some sense of getting a kick out of what we do. I don't think Larry Tisch gets that kick. He looks at it—as any good businessman should—at the profit and loss of the company."

On November 16, three days after the lawyer bashing, *The Wall Street Journal* sucked the ground out from under the bashers with a report that CBS had indeed made offers to its anonymous tobacco executive that might well be construed as inducing him to break his pledge not to talk about his company's business.

CBS had offered to pay the source's legal fees and damages in any libel suit growing out of the broadcast. It seemed to have promised him not to broadcast the program without his approval. And "60 Minutes" had paid him $12,000 as a consultant on another tobacco broadcast.

Safer was furious. In a press release he said Wallace had "deliberately suppressed" before the Charlie Rose program the grounds for the lawyers' concern and information about the payment to the source and the offer to the source of what appeared to be some sort of veto power. He said Wallace had "sandbagged" him and left him "twisting slowly in the wind." Safer sent apologies to Rose and to the CBS lawyers too.

It wasn't over yet. The *New York Daily News* identified the CBS source as Jeffrey Wigand, former vice president for research and development for Brown & Williamson Tobacco Corp. The *News* published parts of the killed interview quoting Wigand as saying B&W Chief Executive Officer Thomas Sandefur had perjured himself when he told a congressional committee that he had no knowledge about how cigarettes were used to deliver nicotine.

B&W filed suit against Wigand for breaking his contractual pledge and notified CBS that it would hold CBS liable for any libel in the transcript. And a B&W spokesman said it did appear to the company that CBS had induced Wigand to break his promise not to speak.

At CBS, peacemaking was going on. The company said the promise to indemnify the source against a libel suit was not unusual; the consulting payment to Wigand was for an unrelated earlier story; and the producer of the interview segment had not promised Wigand a veto over content, but had agreed to hold off broadcasting the interview until Wigand, who has an illness in his family, was comfortable that a lawsuit would not wipe out his resources.

CBS President Eric Ober sent a memo to the staff defending the decision not to broadcast the interview and excoriating the behavior of some individuals who disagreed with the decision. He said they had created a free-for-all resulting in the identification of a confidential source, which he called "one of the most egregious violations of journalistic ethics and tradition."

"It is now time to move on," he said. "Further bickering and self-flagellation are no more positive than revealing confidential sources.

What now? It seems clear that journalism companies—broadcast and print—are financially outmatched by the conglomerates that own them. It's a huge poker game in which the conglomerates can afford to bet high enough that the news organizations can't call. A non-journalism student in a graduate press ethics seminar asked, "Isn't there some way journalists can buy back their integrity? None of his colleagues could imagine a source for the money necessary to buy oneself out of the conglomerate ownership, but the idea is not entirely new.

Marion Tuttle Marzolf, in her book *Civilizing Voices,* reports the suggestion in 1912 of Hamilton Holt, managing editor of the religious journal *Independent,* that since commercial journalists had found that it did not pay to be thorough or impartial, "newspapers could be endowed in the manner of theaters and universities, so that they could say what ought to be said irrespective of anybody and everybody."

The overwhelming stakes, particularly in libel suits, may incline editors and publishers to at last pay serious attention to proposals that offer an alternative to libel to sort out the truth or falsehood of claims and assess actual, not punitive, damages. One such proposal was produced in 1988 by the Annenberg Washington Program in Communications Policy Studies of Northwestern University. Another, the Libel Dispute Resolution Program, was produced by the Iowa Libel Research Project and has a track record as an experimental plan.

Across the nation, state legislatures are beginning to take up a bill called the Uniform Correction or Clarification of Defamation Act, which is designed to establish uniform standards for retractions to pre-empt libel suits and limit damages.

And there is, of course, the possibility that regional news councils or even a national news council is an idea whose time has come and gone and come again.

It is ironic that Mike Wallace should have proposed a new news council in the November/December ethics issue of *QUILL,* an article that appeared just days before he became the center of an ethical maelstrom.

NOTEPAD

A producer for ABC's "20/20" news program was suspended without pay for promising to pay $3,000 for access to chimpanzees as part of a report on the scientific use of the animals, according to a *New York Times* report.

The producer, who wasn't identified, signed a contract last February with the Chimpanzee and Human Communications Institute at Central Washington University in Ellensburg, The *Times* reported in November. The $3,000 was to have been for one day filming.

ABC News executives reportedly also were angered that the contract specified that the institute's co-directors would have veto power over any use of the videotape. Victor Neufeld, executive producer of the program, denied there was any prior approval agreement.

A WINK-TV news team's attempt to remove computer equipment from a state agency's storage area to demonstrate alleged lax security has prompted a formal FCC complaint from Florida Gov. Lawton Chiles, according to the *News-Press* in Fort Myers.

WINK-TV officials said they did not commit a crime and did not lie about their actions. . . .

RELATED WEB SITE

FAIR (Fairness & Accuracy in Reporting): www.igc.org/fair/

CODE OF ETHICS
SOCIETY OF PROFESSIONAL JOURNALISTS

In your opinion, does the Code of Ethics for the Society of Professional Journalists offer sufficient guidance for all of the ethical issues faced by journalists and editors?

PREAMBLE

Members of the Society of Professional Journalists believe that public enlightenment is the forerunner of justice and the foundation of democracy. The duty of the journalist is to further those ends by seeking truth and providing a fair and comprehensive account of events and issues. Conscientious journalists from all media and specialties strive to serve the public with thoroughness and honesty. Professional integrity is the cornerstone of a journalist's credibility.

Members of the Society share a dedication to ethical behavior and adopt this code to declare the Society's principles and standards of practice.

SEEK TRUTH AND REPORT IT

Journalists should be honest, fair and courageous in gathering, reporting and interpreting information.

Journalists should:

- Test the accuracy of information from all sources and exercise care to avoid inadvertent error. Deliberate distortion is never permissible.

- Diligently seek out subjects of news stories to give them the opportunity to respond to allegations of wrongdoing.

- Identify sources whenever feasible. The public is entitled to as much information as possible on sources' reliability.

- Always question sources' motives before promising anonymity. Clarify conditions attached to any promise made in exchange for information. Keep promises.

- Make certain that headlines, news teases and promotional material, photos, video, audio, graphics, sound bites and quotations do not misrepresent. They should not oversimplify or highlight incidents out of context.

- Never distort the content of news photos or video. Image enhancement for technical clarity is always permissible. Label montages and photo illustrations.

Society of Professional Journalists Code of Ethics. Reprinted by permission of Society of Professional Journalists.

- Avoid misleading re-enactments or staged news events. If re-enactment is necessary to tell a story, label it.

- Avoid undercover or other surreptitious methods of gathering information except when traditional open methods will not yield information vital to the public. Use of such methods should be explained as part of the story.

- Never plagiarize.

- Tell the story of the diversity and magnitude of the human experience boldly, even when it is unpopular to do so.

- Examine their own cultural values and avoid imposing those values on others.

- Avoid stereotyping by race, gender, age, religion, ethnicity, geography, sexual orientation, disability, physical appearance or social status.

- Support the open exchange of views, even views they find repugnant.

- Give voice to the voiceless, official and unofficial sources of information can be equally valid.

- Distinguish between advocacy and news reporting. Analysis and commentary should be labeled and not misrepresent fact or context.

- Distinguish news from advertising and shun hybrids that blur the lines between the two.

- Recognize a special obligation to ensure that the public business is conducted in the open and that government records are open to inspection.

MINIMIZE HARM

Ethical journalists treat sources, subjects and colleagues as human beings deserving of respect.

Journalists should:

- Show compassion for those who may be affected adversely by news coverage. Use special sensitivity when dealing with children and inexperienced sources or subjects.

- Be sensitive when seeking or using interviews or photographs of those affected by tragedy or grief.

- Recognize that gathering and reporting information may cause harm or discomfort. Pursuit of the news is not a license for arrogance.

- Recognize that private people have a greater right to control information about themselves than do public officials and others who seek power, influence or attention. Only an overriding public need can justify intrusion into anyone's privacy.

- Show good taste. Avoid pandering to lurid curiosity.

- Be cautious about identifying juvenile suspects or victims of sex crimes.

- Be judicious about naming criminal suspects before the formal filing of charges.

- Balance a criminal suspect's fair trial rights with the public's right to be informed.

ACT INDEPENDENTLY

Journalists should be free of obligation to any interest other than the public's right to know. Journalists should:

- Avoid conflicts of interest, real or perceived.

- Remain free of associations and activities that may compromise integrity or damage credibility.

- Refuse gifts, favors, fees, free travel and special treatment, and shun secondary employment, political involvement, public office and service in community organizations if they compromise journalistic integrity.

- Disclose unavoidable conflicts.

- Be vigilant and courageous about holding those with power accountable.

- Deny favored treatment to advertisers and special interests and resist their pressure to influence news coverage.

- Be wary of sources offering information for favors or money; avoid bidding for news.

BE ACCOUNTABLE

Journalists are accountable to their readers, listeners, viewers and each other. Journalists should:

- Clarify and explain news coverage and invite dialogue with the public over journalistic conduct.

- Encourage the public to voice grievances against the news media.

- Admit mistakes and correct them promptly.

- Expose unethical practices of journalists and the news media.

- Abide by the same high standards to which they hold others.

NOVEL INSIGHTS INTO THE ETHICS OF JOURNALISM
JAY BLACK

Using references and excerpts from novels you will probably recognize, Black identifies some of the most difficult ethical issues in media ethics. What are your general impressions of journalists? Do they correlate with your real-life experiences? Have you had any real-life experiences with journalists? Do you think journalists get a "bad rap" in the popular press, movies, or books?

INTRODUCTION

In the century or so since Kirk Munroe wrote *Under Orders: The Story of a Young Reporter,* as many as three thousand novels have been written with journalists as protagonists. At least one scholarly book has been written on the journalism novel (Howard Good's *Acquainted with the Night*), and several graduate theses have been completed in recent years.

Most of the scholarly and popular writing on the journalist in fiction has focused on a variety of themes: the intrepid reporter—usually male, divorced, and with a drinking problem—who takes on crime and corruption and wins the Pulitzer Prize and/or moves on to edit his own small paper; the gonzo photographer, whose quest to capture "the decisive moment" generally entails personal danger and intrusion into moments of private grief; the small-town journalist, who serves the public interest, whether or not the community appreciates it; the stereotypical editor, typecast in either the fatherly Lou Grant mold or as a curmudgeonly mid-level manager; the Horatio Alger-esque paper carrier, whose work ethic propels him or her to riches; the tough and tormented newswoman, who either gets to the top by practicing "horizontal journalism" or otherwise manages to survive in a male-dominated business; the scandalmonger, who breaks all social rules to pander gossip to the masses; the war correspondent, who puts life in danger to report foreign intrigue; the television journalist, whose glamorous (but often superficial) lifestyle permits movement among the movers and shakers; and the news media owners, who are either community heroes or unconscionable megalomaniacs. Given these stereotypes, it is no wonder the fictional journalist is a ready-made protagonist for novelists who seek to portray interesting characters in a variety of conflict situations. Few occupational roles lead themselves to such treatment, and few novelists can write with insight and passion about their own professions as effectively and naturally as journalists can write about theirs.

Whether journalists should be depicted in gross stereotypes is a question worth raising. Steve Weinberg has written that journalism is seldom the subject of serious literature, and that most journalism novels have given readers a distorted notion of the field. Millions of readers who are interested in journalism but who have limited first-hand experience with how the profession operates have probably formed distorted opinions about the field if their primary exposure is through these books. Some of the books have been bestsellers, in hardback and paperback: Irving Wallace's *The Almighty,* Arnaud De Borchgrave and Robert Moss's *The Spike,* John Grisham's *Pelican Brief,* Arthur Hailey's *The Evening News,* John Katzenbach's *In the Heat of the Summer* and *Just Cause,* and Tom Wolfe's *Bonfire of the Vanities* are examples. The journalistic protagonists in these books are not necessarily the sorts of folks you would want your children to date, let alone emulate. They may be people of action, and they may bring about some social good, but on the whole they are not moral heroes.

Although much has been written about journalism fictional characters, little has been done to systematically analyze their ethics. This short essay limits itself to introducing ethical dilemmas raised in numerous novels in which journalists are central characters and find themselves making "tough calls." I'll introduce some central characters, quote brief passages, and reach some tentative conclusions about how fictional journalists define their professional roles and how they handle conflicts between personal and institutional ethics while dealing with issues of full-disclosure reporting, editorial independence, and harm to sources, audiences, and themselves. The novels used as sources for this paper offer a plethora of insights into questions of accuracy and fairness, objectivity and truthtelling, conflicts of interest, deception, diversity, photojournalism dilemmas, invasion of privacy, relationships with sources, and just about every other interesting dilemma facing journalists. It would take a book-length manuscript to discuss all these topics, so the best I can do at this juncture is to provide a list of fifty novels that are particularly instructive for those wishing to pursue this fascinating literature. Happy hunting.

ROLES AND RULES

Much has been said about the professional role of journalists. In journalism schools, in the trade press, and in scholarly tomes, journalism is depicted as a constitutionally protected commercial enterprise whose primary functions are to (*a*) seek truth and report it fully and accurately, (*b*) while remaining independent of external forces that would control its behavior, (*c*) all the while considering the very real possibilities that much of its activity results in some sorts of harm to individuals and institutions. The task facing journalists, therefore, is to balance those challenges, and to do as much good as possible while minimizing harm; in philosophical terms, to be both beneficent and non-maleficent. At least, that's what real journalists and real journalism students think of their craft. In the world of journalism fiction, it's not always that way. The principles or rules journalists adhere to are certainly not cast in bronze—and generally not in pulp. Moral confusion reigns.

The following excerpts from novels consider the nature of conflicting roles and duties, while raising questions about personal and institutional ethics. (For ease of referencing, each excerpt will be sourced with the quote.)

Statehouse reporter John Cotton, the hero of Tony Hillerman's *The Fly on the Wall,* is one of fictional journalism's most thoughtful characters. Even so, he hasn't completely worked through all of the important questions. One thing he's pretty certain of, however, is that he should not lie to a fellow journalist:

> *Cotton was surprised at himself, and shocked. He was considering whether he should lie. If he did, it would be a professional lie, told to a fellow member of the brotherhood for professional reasons. It would therefore be a violation of taboo. Nothing was written about it in the pressroom rules, and nothing was said about it, ever. But it wasn't done . . . the game had its rules. One evaded. One was secretive. One covered his tracks. But one didn't lie to another newsman. In a profession which risked a hundred mistakes in a working day, and published them on rotary presses, and saw years of being right destroyed by being wrong in one edition, the lie was too dangerous for tolerance. (p. 24)*

The Spike, a cold war right-wing diatribe by Arnaud de Borchgrave and Robert Moss that saw its journalism hero Robert Hockney tossed and turned by first one political faction and then another, describes an interview situation in which Hockney chooses to uphold his newspaper's longstanding policy about off-the-record interviews. His source seems surprised to learn about "rules" for such an enterprise:

> *"If we can go off the record, Mr. Hockney, I might be able to explain a few facts of life to you."*
> *"We have a rule on the paper—"*
> *"That's the first time I've heard of rules in your profession." (p. 199)*

John Katzenbach captured the essence of the journalistic dance in his 1982 novel, *In the Heat of the Summer:*

> *I took down his words, knowing they would find their way to the top of the story. I felt as if I were taking part in an ornate dance, an Elizabethan set filled with dips, bows and flourishes. I knocked on the doors, took down the words. I knew what the neighbors would say; I could have guessed the quotations beforehand. Yet it was an intrinsic part of the ritual of newspaper death. Reporters always ask the neighbors, and the neighbors always say the victims were quiet and kept to themselves. And then the reporters put that in their stories. (p. 193)*

FULL-DISCLOSURE REPORTING

Novelists seem to enjoy waving the banner of the fourth estate, maintaining that journalistic independence is both a curse and a blessing in a system where government and other power institutions are suspect. Damn the torpedoes; full-disclosure reporting ahead!

Arthur Hailey's recent potboiler, *The Evening News,* depicts a well-known anchorman in a personal and professional dilemma. His family has been kidnapped by South American terrorists, and he has pursued the kidnappers and the story simultaneously. At one point a fellow journalist working on the story wonders:

> *Was the public entitled to know whatever an enterprising reporter like himself was able to find out, no matter how the information was obtained?*

Though such questions existed, the plain fact was, Dawson knew, they were none of his business or concern. The rules in the matter were precise and known to all parties involved.

A reporter's responsibility was to write any worthwhile story he found. If he discovered news, his job was not to suppress or modify it in any way, but to write a full and accurate report, then deliver it to the organization that employed him.

At that point what had been written could go to an editor. It was an editor, or editors, who must consider ethics. (p. 402)

Of all the journalism novels that have been written by journalists, rather than by "outsiders" who just happened to select journalism as their story-telling vehicle, several stand out for their emphasis on full-disclosure reporting. Their authors—including Tony Hillerman, who wrote *Fly on the Wall* while still an active journalist—seem to have captured an essential tug of war within the profession. Good examples emerge from John Katzenbach of the *Miami Herald,* Jim DeBrosse of the *Cincinnati Enquirer,* and Jim Wright of the *Bergen (NJ) Record.*

At the conclusion of his murder thriller *In the Heat of the Summer* (which later appeared as a film, *The Mean Season*), Katzenbach has his troubled reporter saying:

I envision the final story—the last story. No more lies, no more half-truths, no more misstatements or misleading information. The real truth: names, places, facts, identities. It will set everything right, I thought. The truth. (pp. 272–73)

A decade later, in his novel *Just Cause,* after Miami journalist Matthew Cowart has been pursuing a story that would win him a Pulitzer prize but turn his life into a living hell, Katzenbach scripts a powerful criticism of journalism:

You know why you won't write that story? I'll tell you why. There are a lot of good reasons, but first off, because you know what you don't have? You don't have any facts. You don't have any evidence. All you have is a crazy combination of events and lies, and I know some editor'll look at all that and think it has no place in the paper. And you know what else you don't have, Mr. Cowart? All newspaper stories are all made up of "according to's" and "police said's" and "spokesmen confirmed's" and all sort of other folks contributing documents and reports, and that's where you get the bones for your story. The rest of the flesh is just the detail that you've seen and the detail that you've heard, and you haven't seen or heard anything important enough to build a story. (p. 354)

The news media's blurring of truth and non-truth, of full-disclosure journalism versus manipulative and selective disclosure, has been captured most effectively by screenwriter Paddy Chayefsky, author of *Network* (novelization by Sam Hedrin). Chayefsky's Howard Beale, "the mad prophet of the airways," yells at his network audience:

Television is not the truth! Television is a goddamned amusement park, that's what television is! Television is a circus, a carnival, a traveling troupe of acrobats and storytellers, singers, and dancers, jugglers, sideshow freaks, lion-tamers and football players! If you want the truth, go to God, go to your guru, go to yourself—because that's the only place you'll ever find any real truth! But, man, you're never going to get any truth from us. We'll tell you anything you want to hear. We lie like hell! (pp. 98–99)

INDEPENDENCE

All else being equal, journalists strive to remain independent of the external forces of control over their activities. This generally means they strive to be free from governmental pressures, but it also entails pressures from various other interest groups and even individual sources who are quick to pollute the channels of communication. Of course, in the world of fiction, some of these conflicts are highly dramatic.

Marvin Kalb and Ted Koppel, two young journalists who teamed up to produce an intriguing tale of Middle East politics (*In the National Interest*), put some harsh comments about journalism into the mouth of a Kissinger-like Secretary of State after the hero shows up with inside information about an upcoming news event which would have had international repercussions:

> "You and your friends in the media think of yourselves as the guardians of our way of life. You know what you are? You're the gravediggers of democracy!" There was icy contempt in his voice.
>
> "There is no such thing as absolute freedom. As soon as a society moves too far in that direction it invites repression. There has to be a limit; and if the press refuses to govern itself, then sooner or later someone else does it for them. That's not a threat. That's one of the immutable laws of history, from which the United States is not exempt. . . . Could you still keep the story off the air?"
>
> "I could," Darius responded coldly, "but I won't." (p. 353)

Former investigative reporter Les Whitten, who worked with muckraker Jack Anderson and later, as a network correspondent, wrote one of the rawest journalism novels. The title, *Conflict of Interest,* says a mouthful. His protagonist, Aubrey Warder, uses seduction, finagling, and even safecracking to bring down the Speaker of the U.S. House of Representatives. After he has been arrested for various missteps, including safecracking, Warder tells a jury:

> "What I'm saying is that the Founding Fathers gave people like me a job to do. It's to keep an eye on the government on behalf of the people. We were told to expose corruption in and outside of government, to tell the people things that the government would rather keep covered up. To set in motion reforms. Of course, this doesn't make the government very happy." (p. 174)

All in all, a journalistic declaration of independence advances a lot of plots in a good many novels. As often as not, it helps set up conflicts which need to be resolved, even if it takes several hundred pages to do so.

MINIMIZING HARM

Telling the truth and remaining independent are hard enough to achieve, but no harder than minimizing the harm caused by the very process of reporting and distributing information. Harm to sources, to subjects, to institutions, to audiences, and even to reporters themselves and their own news media occurs in the world of fiction, just as in reality.

Winston Groom, who went on to fame and fortune with Forrest Gump, tells a fascinating story (*Gone the Sun*) about Beau Gunn, a 40-year-old Vietnam War vet who gets burned out on metropolitan journalism, but comes back to his small southern hometown as editor of the Courier-Democrat. Gunn eventually writes a Pulitzer Prize-winning story involving an old friend charged with murder after having been caught up in an oil-importing scam that involves everybody in town, including Gunn's father. How to do good and minimize harm?

> *A newspaper can be a voice for a whole city. If the newspaper is bad, and if its judgment is bad, if it only represents some of the people, only covers society affairs and business events and fires and crime and disasters, and doesn't get at the root problems, if it doesn't include everybody in its coverage, or slants the news, then it doesn't do any real good, and maybe it does more harm than good.*
>
> *But if a newspaper is good, and if the stories it prints are accurate, true, fair and unbiased, then it assumes a role of leadership in the community and people respect the stories and opinions is that it prints and it gets them to thinking and talking. They don't have to like the stories and opinions, but they've got to respect them and people— at least the majority of them, and I believe this—don't respect arrogance or stupidity or incompetence and, furthermore, they know it when they see it. (p. 192)*

The same issues of beneficence and non-maleficence are treated in novels in which entire metropolitan areas are erupting in violence—and the news media are right at the center of the story. Indeed, as these excerpts show, there may be some question as to whether the media helped cause the rioting.

Edna Buchanan, herself a Pulitzer Prize winner who spent two decades covering the angst of Miami, has turned to the world of fiction to explore some of her passions. The first in a series of Miami journalism novels featuring young Cuban-American reporter Britt Montero is *Contents Under Pressure*. Montero has literally gone through hell to come up with the most powerful story of her career. However, when she returns to the newsroom, she is told that the story will never be released:

> *We have to expose the truth about what happened. The public has a right to know. But, I understand what he was saying. The city had already been through a terrible trauma. The quicker the healing process and rebuilding began, the better for all of us who lived here. My story would bring no one to justice and would only further polarize a divided community. For those reasons, the most important story I ever wrote was never read. (p. 269)*

John Katzenbach (*Just Cause*) has effectively captured the agony of doing good journalism that tries to overcompensate for personal and institutional distress. Editorial writer Matthew Cowart has an encounter with a prison warden who isn't convinced that journalists are capable of causing no harm; a "good story" for a journalist could actually be a matter of life and death for someone else:

> *Everyone always wants the press to get excited about their case. Inmates never think they got a fair shake. They think that maybe if they raise enough of a stink, they'll get a new trial. Happens. That's why prison people like me always hate to see reporters. Hate to see those little pads of paper, those camera crews and lights. Just gets everyone riled up, excited about nothing much. People think it's the loss of freedoms that makes for trouble in prisons. They're wrong. Worse thing by far is expectations getting raised and then smashed. It's just another story for you guys. But for the guys inside, it's their lives you're talking about. (p. 34)*

One could make a case that harm is inevitable in a business that redistributes power among various interest groups, as journalism does. From the above examples, it appears that the costs and benefits of such harm are part of the utilitarian calculus employed by fictional news media. Given that so many of the authors cited have worked as reporters, the line between truth and fiction may be invisible.

CONCLUSION

The image created by this body of literature is that journalism is largely an amoral enterprise. At best, it wallows somewhere in the ethical bog of egoism, subjectivism, and relativism/situationalism. When they broach such ethical constructs as utilitarianism, the authors focus on the hedonic and crass commercialism of the business. In such cases, human profits and losses are calculated just as surely as circulation and advertising gains and losses are calculated by the new cadre of newsroom MBA's.

Occasionally in fiction, the journalist of principle, motivated by virtue and a sense of duty, appears—although often as a foil against his or her own management, and usually at odds with the community. Far more typical is the portrait of the journalist as having more than a touch of sleaze.

If the ethical decision-making processes employed by the journalists of fiction appear convoluted, it may be because even in the real world the profession hasn't done a very good job of figuring these out. Fictional—and real—journalists may not have fully considered the nature of their roles, their obligations, and the consequences of their actions.

Full-disclosure reporting, maintaining independence, and minimizing harm have been proposed as guiding principles for journalists. But how justifiable are some of the means used to reach them? Is it possible to be a truthteller even if it means having to lie and deceive to report that truth? Can one remain independent while encountering and falling prey to conflicts of interest? Can harm be minimized in an environment of ignorance about the ripples caused by reporting? These questions are explored with wit and insight in novels about journalism.

Fifty novels with insights into journalism ethics:

Edna Buchanan, *Contents Under Pressure* (New York: Hyperion, 1992)

Philip Caputo, *DelCorso's Gallery* (New York: Holt, Rinehart & Winston, 1983)

Elliott Chaze, *Mr. Yesterday* (New York: Scribner's, 1984)

Arnaud De Borchgrave & Robert Moss, *The Spike* (New York: Avon, 1980)

Jim DeBrosse, *The Serpentine Wall* (New York: St. Martin's Press, 1988)

Charles Dickinson, *Rumor Has It* (New York: William Morrow, 1991)

Allen Drury, *Anna Hastings* (New York: William Murow, 1977)

Jack Early, *Razzamatazz* (New York: Franklin Watts, 1985)

Loren Estleman, *Whiskey River* (New York: Bantam, 1980)

Howard Fast, *The Pledge* (Boston: Houghton Mifflin, 1988)

John Feinstein, *Running Mates* (New York: Villard Books, 1992)

Richard Ford, *The Sportswriter* (New York: Vintage Books, 1986)

John Grisham, *The Pelican Brief* (New York: Doubleday, 1992)

Winston Groom, *Gone The Sun* (New York: Doubleday, 1988)

Leonard Gross, *Mirror* (New York: Harper & Row, 1981)

Arthur Hailey, *The Evening News* (New York: Doubleday, 1990)

Pete Hamill, *Dirty Laundry* (New York: Bantam, 1978)

Jean Heller, *Maximum Impact* (New York: Forge, 1993)

Sam Hendrin, *Network* (New York: Pocket Books, 1976)

Carl Hiaasen, *Native Tongue* (New York: Knopf, 1991)

———, *Tourist Season* (New York: Warner, 1986)

Tony Hillerman, *The Fly on the Wall* (New York: Avon, 1971)

Sam Hodges, *B-Four* (New York: St. Martin's, 1992)

Dan Jenkins, *Fast Copy* (New York: Simon & Schuster, 1988)

———, *You Gotta Play Hurt* (New York: Simon & Schuster, 1991)

Marvin Kalb & Ted Koppel, *In the National Interest* (New York: Simon & Schuster, 1977)

Jon Katz, *Sign Off* (New York: Bantam, 1991)

John Katzenbach, *In the Heat of the Summer* (New York: Ballentine, 1982)

———, *Just Cause* (New York: Putnam, 1992)

William Kotzwinkle, *Midnight Examiner* (Boston: Houghton Mifflin, 1989)

C. J. Koch, *The Year of Living Dangerously* (New York: Penguin, 1978)

Daniel Lynch, *Yellow* (New York: Walker, 1992)

J. J. Maloney, *I Speak for the Dead* (New York: Charter, 1982)

Graham Masterton, *Headlines* (New York: St. Martin's, 1986)

Peter McCabe, *City of Lies* (New York: William Morrow, 1993)

Al Morgan, *The Whole World Is Watching* (New York: Stein & Day, 1972)

James Paisner, *Obit* (New York: Penguin, 1990)

Cara Saylor Polk, *Images* (New York: St. Martin's, 1986)

Barbara Raskin, *Current Affairs* (New York: Ivy Books, 1990)

Wilfrid Sheed, *The Hack* (New York: Random House, 1963)

Matt & Bonnie Taylor, *Neon Flamingo* (New York: St. Martin's, 1987)

Calvin Trillin, *The Floater* (New Haven & New York: Ticknor & Fields, 1980)

Irving Wallace, *The Almighty* (New York: Dell, 1982)

Donald E. Westlake, *Trust Me on This* (New York: The Mysterious Press, 1988)

Suzy Wetlaufer, *Judgment Call* (New York: William Morrow, 1992)

Les Whitten, *Conflict of Interest* (New York: Leisure Books, 1991)

Tom Wicker, *Donovan's Wife* (New York: William Morrow, 1992)

Tom Wolfe, *Bonfire of the Vanities* (New York: Farrar, Straus, Giroux, 1987)

Jim Wright, *The Last Frame* (New York: Carroll & Graf, 1990)

————, *The Last Man Standing* (New York: Carroll & Graf, 1991)

Chapter 13

ETHICS AND THE ENVIRONMENT

Those who would take over the earth
And shape it to their will
Never, I notice, succeed.
The earth is like a vessel so sacred
That at the mere approach of the profane
It is marred
And when they reach out their fingers it is gone.

LAO TZU

When I was studying law at a law school considered to be rather capitalistically oriented, my law and economics professors would usually point to the environment as the one area where the free market might not provide the *best* result. That's because each one of us, individually, is not so affected by one piece of trash or one scintilla of pollution in the air. To the contrary, if we balance our personal interests, it is often in our self-interest to pollute, rather than to clean up. On the other hand (and we have all heard this argument at one time or another), if we *all* polluted, even a small amount, the world would be a very dirty place in which we would not like to live. And that may be where we stand today.

I conduct a short little experiment in my ethics class where I spill a bit of water on the floor from a soda can. The students can't believe that I am doing this and ignoring it. Then I ask them to go in the hallway just after classes have started and to observe similar behavior by the students. I don't set this up beforehand but, invariably, they *do* see this type of behavior in the hallway. Why does this happen? Do people think that others will pick up after them? Strolling across campus or in your office, do you *always* stop to pick up waste off of the floor? Why do you do this or why do you refrain from doing this?

From the moment a firm begins to produce, service, manufacture, or create, the operations of that firm impact the environment. Imagine the small decisions made by a company: Does it pack its glassware in plastic bubbles or corrugated wrapping? Does it publish a catalogue once a month or once a year? Is that catalogue published on paper or only through the internet? Does it meet with the community before choosing a disposal system? Each of these decisions will have an impact on our physical world, and it is critical to understand the law as it relates to the environment, as well as to be aware of the ethics of each decision.

And our decisions affect not only those around us, but others around the world. In 1991, Saddam Hussein soiled the Persian Gulf with the largest oil spill in history. Exxon has spent an estimated $3.5 billion in trying to clean up after the 1989 tragedy of the Exxon Valdez oil spill in Alaska. A considerable expanse of the former Soviet Union will remain uninhabitable for years as a result of the 1986 Chernobyl nuclear power plant accident.

Although the earth is a natural recycler of wastes—a very effective garbage dump— its ability to successfully neutralize the cumulative refuse of modern society is finite. Some concerns about pollution are centuries old, but the upsurge in population and increased industrialization and urbanization in the last 100 years have concentrated ever-increasing amounts of waste matter in small areas and put much greater pressure on the assimilative capabilities of the planet. Further, because of improved understanding of how various waste materials affect the environment, the general public and especially business decision makers are aware of pollution problems and interested in solving them.

But Who's to Pay?   Both of these stakeholders are understandably concerned, however, about who will pay for the costs of environmental awareness. As history has shown us, left alone, many firms are quite willing to pollute the environment. The additional damage to the environment caused by the acts of one firm may not be severe. Therefore, that one firm may not be persuaded to take action to prevent this damage. The cost of this damage seems outweighed by the cost to ensure that the environment is *not* harmed. In those cases where the acts of one firm do not have an extreme impact on the environment, but the same acts by a number of firms *would* have an extreme impact, it is arguable that the government must step in to regulate those acts. The government believes that it has no choice but to regulate the operations of businesses in order to maintain a clean and healthy environment.

For example, without regulation, a firm may consider that dumping its garbage into a canal is no big deal. In fact, perhaps the slight amount of garbage that this firm dumps *is* no big deal. However, if every firm were allowed to dump this amount, the canal would become excessively and irreversibly polluted. This situation may warrant government intervention. Or consider the possibility that we may all prefer less-costly, though more polluting cars. In this scenario, are the rights of future generations protected? They probably would have preferred that we were more careful so that their air would be cleaner.

Pollution, in this discussion, would be categorized by economists as an "externality." Wilfred Beckerman describes the economic analysis as follows:

> [T]he costs of pollution are not always borne fully, if at all, by the polluter. . . . Naturally, he has no incentive to economize in the use [of the environment] in the same way that he has for other factors of production that carry a cost, such as labor or capital. . . . This defect of the price mechanism needs to be corrected by governmental action in order to eliminate excessive pollution.[1]

Business certainly is not the sole contributor to environmental pollution. Individual citizens are primarily responsible for particulate matter discharged by wood-burning stoves, indoor pollution from cigarette smoking, and air pollution caused by our national one-worker-per-car commuting habits. Most forms of pollution, however, probably do have some business connection—whether direct or indirect.

Are there solutions for these problems which are acceptable to all stakeholders concerned? Most people want a cleaner environment, yet the free market apparently is not of sufficient strength to guide the economy in that direction. The problem is not a failure in pricing system theory, but rather that the pricing system works to perfection, albeit in the wrong directions. This inconvenience can be traced to what economists call the "externality," "free good," or "commons" problem. Simply stated, producers have used the environment as a free garbage dump. In effect, producers can pollute a river and pass the costs (in the form of dirty water, dead fish, disease, and so forth) onto society as a whole. If a good can be obtained at no cost, an economist or a businessperson would be inclined to use as much of the "free good" as possible, and producers have done just that. There is no pricing incentive to minimize pollution if pollution has no direct cost to the company; in fact, the incentive is to maximize pollution. In this instance, the welfare of individuals acting in their own private interests does not coincide with the general good.

---

1. Wilfred Beckerman, "Public Utilities Fortnightly," cited in Robert Solomon, *The New World of Business* (Lanham, MD: Rowman & Littlefield: 1994), p. 319.

Collective Good   Another way in which an economist might examine the problem is as a *collective good.* If the citizens want a clean environment, the market would presumably reflect that desire by paying nonpolluting companies higher prices for their goods. Unfortunately, the benefits of clean air and water are not restricted to those paying for them through higher prices, because equal benefits are bestowed on those persons still trading (at lower prices) with polluting companies. Thus a clean environment benefits everyone equally, regardless of each individual's contribution toward it. A rational utility-maximizing strategy for each person, then, is to patronize cheaper, polluting firms to the exclusion of the more expensive nonpolluters, despite the desire of society for a clean environment. Therefore industries have no incentive not to pollute. Externalities and collective goods are instances of market failure.

And What of the Law?   Obviously, international environmental problems cannot be cured merely by passing a new regulation in this country. Increasingly, the nations of the world are reaching understandings about cleansing the globe. In June 1992, environmental concerns drew together in Rio de Janeiro, Brazil, the largest gathering of heads of state in history. That remarkable assemblage for the Earth Summit testifies to the increasing global recognition of environmental problems and their critical role in international economic development and trade. Consider also the 1990 revision to the Montreal Protocol, a global environmental accord: "Driven by disturbing new evidence of a widening hole in the Earth's ozone layer, representatives of 53 nations agreed . . . to ban major ozone-destroying chemicals by the year 2000."

Similarly, in 1994, 64 nations added teeth to the 1990 Basel Convention (curbing transnational toxic waste shipment) by agreeing to immediately stop dumping toxic waste in developing countries. The United States, feeling, among other things, that certain materials such as scrap metal could properly be sent abroad for recycling if the receiving governments agree, has not ratified the Basel Convention.

Our steady, even spectacular, strides forward in environmental protection legislation have not dispelled the view, particularly among economists and businesspeople, that legislation is sometimes not the best remedy for environmental problems. To them, pollution control is not so much a matter of law as of economics. They believe that with proper incentives, the market will, in many instances, prove superior to legislation in preventing and correcting environmental problems. For example, twenty years ago, 164 pounds of metal were required to create 1,000 soda cans. In 1995, manufacturers have discovered better, more efficient uses of resources and now use only 35 pounds of metal for the same number of cans. In fact, The Heartland Institute, a conservative think tank based in Chicago, reports that air quality was improving as fast or faster before the Clean Air Act as it has since that time.

The general idea of economic efficiency and proper incentives is also well illustrated by New York City's efforts to deal with its daily production of 385 tons of sludge, which cannot legally be dumped into the ocean and which overwhelms local landfill capacity. Bio Gro Systems of Annapolis, Maryland, ships 100 tons of sludge daily by rail from New York City to Colorado and Arizona, where farmers are now on waiting lists to have the potent fertilizers spread on their land. The city pays Bio Gro but the sludge is free to farmers, whose reliance on chemical fertilizers has now been reduced.

Cost-Benefit   From the free market point of view, environmental legislation very often imposes unacceptable costs. *Fortune* asked, "How much is America overpaying for environmental regulations?" In 1990, our total bill for federal air and water legislation was estimated to be $320 billion, of which $79 billion came in direct costs while the balance was the result of reduced job growth, reduced capital formation, and lower savings. According to economists Michael Hazilla and Raymond Kopp, those costs resulted in a 5.8 percent reduction in the gross national product. Some of these costs appear to be excessive. For example, Brookings fellow Robert Crandall has calculated that solid and toxic waste cleanup regulations cost $5 to $9 billion annually. If that money saves half of the 1,100 additional annual cancers that the EPA attributes to the waste, the cost per cancer case prevented would be $10 to $18 million.

Firms may reap results in other ways, as well. The market may support the efforts of environmentally conscious companies precisely *because* they're environmentally conscious. Consider the progress of Patagonia, Inc., the outerwear manufacturer whose sales increased by 20 percent in its last fiscal year. "Its founders and sole owners, Yvon Chouinard and his wife, Malinda, are determined to create a business that is successful in ways far different from what any business school will teach young prodigies." Patagonia has a list of five-year environmental goals (dating to 1994) which include the elimination of all solid waste sent to landfills from domestic facilities and the inclusion of environmental costs in accounting and production systems and decisions. Chouinard justifies his approach as follows:

> *I'm a pessimist about the fate of civilization. Ever since I can remember we've been losing on the environmental front, and all indicators say we are still losing now. Gains we make are wiped out by development or population growth. So, I'm pessimistic and I feel responsible to do all that I can. I figure the best tool I have to help the environment is this company.*

So, in helping the environment, Chouinard has been able to post earnings unmatched by many other firms!

One possible solution to remedy our environmental balance sheet and return us to a true free market would be to leave the risks of unintended (as well as intended) pollution to the insurance industry. A company could simply insure itself against claims of pollution and injured parties would sue the offending firm through its insurance company for restitution. In this way, firms who are more likely to suffer claims would have high insurance premiums, thus encouraging them to reduce their polluting behavior. Firms that did not have a history of polluting would have lower insurance premiums, thus awarding them a benefit for protecting the environment. The government could require a bond from companies that continue to engage in environmentally risky activities, similar to workers' compensation statutes. The end goals of accountability and responsibility would therefore be served.

A Balance?   Of course, unbridled faith in the free market is not likely to be in our long-term best interests. Chile's experience under General Augusto Pinochet from 1973 to 1990 illustrates the risk. Pinochet put his faith in the free market. With privatization and deregulation, he brought Chile the most vibrant economy in South America. However, many argue that Pinochet, a dictator, failed to respect the individual property rights of his citizens. In addition, now that Pinochet is gone, the environmental price of unregulated growth is becoming apparent. Forests, streams, and valleys have been plundered. The result, as described in *Time* magazine, is most apparent in the smog-enshrouded capital, Santiago:

> *A thick layer of contaminants settles almost daily over the city, trapped by cold air and mountains on all sides. The causes of the filth: haphazard development and an out-of-control bus system that Pinochet began deregulating in 1975. Two thirds of the smog's harmful elements come from the 11,000 privately owned buses that spew diesel fumes through the city. The government bought out 2,600 of the worst offenders. But pollution still reached lethal levels for two days in July, forcing the government to shut schools and factories and to warn parents to keep their children indoors.*

The readings that follow present a variety of perspectives on the issue of responsibility and accountability for the environment and the corporate response. Should firms be held to a higher, similar, or lower standard than individuals? What tools might or should a firm use to assist it in its decision-making process? Assuming *no* government regulation, if you were beginning a firm today, how would you handle its environmental responsibility?

Children's book author Dr. Seuss offers his concern for a world without individual or government protection of the environment in his story of the Lorax: The Once-lers have come to the land of the Truffula trees, known for their bright colored tufts. The Once-lers cut down a Truffula trees to knit thneeds, a fine something that all people need.

> "Mister" he said with a sawdusty sneeze,
> "I am the Lorax. I speak for the trees.
> I speak for the trees, for the trees have no tongues,
> And I'm asking you, sire, at the top of my lungs"—
> He was very upset as he shouted and puffed—
> *"What's that THING you've made out of my Trufulla tuft?"*

After the world is turned upside down and the environment is ruined with thneed production, the manufacturer laments:

> Now all that was left 'neath the bad-smelling sky
> was my big empty factory . . .
> the Lorax . . .
> and I.

> The Lorax said nothing. Just gave me a glance . . .
> just gave me a sad, sad backward glance . . .
> as he lifted himself by the seat of his pants.
> And I'll never forget the grim look on his face
> when he heisted himself and took leave of this place,
> through a hole in the smog, without leaving a trace.

> And all that the Lorax left here in this mess
> was a small pile of rocks, with one word . . .
> "UNLESS."
> Whatever *that* meant, well, I just couldn't guess.

The word was explained to the manufacturer/narrator by the Once-ler who tells the reader:

> "UNLESS someone like you
> cares a whole awful lot,
> nothing is going to get better.
> It's not.

Take heed, Dr. Seuss seems to be telling us all, or be wary of what darkness may fall.

SHORT HYPOTHETICAL CASE

After being unemployed for several months, you've just started driving for a local transport company. The company transports and treats chemical waste. Disposal costs have doubled in the past year, putting a squeeze on your firm's profits. You pull in late one evening with a truckload of chemical waste. The supervisor is the only one at the plant. He tells you to drain the truck into a pipe at the back of the lot rather than into the normal holding tank. The tank is already full, he says. You find out later that the pipe dumps waste directly into a nearby creek. What do you do?

Hypotheticals were written by Catherine Haselden and are included in her manuscript "The Ethics Game."

PUBLIC RELATIONS AND CORPORATE ENVIRONMENTALISM

SUSTAINABLE PR

David Shenk

Shenk discusses the notion that the environment can be marketed as a "distinct bottom-line advantage," as opposed to the concept that environmental awareness might really be such a business advantage. Are we simply slaves to marketing programs in connection with the environment because we know so little about the actual impact of businesses on our physical world?

The flighty excess of the Reagan years has given way to an era of stolid pragmatism, and public relations experts—the high priests of the Information Age—are bravely navigating the transition for us. Take the environment. "Gone is the idealistic 'Save the Whales' mentality of the 1980s, a period when companies had money to burn" on conservation, explains *O'Dwyer's PR Services Report.* "Environmental communications has come of age in the lean '90s. . . . Successful PR people will be those who can blend the cold-hearted reality of 1990s economics with the 1970s touching though somewhat naive concern for Mother Earth."

That fanciful '80s notion of "sustainable development" simply does not gibe with quarterly earnings pressure, so PR professionals have come up with a viable alternative which they proudly call "Sustainable PR." "The challenge," reads a Hill & Knowlton ad touting their in-house *Green Team,* "is to make the environment a distinct bottom-line advantage."

Here's how it works. In the '70s, Rockwell International might have foolishly assumed that it would eventually have to *clean up* its 166 separate hazardous waste sites in Rocky Flats, Colorado (including the infamous "Hillside 881," reportedly the most toxic site in the country).

Touching, but very naive. In the '90s, the company opts instead for a more economical demonstration of its deep commitment to the environment: an advertisement coupling the Rockwell logo to an Ansel Adams's photographic celebration of the earth in all its pristine and rugged glory. ("I saw that and went 'Achh!' " one Rockwell employee admits. "It seems kind of contradictory—but that's just my editorial opinion.")

The numbers show that Americans want sustainable *something.* 78% of consumers have demonstrated a willingness to switch to products perceived as environmentally-sensitive, and in recent years the Green product market has skyrocketed to an annual $121.5 billion. With that kind of money at stake, the last thing we want to be is *naive.* The old unsophisticated us may have assumed that adopting a pro-environmental posture in the workplace would require a significant investment—modernized production facilities, recycled paper products, etc.; the new, more cunning us knows that a deep green corporate hue can be as simple as a fresh coat of paint. Does the name *Exxon Valdez* now rub you the wrong way? Exxon's green consultants thought it might, so they've changed it to the more huggable *SeaRiver Mediterranean.* Same single-hulled oil tanker; new, swarthy mien. Look for it off a rocky coast near you.

Does auto exhaust get you down? General Motors and Chrysler would like to try to assuage your guilt when you buy your next Jeep or Geo by planting a tree in your name. Here's hoping this gesture fires your ecological drive: you'd have to plant another 733 trees on your own to make up for the actual amount of CO2 emitted during your average ten-year car life. *Achh!* (But that's just our editorial opinion.)

Luscious images of green rolling hills, sparkling rivers, copper canyons—why would anyone want to interfere with a good-hearted effort to bring a little nature back into the hectic consumer lifestyle? It turns out that the Federal Trade Commission is a real curmudgeon when it comes to marketing regular old GE lightbulbs as "energy-efficient." They ordered the company to cease the false claim. Also, no more will you find the upbeat three-arrow recycling logo on White Castle hamburger boxes, or the "chlorine-free" claim on Mr. Coffee filters. Technically speaking, neither one is. And since Ciba-Geigy's *Basus Flea & Tick Spray* actually does sort of contain some ozone-offending chemicals, the company had to drop the warm and sunny "ozone friendly" label. [From the *Ethics, Inc.* archive: In the '70s, Ciba-Geigy pushed the toxic envelope by testing herbicides on human subjects in Egypt and India].

With the FTC meddling about, the eco image business isn't the sandbox it was in the mid-'80s. "PR pros are less giddy about the growth prospects for environmental PR than they were a few years back," laments an *O'Dwyer's* editorial. But don't count savvy companies out. They may not be interested in actual ecology ("no matter how idealistic a company sounds," reports *O'Dwyer's,* "it puts the bottom line ahead of cleaning up its mess. . . . Does the cost of sick days and hospitalizations due to exposure from the dirt outweigh a payroll?"), but with all these communications professionals about, there's more than one way to maintain a green glow while you thin a forest.

Purchase some credibility outright, for instance. As *O'Dwyer's* details: "Cash-rich companies, PR people say, are funding hard-up environmentalists groups in the belief the imprimatur of activists will go a long way in improving their reputation among environmentally aware consumers." Known as "cause-related marketing," this is Sustainable PR's marketing cousin. "It's a trade," explains Jim Andrews, editorial director of International Events Group, a specialist in the field. "You give money and you use the nonprofit's logo, and you are acknowledged as more than a small line on the cause's annual report. You're almost . . . using *the cause* as a form of media."

Or try your hand at that *SeaRiver* name game. Meet the National Wetlands Coalition, a group of such renowned nature bunnies as Amoco, Arco, Chevron, Conoco, Exxon, Mobil, Shell and Texaco. As the name intimates, these are companies with a genuine interest in Wetlands conservation: *they want to stop it.* During the Bush administration, these faux-ecologists managed to redefine the national definition of wetlands, reducing the amount of land under federal protection by 50%.

The Environmental Conservation Organization (ECO) is another such group with an ironic *nom de green*. Like you and me, this group of real estate developers is disgusted by erosion and pollution. "Efforts to save the environment," its literature proclaims, "should not *erode* fundamental constitutional rights nor *pollute* our free-enterprise economy." Call your congressman now to help conserve the delicate Hardhat ecosystem.

There are many others—the Evergreen Foundation (a timber consortium), the Information Council for the Environment (coal, mining and public utilities), Oregonians for Food and Shelter (pesticide manufacturers), the Sea Lion Defense Fund (the Alaska fishing industry, fighting to *diminish* the Sea Lion's food sources), and a sentimental favorite, the U.S. Council for Energy Awareness (the nuclear power industry).

And, of course, Citizens For the Environment, a "grassroots environmental group that promotes market-based methods for protecting our environment." CFE has no citizen members, per se, unless you count corporate citizens like Amoco, Boeing, Chevron, Coors, GE, GM, Georgia-Pacific, and so on. This group also lobbies against environmental regulations, using the argument that big industry always has been and always will be the most pro-environmental force around.

Let's be open minded about this—maybe they have a point. Perhaps Dupont Chairman Edgar Woolard signaled an abrupt corporate turnaround with his shocking 1990 pronouncement that "we subscribe to the concept of sustainable development as outlined in the report of the World Commission on Environment and Development prepared under the leadership of former Prime Minister Bruntland of Norway." That same year, Dupont released their famous "Applause" commercial with penguins, sea otters, dolphins and gulls all clapping, flapping and squawking joyously to Beethoven's ever-mirthful "Ode to Joy," while a narrator informs us that Dupont has just placed orders for several double-hulled oil tankers. "Dupont. Better things for better living."

Then again, maybe not. Dupont's announcement is touching, but shareholders should be assured that the nation's number one polluter hasn't forgotten how to be cold-hearted in the lean '90s. They still dump chemicals into rivers and oceans, pump ash into the sky and inject toxic waste into underground geologic formations like no other American corporation. Around the time that Woolard announced his new enthusiasm for ecobusiness, he also unequivocally termed his company's 1.6 million pounds of pollution *per day* "safe."

Achh. Seems kind of contradictory. But that's just an editorial opinion.

RELATED WEB SITES

Cascadia Planet: www.tnews.com

Eco-Net: www.igc.org/igc/econet/index.html

"GARNET HILL HONORED FOR RECYCLING EFFORTS"

<small>GARNET HILL</small>

Every time I get a package from a mail-order company, I also receive a small blurb about how their packaging or marketing is environmentally correct. Would this claim encourage you to purchase more from this particular mail order catalog or to feel better about your environmentalism? Perhaps, or perhaps not. But there must be some incentive for firms to publish this material. Perhaps it is for public awareness, so that we (as consumers) become more aware of our impact on our physical world. To that perceived end, Garnet Hill catalog includes the following material in their shipments.

WE THOUGHT YOU WOULD BE INTERESTED

"Garnet Hill of Franconia has been presented with an Environmental Excellence Award for its recycling and waste reduction efforts by WasteCap of New Hampshire. Garnet Hill is a direct mail company specializing in products made from natural fibers. It recycles 64 tons of cardboard and over 4 tons of office paper per year.

"Sponsored by the New Hampshire Business and Industry association, WasteCap of New Hampshire assists companies with solid waste reduction and recycling efforts. Participating companies have significantly reduced purchasing, handling and disposal costs associated with solid waste" (*The Courier,* Littleton, 10/95).

Garnet Hill takes recycling seriously. As one of only four businesses in the state to receive this award, we are proud of our achievement. In addition to the efforts recognized above, we utilize recycled materials in all of our packaging. Our order form and all of our stationery is also printed on recycled stock. We have never used plastic 'peanuts' or plastic packing tape and recently eliminated the use of clear plastic tape over our shipping labels.

We are aware of the environmental challenges that face our industry and are doing whatever we can to reduce the amount of solid waste generated by our day-to-day operations. You can help us in this effort. If you are receiving more than one catalog with the same cover or would like to be removed from our mailing list please let us know. Call (800) 622-6216 and we will be happy to help you help us reduce waste.

Thanks for your patronage. We look forward to serving you again soon.

P.S. Please remember that our shipping boxes can be recycled. They also make great storage containers! The plastic bags containing the merchandise can also be reused in many different ways. They make great ice bags and can be used to store all sorts of household "stuff."

CORPORATE ENVIRONMENTAL RESPONSIBILITY

BUSINESS AND ENVIRONMENTAL ETHICS
W. MICHAEL HOFFMAN

Hoffman highlights the various influences in the relationship between business and its environment. He cites a claim by philosopher Norman Bowie that businesses have an obligation to their environment above and beyond that required by law, then disagrees and offers support for his perspective.

. . . Concern over the environment is not new. Warnings came out of the 1960s in the form of burning rivers, dying lakes, and oil-fouled oceans. Radioactivity was found in our food, DDT in mother's milk, lead and mercury in our water. Every breath of air in the North American hemisphere was reported as contaminated. Some said these were truly warnings from Planet Earth of eco-catastrophe, unless we could find limits to our growth and changes in our lifestyle.

Over the past few years Planet Earth began to speak to us even more loudly than before, and we began to listen more than before. The message was ominous, somewhat akin to God warning Noah. It spoke through droughts, heat waves, and forest fires, raising fears of global warming due to the buildup of carbon dioxide and other gases in the atmosphere. It warned us by raw sewage and medical wastes washing up on our beaches, and by devastating oil spills—one despoiling Prince William Sound and its wildlife to such an extent that it made us weep. It spoke to us through increased skin cancers and discoveries of holes in the ozone layer caused by our use of chlorofluoro-carbons. It drove its message home through the rapid and dangerous cutting and burning of our primitive forests at the rate of one football field a second, leaving us even more vulnerable to greenhouse gases like carbon dioxide and eliminating scores of irreplaceable species daily. It rained down on us in the form of acid, defoliating our forests and poisoning our lakes and streams. Its warnings were found on barges roaming the seas for places to dump tons of toxic incinerator ash. And its message exploded in our faces at Chernobyl and Bhopal, reminding us of past warnings at Three Mile Island and Love Canal. . . .

W. Michael Hoffman, "Business and Environmental Ethics," reprinted by permission of the author.

I

In a 1989 keynote address before the "Business, Ethics and the Environment" conference at the Center for Business Ethics, Norman Bowie offered some answers to the first two questions.

> *Business does not have an obligation to protect the environment over and above what is required by law; however, it does have a moral obligation to avoid intervening in the political arena in order to defeat or weaken environmental legislation.*[1]

I disagree with Bowie on both counts.

Bowie's first point is very Friedmanesque.[2] The social responsibility of business is to produce goods and services and to make profit for its shareholders, while playing within the rules of the market game. These rules, including those to protect the environment, are set by the government and the courts. To do more than is required by these rules is, according to this position, unfair to business. In order to perform its proper function, every business must respond to the market and operate in the same arena as its competitors. As Bowie puts this:

> *An injunction to assist in solving societal problems [including depletion of natural resources and pollution] makes impossible demands on a corporation because, at the practical level, it ignores the impact that such activities have on profit.*[3]

If, as Bowie claims, consumers are not willing to respond to the cost and use of environmentally friendly products and actions, then it is not the responsibility of business to respond or correct such market failure.

Bowie's second point is a radical departure from this classical position in contending that business should not lobby against the government's process to set environmental regulations. To quote Bowie:

> *Far too many corporations try to have their cake and eat it too. They argue that it is the job of government to correct for market failure and then they use their influence and money to defeat or water down regulations designed to conserve and protect the environment.*[4]

Bowie only recommends this abstinence of corporate lobbying in the case of environmental regulations. He is particularly concerned that politicians, ever mindful of their reelection status, are already reluctant to pass environmental legislation which has huge immediate costs and in most cases very long-term benefits. This makes the obligations of business to refrain from opposing such legislation a justified special case.

I can understand why Bowie argues these points. He seems to be responding to two extreme approaches, both of which are inappropriate. Let me illustrate these extremes by the following two stories.

At the Center's First National Conference on Business Ethics, Harvard Business School Professor George Cabot Lodge told of a friend who owned a paper company on the banks of a New England stream. On the first Earth Day in 1970, his friend was converted to the cause of environmental protection. He became determined to stop his company's pollution of the stream, and marched off to put his new-found religion into action. Later, Lodge learned his friend went broke, so he went to investigate. Radiating a kind of ethical purity, the friend told Lodge that he spent millions to stop the pollution and thus could no longer compete with other firms that did not follow his example. So the company went under, 500 people lost their jobs, and the stream remained polluted.

When Lodge asked why his friend hadn't sought help from the state or federal government for stricter standards for everyone, the man replied that was not the American way, that government should not interfere with business activity, and that private enterprise could do the job alone. In fact, he felt it was the social responsibility of business to solve environmental problems, so he was proud that he had set an example for others to follow.

The second story portrays another extreme. A few years ago "Sixty Minutes" interviewed a manager of a chemical company that was discharging effluent into a river in upstate New York. At the time, the dumping was legal, though a bill to prevent it was pending in Congress. The manager remarked that he hoped the bill would pass, and that he certainly would support it as a responsible citizen. However, he also said he approved of his company's efforts to defeat the bill and of the firm's policy of dumping wastes in the meantime. After all, isn't the proper role of business to make as much profit as possible within the bounds of law? Making the laws—setting the rules of the game—is the role of government, not business. While wearing his business hat the manager had a job to do, even if it meant doing something that he strongly opposed as a private citizen.

Both stories reveal incorrect answers to the questions posed earlier, the proof of which is found in the fact that neither the New England stream nor the New York river was made any cleaner. Bowie's points are intended to block these two extremes. But to avoid these extremes, as Bowie does, misses the real managerial and ethical failure of the stories. Although the paper company owner and the chemical company manager had radically different views of the ethical responsibilities of business, both saw business and government performing separate roles, and neither felt that business ought to cooperate with government to solve environmental problems.[5]

If the business ethics movement has led us anywhere in the past fifteen years, it is to the position that business has an ethical responsibility to become a more active partner in dealing with social concerns. Business must creatively find ways to become a part of solutions, rather than being a part of problems. Corporations can and must develop a conscience, as Ken Goodpaster and others have argued—and this includes an environmental conscience.[6] Corporations should not isolate themselves from participation in solving our environmental problems, leaving it up to others to find the answers and to tell them what not to do.

Corporations have special knowledge, expertise, and resources which are invaluable in dealing with the environmental crisis. Society needs the ethical vision and cooperation of all its players to solve its most urgent problems, especially one that involves the very survival of the planet itself. Business must work with government to find appropriate solutions. It should lobby for good environmental legislation and lobby against bad legislation, rather than isolating itself from the legislative process as Bowie suggests. It should not be ethically quixotic and try to go it alone, as our paper company owner tried to do, nor should it be ethically inauthentic and fight against what it believes to be environmentally sound policy, as our chemical company manager tried to do. Instead business must develop and demonstrate moral leadership.

There are examples of corporations demonstrating such leadership, even when this has been a risk to their self-interest. In the area of environmental moral leadership one might cite DuPont's discontinuing its Freon products, a $750-million-a-year business, because of their possible negative effects on the ozone layer, and Procter & Gamble's manufacture of concentrated fabric softener and detergents which require less packaging. But some might argue, as Bowie does, that the real burden for environmental change lies with consumers, not with corporations. If we as consumers are willing to accept the harm done to the environment by favoring environmentally unfriendly products, corporations have no moral obligation to change so long as they obey environmental law. This is even more the case, so the argument goes, if corporations must take risks or sacrifice profits to do so. . . .

Even Bowie admits that perhaps business has a responsibility to educate the public and promote environmentally responsible behavior. But I am suggesting that corporate moral leadership goes far beyond public educational campaigns. It requires moral vision, commitment, and courage, and involves risk and sacrifice. I think business is capable of such a challenge. Some are even engaging in such a challenge. Certainly the business ethics movement should do nothing short of encouraging such leadership. I feel morality demands such leadership.

II

If business has an ethical responsibility to the environment which goes beyond obeying environmental law, what criterion should be used to guide and justify such action? Many corporations are making environmentally friendly decisions where they see there are profits to be made by doing so. They are wrapping themselves in green where they see a green bottom line as a consequence. . . .

The frequent strategy of the new environmentalists is to get business to help solve environmental problems by finding profitable or virtually costless ways for them to participate. They feel that compromise, not confrontation, is the only way to save the earth. By using the tools of the free enterprise system, they are in search of win-win solutions, believing that such solutions are necessary to take us beyond what we have so far been able to achieve.

I am not opposed to these efforts; in most cases I think they should be encouraged. There is certainly nothing wrong with making money while protecting the environment, just as there is nothing wrong with feeling good about doing one's duty. But if business is adopting or being encouraged to adopt the view that good environmentalism is good business, then I think this poses a danger for the environmental ethics movement—a danger which has an analogy in the business ethics movement.

As we all know, the position that good ethics is good business is being used more and more by corporate executives to justify the building of ethics into their companies and by business ethics consultants to gain new clients. . . .

Is the rationale that good ethics is good business a proper one for business ethics? I think not. One thing that the study of ethics has taught us over the past 2,500 years is that being ethical may on occasion require that we place the interests of others ahead of or at least on par with our own interests. And this implies that the ethical thing to do, the morally right thing to do, may not be in our own self-interest. What happens when the right thing is not the best thing for the business?

Although in most cases good ethics may be good business, it should not be advanced as the only or even the main reason for doing business ethically. When the crunch comes, when ethics conflicts with the firm's interests, any ethics program that has not already faced up to this possibility is doomed to fail because it will undercut the rationale of the program itself. We should promote business ethics, not because good ethics is good business, but because we are morally required to adopt the moral point of view in all our dealings—and business is no exception. In business, as in all other human endeavors, we must be prepared to pay the costs of ethical behavior.

There is a similar danger in the environmental movement with corporations choosing or being wooed to be environmentally friendly on the grounds that it will be in their self-interest. There is the risk of participating in the movement for the wrong reasons. But what does it matter if business cooperates for reasons other than the right reasons, as long as it cooperates? It matters if business believes or is led to believe that it only has a duty to be environmentally conscientious in those cases where such actions either require no sacrifice or actually make a profit. And I am afraid this is exactly what is happening. . . .

I am not saying we should abandon attempts to entice corporations into being ethical, both environmentally and in other ways, by pointing out and providing opportunities where good ethics is good business. And there are many places where such attempts fit well in both the business and environmental ethics movements. But we must be careful not to cast this as the proper guideline for business's ethical responsibility. Because when it is discovered that many ethical actions are not necessarily good for business, at least in the short run, then the rationale based on self-interest will come up morally short, and both ethical movements will be seen as deceptive and shallow.

III

What is the proper rationale for responsible business action toward the environment? A minimalist principle is to refrain from causing or prevent the causing of unwarranted harm, because failure to do so would violate certain moral rights not to be harmed. There is, of course, much debate over what harms are indeed unwarranted due to conflict of rights and questions about whether some harms are offset by certain benefits. . . .

Some naturalistic environmentalists only include other sentient animals in the framework of being deserving of moral consideration; others include all things which are alive or which are an integral part of an ecosystem. This latter view is sometimes called a biocentric environmental ethic as opposed to the homocentric view which sees all moral claims in terms of human beings and their interests. Some characterize these two views as deep *versus* shallow ecology.

The literature on these two positions is vast and the debate is ongoing. The conflict between them goes to the heart of environmental ethics and is crucial to our making of environmental policy and to our perception of moral duties to the environment, including business's. I strongly favor the biocentric view. And although this is not the place to try to adequately argue for it, let me unfurl its banner for just a moment.

A version of R. Routley's "last man" example[7] might go something like this: Suppose you were the last surviving human being and were soon to die from nuclear poisoning, as all other human and sentient animals have died before you. Suppose also that it is within your power to destroy all remaining life, or to make it simpler, the last tree which could continue to flourish and propagate if left alone. Furthermore you will not suffer if you do not destroy it. Would you do anything wrong by cutting it down? The deeper ecological view would say yes because you would be destroying something that has value in and of itself, thus making the world a poorer place.

It might be argued that the only reason we may find the tree valuable is because human beings generally find trees of value either practically or aesthetically, rather than the atoms or molecules they might turn into if changed from their present form. The issue is whether the tree has value only in its relation to human beings or whether it has a value deserving of moral consideration inherent in itself in its present form. The biocentric position holds that when we find something wrong with destroying the tree, as we should, we do so because we are responding to an intrinsic value in the natural object, not to a value we give to it. This is a view which argues against a humanistic environmental ethic and which urges us to channel our moral obligations accordingly.

Why should one believe that nonhuman living things or natural objects forming integral parts of ecosystems have intrinsic value? . . . I suspect Arne Naess gives as good an answer as can be given.

> *Faced with the ever returning question of "Why?" we have to stop somewhere. Here is a place where we well might stop. We shall admit that the value in itself is something shown in intuition. We attribute intrinsic value to ourselves and our nearest, and the validity of further identification can be contested, and is contested by many. The negation may, however, also be attacked through a series of "whys?" Ultimately, we are in the same human predicament of having to start somewhere, at least for the moment. We must stop somewhere and treat where we then stand as a foundation.*[8]

In the final analysis, environmental biocentrism is adopted or not depending on whether it is seen to provide a deeper, richer, and more ethically compelling view of the nature of things.

If this deeper ecological position is correct, then it ought to be reflected in the environmental movement. Unfortunately, for the most part, I do not think this is being done, and there is a price to be paid for not doing so. . . .

Furthermore, there are many cases where what is in human interest is not in the interest of other natural things. Examples range from killing leopards for stylish coats to destroying a forest to build a golf course. I am not convinced that homocentric arguments, even those based on long-term human interests, have much force in protecting the interests of such natural things. Attempts to make these interests coincide might be made, but the point is that from a homocentric point of view the leopard and the forest have no morally relevant interests to consider. It is simply fortuitous if nonhuman natural interests coincide with human interests, and are thereby valued and protected. Let us take an example from the work of Christopher Stone. Suppose a stream has been polluted by a business. From a homocentric point of view, which serves as the basis for our legal system, we can only correct the problem through finding some harm done to human beings who use the stream. Reparation for such harm might involve cessation of the pollution and restoration of the stream, but it is also possible that the business might settle with the people by paying them for their damages and continue to pollute the stream. Homocentrism provides no way for the stream to be made whole again unless it is in the interests of human beings to do so. In short it is possible for human beings to sell out the stream.[9]. . .

At the heart of the business ethics movement is its reaction to the mistaken belief that business only has responsibilities to a narrow set of its stakeholders, namely its stockholders. Crucial to the environmental ethics movement is its reaction to the mistaken belief that only human beings and human interests are deserving of our moral consideration. I suspect that the beginnings of both movements can be traced to these respective moral insights.

NOTES

1. Norman Bowie, "Morality, Money, and Motor Cars," *Business, Ethics, and the Environment: The Public Policy Debate,* eds., W. Michael Hoffman, Robert Frederick, and Edward S. Petry, Jr. (New York: Quorum Books, 1990), p. 89.
2. See Milton Friedman, "The Social Responsibility of Business Is to Increase Its Profits," *The New York Times Magazine* (September 13, 1970).
3. Bowie, p. 91.
4. Bowie, p. 94.
5. Robert Frederick, Assistant Director of the Center for Business Ethics, and I have developed and written these points together. Frederick has also provided me with invaluable assistance on other points in this paper.
6. Kenneth E. Goodpaster, "Can a Corporation Have an Environmental Conscience?" *The Corporation, Ethics, and the Environment,* eds., W. Michael Hoffman, Robert Frederick, and Edward S. Petry, Jr. (New York: Quorum Books, 1990).
7. Richard Routley and Val Routley, "Human Chauvinism and Environmental Ethics," *Environmental Philosophy,* Monograph Series, No. 2, eds., Don Mannison, Michael McRobbie, and Richard Routley (Australian National University, 1980), pp. 121ff.
8. Arne Naess, "Identification as a Source of Deep Ecological Attitudes," *Deep Ecology,* ed., Michael Tobias (San Marcos, CA: Avant Books, 1988), p. 266.
9. Christopher D. Stone, "Should Trees Have Standing?—Toward Legal Rights for Natural Objects," in *People, Penguins, and Plastic Trees,* pp. 86–87.

RELATED WEB SITES

Environmental Working Group: www.ewg.org

Greenpeace: www.greenpeace.org

International Environmental Liability Management Association
www.magic.ca/ielma/ielma.home.html

Sierra Club: www.sierraclub.org

House of Representatives Hot Topic—The Environment:
www.house.gov/democrats/ht_environ.html

FORESTS OF THE NORTH COAST: THE OWLS, THE TREES, AND THE CONFLICTS

LISA NEWTON AND CATHERINE DILLINGHAM

You may already be familiar with the basic facts of the next case. It addresses the battle between the logging community of the Pacific Northwest and the animal rights advocates who seek to protect the spotted owl population in that same area. Apparently, the two populations can not co-exist. As you read the case, do any alternatives come to mind for resolving this situation? The authors ask whether this case is, as the media contended, basically a class conflict between the blue-collar loggers and the elite, white-collar professional class that typifies the environmental movement.

The media have characterized the struggle between the loggers and the environmentalists as essentially a class conflict: the working-class lumbermen against the elite professional class that typifies the environmental movement. How does the United States generally handle white-collar versus blue-collar conflicts? Will the lessons learned elsewhere in that type of conflict help us here?

BACKGROUND: THE TRAGEDY OF TREES

"Save a Life, Kill a Tree?" is an article written by Sallie Tisdale; it describes the most recent "trees vs. people" ammunition, the anticancer drug taxol that is found in the bark of the Pacific Yew of the Northwest old-growth forests. "Save a Logger—Eat a Spotted Owl" is a bumper sticker commonly seen throughout this area. A grocery store in northern California recently displayed boxes of Spotted Owl Helper (a takeoff on Hamburger Helper). A recurring theme in this controversy is that something (usually a tree, but sometimes an owl) has to be killed in order to save something of human value; this gives the whole topic an overtone of tragedy. In tragedy, victory is impossible, and reconciliation comes at terrible cost. Simply because the issue will not yield to politically conscious pragmatism (the peculiarly American version of reason), it invites complications from the political and economic left and right and sanctions violence in defense of endangered values. Our first job, then, is to sort out the complications, so that the intersecting ethical dilemmas can be treated independently. Let us consider the issues:

1. *The owl.* The northern spotted owl is threatened with extinction by logging operations in the Northwest Forest. The owl is protected to some extent by the Endangered Species Act . . . , but the issues involved go beyond the law. Why might we have a moral obligation to save an endangered species? On the other hand, why should we care about insignificant faraway birds, anyway? What good is *biodiversity?* And what should we be willing to do to maintain it?

2. *The trees and the business practices that threaten them.* Ted Gup describes the owl as "a fine bird, yes, but . . . never really the root cause of this great conflict." It is the trees themselves—great groves of Sequoia and other cone-bearing trees, some of them more than 2,000 years old, spontaneously likened to the great cathedrals of Europe by many who have seen them—it is the trees that really fire the imagination. Do we have an obligation to preserve these trees, just as a singular treasure for the world?

   We live with a free-enterprise system that generally serves us well. Do we have an obligation either to protect businesses that operate in environmentally sensitive ways, or to require that all businesses do so? The case of Pacific Lumber Company shows a company that preserved environmental values pitted against hostile financial initiatives that were good for the shareholders but bad for the trees. Does the fiduciary duty of the company extend to the environment? Should the trees have a vote at the annual meeting? Do we have an obligation to protect the workers—the loggers, and their peculiarly specialized way of life?

3. *The varied roles of the government.* . . . What is the role of the government in protecting owls, trees, business, and ourselves? What do we want the government's role to be? What should government be empowered to do? at what cost?

All these questions turn on one indisputable fact: the Pacific Northwest Rainforests, ecosystems unlike any others in the world, have been logged for a century to the point of threatened extinction, not only of the species housed there but of the forests themselves. These forests are managed and regulated by an incredible mix of national bureaucracies; the actions of these agencies affect the livelihoods of millions of people and the economies of three states. The loggers and lumber companies are in conflict with the environmentalists; both parties are in conflict with the regulators; the politicians are on all sides of the conflict, depending on their constituencies; and everything ends up in court, where the "lawsuits, motions, and appeals . . . [seem to] have increased faster than the owl population."

THE OWL AND ITS TREES

The currents of the Pacific Ocean provide abundant warmth and moisture to the Northwest Coast of the United States. Through millions of years of evolution, these conditions have allowed the appearance, probably 6,000 years ago, of what we now call "old-growth forests." These are forests with some thousand-year-old stands, forests with trees that are 300 feet tall and ten feet in diameter, trees that are at least twice as massive as those found in tropical rainforests, trees that each contain enough lumber to build two houses. These forests extend from the Alaskan panhandle (Sitka Spruce) south through Washington and Oregon (Douglas Fir, Western Hemlock) to northern California (Redwoods, Ponderosa Pine). . . .

The owl is one of those species that requires unique stable conditions to survive: It appears to be totally dependent upon old-growth forest, and hunts there exclusively. To house the owl, the trees must be dense, and some proportion of them must be over 200 years old. Thus, the future of the northern spotted owl is linked with that of the old-growth forest, and the owl is therefore considered an *indicator* species—that is, a species whose condition will indicate the condition of the entire ecosystem (similar to the canary in the coal mine). Not only does the owl require old growth, it requires a lot of it. Studies have shown that, in northern California, each pair ranged among 1,900 acres of old growth; in Oregon, six pairs averaged 2,264 acres as their range; and six pairs studied in Washington had an average range of 3,800 acres.

ENDANGERMENT AND OBLIGATIONS

The northern spotted owl, then, is clearly endangered. To save it, we must save large numbers of the oldest trees. Given that 90 percent of the forest has been cut down already, virtually all the remaining old growth, whether in private or public hands, must be preserved. Should we do this for the sake of the owl?

Do we have an obligation to preserve endangered species? For starters, what does "preservation" mean in this context? If only the genetic material is in question, we can preserve the spotted owl by capturing a sufficient number of breeding pairs (say, 20), putting them in a climate-controlled zoo, and allowing them to produce baby owls to their hearts' content—and we can do this without gumming up the logging operations. (If no zoos have room for owls right now, we could freeze owl eggs indefinitely and regenerate the species any time it is convenient to do so.) Or does preservation of a wild species always mean preservation in the wild, living as the species has evolved to live, naturally? If this is preservation, then what cost are we expected to absorb to preserve the habitat? Granted that the owl is worth something to us (we would not wish it extinguished, other things being equal), but what is it worth when it affects these other things: jobs, regional economies, and the evolved lifestyle of the North Coast loggers?

The preservation of a species contributes to the biodiversity of the area—this means, literally, the number and variety of species that are living there. For any ecosystem, we assume that the species have evolved as members of a niche and that the destruction of one species, leaving its niche open and its role unfilled, will have an unfavorable impact on the others. For the sake of *all* species, then, we should preserve *each* species. We cannot predict just which of these species will suddenly prove to be dramatically useful to humans—by, say, providing a cure for cancer. . . . This argument was used, but only hypothetically, until the discovery of taxol, a drug that has recently shown better than expected results in treating ovarian and breast cancer; taxol originates in the bark (and perhaps the needles) of the Pacific Yew, which is indigenous to the old growth. The U.S. Forest Service used to consider the Yew a weed, to be removed from a clear-cut and burned; now, of course, there is pressure from many fronts to harvest these trees for the cancer drug. Would we have ever found out about this use for yew trees if the old groves had all been gone? For the sake of the human species, then, we should protect *any* species, no matter how humble, no matter what measures (within the obvious limits of reason) are required to preserve the conditions that species needs to live.

ACTING TO PRESERVE THE SPECIES

Persuaded by such considerations, Congress passed the Endangered Species Act (ESA) in 1973. According to this bill, the National Marine Fishery Service (Department of Commerce) and the Fish and Wildlife Service (Department of the Interior) are empowered to list marine and land species, respectively, as either threatened or endangered; then, these species can no longer be hunted, collected, injured, or killed. The bill also prohibits any federal agency from carrying out or funding any activity that could threaten or endanger said species *or their habitats.* (This latter provision has caused the most controversy with regard to logging in the old-growth forests, but also other projects, such as dams, highways, and other development receiving federal funding.) Therefore, both the Bureau of Land Management (Department of the Interior) and the Forest Service (Department of Agriculture) must consult with the Fish and Wildlife Service before undertaking any action that might threaten a species such as the owl.

This bill is typical of environmental legislation on several counts: (1) It is informed by the best science available, so it is enlightened, far-reaching, and probably the world's most stringent species-protection legislation. To be in noncompliance with the ESA is a criminal act; both civil and criminal penalties are called for, including imprisonment. (2) This bill is also among those most pitifully funded. Until 1988, the yearly funding amounted to about the cost of 12 Army bulldozers. The 1988 amendments doubled the budget, but legislative environmentalists consider that the bill has nowhere near the support it needs to preserve marine and terrestrial species worldwide. (3) Three cabinet-level departments must work harmoniously together for the act to be implemented.

Implementation presents other problems. According to the 1982 amendment of the act, the economic implications of the protection of a species *may not* be considered in determining its status, whether or not it is endangered; that decision must be based "solely on the basis of the best scientific and commercial data." Economic factors *may* be considered after the listing, during the required preparation of a recovery plan for the listed species. (In practice, because of the complexities involved, few plans have been prepared.) The act also calls for a determination of the species' "critical habitat" but allows a year to elapse after the listing for the determination and acknowledges that, because of complications, the habitat might be indeterminable.

When determining the critical habitat, the Fish and Wildlife Service *must* include economic considerations. On two occasions, court-ordered reconsiderations on the basis of economic impact have impelled the FWS to reduce the acreage required to preserve the owl. Additionally, those who feel that their economic interests are damaged by species protection may appeal to the Endangered Species Committee (the "God Squad"). The bureaucratic hurdles to overcome on the way to actual protection of the owl seem daunting even to the most hardened Washington veterans; nevertheless, it *is* legal protection and, as such, the strongest statement that we can make, as a nation, about the value of our most threatened creatures.

THE TALLEST TREES ON EARTH

. . . Unfortunately for those who hope for the survival of these trees, they are the most commercially valuable trees in the United States. The extent of the original forest and of the remaining acreage is very debatable and probably depends on one's definition of "old growth," which is generally described as the largest old trees, living and dead, standing and fallen, within a multilayered canopy. Estimates of the extent of the original forest range from 20 to 70 million acres (depending on what is considered a large tree); some 70 to 95 percent of this forest has been logged over the last century, and the rate of logging has increased dramatically over the last few decades. Estimates are complicated, too, by the fragmentation of the forest by clear-cutting, leaving some stands isolated in a barren landscape.

From the corporate viewpoint, logging just makes good business sense. The woods, as a popular song would have it, are just trees, and the trees are just wood. Humans have always cut and processed timber for lumber—for houses, boats, fences, furniture— virtually since our beginnings on this planet, and the redwoods are eminently suitable for such harvest. The lumber from redwoods is beautiful, durable, light, strong, has good nail-holding capacity, and is insect- and fire-resistant. Each tree yields an average of 12 or 13 thousand board feet—enough to build two houses. The harvest is very profitable but strictly limited. Once those old-growth trees are logged, there will be no more: The trees will be gone forever. The second growth does not share the characteristics of the old growth in its resistance to insects, disease, fire, and decay, nor is it as dense and massive, of course. We might suppose that the twentieth-century remnants of a 2,000-year-old forest were composed of the best survivors of all attacks: The less-resistant trees will have succumbed centuries ago. The old growth is then an irreplaceable asset: It could be argued that it will become more valuable every year into the indefinite future and that it therefore demands careful husbanding and conservative forestry practices. Wise management would seem to require very sparing cuts of the old growth while encouraging plantations of new trees to satisfy demands for ordinary lumber.

TREES, THE ENVIRONMENT, AND THE LAW

Aristotle and Adam Smith both proved, in very different ways, that private property (specifically, land and all resources for production) was better off, more likely to be taken care of, than public property. We accept as established fact that a private owner is the best caretaker of property. The centrality of the right to private property in John Locke's writing depends on that presumption, as do our standard defenses of the American business system.

Is this presumption now generally false? Pacific Lumber's redwoods are clearly not safe in Hurwitz's hands. Do we have a legal right, then, to take the land away from him? We know that, under the doctrine of eminent domain, we can seize the redwoods for a new national park—but can we seize all that land just to continue a more conservative logging operation? What are the business imperatives of a company that logs redwoods? Is it a sufficient discharge of our obligations to replace 2,000-year-old groves with young growth that can be harvested in 40 to 80 years?

Another environmental effect of the logging, presently unmeasurable, is its contribution to global warming. The old growth is a veritable storehouse of carbon, a fact of increasingly intense interest, for carbon dioxide is the most important of the "greenhouse gases" credited with causing the projected global warming. While these trees are alive, they absorb huge amounts of carbon dioxide from the atmosphere in the photosynthetic process. Nature's recycling laws require, of course, that the same amount of gas be returned to the atmosphere, through the trees' respiration and eventual decay, but that happens, as we have noted, over a period of hundreds of years.

When the trees are felled, the photosynthetic carbon dioxide absorption stops and, compounding the crime, when the resulting debris is burned, the stored carbon is abruptly added to the atmosphere as carbon dioxide. The timber industry has claimed that, by cutting old growth and planting young trees with a faster photosynthetic rate, they are actually ameliorating the threat of global warming. To be sure, a rapidly growing tree absorbs more carbon dioxide than a mature tree of the same size, but a small seedling does not approach the chemical activity of the enormous trees in the Northwest Forest, trees that are many times as massive as those found anywhere else in the world. The Northwest old growth "stores more carbon . . . than any other biome—twice as much per unit of area as tropical rainforests."

Incidentally, the claim of the timber companies—that their little plantings are really much better at taking carbon from the air than the mature redwoods—is typical of the self-serving half-truths that tend to harden attitudes in these controversies. This claim, with just enough scientific fact to make it respectable yet clearly in the service of company interests, enrages environmentalists and encourages public cynicism. Should the timber companies be held responsible for global warming—an unintended but predictable, consequence of their operations?

CREATIVE ALTERNATIVES

The strongest indication that the Forest Service and its allied agencies in the federal government might not be the true villains, however, lies in the work they do when the law asks them to think creatively about these forests and their future. Pursuant to the 1960 Multiple Use Sustained Yield Act . . . , the Forest Service, the Bureau of Land Management, and the U.S. Fish and Wildlife Service were asked to describe ways that the owl might be saved and the trees might be put to work for the nation without being cut down. The agencies did a fine job: The combined report of the Forest Service and the BLM, "Actions the Administration May Wish to Consider in Implementing a Conservation Strategy for the Northern Spotted Owl" (May 1, 1990), recommends a drastic cutback in the harvesting of old-growth trees by forbidding export of raw logs, then recommends and describes extensive educational and retraining programs for the loggers who are put out of work by the ban. Technical assistance would make logging and milling more efficient (avoiding the extensive waste entailed by present practices); recreational facilities would make the forests better-known and better-used and create political pressure to conserve the trees. Even more impressive is the FWS report, "Economic Analysis of Designation of Critical Habitat for the Northern Spotted Owl" (August 1991). Going beyond the multiple-use scenario, the report specifically addresses "non-use values," the value to the nation just to have the forests *there:* "Estimates of recreation user demand, benefits of scenic beauty, and benefits of water quality represent only a partial estimate of society's total value for the spotted owl and its associated habitat. The public also is willing to pay for the option of recreation use in the future, the knowledge that the natural ecosystem exists and is protected, and the satisfaction from its bequest to future generations. . . . The average willingness to pay higher taxes and wood product prices reported in a referendum contingent valuation format was $190 per year. The lower limit of the 98 percent confidence range was $117 per household."

These reports place the federal government's environmental services in a new and much better light. Bureaucrats in general, and federal bureaucrats in particular, have been harshly criticized for their role (or lack of same) in the protection of the forests. But these reports on alternate usage of the forests suggest, though, that the idealists who once joined government service to protect the nation's environmental heritage might still be around, waiting only for public opinion to catch up to them. A new agenda for the environment will require a trained corps of experts in science and policy to articulate a national environmental ethic and to frame the plans for implementation. In developing their reports, the Forest Service, the BLM, and the FWS have made an auspicious start.

SUMMARY

The heart of the problem, from an environmental point of view, is the old-growth forest. From the loggers' point of view, the problem is jobs. The owl, the financier, and the government agencies are all bit players in an agonizing twentieth-century drama of loss and conflict. We need not search for villains. Once we all thought that the forests were unlimited. The timber industry's managers watched the old growth disappear before their eyes and did not realize that it could not be restored—that once gone, it would be gone forever; but they were no more ignorant than their regulators, their customers, or their fellow citizens. The environmental movement is not the sole prerogative of Eastern elitists, as the loggers suspect, nor is the timber industry composed of a series of tintypes of Charles Hurwitz, as the environmentalists are convinced.

Protecting the forests will require the abolition of a way of life that has been honored and valued in the immediate past. What, exactly, are we prepared to do to compensate and redirect the people who are stranded by systematic and extensive preservation? On the other hand, are we prepared to spare ourselves that difficult decision by allowing the forests to be destroyed? Once the trees are gone, the industry will die, and the workers will be unemployed anyway, but then it will be *their* problem, not ours. How much are we willing to lose in order to avoid the pain of making this decision now—before it is too late? Our history suggests that we are willing to lose quite a bit.

The most disturbing aspect of our political response to these dilemmas, though, is the hypocrisy of the United States urging Brazil and other Third World countries to halt the cutting of their tropical rainforests to prevent the worsening of global warming, while we cut our forests about twice as fast. To quote an official with the Oregon Natural Resources

Council, "It's interesting that we're telling Third World countries, 'don't cut your forests' [while] . . . we're wiping out our fish runs, we're wiping out our biotic diversity, we're sending species to extinction . . . we're not a Third World country. We're not so poor that we have to destroy our ancient forests. And we're not so rich that we can afford to."

RELATED WEB SITES

The Forest Stewardship Council
   antequera.antequera.com/FSC/

U.S. Environmental Protection Agency: www.epa.gov

Code of Forest Ethics:
   www.wildrockies.org/WildRock/Talus/Campaign/ForEthix.html

Environmental Ethics: Sustainability, Competition and Forestry:
   http://www.ethics.ubc.ca/papers/susdev.html

"LETTER OF THE LAW" ETHICS NOT ALWAYS EQUAL

CHARLES BOUCHARD

Bouchard explains some of the more inconsistent aspects of our present environmental protection regulations. This inconsistency leads to results that, while legal (or "according to the letter of the law"), are not always the intended result. This consequence is not always the most ethical.

Matt Greller is an active environmentalist and often boasts about the state-of-the-art air monitoring and filtration system in the paint department of his steel fabrication and erection business. His company has been successful and has gone after highway bridge projects and other large private industrial jobs.

Recently, the EPA listed his hub city as a "no attainment area" and restricted local manufacturers to using no more than 3.5 pounds of "volatile organic compounds" (VOCs) per gallon of paint. Matt's problem is that many of the highway and bridge jobs he has bid call for coatings well above the 3.5 limit. Because his plant is in the city, he can't paint there, even with his efficient filtration system. Relocating his plant outside of the city is not feasible given the large capital investment he has made. He needs these major contracts to remain successful.

His project manager suggests an easy solution: Do the painting in the field and not in the shop. Since many of the jobs would be outside the local "no attainment area," they would not be restricted to the 3.5 VOCs. For projects located within the city, they could request site variances for short-term field work, which are routinely granted by the EPA. His project manager's opinion is that if there is a loophole in the regulations, they should take advantage of it and remain competitive in their bidding. "It's not our job to make sense of these regulations," he says.

Matt Greller's ethical problem is that his company is bound by a law that, in this case, is defeating its own purpose. If he follows the letter of the law and requests the appropriate variances for outside work, he will actually be adding more pollutants to the atmosphere than if he did the work in his shop and violated the law. What is Matt's ethical responsibility to an ineffective law?

The philosopher Aristotle once noted that laws only apply "for the most part" since the lawmakers can rarely see every contingency and odd circumstance that might arise when they frame laws. He talks about the need for law to "bend" around such unusual circumstances so that the law doesn't defeat its own purpose. He even describes a virtue called "equity" or "epikeia," which allows one to deviate from the letter of the law when one knows the lawmaker would not have intended the law to be binding in this case.

Businessmen who are striving to be ethical always have to try to "see through" laws and regulations to the purpose behind them. In this case, the purpose is a cleaner environment. Anyone who has dealt with government regulations can find holes and inconsistencies in them. It's easy to reduce observance of them to "obeying the law" and ignore the greater value.

But, in this case, protection of the environment is a value in which everyone has a stake. Responsible businessmen know that keeping the air clean is something for which we all share some responsibility.

As an active environmentalist, Matt has to ask himself what is ideal and what is possible. The ideal is to eliminate pollution. Given the needs of business, competitive pressure and regulatory confusion, it may not be possible to do that. But, Matt must avoid the kind of cynicism that would lead him to manipulate the law to his own advantage.

The compromise between these two is what we might call a "prudential decision"—the best choice possible under the circumstances.

Sometimes we have only two choices: yes or no. This is often the case when we are faced with legal questions. But, ethical choices are concerned with realizing values like clean air, productivity, profit and employment goals. These values are not all-or-nothing choices—they are able to be realized in degree. Matt's values of a clean environment and a healthy business are not mutually exclusive, but he must blend them effectively.

Some companies try to escape regulatory inconvenience by subcontracting illegal work to companies that, for some reason or another, do not fall under the same regulations. This would be ethical if local regulations arise from very specific local circumstances. But if such subcontracting is done in order to violate a universal good like clean air or soil, it is quite another story. Managers may escape legal responsibility, but their ethical responsibility is not reduced.

The EPA has an ethical problem, too. The regulations as Matt describes them are based on assigning urban and rural areas different levels of tolerance. Such regulations are one way of taking into account the difference in air quality between urban and rural areas, but they foster the erroneous notion of a "compartmentalized" environment with discrete sections that can be controlled independently of one another.

It's true that at this moment pollutants are at a much higher level in our urban areas than they are in rural areas. But environmental regulations must respect the environment as a whole and seek the lowest levels of pollution possible.

Today all businesses must know more about the environment to survive. Doing the "right thing"—where politics and engineering meet—is only our current best guess. Matt might be in a position to influence the EPA in the formulation of regulations that affect his company.

We would like your thoughts about ethical responses to conflicts that arise from operating a profitable business, responding to our common concern to protect the environment and living with the laws that enforce that protection. Send your comments to: Business Ethics, St. Louis Business Journal, One Metropolitan Square, Suite 2170, St. Louis, 63102.

RELATED WEB SITE

EPA Document Clearinghouse: www.cais.com/tne/neis/superf.html

---

ENVIRONMENT
HARVEY S. JAMES

Harvey James posted the following message to a business ethics list-server. James applies property rights and market analysis to a theory of corporate environmental ethics.

From:	JAMES, HARVEY
To:	Multiple recipients of list BETS-L <BETS-L@LISTSER...
Date:	9/18/96 8:28A.M.
Subject:	Environment

Environmental consciousness is important to business only when it is in the interest of business to be conscious of the environment. So, John Trebnik is correct when he says the answer is simply grounded in economic theory. The important question is when is it in the interest of business to be environmental-friendly.

If a business knows that its customers want strong environmental policies, a business will follow, or lose sales, which is not profit maximizing. For instance, a clothing retailer that sells "outdoor" clothing will not want a reputation for trashing the environment—it's not good for business.

If a business uses "natural" resources for production purposes, then it will want to ensure that the resources are in as good a quality as possible in order to [keep] resource costs low. This also tends to lead to profit maximization. For instance, a logging firm will plant seedlings in order to replenish forest growth in lands the firm owns in order to provide logging opportunities in the future.

The interesting question has to do with when a firm will NOT want to be environmentally conscious. This occurs primarily when the property rights over resources are not clearly defined and enforced. For instance, a factory may dump waste by-products in the local lake because it does not own the lake and the lake owners do not enforce their right to clean lake waters. Hence, discussions of the environmental policies of firms should, in my opinion, be centered around property rights. The rest is, well, academic.

—Harvey S. James, Jr., Ph.D.

"Be right, and then be easy to live with, if possible, but in that order."

Harvey S. James, "Environment," E-mail posted to BETS-L Listserver, September 18, 1996. Reprinted by permission of the author.

Chapter 14

ETHICS IN GLOBAL BUSINESS

American businesses face a challenge of global competition which is   ALEXANDER TROTMAN, CEO,
greater than any time in the history of our country.   FORD MOTOR COMPANY

"When in Rome, do as the Romans." How many times have you heard this phrase? The essence of the rule is that one's actions will be judged according to the norms of the environment in which it takes place. This is not always the case; in many circumstances, we believe that our way is the right way and that alternatives are not acceptable. Consider the decision of Levi Strauss management to take their manufacturing business out of China in protest of China's history of human rights abuses. While it might have been acceptable in the Chinese culture, or at least tolerated, Levi Strauss did not want to be a part of it.

Similarly, there was uproar in mid 1996 when it was discovered that a clothing line sponsored by Kathie Lee Gifford was manufactured under conditions in other countries that appalled many Americans. Chicago Bulls basketball player Michael Jordan was forced to defend his role as spokesperson for Nike shoes when similar conditions were found in foreign Nike plants. (See discussion of The Gap's operations in El Salvador in this chapter.)

On the other hand, the "When in Rome" justification has been used to ethically exculpate American firms who do business in other countries and who have offered what we would consider to be bribes in order to get certain jobs done. Consider what you would do if the only way to obtain a certain permit or contract is to offer a bribe and that "everyone does it." In addition, a firm may contend that if it does not act in ways similar to firms native to that country, it may lose business or be unable to do business there. Does that make it acceptable? Americans generally believe that bribery is wrong or unethical because it allows certain parties to obtain a privilege not afforded to others. On the other hand, most Americans don't believe it is wrong or unethical to eat meat; while individuals in other countries believe that eating meat is wrong and unethical. In the United States, men are limited to one wife. In other countries, that is considered unthinkable and humiliating. Who is "right" in each of these conflicts? Who should answer that question?

Are there any objective rights and wrongs? Is there anything that we would all agree is ethically wrong in the world or ethically right? Western and Eastern concepts of right and wrong may not be that far off. In a recent *Harvard Business Review* article, Wharton professor Thomas Donaldson demonstrates how Western and non-Western values may have a great deal in common. For instance, Donaldson links the Western values of individual liberty and human rights to the Japanese value of kyosei (living and working together for the common good) and the Muslim value of Zakatt (the duty to give alms to the poor).[1]

Donaldson and colleague Thomas Dunfee suggest in their "integrative social contracts theory" that one can differentiate between those values which are fundamental across culture and theory ("hypernorms")[2] and those which are determined within moral

1. Thomas Donaldson, "Values in Tension: Ethics Away from Home," *Harvard Business Review* (September/October 1996) pp. 48–62.
2. Thomas Donaldson and Thomas Dunfee, "Toward a Unified Conception of Business Ethics: Integrative Social Contracts Theory," *Academy of Management Review* 19 (1994), pp. 252, 264 (defining hypernorms as those principles that would limit moral free space, analogizing hypernorms to "hypergoods," "goods sufficiently fundamental as to serve as a source of evaluation and criticism of community-generated norms [within moral free space]").

"free space" and are not hypernorms. Donaldson and Dunfee propose that one look to the convergence of religious, cultural, and philosophical beliefs around certain core principles as a clue to the identification of hypernorms. Donaldson and Dunfee include as examples of hypernorms freedom of speech, the right to personal freedom, the right to physical movement, and informed consent. As you consider these far-reaching rights, do you believe that all reasonable thinkers would agree as to their predominance and worthiness of protection?

In line with Donaldson's and Dunfee's effort to propose a means by which to apply ethical standards across borders, several proposed codes of conduct are presented in this section, including the U.S. Model Business Principles and the Caux Round Table Principles. Consider the similarities and differences between the proposed models of business behavior. If there are differences, do these difference in themselves evidence the fact that there is no general agreement regarding business conduct? If you were to create a model code of conduct for a global firm, would it resemble any of these codes?

Firms often complain that adhering to these codes of conduct are costly, imposing higher costs on them than those imposed on firms in other countries. Therefore, adherence to the codes places them at a competitive disadvantage in comparison to firms in less-regulated countries. Economists have called international labor standards "institutional intervention in competitive markets that impairs the workings of the invisible hand."[3] Free market economists believe that standards reduce efficiency, thereby increasing the cost of labor, lowering the employment of those affected, and benefitting higher cost competitors.[4] On the other hand, standards may be the only way to address a market failure—that is, the market fails to consider the nonfinancial conditions of employment and the nonfinancial impact of these conditions.

Harvard economist Richard Freeman asks whether there is any difference in the actual t-shirt produced by individuals under differing conditions. In other words, is there any difference between a t-shirt manufactured by political prisoners in a labor camp or sexually harassed women in a free trade zone in Central America, and a t-shirt manufactured by workers under normal, acceptable conditions? If the price is the same, perhaps you will prefer the one made under "ethical" conditions. Perhaps you might even pay a slight premium for that shirt. However, the market evidences that, where the price of ethically produced goods is higher, the demand for decent labor standards declines. Fewer and fewer people are willing to pay a premium as the difference in price becomes greater. Freeman argues, therefore, that the market demand will sufficiently, efficiently, and satisfactorily determine labor conditions for manufactured goods.[5]

Beyond compliance to a central code of business behavior, firms must be sensitive to cultural differences in those countries in which they do business. The Campbell Soup Company has learned that paying attention to cultural differences may mean the

---

3. Richard B. Freeman, "A Hard-Headed Look at Labor Standards," *International Labor Standards and Global Economic Integration: Proceedings of A Symposium,* July 1994, p. 26.
4. Ibid.
5. Ibid, p. 27.

difference between reaping a profit and bearing a loss. In many countries, Campbell discovered that other brands' dry soups were highly preferred to Campbell's canned, condensed soups. On the other hand, Campbell's duck-gizzard soup has high sales in Hong Kong and its Godiva Chocolate line sells well in Japan.[6] While answering the soup flavor needs of a country may seem to be trivial in light of other ethical-cultural conflicts, Campbell's was originally viewed as insincere and unresponsive by its foreign consumers—not too trivial to Campbell.

---

6. Joseph Weber, "What's Not Cookin' at Campbell's," *Business Week,* September 23, 1996, p. 40.

ETHICAL PRINCIPLES
GOVERNING GLOBAL BUSINESS

MODEL BUSINESS PRINCIPLES
U.S. DEPARTMENT OF COMMERCE

In an effort to codify the expectations of the American market, the U.S. Department of Commerce (DOC) issued its Model Business Principles in 1995 as guidelines for business conduct in the United States and abroad. While the principles comprise a voluntary code of conduct, the DOC hopes that they will encourage appropriate behavior.

Recognizing the positive role of U.S. business in upholding and promoting adherence to universal standards of human rights, the Administration encourages all businesses to adopt and implement voluntary codes of conduct for doing business around the world that cover at least the following areas:

1. Provision of a safe and healthy workplace.
2. Fair employment practices, including avoidance of child and forced labor and avoidance of discrimination based on race, gender, national origin or religious beliefs; and respect for the right of association and the right to organize and bargain collectively.
3. Responsible environmental protection and environmental practices.
4. Compliance with U.S. and local laws promoting good business practices, including laws prohibiting illicit payments and ensuring fair competition.
5. Maintenance, through leadership at all levels, of a corporate culture that respects free expression consistent with legitimate business concerns, and does not condone political coercion in the workplace; that encourages good corporate citizenship and makes a positive contribution to the communities in which the company operates; and where ethical conduct is recognized, valued and exemplified by all employees.

In adopting voluntary codes of conduct that reflect these principles, U.S. companies should serve as models, encouraging similar behavior by their partners, suppliers, and subcontractors.

Adoption of codes of conduct reflecting these principles is voluntary. Companies are encouraged to develop their own codes of conduct appropriate to their particular circumstances. Many companies already apply statements or codes that incorporate these principles. Companies should find appropriate means to inform their shareholders and the

---

U.S. Dept. of Commerce, U.S. Model Business Principles. (1995)

public of actions undertaken in connection with these principles. Nothing in the principles is intended to require a company to act in violation of host country or U.S. law. This statement of principles is not intended for legislation.

MODEL BUSINESS PRINCIPLES: PROCEDURES

When President Clinton announced his decision to renew China's MFN status last year, he also announced a commitment to work with the business community to develop a voluntary statement of business principles relating to corporate conduct abroad. The President made clear that U.S. business can and does play a positive and important role promoting the openness of societies, respect for individual rights, the promotion of free markets and prosperity, environmental protection and the setting of high standards for business practices generally.

The Administration today is offering an update on our efforts to follow-through on the President's commitment to promote the Model Business Principles and best practices among U.S. companies. The Principles already have gained the support of some U.S. companies. A process is ongoing to elicit additional support for these Principles and to continue to examine issues related to them.

The elements of this process are as follows:

1. Voluntary Statement of Business Principles. The Administration, in extensive consultations with business and labor leaders and members of the Non-Governmental Organization (NGO) community, developed these model principles, which were reported widely in the press earlier this spring. This model statement is to be used by companies as a reference point in framing their own codes of conduct. It is based on a wide variety of similar sets of principles U.S. companies and business organizations already have put into global practice. The Administration encourages all businesses everywhere to support the model principles. (Copies of the model statement are available by calling the U.S. Department of Commerce Trade Information Center, 1-800-USA-TRADE.)

2. Efforts by U.S. Business. As part of the ongoing effort, U.S. businesses will engage in the following activities:

   (a) Conferences on Best Practices Issues. In conjunction with Business for Social Responsibility, a non-profit business organization dedicated to promoting laudable corporate practices, and/or other appropriate organizations, the Administration will work to encourage conferences concerning issues relating to the practices contained in the Model Business Principles. Such conferences can provide a forum for information-sharing on new approaches for the evolving global context in which best practices are implemented. (For further information on Business for Social Responsibility, contact Bob Dunn, President, (415) 865-2500.)

   (b) Best Practices Information Clearinghouse and Support Services. One or more non-profits will work with the U.S. business community to develop a clearinghouse of information regarding business practices globally. The clearinghouse will establish a library of codes of conduct adopted by U.S. and international companies and organizations, to be catalogued and made available to companies seeking to develop their own codes. The clearinghouse would be available to provide advice to companies seeking to develop or improve their codes, advice based on the accumulated experience of other companies. Business for Social Responsibility (described above) is highly respected and is one resource that businesses and NGO's alike can turn to for information on best business practices.

3. Efforts by the U.S. Government. The U.S. Government also will undertake a number of activities to generate support for the Model Business Principles:

   (a) Promote Multilateral Adoption of Best Practices. The Administration has begun and will continue its effort to seek multilateral support for the Model Business Principles. Senior U.S. Government officials already have met with U.S. company officials and U.S. organizations operating abroad as well as with foreign corporate officials to seek support for the Principles. For example, the American Chambers of Commerce in the Asia Pacific recently adopted a resolution by which their members agreed to work with their local counterparts in the countries in which they operate to seek development of similar best practices among their members. The United States also will present the Model Business Principles at the Organization for Economic Cooperation and Development (OECD) and the International Labor Organization (ILO) as part of these organizations' ongoing behavior. Therefore, on an annual basis, the Administration will offer a series of awards to companies for specific activities that reflect best practices in the areas covered by the Model Business Principles. The awards will be granted pursuant to applications by interested companies. NGOs and private citizens will be encouraged to call attention to activities they believe are worthy of consideration. (For further information on the Best Practices Awards Program, contact Melinda Yee, U.S. Department of Commerce, (202) 482-1051.)

   (b) Presidential-Business Discussions. The President's Export Council (PEC), a high-level advisory group of Chief Executive Officers, provides a forum for the President to met regularly with U.S. business leaders to discuss issues relating to U.S. industries' exports and operations abroad.

For further general information about the Model Business Principles, please contact Jill Schuker, U.S. Commerce Department, (202) 482-5151, or David Ruth, U.S. Department of State, (202) 647-1625.

RELATED WEB SITE

Universal Declaration of Human Rights:
www.hamline.edu/robin/Library/A/810

THE CAUX PRINCIPLES

THE CAUX ROUND TABLE

The Caux Round Table consisted of a group of international executives based in Caux, Switzerland. The group shared a belief that business organizations can be a powerful force for positive change in the quality of life for the world. The executives developed their principles based on the Minnesota principles created by the Minnesota Center for Corporate Responsibility in 1992. The Caux Principles are based in the conviction that we can all live together and act for the common good.

The Caux principles are rooted in two basic ethical ideals: kyosei and human dignity. The Japanese concept of kyosei means living and working together for the common good—enabling cooperation and mutual prosperity to coexist with healthy and fair competition. Human dignity relates to the sacredness or value of each person as an end, not simply as the means to the fulfillment of other's purposes or even majority prescription. The general principles in section 2 clarify the spirit of kyosei and human dignity while the specific stakeholder principles in section 3 are concerned with their practical application. After reading the Principles, can you think of any issues that are not addressed?

SECTION 1. PREAMBLE

The mobility of employment, capital, produce, and technology is making business increasingly global in its transactions and its effects.

Laws and market forces are necessary but insufficient guides for conduct.

Responsibility for the politics and actions of business and respect for the dignity and interests of its stakeholders are fundamental.

Shared values, including a commitment to shared prosperity, are as important for a global community as for communities of smaller scale.

For these reasons, and because business can be a powerful agent of positive social change we offer the following principles as a foundation for dialogue and action by business leaders in search of business responsibility. In so doing we affirm the necessity for moral values in business decision making; without them, stable business relationships and a sustainable world community are impossible.

The Caux Round Table, *Caux Principles.* Reprinted with permission from *Business Ethics,* 52 S. 10th St., Suite 110, Minneapolis, MN 55403.

SECTION 2. GENERAL PRINCIPLES

Principle I. The Responsibilities of Businesses: Beyond Shareholders Toward Stakeholders

The value of a business to society is the wealth and employment it creates and the marketable products and practices it provides to consumers at a reasonable price commensurate with quality. To create such a value, a business must maintain its own economic health and viability, but survival is not a sufficient goal.

Businesses have a role to play in improving the lives of all their customers, employees, and shareholders by sharing with them the wealth they have created. Suppliers and competitors as well should expect businesses to honor their obligations in a spirit of honesty and fairness. As responsible citizens of the local, national, regional, and global communities in which they operate, businesses share a part in shaping the future of those communities.

Principle 2. The Economic and Social Impact of Businesses: Toward Innovation, Justice and World Community

Businesses established in foreign countries to develop, produce or sell should also contribute to the social advancement of those countries by creating productive employment and helping to raise the purchasing power of their citizens. Businesses also should contribute to human rights, education, welfare, and vitalization of the countries in which they operate. Businesses should contribute to economic and social development not only in the countries in which they operate, but also in the world community at large, through effective and prudent use of resources, free and fair competition and emphasis upon innovation in technology, production methods, marketing and communications.

Principle 3. Business Behavior: Beyond the Letter of the Law Toward a Spirit of Trust

While accepting the legitimacy of trade secrets, businesses should recognize that sincerity, keeping of promises and transparency contribute not only to their own credibility and stability but also to the smoothness and efficiency of business transactions, particularly on the international level.

Principle 4. Respect for the Rules

To avoid trade frictions and to promote freer trade, equal conditions for competition, and fair and equitable treatment for all participants, businesses should respect international and domestic rules. In addition, they should recognize that some behavior although legal, may still have adverse consequences.

Principle 5. Support for Multilateral Trade

Businesses should support the multilateral trade systems of the GATT/World Trade Organization and similar international agreements. They should cooperate in efforts to promote the progressive and judicious liberalization of trade, and to relax those domestic measures that unreasonably hinder global commerce, while giving due respect to national policy objectives.

Principle 6. Respect for the Environment

A business should protect and, where possible, improve the environment and promote sustainable development.

Principle 7. Avoidance of Illicit Operations

A business should not participate in or condone bribery, money laundering, or other corrupt practices: indeed, it should seek cooperation with others to eliminate them. It should not trade in arms or other materials used for terrorist activities, drug traffic or other organized crime.

SECTION 3. STAKEHOLDER PRINCIPLES

Customers

We believe in treating all customers with dignity irrespective of whether they purchase our products and services directly from us or otherwise acquire them in the market. We therefore have a responsibility to: provide our customers with the highest quality products and services consistent with their requirements; treat our customers fairly in all aspects of our business transactions including a high level of service and remedies for their dissatisfaction; make every effort to ensure that the health and safety of our customers, as well as the quality of their environment, will be sustained or enhanced by our products and services; assure respect for human dignity in products offered, marketing, and advertising; and respect the integrity of the culture of our customers.

Employees

We believe in the dignity of every employee and in taking employee interests seriously. We therefore have a responsibility to: provide jobs and compensation that improve workers' living conditions; provide working conditions that respect each employee's health and dignity; be honest in communications with employees and open in sharing information, limited only by legal and competitive restraints; listen to and, where possible, act on employee suggestions ideas, requests, and complaints; engage in good faith negotiations when conflict arises; avoid discriminatory practices and guarantee equal treatment and opportunity in areas such as gender, age, race, and religion; promote in the business itself the employment of differently abled people in places of work where they can be genuinely useful; protect employees from avoidable injury and illness in the workplace; encourage and assist employees in developing relevant and transferable skills and knowledge; and be sensitive to serious unemployment problems frequently associated with business decisions and work with governments, employee groups, other agencies and each other in addressing these dislocations.

Owners/Investors

We believe in honoring the trust our investors place in us. We therefore have a responsibility to: apply professional and diligent management in order to secure a fair and competitive return on our owners' investment; disclose relevant information to owners/investors subject only to legal requirements and competitive constraints; conserve, protect, and increase the owners/investors' assets; and respect owners/investors' requests, suggestions complaints, and formal resolutions.

Suppliers

Our relationship with suppliers and subcontractors must be based on mutual respect. We therefore have a responsibility to: seek fairness and truthfulness in all of our activities, including pricing, licensing, and rights to sell; ensure that our business activities are free from coercion and unnecessary litigation; foster long-term stability in the supplier relationship in return for value, quality competitiveness, and reliability; share information with suppliers and integrate them into our planning processes; pay suppliers on time and in accordance with agreed terms of trade; seek, encourage, and prefer suppliers and subcontractors whose employment practices respect human dignity.

Competitors

We believe that fair economic competition is one of the basic requirements for increasing the wealth of nations and, ultimately for making possible the just distribution of goods and services. We therefore have a responsibility to: foster open markets for trade and investment; promote competitive behavior that is socially and environmentally beneficial and demonstrates mutual respect among competitors; refrain from either seeking or participating in questionable payments or favors to secure competitive advantages; respect both tangible and intellectual property rights; and refuse to acquire commercial information by dishonest or unethical means, such as industrial espionage.

Communities

We believe that as global corporate citizens, we can contribute to such forces of reform and human rights as are at work in the communities which we are open to. We therefore have a responsibility in those communities to: respect human rights and democratic institutions, and promote them wherever practicable; recognize government's legitimate obligation to the society at large and support public policies and practices that promote human development through harmonious relations between business and other segments of society; collaborate with those forces in the community dedicated to raising standards of health, education, workplace safety and economic well-being; promote and stimulate sustainable development and play a leading role in preserving and enhancing the physical environment and conserving the earth's resources; support peace, security, diversity and social integration; respect the integrity of local cultures; and be a good corporate citizen through charitable donations, educational and cultural contributions and employee participation in community and civic affairs.

RELATED WEB SITES

The Caux Round Table: www.caux.ch/anglais/initer.htm

Caux Principles: www.bath.ac.uk/Centres/Ethical/Papers/caux.htm

INTERNATIONAL ETHICS STANDARDS FOR BUSINESS: NAFTA, CAUX PRINCIPLES, AND U.S. CORPORATE CODES OF ETHICS

PATRICIA CARLSON AND MARK BLODGETT

The authors compare the content of 31 corporate codes of ethics with the Caux Principles. Each of the codes is examined for representative words and phrases taken from the international code. The authors find that there remain areas of inadequate coverage in the corporate codes. The authors then discuss the three major ethical issues of NAFTA, comparing them to the Caux Principles.

NAFTA

This multilateral agreement was executed on January 1, 1994. Some of the main provisions of this unparalleled agreement deal with the elimination of tariff and non-tariff barriers and the facilitation of multinational corporate business operations. Also central to the agreement is a strong position on environmental protection (*San Diego Law Review,* 1994) and intellectual property. The agreement states that each party is to implement the provisions of the agreement so that "there will be a progressive elimination of all tariffs on goods qualifying as North American." It also calls for protection of the environment and intellectual property rights (Litka and Blodgett, 1995, p. 242). NAFTA's ample employment protections are of particular importance since Mexico does not enforce the liberal labor guarantees of its constitution that otherwise bear many similarities to U.S. and Canadian labor laws (Benton, 1993).

NAFTA's provisions deal with some of the most timely issues within the global environment. Do these issues reflect the concerns of businesses as players in a global ethical context? One indication of multinational concern is found in the Caux Round Table Principles of Business Ethics.

CAUX PRINCIPLES

Simultaneous with the implementation of the multilateral agreement (NAFTA) among the U.S., Canada and Mexico to promote free trade by eliminating tariff and non-tariff barriers was the creation of the Caux Principles. Considered to be the first international code of ethics for business, the Caux Round Table Principles originated from a meeting of international business leaders in Caux, Switzerland. These business leaders represented the U.S., Europe and Japan. The Principles are based on an original set of principles known as the Minnesota Principles, developed by the Minnesota Center for Corporate Responsibility (MCCR) affiliated with the University of St. Thomas in the Twin Cities, Minnesota.

The Japanese influence is particularly notable since their concept of *kyosei* "living and working together for the common good" (*Nations Business,* 1996, p. 12) is one of two ethical concepts permeating the Caux Principles. The other concept is "human dignity," defined by the code as the "sacredness or value of each person as an end, not simply as a means to the fulfillment of other's purposes or even majority prescription." (*SBE Newsletter,* 1995, p. 14).

The Caux Principles promote action to further these two main concepts of fairness and respect for others by promoting free trade, environmental and cultural integrity, and the prevention of actions that fall in the category of foreign corrupt practices as defined by U.S. law (bribery, money laundering, etc.). Among the principles that expand upon the concepts of fairness and respect for others, are the following General Principles in Section 2 of the Caux Roundtable Principles for Business:[1]

Principle 2. The economic and social impact of business

Principle 4. Respect for the rules

Principle 5. Support for multilateral trade

Principle 6. Respect for the environment

Principle 7. Avoidance of illicit operations

These principles are further explained as Stakeholder Principles of the Caux Roundtable Principles for Business under the following topics: Customers, Employees, Owners/Investors, Suppliers, Competitors, and Communities. The purpose of this project was to examine codes of ethics from major corporations to determine whether they include the provisions of the Caux Principles. The following sections show the analysis of the data from the corporate codes of ethics and discuss the implications of the findings for responsible corporations acting in the international arena.

---

[1]The authors did not test the more general Caux principles 1 or 3 in this project, since more extensive resources would be required. The authors investigated Caux Principle 3 in a previous project.

METHODOLOGY

The project was carried out in a large northeastern city during the months of February and March, 1994. Codes of ethics were solicited from businesses represented in the area, as evidenced by their presence in the yellow pages. The businesses were chosen based on two criteria: size and industry. Since larger businesses were considered most likely to have formal codes of ethics, the sample was limited to businesses with national prominence (national chains) or those easily recognizable as locally prominent. The industries selected were: retail (fast food, grocery stores, department stores), financial services, utilities and health services.

Each business was contacted to determine the name of the person to whom a follow-up letter should be addressed. Once the name of the person was known, a letter soliciting the company code of ethics was sent by the researchers. A follow-up phone call to those businesses who had not responded within a 2 month time period resulted in a response rate of 84%; 37 letters were sent, 31 codes were received.

Each corporate code of ethics was read by one of the researchers, and references to important concepts were noted. The researchers each read a subset of the other researcher's codes so that the coding would be uniform.

Salient concepts were decided upon before the coding process by combining principles mentioned in NAFTA with those from the Caux Principles. NAFTA is essentially an international trade agreement, which addresses the main issues of multinational trade, environmental protection, intellectual property, and employment, among others. The Caux Principles contain a broad statement of ethical principles encompassing and enlarging upon these NAFTA provisions. The final coding scheme consisted of five all-encompassing concepts from the Caux Principles (see Table 1).

TABLE 1

Data Collection Coding Table

Caux Principle	Name of Principle	Evidence in Corporate Codes of Ethics
Principle 2	The economic and social impact of business	Importance of ethnicity, employee culture, equal opportunity, equal conditions
Principle 4	Respect for the rules	Intellectual property, copyright, trade marks
Principle 5	Support for multilateral trade	Trade, relationship with suppliers, free trade
Principle 6	Respect for the environment	Improve or promote sustainable development, prevent waste, environmental protection
Principle 7	Avoidance of illicit operations	Corrupt practices, bribes, arms, other corrupt practices

DATA

The typical composition of the codes of ethics includes three parts: (1) a cover letter, (2) a general statement at the beginning of the code, (3) a list of compliance situations in which ethical dilemmas may arise. A cover letter was included with 62% of the codes of ethics. The cover letter is always from the Chairman of the Board and/or the Chief Executive Officer (CEO). The letter contains broad general statements about the importance of the code of ethics, and, in many cases, it is this document that instructs the employee about correct behavior when a situation is not specifically mentioned in the code of ethics. It is interesting to note that fully 38% of the companies attached so little importance to the code of ethics that no cover letter from upper management was included.

The general statement that prefaces the formal code of ethics usually consists of from two to six short paragraphs that include information about the importance of the code, who is held to obey the code, and it often contains information about the person who should be contacted when situations not covered in the code of ethics arise.

The final and longest part of the code of ethics (consisting of from 5 to 10 pages) is a list of compliance situations which could present an ethical dilemma to employees. The lists that are most helpful to employees are those that, in addition to listing the situations in formal terms, also give examples of actual situations (the examples are adapted to the particular industry). Some companies have only the lists without explanation or examples of situations. All of these sections were searched for references to the international ethics principles from the Caux Principles.

Each of the codes of ethics was examined for evidence of the five coding categories from Table 1. The data collected is shown in Table 2.

ANALYSIS

The primary objective of the study consisted in determining whether corporate codes of ethics contain any references that show an awareness of international ethical issues. This type of concern would be manifested by statements alluding to any of the General Principles of the Caux Roundtable Principles for Business as shown in Table 1 above. The data collection resulted in the [Table 2] data set.

TABLE 2

Data Set

	The Economic and Social Impact of Business	Respect for the Rules	Support for Multilateral Trade	Respect for the Environment	Avoidance of Illicit Operations
Number of Codes of Ethics	15	8	11	4	31

From the frequencies reported in the data set . . . the areas of major concern in corporate codes of ethics are evident. All of the codes of ethics contained references to illicit operations such as bribery and corrupt practices. Fully half of the codes of ethics contained references to the economic and social impact of business such as equal opportunity for all employees, the importance of ethnicity, and equal conditions of work. Nearly one third of the companies were concerned about multilateral trade and relationships with suppliers. However, a majority of the companies did not mention intellectual property, copyright, and trademarks; only four companies included statements about respect for the environment.

When the information from Table 2 is considered, several concerns of business become apparent:

1. Businesses are very aware of the importance of instructing employees about one of the concepts—avoiding corrupt practices.
2. Businesses seem fairly aware of the importance of instructing employees about proper actions concerning two other concepts.The economic and social impact of business and support for multilateral trade are mentioned by at least one third of the codes of ethics.
3. Businesses are, however, for the most part, not instructing employees about actions regarding two important concepts—respect for the rules (illustrated by respect for intellectual property, copyrights, etc.) and respect for the environment—which are mentioned in only a few of the codes.

Organizations are apparently doing a good job of informing employees about only one out of the five principles, and they are doing an "OK" job for two more principles. What impact could the resulting lack of information have on employee actions in a domestic or an international setting? The importance of this question is discussed in the following section.

CONCLUSIONS AND RECOMMENDATIONS

The data show that employees are not informed about corporate preferences for action at least 50% of the time for four of the principles tested. In this scenario, corporations run the risk that employees will not know how to respond when faced with certain situations. This might lead to two undesirable results:

1. Employees might not act when action should be undertaken.
2. Employees might act in an inappropriate manner.

How important is correct action? From a societal point of view, the Caux Principles tell us that correct action is important and NAFTA tells us that correct action is important. Making incorrect choices concerning employment, trade, intellectual property or environmental protection will lead us to undesirable consequences such as child labor, unfair trade practices, pirating of copyrights, and environmental pollution. These actions have undesirable consequences at a societal level.

How important is correct action at an organizational level? In today's society organizations are expected to be responsible citizens at home. In our global economy organizations must also be responsible citizens abroad. This responsibility is enforced by laws and sanctions which organizations must respect or suffer the consequences in legal action.

Universal adoption of ethical standards such as the Caux Principles will enhance corporate codes of ethics as well as international treaties. From a practical point of view, when these ethical standards are translated into behavior, our global environment will be more desirable and organizations will be required to spend less time preparing for and carrying out litigation.

As members of the "local, national, and global communities in which they operate, businesses share a part in shaping the future." (*Society for Business Ethics Newsletter,* 1995). When corporations are actively promoting kyosei (living and working together for the common good) and human dignity (sacredness or value of each person) the result is a world society where employees, intellectual property, and the environment are respected, trade is enhanced, and business profits.

BIBLIOGRAPHY

1. Benton, Janine, "Extraterritorial Application of the ADA," *George Mason Independent Law Review,* vol. 2, no. 1, 1993, pp. 218–19.
2. Litka, M., and M. Blodgett, *International Dimensions of the Legal Environment of Business,* 3rd ed., South-Western College Publishing, Cincinnati, Ohio, 1995.
3. *Nation's Business,* vol. 84, no. 4, April, 1996.
4. *San Diego Law Review,* vol. 31, no. 4, Fall, 1994, pp. 1025–1055.
5. *Society for Business Ethics (SBE) Newsletter,* "Caux Roundtable Principles for Business," vol. 6, no. 1, May, 1995.

INTERNATIONAL LABOR STANDARDS: THE PERSPECTIVE OF BUSINESS

FRANK P. DOYLE

The following two items present a triangular perspective on the issue of international labor standards. The first item presents the corporate perspective; the second presents the perspective of labor. Consider whether international labor standards are a realistic solution given the cultural differences between nations.

. . . I have to say that the issue of international labor standards is one that concerns the business community. In the past, our concerns have led many of us to resist discussion of the issue. Today, we are increasingly aware that we must participate in the debate.

Let me start by being candid about our concerns. We are concerned, in fact, about protectionism—the inhibition of free markets. Realistically, I think that we can say that there are at least some forces in the world that engage in a form of deliberate protectionism. It's not such a horrible conclusion when you consider that political leaders and labor leaders represent people whose jobs are being threatened. And people whose jobs are being threatened turn to their leadership and say do something about it.

The fact that this kind of protectionism becomes a temptation for some is just realistic. We should acknowledge it, talk about it, and put it in its place.

I think, however, there is a more subtle, and perhaps more widespread, form of protectionism that flows from seeing the world through the filter of our own experience. In ways discussed earlier today, there are issues one might assume would find universal agreement—child labor being a classic case—and yet the definition of what constitutes child labor varies radically around the world. The alternatives to child labor in many less developed nations may be even more horrible.

Finally, let me tell you why I think the debate must be engaged. This time, and I've said this to business audiences, something real may happen. I distinguish today from the rhetorical past where lots of things were advanced, but when push came to shove, and it was trade, exports, and jobs versus the realities of what was going on in some other nation, we would duck our heads and go forward in trade. We have been unwilling to make the tradeoff, sacrificing U.S. export jobs for imposing and measuring other societies, except in

Frank P. Doyle, "International Labor Standards: The Perspective of Business," from *International Labor Standards and Global Economic Integration: Proceedings of a Symposium* (July 1994).

the most egregious cases. The only case I can think of where such efforts had a long-term effect was in South Africa. . . .

What happens when a network of unilateral, often conflicting, sanctions and values are created around the world? I've used the example of the days when conflicting state initiatives eventually caused many in the United States to say that federal preemption looked pretty good. I raise the analogy to point out that we may now be facing an impenetrable network of unilateral or coerced bilateral agreements that will be far more burdensome and far more damaging to world trade than a rational set of carefully negotiated standards of conduct that apply to everyone.

Unilaterally imposed solutions on worker rights usually don't work. Developing countries have vigorously opposed, and will vigorously oppose, intrusions on their sovereignty. The United States should not over-estimate its current or future ability to act unilaterally. We are a less dominant part of the world economy today than we were ten years ago, and ten years from now, other nations—China being a case in point—may become more important in the future. China is now a less leveraged economy in world terms than we are; but who can say where they will be twenty years from now. This argument suggests that where there are leverage shifts, partnership rather than dominance becomes the defining element in world politics and, therefore, in world trade.

So I would suggest that effective worker rights standards must be negotiated between equal partners, and accepted as mutually advantageous. Standards imposed by the more powerful on the weak are not likely to have a long life.

Where, then, do I stand on the question of what's the most appropriate forum, and what's the role of the ILO? My conclusion is that the ILO is equipped to deal with worker rights issues, and the World Trade Organization is far less so. . . .

We must reevaluate the work of the ILO and ask it to use its resources to reach consensus on workable, universally accepted labor standards that are as applicable to developing countries as they are to the developed world. . . .

The new agenda will have to recognize the fact that worker rights that don't promote employment growth and economic development are not in the best long term interest of workers.

I close by saying that those who suggest that there are easy and obvious answers do not understand the highly complex, fast changing, economic world, and the competitive nature of doing business in a world economy.

INTERNATIONAL LABOR STANDARDS: THE PERSPECTIVE OF LABOR

Thomas R. Donahue

I come to you at a moment when I think most of what can be said about international labor standards has been said, and most of the ideas have been discussed. I listened to Frank Doyle, and note that he speaks for the best of the business community. I wish that all of the business community was as engaged in this subject. We can argue about the details, and we can argue about how this ought to be done, but he speaks in a way that says to the business community: this is an idea whose time has come. This is an idea that needs to be advanced.

On the subject of protectionism—just to clarify before I begin—I'm for it. As I define it, and as I think Frank began to define it, protectionism is a principle of self-interest that drives action. Anybody in this room who doesn't practice it should be very careful crossing the street, because they may be killed by a car.

The rest of the debate about protectionism has become too much of a screen for denial of change, denial of an honest evaluation of what is competitive and what is not, and I think we ought to put it to rest.

If protectionism is defined as closing markets, then I'm against it. If it is defined as limiting trade and attempting to return to an earlier era, I'm against it. So too is the Federation.

As for international labor standards, let me say that the Federation has argued for them for more than 100 years. We have consistently supported the International Labor Organization's (ILO's) development of those standards. We have sought, wherever possible, to advance international labor standards, and in particular to advance the opportunity for workers to improve their own conditions through their own actions. We have pressed for unilateral action through our efforts on the Generalized System of Preferences (GSP), the Overseas Private Insurance Corporation (OPIC), the Caribbean Basin Initiative (CBI) legislation, and in a variety of other forums.

The conversation in every meeting of this type, or any discussion of international economics, always somehow begins with the phrase, "the global village." If they gave a Pulitzer Prize for the metaphor of the year, that ought to be the winner for 1993, 1994, and 1995, I suspect. . . .

When they talked about comparative advantage, they talked about country size, natural resources, climate, or geographic location as determining a country's unique comparative

Thomas R. Donahue, "International Labor Standards: The Perspective of Labor," in *International Labor Standards and Global Economic Integration: Proceedings of a Symposium* (July 1994).

advantage. But that's not the case today. For more and more countries, the advantage, which they will preserve at almost any cost, is not unique or distinctive. It is a workforce that is poor, desperate, and vulnerable to exploitation, and an environment that an individual nation is, at best, slow to protect.

There are plenty of examples of this. I shall not bore you with them beyond noting one of the most blatant examples. It is the case of the Mexican maquiladoras along our southern border. Over 600,000 people work at wage rates which are, on average, $1 an hour less than the average manufacturing rates in the interior of Mexico. One has to ask, why? What forces have conspired to provide a large, exploited workforce in an environment that creates conditions that the *Wall Street Journal* called "a social and economic inferno?"

Why are those people denied their rights? Because the day that the maquiladoras pay higher wages, is the day that they begin thinking about moving someplace else. That's the terror that we have to get over, that we have to put behind us, and I submit the only way we will do that is with the adoption of a set of international standards and provisions for their enforcement.

The debate takes a funny turn. Some claim that it now becomes another North/South issue. Nothing could be further from the truth. This is not a North/South issue nor is it a developed versus developing country issue. I could show you a stack of letters about two inches high from organizations representing workers all around the world, pleading for the development and enforcement of international standards on worker rights. I don't have a lot of letters from corporations urging that, but workers are very clear on this issue. They want development and enforcement of a scheme of international labor standards.

In Morocco two weeks ago, the only discussions on this issue implied that this is another developed/undeveloped country argument over protectionism. That particular charge was fueled, I think, by the careless remarks of the GATT Director-General a week or so earlier in his discussions of comparative advantage and the charge that the developed nations are trying to protect themselves by insisting on imposing their wage standards, their occupational safety and health standards, their environmental standards, and so forth upon less-developed countries.

Obviously, this is false. Anybody who thinks that less-developed nations can quickly create unions which would be strong enough to achieve the conditions achieved in the developed nations needs to rethink that view.

Rather, what we argue for is the creation of conditions in which the workers of less-developed nations can form unions and affect their society in their way and at their levels, to improve the life circumstances of working people.

We think that the ILO standards that are already in place are the ones that ought to be applied. We don't have to search for a new consensus. Standards on freedom of association, on collective bargaining, on non-discrimination in employment, on forced labor, and on child labor are a very good beginning. We ought to be very clear to all of the naysayers in the developing nations that this is what we're talking about. . . .

I don't think that we need an elaborate new structure. The ILO standards are in place. However, I think what is essential is to link these standards to an action mechanism that will bring reality to the discussion. I remember very early in my career being asked by an employer to take down a picket line while we negotiated a contract. An older hand whom I was with said, "You can't do that. Don't be silly. That's the only thing that turns discussion into negotiation." Only an enforcement mechanism will turn discussion into negotiation. . . .

MULTICULTURAL PERSPECTIVE

FUNDAMENTAL INTERNATIONAL RIGHTS

THOMAS DONALDSON

Donaldson identifies some of the items that should appear on a list of fundamental international rights. Donaldson defines a fundamental international right as satisfying three conditions: the right must protect something of great importance, the right must be subject to substantial and recurrent threats, and the duties associated with the right must be limited in light of fairness and affordability.

. . . Though probably not complete, the following list contains items that appear to satisfy the three conditions and hence to qualify as fundamental international rights:

1. The right to freedom of physical movement
2. The right to ownership of property
3. The right to freedom from torture
4. The right to a fair trial
5. The right to nondiscriminatory treatment (freedom from discrimination on the basis of such characteristics as race or sex)
6. The right to physical security
7. The right to freedom of speech and association
8. The right to minimal education
9. The right to political participation
10. The right to subsistence

This is a minimal list. Some will wish to add entries such as the right to employment, to social security, or to a certain standard of living (say, as might be prescribed by Rawls' well-known "difference" principle). Disputes also may arise about the wording or overlapping features of some rights: for example, is not the right to freedom from torture included in the right to physical security, at least when the latter is properly interpreted? We shall not attempt to resolve such controversies here. Rather, the list as presented aims to suggest, albeit incompletely, a description of a *minimal* set of rights and to serve as a beginning consensus for evaluating international conduct. If I am correct, many would wish to add entries, but few would wish to subtract them.

The list has been generated by application of the three conditions and the compatibility proviso. Each reader may decide whether the ten entries fulfill these conditions; in

---

Thomas Donaldson, *Fundamental International Rights*, reprinted by permission of Oxford University Press, Inc.

doing so, however, remember that in constructing the list one looks for *only* those rights that can be honored in some form by *all* international moral agents, including nation-states, corporations, and individuals. Hence, to consider only the issue of affordability, each candidate for a right must be tested for "affordability" by way of the lowest common denominator—by way, for example, of the poorest nation-state. If, even after receiving its fair share of charitable aid from wealthier nations, that state cannot "afford" kidney dialysis for all citizens who need it, then the right to receive dialysis from one's nation-state will not be a fundamental international right, although dialysis may constitute a bona fide right for those living within a specific nation-state, such as Japan.

Even though the hope for a definitive interpretation of the list of rights is an illusion, we can add specificity by clarifying the correlative duties entailed for different kinds of international actors. Because by definition the list contains items that all three major classes of international actors must respect, the next task is to spell out the correlative duties that fall upon our targeted group of international actors, namely, multinational corporations.

This task requires putting the "fairness-affordability" condition to a second, and different, use. This condition was first used as one of the three criteria generating the original list of fundamental rights. There it demanded satisfaction of a fairness-affordability threshold for each potential respecter of a right. For example, if the burdens imposed by a given right are not fair (in relation to other bona fide obligations and burdens) or affordable for nation-states, individuals, and corporations, then presumably the prospective right would not qualify as a fundamental international right.*

In its second use, the "fairness-affordability" condition goes beyond the judgment *that* a certain fairness-affordability threshold has been crossed to the determination of *what* the proper duties are for multinational corporations in relation to a given right. In its second use, in other words, the condition's notions of fairness and affordability are invoked to help determine *which* obligations properly fall upon corporations, in contrast to individuals and nation-states. The condition can help determine the correlative duties that attach to multinational corporations in their honoring of fundamental international rights.

SAMPLE APPLICATIONS

Discrimination

The obligation to protect a person from deprivation of the right to freedom from discrimination properly falls upon corporations as well as governments insofar as everyday corporate activities directly affect compliance with that right. Because employees and

---

*It is worth noting that fundamental international rights are not the only type of rights. In addition there are legal rights and nation-specific moral rights. For example, the right to sue for damages under the doctrine of strict liability (where compensation can be demanded even without demonstrating negligence) is a legal right in the United States, although it would not qualify as a fundamental international right and is not a legal right in some other nation-states. Similarly, the right to certain forms of technologically advanced medical care such as CAT scanning for cancerous tumors may be a nation-specific moral right in highly industrialized countries (even when it is not guaranteed as a legal right) but could not qualify at this point in history as a fundamental international right.

prospective employees possess the moral right not to be discriminated against on the basis of race, sex, caste, class, or family affiliation, it follows that multinational corporations have an obligation not only to refrain from discrimination, but in some instances to protect the right to nondiscriminatory treatment by establishing appropriate procedures. This may require, for example, offering notice to prospective employees about the company's policy of nondiscriminatory hiring, or educating lower-level managers about the need to reward or penalize on the basis of performance rather than irrelevant criteria.

Physical Security

The right to physical security similarly entails duties of protection. If a Japanese multinational corporation operating in Nigeria hires shop workers to run metal lathes in an assembly factory, but fails to provide them with protective goggles, then the corporation has failed to honor the workers' moral right to physical security (no matter what the local law might decree). Injuries from such a failure would be the moral responsibility of the Japanese multinational despite the fact that the company could not be said to have inflicted the injuries directly.

Free Speech and Association

In the same vein, the duty to protect from deprivation the right of free speech and association finds application in the ongoing corporate obligation not to bar the creation of labor unions. Corporations are not obliged on the basis of human rights to encourage or welcome labor unions; indeed they may oppose them using all morally acceptable means at their disposal. But neither are they morally permitted to destroy them or prevent their emergence through coercive tactics; for to do so would violate their workers' international right to association. The corporation's duty to protect from deprivation the right to association, in turn, includes refraining from lobbying host governments for restrictions that would violate the right in question, and perhaps even to protesting host government measures in countering the well-documented tendency of multinationals to mask immoral practices in the rhetoric of "tolerance" and "cultural relativity." According to this algorithm, no multinational manager can naively suggest that asbestos standards in Chile are permissible because they are accepted there. Nor can a manager infer that the standards are acceptable on the grounds that the Chilean economy is, relative to the multinational's home country, underdeveloped. A surprising amount of moral blindness occurs not because people's fundamental moral views are confused, but because their cognitive application of those views to novel situations is misguided.

What guarantees that multinationals possess the knowledge or objectivity to apply the algorithm fairly? As Richard Barnet quips, "On the fifty-sixth floor of a Manhattan skyscraper, the level of self-protective ignorance about what the company may be doing in Colombia or Mexico is high." Can Exxon or Johns Manville be trusted to have a sufficiently sophisticated sense of "fundamental rights," or to weigh dispassionately the hypothetical attitudes of their fellow citizens under conditions of "relevantly similar economic development"? My answer to this is "perhaps not," at least given the present character of the decision-making procedures in most global corporations. But this only serves to underscore the need for more sophisticated, and more ethically sensitive, decision-making techniques in multinationals. And I would add that from a theoretical perspective the problem is a contingent and practical one. It is no more a theoretical flaw of the proposed algorithm that it may be misunderstood or misapplied by a given multinational, than it is of Rawls's theory of justice that it may be conveniently misunderstood by a trickle-down Libertarian.

What would need to change in order for multinationals to make use of the algorithm? Most of all, multinationals would need to enhance the sophistication of their decision making. They would need to alter established patterns of information flow and collection to accommodate moral information. They would need to introduce alongside analyses of the bottom line, analyses of historical tendencies, health, rights, and demography. And they might even find it necessary to introduce a new class of employee to provide expertise in these areas. However unlikely such changes are, I believe they are within the realm of possibility. Multinationals, the organizations capable of colonizing our international future, are no doubt also capable of applying—at a minimum—the same moral principles abroad that they accept at home.

BUSINESS ETHICS IN THE MIDDLE EAST
Dove Izraeli

To provide some basis for a multicultural perspective, the following items identify some of the key issues in business ethics facing other countries. Israeli details ethical issues facing businesses in the Middle East, while Guoxi discusses the ethical environment of business in mainland China.

INTRODUCTION

The idea of preparing a report on Business Ethics in the Middle East was initiated by the organizers of [the first] World Congress [of Business, Economics, and Ethics]. When the program chairperson, Dr. George Enderle, approached me to prepare the report, I immediately agreed to do so with the thought that gathering the material would provide me an opportunity to cooperate with Palestinians and scholars from other Middle Eastern countries working in the same field. I also welcomed the invitation because it focused on the interface of my three fields of specialization: Middle East Studies, Business (marketing and management), and Business Ethics. It also related to the peace process, which for me, like for many Israelis, is a life's dream coming true. Although I knew very little about the field of Business Ethics in other countries of the Middle East, I assumed that in this age of modern technology and internet, the search for information would be fairly straightforward and that my major task would be to plow through the material, analyze and evaluate it, discuss the main ideas with Arab scholars and others acquainted with the issues and report my findings for further discussion and research.

To my dismay, despite considerable effort on my part, the material gathering stage revealed very few research articles and despite my requests for information and contacts over the internet and netscape, I received few relevant responses. The purpose of this report, therefore, is to report on what I did find from secondary sources and personal interviews and suggest an agenda for future development. I wish to put special emphasis on the new challenges and opportunities generated by the peace process in the Middle East.

1. The Concept of Business Ethics in the Middle East

There is no commonly used term in either Arabic or Hebrew for the concept of Business Ethics. This suggests that the very concept is still unfamiliar for most people and approximate equivalents have to be constructed.

---

2. Stereotypes about Business Ethics in the Middle East

There are many negative stereotypes of the level of Business Ethics in the Middle East. People from different countries whom I interviewed about their opinions and thoughts on the subject of Business Ethics in the region often responded with a chuckle or smile, a knowing wink and a derogatory wave of the hand. This was followed by a short explanation that these concepts are a contradiction in terms: business does not go with ethics and that Western norms of Business Ethics did not apply in the Middle East. Sometimes this would be followed by stories of their personal experiences of unethical behavior in business or of stories reported in the newspaper of business ethical misdeeds. Many referred to the practice of bakshish, translatable as tip or bribe, as an example of widespread corruption.

The responses I received were clearly stereotypical and influenced by prejudice and ignorance. But the Middle East is not unique in this respect. The media of all countries have reports of business scandals and I have found that in most countries people tend to consider that ethics and business are contradictory terms—an oxymoron. Such cynical and unfounded beliefs, however, are in themselves problematic in that they undermine the trust so important in business and economic development.

3. Business Ethics in the Academia

Apart from in Israel which I will return to, to the best of my knowledge Business Ethics is not institutionalized in the Academia in the Middle East. I was told by my interviews and my own search supported this finding that Business Ethics courses are not taught, very little research is being conducted, there are not any specific publications on the issues, nor any regular training on Business Ethics.

In Israel there is at least one elective Business Ethics course taught in all the business schools but in none is it compulsory. There is an Israeli text and reader on Business Ethics and a modest publication that appears at irregular intervals. In 1995 the Israeli Network for Social Responsibility established the Academic Forum for Ethics and Social Responsibility—a national network of academics from a variety of disciplines concerned with ethical issues in their respective fields. . . .The network held a founding conference in 1995 and provides an arena for stimulating interest in the teaching and research of ethics in different disciplines, including business and academic exchanges.

An Israeli initiative in cooperation with the Academia is the International Jerusalem Conference on Ethics in the Public Service, the third of which took place in Jerusalem in 1995 with participants from the Palestinian Authority. Unfortunately, repeated attempts to involve participants from other countries in the Middle East have not been successful to date. Hopefully with the progress of the peace process there will be more readiness on the part of other countries to participate.

An initiative outside the Middle East provides an interesting example of the way the Academia in countries with more developed Business Ethics programs may provide an impetus for the development of interest in the subject in the Middle East. I refer to the *Middle East Business Review*—a new journal out of the University of London whose first issue is announced in Netscape as scheduled to be published in Spring 1996. Although Business Ethics was not included in the subject areas to be covered, I expect that the review potentially provides a locale for publishing in this area as well. I would like to add that Israel unfortunately was not listed among the 14 Geographical areas of the Middle East to be included.

4. Business Ethics in the Private Sector

I found no Business Ethics initiatives in the private sector. None of the local companies have ethical codes although there are some beginnings among firms involved in multinational business. There are no business initiatives against corruption even though, with the growth of business, white collar crime is on the increase in all countries. With few exceptions, there are also no business initiatives in the training of employees or managers on Business Ethics.

5. Corruption

5.1 Government against Corruption   Most governments in the Middle East have agencies whose specific purpose is to combat corruption among government officials. For example: the Central Audit Agency and Administrative Control Agency in Egypt, the State Comptroller and Ombudsman and special police units to combat white collar crime in Israel. These agencies which focus on corruption in government administration have indirect relations to Business Ethics in so far as business is sometimes involved as culprits in the use of corruption for promoting its interests.

5.2 Comparative Measures of Corruption   The Berlin-based Transparency International Organization and Gottingen University recently published the results of an international poll, conducted in 54 countries using its Corruption Perception index. The 54 countries were rated on corruption defined as the misuse of public power for private benefits. These misuses include bribing public officials, taking kickbacks in public procurement or embezzling public funds. The index score was based on 10 international surveys of businessmen and reflects their impressions and perceptions and not necessarily the reality of the level of corruption of the country. The 54 countries were ranked according to their corruption index score from 1 (most corrupt) to 54 (least corrupt). The scores ranged from 0 (highest level of corruption) to 10 (lowest level). The scores and rank order for the five countries of the Middle East included in the survey are listed below:

Country	Score	Rank
Kuwait	2.58	8
Egypt	2.86	14
Turkey	3.54	22
Jordan	4.89	25
Israel	7.71	41

SOURCE: Yediot Ahronot 4.6.96 pp. 10–11 (Hebrew daily)

6. Business Ethics and the Ecology Movement

One of the interesting recent developments in the Middle East is the cross national cooperation in the field of ecology and the establishment of a roof organization for the ecology/environmental organizations in Egypt, Jordan, Israel and Palestine. The business community is in many cases represented in the organizations both in the participating countries and in EcoPeace, the roof organization.

The disastrous ecological consequences of the Gulf War was an important consciousness raising experience concerning the importance of guarding the environment and catalyst for a variety of initiatives. The Peace process was the catalyst for the establishment of EcoPeace. In March 1995, EcoPeace, a Middle Eastern Environmental NGO Forum began intensive activity serving as a linking organization among the ecological organizations in Egypt, Jordan, Israel and Palestine around issues which require cooperation across borders. EcoPeace provides an interesting model for the possibilities of cross national cooperation in this region. The first major project of EcoPeace is associated with the development of sustainable tourism for the Dead Sea area. EcoPeace has already held a number of conferences in those countries, with the purpose of gathering information, preparing development programs and putting pressure on government and business to give greater priority to ecological considerations. Its projects initiated in 1995 include: a Gulf of Aqaba Task Force, Development Projects Inventory and Review, Regional Experts Inventory, a Regional Environment Journal, a Capacity Building Program and a Regional Environmental Emergency Fund.

7. Cultural Issues in Business Ethics

Business Ethics are culture specific and what is considered normative in one culture may be considered unethical in another. In Arab countries favoritism, nepotism and personal connections have a significant impact on managers' decisions (for a review of research see Atiyyah, 1992). This is usually explained in terms of cultural factors such as strong kinship ties and obligations that expect individuals to give preference to family. David Weir (1993) suggests that there is a distinguishable Arab managerial paradigm built on the notion of 'trading' and that emphasizes kinship and networked market orientation. In Israel political patronage is fairly widespread. The close ties between the various elites including economic and political elites also result in favoritism.

The subordinate position of women in the work force and in business organizations is another cultural issue where normative standards of equality prevalent in most industrialized countries are not accepted in many Arab countries. Atiyyah (1992) notes that only 15% of Arab women in Arab countries above the age of 15 are actually in employment. The proportion of Arab women employed in Israel is not very much higher.

8. Looking to the Future

In conclusion I would like to consider some of the trends that I believe will impact on developments in Business Ethics in the coming decade and some of the developments that are needed in a global economy.

8.1 The Globalisation of Business   The entry of multinational corporations which have developed codes of ethics and training programs in business ethics may further influence such developments through the implementation of similar policies in their Middle East subsidiaries.

There is the beginning of interests in the globalisation of business in the Middle East. The first conference on the Globalisation of Arab Business, being organized from the UK, will be held in Kuwait in Sept. 1966. An awareness of and commitment to business ethics is especially important in international business where institutionalized safeguards are less established and transactions are between people from different cultures. The success of globalisation is dependent on the establishment of a universe of meaning and of discourse on normative patterns of behavior.

8.2 The Need for Incorporating the Stakeholder Concept   Business people in the Middle East have a very narrow and limited conception of who the stakeholders are in their organizations. It is usually limited to the stockholders. The need to establish a wider view of stakeholders as including workers, suppliers, consumers and the public at large as a necessary condition for the development of Business Ethics in the Middle East.

8.3 The Need for Understanding the Philosophical and Normative Underpinning of Business Ethical Behavior in the Middle East   Most concepts and courses on Business Ethics were developed in western Christian dominated countries. This leads to ethnocentric perspectives about ethical standards. There is a need to examine in what ways and to what extent the normative ideas about business behavior in the various cultures of the Middle East are similar to or different from those of the West.

8.4 The Peace Process   The peace process in the Middle East is still in embryo and years of hostility are not erased with the signing of treaties. Common business interests can be an important leverage for increasing trust and mutual understanding and the strengthening of business ethics would be an important catalyst in this process.

REFERENCES

1. Al-Alfy, Hassan. "Acquired Expertise in Adopting Practical Measures to Combat Bribing Government Officials." Unpublished paper presented at the 9th International Congress for Crime Prevention and Treatment of Offenders, Cairo, Egypt, May 4, 1995.
2. Atiyyah, Hamid S. "Research note: Research in Arab Countries, Published in Arabic." *Organization Studies* 13:1 pp. 105–110. 1992.
3. Izraeli, Dove. "Business Ethics in Israel," in E. Freeman and P. Verhane (eds.) *Business Ethics Dictionary and Encyclopedia.* Cambridge, MA: Blackwell, 1996.
4. Weir, David. "Management in the Arab World." Paper presented at the first Arab Management Conference, Bradford University, Bradford, U.K., July 6–8, 1993, pp. 604–623.

MAJOR ISSUES OF BUSINESS ETHICS IN MAINLAND CHINA

Gao Guoxi

The author discusses the emergence of business ethics as an area of study in China and offers his prescription for further study and action.

By now the major issues that need more attentions in the business ethics field in mainland China are the following: The academic discipline of business ethics requires the approval and support of entrepreneurs and enterprises; Equal treatment of technical and human aspects in management; The relationship between justice and efficiency in business organizations; Benefits and social obligation of business; The Corporate Identity System and its relationship between image creation and management practice; The scope of power of top management and its constraints; The ethical rationality of autonomous corporate management and macro-economic policy by the government.

The emergence of business ethics in mainland China represents a great challenge to this old and fresh continent and brings vital strength to the fields of ethical theories and business practices. While business ethics is still at its beginning, there are four major tasks for both scholars and entrepreneurs:

First, the in-depth investigation of the moral status and level of business activities in mainland China in order to adequately grasp the ethical problems involved in those activities. In the course of the reform and opening process the practices of life provide a particularly suitable atmosphere for the development of business ethics. With the help of surveys, personal interviews, and other techniques the actual situation is to be described and analyzed in objective and scientific terms. . . .

Second, the introduction of recent achievements in the field business ethics from outside China. It is of great importance to business education and practice under the conditions of the contemporary market economy. Nowadays academics as well as entrepreneurs are increasingly aware of this urgent need. They are realizing that theory and practice of business ethics in western countries are not only suitable to those countries, but also offer many experiences and insights to market economies in general. Hence an important project of the Centre of Applied Ethics is to introduce western business ethics to readers in China. Accordingly, various western approaches to business ethics were compared and published in the widely-known journal "Social Sciences Abroad."

Third, on the basis of a thorough understanding of the actual situation in China and the contribution from business ethics outside China, a kind of prolegomena of business ethics is to be developed that can operate effectively in the Chinese situation.[1]

Fourth, according to the normative and practical orientation of business ethics, cooperation between business practitioners and academics is crucial in order to develop operational guidelines for business practice which integrate both "good ethics" and "good business." This objective of business ethics is of paramount importance, yet very difficult to achieve because the successful integration depends not only on theoretical clarification and reasoning but also on the competence of and support of business people. . . .

Business ethics in mainland China is a new challenge to both academics and entrepreneurs which involves the following major issues:

1. Business ethics requires the approval and support of entrepreneurs and enterprises

Frankly speaking, without the support of business, business ethics remains a merely academic undertaking and cannot achieve its important tasks. As the investigation of the Centre for Applied Ethics on "Ethical Perceptions of Business People in East China" reveals, the enterprises which recognize the importance of business ethics are at a low percentage. Only a few companies realize that they should pay attention to the moral dimension of management. Some enterprises use business ethics as a tool for marketing or window-dressing. Therefore, it is important to develop rules and regulations on the basis of the appropriate roles and essential personal characteristics of business people. These guidelines should be neither purely external obligations nor arbitrary.

To implement business ethics in mainland China today, one has to pay more attention to the discipline of business codes of conduct. These operating rules and guidelines should be set up and enforced by established institutions and associations. However, the prevailing view in China is that, at present, the development of the economy be the most urgent objective. So most factories and districts strive for beneficial economic results. In contrast, ethics in business is not considered urgent to them.

This situation represents a great challenge for business ethics. To sensitize and educate business people is a very difficult task because many people in developing countries believe that the first and most important thing is to develop the economy while they lose sight of other essential things. The economy overrides everything at the first stage of development in a market economy. This prejudice strongly influences many people, including governors, entrepreneurs, and workers.

2. Equal treatment of technical and human aspects in management

Nowadays in China the two aspects of management and corporate life—technical and human resources—are not handled in a balanced way. In fact, technical considerations prevail in most enterprises which seek to increase their "utility." Certainly, there are also some companies which are sensitive to ethical issues and aspire for higher ethical standards; they anticipate the future of business in China.

3. The relationship between justice and efficiency in business organizations

Employees in enterprises are most concerned about the problem of distributive justice which has a direct impact on their activities in the workplace and their opinion about their organizations in the society. The criterion to measure the ethical level of the enterprise is to what extent the organization of labor is rational.

Along with the reform of the system of labor arrangements, many problems have arisen. For example, when a certain unit (such as a corporation, a workshop, or a group) plans to reorganize its labor force, who should stay and who should be laid off? How should this question be dealt with by the social security system that is now in the process of radical transformation: by the old or the new system? If priority of employment is given to young workers, efficiency may be improved; however, the financial resources of the units were created by the older workers who have not reached the age of retirement yet and who would lose their investments. So the dilemma seems unavoidable: Either we seek justice and reduce efficiency or we choose efficiency and abandon justice. More-over, the way of handling the lay-off issue will certainly affect the motivations and activi-ties of the employees. In short, the principle of justice in enterprises needs to be investi-gated seriously: what do equal opportunity and just distribution according to work mean? Does the principle of justice in enterprises include only these two aspects? Furthermore, a host of difficulties remains when tackling with the implementation of more just and more efficient organizations.

4. Benefits and social obligations of business

Business is the most important institution nowadays to provide the livelihood of peo-ple. In different forms of business organizations human beings spend a great deal of their time, do their work, and earn their living. However, business could not exist without the support of society that is necessary for the existence and development of business. Be-cause business organizations exist in, and benefit from, society, they also have social obligations and should give something back to the society. This, however, does not just emerge spontaneously. Thus business ethics as a conscious endeavor is needed to advo-cate, promote, apply, and cultivate a balanced relationship between business and society. Committed entrepreneurs with their foresight, sagacity and unique mission play a critical role in this process which aims beyond the narrow benefits of business.

In contrast, enterprises may solely strive for accumulation of wealth and self-devel-opment and limit their responsibilities to maximizing their profits (and minimizing their losses) while denying any responsibility to society. They only seek their own interests and do not bring themselves into the whole social system. Therefore, the relationship be-tween maximizing corporate profits and corporate social responsibility is a very impor-tant problem. For sure, enterprises should seek profits, but they should achieve it in an ethical way.

In ancient China the benefits produced by business (profit) were called "Li" while morality was called "Yi." Under normal conditions of the market economy both benefits and morality are the roots of the enterprise's existence and development. Only with this balanced view the far-reaching importance of business ethics becomes understandable. The market economy is a kind of productive system in which the production for oneself is intrinsically interwoven with the production for others. Only through the production "for-others" can one produce "for oneself." This mutually dependent "metabolism of commodities" was characterized by Karl Marx as a relationship in which "individuals exist for others, but the others also exist for them." So the question arises as to what is the difference between the cooperation of enterprises in society and the selfish pursuit of cor-porate interest. How can the former be promoted and the latter be prevented? . . .

7. The ethical rationality of autonomous corporate management and macro-economic policy by the government

The aim of the macro-economic policy of the government is to determine the model of adjusting and controlling the markets according to economic and social criteria so that the enterprises are led by the markets. Although the role of government for macro adjustment and control by legislation and policies is indispensable, the market economy and government control cannot function without the moral support of the people and their adjusting values to the new situation. Only if the whole economy, the legislation, the governmental policies, and the conduct of enterprises are based on a common morality and value-orientation, the processes of adjusting and controlling the market economy can be realized in a conscientious, effective, and forceful way. Therefore, common criteria for value-orientation and codes of conduct are needed.

In spite of laws and regulations, the market economy leaves broad free space to the economic actors, which, in turn, involves ethical responsibility. To the extent one can make free choices, one bears ethical responsibility accordingly. While the market economy in the West has developed as a contract economy over a long period of time, the situation in China differs considerably. The contract economy in the West has been based on a developing civil society in which the contractual economic relationship among citizens is of far-reaching importance. By contrast, before the reform and opening in mainland China, social life was predominantly political. Over thousands of years the political social life has become a strong and pervasive tradition that covered all aspects and levels of social life while civil society did not flourish at all.

Against this historical backdrop, the support by the government to launch and foster the process of contractual relations is necessary. At the same time, however, the very idea of the contract economy requires to reduce as far as possible the control and interference of government. Hence, it demands a great amount of care to deal with the relationship between the government that tends to interfere and business that claims more autonomy.

What is necessary is that each market participant aims at striking a balance between both: to have the courage to resist the unreasonable interference of government, and, at the same time, to respect the reasonable authority of government. The enterprise as "social person" and market participant unavoidably faces the question of social morality that cannot be answered by the rules of the market and the laws of the state exhaustively. The rules of the market are but one kind of norms which need longstanding practice to become an internally accepted moral order. The laws basically contain minimal requirements. So a wide field of human behavior remains that is influenced and guided by norms of morality and habits.

Admittedly, there are many and great difficulties to develop business ethics in China. However, the society seems to expect that China will move towards a relatively comprehensive understanding and practice of business ethics.

ENDNOTE

1. In line with this, the Centre for Applied Ethics is preparing a series of books on applied ethics, including business ethics. It will not only analyze the situation of applied ethics in China, but also introduce the recent initiatives and achievements in the field of applied ethics abroad. However, the work is still at the first and second level mentioned above and is far from covering a comprehensive view on applied ethics in China.

ETHICS OF HOPE VERSUS ETHICS OF DISILLUSIONMENT

Tadeux Borkowski

Polish Professor Borkowski asked his students at the Jagiellonian University in Krakow to draft brief case studies highlighting specific instances of ethical breaches or dilemmas. Their perceptions and descriptions follow.

MARIUSZ ZAWADZKI

In 1988 the modern tannery started its work in Kracow. Due to industry restructuring starting in 1990 the financial situation got worse and worse each year. This situation was a result of breaking contracts with the eastern market which was the main buyer of the Kracow tannery products. In this difficult time the enterprise was transformed into a company belonging to the State treasury. After four years Jan Nowak became the main technology manager. He was an employee respected by the worker and managers, with long experience. Under his management, due to the introduction of many innovative reforms in manufacturing and sales the firm became profitable. One year after Jan Nowak became a technological manager, there was a failure of the main silo. The damage was due to faulty construction and was not a result of Nowak's neglect. In this silo there was stored acids necessary for technological treatment of leather. The damage to the silo involved a breakage in the middle of its acid-resistant surface. The acids being under pressure caused a quick corrosion of the outside of the container. The board of directors under Jan Nowak's chairmanship had two options:

The first was to replace the silo with a new one.

The second option was to lower the level of the acid to a point below the location of the damage, but in this case redundant acids had to be put into a river, due to a lack of a suitable container.

The first of the options would result in at least a three-month standstill, which in practice meant a collapse of the firm and sacking of all employees.

The second option would result in two-week standstill and biological contamination of a nearby river and ground waters within an area of several kilometres.

The question was: Should the management and the main technologist decide to deprive all employees of financial means and cause a collapse of the enterprise now that the firm had become profitable and started to prosper in the free market economy? Or, perhaps should they contaminate the river and ground waters which would be used by local inhabitants, in this case preventing the firm from bankruptcy and giving work to 600 people. The manager knew that fines for environment contamination were relatively low and could be spread over time, and the firm had no time to spare. What should Jan Nowak do?

The solution to this problem occurred by chance. The fire brigade unit located in the same street got for testing some equipment for chemical life-saving which included a container for storing acids. This container was made available for the period required to repair the silo.

PIOTR KISIEL

I met a problem of unethical behaviour working in one of the shops in Kracow last year. It concerns many small shops, firms, and restaurants. For employers the main problem is the social security system not reformed for years. The owners do not want to employ workers permanently or in the column 'payment' put down a much lower amount. This happens because an employer must pay a tax of as much as 48% of the employee's pay. So, if a worker earned 1000 zloty, for example, then the cost of his/her employment would be about 1500 zloty, which would be a much higher sum. We must remember that as a rule in a small firm there is more than one employee. This can amount to astronomical sums which the firm's owner must pay for old age pensioners.

It seems that in the present government coalition there is not enough courage for radical changes in the whole system of social security. If the rates were lowered, the illegal employment would be diminished, because most of the owners would decide to reveal the real salaries of the employees. Then payments into the social security budget would certainly increase and the problem of old age pensioners would be solved.

On the other hand, very often it is in the interest of employees, young people, dropouts to work illegally. They are registered in the employment office as unemployed, and in spite of that they work. They receive double income. We must remember that unemployment benefits are paid from our taxes and with the higher unemployment rate the government will not lower taxes. One of the elementary principles of economy says that taxes 'kill' entrepreneurship and too high taxes increase black market.

This problem is difficult to solve, but the act allowing clerks to examine citizens' bank accounts will only increase it.

MAGDALENA KUBICKA

In a shop selling household goods "Domar," a new shop assistant, was employed for a probation period. Apart from her, two other girls, Beata and Agnieszka, worked there as well. Work went on well. The new shop assistant got involved in the work very quickly, and the two girls helped her, because they had worked there for a few years. One day after work, when the owner counted the money, it turned out that a large sum of money was missing. Neither of the girls admitted to having taken the money. The whole affair ended with a warning and withholding the amount out of their salaries.

A few days later Beata noticed that it was her friend who was stealing the money. Next time when it turned out that the money was missing, the owner started to suspect the new shop assistant. Her explanations did not convince him and he decided to sack her. His suspicions seemed to be true because earlier such situations did not take place. Only Beata knew he was mistaken, and she had a great dilemma. She didn't know what to do. Should she tell the truth and lose a friend, or should she say nothing and in this way allow the innocent girl to be sacked?

LABOR CONFLICTS:
U.S. STANDARDS VS. OTHERS?

LEVI STRAUSS & CO.
AND CHINA

Timothy Perkins, Colleen O'Connell, Carin Orosco,
Mark Rickey, and Matthew Scoble

*What should a firm do about human rights violations in a country
where it is doing business? Levi Strauss & Co. has been continually
praised for its response to human rights violations in China. Consider whether its choice would have been the same (or whether it
would have had the same flexibility in its decision making) if it was
merely a start-up firm rather than a well-entrenched success story.*

PART A

The market that is the People's Republic of China consists of more than 1 billion consumers and offers low production costs, but its human rights violations have long been
condemned by international bodies. In 1993, Levi Strauss & Co. (LS&Co.) faced one of
its more difficult decisions in a long corporate history. Would it continue to conduct business in this enormously promising market or honor its relatively high ethical standards
and withdraw?

Levi Strauss: History and Ethical Stance

Founded in the United States in 1873, LS&Co. enjoyed consistent domestic growth for
generations and began overseas operations during the 1940s. The company became the
world's largest clothing manufacturer in 1977 and achieved $2 billion in sales by the end
of the decade. Having offered stock to the public during the 1970s to raise needed capital,
management decided fourteen years later to reprivatize in a $2 billion leveraged buyout,
the largest such transaction to date. Management's reasons included its heightened ability
to "focus attention on long-term interests (and) . . . to ensure that the company continues
to respect and implement its important values and traditions."[1] By 1993, LS&Co. produced merchandise in 24 countries and sold in 60.

LS&Co. has been a leader among U.S.-based corporations in recognizing the importance of business ethics and community relationships. Two 1987 documents developed

by management summarize the unique values operating at LS&Co. The Mission Statement
. . . affirms the importance of ethics and social responsibility, while the Aspirations Statement . . . lists the values intended to guide both individual and corporate decisions.

CEO Robert Haas frequently explains the importance of the Aspirations Statement as
a way employees can realize the company Mission Statement and otherwise address factors that did not receive adequate consideration in the past. Efforts to take the values seriously have led to specific changes in human resources policies and practices. For instance, LS&Co. extends liberal domestic partner benefits, offers flexible-work programs,
and has established child-care voucher programs. A series of classes for senior managers
focuses on the Aspirations Statement. The company has also earned a reputation as an industry leader in facing controversial social issues. It was one of the first companies to establish programs to support AIDS victims.

In 1990, the company closed a Docker's plant in San Antonio, Texas, transferring
production to private contractors in Latin America where wages were more competitive.
LS&Co. provided a generous severance package for the laid-off workers that included
90-day notice of the plant closing and extended medical insurance benefits. LS&Co. also
contributed $100,000 to local support agencies and $340,000 to the city for extra services
to the laid-off workers.[2] Despite these efforts, the company received serious criticism for
relocating the plant.

Ethical Standards for International Business

In early 1992, LS&Co. established a set of global sourcing guidelines to help ensure that
its worldwide contractors' standards mesh with the company values. A group of 10 employees from different areas of the company spent nine months developing the guidelines. The group used an ethical decision-making model that ranked and prioritized all
stakeholders to help design the guidelines. The model examines the consequences of each
action and suggests a decision based on a balance between ethics and profits.

The ensuing guidelines, "Business Partner Terms of Engagement," . . . cover environmental requirements, ethical standards, worker health and safety, legal requirements,
employment practices, and community betterment. Contractors must: provide safe and
healthy work conditions, pay employees no less than prevailing local wages, allow
LS&Co. inspectors to visit unannounced, limit foreign laborers' work weeks to a maximum of 60 hours, and preclude the use of child and prison labor.[3]

In addition, the company established "Guidelines for Country Selection." . . .
These guidelines cover issues beyond the control of one particular business partner. Challenges such as brand image, worker health and safety, human rights, legal requirements,
and political or social stability are considered on a national basis. The company will not
source in countries failing to meet these guidelines.

The question would soon be raised: Does China meet these guidelines?

Human Rights and Labor Practices in China

China is ranked among the world's gravest violators of human rights, although Chinese
officials do not regard their actions as such. The U.S. State Department says that China's
human rights record falls "far short of internationally accepted norms."[4] Two more-

egregious violations include arbitrary arrest and detention (with torture that sometimes results in death). Despite laws prohibiting arbitrary arrest and providing limits on detention, a commonly referenced clause states that family notification and timely charging are not required if such actions would "hinder the investigation."[5] Judicial verdicts are believed by many observers to be predetermined.

Chinese prison conditions are deplorable, and a long-standing practice holds that all prisoners, including political, must work. Chinese officials say that the fruits of prison-labor are used primarily within the prison system or for domestic sale.

Personal privacy is severely limited in China. Telephone conversations are monitored, mail is often opened and examined, and people and premises are frequently subjected to search without the necessary warrants. China has also engaged in forced family planning, with monitoring of a woman's pregnancy occurring at her place of employment.[6] Official rights to free speech and assembly are extremely restricted, as the world witnessed during the Tiananmen Square massacre in 1989.

Regarding labor conditions, China's leaders have refused to ratify the 10 guidelines prohibiting use of forced labor for commercial purposes established by the International Labor Organization Convention. Although China has regulations prohibiting the employment of children who have not completed nine compulsory years of education, child labor is widespread, especially in rural areas. Surveys show a recent increase in the dropout rate among southern Chinese lower-secondary schools, presumably because the booming local economy lures 12 to 16-year-olds away. At the time of LS&Co.'s deliberations regarding China, no minimum wage existed and safety conditions were found to be "very poor."

LS&Co. in China

This combination of government practices and labor conditions increased pressure within LS&Co. to rethink its decision to operate in China. 1992 operations in the country generated some 10 percent of the company's total Asian contracting and 2 percent of worldwide contracting. Its Chinese operations produced approximately one million pants and shirts in 1993 and operated directly or indirectly through some 30 Chinese contractors. Over one-half the goods produced in China were shipped to Hong Kong to be refined for sale in other countries. These contracts were estimated to be worth $40 million.

LS&Co. is only one of thousands of foreign firms operating in China. The other companies, especially prominent *Fortune 500* companies with factories or manufacturing contracts in China, are cognizant of the human rights and labor conditions. Most of these companies lobbied President Clinton to renew China's Most Favored Nation (MFN) trading status, arguing that the continuing presence of U.S. companies would have a positive influence on reform. According to this viewpoint, investments made by companies such as LS&Co. could transform working conditions and thereby accelerate movement toward the social, economic, and political standards favored by the United States and other western countries.

Should Levi Strauss Stay or Leave?

In assessing the objectionable conditions in China, LS&Co. management felt it could not improve the situation because the violations were well beyond what could be remedied strictly through company communication and cooperation with contractors. At issue were practices that had to be addressed on a larger, national scale.

Leaving the country would expose LS&Co. to the high opportunity cost of forgoing business in a large emerging market. Some managers and employees felt the company would be supporting a repressive regime if it remained in China, while others argued that LS&Co. is a profit-making business enterprise, not a human rights agency. This latter group saw as positive management's acknowledged responsibility to society, but it felt the company also needed to consider its responsibilities to shareholders and employees. Some employees argued that staying in China would enable LS&Co. to improve conditions for Chinese citizens. But other stakeholders countered that remaining in China would violate the company's own guidelines about where it would and would not conduct business.

Important issues that complicated the decision include: the possibility that China might not accept LS&Co. back if the company left until conditions improved. If the company ceased production in China, it might be difficult for it to sell product there due to high tariffs imposed on imported apparel. But, some voices argued, continuing to manufacture in China would have a damaging impact on Levi's reputation, possibly putting at risk its valuable brand image.

PART B

To address the many issues regarding LS&Co.'s continued operations in China, the company organized a China Policy Group (CPG). Composed of 12 employees who together devoted approximately 2,000 hours to reviewing the China situation, the CPG consulted human rights activists, scholars, and executives in its attempt to fully address the critical issues.

The group examined all the issues highlighted in Part A and found itself divided on the question. In March 1993, the CPG delivered a report to LS&Co.'s Executive Management Committee. On April 27, after a half-day of deliberation, this most-senior management group remained undecided over what to do.

Robert Haas Acts

Confronted by the indecision of the Executive Management Committee, LS&Co.'s CEO and Chairman, Robert Haas, ended the stalemate by recommending the company forgo direct investment in China and end existing contracts over a period of three years due to "pervasive violations of basic human rights."[7] He maintained that the company had more to gain by remaining true to its ideals than by continuing to produce in China.

Reactions to the Decision

LS&Co. did not publicly announce its decision, but the news hit the airwaves with a speed and volume that surprised all involved. John Onoda, LS&Co.'s vice president of corporate communications, explained: "We never intended to get in the spotlight. . . . It was leaked and got out in 20 minutes."

Many people were highly skeptical of the company's stated intentions. Some asserted it was only a public relations ploy engineered to make the company look good. "I don't see broad support of it," claimed Richard Brecher, director of business services at the U.S.-China Business Council. "[It] would be regarded much more seriously if Levi's had made direct investment in China."

In one respect, Brecher is right. The company did not directly invest in China; it produced its merchandise through Chinese contractors. In fact, on the sales side, LS&Co. jeans continue to sell in China through Jardine Marketing Services. Moving production contracts to other countries in Asia raised costs between four and ten percent, depending on which location was chosen. LS&Co. recognized this cost and considers it the price it must pay to uphold its integrity and protect its corporate and brand images.

Vice President Bob Dunn explained, "There's the matter of protecting our brand identity. Increasingly, consumers are sensitive to goods being made under conditions that are not consistent with U.S. values and fairness."[8] Linda Butler, director of corporate communications for LS&Co., iterated this sentiment when she affirmed that it was "better for us to honor our company's values."[9] Some even believe that the decision may ultimately prove profitable to the company. As one person claimed, "In many ways, it strengthens the brand. . . . This is a brand that thinks for itself, and these are values which people who buy the brand want for themselves. They're a badge product for youth who want to say 'I'm different.' "[10]

Impact in China

China's leadership showed no interest in the company's decision. One Chinese foreign ministry official was quoted, "At present there are tens of thousands of foreign companies investing in China. If one or two want to withdraw, please do."[11] Coincidentally, the LS&Co. decision-making process occurred as the United States considered extending China's MFN status. U.S. Trade Representative Mickey Kantor voiced his support for LS&Co. by stating, "As far as what Levi Strauss has done, we can only applaud it; we encourage American companies to be the leader in protecting worker rights and worker safety and human rights wherever they operate."[12]

More recently President Clinton renewed China's MFN trading status without requiring steps to improve human rights.[13] Clinton explained, "I believe the question . . . is not whether we continue to support human rights in China, but how we can best support human rights in China and advance our other very significant issues and interests. I believe we can do it by engaging the Chinese."[14]

The position of the Clinton administration is that the United States should continue trading with China and hope that economic involvement will contribute to improvement in the conditions of Chinese citizens. As one might surmise from the case, LS&Co. takes a different position.

ENDNOTES

1. *San Francisco Chronicle,* July 16, 1985, p. 51.
2. *The 100 Best Companies to Work for in America,* p. 502.
3. *Across the Board,* may 1994, p. 12.
4. *Far Eastern Economic Review,* April 14, 1994, p. 60.
5. *U.S. News & World Report,* August 2, 1993, p. 49.
6. Levi Strauss & Co. executive John Onoda, interview, February 1, 1995.

7.   The CPG defined "pervasive human rights violations" as meaning when "the greater majority of the population are denied virtually all human rights. Most human rights violations are severe. Government has taken few or no actions to improve human rights climate and positive change is unlikely or, at best, uncertain."

8.   *Wall Street Journal,* May 5, 1994, p. A18.

9.   *Far Eastern Economic Review,* April 14, 1994, p. 60.

10. *Wall Street Journal,* May 5, 1994, p. A18.

11. *Far Eastern Economic Review,* April 14, 1994, p. 60.

12. *The New Republic,* June 14, 1993, p. 8.

13. *U.S. Department of State Dispatch,* May 30, 1994, p. 345.

14. Across the Board, May 1994, p. 12.

RELATED WEB SITE

Levi Strauss & Co.: www.levi.com

THE DENIM REVOLUTION: LEVI STRAUSS & CO. ADOPTS A CODE OF CONDUCT

Deborah Leipziger

Leipziger details the efforts of Levi Strauss & Co. to create and implement its global sourcing guidelines.

Let me introduce you to Shilpi, a thirteen-year-old girl from Bangladesh. Shilpi is part of a unique agreement with Levi Strauss & Co.: the clothing manufacturer pays for her to go to school! How did such an agreement come about?

When Levi Strauss & Co. discovered that its contractors in Bangladesh were employing children like Shilpi, senior management realized that it would need to be compassionate toward the children and their families, while maintaining their Global Sourcing Guidelines. Having recently adopted guidelines that prohibit child labor worldwide, by its own facilities and by suppliers, Levi Strauss & Co. considered the issue to be clear-cut. But then an interesting fact came to light. Some of these children were the sole wage-earners in their families. If fired, their families would very likely starve and the children would resort to begging and prostitution.

Levi Strauss & Co. was challenged to balance its commitment to ethical work standards with its effect for these families. The company made a courageous decision: pay for the children to go to school until their 14th birthday, and then give them the opportunity to come back and work at the factory. The company even paid for tuition, books, and uniforms.

After conducting a study of 800 transnational corporations, CEP [Council on Economic Priorities] and New Consumer have selected Levi Strauss & Co. as one of 20 corporations promoting ethical practices in developing countries. Interviews with senior management have been conducted at Levi Strauss & Co. headquarters and, in the near future, will be conducted with contractors in Costa Rica and Guatemala. CEP's Transnational Corporations Project is writing a case study on Levi Strauss & Co. and its code for contractors, known as the Global Sourcing Guidelines.

Global Sourcing Guidelines

While many transnational companies seek low-wage havens where occupational safety and environmental standards are not enforced, Levi Strauss & Co. will produce clothing only where strict safety and environmental standards are upheld and where employees are treated ethically. Under its Global Sourcing Guidelines, Levi Strauss & Co. requires that its contractors abide by the following criteria:

•   Child labor is prohibited;

•   Prison labor is prohibited:

•   The work environment must be safe and healthy;

•   Water effluence must be limited to certain prescribed levels;

•   Employees cannot work more than sixty hours a week and must be allowed one day off in seven;

•   Business partners must comply with legal business requirements.

After conducting audits of all of its 700 contractors' facilities, Levi Strauss & Co. concluded that 5 percent of them had to be dropped. Twenty-five percent needed to make improvements and the rest were in compliance.

Levi Strauss & Co. recognizes that there are certain factors that contractors cannot control, including human rights violations. Thus, Levi Strauss & Co. is the only company to have adopted Country Selection Guidelines, which include the following country selection criteria: impact on brand image, adoption of health and safety requirements, commitment to human rights and legal requirements, and the level of political or social stability.

Since the adoption of the guidelines, Levi Strauss & Co. is phasing out sourcing from China and has already left Myanmar (Burma) due to pervasive human rights abuses.

Implementing the Global Sourcing Guidelines

Levi Strauss & Co. has a long-established reputation for contracting from the best factories in each country where it operates. But management realized that this was not enough; a factory can be the best in all of Bangladesh and still not meet the Levi Strauss & Co. standards. Once Levi Strauss & Co. decided that a code of conduct was necessary for its factories, the real challenge became one of implementation: how to audit over 700 contractors and their subcontractors in over 60 countries. The company had not even been aware that some contractors had many subcontractors.

Many questions still needed to be resolved. For example: How clean should a factory be? How much improvement is warranted? While it was decided that audits should be standardized, there was a commitment to take local social and cultural customs into account. For example, in some cultures, toilet seats are not used, so if no toilet seats were found in a factory in this culture, no changes were necessary. However, if a factory in a country with a tradition of providing toilet seats failed to do so, seats would be required. A similar situation occurs with air conditioning—it would not be required if there were adequate ventilation. There is a base standard, but social and cultural factors are applied. Despite these differences, Levi Strauss & Co. still seeks to balance U.S. values with cultural differences in developing countries.

Audits were first conducted in Asia, where most of the company's contractors in developing countries are situated. Levi Strauss & Co. had already formulated the Sourcing

---

LEVI STRAUSS & CO. GUIDELINES FOR COUNTRY SELECTION

The following country selection criteria address issues which we believe are beyond the ability of the individual business partner to control.

1. Brand Image

We will not initiate or renew contractual relationships in countries where sourcing would have an adverse effect on our global brand image.

2. Health & Safety

We will not initiate or renew contractual relationships in locations where there is evidence that Company employees or representatives would be exposed to unreasonable risk.

3. Human Rights

We should not initiate or renew contractual relationships in countries where there are pervasive violations of basic human rights.

4. Legal Requirements

We will not initiate or renew contractual relationships in countries where the legal environment creates unreasonable risk to our trademarks or to other important commercial interests or seriously impedes our ability to implement these guidelines.

5. Political or Social Stability

We will not initiate or renew contractual relationships in countries where political or social turmoil unreasonably threatens our commercial interests.

Guidelines when a scandal broke over a large clothing supplier in Saipan, a U.S. territory in Asia with a minimum wage far lower than that in the U.S. A large manufacturer that made clothes for Levi Strauss & Co. was found to be in violation of various U.S. laws. Because it had clear guidelines, Levi Strauss & Co. was able to withdraw immediately, while other companies took months deliberating alternatives.

While praise for the Global Sourcing Guidelines is widespread, there is some criticism. According to a labor analyst, Levi Strauss & Co. should provide a "living wage" for its workers in developing countries. A "living wage" would ensure that families could purchase an adequate level of food, clothing, and shelter. According to Dave Samson of Levi Strauss & Co., the company pays wages in the top third of the clothing sector in every country where it operates.

Results

After one year of conducting audits, 5 percent of the contractors were dropped. Many others made improvements, some with help from Levi Strauss & Co. For example, in the Dominican Republic, there are no building codes to ensure that factories are fireproof. Levi Strauss & Co. located an expert who assisted the contractor in fireproofing his factory. Another factory had only one exit for hundreds of employees. Levi Strauss & Co. required that the owner build another door. Contractors were required to clean toilets, insulate wires, and eliminate exposure to toxic chemicals.

For Levi Strauss & Co., the costs of implementing the Global Sourcing Guidelines have been significant. These include: the cost of excluding contractors that are not in compliance, the increased cost of goods, staff time for audits, penalties for cancellations, financial incentives for contractors to upgrade the facilities, training and travel, and staff resources for human rights reviews.

By applying guidelines for country selection, Levi Strauss & Co. has forgone the world's largest market: China. The company may also have limited access to countries in the future, because of pervasive human rights abuses.

"We believe companies have an obligation to see that workers are treated with respect and provided with a safe and healthy work environment regardless of where they reside in the world," says Bob Dunn, Vice President for Corporate Communications.

Says Dunn, "we also feel that it is important to put your stake in the ground on issues that you stand for such as human rights. We also understand that there is a cost involved in choosing to operate in an ethical way. We did not implement the Global Sourcing Guidelines for marketing gain, but rather because it was consistent with our corporate values." . . .

INNERSCREEN, INC.

JACK RAISNER

In the Innerscreen case study, Raisner asks us to consider the balance between domestic and foreign interests. What are the issues facing the CEO at the end of the case? Why should we be concerned about what happens in maquiladoras? What is the real issue to be determined here?

It becomes clear by early May that Innerscreen, Inc., has the hottest-selling toy on the market and is booking record pre-Christmas orders. The toy, called "Star Trek Simulator," is a virtual reality computer with special headset and gloves. The player can enter the Starship Enterprise and become a character in improvised sequences of Star Trek adventures. Besides visiting unknown galaxies, the player can ask Mr. Spock (old series) virtually *any* question and get a logical answer.

Prior to Innerscreen's annual May shareholder meeting, it also becomes clear that Innerscreen may fail to ship many of these orders due to insufficient assembly capacity. Although Innerscreen has some high-end manufacturing capability in the U.S., until now, the Star Trek simulator has been assembled from domestic and foreign-made parts by sub-contracted factories in Singapore and Taiwan. It is too late to book additional capacity in the Far East. Innerscreen must immediately find additional assembly facilities elsewhere to fulfill its requirements. Factories in Guatemala have been suggested.

The May 15, Innerscreen, Inc., annual shareholder meeting is about to start. Excitement over the "Star Trek" product team has focused the attention of major investors and the national business media on the meeting. But rumors that Innerscreen's production may be moved to Guatemala have brought a wave of criticism. A human rights activist whose "open letter" to Innerscreen's CEO was printed in the local newspaper warns that Guatemala is the most repressive country in the Western Hemisphere and that slave-labor conditions exist there (owners lock women and underage laborers inside factories to work 20 hour days, seven days a week—and pay them *less* than the minimum wage of $1.59 a day).

Prior to the shareholder meeting the CEO asks the "Star Trek" product team to confirm its delivery schedule so that he can make a rosy, though not inaccurate, report at the meeting.

According to Innerscreen's production manager, who found the available assembly capacity in "maquiladoras" (assembly factories) in Guatemala, the orders can be met if assembly is done by Innerscreen's own factories in the United States, or moved to Guatemala, or split between the two sites. Innerscreen's own unionized U.S. facilities can be rapidly retooled to meet the assembly demand. Due to record unemployment in the industry, the union, in an unprecedented give-back, will provide "special employees" at $9 per hour with limited benefits (instead of the regular $14 per hour with full benefits). The domestic assembly cost to Innerscreen would be $34 per machine, as compared to the present $6 per machine cost in the Far East (landed in U.S.); the average wage in Manilla is $2 per hour. The additional $28 expense for domestic assembly would wipe out 85% of the projected net profit for Innerscreen and would mean the Christmas season would more or less be a "wash" for Innerscreen investors.

In Guatemala, on the other hand, the landed cost of contracting production out to "maquiladoras" would be $3 per machine. (The wage of the average worker is $1.40 per day.) There may be some upfront capital costs, however, to equip the maquiladoras. This investment would be absorbed if Innerscreen decided to shift production year-round there. Indeed, many competitors are "locking in" contracts with the few Guatemalan "cartels" that can provide semi-skilled workers and facilities capable of electronic assembly. These competitors are already projecting low-priced "knockoff" virtual reality simulators for 1996 based on the lower assembly costs.

The CEO is about to take the stage at the meeting. He visits the product team to get its final recommendation. The activist has been invited to negotiate an arrangement whereby the issue will not be raised at the meeting. The product team includes the:

1. production manager, who has just returned from Guatemala;
2. financial manager;
3. the marketing manager; and
4. the general counsel.

The CEO has just entered the room. A Star Trek simulator sits on the table, and Mr. Spock is following the discussion closely.

EL SALVADOR AND THE GAP

TEE-SHIRTS AND TEARS: THIRD WORLD SUPPLIERS TO FIRST WORLD MARKETS

Laura B. Pincus

It is important to note that these conditions do not exist only in foreign markets. U.S. Secretary of Labor Robert Reich made the following remarks in a keynote address at a conference on international labor standards:

> *I have had occasion over the past year to study a country in which many workers who have tried to organize themselves have been fired for their activities. It is a country in which there are sweat shops of the worst Third World variety. In fact, there are sweat shops in which young children are working.*
>
> *It is a country in which many workers are still exposed to hazards that kill and maim them. In this country just a week ago today, I had occasion to visit a plant to serve papers on a plant manager and a company—a very, very large company—where one worker was killed recently. Other workers had been maimed, suffering lost fingers and mangled arms, and yet the company still, still, refused to change its ways and come into compliance.*
>
> *The country I'm talking about is, obviously, the United States. I issue a warning to all of us—a warning to all Americans dealing with the issue of international labor standards. We must guard against too much self-righteous indignation.* (Robert B. Reich, *"Keynote Address,"* International Labor Standards and Global Economic Integration: Proceedings of A Symposium, *July 1994, p. 1)*

The hottest places in hell are reserved for those who, in a period of moral crisis, maintain their neutrality. DANTE

Recent media attention has heightened our awareness of labor conditions in third world countries. While Americans otherwise may have been able to write off substandard labor conditions as another case of cultural variations, these recent cases garnered domestic interest as a result of the parties involved. Their names are about as American as Apple Pie. The Gap. Kathie Lee Gifford. Even Michael Jordan. These are the contractors, the investors, the spokespeople who represent "sweatshops" where, allegedly, young girls are allowed only two restroom visits per day and, allegedly, the days sometimes consist of twenty-one straight hours of work.

LABOR CONDITIONS IN THE UNITED STATES

America's garment industry today grosses $45 billion per year and employs more than one million workers.[1] Uproar began in the Fall of 1995 when Secretary of Labor Robert Reich announced the names of several large retailers who may have been involved in an El Monte, California, sweatshop operation. Notwithstanding the fact that the retailers are not liable for the conditions if they have no knowledge of them, the companies involved in this situation agreed to adopt a statement of principles which would require their suppliers to adhere to U.S. federal labor laws.[2]

Reich followed this announcement with an appearance on the *"Phil Donahue Show"* where he discussed a situation at another plant that employed Thai workers at less than $1.00 per hour and kept its workers behind a barbed wire fence. Retailers respond that it is difficult, if not impossible, to police their suppliers and subcontractors, who may total more than 20,000 in some cases. And the pressures of the situation are only becoming worse. The apparel industry, which has borne the brunt of Reich's focus, is highly competitive, and extremely labor-intensive. Competition from companies in other countries that do not impose similar labor condition requirements is fierce. Consequently, one is not surprised to learn that a 1994 Labor Department spot check of garment operations in California found that 93 percent had health and safety violations.[3]

Manufacturers may have a bit more to be concerned about than retailers. Reich has recently involved a little-used provision in the Fair Labor Standards Act that holds manufacturers liable for the wrongful acts of their suppliers and that allows for the confiscation of goods produced by sweatshop operations.

Reich has now appealed to the retailers and manufacturers alike to conduct their own random spot checks. "We need to enlist retailers as adjunct policemen. At a time when business says to government, "Get off our back. We can do it ourselves," we're giving them the opportunity," Reich notes.[4] In June 1995, Reich established a consortium to police working conditions made up of manufacturers. The group, called Compliance Alliance, will police contractors conducting regular audits and will identify firms that pay less than minimum wage or otherwise violate the provisions of the Fair Labor Standards Act.[5] . . .

The Clinton Administration's voluntary Model Business Principles, published in May 1995, are relevant to this discussion. The principles encourage all businesses to adopt and implement voluntary codes of conduct for doing business around the world and suggest appropriate code coverage. . . .

AMERICAN ATTENTION DRIFTS
TOWARD OTHER COUNTRIES

Neil Kearney, general secretary of the International Textile, Garment and Leather Worker's Federation, describes the garment work place as follows:

> *The reality today is that most of the 30 million jobs in the fashion industry around the world are low paid, often based in export processing zones where worker rights are usually suppressed. Wages are frequently below the subsistence level and falling in real terms. . . .*
>
> *Management by terror is the norm in many countries. Workers are routinely shoved, beaten, kicked, even when pregnant. Attempts to unionize are met with the utmost brutality, sometimes with murder.*[6]

Once the American public considered its own conditions, it looked to other countries to see how labor was treated there. Following Reich's slap on the hand to American manufacturers, media attention turned toward the conditions in Third World countries and toward American responsibility for or involvement in those conditions. In 1970, there were 7,000 multinational companies in the world. Today, there are more than 35,000.[7] The topic of conditions in those multinationals was destined for afternoon talk shows once it was announced that television personality Kathie Lee Gifford endorsed a line of clothing that had been made for Wal-Mart in Honduran sweatshops. These operations employed underage and pregnant women for more than 20-hour days at $.31 per hour. The conditions were extremely hot and no worker was allowed to speak during the entire day.

The situation was brought to the attention of the press by Charles Kernaghan, director of the National Labor Committee, based in New York City. Kernaghan informed Gifford, and the press, of the conditions in the plant and asked her to respond. Gifford's immediate response was to immediately break off her relationship with the company.[8] Unfortunately, this is not what is always best for the exploited workers. Instead, Kernaghan impressed upon her the need to remain involved and to use her position and reputation to encourage a change in the conditions at the plants.

These arguments may remind the reader of those waged several years ago regarding divestment from South Africa. Proponents of investment argued that the only way to effect change would be to remain actively involved in the operations of the South African business community. Others argued that no ethical company should pour money into a country where apartheid conditions were allowed to exist. The same arguments can and have been made about conducting business in Third World countries, and Gifford found herself right in the middle of them.

THE EL SALVADORAN LABOR ENVIRONMENT

El Salvador is a country that has been ravaged by internal conflicts culminating in a civil war that lasted for many years. In 1992, with the advent of peace, the country sought to rebuild what it had lost during wartime and is now considered one of the fastest growing economies in Latin America.[9] The objective of the El Salvadorans involved in the rebuilding process was to help the poor to overcome the conditions of poverty, dependence, and oppression that they had experienced during the conflict. While the objectives of private investors may be different, all seem to share a common interest in social stability and development. Economist Louis Emmerij notes that the leading cause of social unrest is "the lack of sufficient and renumerative employment opportunities, bad living conditions and the lack of perspective and hope."[10]

In developing countries like El Salvador, long-term strategies for improving a poor household's ability to generate disposable income on a sustained basis must consider if households have the skills, education, and know-how to allow them to operate in the market. These strategies include support for training and education, access to markets, and access to technology and credit. A large part of the labor problem in the *maquiladores* is the lack of agreement between the workers and management as to the minimum level of productivity expected per day, the level of compensation for a worker who achieves that level, and who should assume the burden of training in order to increase productivity.

Yet, low wages are the prime magnet for multinational firms coming to El Salvadore. In 1990, a glossy full-colored advertisement appeared in a major American apparel trade magazine showing a woman at a sewing machine and proclaiming, "Rosa Martinez produces apparel for U.S. markets on her sewing machine in El Salvador. *You* can hire her for 57 cents an hour." One year later, the same ad announced that Rosa's salary had gone down—"*You* can hire her for 33 cents an hour."[11] It appears that the publicists felt that Rosa's salary originally looked too high in the eyes of the market players.

Critical to understanding these conflicts is an understanding of the Salvadoran culture itself. Salvadoran workers are not exempt from the consequences of their history. When they enter the workplace, they expect to be exploited and do not trust management. In addition, as a result of the repressive conditions in El Salvador during the war, the society suffers from a general lack of candor and a tendency on the part of individuals to protect themselves by not telling the truth.[12] But this quality is different from the deception that occurs in American business dealings. In this situation, it serves as a means of self-protection in a culture that offers little else. Moreover, the government does not protect individual and business interests, thereby allowing cartels to develop, flourish, and continue.

The author of this case had the opportunity to travel to El Salvador in 1996 in order to observe a class in financial administration at an El Salvadoran university. During the course of a quiz in the class, the professor had reason to leave the classroom for a moment. Upon his return, he found that the students were now collaborating on the answers to the quiz. During the discussion that later ensued regarding the students' actions, the students articulated a need to help each other to succeed. They felt that they should bind together in order to help them all to move forward. If this meant helping a colleague who did not have time to study because he had to work to support his family, in addition to attending school, that seemed acceptable, if not necessary and ethical.[13]

During that same course, the graduate students (most, if not all, of whom worked full-time in professional positions) were asked to identify the principal barriers to trust in Salvadoran business relationships, and the means by which those barkers could be broken down. Students responded as follows (translated from Spanish):

> One barrier is that the big businesses are formed at the level of families and friends that form a close nucleus, prohibiting others from entering.

The government does not enact laws to guarantee business interests and growth without the intervention of stronger, "bully" businesses.

There is a failure of information—only certain people have access to the most important, business-related information. There is no requirement that business share information, even at a level that would mimic the American SEC requirements.

Create legal mechanisms that sanction companies violating the rules. These sanctions *do not* exist. Companies use illicit means to take advantage of their competitors and employing the same means is the only way to compete.

The period since the war has seen an increase in vandalism at an individual and corporate level, making it difficult to carry on a business.[14]

Consider the expectation of conflict in this scenario recounted by Fr. David Blanchard, Pastor of the Our Lady of Lourdes Church in Calle Real Epiphany Cooperative Association:

> *In February of 1994, the cooperative had a serious labor conflict. The women became quite adept at sewing lab coats. But in February 1994, when the only contract available was for sewing hospital bathrobes, a serious labor conflict arose. Unfortunately, the women who were elected by their peers to negotiate with the contractor made some serious errors in judgment when they calculated the time required to sew this item.*
>
> *At the time, some women were earning 80 colones daily (twice the minimum wage). Most were making 50 colones. Only a few apprentices were making less than the minimum wage.*
>
> *With the transition to sewing bathrobes, production, and therefore income, was cut in half. Six of the highest wage earners subsequently staged a sit-down strike at their machines, claiming that they were being oppressed.*
>
> *Father Blanchard asked, "Who negotiated your contract?"*
>
> *"Our representatives," they said.*
>
> *"Who elected your representatives?"*
>
> *"We did."*
>
> *"Who will suffer if this work is not completed?"*
>
> *"We will."*
>
> *These women had entered this project with no prior skills. They had received high-quality and expensive technical, legal and social training. They were all self-employed, but when their wages plunged, they felt oppressed, frustrated and angry, and ended up leaving the cooperative. . . . Some of these women will continue to suffer in poverty. It is certain that they are victims. But they are the victims of hundreds of years of oppression and not of the immediate circumstances sewing hospital bathrobes. They responded to the problems created by the lack of education and their lack of abilities by generating conflict.[15]*

Blanchard remarks that Salvadoran industrialists and managers are even more strident in generating conflict in the workplace. For instance, consider the case of the Mandarin factory and many other similar plants throughout El Salvador.

THE MANDARIN PLANT AND ITS LABOR CONDITIONS

The San Salvador Mandarin International plant was established in order to assemble goods to be shipped to the United States under contract with major U.S. retailers such as The Gap and Eddie Bauer. The plant was built in the San Marcos Free Trade Zone, a zone owned by the former Salvadoran Army Colonel Mario Guerrero and created with money from the Bush Administration's U.S. Agency for International Development (USAID). David Wang, the Taiwanese owner of the plant, subsequently hired Guerrero as its personnel manager. In addition, the company also hired ex-military, plain-clothed armed guards as security for the plant.[16] Factories in El Salvador, as in the United States, need protection for workers, for personal property, and for real property.

While personnel managers are not security guards, such appointments have become commonplace with Salvadoran industrialists precisely because they expect conflict in the workplace. However, in many situations, their personnel managers generate the conditions of conflict and attempt to control the conflict through the same methods employed during wartime.[17] For example, Colonel Guerrero himself told the workers at one point, "I have no problem, but perhaps you do; either the union will behave, leave, or people will die."[18]

While The Gap was one of the first companies to have a code of conduct for overseas suppliers (along with Reebok), this strategy might not be effective in the El Salvadoran business environment. Charles Kernaghan, director of the National Labor Committee in Support of Democracy and Human Rights in El Salvador (NLC), believed that a preexisting code of conduct was practically useless and stated the following in an interview with *Business Ethics* magazine in June, 1996:

> *Consider the history of El Salvador's military, which specialized in the killing of nuns and priests and trade unionists. It is laughable to think that these same people will carry out a company's code of conduct. And there were no legal avenues to challenge any violation because the ministry of labor there is so ill-funded and ill-trained. So you can't depend on the laws. And the women were afraid to speak out.*[19]

After a bitter union-management struggle regarding working conditions and the termination of 100 union workers, the union and management reached an agreement. Unfortunately, the Mandarin did not abide by this agreement.

As North Americans became more and more aware of the working conditions in El Salvador, they began to take action against the retailers. On August 16, 1995, more than one hundred workers from UNITE (Union of Needles Trades and Industrial & Textile Employees) demonstrated in front of a Gap outlet store in downtown Toronto in protest of the working conditions at Gap suppliers. At the same time, thousands of miles South of Toronto, Guerrero claimed that "the working conditions here are good for us and good for the Salvadoran workers, but bad for those seeking to keep jobs in the United States. . . . [Without the jobs in the maquilas,] young women would have few other work options apart from prostitution or crime."[20] The story becomes further blurred, however, when Guerrero's comments are compared with an earlier statement by Mandarin owner David Wang in connection with the wages paid to Mandarin workers: "If you really ask me, this is not fair."[21]

> "Workers wages make up less than 1% of the retail cost of GAP shirts. Is it any wonder that the company made $310 million in 1994, and paid its CEO Donald Fisher $2 million plus stock options?[22]
>
> From Gap Sourcing Principles & Guidelines: "Workers are free to join associations of their own choosing. Factories must not interfere with workers who wish to lawfully and peacefully associate, organize or bargain collectively. The decision whether or not to do so should be made solely by the workers.[23]

Based on claims of a violation of its sourcing principles and in an effort to ameliorate the situation, the Gap decided to discontinue its relationship with the Mandarin (following in the footsteps of other previous Mandarin contractors such as Eddie Bauer, Liz Claiborne, J. Crew, and Casual Corner); however, this action prompted strong cries of concern from labor activists. Contrary to the intentions of the Gap, this resolution was viewed as irresponsible and lacking in accountability.[24] Those concerned with the rights of workers in El Salvador contested the Gap's decision, claiming that this would be the worst possible solution to the problems in a country where 60 percent of the labor force is unemployed.[25] As a result of other pullouts, the Mandarin has had to cut its work force from 1,300 to 300, and 32 other maquilas have already shut down.[26] "Instead of acting responsibly and seeing that conditions are improved at Mandarin, the Gap is trying to wash its hands and to shift production to other maquilas in other countries with equally bad conditions."[27]

The Gap's original perspective is not without its supporters. Joan Spero, business executive and Secretary of State for Economic Affairs explains: "A world community that respects democracy and human rights will provide a more hospitable climate for American trade and commerce. . . . Repression fosters instability in the long run and puts investment at greater risk of expropriation and loss."[28] Consider as well the following comments of John Duerden, former president of Reebok:

> As a public company, we have an ethical responsibility to build value for Reebok's shareholders—but not at all possible costs. What we seek is harmony between the profit-maximizing demands of our free-market system and the legitimate needs of our shareholders, and the needs and aspirations of the larger world community in which we are all citizens.[29]

"A VICTORY FOR ALL OF US WHO ARE DETERMINED TO ELIMINATE SWEATSHOPS AT HOME AND ABROAD."[30]

The situation took a drastic turn in December 1995 when Reverend Paul Smith called a meeting between the Gap senior vice president for sourcing, Stan Raggio, the Gap sourcing guidelines director, Dottie Hatcher, Gap consultant James Lukaszewski, Reverend David Dyson of the Interfaith Center for Social Responsibility, and Charles Kernaghan (NLC). The Gap was feeling pressure from all sides. On the one hand, labor, religious, consumer, solidarity, children's, and women's groups were arguing for dramatic changes in working conditions. On the other hand, the National Retailers' Federation contested the complaints and encouraged the Gap to ignore the demonstrations.

The Gap responded to the consumers, issuing a letter stating that it is "committed to ensuring fair and honest treatment of the people who make [its] garments in over 40 countries worldwide,"[31] and, in the words of the NLC, "took a major step forward in accepting direct responsibility for how and under what conditions the products it sells are made."[32] As a result of the meeting, the Gap agreed to implement an independent monitoring system in El Salvador, using the Human Rights Ombudsperson in El Salvador to monitor factories' compliance with its labor guidelines, as long as the Mandarin agreed to rehire the fired union activists.

The NLC and others saw this decision by the Gap as a benchmark against which all other multinational retailers will be measured. Says Kernaghan, "The message is clear: if you make it, you are responsible."[33] Not everyone agrees with Kernaghan's assessment. Larry Martin of the American Apparel Manufacturer's Association believes otherwise: "They've [labor] given us a black eye that most of us don't deserve. Most of us monitor contractors we use here and offshore."[34] One might understand Martin's concerns for the rest of American retailers when one considers the comments of U.S. Labor Secretary Robert Reich: "This raises the question for other big retailers who haven't moved in this direction—why not?"[35]

Most recently, the Salvadoran minister of labor established a government commission to review conditions in the free trade zone and indicated that foreigners would no longer be permitted to monitor the implementation of work codes in El Salvador.[36] This begs the question of why the Gap doesn't simply allow the El Salvadoran government to monitor the work conditions of the plant? Father Blanchard offers the following response:

> *We must consider what are the global consequence for disbanding this effort after less than one month in existence.*
>
> *For example, recently we have learned that the Commerce Department of the United States has informed the international fishing industry that it will not allow the importation of shrimp that are caught with nets that also snare turtles. All fisherman who use nets, and who wish to sell their produce in the United States, must use turtle-free nets. What is more, the industry must allow independent monitoring by outside agencies.*
>
> *Salvadoran law permits the use of turtle-snaring nets. The United States has no authority to control the Salvadoran shrimp industry (one of the largest sources of external revenue for the Government of El Salvador). It has complete authority to determine the conditions under which shrimp may be imported into the United States.*
>
> *The question remains: why not simply rely on the government of El Salvador to supervise compliance, especially given the importance of the shrimping industry in this country.*
>
> *The answer lies in norms for the modernization of government and general guidelines for development being promulgated by the World Bank, the InterAmerican Development Bank and other loaning agencies. Governments that contribute to international loaning agencies insist on down-scaling government and allowing compliance to be monitored by the private sector in alliance with independent monitoring groups. In this scheme, Congress passes the law defining the kinds of nets that are required in the shrimp industry; people concerned about the welfare of turtles contribute to organizations like the International Wildlife Fund to guarantee that these laws are enforced; organizations like the International Wildlife Fund in*

turn collaborate with the fishing industry to guarantee that the norms are followed. When all is said and done, if nobody cares about the welfare of turtles, the laws are not passed and compliance never takes place.

What is good for turtles is also good for human beings.[37]

ENDNOTES

1. Department of Labor, "No Sweat Initiative: Fact Sheet," http://www.dol.gov/dol/esa/public/forum/fact.htm.

2. Susan Chandler, "Look Who's Sweating Now," *Business Week,* October 16, 1995, pp. 96, 98. (In March, 1996, 72 Thai workers at the El Monte sweatshop were awarded more than $1 million in back wages in connection with the scandal. George White, "Sweatshop Workers to Receive $1 Million," *L.A. Times,* March 8, 1996, p. B1.)

3. Ibid., p. 98. The study also found that 73 percent of the garment makers had improper payroll records, 68 percent did not pay appropriate overtime wages, and 51 percent paid less than the minimum wage.

4. Ibid, pp. 96, 98. Self-inspection may also be necessitated by the drop in the number of inspectors assigned by the Labor Department to investigate wage and hour law violations. Since 1989, that number has fallen from almost 1,000 to less than 800. Also see Andrea Adelson, "Look Who's Minding the Shop," *New York Times,* May 4, 1996, p. 17.

5. Stuart Silverstein, "Self-Regulatory Group to Police Clothes Makers' Work Conditions," *L.A. Times,* June 20, 1995, p. D1.

6. http://www.dol/gov/dol/opa/public.forum/kearnery.txt.

7. Douglass Cassel, "Human Rights Violations: What's a Poor Multinational to Do?" Remarks before the Chicago Council on Foreign Relations, February 7, 1996, p. 10.

8. "Gifford Counters Sweatshop Charges," May 2, 1996, p. 40 (Reuters).

9. Michael McGuire, "Lost in the Junkyard of Abandoned U.S. Policy," *Chicago Tribune,* April 7, 1996, sec. 2, pp. 1, 4.

10. Louis Emmerij, *Social Tensions and Social Reform: Toward Balanced Economic, Financial and Social Policies in Latin America* (Washington, DC: Social Agenda Policy Group, Inter-American Development Bank, 1995), p. 7, *cited in* letter from Fr. David Blanchard, pastor, O.L. Lourdes in Calle Real Epiphany Cooperative Association, to Aaron Cramer, Director, Business and Human Rights Program, Business for Social Responsibility, February 6, 1996, p. 2.

11. Bob Herbert, "Sweatshop Beneficiaries," *New York Times,* July 24, 1995, p. A13.

12. Blanchard letter, p. 8, citing research by Fr. Ignacio Martin-Baro, a social psychologist and one of the six Jesuit priests slain in November 1989 at the University of Central America in El Salvador. The war has additional effects on the people of El Salvador, even if they were not alive at the time of the recent conflicts. For example, one American student recorded in his journal, "9/3/95: One of the little children handed me an old bullet that he must have found. I imagine there must be many bullets out there in the field. I just wanted the day to be over, for me and for this little boy." Student manuscript in possession of the author.

13. First-hand experience of the author, February 1996.

14. Student manuscripts in possession of the author (June 1996).

15. Blanchard letter, p. 5.

16. Terry Kelly, "The GAP: Brutality Behind the Facade," part of *World History Archives,* located at http://neal.ctstateu.edu/history/world.history/archives/canada/canada002.html, p. 1 (1995).

17. Blanchard letter, p. 6.

18. Kelly, "The GAP," p. 2.

19. Mary Scott, "Going After The Gap," *Business Ethics,* May/June 1996, p. 20.

20. Letta Taylor, "Salvadoran Clothing Factory Accused of Worker Abuse," *Roanoke Times and World News* (December 31, 1995) p. D4.

21. Bob Herbert, "Not a Living Wage," *New York Times,* October 9, 1995, p. A17.

22. Kelly, "The GAP," p. 2.

23. Gap, Inc., *Code of Vendor Conduct,* sec. VIII, 1996. See also Christian Task Force on Central America, "Urgent Action El Salvador," http://www/grannyg.bc.ca/CTFCA/act1295a.html (November 29, 1995) p. 1.

24. Letta Taylor, "Salvadoran Clothing Factory Accused of Worker Abuse," *Roanoke Times and World News,* December 31, 1995, p. D4; Joanna Ramey, "Worker Rights Groups Slam Gap for Ending El Salvador Contract," *Women's Wear Daily,* November 30, 1995.

25. Letta Taylor, "Salvadoran Clothing Factory," p. D4.

26. Ibid.

27. Christian Task Force on Central America (CTFCA), "Urgent Action El Salvador," http://www/grannyg.bc.ca/CTFCA/act1295a.html, Nov. 29, 1995, p. 2.

28. Quoted by Douglass Cassel, "Human Rights Violations: What's a Poor Multinational To Do?" remarks before the chicago Council on Foreign Relations, Feb. 7, 1996, pp. 9.

29. Quoted by Cassel, "Human Rights Violations," p. 9.

30. Words of Jay Mazur, UNITE President, in National Labor Committee, "Gap Victory," http://www.alfea.it/coordns/work/industria/gap-victory.html, Feb. 1996.

31. CTFCA, "urgent Action El Salvador."

32. National Labor Committee, "Gap Agrees to Independent Monitoring Setting New Standard for the Entire Industry," http://www.alfea.it/coordns/work/industria/gap.agrees.html.

33. Quoted in Industrial Workers of the World, "Unions Win Victory in Gap Battle," *The Industrial Worker,* http://fletcher.iww.org/~iw/feb/stories/gap.html, February, 1995. See also Mary Scott, "Going After The Gap," *Business Ethics,* May/June 1996, pp. 18–20 ("What the Gap has done is historic. It will be a good pilot project to see if third party monitoring works," said Conrad McKerron, social research director of Progressive Asset Management).

34. Quoted in Paula Green, "The Gap Signs Accord on conduct code with U.S. Labor Group," *The News-Times,* http://www.newstimes.com/archives/dec2295/bzf.htm, 12/22/95, p. 2.

35. Quoted in United Auto Workers, "The Gap Agrees to Improve conditions in Overseas Plants," *Frontlines,* http://www.uaw.org/solidarity/9601/frontlinesjan96.html, January 1996, p. 1.

36. Memo from Fr. David Blanchard to Mark Annerm Coordinator, Independent Monitoring Team, April 19, 1996, p. 4.

37. Ibid., pp. 5–6.

RELATED WEB SITES

The Gap: http://www.gap.com

NIKE: http://www.nike.com

LIST OF FASHION TRENDSETTERS

U.S. DEPARTMENT OF LABOR

The retailers listed below have all pledged to help eradicate sweatshops in America and to try to ensure that their shelves are stocked with only "No Sweat" garments.

Abercrombie and Fitch	Dana Buchman
Lands End	Nordstrom
Baby Superstore	Elisabeth
Lane Bryant	Old Navy Clothing Store
Banana Republic	Express
Lerner New York	Patagonia
Bath & Body Works	Galyans Trading
Levi Strauss and Company	Penhaligon's
Bergner's	GapKids
Limited Too	Structure
Boston Stores	Gerber Childrenswear
Liz Claiborne Inc.	Superior Surgical Mfg.
Brylane	Guess Inc.
Mast Industries	The Limited
Cacique	Henri Bendel
NFL Properties	The Gap
Carson Pirie Scott	Jessica McClintock
Nicole Miller	Victoria's Secret Catalogue and Stores

This list is based on the voluntary efforts of the listed companies. They have agreed to: demonstrate a commitment to labor laws; cooperate with law enforcement agencies when violations of the law are found; and monitor working conditions, for example by

List of Fair Labor Fashion Trendsetters from Dept. of Labor, Released Dec. 5, 1995, in "GAP Stores Added to Fair Labor Fashion Trendsetter List," 12/20/95, http://gatekeeper.dol.gov/dol/opa/public/media/press/opa/opa95528.htm.

contracting with suppliers who monitor contractors or by conducting site visits of suppliers. (Companies not on this list also may follow these practices.)

The Trendsetters List is still open. Any company interested in joining the list may contact the U.S. Department of Labor at: Trendsetters, 200 Constitution Ave., NW, Washington, DC 20210. The Trendsetters List is not a "Where To Shop" list. A company's inclusion on the list does not constitute an endorsement by the U.S. Department of Labor.

Help End
Sweatshop Conditions
for American Workers
Robert B. Reich, Secretary
U.S. Department of Labor

Help End Sweatshop Conditions for American Workers.

Sweatshops still exist for many garment workers in America—sweatshops where workers earn less than 70 cents an hour and live in slavery-like conditions.

As Secretary of Labor, I am committed to ending this shameful practice. Even though many retailers and manufacturers have agreed to help eradicate sweatshops, it's going to take more.

Consumers like you can make a difference. You can exercise your right as a consumer to avoid buying sweatshop-made clothing. Please carry this card with you as a guide to "No Sweat" shopping.

Thank you for your support.

Robert B. Reich, Secretary
U.S. Department of Labor

Three Clues for Consumers That Your Clothing is NO SWEAT.

 You can ask your retailers questions about where and how the garments are made. Garment workers are required to be paid at least the minimum wage and overtime.

 You can ask your retailers whether they independently monitor garment manufacturers to avoid buying from sweatshops. Many retailers have voluntarily agreed to conduct site visits of suppliers to monitor working conditions.

 You can ask your retailers whether they support "No Sweat" clothing. Commitments from retailers to avoid buying sweatshop-made clothing can go a long way toward eradicating sweatshops in America.

"Help End Sweatshop Conditions for American Workers," Robert Reich Poster, http://www.dol.gov/dol/esa/public/nosweat/card.htm.

REFORM OF THE ARGENTINE INSURANCE INDUSTRY

JUAN CAMBIASO

This case poses the following questions: What can be done to over-come structurally embedded corruption and bribery in certain cul-tures or environments? Often, business people will express to ethi-cists the following concern. They plan to expand into a foreign country but learn that bribery is an accepted and expected manner of obtaining certain required permits or licenses. They ask what they are expected to do? Impose our country's standards in a foreign cul-ture and perhaps forgo doing business in that country? Consider your response as you read this case.

PART A

The structure of the Argentine insurance industry, with a national governmental body providing legally required reinsurance to all insurers, has created numerous opportunities for corruption. It also has raised important questions, such as: Should a responsible for-eign insurer be permitted to participate? How could a concerned citizen or business leader seek to change the corrupt system?

Background

In 1952 the National Institute of Reinsurance (INDER) was created as a governmental body wholly owned by the Argentine National State. INDER enjoyed a monopoly in the Argentine reinsurance business. (*Reinsurance* is a contract by which an insurance com-pany procures a third party, like INDER, to insure *it* against a loss of liability.) Shortly after the creation of INDER, it became evident that this body would be run as a bureau-cratic agency to benefit local insurance companies rather than as a business minding its own legitimate interests.

This business approach, together with the fact that insurance companies were forced to buy reinsurance only from INDER, meant that INDER would not reject any reinsur-ance coverage. All risks, including bad ones, were passed to INDER, yet the insurance companies continued to charge their clients for assuming bad risks. INDER even agreed in some cases to pay losses that were not covered by insurance. Insurers, naturally, found the business very profitable.

Opportunities for Corruption

This system, in addition to supporting an insurance industry that was inefficient and costly to taxpayers, fostered a number of opportunities for corruption:

- Customers were overcharged for risks the local insurer would never have to assume.

- Customers were motivated to, for example, repair a car beyond the minor damage that had occurred, because INDER paid for the repair. Many other similar abuses were customary.

- Forging insurers, who were not entitled to INDER preferences, used local names to conceal their holdings in local insurers so they could gain the preferences.

- INDER officials required or were offered bribes to ensure special treatment in individual cases.

PART B

The opportunity of waste and corruption under INDER continued to create problems. By 1990 the attraction of such a profitable industry had spawned as many as 250 insurance companies. At this time, however, the Superintendent of Insurance Companies finally stopped authorizing new entrants.

It had become evident that, in addition to encouraging corruption, the system was very costly to taxpayers. Although much of the insurance industry resisted any change, the government finally took a series of steps designed to eliminate the problems:

- INDER was closed

- INDER's monopoly on reinsurance was replaced by a market open to all reinsurance companies.

- Separate treatment for local and foreign companies was eliminated, enabling large international insurers to participate in a very competitive market.

- Capital and liquidity requirements for insurance companies were raised; this helped ensure that only companies with a commitment to put substantial capital at risk would enter the market.

- The Superintendent of Insurance Companies began hiring and training qualified professionals to monitor the market closely.

In addition, the government confronted the problem of unsettled claims from the past. The information available was so poor and unreliable that cost projections for settling these claims spanned an extremely wide range of estimates. It appeared that any settlement could only be based on the arbitrary decision of a powerful bureaucrat, which raised new fears about corruption.

To move ahead, the government adopted a policy requiring a court decision for a party to collect on a reinsurance claim. The reputation of the judiciary for integrity made this solution the one least subject to corruption. Although insurance companies sometimes feel they are poorly treated, this decision enabled the government to implement its reforms and put its biggest INDER problems behind it.

Today's Argentine insurance market includes approximately 150 companies, only a few of which are financially strong and highly professional. Some experts estimate that approximately 100 companies are too small or too weak to survive. In response, customers buy primarily from the larger and stronger companies.

Supporters of the government argue that the problem of systemic corruption has been swept away merely by destroying a monopoly and deregulating an industry. They believe that competition among sound, professional companies in a free and transparent market will ensure that corruption does not return.

THE SOCIALLY
RESPONSIBLE
INVESTOR AND
GLOBAL INVESTING

Peter D. Kinder[1]

Kinder defines a socially responsible investor as one who incorporates ethical or religious considerations in the investment decision-making process. Kinder describes how many investors of this type are troubled by Nike's use of poorly paid East Asians to manufacture its sneakers. Few, though, equate their own personal global investing with these types of practices or understand the moral questions global investing poses.

LOBBYING THE CORPORATION

Social investors tend to use their investments to both make money and effect positive social change. Most financial professionals, however, think of SRI [socially responsible investing] in terms of eliminating from a portfolio, say, tobacco companies. Portfolio purges offer the satisfaction of consistency: one's money is not working counter to one's ethics.

Moving toward consistency oneself can persuade others to do so. But, most social investors are more pro-active. They use their conventional investments (stocks, bonds, mutual funds) to lobby corporations.[2] Corporations are quasi-governmental organizations. Their constituents use the same types of tools to change their policies as citizens use to change government policies. These tools include: persuasion (*i.e.*, lobbying) of officials, use of the press, and the vote at annual meetings. Corporations in the U.S. respond because of their own internal values, the press of public opinion, and the like.

Most social investors do their lobbying by proxy. Research organizations, like ours, that serve money managers raise the issues that concern social investors with corporate officers. Screened mutual funds, like the Domini Social Equity Fund, that vote their proxies and report their votes to the public and the corporations achieve the same end. In addition, most research organizations and screened funds support U.S. shareholder activists, such as

---

"The Socially Responsible Investor and Global Investing," by Peter D. Kinder. Reprinted by permission of the author.

1. Peter D. Kinder is the president of Kinder, Lydenberg, Domini & Co. Inc. (KLD) of Cambridge, Massachusetts, which provides social research on securities issuers to institutional investors. Among his publications is *Investing for Good* (HarperBusiness, 1993).
2. Credit for this insight must go to Berkeley professor David Vogel, whose brilliant *Lobbying the Corporation* (New York: Basic Books, 1977) traced the early history of SRI.

the Interfaith Center on Corporate Responsibility who use the proxy process to engage corporations in dialogue on, say, the CERES Principles on environmental performance.

THE PRACTICAL DIMENSION

"Can Mexico Cope?" asked *Business Week* on its cover the week the bottom dropped out of the peso—and Mexican stocks and bonds. A better question would be, "Will investors ever learn?" Since the 16th century, each generation, it seems, has had its South Sea Bubble (1720), Balkan railway bonds (1920s), or South American debt crisis (1980s).

Ignorance Is Its Own Reward

Each off-shore investment debacle affords the same lessons:

• Investors know little about the countries—and still less about the non-U.S. companies—in which they are investing; and

• Cultural and legal barriers restrict the quantity and quality of information available to them about securities issuers outside the United States.[3]

Investor ignorance is the rule, especially in the U.S. where knowledge of a foreign language is a rarity. Lack of background rarely deters the speculator. But, it should give pause to an *investor,* especially a social investor who is supposed to hold his/her companies to a higher standard. Little short of an unlikely revolution in American education will produce investors prepared for global markets.

TYPICAL PORTFOLIO SCREENING CATEGORIES

Qualitative Screens	*Exclusionary Screens*
Product Quality/Consumer Relations	Product (Alcohol, Tobacco, Gaming)
Environmental Performance	Nuclear Power
Community Relations	Military Weapons
Diversity	Life Ethics
Employee Relations	
Off-shore Operations	

N.B.: Each category can contain several screening areas. Those for the Domini 400 Social Index's nine categories exceed 80. However, few if any social investors will screen in all of these categories, much less the subcategories.

But even if one has the will to educate oneself, substantial barriers exist for socially responsible investors. They must worry about the lack of reliable non-financial information. They need this data to evaluate the social records of companies and governments. It is not a question of looking harder for data; they do not exist. For one thing, no securities regulator

---

3. A third lesson, which exceeds the scope here, is: They must factor currency risks into every investment decision involving a non-U.S. securities issuer.

outside the United States requires the level of reporting—either financial or non-financial—as our Securities and Exchange Commission (SEC) does. Worse, one does not have to go far from the U.S. to find regulators untroubled by corporate Baron Munchausens.

Libel's Huge Impact

For social investors, the lack of government-required data is of less importance than the restrictions on information imposed by libel laws—laws designed to protect individuals and corporations from public disparagement.[4] Outside the U.S., stringent libel laws inhibit every type of publication from *The Financial Times* to environmental groups' newsletters. One can't rely on the journalist's nose for scandal or the green's sense of outrage to lead to publicity about corporate or government misfeasance. Some governments, such as Taiwan's, have even tried to apply criminal libel laws to U.S. journalists writing here.

No country protects the press as ours does.[5] For instance, truth is *not* an absolute defense in a libel action anywhere except here. Placing an individual or company in a bad light suffices. When big-time thief Robert Maxwell drowned in 1994, he left pending a dozen or so actions against British journalists. And, he was winning them! The situation gets worse as one goes east. Because of the close links between governments and corporations, corporate affairs can fall under official secrets acts. The line Americans perceive (wrongly) as separating corporations from government does not exist in Korea, Thailand, and Indonesia, among others.

THE MORAL DIMENSION

Issues of information access do not seem to have an ethical dimension. After all, every society should have the right to define how it wishes its citizens treated in the press. Or, should it? "First Amendment" issues lack the emotional force of, say, child labor. But, the First Amendment is first in our Constitution for a reason: It goes to the heart of the American view of the relationship between individuals and their government.

Cultural Imperialism or Universal Values?

If our First Amendment values conflict with the information and libel norms of other countries, which should give way? To say the least, no consensus exists on the question. Malaysia's Prime Minister, Mahathir Mohamad, recently asserted, "Asian values are universal values. European values are European values."[6] In accord is Harvard professor and political "realist" Samuel P. Huntington, who has written, "What is universalism to the West is imperialism to the rest."[7]

---

4. The aggressive U.S. business press (largely unfettered by libel laws) allows the SEC to operate with a minimum of intrusion in the day-to-day operations of the firms it regulates. Even so, the SEC has been underfunded and shorthanded for years. One wonders whether the concentration of the press in "happy news" companies such as Disney, TimeWarner, and Gannett will erode the protection investors have enjoyed since 1934.
5. This protection, while always substantially greater than elsewhere, only reached its present level in the early 1960s, when the Supreme Court subjected libel actions to the First Amendment's strictures.
6. "Friends Apart," *The Economist,* March 9, 1996, p. 33.
7. Samuel P. Huntington, "The West: Unique, Not Universal," *Foreign Affairs,* Nov.–Dec. 1996, p. 40.

These arguments resonate with social investors because they tend to have a deep skepticism about imperialism derived from the Vietnam War and U.S. adventures in Central America. But in the end, most social investors stand on their western values, on the humanism bred of the Enlightenment. The logic of holding corporations accountable dictates that the public should be able to learn what they are doing wrong—and right.

"All Politics Is Local"

As noted earlier, the opportunities to change corporate behavior are far more limited—where they exist at all—outside the United States. Even in Canada and the United Kingdom, corporate laws keep almost all such issues off the ballot at the annual meeting, So, if you cannot use your money to achieve your social goals, why invest in non-U.S. securities issuers? Perhaps a better question is, if you cannot influence the system—since you are not a constituent of it—in which a corporation operates, why waste your efforts?

In my view, social investors wishing to invest outside the U.S. should focus on micro-enterprise loan funds, such as ACCION International and Working Capital, that fund the smallest of businesses. Investors don't get the eye-popping returns they would by hitting an emerging market at the right moment. But, the loan funds have a reputation for safety of principal and payment of interest. And, they fund social change of the most positive sort—the creation of small businesses that lead to nets of entrepreneurs.

But, as Former U.S. House Speaker Tip O'Neill once observed, "All politics is local." And, we in the U.S. need the same type of investments. Krista Kallio of Access Capital in Cambridge, Mass., pointed out at a conference not long ago, that investors looking to less developed countries for investment opportunities should put our cities and some rural regions in the same category.

Adam Smith best stated the argument for investing at home in a passage from *The Wealth of Nations* what is usually quoted partially and out of context:

> *By preferring the support of domestick [industry] to that of foreign industry, [the merchant] intends only his own security; and by directing that industry in such a manner as its produce may be of the greatest value, he intends only his own gain, and he is in this, as in many other cases, led by an invisible hand to promote an end which was no part of his intention. . . . By pursuing his own interest he frequently promotes that of the society more effectually than when he really intends to promote it.*[8]

All things being equal, Smith argued, you should buy goods locally to strengthen your society. When things aren't equal, buy from foreign sources and pay with goods you produce better than they. But, foreign securities were not one of the things he had in mind. In fact, Smith's "invisible hand" argument responded to arguments for laws restricting the export of capital. Such laws, Smith urged, were unnecessary since shipping capital to potential national or colonial competitors so obviously ran counter to the merchant's interests.

---

8. Adam Smith, *The Wealth of Nations* [5th ed. 1789] [Glasgow ed.] (Indianapolis: Liberty Classics, 1981), v.1, p. 456.

Few people today realize how profoundly wrong Adam Smith got the "invisible hand" argument. Fewer still appreciate the political context in which Smith offered legislators his advice on what types of economic laws Britain should have. The first edition of *The Wealth of Nations* appeared in 1776; the last revision he supervised appeared in 1789. From those dates, contemporary Americans will not be surprised to learn that relations with colonies dominated the British legislative agenda.[9] But, it was not just North America that absorbed Parliament.

Burke's Law

In the 1780s, Smith's great admirer, Edmund Burke, served as prosecutor of an impeachment proceeding in the House of Lords against Warren Hastings. Hastings headed the British East India Company and ruled—backed up by a large private army—much of the Indian subcontinent. An Irishman, Burke's first-hand knowledge of colonial oppression led him to take up the cause of the Indian people whom the Honourable Company (as it was known) regarded as mere sources of plunder.

In his defense, Hastings claimed he was maximizing shareholder value—an anachronistic but accurate description of his position. His responsibilities, he argued, were to the Honourable Company's owners, not to the Crown or the Indian people. Hastings also defended his actions as meeting local (that is, Indian) norms, just like today's retailers who support China's prison industries. In an age where cultural relativism is often the first line of defense for western transnationals, Burke's words on this subject bear quoting:

> [The] laws of morality are the same everywhere, and . . . there is no action that would pass for an act of extortion, of peculation, of bribery, and of oppression in England, that is not an act of extortion, of peculation, of bribery and of oppression, in Europe, Asia, Africa, and all the world over.[10]

Burke speaks for me and for most social investors. But, I would go further. We Americans have an obligation to live our values at home. We have a positive duty to use our investments to benefit our neighbors first. By living our values at home, we will be in a position to export them. But until our people are living and working with dignity, we cannot expect the world to take seriously our moralizing.

---

9. For this reason, the chapters of *The Wealth of Nations* on colonies are critical to understanding Smith's political, economic, and, most importantly, moral theses. Because of their subject matter, few scholars and fewer students read them. Yet, there one finds Smith's mordant comments on what we now call "corporations."

10. Conor Cruise O'Brien, *The Great Melody* (Chicago: University of Chicago Press, 1992), p. 370. In the end, Warren Hastings outlasted his opponents, just as Harold Geneen of ITT would survive the South American bribery scandals of the Nixon era.

COMPARATIVE ETHICS

TRANSPERENCY INTERNATIONAL 1996 CORRUPTION RANKINGS

The Corruption Perception Index represents the average scores which countries have been given by international business people and financial journalists. Transperency International reminds readers that the Index is not an assessment of the corruption level in any country, but rather is an attempt to assess the level at which corruption is perceived by business people as impacting on commercial life.

. . . The index has been prepared using seven surveys, including three from the World Competitive Report from the Institute for Management Development in Lausanne (1992–1994), three from the Political & Economic Risk Consultancy Ltd, Hong Kong (1992–1994) and a 1980 survey from Business International, New York. The index only incudes countries for which a minimum of two scores (and in some cases as many as 7) exist. As the Index matures, the older surveys will be dropped off.

In the index there are three figures given for each country. The first is its overall integrity ranking (out of 10). A ten equals an entirely clean country while zero equals a country where business transactions are entirely dominated by kickbacks, extortion, etc. No country scores either ten or zero.

The second column indicates the number of surveys in which the particular country has been included (i.e., from 2 to 7: the greater the number the more reliable the assessment).

The third column indicates the variance of the rankings. A high number indicates a high degree of deviating opinions. On the one hand, a variance of 0.01 for Denmark, for example, represents an almost perfect concordance. On the other hand, the variance of 5.86 for Argentina indicates a high disagreement among the polls, with some placing the country much higher and others much lower on the overall scale. . . .

For an up-to-date assessment of the TI Corruption Index, you can also consult the Internet at http://www.gwdg.de/~uwvw/icr.htm.

Transperency International 1996 Corruption Rankings from *1996 Annual Report,* Chapter Six, 1995 TI Corruption Perception Index, and excerpts from press release, "1996 TI Corruption Perception Index," June 2, 1996. Reprinted by permission of Dr. Johann Lambsdorff.

Country	Score	Surveys	Variance
1 New Zealand	9.55	4	0.07
2 Denmark	9.32	4	0.01
3 Singapore	9.26	7	0.21
4 Finland	9.12	4	0.07
5 Canada	8.87	4	0.44
6 Sweden	8.87	4	0.11
7 Australia	8.80	4	0.54
8 Switzerland	8.76	4	0.52
9 The Netherlands	8.69	4	0.63
10 Norway	8.61	4	0.78
11 Ireland	8.57	4	0.61
12 Untied Kingdom	8.57	4	0.17
13 Germany	8.14	4	0.63
14 Chile	7.94	3	0.97
15 USA	7.79	4	1.67
16 Austria	7.13	4	0.36
17 Hong Kong	7.12	7	0.48
18 France	7.00	4	3.32
19 Belgium/Luxembourg	6.85	4	3.08
20 Japan	6.72	7	2.73
21 South Africa	5.62	4	2.35
22 Portugal	5.56	4	0.66
23 Malaysia	5.28	7	0.36
24 Argentina	5.24	2	5.86
25 Taiwan	5.08	7	1.03
26 Spain	4.35	4	2.57
27 South Korea	4.29	7	1.29
28 Hungary	4.12	3	0.69
29 Turkey	4.10	4	1.33
30 Greece	4.04	4	1.65
31 Colombia	3.44	2	1.12
32 Mexico	3.18	4	0.06
33 Italy	2.99	4	6.92
34 Thailand	2.79	7	1.69
35 India	2.78	5	1.63
36 Philippines	2.77	5	1.13
37 Brazil	2.70	4	3.11
38 Venezuela	2.66	4	3.18
39 Pakistan	2.25	4	1.62
40 China	2.16	4	0.08
41 Indonesia	1.94	7	0.26

FREQUENTLY ASKED QUESTIONS

Has Worldwide Corruption Increased or Decreased?

Evaluations about worldwide trends are likely to bring about biased opinions. Cultural settings are likely to differ considerably between time and between different surveys and differing perceptions may be due to a change in awareness rather than real corruption. Since such trends are difficult to assess they have bene neutralized in our data. All surveys are normalized to the same mean and variance, hence only their comparative cross-country information is used. This implies that with our data no "world-wide-trend" can be determined. In fact, a worse score of one country may be due to a situation, where all other countries have improved and vice versa. This procedure has also been applied to the historical data. . . .

Why Does Your Ranking Not Produce Objective Figures?

An objective approach is almost impossible. On the one hand, corruption involves concealed actions and data are not revealed publicly. There exist objective data created by the justice system and the media. However, these data rather give an impression on how effective the media is in discovering and reporting about scandals and how independent and well trained the judiciary is in prosecuting. An efficient and incorruptible jurisdiction may bring about high numbers of convictions. Instead of acknowledging this, "objective" data would "punish" such a country with a bad score. . . .

Is Corruption Part of the Culture in Some Countries?

No. Time and again people seeking to find excuses for paying bribes attribute their actions to local foreign cultures. TI is firm in the view that paying bribes is wrong and has no basis for ethical or legal support in any society. That bribery may be tolerated in some countries more than in others may say a lot more about the politics and the legal system, than about deeper matters. In all environments corruption is an illegitimate behaviour. Neither is it sensed as legitimated by those delegating power to politicians and public officials. Nor can politicians or public officials claim to be legitimately empowered to corrupt acts. Therefore corruption is necessarily accompanied by secrecy. Corruption cannot prosper in highly transparent environments.

How Can You Compare between Countries?

Corruption is defined by some researchers as a particular public reaction to political/ administrative behaviour rather than as an illegitimate act as such. Looking for appropriate definitions, this approach assigns a much more active role to the public perception and reactions towards corruption. A high degree of observed corruption may in such an approach reflect a high standard of ethics and a rigid application of rules rather than a high degree of real misbehaviour. Across-country comparison of levels of corruption would hence not be applicable since the underlying standards of ethics may not correspond between countries. However, the sources we included put a high effort on comparative judgements. People working for internationally operating firms and institutions are able to provide a comparative judgement and apply the same internalized definition to different countries. In this perspective a cross-country approach can contribute to a valid comparison of real degrees of corruption. . . .

RELATED WEB SITE

Internet Corruption Perception Index: www.gwdg.de/~uwvw/icr.htm

---

A PRESIDENTIAL DILEMMA: AMERICA GO GLOBAL OR AMERICA STAY HOME?

Ian Spaulding, Lori McDonough, and Lawrence Ponemon

The "Presidential Dilemma" demonstrates the difficulty of weighing personal beliefs against professional and global obligations. KPMG Peat Marwick presents this dilemma through its Website in an innovative manner through which one can judge her or his personal solution against other Website visitors. After choosing one of the four options to President Smith, the site takes you to a choice page that asks you your motivation for the choice, then explains how similar your choice was to that of others. In choosing your option and motive, would you have assumed that you were in the majority or minority, and were you correct in your assumption?

INTRODUCTION

Increasingly in the business world, U.S. companies pursuing a worldwide presence have to pay close attention to the ramifications of the global market—political, economic, and cultural.

Additionally, in a global context, executives sometimes have to choose between their personal beliefs and generally-held societal beliefs that they have a professional obligation to uphold.

The following hypothetical dilemma of an imaginary president in an election year has been chosen not just for its relevance to today's political realities, but because it pertains to these current business issues.

PRESIDENTIAL DILEMMA—BACKGROUND

Sam Smith is President of the United States. He is a moderate member of a conservative political party. In his youth, he observed people in poverty and the suffering it caused. As a result, Smith has resolved to use whatever power he acquired in his political career to help alleviate that suffering. At the same time, he sincerely believes that no Americans, rich or poor, can benefit without a safe and secure country, so Smith has always advocated a strong military defense.

Ian Spaulding, Lori McDonough, Lawrence Ponemon, all of KPMG Peat Marwick LLP, "A Presidential Dilemma: America Go Global or America Stay Home?" from http://www.us.kpmg.com/ethics/november96/story2.html

The President is increasingly being viewed as "too soft" by the more conservative members of his party. His first term in office is nearing an end and he wants desperately to be re-elected. However, a more conservative challenger is gathering increasing support as a possible rival for the nomination.

Abroad, a powerful dictator, Malaan, has emerged in South Asia. Malaan has nuclear weapons and has begun an aggressive policy towards mainland China, even claiming that part of the Chinese empire rightfully belongs to his country. The angry Chinese have responded with their own aggressive rhetoric. This situation has made the U.S. military as well as the senior leaders of Smith's party very nervous.

At home, Smith is presiding over a recessionary economy. A surge in corporate downsizing has put unemployment statistics in double digits, and white-collar workers from the upper- and middle-classes are competing for minimum-wage jobs traditionally held by those from other groups. As a result, poverty levels are escalating out of control with heavy demands being placed on social services, i.e., food stamps, shelters, etc. Smith's opposing party is taking an isolationist, "America First" stance, claiming that the top priority of the nation is to deal with the economic emergency. This party strongly opposes any substantial increase in military aid, at least until the economy recovers.

SITUATION

The Pentagon is demanding a massive increase in military aid (though short of sending in ground troops) to contain the threat posed by Malaan. If Smith supports the Pentagon, his opposing party has vowed to fight the measure on the floor of the Senate, possibly leading to a humiliating defeat for Smith. Meanwhile, civil rights groups are protesting outside the White House, demanding more domestic aid. Finally, advocates of fiscal responsibility from both parties are protesting any increases in funding that might prevent a balanced budget.

If he could act solely in accordance with his personal values, Smith would fully fund both the military and domestic initiatives—but he knows that there is not nearly enough money to pursue that option.

ETHICS COMMENTARY

In business, as in government, the single most important factor about resources is that they are limited. This fact necessarily restricts the options of the most powerful executives, be they CEOs or Presidents. And the fact of limited options means that ethical choices, no matter how painful, are sometimes necessary.

President Smith's dilemma is actually four separate dilemmas, all of them relevant to the ethics of business management:

- the problem of how to expand one's global presence at the least possible expense to one's domestic stakeholders

- the problem of reconciling one's personal beliefs with commonly-held societal beliefs that one has a professional obligation to uphold

- the problem of fiscal restraint versus fiscal risk, and of achieving an ideal balance between the two

- the problem of reconciling ideals to the practical compromises required to exercise and retain power

PRESIDENT SMITH'S OPTIONS

Imagine that you are President Sam Smith. The following options are possible actions you might pursue to deal with the situation described above. Please click on the option you would choose. An analysis of the possible motives of that option will then appear. Select the button that most corresponds with your motive for choosing that option. The results of all the choices will be tabulated and a discussion of the results will appear in a future ethics page.

Option I   As President, you give the Pentagon all the money it demands to deal with Malaan, then go on television to get the nation's support behind this expensive defense initiative.

Option II   As President, you refuse the Pentagon's demand, choosing instead to back a multi-billion-dollar law providing aid to lower-income people hurt by the recession.

Option III   As President, you refuse to support either initiative; instead, you go on television calling for fiscal austerity to achieve a balanced budget to secure America's future.

Option IV   As President, you compromise, agreeing to provide the extra military spending, but for an amount considerably lower than requested, while at the same time agreeing to some government help to the poor at a level substantially below what your administration's critics are demanding.

YOUR ETHICAL DECISION AS PRESIDENT

You Chose Option I—You Comply with the Pentagon's Request for Funds

How this dilemma was answered by others in this survey:

Option I   **17% chose Option I**

As a motive, the choices were:

Motive 1.   In supporting the Pentagon, you place a higher value on your belief in a strong defense than on your belief in aiding the poor.

Motive 2.   In supporting the Pentagon, you decide to defer your dream of helping the poor in order to consolidate your position within your party, ensuring renomination.

You Chose Motive 1—In Supporting the Pentagon, You Place a Higher Value on Your Belief in a Strong Defense Than on Your Belief in Aiding the Poor

How this dilemma was answered by others in this survey:

Motive 1.   **12% chose Option I AND Motive 1**

Motive 2.   **5% chose Option I AND Motive 2**

YOUR ETHICAL DECISION AS PRESIDENT

You Chose Option II—You Refuse the Pentagon's Request for Funds, Giving Money to the Poor Instead

How this dilemma was answered by others in this survey:

Option II   11% chose Option II

As a motive, the choices were:

Motive 1.   In opposing the Pentagon, you place a higher value on your belief in helping the poor than on your belief in a strong defense.

Motive 2.   In opposing the Pentagon, you decide to appeal to large numbers of the electorate in their time of need, defying the right wing of your party.

You Chose Motive 1—In Opposing the Pentagon, You Place a Higher Value on Your Belief in Helping the Poor Than on Your Belief in a Strong Defense

How this dilemma was answered by others in this survey:

Motive 1.   **8% chose Option II AND Motive 1**

Motive 2.   **2% chose Option II AND Motive 2**

YOUR ETHICAL DECISION AS PRESIDENT

You Chose Option III—You Refuse the Pentagon's Request for Funds and Also Refuse Any Additional Aid to the Poor, in Order the Help Balance the Budget

How this dilemma was answered by others in this survey:

Option III   13% chose Option III

As a motive, the choices were:

Motive 1.   In opposing both the Pentagon and social welfare groups, you are placing the value of the nation's future fiscal health above your personal values, however strongly felt.

Motive 2.   In opposing both the Pentagon and social welfare groups, you are trying to buy time hoping that either the economic or the geopolitical crisis will blow over, making a final decision easier.

You Chose Motive 1—In Opposing Both the Pentagon and Social Welfare Groups, You Are Placing the Value of the Nation's Future Fiscal Health above Your Personal Values, However Strongly Felt

How this dilemma was answered by others in this survey:

Motive 1.   10% chose Option III AND Motive 1

Motive 2.   2% chose Option III AND Motive 2

YOUR ETHICAL DECISION AS PRESIDENT

You Chose Option IV—You Work Out a Compromise by Which You Give Something to the Pentagon and Something to the Poor

How this dilemma was answered by others in this survey:

Option IV   56% chose Option IV

As a motive, the choices were:

Motive 1.   In choosing not to choose between two of your most deeply-held values, you satisfy your own conscience.

Motive 2   In giving a little to both sides, you place the abstract value of compromise above the complete satisfaction of your personal values.

Motive 3.   In not totally denying the needs of social interest groups, you hope to win over a least some liberal voters while retaining the loyalty of your party's right wing—and are willing to risk the possibility that no one will be happy.

You Chose Motive 1—In Choosing Not to Choose between Two of Your Most Deeply-held Values, You Satisfy Your Own Conscience.

Motive 1.   8% chose Option IV AND Motive 1

Motive 2.   36% chose Option IV AND Motive 2

Motive 3.   9% chose Option IV AND Motive 3

CONCLUSION

The following are some of the general conclusions that may be drawn from this dilemma:

- In business, we often have to choose between personal values and professional obligations.

- In a globally-oriented organization, a balance must be struck between the cost of international expansion and the price of maintaining the core domestic business.

- The desires and needs of the most crucial stakeholders in the organization (stockholders, managers, staff) have to be taken as seriously as the actions of one's current or potential competitors.

- An American organization operating abroad cannot expect to think or act in a vacuum; rather, it must understand the political, societal and business culture of the countries in which it does business.

RELATED WEB SITE

A Presidential Dilemma: ww.us.kpmg.com/ethics/november96/story2.html

RE-EDUCATION
THROUGH LABOR
DAVID SHENK

Do you think it is just a Western concept to protect employees from torturous conditions? Shenk satirizes the concern that American firms are imposing their "Western" standards on other countries when they seek to improve working conditions. Should we instead stay out of other countries' business? Keep our standards to ourselves and simply accept that which occurs elsewhere as culturally defined? Does Shenk go too far?

One is nibbling on one's morning scone, sipping one's latte and skimming the *Journal* when one notices that financial news has uncomfortably veered away from housing slowdowns and rocky pharmaceutical stocks. "To have Western standards," declares Chrysler Chairman Robert J. Eaton. "That's absolutely ridiculous." One's hands begin to shake. Multicultural creep on the Dow?

Oh, *phew,* nothing like that. Eaton is just pulling the proverbial rug out from under a Chinese employee, Gao Feng, who was arrested on suspicion of being a Christian and then, upon his release, fired for missing work without a reasonable explanation. "We can't assume [Gao] is 100% right and the government is a 100% wrong," explains Eaton, demonstrating his American verve for due process and the democratic way. "We're a minority shareholder in a [joint-venture] company. We can't dictate."

Eaton is gearing up for his late-summer trip to China with twenty-three other top corporate executives and Commerce Secretary Ron Brown. It's the glorious consummation of the recent Clinton directive to de-link human rights policy from trade policy. After years of a forced interest in China's human rights policy, American business is now free to stop worrying about the prisoners of conscience and "re-education through labor." Clinton has decided to let business be business.

But somehow there are still all these pesky media distractions. First the truant Christian is demanding his job back, *loudly,* and then comes an all-too-credible report that Chrysler's joint venture company, Beijing Jeep, has been quietly—but not quietly enough—contracting out work to Beijing Autoworks Industrial Corporation, a known prison labor outfit. "What is a labor camp?" says Franc Krebs, president of Beijing Jeep, in response to the charge. "I've never been able to find one myself." After the allegations are specifically articulated—*Oh, THAT labor camp*—Krebs adopts Eaton's I'm-no-authoritarian rap. "We have kind of a distant relationship with BAIC," he says. "I don't go into his shop and tell him how to run it."

To go into another man's shop and demand a halt to the use of electric whips and "punishment beds"? To insist on protection from 180-degree flames and bandages for open baton wounds? How *Western;* how absolutely ridiculous.

"We're businessmen and we're playing our role," insists Hewlett-Packard's Jim Whittaker. "Certain issues are really government-to-government issues, and are being dealt with, some more successfully than others. It's the federal government that should be reflecting the human rights policies. I don't believe U.S. business should be a message carrier or an arm of the federal government."

For strict non-partisan, however, with only a vague sense of the human rights climate in China ("there have been ups and downs; things seem to be improving, and then things are not improving and so on"), Whittaker is terrifically eloquent on the plight of the Chinese *leadership.* "The Premier was over in Europe," he says. "He canceled a number of meetings because of protesters, and I guess he got a little upset, and he challenged publicly all European leaders. He said, 'I'll gladly exchange you my job. I'm trying to run a 1.2 billion-person economy and we want to grow, but we don't want to be unstable. It's a real challenge.' "

Instability is the hobgoblin of all great institutions, which perhaps explains the palpable empathy for the Chinese government emanating from American corporations. "China is striving to become a full and respected member of the international community of nations," declared a consortium of nine multinationals (AT&T, Boeing, Chrysler, Digital, Kodak, GE, Honeywell, Motorola, TRW) in a letter sent last spring to the White House. The U.S. Association of Importers of Textiles and Apparel similarly told Congress, "We have seen dramatic progress in China, both in its economy and in its human rights environment." The National Retail Federation's Robert Hall trumpeted its analysis that "the new engagement policy is clearly working."

Don't assume that these people are actual fools. Sounding dumb may just be their *strategy.* "Human rights begin with the basics," reads a Washington State Business Coalition press release, "including basic foods like those exported from Washington to China. 'Imagine if 1.2 billion Chinese each had an apple a day,' said Tom Mathison, president of Stemilt Growers."

Yes, of course. It *must* be a tactic. They must be concocting this prattle for a reason. Otherwise, why would they say such things when anyone is able to read Amnesty International's blunt analysis that "there has been no fundamental change in the government's human rights policy" in the past five years; that with as many as 40,000 executions last year, China was once again the gold medalist in rolling heads; that many of those not killed on the spot are held indefinitely without being charged or tried, without legal representation, and are frequently treated to lengthy beatings, electric shock, psychiatric torture, excruciating labor and solitary confinement in cells about the size of a first class airline seat.

". . . Feng Haiguang was subjected to two more beatings, where police electric whips and electric batons were used," recounts one prisoner in a letter smuggled to Amnesty. "Five political prisoners were locked up in [tiny] punishment cells, and each ordered to deliver at least 10,000 bricks per day."

The reason is, *it pays not to know.* Eaton et al. could easily keep up to speed on detailed reports of abuse, such as ". . . this caused Jiang's toe-nails to split, reducing his toes to bloody stumps"; but in this case the ignorance is profitable. "They have chosen not to be fully knowledgeable," says a senior Congressional staffer familiar with the issue, "because if they were fully knowledgeable, they might not be willing to do some of things that they're doing. Someone comes up and says, 'Did you know that the person who's producing these textiles is doing prison labor?' They say, 'No, we didn't know that. How could we know that? We're not responsible for all of our little production subsidiaries.' "

Meanwhile, back in Washington, the corporate interest in government-to-government dealings is quite active. "I've never seen the kind of intensive corporate presence on Capitol Hill that we saw this past spring, leading up to the MFN decision," says Mike Jendrzejczyk, Washington director of Human Rights Watch. "Congressional offices were being deluged by CEOs, presidents of banks, you name it."

"The pressure up here was incredible," confirms the Congressional staffer. "It was just amazing, really. There's money on the line—that's what this is all about."

A lot of money. *A lot.*

"We estimate that in ten years our cumulative sales to China will reach $158 billion assuming normalized relations," the nine CEO coalition wrote to Clinton, pressing for a "long term solution to the China MFN and human rights conundrum." Other lobbyists explained that early in the next century China is likely to become the world's biggest market.

Those sorts of dollar figures naturally make a person a little giddy; one might forget for a moment about international standards of decency and one might say a few things that, to western ears, seem absolutely ridiculous. "Low and middle income American families," warned Macy's chairman Myron E. Ullman III last spring, "will face higher prices and shortages of many familiar items" if Clinton insists on drawing a line in the sand on behalf of the persecuted Chinese democrats and intellectuals. What items of critical importance was he speaking of? National Retail Federation's Robert Hall later clarified that they foresaw "a heavy burden on American consumers" due to tariffs on footwear, toys and men's trousers.

Ridiculous, but it worked. American access to slave-labor slacks remains unimpeded, for the first time in years a President has had to the courage to stand up and guarantee business that such vital access to cheap labor will not be sacrificed in the name of rigid Western standards of free speech, press, religion and so on (ad nauseam). With this key victory in hand, American business is pressing for more. "Now they're trying to get OPIC [Overseas Private Investment Corporation] guarantees to go into China," says the senior Congressional staffer. "Why the American taxpayer should have to underwrite these business risks is beyond me."

Now, imagine not 1.2 billion apple eaters per day, but *5 billion.* Imagine the whole world, de-linked. "If we can trade with China and other countries in Asia where there are human rights problems," says Irwin Jay Robinson, president of the Vietnam American Chamber of Commerce and an important leader in the new incorporated version of multicultural creep, "there is no reason to single out Vietnam." Lobbyists representing foreign ventures in Indonesia, India, and other non-western countries agree: Human rights begins with the basics. Let's be reasonable, and not too western.

Index

Journal of Business Ethics, 91–99
Jung, Carl, 119
Just Cause (Katzenbach), 677, 679, 681

K

Kalb, Marvin, 680
Kaldor, N., 53n
Kamm, Judith Brown, 608n
Kant, Immanuel, 6–8, 15–20, 21–24, 176, 384, 386, 389, 390, 392, 393, 393n, 568, 569, 596
Kanter, Donald L., 124–125
Kantor, Mickey, 753
Kaplan, 611–612
Kaplan, Jeffrey M., 320–323
Katsh, S., 181n
Katzenbach, John, 677, 678, 679, 681
Kay, Tom, 385–386
Kearney, Neil, 763
Kellogg Co., 497–498, 501
Kelly, Marjorie, 528, 545–550
Kelly, Terry, 769n
Kelman, Stephen, 35–43
Kennedy, Edward M., 508, 509, 513
Kennedy, John F., 358–359
Kennedy, S. D., 661n
Kent, Christina, 490n
Kernaghan, Charles, 763, 766, 767, 768
Kerstein, J. J., 649n
Kettinger, William, 602n
Kezios, Susan, 530–531
Kilminster, Joe, 366–367
Kilpatrick, William, 111, 112
Kimble, Dick, 344
Kinder, Lydenberg, Domini & Co., 280–285, 583

Kinder, Peter D., 776–780
King, Martin Luther, Jr., 481
Kinsman, Jerry, 535, 541
Klonoski, Richard, 635n
Kodak, 791
Koehn, Daryl, 206–215, 469–475
Koestenbaum, Wayne, 226, 226n
Kohlberg, Lawrence, 72–74, 110–115, 117, 119, 120, 121, 153
Kolata, Gina, 197n
Kopp, Raymond, 689
Koppel, Ted, 680
Kossovsky, Nir, 193
KPMG Peat Marwick, 113
Krebs, Franc, 790
Kuhn, J., 273

L

L.A. Gear, 482
Landau, H., 450n
Lao Tzu, 243, 300, 329
LaPuma, John, 643–650, 649n
Larson v. *General Motors Corp*, 347
Lauria, Thomas, 490
Law, The (Bastiat), 426–427, 428
Lawlor, E. E., 448n, 649n
Lazard Frères, 591
Lear, Norman, 220n, 220–221
Lecker, Martin J., 116–121
Lee, Dwight, 75, 75n
Legal profession, 666–668
LeGuin, Ursula K., 60–62
Leighton, L., 450n
Leipziger, Deborah, 755–758
Lennox, D., 92
Leopold, Nathan, 63–67

Leveraged buyouts (LBOs), 578–580
Leviathan (Hobbes), 10–11
Levine, Dennis B., 578, 588–593
Levinsky, N. G., 649n
Levinson, D. F., 650n
Levi Strauss & Co., 303, 399, 717, 749–758
Levi Strauss & Co. (Edwards and Lunday), 303
Liedtka, J., 181n
Likert, Rensis, 223–225, 227–228
Liman, Arthur, 588–589
Lincoln Electric, 304
Lissack, Michael, 621–623
List, W., 453n
Litka, M., 727, 732n
Liz Claiborne, 767
Locke, John, 12–14, 596, 597, 708
Lockheed, 137
Lodge, George Cabot, 698–699
Loeb, Richard, 63–67
Logan, John, 602n
Lopez de Arriortua, José Ignacio, 334–335
Loss, Louis, 595
Lubin, Joseph, 120
Luce, R. D., 53n
Luck v. *Southern Pacific Transportation Co.*, 468n, 631n
Ludington, Jack, 208, 209
Ludwig, Dean C., 398n
Lukaszewski, James, 767
Lunday, Jason, 303–305
Luther, Martin, 222–223
Lutz, William, 376
Lying, 566–576
Lynch, Peter, 544

Perception

Hitler
slavery
republicans / democrats
Mormons + Baptists
Union / Confederate
etc.